WOMEN'S MINDS
WOMEN'S BODIES

The Psychology of Women in a Biosocial Context

Joan H. Rollins
Rhode Island College

PRENTICE HALL, Upper Saddle River, New Jersey 07458

Library of Congress Cataloging-in-Publication Data

Rollins, Joan H.
    Women's minds/women's bodies : the psychology of women in a
biosocial context / Joan Rollins.
        p.   cm.
    Includes bibliographical references and index.
    ISBN 0-13-720343-8
    1. Women—Psychology.   2. Mind and body.   I. Title.
HQ1206.R64   1996   95-26469
                                                CIP

For permission to use copyrighted material, grateful
acknowledgment is made to the copyrightholders listed
on page xi, which are hereby made part of this
copyright page.

Senior editor: Heidi Freund
Editorial assistant: Jeffrey Arkin
Marketing manager: Michael Alread
Editorial/production supervision: Bob Moschetto
Senior managing editor: Bonnie Biller
Cover design: Bruce Kenselaar
Manufacturing buyer: Tricia Kenny

 © 1996 by Prentice-Hall, Inc.
Simon & Schuster/A Viacom Company
Upper Saddle River, NJ 07458

Printed in the United States of America

10 9 8 7 6 5 4 3 2 1

ISBN 0-13-720343-8

Prentice-Hall International (UK) Limited, *London*
Prentice-Hall of Australia Pty. Limited, *Sydney*
Prentice-Hall Canada Inc., *Toronto*
Prentice-Hall Hispanoamericana, S.A., *Mexico*
Prentice-Hall of India Private Limited, *New Delhi*
Prentice-Hall of Japan, Inc., *Tokyo*
Simon & Schuster Asia Pte. Ltd., *Singapore*
Editora Prentice-Hall do Brasil, Ltda., *Rio de Janeiro*

CONTENTS

Preface   vii

Credits   xi

CHAPTER 1   *Feminist Reconstruction of Psychology*   1

FEMINISM, 1   FEMINIST EPISTEMOLOGICAL POSITIONS, 6   ANDROCENTRIC BIAS IN PSYCHOLOGY, 11   FEMINIST RESEARCH METHODS, 13   FEMINIST TRANSFORMATION OF PSYCHOLOGY, 15   REFLECTIONS, 20   KEY TERMS, 20   SUGGESTED READINGS, 21

CHAPTER 2   *Biology and Gender*   23

HEREDITY AND ENVIRONMENT, 23   SEX HORMONES IN HUMANS, 26   HORMONAL INFLUENCES ON ANIMAL BRAINS, 29   HORMONES AND HUMAN BEHAVIOR, 31   THE HUMAN BRAIN, 35   SEX CHROMOSOME ANOMALIES, 40   SOCIOBIOLOGY, 43   THE MENSTRUAL CYCLE, 46   REFLECTIONS, 56   KEY TERMS, 56   SUGGESTED READINGS, 57

CHAPTER 3   *Cognitive Gender Differences, School Achievement, Motivation, and Attributions for Achievement*   59

STATISTICAL ANALYSIS, 59   INTELLIGENCE, 62   MATHEMATICS ABILITY, 63   VERBAL ABILITY, 67   VISUAL SPATIAL ABILITY, 69   WOMEN'S WAYS OF KNOWING, 72   GENDER IN THE CLASSROOM, 73   ACADEMIC DECISION MAKING, 76   GENDER AND ACADEMIC ACHIEVEMENT, 78   HISPANIC FEMALE STUDENTS, 79   ACADEMIC ACHIEVEMENT OF AFRICAN AMERICAN WOMEN, 80   ASIAN AMERICAN FEMALE STUDENTS, 81   RE-ENTRY WOMEN, 82   GENDER DIFFERENCES IN COMPUTER COMPETENCE, 83   GIFTED WOMEN, 84   SUCCESS AND FAILURE, 85   REFLECTIONS, 90   KEY TERMS, 90   SUGGESTED READINGS, 91

CHAPTER 4   *Gender Stereotypes, Sex Role Orientation, Gender Differences in Personality, Language, and Nonverbal Behavior*   93

STEREOTYPES OF MALES AND FEMALES, 94   MASCULINITY, FEMININITY, AND ANDROGYNY, 99   GENDER DIFFERENCES IN PERSONALITY, 103   GENDER DIFFERENCES IN LANGUAGE, 113   NONVERBAL BEHAVIOR, 116   REFLECTIONS, 120   KEY TERMS, 121   SUGGESTED READINGS, 121

CHAPTER 5   *Gender Construction Across the Life Span*   123

THEORIES OF GENDER DEVELOPMENT, 123   GENDER CONSTRUCTION IN CHILDHOOD, 131   MEDIA AND LANGUAGE, 134   ADOLESCENCE, 137   YOUNG ADULTHOOD, 145   MIDDLE AGE, 146   AGING AND GENDER, 151   REFLECTIONS, 154   KEY TERMS, 155   SUGGESTED READINGS, 156

CHAPTER 6   *Women and Work*   157

WOMEN'S LABOR FORCE PARTICIPATION, 158   WOMEN'S INCOME, 162   OCCUPATIONAL GENDER SEGREGATION, 165   WOMEN IN THE PROFESSIONS, 170   WOMEN MANAGERS, 176   REPRODUCTIVE HAZARDS, 180   AFFIRMATIVE ACTION AND COMPARABLE WORTH, 181   TARGET HIRING, 182   COMPARABLE WORTH, 182   ENTREPRENEURIAL WOMEN, 183   SEXUAL HARASSMENT, 183   DUAL-EARNER COUPLES, 187   THE UNPAID WORK OF WOMEN, 190   DISPLACED HOMEMAKERS, 193   REFLECTIONS, 194   KEY TERMS, 194   SUGGESTED READINGS, 195

CHAPTER 7   *Violence Against Women*   197

RAPE, 197   PORNOGRAPHY, 212   INCEST, 215   PROSTITUTION, 219   BATTERING, 220   THEORIES OF BATTERING, 229   WOMEN AND CRIME, 233   REFLECTIONS, 235   KEY TERMS, 235   SUGGESTED READINGS, 236

CHAPTER 8   *Mental Health*   237

UTILIZATION OF MENTAL HEALTH SERVICES, 237   COMMUNITY MENTAL HEALTH, 238   DEPRESSION, 240   EATING DISORDERS, 245   ANXIETY DISORDERS, 252   SUICIDE, 254   ALCOHOL AND DRUG ABUSE, 255   PSYCHOTHERAPY, 258   PSYCHOPHARMACO-THERAPY, 267   MULTIPLE ROLES AND MENTAL HEALTH, 271   REFLECTIONS, 273   KEY TERMS, 274   SUGGESTED READINGS, 275

CHAPTER 9   *Physical Health*   277

THE WOMEN'S HEALTH MOVEMENT AND PUBLIC POLICY, 277   GENDER, MARITAL STATUS, AND RACE DIFFERENCES IN PHYSICAL HEALTH, 278   CORONARY HEART DISEASE, 280   CANCER, 281   SMOKING, 288   FERTILITY-RELATED BEHAVIOR, 289   CONTRACEPTIVES, 290   ABORTION, 294   MENOPAUSE, 298   DIETHYLSTILBESTROL (DES), 304   OSTEOPOROSIS, 304   HYSTERECTOMY, 305   SEXUALLY TRANSMITTED DISEASES, 307   PREVENTIVE HEALTH, 311   REFLECTIONS, 314   KEY TERMS, 315   SUGGESTED READINGS, 316

CHAPTER 10   *Intimate Relationships*   317

FEMINIST ANALYSIS, 317   FRIENDSHIP, 318   DATING RELATIONSHIPS, 322   NEVER-MARRIED WOMEN, 331   MARRIED AND COHABITING COUPLES, 332   MARITAL CONFLICT, 338   DIVORCE, 339   REMARRIAGE, 344   REFLECTIONS, 345   KEY TERMS, 346   SUGGESTED READINGS, 346

CHAPTER 11   *Female Sexuality*   347

THE SOCIAL CONSTRUCTION OF FEMALE SEXUALITY, 347   HUMAN SEXUAL RESPONSE, 351   SEXUAL SURVEYS, 354   SEXUAL ORIENTATION, 364   SEX AND THE REPRODUCTIVE LIFECYCLE, 368   SEXUAL DYSFUNCTION, 371   REFLECTIONS, 374   KEY TERMS, 374   SUGGESTED READINGS   375

CHAPTER 12   *Pregnancy, Childbirth, Breast-Feeding, and the New Reproductive Technologies*   377

PREGNANCY, 377   PRENATAL SCREENING, 384   SUBSTANCE ABUSE DURING PREGNANCY, 386   BABIES AT RISK, 389   MIDLIFE CHILD-BEARING, 391   CHILDBIRTH, 392   PSYCHOSOCIAL ASPECTS OF PREGNANCY AND CHILDBIRTH, 396   POSTPARTUM ADJUSTMENT, 398   MOTHER–INFANT BONDING, 400   BREAST-FEEDING, 401   INFERTILITY AND REPRODUCTIVE TECHNOLOGY, 406   REFLECTIONS, 411   KEY TERMS, 411   SUGGESTED READINGS, 413

CHAPTER 13   *Mothers and Children*   **415**

THEORIES OF MOTHERHOOD, 415   MOTHERING, 421   MATERNAL EMPLOYMENT, 425
CHILDCARE, 427   SINGLE-PARENT FAMILIES, 432   LESBIAN MOTHERS, 439   STEP-
MOTHERS AND NONCUSTODIAL MOTHERS, 440   MOTHERS IN MINORITY SUB-
CULTURES, 443   THE POSTMODERN FAMILY, 448   REFLECTIONS, 449   KEY TERMS, 450
SUGGESTED READINGS, 450

CHAPTER 14   *Women and Power/Empowering Women*   **451**

THE RIGHT TO VOTE, 451   WOMEN IN POLITICAL OFFICE, 453   WOMEN IN EUROPEAN
POLITICS, 455   POWER, 457   THEORIES OF POWER, 458   INFLUENCE STRATEGIES, 458
THE POWER MOTIVE, 461   POWER IN INTIMATE RELATIONSHIPS, 462   LEADERSHIP, 467
SUCCESSFUL WOMEN LEADERS, 471   EMPOWERING WOMEN AND MINORITIES, 472
WOMEN AND POVERTY, 473   HUMAN RIGHTS VIOLATIONS AGAINST WOMEN, 475
REFLECTIONS, 476   KEY TERMS, 477   SUGGESTED READINGS, 477

References   **479**

Author Index   **517**

Subject Index   **531**

This book is dedicated to the memory of my mother,
Helena Golen Heller,
for her love, and for her encouragement of my academic endeavors,
and to the memory of my father,
John Heller,
a kind, gentle, loving, family man with a ready smile and sense of humor.

PREFACE

Women's Minds/Women's Bodies is written from the perspective that mind and body are one. Psychological, biological, social and cultural factors interact from the time of conception. This book includes chapters on Physical Health, Biological Gender Development and on Pregnancy, Childbirth, Breast-feeding and the New Reproductive Technologies because the biological and psychosocial constantly interact. The biological and medical aspects are cast in a new light in this text, not as fixed or overriding determinants of behavior, but as one element in a causality that is conceptualized as a psychedelic mosaic.

Feminist psychologists have been wary of including biological materials because in the history of science biological explanations have been used to justify the oppression of women. The complexity of the biological research is constantly oversimplified by the media who jump to conclusions about a biological basis for gender differences when often the research shows only marginal or inconsistent results. Environment also alters biology. Furthermore, many categories including sex, are continuous rather than dichotomous.

Chapters on Feminist Reconstruction of Psychology; Cognitive Gender Differences, School Achievement, Motivation, and Attributions for Achievement; Gender Stereotypes, Sex Role Orientation, and Gender Differences in Person-

ality, Language, and Nonverbal Behavior; Gender Construction across the Life Span; Women and Work; Violence Against Women; Mental Health; Intimate Relationships; Female Sexuality; Motherhood; and Women and Power/Empowering Women are interdisciplinary integrations of psychology, sociology, economics, political science and feminism. It is clearly a psychology text, however, because the focus of the book is the understanding of women's experience and behavior.

Women's Minds/Women's Bodies brings women to center stage. In the history of psychology, women were infrequently included as researchers or participants, so that much of the research in most subject areas of psychology, from experimental psychology to personality and social psychology, has been conducted with an androcentric bias. Men are frequently included in this book because they are important in the lives of women, as family members, lovers, and friends, (and unfortunately, also as rapists, batterers and murderers), as power holders in the more public arena of work, and in the institutions of society such as the economic, health care, political and judicial systems. This book has the feminist goal of empowering women by providing them with a knowledge base that can help them make better choices in their lives.

The experience of being a woman varies from one racial/ethnic group to another in American society. Perspectives of and research with women of color has been integrated throughout the text. Gender is defined by power relations both vis a vis the men in one's own racial/ethnic group and vis a vis White men who have the dominant power in society. For this reason, generalizations can not be applied across all groups of women. For example, gender differences in cognitive abilities are not consistent across racial/ethnic groups. Patterns of submissive nonverbal behaviors exhibited by women in the presence of men are found only for White and not Black women. The experience and behavior of women are shaped by their particular socio-cultural history as well as gender.

This book points out the many problems that still face women in American society. Poverty of women and children continues to be on the rise. Full-time working women still earn less than three quarters of the wages of full time working men. Despite the fact that the majority of mothers of children under six are now working, the U.S. has no federally funded system of day care, and many mothers have difficulty finding quality, affordable childcare. Solutions are discussed.

ABOUT THE AUTHOR

Even a textbook reflects the perspective of the person who writes it. A thumbnail sketch reveals that I am a middle-aged, middle-class, heterosexual, White woman who is the divorced mother of two grown daughters and one son, and grandmother of one baby girl. I am a member of the First Unitarian Church of Providence (although I was christened a Catholic and as a child received communion and confirmation in that faith). Politically, I am a registered Independent.

I consider myself a liberal or egalitarian feminist, but multiple feminist perspectives contribute to illuminating the discussion of women throughout the book. African American feminism makes valid criticisms of liberal feminism which has not sufficiently worked to eradicate race and class oppression as well as sexism. I also agree with African American feminists that men and women

must work together to make a more humane society for people.

I am basically a feminist empiricist, which is why this book is a review of a great deal of empirical literature, but strongly believe that qualitative methods are a necessary component of an empirical approach. Quantitative methods can only provide a partial picture of the psychology of women, which is why first person accounts of individual women, including myself, and women in group contexts are included to convey the personal and lived experiences of women that the research addresses in statistical and abstract ways.

At the same time that I value scientific research, I am a social constructionist who is aware that the problems studied, questions asked and interpretations given reflect the points of view of the researcher and that science is not a purely objective or value free process. For this reason, I have included different theoretical perspectives and research derived from those perspectives, which at times led to conflicting findings. The research methodology used to determine the findings reported, as well as the number of participants, and their ethnic/racial characteristics are more often reported in this book than they are in most texts, because I think that it is important information to have in evaluating the findings.

PEDAGOGICAL FEATURES OF THE TEXT

This book was designed to be reader friendly without sacrificing complexity or comprehensiveness. For pedagogical reasons, a summary appears at the beginning of each section throughout the chapters, which can serve as a cognitive organizer for the reader. The students in my Psychology of Women class, who used a draft of this book as a text, were unanimous in support of this device as an aid to learning.

The Reflections section which closes each chapter provides some of the author's conclusions about the material presented and/or experiences relevant to the chapter and raises questions for thought and discussion. Within the chapter text, Key Terms are printed in boldface type and the definitions for these terms appear at the end of each chapter.

One of the theoretical premises of psychology of women is that experiential learning is equally as valuable as abstract knowledge. The Experiential Exercises at the end of each chapter are designed to motivate readers to learn about some of the topics on a first hand basis. Whenever I assign a library research paper in my Psychology of Women classes, I ask students to interview two people whose experiences are relevant to the topic and to attach a summary of those interviews at the end of the paper. For example, if the student writes a paper on teenage pregnancy, she would interview two teenagers who are or have been pregnant and how they dealt with the situation.

ACKNOWLEDGMENTS

Unlike most academic women of my generation, I have been privileged to have women as professors in both my undergraduate and graduate education. I did my undergraduate work at Goucher College, at the time a women's college, where all of my professors in psychology were women. I owe special thanks to Sonia Osler, a clinical psychologist, who was my advisor for four years as well as my professor in three courses. From Dr. Osler I learned about the more human, caring side of psychology. I received my M.A. degree in psychology at Fordham University taking mostly courses in experimental and physiological psychology, and two courses with Anne Anastasi, a role model who demonstrated the level of excellence that a woman psychologist could achieve. I received my Ph.D. from the University of Oklahoma, focusing on social psychology with a minor in sociology, where I was officially research assistant to Muzafer Sherif at the Institute of Group Relations, but in actuality was research assistant to Carolyn Sherif, who was also my unofficial dissertation advisor. Carolyn Sherif was a very supportive mentor, who encouraged my academic aspirations at a time when few women were in

doctoral programs, let alone with two preschool children as I had during that time. I have spent my entire teaching career at Rhode Island College, where a little better than one-third of the faculty and two-thirds of the students have been women over the years, and the atmosphere has been supportive for the advancement of women. I owe a special thanks to the students in my psychology of women classes, without whom this book would not have materialized.

Although my main area of teaching has been social psychology, I have been teaching psychology of women classes for the past seventeen years to mostly junior and senior psychology majors at Rhode Island College. I have learned a great deal from my students who represent a diversity of cultural backgrounds and ages.

This book was originally to have been co-authored by myself and my colleague Victoria Lederberg, but her political career precluded her from doing any of the library research or writing of the book. Victoria Lederberg is currently Associate Justice of the Supreme Court of Rhode Island. I wish to thank Susan Finnemore Brennan (the acquisitions editor at Prentice Hall) who had faith in my ability to write this text on my own. Thank you also to Heidi Freund, Managing Editor for Psychology, who exhibited patience in answering my many questions and guided me to complete the book.

I wish to thank Gita Brown for her cogent editorial comments on the first nine chapters and for checking references against the text, Danielle Clark for checking references, and Heather Annis for checking references in the final manuscript and for correcting miscellaneous errors. Mary Satterfield helped write the preliminary draft for key terms for the chapters on pregnancy, motherhood, and violence against women. I wish to thank Ken McNichols for his moral support during the last year of writing, and for his practical support in doing preliminary drafts of graphs, tables and figures for the text based on my rough sketches.

A special thanks is owed to the former students who wrote the group observations and to the people who allowed me to interview them for the Focus on Women boxes. As a condition of providing me with written permission to use these observations and interviews, they all requested anonymity.

I wish to thank the reviewers of the first five chapters, who helped me steer a clearer course, and those reviewers who had the endurance to review the entire manuscript: Vita C. Rabinowitz, Hunter College; Donna Castaneda, San Diego State University; Elizabeth Paul, Trenton State College; Lauren Perdue, Potsdam College; Anne Peplau, University of California, Los Angeles; Beverly J. Weiss, Framingham State College; Abigail Stewart, University of Michigan; Alice H. Eagly, Purdue University; Joyce Lynn Carbonell, Florida State University; and Kay Deaux, City University of New York.

I have done all of the library research for and writing of the text myself. Any omissions or errors are entirely my own. The Rhode Island College and Brown University Sciences and Rockefeller libraries have been invaluable resources. I owe a special thanks to the government documents librarian at Rhode Island College, Frank Notariani, reference librarian Carla Weiss, and former and current interlibrary loan clerks, Linda Green and Myra Blank.

Last, but not least, I wish to thank my daughters Diane Jeffery and Valerie Rollins, my son Michael Rollins and my sister Edith Heller for their love, encouragement and moral support during the writing of this book.

Joan H. Rollins

CREDITS

Page 1: Epigraph: Rose, H. (1986). A feminist epistemology for the sciences. In R. Bleir (Ed.), *Feminist Approaches to Science* (pp. 57–76). New York: Pergamon.

Page 23: Epigraph: Halpern, D. F. (1992). *Sex Differences in Cognitive Abilities* (2nd ed.). Hillside, NJ: Lawrence Erlbaum.

Page 36: Figure 2.1: Turner/Rubinson, *Contemporary Human Sexuality.* Reprinted with permission of Prentice Hall, One Lake Street, Upper Saddle River, NJ 07458.

Page 59: Epigraph: Hall, G. S. (1905). *Adolescence,* vol. 2. New York: Appleton.

Page 64: Table 3.1: Hyde, J. S., Fennema, E., & Lamon, S. J. (1990). Gender differences in mathematics performance: A meta-analysis. *Psychological Bulletin, 107,* 139–155.

Page 68: Table 3.2: Hyde, J. S., & Linn, M. C. (1988). Gender differences in verbal ability: A meta-analysis. *Psychological Bulletin, 104,* 53–69.

Page 70: Table 3.3: Linn, M. C., & Petersen, A. C. (1985). Emergence and characterization of sex differences in spatial ability: A meta-analysis. *Child Development, 56* 1479–1498. Linn, M. C., & Petersen, A. C. (1986). A meta-analysis of gender differences in spatial ability: Implications for mathematics and science achievement. In J. S. Hyde & M. C. Linn (Eds.), *The Psychology of Gender: Advances Through Meta-analysis* (pp. 67–101). Baltimore, MD: Johns Hopkins University Press. Voyer, D., Voyer, S., & Bryden, M. P. (1995). Magnitude of sex differences in spatial abilities: A meta-analysis and consideration of critical variables. *Psychological Bulletin, 117,* 250–270.

Page 71: Figure 3.2: Halpern, D. F. (1992). *Sex Differences in Cognitive Abilities* (2nd ed.). Hillsdale, NJ: Lawrence Erlbaum.

Page 80: Box: Castellano, O. (1992). Canto, locura y poesia. In M. L. Andersen, & P. H. Collins (Eds.), *Race, Class and Gender: An Anthology* (pp. 376–385). Belmont, CA: Wadsworth.

Page 93: Epigraph: Gilligan, C. (1982). *In a Different Voice: Psychological Theory and Women's Development.* Cambridge, MA: Harvard University Press.

Page 106: Table 4.1: Eagly, A. H., & Carli, L. L. (1981). Sex of researchers and sex-typed communications as determinants of sex differences in influenceability: A meta-analysis of social influence studies. *Psychological Bulletin, 90,* 1–20. Eagly, A. H., & Crowley, M. (1986). Gender and helping behavior: a meta-analytic review of the social psychological literature, *Psychological Bulletin, 100,* 283–308. Eagly, A. H., & Steffen, V. J. (1986). Gender and aggressive behavior: A meta-analytic review of the social psychological literature. *Psychological Bulletin, 100,* 283–308. Eaton, W. O., and Enns, L. R. (1986). Sex differences in human motor activity level. *Psychological Bulletin, 100,* 19–28. Feingold, A. (1994). Gender differences in personality. *Psychological Bulletin, 116,* 429–456. Hyde J. S. (1986). Gender differences in aggression. In J. S. Hyde and M. C. Linn (Eds.), *The Psychology of Gender: Advances Through Meta-analysis* (pp. 51–66). Baltimore: John Hopkins University Press. Thoma, S. J. (1986). Estimating gender differences in the comprehension and preference of moral issues. *Developmental Review, 6,* 165–180. Walker, L. J. (1984). Sex differences in the development of moral reasoning: A critical review. *Child Development, 55,* 677–691. Walker, L. J. (1986). Sex differences in the development of moral reasoning: a rejoinder to Baumrind. *Child Development, 57,* 522–526.

Page 117: Table 4.2: Hall, J. A. (1987). On explaining gender differences: The case of nonverbal communication. In P. Shaver & C. Hendrick (Eds.), *Sex and Gender* (pp. 177–200). Newbury Park, CA: Sage. Hall, J. A., & Halberstadt, A. G. (1986). Smiling and gazing. In J. S. Hyde & M. C. Linn (Eds.), *The Psychology of Gender: Advances Through Meta-analysis* (pp. 136–158). Baltimore, MD: Johns Hopkins University Press.

Page 123: Epigraph: Reid, B. V., & Whitehead, T. L. (1992). Introduction. In T. L. Whitehead, & B. V. Reid (Eds.), *Gender Constructs and Social Issues* (pp. 1–9). Urbana, IL: University of Illinois Press.

Page 157: Epigraph: Amott, T., & Matthaei, J. (1991). *Race, Gender and Work: A Multicultural Economic History of Women in the United States.* Boston, MA: South End Press.

Page 169: Box: Caswell-Patterson, S. (1995, September 21). No liberation in sight for blue-collar women. *Hersi (47), The Providence Journal Bulletin,* p. 19.

Page 197: Epigraph: Hall, J. D. (1993). *The Mind That Burns in Each Body:* Copyright 1983 by Snitow, et al. Reprinted by permission of Monthly Review Foundation.

Page 208: Box: Judith Kinzel, Director of Advocacy Services, RI Rape Crisis Center.

Page 232: Box: Anne Grant, Women's Center of Rhode Island Newsletter (Vol. 1, No. 3, Summer 1989), p. 1ff.

Page 237: Epigraph: McGrath, E., Keita, G. P., Strickland, B. R., & Russo, N. F. (eds.) (1990). *Women and Depression: Rick Factors and Treatment Issues.* Washington, DC: American Psychological Association.

Page 277: Epigraph: Whatley, M. H., & Worcester, N. (1989). The role of technology in the co-optation of the women's health movement: The cases of osteoporosis and breast cancer screening. In K. S. Ratcliff, M. M. Ferree, G. O. Mellow, B. D. Wright, G. D. Price, K. Yanoshik, & M. S. Freston (Eds.), *Healing Technology: Feminist Perspectives* (pp. 199–220). Ann Arbor, MI: The University of Michigan Press.

Page 347: Epigraph: Vance, C. S. (1984). Pleasure and danger: Toward a politics of sexuality. In C. S. Vance (Ed.), *Pleasure and Danger: Exploring Female Sexuality* (pp. 1–27). Boston: Routledge & Kegan Paul.

Page 352: Figure 11.1: Turner/Rubinson, *Contemporary Human Sexuality,* copyright 1993, (pp. 62–63), reprinted with permission of Prentice Hall, One Lake Street, Upper Saddle River, NJ 07458.

Page 360: Table 11.1: Oliver, M. B., & Hyde, J. S. (1993). Gender differences in sexuality: A meta-analysis. *Psychological Bulletin, 114,* 29–51.

Page 377: Epigraph: Davis-Floyd, R. E. (1994). The technocratic body: American childbirth as cultural expression. *Social Science & Medicine* (p. 38, pp. 1125–1140).

Page 415: Epigraph: Lowinsky, N. R. (1992*). Stories From the Motherline: Reclaiming the Mother-Daughter Bond, Finding Our Feminine Souls.* Los Angeles: J. P. Tarcher.

Page 451: Epigraph: Newman, J. (1994). *Perception and Reality: A Study Comparing the Success of Men and Women Candidates.* Washington, DC: National Women's Political Caucus.

CHAPTER 1

Feminist Reconstruction of Psychology

A feminist epistemology derived from women's labour in the world must represent a more complete materialism, a truer knowledge. It transcends dichotomies, insists on the scientific validity of the subjective, on the need to unite cognitive and affective domains; it emphasises holism, harmony, and complexity rather than reductionism, domination, and linearity.

Hilary Rose, 1986

The study of the psychology of women can be traced to the second wave of the feminist movement that dates from the 1960s. The philosophical base of feminism, however, has its roots in the eighteenth century during the Enlightenment when the American Declaration of Independence (1776) and the French Declaration of the Rights of Man (1789) proclaimed that people have certain inalienable rights that government may not infringe upon (Donovan, 1985). It was during that time that the first major work of feminism was completed: *A Vindication of the Rights of Woman* (1792) by Mary Wollstonecraft, an Englishwoman. She argued for educational, political, and economic equality for women.

In the nineteenth century, John Stuart Mill, in his essay "The Subjection of Women," took a similar position:

That the principle which regulates the existing social relations between the two sexes—the legal sub-

ordination of one sex to the other—is wrong in itself, and now one of the chief hindrances to human improvement; and that it ought to be replaced by a principle of perfect equality, admitting no power or privilege on the one side, nor disability on the other. (Mill, 1869/1970, p. 125)

Unlike the other men of the liberal tradition, Mill argued that women ought to be able to own property, to vote, to receive an education, and to enter any profession for which they were qualified.

FEMINISM

The First Feminist Movement

The opening shot of the first feminist movement was fired in 1848 at the Seneca Falls Convention when women demanded the right to vote.

The **first feminist movement** was the suffrage movement, which began at the Seneca Falls Convention in 1848, when women first demanded the right to vote, and culminated when the Nineteenth Amendment to the Constitution was ratified in 1919. "Some suffragists promised a new era of political morality, the abolition of poverty, social injustice and civil strife, and world peace. Antisuffragists warned that voting would corrupt and unsex women and destroy the home and family" (Hartmann, 1989, p. 1). Although the door had been opened to women to participate in the entire spectrum of public affairs, the optimistic predictions of the suffragettes have not come about, but neither have the dire warnings of the antisuffragists.

The Second Wave of Feminism

The seeds of the second wave of the feminist movement were sown when 4 million women who had gone to work during World War II suddenly lost their jobs at the end of the war.

The awakening of consciousness of American women began at the end of World War II when 36.7% of the labor force were women. The returning GIs claimed their jobs, suddenly putting 4 million American women out of work. Despite the slogan, "A woman's place is in the home," which was given revived popularity at the time, a survey by Roper for *Fortune* magazine showed that two women in three would have liked to have kept their jobs (Castro, 1990). Although most women retreated peacefully to their kitchens, the groundwork had been laid for the *second wave of feminism.* A small, elite women's movement, which took no position on issues other than women's rights, did continue in the late 1940s and during the 1950s, and emerged again full blown in the 1960s (V. Taylor & Rupp, 1991).

The second wave of feminism swept to center stage with the Equal Pay Act of 1963, Title VII of the Civil Rights Act of 1964, and Betty Friedan's book The Feminine Mystique *in 1963.*

Two federal initiatives on behalf of employed women—the **Equal Pay Act of 1963,** which required equal pay for equal work, and **Title VII of the Civil Rights Act of 1964,** which applied to wages as well as to all aspects of employment including hiring and promotion—sparked the second feminist movement (Hartmann, 1989). The mass movement usually precedes the legislation. In this case, however, the improbable combination of a southern president, Lyndon Baines Johnson, responding to the Black freedom struggle, conservative lawmakers who hoped to sabotage the Civil Rights Act, and a small group of women activists led to the passage of this legislation (Hartmann, 1989).

Betty Friedan's *The Feminine Mystique*, published in 1963, was a call to arms for housewives no longer to seek identity through the possession of objects or even beloved persons—"Bill's wife," "Johnnie's mother"—but rather to seek their own identity through their development as full human beings. Growing out of federal commissions on the status of women, the first of which was appointed in 1961 by President Kennedy, the National Organization for Women (NOW) was founded in 1966 as an avowedly feminist organization to combat sexual discrimination in all areas (social, political, economic, and psychological) (Castro, 1990). Shortly thereafter, two other liberal feminist organizations were founded: the Women's Equity Action League (WEAL) in 1967, and the National Women's Political Caucus (NWPC) in 1971 (V. Taylor & Whittier, 1993). Although Betty Friedan's book is heralded as paving the way for the second wave of feminism, it spoke only for a select group of college-educated, middle- and upper-income, married White women.

The voices of minority women have only more recently begun to be heard in the feminist movement. That is not to say that minority women were also not concerned with issues of gender because they did not join the White dominated feminist organizations:

In 1970, for example, women from forty-three tribes organized the North American Indian Women's Association. Six hundred Mexican-American women gathered at the first national Chicana conference in 1971 and adopted strong resolutions criticizing the Catholic Church and calling for free legal abortion. 1972 saw the founding of the Conference of Puerto Rican Women, and in 1973 Eleanor Holmes Norton and others organized the National Black Feminist Organization. (Hartmann, 1989, pp. 70–71)

The specific problems of leisure class White women are a far cry from those, for example, of the single Black mother trying to raise her children in poverty. hooks takes issue with privileged White feminists speaking for minority women because she thinks they do not fully understand the interrelatedness of sex, race, and class oppression, nor its serious effects (hooks, 1990; 1993). In the 1990s Black feminists are finally being heard. They are leading a liberation movement that attempts to liberate women from oppression based on race and class as well as gender.

Egalitarian (Liberal) Feminism

Egalitarian (liberal) feminism is a reformist movement. The focus of egalitarian feminism is the rights and opportunities for women, particularly in the workplace.

In 1972, Congress passed the Equal Rights Amendment (ERA). The campaign to ratify this amendment mobilized many women into feminism, and brought liberal feminists into the political mainstream. Liberal feminists argue that the physiological differences between men and women do not justify providing women and men with unequal opportunities. NOW represents what has come to be called **egalitarian** or **liberal feminism,** which seeks "true equality" between men and women. The focus of NOW's activities was to eliminate barriers to women's paid work.

Following Friedan's prescription, the NOW *Statement of Purpose,* and the NOW *Bill of Rights* assert above all women's full right to work, that is, the right to all types of work and to all the benefits connected with these types of work. (Castro, 1990, p. 47)

An ancillary of the right to work is the availability of women to work, which creates demands for childcare centers and for contraception and abortion services.

Liberal feminism is what sociologists would consider a reform social movement that seeks to bring about change within the existing social framework by reforming rather than overturning the basic institutions of society. "The reform movement advocates a change that will implement the existing value scheme more adequately than present conditions, but the revolutionary movement urges replacement of the existing value scheme" (Turner & Killian, 1972, p. 257). Liberal feminists are not saying women have to work; rather, they say that they have a right to that alternative without discrimination. By the end of the 1970s, NOW had broadened its stance, linking a wide range of social issues such as the threat of nuclear energy to the species, lesbian and gay rights, and homemakers' rights, as well as legal and economic equality.

The defeat of the ERA in 1982, however, ushered in a conservative backlash during which time rights won by feminists were challenged— from affirmative action to legal abortion (V. Taylor & Whittier, 1993). Even the Women's Studies programs that had been established at colleges and universities during the 1970s, came under attack during the late 1980s and early 1990s as "political correctness" was ridiculed. V. Taylor & Whittier suggested that the women's movement was in abeyance or a "holding pattern" during the early 1990s.

Radical Feminism

Radical feminism is a revolutionary movement. There are three directions within radical feminism: radical feminism, political lesbianism, and Marxist feminism.

Feminism has primarily been reformist, seeking legal remedies for sexism in a structure that it sees as committed to social justice. **Radical feminism** criticizes the legal reformist remedies for racism, sexism, homophobia, and classism because of the pessimism with which it views the reform of the system from within. Radical feminism is a revolutionary movement that seeks to overturn the basic institutions of society.

Radical feminism is represented by a wide variety of small militant groups. Unlike NOW, these groups exclude men. Radical feminism sees the oppression of women as a result of the universal value system of patriarchy. "Patriarchy is a system of structures and institutions created by men in order to sustain and recreate male power and female subordination" (Rowland & Klein, 1990, p. 277). Economic, political, legal, and religious structures have all been dominated by men.

Political lesbians believe that heterosexual love is women's identifying with the oppressor. Lesbian separatists want to separate from men and create communities of women.

Political lesbianism, is represented by groups in the United States such as the Furies and Radicalesbians, who coined the phrase "woman-identified woman." Revolutionary feminists argue that lesbianism is a necessary political choice because male sexuality acts to control women's lives. Since sexuality is socially constructed, women can become lesbians for political reasons (Hester, 1992).

In 1979, the Leeds Revolutionary Feminist Group in England presented a paper, "Political lesbianism: The case against heterosexuality," that argued that lesbianism is an act of resistance against male supremacy. In recognition of the power imbalance between men and women, the paper emphasized woman identification and withdrawal from sex with men. Sexism is the root of all oppression, and giving love and support to men maintains that system of male oppression (Bunch, 1993). Thus, political lesbians define lesbianism as a political choice. Further, heterosexual women are accused of impeding the progress of the women's movement.

Straight women are confused by men, don't put women first. They betray lesbians and in its deepest form, they betray their own selves. You can't build a strong movement if your sisters are out there fucking with the oppressor. (R. M. Brown, 1976, p. 114)

Heterosexual love is seen as women's identifying with the oppressor, and heterosexual marriage is seen as a form of prostitution whereby a woman trades sex for economic support. "The lesbian version of feminist sisterhood is presented as the only possible way to achieve love, since lesbian love unites two equal persons, equal by virtue of the fact of their common oppression by men" (Castro, 1990, p. 106).

Emerging out of radical lesbian feminism is the concept of separatism. Women would recreate both themselves and a women's culture (Molina, 1994). Radical lesbian feminists wish to separate from roles, relationships, and activities that are male defined and male dominated (Frye, 1993). They wish to have their own communities. Tension between heterosexual and radical lesbian feminists arises in particular over this issue of separatism.

The open hostility of radical lesbian feminists to heterosexual feminists and the call for complete separation from men has served to keep this a minority position (Echols, 1989). Separatism is a rational solution for radical lesbian feminists because it removes them from the violence and oppression of men. It fails as a plausible resolution to the male–female power imbalance, however, because it does not make sense for heterosexual women who love men and want men in their lives. This is a movement on the margins of feminism. It should also be noted that most lesbians believe that lesbianism is not a political choice, but rather a biological given, and do not support separatism.

Although most African American women espouse a feminism that includes men, some vocal support for separatism comes from African American radical lesbian feminists. "As lesbian separatists, we believe that the first and most basic step necessary to attend to ourselves and our safety as women in the present world is to separate from men to the extent that is possible" (J. Anderson, 1994, p. 437). These views, however, are the complete opposite of those of most African American women who emphasize cooperative humanitarian goals of men and women.

Marxist feminism sees women's oppression as arising out of capitalist society.

Marxist feminist radicalism is based on an anticapitalist premise. It is a reflection of Marxist ideology. It sees the oppression of women as arising out of a class society based on private property. Capitalism has profits from the low wage work of women in factories and corporations around the world. The family is seen as a way of conserving and passing on private property—and of confining women to domestic slavery, the unpaid care of children, old people and the handicapped. Keeping women in a subservient role is the least costly means for a capitalist society to take care of the nonproductive members (Donovan, 1985).

Socialist feminists argue that liberal feminists are fighting for women to pursue self-interest in a capitalist system. Socialist feminists also depart from Marxist feminists, arguing that gender oppression has not been recognized by Marxism.

Socialist feminists contend that liberal feminists are fighting for a world in which women will learn to pursue self interest in a capitalist system, competing for profits regardless of the good of society. According to **socialist feminism,** Marxist feminists have not paid enough attention to women's issues, pointing out that women have been oppressed as women, and not only as workers (Hunter College Women's Studies Collective, 1983).

Socialist feminists believe that patriarchy predated capitalism. They argue that men maintain power over women and exploit their labor both in the workplace and in the domestic sphere (Hartmann, 1989). Catherine MacKinnon (1987; 1992) takes socialist feminism a step further, claiming that sexuality is central to feminism as work is to Marxism. Patriarchy expropriates wom-

ens' bodies. Her position is that rape, pornography, and domestic violence are at the core of women's oppression.

African American Feminism

African American feminists criticize the feminist movement as being too oriented to White, middle-class concerns. Black feminists are seeking ways for men and women to work together to eliminate racism, class privilege, and sexism.

The triple oppression of minority women is reflected in their oppression as women and in their oppression as workers and as members of a particular race. Blacks share a history of oppression, whether they live in parts of Africa, the Caribbean, South America, or North America. Black women also share a history of patriarchal oppression with all women. Sojourner Truth, an ex-slave, noted after the Civil War that "there is a great stir about colored men getting their rights, but not a word about colored women" (Sojourner Truth, as cited in Donovan, 1985, p. 2).

African American Feminism criticizes the contemporary feminist movement as being too one-dimensional, dominated by a White middle-class view of the world, ignoring the role of class and race hierarchies in the oppression of women. Although hooks (1993) questions how many White racist women can call themselves feminists, she says that the contradiction should not lead Black women to ignore feminism. hooks instead chooses to "re-appropriate feminism for the liberation of all people" (hooks, 1993, p. 167).

Black feminists attack the antimale stance of radical feminists.

> They were not eager to call attention to the fact that men do not share a common social status; that patriarchy does not negate the existence of class and race privilege or exploitation; that all men do not benefit equally from sexism. They did not want to acknowledge that bourgeois white women, though often victimized by sexism, have more power and privilege, are less likely to be exploited or oppressed, than poor, uneducated, non-white males. (hooks, 1984, p. 68)

Unlike White women and men, Black women and men have had to struggle together to resist racist oppression, providing them with a tie of political solidarity.

African American women have been recognized as playing a significant and valuable role in Black institutions not accorded to White women in White institutions. That is not to say, however, that sexism and male–female antagonism does not exist among Blacks. Black men have made scathing criticisms of their treatment in books by Black women writers such as Alice Walker's *The Color Purple* (1985), Toni Morrison's *Beloved* (1987), and Gloria Naylor's *The Women of Brewster Place* (1982). Black women have demanded an agenda that does not subject them to sexism in the name of Black liberation struggle (hooks, 1990).

Black women, however, are saying to Black men that "'we are not one another's enemy,' 'we must resist the socialization that teaches us to hate ourselves and one another'" (hooks, 1984, p. 70). Rather than separating from men, Black women are seeking ways for men and women to work together to eliminate racism, class privilege, and sexism.

African American women historians have not analyzed race along a gender (male–female) dichotomy as is the case with European American feminists. Many Black women scholars still do not isolate gender from the context of race and class. Gender identity is linked to and even determined by racial identity. For a long time women's studies universalized women's culture, without acknowledging White women's complicity in racial oppression. The issue of the social construction of race and refutation of biological and genetic explanations of racial differences was at the core of Black scholarship earlier in this century. What Higgenbotham (1992) calls the "metalanguage of race" has impregnated myriad aspects of life, from such everyday aspects as "good" and "bad" speech patterns and type of hair to its construction of social and power relations. It is therefore ironic that White women who speak of the social construction of gender should have ignored race for so long. Blacks' self-representation is antithetical to that of Whites, meaning that Blacks view of themselves may be the opposite of the White stereotype. The meanings of race and of gender are constantly being transformed by political conflict.

FEMINIST EPISTEMOLOGICAL POSITIONS

Feminist Criticism of Science

Science is not value-free.

Science is rooted in the tradition of logical positivism, the goal of which is to use empirical methods to investigate the world (including people) in an objective and value-free manner, finding universal truths that may be replicated by other scientists (Peplau & Conrad, 1989). Is that true? Is science objective and free of biases? Biologist Ruth Hubbard has stated, "Science is made by people who live at a specific time in a specific place and whose thought patterns reflect the truths that are accepted by the wider society" (Hubbard, 1979, p. 8).

There is a continuum of criticism of androcentric (male centered) science that represents differing levels of challenge to science. Liberal feminists point out the history of discrimination against women in science. Many structural barriers have historically existed for women in academic areas, particularly science. Prior to the twentieth century, all but a few privileged women were officially barred from universities and all women from prestigious scientific academies (Schiebinger, 1987). It was not until 1945 that the Royal Society of London, the oldest continuing scientific academy (founded in the 1660s), admitted a woman, and not until 1979 that the Academie des Sciences (founded in 1666 in France) admitted a woman. Even so qualified a scientist as the Nobel prize winner Marie Curie was not admitted to Academie des Sciences. The women who do contribute to a field, even in this century, are often overlooked.

The next and slightly more radical criticism is that the predominance of men in science has led to a bias in the problems selected for study, particularly in the health sciences. Little research has been conducted on menstrual cramps, for example. These criticisms, however, do not aim at the scientific method itself. Criticisms somewhat toward left of center claim bias in the actual conducting of experiments in design and interpretation. More radical still are the criticisms of even the "hard" sciences and questioning of the assumptions of objectivity and rationality underlying the scientific method (Keller, 1987).

Feminists raise many issues about science, technology and theories of knowledge (epistemology). Although science generates useful information about the world, science is also political. It is not the impartial, value-free, disinterested discourse that conventional mythology holds (Harding, 1993). It is a challenge to feminism to bring into play the progressive elements of science while minimizing the regressive aspects. Science must also decenter White, middle- and upper-class, heterosexual, Western men and women. Another bias in science has been the conception that the natural sciences with their emphasis on quantitative methods should also be the standard for social sciences.

Feminist Empiricism

Feminist empiricism accepts the scientific method but tries to eliminate androcentric bias.

Feminist empiricism accepts mainstream scientific experimentation, observation, and recording; however, it believes that social inquiry has been biased from a male point of view in the questions asked and the interpretations made, leading to distortions in knowledge. "One corrective that feminist empiricism proposes is an acceptance and acknowledgment of the context in which the research is carried out and an awareness of how characteristics of the researcher may bias the research process" (K. R. Allen & Baber, 1992, p. 3). Feminist empiricists have faith in the scientific method, but present guidelines for

eliminating bias in the conducting of scientific research. Suggestions given by empiricists include specifying the circumstances in which gender differences are found, seeking gender similarities as well as differences, and assessing the impact of the gender of the experimenter (Riger, 1992).

"Feminism is, among other things, a response to the fact that women either have been left out of, or included in demeaning and disfiguring ways in what has been an almost exclusively male account of the world" (Lugones & Spelman, 1983, p. 573). Feminist empiricists want to conduct research so that "the woman's voice" is no longer missing or distorted by androcentric research.

A serious criticism of the feminist empiricist point of view is that there is not yet a feminist practice in the conduct of scholarship

> because the women's movement must of necessity develop itself within a patriarchal culture of such a depth and pervasiveness that, even in reacting to or resisting its oppressive nature, the women's movement continually "reinfects" or contaminates itself with it. All of us, women and men alike, are "soaked" in it. (Shotter & Logan, 1988, p. 68)

Can we in fact remove patriarchy from science and psychology or is it too pervasive in our lives to separate from science, particularly from psychology?

Qualitative versus Quantitative Methods

A lively debate has been going on among feminists about the value of qualitative versus. quantitative methods.

Some feminists have proposed that qualitative methods such as interviews and personal documents constitute feminist research, while quantitative methods such as laboratory experiments and psychological tests do not (Graham & Rawlings, 1980, as cited in Peplau & Conrad, 1989). Peplau and Conrad (1989) argue, however, that qualitative data are not inherently more feminist than are quantitative data. Sexist bias can influence verbal descriptions of personal interviews and participant observations just as it can distort statistical analysis. On the other hand, statistical techniques such as meta-analysis can enhance feminist research, as have a number of meta-analytical studies that show disappearing gender differences in verbal and mathematical performance (Hyde & Linn, 1988).

A lively debate has been going on among feminists about the value of quantitative versus qualitative methods in social science research. "Much of the debate has concerned the claim that quantitative research techniques—involving the translation of individuals' experience into categories predesigned by the researchers—distort women's experience and result in a silencing of women's own voices" (Jayaratne & Stewart, 1991, p. 85). Feminists have a skepticism about quantitative research because of its past use to maintain women in a position of subjugation. The public has great respect for quantitative research, and it has been used frequently in biased ways against women. For example, the research reporting that husbands and wives are equally likely to be violent, which was used as an excuse for not providing shelters for battered women, only later revealed large differences in "violence" related to self defense and the amount of physical harm caused. Therefore, although we need to be critical of biases in research, and strive to incorporate more qualitative methods, we should not go to the other extreme by no longer using quantitative methods.

Feminist Standpoint Theory

Feminist standpoint theory posits that a person's view of reality is based on their particular position in society (race, class, gender, etc.).

Feminist standpoint theory is rooted in the view that a person's understanding of reality is a product of a particular position in society (race, class, gender, etc.). More oppressed individuals, according to this theory, potentially have a more complete and less distorted view of reality be-

cause an understanding of the dominant culture as well as their own culture is necessary to survival. A feminist standpoint, however, is not something a woman has by virtue of being a woman; rather, it is something that she must develop through intellectual and political struggles against inequality (K. R. Allen & Baber, 1992).

Contemporary social science is an androcentric ideology that frames questions in terms of dualisms: "culture vs. nature; rational mind vs. prerational body and irrational emotions and values; objectivity vs. subjectivity; public vs. private—and then links men and masculinity to the former and women and femininity to the latter in each dichotomy" (Harding, 1986b, p. 136). According to feminist critics, this dichotomizing represents an ideology that structures thinking that is reflected in social institutions, including science.

Essentialism is the point of view that women and men do differ because of socialization and that women are at least equal to and possibly superior to men.

Essentialism has been put forth by some feminists (Belenky, Clinchy, Goldberger, & Tarule, 1986; Chodorow, 1978; Gilligan, 1982; J. B. Miller, 1986) who suggest that males and females have different characteristics in thinking, relating, and moral development. These traits within women are presented as distinctly feminine and are at least equal to or even superior to those that characterize men. These psychologists are termed *cultural* feminists because they see these characteristics as a result of different socialization of males and females, not as biologically innate.

These theorists help to validate feminine qualities. They use primarily qualitative methods that allow the women to speak for themselves. Nevertheless, there are some serious flaws in their approach. One is the assumption of the universality of these qualities, although their research was typically carried out with small samples of White women. Another is the absence of empirical support for the gender differences they claim (Mednick, 1989).

Feminist Postmodernism

Feminist postmodernism is deconstructive, challenging existing beliefs about women and men, and viewing gender as a social construction.

Feminist postmodernism questions the existence of a single truth or reality. It questions whether one group of people have special insight that makes their perceptions of the world uniquely superior (Gergen, 1988). "Postmodernism is 'deconstructive,' challenging and exposing existing beliefs and concepts that are accepted as natural or absolute." (K. R. Allen & Baber, 1992, p. 4). Viewing gender as a social construction allows the questioning of power and domination in the lives of women. **Feminist epistemology** offers a deconstruction of the assumptions of inferiority of women as they occur in our thinking about men, women, and society on a daily basis (Young-Eisendrath, 1988).

Social Construction of Gender

Feminist postmodernism states that gender is socially constructed in social interaction.

The underlying assumption of the research on gender differences in psychology has been that gender resides within the individual. Historically, in psychology, gender differences were regarded as fundamental to human nature (Bohan, 1993). From a feminist psychological point of view, "focusing on gender differences marginalizes and obscures the interrelatedness of women and men as well as the restricted opportunities of both. It also obscures institutional sexism and the extent of male authority" (Hare-Mustin & Marecek, 1988, p. 462).

This dimorphism was not questioned until the second feminist movement in the 1960s. Feminist psychological theory and research argued instead that gender is socially constructed. "The constructionist argument is that gender is not a trait of individuals at all, but simply a construct that identifies particular transactions that are under-

stood to be appropriate to one sex" (Bohan, 1993, p. 7). Gender, then, is not a characteristic of a person, but rather of the interaction between persons. The example used by Bohan is that describing an interaction between persons as "friendly" is quite different than describing a person as "friendly." Support for this position is found in the work of Nancy Henley (1973), who found that women in positions of power have patterns of nonverbal communication that are considered "masculine."

Personal and Interpersonal Construction of Gender

Gender is created by idiosyncratic psychological feelings and fantasies and interpersonal interactions as well as by culture.

Individual psychological processes also underlie the construction of gender, in addition to cultural, linguistic, or political forces (Chodorow, 1995; Mahoney & Yngvesson, 1992). Theorizing from the perspective of a psychoanalytic feminist, Nancy Chodorow (1995) provides examples from clinical practice of idiosyncratic gendered selves created by unconscious feelings and fantasies that are evidence for the variability of people's constructions of gender. She agrees, however, that gender cannot be viewed independently of culture. The capacities and processes for the creation of personal meaning that psychoanalysis describes contribute to gendered subjectivity as do cultural categories and the enactment or creation of social or cultural roles" (Chodorow, 1995, p. 542). One does not have to be a psychoanalyst to acknowledge the role of individual life history and one's emotional meanings in forming gender identity.

The development and expression of gender is also mediated by interpersonal interactions and situational contexts (Harding, 1986a). For example, interaction between a husband and wife can be quite egalitarian in some marriages, whereas in other marriages the husband is dominant and the wife submissive in their interactions. The meanings associated with these interactions also vary from one individual to another. One woman in a submissive role may feel anger and bide her time until she is financially capable of leaving the marriage. Another woman in a submissive role may feel she is conforming to an appropriate gender role and accept her husband's dominance. Each individual creates her own gender within the context of interpersonal relationships and culture.

Poststructuralism

Poststructuralism states that we do not discover reality, we create it.

Poststructuralism, a movement within postmodernism, says that science does not mirror reality, but rather creates it (Riger, 1992). Poststructuralists would say that "facts" produced by scientific research represent the version of reality of those with power, not some kind of "pure" knowledge. Within psychology, poststructuralism is known as social constructivism. "Constructivism asserts that we do not discover reality, we invent it (Watzlawick, 1984). Our experience does not directly reflect what is 'out there,' but is an ordering and organizing of it" (Hare-Mustin & Marecek, 1988, p. 455). Deconstruction, taken from an approach to literary interpretation that examines the variety of meanings of a text, looks below the surface as well as at what the text does not say. It can be applied to scientific texts and to psychotherapy as well. Therapists question, explain, and disregard meanings within the clients' frames of reference (Hare-Mustin & Marecek, 1988).

The danger of postmodernism to feminism is that it becomes a short slide into the position that every viewpoint is equally valid—a depoliticized relativism. K. R. Allen & Baber (1992) believe that postmodernism, however, can serve to identify the experiences of a wide variety of women leading to a more inclusive feminist agenda, rather than one based on a privileged subgroup.

Afrocentric Feminist Epistemology

Black feminist thought values common sense, personal experience, and the ethic of caring as central in assessing knowledge claims. Etic (objective, behavioral approaches) may not reveal cultural diversity as well as do emic (subjective, phenomenological) approaches.

Feminist theory and pedagogy is criticized by women of color as being racist.

Women of color have engaged in trenchant critiques of Second Wave feminism as a politic formed primarily by and for white women; feminist courses have been implicated in this critique on the ground of assisting in the reproduction of a white-dominated feminism. (Weir, 1993, p. 19)

Women of color are contributing to deracializing feminist theory and research.

African American feminist thought is that which is produced by Black women that arises from the historical and material conditions that shaped their lives. Patricia Hill Collins (1989) describes the contours of an **Afrocentric feminist epistemology:**

1. The wisdom of good common sense is valued, and the personal experience of a Black person is highly valued as the basis for knowledge;
2. New knowledge is rarely worked out in isolation and is usually developed in dialogue with others in the community;
3. The ethic of caring places personal expressiveness, emotion, and the capacity for empathy in a central position in assessing knowledge claims.

Research has found that **etic** (objective, behavioral) and **emic** (subjective, phenomenological) approaches may reveal cultural diversity in findings that using only objective, controlled methods may not (Landrine, Klonoff, & Brown-Collins, 1992). One hundred and thirty-eight undergraduate women—71 White, 35 Black, 13 Latina, and 19 Asian American—completed seven items from the Bem Sex Role Inventory (for example, "I am assertive") by attributing these phrases to themselves using seven point scales. After rating themselves on these attributes, participants were instructed to circle the definition that best matched what they had in mind while rating themselves. The etic, or quantifiable data, showed no statistically significant difference in the ratings among racial groups. The emic, or qualitative data, however, showed that White women and minority women had different meanings of the terms in mind while rating themselves.

> Latinas and Asian women were most likely to define assertive as "say whatever's on my mind"; white women were most likely to define it as "standing-up for myself," and black women were most likely to define it as "say whatever's on my mind" or as "aggressive." (Landrine, Klonoff, & Brown-Collins, 1992, p. 160)

The researchers conclude that although this is a simple study, it does demonstrate cultural differences in the interpretation of words and the necessity of collecting both etic and emic data.

The Black women's literary tradition is a source that can be tapped to understand the customs, mores, and opinions of the Black community. It is the source for understanding the ethical values of Black women. The stereotypes and caricatures of Black women are replaced by a glimpse of the magnitude of the Black personality (K. G. Cannon, 1993). The patterns and themes of Black women's writings reflect historical and sociological facts of the Black community. The suppression of education of Blacks led to an oral tradition that has obligated Black women writers to document the Black experience and wisdom.

Lesbian Epistemology

Nonradical lesbian feminists seek an epistemology based on a lesbian and gay male reality.

Lesbians want to make feminist theory and the construct of woman inclusive of all women.

They are critical of liberal and socialist feminists for excluding lesbians. Nonradical lesbian feminists seek an epistemology based on a lesbian and gay male reality. According to Laura S. Brown (1989), there are common elements in the lesbian and gay realities. The first of these is a biculturalism, a state of simultaneously being a participant in both the heterosexual and the lesbian and gay worlds. Second, lesbian and gay reality exists within the context of marginality in heterosexual culture. This experience of the world as outsiders can allow lesbians and gay males to see the world differently and to challenge long held assumptions. For example, under patriarchy, family is only considered to be appropriate with a mother and a father. Creativity is normative in the lesbian and gay world because clear rules about what is normative for heterosexual couples are lacking (L. S. Brown, 1989). The lesbian perspective is unlike the liberal feminist perspective because it is not reactive. It is self-created and self-authorized (N. Hart, 1990).

ANDROCENTRIC BIAS IN PSYCHOLOGY

Historical Androcentric Bias in Psychology

There are many ways in which androcentric (male) bias has colored the science of psychology. Historically, psychologists focused on gender from the point of view that differences were innate.

An androcentric bias was evident from the early days of psychology. For many decades in psychology the male was norm, and research and theory focused on men's experience and behavior (P. T. Reid, 1991). From the early days of psychology, the origin of which is usually dated from the founding of the first psychological laboratory in 1879 by Wilhelm Wunt at Leipzig, Germany, the study of sex differences also was a topic of research (Anastasi, 1958). Inspired by evolutionary theory, researchers compared the sizes of male and female brains and concluded that male brains weighed more and were therefore superior. Scientists were soon clever enough, however, to conclude that women's brains were proportional to their height and weight. The argument, then, was that women had smaller frontal lobes and larger parietal lobes, which was then said to be the cause of women's intellectual inferiority. When some researchers reported that the parietal lobe might be associated with higher intelligence, researchers suddenly found that women's parietal lobes were *smaller* than men's. "Today, many researchers are splitting brains instead of weighing them, but they are no less determined to find sex differences" (Tavris, 1992, p. 44).

The androcentric bias so central in biology and psychology refers to the initial tendency of man to see himself as the center of the universe, then when scientists could no longer hold to that view, as central to the species. Darwin argued that men's greater intellectual powers—observation, reason, invention, or imagination—were greater than women's, having been demonstrated by the fact that far more men than women were eminent in history, science, philosophy, and many other fields (Hubbard, 1979). Darwin, of course, does not mention the fact that women were barred by discrimination from education and membership in learned societies and other positions that would allow them the prerequisite resources.

Mechanistic Psychological Research

The historical, sociocultural, and situational context must be taken into account in research.

One of the problems of traditional psychology is that it has attempted to imitate the more prestigious physical sciences (C. W. Sherif, 1979). The ideology of technology that permeates our society has led to a way of thinking about the world and ourselves in mechanistic terms (Rothman, 1989). Consistent with that ideology is research conducted on humans as if they were automa-

tons. The realization is lost, however, that there are unique problems in the study of human individuals that are quite different from those, for example, of analyses of a chemical interaction in a test tube.

The isolation of variables ignores the context as a causative agent in behavior. In order to understand behavior fully we must know historical background and sociocultural context as well as immediate factors such as the genders of the researcher and participant. Research itself is an interpersonal, cultural event that influences the responses of those being studied. Further, the hierarchical arrangement of patriarchal society is replicated in the psychological laboratory (C. W. Sherif, 1979).

Bias in the Research Process

Bias has entered every stage of the research process from the selection of the research topic and of participants to the dissemination of the research findings.

Many criticisms of psychology have appeared in feminist writings (Jayaratne & Stewart, 1991; Riger, 1992). At each stage of research male bias has entered into the research process. It begins with the selection of the topic, with an absence of topics central in the lives of women such as pregnancy, rape, and housework, and framing research questions to ensure that women are relegated to an inferior position. For example, researchers have developed models of why women are poorer at visual spatial tasks, rather than asking in what particular situation women do and do not exceed male performance and what the variables are in both situations. The research design with women's invisibility as both researchers and participants of research permits further bias. Sex-of-experimenter effects that contaminate research findings in virtually every area are not considered. Research designs also emphasize hierarchical distance between researcher and participant and may exploit the participant through deception and inadequate debriefing. There is an emphasis on between gender differences and a lack of attention to within gender differences. Male behavior may be considered the norm with female behavior interpreted as deficient when compared with a male standard. Individual's reactions are abstracted from their social and historical context, thereby attributing causes to internal rather than external factors. The quantitative data collected may be simplistic and superficial. Overgeneralization of the data also occurs too frequently, cloaked, however, as scientific fact. On the other hand, inadequate dissemination and underutilization of the data also often occurs (Jayaratne & Stewart, 1991).

FEMINIST RESEARCH METHODS

Feminist Perspective in Research

Feminist research is a perspective that is guided by feminist theory and uses a multiplicity of interdisciplinary methods.

The first book on feminist research, *Feminist Methods in Social Research* by Shulamit Reinharz, appeared in 1992. In this book Reinharz examines the full range of **feminist research methods.** She identifies 10 themes of feminist methodology:

1. Feminism is a perspective, not a research method.
2. Feminists use a multiplicity of research methods.
3. Feminist research involves an ongoing criticism of nonfeminist scholarship.
4. Feminist research is guided by feminist theory.
5. Feminist research may be transdisciplinary.
6. Feminist research aims to create social change.
7. Feminist research strives to represent human diversity.
8. Feminist research frequently includes the researcher as a person.
9. Feminist research frequently attempts to develop special relations with the people studied (in interactive research).
10. Feminist research frequently defines a special relation with the reader. (Reinharz, 1992, p. 240)

The ideals of feminist scholarship are to conduct research that works for the emancipation of women and to achieve a more egalitarian society (Acker, Barry & Esseveld, 1991). This may sometimes require turning the problem inside out. J. Ladner (1987) points out that the focus of research on the Black community has been on the problems of drug addiction, poverty, crime, unemployment, dilapidated housing and the "sick" inhabitants. Little has been written about the strength of the people. Most research has instead focused on the alleged deviant attitudes and behavior of Blacks.

> There must be a strong concern with redefining the problem. Instead of future studies being conducted on problems of the Black community as represented by the deviant perspective, there must be a redefinition of the problem as being that of institutional racism. If the social system is viewed as the source of the deviant perspective, then future research must begin to analyze the nature of oppression and the mechanisms by which institutional forms of subjugation are initiated and act to maintain the system intact. (Ladner, 1987, p. 77)

What social scientists should be investigating is how social policy creates pathology. It requires refocusing one's perspective from the deviant personality to oppression by the social system. Framing of the question needs to be turned inside out. For example, the focus of research might be how the criminal justice system and the welfare system structure the lives of ghetto inhabitants.

Feminist Principles for Research

Many factors are taken into account by feminist scholars that are not yet a part of mainstream theorizing and research. (I may be optimistic to say "not yet.") According to J. Meyer (1988) the following principles would be useful for social science theorizing and research.

1. The investigator should take stock of the material context. That would include factors such as the distribution of scarce resources like schooling and the presence of institutional hierarchies.

2. The investigator should take account of the normative context for social processes. This means that the researcher should be aware of the historical and cultural background in which behavior takes place. For example, when studying marriage, factors such as unemployment rate and cultural norms about marriage need to be taken into account.

3. The investigator should give the subjective experience a legitimate place in social science. Many well-known experiments in social psychology such as Milgram's famous 1965 study of obedience to authority, omit the participants' subjective experiences leaving interpretation solely to the experimenter. This interpretation would include how the researcher's subjective experience influenced her selection of the particular topic, hypothesis, and so forth.

4. The researcher should be aware of the impact of the research on society. There is a responsibility to state the relevance of the research to groups and problems in society. (J. Meyer, 1988).

Feminist research recognizes the value orientation of the research and the interconnection of scientist and participant.

Gergen (1988) points out empiricist shortcomings in the social sciences which feminist thinkers reject:

1. the independence of scientist and subject;
2. the decontextualization of the subject matter from the field in which it is embedded, physically and historically;
3. value-neutral theory and practice;
4. the independence of "facts" from the scientist;
5. the superiority of the scientist over other people (Gergen, 1988, p. 94).

For feminist researchers, scientist and participant are interconnected. The value orientations of scientific endeavors are recognized and formed with a specific value in mind.

This is not just the historically crude perception that men are inherently superior to women but a more treacherous underpinning of that perception: a definition of males and male experience as a neutral standard or norm, and females and female ex-

perience as a sex-specific deviation from that norm. It is thus not that man is treated as superior and woman as inferior but that man is treated as human and woman as "other." (Bem, 1993, p. 2)

Feminist research is then more than a methodology. It is a research perspective that seeks to correct traditional androcentrism or male centeredness. Androcentrism is a way of reproducing male power, or more specifically, the power of White, heterosexual males. Table 1.1 is a summary of feminist research at each stage of the process.

TABLE 1.1 Feminist Research

I. Formulating the Hypotheses

    A. The historical and sociocultural context is taken into account.

    B. Topics are selected which are relevant in the lives of women.

    C. Questions are worded to incorporate the frame of reference of the participant.

II. Designing the Research

    A. Participants are chosen who are of the population to which the results will be generalized.

    B. Researchers are chosen who have characteristics similar to those of participants, such as sex, age and race.

    C. Measures of the sociocultural context are incorporated into the research design.

    D. Both qualitative and quantitative data are collected.

III. Performing the Research

    A. Researchers who do not know the hypotheses interview participants and run experiments.

    B. Researchers develop a special relationship with participants, enabling them to better understand their participants' frame of reference.

IV. Analyzing and Reporting the Data

    A. Both statistical significance and practical significance are reported and discussed.

    B. Nonsignificant findings, such as of no gender differences on a behavioral measure, are also reported.

    C. When communicating findings it is pointed out that a gender difference is only an average group difference which does not apply to any individual.

    D. A title is chosen for the report which does not sensationalize or overgeneralize the results.

Collaborative research has been used as a model for feminists in both the humanities and social sciences.

Collaborative research is an approach that has been developed as a model by feminists in both the humanities and the social sciences. An example was a research project conducted between 1976 and 1979 in Cologne, Germany, in which a research group of 15 women applied a variety of methods to provide empirical proof of the need for a house for battered women. The city had requested such proof before acquiring a house. The social scientists working on the project became participants in all aspects of it. Intensive individual and group discussion took place between the researchers and the battered women. The goal of these discussions was to raise the consciousness of the battered women and to have them understand that the male violence of which they were victims was part of social and historical conditions (Mies, 1984, as cited in Reinharz, 1992).

Conventional Methods

At times, conventional methods are better able to provide documentation that can help to bring about change in society on women's behalf.

Nevertheless, there are times when adherence to the most conventionally rigorous procedures is necessary in order to provide documentation that can be used to bring about change on women's behalf. An example of this approach was Diana E. H. Russell's (1982) study of the incidence of rape. In order to be able to generalize to a larger population, she constructed a scientifically selected sample. She also matched demographic characteristics of interviewers and interviewees to obtain sensitive information. She hired White, Black, Asian, and Latina interviewers of varying ages and class backgrounds who displayed empathetic attitudes to rape victims. They were given sixty-five hours of paid training, including consciousness raising about rape and incestuous abuse. Twenty-two percent of the interviews were also verified (i.e., follow-up calls were made to check that the interview had actually taken place) (Reinharz, 1992; D. E. H. Russell, 1982).

FEMINIST TRANSFORMATION OF PSYCHOLOGY

Sexism in Psychology

Although feminists have pointed out sexist bias in psychology, an examination of studies in eight psychology journals found that even though sexist language has been eliminated, sexism still exists in the literature.

In the field of psychology, sexism was pointed out by feminists in the early 1970s who encouraged their colleagues to examine sexist bias at several levels. Psychological journals instituted policies, such as anonymous reviewing of articles submitted for publication. The journals also advocated changes in research methodology to include participants of both sexes, to eliminate sexist language, and to avoid generalizing from male samples to the general population. To assess changes in sexism in psychological research, Gannon et al. (1992) reviewed 4,952 articles published in 1970, 1975, 1980, 1985, and 1990 in two journals from each of four areas in psychology: developmental, social, clinical, and physiological. The examination of these studies found that sexism had diminished but was not eliminated during the twenty-year period.

In the journals examined, sexist language has been virtually eliminated, the percentage of studies that included only male participants has decreased, the percentage of studies authored by women has increased and the percentage of studies in which data based on participants of one sex were generalized to people of both sexes has decreased. (Gannon et al., 1992, p. 394)

There has, however, been a lack of change in the hypothesizing and testing of sex differences. The two social and physiological journals reviewed contained more evidence of sexism than the two clinical and developmental journals.

Even feminist journals such as *Psychology of Women Quarterly (PWQ)* and *Sex Roles (SR),* however, continue to print articles based on research conducted by traditional methodological norms. Content analysis of 228 research articles in *PWQ* for 1976–1978 and 1986–1987, and for *SR* for 1976–1977 and 1986–1987 found that not a single study showed participants to play any role other than research source, usually no report of informed consent, and neglect of debriefing, no report of gender of experimenter, and only two studies that showed data to be put to some socially constructive use, reliance primarily on undergraduate participants, and the continued use of the term *subject* by most authors conveying a hierarchical model (R. T. Walsh, 1989). Feminist psychologists have also been socialized by patriarchal institutions of higher education, necessitating a conscious process of change in the direction of democraticizing the research relationship and human-centered report writing.

Feminist Psychology

Feminist psychology emphasizes the importance of multiple methods and a greater reliance on qualitative methods. A debate is going on in feminism about the value of quantitative versus qualitative methods.

Feminist psychologists are having an impact on all areas of psychology. Feminist contributions to psychology include the recognition that psychology, like other sciences, is not value-free and that there are unacknowledged biases at all stages of scientific (including psychological) research. Although some feminists urge the abandonment of the experiment, others emphasize the importance of multiple methods, including the experiment, and a greater reliance on qualitative methods (Lott, 1991).

Even when qualitative methods are used, however, data may still be biased. For example, studies employing volunteer samples may be vulnerable to race and class bias. L. W. Cannon, Higgenbotham, and Leung (1991) found it more difficult to recruit Black women when they wanted a sample of 200 Black and White professionals, managers, and administrators in the Memphis, Tennessee, area. A greater reliance on personal contact and less reliance on occupational mailing lists and media solicitations were necessary in order to find Black women.

> Some social psychological and structural factors militated against Black women's participation. These factors were skepticism about the purpose of the research, worries about protection of anonymity, and structural obstacles such as less free time. (L. W. Cannon et al., 1991, p. 113)

It was necessary to inform Black women that the research team was biracial and to make sure that only Black women interviewed Black respondents and White researchers interviewed White participants.

Feminist research in psychology is a perspective rather than a methodology, the goal of which is the empowerment of women. Feminist research emphasizes the importance of the social context.

Feminist emphasis on the importance of social context has been at odds with psychology's tendency to focus on the isolated individual. Ignoring social context in research can contribute to a number of systematic biases in research.

> First, psychology focuses on the person as he or she exists at the moment. Such a focus leads the researcher away from the person's history or social circumstances. Second, the cultural context in which psychology is practiced (at least in the United States) is dominated by an individualistic philosophy. (Riger, 1992, p. 732)

Two outcomes of this approach are that certain social assumptions, such as male dominance, are not examined and are taken for granted, and an emphasis is placed on the individual's free choice because we are not aware of the social influences operating on the individual.

A greater emphasis on context, however, is appearing in psychology. An article on family psychology views the family and culture as contexts that both emphasize embeddedness of the individual (Szapocznik & Kurtines, 1993). In their work with Hispanic families, Szapocznik & Kurtines realized that what was also required was adjusting their thinking to understand families within a multicultural framework. America, like the world, is becoming increasingly culturally diverse, as peoples of different cultures are living at the interface between cultures and customs. In clinical psychology, feminist criticism of the mental health establishment has included sexist diagnoses, the misuse of medication, and sexual misconduct in therapy. Feminists also call attention to psychological problems arising from gender inequality and physical and sexual abuse of women. They have criticized the blatant sexism of psychoanalysis and other traditional models of therapy. Feminist therapy is not a method of therapy per se but an underlying perspective that recognizes that many of women's dissatisfactions are rooted in social injustice (Marecek & Hare-Mustin, 1991).

Feminism has influenced the progression of developmental psychology by leading to the understanding that many gender differences are shaped by differing socialization of males and females. It has led to a reconceptualization of theories to explain children's socialization. Understanding the role of fathers, daycare, and other socializing forces, for example, has led to a lessening of mother blame in the literature (P. T. Reid, 1991). My own field of social psychology has become increasingly reliant on the experimental method. In 1985, 78% of studies published in major social psychology journals were experiments conducted in laboratories (Reinharz, 1992). Carolyn Sherif (1979), in an influential chapter, "Bias in Psychology," pointed out that much of the research in psychology relies on the isolation of variables and the manipulation of independent variables, in order to seek lawfulness in the relationship of independent and dependent variables, which are statistically analyzed. This paradigm ignores much of what is important for understanding human behavior, including historical background or even sex of the researcher and the participant.

Can men be feminist researchers?

Men can be feminist researchers if they adhere to the goals of feminism; to change society to empower women. The primary value of feminism is as a set of questions that challenge the patriarchal assumptions in science and society, rather than as a basis for a unique method (Reinharz, 1992; Riger, 1992). In this process the scientist is no longer reified as the only expert, and an interactional conceptualization of the problem by researcher and participant needs to be developed. Not all research conducted by women or with female participants is feminist research.

Is psychology of women failing in the goal of empowerment of women? Women can be empowered either by the individual making changes in her life or by making changes in society.

Criticism by feminists of the field of psychology of women is that it is failing in the goals of feminist research. The reason is seen to be that psychology as a discipline focuses on the individual at a particular moment in time. Efforts are made by psychologists to change individuals rather than society, the result of which is to maintain the status quo in society (A. S. Kahn & Yoder, 1989). Psychologists seem to overlook the fact that changes in society can be a mechanism for changing behavior. On the other hand, feminists who claim that a focus on the individual leads to blaming the victim fail to look at the other side of the coin, which is that a focus on the individual also has a message of hope, that the individual can change her life at any point in time, to fight against the oppression of social forces. This fight may start alone, but she can also involve and organize others to join her. A. S. Kahn and Yoder (1989) feel that the goal of psychology of women to change society so that women are empowered, not only has not been met, but that it no longer even exists as a goal.

In summary, a psychology of women that assumes that women and men are naturally different (alpha bias) or that differences are caused by factors internal to individuals (i.e., biological or socialized) is necessarily supportive of the status quo and, hence, antithetical to a women's movement. In contrast, we believe that a psychology that assumes apparent gender differences are the result of differential social forces supports a women's movement by identifying targets for social change. (A. S. Kahn & Yoder, 1989, p. 428)

It also needs to be kept in mind that a gender difference is only an average group difference and any individual of either gender may have a behavior pattern more typical of the other gender.

Adopting a White, privileged, heterosexual, physically able, female as representative of all women is another pitfall that must be avoided in the rebuttal of androcentrism (Yoder & Kahn, 1993). Researchers must be watchful of limited inclusion and biased treatment of minority women. Many pitfalls also exist in the use of minority women as comparison groups who are then compared unfavorably with the normative female group. Studies designed to focus on women of a minority group alone are a way to avoid this trap. It is also important to focus on the structural factors impinging on minority women, such as lack of employment opportunities in inner cities.

Causality

Causality is a psychedelic mosaic—with biological, individual, and social forces interacting at every moment in time.

A trend in science away from reductionism is chaos theory, which is interdisciplinary and makes claims about the universality of complexity (Gleick, 1987). The illusion of deterministic predictability of Newtonian physics is no longer accepted in the "hard" sciences, nor should it be in psychology.

Concepts from chaos theory that are particularly relevant to psychology are nonlinear dynamics and self organization (Barton, 1994). Nonlinear dynamics refers to the way systems change, whether the changes being described are

the forces that act on the fertilized egg that lead to the development of a human infant or the forces acting within the family after that infant is born. Linear equations cannot describe the sudden jumps that occur resulting from the constellation of forces. Self organization is a process of instability that creates new neurological structures and behaviors.

Chaos theory is compatible with what feminists have been saying for a long time, that psychologists have reduced behavior to quantitative methods that distort the complexity of the behavior being studied. To leave out any of the interacting factors in studying behavior, whether those are biological or societal is to have an incomplete understanding of the context, and be less capable of bringing about changes to improve the lives of women. Causality is a psychedelic mosaic—with biological, individual and social forces interacting at every moment in time. Behavior is complex, and to underestimate that complexity is to impede change.

Psychology is beginning to understand the importance of a multilevel, integrative approach to the study of mental and behavioral phenomena that includes the reciprocal influences of neurochemical events and social events. For example, it has been discovered that testosterone levels promote sexual behavior in male primates, but also that the availability of sexually receptive females has been found to increase primates' testosterone levels (Cacioppo & Berntson, 1992).

Author's Framework

The author's framework for writing this book recognizes the similarities between women and men and the need for cooperation between women and men in solving the problems of society. Psychology of women must be inclusive of all women.

While this book does have the overall goal of empowerment of women, much of the research cited in it was not conducted based on feminist research principles. The following statements represent the author's frame of reference while writing the book.

Cathy

Many young women do not label themselves feminists because they think it means rejecting men. CATHY © Cathy Guisewite. Reprinted with permission of UNIVERSAL PRESS SYNDICATE. All rights reserved.

1. Men have been considered the norm and women "other," and often, in the literature, normal events in women's lives such as menstruation have been considered pathological.
2. The similarities between men and women are far greater than the differences.
3. Gender is socially and individually constructed (i.e., what is considered "natural" or appropriate behavior for men and women is based primarily on socially constructed theories about men and women and not on their biological capacities). Each woman also has unique experiences that shape her view of what it means to be a woman. What is considered natural for the behavior of women has varied from one historical period to another, from one culture to another, and, even within a particular time and place, from one group of women to another (i.e., African American slave women were considered strong while White women were considered delicate).
4. Behavior is a product of multiple causality that is bidirectional. Heredity and environment interact from the time of conception, influencing the behavioral outcome. Because individual differences in a particular characteristic may be partially inherited does not mean that gender differences in that characteristic are at all inherited.
5. Women and men are neither superior nor inferior to the other.
6. A psychology of women needs to encompass the experiences of women of color and of all social classes, as well as of White middle-class women who have been the focus of most of the research.
7. Women and men must work together to solve the problems of society. They must work in cooperation to eliminate violence against women and to improve structural supports in society for raising children, eliminating poverty and providing equality of opportunity for women and minorities.
8. The goal of feminist psychology is emancipation and empowerment. It attempts to understand gender in order to provide women with choice and autonomy and eliminate gender-based discriminatory barriers.

A feminist psychology further recognizes that categorization and dichotomous thinking about nature versus nurture, male versus female, homosexual versus heterosexual, Black versus White, disabled versus able bodied, mind versus body are nothing more than convenient mental categories that distort the essence of persons. Unfortunately, where they represent categories of persons, they have also become institutionalized as the basis for power and privilege, which translates into differential treatment in everything from access to a good education to medical care to police protection. This book attempts to obliterate dichotomies as much as possible, notwithstanding the research literature that has primarily been structured in terms of dichotomous thinking—at least where it even recognizes the "other."

REFLECTIONS

Do you consider yourself a feminist? I think it is important to understand the diversity of viewpoints within feminism. I have heard students say that they are not feminists because they do not hate men. Radical political lesbian feminists who want separatism from men are actually only a very small minority within feminism. It is the equating of radical feminism with feminism by the media that has led many women to shy away from calling themselves feminists.

On the first day of my Psychology of Women class last fall, I asked how many people in the class considered themselves feminists. Only two women raised their hands. By the end of the semester most of the class considered themselves feminists because they agreed with feminism's basic premise of the equality of men and women, and that they should be treated equally by the institutions of society—educational, political, health, justice, and business institutions. Although radical feminists may alienate many mainstream women from feminism, radical feminists have made valuable contributions to society, particularly by pointing out the exploitation of women in society through pornography, rape, and violence.

Feminist criticism of resesarch in psychology is contributing to a strengthening of the field by encouraging research on more diverse populations (gender, age, race, class), and the use of both subjective and quantifiable methods and by taking into account the historical and cultural context of the behavior. I am more optimistic than A. S. Kahn and Yoder (1989), and believe that the field of psychology of women is contributing to the empowerment of women.

Experiential Exercises

1. Attend a NOW meeting.
2. Ask five males and five females if they are feminists. How do they define feminism?
3. Read the sections in psychology journals that provide instructions for authors submitting articles for publication. Do the instructions indicate that blind review of the article will be conducted (that is the article will be submitted to reviewers without the author's name and institutional affiliation)?
4. Talk with Black, Hispanic, or Asian women about their experiences of race and gender discrimination.

KEY TERMS

African American Feminism   A movement seeking ways for men and women to work together to eliminate racism, class privilege and sexism.

Afrocentric Feminist Epistimology   Black feminist thought values common sense, personal experience, and the ethic of caring as central in assessing knowledge claims. Emic (subjective) approaches may reveal cultural diversity better than etic (quantitative) approaches.

Egalitarian or Liberal Feminism   Liberal feminism seeks equality between women and men. It is a reform movement that has as its focus a woman's full right to work and seeks ancillary services such as childcare centers, and contraception and abortion services which make it possible for women to work.

Emic Approaches   Objective, quantitative, controlled research methods.

Equal Pay Act of 1963   A law that requires equal pay for equal work.

Etic Approaches   Subjective, qualitative research approaches.

Feminist Empiricism   An epistemology that accepts the scientific method but tries to eliminate androcentric (male centered) bias in scientific research.

Feminist Epistemology   Feminism raises many issues about science, technology, and theories of knowledge (epistemology)—that science is not the impartial, value-free, disinterested discourse that conventional mythology holds it to be.

Feminist Postmodernism   A theory that questions the existence of a single truth or reality. Feminist postmodernism deconstructs the assumptions of the inferiority of women.

Feminist Research Methods   A perspective that supports use of a multiplicity of research methods, encourages transdisciplinary research, aims to create social change which empowers women, strives to represent cultural diversity, frequently involves an interactive relationship between the researcher and the people studied and takes account of the historical and cultural context in which the behavior is embedded.

Feminist Standpoint Theory   A theory that posits that a person's view of reality is based on their particular position in society (race, class, gender, etc.). A feminist standpoint is developed through intellectual and political struggles against inequality.

First Feminist Movement   The suffrage movement that began in 1848 and culminated with the passage of the Nineteenth Amendment to the Constitution, which gave women the right to vote.

Lesbian Epistemology   Radical lesbian feminists want to make feminist theory and the construct of woman inclusive of all women, including lesbians, but do not want to accommodate to men and male institutions. Nonradical lesbian feminists seek an epistemology based on a lesbian and gay male reality.

Marxist Feminist Radicalism   Sees the oppression of women arising out of a class society based on private property.

Political Lesbianism   Identification with women including the choice of lesbianism and withdrawal from heterosexual love.

Poststructuralism   A movement (also known as social constructivism within psychology) within postmodernism that says that science does not mirror reality, but that "facts" produced by scientific research are the version of realty of those with power.

Radical Feminism   A revolutionary movement with three directions: radical feminism, which sees the oppression of women as universal because of patriarchy (a system that seeks to sustain and recreate male power and female subordination); political lesbianism, which argues that lesbianism is a necessary choice in order to resist male supremacy; and

Marxist feminism, which sees women's oppression as arising out of capitalist society.

Second Wave of Feminism   A movement ushered in with the Equal Pay Act of 1963 and Betty Friedan's book *The Feminine Mystique* (1963). The goal of the movement was to combat discrimination against women in all areas (social, political, economic, and psychological).

Socialist Feminism   A movement that contends that liberal feminists are fighting for a world in which women will learn to pursue self interest in a capitalist system and that Marxist feminism has not paid enough attention to women's issues. This movement sees the source of women's oppression as in both patriarchy and capitalism.

Title VII of the Civil Rights Act of 1964   A law that requires equality for women in all aspects of employment including hiring and promotion.

SUGGESTED READINGS

hooks, b. (1990). *Yearning: Race, gender, and cultural politics.* Boston: South End Press. This is a powerful book of essays about Black feminism, gender relations, and the politics of race.

Reinharz, S. (1992). *Feminist methods in social research.* New York: Oxford University Press. This is the first text on feminist research methods. It is a readable overview of the feminist approach to social science research.

Riger, S. (1992). Epistemological debates, feminist voices: Science, social values, and the study of women. *American Psychologist, 47,* 730–740. Riger's article provides an excellent summary of feminist criticisms of psychological research that she says reflect three epistemological positions: feminist empiricism, feminist standpoint epistemologies, and postmodern feminism.

CHAPTER 2

Biology and Gender

Nature and nurture are like Siamese twins who
share a common heart and nervous system.
Diane F. Halpern, 1992

The biological research on gender differences is
highly touted in the media, before replication.
When a gene is discovered or thought to be discovered, it is treated as if biology acted as the
sole determinant rather than as a variable in interaction with psychosocial factors. The biological basis of gender development is a political
question because of the interpretations that have
been placed on biological causes. The most outrageous of these was that biology justifies the
inequality of the sexes (Lambert, 1987). Historically, scientists tried to prove that biological
differences in the brain and nervous system, resulted in the intellectual inferiority of women (as
well as minorities) (Fausto-Sterling, 1992; Gould,
1981).

HEREDITY AND ENVIRONMENT

*Because a characteristic is partially inherited
does not mean it is fixed. Heredity and environment interact from conception to death.*

The reason that the study of gender differences is such a "hot" topic is that there are political implications of taking a hereditary versus an
environmental position. Ideologically, a hereditary position has been considered a conservative
position which serves to reinforce and explain
the status quo, and the environmental explanation a liberal position. This reasoning, however,
is due to a misunderstanding of the nature of
heredity and environment. Since heredity and
environment are constantly interacting, the environment can modify heredity from the time of
conception to death. For example, the woman
who drinks during pregnancy is environmentally
lowering her child's hereditary potential for average or perhaps even gifted intelligence. On the
other hand, environment can correct a hereditary
predisposition for retardation and microcephaly
(small head), such as in the case of phenylpyruvic
amentia (PKU). PKU, which is caused by a recessive gene, is an enzyme deficiency that can be detected by a simple urine test at birth, and if the
child follows a prescribed diet will develop normal intelligence and growth (Schaefer et al.
1994). Without the prescribed diet, the child will
become retarded. Hence, the environment in the
first case can lower a hereditary predisposition
for normal intelligence, and in the second case
can correct a hereditary predisposition for retardation.

The heredity of behavioral characteristics operates within a reaction range. For example, someone with the same hereditary potential may develop an IQ of 110 on the Stanford Binet, while her identical twin sister who was adopted at birth into a much more stimulating environment might develop an IQ of 125 as measured by the same test. There are a range of behavioral characteristics that can emerge from the same hereditary potential depending on the environmental context.

Genotypes and Phenotypes

Genotypes and phenotypes for a given characteristic may differ from one another.

A **genotype** is the hereditary information transmitted by the genes on chromosomes. A **phenotype** is the observable characteristic in question as manifest in the individual at a given time. A phenotype results from the interaction of the gene(s) with the environment. The genotype and phenotype for a given characteristic are not necessarily the same. For example, my phenotype for eye color is brown. My genotype includes both brown and blue genes, as well as green and gray. I know this because I have three children, only one of whom has brown eyes. The other two children have blue/gray eyes. Their father has blue eyes, but since brown is dominant over blue, in order for two of our children not to have brown eyes, my genotype must include blue/gray genes. Environmental interventions sometimes influence eye color. Some people wear contact lenses that change the apparent color of their eyes. Human behavior is much more complex than eye color, with phenotypes always reflecting both environmental and biological characteristics.

Environmental Selection

Since individuals select their environments, heredity contributes to what have been considered environmental influences. Arduous practice contributes to what have been considered hereditary influences.

Current theorizing on heredity and environment also points out that individuals may select their environment, when possible, to be favorable to their hereditary dispositions, so that environmental determinants may be reflective of hereditary predispositions as well. "Thus, how parents bring up their children is going to be affected by their own qualities as individuals, and those qualities are going to include a substantial genetic component." (Rutter, Silberg & Simonoff, 1993, pp. 442–43). Therefore, some of the variance traditionally attibuted to the environment is, in fact, due to heredity.

On the other hand, there has been a traditional view that individuals displaying exceptional performance in a field possess an innate talent. This is not consistent with the research evidence. Differences between expert and less-accomplished performers in a variety of fields, such as athletic and musical performance, reflect acquired knowledge and skills that are the result of arduous practice. Physiological adaptations such as lung capacity are affected by training (Ericsson & Charness, 1994). Anatomical changes such as muscular development can also result from intense physical activity. The point of this is that heredity contributes to what have been considered environmental influences, and the environment contributes to what have been considered hereditary influences.

Rearrangement of Genes

Genes may rearrange themselves on chromosomes creating new effects on development.

Genes are also more fluid and mobile than is popularly realized, and are subject to rapid rearrangement. Some genes may move to other locations, creating new effects on development (Gould, 1987). The traditional idea of one-way flow of information from the genetic code has to also be revised.

A substance called "reverse transcriptase" can read RNA into DNA and insert new material into genetic programs by running backward along the supposedly one-way street of the central dogma. A class of objects, called retroviruses (and including the cause of AIDS), used this backward path, placing new material into chromosomal DNA from the outside. (Gould, 1987, p. 159)

Much of the research on this new revolution in genetics is due to the work of Barbara McClintock, who in the 1950s discovered the transposable elements in maize and was for many years ignored by the scientific community, finally winning the Nobel prize when in her eighties (Gould, 1987).

Hereditability of Individual and Group Differences

The degree of variance in a behavioral characteristic due to heredity and due to environment varies from one individual to another.

Another caution light to heed in our discussion of gender differences is that hereditability of individual differences for behavioral characteristics does not provide evidence for hereditability of group differences for those characteristics. For example, one of the major changes that occurred in developmental psychology in the 1980s was the accumulating evidence and belief among scientists and educators that individual differences in IQ scores are partially inherited (Plomin, 1989). Analysis of adoption studies now clearly shows that both heredity and environment contribute to the development of intelligence (Turkheimer, 1991).

Disagreement arises, however, over what proportion of the variance in intelligence is due to heredity and what proportion is due to environment. I do not think that this is an answerable question, however, because the amount of variance due to heredity and environment differs from one individual to another. For example, take the case of the person with untreated PKU discussed in the beginning of this chapter. If not treated by proper diet, most of the variance in intelligence of a person born with that enzyme deficiency will be due to heredity. If detected at birth and treated by proper diet, most of the variance in that person's intelligence will be due to

environment. In the case of the baby born with alcohol fetal syndrome, a higher proportion of his/her intelligence will be due to environment because the environment in that case severely restricted the infant's genetic potential for normal intelligence.

There is no evidence of hereditability of group differences such as gender or race differences in intelligence. "Measures obtained on one population (e.g., race) cannot be generalized to other populations or to differences between populations. Such differences are phenotypic differences" (Kimble, 1993, p. 21). Anne Anastasi, author of the classic book, *Differential Psychology* (1958), has been saying for many years that psychologists are asking the wrong question about heredity and environment. She still found it necessary to make the same point in the 1980s:

Rather than asking which differences are hereditary and which acquired, or how much of the variance is attributable to heredity and how much to environment, it would be better to investigate the modus operandi of hereditary and environmental influences in the development of individual differences. What is the chain of events whereby particular hereditary and environmental factors interact to produce the behavioral differences observed at any given stage of individual development? (Anastasi, 1985, p. 19)

Bronfenbrenner and Ceci (1994) have formulated the bioecological model as a response to Anastasi's challenge. Their model allows for non-additive synergistic effects in the heredity–environment interaction. They propose that genotypes are transformed into phenotypes by proximal processes, which are forms of interaction in the immediate environment such as mother–child play behavior. Proximal processes, when highly favorable, serve to maximize genetic potential. The proximal processes take place in a broader context of social class, race, ethnicity, subculture, or culture. Measures of hereditability provide information only about actualized genetic potential, with the amount of unactualized potential remaining unknown. In other words, we have no idea what the upper limit of an individual's genetic potential is, for example for intelligence, because no one ever grows up and lives his/her life in an ideal environment and reaches their full potential. The implications of Bronfenbrenner and Ceci's model is that the greater the environmental enrichment the more genetic potential can be realized.

Genetics of Sex Determination

The sex of the child Is determined by an X chromosome from the mother's egg and an X or Y from the father's sperm (XX is a girl; XY is a boy). The X chromosome has over 300 genes, whereas the Y only causes the development of testes in the embryo.

Every cell in the normal human body (except for the egg or sperm cells which have 23 single chromosomes) contains the identical 23 pairs of chromosomes, a total of 46 chromosomes. One of each of a pair of chromosomes is inherited from the father and the other member of the pair is inherited from the mother. Each chromosome carries a large number of genes, depending on its size, up to thousands of genes. Twenty-two of these chromosome pairs are called autosomes, which interact with the environment to determine a wide variety of the individual's characteristics. The twenty-third set of chromosomes are the **sex chromosomes,** XX in females and XY in males. The baby will be a boy if it receives an X from the mother's egg and a Y from the father's sperm (XY), and it will be a girl if it receives an X from the mother's egg and another X from the father's sperm (XX). More than 300 genes are located on the X chromosome, whereas the Y chromosome appears to be specialized primarily for the development of the male sex organs in the embryo (Goodfellow, Davies, & Ropers, 1985). If an abnormal recessive gene appears on one of the X chromosomes, females usually have a dominant normal gene to override the effects of the recessive gene (Otten, 1985). Since the male has only one X chromosome, he will express that X chromosome whether it is dominant or recessive.

Sex-linked genes are those that are carried on the X or Y chromosome. Among the disabilities that are linked to the recessive X chromosome, and which are therefore much more prevalent in males, are hemophilia, color blindness, muscular dystrophy, and several forms of mental retardation. For example, a father who is color blind cannot pass the gene for color blindness on to his son because the gene is on the X chromosome and the father only passes on a Y chromosome to a son. The father can, however, contribute the gene for color blindness to his daughter because it is on the X chromosome and she receives one X from her father. She would not be color blind, however, unless she also received a gene for color blindness on the X chromosome that is transmitted to her by her mother because the gene for color blindness is recessive.

Certain genes are sex limited. They are located on autosomes. They are frequently dependent on the level of hormones in the bloodstream for the gene to be turned on. For example, male pattern baldness is genetic, but requires a certain level of the male sex hormones in order to appear (Hoyenga & Hoyenga, 1993).

SEX HORMONES IN HUMANS

Endocrine Glands

The endocrine glands regulating sexual and reproductive functions are the hypothalamus, pituitary, ovaries in females and testes in males, and the adrenal gland.

In order to have a meaningful discussion about sex differentiation, it is first necessary to describe the major **endocrine glands.** Endocrine glands produce chemical substances called hormones, which are secreted directly into the bloodstream. Certain tissues in the body are target tissues for specific hormones. Before that hormone can exert its effect, however, it must bind with a receptor molecule on or inside the cell. Cause and effect sequences are not linear; rather, depend on the interaction of the hormones of the endocrine system with environmental stressors that also influence hormone secretion (Becker & Breedlove, 1992).

The hypothalamus, a small area at the base of the brain just above the roof of the mouth, is the regulatory center for hormones released by the pituitary. The master gland is the pituitary, which is a two-lobed structure adjacent to the hypothalamus. The anterior lobe of the pituitary secretes six hormones: adrenocorticotropin (ACTH), **follicle-stimulating hormone (FSH), luteinizing hormone (LH),** thyroid stimulating hormone (TSH), prolactin, and growth hormone (GH). ACTH acts primarily on the adrenal cortex (which is the outer layer of the adrenal gland, which is located just above the kidneys), FSH and LH act on the ovaries and testes, TSH acts on the thyroid, prolactin acts on mammary glands in the breasts, and GH acts on bone cells (Becker & Breedlove, 1992).

Sex Hormones

Sex hormones are androgens in males and estrogens and progesterone in females.

Sex hormones are secreted by the **gonads, ovaries,** in the female and **testes** in the male, and by the adrenal glands. **Androgens** are the general name for male sex hormones, which include several types of testosterone. Estrogen refers to a class of hormones secreted by the ovaries, which also secrete progesterone. Most of a female's androgens and a male's estrogens are secreted by the adrenal cortex, although the ovaries secrete small amounts of androgens and the testes small amounts of estrogens (Becker & Breedlove, 1992). Androgens can also be converted to estrogen in the woman's body. "After menopause, the conversion of androgen to estrogen in adipose (fat) tissue may offer some protection against the serious consequences of estrogen loss such as osteoporosis (loss of bone tissue). Research has suggested that obese women are less likely than lean women to develop osteoporosis after menopause" ("A preview/review," 1992, p. 8).

Hormonal Effects on Sexual Differentiation

The embryonic testes secrete testosterone which promotes development of male reproductive organs. In the absence of testosterone, female reproductive organs develop.

In the first several weeks of embryonic development, the tissues of the two sexes do not differ. A gene on the Y chromosome within the **zygote** (fertilized egg) transforms the gonadal tissue into a testis. In the absence of the Y chromosome, ovaries will develop. Once the ovaries or testes develop, somatic and central nervous system differentiation is controlled by hormones secreted by the gonads. **Testosterone,** secreted by the male embryo testes, promotes development of the Wolffian duct system that is the precursor of the male reproductive system. The testes also secrete, during a brief period, antimullerian hormone, which prevents development of the Mullerian structures that differentiate into the uterus, fallopian tubes and ovaries (Yahr, 1988). Whether or not estrogen is necessary to early female development is still being debated (Micevych & Ulibarri, 1992). The embryo differentiates as female when exposed to lower levels of testosterone during this critical period (Finegan, Bartleman, & Wong, 1989; Jost & Magre, 1984).

Significant sex differences have been observed in levels of testosterone in amniotic fluid (the fluid in the sac surrounding the embryo) obtained by amniocentesis (insertion of a needle into the amniotic sac) from 32 male and 33 female fetuses at 14 and 20 weeks from the date of the last menstrual period (Finegan, Bartleman, & Wong, 1989). It is interesting, however, that 25% of the males and 9% of the females had levels of testosterone in the overlap range. This means that fetal chromosomal sex does not entirely determine fetal hormone levels. Other research has found that at birth there are no significant sex differences in testosterone levels. The clitoris and the penis, so also the clitoral hood and the penile foreskin, develop from a single set of precursors. In contrast to the Biblical myth of Eve developing from Adam's rib, the female is the biological norm and testosterone must be added at a critical period to create man (Money, 1988).

Environmental Effects on Sexual Differentiation

Prenatal environmental factors also influence sexual differentiation.

When discussing sexual differentiation in humans, for whom chromosomes determine sex, the sexual phenotype depends both on the genotype and on factors in the environment. "The environmental factors that induce sexual differentiation are usually chemicals such as hormones, that originate elsewhere in the organism, but they can arise externally" (Yahr, 1988, p. 197). A woman may be given hormones during pregnancy, for example, to prevent miscarriage that may influence the external genitalia of her offspring as well as its later behavior.

Hormone Levels

Male and female hormones are secreted in both sexes. Estrogen and progesterone levels in males overlap with female levels at the lower end of the menstrual cycle. Testosterone levels in males are 10 to 20 times greater than in females.

Contrary to our dichotomous thinking about the sexes, male and female hormones are secreted by both sexes, but in different concentrations. Hormone levels in males and females overlap for some hormones as measured in picograms per milliliter in blood (Hoyenga & Hoyenga, 1993). Females' estrogen levels are between 35 and 50 picograms per milliliter of blood, or somewhere between 193 and 400, depending on the stage of the menstrual cycle. The male range for estrogen is between 19 and 56, which overlaps with the lower female range. Progesterone also varies with the menstrual cycle, and ranges from 200 to 500 during the early phases of the menstrual cycle, or may go as high as 14,000 after ovulation. Male progesterone falls within the 200–500 range, which is the same as for

females in the lower end of the cycle. After menopause, the estrogen level in females is only from 10 to 34 picograms per milliliter of blood, with progesterone about 88.

After puberty, there is no overlap in male and female levels of the male hormone testosterone. At their lowest level during the menstrual cycle, testosterone levels in the female range from 200 to 400 picograms per milliliter of blood, and at the highest levels from 285 to 440. In males the range of testosterone is from 5,140 to 6,460 picograms per milliliter of blood.

Hormones, Body Structure, and Environment

Testosterone at puberty increases male musculature and female fat accumulation on the breasts and hips. People respond differently to people of different body types.

The surge of testosterone at puberty stimulates the growth of large muscle in males; estrogen increases the accumulation of fat on the breasts and hips in females. The average adult male is 40% muscle and 15% fat, whereas the average female is 23% muscle and 25% fat (Kenrick, 1987). Differences in male and female behavior are in part due to the differential response of the people in the environment to different body types.

Western society has also placed much higher value on male muscular development and athletic prowess than on that of females. Females have typically been given less physical training than males. Highly trained female athletes have increasingly approached records set by males. Gertrude Ederly astounded the world by becoming the first woman to swim the English Channel in 1926—and by breaking the men's record by two hours! Between 1964 and 1984, women marathon runners decreased their running times by more than an hour-and-a-half, while men's times decreased by only a few minutes during that period. There have been similar trends in shorter running events as well (Fausto-Sterling, 1985). Obviously, the variations among men in athletic prowess is far greater than the difference between the sexes.

HORMONAL INFLUENCES ON ANIMAL BRAINS

Prenatal Hormones

Prenatal hormones organize mammalian brains into male and female patterns which in turn organize behavior. After an organizational period, hormones presumably do not cause changes in the structure of the brain or central nervous system.

There appear to be sensitive periods for growth and development during certain prenatal, immediate postnatal, and pubertal times when hormones may have greater effects on the individual's later adult behavior (Corbier, 1985; Epple, Alveario, & St. Andre, 1987; Brand & Slob, 1988; De Jonge, Muntjewerff, Louwerce, & van de Poll, 1988). Prenatal hormone theory posits that prenatal hormones not only trigger the development of male and female reproductive organs during a critical prenatal period; "they also irreversibly organize mammalian brains into a male or female pattern, and these hormonally organized brains, in turn, organize mammalian hormone function and mammalian behavior into a male or female pattern" (Bem, 1993, p. 23).

Most of the research on hormonal effects on brain organization has been conducted on animals rather than humans (for obvious reasons) and has clearly demonstrated the occurrence of differential brain organization by sex. For example, rhesus monkeys display behavioral sex differences as young juveniles, even when they have been castrated neonatally (right after birth) or during infancy and no longer have gonads (Goldfoot & Wallen, 1978). They still display mounting behavior just as frequently as intact males. On the other hand, when the testes are removed during fetal development, severe deficiencies in adult male behavior are observed. In one study, a male baboon castrated in utero showed female-like behavior, and was unable to display male sexual

behavior in response to later testosterone treatment (Bielert, 1984). After the organizational period, the influence of hormones presumably does not cause structural changes in the brain or nervous system. For primates, the sensitive period for organizational effects in the central nervous system is the prenatal period.

A second mode by which hormones affect behavior is activational (i.e., transient). These would be hormonal effects which would be reversible when the hormonal level changes, for example, changes in sense of smell during different phases of the menstrual cycle. Organizational and activational effects are no longer viewed as a dichotomy, but rather as a continuum (Hoyenga & Hoyenga, 1993).

Female monkey fetuses exposed to androgens early in prenatal development showed behavior more similar to normal male monkeys than female monkeys exposed to androgens late in prenatal development.

Can behavioral masculinization be independent of genital masculinization? To answer this question, genetic female monkey fetuses were exposed to testosterone proprionate either early or late in gestation (Goy, Bercovitch, & McBrair, 1988). The early and late androgenized females (EAFs and LAFs, respectively) were raised with normal males and females, whose behavior served as criteria for evaluating the degree of behavioral masculinization. The EAFs showed behavior more similar to normal male monkeys than the behavior of LAFs. The EAFs showed more mother-mounting, more peer-mounting, and less mother-grooming than did normal females, but they did not differ from normal females in the amount of rough play. Unlike males, however, they did not manifest a preference for initiating play with male partners. They also showed a statistically significant delay in puberty. Mothers of EAFs inspected their offspring's genitalia as often as did mothers of normal male monkeys. LAFs, like females, groomed their mothers, did not mount their mothers, and did not initiate play with male peers. Unlike females, however, they did show elevated rough play and mounting with females. Their mothers did not inspect their genitalia as often as mothers of males did. "Rather than assessing masculine development on the basis of isolated behaviors, this study has demonstrated that masculinity is a constellation of activities whose expression depends upon age, social environment, and neurobiological development in utero" (Goy et al., 1988, p. 569).

Postnatal Hormones

In some species such as marmosets, the hormonal effects on the brain occur during the immediate postnatal period rather than prenatally.

In some species, such as marmosets, the hormonal effects on the brain may occur during the immediate postnatal period rather than prenatally. Activation of masculine copulatory behavior was achieved by testosterone propionate (TP) replacement in male marmosets castrated in infancy (days 1–7) (Dixson, 1993). The castrated males showed high levels of aggression with normal female marmosets and evoked aggression from them and displayed low levels of aggression with intact males. The castrates behaved in a socially feminine manner (normal adult females engage in aggression with other females, whereas aggression is infrequent between females and intact adult males). Testosterone treatment was able to reverse these aggressive patterns, indicating postnatal neural changes in response to testosterone replacement.

Hormones and Aggression

Animals castrated as adults continue to show aggressive behavior. In species of mammals that are seasonal breeders, there is a correlation between hormone levels and the frequency and intensity of fighting behavior. Testosterone appears to increase aggression in male vertebrates, but learning and experience modify aggressive responses.

When males are castrated as adults, they continue to show intense aggression toward strange male animals of their own species (Epple, 1978).

It has long been known that domestic animals castrated before puberty are more docile (Archer, 1988). In species of mammals that are seasonal breeders, there is a correlation between their changing hormones and the frequency and intensity of fighting behavior. For example, in red deer who breed in the autumn, testosterone levels in the stag are at their peak in the autumn, as is antler growth and aggressive behavior. Animals castrated in late summer showed less fighting behavior. The loss of the deer's hard antlers as a result of the castration could also account for the decrease in fighting (Monaghan & Glickman, 1992).

Aggressive encounters, in turn, have been found to alter testosterone levels in male monkeys. Within 24 hours after an attack and defeat, testosterone levels of defeated males were only 10–15% of baseline.

The influence of testosterone and other androgens on aggression in male vertebrates has been studied extensively (Brain, 1977, 1979, 1981a). In general, androgens increase aggressiveness, although this may be overridden by habit or experience, and the precise influence varies widely between different species . . . and the sexes (Archer, 1976a; Floody, 1983). (Archer, 1988, p. 136)

Social context also plays an important role in modifying the effect of testosterone on aggression. Although cynomolgus monkeys who received injections of testosterone showed a significant increase in aggression, the incidence of aggression was much greater in monkeys who were high in the dominence hierarchy as compared to those who were low in the dominance hierarchy (Rejeski, Brubaker, Herb, Kaplan, & Koritnik, 1988). Therefore, although testosterone appears to increase aggression in male vertebrates, there is no direct relationship between testosterone levels and aggression because learning and experience and the social context can modify aggressive responses.

There is an inverse relationship between aggression and the central nervous system transmitter serotonin.

Evidence is accumulating that there is an inverse relationship between aggression and the central neurotransmitter serotonin. In animal research, reduction of serotonin levels is associated with aggression (Bonson & Winter, 1992). In a series of experiments, TP caused an increase in dominant behavior in male rats. Subsequently, the administration of the serotonergic antagonist (block) quipazine reversed the dominance in rats given TP as well as in naturally dominant rats. "These results indicate that androgen-induced aggression may involve a complex alteration in serotonergic neurotransmission" (Bonson & Winter, 1992, p. 809).

The research findings for animal data are much more clear-cut than they are for humans. However, animal data cannot be directly generalized to humans. The human studies that have been done lack experimental rigor because humans cannot be assigned randomly to conditions in which their pre- and postnatal hormone levels are manipulated. Although we have extensive research supporting prenatal effects of hormones on organizing the brains of animals, we do not have such conclusive data on humans.

HORMONES AND HUMAN BEHAVIOR

Sex Hormones and Aggression

Criminals who have committed violent crimes have higher testosterone levels than other criminals. Socioeconomic level mediates the relationship between testosterone levels and aggression.

A number of studies of criminal and delinquent populations have found higher levels of testosterone in those criminals who have committed violent crimes (Dabbs, Frady, Carr, & Besch, 1987; Dabbs, Ruback, Frady, Hopper, & Sgoutas, 1988). Two hypotheses have been proposed to explain the relation between testosterone and antisocial behavior. One is that higher levels of testosterone cause antisocial behavior. The other is that high testosterone levels are associated with a constellation of dominance, com-

petitiveness, and sensation seeking that can lead to either antisocial or prosocial behavior, depending on the individual's resources and background. Analysis of archival data from a study of 4,462 male U.S. military veterans (mean age of 37) found a significant relationship between high testosterone levels and antisocial behavior.

> Individuals higher in testosterone more often reported having trouble with parents, teachers, and classmates; being assaultive toward other adults; going AWOL in the military; and using hard drugs, marijuana, and alcohol. They also reported having more sexual partners. The overall picture is one of delinquency, substance abuse, and a general tendency toward excessive behavior. (Dabbs & Morris, 1990, p. 209)

Socioeconomic level (as measured by both household income and education) was a moderating variable. Except for marijuana use, the other behaviors were only related to testosterone levels in low-socioeconomic men. Testosterone levels also were lower in men of high socioeconomic level. Two hypotheses can be put forth to explain these results. One is that environmental factors, such as higher levels of education, can modify the effects of testosterone on aggressive behavior. The other hypothesis is that males who have high levels of testosterone are less likely to continue their education to college and beyond. There was no evidence in this research, however, of high testosterone levels leading to prosocial behavior; future research needs to further test that possibility.

Clinical treatment with antiandrogens of men convicted of violent sexual crimes show significantly lower recidivism than in those individuals who did not receive drug treatment. The men given the drug also reported fewer sexually deviant, aggressive fantasies. "Researchers have concluded that the antiandrogens act to reduce an individual's motivation to engage in deviant behaviors, thus allowing for the adaptation of socially acceptable alternatives" (Monaghan & Glickman, 1992, p. 283).

It has been hypothesized that aggression induced by androgens could be mediated by the serotoninergic system in humans as well as animals. Serotonin is one of the chemical transmitters that is necessary for communication between neurons in the brain. In humans, reduced levels of a peripheral serotoninergic marker in blood was found to significantly differentiate suicide attempters and aggressive patients from healthy controls (Marazziti et al., 1993). In addition, suicide attempters had significantly lower levels of the serotoninergic marker than did aggressive patients. This may be partly a consequence of the complexity of the nervous system and the implication of serotonin in a broad range of behavioral disorders, including depression (B. L. Jacobs, 1994).

Sex Hormones and Cognitive Functioning

Curvilinear relationships have been found between performance on spatial tasks and estradiol and testosterone levels in males and females.

Nyborg (1982, 1988, 1990) has developed a theory called "The General Trait Covariance—Androgen/Estrogen (GTC-A/E) Balance Model," which is based on the assumption that there is a negative correlation between spatial ability and verbal ability when general intelligence is statistically controlled for, and that a range of hormones is optimal for spatial abilities. According to Nyborg, estradiol, a hormone secreted by the ovaries, is the critical hormone for spatial ability. The brain also converts androgens, a process called "aromatization" to other hormonal forms for use by the brain, one of which is estradiol.

When Turner's syndrome women, who have very poor spatial and mathematical skills, are treated with cyclic estrogen/gestagen for a period of one year they show large increases in mathematical and spatial performance, bringing them to a level equal to that of their age matched sisters (Nyborg, 1984). According to Nyborg's theory the optimal range of estradiol is a midrange, and most men do not have enough while most women have too much estradiol for optimal spatial ability. "According to this model, normal fe-

males (E–H) typically overshoot the range of estradiol values for the full expression of spatial ability at puberty. This explains the common female teenage regression in spatial ability and mathematical achievement (Nyborg, 1983)" (Nyborg, 1988, p. 207). Nyborg's argument is reductionist in that it fails to take into account that during the teenage years, many sociocultural factors are impacting on females, which influence them to opt out of math classes and not show skill in mechanical fields.

Several studies have reported a curvilinear relationship between testosterone levels and cognitive function in humans. Men with higher testosterone levels display relatively poorer performance on spatial tasks such as the Minnesota Paper Form Board Test (MPFB) (Shute, Pellegrino, Hubert, & Reynolds, 1983) and paper folding (Gouchie & Kimura, 1991) whereas the reverse is true for females (i.e., higher levels of testosterone are associated with better spatial performance). Participants in the latter study were divided into high and low free testosterone groups as measured in saliva. Gouchie & Kimura (1991) suggest an optimal level of testosterone for maximal spatial ability, perhaps falling somewhere in the low male range. There was no correlation with testosterone for either males or females for perceptual speed tasks, the tongue twister, or vocabulary tests, tasks at which men are not usually better than women. On mathematical reasoning, there was a trend for low-testosterone men to test higher, although not significantly so as compared with high-testosterone men. No relation was found between testosterone and mathematical reasoning in women.

Contrary to the curvilinear findings already cited, other research on men finds a significant positive correlation between androgen levels with measures of spatial ability and field independence-dependence and a negative correlation with measures of verbal production.

Blood and saliva samples were obtained from 117 men between the ages of 20 and 30, after which radioimmunoassay was used to determine the concentrations of the participants' androgens (K. Christiansen & Knussmann, 1987). The men were also administered standardized tests of verbal and spatial abilities that were repeated with a parallel form on a separate occasion. The sex hormones were also obtained on both occasions. The results show a significant positive correlation between androgen levels and measures of spatial ability and field dependence–independence, and a significant negative correlation with measures of verbal production.

According to the Geschwind-Behan-Galaburda model of cerebral lateralization, high levels of prenatal testosterone slows left hemisphere growth and allows right hemisphere dominance. Other consequences include language disturbances, immune system disorders and neural crest disorders.

An influential theory, the Geschwind-Behan-Galaburda (GBG) model of cerebral lateralization postulates that the critical time period for the influence of testosterone on cognitive abilities is during prenatal development (Geschwind & Behan, 1982; Geschwind & Galaburda, 1987). According to GBG theory, high levels of prenatal testosterone (which would be more likely in males), slow the growth of the left hemisphere, allowing the right hemisphere dominance. GBG is a complex and wide ranging theory which says that other organs of the developing fetus such as the thymus gland (which regulates the immune system) are also affected by high levels of testosterone. The predicted consequences of high levels of prenatal testosterone fall into five categories: (1) anomalous dominance (left-handedness or ambiguous handedness); (2) greater development of right hemisphere cognitive abilities especially those involving spatial ability, music, and mathematics; (3) deficits in left hemisphere abilities such as language disturbances (i.e., dyslexia); (4) disorders of the immune system such as allergies, arthritis and thyroiditis; and (5) neural crest disorders (i.e., thyroid, neural, thymus and cardiac abnormalities). Further, GBG theory states that these neuropsychological and

biological phenomena are intercorrelated. So, our prototype individual exposed to high levels of testosterone in utero would be male, left-handed, have high levels of mathematical, visual spatial and musical ability, do poorly in language and perhaps be dyslexic or a stutterer, suffer from allergies, and have abnormal facial development such as cleft palate.

Bryden, McManus, and Bulman-Fleming (1994) concluded that the GBG model is not well supported by the scientific evidence, after an extensive review of the literature on intercorrelations among the variables relevant to the model. A meta-analysis of the relation between handedness and immune disorders found only a slight overall relationship. Some immune disorders (allergies, asthma, and ulcerative colitis and Crohn's disease) were related to a high incidence of left-handedness and two (arthritis and myasthenia gravis) were related to a lower incidence of left-handedness. There is an increased incidence of immune disorders in those with developmental language difficulties. "Although handedness and language lateralization are at least moderately correlated, the evidence that the two are also correlated with the lateralization of spatial function is weak" (Bryden et al., 1994, p. 155). There is almost no empirical support for the GBG model in relation to neural crest disorders.

Research on the influence of hormones on cognitive abilities is in its infancy. Sex hormones do appear to play some role in cognitive abilities. Research, however, does not clearly support any one theory. There is probably a basic hormonal level required for normal visual spatial abilities. Learning and environment are nevertheless more important determinants of spatial ability given the requisite hormonal substrate. Just as a certain minimum level of vitamins are necessary for normal body function, a certain level of hormones are probably necessary for normal cognitive functioning.

Sex Hormones and Personality

Feminine sex-typed women have the lowest concentrations of testosterone, with undifferentiated women having the highest concentrations. Female personality is sensitive to small increments in testosterone at puberty.

Greater precision in measuring hormones during the 1970s made possible the study of hormones and human behavior. Attention has primarily focused on sex hormones and sexual and aggressive behavior, although research has also tentatively found relationships between sex hormones and personality.

A number of research studies have found that testosterone levels correlate with variations in normal personality functioning as measured by psychological tests. Among a sample of 84 female college students, mean testosterone concentration scores (as measured in saliva) were higher for females who were undifferentiated (on Bem's and Baucom's sex role scales) than they were for either the masculine-sex-typed or feminine-sex-typed women (Baucom, Besch, & Callahan, 1985). Feminine-sex-typed women had the lowest concentrations of testosterone of any of the groups of women. "Adjectival correlates indicated that females with higher testosterone concentrations perceive themselves as self-directed, action-oriented, resourceful individuals; women with lower testosterone concentration view themselves as conventional, socialized individuals, possessing a caring attitude coupled with an anxious dejected mood" (Baucom et al., 1985, p. 1218).

Other personality factors, as measured by a standardized scale, the Adjective Check List Scales, were found to correlate with blood levels of testosterone for both female and male adolescents in grades 8, 9, and 10 (Udry & Talbert, 1988). The common list of adjectives associated with higher testosterone for both girls and boys were: cynical, dominant, original, outgoing, self-centered, sensitive, sexy, understanding, enterprising and pleasant. Although female testosterone values have a much lower mean, the increases in female testosterone levels from prepuberty to adult levels have about the same effect on the personality dimension as the much greater increase in male testosterone during the same period, because of a much greater sensitivity of female personality to testosterone. "The net ef-

fect, given the typical increases in T experienced by each sex, is that T should not increase sex differences in personality at puberty, contrary to our first expectations" (Udry & Talbert, 1988, p. 294). Differences in the adjectives related to testosterone concentrations in this study and that of Baucom et al. (1985) could be due to the different age groups in the samples (pubertal vs. college students) or in the method of measuring testosterone (blood vs. saliva). Further research needs to clarify the relation between personality and testosterone concentrations.

Sex Hormones and Occupation

Some occupations have been found to be related to testosterone levels for both males and females.

Factors both internal and external to the individual lead one to an occupational choice. External factors might be opportunities for higher education, parental influence, or demands such as a family situation requiring one to stay on the family farm to help run it. Some psychologists have suggested that the hormone testosterone could be related to occupational choice because of its association with personality and antisocial behavior. Among females, it was found in a sample of 55 normal women, that women in professional, managerial, and technical occupations have higher levels of all androgens (Purifoy & Koopmans, 1980). The same hormonal pattern was correlated with previous occupation for retired women. Further, one of the androgens that is found in higher concentrations in women than in men was significantly associated with job complexity related to people. On the other hand, testosterone significantly correlated with job complexity related to things. "These data most likely reflect biological and environmental causes in a hormone-behavior feedback relationship" (Purifoy & Koopmans, 1980, p. 179). Genetic potential for relatively higher levels of testosterone may be related to those personality characteristic such as drive and persistence that enable the possessor to succeed in longer periods of training and maintain a career orientation. Those careers providing a higher level of positive social stimulation might stimulate adrenal androgen secretion.

Salivary testosterone concentrations in 92 men in seven occupational groups and unemployed men showed actors and football players to be significantly higher in testosterone levels than were ministers (Dabbs, de La Rue, & Williams, 1990). The actor–minister difference was followed up in an examination of archival data from 4,462 military veterans. The ministers were low and the entertainers significantly higher in testosterone, although they did not differ significantly from the set of other occupations. The authors of the study conclude that previous research has found ministers to score high on the Social Service Scale while actors score high on the Men's Adventure scale of the Strong Vocational Interest Blank. Ministers have also been found to be more social while actors are more enterprising.

THE HUMAN BRAIN

The Left and Right Hemispheres

The left and the right hemispheres (halves) of the brain are responsible for different functions. The left hemisphere is specialized for verbal functions and the right side for nonverbal or spatial functions. The two hemispheres work as a unit.

A large number of research studies have demonstrated that the left and right hemispheres (halves) of the brain, although structurally apparently identical, are responsible for the control of different functions. This is referred to as **brain lateralization.** The left hemisphere is specialized for verbal functions—language, speech, and reading and writing. Higher volitional movements are also controlled by the left side of the brain. The right side of the brain is specialized for nonverbal or spatial functions such as drawing complex figures and recognizing complex figures, such as a face. The right side is also the side of the brain used to compose music. "Furthermore, in the normal state, the two hemispheres appear to work closely together as a unit, rather than one being

turned on while the other idles" (Sperry, 1982, p. 1225). Figure 2.1 shows a drawing of the two hemispheres of the brain and the corpus callosum that connects the two hemispheres.

The corpus callosum is the part of the brain that carries information from one hemisphere of the brain to the other. Some researchers find the splenium of the corpus callosum to be larger in females than in males.

The part of the brain that carries information from one hemisphere of the brain to the other is called the **corpus callosum.** There is no sex difference in the overall cross sectional area of the corpus callosum. At the end nearest the back of the head, the corpus callosum is shaped like a bulb. This area is called the splenium. Some researchers have described the splenium of the corpus callosum as being larger in the female than the male (de Lacoste-Utamsing & Holloway, 1982). Despite the expenditure of considerable research effort, some researchers have replicated this finding whereas most others have failed to do so. Even if there is a real difference in the size of the splenium in male and female brains, we do not know what significance, if any, this difference would have for cognitive functioning (Fausto-Sterling, 1992).

Brain Lateralization in Males and Females

Some support has been gained for the theory that male brains are more asymmetric (specialized on one side) whereas there is greater bilateral processing in female brains, particularly for language.

The view that male brains may be functionally more asymmetric (specialized on one side) than female brains has gained some support. Research on sex differences in asymmetry in the developing fetal brain has found that volumetric asymmetries are found in the developing male brain that favors the right hemisphere, whereas the two hemispheres in the developing female brain are more likely to be the same size or have a slightly

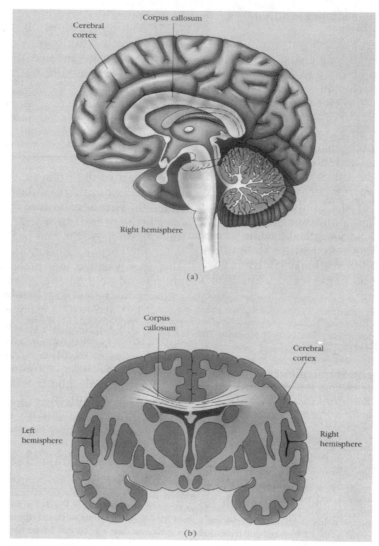

FIGURE 2.1   The Cerebral Hemispheres and the Corpus Callosum

larger left than right hemisphere (de Lacoste, Horvath, & Woodward, 1991).

Most studies of **lateral asymmetry** of cortical function have been based on brain lesions, confirmed after autopsy. Questions about this type of research arise relating to whether the individual's brain function was normal in the area studied. New techniques have been developed that "investigate the localized functioning of the brain by measures of local metabolism or blood flow during a particular behavioral or cognitive task" (F. B. Wood, Flowers, & Naylor 1991, p. 103). Regional blood flow was measured directly during performance of two tasks, a recognition memory task and a spelling task. To examine lateral asymmetry in localized areas of the hemispheres, difference between left and right brain blood flow at similar sites in the two hemispheres were measured. Sex differences were then calculated. Sex differences were found in brain response during spelling. In males, a tightly coupled activation of Broca's area (an area of the frontal lobe responsible for language production) with Wernicke's (an area of the temporal lobe responsible for language understanding) was found. A different and much more complicated picture is found for females. When Wernicke's area is activated in females, there is no similar activation with Broca's area.

> Instead, there is a bitemporal coupling, that is, as left temporal regions are activated so are right temporal regions. This could be interpreted as providing some support for greater bilateral representation of verbal skills in females. There is also a unique coupling between the left temporal region and a more posterior and inferior region of the left hemisphere. Thus, in females, it is as if this task recruits more cross-hemispheric activation and also more posterior (possibly more purely perceptual) activation than with males. (F. B. Wood et al., 1991, p. 111)

Sex differences also exist in the functional organization of the brain during phonological (rhyming) tasks, according to research using magnetic resonance imaging conducted with 38 right handed participants (19 females and 19 males) (Shaywitz et al., 1995). During rhyming tasks brain activation in males is lateralized to the left, whereas in females the pattern of activation is more diffuse, involving both the left and right frontal lobes. "Our data provide clear evidence for a sex difference in the functional organization of the brain for language and indicate that these variations exist at the level of phonological processing" (Shaywitz et al., 1995, p. 607). Other language tasks (semantic category and letter recognition tasks) did not, however, show a gender difference in functional organization of the brain during processing. This research tends to lend support for the theory that for some language tasks processing in female brains is con-

ducted bilaterally to a greater extent than it is in male brains.

Shift of cerebral asymmetry during the menstrual cycle has been found for face perception (Heister, Landis, Regard, & Schroeder-Heister, 1989). During menstruation, a large right-hemisphere superiority was found for face perception, whereas during the premenstrual phase (before the drop in progesterone) there was a small left-hemisphere superiority. Verbal processing, however, showed a left-hemisphere superiority throughout the menstrual cycle. This research supports a dynamic rather than a static concept of cerebral dominance.

Damage to an area of the brain may have consequences for specific functions which may effect males and females differently.

Studies of individuals following brain injury have shown that damage to one area of the brain may have consequences for specific functions that may affect males and females differently. For example, women are more likely than men to suffer aphasia (speech disorders) most often if damage is in the anterior (front) part of the cerebral cortex, whereas aphasia is most common in men who have damage to the posterior (back) area (Kimura, 1993). Some researchers have suggested greater brain asymmetry in men than in women based on the observation that women suffer speech disorders less frequently than men when damage has occurred to the left hemisphere. The explanation could be, however, that because the anterior of the brain is less likely to suffer damage, women's speech functions are less likely to be affected.

Hemispheric control of spatial visualization appears to vary by level of ability rather than by sex.

J. Levy (1972) has proposed a theory that spatial abilities are related to increasing lateralization to the right cerebral hemisphere. Levy further states that males do better in spatial performance than females because of greater right-hemisphere lateralization. To test this hypothesis, Bowers and La Barba (1988) presented 150 male and 150 female undergraduates with spatial problems to solve while simultaneously doing a finger tapping exercise in the first phase and a vocalization task during the second phase of the experiment. The students had been previously divided into top and bottom quartile groups on the basis of scores on spatial visualization and spatial orientation items from the Guildford-Zimmerman Aptitude Survey. The results of this study present a more complicated picture of brain processing of spatial tasks than that proposed by Levy. The results of the first phase of the experiment indicated right-hemispheric control of the spatial visualization component for both males and females of both high and low ability levels. The purpose of the vocalization in the second phase was to assess the role of verbal mediation in performing the spatial tasks. In the second phase, both high-ability males and females showed left-hemispheric lateralization in the processing of spatial orientation tasks, whereas low-ability males and females showed right-hemispheric control. Although no verbal component was found to mediate the spatial orientation component, a verbal mediation strategy was possibly used by high-ability females and low-ability males.

There are both cognitive and structural brain differences in right and left handers.

Handedness also interacts with laterality and sex in the function of the frontal and posterior cortices. E. Goldberg, Podell, Harner, Riggio, & Lovell (1994) designed a Cognitive Bias Task (CBT), a measure of preferences for geometric designs, to quantify cognitive selection mechanisms in the frontal lobes. Their research with both healthy right- and left-handed males and females, and with patients suffering frontal and posterior cortical lesions, demonstrated that frontal lobe functions are more lateralized in males than they are females, and that right-handers and left-handers also differ in fundamental aspects of cortical geometry. Healthy female non–right handers are more similar to males in

the CBT scores. The effect of handedness, however, is minimal for males. The lesions had differential effects depending on handedness. "In both genders right frontal lesions shift response toward context-dependence in right-handers, and toward context independence in non–right-handers, relative to healthy controls" (E. Goldberg et al., 1994). Handedness was also found to interact with the frontal-posterior in females on the CBT task to a greater extent than it did with the left-right cortical axis. Other researchers have also found both cognitive and structural brain differences in right- and left-handers (Habib et al., 1991; O'Boyle & Benbow, 1990; Wittleson, 1985; 1989). More males than females are left-handed, thus it is not surprising that cognitive patterns of left-handers are more similar to the male pattern than the female pattern. "Reading disabilities, stuttering, and some categories of mental retardation are more prevalent in males than in females and in left-handers than in right-handers" (Halpern, 1992). The E. Goldberg et al., (1994) experiment points to greater anterior–posterior interaction in the female brain and greater frontral lobe lateralization in the male brain.

Antecedents of Brain Lateralization

Brain lateralization can be a result of genetics. Testosterone levels can also alter lateralization patterns in the developing fetus.

The theory of brain lateralization that is most accepted is genetic, but other important influences can alter the lateralization patterns in the developing fetus, the most important of which is the chemical environment. Testosterone has been found to induce changes in the structure of nuclei in the hypothalamus and limbic system of rats and monkeys (Geschwind & Galaburda, 1987).

There are a number of critically weak links in the argument that sex differences in brain lateralization underlie cognitive gender differences. Cognitive differences in mathematical and verbal abilities have been declining over the last 30 years, and average differences in these abilities are small. It is not plausible that brain structure of males and females would have changed in that brief period of time. As we shall see in Chapter III, patterns of cognitive gender differences vary in different cultural contexts. Fausto-Sterling (1985) points out that data show that basic patterns of male and female brain symmetry are more alike than they are different. "If there are any differences they are so small that intrasexual variation swamps them" (Fausto-Sterling, 1985, p. 221). The meaning of her statement is that there are far greater differences within the group of men or within the group of women than there is between men and women. Further complicating the picture is that lateralization in male and female brains also differs for right- and left-handers. "The lack of consistent behavioral evidence of sex or handedness differences in interhemispheric interaction . . . also suggests that more work is necessary to determine whether these relations have functional significance and, if so, what it is (Hoptman & Davidson, 1994, p. 200).

Both biological and psychosocial factors most likely influence cognitive functioning. For example, on Piaget's Water Level Test it has been found that far fewer females are able to draw in the horizontal line representing the water level in the glass. To perform the task correctly individuals must know that the water level remains horizontal even when the glass is tipped. Although some authors suggest that this is the result of biological factors (Halpern, 1992) we shall see in Chapter IV that females with a male sex role orientation do better on this task than do females with a feminine sex role orientation suggesting the influence of psychosocial factors.

Environmental Influence on Brain Structure

Environmental factors also influence brain structure. Cortical neurons become larger in a stimulating environment and diminish in an impoverished environment.

While giving emphasis to the effect of sex hormones on the brain, we should also note the influence of environmental factors on brain development. "Nutrition, exercise, physical contact with other humans, exposure to varying sorts of visual and cognitive stimuli, all these and more influence brain structure" (Fausto-Sterling, 1985, p. 74).

Prenatal stress has been experimentally manipulated in animal studies. It has been found to be interrelated with the size of the sexually dimorphic part of the preoptic hypothalamus (SDN-POA) and adult hormone levels (R. H. Anderson, Fleming, Rhees, & Kinghorn, 1986). Research on humans also finds prenatal stress to affect babies both physiologically and behaviorally (Van den Bergh et al., 1989). Research on rats who were reared in either enriched or impoverished environments were found to have brains that differed in cortical thickness and weight, branching of dendrites (parts of neurons) and number of glial cells (tissue that nourishes the brain) and cell size (M. C. Diamond, 1988). So, cortical neurons become larger in a stimulating environment and diminish in size in an impoverished environment. These changes in the brain occur at any age, from the prenatal period to old age, in response to the environment.

The offspring of mother rats who were protein deprived during pregnancy show greater changes in brain structure if they are given enriched living conditions as well as protein-enriched diets as compared with rats only given enriched diets. According to Marian C. Diamond, "we must not give up on people who begin life under unfavorable conditions. Environmental enrichment has the potential to enhance their brain development too, depending upon the degree of severity of the insult" (1988, p. 164).

The Brain and Homosexuality

Male homosexuality has been recently linked to an area of the hypothalamus, and of the X chromosome.

Homosexuality, a preference for sexual partners of the same sex, is based on the criterion of whether two sexual partners have the same genital and overall body conformation (Money, 1988). It is not based on chromosomes, so the androgen-insensitive male who has sexual relations with males is heterosexual. In more recent years controversy has swirled about the question of whether homosexuality is the result of psychosocial factors or of biological destiny.

Although many studies have looked for differences between homosexual and heterosexual men or women in amounts of adult levels of androgen or estrogen, none have been found (Meyer-Bahlburg, 1984). Neither have any differences between heterosexual and homosexual men or women been found in any measures of cognitive abilities (Tuttle & Pillard, 1991). In 1991, in research widely publicized by the media, LeVay reported that a nucleus of the hypothalamus that is usually larger in males than in females, was larger in heterosexual men than homosexual men as determined in postmortem examination. LeVay suggested that this finding indicates that homosexuality has a biological basis.

A team of geneticists at the National Cancer Institute also suggested a biological basis in a report linking male homosexuality to a small stretch of DNA on the X chromosome (Hamer, Hu, Magnuson, Hu & Pattatucci, 1993). Studies of the X chromosomes of a population of families in which there were two homosexual brothers and no transmission of homosexuality through fathers or to females, but same-sex orientation found in maternal uncles and male cousins of these men, suggested X linkage. Laboratory analysis of the DNA of the homosexual brothers revealed that 33 of the 40 brothers had coinherited genetic information on the sexual orientation-related locus on the X chromosome. There were seven pairs of brothers (36%) who did not coinherit all of the genetic markers at this point (Xq28) of the X chromosome. "Given the overall complexity of human sexuality, it is not surprising that a single genetic locus does not account for all of the observed variability" (Hamer et al., 1993, pp. 325–326).

A twin study conducted with gay men found that there was a concordance rate of .50 between identical twin brothers (in 50% of the cases both identical twin brothers were gay). The concordance rate dropped to .24 if the twins were frater-nal; to .11 for adoptive brothers; and to .09 for nontwin biological brothers (Bailey & Pillard, 1991). Fausto-Sterling (1992) points out that their research also supports an environmental hypothesis for the causality of homosexuality in order to explain the 50% of identical twins who were not also gay.

Similar results were found for lesbians, with 34 of 71 identical twins either homosexual or bisexual as compared with 6 of 36 fraternal twins and 2 of 35 unrelated adoptive sisters (Bailey, Pillard, Neale, & Agyei, 1993). An approximate 50% concordance rate of homosexual or bisexual behavior for identical twins in both the male and female samples does provide evidence that homosexuality or heterosexuality is partially inherited.

SEX CHROMOSOME ANOMALIES

Klinefelter's Syndrome

The Klinefelter's male has at least one extra X chromosome. Although they may have normal or above normal intelligence, they are likely to have IQ scores that are lower than normal.

A male with **Klinefelter's Syndrome** has at least one extra X chromosome (XXY, or XXXY). It occurs in slightly over 1 out of 1,000 male births. A comparison study of babies with the chromosome abnormalities who were studied longitudinally in comparison with their own normal siblings or babies born at the same time found more learning disabilities and speech impairments in the Klinefelter's males. Although the average IQ scores of Klinefelter's males are lower than normal, (with particularly low verbal scores) some may have above normal IQs and may even be gifted (M. E. Porter, Gardner, DeFeudis, & Endler 1988). They do, however, generally have more difficulty with social skills and in interpersonal relationships.

Men with Klinefelter's syndrome have underdeveloped penis and testes, do not produce sperm, and are therefore sterile. They also have some feminization of appearance with contoured hips and some breast development. They have little facial and pubic hair, and their voices are rather high-pitched.

Klinefelter's males are at increased risk of being in prisons or mental institutions. A Japanese study of male juvenile delinquents found that the expected frequency for XXY men to be in prison (based on their frequency at birth) was 01.2, but 2.9% were delinquent (Nanko, Saito, & Makino, 1979). When IQ is controlled for, however, they do not commit more crimes.

XYY Males

XYY males are more likely to be in prisons and mental institutions than their frequency at birth would predict.

Controversy surrounds the reports that both XXY and **XYY men** are more likely to be found in both prisons and high-security mental institutions. A study in Japan found that although the frequency at birth of XYY men is 0.9 per 1,000, they were found among male juvenile delinquents to be 3.6. per 1,000 (Nanko, Saito, & Makino, 1979). The effect related to both an extra X or an extra Y chromosome in males is lowered intelligence (Witkin et al., 1976). Since men of lower than average intelligence are more likely to be in prison than are men of normal or high intelligence, the greater incidence of XXY and XYY men with lower than average intelligence accounts for their greater liklihood of being in prison.

XXX Females

XXX females are developmentally delayed and are in prisons in disproportionate numbers.

XXX females have an extra X chromosome. As babies they are placid and somewhat unresponsive. They are developmentally delayed in walking, talking, and social skills. They also appear in prison in disproportionate numbers as do XXY and XYY men (Hook, 1979).

Turner's Syndrome

The Turner's Syndrome person (always a female) has only one sex chromosome, an X. She is short, infertile, and has a feminine sex role.

The person (always a female) with Turner's Syndrome has only one sex chromosome present, an X. This usually comes from the mother. Over 95% of fetuses with a single X chromosome result in miscarriage. Turner's syndrome females have very low levels of sex hormones both prenatally and at puberty. These females are short of stature (usually about 4½ feet tall), with webbed neck and shieldlike chest. At puberty they remain immature, with a failure to develop breasts and lack of pubic hair. Although they have female external genitalia, and therefore labeled female at birth, they do not have any sex hormones. Their gonads are not fully developed and begin degenerating before birth; by puberty they are only rudimentary forms. They are infertile. Turner's syndrome females have an unusual pattern of cognitive deficits. Although they have normal verbal intelligence, they have particular difficulty in visualizing objects in three-dimensional space (J. Downey, Ehrhardt, Gruen, Bell, & Morishima, 1987; Money, 1988, Money, 1993).

Turner's Syndrome girls have a female gender identity, and are described in childhood as being even more feminine than normal girls. They are less athletically skilled, fight less, and have a greater interest in dolls. As adults, they are less socially skilled and are less likely to have sexual experiences than matched women. They have fewer symptoms, however, of psychopathology (J. Downey, Ehrhardt, Gruen, Bell, & Morishima, 1987; Ehrhardt, Greenberg, & Money, 1970).

Androgen Insensitivity Syndrome

The androgen insensitive individual has XY chromosomes. An X linked recessive gene blocks the effect of testosterone. They have a male genotype but a female phenotype.

The individual born with **androgen insensitivity syndrome** is gynotypically a man but phenotypically a woman. In other words, although she appears to be a normal female, chromosomally she is 46, XY. An X linked recessive gene blocks the uptake or utilization of the hormone testosterone, which is secreted by the testes, which also secrete antimullerian hormone that stops the formation of the uterus and fallopian tubes. The testes are undescended, so that at birth the baby is labeled a female. Although a vagina may be present it lacks depth. The vulva develops normally and at puberty breasts and a feminine body contour develop because of the estrogen, unopposed by testosterone, which is secreted in males by the adrenal cortex. If the pubertal hormones are inadequate, feminization is successful with hormonal treatment. Nine androgen insensitive women studied by V. G. Lewis and Money (1983) were found to be exclusively heterosexual as women in their sex lives, ideation, fantasies, and thoughts.

Adrenogenital Syndrome

Genetic females exposed in utero to high levels of testosterone are more "tomboyish." Explanations other than testosterone in utero have been put forth to explain their behavior.

Money and Ehrhardt (1972) in a widely quoted study, followed up 25 genetic females exposed in utero to high levels of testosterone. Fifteen of the girls in their study had **adrenogenital syndrome**—adrenal glands that produced too few adrenocorticoids and high levels of adrenal testosterone (CAH). The high levels of androgens are produced too late in fetal development to affect the internal reproductive organs, so the woman has normal ovaries, fallopian tubes, and uterus. They have masculinized external genitalia, however, such as an enlarged clitoris. Ten of the girls in the study had mothers who received progestins during pregnancy, which masculinized their external genitalia. The fifteen girls with CAH received cortisone treatment throughout their lives to help their adrenal glands to function. All of the 25 girls had to have one or more

surgeries to reduce the size of their external genitalia and make them more normal in appearance.

These girls were studied when they were between the ages of 5 and 16. Money and Ehrhardt compared self reports and mothers' reports of behavior of a sample matched for age and socioeconomic level. The researchers concluded that the masculinized girls were more "tomboyish" than the matched controls. They had a higher activity level, preferred to play with boys and boys' toys, less interest in dolls, and infant care, and less interest in future marriage and more in careers. Money and Ehrhardt attribute this tomboyish behavior to "a masculinizing effect on the prenatal brain" (1972, p. 103).

Bem (1993) offers a number of alternative explanations for the observations. The cortisone that the girls took is known to increase activity level. Because of the surgeries and continuing cortisone therapy, they may be compensating for a sense of inadequacy and uncertainty about the future. They may have been reacting to the masculinized genitalia by acting more "boyish" than other girls. She states that this and other "experiments to date provide very little support for the theory that prenatal hormones differentially organize male and female brains" (Bem, 1993, p. 26). Bem does state, however, that although there is little support in humans, there is much support in other primates for differential brain organization in males and females.

A study of rough-and-tumble play and sex of preferred playmate of 3–8-year-old boys (11) and girls (27) with CAH and unaffected 3–8-year-old boys (18) and girls (15) who were relatives was in partial agreement with the Money and Erhardt study (Hines & Kaufman, 1994). The unaffected boys engaged in more rough-and-tumble play than did the unaffected girls; however, the CAH girls were similar in their play behavior to the unaffected girls. CAH boys showed reduced levels of rough-and-tumble play. Unaffected girls and boys and CAH boys showed preference for same sex playmates. In contrast, girls with CAH showed a preference for male playmates intermediate to that of male and female relatives. Preference for male playmates by CAH girls did not correlate with degree of virilization at birth.

In yet another study, the toy preferences of CAH girls differed from those of their unaffected female relatives and showed no difference from those of their unaffected male relatives (Berenbaum & Hines, 1992).

Based on the research on CAH females, I think that there is some relation between the prenatal hormone environment and sex-typical behaviors, although this is not uniform. Not all CAH children have had the same level of hormones or at the same prenatal periods, perhaps diluting some of the results. Also, behavior in humans is always influenced by the environment as well as biology.

Alpha Reductase Deficiency

5 alpha reductase deficiency is a rare enzyme disorder that prevents masculinization of genitals of male babies with the disorder. Although reared as females until puberty when their genitals develop, they assume normal male sex roles as adults.

Cases of genetic males, suffering from a rare enzyme deficiency (**5 alpha reductase deficiency**) that prevented prenatal testosterone from masculinizing their genitals and who were reared as females until puberty, then later reared as males were discovered in the Dominican Republic (Imperato-McGinley, 1979; Imperato-McGinley, Peterson, Gautier & Sturla, 1979). At birth their genitals vary from normal female to partially masculinized. The genitals begin to masculinize at puberty in response to the surge of testosterone. A normal size penis develops allowing for sexual relations. In the Dominican Republic this disorder is often recognized at birth and boys are labeled as guevedoces (penis at 12) or as machi-hembra (man–woman), which may lead to their being raised as a Turnim-man (a baby who looks like a female but will become a man at puberty).

Interview data on the psychosexual development of these individuals provides evidence that 19 of the 34 affected individuals from two villages in the Dominican Republic were unambiguously raised as females. "At puberty, the affected males develop an increase in muscle mass, deepening of the voice, skeletal growth, rugation and hyperpig-mentation of the scrotum and growth of the phallus" (Imperato-McGinley, 1979, p. 643). Sixteen of the 18 for whom postpubertal data was obtained had successfully changed to a male gender identity and male gender role. Imperato-McGinley and her colleagues conclude that the formation of a male gender identity is induced by androgens at a critical period in utero, neonatally, and at puberty.

Gender and Biology

A review of the sex chromosome anomalies reveals genes and hormones and sex role socialization to play a role in gender identity and gender role orientation.

> Simply put, the impact of any biological feature depends in every instance on how that biological feature interacts with the environment in which it is situated. That is why there is a technical distinction between a genotype and a phenotype in the first place. That is also why biologists never specify a one-to-one correspondence between biology and behavior but always specify a norm, or range, of reaction. (Bem, 1993, p. 22)

Humans also radically change their environment, which in turn changes them. The dramatic changes in technology such as jet planes, in vitro fertilization, and computers, are just a few of the important technological developments that have greatly impacted on people's relationships.

SOCIOBIOLOGY

Sociobiology, based on Darwin's theory of evolution, claims that gender differences in behavior are the result of biologically programmed universal traits that have survived evolutionary history because they are adaptive.

Sociobiology was first proposed by a Harvard entomologist, Edmund O. Wilson, in a lengthy tome, *Sociobiology: The new synthesis* (1975). E. O. Wilson defined sociobiology as "the systematic study of the biological basis of all social behavior" (E. O. Wilson, 1975, p. 4). Sociobiology draws heavily on Darwin's theory of evolution, which noticed that far more young are produced in each species than survive. According to Darwin, there is survival of the "fittest," the strongest, fittest, most aggressive animals.

Sociobiology defines fittest somewhat differently than Darwin did. The fittest animals, according to sociobiology, are those who contribute the most genes to the next generation. Sociobiology seeks traits that characterize all people, and certain animals. They argue that this universality is evidence that the traits in question are adaptive. These traits become universal because they are inherited and individuals who inherit them leave more descendants than do those who do not inherit these traits.

Sociobiology has tried to explain gender differences by looking at adaptive behaviors, behavior that is universal cross-culturally and cross-species, because the genes producing these behaviors have survived. Sociobiologists therefore claim the survival of the fittest in terms of behavioral traits as well as physical characteristics. One prominent gender difference in terms of sociobiology is the degree of parental investment in offspring. Why is it that the female of the species is the one who does most of the childcare? According to sociobiology it is because the female egg is more precious than the male sperm since females produce relatively few eggs over the course of their reproductive lives, only one per month, compared with the 200,000–500,000 sperm in a single ejaculation. The goal of human life for sociobiology is the survival of the individual's genes. Males try to impregnate as many women as possible, so are naturally promiscuous. Females on the other hand, want to mate with a genetically potent male and to take good care of their offspring until they survive to reproduce and carry on the genes. It then becomes adaptive behavior for the female to be faithful to a male who will help provide for her and the offspring and to be nurturing. The human female's interest in sex during all phases of the menstrual cycle and the female orgasm have evolved, sociobiologists say, to maintain male–female pair bonding. Thus, from the differences in size and number between egg and sperm sociobiology postulates major social consequences such as female fidelity, male promiscuity, women's nurturing and investment in the care of children, and even the distribution of labor by gender (Hubbard, 1990).

The Parental Investment Model

Fiengold tested the parental investment model, finding that females place more emphasis on socioeconomic resources, but this data could also support a cultural model.

A test of the parental investment model was conducted by Feingold (1992a) by means of a meta-analysis of mate selection research using North American samples. Women placed more emphasis than did men on socioeconomic status, ambitiousness, character, and intelligence. The largest gender differences were for those characteristics particularly related to progeny survival, status and ambitiousness. Although this research supports the sociobiological model of parental investment, it is also amenable to explanation by other models such as a cultural model. Since males have in the past usually paid for dates (greater male investment) the research could be skewed by gender dating roles, so that if a man paid, he would be more likely to require an attractive companion. In contrast, on dates on which the bill is split or the woman pays, she may require a more attractive date. We do not yet have any research testing that situation.

Male Reproductive Success and Resources

In most mammalian species, male reproductive success is directly related to position in the dominance hierarchy. In industrial societies, there is an inverse relationship between cultural success and fertility.

In over 50 nonmammalian and mammalian species, including nonhuman primates, animals assort themselves into dominance hierarchies

(Perusse, 1993). In four out of five of these species there is a direct relationship between position in the dominance hierarchy and male reproductive success. Among humans, the term *cultural success* has been used to refer to individuals who derive status from resources, power, or prestige. A relationship between reproductive and cultural success has been found by studies of a number of horticultural, agricultural, and pastoral societies. In industrial societies, across countries, and across continents, however, an inverse relationship has been demonstrated between fertility and the two most frequent measures of success in industrial societies—occupation and income. In the United States in particular, there is a sharp decline in fertility from very-low to very-high income (i.e., the weathier the man, the fewer the children he fathers).

Perusse (1993) collected data on 343 French Canadian males, via anonymous self answered questionnaires to test hypotheses to explain the absence of a positive relationship between social success and fertility in industrial societies. It was found that although social status was not related to fertility, it was strongly related to mating success, which integrates both the number of partners and the number of sexual relations per partner. Two factors are preventing high-income men from reproducing—monogamy and contraception. Monogamy prevents many conceptions because, for example, 100 instances of coitus with a single partner in a year would result in .95 possible conceptions as opposed to 2.28 with 20 relations with each of five partners. "Unmarried high-status French-Canadian males copulate more often with more females than unmarried low-status French Canadian males" (Perusse, 1993, p. 293). In modern society, where agreement of both partners is usually necessary for mating to take place, the data also probably reflect females' greater willingness to mate with high-status males due to sensitivity to acquisition of greater parental resources. The authors cite this data as support for evolutionary theory of mate selection. An alternative hypothesis is that females achieve higher social status themselves by mating with a male of higher status. This re-

search can also be said to disprove their hypothesis because high status was inversely related to fertility, showing that socialization can influence fertility behavior patterns.

Criticisms of Sociobiology

Serious criticisms of sociobiology include reductionism, extrapolation from lower forms of life such as insects to humans, failure to take into account the effect of environment on genes, distortion of universality of behavioral traits, and underestimation of the effect of culture on behavior.

Despite the superficial plausibility of sociobiology, there are serious criticisms that have been articulated. First of all, it is a reductionist theory, trying to explain the complexities of social behavior in terms of biological structure, and explaining phenomena on one level by explanations on a lower level. Entomology is the study of insects, and Edmund Wilson used many examples in his book from insect life, often extrapolating to humans. The higher an organism is on the phylogenetic scale, however, the greater the role of learning in behavior. Therefore, to extrapolate from insect to human behavior is absurd. Sociobiology is a form of biological determinism. Sociobiologists claim a genetic basis for all kinds of social behavior without any evidence of such genes.

Fausto-Sterling (1985) criticizes much of the research on biological gender differences as "inadequate research and inappropriate model building."

Any biological theory about human behavior that ignores the complex of forces affecting behavior as well as the profound two-way interactions between mind and body is scientifically hopeless. Yet the continued appearance of such ideas in both the scientific and popular literature attests to their tenacity. Their often unself-conscious coupling with (usually retrogressive) social programs helps to explain their continued presence and to underline the political nature of their formulation. (Fausto-Sterling, 1985, p. 221)

Finally, it should be kept in mind that most of the research on biological sex differences has been conducted on animals. We must always be careful in extrapolating animal brains and behavior to human brains and behavior. Laboratory rats are not just little people with white fur coats. They are at a much lower level phylogenetically. The higher the animal on the phylogenetic continuum, the greater the role of learning and environment and the lesser the role of biological determination in behavior.

THE MENSTRUAL CYCLE

The menstrual cycle is regulated through a negative feedback loop—by gonadotrophin releasing hormone (GnRH) from the hypothalamus, two gonadotropic hormones produced by the pituitary—FSH and LH, and two gonadal hormones—estrogen and progesterone.

I include the **menstrual cycle** in this chapter on biology because it is a phenomenon that is biological in nature and experienced only by female, not male, members of the human species. At the same time, it illustrates the importance of sociocultural influences on the way that men and women are differentiated in society (Richardson, 1992). Nicolson (1992) points out that the framing of the research on psychological effects of the menstrual cycle coincides with the implicit construction of the female mind and body as described by nineteenth-century medicine. "Clinical and medical writers do not appear to have seriously challenged the notions of female psychology that predominated in nineteenth-century medical texts. Women were portrayed there as illogical and weak and particularly as being vulnerable to their reproductive cycles" (Nicolson, 1992, p. 178).

The menstrual cycle (Figure 2.2) is regulated by the brain (the hypothalamus and pituitary), the ovaries, and hormones by means of a negative feedback loop (Asso, 1983). The days of the menstrual cycle are numbered beginning with the day of the onset of bleeding. The menstrual cycle can be divided into five phases: (1) Menstrual phase—Days 1–5, during which the lining of the uterus (endometrium) is sloughed off due to estrogen reaching its lowest level in the blood, stimulating the hypothalamus to release Gonadotrophin Releasing Hormone (GnRH), which stimulates the pituitary to release Follicle Stimulating Hormone (FSH); (2) Follicular phase—Days 6–12, during which FSH arrives at the ovaries, stimulating the growth of a group of follicles that become an important source of estrogen that in turn has a negative feedback effect on the hypothalamus and the pituitary to reduce FSH and begin secreting luteinizing hormone (LH); (3) Ovulatory phase—Days 13–15, during which one follicle grows rapidly, is then stimulated by high levels of LH to rupture and release an ovum; (4) Luteal phase—Days 16–23, during which the corpus luteum forms in the cavity from the ruptured follicle and produces progesterone, which acts on the pituitary to inhibit production of LH; (5) Premenstrual phase—Days 24–28, during which estrogen and progesterone are low, stimulating hypothalamic release of GnRH to the pituitary starting the cycle over again (Asso, 1983; Richardson, 1992). The average length of the menstrual cycle is 28 days, with the normal cycle ranging from 20 to 40 days.

Menstrual Synchrony

Menstrual synchrony occurs among women who interact with one another.

Barbara McClintock (1971) was the first to identify the phenomenon of **menstrual synchrony**—the finding that in a college dormitory the menstrual cycles of roommates become increasingly synchronized (the menses beginning on the same day). A number of other studies have since supported the finding of menstrual synchrony. In an examination of menstrual synchrony conducted in Israel, (A. Weller & Weller, 1993) found a significant degree of synchrony in menstrual onset in 82 mothers and their daughters living in the same home, 47 pairs of women sharing a room in a private residence, and 93 pairs of women roommates in a dormitory.

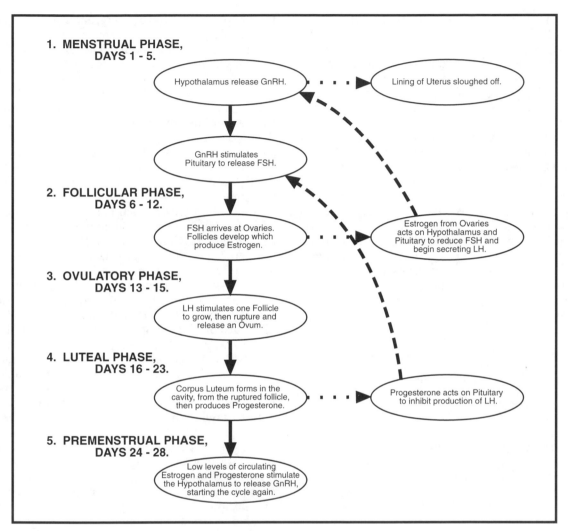

FIGURE 2.2   The Menstrual Cycle

The finding of menstrual synchrony is fascinating because it is an excellent example of the social altering biology. Most of the research on the menstrual cycle has been looking at it the other way around, how biology shapes behavior (Lander, 1988). Why does menstrual synchrony occur? To test the hypothesis that it is because of pheromones, chemicals used by members of a species to communicate with one another, an experiment was conducted in which underarm perspiration from one woman was applied to the upper lip of other women; alcohol was used in the control group. After four months, the women in the condition where sweat was applied to the upper lip showed a significant shift toward the donor in the timing of their menstrual cycles (M. J. Russell, Switz, & Thompson, 1980).

L. Weller and Weller (1993) reviewed published studies, concluding that menstrual synchrony occurs often, but not always. It is also related to degree of exposure of the women to each other. The evidence points to pheromones as the cause, but is not conclusive. One study of 29 cohabiting lesbian couples found no evidence for menstrual synchrony (Trevathan, Burleson, & Gregory, 1993). In fact, the onset of menstruation dates for the dyad members were randomly distributed. In contrast, another study of 20 lesbian couples found menstrual synchrony to be very frequent (A. Weller & Weller, 1992). Menstrual synchrony was related to more frequent mutual activities, stronger friendship, and menstrual regularity. Personality factors as well as psychosocial and biological factors have also been found to be able to predict individual differences in menstrual synchrony (Jarett, 1984).

Menstrual Cramps (Dysmenorrhea)

Menstrual cramps are caused by prostaglandins and can be successfully treated by antiprostaglandins.

Menstrual cramps, which are called **dysmenorrhea,** are experienced by some women every month, by some women some months but not others, and never by other women. Also, the same woman may experience dysmenorrhea at some times during her reproductive lifetime but not at other times. When I was in high school and college, I had dysmenorrhea on the first day of my menstrual period during most months, a few months a year so severe I would experience nausea and vomiting. After my first child was born (when I was 23 years old), I no longer had dysmenorrhea. A few years after my third child was born (13 years after the first), I again begin to experience painful cramps on the first day of my period. My gynecologist recommended a hysterectomy, since he said I was not planning to have any more children. I said, "No thanks," and left the HMO in which he practiced and took a health plan that gave me greater freedom of choice of a doctor.

I also then happened to read Dr. Penny Wise Budoff's (1981) book, *No More Menstrual Cramps and Other Good News,* in which she said that menstrual cramps are not "all in your head" but are thought to be caused by **prostaglandins.** Prostaglandins are hormone-like substances, produced by the lining of the uterus and other tissues in the body, that cause smooth muscle to contract. The intense uterine contractions caused by high levels of prostaglandins cause pain. Contractions may cut off some of the oxygen carrying blood to the uterus, which increases the pain. In addition, prostaglandins increase sensitivity of nerve endings. Cramps are produced by the intense uterine contractions, lack of oxygen, and greater nerve sensitivity.

Cross-cultural research with 5,322 women who had borne a child but were not pregnant nor breast-feeding at the time of the study found an incidence of dysmenorrhea in about 60% of these women, the incidence not differing by culture (World Health Organization, as cited in Richardson, 1992). After reading Dr. Budoff's book I went back to the obstetrician/gynecologist who had delivered my last child and asked him for an antiprostaglandin prescription. He gave me a prescription for Anaprox. At the beginning of cramps, I would take two pills and the cramps would disappear within a half hour. A few years later, I no longer needed to take Anaprox because I no longer had cramps on the first day of my period. Other trade names for antiprostaglandins are Ponstel and Motrin. Aspirin is a weak antiprostaglandin, which is why it works to relieve mild cramps. Dr. Budoff was the first to use antiprostaglandin drugs in the treatment of menstrual cramps. She found 85% of women treated reported a significant reduction of cramps, nausea, vomiting and dizziness (Budoff, 1982). Other researchers have corroborated the effectiveness of treatment with prostaglandins. General agreement exists among researchers that primary dysmenorrhea is a physical rather than a psychological problem (Richardson, 1992). Nevertheless, psychosocial factors also play a role in menstrual distress.

Sex Role Attitudes and Menstrual Distress

Research on women's sex role behavior or attitudes toward the role of women and menstrual distress has led to inconsistent results.

Numerous research studies have attempted to find a relationship between women's sex role behavior (masculinity–femininity–androgyny) and menstrual distress. The literature is remarkable for its inconsistent results. Similarly, the research on attitudes toward the role of women in society in relation to menstrual distress has been plagued with conflicting results. Research with college women, however, found an interaction between sex role behavior, attitudes toward the role of women in society and menstrual distress, which could explain some of the inconsistency in previous research (Heilbrun, Friedberg, Wydra, & Worobow, 1990). Masculine women who preferred a contemporary role for women in society, and feminine women who preferred a traditional role for women, both suffered greater menstrual and premenstrual distress. On the other hand, feminine women who supported contemporary attitudes toward the role of women and masculine, traditional women reported less distress associated with the menstrual cycle. The researchers hypothesize that these "pure" contemporary or traditional types of women are less flexible in meeting *both* the instrumental/academic and expressive social demands made on college students and thus have greater stress that has been consistently found to relate to menstrual distress.

Cognition and the Menstrual Cycle

Objectively measured complex cognitive performance does not change in any significant way with the menstrual cycle in women in general.

Complex cognitive functions, such as women's abilities to solve problems, form concepts, and think creatively are not affected by the menstrual cycle. Golub (1976) found that the cycle does not affect the following tasks: classifying figures into groups; thinking logically; creatively thinking of ways to use objects; creative free association; or solving word jumble problems. No effects of the menstrual cycle have been found for medical school exams (Walsh et al., as cited in Sommer, 1992), introductory psychology exams (Asso, 1986; B. Bernstein, 1977; Sommer, 1983), or honors degree psychology exams (Asso, 1986). A more recent survey of the literature by Sommer (1992) concluded that the process of menstruation has no substantive effect upon academic performance, abstract thinking, immediate and short-term memory, visuospatial ability, frustration tolerance and flexibility in working on various puzzles and problems, and simple speed decisions.

Some research finds that selected cognitive and motor functions (speech articulation, manual dexterity, verbal fluency, and the rod and frame test) vary with the menstrual cycle.

Some research, however, has found variations in certain cognitive as well as motor abilities for women during the menstrual cycle (Hampson, 1990a, 1990b; Hampson and Kimura, 1988). They selected cognitive abilities to study where gender differences have been found. During the ovulatory phase (midcycle) when hormone levels are high, women perform significantly better on speech articulation, manual dexterity, and verbal fluency than during the menstrual phases when hormone levels are low. Performance on spatial tasks (the rod and frame test) however, are poorer during the menstrual phase when hormone levels are low than they are during the midleuteal phase. Control groups of postmenopausal women who were on hormone replacement therapy showed the same variations as did the menstruating women. Postmenopausal women not on hormone replacement therapy did not show the fluctuations in task performance. Sommer's (1992) literature review, however, concluded that eight studies of visuospatial ability, including tasks of localization and orientation of visual stimuli found no menstrual cycle effects.

According to Sommer, although there may be a cycle–phase effect for articulation, the pattern is not consistent among research studies for other types of abilities.

Reaction Time and Attention

Simple reaction time does not change with the menstrual cycle, but choice reaction time is faster during the ovulatory phase, as is performance on repetitive tasks.

Most studies show that during the menstrual cycle women do not change how quickly they react without making any choices, which is known as "simple reaction time" (S. Hunter, Schraer, Landers, Buskirk, & Harris, 1979; Sommer, 1983). On the other hand, results for choice reaction time, where a choice must be made how to react, show that women have greater speed in the ovulatory phase and react more slowly during the paramenstruum (B. K. Jensen, 1982; Slade & Jenner, 1980). Women perform better at boring, repetitive tasks that make attention difficult during the ovulatory phase (Komnenich, Lane, Dickey, & Stone, 1978). Attention therefore, is apparently better during the ovulatory phase.

Perceptual Abilities

Sensitivity to smell and faint light is greater during the ovulatory than the menstrual phase of the cycle.

According to Parlee (1983) variations in some perceptual abilities do occur in cyclical fashion with the menstrual cycle. Sensitivity to smell of certain compounds is greatest during ovulation and less acute during menstruation. Women are also most likely to detect faint light during the ovulatory phase.

Premenstrual Syndrome

Premenstrual syndrome refers to a set of psychological and physical symptoms that occur during the week prior to menstruation.

People in American society believe that women experience a variety of psychological and physical symptoms during different phases of the menstrual cycle (Brooks-Gunn & Ruble, 1980). In 1931, a physician, Dr. Robert Frank, coined the term premenstrual tension to denote a constellation of symptoms which occur during the week prior to menstruation and which end with the onset of menses. Dr. Katharina Dalton, a British physician first used the term **premenstrual syndrome** (PMS) in 1953, identifying the same sorts of physical and emotional symptoms that Dr. Frank had observed—headache, backache, abdominal and back pain, fatigue, and nausea (M. Rodin, 1992).

Disagreement exists among researchers as to when the premenstrual period actually occurs.

When does the premenstrual period actually occur? Is it the last six days of the luteal phase and the first two days of menstruation? Is it only the few days prior to menstruation, ending with the onset of menses? Does it begin with ovulation with a gradual increase in severity of symptoms continuing through the third day of menstruation? All of these phases of the menstrual cycle have been included as the time period during which PMS symptoms are attributed to PMS rather than some other cause (M. Rodin, 1992).

The popular press paints a picture of the premenstrual woman as a "menstrual monster."

The popular press has painted a picture of the premenstrual woman that is clearly negative and extremely variable. According to Chrisler and Levy (1990), the media have constructed a "menstrual monster." A content analysis of descriptions of premenstrual syndrome in magazine articles that appeared during the years 1980–1987 revealed "a strong bias in favor of reporting negative menstrual cycle changes." Not one symptom appeared in all of the articles, and 131 different descriptive terms were used of the physical symptoms and behavior of the premenstrual woman.

> *Political considerations influence whether PMS should be included as a diagnostic category of mental illness.*

Political considerations also enter into whether PMS is a category of diagnostic mental illness. An illustration of the politics of PMS occurred when Edgar Berman, Hubert Humphrey's personal physician, declared that "women's raging hormonal influences" made them unfit for political office (Tavris, 1992). Feminist psychologists have strongly opposed the inclusion of a category of premenstrual syndrome in the Diagnostic and Statistical Manual of Mental Disorders III-R (DSM-III R) and more recently in DSM-IV (American Psychiatric Association, 1987; K. Hood, 1992; M. Rodin, 1992). Premenstrual syndrome could possibly be used to justify discriminatory treatment of women. "For example, an employer may accuse a woman of being unable to make correct judgements for two weeks out of the month . . . as justification for taking action against the woman" (M. Rodin, 1992, p. 53). Nevertheless, The American Psychiatric Association included a category for premenstrual syndrome in Appendix A of the DSM III-R (1987) and in Appendix B of DSM IV (1994), which includes diagnoses that are tentative and merit further clarification.

A work group of The American Psychiatric Association reanalyzed data from prospective, daily symptoms ratings to evaluate individual symptoms required for the present diagnosis and to explore the association between premenstrual syndrome and other mental disorders (Hurt et al., 1992). Data from 670 women seeking treatment for premenstrual syndrome at five U.S. cities revealed that depending on the assessment method used for evaluating changes in symptom severity, 14–45% of the women met the criteria for premenstrual syndrome. This variability in the frequency of diagnosis based on the same symptoms, underscores the need for a uniform method for evaluating symptoms. Only a weak association was found between a past history of major depressive disorder and premenstrual syndrome, so the researchers concluded that pre-menstrual syndrome is not synonymous with another mental disorder.

The American Psychological Association wrote a letter protesting the inclusion of "premenstrual dysphoric disorder" (the term used for premenstrual syndrome) in the DSM-IV. Nevertheless, on May 22, 1993, the American Psychiatric Association's Legislative Assembly voted to include Premenstrual Dysphoric Disorder (PMDD) in Appendix B of the fourth edition of the Diagnostic and Statistical Manual of Mental Disorders (DSM-IV) (Caplan, 1993).

> *A number of methodological issues have led to the confusion in menstrual cycle research.*

A number of methodological issues are pertinent to menstrual cycle research. Many of the studies have only examined the premenstrual phase, which could provide a biased view of mood changes during the menstrual cycle. In fact, if there are different durations during which women suffer premenstrual syndrome, then that could account for some of the contradiction in the research. Negative affect symptoms have been the focus of most of the research with positive affect being studied only infrequently. Most studies have also been retrospective, which opens up the possibility that memory of symptoms could be influenced by beliefs about changes that ought to be occurring in the menstrual cycle.

> *Retrospective research is influenced by the woman's belief that she should have symptoms during menstruation, even though daily diaries show that she did not experience them at the time.*

The problem with retrospective research is that the women's implicit theories of menstruation intrude on their recollections. Research finds that women who believe that menstruation has a severe impact on them recall the menstrual state as being worse than they had initially reported it on a daily questionnaire (McFarland, Ross, & DeCourville, 1989). Their recollections were biased so as to be consistent with their menstrual theories. On average the women did experience some physical changes during the menstrual period, but they exaggerated the magnitude of the ailments in their recollections. Negative affect, according to their daily questionnaire, was not associated with the menstrual phase, contrary to their later recollections. The authors point out that the apparently false belief that affect is influenced by menstruation, serves to validate the negative stereotype of women being unfit for responsible positions because they are unreliable and overemotional during the premenstrual and menstrual phases.

Based on two experiments that examined both expectations and bodily sensations during the premenstrual phase, it was found that the higher a women's retrospective reports of premenstrual distress, the more symptoms she reported during the lab in her premenstrual phase (Klebanov & Jemmott, 1992). When on a random basis, some women were told they were in the premenstrual phase and others that they were in the intermenstrual phase, women who were told they were in the premenstrual phase reported more symptoms than women who were told they were intermenstrual. In summary, although actual physical symptoms may increase for some women as they approach menstruation, expectations can lead women to report more symptoms of premenstrual syndrome.

In a well-designed study of mood and the menstrual cycle, little support was found for negative mood swings associated with the menstrual cycle.

Typically, retrospective research on mood and the menstrual cycle has reported heightened feelings of well being during the ovulatory phase of the menstrual cycle and more negative mood swings during the premenstrual and menstrual phases. In a recent, very well-designed study of premenstrual syndrome 60 women and 10 men from the community provided daily data for 12–18 weeks on mood fluctuations (McFarlane & Williams, 1994). Participants were blind to the fact that the focus of the study was the menstrual cycle. Data were analyzed in relation to the lunar cycle and day-of-the week, as well as menstrual cycle. "Cyclicity was the norm; two thirds of both the women and men had one or more menstrual or lunar phases or days of the week that were markedly positive and/or negative, relative to their own range, but few experienced sterotypical cyclicity (PMS, Monday blues, full moon)" (McFarlane & Williams, 1994, p. 339). The data, therefore, did not support the stereotype that most women suffer from negative premenstrual mood. The majority of the women in the study (51.7%) said they have PMS. McFarlane and Williams think that perhaps these women attribute mood swings to the menstrual cycle because they knew they experienced cyclical changes in mood and labeled it with the PMS stereotype. Only 11.7% actually met the criteria for PMS. Of those 11.7%, about half actually labeled themselves as having PMS.

Positive portrayal of the menstrual cycle can change negative attitudes and reporting of negative menstrual symptoms.

A Menstrual Joy Questionnaire (MJQ) (consisting of 10 positive experiences) and the Menstrual Attitude Questionnaire (MAQ) were administered to 50 undergraduate students in a counterbalanced design—half of the students completing the MJQ first and the other half the MAQ first, and all students completed the Menstrual Distress Questionnaire (MDQ) a week later (Chrisler, Johnston, Champagne, & Preston, 1994). Students who responded to the MJQ first reported more positive cyclic changes on the MDQ and more positive attitudes on the MAQ. "The major contribution of the present studies is to provide evidence for what many of us have long suspected—that the portrayal of the menstrual cycle by authorities and in popular culture affects the way women think about their bodies and their cyclicity" (Chrisler et al., 1994, p. 386). This research supports the view that new approaches are needed to menstrual education in which positive aspects of menstruation are included.

> *Women who use oral contraceptives are higher in positive affect during the menstruation, follicular, and ovulatory phases than women who do not use hormonal contraceptives.*

Emotional changes during the menstrual cycle were studied by comparing 30 women who had not used hormonal contraceptives during the preceding 12 months with 20 who were regular users of the Pill (Almagor & Ben-Porath, 1991). Scores on measures of negative and positive affect did not differ for the premenstrual phase of the menstrual cycle for either group as compared to the other. Users of oral contraceptives, however, were higher in positive affect scores during the menstruation, follicular, and ovulatory phases, but not in the luteal and premenstrual phases. "This difference suggests that during these periods users of oral contraceptives may feel more attentive, interested, alert and enthusiastic and less sleepy and tired than non-users of oral contraceptives (Almagor & Ben-Porath, 1991, p. 725). Since oral contraceptives provide a more constant dose of estrogen and progesterone throughout the cycle, the difference between the two groups in mood during the luteal and premenstrual phases suggested to the researchers that differences in hormone levels may play a role in mood differences between the two groups.

Physical symptoms are more consistent between consecutive menstrual cycles than are emotional experiences (Anne Walker, 1994). This conclusion is based on research on 109 women of reproductive age who completed daily diaries of mood and physical well-being for two consecutive menstrual cycles. "Only 5.4% (nonsteroidal contraceptive users) and 7.8% (oral contraceptive users) of Cycle 2 emotional score variance could be accounted for by Cycle 1 scores compared with 15% and 22%, respectively, for physical scores" (Anne Walker, 1994, p. 271). The implications of this study are that biological determinism cannot account for intercycle variability, particularly in moods, and that external psychological and social factors have to be integrated into models of mood and the menstrual cycle.

> *Two to eight percent of women suffer from severe premenstrual symptoms which disrupt their daily lives. Black and White women are equally likely to suffer from premenstrual syndrome.*

While most women do not suffer from debilitating effects during the premenstrual phase, for perhaps 2–8% of women, premenstrual symptoms are so severe they profoundly disrupt daily life and the women seek treatment. A comparison of White and Black community samples of women seeking help from a premenstrual syndrome clinic found no significant differences in the severity or prevalence of premenstrual symptoms (Stout, Steege, Blazer, & George, 1986).

> *Factor analysis has identified three premenstrual factors: increased well being; physiological depression, and anxiety–volatility.*

Three premenstrual factors were identified by factor analysis of the scores on the Premenstrual Assessment Form of 109 18–41-year-old women seeking treatment for premenstrual complaint (Cumming, Cumming, Krausher, & Fox, 1991). Increased well being, one of the factors, was unrelated to the other two factors, physiological depression (depression with physical symptoms) and anxiety–volatility, which had some overlap with each other.

> The two negative subsyndromes which emerge from the analysis do fit with general clinical experience, i.e the broad delineation of symptomatic women into those women who become depressed prior to menses (Factor 1) and those who become predominantly anxious with an element of low mood (Factor 2). (Cumming et al., 1991, p. 719)

Women who suffer from premenstrual syndrome are thus not a homogeneous group, with differences in the psychological symptomatology also related to the two psychological subtypes. Physical symptoms are much more related to depressive style, whereas the anxious–volatile group who are more prone to lability and impulsivity are much less likely to report physical symptoms.

Women who suffer from PMS are not neurotic. High estradiol levels may cause PMS in a few women.

In current medical practice, PMS is seen as a combination of mental and physical symptoms that arise in the luteal phase of the menstrual cycle and disappear after the onset of menstruation. Backstrom and Hammarback (1991) identified three PMS subgroups of women. The "Pure PMS" group had significant cyclical symptoms during the luteal phase and no symptoms during the follicular phase. The "Premenstrual aggravation" group had symptoms always present, but an aggravation of the symptoms premenstrually. The "Non PMS" group did not suffer from cyclical symptoms. Psychiatric histories and the neurosis scores on a personality test found that the "Pure PMS" group had the lowest neurosis scores and a lower frequency of women with an earlier psychiatric history than did women in the other two groups.

Is there a higher incidence of crime among women during the premenstrual and menstrual phases? Does behavior actually change during the premenstrual phase of the cycle?

Katharina Dalton (1980) reported on three women in England who were successful in pleading that the violent crimes they committed were due to premenstrual tension. Dalton has been widely quoted in the media as indicating that there is an increase in women committing crimes of violence during the premenstrual and menstrual phases. In one study conducted by d'Orban and Dalton (1980), 44% of a sample of 50 women charged with crimes of violence committed the crime during the premenstrual and menstrual phases. However, this is not greatly increased over what would be expected by chance during this time.

After doing comparative research on female rodents, in which she found that female rodents increase their attacks on other females when in the postovulatory phase of low progesterone,

Hood (1992) designed a longitudinal observational study of female college students who were told the study assessed health and mood states. Participants were videotaped while discussing controversial issues during weekly 30-minute meetings over a 40-day period. During this time students returned a daily questionnaire. Interactions were coded in order to quantify changes in assertive statements, participation style, and nonverbal behavior. There was no evidence of premenstrual syndrome in these behavior samples. In other words, students were no more assertive, as had been predicted, during the premenstrual phase of their cycle. In analyzing mood items from their daily self report, it was found that two items showed significant effects of menstrual phase. These items were in the opposite direction predicted, in other words students found it easier to cope and felt more physically well during the premenstrual phase (Hood, 1992).

Progesterone is no more effective than placebo in reducing symptoms of premenstrual syndrome.

Katharina Dalton (1977) advocated progesterone as a treatment for premenstrual syndrome. No significant difference in premenstrual symptom severity has been found, however, for women in a double blind, placebo-controlled crossover treatment study, in which 168 women received either progesterone or placebo for eight months (Freeman, Rickels, & Sondheimer, 1992). Although there was a significant reduction of symptoms from first evaluation, there was no significant difference between those receiving progesterone or placebo. One year after the end of the study, 129 of the patients were followed up to determine symptom severity and medication use. At the time of follow-up only 27% of the women were taking medication for PMS. There was no significant difference in symptom severity score of the women taking medications compared with those taking no medications. It can be concluded that progesterone is not an effective treatment for PMS.

Alprazolam (Xanax), a drug with both antianxiety and antidepressant effects, significantly reduces psychological symptoms of premenstrual syndrome among women seeking treatment.

Alprazolam (Xanax), a drug shown to have both antianxiety and antidepressant effects, was compared with placebo in the treatment of 30 women who were self-referred or referred by health professionals for premenstrual symptoms to a university-affiliated clinic (W. M. Harrison, Endicott, & Nee, 1990). Patients completed daily ratings as well as retrospective ratings using the Premenstrual Assessment Form scale. There was a significant reduction of depression and anxiety as well as irritability in the xanax as compared to the placebo treatment conditions.

Nutrition and exercise may also be effective in reducing PMS.

Before a woman resorts to pharmacological therapy for PMS, she should first try diet and exercise. If improvement does not occur after a few months, pharmacologic therapy can then be tried. Eating whole fresh foods, such as whole grains, legumes, seeds, nuts, vegetables, and fruits and avoiding highly processed foods and those high in refined sugar and fat, and decreasing intake of salt and caffeine may be helpful (Abraham & Rumley, 1987). High-dose calcium supplements (1,300 milligrams per day) have also been found to alleviate both mood swings and physical discomforts of women randomly assigned to the high-dose rather than low-dose (600 milligrams daily) condition ("Calcium subdues menstrual blues," 1991). Eating foods high in calcium such as skim milk, lowfat yogurt, and broccoli during the premenstrual period should also be tried before medication. Another research study indicated that low levels of zinc as measured in blood were related to PMS (as cited in "Calcium subdues menstrual blues," 1991). The relation of PMS to these deficiencies could explain why a small percentage of women suffer from PMS. Exercise may also be helpful in reducing PMS.

Having a hysterectomy reduces both physical and psychological symptoms of PMS.

Does having a hysterectomy ameliorate premenstrual symptoms? Yes. Having a hysterectomy (removal of uterus only) reduced both psychological and physical symptoms by 66% in mean premenstrual syndrome severity of 12 women who kept a daily symptom record before and after hysterectomy (Metcalf, Braiden, Livesey, & Wells, 1992). Only one of the women had persistent and unfailing mood-related PMS after the hysterectomy. The authors conclude that a uterus is not essential for the experience of premenstrual syndrome, but that either uterine or psychological factors account for PMS in most women. In any case, removal of the uterus often results in improvement of symptoms.

Some women use PMS as a method of self-handicapping.

Are some women simply faking it in order to derive certain benefits. Self-handicapping, as proposed by social psychologists, explains performance by reasons that enhance the opportunity to externalize (or excuse) failure and to internalize (or accept credit for) success. For example, a student might go to a party the night before an exam; then, when he/she does not do well, explain the failure as due to having gone to a party the night before the exam. Self-handicapping has been investigated in relation to premenstrual syndrome. Students who report a higher degree of PMS symptoms also claim symptoms as a self-handicap more than low PMS students to obscure the impact of a potentially poor performance (B. L. Beck, 1991).

After reviewing the mind-boggling literature on premenstrual syndrome, what do I think? I think that women are influenced by the media and others around them to believe that they should suffer from PMS every month and therefore focus attention on the minor changes that herald the onset of the menstrual period. A very small percentage of women suffer from psychological and/or physical premenstrual symptoms which disrupt their daily lives and require treatment. For those women who do suffer severe symptoms, treatment with progesterone is of no greater value than treatment with placebo; however, if all else fails, an antianxiety antidepressant, is likely to provide relief. Most women can be relieved of symptoms through diet and exercise, and the realization that women do not turn into menstrual monsters.

REFLECTIONS

A review of the research on sex differences in behavioral genetics and neuroendocrinology and of the effect of the menstrual cycle on behavior does not provide any scientific basis to justify the inequality between the sexes found in the world. Biology does not preordain behavior. Behavior can go in myriad directions depending on the sociocultural and historical context. Behavior is affected by an ecology, and events. That does not mean that we should stop looking at biological factors. Biology is a piece of the puzzle, but we should not reduce our thinking to biological determinism. The environment can also change biology.

Although there are some biological sex differences in brain organization and endocrine levels, it is not clear what implications these differences have for behavior other than reproductive behavior. Behavioral genetics and behavioral endocrinology have become burgeoning sciences. Feminists cannot dismiss this research, but must work to integrate it in conjunction with cultural and psychosocial factors. They also need to be vigilant for distorted media reports which overgeneralize the biological research, in order to provide alternative interpretations.

What is the relationship between testosterone levels and aggression? How can that relationship be moderated by social environmental factors? Why are feminist psychologists so sensitive to research purporting to find sex differences in the brain? Is premenstrual syndrome a socially constructed, rather than a biological, disorder? Why has there been such a long history of research trying to find a relationship between mood and/or cognition and the menstrual cycle?

Experiential Exercises

1. Plot your daily moods for a few months. If you are a menstruating female, then compare your mood fluctuations with your menstrual cycle, with weekends, and with events such as holidays. If you are a male or postmenopausal female, compare your mood fluctuations with weekends, and with events such as holidays.
2. Observe a litter of puppies at play. Can you distinguish the male puppies from the female puppies by their play behavior?

KEY TERMS

Adrenogenital Syndrome (CAH)   Genetic females exposed in utero to high levels of testosterone, produced too late to affect the internal reproductive organs, do have somewhat masculinized external reproductive organs and more tomboyish behavior.

5 Alpha Reductase Deficiency   Cases of genetic males suffering from a rare enzyme disorder that prevents prenatal testosterone from masculinizing their genitals. Masculine genitals, including a normal size penis, develop at puberty in response to the surge of testosterone. Although raised as females until puberty, they develop a male gender identity and male gender role after puberty.

Androgen Insensitivity Syndrome   This individual is a genetic male who is insensitive to testosterone. She/he appears to be a normal female, but has a male genotype. She/he exhibits normal female behavior.

Androgens   Male sex hormones. They are found in relatively larger concentrations in males than they are in females. Androgens are secreted by the male embryo's testes and cause the male internal organs and genitals to develop.

Brain Lateralization   The left and right hemispheres (halves) of the brain are somewhat responsible for the control of different functions. The left hemisphere is specialized for verbal functions. The right side of the brain is specialized for nonverbal or spatial functions.

Chromosomes   Genes are grouped into chromosomes. Every cell in the human body (except for the egg or sperm cells, which have 23 single chromosomes) contains 23 pairs of chormosomes, a total of 46 chromosomes.

Corpus Callosum   The part of the brain that carries information from one hemisphere of the brain to the other.

Dysmenorrhea   This is the medical term for menstrual cramps.

Endocrine Glands   Glands that produce chemical substances called hormones that are secreted directly into the bloodstream.

Follicle Stimulating Hormone   A hormone, released by the pituitary, which stimulates follicles in the ovary to grow. The ovarian follicles become an important source of estrogen.

Genotype   The hereditary information transmitted by genes on chromosomes.

Gonadotrophin Releasing Hormone (GnRH)   This hormone, released by the hypothalamus, causes the pituitary to release luteinizing hormone (LH) or Follicle Stimulating Hormone (FSH).

Gonads   Endocrine glands that secrete sex hormones.

Homosexuality   A preference for sexual partners of the same sex, based on the criterion of whether two sexual partners have the same genital and overal body conformation.

Klinefelter's Syndrome   Males that have an extra X chromosome. They have some feminization of appearance. They are likely to have lower than normal IQ scores and be at increased risk of being in prisons or mental institutions.

Lateral Asymmetry   The theory that male brains may be functionally more specialized on one side whereas there is greater bilateral processing in female brains, particularly for language.

Luteinizing Hormone (LH)   A hormone secreted by the anterior pituitary. LH acts on the ovary, stimulating a follicle in the ovary to rupture and release an ovum.

Menstrual Cycle   The menstrual cycle occurs on average every 28 days in the human female of reproductive age. There are five phases in the menstrual cycle: (1) menstrual phase; (2) follicular phase;

(3) ovulatory phase; (4) luteal phase; and (5) premenstrual phase.

Menstrual Synchrony   When menstruating women live in close interaction with one another, the phases of their menstrual cycles tend to coincide.

Ovaries   Female gonads that secrete estrogen and progesterone, the female sex hormones.

Phenotype   An observable characteristic as manifest in the individual at a given time, which results from an interaction of the gene(s) with the environment.

Premenstrual Syndrome   This refers to a set of psychological and physical symptoms that occur in some women during the week prior to menstruation and which end with the onset of menses.

Prostaglandins   These are hormone-like substances produced by the lining of the uterus and other tissues in the body, which cause smooth muscle to contract. The intense uterine contractions caused by high levels of prostaglandins cause pain.

Serotonin   A central nervous system neurotransmitter. Reduction of serotonin levels is associated with aggression.

Sex Chromosomes   The twenty-third set of chromosomes that determine the sex of the individual (XX in females, and XY in males).

Testes   The male gonads that secrete androgens.

Testosterone   The primary androgen.

XXX Females   Females that have an extra X chromosome are delayed in walking, talking, and in social skills. They also are more likely to be in prison than XX women.

XYY Males   Males that have an extra Y chromosome are taller than average and have lower average intelligence.

Zygote   A fertilized ovum.

SUGGESTED READINGS

Becker, J. B., Breedlove S. M., & Crews, D. (Eds.). (1992). *Behavioral Endocrinology.* Cambridge, MA: MIT Press. This edited volume contains 16 chapters that provide an encyclopedic treatment of behavioral endocrinology. It serves as an excellent reference work on the topic.

Bem, S. L. (1993). *The lenses of gender: Transforming the debate on sexual inequality.* New Haven, CT:

Yale University Press. Sandra Bem offers social psychological explanations for gender inequality, critically reviewing and refuting biological explanations.

Fausto-Sterling, A. (1992). *Myths of gender: Biological theories about women and men* (Rev. Ed.). New York: Basic Books. Anne Fausto-Sterling is a professor of biology at Brown University who presents a well-researched critique of the theories on gender differences in the brain.

Richardson, J. T. E. (Ed.). (1992). *Cognition and the menstrual cycle.* New York: Springer Verlag. This book summarizes the literature on menstrual cycle research relating to moods, cognition, and behavior, with the primary focus on cognition.

CHAPTER 3

Cognitive Gender Differences, School Achievement, Motivation, and Attributions for Achievement

The woman who uses her brain, loses her mammary function first and has little hope to be other than a moral and medical freak.

G. Stanley Hall, 1904

At the turn of the century, psychology took over from biology the scientific search for an understanding of the nature of males and females. "In psychology, the questions would be examined empirically, the focus would be psychological and hence would differ from dubitable work in biology; and inquiry would be open-minded as to the true causes—nature or nurture—of sex related difference" (Morawski, 1987, p. 46). Despite the enthusiastic early work of some psychologists, it became clear by the 1920s that the work was inconsistent and inconclusive. It was not until the impetus provided by the Women's Movement in the 1960s that gender differences became a widely researched topic in psychology. This book uses the word *sex* to refer to two biological categories of persons—females and males. Differ-

ences in behavior between males and females are called gender differences.

STATISTICAL ANALYSIS

The Normal Curve Distribution

The normal curve distribution provides a good description of most behavioral characteristics. Most scores cluster around the mean, with fewer and fewer cases falling at either end.

Most behavioral characteristics in psychology approximate the normal probability curve. The graph of this distribution approximates a symmetrical, bell-shaped curve (See Figure 3.1). The

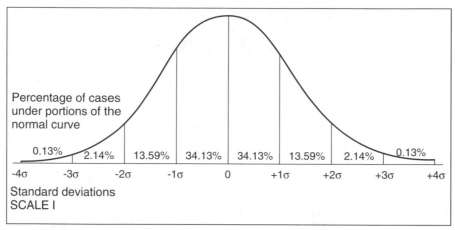

Percentage of cases
under portions of the
normal curve

0.13% 2.14% 13.59% 34.13% 34.13% 13.59% 2.14% 0.13%

-4σ   -3σ   -2σ   -1σ   0   +1σ   +2σ   +3σ   +4σ

Standard deviations
SCALE I

FIGURE 3.1 Normal Curve Distribution

frequencies concentrate around the mean (average score), with fewer and fewer cases falling at either end. The **standard deviation** of the scores should also to be taken into account when comparing gender differences. The standard deviation is a measure that tells us how much the scores in the distribution deviate from the mean, or how much variability there is in the scores. A small standard deviation would mean that the scores are close to the mean, whereas a large standard deviation would indicate that the scores are widely scattered. If you measured the height of women on a basketball team and they all measured between 5'10" and 6' tall, there would be a small standard deviation for height in that group. If you then measured women in Sorority Alpha and they were of a wider range of heights, from 4'10" to 5'10" tall, with women measuring across the continuum, the standard deviation for height for the sorority women would be larger than for the women on the basketball team.

If the distribution is the normal curve type, 68.2% of the cases will fall within one standard deviation of the mean, 95.4% of the cases within two standard deviations of the mean, and 99.7% of the cases within three standard deviations of the mean. It should also be kept in mind that if there is a very large number of individuals in the sample, then there may be a statistically signifi-

cant difference between the means for males and females even when the average scores are not very far apart. A difference can be statistically significant but have little practical significance.

A useful concept in studying gender differences is percentage overlap, which is a measure of the percentage of members of Group A who reach or exceed the median (point above which and below which half of the scores fall) of Group B. So even when a mean difference between the scores of two groups is statistically significant, nearly all of the individuals within both groups may fall within the same range of scores and there may be extensive overlapping of scores.

Meta-Analysis

Meta-analysis is a quantitative technique that combines the data from different studies to calculate the difference between the means for two groups such as males and females.

A major methodological breakthrough that has had significant impact on the study of gender differences in the 1980s and 1990s has been the development of **meta-analysis** (R. Rosenthal, 1991). It consists of quantitative techniques for the analysis of results from different studies testing the same hypothesis; for example, the hypothesis that females score higher on tests of verbal ability than do males.

Therefore, the first step in conducting a meta-analysis would be to do a search of the literature for all of the studies that tested for gender differences in verbal ability. We have a large number of studies that include thousands of people who have been tested in this area. For each study the relevant data is extracted and coded, then the magnitude of the finding or gender difference is calculated. In meta-analysis of a gender difference, the most commonly used measure of the difference is the effect size "d", which is the difference between the means in standard score form, divided by the standard deviation. The effect sizes or d values are then averaged across all of the studies included in the meta-analysis, to yield an overall d value. The d statistic is a measure of how far apart or how much difference there is between the means for males and females from all of the studies combined. The effect size is compared with 0.00, which would be the result if there was no difference between the groups being compared. For example, if the effect size $d = 0.25$, that is one quarter of a standard deviation; if $d = 0.50$ that is one half of a standard deviation, and so on (Hedges & Becker, 1986; J. E. Hunter & Schmidt, 1990).

Although there is a difference of opinion on what constitutes a large or a small effect size, J. Cohen (1977) suggests that for the d value, 0.20 is small, 0.50 is medium, and 0.80 is a large difference. One common practice is for researchers to report d as a plus (+) value when males score higher on a measure and as a minus (−) value when females score higher. That practice will be followed in this book.

When the research literature has tested the hypothesis of interest as a correlation rather than as a difference, the correlation coefficient "r" is the effect size calculated by meta-analysis. Meta-analysis of correlations is usually of the distribution of correlations between a given independent and dependent variable (J. E. Hunter & Schmidt, 1990). For example, a meta-analysis of correlations could be conducted for the relation between college performance and SAT scores. The data could also be examined by gender to see if the correlation between college performance and SAT scores, for example, differed for men and women.

Robert Rosenthal (1984) developed techniques for combining the probability level (p values) across studies. It can then be determined if the d (effect size) for all the studies combined reaches the .05 level of significance, which means that the difference between males and females on the characteristic being measured would occur by chance 5 or fewer times out of 100.

If there are large variations in the d values calculated from different studies, the effect size d, in that meta-analysis would not be homogeneous (consistent). For example, there might be two different types of abilities being measured by mathematics studies, computation and problem solving, one of which may show a gender difference in favor of females and the other a gender difference in favor of males. Separate meta-analyses would then be done on subsets of the studies, in order to obtain homogeneity (Hedges & Olkin, 1985). That part of the analysis may take a little detective work to determine what characteristics of the studies are related to the variations in the research findings.

Meta-analytic methods provide advantages over narrative reviews in that they are less subject to the reviewer's own biases in drawing conclusions. They also help avoid the problem that occurs when a particular study finds a gender difference that catches the attention of psychologists and even the general public, often ignoring replications (independent repetitions of the research by other scientists) that may not find the gender difference at all. "These techniques . . . provide explicit and statistically justified methods of drawing conclusions from the large numbers of studies that had been conducted in various areas of sex-difference research" (Eagly, 1987, p. 36). Meta-analysis, however, is going to reflect the biases of the studies on which it is based. If a meta-analysis uses only published studies, it may be weighted in the direction of finding a gender difference because it has typically been the case that research has been more likely to be published if a significant difference is found. Techniques are also available to calculate the number of nonsignificant studies one would have to find in order to render the meta-analytic findings no longer statistically significant (R. Rosenthal, 1984). Literary reviews also face the same problem of not having available nonpublished studies. If the meta-analysis does include unpublished as well as published studies, then it is open to the criticism that the unpublished studies have not had to go through peer review and may not be as methodologically rigorous.

INTELLIGENCE

Who are more intelligent, men or women?
Neither.

When Samuel Johnson was asked which are more intelligent, men or women, he replied, "Which man, which woman?" Typically, on psychological measures there are small average differences between the sexes and large individual variations within each group (Anastasi, 1958). When IQ tests were initially developed, it was clear that boys did better on some subtests, while girls did better on others. The tests were constructed to eliminate items showing a gender difference and to balance subtests so that there would be no difference in mean IQ scores for males and females. Thus, one of the reasons why there are no gender differences in intelligence test scores is because of the way intelligence tests were constructed (Anastasi, 1958). The research on gender differences in intelligence has focused instead on separate abilities rather than global intelligence.

Variability in Intelligence

A highly controversial theory is that males have greater variability in intelligence. The data does support the conclusion that more males are retardates than females.

One of the controversial long-standing theories of gender differences in intelligence is the variability hypothesis, which originated when Charles Darwin first suggested it in 1868. This hypothesis states that there is greater general variability in male than in female intelligence (i.e., there are more male retardates and male geniuses), whereas females cluster closer to the mean. Biologically deterministic explanations were given for the variability. Beginning with Galton's study of hereditary genius, scientists compiled lists of persons who had achieved eminence. Because few women appeared on these lists, they were used to support the belief of the innate inferiority of women (Shields, 1987). "Few scientists questioned whether nurture might be as important as nature in determining the course of development" (Shields, 1987, p. 198). Never mind that it was not until the 1880s that women were even admitted to any graduate school, which means that women did not have the opportunities to be trained in scientific and other academic fields. Even highly gifted women who were studied longitudinally in the twentieth century were more likely to be housewives and secretaries than employed in academic, scientific, or other professional fields (Terman & Oden, 1947).

Research does support the finding that mental retardation is more prevalent in males than in females (Halpern, 1992). Vandenberg (1987) presents evidence that the phenomenon of more male than female retardates may be caused by the "fragile X syndrome," which is a fragile site in an area of the X chromosome that does not stain as this area normally does when prepared for viewing by an electron microscope that has revealed a defect in this area. The fragile X has been associated with severe mental retardation, although it is occasionally mild, or intelligence is normal. Since females have two X chromosomes, they would be less affected by a fragile X chromosome, or other forms of retardation associated with the X chromosome. The fragile X syndrome is considered to be a major genetic cause of mental retardation.

Research by Feingold (1992b) on gender differences in variability on the national norms of several standardized test batteries "consistently found that males were more variable than females in general knowledge, mechanical reasoning, quantitative ability, spatial visualization, and spelling. There was essentially homogeneity of variance for most verbal tests, short-term memory, abstract reasoning, and perceptual speed" (p. 74). Feingold notes, however, that other research finds greater male variability in some nations and greater female variability in other nations, which argues against a biological hypothesis to account for greater male variability.

MATHEMATICS ABILITY

Gender Differences in Mathematical Ability

Gender differences in mathematics are disappearing, except in the highest range of scores.

The 1980 article by Benbow and Stanley in *Science* reporting gender differences in mathematics based on scores on the mathematics section of the Scholastic Aptitude Test (SAT-M) given to 9,927 intellectually gifted junior high school students over a period of several years, was perfect grist for the media mill. The media is much more interested in gender differences than similarities, and whatever differences exist tend to be exaggerated. The smallest mean gender difference for any year studied was 32 points in favor of boys in the 1979 sample. Because Benbow and Stanley tested junior high students, they claimed their study refuted Fennema and Sherman's (1977) hypothesis that males scored higher than females on the SAT-M because boys took more math courses in high school. Benbow and Stanley argued that junior high boys and girls had essentially the same amount of training in mathematics. Do teachers, however, ask girls as pointed questions and give them as much individual help in mathematics? Are little boys more likely than girls to work with their fathers in tasks requiring math skills such as building models?

In follow-up talent searches in 1980, 1981, and 1982, which tested 39,820 high-ability students, the gender difference in mathematical ability in favor of boys was again most pronounced at the highest levels (scores of over 700), where boys outnumbered girls by 13 to 1 (Benbow & Stanley, 1983). Although Benbow and Stanley (1980) suggested a biological explanation for the gender difference, they offered no genetic or biological data to support such a view. As was seen in Chapter II, the research trying to link biological and cognitive abilities is very contradictory.

What about the other 98% of the school age population, do boys score higher than girls in mathematics? Research documents a decline in gender differences in mathematical ability and concludes that males do not score higher than females in mathematics in the general population. Feingold (1988) examined the norms from the four standardizations of the Differential Aptitude Tests (DAT) conducted between 1947 and 1980 and four standardizations of the Preliminary Scholastic Aptitude Test/Scholastic Aptitude Test (PSAT, SAT) conducted between 1960 and 1983. Analyses of the norms from the mathematics tests of the SAT and PSAT show that girls have narrowed the gender difference in quantitative abilities over the years, cutting them to almost one-third of the difference between 1960 and 1983. "The important exception to the rule of vanishing gender differences is that of the well-documented gender gap at the highest levels of performance on high school mathematics has remained constant from 1960 to 1983" (Feingold, 1988, p.101).

The most thorough and current meta-analysis of gender differences in mathematical performance was conducted by Hyde, Fennema and Lamon (1990), based on data from 100 studies representing the testing of over 3 million individuals. They found a weighted mean effect size of +0.20 (weighted means are calculated when subgroups are of unequal size). When averaging over all studies, except the SAT scores, the gender difference was +0.15, a small gender difference favoring males. For the general population the average effect size of $d = -0.05$ (excluding SAT scores, and selective samples such as those on gifted adolescents) was a negligible difference favoring females.

Since overall the effect sizes were nonhomogeneous, further analyses were conducted that showed three variables to account for 87% of the variance: age, selectivity of the sample, and cognitive level of the test (see Table 3.1). Gender differences in mathematics slightly favor girls in elementary school and middle school. With increasing age gender differences favor males, beginning at ages 15–18 ($d = +0.29$, excluding SAT exams), increasing at ages 19–25 ($d = +0.41$), and again increasing for adults 26 and older ($d = +0.59$). In understanding mathematical concepts, no gender differences appear at any age level. Gender differences in problem solving are not consistently found until the high school and college level, when there is a moderate gender difference favoring males. As Hyde et al. (1990) point out, it is in the high school and college years that females begin to select fewer mathematics courses than do males, but this still does not account for all of the difference. Men are also more likely to enter occupations requiring the use of mathematics and therefore have more practice with mathematics on a daily basis.

The more selective the sample, the larger the gender difference favoring males ($d = +0.54$ for students at highly selective colleges, and graduate students). A trend was also apparent in a decline in gender differences in more recent studies. For studies published after 1973, $d = +0.14$ as compared with studies published in 1973 or earlier for which $d = +0.31$. Hyde et al. (1990) conclude that there is little support for a global gender difference in mathematics.

When Hyde et al. (1989) computed a meta-analysis by ethnicity, excluding SAT scores, Blacks and Hispanics showed essentially no gender differences in math performance. Among Asian Americans, the females showed a slight advantage in mathematical performance ($d =$

TABLE 3.1 A Meta-Analysis of Gender Differences in Mathematics Ability

Mathematics Ability	Weighted Mean d	Effect Size k	Study
All Studies (SATs Excluded)	+0.15	254	Hyde, Fennema & Lamon (1990)
Subtests			
Computation	−0.14	45	
Concepts	−0.03	41	
Problem Solving	+0.08	48	
Ethnicity			
Black	−0.02	21	
Hispanic	−0.00	20	
Asian American	−0.09	4	
White	+0.13	13	
Selectivity of Sample			
General	−0.05	184	
Moderately Selective	+0.33	24	
Highly Selective	+0.54	18	
Precocious	+0.41	15	
Selected for Low Performance	+0.11	12	
Age Group			
5–10	−0.06	67	
11–14	−0.07	93	
15–18	+0.29	53	
19–25	+0.41	31	
26 and older	+0.59	9	

Note: k represents the number of effect sizes on which each mean is based.

−0.09). There was a small gender difference ($d = +0.13$) favoring males only for White Americans.

Gender differences that appear on the SAT-M have practical implications to the extent to which they are used to determine college admissions and scholarship money. Do actual gender differences in college performance in math courses warrant exclusion of women students from colleges based on SAT-M scores?

Gender Differences in Mathematics Grades

Although males get higher SAT-M scores, females get equal or slightly higher grades in math classes.

Despite the higher SAT-M scores of males compared with females, women get equal or higher grades in math classes in college than do men. Females' superiority in math grades in school and college is supported by ample evidence (Bridgeman & Wendler, 1991; deWolf, 1981; Stockard & Wood, 1984). Men and women enrolled in the same classes in algebra, precalculus, and calculus with analytic geometry at nine colleges and universities were found to have SAT-M scores that differed by one-third of a standard deviation or more, favoring men (Bridgeman & Wendler, 1991). Nevertheless, the females' grades were equal to or slightly better than those of their male classmates in math. Bridgman and Wendler point out that the higher math course grades of women are not due to social skills or attending class and doing homework on time because the grades reported in their research were solely based on classroom tests. Is it fair to award scholarships to men on the basis of SAT-M scores when women do just as well in math classes?

A number of hypotheses have been put forth to account for girls' higher math grades, but lower rates of taking more advanced math classes (Kimball, 1989). These include girls' lesser experience with extracurricular math and science; a rote approach to learning math; attribution of their success in math to effort rather than ability (which does not increase their confidence for future challenges); their tendency to do better in familiar situations (classwork); and sex role conflict.

Gender Differences on the SAT-M

Gender differences in spatial ability do not account for gender differences in mathematics. Prior mathematics knowledge and problem-solving strategies can account for gender differences in mathematics.

Interest has been generated as to why gifted male adolescents perform better on the SAT-M than gifted female adolescents. One hypothesis that has been put forth to explain gender differences in math is that it is related to male superiority in spatial tasks. "Examination of the nature, magnitude and age of first appearance of gender differences in mathematics, science, and spatial ability fails to reveal a consistent pattern" (Linn & Petersen, 1986, p. 87). It thus becomes difficult to see how spatial ability could account for the gender differences that appear in mathematics.

A more recent explanation for gender differences on SAT-M items uses a cognitive process approach (Byrnes & Takahira, 1993). This theory was supported in a sample of 59 female and 49 male eleventh- and twelfth-grade students by the finding that 50% of the variance in SAT scores could be explained by prior knowledge and assembling strategies. For example, in order to solve a problem that involved finding the midpoint of a tangent, the student must know what a tangent is and the formula for finding it as well as to be able to compile or assemble the procedures together in an effective fashion. Although 4% of the variance could be explained by gender, this finding washed out when prior knowledge and strategies were included. Further research needs to investigate why female senior high school students have less adequate prior mathematics knowledge and strategies even when they have taken the same number of courses and performed as well in them.

Social and Attitudinal Factors

Social and attitudinal factors influence females' math performance. Males stereotype math as a male domain. Females are less likely to enroll in math courses, which becomes a "critical filter" for careers that require math.

As noted earlier, the Benbow and Stanley (1980) research of male superiority in mathematics has been greatly exaggerated by the media and, in turn, had an impact on parents, teachers, and students themselves. Based on a two-year longitudinal study of average and above-average students in seventh through ninth grade, Eccles and Jacobs (1986) concluded that social and attitudinal factors have greater influence on math achievement than does mathematical aptitude. Questionnaires were sent to parents in April, 1980, who had provided information in 1978–1979 on their children's mathematical ability (J. E. Jacobs & Eccles, 1985). In the 1980 questionnaire they also asked parents if they had read or read about the Benbow and Stanley study. The results indicated that mothers of girls who had read about the Benbow and Stanley study had lower estimates of their daughters' mathematical ability than they had during 1978–1979, and lower estimates than mothers of girls who had not read about the study. Clearly, J. E. Jacobs and Eccles' research indicates the impact of media reports on expectations of mothers of girls even when the research was not relevant to them, because the study was only describing results for mathematically gifted children.

Our data suggest that social and attitudinal factors have a greater influence on junior and senior high school students' grades and enrollment in mathematics courses than do variations in mathematical aptitude. Further, our data suggest that sex differences in mathematics achievement and attitudes are largely due to sex differences in math anxiety; the gender-stereotyped beliefs of parents, especially mothers; and the value students attach to mathematics. (Eccles & Jacobs, 1986, p. 370)

Educator Sheila Tobias (1976, 1978) brought the country's attention to the concept of "**math anxiety**" that she says is a conditioned anxiety to mathematics that females in our society acquire, leading them to avoid math classes, and to fear quantitative concepts. Anastasi (1985) points out the tendency of researchers in differential psychology to continue to separate affect and cognition. Research with school children and college students demonstrates the lower achievement and intelligence test scores of students with test anxiety. Moreover, intervention has been effective in improving both test performance and school work.

Males hold much more stereotyped views about math as a male domain than do females ($d = +0.90$). That was the result of a meta-analysis of gender differences in math attitudes/affect based on the testing of 63,229 persons (Hyde & Fennema, 1989; Hyde, Fennema, Ryan, Frost, & Hopp, 1990). The overall gender differences are small in areas such as confidence, math anxiety, usefulness of mathematics, attitudes toward math success, effectance, and mother's attitude. Hyde and Fennema (1989) are particularly concerned about the males in positions of power who believe math is a male domain and the teachers, guidance counselors, and mentors who may discourage girls and women from achieving their mathematics potential. Based on this research, and that on gender differences in mathematics ability, Hyde et al. (1990) believe that the underrepresentation of women in mathematics-related fields is not due to differences in abilities and intrapsychic factors, but rather to sex discrimination in education and employment.

Studies have shown that females have less investment in mathematics. They are less likely to perceive math as useful to them, to enroll in math-related courses, or to choose careers that require math (J. M. Singer & Stake, 1986). Of course, choices of careers become considerably limited because mathematics has been called a "critical filter" (Sells, 1978; 1980) keeping women out of many fields in science, engineering, and even business and economics because females do not take the required mathematics courses. In fact, a study by Sells at the University of California at Berkeley found that 57% of the men who were freshman in 1972 had taken at least 3½ years of high school mathematics in comparison to only 8% of the freshman women (Sells, 1980).

Although a later study by J. M. Singer and Stake (1986) found females taking more mathematics in high school and college, women are still less likely to select career goals requiring mathematics, and continue to select more traditional female occupations. The college women in the study, however, did not have greater math anxiety, lower self-assessments of math ability, or consider mathematics any less useful than did the men. The women also tended to deny that math is a male domain. The women's general performance self-esteem, however, was not enhanced by participation or success in math, as was the performance self-esteem of the men.

> Why wasn't the women's performance self-esteem positively affected by math involvement and success? The most obvious explanation is that the women viewed mathematics as a male activity that was not important in determining their success in becoming capable women. (J. M. Singer & Stake, 1986, p. 349)

Women may have held more traditional attitudes on a deeper level in which their internalization of stereotypes about mathematics as a male domain may influence their lack of association of mathematics with their own performance self-esteem. In the light of changing sex role norms, females may now be consciously accepting that mathematics is of importance, but on a less-conscious level have not yet really internalized the message. The result is that fewer females than males in the 1990s are taking mathematics courses in college. When my daughter, as a freshman at the University of Rhode Island in the spring of 1992, enrolled in a course in calculus with analytic geometry she was only one of three women in a class of approximately 70 students.

VERBAL ABILITY

Gender Differences in Verbal Ability

Gender differences in overall verbal ability are also disappearing. The largest gender difference in verbal ability is a moderate difference in quality of speech production.

Are gender differences in verbal ability disappearing? The earlier classic texts on differential psychology all concluded that females were superior to males in verbal ability from early childhood through adulthood (Anastasi, 1958; Tyler, 1965; Maccoby; 1966). After reviewing 85 studies Maccoby and Jacklin (1974) said that the sexes are very similar in verbal ability until about age 11, after which time girls score higher on "high-level" verbal tasks such as analogies, comprehension of difficult written material, and creative writing, as well as "lower-level" measures such as fluency.

The research by Feingold (1988) found that when the Differential Aptitude Tests (DAT) and the PSAT/SAT were first normed in 1947 and 1960, respectively, girls scored higher on the DAT tests of spelling and language use and boys scored higher on Verbal Reasoning. Girls scored higher on the PSAT-Verbal and the SAT-Verbal. By 1980 boys had closed the gap on the PSAT-Verbal and girls had closed the gap on the DAT Verbal Reasoning, whereas girls still scored higher on measures of spelling ($d = -0.51$) and language use ($d = -0.40$). Until 1972, the gender differences on the SAT-Verbal favored females; since 1972, this has been no longer been true.

Data analysis of all persons taking the SAT in 1993 found males to slightly outperform females on the SAT-Verbal (for males, $M = 428$, and for females $M = 420$) (U.S. Bureau of the Census, 1994). This difference favoring males could be due to differences in characteristics of the samples of males and females. More females take the test than males. Background data indicates that males who take the SAT are more likely to come from homes of slightly higher socioeconomic level as measured by parental income, father's education, and attendance at private schools (Feingold, 1988).

Halpern (1989) argues that Feingold's (1988) normative sample for the DAT is not comparable for males and females, even though unlike the PSAT and SAT, Feingold claims it was normed on "representative samples" of high school students. She says that what Feingold and others fail to consider is that "sex ratios in high school dropout rates beginning as early as eighth grade have also been changing, and any test normed on high school students reflects these changes" (Halpern, 1989, p. 1156). Prior to 1980, more girls dropped out than boys. Between 1970 and 1980 the gap narrowed. Since 1980, more boys drop out than girls, leaving a biased sample of higher ability males in school. Boys are overrepresented in the extremely low end of the verbal abilities distribution in high schools. Students in special classes or those with dyslexia do not usually take standardized written exams. The written exams also do not measure fluent speech, and we know that male stutterers outnumber female stutterers three

or four to one. Those factors additionally contribute to a biased sample of higher-ability males taking standardized tests in high schools.

Hyde and Linn (1988) conclude that gender differences in verbal ability no longer exist. Their meta-analysis of 165 studies of gender differences in verbal performance yielded a very small difference, $d = -0.11$ Homogeneity analyses found the effect sizes to be heterogeneous. Partitioning verbal abilities into more homogeneous subgroups yielded effect sizes almost all of which were small (see Table 3.2). The largest gender difference in verbal ability was for speech production ($d = -0.33$), and the next largest for anagrams ($d = -0.22$), both of which favored females. Hyde and Linn note that most of the studies of speech production use quality of speech rather than quantity as the dependent measure. Studies of total talking time show that males exceed females.

Contrary to Maccoby and Jacklin (1974), who said that gender differences in verbal ability emerge around age 11, no striking gender differences in verbal ability by age were found. Gender differences, however, were found to be smaller

TABLE 3.2   A Meta-Analysis of Gender Differences in Verbal Ability

Verbal Ability	Weighted Mean d	Effect Size k	Study
All Studies (SATs Excluded)	−0.11	119	Hyde & Linn (1988)
Type of Test			
Vocabulary	−0.02	40	
Analogies	+0.16	5	
Reading comprehension	−0.03	18	
Speech production	−0.33	12	
Essay writing	−0.09	5	
Scholastic Aptitude Test	+0.03	4	
Anagrams	−0.22	5	
General/mixed	−0.20	25	
Age Group			
5 and under	−0.13	24	
6–10	−0.06	29	
11–18	−0.11	39	
19–25	−0.06	18	
26 and older	−0.20	9	

Note: k represents the number of effect sizes on which each mean is based.

for studies published more recently as compared with earlier research. The effect size for studies of verbal ability published prior to 1974 was $d = -0.23$, which was twice as large as the effect size for studies published after 1974, $d = -0.10$, indicating a decline in the magnitude of gender differences. This may reflect changes in American society in less-stereotyped expectations for differential performance of males and females.

VISUAL SPATIAL ABILITY

There are three categories of visual spatial ability—spatial perception, mental rotation, and spatial visualization.

Visual spatial ability helps us to get around in the world. Activities from children playing on a jungle gym or building with blocks to adults driving a car or becoming a mechanic or architect or engineer all are all heavily dependent on spatial ability. The problem of reorienting myself spatially became crucial to me when I was visiting Ireland several years ago and rented a car. Suddenly, the passenger seat and rear-view mirror were to my left. I was driving down the left side of the street and when I went around a corner or a rotary, I would ask for help from my teenage daughter who was traveling with me, "Quick Valerie, which side of the street should I be on?" Fortunately, we returned the rental car a week later without having had any mishaps. Do men fare any better than I did? I do not think so, because it was about that time that the American actor Matthew Broderick had an accident in Ireland in which, while driving his rental car on the wrong side of the road, he smashed head on into a car driven by two Irish women who were instantly killed. Anecdotes aside, can we really account for the dearth of women mechanics, engineers or architects on the basis of a female disadvantage in visual spatial ability?

Maccoby and Jacklin (1974) concluded that "male superiority in visual-spatial tasks is fairly consistently found in adolescence and adulthood,

but not in childhood" (p. 351). To test for gender and age differences in visual–spatial ability, Linn and Petersen (1985; 1986) conducted meta-analyses. In order to provide cohesion and make replication possible, broad categories of spatial ability were formed: **spatial perception** that requires subjects to locate the horizontal or the vertical despite distracting information (such as a tilted glass or a tilted frame); **mental rotation**, which requires the subject to rapidly and accurately mentally rotate a two- or three-dimensional figure; and **spatial visualization** that requires complicated multistep analysis of spatially presented information.

A recent meta-analysis of gender differences on spatial tasks that provided a nearly exhaustive review of the published literature for nearly 50 years up to 1993 concluded that gender differences are clearly established in some areas of spatial abilities (Voyer, Voyer, & Bryden, 1995). The overall analysis of 286 studies yielded a mean weighted d of $+0.37$. Although there was a tendency for participants who were born more recently to show smaller gender differences in spatial abilities in comparison to participants who were born earlier (thus showing an effect of changing attitudes toward women), this result was not statistically significant (Voyer et al., 1995). These meta-analyses cannot provide any answer as to the causes of gender differences in spatial abilities.

Spatial Perception

Gender differences in spatial perception favoring males appear in childhood and increase after age 18.

Women were labeled as field dependent and men as field independent by Witkin and his colleagues (1962) because of differential performance on the rod and frame test, which is frequently used to measure spatial perception. Spatial perception requires the individual to distinguish the vertical or horizontal when it appears in a context of distracting information. On the rod and frame test, the individual, who is seated in a dark room, is asked to adjust a luminous tilted rod to the true vertical. The rod is inside of a luminous tilted frame that serves to provide misleading cues. It is not purely a visual task because kinesthetic cues relating to body position, body motion, and gravity also come into play. Research has shown that males are better able to adjust the rod to the upright position, whereas females are more likely to have the rod tilting, influenced by the tilted frame. Their performance was interpreted as fitting in with the stereotype of females being more dependent and males as more independent. Another way of interpreting this same result is to see females as "context sensitive" and males as "context insensitive."

Both Voyer et al. (1995) and Linn and Petersen (1985; 1986) in their meta-analyses found a mean effect size of +0.44, for spatial perception, but that the unbiased effect sizes were not homogeneous (see Table 3.3). Partitioning by age, Linn & Petersen found the average effect size was +0.64 for those 18 years of age and older, which was significantly larger than for those in the two younger age groups, which were both +0.37. Linn and Petersen's overall conclusion, based on their meta-analyses, was that gender differences in spatial perception favoring males appeared as young as seven or eight and persist, increasing after age 18 and continuing throughout adulthood. No clear explanation can account for the much larger gender difference in spatial perception after age 18.

Mental Rotation

Gender differences favoring males are found for mental rotation.

Mental rotation involves rapidly mentally rotating a two- or three-dimensional figure. The 29 effect sizes that Linn and Petersen (1985, 1986) obtained for mental rotation were not homogeneous. Homogeneity was achieved by subdividing by task. The Vandenberg version of the

Table 3.3 Meta-Analyses of Gender Differences in Spatial Abilities

| | *Weighted Estimator of Effect Size* | |
Category of Tests	*Voyer, Voyer & Bryden (1995)*	*Linn & Petersen (1985, 1986)*
Spatial Perception		
All ages	+0.44*	+0.44*
Under 13 years	+0.33*	+0.37*
13–18 years	+0.43*	+0.37*
Over 18 years	+0.48*	+0.64*
Mental Rotation		
All ages	+0.56*	+0.73*
Under 13 years	+0.33*	
13–18 years	+0.45*	
Over 18 years	+0.66*	
Vandenberg version of the Shepherd-Metzler mental rotation test		+0.94*
Primary Mental Abilities–Space test	+0.44*	+0.26
Spatial Visualization		
All ages	+0.19	+0.13
Under 13 years	+0.02	
13–18 years	+0.18	
Over 18 years	+0.23*	

*P < .05

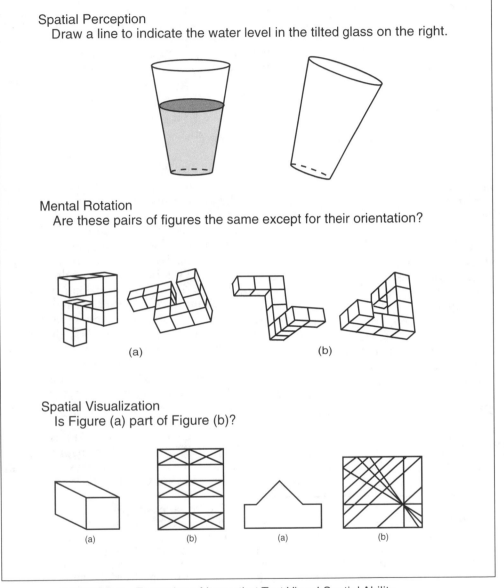

FIGURE 3.2 Examples of Items that Test Visual Spatial Ability

Shepard-Metzler mental rotations test yielded effect sizes that averaged +0.94, which was much larger than the effect size for the Primary Mental Abilities-Space test and related measures, which averaged +0.26. Voyer et al. 1995 found an effect size of $d = +0.56$ for mental rotation. Mental rotation is difficult to test before age 13 because of the high level of concentration this type of task requires, but gender differences favoring males are found at whatever age it is measured, although differences are not significant before age 12.

Spatial Visualization

No gender differences emerge for spatial visualization.

Spatial visualization is frequently measured by the embedded-figures test, which requires the individual to disembed a figure from a complex background. Spatial visualization tasks also include hidden figures, paper folding, the paper-form board, and the spatial relations subtest of the DAT. Linn and Petersen (1985) and Voyer et al. (1995) concluded that no gender differences exist for spatial visualization based on meta-analyses which yielded $d = +0.13$ and $d = +0.19$ respectively.

Mechanical Reasoning

Large gender differences favoring males are found for mechanical reasoning.

A cognitive gender difference that has components of both math and visual spatial ability is mechanical reasoning. Feingold (1988) reported a large gender difference in mechanical reasoning ($d = +0.98$) calculated from DAT scores. The gender differences in mechanical reasoning may be influenced by boys having more problem-solving experiences in classes such as physics and chemistry, in which they are more likely to enroll than girls, and from experiences such as learning to fix cars and other machinery. When I took a mechanical reasoning test in a psychological test-

ing course as an undergraduate at a women's college, I obtained the highest score in the class. I had taken an excellent physics course my senior year in high school, and also had some early experiences boys are more likely to have, such as learning to drive a tractor at age seven on my grandfather's farm and working around the farm every summer with my uncle.

WOMEN'S WAYS OF KNOWING

So far this chapter has dealt with cognitive abilities from a quantitative point of view. While this represents the mainstream approach within psychology to studying cognitive gender differences, another qualitative approach has been used to study women's cognitive development. In their book *Women's Ways of Knowing,* Belenky, Clinchy, Goldberger, and Tarule (1986) conducted in-depth interviews with 135 ordinary women, 90 of whom were enrolled in academic institutions, to learn the stages women go through in their acquisition of knowledge. They did not study men, so we have no basis for making comparisons about gender differences, but that is okay. We do not need always to be comparing women to men. We can study women in their own right to develop a better understanding of their intellectual processes.

The Belenky et al. (1986) research shows how intimately affective and cognitive processes are intertwined. Women's ways of thinking were grouped into five categories:

silence, a position in which women experience themselves as mindless and voiceless and subject to the whims of external authority; *received knowledge,* a perspective from which women conceive of themselves as capable of receiving, even reproducing, knowledge from the all-knowing external authorities but not capable of creating knowledge on their own; *subjective knowledge,* a perspective from which truth and knowledge are conceived of as personal, private, and subjectively known or intuited; *procedural knowledge,* a position in which women are invested in learning and applying objective procedures for obtaining and communicating knowledge; and *constructed knowledge,* a position in which women view all knowledge as contextual, experience themselves as creators of knowledge, and value both subjective and objective strategies for knowing. (Belenky et al., 1986, p. 15)

Belenky et al. state that the implications for education of their research is that educators should help women develop their own authentic voices by allowing them to evolve their own patterns of work and emphasize connection, understanding, collaboration and respect over assessment, separation and debate. Educators should listen to women's voices.

GENDER IN THE CLASSROOM

Teacher Attention in the Elementary School Classroom

Teachers give more attention to boys—both positive and negative, in the elementary school classroom. Science teachers ignore girls, and when they do direct questions to girls, they ask them lower-level questions than they ask boys.

Teachers check boys' work more often, call on them more during lessons, criticize and punish boys more for misbehavior, give boys instructions more, and monitor their behavior more (Brophy, 1985). This difference in directing communications to boys is even more pronounced for informatives—additional information, such as explanations for role expectations, causal attributions, and sanctions (Eccles & Blumenfeld, 1985). Is this due to bias on the part of teachers, or is it because boys behave differently from girls in the classroom?

In general, the data suggest that differences between boys and girls and patterns of interaction with their teachers are due to differences in the behavior of boys and girls themselves (and the effects of this behavior on the teachers) rather than to any consistent tendency of teachers to treat the two sexes differently. (Brophy, 1985, p. 120)

According to research by Myra and David Sadker (1986, 1994), it is in part that boys de-

mand more attention, as well as that teachers give boys more attention when boys call out of turn, whereas they ignore girls when they do the same thing. The Sadkers observed sex bias in classroom interactions in more than 100 fourth-, sixth-, and eighth-grade classrooms in four states and the District of Columbia. The classes were in rural, suburban, and urban schools, and included schools that were predominantly all White, all Black or integrated.

At all three grade levels and in all subjects, we found that male students were involved in more interactions than female students. It did not matter whether the teacher was black or white, female or male; the pattern remained the same. Male students received more attention from teachers. (Sadker & Sadker, 1986, p. 512)

Boys do demand more teacher attention. Boys are eight times more likely than are girls to call out an answer or make a comment without raising their hands. Teachers react differently, however, to a boy or a girl who calls out an answer without raising his/her hand and waiting to be recognized. Teachers will accept the answer from a boy, but tell the girl to wait to speak until she is called. "Boys are being trained to be assertive; girls are being trained to be passive—spectators relegated to the sidelines of classroom discussion" (Sadker & Sadker, 1986, p. 513).

Research focusing on the quality and quantity of elementary school science classroom interactions in relation to gender raised the question, "Are females invisible students?" (Barba & Cardinale, 1991). While the question may be overstated, the evidence shows that girls have fewer interactions with science teachers, including fewer questions directed to them. Teachers were significantly more likely to ask boys high-level questions and girls low-level questions. "By asking female students low-level questions, the observed science teachers provided cues to those students that they were low-ability students" (Barba & Cardinale, 1991, p. 309). Girls were more likely to give on-task responses (relevant to the question whether or not correct) 71% of the time as compared with boys' 29% of the time.

Doonesbury

Teacher Expectations

Teacher expectations for performance are lower for Black boys than for Black girls.

Teachers have been found, however, to have higher expectations for performance of African American girls than for African American boys (S. I. Ross & Jackson, 1991). Teachers from integrated school districts predicted lower academic performance for both the current school year and in the future for Black fourth-grade boys as compared with Black fourth-grade girls on the basis of 12 case histories, even when students had equivalent qualities. Teachers had the lowest expectations and least preference for nonsubmissive, independent Black boys.

Teacher and Peer Contacts

A study in integrated classrooms found that White girls and Black girls have more teacher contacts than White boys and Black boys. In peer interactions, girls give boys more support and receive more aggression from them.

Race effects and gender effects in classroom interactions of 139 first-grade students in six desegregated classrooms over a period of five to six months were not what would be predicted based on the studies just cited by Brophy (1985), the Sadkers (1986), and Barba and Cardinale (1991) (L. Grant, 1985). White girls were most likely to approach the teacher, and Black boys approached the teacher least often, with some fluctuation in the pattern for White boys and Black girls.

White and Black boys were most likely to challenge the teachers in all of the classrooms. Their challenges were of a different nature, however, with White boys more likely to challenge information and Black boys more likely to challenge application of rules. In examining the proportion of teacher–student and peer interactions, it was clear that White females had the highest ratios for teacher as opposed to peer interactions. Neither White boys nor Black boys had more contacts with teachers than they did with peers. Black girls ranked after White girls in teacher contacts. In all but two of the classrooms peer interactions were more common than teacher contacts. Black girls were the most frequent recipients of teacher praise for behavior, with White girls also above the mean for receipt of praise. White boys are slightly below the mean in most classrooms for praise, while Black boys are least likely to be recipients of praise in all of the rooms.

Girls, and particularly White girls, are more disadvantaged in peer interchanges. Girls give boys more emotional and academic support than they receive from them. Girls are more likely to be victims of verbal and physical aggression. Black girls are more likely to retaliate rather than back down in the face of these attacks than are White girls. Power and status differentials are greater among White than Black boys and girls. This research indicates that children's schooling experiences systematically differ by race–gender status (L. Grant, 1985).

Intellectual and Social Skills Related to Academic Performance

Intellectual skills and social skills both affect academic performance.

Intellectual skills and social skills were both found to directly affect academic performance of elementary school children (Serbin, Zelkowitz, Doyle, & Gold, 1990). Girls scored significantly higher than boys in academic performance, which was found to be due largely to their greater social responsiveness and compliance with adult direction. Boys' performance on the Block Design subscale of the Wechsler Intelligence scales for children (a standardized visual–spatial test) was also a predictor of academic success.

Mother's occupation level was related to children's academic success because of the amount of intellectual stimulation children receive via the toys they are given that allow them to practice visual–spatial skills. The higher the status of the mother, the more male toys were found in the homes of both boys and girls. In other words, mothers who have higher occupation level buy toys such as erector sets and Lego blocks for both their sons and daughters.

Father's education level was related to academic outcome via socializing the child in the behavioral–social style involving both social sensitivity and compliance, which enables the child to succeed in the classroom. Girls had higher levels of social responsiveness. The implications of the Serbin et al. (1990) study are that current socialization practices can be improved to provide each sex with specific cognitive and social skills needed to succeed in the classroom.

Gender in the College Classroom

The college classroom is a "chilly" climate for women, but it is improving.

In an influential report entitled "The Classroom Climate: A Chilly One for Women?," which was issued by the Project on the Status and Education of Women, R. M. Hall and Sandler (1982), raised the issue of whether men and women are treated differently in the college classroom and related learning situations. Many of these biases may be subtle and therefore go unnoticed. Nevertheless, these patterns may leave women students feeling less confident about their academic abilities than their male classmates. R. M. Hall and Sandler describe many verbal and nonverbal inequities that occur in the college classroom that include:

- comments that disparage women in general
- comments that divert discussion of a woman student's work toward a discussion of her physical attributes or appearance
- calling directly on men students but not on women students.
- calling men students by name more often than women students
- addressing the class as if no women were present
- waiting longer for men than for women to answer a question before going on to another student
- making eye contact more often with men than with women
- favoring men in choosing student assistants
- making direct sexual overtures (R. M. Hall & Sandler, 1982, pp. 6–9).

R. M. Hall and Sandler note that certain women may be especially affected, graduate students, women in traditionally "masculine" fields, minority students, and older women students.

In a more recent assessment of the "chilly climate" for women in the college classroom, student perceptions of student–teacher interactions were obtained at a state university and a small liberal arts college (Crawford & MacLeod, 1990). Gender was found to be related to class participation, with males participating more than females, only in the college survey. This difference, however, was not due to teacher discrimination. Female teachers were better than male teachers at creating a classroom climate that encouraged student questions and discussions, regardless of the gender of the student. It should be hoped that things have changed because this more recent research did not find as inhospitable a climate for women in the college classroom as was previously reported.

ACADEMIC DECISION MAKING

Eccles has developed a model of academic decision making that explains gender differences by focusing on expectations for success and positive values. Jacob's extension of this model shows that parents' stereotyping influences children's beliefs about their mathematical ability.

Three theoretical approaches have emerged to explain women's lack of parity in professional and executive positions: structural barriers; normative barriers; and cognitive differences (Fiorentine, 1988). Structural barriers refer to sex discrimination that, for example, forces women into secondary jobs such as lecturers in the academic world rather than into tenured positions. The normative approach emphasizes that the pursuit of a high status career runs counter to social norms for females and exposes them to social rejection and the inability to fulfill their role expectations of wife and mother. The cognitive differences approach looks at cognitive mediating variables, such as lesser confidence of females in their ability to perform successfully in high-level careers due to cultural stereotypes, which do not depict females in these positions. Another result of the lower level of confidence may be differences in causal attributions for the successes and failures of males and females.

Eccles (1985, 1987) has developed a cognitive model for decision making by females for education and careers in order to explain the persistence of women's concentration in female-dominated occupations (see Figure 3.3). According to Eccles, although approximately 4 million women

entered the work force since 1970, 3.3 million are concentrated in female dominated supportive occupations such as secretaries, nurses, bookkeepers, and cashiers. Why are women so underrepresented in certain professions, particularly the physical sciences and engineering and high-level management positions?

Although she acknowledges institutional barriers, Eccles believes that psychological factors also contribute to limiting women's professional and educational attainments by influencing the training and skills they seek and acquire. Eccles has developed a complex model based on both her own research with her colleagues and that of others reported in the literature. The model of women's educational and occupational decision making focuses on choice rather than negatively motivated dynamics such as fear and avoidance. The gender differences in educational and vocational choices result from expectations for success (perceived likelihood of success in the course or career) and values (positive values, for example, about mathematics courses and careers such as chemistry that require mathematics). Generally, the data supports the model (Figure 3.3).

A girl's expectations and values are shaped in the socialization process. Gender role socialization includes socialization of expectations for performance in different school subjects (parents expect girls to be better at English than mathematics). Parents, friends, teachers, and/or counselors provide boys and girls with different feedback on the importance of preparation in different school subjects and with different information on occupational opportunities.

Last year, I had a student in my Psychology of Women course who said that she had received the highest score in her high school on a standardized test of mechanical aptitude. She was at the time planning to major in engineering in college. Her high school guidance counselor had insisted that there must have been a mistake with regard to her mechanical aptitude score, and he urged her to consider a career other than engineering. At the time she took my course, she was a college junior majoring in elementary education.

Values can be subdivided as mediators of achievement-related choices. Evidence from var-

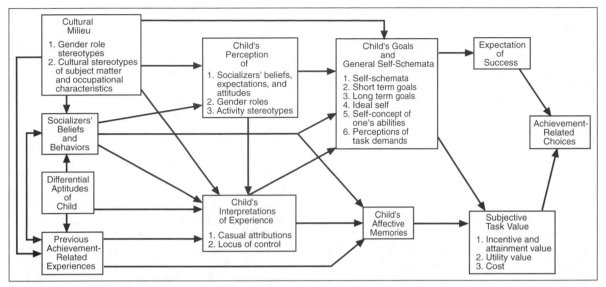

FIGURE 3.3   Eccles Model of Achievement-Related Choices
Source: Eccles, J. S. (1987). Gender roles and women's achievement related
decisions. Psychology of Women Quarterly, II, p. 139.

ious sources supports the hypothesis that even among high-aptitude college-bound students, gender differences in enrollment in advanced mathematics courses is due to the lesser value placed on mathematics by the girls who feel it is less important, less useful, and less enjoyable than do the boys.

One's self-schema influences the task value through the intrinsic value (pleasure) derived from the activity and extrinsic value (demonstration of the characteristics associated with the task). Perceived costs associated with the task include factors such as fear of failure or negative consequences of success and loss of time and energy for other activities.

Gender role socialization shapes an individual's personal values and goals. Females are socialized to rate social values and helping people as important. It is therefore not surprising that females select occupations that involve helping relationships and allow more time for family and friends. According to Eccles, there are also differences in motive and goal density—in the single-minded purpose to which an individual pursues one goal. Women are more likely to diversify

their lives and to integrate achievement and affiliative needs. Gender role socialization defines which educational and vocational activities males and females should find of interest. Similarly, gender roles for men and women define successful performance differently. For example, Eccles says that males may define success as a parent as an extension of their occupational role through their provider function and may devote more effort toward career goals when they become a parent. Females, however, may show decreased commitment to career goals after parenthood because of their role prescription for high levels of involvement in their children's lives. The same motives and goals may be manifested differently by men and women. Men and women with high need for achievement, for example, may excel precisely at those activities considered gender role appropriate.

Eccles points out that there are long-term costs for women in the choices they make because society gives lesser economic rewards to women who choose "feminine" vocations. These costs are further magnified by the high rates of divorce, spousal abuse, and failure to pay child support, which leaves many women in the role of family providers. She points out some solutions for this inequity in economic remuneration in the workplace, such as comparable worth and making male and female occupations equally rewarding economically. Another solution is to have parents, teachers, and counselors broaden the range of educational and vocational options that females are encouraged to consider. Boys' interest in family and child-rearing tasks also need to be encouraged.

J. E. Jacobs (1991) added to the Eccles et al. expectancy socializer model by including the parents' mathematical gender stereotypes as an influence on their beliefs about their child's mathematical ability and expectations for future success. In addition, the study included the child's performance as measured by current mathematics grades.

Analysis showed that children receive indirect messages from their parents about their ability.

> The influence of the child's gender on parents' beliefs about their child's mathematics ability and future success in mathematics depended on their level of stereotyping: stronger gender stereotypes were related to higher specific beliefs for parents of sons relative to the ability beliefs of parents of daughters. (J. E. Jacobs, 1991, p. 525)

Despite the fact that girls had higher math grades, boys had higher mathematics ability beliefs and future expectancies. This would indicate that their beliefs about their mathematical self-perceptions are formed on the basis of more than their own and their peers' actual math performance.

GENDER AND ACADEMIC ACHIEVEMENT

Women are beginning to surpass men in academic achievement. More girls than boys graduate from high school and more women than men receive baccalaureate degrees. Men still predominate in science, engineering, and management training. Two-thirds of doctorates are awarded to men.

Affirmative action in higher education was mandated in 1972 by the Higher Education Guidelines to Executive Order 11246 that were issued by the Office for Civil Rights of the Health, Education, and Welfare Department. The purpose of affirmative action in higher education is to ensure entrance into and fair and equitable treatment of social groups who have been systematically discriminated against in access to and promotion within higher education (McComb, 1989).

Women are beginning to surpass men in academic achievement. More girls than boys graduate from high school and go on to colleges and universities (U.S. Dept. of Labor, 1993). More women than men now receive baccalaureate degrees. Of the total baccalaureate degrees awarded in 1991, 53.9% were earned by women. The proportion of baccalaureate degrees being awarded to women will continue to rise because 55% of first-time, full-time college freshmen in 1993 were women (U.S. Bureau of the Census, 1994). Men still dominate in certain fields, however, such as mathematics, engineering, and physical and biological sciences. Currently, more women receive master's degrees than men.

In the adult population, however, there is still a cumulative deficit in women's education. In 1993, 24.8% of men but only 19.2% of women over 25 had baccalaureate degrees (U.S. Bureau of the Census, 1994). For Whites, 25.7% of men versus 19.7% of women over 25 were college graduates.

Men still outnumber women in professional schools and Ph.D. programs. In 1991, 25,000 doctoral degrees were granted to men in the United States, compared with 15,000 awarded to women. There is still considerable sex segregation of some of the fields in which doctorates are awarded. For example, women received the majority of doctorates in home economics (75.7%), psychology (61.2%), education (58.1%), health sciences (57.0%), letters (55.4%), foreign languages (53.6%), and public affairs (55.8%). On the other hand, only 9.2% of the doctorates awarded in engineering, 13.6% in computer and information sciences, 19.7% in physical sciences, and 25.7% in business and management were given to women (U.S. Bureau of the Census,

1994). Although women are still in the minority as professional degree recipients, they have made dramatic gains between 1960 and 1991 in the professions. In dentistry women went from fewer than 1% of dental school graduates to nearly one-third (32.1%). The percentage increase of women law school graduates from 2.5% in 1960 to 43% in 1991 was equally dramatic (U.S. Bureau of the Census, 1994).

In 1960, only 5.5% of medical degrees were awarded to women. By 1991, however, women were 36% of all medical degree recipients (Foreman, 1993). Performance in medical school between men and women is virtually identical. Women, however, report more depression and anxiety and failed relationships as a result of the medical school grind than do men. A number of factors are related to women's experience of more stress, such as lack of role models among medical faculty, and less help at home. As of 1987, only 19% of medical school faculty were women, with only 53% of the women faculty holding M.D. degrees. Women medical students also tend to come from less affluent homes than do their male counterparts, and, as a result, come into and leave medical school with higher debt. The problem of debt is even greater for Black women students who graduated an average of $7,000 more in debt than did White women (Bickel, 1990).

Although women now exceed men in the number of doctorates awarded in psychology, there are still large differences within psychology in the subfields in which women are receiving these doctorates. For example, 78% of the doctorates awarded in 1989 in developmental psychology, 65% in school psychology, 57% in counseling and 56% in clinical were awarded to women, whereas only 13% of those in comparative psychology were awarded to women (Fowler, 1991).

HISPANIC FEMALE STUDENTS

Hispanic females have a higher high school dropout rate than non-hispanics. Hispanic females attending college who prefer endogamy and have a high ethnic identification experience more psychological distress.

Education is one of the most important ways for women to gain socioeconomic mobility and independence. It is particularly true for minority women who otherwise lack the social contacts with individuals of power and status in the community who might assist their economic advancement through business or marriage.

In general, Hispanics have less education than does the rest of the population in the United States. As of 1993, only slightly more than half of all Hispanic women (53.2%) had completed high school, as compared with four-fifths (80%) of women of all races. Hispanic women have a higher high school dropout rate (29.6% of women 18–24 who have not completed high school and are not enrolled) than any other group of women (12.7% for women of all races) (U.S. Bureau of the Census, 1994). When Hispanics do attend college, they are less likely to complete college than are White students—31.8% of Mexican Americans and 28% of Puerto Ricans who begin college finish, as compared with 61% of Whites (Cardoza, 1991). In the population over 25 years of age, 9.5% of Hispanic men have Baccalaureate degrees, compared with 8.5% of women.

College aspirations were the strongest predictor of college attendance and persistence among a longitudinal sample of 1,252 Hispanic women (Cardoza, 1991). Having a role model—a mother who had completed four or more years of college—was also predictive of college persistence and attendance. Women who were married and/or had children were much less likely to attend college than the less "traditional" single women. If Hispanic women married in college, they were much less likely to continue.

High school preparation for college was also a significant predictor of college attendance and success—whether or not students had taken college preparatory courses, the SAT or ACT, and their high school grade point average. This finding has implications for high school teachers and guidance counselors. Is sufficient attention given to counseling Hispanic young women to take college preparatory courses and college entrance examinations? Surprisingly, unlike for non-Hispanics, socioeconomic status of the Hispanic young woman's family was not a variable related

Hispanic Woman Scholar

I wanted to prove to anyone who cared to ask (though by now I was convinced no one gave a damn) that I, the daughter of a laborer-farmworker, could dare to be somebody. Try to imagine what it is like to be always full of rage—rage at everything: at white teachers who could never even pronounce my name (I was often called anything from 'Odilia' to 'Otilia' to 'Estela'); rage at those teachers who asked me point-blank, 'But how did you get to be so smart? You are Mexican, aren't you?'. . .

From age thirteen I was also angry at boys who hounded me for dates. When I'd reject them they'd yell, 'So what do you plan to do for the rest of your life, fuck a book?' I was angry at my Chicana classmates in high school who, perhaps jealous of my high grades, would say, 'What are you trying to do,

be like the whites?' I regret to say that I was also angry at my parents, exasperated by their docility, their limited expectations of me. Oh, I knew they were proud; but sometimes, in their own misdirected rage (maybe afraid of my little successes), they would make painful comments 'Te vas a volver loca con esos jodidos libros' (You'll go nuts with those fucking books') was my mother's frequent statement. Or the even more sickening, 'Esta nunca se va a casar.' (Give up on this one; she'll never get married.') This was the tenor of my adolescent years. When nothing on either side of the two cultures, Mexican or Anglo-American, affirms your existence, that is how rage is shaped.

Olivia Castellano (1992), Professor

to college attendance. There was also little or no effect of Spanish language use on college attendance (see Box 1).

Research indicates that traditional concepts of women's family role persist among educated Chicano males. Preference for endogamy (marriage within one's own ethnic group), high ethnic identification, and perceptions that Mexican American males feel threatened by educated females (the double-bind factor) were significantly related to psychological distress for Chicana females attending five colleges and universities in California (Gonzalez, 1988). For those Chicana women low in endogamy and ethnic identification, however, perceived threat to males is not associated with psychological distress.

A college education and professional career for Chicana women are contrary to long-held sex role expectations in their culture.

They experience conflict as their behavior is changing more rapidly than their sex role attitudes and the attitudes of their male counterparts. Their professional and academic obligations place them squarely in the dominant society's work world, yet many of their values regarding marriage choices and appropriate sex roles originate in the world of their parents and family. (Gonzalez, 1988, p. 378)

For the Chicana woman, therefore, maintaining strong ties to the ethnic community and achieving academically creates conflict and stress.

ACADEMIC ACHIEVEMENT OF AFRICAN AMERICAN WOMEN

College and Graduate Training

African Americans are the only group for which the percentage of college graduates in the population is similar for men and women. Since the 1970s, Black women have been surpassing Black men in college and graduate training.

Blacks have a significantly lower rate of high school graduation than do whites. Although more Black females complete high school than do Black males, the high school dropout rate for Black women between the ages of 14–34 is 15.4%, which is significantly higher than that for White women, which is 11.1% (Wilkerson, 1988).

Black women under age 44 are very similar to White women in their rate of having completed four years of college. For every ethnic group except Blacks, the percentage of college graduates in the population is greater for males than for females. Among Blacks, the percentage of college graduates in the population is slightly higher among women (12.4% of Black women versus 11.9% of Black men) (U. S. Bureau of the Census, 1994).

The late 1980s and early 1990s saw an increase in the number of Black women enrolled in undergraduate and graduate schools as compared with Black men (U. S. Bureau of the Census, 1994). The priority of education of Black women within the African American community has been the result of several social and economic factors (Coleman-Burns, 1989). Unlike Whites, where the social position of the child was determined by the father's position, the Black child's status was historically determined by the mother, and her education would raise the status of the child. Second, Black women who were educated could gain a higher and more prestigious employment than the Black male. Black males were always relegated to positions below White males. Third, Black women, like all women, have been viewed as carriers of the culture to their children. Black women had high status within the Black community in the hope that "the educated mother could impart to her oppressed children the seeds of liberation" (Coleman-Burns, 1989, p. 154).

Planning Careers

Black women are more likely than White women to plan careers in male-dominated professions.

Black women at a midwestern university were somewhat more likely to aspire to male occupations (71%) than were the White women (61%) (Murrell, Frieze, & Frost, 1991). Women planning male-dominated careers were found to score higher on career and educational aspirations than were women who desired careers in female-dominated occupations. Perhaps, in anticipation of the double discrimination of racism and sexism that they face in the workplace, Black women who planned careers in male-dominated professions had high-level aspirations and planned

more education than was necessary for the particular occupation. Although there were no differences between Blacks and Whites on items relating to beliefs about traditional roles of women and men, Black women perceived less conflict in combining the roles of career and family than White women. Regardless of race, those choosing female careers had more traditional attitudes toward the roles of men and women.

ASIAN AMERICAN FEMALE STUDENTS

Women are a larger percentage of scholarship winners among Asian Americans than among Whites. Asian American men have higher educational attainment than Asian American women. Asian American immigrant women are now achieving higher educational attainment than Asian American immigrant men.

Asian American students have higher high school grade point averages, SAT scores, and proportionately more winners and finalists in the National Merit Scholarship Program, Presidential Scholars and Westinghouse Science Talent Search Program than White Americans. Among these young scholars, Asian American women account for a larger percentage than do White women of their group. For example, between 1975 and 1983 almost half of the Asian American winners in the New York region's Westinghouse Science Talent Search were women as compared to only one quarter of the White winners (Brandon, 1991).

The difference in educational attainment in the population is largest for Asians (43.2% of men versus 35.5% of women held four-year-college degrees in 1991). Nevertheless, the percentage of Asian women who hold baccalaureate degrees is higher than the percentage of White men with college degrees (U.S. Bureau of the Census, 1994). In more recent years, more Asian American immigrant women than men are attending college.

A follow-up survey in 1986, of a national probability sample of tenth and twelfth graders in

1980, found that Chinese and Filipino Asian American women's education attainment was significantly higher than that of Asian American men (Brandon, 1991). Among Chinese Americans, 66% of the females compared with 40.4% of the males had attained a two-year degree or more, and among Filipinos 44.2% of the females and 20.8% of the males had two-year degrees or more. The gender difference in educational attainment was only found between males and females whose home language was not English—in other words, immigrants and the children of immigrants.

"Within the University of California system, which enrolls the largest number of Asians in the United States, fully 26% of Asian-American high school students (not including foreign students) in 1985 qualified for entry, whereas only 13% of non-Asian students did" (Sue & Okazaki, 1990, p. 914). Growing evidence of discrimination in admissions against Asian Americans at some of the most prestigious universities such as Harvard, Brown, and the University of California at Berkeley brought about an investigation by the U.S. Department of Education (Amott & Matthaei, 1991).

Southeast Asian Women

Early marriage and childbearing among Southeast Asian high school students does not prevent educational achievement.

Unlike other racial and ethnic groups, early marriage and childbearing of Hmong female high school students has not been found to be an impediment to educational expectations and achievement (Hutchison & McNall, 1994). The Hmong, who fled their Laotian homeland following the Vietnam War, have a tradition of early arranged marriages. The Hmong in the United States have a higher fertility rate than any other refugee or immigrant group. A random sample of enrolled ninth-grade students in the St. Paul, Minnesota, Public School District were surveyed each year through the twelfth grade. "In the senior year of high school, more than half of the Hmong girls reported that they were married and

more than one-third reported that they had given birth to one or more children" (Hutchison & McNall, 1994, pp. 582–83).

Significant in relation to other ethnic groups in which high school girls who become mothers are more likely to drop out of high school and have lower educational aspirations, there was no difference between the married and single Hmong females in educational aspirations or expectations. The Hmong have strong social support in the form of traditional clan and family units. Change in traditional patterns is also evident in that 47% of the Hmong girls were still single by their senior year. A Hmong woman student in my social psychology class last year said that she was still single although her parents had arranged a marriage several years ago between her and her uncle's son, her first cousin. They were, however, willing to wait for her to graduate from college before she got married. She said that she did not want to marry her cousin and was seeing another Hmong man she intended to marry. She had not yet found the courage to tell her mother of her decision (her father was dead).

RE-ENTRY WOMEN

The student population of re-entry women in higher education has been increasing.

Re-entry women are women who have returned to higher education to complete or begin a degree program after an interruption in their education to assume adult responsibilities. Eighty percent of the growth of total enrollment in institutions of higher education from 1970 to 1985 was due to the enrollment of women. The percentage of women enrolled who were 25 years and older increased from 25.8% of the female student population to 30.6% during this period. On the other hand, the percentage of men 25 and older decreased from 45.8% to 38.7% of the total male enrollment (Chamberlain, 1988).

The population of re-entry women has changed over the years. The women were younger in the early 1980s than they had been in 1964, with only one-sixth of the women aged 40 or over in 1983 compared with one-third in the 1960s. The number of women who are employed has increased from less than one-third in the 1960s to more than three-fifths in the 1980s. The number of married women has dramatically decreased from nearly 80% in the mid-1960s to roughly 35% in the 1980s. The picture of the returning woman has shifted from that of a woman married to a professional man with a stable income, to a self-supporting woman (Chamberlain, 1988). The returning women, however, have not changed in one dimension—the seriousness with which they approach a college education. A disproportionate number of the best students I have had in my classes over the years have been re-entry women. Many of them were juggling families and jobs as well as school.

GENDER DIFFERENCES IN COMPUTER COMPETENCE

Computer Attitudes, Usage, and Expectancies

Males have more exposure to computers and feel more comfortable with computers than females. Women inexperienced with computers have less confidence and lower expectations for success than men inexperienced with computers

Computer use is widespread in society and a necessary component of scientific and technical fields and a useful tool in all academic fields. Males have been found to have more favorable attitudes toward computers, to have greater participation with computers, and to perceive themselves as more competent in computer tasks than females (Dambrot, Watkins-Malek, Silling, Marshall, & Carver, 1985; Fetler, 1985; Hawkins, 1985). For example, a study of summer camps offering training in programming for microcomputers found three times as many boys as girls enrolled (Hess & Miura, 1985). Males have been found to use computers more for playing games and programming but not for tool usage such as word processing or other applications (Lockheed, 1985).

According to Kramer and Lehman (1990), the gender-related differences in learning and computer usage may be related to the computer's being linked to mathematics and science departments within primary and secondary education. Kramer and Lehman suggest that the sociocultural context of computing for females needs to be examined, as well as girls' styles of learning and the content and context of computing. Current gender differences in computer usage have raised questions of whether lesser computer literacy will be a further stumbling block for women in entering careers in science, mathematics, and engineering.

Women who have not had previous experience with computers, have less confidence and lower expectations for success than men inexperienced with computers. In one study, there were no differences between low-experience men and women working alone on Zork, a computer game similar to the ones found in arcades, or the scores they obtained on the computer game (Robinson-Stavely & Cooper, 1990). When low-experienced participants worked in the presence of the confederate, however, the men scored significantly higher than the women. On the other hand, the participants high in computer experience did not differ in their performance by gender or by the presence or absence of another person in the room.

A survey of undergraduates found that men's expectations for success on the game of Zork were higher than women's. In a second experiment, expectations for success were explicitly manipulated for male and female participants who were low in computer experience and had never before played the game of Zork. In this experiment, the presence of another person resulted in facilitation for positive expectancy participants and impairment for negative expectancy participants, relative to those working alone. It was found to be difficult to induce positive expectancies, particularly for women, and several women had to be eliminated from the experiment who did not develop a positive expectancy for performance on the computer game.

It suggests that the presence of others has debilitating effects on women who are inexperienced users, with the potential to discourage or limit their use of computers. But it also suggests than an emphasis on positive expectancies could eliminate these unwanted effects. (Robinson-Stavely & Cooper, 1990, p. 182)

The educational implications are that women should be able to work on computers alone in a room, and positive expectations for their performance should be developed.

In contrast, a study by E. G. Hall (1990) found no significant gender differences in initial expectancy scores for three competitive video games for male and female undergraduate students, when initial skill level was controlled. The participants competed in three games, two of which they lost. They were then asked to rate themselves on how well they expected to do against the same opponent on another game. Again, no significant gender differences were found on the postcompetition expectancy scores. "The present findings suggest that initial performance expectancies, as well as postcompetition expectancies, are more significantly related to skill level than to subject gender or opponent gender" (E. G. Hall, 1990, pp. 37–38). Since this was a computer task, the implications are relevant to computer learning and indicate that bringing women up to skill level with men in computer usage can eliminate their lower expectations for success in that field.

In one study, when masculinity–femininity and computer ownership and usage were controlled for, the gender difference in computer attitudes, aptitude, and self-efficacy was no longer significant (Ogletree & Williams, 1990). Implications of this research are that gender roles need to be broadened so computer usage is seen as part of the feminine role as well as the masculine, and females need to be given at least equivalent computer experience.

GIFTED WOMEN

Gifted women have been much less prominent in achievement than gifted men. The current generation of gifted women, however, are obtaining advanced degrees and entering higher level positions.

Noble (1987) argues that sexism obscures the recognition and expression of giftedness in women. This is due to society's ambivalence toward highly capable women. Women are seen as important primarily in relationship to boys and men. "Many studies suggest that, unlike gifted males and females not identified as gifted, almost all gifted women have found it necessary at some time in their lives to hide their abilities in order to survive socially" (Noble, 1987, p. 371). The fact that men have been more prominent in areas of high achievement than women is a reflection of differing socialization opportunities and expectations, not of differing abilities.

Terman's classic study of 1,528 gifted children, first identified in the 1920s by standardized IQ tests and followed up for the rest of their lives, showed that the gifted women in the sample, relative to the gifted men, were much less likely to make high-level professional and public contributions. On follow-up, in the 1940s, 42% of the gifted women were full-time housewives. Of the 48% who were employed, the largest category were secretarial and clerical office workers (35%). Among the gifted women, only 10% were in professions requiring advanced degrees such as medicine, law, college teaching, or scientific research, as compared with 45% of the men. Even among the most gifted women, those with IQ scores of 170 and above, two-thirds were housewives and office workers (Terman & Oden, 1947). When a woman does get the training necessary for the full flower of her native genius, society often discounts her contributions because she is a woman.

Are gifted women of the current generation achieving greater fulfillment of their potential? To answer this question, and also to examine the characteristics of gifted women at midlife today compared with the characteristics of gifted women of previous generations, Schuster (1991) analyzed data from four longitudinal studies of gifted women. Comparisons of four cohorts—women born in 1910, the early 1920s, the 1920s and 1930s, and in 1940, show that for each of these successive cohorts a larger proportion of women are obtaining advanced degrees and are entering careers that make use of their abilities. A somewhat higher percentage of both home-makers and professionals in the 1940 cohort felt that they were living up to their potential as compared with the 1910 cohort. The researchers judged 48% of the 1920 cohort to have good to high levels of achievement, in comparison with 62% of the 1940 cohort.

When the 1920 and 1940 birth cohorts were asked to describe their life satisfaction, 72% of the 1920 birth cohort rated their life satisfaction as good to high. Somewhat fewer, 57% of those born in 1940, indicated good to high satisfaction. Schuster (1991) accounts for this decline by the fact that one-quarter of the 1940 birth cohort were divorced at midlife compared with only 6% of the 1920 cohort who were divorced or widowed. The divorced women tended to have generally lower life satisfaction. The same proportion of women in both cohorts expressed nearly identical high career satisfaction (1920, 79%; 1940, 80%).

SUCCESS AND FAILURE

Fear of Success

According to a widely quoted article by Horner in 1969, women fear success. Despite the popularity of the concept in the media, the many research studies conducted since then have found that women do not fear success any more than do men.

In a 1969 article in *Psychology Today,* which caught the attention of newspapers and magazines as well as psychologists, Matina Horner wrote about the motive to avoid success among bright college women. As stated previously in this chapter, the media loves to report on gender differences, ignoring research that finds no differences. The popularity of her concept of "**fear of success**" in women propelled Horner from a position as an assistant professor of psychology at Bryn Mawr College to becoming the president

of Radcliffe College at the age of 32 (she certainly did not exhibit any fear of success).

Let's take a look at how Horner developed the concept of fear of success. David McClelland and John Atkinson had been developing a major theory of achievement motivation during the 1950s and 1960s that they applied cross-culturally and historically as well as in contemporary life (J. W. Atkinson, 1958; J. W. Atkinson & Feather, 1966; McClelland, 1961). When they begin their research, they found the theory to be highly predictive of the behavior of men in laboratory settings, but not of women, who under competitive conditions did not show an increase in achievement motivation as did men. Faced by the contradictory research with females, and rather than investigating further, they ended research on women and subsequently only studied men. Horner wanted to find out why women behaved "inconsistently" in achievement situations.

For her doctoral dissertation at the University of Michigan, Horner devised a projective method to measure achievement motivation in men and women (Horner, 1968). In 1964, 90 female and 88 male students at the university were asked to write an imaginative story in response to a lead sentence: "After first term finals, Anne (John) finds herself (himself) at the top of her (his) medical school class." More than 90% of the men responded positively to the cue. On the other hand, 65% of the women wrote stories that were filled with negative consequences for Anne, reflecting the belief that high achievement in women is associated with a loss of femininity and social rejection. For example:

Anne is an acne faced bookworm. She runs to the bulletin board and finds she on top. "As usual" she smarts off. A chorus of groans is the rest of the class's reply.... "Well it certainly paid off. All the Friday and Saturday nights with my books, who needs dates, fun—I'll be the best woman doctor alive." And yet, a twinge of sadness comes through—she wonders what she really has. But, as is her habit, she promptly erases that thought, and goes off reciting aloud the 231 bones in her wrist. (Horner, 1978, p. 58)

Some of the stories were rather bizarre. In one, Anne was badly beaten by her classmates. Others reflected a denial of reality that Anne could really be first in her class. One story said Anne was a code name for a nonexistent person.

The next step in Horner's research was to see if the fantasy responses that indicated a fear of success in young women related to performance in achievement situations. She found that those who were high in fear of success performed significantly less well in competitive achievement conditions than they did under noncompetitive situations, particularly against men.

Women high in fear of success nevertheless did succeed. Nine years later, Hoffman (1977) conducted a follow-up study of the same women that Horner had tested on fear of success. She found that the women who had scored high or low in fear of success did not significantly differ in either educational or occupational attainments. A high percentage of these women obtained master's and doctorate degrees.

The research conducted since Horner's original work, has not supported substantial gender differences in fear of success. Paludi (1984) reviewed 64 studies of fear of success, finding a range between 6% and 93% of the females in the studies showing a fear of success (median = 49%), and a range between 7% and 95% of the males showing a fear of success (median = 45%). Based on Paludi's review, it can be concluded that the motive to avoid success is found equally in women and men.

The research by Horner seems instead to be a fear of being successful in a "gender inappropriate" role. When Cherry and Deaux (1978) asked students to complete sentences about Anne and John, who were at the top of either their medical school or nursing school class, high fear of success stories were written about Anne in medical school and John in nursing school, by both men and women. Both men and women are aware of the negative consequences that someone may face who deviates from the cultural norms. As Mednick (1989) points out, the popularity of the concept has continued long after being refuted.

Piedmont (1988) has developed an interactional model of achievement motivation and fear of success. Based on research with a sample of college students, he reports that fear of success only occurs with women who have both high fear of success and high achievement motivation, and only when situationally aroused. So fear of success does not apply to most women, which is why there is so much conflicting research in the literature.

Estimates of Ability and Expectations for Performance

Males have higher estimates of their abilities than females do of theirs. Generally, females have less self-confidence—lower expectations for performance on a task than do males. Receiving positive feedback or having a high level of skill on the task improves females self-confidence.

Research on self perceptions of intelligence and self-confidence among boys and girls in grades three through eight found that third-grade girls were significantly more likely to describe themselves as "smart" than third-grade boys, but "smart" was used more by boys than girls in the fifth, sixth, seventh, and eighth grades. No gender differences were found in use of the label "self confident" in the third grade, but by the fifth, sixth, seventh, and eighth grades, boys outnumbered girls in saying they were "self-confident." Thus, the further girls advance through the elementary grades the less intelligent and self-confident girls perceive themselves, thereby perhaps leading them to give lower expectations for success.

Studies of adults have also found men to be prone to higher estimates of their abilities. When 2,000 people were asked to estimate their IQs, men gave significantly higher estimates than women (Hogan, 1978). When college students are asked at the beginning of a course to estimate the grade they will get for the semester, female college students tend to predict lower grades than the males do. In spite of their lower expectancy for grades, the women's grades tended to be somewhat higher than the men's (V. C. Crandall, 1969).

Although women may not fear success, they often do not expect success. Generally, it has been found that people who expect to do better on some task actually do better, or that individuals who have low expectations for their performance may avoid a task they see as challenging. Although there are mixed results, many studies have found that females have less self-confidence—lower expectations for performance on a task than do males. As early as first grade, boys were found to have higher expectations for their performance in mathematics even though their grades or aptitude scores were no higher than that of girls (Entwisle & Baker, 1983).

Elementary school boys gave higher estimates of how well they expected to perform on six intellectual tasks, such as brain teasers, mazes, and memory tasks, than did girls (V. C. Crandall, 1969). Although this research is often described as indicating that females have less self-confidence than males, it was found that females tend to be more accurate in their estimates and males to inflate their performance.

This pattern of females underestimating and males overestimating their performance is not found, however, in all situations. A review of the literature concluded that when a task is described as feminine or neutral, women do not differ from men in their performance estimates (Lenney, 1977). When the participants in the studies are given clear feedback about how well they did on a task, women have been found to give even higher estimates than men of how well they will do. When the feedback is nonexistent or ambiguous, women are less likely to say they have done as well as men say they have done. When men and women are told their performance will be compared with that of others or that they are competing against others, women tend to lower their expectations for their performance.

When participants worked on three tasks involving creativity in a laboratory experiment, McCarty (1986) did not find that clear feedback eliminated the gender difference in self-confidence. Men had much higher expectations for success before beginning the task and when there was no feedback. It is surprising that, in contrast to Lenney's article, this confidence gap did not

disappear when participants were told either that they had done very well, or quite poorly. Men gave significantly higher estimates of their future performance than did women after receiving either positive or negative feedback. Finally, men who received no feedback during the experiment displayed levels of confidence as high as women who had received strong positive messages about their performance. The positive feedback did bring women up to the level of confidence that men had initially. This finding underlines the importance to women of receiving encouraging feedback in a task situation. Teachers and supervisors of women should make every effort to provide them with positive feedback when warranted.

Accuracy of Self-Evaluations in Performance

Women have innacurately low self-evaluations on masculine and unfamiliar, neutral tasks. Women are more influenced by the evaluations of others than are men.

Are women more accurate than men in their self-evaluations of performance? In an experiment involving feminine, masculine, and unfamiliar neutral tasks, "men tend either to be accurate or to overestimate, whereas women tend either to be accurate or to underestimate" (Beyer, 1990). Women's underestimations were task specific, on those tasks on which they had initially low confidence and expected not to do well, masculine tasks, and unfamiliar neutral tasks. Beyer goes on to point out the potentially serious implications of women's underevaluations of their performance. The implications of this pattern for women's lives is that "a woman's misperceptions regarding her competence may lead to low expectancies for future performances and dissuade her from pursuing a career in certain masculine gender-typed-domains, whereas a man of equal ability might not doubt his competence for a moment" (Beyer, 1990, p. 968).

Based on a literature review T. Roberts (1991) concludes that women are more responsive to evaluative feedback they receive than are men.

Roberts says the evidence does not support the hypotheses that lower self-esteem in women, or greater attention to social cues, or that women are more prosocial accounts for their greater yielding to evaluative influence. The explanation that Roberts' research strongly supports is that women, unlike men, perceive the evaluative feedback to be reality based, and therefore an accurate assessment of their ability.

T. Roberts (1991) explains that women have lower status than men in society and social situations and therefore actually lack information about their own capabilities and need to turn more to others as sources of information about their capacities and limitations. Boys also receive more criticism from teachers than girls, but this is directed toward nonintellectual behaviors such as misconduct. A second explanation is that boys' peer groups are more competitive and involve a far greater amount of negative feedback than do girls' groups, and boys may learn to discount it. Girls may learn that evaluative feedback is most often related to their ability and they should take it seriously. Roberts further makes the point that whenever gender differences arise, men's behavior is considered normative, and women's behavior maladaptive. "Indeed, one could argue that in different kinds of achievement situations, or in different stages of the same endeavor, each of these strategies is optimal" (T. Roberts, 1991, p. 306). In a training situation, for example, it is important to be responsive to the feedback from one's coach or teacher. Alternatively, in the event itself, it is important to focus on the task at hand, and to remain self-confident regardless of others' opinions.

Research with undergraduates (30 women and 30 men) found that women's private self-evaluations reflected others' evaluations to a greater extent than did the men's (T. Roberts & Nolen-Hoeksema, 1989). Women also perceived others' evaluations of them to be more accurate than did the men, and were more influenced by those evaluations than were the men.

Attributions for Success and Failure

Although some intriguing studies in the 1970s found women to attribute their success more to luck and men to attribute their success to ability, meta-analysis of attribution studies find no gender differences.

Think for a minute about the grade you got on the last exam you got back. Why do you think you got the grade you did? Did you get an *A*? If so, did you say it was because you were lucky? Or, maybe it was because you studied very hard for the test. Or do you think you're smart and can get good grades and study much less than your friends do? The way you answered the question tells us something about the kind of attributions you make for your academic behavior.

For a number of years, since Fritz Heider's theorizing (1958), social psychologists have been studying the attributions people make for their own and other's behavior. In other words, how do people decide what are the causes of their own and others' behavior. They ask why Michelle got an *A* on the exam, or why Michael failed it. Three dimensions of causality form the basis for attributions, whether the cause is internal to the individual or external, whether it is stable or unstable, and whether it is controllable or uncontrollable (Weiner, 1986). A student's success or failure in an achievement situation can usually be attributed to one of four causes: ability, luck, effort, or task difficulty. Ability and effort are internal factors, whereas luck and task difficulty are external factors. Ability is a stable factor, relatively unchanging. On the other hand, effort and luck are unstable factors that may change from one exam to the next. Task difficulty may be stable such as in the case of SAT exams, which are relatively equivalent from year to year in the task difficulty, or more unstable such as exams made up by different teachers. An unstable, internal cause such as effort is generally seen as controllable (i.e., a student can study hard for an exam or not at all). A stable, internal cause such as ability is usually seen as uncontrollable. An external, unstable cause like luck is not usually seen as controllable. An external, stable cause such as course difficulty is in many circumstances not seen as controllable, although it might be seen as controllable if the person can choose the level of course difficulty.

The causal attributions that one makes for his/her own success and failure can have implications for future goals and achievement motivation. If I got an *A* on an exam in calculus, and I said that was because I have high math ability, I am likely to take other math courses and to aspire to a career in which mathematics is a necessary requirement, such as science or engineering. On the other hand, if I failed the calculus exam, and if I attributed that grade to my low math ability, I might drop the course, not take any other math courses and set as my goal a career requiring no mathematics.

Research in the 1970s found that women tend to attribute success to luck (an unstable, external attribute), whereas men attribute it to ability (a stable, internal attribute). Three psychologists happened to notice that at amusement parks men tend to play games of skill such as tossing a ring around the neck of a bottle, whereas women more often played games of chance such as bingo (Deaux, White, & Farris, 1975). They then set up a laboratory experiment in which they found that 75% of the men chose a skill game, whereas 65% of the women chose a luck game.

In a field study, Deaux (1979) found that among male and female first-level managers, men were significantly more likely to see their success as due to ability than were women. Unlike previous laboratory research, however, no gender differences in attributions to luck, effort, or task were found. In an "employee testing" simulation, sex of employee by itself did not influence self-attributions of causality for performance. Both males and females, however, when supervised by someone of the same sex attributed successful performance more internally than unsuccessful performance. This study has implications for the workplace, indicating that women supervised by other women may be more likely to attribute their success to their own internal characteristics, such as ability.

Reviews of the literature that addressed gender differences in ratings for causal attributions for success and failure concluded that there are conflicting results in the area of self-attributions (McHugh, Frieze, & Hanusa, 1982; Sohn, 1982). On the basis of a meta-analysis of 21 published studies using adolescent or adult participants, it was concluded that ". . . although it does appear that women have a very slight tendency to attribute failure to luck more than do men, and men make somewhat stronger informational attributions to ability, there are no strongly supported sex differences in attributions." (Frieze, Whitley, Hanusa, & McHugh, 1982, p. 341). Again, we find a gender difference played up by the media that turns out not to be a very robust difference at all.

Among third graders and junior high school students who completed questionnaires before and after they took a mathematics exam, girls rated their ability lower and expected to do less well than the boys (Stipek & Gralinski, 1991). Girls were less likely than boys to attribute success to high ability, but more likely to attribute failure to low ability rather than luck. Girls had less pride then boys when they did well on their exam, but were more likely to hide their paper after failure. Girls also showed less belief that success could be achieved by effort, and a greater desire to avoid future mathematics tasks. Since these gender differences appeared by third grade, the authors suggest early intervention to improve girls' mathematics achievement related beliefs.

Among high school students about to enter the premed program at SUNY Stony Brook, there were no differences in attributions made by male and female students about their high school performance being due to ability, task difficulty, or effort, although females were slightly more likely to attribute their high school grades to luck (Fiorentine, 1988). These attributions remained stable over the course of their premed career, with no gender differences in the use of attributions to ability, effort, task difficulty, or luck, even though the female students in the sample earned lower grades in the required courses. Nor did females have lower expectancies for success in the premed program when asked to estimate their grade point average at the completion of the program. We must keep in mind, however, that female premed students are a highly select sample of young women.

The female premed students did, however, rate themselves lower on a variety of academic and social skills, and had lower levels of confidence in their ability to perform the role of physician. The persistence gap of females being less likely to stay in the premed program was accounted for to a great extent by males having higher grades and more confidence in their ability to perform the role of doctor. If we are looking for psychological factors as one cause of the achievement gap between men and women, it appears that self-confidence or the expectation for success along with values rather than attributions for success and failure may hold the key.

REFLECTIONS

It is amazing to me that the media has played up gender differences in cognitive abilities—particularly when the report is unfavable to women—but has ignored the research showing that cognitive gender differences are disappearing. Did you ever read in the popular press the fact that girls get better grades than boys in math classes in high school and in college? The media has also ignored the major revolution going on in society, the gender reversal in education. More women than men now graduate from high school, go on to college, are enrolled in master's programs and in some fields such as psychology make up the majority of doctoral students. How will these changes in education influence male–female relationships? What impact will this new generation of educated women have on society? on politics? on the professions? on war and peace?

Experiential Exercises

1. Observe who answers more of the professor's questions and volunteers more comments in your college classes, men or women.
2. Ask some of your male and female college friends how many college math classes they have taken. Ask them why they did not take more math classes.
3. In the beginning of the semester in your classes, ask your male and female classmates what grade they expect to get in the class. Is there a gender difference? At the end of the semester, ask them what grade they got in the class.

KEY TERMS

Affirmative Action   Affirmative action in higher education was mandated in 1972 by the Higher Education Guidelines to Executive Order 11246 that were issued by the Office for Civil Rights of the Health, Education, and Welfare Department. The purpose of affirmative action in higher education is to ensure entrance into and fair and equitable treatment of social groups who have been systematically discriminated against in access to and promotion within higher education.

Fear of Success   Horner's theory that women have a fear of high academic and occupational achievement. Reviews of the literature on this concept conclude that the motive to avoid success is not found more frequently in women than it is in men.

Math Anxiety   A conditioned anxiety to mathematics that females in our society have acquired leading them to avoid math classes and to fear quantitative concepts.

Mental Rotation   The rapid mental rotation of a two- or three-dimensional figure, or the ability to visualize how a flat object will appear when it is folded, or a solid object when it is unfolded.

Meta-analysis   A statistical technique that combines the data from different studies testing the same hypothesis in order to determine whether there are significant overall effects. In meta-analyses of gender differences, the most commonly used measure of the difference is the effect size d, which is the difference between the means in standard score form, divided by the standard deviation.

Re-entry Women   Women who have returned to higher education to complete or begin a degree program after an interruption to assume adult responsibilities.

Spatial Perception   The ability to locate the horizontal or the vertical while ignoring the context. Two frequently used measures of spatial perception are the rod and frame test and the water level test.

Spatial Visualization   A multistep process of analyzing visual spatial information. Spatial visualization tasks include the embedded-figures test which requires the individual to disembed a figure from a complex background, paper folding, and the paper form board.

Standard Deviation   The extent of variability of the scores around the mean.

Visual Spatial Ability   There are three categories of visual spatial ability—spatial perception, mental rotation and spatial visualization.

SUGGESTED READINGS

Hyde, J. S., Fennema, E., & Lamon, S. J. (1990). Gender differences in mathematics performance: A meta-analysis. *Psychological Bulletin, 107,* 139–55. Meta-analyses are described in this article that were conducted on samples according to age, ethnicity, selectivity of sample, date of publication, and type of mathematical task.

Hyde, J. S., & Linn, M. C. (1988). Are there sex differences in verbal abilities?: A meta-analysis. *Psychological Bulletin, 104,* 53–69. To date, this is the definitive meta-analysis on gender differences in verbal abilities.

Roberts, T., (1991). Gender and the influence of evaluations on self-assessments in achievement settings. *Psychological Bulletin, 19,* 297–308. This is a thorough review of the literature on gender differences in response to evaluative feedback. The author interprets the findings in terms of gender differences in status in the society.

CHAPTER 4

Gender Stereotypes, Sex Role Orientation, Gender Differences in Personality, Language, and Nonverbal Behavior

Qualities deemed necessary for adulthood—the capacity for autonomous thinking, clear decision-making, and responsible action—are those associated with masculinity and considered undesirable as attributes of the feminine self. The stereotypes suggest a splitting of love and work that relegates expressive capacities to women while placing instrumental abilities in the masculine domain.

Carol Gilligan, 1982

Stereotypes are shared beliefs in a culture about what characteristics members of a group possess and how they behave. Stereotypes are a part of culture, social and personality systems.

When we know the sex of a person, even of a newborn, we then think that we know certain traits and characteristics of the person. Most of our ideas about how males and females behave, however, are not based on scientific evidence, but on stereotypes. Stereotypes are shared beliefs in a culture about what characteristics members of a group possess and how they behave. Stereotypes exist about males and females, members of racial, ethnic and religious groups, people in certain occupations, and even about people with certain color hair,—"red heads have hot tempers."

Stereotypes are a part of culture. They are shared symbols, beliefs, and values. Stereotypes are preserved over long periods of time because they are maintained by certain systems of action

(Parsons, 1961). These include inculcation of stereotypes within the family and by the mass media. Stereotypes are also components of social and personality systems. Stereotypes often result from conflict and power relations between groups rather than from actual characteristics of group members. For the social system, stereotypes help to maintain the position of power and privilege of the dominant group. Stereotypes of Blacks and women have been similar because both groups have been powerless in society, and certain characteristics are attributed to powerless people. For example, both Blacks and women have been seen as emotional rather than rational. This stereotype helps maintain the status quo because, after all, who would entrust a position of power and responsibility to someone who is emotional rather than rational. Stereotypes are internalized by both the dominant group and by the groups that are targets of the stereotypes (R. Brown, 1965).

STEREOTYPES OF MALES AND FEMALES

Masculine characteristics are seen as more desirable than feminine characteristics. The male valued adjectives form a "competency" cluster and the female valued adjectives form a "warmth and expressiveness" cluster. The research is conflicting about how much stereotypes of women have changed during the past couple of decades.

The classic research on stereotypes of men and women was conducted by Broverman and her colleagues in the late 1960s and early 1970s (Rosenkrantz, Vogel, Bee, Broverman, & Broverman, 1968; Broverman, Vogel, Broverman, Clarkson, & Rosenkrantz, 1972). Participants indicated on questionnaires, which listed a series of bipolar traits (very aggressive—not at all aggressive, very illogical—very logical, very sneaky—very direct, etc.), the extent to which a normal male, a normal female, and they themselves possessed each of the traits. A trait was characterized as a stereotype when at least 75% of the individuals of each sex agreed as to which pole of the trait was most

characteristic of a male or a female. Responses to the sex role questionnaire were obtained from 599 men and 383 women ranging in age from 17 to 60 and heterogeneous as to educational background. Agreement as to stereotypical traits of men and women did not differ by age, sex, marital status, religion, or education level of those completing the questionnaires.

Masculine characteristics are seen as different from feminine characteristics, and they are also seen as more desirable than feminine characteristics. Additional samples of men and women were given the questionnaire with the instructions to indicate the most desirable point for an adult (sex unspecified) on each bipolar scale. The point considered most socially desirable for an adult was closer to the masculine pole on the 29 stereotypic items, based on social desirability ratings by previous samples.

Further analyses revealed the male valued cluster of items to be a "competency" cluster consisting of attributes such as being independent, objective, active, competitive, logical, skilled in business, worldly, adventurous, able to make decisions easily, self-confident, always acting as a leader, and ambitious. Female valued stereotypic attributes are referred to as the "warmth and expressiveness" cluster. It consists of attributes such as gentle, sensitive to the feelings of others, tactful, religious, neat, quiet, interested in art and literature, and able to express tender feelings.

Because of the major changes in the roles of women that have taken place over the last couple of decades, it is reasonable to think that stereotypes of men and women would have changed as well. A 1988 replication of a sex stereotype study conducted in 1972 with undergraduate students found a high correlation (.90) across the 16-year period for the association of each adjective with men or women (Bergin & Williams, 1991). In other words, the same adjectives were still being used to describe men and the same adjectives used to describe women. There also were no changes in the affective meaning (Favorability, Strength and Activity) associated with the male and female stereotypes. Further analysis revealed, however, that women were seen as less childlike in 1988 than they had been in 1972, and there was a trend toward more adult descriptions. The male stereotype, on the other hand, decreased in terms of adult and parental connotations and increased in childlike connotations. It should be kept in mind that this study asked participants to report on characteristics associated with men and women in their culture rather than describing their own beliefs.

Another study, however, comes to very different conclusions. Eagly, Mladinic, and Otto (1991) asked undergraduate students to rate men and women along with several other groups—Republicans, Democrats, prostitutes, Europeans, rapists, clowns, soldiers, Latin Americans, tennis players, and grandparents. In addition to the rating scales, they completed free response measures, which assessed beliefs about each group and emotions they typically felt toward the group. In contrast to previous research, Eagly et al. found that respondents' evaluations of women were more positive than their evaluations of men. Women were evaluated more favorably than men on both belief and attitudinal measures. This more positive evaluation of women was found for both male and female respondents. There was no significant difference, however, in emotional reactions to men or women. The researchers cite three possible reasons for their results in contrast to previous results. One is that more adequate methods of assessment were used in comparison to previous research. Second, the change in the status of women may cause young people now to evaluate women more favorably than they had in previous years. Third, this research only assessed attitudes and beliefs toward the general category of women. It is possible that attitudes toward subtypes of women would be less favorable.

Stereotypes of Black and White Women

The white, middle-class woman is the woman people have in mind when stereotyping women. Black women and lower-class women are described differently from the stereotype of women.

When people are asked to indicate characteristics of men and women on bipolar rating scales, what man and what woman do they have in mind? To answer this question, Landrine (1985) asked 44 undergraduates to rate middle-class Black, middle-class White, and lower-class White female stimulus persons on 23 adjectives. The stereotypes of White women and of middle-class women were closest to findings of other studies of stereotypes of women. The Black female stereotype, compared with that for a White woman, was dirty, hostile, and superstitious. White women were rated higher than Blacks on being neat, non-aggressive, passive, dependent, and emotional.

Lower-class women were rated significantly higher than middle-class women on confused, dirty, hostile, illogical, impulsive, incoherent, inconsiderate, irresponsible, and superstitious. In contrast, the stereotype of the middle-class woman received significantly higher ratings than the lower-class female on ambitious, competent, happy, intelligent, self-confident, vain, and warm. The White middle-class woman is implicit in the stereotype of women.

Stereotypes as Multicomponent Social Categories

Gender stereotypes are multicomponent social categories. Research has yielded several different clusters or types for men and women: personality, role behaviors, occupation, and physical appearance.

The approach to stereotypes has changed from viewing them as negative evaluations, which was an outgrowth of the research on racial and ethnic stereotypes, to conceptualizing them as social categories within the theoretical framework of social cognition research (Six & Eckes, 1991). Research on **gender stereotypes** in the 1980s and 1990s has found them to be more complex than originally described. Six and Eckes view gender stereotypes as multicomponent social categories. Their research has yielded nine clusters or types for women and nine types for men. Examples of these clusters for males are: Cluster I—aggressive, vicious, intolerant, opinionated; Cluster VI—cheerful, likeable, sympathetic, tolerant, relaxed manner, sees the good in people, sloppily dressed. Examples of these clusters for females are: Cluster I—above the common herd, strenuous, smoker, exaggerates, untidy; Cluster VI—risk-loving, likes thrills. "In sum, these studies provide further evidence not only for the multicomponent nature of gender stereotypes, but also for subcategories of gender stereotypes defined by traits and role behaviors, including sexual behavior and physical appearances" (Six & Eckes, 1991, p. 69).

Deaux and Lewis (1984) describe four components of gender stereotypes: (1) personality characteristics; (2) role behaviors; (3) occupations; and (4) physical appearance. These four components are relatively independent of one another. At the same time, information from one component will be used to shape judgments about other components. Role or trait information has been shown to shape other judgments such as occupation and even sexual orientation.

A male who is described by such traits as emotional, gentle, understanding of others and kind, for example, is given a .40 chance of being homosexual. Similarly, a mean estimate of .39 for being homosexual was obtained when a male was described as being a source of emotional support, managing the house, taking care of children, and decorating the house. Although estimates of heterosexuality were higher in each case, it is still notable how strongly the estimates shifted in the face of quite minimal information. (Deaux & Lewis, 1984, p. 998)

Specific information, therefore, may outweigh the gender label. Also, the components are not equivalent in their influence. For males, occupation and physical appearance had the greatest influence on one another (as opposed to trait or role behavior information). For females, either trait or physical information led to an increased probability of judgments of a person having feminine characteristics. The effects of physical appearance are more pervasive than those of the other components.

Stereotypes and Evaluations

The more we know about a person, the less important stereotypes are in evaluating her/him.

Children rely less on stereotypes in perceiving people as they get older. Even though men and women may be given similar subjective ratings, women may be given lower objective ratings in areas stereotyped as masculine.

Which is more important in evaluating a person, their gender or their behavior? Gender stereotypes play a lesser role based on the more information we have about the person. Gender stereotypes are more important when we are judging strangers or when gender is all that we know about the individual. Locksley and her colleagues (Locksley, Borgida, Brekke, & Hepburn, 1980) conducted a series of studies in which they said their research found that individual behavior could override stereotypes. For example, male and female target persons who behaved assertively were judged equally assertive, ignoring the widespread stereotype that males are more assertive than females.

The use of individuating information increases from childhood to adulthood. Kindergartners, third graders, seventh graders, tenth graders, and college students were interviewed/surveyed, presenting them with descriptions of boys and girls who possessed characteristics that fit their gender stereotype or were opposite of them (Biernat, Manis, & Nelson, 1991). They were then asked about their perceptions of the male and female targets. The use of gender labels remains stable, but at the same time the behavior of the target persons becomes more important in their descriptions of them as the children get older.

An alternative hypothesis has been proposed by Biernat, Manis, and Nelson (1991) who suggest that people may use different standards when rating the stereotypic traits of males or females so that although subjectively, for example, they both may be rated as "very superior" the male may have a higher objective rating than the female. They conducted studies with undergraduate students where they found differences in ratings using subjective and objective rating scales. On objective scales men were rated as earning more money than women. When using subjective scales, the end anchors were psychologically adjusted so that a woman could be earning less than a man and still be rated very financially successful, whereas the man had to earn much more than the woman to receive that label.

In a more recent test of what they call the shifting standards model, Biernat and Manis (1994) extended their work to traditional social stereotypes about Blacks and women. "When judgments are made with respect to attributes that are associated with widespread stereotypes, objective assessments consistently reveal bias effects based on group membership, whereas subjective ratings will reveal these effects less clearly (or not at all)" (Biernat & Manis, 1994 p. 19). For example, although women were given higher objective ratings in verbal ability than were men, the subjective ratings were not significantly different from each other.

Meta-analysis reveals no overall gender differences in the evaluations of males and females. But female employment applications are judged less favorably than those of males. The written work of females is also somewhat undervalued.

Stereotypes about males and females influence our judgments of their work and behavior. The first study of sex bias in performance evaluation was conducted by Phillip A. Goldberg (1968), who gave female college students six professional articles to evaluate. The same article was given to half the students with a female author's name (Joan T. McKay) and the other half of the students with a male author's name (John T. McKay). Although P. A. Goldberg concluded from this research that women were prejudiced against women, the articles were rated more positively and the author more competent when the article was presumably written by a man rather than by a woman, for only three of the six articles. Remember the evaluators were all females, who had apparently internalized the cultural stereotypes of males being more competent than females.

Although P. A. Goldberg's study has been cited widely in the scientific and popular literature, few texts have reported the studies that have not found gender biases in evaluations (Swim,

Borgida, Maruyama, & Myers, 1989). In order to test for the strength of evaluative biases against women, Swim et al. conducted a meta-analysis of 106 studies of evaluations of the work of women and men, finding that the effect size was so small as to be almost zero ($d = +.07$). There were differences in evaluations of males and females depending on the kind of material being evaluated. When employment applications were being evaluated the effect size was larger ($d = +0.25$), than it was for written work ($d = +0.14$).

When raters knew only whether the person being evaluated was a male or a female, the gender bias in their evaluations was larger ($d = +0.38$). When a paragraph or more of information about the person was included, the effect size was much smaller ($d = +.08$). A weakness of most of the studies included in the meta-analysis is that they were analog studies that were conducted with college students. They were not evaluations of people in the context of a situation where a person's life would be affected by the evaluations (Swim et al., 1989).

Biases were found to be complex in nature and limited in scope in a literature review of published studies using P. A. Goldberg's original paradigm, [in which the sex of the person is varied while the work that is evaluated is kept identical] (Top, 1991). In 10 of the 35 experiments reviewed, there was a significant difference in evaluation of work by sex of the stimulus person. In all but two of the cases, the male stimulus person received more favorable evaluations. Often, however, there was not a significant difference in evaluations by sex of stimulus persons.

In general, male and female judges agree in their evaluations of the work of men and women. When differences do emerge, female judges show more favorable attitudes toward women's performance than male judges. There is a tendency for more bias against women in "masculine" or sex-neutral fields than in feminine ones. It appears that work is evaluated more favorably when the stimulus person of either sex is attractive. For both sexes, married persons and childless persons are evaluated as more competent.

Antifemale bias does not occur when a female's work is recognized as successful such as paintings labeled as prize-winning (Pheterson, Kiesler, & Goldberg, 1971). There is some conflicting research on this point. The few studies done on experimenter effects found a tendency to give higher ratings to a stimulus person of the same sex as the experimenter.

Conclusions about the extent of bias against the work created by women are difficult to draw from this research. Most of the research was conducted with college students in a laboratory, not with real judges in a field setting. A review of the literature by Top (1991) found the results to be diverse and ambiguous.

Gender Diagnosticity

Gender diagnosticity is a new approach that assesses gender-related differences that actually discriminate between men and women.

In the 1990s, a new approach is emerging to study gender related individual differences, called **gender diagnosticity**. "Gender diagnostic probabilities assess gender-related individual differences in terms of behaviors that actually discriminate between men and women within a given population rather than in terms of gender stereotypes" (Lippa, 1991, p. 1000). For example, one might ask what the probability is that an individual is male or female based on the wearing of pants. If we know that 30% of the women wear pants and 99% of the men, in a population where there are an equal number of men and women, we can compute the probability that an individual is female based on the wearing of pants. Lippa (1991) computed gender diagnostic probabilities for male and female college students from ratings of occupations, school subjects, everyday activities, and amusements and hobbies. The results of his study shows a high degree of reliability.

In three experiments, the formation of stereotypes were studied in relation to behaviors regarding friendliness and intelligence performed by a red group and a blue group, either group alone or both groups. The results of the experiments suggest that "when forming impressions of social groups, individuals form group stereotypes by using the central tendency and variability of different attribute dimensions as criteria for determining which dimensions are most diagnostic (i.e., provide the most information about differentiating the groups," (Ford & Stangor, 1992, p. 364). Ford and Stangor conclude that people tend to gather information about real differences between groups, and that in some cases these categories serve as the basis for stereotype formation. Of course, the history of social psychology is replete with examples of how stereotypes form on the basis of the nature of relations between groups (i.e., competitive or cooperative) rather than on the basis of the characteristics of the members of the groups involved (Sherif, Harvey, White, Hood, & Sherif, 1961).

Accuracy of Stereotypes

Research is conflicting on the accuracy of stereotypes.

Adults were asked to estimate the prevalence of 30 socially desirable traits in men and women (C. L. Martin, 1987). Undergraduates were then asked to rate themselves on the same traits, providing group norms for these characteristics in men and women. Carol L. Martin found that there were only a few large gender differences on traits, and many small gender differences when men and women rated themselves. The stereotypes, however, were much more extreme, with people assuming large gender differences for almost every trait. Thus, this study found stereotypes to greatly exaggerate the differences that do exist between the sexes.

On the other hand, a test of the accuracy of gender stereotypes, in which Janet Swim (1994) compared meta-analytic and perceived effect sizes for a number of cognitive and behavioral characteristics, found sterotypes to be highly accurate.

If a perceived and meta-analytic effect size was not statistically different, the perception was labeled accurate. . . . If a perceived effect size differed significantly from its corresponding meta-analytic effect size and in the stereotyped direction, it was labeled an *overestimate*. If a perceived effect size differed significantly and in the nonstereotyped direction, it was labeled an *underestimate*. (Swim, 1994, p. 25)

The results show that the college student participants did not uniformly overestimate gender differences. In fact, the participants were accurate or underestimated gender differences in six areas (restlessness, mathematical abilities, helping in emergencies, happiness, influencibility, and gazing during conversations). There were overestimates of stereotypes in only two areas: men's aggressiveness and women's verbal abilities. As the author points out, however, even if a stereotype is accurate for a group average, then that does not mean that the stereotype will be accurate for individuals because variability among women or among men is not taken into account by the stereotype.

MASCULINITY, FEMININITY, AND ANDROGYNY

> *Agency is identified with masculinity and communion with femininity. Sex role orientation scales have been developed on which a man or woman can be masculine, feminine, androgynous, or undifferentiated.*

According to D. Bakan (1966), two modes of existence characterize all living organisms—agency and communion. Agency reflects a sense of self and is manifest in self-assertion, self-enhancement, and self-protection. Communion, on the other hand, entails selflessness, a concern for others, and group participation. He further identifies agency with males and **masculinity** and communion with females and **femininity**. Not all men or all women, however, have the same personality characteristics or display the same behavior in social situations.

The early tests of masculinity and femininity, such as the 910 item test developed by Terman and Miles (1936) and the Male–Female scales incorporated in standardized psychological scales such as the Personality Research Form, conceived of masculinity and femininity as separate spheres—opposites of each other. With the feminist movement in the 1960s came a critique of these scales and their method of construction. In a review of the literature on sex role research, Constantinople (1973) concluded that masculinity and femininity were not opposite ends of a unidimensional continuum. Sandra Bem (1974) conceptualized the additional sex role category of **androgyny** to indicate someone who has both masculine and feminine characteristics. She developed the Bem Sex Role Inventory (BSRI), which assumed masculinity and femininity to be independent dimensions. Hence, an individual could score high on masculinity and high on femininity, and be "androgynous." A woman who demonstrated neither stereotypical masculine or feminine characteristics would be considered **undifferentiated**. The BSRI scores on the masculinity and femininity scales could place people in one of four categories:

1. Feminine—people who score high on the femininity scale, and low on the masculinity scale.
2. Masculine—people who score high on the masculinity scale and low on the femininity scale.
3. Androgynous—people who score high on both the masculinity and the femininity scales.
4. Undifferentiated—people who score low on both the masculinity and the femininity scales (Bem, 1974).

Shortly after Bem's scale appeared, Spence, Helmreich, & Stapp (1975) developed the Personal Attributes Questionnaire (PAQ) to measure sex role orientation. Since then, a great deal of research has been published using one or both of these scales. Certain assumptions are shared by these scales: (1) Masculinity and femininity are not mutually exclusive; (2) Masculinity and femininity are unrelated to biological sex and sexuality; (3) The categories are derived from stereotypes about gender differences; (4) These sex-typed characteristics reflect individual traits; (5) To be masculine is to be direct, instrumental, and independent, whereas to be feminine is to be indirect, expressive, and dependent; (6) Someone who is androgynous scores high in both masculine and feminine characteristics; (7) Placement in the category of masculine, feminine, or androgynous is predictive of behavior (not defined in the model); (8) It is desirable to be androgynous because androgynous persons are more flexible and better adjusted; (9) Androgyny theory fits in with current psychological theories such as trait theory (Morawski, 1987).

The concept of androgyny came along at a time in history when women were entering the workforce in larger numbers than ever before and asked to take on more instrumental roles, yet continued to fulfill their traditional emotional and expressive roles of nurturing wife and mother within the family. The concept of androgyny fit in with the new roles of women, and was picked up by the popular culture.

Sex Role Orientation and Psychological Adjustment

Are androgynous men and women better adjusted than "hairy chested" men and "fluffy" women? No. Masculine men and women are better adjusted then androgynous, feminine, or undifferentiated men or women.

The development of the sex role orientation scales has served to generate more research than any other area of psychology of women. Other chapters will also include some of this research where pertinent. One of Bem's assumptions was that androgynous people were better adjusted psychologically than were masculine men or feminine women. Are they?

Whitley (1983) conducted a meta-analytic review to test three models of the relationship between psychological well being and sex role orientation. The congruence model proposes that when one's sex role orientation is the same as one's gender (masculine men and feminine women) psychological well being is fostered. Bem's androgyny model argues that well-being is maximized when both men and women incorporate a high degree of masculine and feminine characteristics in their sex role orientation. The

masculinity model hypothesizes that well being is a function of a masculine sex role orientation for both men and women. Whitley's meta-analysis included 35 studies that used the PAQ or the BSRI as a measure of sex role orientation, and self-esteem as a measure of psychological well being. The meta-analysis found the most support for the masculinity model—both men and women who are masculine tend to have high self-esteem. Femininity and androgyny were also related to self-esteem, but the relationship was much weaker than for masculinity.

The mean correlation between self-esteem and masculinity was so large (.53) in Whitley's 1983 study that he thought the two measures might be tapping the same construct. To test this possibility, Whitley (1988) conducted a study using both a trait and a behavioral measure of self-esteem, and of masculinity and femininity. Just as stereotypes have different components, sex role orientation can have a number of dimensions.

Sex as a qualification for a position in society (e.g., nursing as a woman's profession and engineering as a man's), a set of behaviors associated with or restricted to one sex or the other (e.g., men's and women's clothing), and a set of personality traits associated with one sex or the other (e.g., nurturant women and aggressive men). However, the most commonly used sex role orientation measures—the Bem (1974) Sex Role Inventory (BSRI) and Spence, Helmreich, and Stapp's (1975) Personal Attributes Questionnaire (PAQ)—assess sex role orientation only in terms of personality traits. (Whitley, 1988, pp. 419–20)

Whitley measured behavioral masculinity and femininity in the following areas: leisure activity; preferences; vocational interests; social interaction; and marital (or primary relationship behavior), as well as trait sex role orientation. Self-esteem was measured by both self-ratings on bipolar adjective scales and behavioral measures. Although there was a statistically significant correlation between trait and behavioral measures of masculinity, they were found to show little convergence (i.e., they are not measuring the same thing). In other words, a man may be in a masculine occupation such as engineering, yet have feminine personality traits such as nurturance.

The convergence correlation for trait and behavioral measures of femininity were not statistically significant—indicating even more divergence between trait and behavioral measures of sex role orientation for femininity. The trait measures of masculinity were more highly correlated with self-esteem than were the behavioral measures. In fact, trait masculinity could not be distinguished from self-esteem. Whitley suggests that it is possible that the research findings regarding differences between masculine, feminine, and androgynous people are a reflection of differences in self-esteem.

In another test of sex role orientation and psychological adjustment, O'Heron and Orlofsky, (1990) examined the relationship between sex role trait and behavior orientations, gender identity, and psychological adjustment. The key questions asked in this research were whether deviation from sex role stereotypes in either personality traits or one's interests and behaviors causes one to become maladjusted. On the other hand, might some deviations, such as to be androgynous, actually be of value in adjustment? The results indicate differing effects for stereotypic and nonstereotypic sex role orientations for men and women.

Men who were low in masculine traits and behaviors had higher levels of depression, anxiety, and social distress, and scored lower on gender-identity and gender-adequacy scales than did other men. However, androgynous men, those possessing both masculine and feminine characteristics, did not exhibit gender identity confusion or maladjustment. "Therefore, not all deviations from traditional sex role standards leave the individual vulnerable to psychopathology; men who exhibit stereotypically feminine traits and interests or behaviors are not psychologically disadvantaged as long as they also manifest masculine characteristics and behaviors" (O'Heron & Orlofsky, 1990, p. 140).

In contrast to the findings for men, cross-sex-typed women were not less well adjusted.

"Rather, consistent with findings from other research, it is the absence of masculine-instrumental traits (in sex typed and undifferentiated women) that was connected with lower levels of adjustment" (O'Heron & Orlofsky, 1990, p. 141). Although women who scored high on masculine traits and behaviors described themselves as less feminine than sex-typed women, it did not affect their feelings of adequacy as women, nor was there a relationship to their gender identity scores. Perhaps, the feminist movement that has greatly expanded the options for the roles of women in society have left women much freer than men to expand the range of traits and behaviors that they can display. Whereas the range of options for men has not yet changed so significantly.

Research, however, has found a positive relationship between well being and both instrumentality and expressiveness on the Short Bem Sex Role Inventory (SBSRI) (Hunt, 1993). Only the expressiveness scale was related to affect intensity overall, in particular to positive affect intensity. The Expressiveness scale of the SBSRI consists of the traits: affectionate; sympathetic; sensitive to needs of others; understanding; compassionate; eager to soothe hurt feelings; warm; tender; love children; gentle. The following traits are found on the Instrumental Scale of the SBSRI: defend my own beliefs; independent; assertive; strong personality; forceful; have leadership abilities; willing to take risks; dominant; willing to take a stand; aggressive. Hence the items are a narrower range than the traits used to distinguish Femininity and Masculinity on the original BSRI.

Nearly 20 years after its initial development, Ballard-Reisch & Elton (1992) re-examined the BSRI as a measurement construct. Their results showed that the structure of the original factors (Masculinity and Femininity) were highly reliable. Whether or not the items are really measures of masculinity and femininity, however, is questionable. "The assumptions that masculine and feminine items of the BSRI are both positive and perceived as relating to one gender orientation were not supported in this study" (Ballard-Reisch & Elton, 1992, p. 304). It is possible that society has changed in perceptions of socially desirable characteristics for males and females during the past couple of decades.

Sex Role Orientation and Cognitive Abilities

The more feminine the woman, the poorer her performance on Piaget's water-level task. Males and females who describe themselves as more masculine and less feminine do better on spatial and mathematical tasks.

Sex role orientation is related to cognitive functioning as well as to expectations and attributions for achievement. Feminine women do not perform as well as masculine women and men on Piaget's water-level task, which is a problem that requires both knowledge of physics and spatial perceptual abilities (Kalichman, 1990). Male and female undergraduates took a paper and pencil water-level task consisting of bottles tilted at 15, 30, and 60 degrees off of the horizontal. Their task was to draw a line representing where the water line would be in each of the bottles.

Sex was significantly related to performances with males more accurate than females. The Femininity scale of the BSRI was inversely related to performance. The authors say it is because women with feminine identities are least likely to engage in activities which contribute to accurate spatial performance. They did not find, however, any relationship between scores on the Masculinity scale of the BSRI and performance on the water-level task. Manual skills reflected by a career interest inventory did account for a significant proportion of the variance in women's task performance. According to Kalichman, the proportion of men and women passing and failing the water-level task approximates that which would be predicted by an X-linked recessive genetic model. It is not a perfect fit and moderated by such factors as personality and selection of activities and interests.

As noted in Chapter III, math is stereotyped as a male domain. Signorella and Jamison (1986) conducted a meta-analysis to determine if individuals will perform better on cognitive tasks when the masculinity and femininity in their self-concepts is consistent with the gender stereotyping of the task. They found that on spatial and mathematical tasks, persons who describe themselves as more masculine/and or less feminine do better than persons who describe themselves as more feminine and/or less masculine. The results from the meta-analysis showed that for girls and women in particular, there was a robust relationship between higher masculine and lower feminine scores, and better performance on spatial perception and mathematics tasks. For males, the relationship between more masculine and lower feminine self concept and better spatial and mathematical performance held only for adults. For both males and females, gender self-concept was more related to spatial perception than to mathematics performance. Finally, there was no evidence for a relationship between gender self-concept and performance of verbal tasks.

The findings by Signorella and Jamison (1986) are consistent with the expectancy-value model developed by J. S. Eccles and her colleagues (discussed in Chapter III). If spatial perception and mathematics are seen as stereotypically masculine, then someone who is more feminine and less masculine would place less value on those endeavors and have lower expectations for successful performance in those areas.

Sex Role Orientation and Attributions for Success and Failure

Masculine and androgynous individuals make attributions to effort and teacher performance more when successful than unsuccessful as compared with feminine and undifferentiated women. Highly instrumental women attribute success to ability and failure to external causes.

Expectations for and attributions for achievement in an economics class were also found to relate to sex role orientation as well as to sex (Basow & Medcalf, 1988). As reported in Chapter III, males had a higher preexam expectancy for success than females. Masculine and androgynous individuals made attributions to effort and teacher performance significantly more when successful than when unsuccessful as compared with feminine and undifferentiated individuals. Feminine and undifferentiated individuals tended not to differ in attributions when successful or unsuccessful.

The effects of success and failure on attributions about performance and on actual performance were compared for female students who were divided into a high-instrumental and a low-instrumental group based on their responses to the PAQ (Welch, Gerrard, & Huston, 1986). Women who score high on instrumental personality attributes were found to attribute success to ability and failure to external causes. On the other hand, women who perceive themselves as low on instrumental attributes tend to attribute failure to ability and success to external causes. Patterns of performance also differed, with the high-instrumental group improving performance after success and not showing a deterioration in performance after failure. "Women scoring high and low on instrumentality did not respond differently as a function of gender appropriateness of the task, suggesting that sex role identity per se was not the variable mediating their differential performance and attributions" (Welch et al., 1986, p. 231). Higher perceived ability and higher performance expectations did account for the superior task performance of high-instrumental women. When there was no feedback about performance, however, high- and low-instrumental women did not differ in performance, so they do not differ in their ability to perform the task. The pattern of attributions and task performance for low-instrumental women could seriously impair their educational and career achievement.

Race and Sex Role Orientation of Women

Black women are more likely to be androgynous than any other sex role orientation. Although they are more likely to be androgynous than are White women, Black women hold more traditional sex role attitudes.

Binion (1990) studied the relationship between masculine and feminine personality attributes (as measured by the PAQ), sex role attitudes

and parental socialization of middle class, Black women in relation to a comparison group of White women. Black women were more likely to identify themselves as androgynous (36.6%), than as feminine (17.9%), masculine (23.6%), or undifferentiated (22.0%). Racial comparisons show White women much less likely to be androgynous (15.6%), and more likely to be undifferentiated than the Black women. Despite the fact that the majority of Black women were androgynous or masculine, Black women held more traditional sex role attitudes than White women.

The Black androgynous women were found to identify more closely with both parents while growing up, while feminine women identified closely with the mother, and masculine women with the father. Overall, the women were, however, more closely identified with their mothers than with their fathers. Among the Black women, the masculine women were more likely than the androgynous to be married, while the androgynous were more likely than the masculine to have never married. The androgynous and feminine women were significantly more likely to have children, but the masculine women who were mothers had more children. The masculine and undifferentiated women were significantly more liberal in their sex role ideology than were androgynous or feminine women.

> These results suggest that for Black women masculine traits are not antithetical to beliefs about the desirability or legitimacy of certain stereotypic feminine role expectations. Regardless of the sexual identity category, the Black women in this sample are all heavily invested in the mothering role. (Binion, 1990, p. 503)

These findings reflect the historical role of Black women as having to work outside of the home as well as play a nurturing role in the family.

GENDER DIFFERENCES IN PERSONALITY

Now that we've looked at stereotypes about men and women, we want to know what gender differences appear in the research literature. Are men and women really different in personality? The answers to these questions are more complex than they may appear on the surface. Do men and women differ on the characteristic under consideration in both laboratory and field settings? Are the same gender differences that are found between White men and women found between Black men and women? For the most part, we have not done sufficient research with minorities to answer that question. Do the differences on the behavior being studied occur at all age levels? Gender roles are changing and with them the social behavior of men and women. Do current studies report the same gender differences that previous research found?

Aggressiveness

Based on psychological research in both laboratory and field settings, statistics for violent crime, and cross-cultural and historical reviews, the evidence is clear that males are, on average, more aggressive than females across the life span.

Psychologists define aggression as behavior with the intention of inflicting harm on a person or animal. Aggression may be a physical act, such as a shove, a punch in the nose, or strangling someone, or, in the psychology laboratory, administration of an electroshock. Verbal aggression is calling someone a derogatory or obscene name or telling them something intended to inflict psychological pain.

Hyde (1984b) conducted a meta-analysis on gender differences in aggression that she then updated (1986), using newly derived statistical techniques on homogeneity tests that enabled her to separate out the effects of different types of studies. The meta-analyses conducted by Hyde indicated that several factors were sources of variation in effect size, including age, kind of aggression, method of measurement, and design. For example, gender differences in aggression were larger among preschoolers than they were among college students. Also, larger differences are found in naturalistic–correlational studies

than in experiments. Hyde interprets gender differences in naturalistic-correlational situations as reflecting spontaneous aggression, whereas in experimental laboratory situations, aggression is stimulated in some way. She says this might be interpreted as indicating that females exhibit less spontaneous aggression, but have the capacity for aggression that increases relative to males in a laboratory situation, when something is done to provoke the aggression. Another possibility is that the demand characteristics of the laboratory situation may lead women to believe aggressive behavior is expected. Also, there may be more inhibitions for men in a laboratory situation with the experimenter watching than in the real world.

Hyde (1986) found that overall males were found to be more aggressive than females ($d = +0.50$). The gender difference in physical aggression ($d = +0.60$) was found to be larger than for verbal aggression ($d = +0.43$), although the difference between the two effect values was not significant. Males were also found to be more aggressive following exposure to a model—the mean effect size is $+0.49$ for imitative aggression. As Hyde points out in her analyses, which found some variation as to type of aggression, the means for the males and the females are about one-half standard deviation apart. Hyde states that her meta-analytic studies do not have any implications—biological or environmental—for the causes of the gender differences.

Eagly and Steffen (1986) and Eagly (1987) conducted meta-analyses on 63 studies of aggressive behavior, studies of male and female adolescents or adults from the United States or Canada who were not from specialized populations (e.g., criminals, mental hospital patients). The mean weighted sex-of-subject effect size was $+0.29$—less than one-third of a standard deviation in the direction of greater aggression by men than by women. Eagly (1987) notes that her mean sex-of-subject effect size is smaller than that reported by Hyde (1984b; 1986), probably because she eliminated studies with children, whereas Hyde had a preponderance of such studies, and the gender differences in aggression have been found to be larger among children than among adults.

Eagly and Steffen (1986) found that the gender difference in aggression was greater for physical than psychological aggression, similar to Hyde's (1984b; 1986) findings. Aggression differences between males and females were also greater in semiprivate (target and/or experimenter present) than in public situations. Women were particularly less likely to be aggressive in situations where the behavior would likely cause harm to the target, would create guilt and anxiety in oneself, or could be dangerous to oneself.

Men were also more likely than women to be the target of aggression. Aggression was more likely to be directed at men in the laboratory rather than field settings, in semiprivate rather than public contexts, when aggression was required rather than a free choice, and when there was greater rather than minimal provocation. The meta-analyses on aggression specifically eliminated studies done on criminal and mental patient populations, thereby reducing the difference between men and women in aggression. In the real world, rates of violent crime of men and women clearly show much higher levels of aggression in men. Women accounted for only 10.4% of arrests for murder and 13.3% of arrests for aggravated assault in the United States in 1990 (J. K. White & Kowalski, 1994). Male offenders are also more likely to be involved in repetitive criminal activity (Chapman, 1988).

Among other vertebrate species males are found to be more aggressive. "In all mammalian species, from mouse to man, the male is the more aggressive species" (Moyer, 1974, p. 335). Among humans, the historical and cross-cultural data also support a conclusion of males being more aggressive than females. "Since history has been recorded, males have committed more crimes of violence than have females in all nations and all communities within those nations" (Moyer, 1974, p. 335). In summary, based on psychological research in both laboratory and field settings, statistics for violent crime in the United States, and cross-cultural and historical reviews, the evidence is consistent in leading to a conclusion that males are more aggressive than females across the life span.

To say that men are more aggressive than women, however, is not the same as saying that women are nonaggressive. A laboratory experiment has demonstrated that women have an equal potential for being aggressive given the appropriate circumstances (Lightdale & Prentice, 1994). In the experiment that involved playing video games defending against bombs being dropped by another participant, and then aggressing against the other, women were found to be equally as aggressive as men only in a deindividuation condition in which the participants were playing the game against a person they did not see or hear.

> In the absence of social expectations and obligations, women were at least as aggressive as men in an aggression-eliciting situation. Given these results, the case for innate or immutable sex differences in aggression is not compelling enough to eclipse alternative theories. (Lightdale & Prentice 1994, p. 42)

In another article, J. K. White and Kowalski (1994) say that the nonaggressive woman is a myth that serves to perpetuate women's subordination to men. Rather than asking who is more aggressive—women or men—we should be analyzing the cultural, social, and psychological circumstances surrounding incidents of aggression by women or men.

Helping Behavior

Statistics for awards for saving human lives, and psychological research in the laboratory and field settings are consistent in showing that men are more likely to help someone in distress.

If men are more likely to hurt other people, are men also more likely to help other people? Eagly (1987) notes that of the 6,955 Carnegie medalists who received awards for heroism displayed in saving human life, only 616 (8.86%) have been awarded to women. This is consistent with the male sex role that expects heroic behavior from men. The male sex role expects risky

TABLE 4.1   Meta-Analyses of Gender Differences in Personality and Social Behavior

Characteristic	Effect Size *d*	Study
Aggression		Hyde (1986)
Overall Agression	+0.50	
Physical Agression	+0.60	
Verbal Agression	+0.43	
Imitative Agression	+0.49	
Adolescents and Adults	+0.29	Eagly & Steffen (1986)
Activity Level	+0.49	Eaton & Enns (1986)
Infancy	+0.29	
Preschool	+0.44	
School Age & Older	+0.64	
Helping Behavior		Eagly & Crowley (1986)
Overall	+0.13	
Overall (weighted)	+0.34	
Off Campus Location	+0.50	
On Campus	−0.04	
Under Conditions of Surveillance	+0.74	
No Surveillance	−0.02	
Other Help Available	+0.42	
Other Help Unavailable	+0.20	
Self Esteem		Feingold (1994)
Children	−0.10	
Adolescent & Adult		
United States	+0.19	
Canada	+0.04	
Other Countries	+0.17	
Assertiveness		Feingold (1994)
Studies reviewed by Maccoby & Jackin (1974) and by Hall (1984)	+0.10–+0.16	
Personality Inventories	+0.46	
Influenceability		Eagly & Carli (1981)
Overall Influenceability	−0.28	
Group Pressure	−0.32	
Persuasion	−0.16	
Anxiety		Feingold (1994)
Overall Anxiety	−0.30	
General Anxiety	−0.18	
Social Anxiety	+0.14	
Personality Inventory Anxiety	−0.30	
Empathy		Feingold (1994)
Tendermindedness	−0.97	
Moral Reasoning	+0.05	Walker (1986)
	−0.20	Thoma (1986)

acts of rescuing others, as well as more courteous and protective behaviors, typically directed toward women. On the other hand, the helping expected of women consists primarily in caring for others, typically in close and long-term relationships (Eagly, 1987). The female role prescription actually cautions women about even helpful interactions with strangers.

Eagly and Crowley (1986) conducted a meta-analysis of gender differences in helping behavior, limiting the studies for inclusion to those whose research subjects were male and female adolescents and adults from the United States and Canada who were not from specialized populations. A study was also omitted if it did not report the sex distribution of the nonhelpers in the situation.

The social psychological studies of helping have been confined to short-term encounters with strangers. The results of the meta-analysis showed the mean weighted sex-of-subject effect size was +0.34, or approximately one-third of a standard deviation in the direction of greater helping behavior by men than by women. It can be concluded that men are more likely to help a stranger in distress than are women.

Future research needs to be done on behavior in the context of family or of other close interpersonal relationships to determine if there is a gender difference in helping behavior within the sphere of intimate relationships.

> "The female gender role may prescribe that women help only certain people in certain ways. Women are expected to care for the personal and emotional needs of others, to deliver routine forms of personal service, and, more generally to facilitate the progress of others toward their goals." The demand for women to serve others in these ways is especially strong within the family and applies to some extent in other close relationships, such as friendships. (Eagly and Crowley, 1986, p. 284)

The research on altruism has clearly not studied helping behavior within families and close relationships, but only from an androcentric conceptuaslization of helping as bravery in a dangerouse situation.

Affiliation

Although there is some conflicting research, it appears that females have a higher need for affiliation and intimacy than males. Adolescent girls actually spend more time with others than do boys.

Affiliation motivation is the need to establish and maintain positive relationships with others. Some of the research is conflicting on the difference in the strength of the need for affiliation in males and females. No gender differences in need

for affiliation were found in a review of the literature that used a projective technique, the Thematic Apperception Test (TAT), which involves a person telling a story about what is happening in an ambiguous picture as the measure of affiliation (A. J. Stewart & Chester, 1982). However, another literature review of studies using either the TAT or the Edwards Personal Preference Inventory, found women to score higher on affiliation orientation (Minton & Schneider, 1980). A study of intimacy motivation in 1,500 college students found higher intimacy motivation in women than in men (McAdams, Lester, Brand, McNamara, & Lensky, 1988).

High school girls have reported having about twice as many interpersonal thoughts as do boys (Wong & Csikszentmihalyi, 1991). Both boys and girls high in affiliation motivation wished to be with friends more often and wished to be alone less often compared with less-affiliative ones. Regardless of affiliative orientation, girls actually spent more time with friends and less time in solitary activities than did boys. The highly affiliative girls, however, spent more time at parties, going out with friends, and talking with people than did the less affiliative girls.

> Affiliative girls reported better experiences in both friends and alone situations than did other girls, but affiliative boys felt worse than other boys in both situations. Adolescents who have gender appropriate characteristics might be better adjusted. (Wong & Csikszentmihalyi, 1991, p. 161)

Affiliation motivation is seen as more appropriate for the female gender role than it is for the male gender role in our society. As a result, boys with a high need for affiliation are probably aware that they do not fit the gender role, and are uncomfortable with their desires and needs both when they are alone and when with others.

Sociability

In early childhood the two sexes are equally interested in social stimuli. Adult male friendships tend to be more instrumental and female friendships more expressive.

It is difficult to conceptually differentiate affiliation motivation from sociability, but affiliation motivation is generally referring to a need to be with other people, and sociability refers to actual group participation. I have placed them in different sections simply on the basis of the terminology used in the studies. Some psychologists have hypothesized that from early infancy through adulthood, males are more interested in objects and females are more interested in persons. Research on infancy has focused on whether girl babies look at faces rather than objects more than boys do. In their review of the literature Maccoby and Jacklin (1974) concluded that the "the two sexes are equally interested in social (as compared with nonsocial) stimuli." They also found no evidence for any gender differences in learning through imitation of models, willingness to remain alone, responsiveness to social reinforcement, or being more dependent on their caretakers. A meta-analysis of U.S. norms for 13 personality inventories finds a small gender difference indicating greater female gregariousness (Feingold, 1994).

Dependency

Contrary to the stereotype, there is no consistent evidence that females are more dependent than males.

A great deal of media attention was given to Collette Dowling's book, *The Cinderella Complex* (1981), in which she argued that even women who appear to be competent and successful in their careers harbor a secret desire to be taken care of by a man. According to Dowling, they long for a knight in shining armor to come and rescue them. The only reason I mention Dowling's unsubstantiated claims here is that a popular book like that shapes stereotypical beliefs in society. Are women really more dependent than men? Research in the real world shows that men who are bachelors have a higher rate of mental illness than never-married women. Men remarry more quickly after divorce; those who do not remarry have a higher rate of mental illness than divorced women (see Chapter VIII).

Men who are widowed often find it much more difficult to cope with life alone than do women who are widowed; in fact, widowed men have a much higher mortality rate than do widowed women (see Chapter IX).

A number of different definitions of dependency have been put forth. I will define it here as the need to be nurtured, helped, and taken care of by others. Different methods have been used to measure dependency—observation of assistance, attention or reassurance on the part of children, or remaining close to or in physical contact with a parent or other adult such as a teacher. Other studies have used ratings, projective tests, or self-report scales. Different research methods have produced discrepant evidence (Minton & Schneider, 1980).

Maccoby and Jacklin's (1974) review found most studies to show no gender differences in dependency in children. The few that did found a pattern of girls showing more attachment than boys, with girls seeking to be closer to parents when they were in the room with them, but boys showing greater resistance to separation from their parents.

Self-Esteem

Males have slightly higher self-esteem than females.

Feingold's (1994) meta-analysis of the studies reviewed by Maccoby and Jacklin (1974) found a slight gender difference ($d = -0.10$) in self-esteem favoring female children, and a slight gender difference ($d = +0.10$) favoring adolescent and adult males. A replication of a meta-analysis by J. A. Hall (1984) by Feingold found an effect size of $+0.19$ for the United States, $+0.04$ for Canada, and $+0.17$ for other countries in self-esteem, "indicating no notable gender difference on that trait" (Feingold, 1994, p. 437).

Assertiveness

Males are somewhat more assertive than females.

Across three meta-analyses, one based on studies of adolescents and adults reviewed by Maccoby and Jacklin (1974), J.A. Hall's (1984) meta-analysis, and a replication of J. A. Hall's meta-analysis, males were higher in assertiveness than females, although the effect sizes were small ($ds = +0.10$ to $+0.16$) (Feingold, 1994). Gender differences in assertiveness were in the moderate range ($d = +0.46$), however, when the meta-analysis was calculated from standarized personality inventories.

Activity Level

Boys are more active than girls during childhood and possibly during adolescence, and into adulthood.

Activity level can be defined as "... the individual's customary expenditure of energy through movement" (Eaton & Enns, 1986, p. 19). Eaton and Enns (1986), who found males to be more active than females ($d = +0.49$). Ninety percent of the studies had samples of mean ages of 15 or less. Gender differences did appear in the 14 infancy studies (0–11 months), $d = +0.29$. For preschool and older subjects, the mean effects, for these two older groups were $d = +0.44$ and $d = +0.64$. Situational factors were also found to be mediating variables in gender differences. Greater gender differences in activity level tended to be found in low- rather than high-stress situations and in familiar rather than novel settings, as well as when peers were present and when the situation was unrestricted.

Are gender differences in activity level due to girls being more mature and therefore less active than boys? The relative physical maturities and activity levels of 83 5–8-year-olds were assessed (Eaton & Yu, 1989). When maturity was added as a predictor of activity level variance, the significant predictive contribution of sex remained. Thus, although relative physical maturity accounts for some of the gender difference in activity level, the sex effect is also significant.

A meta-analysis of gender differences in activity level is in sharp contrast to that of Eaton & Enns. U.S. norms for 13 personality inventories

for activity level found what Feingold (1994) calls trivial ($d = -005$ to $+017$). Eaton and Enns' sample of studies were primarily observational studies of children, whereas Feingold's meta-analysis was based on self-report primarily of high school samples and older. I think we can conclude that males have a higher expenditure of energy through movement during childhood. Before drawing conclusions about gender differences in activity level of adolescents and adults further observational studies should be conducted.

Morality

Gilligan claims that men have a view of morality that focuses on abstract principles of justice, whereas women's morality speaks in a voice of caring and connectedness.

Theories of moral development assumed the male to be the normative model with afterthoughts given to moral development of the female. The classic early work, Jean Piaget's *The Moral Judgment of the Child* (1932/1965), focuses on moral development through the learning of rules of boyhood games such as shooting marbles. Girls, he observed, were more tolerant in their attitudes toward rules. Boys were governed by equity (you get out what you put in), which Piaget saw as a more advanced moral standard than equality (share and share alike), which was preferred by girls (Piaget, 1932/1965).

Kohlberg (1969) extended the work of Piaget, discovering six levels of moral development and three stages from an egocentric, through a societal, to a universal ethical conception of justice. Kohlberg's six stages were primarily based on a study of 84 boys whose development Kohlberg followed for over 20 years.

Carol Gilligan captured the nation's attention (her picture was even on the cover of Time magazine) when she proclaimed in her book, *A Different Voice* (1982), that males and females are guided by different conceptualizations of morality. She said that subsequent research showed that groups not included in Kohlberg's original sample, and that includes women, rarely reach stage six. According to Gilligan, this is not because women are deficient in moral judgment, just different in their conception of morality. She says that women speak in a voice of caring and connectedness, and men speak in a voice of abstract justice.

> The moral imperative that emerges repeatedly in interviews with women is an injunction to care, a responsibility to discern and alleviate the "real and recognizable trouble" of this world. For men, the moral imperative appears rather as an injunction to respect the rights of others and thus to protect from interference the rights to life and self-fulfillment. (Gilligan, 1982, p. 100)

Gilligan primarily based her theory on three studies. In the first, 29 pregnant women were interviewed during the first trimester of pregnancy at a time when they were considering abortion. In addition, she interviewed 25 college students, both men and women who were randomly selected from students who as sophomores had signed up to take a course on moral and political choice. The students were interviewed as seniors and again five years later. A third study involved a matched sample of males and females at nine different ages from 6 to 60.

Other research has found that men and women are more alike than they are different in their moral reasoning (Ford & Lowery, 1986; Friedman, Robinson, & Friedman, 1987). Both men and women are concerned with caring and relatedness and with principles of justice in resolving moral conflicts. Research has also not found that females score lower than males on Kohlberg's measure of moral reasoning (Greeno & Maccoby, 1986; L. J. Walker, 1984).

Few significant gender differences in moral reasoning were obtained in a study testing Gilligan's theory with 202 male and female college students who described how they resolved three important moral conflicts in their lives (Ford & Lowery, 1986). Women were more consistent, however, in their use of relationship, care and responsibility, whereas men were more consistent in their use of fairness, justice and rights. More feminine males use a care orientation to a greater extent than less feminine males.

Similarly, Friedman et al. (1987) found no significant differences between men and women in their use of a justice or a caring orientation. Neither was there a relationship between the PAQ scores and moral judgments, so that students who scored masculine, feminine, or androgynous did not differ in their moral judgments. "Finally, while this study fails to support Gilligan's (1977, 1979, 1982) claims for sex differences, it does provide preliminary evidence for a basis of moral judgments that is distinct from Kohlberg's" (W. J. Friedman et al., 1987, p. 46). Some men as well as some women utilize a care justification for morality. Gilligan discovered an important basis for moral judgment—caring and connectedness. Caring, however, is an important factor in understanding the moral reasoning of both men and women.

Meta-analytic studies have also failed to confirm a gender "inferiority" of females in moral reasoning as defined by Kohlberg's stages. A meta-analysis by Lawrence J. Walker (1986), testing the hypothesis that males are more advanced in moral reasoning than females, obtained an effect size that was almost zero. Thoma (1986), who conducted a meta-analysis of 56 studies that used Rest's (1979) objective test of comprehension and preference of moral issues, Defining Issues Test, found that although females scored significantly higher than males at every age and educational level, gender accounted for less than one-half of 1% of the variance in moral reasoning.

Martha Mednick (1989) notes that "The belief in a 'different voice' persists; it appears to be a symbol for a cluster of widely held social beliefs that argue for women's differences, for reasons that are quite independent of scientific merit" (Mednick, 1989, p. 1120). She says that Gilligan's theory is part of a cluster of theories that emphasize women's special, perhaps even superior, nature, and direct the focus of explanation of gender differences intrapsychically. "An intrapsychic emphasis places the burden of change entirely on the person and does not lead scientific inquiry to an examination of cultural, socio-economic, structural, or contemporaneous situational factors that may affect behavior" (Mednick, 1989, p. 1120). These theories propose personality traits as the cause of gender differences, and postulate the cause of these differences as either biological/genetic factors or an early female socialization process.

On the other hand, Mednick points out that there are other theorists and researchers, mostly social psychologists, who emphasize the necessity for studying gender in social and historical contexts (Sherif, 1979). It is conceivable that the individual's position in the power structure is a greater determinant of autonomy or relatedness than is gender (Hare-Mustin and Marecek, 1986). Gilligan's "different voice," however, appeals to the popular culture in its dichotomous thinking that perceives women and men in terms of stereotypes that emphasize difference.

Influenceability

Research on influenceability finds females to be somewhat more easily influenced than males. The gender difference is larger for group pressure conformity experiments than for persuasion studies.

Social psychology textbooks typically state that females are more easily influenced than males. Do meta-analytic studies reach this conclusion? Meta-analyses have been conducted on gender differences in two types of influenceability: persuasion studies and conformity studies. Persuasion studies typically present the subject with an argument and a pretest, then a posttest measure of attitude. In conformity studies, the subject is exposed to confederates whose responses support a particular position or choice of the "correct stimulus." The subject must then take a position or make a choice. Sometimes the naïve subject is in face-to-face interaction with the confederates, but, at other times, the responses of others are communicated to the subjects via audio or visual-display equipment.

Eagly and Carli (1981) found females to be more influenceable, but the difference is small, $d = -0.28$ and for the other conformity studies $d = -0.28$. The group pressure designs yielded a $d = -0.32$. For persuasion studies, $d = -0.16$. These results were significant, indicating more fe-

male conformity for all three study paradigms. Eagly and Carli also found a lack of gender differences in interest in and knowledge about the topic of the persuasive message (as indicated by a group of undergraduates), which suggests that the greater conformity or influenceability of females was not due to their lesser knowledge of or interest in the content of the material presented in these research studies.

There was, however, a correlation between sex of author and gender difference in influence with all three paradigms, showing that male researchers found women to be more easily influenced than did female researchers. The bias due to sex of the researcher may have operated in several ways, such as through design of tasks at which males had more knowledge and experience, or through conveying expectancies nonverbally in some way to research participants. Because most of these studies were of college students in laboratory situations, we do not know the extent of generalizability to real-world circumstances.

To discover the process by which influence occurs, Carli (1989) examined gender differences in influence strategies in laboratory groups. She found that gender differences were larger in same-sex than in mixed-sex groups. The gender of the partner was a determinant of interaction patterns. Participants exhibited a higher percentage of task disagreements with men and agreements with women. "Because influence was found to be positively associated with agreement and negatively associated with disagreements, subjects, regardless of gender, used an interaction style that was stereotypically masculine although less influential when interacting with men" (Carli, 1989, p. 574). Thus, women apparently conform more because their partners use more agreement with them, which is actually more persuasive.

Emotion

Very little research has been conducted on gender differences in emotion. Women cry more than men.

Stereotypically, women are seen as more emotional, and less rational than men. Very little research on gender differences in emotion has been conducted.

> The sex-differences model is particularly unproductive if applied to emotion. It limits us to asking about the quantity of emotion expressed and experienced, thereby implying that psychologically relevant emotion should be viewed exclusively as capacities of the individual, not as functions of the circumstances in which the individual is behaving. (S. A. Shields, 1987, p. 232)

In addition to the problem of not adequately taking into account the circumstances in which the emotion is expressed is the problem that not all emotions are created equal in the public's view. Stephanie A. Shields (1987b) points out that there is an emotional double standard. Anger is an acceptable emotion for males to express, but not for females to express, whereas emotions such as happiness, sadness, and fear are more associated with and acceptably expressed by females. In fact, men have been found to rate themselves higher on anger and contempt, whereas women rate themselves higher on positive emotions (e.g. happiness and joy) and negative inwardly directed emotions (e.g. shame, fear and guilt) (L. H. Brody & Hall, 1993; LaFrance and Benaji, 1992). Many political reporters said that Senator Edmund Muskie's chances for the 1978 Democratic presidential nomination evaporated when he cried publicly during the New Hampshire primary campaign.

Crying was also seen as a kiss of death for future presidential aspirations for Congresswoman Patricia Schroeder who cried on her husbands's shoulder when withdrawing from the 1988 Democratic presidential primary campaign. Crying is seen as a stereotypical female behavior, and the presidency of the United States as a masculine position. Rep. Schroeder might have been forgiven for the crying had she not also exhibited the stereotypical feminine dependency behavior of crying on her husband's shoulder.

In a study of British university students, (Bindra, 1972), females reported crying longer and more intensely than males. Similarly, self-reported crying behavior of 307 female and 285 male California university students (Lombardo, Crester, Lombardo, & Mathis, 1983) found that females reported crying significantly more frequently and more intensely than males. When asked which sex cries more frequently, 87% of the sample said "women cry more." Similarities, however, were found in the types of interpersonal relationships that they saw as making crying most likely; the types of stimulus situations that are most conducive to crying; and the adjectives chosen as most descriptive of the postcrying affect. Thus, although females cry more often than males, the same types of interpersonal relationships and situations evoke crying in men and women, and for both sexes the predominant feelings afterwards are of relief and a sense of being better able to carry on.

Anxiety

Women show a tendency toward general anxiety and men show a slight tendency toward greater social anxiety.

A recent meta-analysis of studies reviewed by Maccoby and Jacklin (1974) found that females scored higher than males on measures of anxiety ($d = -0.30$) (Feingold, 1994). A replication of J. A. Hall's 1984 meta-analysis found within the subset of U.S. studies, a higher mean effect size for females for general anxiety ($d = -0.18$), but higher for males for social anxiety ($d = +0.14$). Females scored higher than males on the meta-analysis of personality inventory norms for anxiety ($d = -0.30$). Overall, it can be concluded that females show a tendency toward greater general anxiety, but that males show a slight tendency toward greater social anxiety.

Empathy

Self report measures show large gender differences in empathy favoring females. When measures such as physiological or facial/gestural are used, no gender differences are found.

Empathy has most often been defined in affective terms as vicarious emotional responding to another (Eisenberg & Lennon, 1983). Defined in this way, it reflects the sex role stereotype that females are more responsive to another's emotional state and express more sympathy. The expectation is thus that females would have more empathy than males.

Meta-analyses of gender differences show that the method of assessing empathy was highly related to gender differences in empathy (Eisenberg & Lennon, 1983). When self-report measures were used asking subjects to rate themselves there was a large gender difference favoring females. (Eisenberg & Lennon, 1983). Meta-analyses calculated from U.S. norms for 13 personality inventories found that females score much higher than males on tendermindedness ($d = -0.97$) (Feingold, 1994). Somewhat more reflexive crying behavior was exhibited by female than by male infants. When methods of measurement were either nonobtrusive measures such as physiological or facial/gestural measures, however, no gender differences were found.

GENDER DIFFERENCES IN LANGUAGE

Because men have more power than women, men engage in more assertive speech. Women's more submissive position is reflected in speech that includes more hedges, adverb phrases, intensifiers, and tag questions. This is a style considered to be feminine regardless of speaker.

The linguist Robin Lakoff (1973, 1975) originally noted that because men generally have more power than women, then men would engage in more assertive speech. She further argued that women's lower status relative to men would be evidenced by less swearing, being more polite, and using more hedges, intensifiers and tag questions in their speech. Hedges are adverbs or adverb phrases added to a sentence such as "sort of, perhaps, maybe, etc." Intensifiers are words like "so" added in a sentence. For example, "She is so beautiful." A tag question is one that is tacked on to the end of a declarative statement. A woman might say, "This is a good meal, isn't it?" According to Henley, use of "women's speech" puts women at a disadvantage, making them less creditable and influential.

Ratings of pairs of sentences, one of which ended in a tag question, confirmed Lakoff's "women's style" as more feminine, consistent with gender stereotyping of speech (Quina, Wingard, & Bates, 1987). Regardless of the gender of the speaker, the feminine linguistic style was rated lower in competence, but higher in social warmth than the nonfeminine style.

When speaking to men, women's language is more tentative than when speaking with women. Women speak in a more competent manner when speaking to their boss. Men speak in a more competent manner to peers. Not all research supports gender differences in language style.

Carli (1990) observed mixed-sex and same-sex dyads in discussion of a topic on which they disagreed. A measure of each individual's tentative language was completed, including each person's use of qualifiers (i.e., "I may be wrong, but,"), hedges, and tag questions. The results show that when speaking to men, women's language is more tentative than when speaking with women. Women had a greater influence on men when their language was tentative, but less influence on women. Men, however, were equally influential whether or not they used tentative language.

In a second study, Carli (1990) asked students to rate the speaker of an audiotaped persuasive message presented either by a man or a woman. A female speaker was more influential when speaking tentatively to a male audience, although she was evaluated as being less knowledgeable and competent than a woman speaking assertively. Men perceived a tentative female speaker as more trustworthy and likeable than an assertive woman, whereas women perceived her as less likeable and trustworthy.

In a laboratory study, with male and female MBA candidates pretending to have conversations with a peer, supervisor, and subordinate, women's voices were judged as sounding more competent when they talked to their bosses or subordinates than to their peers (Steckler & Rosenthal, 1985). Men, on the other hand, were judged more competent when they talked to their peers and subordinates than when speaking to their bosses. These reactions on the part of women may be associated with stereotypes of women managers. A woman may particularly want to make an effort to sound competent to people who may have doubts about her competence.

> Her boss, who is likely to be male, may hold traditional stereotypes as to how she will behave, and she may make a special effort to compensate, to impress upon her boss that she is businesslike and competent, contrary to established stereotypes of women (Bowman, Worthey, & Greyser, 1965; Broverman et al., 1972). Her subordinate, who is likely to be female, may also challenge her authority, or not cooperate with her as she would a male boss (Kanter, 1972) and so the female manager may feel the need to assert her authority particularly strongly in communicating with her subordinate. (Steckler & Rosenthal, 1985, p. 162)

A man's expressing greater competence when talking to peers may reflect competition between male peers, whereas he wants to show his boss and subordinates that he is not competing with them.

Some research, however, conflicts with these studies. A study conducted with British university students found female speech to be more masculine and less feminine in mixed-sex groups of four than in same-sex dyads (Hogg, 1985). Finally, a study found no gender differences at all in male and female language. Male and female undergraduate students participated in same-sex or mixed-sex dyads to discuss suggestions for a new orientation handbook (Simkins-Bullock & Wildman, 1991). Audiotapes of the discussion were evaluated on variables that previous research suggested represented either "powerful" or "less powerful" linguistic features. This study, in contrast to the one previously cited, found that there are no systematic differences in use of either "powerful" or "less powerful" linguistic styles by men and women. Powerful people use powerful language features and the reverse is true for powerless people regardless of sex. The conflicting research in this area needs to be resolved by a meta-analysis, which could determine the extent of overall gender differences in language style, and circumstances under which these differences are likely to occur.

Children's Language

Gender differences in children's language show boys to use more imperatives and to be more judgmental. Girls are more expressive in their speech.

Gender differences in language style have been found for boys and girls as well as among adult men and women. Children in kindergarten through the sixth grade, ages 5 through 12 years, were brought into the laboratory and a rabbit was put in the child's arms. It was surprising that there were no age differences in the styles used in talking to the animal. Boys and girls, however, spoke differently to the rabbit. Girls' speech was more complex in talking to the animal than that of the boys. The girls were more affectionate and expressive in their speech than the boys, as measured by judges' ratings and by variability in the fundamental frequencies in their voices. Girls also asked more questions. Boys used more imperatives and annoyed utterances. "Among adults, these differences are often stereotypically interpreted as men's dominance and women's submission" (Levin & Hunter, 1982, p. 70).

Systematic differences in linguistic style in written language has also been found for children and adolescents. Mulac, Studley and Blau (1990) obtained essays written by male and female students in grades 4, 8, and 12 who were enrolled in the largely white, middle-class Santa Barbara County Public School System. By the fourth grade, there was a discernable difference in written language. Based on previous research, 19 language features were selected for analysis. "The discriminant analysis of fourth graders' essays correctly identified the gender of 87% of the students on the basis of 10 language features" (Mulac, et al., 1990, p. 460). Despite crossover of some characteristics of girls' language in the fourth grade that became more characteristic of boys' speech in later grades, four language features were consistent in the essays of either male or female writers across grade levels.

Judgmental phrases ("It is important") were found to be indicative of males for all three grade levels. In addition, three variables were predictive of female writers for at least two grades: references to emotion ("she'll be hurt"), fillers ("Well . . . "), and progressive verbs ("giving"). Despite the differences, these spontaneous essays indicate a great deal of overlap of male and female styles. When untrained university students were given the essays to see if they could guess the sex of the writers, they were not able to do so with anything better than chance accuracy. This meant that the differences that were found in language usage were the result of language differences in the written essays and not of sex role stereotypes. Attributional ratings by untrained observers on the basis of their essays found boys in the fourth, eighth and twelfth grades to be rated as stronger and more aggressive (Dynamism) and girls in the fourth grade to be perceived as higher in social status and literacy (Sociointellectual Status) as well as nicer and sweeter (Aesthetic Quality). Therefore, the differences in language usage were found to affect the judgment of observers about the child without their knowing the sex of the essay writer.

Talking in Groups

Men in mixed sex groups talk more than women, and speak in longer utterances. Men act as if they have more power.

Contrary to long held stereotypes that depict women as talking constantly, the weight of the evidence is that men talk more than women (D. James & Drakich, 1993). A review of the literature of 56 studies of mixed-sex interaction found

that in 26 (42.9%) of the studies men talk more than women; in a further 10 studies (17.9%) men talked more than women in some situations with no difference in the other situations; in 3 studies, (5.4%) sometimes men and sometimes women talked more; in 16 studies (28.6%) no significant difference between the sexes in overall amount of talk was found; and in only two studies (3.6%) were women found to talk more than men overall.

> Much evidence suggests that men learn that it is important for them to assert status and to appear a leader in interactions, while women learn to concentrate on using talk in such a way as to establish and maintain harmonious relationships with others. It has been suggested that taking and holding the floor for long periods follows logically from this as a male speech strategy, since this can function as a way of gaining attention and asserting status, while by contrast, being careful not to take up a disproportionate amount of talking time follows logically from the female speech style, since this emphasizes cooperation, support, and equality among interactants. (D. James & Drakich, 1993, p. 285)

Another approach to explaining differences in amount of talk is expectations states theory. The differences in amount of talking by men and women in different contexts (although men talk more in the public sphere, women are perceived to talk more in the private sphere) can be explained in terms of the difference in status of men and women and expectations about areas of competence of men and women (Berger, Fizek, Norman, & Zelditch, 1977).

A study conducted by Zimmerman and West (1975) recorded conversations in coffee shops, drug stores, and other public places in a university community. They found few overlaps of conversation and interruptions in same-sex pairs, but a drastically different pattern in cross-sex pairs, with almost all of the interruptions and overlaps by male speakers. The findings from a laboratory experiment with students reached the same conclusions (Mulac, 1989). Men in mixed-gender dyads talk more than men or women in same-gender dyads, who in turn talk more than women interacting with men. Men speak in longer utterances than women, regardless of whether they are interacting with other men or with women. When there was a control for interactant gender, individuals who talked more and in longer utterances were rated higher in Dynamism, which is an operational measure of power. In other words, the men acted as if they possessed more power than the women.

Before we jump to conclusions that men interrupt women more, we need to look at an overview of research results on interruptions from 21 studies (D. James & Clarke, 1993). In terms of the number of interruptions initiated by males versus females in dyadic interaction, 13 studies found no significant difference between the sexes in number of interruptions, two studies found women to interrupt more and six found men to initiate more interruptions overall.

According to D. James and Clarke (1993), one reason for the lack of gender differences or conflicting results may be because interruptions may have more than one function in interaction. Interruptions may be dominance associated, or they may be cooperative interruptions which function to indicate support, collaboration and solidarity. Three studies of all female groups tend to support the hypothesis that interruptions in all female groups are primarily of the collaborative type.

NONVERBAL BEHAVIOR

Smiling

Women smile more than men.

Studies of social smiling from both laboratory and field settings, with the former greatly predominating, indicate that for children ages 2–12 there is virtually no evidence for a gender difference. The picture changes dramatically for adults, however, where "all the indices show that women engage in more social smiling than men" (J. A. Hall, 1984, p. 142). The results of the meta-analysis for adults was nonhomogeneous. Women's smiling increased significantly relative to that of

men when they were interacting with others rather than alone, and when telling the truth rather than lying. Smiling in women may be related to oppression of women both as a proximal and distal cause.

> If a woman smiles to appease her violent husband, then oppression plays a very significant and direct role in her nonverbal behavior; but if she smiles because it is an ingrained habit shared by most others of her gender, a habit that is engendered by gender-role expectations that stem only historically from oppression, than oppression plays a remoter role in her behavior, one that may be of little importance either in her own motivation or in the reaction of others. (J. A. Hall, 1987, p. 184)

In order to test Henley's (1977) hypothesis that women smile more than men because of having a lower status position, Deutsch (1990) recruited 40 male and 40 female undergraduates to play the role of either interviewer (high power) or interviewee (low power) in simulated job interviews with either male or female partners. Overall, applicants smiled more than interviewers, which indicates that low status persons smile more than high status persons. When a man was the interviewer, he smiled significantly less than either a male or a female applicant. This difference in smiling, however, disappeared when a woman was the interviewer and a man the applicant. When a woman interviewed a female applicant, the greater smiling on the part of the applicant did not quite reach significance. The author interprets her findings in terms of Berger's expectation states theory.

Gaze

One of the largest gender differences reported in the literature is for gazing behavior.

Most of the research on gazing also was based on laboratory interactions, with only an occasional study in naturally occurring situations. Judith A. Hall & Amy Halberstadt's (1986) meta-analysis found a gender difference in overall

TABLE 4.2 Meta-Analyses of Gender Differences in Nonverbal Behavior

Nonverbal Behavior	Effect Size d	Study
Smiling		Hall & Halberstadt (1986)
Children	0.04	
College Students	−0.70	
Adults	−0.41	
Gazing		Hall & Halberstadt (1986)
Elementary School	−0.47	
College Students	−0.70	
Adults	−0.54	
Approach		Hall (1987)
Women Approaching Others	−0.54	
Others Approaching Women	−0.86	

magnitude above −0.60 in standard deviation units—in the range that they say J. Cohen (1977) would call visible to the naked eye. Among both children and adults, females gaze more than males do. "Thus the gazing gender difference seems unusually resistant to a range of situational manipulations that tapped all three factors of positive affect, status, and social tension" (J. A. Hall & Halberstadt, 1986, pp. 144–45). Gender differences favoring females did increase in size when individuals were conversing rather than building with blocks together, close rather than far apart, and concealing information in an interview. Although accounting for only some 10% of the variance in gazing behavior, these gender differences are larger than they are for most others reported in the literature.

Racial differences as well as gender differences occur in gazing. Black women have a tendency to gaze at each other less often than do White women when interacting in same-sex pairs (A. Smith, 1983). Future research needs to take into account racial as well as gender differences, rather than lumping together all females.

Visual behavior is important in influencing others and establishing and maintaining social power. One way power is measured nonverbally is in terms of visual dominance behavior. The visual dominance ratio is the percentage of looking while speaking divided by the percentage of looking while listening. A relatively high visual dominance ratio is characteristic of persons high

in power, who typically gaze more while speaking and less while listening (Dovidio & Ellyson 1985; Exline, Ellyson, & Long, 1975). In same-sex dyads, a high visual dominance ratio is consistently found.

Since women have typically had lower status in society, do women in high-status positions display high or low visual dominance behavior? In a laboratory experiment, Ellyson et al. (1991) examined visual dominance behavior of women in three different leadership conditions in mixed-sex dyads. Women leaders with established structural power roles displayed higher visual dominance than did women in the intermediate power and the unstructured (control) condition. Women in the intermediate power roles displayed significantly less visual dominance than did men in that condition. The men with intermediate power displayed as much visual dominance as did women in firmly established power positions. It appears that because women are culturally considered less legitimate candidates for leadership, they do not display visual dominance associated with higher power positions unless they have a clear mandate for the exercise of that power role.

Touch

Men touch women more than women touch men with the hand (not all research supports this finding). Women touch children more than men do. There are no gender differences in touch among children. Women touch men more, but not with the hand.

Gender differences in nonverbal behavior and more specifically in touch were brought to public as well as to psychologists' attention by Henley (1973, 1977). Based on research observations of male and female touching behavior in public places, Henley concluded that men touch women more than women touch men. Henley proposed that this gender asymmetry in touch is an expression of men's higher status and power in society. She also said that women's other nonverbal behaviors, such as smiling, can also be interpreted in terms of their subordinate position, as a means of conveying submissiveness and appeasement.

The literature in the area of touching is not standard methodologically, so it is not conducive to meta-analysis. J. A. Hall (1984) reports the main conclusion to be drawn from the literature is that adult women initiate more touch, but this finding is ambiguous because it may be based primarily on women touching other women. Methodological problems make it difficult to interpret some of the data because a number of studies counted total frequency of touches without controlling for proportions of same-sex and opposite sex dyads available for observation.

A field study by Major, Schmidlin & Williams (1990) was designed to replicate Henley's original study and to go further by systematically considering four factors that might serve to clarify the literature: (1) the intentionality of touch; (2) the age of the participants; (3) the nature of the relationship between the participants; and (4) the setting or context in which touch was observed. People were observed interacting in public settings such as shopping malls, and recreational settings as well as in greeting and leave-taking situations such as airports and bus stations.

The results show that gender asymmetry, male to female touch, was observed to be significantly more prevalent among adults, but not among children. Cross-sex touch was more prevalent among adults, but not when children were involved. Touch between females was more prevalent than touch between males among Whites, but male to male touch, and female to female touch did not differ significantly among Blacks. Further, female adults were significantly more likely to touch children than were male adults. The setting also had a strong influence on the touch patterns. There was no significant difference in male or female initiation of touch in greeting and leave-taking settings.

Although the results of this research are in accord with Henley's main finding of greater male to female touch for adults, it does not necessarily tell us that the reason is because of men's greater power in society. Further research observing males and females of different status in organizational hierarchies in their touch behavior would need to be done to provide some indication of the role of status in touch behavior.

The complexities of the research in this area are borne out by observations of 4,500 dyads in public places in Boston, in which it was found that each sex touched the other intentionally with equal frequency (J. A. Hall & Veccia, 1990). Men touched women more with the hand, but women touched men more for touches not initiated with the hand. For example, men would put their arm around a woman companion, whereas women would put their arm through a male companion's arm. Men were also more likely to initiate a new touch, with women predominating for in-progress touches. Although J. A. Hall and Veccia did not record race of individuals being observed, they say that most of them were White. This research focused on dyads, which meant two individuals involved in a relationship, so part of the discrepancy between this study and that of Major et al. may be in terms of relationship variables.

In order to determine the interaction of gender with other status variables, J. A. Hall and Veccia (1992) obtained observational data at the 1989 convention of the American Psychological Association (APA). Status of the man or woman initiating the touch was obtained from the name tag and APA directory. Rather than observing a dyad over a period of time, 70 touches made by different individuals were recorded. Of these, men initiated 40 touches (57%) and women initiated 30 touches in mixed-sex dyads (43%). Men initiated 58% of the touches with the hand. Although in the direction of greater male to female touches, the data was not statistically significant. In examining some of the more specific status factors, it was found that for men and women whose age appeared to be in the same decade, men touched women significantly more often (65% of touches). When either the man or the woman was older, there was no gender asymmetry. There was no relation between an overall composite index of status and touch initiation. One of the serious limitations of this study was small sample size.

Interpersonal Distance

Women have a smaller personal space than men have.

Did you ever notice how closely you stand to someone with whom you are talking? The distance that people feel comfortable keeping between themselves and others is referred to as personal space. It is conceptualized as an invisible bubble that each of us carries with us. Of course, it makes a difference who the person is who is approaching you. Obviously, you would stand closer to your boyfriend or girlfriend than to a stranger who asks you directions on the street. The sex of the person you are interacting with also has been found to make a difference. Women tend to stand closer when talking to another woman than men do with members of the same sex (Heshka & Nelson, 1972).

Participants in another study seated themselves closer to a female stimulus person (4.6 feet) than to a male (8.5 feet) (Wittig & Skolnick, 1978). When someone approaches, the sex of the person makes a difference, with women being allowed to approach more closely than men (J. A. Hall, 1987). Meta-analysis found that the gender differences in women approaching others is $d = -0.54$. Others also approach women more closely than they do men, $d = -0.86$.

The results cited are specific to American culture. Cultural factors also play a role. North Americans and Northern Europeans engage in social interactions at greater distances from one another than do Southern Europeans or Middle Easterners (E. T. Hall, 1966). In particular, the gender differences in the Middle East would not be the same, since men typically stand at very close distances when talking with one another.

Decoding Cues of Nonverbal Behavior

Women are better than men at decoding cues of nonverbal behavior.

Robert Rosenthal (1979) and his colleagues conducted an extensive research project on people's abilities to decode or judge the meanings of nonverbal expressions of the face, body, and voice. A measuring instrument, called the Profile of Nonverbal Sensitivity, or PONS test, was given to over 10,000 people from childhood through middle age, and to people from 11 cultural groups. Participants were judging the nonverbal behaviors of a female in a 45-minute film. Although age, personality, and practice have also been found to relate to PONS scores, females score higher than males across age groups and across cultures (except for the one study conducted in West Germany showing males to have performed slightly better). One critique of the research by Rosenthal et al., is that the stimulus person was female, perhaps giving females an advantage in decoding the nonverbal behavior.

Females are particularly better than males at decoding facial cues, followed by body cues, and the gender difference is least pronounced for vocal cues. Judith A. Hall (1978) analyzed 75 studies of gender differences in accuracy of decoding nonverbal cues and concluded that females are better visual and auditory decoders than males at all age levels. In their review and meta-analysis of this literature, Eisenberg and Lennon (1983) also conclude that women are better than men at decoding overt nonverbal cues, but that there are few consistent gender differences among children. Although girls seem to be better at decoding auditory cues, there is little difference in decoding visual nonverbal cues. Males particularly appear to be better, with increasing age, at decoding deceptive or covert cues. According to Henley (1977) female's greater decoding skills could be a survival mechanism, useful when dealing with the dominant group.

The Existence of Gender Differences

Although men and women are more alike than they are different, gender differences exist in certain personality characteristics and social behaviors.

When Maccoby and Jacklin's book reviewing the literature appeared in 1974, they concluded that gender differences existed in only one social behavior, aggression. Since the appearance of their book, feminists and psychologists have continued to debate whether or not gender differences exist. Now that many meta-analytic reviews have been conducted on a number of areas of personality and social behavior, it is clear that gender differences do exist.

The differences are based on research largely conducted on middle-class American Whites, and may not be found for Blacks or other racial and cultural groups. It should also not be lost sight of that there is more variation within gender than between genders. That does not mean that the gender differences are inconsequential. "We maintain that sex-difference findings are not particularly small and suspect that many differences are large enough to be noticeable in natural settings and to have nontrivial implications for daily life" (Eagly & Wood, 1991, p. 308).

According to Eagly and Wood (1991), there has been some difficulty in psychology, and among feminist psychologists in particular, in digesting some of these differences, especially those that tend to support some stereotypes of men and women. They point out, however, that finding gender differences serves to resolve some contradictions existing in understanding of psychological phenomena.

On the one hand, gender roles and stereotypes as well as the oppression inherent in women's subordinate status were believed to be powerful forces that shape people's thoughts and behavior. On the other hand, psychological research had presumably established that the behavior of men and women is essentially equivalent. Either the power of roles, stereotypes, and oppression was much weaker than feminists had maintained, or the generalizations about the equivalence of male and female behavior were erroneous. As we have shown, it is the consensus views about the equivalence of the sexes that have turned out to be in error. (Eagly & Wood, 1991, p. 309)

The task ahead now is no longer to see if there is a difference, but to explain the differences that exist. Meta-analysis also makes it possible to examine mediating variables for the gender differences, by partitioning samples to determine for example, whether differences occur for a particular behavior in laboratory as well as field settings, or at different age levels, or for all kinds of measures used, and so on. Thus, psychologists still have a great deal of work cut out for them in figuring out how these differences come about. What factors in the biology, socialization, culture, or in the situation create the differences and through what processes?

REFLECTIONS

Certain gender differences in personality and social behavior exist at a given time for a given subcultural group of males and females. That means that when we find a mean difference in the personality or behavior of males and females, it may only apply to a certain group such as White middle class Americans at a given time. As the opportunities and social roles of men and women become more equivilent, that difference may no longer exist in 10 years. Other gender differences such as aggression may have existed historically, cross-culturally, and cross-species, but that does not mean that that difference cannot also be eliminated in the future. What gender differences do you think will be eliminated in the future?

Which ones do you think will still be with us 10 or 20 or 50 years from now? What new gender differences do you think might arise in the future? What are the processes through which gender differences develop?

Experiential Exercises

1. Observe children playing at a public playground. Do the boys and girls differ in the types of activities in which they engage, the roughness of play, and the level of physical activity?
2. Observe a meeting of a college or community group. Who does more talking, men or women? Who interrupts and who gets interrupted more often, men or women?
3. Observe the nonverbal behavior of men and women in a public place. Is the distance between two men talking to one another the same as the distance between two women? Who touches whom more often, men or women?

KEY TERMS

Androgyny   The possession by an individual of both masculine and feminine characteristics.

Diffuse Status Characteristics   Characteristics of the individual that are associated in the culture with status, such as sex, age, race, social class, and ethnicity.

Expectation States Theory   A theory that postulates that members of a group working on a task take into account diffuse status characteristics and specific status characteristics of individuals when allocating status. Individuals with higher status have more power and influence in the group.

Femininity   A concept derived from sterotypes about gender differences. To be feminine is to be indirect, expressive, and dependent.

Gender Diagnosticity   Gender related differences that actually discriminate between men and women.

Gender Stereotypes   Shared beliefs in a culture about what characteristics males and females possess and how they behave.

Masculinity   A concept derived from stereotypes about gender differences. To be masculine is to be direct, instrumental, and independent.

Specific Status Characteristics   Qualities of an individual that are directly related to her/his ability to perform a specific task in a situation.

Undifferentiated   Possession by an individual of neither masculine or feminine characteristics.

SUGGESTED READINGS

Feingold, A. (1994). Gender differences in personality: A meta-analysis. *Psychological Bulletin, 116,* 429–456. This article reports on four meta-analyses conducted to examine gender differences in personality.

Lightdale, J. R., & Prentice, D. A. (1994). Rethinking sex differences in aggression: Aggressive behavior in the absence of social roles. *Personality and Social Psychology Bulletin, 20,* 34–44. The laboratory experiment reported in this article supports a gender role theory of gender differences in aggression.

Tannen, D. (Ed.) (1993). *Gender and conversational interaction.* New York: Oxford University Press. This is an edited book reporting on research on gender differences in conversation. Deborah Tannen's books written for the more popular market are based on research reported in this book.

CHAPTER 5

Gender Construction Across the Life Span

The sense people have of their gender, of being a man or a woman, is culturally constructed; that is, gender is a cognitive and symbolic construct that helps individuals develop a sense of self, a sense of identity that is constructed in the process of interacting with others within a given human community.

Barbara V. Reid & Tony L. Whitehead, 1992

One of the premises of this book is that gender is socially constructed. In this chapter we will look at how this happens across the life span. Gender concept—the factors that make up one's beliefs, feelings, and behavior related to what it means to be a woman—will differ at different times during a woman's life. In other words, while gender identity, (i.e., knowing that you are female rather than male) remains stable from early childhood, gender concept comes to mean different things to a woman at different stages of her life (i.e., childhood, adolescence, young adulthood, middle age, and aged). For example, when many women of my generation were young adults an important part of their gender concept was deferring to a man in important decisions and being non-assertive. By middle age, a changing world, exposure to the women's liberation movement, and perhaps a career have all been experiences changing their gender concept of what it means

to be a woman. At age fifty, they may now consider assertiveness as consistent with their female gender concept.

THEORIES OF GENDER DEVELOPMENT

Theories of gender development can be divided into two broad categories: biological hypotheses and psychosocial hypotheses. In Chapter II, we examined biological theories of gender differences. This chapter deals with theories of how children learn gender roles—psychoanalytic theory, social learning theory, cognitive development theory, gender schema theory, and gender identity theory. Social roles theory and gender role theory have been put forth to account more specifically for gender differences, particularly for adult behavior. Expectations states theory has not been put forth specifically as a theory of gender differences, but as a theory to explain differences in social interaction resulting from power or status differences. Since gender differences are one category of status, expectation states theory can explain the different patterns of interaction of men and women in nonverbal behavior, language, dominance, and group interaction.

Psychoanalytic Theory

It is during the third stage of psychosexual development that Freud differentiated the development of boys and girls. Boys resolve the Oedipus stage by identifying with the father because of castration anxiety. Girls go through the Electra stage and then identify with the mother, but develop penis envy and a weak superego.

Freud has had a major impact on psychology and the culture of the twentieth century. Although there is much to criticize about **psychoanalytic theory**, particularly from a feminist perspective, Freud made major contributions to the understanding of the unconscious mind and is the father of psychotherapy. Freud began writing in the late nineteenth century, and his theory reflects the biological determinism of the time. For Freud, early childhood development was critical for the personality of the adult.

In psychoanalytic theory, the source of psychic energy for the individual are instincts that drive the individual to take certain actions. There are two categories of instincts—the life instincts and the death instincts. The psychic energy of the life instincts is the libido, which is an expanded form of sexuality, the goal of which is pleasure.

Freud conceptualized personality as having three structures—the id, ego, and superego. The id is the reservoir of the instinctual needs of the individual, and of psychic energy—the libido. The ego is the rational part of the personality that operates according to the reality principle. The ego tries to help the id attain its pleasures within the constraints of the environment. The third structure in the personality is the superego, which is the moral center formed through a process of in-ternalization of parental and societal values and rules.

Freud formulated psychosexual stages of development through which children pass and viewed these stages as critical for adult personality. Each child passes through these three stages in the same sequence—the oral, anal, and phallic stages (Freud, 1938). During each stage, the libido is focused on a specific erogenous zone of the body. The oral stage lasts from birth to some time during the second year of life. The erogenous zone of the oral stage is the mouth, the lips, tongue, and cheeks. The sensations of biting, sucking, tasting, and swallowing provide the sexual satisfactions (broadly defined) of this stage.

The second psychosexual stage is the anal stage, during which toilet training occurs. The demands of the parents cause the child to delay the gratification of defecation. Conflicts may arise between parent and child during this stage, with implications for later personality. According to Freud, both boys and girls pass through both the oral and anal stages in a similar manner.

It is in the third psychosexual stage—the phallic stage—that Freud differentiated the development of boys and girls. The genitals become the erogenous zone of the phallic stage. It is during the phallic stage that the boy goes through the Oedipal complex, which he named for the Greek myth described in the play *Oedipus Rex* in which Oedipus kills his father and marries his mother, not knowing his relationship to them (Freud, 1925/1989).

During the phallic stage, the child develops an unconscious incestuous desire for the parent of the opposite sex. The Oedipus conflict refers to the boy's conflict between his sexual longings for the mother and his fear of the father, whom he perceives to have a special relationship with the mother. He fears that his father will cut off his penis, which Freud termed castration anxiety. So strong is this fear that the boy represses his sexual desire for his mother, and replaces his sexual desire for the mother with identification with the father, which provides the boy with a certain amount of vicarious satisfaction. He tries to become like the father, copying his mannerisms, behavior, and, most importantly, his moral values.

His superego forms as a means of resolution of the Oedipus complex.

The Electra complex is less clearly developed according to Freud. The girl's first love object, like the boy's, is the mother. She switches to the father as a new love object when she discovers she does not have a penis. She blames the mother for the castration and therefore transfers her love to the father. Girls develop penis envy (believing that at one time they did have a penis but it was cut off). The desire for a penis was also called the masculinity complex by Freud. This view of themselves as castrated males results in inferior feelings about their own bodies. Although the girl does come to identify with her mother, the resolution of the Electra complex is less clear cut, leading to what Freud said is a poorly developed superego in women. The girl's desire for a penis becomes transformed into her desire to be impregnated by the father. Penis envy is later transformed into maternal urges, particularly the desire for a son who brings with him the longed-for penis (Freud, 1948).

Following the first three stages of psychosexual development is the latency period, which lasts about five or six years, during which time the sex instinct is largely dormant. The fourth and final stage of psychosexual development is the genital stage, which begins at puberty. During this stage, the girl must renounce the clitoris in favor of the vagina as the primary source of sexual pleasure in order to become a mature woman.

Freud posited that females have a more passive orientation, whereas males have an active one. As a result, Freud hypothesized that there are gender differences in defense mechanisms used by males and females. Females are more likely to use repression, especially for sexual impulses, and to turn aggression inward (masochism).

Feminist Criticisms of Freud

Feminists believe that women envy men's power, not their penises. Historical evidence indicates that men envy women's capacity to give birth. Feminists believe that gender is socially constructed, and that biology is not destiny.

Most major feminist theorists have been very critical of Freud's theories. One area of criticism is Freud's biological determinism, which is summed up in his statement, "biology is destiny." Kate Millett, in her book, *Sexual Politics* (1970), charges that Freud's message infers that female inferiority is organic and therefore unalterable. She said that if women do envy men, it is not because of their penises, but rather because of their power in society. Millet is a social constructionist who believes the development of gender to be cultural rather than biological.

Feminists are also critical of what they call Freud's "phallocentric" views, that the clitoris and vagina are inferior to the penis. Scientific research has not demonstrated penis envy among women. Sally G. Allen and Joanna Hubbs (1987) have traced "pregnancy envy" in the male to seventeenth-century alchemical treatises. "The alchemist, who exemplifies the primordial striving for control over the natural world, seeks nothing less than the magic of maternity conferred on the 'lesser' half of the species" (S. G. Allen & Hubbs, 1987, p. 82). Pictorial emblems of the seventeenth century, for example, depict the birth of Athena from the head of Zeus.

Freudian theory posits that women who strive for accomplishments outside of the home are driven by penis envy.

Psychoanalysis thus became a central brainwashing device to keep women passive. The catchword of the 50s became "adjustment" which meant, in essence, acceptance of a role with which one is dissatisfied. What Friedan called the "feminine mystique" could equally be called the Freudian mystique. It told women that it was normal to be passive and dependent and abnormal to have intellectual ambitions. (Donovan, 1985, p. 105)

One of the problems with Freudian theory is that many of its premises are difficult if not impossible to test scientifically because the processes are largely unconscious. Another general criticism is that psychoanalytic theory was based on work with clinical patients rather than normal people. Hence, Freud's theory of female development may fit neurotic women but not normal women.

Karen Horney

Karen Horney, a psychoanalytically trained therapist, rejected Freud's biological determinism. She said that if women feel inferior, it is because of the way they are treated in society, not because of biological destiny.

Psychoanalytic theory was modified by a number of Freud's followers. Karen Horney (1885–1952) was a woman who made revisions of Freud's theory, particularly with regard to female psychology. She departed from Freud in the belief that personality was dependent on biological forces and developed a more social psychological theory. She believed that sex was not the primary motivating force for people, but rather a need for security. Horney was the mother of three daughters. Based on her own sense of pleasure and pride she had felt in childbirth, she developed the idea of womb envy among males.

> When one begins, as I did, to analyze men only after a fairly long experience of analyzing women, one receives a most surprising impression of the intensity of this envy of pregnancy, childbirth, and motherhood, as well as of the breasts and the act of suckling. (Horney, 1967, pp. 60–61)

She further speculated that men have to compensate for their womb envy through achievement in work and the disparagement and belittling of women. If women feel unworthy, it is for social and cultural reasons, rather than because of any biological inferiority. Horney further developed a more modern view of women, encouraging them to pursue careers. She herself received an M.D. degree from the University of Freiburg, having begun her medical studies there only six years after women first gained admission to medical school in Germany (Horney, 1980).

Social Learning Theory

Social learning theory assumes that boys and girls learn gender roles through modeling and imitation of the same sex parent as well as reinforcement for "appropriate" sex role behavior and punishment for "inappropriate" sex role behavior.

Social learning theory, a major theoretical orientation in psychology, uses the concepts of reinforcement, modeling, imitation, and identification to explain gender learning (Bandura, 1977). Boys and girls are given rewards and punishments for different behaviors, depending on the appropriateness of the behavior to their gender roles. A great deal of research has been amassed that people (and animals) perform a behavior more frequently when they have been rewarded for it and less frequently when they have been punished for it. Research studies have documented differential reinforcement of children based on gender (A. C. Huston, 1983; M. O'Brien & Huston, 1985). Therefore, when a little boy picks up his sister's doll to play with it, his father may grab it away and say, "Boys don't play with dolls." On the other hand, his sister may be rewarded by such an exclamation as, "What a cute little mother."

The concept of observational learning or modeling is important in social learning theory. Social learning theorists also use the concept of identification, which is a form of imitation in which the child copies patterns of behavior of a person with which he or she identifies. The theory assumes that children learn gender roles by imitating the same sex parent or the same gender adults more than those of the opposite sex. The research does not always support this premise (Raskin & Israel, 1981).

A study by Bussey and Bandura (1984) found that children as young as three years old, who had not even achieved gender identity, patterned their behavior after same sex models when asked to reenact the various behaviors displayed by male and female models. The effect of same sex modeling was stronger for boys than for girls. When the female models commanded power, however, boys imitated male and female models equally. Girls displayed more cross-gender modeling in all the conditions, and were less affected by the power manipulation than were boys.

The Cognitive Developmental Model

Between the ages of three and six, the child develops gender constancy, the idea that gender is fixed and unchanging. Experimental research demonstrates that cognitive classification skills affect gender stereotyping.

Based on the work of Jean Piaget (1952), who proposed stages of intellectual development, Kohlberg (1966) developed a **cognitive developmental model** of learning gender roles. According to Kohlberg, it is between the ages of three and six that a child attains "gender constancy," which is an understanding that gender cannot be changed by, for example, changing clothing or hair style.

Kohlberg argued that young children actively seek to cognitively process the world—to find patterns and categories that exist in the world. When they definitely label themselves as male or female, they then construct a self consistent with their gender. "Basic self-categorizations determine basic valuings. Once the boy has stably identified himself as male, he then values positively those objects and acts consistent with his gender identity" (Kohlberg, 1966, p. 89).

Both boys and girls at about the age of six see gender identity largely in physical terms. They know what gender category they belong to but don't really have an identity with that category. Mixed-sex friendships are still quite common among five and six year olds. When they get closer to the age of 9 or 10, social behavior becomes the primary determinant of sex, and friendships are almost entirely limited to the same sex. By age 11, however, a "romantic" opposite-sex friend is also becoming acceptable.

Developmental increases in cognitive functioning also influence the child's gender beliefs. For example, young children have been shown to have very rigid gender stereotypes that become less so with age (Stangor & Ruble, 1987). Is this due to their level of cognitive functioning? Cognitive developmental theory hypothesizes that one cognitive ability relevant to gender stereotyping is multiple classification. Although older preschoolers are able to sort consistently along one dimension, they are unable to sort the same object along two or more dimensions (e.g., color and shape) simultaneously. To evaluate the importance of multiple classification for gender stereotyping, an experiment was conducted in which 5–10-year-old children were matched on pretest measures of gender stereotyping and multiple classification skill, and then given multiple classification training for either social stimuli or nonsocial objects or a rule-training intervention where they were taught the irrelevance of gender in performance of sex-typed occupations (Bigler & Liben, 1992). Children who had acquired multiple classification skill as a result of training with social stimuli or rules for occupational sorting showed more egalitarian responding on a gender stereotyping measure and superior memory for counterstereotypic occupational portrayals embedded in stories. In addition children given classification training with objects showed superior memory for the counterstereotypic information in the stories despite no change on the gender stereotyping measure. These results support the cognitive developmental model by demonstrating that receiving multiple classification training can increase egalitarian gender attitudes.

Gender Schema Theory

Gender schemas develop that are used to process information about the social world. Boys and girls guide their own behavior according to expectations implicit in gender schemas.

The term *schema* refers to a structured set of cognitions about particular people, social roles, objects, groups, or common events (Fiske & Taylor, 1991). Schemas are used to interpret the environment and process information. Sandra Bem (1981) developed **gender schema theory** to describe the process whereby gender typing is developed. The child develops a gender schema, based on what males and females look and act like in the social world. She further states that the child uses this cognitive structure, the gender schema, to process incoming information, filtering and interpreting it through the gender schema. This process leads to the child's becoming sex typed.

> As one aspect of their imposing a gender-based classification system on reality, children evaluate different ways of behaving in terms of the culture's definitions of gender-appropriateness, and then reject any way of behaving that does not match their sex. (Bem, 1987, pp. 264–265)

Bem also accepts the idea that some people are nonsex-typed or gender aschematic and relatively uninfluenced by gender stereotypes and expectations.

Multifactorial Gender Identity Theory

According to Spence (1993) gender identity incorporates a number of categories including attitudes, preferences, behaviors, and roles that are more or less independent. The factors associated with the gender-based-self-image are not all necessarily associated with gender.

The new kid on the block in gender theories is Spence's (1993) **multifactorial gender identity theory**.

> According to this conception, the various categories of attributions, attitudes, preferences, and behaviors that empirically distinguish between men and women in a given culture do not contribute to a single underlying property but instead to a number of more or less independent factors. (Spence, 1993, p. 625)

The specific gender-relevant characteristics and the gender roles occupied are heterogeneous within each sex. Nevertheless, gender identity (a clear concept of being male or female), developed in early childhood remains a core part of the individual's self-image throughout the life span. Any individual, however, does not display all of the gender-congruent characteristics expected of their sex by their society. They also may possess some of the characteristics more closely associated with the other sex. Spence criticizes Bem's Gender Schema Theory on the grounds that it is unifactorial, "that a single bipolar factor underlies all specific manifestations of gender-linked attributes and behaviors." (Spence, 1993, p. 625). The bipolar factor referred to is masculinity-femininity. Spence, on the other hand, proposes that an individual's summary judgments of their gender-based self-image better fits a multifactorial theory that incorporates attributes, interests, attitudes, roles, and behaviors, not all of which are associated with their sex. Over time, individuals also incorporate roles they occupy into their sense of self, some of which are related to gender such as becoming a father or mother.

Social Identity Theory

Social identity theory explains gender in terms of social identity as derived from social groups to which one belongs, and the power and status relations between these groups.

Some theorists explain gender identity in terms of social identity theory (SIT) as developed by social psychologists Tajfel and Turner (1986). They are concerned with identity that is derived from social groups which stand in status and power relations to one another. Gender is one such social group. A number of theorists have applied SIT to gender. SIT attempts to explain changes in personality and development, as well as the relations between the sexes in adolescence and beyond in terms of more social psychological processes than most theories do. "The focus is not so much on cognitive, moral or sexual development, as on the way that social context and intergroup relations between the sexes may shape gender identity over time" (D. Abrams, 1989). When relating to members of the opposite sex, people can display both personal and social categorical behavior. Social identity theory proposes that people seek identity with groups that provide a positive self-identity.

If the ingroup has low status, SIT suggests that a number of different strategies are possible that are aimed at achieving a positive social identity. These three strategies are: individual mobility (i.e., physical or psychological dissociation from the low-status group); social creativity (i.e., changing the terms of intergroup comparison so that the ingroup is viewed more positively); and social competition (i.e., challenging the status quo and attempting to change the position of the ingroup) (Breinlinger & Kelly, 1994).

Research by Breinlinger and Kelly (1994) tested the theory that distinct subgroups of women could be identified according to their acceptance of one of the three strategies as a means of dealing with being part of a subordinate group. Fifty women between the ages of 22 and 69 sorted 51 statements derived from each of these strategies using a Q technique that combines quantitative data with interviews. The findings provided partial support for SIT, but were more complex than predicted. Factor analysis found four main factors, two of which were predicted— social competition and individual mobility. Another factor that emerged was a mixture of social competition and individual mobility, which Breinlinger and Kelly state are "ideologies that might seem diametrically opposed and logically inconsistent." The fourth factor reflected social creativity and other strategies. Strength of identification with feminism as a measure of identification with own sex group was not related to choice of a strategy.

Gender identity is formed both in individual interactions as well as in relation to reference groups, such as family, school, church, occupation, social class, and race or ethnicity.

Gender identity is formed in relation to one's reference groups. The meaning and status of gender may vary in different reference groups. Gender may have a different meaning and vary in status for women in different types of families (husband dominant, egalitarian, wife dominant),

different occupations, and different social class and racial or ethnic groups.

> When human groups classify people into different social categories, their members invariably form a set of social norms evaluating people in the different categories, standardizing a set of beliefs about them (which have been referred to as "social stereotypes") and prescribing rules for relationships between those in different categories. Such norms seldom specify exact behaviors, but prescribe ranges for individual differences, i.e., a latitude for acceptable conduct and activities as well as a latitude for objectionable conduct and activities. (C. W. Sherif, 1982, p. 377)

Gender identity is therefore formed both in individual interactions as well as in relation to organized patterns of institutional contexts such as family, school, church, occupation, social class, and race or ethnicity. Each of these contexts sends normative messages about what is appropriate behavior as well as evaluations of that behavior for males and females. The self system is linked to the individual's reference persons and reference groups. The individual internalizes the norms of her or his reference groups. Gender categorization is complex because gender is related to power in all societies and institutions; however, one must be cognizant of the great array of differences in power of different groups of women by virtue of ethnicity, social class, religion, education, and other institutionalized versions of the roles of men and women.

Social Roles Theory

Eagly's social roles theory accounts for gender differences through socialization in different social roles, such as work roles, family roles, and gender roles.

Eagly (1987) has developed a social roles theory of the causes of gender differences. "Social roles are regarded as the proximal predictors of adult sex differences" Eagly, 1987, p. 9). In her theory, the social behaviors for which gender differences are evident are embedded in social roles. Social roles are structural—people occupying the same social roles within organizations or other structures such as families. Social roles are broader than gender roles because they encompass other roles such as family and work roles. Explicit skills and beliefs are learned through enactment of specific roles (i.e., a teenage girl who babysits learns nurturing skills). Attitudinal learning also occurs during role enactment. Occupants of military roles acquire beliefs about aggression that lead to beliefs that tend to legitimize aggression. "Whatever the ultimate causes of the division of labor, it shapes gender roles in such a way that women are expected to behave relatively communally and men relatively agentically" (Eagly, 1987, p. 31).

Gender roles establish expectations for behavior in a variety of areas such as work and family as well as molding personality.

Gender role theory states that people have a role in society based solely on gender. Gender role is defined in terms of those expectations for appropriate behavior for males and females. There is a greater scope and generality of gender roles than of most other social roles because gender expectations mold personality characteristics as well as work and family positions. Females may learn that being submissive, whereas males may learn that being assertive, is appropriate gender role behavior in a variety of situations from family to work.

Gender role theory can account for gender differences in helping behavior. For example, gender role theory would predict gender differences in helping would be larger when "(a) women perceived helping as more dangerous than men did; (b) an audience witnessed the helping act; and (c) other potential helpers were available" (Eagly, 1987, p. 66). These predictions were confirmed by the analyses.

Gender role theory was used by Lightdale and Prentice (1994) (see the previous section on aggression) to explain the similar levels of aggression by college women and men in a deindi-viduation condition. Anonymity served to reduce social expectation and by removing gender roles, allowing the individual to respond in terms of his/her own personal dispositions. When the need to perform in accord with their gender roles was removed, male and female aggressive behavior merged. The implications of gender role theory is that as gender role expectations change, behavior will also change.

Expectation States Theory

According to expectation states theory, sex is a diffuse status characteristic that confers lower status on women than on men. Many gender differences in social behavior associated with women are the same as those associated with lower status of powerless people.

According to Joseph Berger and his colleagues (Berger, Cohen & Zelditch, 1972; Berger, Webster, Ridgeway, & Rosenholtz, 1986), status differences develop when a group is working on a task that it considers to be important. Because the group wants to succeed, it pays attention to those characteristics of the members that it considers relevant to goal achievement. **Expectation states theory** postulates two types of cues when allocating status in groups, **diffuse status characteristics** and **specific-status characteristics.** Diffuse status characteristics are general qualities of the person that culture associates with his/her competence, ability, or value such as sex, wealth, age, attractiveness, occupation, and education. Specific-status characteristics are qualities that have been demonstrated to be specific to the task at hand, such as having a very good singing voice for a member of the church choir.

In our culture, and most other cultures of the world, sex is a diffuse status characteristic that confers lower status on women than men. Women are therefore expected to act like lower status members. Many of the gender differences found in social behavior are also differences associated with people in lower status or more powerless positions.

Expectation states theory exemplifies what has come to be recognized as a status approach. Two major criticisms have been leveled at these approaches. One is that women's greater expressiveness in interaction such as smiling and positive socioemotional behavior reflects more than a status dimension in interaction. It may reflect greater interpersonal warmth and caring. Second, why, for example, did Carli (1989) find greater gender differences in same-sex than in mixed-sex pairs if interaction is influenced by status characteristics? Carli concluded that both men and women show less sex-stereotyped behavior when interacting with individuals of the opposite gender.

GENDER CONSTRUCTION IN CHILDHOOD

Socialization by Adults

From the time a baby is born, thoughts and actions regarding that child are different depending on whether it is a boy or a girl. A meta-analysis, however, found only one area where boys and girls are socialized differently—encouragement of sex-typed activities in play and household chores.

The first question you are likely to ask when you hear that a friend, relative or colleague has just given birth to a baby is, "Is it a boy or girl?" From that moment on our thoughts and actions regarding that baby are likely to be different depending on whether it is a boy or girl. A number of research studies have demonstrated the differential treatment of male and female infants. In laboratory experiments the typical design is to dress an infant in either pink or blue or yellow (sex unspecified) and then ask unfamiliar individuals to play with the child and watch the interaction. A review of 23 studies along these lines found that young children were more stereotypical than adults in their responses to the infant's gender label (M. Stern & Karraker, 1989). Adults show greater sex stereotyping in their interactions with the infant than they did in their ratings.

Toy choices were particularly influenced by gender label, with girls being given dolls and boys footballs or hammers.

Are there systematic differences in the way parents socialize boys and girls? A meta-analysis of 158 North American studies testing the hypothesis that parents rear boys and girls differently found that only 1 of 19 areas of childrearing displayed a significant effect size for both parents: the encouragement of sex-typed activities in play and household chores for which $d = .34$ (Lytton & Romney, 1991). The effect size for most of the socialization areas were generally small and nonsignificant. A meta-analysis of the 17 studies conducted in other Western countries obtained a significant effect size ($d = +.32$) in the direction of parents using more physical punishment on sons than on daughters. The difference between mothers and fathers was significant only in terms of restrictiveness, in the direction of fathers restricting girls more than boys. Differential treatment by parents was also found to decrease over age, being the greatest during early childhood. The authors conclude that the gender differences that have been found in other meta-analytic studies (i.e., in aggressiveness and high mathematical reasoning ability) are "not due to parents directly and systematically reinforcing stereotypical behavior or abilities in their children" (Lytton & Romney, 1991, p. 287). Their conclusion is too broad, however, since there was a significant difference in socialization of girls and boys for play and household chores.

Gender Differences in Play and in Playmate Preferences

Gender differences in early childhood styles of play and playmate preferences may result from both socialization and innate factors.

Gerianne M. Alexander and Melissa Hines (1994) explored the play styles (masculine or feminine) and gender labels on playmate selection with 60 children between the ages of four and eight years, using a novel interview approach in which the child's gender label and the child's play styles were presented as independent dimensions. Boys and girls both showed strong preference for a playmate of the same sex when the children they had to choose between differed only in regard to their gender labels. Children also showed preferences consistent with established gender differences in play styles (activity level, toys, rough-and-tumble play). When gender and play styles were presented as competing dimensions, boys and older girls selected playmates on the basis of play styles. Younger girls, however, preferred girls with masculine play styles over boys with feminine play styles. Alexander and Hines say that "our findings for boys appear to contradict both cognitive-social and gender-schema theories of the role of gender group identification in boys' selection of playmates" p. 878). The authors state that biological factors need to be taken into account in that prenatal testosterone levels may account for boys greater preference for rough-and-tumble play.

Support has been found for gender schema theory, however, in the way in which boys and girls (aged 48–69 months) comprehended, encoded and demonstrated recall of gender-linked toys (G. D. Levy, 1994a). Low gender schematic children were more consistent in their recall of all items, suggesting that gender roles served as a filter for information processing of high gender schematic children.

In another study with boys and girls (aged 44 to 81 months) G. D. Levy (1994b) found that although all children more accurately classified same sex indoor and outdoor toys, children high in gender schematicity demonstrated greater clustering of their recall by gender type of toy.

Children's Narrative Fantasies

Girls and boys tell more stories about their own sex. Girls' themes deal more with nurturance and boys' themes with aggression.

Differences have also been found in narrative fantasies of 3–5-year-old children (Libby & Aries, 1989). Both boys and girls tell more stories about their own sex. Girl's fantasies involved girls tak-ing care of and responding to the needs of others, whereas boy's fantasies involved characters coping with aggressive drives. The different issues that boys and girls are dealing with at this age can help explain why boys and girls increasingly show sex segregation in their play during this time (Feiring & Lewis, 1987).

Racial and Gender Differences in Children's Nurturing of Infants

Research with White Americans finds girls to show greater responsiveness to infants and young children than boys. Among African Americans, no gender differences are found in responsiveness to infants.

Research on responsiveness of boys and girls to infants and young children have shown girls to show greater responsiveness. This research has largely been conducted with White American children. The African American family has been found to differ from the White American family in several respects. African American families have a less-stereotyped gender role differentiation. Historically, African American women have worked outside of the home as well as had a family. In an experiment designed to test preadolescent children's responsiveness to an infant, male and female African American and European American children were photographed with an infant (P. T. Reid & Trotter, 1993). As predicted by gender stereotypes, White girls stood closer to the infants and showed more attraction to the infants than did White boys. For African American children, however, there were virtually no gender differences. "This finding is extraordinary in light of the numerous studies with White children showing strong gender differences. Indeed, it leads us to reject the notion that social preferences for infants are *necessarily* linked to gender" (P. T. Reid & Trotter, 1993, p. 179). This study serves as a caution light in interpreting gender differences reported in this book, for which the research base is largely European American. The findings may apply only to middle class White Americans on whom most of the research was conducted.

In both laboratory and natural situations, 2-year-old boys spend more time playing with male toys and 2-year-old girls spend more time playing with female toys.

Children have established gender identity by between two and three years of age and have learned some of the culturally approved sex role behavior. Parents buy toys they consider sex role-appropriate for boys and girls. Lewis & Michaelson (as cited in M. Lewis, 1987) asked 62 mothers of boys and 68 mothers of girls to report on which of a set of 10 toys were likely to be found in their two-year-old child's home. Male children were found to have significantly more toy guns, blocks, and trucks available to play with, while girls had more dolls and toy pianos. The difference between the numbers of male and female "appropriate" toys in the home was greater for boys than for girls.

In a 15-minute laboratory observation of the children's toy-play behavior, it was found that boys played significantly longer with male toys (136.50 seconds) than with female toys (118.20 seconds), whereas girls played significantly longer with female toys (139.50 seconds) than with male toys (84 seconds). A follow-up measure of these same children at age six found no relationship between the children's two-year old toy-play behavior with the six year old's school adjustment scores or psychopathology scores. More female toy-play at two years, however, was significantly related to number of female friends at age six. For boys, although there was a trend in the direction of more male toy-play at two being related to more male rather than female friends at age six, the relationship was not significant.

Boys play in larger groups than do girls. Girls are more passive when interacting with boys as compared to interacting with girls.

The pattern of social interaction in childhood does seem to differ for boys and girls with boys spending more time in larger groups, and girls spending more time in dyads or smaller groups.

Maccoby and Jacklin (1974) concluded that the belief that girls are more social than boys is unfounded. According to research by Maccoby (1990), however, the reason that we do not find differences in sociability between males and females is in part illusory, she says, because social behavior is never a function of the individual alone. Rather, it is the result of the interaction of two or more persons.

Individuals behave differently with different partners. There are certain important ways in which gender is implicated in social behavior—ways that may be obscured or missed altogether when behavior is summed across all categories of social partners. (Maccoby, 1990, p. 513)

Research by Maccoby (1988; 1990) has found that young children (33 months old) were much more active socially when paired with a same-sex partner. Girls were much more passive, watching, rather than actively participating, when interacting with boys as compared with interacting with girls. She concludes that social behavior is situationally specific and depends on the gender of the other person.

Preference for playing with other children of the same sex is evident by age three, increases in strength by school age, and is sustained at a high level between 6 and 11. Maccoby (1990) believes that there are two factors underlying this same-sex preference. One is that girls find the rough-and-tumble play style of boys, their competitiveness and concern with issues of dominance, to be aversive. Second, boys are not responsive to girls' influence attempts, although they modify their behavior in response to a male partner's prohibitions. A number of studies have pointed out that girls prefer to sit closer to the teacher. Research Maccoby cites by Greeno, however, shows that this is not a general trait of girls. The previous studies were all conducted in mixed-sex nursery schools. When only girls are present, the girls do not move in the direction of the adult. Boys in all-boy groups actually sit closer to the adult than girls when only girls are present, but when boys are present girls move closer to the adult.

Just as with adults, it must be kept in mind that there are individual differences in gender typing in children. Observations of 57 Canadian preschoolers for 4–6 months during free play at school revealed stable individual differences for gender segregation, use of masculine and feminine toys and teacher proximity among boys and for feminine toy play and teacher proximity among girls (Powlishta, Serbin, & Moller, 1993). I noticed that my younger daughter was less sex typed in her toy preferences and interests as a child than her older sister had been.

Girls Who Are Tomboys and Boys Who Are Feminine

Among preteens, girls who are tomboys are most popular, whereas boys who are feminine are least popular. Boys who are feminine at age 12 are less well adjusted at ages 31 and 41. More feminine girls, however, are not less well adjusted at ages 31 and 41.

Tomboys, or girls who enjoy masculine activities and play, are often popular with preteen peers, whereas boys who engage in feminine activities and play are usually not accepted. Fifth and sixth grade children in Israel watched a video of a child playing a gender-appropriate game with members of the same sex, or a gender-inappropriate game with members of the opposite sex. Variances in the child's gender-related behavior was related to preadolescent's inferences and judgments about the child (T. E. Lobel, Bempechat, Gewirtz, Shoken-Topaz, & Bashe, 1993). The child's stereotypic or counterstereotypic behavior was found to influence the attribution of masculine or feminine traits to a greater extent than did biological sex. The girl who played a masculine game with the boys was the most popular, whereas the feminine boy was the least popular.

A longitudinal study of gender characteristics and adjustment across the life span found that men whose interests and traits at age 12 were typical of females had poorer social–personal adjust at ages 31 and 41 (Aube & Koestner, 1992). Adolescent femininity, however, did not predict poorer adjustment at ages 31 and 41 for women.

Feminine expressive traits at age 31 were not related to adjustment at age 41 for either men or women. Lack of masculine characteristics in adolescent boys may contribute to poorer adjustment because of the power disparity between men and women in American society. Females who behave in a more masculine way can be viewed as minimizing distinctions that lower their status and power since men have more power in society, and therefore do not suffer lowered adjustment as a result of deviation from the female stereotype. Males who endorse nontraditional gender-related interests and undesirable feminine traits (i. e., complaining, meek, nervous, worrying) suffer a more negative reaction from peers than girls who do so. The research supports a multidimensional view of gender. Feminine interests and undesirable feminine traits at age 12 were not related to instrumental traits, were negatively related to expressive traits, and were positively related to undesirable feminine traits at age 31. "Furthermore, interests, undesirable feminine traits, instrumental traits, and expressive traits all had different relations to the adjustment measures, underscoring the importance of considering multiple dimensions of gender in research" (Aubé & Koestner, 1992, p. 491).

MEDIA AND LANGUAGE

Comic Strips

Men are more likely to be main characters in comic strips and to be shown in the workforce than are women. Women are much more likely to be shown taking care of the home and children. Women are also portrayed as more passive than men and in more negative ways in the comics.

I learned to read from comic strips and was an avid reader of comic books through elementary school. What messages about gender are conveyed to children (and adults) who read them? In a review of four popular Sunday comics, Brabant (1976) observed that wives were portrayed as staying at home and cooking and cleaning. Men were either working or engaging in leisure activities such as playing golf. Ten years later in reviewing three of these same comics, the reviewers noted a lessening of differences in the roles played by men and women; however, women were still much more likely to be shown taking care of the home and children and engaging in less leisure activities than the men (Brabant & Mooney, 1986). Women were also more likely to be passive onlookers. Another analysis of the Sunday comics in the 1980s found more women to be employed than in the earlier comics, but that they were more often portrayed in negative ways. Wives were highly critical of their husbands and also controlling of husbands, who are portrayed as ineffectual and weak (Mooney & Brabant, 1987). Content analysis of 100 randomly selected comics concluded that men were much more likely to be main characters and to be shown in the workforce more frequently than women (Chavez, 1985).

Books and Magazines

Children's books of the 1970s portrayed males and females in gender-stereotyped roles and males as the central figures. Major changes in the direction of more equal treatment of males and females took place in the 1980s.

A number of content analyses of children's books conducted during the 1970s documented the gender-stereotyped roles assigned to girls and women. One such study by Lenore Weitzman, Eifler, Hokada, and Ross (1972) examined the content of children's books that had won the prestigious Caldecott medal between 1967 and 1971. The focus of attention of the majority of the books were boys and men. The gender ratio was 11 to 1, male to female characters. Boys were action figures, whereas girls were more peripheral to the stories. Male animal characters were overwhelmingly represented (95:1) compared with female animal characters. Another content analysis of Caldecott medal winning books published between 1972 and 1979 found a significant improvement in the sex ratio with males outnumbering females by only 1.8 to 1 (Kolbe & LaVoie, 1981).

Males were also central characters in children's elementary school readers. A content analysis of 134 elementary readers from 13 publishers found portrayals of females and males to be equally stereotyped.

> This study *Dick and Jane as Victims,* found that males were portrayed more often, in more roles, and as being more active than females, who were often shown in passive or domestic roles (Women on Words and Images, 1975). A study of 84 additional readers done by the same group in 1975 found similar results (Women, 1975). (Purcell & Stewart, 1990, p. 177)

To determine if the stereotypical portrayal of males and females had changed in the 1980s, a content analysis of 62 children's readers in use in 1989 was conducted (Purcell & Stewart, 1990). While the earlier study showed a ratio of 7:1 of male–child-focused to female–child-focused stories, the 1989 replication found nearly a 1:1 ratio. The male–adult-centered stories had also declined from a ratio of 3:1 to a more nearly equal 4:3. Books also influence children's gender attitudes and behavior. After exposure to a gender stereotypic picture book preschool children both girls and boys are more likely to select a gender-stereotypic toy with which to play. When exposed to a nongender-stereotypic book, they are more likely to choose a non-gender stereotypic toy (Ashton, 1983).

The magazine Seventeen *still devotes most of the editorial content to traditional feminine topics of beauty, fashion and home.*

What messages are conveyed to teenage girls in the magazines they read? A review of the editorial content of *Seventeen* magazine in the years 1961, 1972, and 1985 found that about 50% of the magazine for each of the years was devoted to the category, Appearance (beauty and fashion), with the category, Home, accounting for another 10% (K. Pierce, 1990). Feminist messages of self-reliance and independence increased between 1961 and 1972, from 7.5% to 16.6%, but declined again to 6.8% in 1985. Pierce speculates that the decrease in feminist messages reflects the decline in coverage of the feminist movement after the 1960s and early 1970s was followed by *Seventeen.*

Television

Television still portrays women in stereotypical roles, and uses males as narrators. Rock music videos also depict women as victims of rape and violence. Males who view these videos develop a greater acceptance of sex role stereotypes and violence against women.

For the most part women are portrayed in traditional and stereotypical ways on television (M. Butler & Paisley, 1980). In the popular TV show setting of hospitals, 99% of nurses were women and 95% of doctors were men (Kalisch & Kalisch, 1984). When women did appear as a doctor, their role was still stereotyped with a woman physician playing a more peripheral role. On television commercials, the male narrator was just as typical in 1985 (91% of commercials) as he had been in 1971 (89% of commercials). Some recent changes have been made in the direction of fewer stereotypical roles in commercials, however, such that men are now portrayed more frequently in their family role as husband or father (Brell & Cantor, 1988).

Television is not just an innocuous baby-sitter for young children, it influences children's perceptions of the world. Attitudes toward women of third and eighth grade children were affected by watching commercials of either traditional (housewives and mothers) or nontraditional (professional and business) women (Pingree, 1978).

Many adolescents spend a considerable amount of time viewing rock music videos. High school students in one study were found to watch music videos an average of two hours per day (Sun & Lull, 1986). Women are portrayed stereotypically as emotional, frivolous, and passive, while men are seen as "cool" and aggressive. Some of these videos depict scenes of rape and other forms of violence against women (Hansen & Hansen, 1988). Adolescents who are frequent viewers of rock videos show an acceptance of rape myths (D. L. Peterson & Pfost, 1989). An experiment, which exposed undergraduate males to

heavy-metal rock music for 17 minutes in a laboratory setting, produced measurable attitudinal shifts in the direction of increased sex role stereotyping irrespective of the lyrical content of the music (St. Lawrence & Joyner, 1991). Sexually violent depictions and heavy-metal rock music increases acceptance of violence toward women and contributes to sex role stereotyping. Parents need to play a greater role in steering adolescents toward more wholesome media.

A comparison of one week of primetime network television in 1979 and 1989, revealed that explicit intercourse, which had not been shown in 1979 was shown in 1989. These depictions were only rarely accompanied by any mention of contraception, safe sex or sexually transmitted disease. The lovers were most often unmarried, with White males typically initiating sexual acts (S. Sapolsky & Tabarlet, 1991). The media should show greater responsibility in addressing issues such as contraception in its programs.

Language and Gender Messages

Language conveys gender messages. The English language conveys a message that males are the norm.

The pronoun *he* is often used to refer to both males and females in the English language. Does the use of the generic masculine in language influence the way males and females think about themselves and gender? A pronoun in a sentence cue was varied to be either he, or he or she or they and presented to children in kindergarten, first, third, and fifth grades (Hyde, 1984a). When the cue was *he,* only 12% of stories were written about females, in contrast to 42% when the pronoun was *he* or *she,* and 18% when the pronoun was they. Most children seemed to be unaware that the pronoun he could be a generic term. Children gave women the low ratings for ability to perform the fictional job of *wudgemaker* when the pronoun in the job description was he.

A review of the literature by Nancy Henley (1989) examined the question of whether the generic he and man are interpreted as referring to women as well as men. After reviewing the findings of 20 studies, with participants ranging in age from six to adult, she concluded that males came to mind more frequently than did females when masculine pronouns (he) or nouns (man) are used. This was true for stories told, pictures drawn, names used for persons referred to, or answers to questions about the people involved.

ADOLESCENCE

Puberty

Puberty is a period of rapid height and weight gain during which sexual maturity is achieved. Early maturing girls date earlier and are more likely to engage in sex and drink at earlier ages than late maturing girls.

Puberty is the several years during the person's life when physical and sexual maturity is being attained. Puberty is the time of most rapid physical growth, produced by the effect of hormones on the growth centers of the long bones. There is also a rapid gain in weight for girls during this time. The growth spurt begins earlier in girls, as early as nine, and most girls attain their adult height by age 14 to 16. The most important physical event of puberty for girls is menarche—the first menstrual period. The average menarche is now 12.8 years in the United States. Age at menarche has been declining as nutrition has improved. It was about 15½ to 16½ years in Britain during the 1800s. Even now in Bangladesh age at menarche is just under 16. (Frisch, 1983; Golub, 1992). Menarche does not usually occur until after the growth spurt has been achieved. In many societies menarcheal rites signify the new status of the girl in the community (Paige & Paige, 1981). In our culture, a girl typically only tells her mother and close girlfriends about the event.

Other physical changes are also occurring in the body during puberty, such as the development of secondary sex characteristics (body hair, larger, rounder breasts, hips and buttocks, and voice changes). Variation in the timing of puberty can make a difference in the social and sexual behavior of adolescents. Early maturing girls are likely to date earlier and be sexually active at an earlier age than girls who are late maturers (Brooks-Gunn, 1988; Crockett & Petersen, 1987). They also may engage in other more adult behavior at an earlier age such as smoking and drinking (Magnusson, Strattin, & Allen, 1985).

Girls' Loss of Voice

According to research by Gilligan and Rogers, girls lose "voice" as they move from preadolescence to adolescence.

Carol Gilligan has spent considerable time studying adolescent girls in which she compared early and later teenage years. As the girls get older they start losing confidence and begin adopting the passive, submissive feminine stereotype (Gilligan, Lyons, & Hammer, 1990). Feminist methodology, a voice-centered, relational approach to research, guided the study of girls at the Harvard Project on Women's Psychology and Girls' Development. Based on interviews with preadolescent and adolescent girls who attended both private and public schools, and who were diverse in ethnicity, race, and class, Annie Rogers (1993) concluded that girls lose "not only clarity, self-confidence, and voice—but also their courage—as they come of age in androcentric cultures" (Rogers, 1993, p. 272). She uses the old meaning of the word courage: "to speak one's mind by telling all one's heart." The younger girls have an outspokenness and authentic relationships. Rogers notes that other researchers have found girls to lose ground on standardized tests of intellectual ability and in their capacity to think critically during adolescence. She identifies these changes as girls enter adolescence as a loss of voice, of resiliency, and of self-confidence.

Racial and Gender Friendship Patterns in Junior High

Junior high school friendship patterns differ more by gender among Whites than among Blacks. Black female adolescents, however, do have a greater attachment to their families than do Black males.

Most of the research treats adolescents as a homogeneous group, having been conducted on White, middle class adolescents. Nevertheless, there is great diversity among adolescents in the United States based on race, ethnicity, family constellation, physical abilities, type of school attended (or whether they are in school), and socioeconomic status, as well as gender.

Gender differences in friendship patterns of junior high school students do not appear to be as pronounced among African Americans as among European Americans (D. L. Coates, 1987; DuBois & Hirsch, 1990; D. Stewart & Vaux, 1986). A study of a sample of 292 male and female junior high school students found that Black boys and Black girls did not differ significantly on the extent to which they talked about personal problems with school friends (DuBois & Hirsch, 1990). White girls, however, talked about personal problems with school friends to a greater extent than did White boys or Black girls. Perceived availability of help from best school friends did not differ for Black boys or Black girls, but White girls did indicate more perceived availability of help than did White boys. Generally, it appears that White girls have more intimate relations with their friends than do White boys. White boys are also less intimate with their friends than are Black boys.

In another study of 390 Black adolescents, although Black girls indicated they had more frequent contact with their network members, there were no differences in the actual number in the male and female networks (D. L. Coates, 1987). Black girls did have a greater attachment to their families than did Black boys, as indicated by the fact that more girls than boys (26% compared with 19%) nominated family members exclusively as role models, and indicated parents as preferred sources of material aid as compared with males.

Romance and Adolescence

Adolescent romance is a conservative and patriarchal ideology.

Romance is one of the ways through which adolescent femininity is constructed. A feminist analysis of adolescent romance is that it is a conservative and patriarchal ideology (Leahy, 1994). Girls are expected to develop "femininity" during their adolescence. Girls lose initiative as they wait for boys to do the calling and asking. Their role becomes making themselves into what the media considers to be sexually attractive in order to receive the attention of boys. Dating begins at an earlier age than in the past and the median age to begin going steady was found to be 16 among White adolescents in the Detroit area (Thornton, 1990). Sexual pressures are exerted in dating relationships for which girls may not be emotionally ready.

Independence in Relationship

Adolescent girls develop a sense of self determination that includes maintaining personal attachments.

Theorists of adolescence have emphasized the need to develop independence and autonomy during adolescence (Erikson, 1968). Feminist theorists, however, have indicated the importance of relational ties throughout the lifespan for females (Chodorow, 1978; Gilligan, 1982). Based on in-depth interviews with girls at a private school for girls, Lori Stern (1990) explored how adolescent girls navigate the need to develop independence with the importance of relationships and connection. These girls appear to be able to integrate a conception of self that includes both increasing individualism and of inclusion.

A complex understanding of relationship is revealed as they describe how their increased individual capabilities (resembling "independence") are used not to foster breaking away but to be funneled back into the relationship. These young women's discussions of separation and independence uncover a basic premise that assumes the presence and importance of relationships. Thus, separation is not pitted against connection but involves a redefined ability to respond to (and consequently connect with) the other. (L. Stern, 1990, p. 85)

Self determination does not preclude them from taking others into account, or maintaining personal attachments. Independence involves not the separation from relationships but a reframing and renegotiation of relationships.

Gender and Ego Development in Adolescence

Large effect sizes favoring female ego development are found for junior high and high school students. These differences disappear among older adults.

Ego development across the life span has been examined by a meta-analysis of 65 studies using the Washington University Sentence Completion Test of ego development (L. Cohn, 1991). It is a semiprojective measure consisting of 36 sentence stems that are completed by respondents. Low scores on the scale are given for responses that show little time perspective, impulse control, or self-reflectiveness. Responses signifying psychological insight and cognitive complexity are scored high. Construct validity has been demonstrated by low ego levels being associated with impulsiveness, adolescent pregnancy, authoritarianism, lower levels of moral reasoning, less empathy, and delinquent behavior. Moderately large effect sizes favoring female ego development were found for junior and senior high school students. The differences declined during college years, and disappeared among older adults.

Gender Differences in Adolescents' Use of Defense Mechanisms

Females show greater use of internalizing defenses (turning against the self) and males show greater use of externalizing defenses (projection and aggression).

Levit (1991) tested Freud and Erickson's theories about male and female differences in **defense mechanisms** regarding males' greater use of externalizing defenses (projection and aggression) and females' greater use of internalizing defenses (turning against the self) with 66 high school students (31 boys and 25 girls) aged 14–19. The research data supported the hypotheses. Sex role

identity (as measured by the Bem Sex Role Inventory (BSRI) and the Agency and Communion Scales were found to contribute significantly to the prediction of the defense mechanisms. Girls' higher scores on femininity, which correlated significantly with almost all of the defenses, leads to the explanation that femininity accounts for the underlying observed gender differences in defenses.

Ethnic Differences in Identity Development

The identity search is more complex for minority youth.

The norms, values, and behavioral routines vary for different racial and ethnic groups within American culture. When the individual is a member of a minority group, the ethnic group becomes a focus of the search for identity (Rotheram-Borus, and Wyche, 1994). Minority youth are socialized into gender roles that differ from that of mainstream European American culture. The influence of these gender roles also vary with the adolescent's acculturation, and the acculturation of his or her parents. Therefore, the process of identity formation is more complex for minority youth than it is for European Americans.

> Specifically, minority youths are faced with the choice of identifying themselves as (a) multiculturally synthesized (i.e., personally identified and competent to interact effectively with one or more groups), (b) multiculturally competent but oriented to the mainstream, (c) multiculturally competent but oriented to their own ethnic group, (d) strongly ethnically identified with their own ethnic group or monocultural, or (e) closely affiliated and adoptive of mainstream European-American values, attitudes, feelings, and behaviors. (Ramirez, 1983; Rotheram-Borus & Wyche, 1994, pp. 71–72)

Community and family factors play a role in shaping this identity. The identity search of the minority adolescent is influenced by the political and social climate, the cross-ethnic tension in the community and school, and the ethnic identities of family and peers.

Poverty

Large numbers of adolescents are growing up in poverty—one out of 10 White, and approximately four out of 10 Hispanic and Black adolescents.

In the United States in 1988, one out of five adolescents were growing up in poverty—11% for Whites, 37% for Hispanics, and 44% for Blacks (Jessor, 1993). Concomitant with poverty is a greater risk of exposure to adverse conditions such as abuse, violence, and easy access to drugs. Estimates are that there are approximately 1.5 million 11–18 year olds who are homeless in the United States, which is accompanied by multiple psychological and physical health problems (Kazdin, 1993). These include youth who are part of homeless families, runaways, and throwaways (those who are thrown out of their homes). Research on adolescents engaging in delinquency finds that for both females and males attachment to deviant peer groups was most directly related to delinquency and later drug use.

Teenage Sexual Activity and Pregnancy

A topic that I feel should be a major feminist issue, but one that has been more peripheral on the feminist agenda, is that of teenage pregnancy. I am including the topic in this chapter on life span development because of the profoundly negative way becoming a mother as a teenager often impacts on the rest of a woman's life and on the lives of her children. If we wanted to make one change in society that would empower women more than any other, it would be to have teenage pregnancy prevention programs in all of the middle schools, junior high schools, and high schools in the United States. We should not place blame on adolescent girls, but instead we should structure our educational system so that it provides opportunities to work toward future career goals.

Initiation and frequency of female adolescent sexual activity are related to the social context within which the adolescent lives.

Many factors within the social context in which adolescents live contribute to the likelihood of first intercourse and frequency of sexual behavior. Measures of the social context within the census tract and within the county were related to the likelihood of first intercourse and frequency of subsequent sexual behavior of 566 Black and 1,286 White adolescents from a national probability sample (Billy, Brewster, & Grady, 1994). On an individual level, White women were more likely to have ever engaged in nonmarital sexual intercourse who had an earlier age at menarche, less religiosity, a mother who worked full-time, a mother with lower level of education, lower income level, having birth control instruction, and who were living in a household with only one parent at age 14. Census tract and county level variables positively related to the likelihood of sexual activity of White adolescent women were: the percentage of female labor force participants employed full-time; the ratio of males 15 or over to females; the percentage of adult females who are separated or divorced; the total crime rate; the number of high school drop outs not in the labor force; and the number of family planning service clients under age 20. Decreases in sexual activity for White adolescent women were related to living in a census tract with a higher percentage of African Americans and immigrants, higher median housing values and a higher percentage of conservative religious adherents.

Unlike for White females, age at menarche, mother's employment status and family planning visits had no relationship to young Black women's initiation to sexual activity. Similar to Whites, mother's educational attainment and religiosity had a negative effect on sexual activity for Black adolescent women, and living with only one parent while growing up was related to increased likelihood of sexual activity. At the census tract and county levels, increases in the likelihood of sexual activity were found with increases in the sex ratio among Blacks, the proportion of the teenage population that were not in school or other productive activity, the percentage of women employed full-time, and the percentage of the female population 15–19 using family planning services. Community factors negatively related to sexual activity were percentage in the census tract who were foreign born and the percentage in the county living in urban areas. What this research demonstrates is that the community context in which the adolescent lives influences the age at which she initiates sexual intercourse and the frequency of her sexual behavior.

Becoming a teenage mother is associated with many negative consequences for mother and child.

Only 57% of teen mothers began prenatal care in the first trimester as compared with 76% of all mothers; therefore, their infants are at increased risk of illness, developmental delays, and even death (Ventura, 1994). Becoming a teenage mother has been associated with many negative consequences for both mother and child, which include more difficult pregnancies putting their babies at higher risk, higher rates of divorce if they do marry, higher high school drop out rates, high rates of unemployment, poverty, and dependence on welfare, and a greater likelihood that their daughters will also be teenage mothers. "The burden of public expenditures may be what is driving public concern with adolescent parenting, but clearly the private costs—the poor life prospects for these mothers and their children—are substantial, also, and merit concern" (Kamerman & Kahn, 1988, p. 116).

To control for the fact that teenage mothers come from more deprived backgrounds to begin with, a study based on census data from 1970 and 1980 examined the socioeconomic effects of an unplanned birth on teenage mothers by comparing the outcomes for those mothers whose first birth was to twins with those of teenage mothers whose first birth was to a single infant (Groggar & Bronars, 1993). This method uses a random fertility event—the birth of twins—to determine the socioeconomic consequences of teenage child-

bearing. Black women who have an unplanned child are significantly less likely than women who have not to have lower rates of high school graduation as well as labor-force participation and significantly higher rates of poverty and welfare recipiency. Ten years after giving birth they are also less likely to be currently married than are women who have not had an unplanned birth. White women who have an unplanned teenage birth also have significantly higher rates of poverty and welfare recipiency, as well as lower family earnings and household income.

Rates of teenage pregnancy have continued to rise in the United States since 1970. High rates of teenage abortion lowered the rate of adolescent childbearing during the 1970s and early 1980s, but the teenage birthrate rose by 24% between 1986 and 1991.

The United States has higher rates of teenage pregnancy than 27 out of 30 industrialized nations. The legal abortion rate for U.S. teenagers is higher than it is for any other developed country for which there is data (E. F. Jones, 1986). When I was on a panel on teenage pregnancy at the International Interdisciplinary Congress of Women in the Netherlands in 1984, a woman on the panel from Sweden said that the rate of teenage pregnancy in Sweden was far lower than that of the United States because they begin sex education and teach about contraception in the public schools as young as seven years of age.

Polls in the United States show that 8 out of 10 people favor sex education in the schools (E. F. Jones, 1986). Nevertheless, only a little more than half of high school students receive information about contraceptives by the time they graduate from high school (Zelnik & Kim, 1982). Since most parents do not talk to their teenagers about sex or contraception, sex education comes too late for the one out of every five American girls who have intercourse by age 15 (G. L. Fox, 1983). Lack of knowledge about contraception is only one factor leading to teenage pregnancy.

Adolescent pregnancy and parenting has been seen as a major problem for American society only since the mid-1970s. The pregnancy rate for teenage women has continued to rise since 1970 because of an increase in sexual activity among teenagers. Childbearing among teenagers, however, declined during the 1970s and early 1980s due to legalization of abortion, but rose again in the late 1980s and early 1990s. "About 30 percent of all abortions performed in the United States are to adolescents; and about 40 percent of all teenage pregnancies are ended by abortion" (Kamerman & Kahn, 1988, p. 114). Given the strong religious and political opposition to abortion among some groups, some teens do not consider abortion, or cannot afford to pay for it (Figure 5.1).

Notwithstanding the high rate of abortions to adolescents, the 1991 birthrate was 62.1 births per 1,000 teenagers aged 15–19, 24% higher than it had been in 1986. This increase in the birthrate occurred in spite of a 9% decline in the number of women aged 15–19 during this time. Among these births to 15–19-year-old women, 25% of the births were the mother's second or higher-order birth. The 1991 birth rate for Black, Hispanic, and White teens aged 15–19 was 118.9, 106.7, and 43.4 respectively, per 1,000 (Ventura, 1994). National concern about teen mothers has escalated because half of teen mothers go on welfare within one year after the birth of their child and 77% of teen mothers go on welfare within five years (Rodriquez & Moore, 1995).

Teenage mothers come from more disadvantaged backgrounds than nonmothers.

What do we know about teen parents and why children in the United States are having children? A comparison of childhood backgrounds of 39 teenage mothers and 35 nonmothers attending a clinic found that teenage mothers had experienced foster care, family violence, parental substance abuse, and lower educational achievements to a greater extent than did nonmothers (Oz & Fine, 1988). The boyfriends of the teenage mothers had higher rates of alcohol abuse, violence, and lower educational achievements as compared with the boyfriends of nonmothers.

A comparison of the life-course patterns of 30 adult women who became mothers as teenagers with 237 adult child-bearing mothers found the adolescent mothers had lower levels of completed education than did adult mothers, and their children exhibited more learning problems (East & Felice, 1990). Both the women who became mothers as adolescents and the children's fathers felt that they provided less esteem-enhancement support for their children than did the older parents.

Often overlooked, is the role of physical and sexual abuse as a factor in adolescent pregnancy. Sixty-eight percent of a sample of 535 young women from the state of Washington, who became pregnant as adolescents, had experienced molestation or rape prior to their first pregnancy. "Compared with adolescent women who became pregnant but had not been abused, sexually victimized teenagers began intercourse a year earlier, were more likely to have used drugs and alcohol and were less likely to practice contraception" (Debra Boyer & Fine, 1992, p. 4). Counseling should be a component of teenage pregnancy prevention programs.

Research on the high rate of teenage pregnancy in the District of Columbia among primarily African American teenagers attributes teenage pregnancy to at-risk behaviors that include "(1) early sexual activity with multiple partners, often without effective use of birth control; (2) drug abuse; and (3) lack of appropriate information on birth control advice and devices" (Ladner, & Gourdine, 1992, p. 207). Reasons underlying these proximal causes, according to Ladner and Gourdine, are the legacy of slavery among certain sectors of the African American community that is manifest in poverty and unequal opportunities for jobs, education, and housing.

White adolescents are more likely to be sexually active than Mexican American adolescents, but Whites are more likely to use contraceptives. Although the pregnancy rates are similar for the two groups, Mexican American adolescents are more likely to give birth because Whites are more likely to have an abortion.

A probability sample of Los Angeles County Mexican American and non-Hispanic White females aged 13–19 years revealed that the overall rate of ever having had sexual intercourse is significantly greater among non-Hispanic White than among Mexican American teens (Aneshensel, Fielder, & Becerra, 1989). The age of first intercourse is also significantly younger among non-Hispanic White teens than it is among Mexican American adolescents.

Mexican American females also had fewer partners than did the White adolescents, with 74% of those who had experienced intercourse reporting only one partner. For White adolescents, teenagers living in families with the lowest income levels have the highest rates of sexual intercourse, with little difference in rates of sexual activity among middle- and upper-income females. For Mexican Americans, middle-income teens have the lowest rates of sexual intercourse, and upper-income adolescents the highest rate. Within middle- or high-socioeconomic strata there is no significant ethnic difference in rates of sexual intercourse.

Several lifestyle indicators are related to sexual activity for both ethnic groups. Adolescents who changed residence more frequently, and those who lived in a single parent home, were more likely than nonmovers and those living with both parents to have had intercourse. Instability in the parental marriage was a greater risk factor for sexual intercourse for White than for Mexican American teens.

Among those who have ever had sexual intercourse, the rate of ever using contraceptives is significantly higher among Whites (80.6%) than it is among Mexican American (48.5%) adolescents. Although the overall pregnancy rate for the two ethnic groups is similar, among those who have ever had sexual intercourse, one in two Mexican Americans have been pregnant compared with only one in four Whites. Mexican Americans are more likely than Whites to ever have had a live birth because white adolescents are much more likely to have an abortion when pregnant than are Mexican Americans.

Changes are occurring among acculturated Mexican American teenagers in reproductive be-

havior. Among a sample of 12 to 18 year olds attending an obstetric clinic for teens, acculturated adolescents were younger at first age of intercourse and less likely to be married to the father of their child than immigrant adolescents. (Reynosa, Felice & Shragg, 1993).

White teenagers no longer give up their babies for adoption. Black teenagers have never given up their babies for adoption.

One reason for the alarm about teenage pregnancy is probably due to the fact that prior to 1970 most mothers who became pregnant as teenagers either married the father or gave the baby up for adoption (Kamerman & Kahn, 1988). "By the early 1980s, close to two thirds of all White teen mothers (delivering first births) were unmarried when they became pregnant, and almost all Blacks (97%) were single (Furstenberg, Brooks–Gunn, & Chase-Lansdale, 1989, p. 313).

There is a scarcity of research bearing on the issue of why teenagers do not place their babies for adoption. Formal adoption was never widely practiced among Blacks. A study among Whites found more negative consequences for those who kept their children as compared with those who gave them up for adoption (McLaughlin, Manninen, & Winges, 1988).

Unmarried women were much less likely to relinquish a child for adoption in the 1980s than they had been in the early 1970s. Nine percent of children born to never-married women were placed for adoption prior to 1973 in contrast to 4% during 1973–1981 and 2% during 1982–1988. The rate of relinquishing children for adoption has always been low for Black women; only 1.5% of Black babies born to never-married women were placed for adoption prior to 1973 as compared with 19.3% of similar White babies. During 1982–1988, 1.1% of Black babies were placed for adoption compared with 3.2% of White babies, which represents a dramatic drop in relinquishment of White babies, but only a slight change for Black babies. Several factors are related to a White mother's placing her child for adoption: a higher educational level; being in school at the time of the pregnancy; the sex of the child (girls are twice as likely to be placed for adoption as boys); being older; and having no labor force experience. These findings are based on data on the fertility and fertility-related behavior of U.S. women aged 15–44 from the 1982 and 1988 cycles of the National Survey of Family Growth (NSFG), which are area probability samples of the U.S. population (Bachrach, Stolley, & London, 1992).

Given the profound stresses of having a baby while a teenager, why do some young women make this choice? First of all, most teenagers do not deliberately plan the pregnancy. Although the use of condoms doubled during the 1980s, as of 1990, 60% of teenage pregnancies were unplanned (Rodriquez and Moore, 1995). Some do plan the pregnancies. Two of the students in my psychology of women class this semester told me that in the few years since they have been out of high school it has become the "in" thing at their former high schools to become pregnant and have a baby. These students are from all-White schools in Rhode Island.

A cognitive model can help explain teenage pregnancy.

Thoughts about relationships—wanting the affection and attention of the boy—encourage sexual risk taking according to a cognitive model of teenage pregnancy that has been developed by Norris (1992). The brakes on teenage pregnancy, according to this model, are values and goals and thoughts about the impact of an unwanted pregnancy on one's immediate and near-future life circumstances. In an experiment, Norris and Devine (1992) found that making pregnancy concerns highly accessible (by priming), led to risk avoidant responses on a story completion task for undergraduate men and women who had chronic concerns about an unplanned pregnancy due to frequent sexual activity.

Teenage pregnancy is adaptive for the girl living in poverty, with inadequate education and job training and what she perceives to be a bleak future. Values also play a role, and peer values may influence girls to become caught up in a peer cul-

ture that supports pregnancy and childbirth. The solution is excellent education, opportunities for the future, and programs such as the one described in the next section, as well as after school programs which provide recreation and skill training. Discussion group participation helps cognitively access the concerns about bearing a child as a teen (J. P. Allen, Kupermine, Philliber, & Herre, 1994).

A school-based clinic program found that dispensing contraceptives combined with education about pregnancy risk avoidant behavior, decreased the pregnancy rate and increased the age of first intercourse.

Accessibility of a construct has been shown by a number of studies to be related to behavior. A school-based clinic program, which dispensed contraceptives and educated about preventing pregnancy, in an urban junior high school and a senior high school produced a 30.1% decrease in pregnancy rates after 28 months, as contrasted with a 57.6% increase at control schools that had no pregnancy prevention program (Zabin, Hirsch, Smith, Streett, & Hardy, 1986; Zabin et al., 1988). Median age at first intercourse also increased for both male and female students from 15 years and seven months to 16 years and two months thereafter, and the percentage of sexually active students declined significantly from the baseline data collected during the three years preceding the program.

Two teams consisting of a nurse and social worker delivered most of the services. The program involved many features specifically designed to increase students awareness of negative consequences of unprotected sex including group education and discussion. Announcements and signs for program activities were prominently displayed, and peer counselors wore T shirts and large buttons with the words, "Ask me about the Self Center" around school. Thus, there are effective programs for teenage pregnancy prevention. The state and federal governments should provide funding for such programs throughout the country.

Adolescent Females' Ideal Self-Image

Adolescents anticipate adult roles, particularly occupational roles, when asked about their ideal self-image. Girls are likely to mention wanting to get married and family roles, whereas athletics and owning a sportscar are more important for boys.

Students from the fifth, eighth, and eleventh grades (55 male and 53 female) most frequently described their ideal self-image as occupational (Bybee, Glick, & Zigler, 1990). Twice as many girls (54%) as boys (26%) also mentioned wanting to get married, and nearly three times as many girls (35%) mentioned family relationships (35%) as did boys (13%). Boys desired athletic abilities, wanting to be a professional athlete, and owning a sportscar more than girls. Many students also expressed a desire for wealth (36%). At higher grade levels children were less likely to mention intellectual abilities and physical appearance. They more frequently mentioned wanting to go to college, get married, and have children.

Although commonalities are found in different cultures for the role of the ideal woman (a woman cooking is seen as cooking for her family and a woman in an office is seen as hard-working), cultural differences emerged in a study using the emic approach in Guatemala, the United States, and the Philipines (Gibbons et al., 1993). Contentment was a theme for Filipino and U.S. adolescents, whereas Guatamalan adolescents had themes of betterment, hope and family.

YOUNG ADULTHOOD

Most of the research in this book has focused on adults in their twenties, and thirties, and forties—the research on dating and marriage, motherhood, pregnancy, and childbirth, dual career couples, women and work, and female sexuality. It is therefore particularly appropriate to discuss here the transition to adulthood, the disengagement from parents. Independence from parents needs to take place in a gradual, constructive way. Going away to college generally assists in that transition.

The College Experience

The tasks of the college experience are succeeding academically, making friends, and learning to live independently from one's family.

Although a great deal is known about college students because of their availability for research studies, little has been written about the social context and the impact of the college students' life stage on the research. Three main life tasks have been delineated for this group: (1) succeeding academically, (2) making friends, and (3) learning to live independently away from one's family. A questionnaire administered to 132 college students found that ego identity in students was related to four measures of leaving home: economic independence, living apart from one's parents, perception of personal control, and emotional attachment to parents (S. A. Anderson & Fleming, 1986).

Both Black and White women at two southern universities were found to lessen their career commitment during college. The peer cultures pressured them into assessing themselves in terms of heterosexual relationships.

The peer culture has been found to have a profound influence on the woman in college—both in terms of her relationships as well as her career commitment (Eisenhart & Holland, 1992). A longitudinal study (1979–1987) of college women at two Southern universities revealed that a number of these women lessened their commitment to careers during college. The researchers used participant observation and interviews (an ethnographic approach) to study the social world of 12 Black women at Bradford University, a historically Black university, and 11 White women at Southern University over a three-semester period. These women were again contacted when their class was graduating from college, and once more four years later. In addition, they administered a survey to 362 women at the two universities. All of the women in the intensively studied sample had strong academic records in high school. During preliminary interviews near the beginning of the respondents' freshman year, all of these women expressed definite interest in pursuing a career.

The ethnographic study revealed the important role of their informal peer groups in creating the meaning of gender for these women. The peer cultures at both schools encouraged the young women to assess themselves in terms of heterosexual romantic relationships. Schoolwork and career plans of the women were of little consequence in a peer culture that evaluated the women based on their attractiveness to men and their success in their romantic relationships. Whereas men had several sources of prestige in the peer culture such as sports or campus offices, the main indicator of prestige for women was relationships with men. Women's relationships with other women were considered secondary to those with men. Schoolwork and career-related matters were also relegated to a peripheral concern in the peer system. Schoolwork was considered too demanding, and students had many conflicts about time spent studying versus with peers. Three distinct orientations to schoolwork organized around motives for doing schoolwork were described as: (1) "getting over" and enjoying peers—in other words get the work done in order to stay in school and get the credentials, but the emphasis was clearly on the peer relationships; (2) "doing well" and succumbing to peers—trying to do well in both areas, but this group was vulnerable to reducing career commitment; and (3) learning from experts and managing peers—placing primary emphasis on learning from professors, and containing peer and romantic relationships so as not to interfere. From both the ethnographic and survey research it appeared that at Bradford, "getting over" appeared to predominate. At Southern University the "doing well" model fit the pattern. Only four students in the ethnographic study fell in the "learning from experts" category. All four of these women graduated and went to graduate school. This research

highlights the fact that peer culture, with its emphasis on romantic involvement, promotes a system that has important influence on women's career decisions.

This section has been a very narrow view of young adulthood. Other young women enter the world of work right after high school, or drop out of school to become a teenage mother. We need more research on the process of becoming adults among young women who do not go to college, as well as a broader spectrum of research on students at different colleges.

MIDDLE AGE

Personality at Midlife

Psychological science provides little in the way of theoretical explanation of women at midlife.

> An overview of women's adult development in textbooks and the professional literature indicates that (a) the prevailing focus of concern is the woman as a biological creature, especially as a mother; (b) the proposed lifecycle trajectory is one in which the woman's life goes into decline after approximately age 40; and (c) little attention is paid to the particular character of women's life narratives. (Gergen, 1990, p. 471)

A longitudinal study of women graduates of Mills College finds that they increase in competence and self confidence and decline in succorance (the need for help and support from others) between the ages of 27 and 52. These changes were not tied to motherhood or work.

Several articles on women at midlife have been based on a longitudinal study of women graduates of Mills College, California. Two thirds of the 1958 and 1960 senior classes at Mills College participated in the research. They were contacted again at ages 27, 43, and 52. When the women were age 27 and 52, their male partners also provided data relevant to the study. It must be kept in mind that these are college-educated, mostly White, upper–middle-class women, and that the findings of this research may not apply to the general population of women.

The personality of the Mills College women and their partners were found to change throughout their lives together (Wink & Helson, 1993). Adjective Check List (ACL) data found the women at age 27, which the researchers called the early parental period (although not all were mothers), to be "less goal oriented, more facilitative in interpersonal relationships, and more in need of emotional support from others" (Wink & Helson, 1993, p. 603). The women at this time scored significantly lower than did their partners on the Competence Scale and higher than their partners on the Affiliation and Succorance scales of the ACL. There was also a tendency for women to score lower on the Self-Confidence scale. This data was corroborated by that from the Marital Tensions Checklist, which showed women at age 27 to rate themselves as not feeling responsible enough, wanting too much affection, and being jealous as compared with their ratings at age 52. On the other hand, during the Postparental period (age 52), there were no longer any significant differences between women and their partners. Data from 21 matched couples who were tested when the woman was age 27 and were still together when she was 52 revealed that women changed significantly on Competence, Self-Confidence, and Succorance, and partners increased significantly in Affiliation. The changes in the women could not be attributed to motherhood because both women who were and were not mothers increased significantly on Competence and Self-Confidence and decreased on Succorance. There was a trend only on the measure of Forcefulness to significance with women without children showing a greater increase. Higher status work was found to contribute to an increase in Forcefulness in women, and a decrease in Succorance.

Data had also been collected from the mothers and fathers of the Mills College women, when the parents were in their early fifties. Compared with the husbands, the mothers scored somewhat lower on Self-Confidence and higher on succorance and were also less goal oriented, less confi-

dent, and indicated a need for more emotional support. The daughters scored higher on Competence, Forcefulness, and Individuality, and lower on Succorance than did their mothers at the same age. "The findings thus indicate that within the Mills sample women's normative personality change was not tied to motherhood or status of work but that cohort was a significant factor" (Wink & Helson, 1993, p. 604).

A person-centered perspective on the personalities of the Mills College women at midlife yielded four prototypes: Individuated, Traditional, Conflicted, and Assured (York & John, 1992). The Individuated woman is characterized by openness, high aspirations, high intellectual capacity, assertiveness, wide interests, warmth, introspection, independence, and aesthetic sensitivity. The Traditional woman is protective, dependable, giving, overcontrols needs, has conservative values, is sympathetic, has a feminine style and is guilt prone. The Conflicted prototype is a more undesirable pattern that correlates negatively with emotional stability and agreeableness. The Conflicted prototype is made up of characteristics such as being anxious, hostile, defensive, distant, aloof, fearful, and questioning of self-adequacy and lacking meaning. The fourth prototype—the Assured woman—is rational, objective, behaves assertively, is satisfied with self, is distant, aloof, power oriented, critical, skeptical, productive, and values independence. The Assured prototype scores high on scales measuring masculinity. Future research needs to address the issue of whether women with different prototypes have differing life patterns in areas such as relationships and work, and whether there are differences in the patterning and change across the life span of their personality development.

Adjustment at Midlife

A woman in her early 50s is in her prime of life according to a study of Mills College alumnae. There also seems to be a rewriting of the life story at midlife.

Participants in the Mills College Longitudinal Study were asked in their middle 50s to describe their most difficult time since college (Helson, 1992). The most critical period in their lives, for most women, was in the late 30s and early 40s. Why should what the author's term, *rewriting the life story,* have occurred for women at this age? In reading this study, it occurred to me that this was also the most difficult time of my life. I went through a divorce at age 41. Helson explains that the crisis occurs around age 40 because "the experience of dependence and restriction associated with marriage and motherhood, followed by a lessening of that dependence and restriction as children grow up and the resistance of partners to a change in roles in which they lose power" (Helson, 1992, p. 344).

The early 50s is a woman's prime of life according to a comparison of Mills College alumnae cohorts who returned questionnaires (V. Mitchell & Helson, 1990). Fifty percent of the women at age 51 described their lives as "first-rate." In comparison, 32% of 26–36-, 37% of 41–46-, 43% of 56–61-, and 34% of 66–76-year olds rated their lives as "first rate." A smaller longitudinal sample also rated the early 50s very favorably. "Conditions distinguishing the early 50s from earlier and/or later periods of the middle years included more 'empty nests,' better health, higher income, and more concern for parents" (V. Mitchell & Helson, 1990, p. 451). All but the latter was related to higher quality of life.

Is the life course any different for women from working-class backgrounds who go to an Ivy League university as compared with those from middle- and upper-class backgrounds? Retrospective experiences at Radcliffe and later life events of women from working-class origins who graduated in from Radcliffe College in 1947 and 1964 were compared with women of middle- and upper-class backgrounds graduating at the same time (A. J. Stewart & Ostrove, 1993). The large majority of working-class women in both the class of 1947 (67%) and of 1964 (75%) reported feelings that the researchers characterized as a sense of alienation compared with about half of middle-class and only 15% of upper-class stu-

dents who felt this way. The values most evident at Radcliffe when these women were students there were upper-class, explaining why upper-class women felt most at home there. Nevertheless, the midlife educational and occupational attainment of the working-class women who attended Radcliffe did not differ from those of the women from more privileged backgrounds.

The larger social changes occurring in society affected the women of the class of 1964 more than those of the class of 1947, regardless of social class background. The women of the class of 1964 were equally as likely to marry as those in the class of 1947, but were more likely to divorce. The women of 1964 were more likely to continue their education beyond college and pursue careers, but were less likely to participate in community organizations. Women of working-class backgrounds viewed their mothers as negative role models, while middle-class women perceived their mothers as positive role models, and upper-class women did not perceive their mothers as role models at all. Marriage was perceived as having sex-linked stresses and strains by women of working-class origin, with upper-class women having the most positive views of marriage, and middle-class women in between in attitudes toward marriage.

Psychological Effect of Menopause

There is no evidence that menopause causes depression or other psychiatric disturbance in women.

Because 40% of first depression in women also occur between 40 and 60, depression became associated with menopause, even being labeled "involutional melancholia" (McKinlay, McKinlay, & Brambilla, 1987). It was then assumed that estrogen deficiency caused physiological and psychological effects that lead to depression. An alternative hypothesis has also been put forward: the social circumstances perspective, which says that during the middle years, 45–55, women experience more personal changes than at other times, such as caring for elderly parents, death of

Sylvia

The popular culture emphasizes negative symptoms of menopause.
Copyright 1995 by Nicole Hollander

parents, illness or death of a spouse, unemployment, children leaving home, midlife crisis of a spouse, divorce or separation, and moving. Change has also been associated with depression.

Research on a random sample of 2,500 women in Massachusetts aged 45–55 years who were followed up for 27 months did not support menopause as a cause of depression (McKinlay, McKinlay, & Brambilla, 1987). Women who were going through menopause or had recently gone through menopause were no more depressed than women who had not yet gone through menopause. The only women who showed an increase in reported depression were women who had recently undergone a surgical menopause (hysterectomy with removal of ovaries). These women, however, had poorer health before the surgery and had been higher users of medical care. Review of the psychiatric literature by Ballinger (1990) found that there was no scientific basis for the belief that menopause is a high-risk time for mental illness.

Studies of women admitted to hospitals and mental health centers show no increased incidence of psychiatric disorders related to the menopause. Similarly, general population surveys also find no major effect of menopause on common psychiatric symptoms. Also, the failure to find any significant therapeutic effect of estrogen on symptoms of depression or anxiety is well established in clinical studies of estrogen therapy.

On the other hand, antidepressant medication has been found to be superior to placebo in the treatment of depression, irritability, headache, and insomnia in women attending menopausal clinics.

Social psychological factors such as changes in family structure, taking care of elderly parents, involvement in outside work, and dealing with adolescent children have more impact on mental health at this time than the physiological changes of the menopause. Moreover, Western culture conveys negative expectations of the menopause and the conviction that it presages a marked deterioration in physical and mental health. "It is a tribute to the power of culturally determined attitudes, media pressure and the promotion of oestrogen sales that this menopause myth persists, despite all the evidence to the contrary" (Ballinger, 1990, p. 784). If anything, the literature shows a drop in the prevalence of minor psychiatric disorder in the 10 years following menopause.

In a longitudinal study of 541 initially premenopausal healthy women, at two-and-a-half year follow-up it was found that natural menopause led to few changes in psychological characteristics. An increase in hot flashes was the only symptom reported for women who did not use hormone replacement therapy along with a decline in private self-consciousness (Matthews et al., 1990).

Natural menopause did not adversely affect Type A behavior, anxiety, anger, total symptoms, depression, public self-consciousness, perceived stress, or job dissatisfaction scores. It did not adversely affect reports of recent symptoms of body worry, excitability, aches in neck and skull, depression, nervousness, and difficulty sleeping. (Matthews et al., 1990, p. 349)

No differences existed between those women who used hormone replacement therapy and those who did not at baseline (the beginning of the study). At the follow-up, hormone users reported more worry about their body, but little change in joint pain and hot flashes. The best conclusion is that menopause is a benign condition for the majority of healthy women. Nevertheless, psychiatric symptoms such as depression, irritability, lack of confidence, and poor concentration are still listed by standard gynecological textbooks as specific symptoms of menopause. I wrote this book while going through menopause (without hormone replacement therapy). I was not aware of depression, irritability, lack of confidence, sleeplessness, or of inability to concentrate.

Research on the influence of sociocultural paradigms on attitudes toward menopause of 581 women and men between the ages of 18 and 85 indicated that conceptualizing menopause within a medical context elicited significantly more negative and fewer positive attitudes than did describing their attitudes in the context of life transitions or of aging (Gannon & Ekstrom, 1993). The paradigm was experimentally manipulated by the framing of the interview.

Women's Attitudes toward Aging

A New Woman *magazine survey of women's attitudes toward aging finds young women more fearful of growing old than older women. The best part of growing older, according to women over 50, is a firm sense of self.*

A 1993 *New Woman* magazine survey on women growing older was answered by more than 6,000 magazine readers. Among women over 50, 48% said they felt young, 48% middle aged, and only 4% felt old. Although respondents in their 20s said they thought they would feel old when they reach 52, women in their 50s did not expect to feel old until 69, and women in their 60s until they were 71 (Perlmutter, Hanlon, & Sangiorgio, 1994).

Younger women are more fearful of growing old than are older women. Actually 54% of women in their 20s compared with only 23% of women over 60 admit to a fear of growing old. When asked what makes a woman feel old, they replied "lack of enthusiasm" (39%), "declining health" (25%), "how she looks" (19%), "lack of energy" (11%), and a "conservative attitude" (7%).

The women over 50 had positive views of older women. Fifty percent said that feeling a firm sense of self is the best part of aging. When asked, "How do you feel about life as a whole?" 26% of women over 50 were "delighted, pleased" and 37% were "mostly satisfied," as compared with 17% and 28%, respectively, of women under 30.

The Sandwich Generation

Middle-aged married mothers caring for their mothers report it as only an infrequent source of conflict.

One area of potential strain for middle-aged women is the conflict of responsibilities engendered by caring for aging parents and those toward their husbands, children, and employers. Daughters are the primary source of caregiving for widowed mothers. In one study, this dilemma of middle-aged, married mothers caring for their physically impaired mothers was found to be only an infrequent cause of conflict (A. J. Walker, Pratt, & Wood, 1993). Those women who did report frequent conflict between their obligations as caregivers and those in their other roles had poorer relationships with their mothers. This research is consistent with the research on women and multiple roles that has been found to support the expansion hypothesis that multiple role occupancy provides mental health benefits (see chapter VIII).

AGING AND GENDER

America is an aging nation. The population 65 and older was 10 times larger in 1990 than it had been in 1900. The over 65 population grew by 22% during the 1980s (U.S. Bureau of the Census, 1992, May). One in eight Americans is now over age 65. Many more women than men live to older ages. Between the ages of 65 and 69, there are only 81 men for every 100 women. Women, particularly, are living into their 70s and beyond. Older women are much more likely to live in poverty than older men. Of women 65–74 years old, 10% of White women compared with 5% of White men and 34% of Black women compared with 25% of Black men and 23% of Hispanic women compared with 18% of Hispanic men live in poverty (U.S. Bureau of the Census, 1992, December) (Figure 5.1).

Retirement

Women are less likely to receive pensions than men and have a 60% chance of being poor in retirement. Women who consider themselves both retired and homemakers have less depression than women who only identify themselves with a single role.

A lower income for women than men follows women into retirement. "Women have a 60 percent chance of being poor in old age, a situation intensified by their longevity because women live an average of 79 years (Hewlett, 1986)" (Perkins, 1992, p. 526). Little research has been conducted on women in retirement, perhaps because of the belief that employment is ancillary for women, making retirement an easier transition for them. Women are less likely to receive pensions than men because of their lesser years in the workforce and lesser affiliation with unions, segregation in low-wage occupations, and discrimination involving training, promotion, and raises. Preretirement planning could help alleviate some of women's serious financial problems. The feminist movement has not sufficiently dealt with the double whammy of ageism and sexism.

What is the effect of multiple role identities on retired women? Life satisfaction, depression, and self-esteem were compared for 864 Black and 622 White women over age 60 (from a national probability sample) who considered themselves retired only, homemakers only, or retired and homemaker (Adelmann, 1993). Women who said they were both retired and homemakers had higher self-esteem and lower depression than women who only identified themselves with a single role. Women also had lower depression scores who had higher levels of education, were married, had better health, were older and who engaged in hours of do-it-yourself activities. Age, education, health, do-it-yourself activity, and volunteer activity were significantly related to higher self-esteem. Even after the adjustment for covariates, homemakers still had significantly lower self-esteem and higher depression scores than the dual role group. This study demonstrates that multiple-role identities persist after retirement and have implications for women's well-being.

Perceptions of Aging Women

The image of aging women is improving.

Although aging men have traditionally been treated more kindly by society than have aging women, there are hopeful signs that images of aging women are improving. One study asked college students and adults in the community to list the characteristics of 35-year-old and 65-year-old men and women. This research found a similarity in the evaluations of 65-year-old men and women (Kite, Deaux, & Miele, 1991). Age differences were greater than gender differences in evaluations.

In a replication of a life span sex role orientation study conducted 10 years earlier, it was again found that there was an increase in the number of feminine women and masculine men in the oldest age category (61 years and older) (Hyde, Krajnik, & Skuldt-Niederberger, 1991). Over half of the women in the sample, which ranged in age from 24 to 81, were categorized as being feminine, with over 70% of women over 61 so classi-

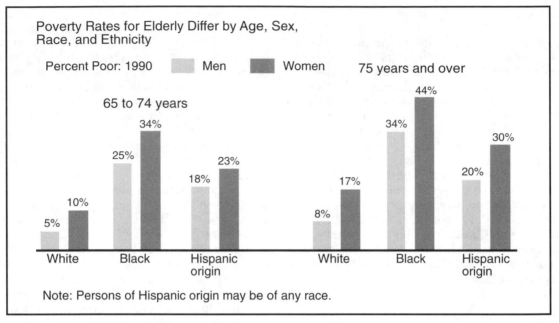

FIGURE 5.1 *Source:* U.S. Bureau of the Census. (1992, December). *Census and You, 27* (12), p. 6.

fied. In the part of their study in which the same individuals were recontacted 10 years later, masculinity, femininity and androgyny were found to be quite stable, with 54% of the people remaining in the same category over a period of 10 years.

Widowhood

Widowhood is one of the most stressful life events. Widows cope better than widowers, due primarily to the larger social networks that women have.

The proportion of widowed in the population is much greater among females because of the cultural pattern of younger women marrying older men, higher mortality rates among men, and the greater likelihood of remarriage among men. There are both health and social consequences of bereavement. The first phase of widowhood is the grieving process. Grief is an emotional response to the loss of someone with whom there is a relationship of attachment. The loss of a child or of a spouse are causes of intense grief. Grief is characterized by a sequence of phases identified as shock, protest, and despair, followed by a long period of recovering. Recovery from grief is exhibited by a return to energy in everyday life, freedom from pain and discomfort, ability to feel pleasure, hopefulness regarding the future, and ability to function adequately in terms of social roles and as a member of the community (R. S. Weiss, 1988). Younger widows (those under 65) initially show more intense grief responses than do widows over 65, but 18 months later the older widows expressed greater loneliness and anxiety and an increase in physical symptoms (Sanders, 1980).

In a study of widows between the ages of 60 and 89, the widows who were lonely were those who had few social supports (Rook, 1987). Asymmetrical social exchange patterns (in emotional support, instrumental support, and companionship) that either overbenefitted or underbenefitted the women were associated with greater loneliness. Nonreciprocal exchanges probably reflect lack of intimacy in the relationship with others in their social network. The widows' exchanges with their friends were much more likely to be reciprocal than were those with adult children. Although reciprocity was related to satisfaction in friendships, it was unrelated to positive feelings in relations with their adult children. Women's satisfaction with their children was related to the amount of instrumental support provided by the children.

A number of studies point to the low socioeconomic status of many widows as the primary factor in poor adjustment (L. A. Morgan, 1976; Sanders, 1980). Other risk factors have been found that prolong grieving and hinder recovery. These include circumstances surrounding the death including sudden unexpected death, suicide, and stigmatized death, particularly AIDS. Circumstances of the widow after the death can also exacerbate the loss experience: lack of social support; other concurrent crises such as loss of employment or problems with children, and loss of physical health (Sanders, 1988). Research by Stroebe and Stroebe (1983), points out that widowers have a higher mortality rate than widows during the first six months after the death of a spouse. This was attributed to the larger support networks that women have.

Support networks were also found to be the strongest predictor of life satisfaction among widows living in retirement communities (Hong & Duff, 1994). Married women were happier than widowed women. Widows had higher life satisfaction in communities in which the majority of residents were widows, rather than marrieds. Widows were less likely to participate in group activities in communities in which the majority of residents were married.

The Oldest Old

Many more women than men survive to age 85 and older, but are more likely to be ill and live in poverty.

A rapidly growing segment of the population is the oldest old—those 85 years of age and older. National surveys find that although far fewer men survive beyond 85, for those who do the picture is brighter than for women in this age group. Among Whites, 48.7% of men but only 10.3% of women are still married. Women are also more likely to suffer from functional impairment due to chronic diseases than are men, who are more likely to have acute and fatal diseases. Women in this age group are more likely to be living below the poverty level (23% of women, compared with 16% of men) (Barer, 1994).

Longitudinal research in the San Francisco Bay Area is being conducted with White and African Americans 85 years old and older (47 men and 153 women) (C. L. Johnson, 1994). Despite the fact that African Americans are significantly more disadvantaged than are Whites in their socioeconomic status, and African Americans perceive their health as worse than do Whites, they express significantly more contentment with their lives than do Whites. Johnson concludes that this may be due to higher expectations on the part of Whites that are less congruent with the realities of life in advanced age.

Residence of the Elderly

The majority of elderly Americans live in their own homes.

Contrary to stereotypes, only 6% of those over 65 live in nursing homes. The majority of Americans over 65, and even over 85, are homeowners living in their own homes. A U.S. Census Bureau survey in 1991 found that among Whites over 65, 79% were homeowners, compared with 64% for Blacks and 59% for Hispanics. Elderly married couples are most likely to live in their own homes (91%), whereas the ownership rate for persons living alone is 64% (Eskey, 1993).

Nursing homes can be structured to improve the lives of the residents by having reminiscing-type group sessions and allowing residents to make decisions.

Elderly nursing home residents were found to benefit from participation in reminiscing-type

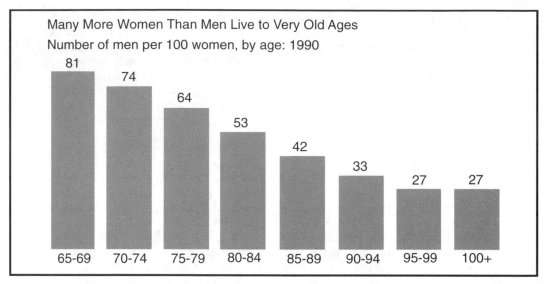

FIGURE 5.2 *Source:* U.S. Bureau of the Census. (1992, December). *Census and You, 27* (12), p. 6.

group sessions (C. M. Brody, 1990). Eight groups of five to eight women that focused on life review met for periods of from six weeks to six months. Although the study was more qualitative than quantitative, over the course of time, more inter-action and self-confidence of participants was noted, as well as increased self-awareness and empathy for others.

Ellen Langer and Judith Rodin (1976) con-ducted a field experiment in a nursing home in which a randomly selected group of residents were encouraged to make decisions and take re-sponsibility for caring for themselves. They were told they could rearrange the furniture, were given a plant to take care of if they wanted one, and given a choice of whether to see a movie, and if so, on which of two nights. Residents in a com-parison group received a communication stress-ing the staff's responsibility for caring for them.

Residents were evaluated after a few weeks and 18 months later. After only a few weeks, the responsibility-induced group reported feeling happier and participated more frequently in ac-tivities and social interaction. The most striking

finding was that during the 18-month period following the intervention, only 15% in the re-sponsibility induced group had died, whereas 30% in the comparison goup had died (J. Rodin & Langer, 1977). Most nursing homes are highly regulated and structured with little opportunity for decision making, restricting residents' sense of control over their own lives. J. Rodin and Langer suggest that decline in the elderly can be slowed by manipulations that provide an in-creased sense of effectance.

REFLECTIONS

Several theories have been put forth to account for gender socialization. That does not mean that one theory must be right and the others wrong. Nor does that mean that the theories are all equally valid. Little or no empirical support has been found for some of the theories such as Freud's psychoanalytic theory. Which theory of gender socialization makes the most sense to you? Why? Any theory must also account for the fact that gender role concept may change throughout life. As a social psychologist, social roles theory and social identity theory make a lot of sense to me. These theories can account for changing gender role identity throughout life as one changes reference groups and moves to different role positions.

Contrary to stereotypes of the "empty nest" or the menopausal shrew, middle-age may be the best time of a woman's life. One of women's biggest problems in old age is having a less-adequate income than have men. Society has not valued the contributions of women equally to those of men, whether as housewives or in the world of work, where women earned less and are less likely to have pensions. As a result poverty remains one of the biggest problems for elderly women, much more so for minority women than for White women.

Experiential Exercises

1. Observe children in a day care center. Do the boys and girls select different toys with which to play? Do boys and girls play in a different way with each other.
2. Visit an elderly woman in a nursing home. Engage her in a discussion about her life story, and her gender role behavior at different stages in her life.
3. Talk with a middle-age woman about menopause and how she is coping with that stage of her life. Is she depressed, irritable, or having difficulty concentrating, or is it the best time of her life?
4. Discuss dreams and aspirations with teenage girls.

KEY TERMS

Cognitive Developmental Model   Based on Piaget's intellectual stages of development, according to Kohlberg, once a child develops gender constancy (between three and six years of age) and definitely label themselves as male or female, they then construct a self consistent with their gender.

Defense Mechanisms   Psychological means of dealing with anxiety. Females show greater use of internalizing defenses (turning against the self) and males greater use of externalizing defenses (projection and aggression).

Diffuse Status Characteristics   General qualities of a person which that culture associates with his/her competence, ability, or value such as sex, wealth, age, attractiveness, occupation and education.

Ego Development   It is a concept that signifies psychological insight and cognitive complexity. Low scores indicate little time perspective, and a lack of impulse control or self relfectiveness.

Expectation States Theory   A theory that considers characteristics of persons that contribute to their status and power in a group. The group pays attention to two types of cues that it considers relevant to its goal achievement, diffuse status characteristics and specific status characteristics.

Gender Identity Theory   Gender identity is formed in relation to one's reference groups—to organized patterns of institutional contexts such as family, school, and church. The individual internalizes the norms of her reference groups.

Gender Schema Theory   The child develops a gender schema, based on associations of what males and females look and act like. The child uses this gender schema to process incoming information, leading the child to become sex typed.

Multifactorial Gender Identity Theory   Spence proposes that an individual's summary judgments of their gender-based self-image incorporates a number of categories including attitudes, preference, behaviors, and roles that are more or less independent, not all of which are associated with their sex.

Psychoanalytic Theory   According to Freud, at the third stage of psychosexual development, the phallic stage, boys resolve the Oedipus complex by identifying with the father because of a fear of castration. Girls resolve the Electra complex by identifying with the mother, but develop penis envy because they think they have already been castrated. At puberty, girls enter the genital stage during which they develop a vaginal, passive sexuality.

Puberty   A period of rapid height and weight gain during which sexual maturity is achieved. The most important physical event of puberty for girls is menarche—the first menstrual period.

Social Learning Theory   Assumes that boys and girls learn gender roles through modeling and imitation of the same-sex parent as well as reinforcement for "appropriate" sex role behavior and punishment for "inappropriate" sex role behavior.

Specific Status Characteristics   Qualities that have been demonstrated to be specific to the task at hand.

The Sandwich Generation   Middle-aged women caring for their aging parents as well as for children and often husbands and meeting demands of employers.

SUGGESTED READINGS

McKinlay, J. B., McKinlay, S. M., & Brambilla, D. (1987). The relative contributions of endocrine changes and social circumstances to depression in mid-aged women. *Journal of Health and Social Behavior, 28*, 345–63. This study shatters the myth that menopause causes depression.

Norris, A. E. (1992). Cognitive analysis of contraceptive behavior. In Kenney, N. J., Brot, M. D., Moe, K. E., & Dahl, K. (Eds.), *The complexities of women: Integrative essays in psychology and biology* (pp. 154–164). This article presents a cognitive model for risking pregnancy or avoiding pregnancy.

Rotheram-Borus, M. J., & Wyche, K. F. (1994). Ethnic differences in identity development in the United States. In S. Archer (Ed.), *Interventions for adolescent identity development* (pp. 62–83). Thousand Oaks, CA: Sage. This book chapter is an excellent assessment of the impact of ethnicity on gender roles and identity search of adolescents. Interventions are suggested for making the identity search easier for minority youth.

CHAPTER 6

Women and Work

Women throughout the United States have not experienced a common oppression as women. The processes of gender, race-ethnicity, and class—intrinsically interconnected—have been central forces determining and differentiating women's work lives in U.S. history.

Theresa Amott and Julie Matthaei, 1991

Massive postwar changes in the U.S. economy have transformed the labor force from jobs dominated by the production industry into new service occupations. In the process, the labor force changed from one that was male dominated to one of a more equal male and female mix.

Reproductive Labor

Much of women's work is in the area called social reproduction—taking care of people in the family. This is also true of their occupations outside of the home.

Much of both paid and unpaid women's work is in the area called **social reproduction** or **reproductive labor.** Women take care of people both within the family and in jobs they do outside of the home.

The term social reproduction is used by feminist scholars to refer to the array of activities and rela-

tionships involved in maintaining people both on a daily basis and intergenerationally. Reproductive labor includes activities such as purchasing household goods, preparing and serving food, laundering and repairing clothing, maintaining furnishings and appliances, socializing children, providing care and emotional support for adults, and maintaining kin and community ties. (E. N. Glenn, 1992, p. 1)

Before the industrial revolution, women engaged in the production of foodstuff, clothing, and other goods, as well as most of what is called reproductive labor. Industrialization transferred the production of basic goods to capitalist industry. A division of labor occurred in which men were largely responsible for production outside the home, while women were responsible for housework. Gradually, more and more of household "productive" labor was taken over by industry, with household work becoming almost exclusively reproductive.

In the second half of the twentieth century, with more and more women employed outside of the home, social and emotional needs have also become increasingly relegated to commercial services. These services include taking care of children, the elderly, and mentally and physically disabled people, as well as services for everyone, such as health care and food preparation and service in restaurants. The increasing transfer of social reproduction to the marketplace since World War II has led to the employment of women in service work such as childcare, food preparation, and health care services. Because women have more recently also been closing the education gap and increasingly attending graduate and professional schools, more and more women are employed in managerial and professional positions.

WOMEN'S LABOR FORCE PARTICIPATION

Rates of Labor Force Participation

Labor force participation rates for men and women have been converging.

There was a dramatic increase in women in the labor force between 1950 and 1980, from 34% to 55%. The rate of increase slowed to a crawl, however, during the 1980s, reaching a **labor force participation rate** of 57.5% for women 16 years and older in 1990 (Fullerton, 1992). The proportion of women in the labor force varies state by state, with highs in 1990 of about 67% in Alaska and about 65% in Minnesota and New Hampshire to only 43% in West Virginia, 49% in Louisiana, and 51% in Alabama (U.S. Department of Labor, 1991, July). By 1990, men 16 years and older made up 54.7% of the labor force, whereas women over 16 were 45.3% of the labor force.

Racial-Ethnic Women's Labor

Women's work has been structured hierarchically by race and ethnicity as well as by gender.

Women's work lives in U.S. history have, however, been differentiated both by gender as well as by race-ethnicity and social class. The experi-

ence of oppression of women has been quite different for White women and women of color. "In the process of invasion and conquest, Europeans imposed their notions of male superiority on cultures with more egalitarian forms of gender relations, including many American Indian and African tribes" (Amott & Matthaei, 1991, p. 16). White men treated women of color in terms of a very different concept of femininity than they did White women. "Black female slaves were forced to perform the same inhuman fieldwork as Black male slaves and were expected to do so even in the final weeks of pregnancy. They were routinely beaten and abused without regard for the supposed biological fragility of the female sex" (Rothenberg, 1988, p. 180).

In the latter half of the nineteenth century and continuing during the first half of the twentieth century, racial-ethnic women were employed to clean house, care for children, cook, and do laundry for White, middle- and upper-class women. In the northeast the domestic servants were primarily Irish and German immigrant women until World War I. African American women in the South and Mexican American women in the Southwest were almost exclusively the servants. In California and Hawaii, Asian immigrant men filled the roles of cooks and other domestic help, but with increasing immigration of Japanese women in the twentieth century, Japanese American women became servants. The White middle-class women employing the racial-ethnic women denied the roles of these minority women as wives and mothers in their own right, since these women worked long hours taking care of their employers' children while they had little time to spend with their own.

Representatives of women and work in U.S. history have included household servants descended from African slaves, Chinese women imported for purposes of prostitution, European American factory workers, and Puerto Rican feminist union organizers (Amott & Matthaei, 1991). The experience of women and work in this country is very diverse, this diversity frequently determined by racial-ethnic background.

The race and gender hierarchy is also evident in the public settings that now employ service workers (E. N. Glenn, 1992). For example, in health care, doctors who are disproportionately white and male delegate the enforcement of hospital rules and patient care to registered nurses, who are largely White females. In institutional settings, White males are still the privileged group who benefit from the labor of female subordinates, with White women insulating them from conflict with racial-ethnic subordinates. The licensed practical nurses, who are often supervised by the registered nurses, are disproportionately women of color. At the bottom of the hierarchy are nurses' aides, housekeepers, and kitchen workers, who are overwhelmingly minority women. The orderlies and cleaners are primarily men of color.

The social construction of race and gender in women's reproductive work provided White women with more privileged positions in the domestic sphere, while remaining subordinate to their husband's positions.

> While research in the 1960s and 1970s focused on the significance for women's oppression of unpaid domestic labor, since the 1980s scholars have devoted more attention to the role of paid domestic service in oppressing minority and working-class women. The growing interest in paid domestic labor reflects a recognition among some feminists that the employment of domestic workers in private households is a crucial means through which asymmetrical race and class relations among women are structured. (A. B. Bakan & Stasiulis, 1995, p. 303)

More recently, citizenship status has also become a dimension pertaining to relations with household workers. The employers typically have full citizenship rights while the domestic workers are often illegal aliens, which greatly restricts their rights and privileges vis-á-vis their employers. The widespread practice of employment of illegal aliens as childcare workers among the upper middle class was brought to the nation's attention when President Clinton rescinded his nomination of Zoe Baird as attorney general of the United States because of her failure to pay social security taxes for the illegal alien she employed as a nanny.

> *Black women have been disproportionately employed as compared with White women. At the present time employment rates are the same for Black and White women. Black women, however, have more than twice the unemployment rate of white women.*

The narrowest gap in the labor force participation rate by sex is for African Americans: 58.0% of Black females compared with 69.7% of Black men were in paid employment in 1992 (U.S. Bureau of the Census, 1994). African American women have made considerable progress in recent years, and Black women work in almost every job category. Until recently, Black women were disproportionately employed compared with White women. In 1900, 41% of Black women as compared with only 16% of White women were in the labor force (Amott & Matthaei, 1991). The higher labor force participation rate among Black married women, compared to White married women, results from a tradition of two earner families among Blacks because of the historic and present lower earnings of Black men compared with White men (Woody, 1992).

Actually, as with the social and economic conditions for African Americans in the United States, the work participation of Black women have their roots in Africa. "Leadership in the community and in the home, prominence in the world of work, independence and pride in womanhood are usually pointed to as evidence of the strength of African American women" (N. J. Burgess, 1994, p. 397). The phenomenon of Black women in the world of work represents continuity with African traditions where women did take on the roles of farmers, craftswomen, and entrepreneurs.

By 1992, however, the rate of Black women's participation in the labor force (58.0%) was identical to that for White women (57.8%). Two reasons appear for the closing of the gap between White and Black women's participation in the paid labor force. One is the increasing numbers of White married women entering the labor force, while the other is the higher **unemployment** rates of Black women who would like to be

TABLE 6.1 Civilian Labor Force Participation Rates by Race, Hispanic Origin, and Sex

	1970 (%)	1980 (%)	1992 (%)
White			
Female	42.6	51.2	57.8
Male	80.0	78.2	76.4
Black			
Female	49.5	53.1	58.0
Male	76.5	70.3	69.7
Hispanic			
Female	N/A	47.4	52.6
Male	N/A	81.4	80.5

Note: Persons of Hispanic origin may be of any race

Source: Abstracted from U.S. Bureau of the Census (1994). *Statistical Abstract of the United States 1994,* Washington, DC: U.S. Government Printing Office.

employed. In 1993, the unemployment rate was 12.0% for Black women compared with only 5.7% for White women (U. S. Bureau of the Census, 1994).

> Unemployment is an extremely serious problem among black women and has reached particularly high, even crisis, levels among teenagers and young adults. While the unemployment problem and the problem of underemployment among black women have taken a back seat to those problems of males, the accelerated rate of women heading black families indicates that a far more serious look is appropriate. (Woody, 1992, p. 49)

Ironically, it is Black single women for whom unemployment and **underemployment** (only part-time or employment below the level of job skills) rates are the highest. Black married women with a husband present had lower unemployment rates in 1991 (6.1%) as compared with Black female head of households (11.5%) (U.S. Department of Labor, 1991).

Although Hispanic women currently have lower labor force participation rates than White or Black women, hispanic women will be an increasing proportion of the U.S. labor market.

Hispanic women, in 1992, had a lower labor force participation rate than White or Black women in contrast to Hispanic men who had the highest rate of any racial-ethnic group of men. Hispanic women represent several different ethnic groups, all of which were influenced by Spanish settlers and are Spanish speaking. Hispanics are a rapidly growing segment of the U.S. population, who by 1988 represented 8% of the population. They come from Mexico, Puerto Rico, Cuba, Central and South America and Spain. Mexican Americans, also called Chicanos-Chicanas, are the largest group, accounting for 62% of the Hispanic population in the United States. People from Puerto Rico represent 13% of all Hispanics, those from Central and South America 12%, Cubans 5%, and people from Spain or whose families have been here for generations representing about 8% (Bonilla-Santiago, 1990).

Hispanic women will continue to be an increasing proportion of the U.S. labor market because of their relatively young average age compared with the rest of the U.S. female population and because of high fertility and immigration rates. Mexican American women had average annual earnings in 1987 of $7,912, which was considerably lower than that of Cuban-born women, who were the highest earners among Hispanic women ($11,327 per year). Cuban-born women are as likely to be professionals or managers (27%) as non-Hispanic women workers (26%), and much more likely than Hispanic women workers in general (16%) (Bonilla-Santiago, 1990). Improvements in the occupational and socioeconomic condition of Hispanic women is most likely to occur with increased educational and vocational opportunities as well as the lifting of barriers to **discrimination** in employment.

Native American women have a low rate of labor force participation. Historically, and currently, Native American women have played an important role in their society.

The participation of Native American women in the labor force rose from 35% in 1970 to 48%

in 1980. Those who did hold full-time year-round jobs earned nearly 89% of the earnings of White women. Since the 1950s Native Americans have been split between living in urban areas and on reservations. Employment rates and incomes are higher in urban areas.

> Relocated urban women were in the lead of economic and cultural reorganization in the new, multination urban communities. They formed craft circles, building on their traditional arts of quilting, beading, and making ceremonial garb; held fairs to sell their work; and used the money earned to fund American Indian centers and to ship the bodies of their dead home for burial. (Amott & Matthaei, 1991, p. 51)

Many Native Americans, however, return to the reservations and their extended families and their cultures. American Indian women have historically occupied an important role in their society. In 1980, about 70 chiefs or chairs of the 482 federally recognized Indian nations were women.

Age, Marital Status, Children, and Employment

Unlike men, the more children a woman has, the less time she spends in the labor force. Married women with a young child are more likely to be in the paid labor force than single mothers.

The gap in labor force participation rates peak during the child-bearing and child-rearing years of ages 20–44, but labor force participation converges considerably for men and women over 45 (primarily due to a decline in men in the labor force after age 44). The age group in which the highest percentage of women participate in the labor force is 35–44 years. The labor force participation rate is highest for never-married women (U.S. Bureau of the Census, 1994).

The more children men have, the more time they spend in paid employment; the reverse is true for women. This gap in paid employment, however, has been narrowing. In 1975, women with no children spent 77.2% as much time in paid labor as did men, whereas in 1987 women with no children spent 85.4% as much time as men in paid labor. In 1975, women having two or more children spent 67.4% as much time as men in paid labor, but that had increased to 75.5% as much time in 1987 (Shelton, 1992).

A more surprising finding is that married women (59.6%) with young children under six were more likely to be in the paid labor force in 1993 than were single women (47.4%) with that age children. Black married women (70.9%) with a child under six were much more likely to be in the paid labor force than were White married women (58.6%) with that young of a child (U.S. Bureau of the Census, 1994). College-educated women return to work sooner after childbirth than women with less than a high school education. Among college-educated women 72% were in the labor force in June 1992 who had given birth in the previous year as compared with only 30% for mothers who had less than a high school education (U.S. Bureau of the Census, 1993, August) (see Figure 6.1). These differences could possibly be due to greater job commitment and greater financial resources to obtain childcare of college-educated women. Women increasingly find it necessary to pay someone to care for their children when they are at work, and childcare costs keep rising. The percentage of family income spent on childcare when the mother works is obviously higher the lower the family income (U.S. Bureau of the Census, 1992, November).

Women with college degrees are two-and-a-half times as likely to be employed as women with less than a high school education.

Women's labor force participation rate differs drastically by educational status, much more so than does men's. In 1993, only 28.3% of women with less than a high school education were in the labor force, whereas 74.9% of women who were college graduates were in the labor force. For men the gap is narrower in labor force participation rates for those who dropped out of high school (52.8%) as compared with those who have

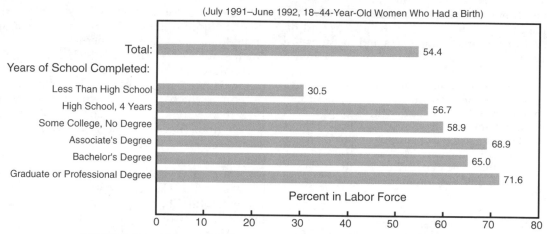

Women Who Have Had a Child in the Last Year and Their
Percentage in the Labor Force by Educational Attainment.

(July 1991–June 1992, 18–44-Year-Old Women Who Had a Birth)

FIGURE 6.1   Educated Mothers Return to Work Sooner. *Source:* U.S.
Bureau of the Census, (August, 1993) *Census and You 28* (8), Washington, DC:
U.S. Government Printing Office.

a bachelor's degree (86.3%) (U. S. Bureau of the Census, 1994).

Part-Time Employment

Women are overrepresented in part-time employment. Two-thirds of Native American women who are employed hold part-time jobs.

There are differences that are obscured by the data on labor force participation rates, however, because the labor force includes part-time as well as full-time employees, and women are more overrepresented in **part-time employment**. In 1987, of those in the paid labor force, 84.2% of men were employed full-time as compared with 69.3% of women.

Part-time employment is an important part of the contemporary labor force. Many workers hold part-time jobs because they cannot find full-time jobs. In February 1991, the number of persons working part-time for economic reasons, sometimes called the underemployed, increased to 6.1 million (U.S. Department of Labor, 1991, March). Among Native American women work-

ers, nearly two-thirds of these women were in part-time jobs in 1980 (Amott & Matthaei, 1991).

In a vignette study, judgments made about the sex role (in) appropriateness of an occupational role showed that both full- and part-time jobs are rated as more suitable for a male or a female applicant according to the traditional patterns of employment for the occupations (Ward, 1991). For example, men were rated as more suitable applicants for the jobs of plumber, bus driver, and cabinet maker, whereas women were rated as more suitable for jobs such as secretary and telephone operator.

WOMEN'S INCOME

Education and Income

The higher the education level, the higher the income.

The single most important determinant of income in U.S. society is education. In the spring of 1990, the average monthly earnings for adults

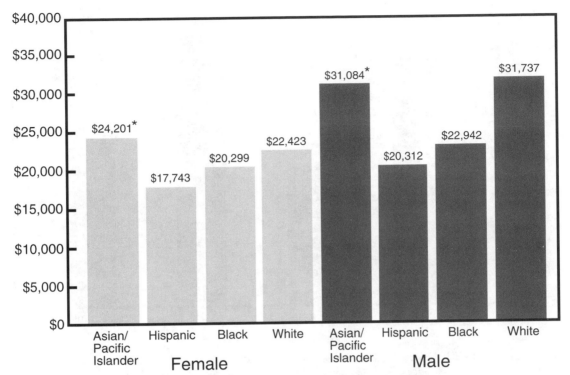

FIGURE 6.2   Median Annual Income of Year-Round Full-Time Workers by Race and Hispanic Origin, 1992. *Source:* Abstracted from Statistical Abstract of the United States: 1994, U.S. Bureau of the Census (1994). Washington, DC: U.S. Government Printing Office. *Current Population Survey Data, March 1993. Unpublished, U.S. Bureau of the Census.

who were holders of professional degrees was $4,961 as compared with $492 for adults without a high school diploma. For individual's whose highest degree is a bachelor's, income varies with major. The male dominant fields of engineering and mathematics/statistics have the highest average monthly salaries ($2,953 and $2,569 respectively), whereas the females dominate field of home economics is the least well paid ($906) (U.S. Bureau of the Census, 1993, April).

The Gender Gap in Pay

In 1992, full-time working women earned 71.5 cents for every dollar earned by full-time working men.

Since 1978, the **gender gap in pay** has narrowed. The weekly wage and salary earnings of full-time working White women was 60.8% of the earnings of White males in 1967, and were still the same in 1977, 60.6%. By 1992, the gender gap had decreased, however, and the median annual income of White full-time working women was 70.7% of the income of White full-time working men. The gap has also narrowed for Black women, who were earning 70% of what Black men were earning in 1967, and by 1992 were earning 88.5% of what Black men earned. Hispanic women earned 87.4% of what Hispanic men earned in 1992. If earnings of White men are used as the standard, however, then in 1992 Black women earned only 64.0% of what White men did, and

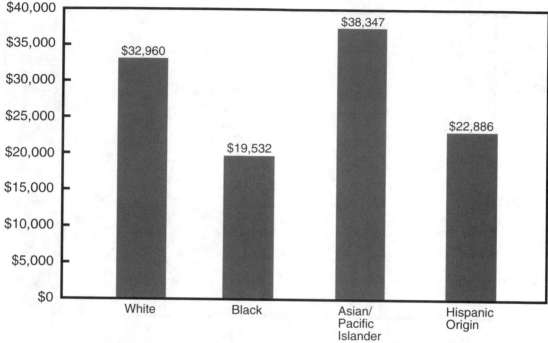

FIGURE 6.3 Median Household Income by Race and Ethnicity of Householder, 1993. *Source:* U.S. Bureau of the Census (1994, November) *Census and You, 29,* (11). Washington, DC: Government Printing Office.

Hispanic women earned only slightly more than half (55.9%) of what White men earned. Based on median income of full-time workers in the United States, in 1992 women earned 71.5% of what men earned (England, 1992; U.S. Bureau of the Census, 1994).

Income of Hispanic Women

Low educational level and discrimination has placed Hispanic women in the lowest occupational and income level of any racial-ethnic group of women.

Both low educational level and discrimination in the labor market has led to Chicanas having the lowest income levels for any racial-ethnic group in the United States. Although the proportion in the labor force continued to grow in the 1980s, they are still concentrated in seasonal and low-paid jobs. It is the legacy of child labor and disruption of schooling brought about by migrant farm work (Amott & Matthaei, 1991).

Selective migration from Puerto Rico has led to lower educational and income level of Puerto Rican women workers on the mainland than in Puerto Rico. The increasing number of single-mother Puerto Rican families has contributed to low average income levels for Puerto Rican women (Amott & Matthaei, 1991).

Income of African American Women

Recent Black women college graduates earn more than White women who are recent college graduates.

A college education has an increasingly important effect on the income of Black women. Black women who have been out of college from one to five years earned more in 1991 than White women or Black men who were recent college graduates. "The median income for college graduates age 25 and younger was about $18,000 for white men, $17,000 for black women, $16,000 for white women and $16,400 for black men" (Roberts, 1994, p. 15). The income of Black women overall was 90% of that of White women in 1991, ($18,720 for Black women and $20,790 for White women) (U.S. Bureau of the Census, 1994).

Income of Asian American Women

High educational achievements have led to business and professional success for Asian American women. Newer immigrants such as Vietnamese and Hmong, however, struggle economically.

The Asian American population was about 3% of the total U.S. population in 1988. It includes peoples who themselves or whose ancestors came from China, Japan, the Philippines, Vietnam, Cambodia, Korea, Thailand, India, Pakistan, Bangladesh, Laos, Malaysia, Burma, Indonesia, and other smaller countries. The three largest groups in the United States are, in descending order of population, the Chinese, the Filipinas/Filipinos, and the Japanese (Amott & Matthaei, 1991).

Asian American women have a bipolar distribution of income, with groups such as Chinese and Japanese American among the most successful of American business and professional women and others such as the Vietnamese and Hmong struggling at the bottom of the economic hierarchy. Although Asian American households have the highest median income of any racial-ethnic group, the "model minority" is a myth when applied to all Asians. It has a double-edged quality that masks the persistence of poverty, sexploitation, and anti-Asian discrimination in American society (Amott & Matthaei, 1991). Asian and Pacific Islander families immigrating since 1980,

were three times as likely to be below the poverty level in 1990 as those who immigrated prior to 1980 (21% versus 7%) (U.S. Bureau of the Census, 1994, February).

A phenomena leading to occupational success in American society for Asian women as well as men has been the high educational achievements of Asian Americans (see Chapter III). The traditional emphasis on male education has been transformed among Asian American groups to include females as well. As a result, a higher percentage of Chinese American women hold college degrees than do White women, and the median earnings of employed Chinese American women is greater than the earnings for White women (Amott & Matthaei, 1991).

Like Chinese American women, Japanese American women are better educated than European American women, and, in substantial percentages, have progressed to jobs in the managerial and professional tiers; however, they also earn less than comparably educated White women. Both Chinese and Japanese American women have earnings far less than those of the men in their ethnic groups. Overall, Asian/Pacific Islander American women still receive less monetary return for their education than do White women (see Figure 6.2).

OCCUPATIONAL GENDER SEGREGATION

Female Occupations

Occupational gender segregation still exists. One-third of women are in six occupations. The "women's" professions of nursing and teaching have less autonomy than other professions.

One of the reasons for the lower wages of women is sex segregation of the workforce and that women in "women's jobs" earn less than men in "men's jobs." Despite some decline in **occupational gender segregation** between 1900 and 1970, and a more rapid decline during the 1970s, women still tend to be concentrated in "female" occupations. Elementary school teaching was still

90.3% female and nursing 89.7% female in 1990 (U.S. Department of Labor, 1990). The professions of teaching and nursing have long been considered the top of the female employment hierarchy. Nevertheless, they lack the autonomy of male-dominated occupations. "Unlike doctors and lawyers, teachers and nurses have no control over accreditation, do not set their own fees, have little latitude in how they do their work, and are closely supervised" (Ferree, 1987). The pay is also lower. The sex division of labor occurs in both the private (home) and public (paid employment) spheres of life.

> The sex division of labor results from a gender hierarchy in which women work longer hours for less money. The clearest expression of this is the uncounted, unpriced, and unpaid housework assigned to women in both capitalist and socialist economies. This unequal exchange is also apparent in the wage gap; women working in jobs of comparable worth earn significantly less than men. (Ciancanelli & Berch, 1987, p. 246)

In 1989, the six most prevalent occupations for women were secretaries, schoolteachers (excluding college teachers), semi-skilled machine operators, managers and administrators, retail and personal sales workers, and bookkeepers and accounting clerks (U.S. Department of Labor, 1990).

Theories of Gender Segregation

Four theories have been proposed to account for gender segregation in American society: gender role socialization; human capital; discrimination; and structured mobility ladders.

Four major theories of the causes of gender segregation have been proposed: gender role socialization; human capital; discrimination; and structured mobility ladders (England & McCreary, 1987). Theories that explain how differential gender role socialization of males and females occurs were described in Chapter IV. Some feminists criticize explaining gender segregation by gender socialization as tantamount to "blaming the victim." In support of socialization

theory, aspirations can be limited by expectations of what positions will be open to women. As was explored in Chapter III, J. S. Eccles (1987) model proposes that career choice is mediated by values and expectancy for rewards and costs. Undergraduate male and female students, who rated 18 job characteristics in terms of importance for career selection, demonstrated a gender difference in occupational values (Bridges, 1989). One of the most important characteristics for career selection of the women was helping others through one's career. This value can help explain the concentration of women workers in service occupations such as nursing, teaching, and social work. Job scheduling factors are also more important to young women than they are to young men.

In comparison to males, females also rated personal rewards, job availability, job security, ease of reentry to the profession, and sex discrimination as important factors for career selection. More surprising, however, were the findings that there were no gender differences in the rating of the importance of salary or in occupational prestige ratings. Also unexpected was the finding that more females than males rated same-sex appropriateness of occupation as important.

Some of the factors rated as important by college students may not be as important at different stages of a woman's life. A young woman, Cindy, whom I have known since she was in college, told me that she took a job in college teaching this year at less than half the salary she had been making in industry. Cindy has a Ph.D. in chemistry, but is married and wants to start a family and she believes college teaching would allow more time at home.

Economic theory of human capital looks at people as investments. Human capital can appreciate through educational investment or on-the-job training, but it can also depreciate through nonuse, such as when a woman stays out of the labor force to be a full-time homemaker. A woman who stays out of the labor force may have to take a lower job when she returns than she had before. Research nevertheless shows that male jobs generally pay more at every level of education and experience than do female jobs, indicating that the same investment pays bigger dividends for men than for women. Women's concentration in lower-paying jobs cannot be accounted for by differences in education and experience. For example, in 1989 the earnings ratio of women to men for selected occupations was: engineers—85.7%; psychologists—83.1%; computer programmers—83.1%; elementary teachers—90.3%; nursing aides, orderlies—82.7%; bus drivers—82.5%; general office clerks—91.6% (U.S. Department of Labor, 1990).

Discrimination in hiring, placement, and promotion of women is another explanation for gender segregation. The numerous class action lawsuits that have been won by women attest to the persistence of discrimination as an important cause of women's lower wages. Sex discrimination in the workplace is a way of preserving the status quo in society. The traditional norms of society are internalized by both men and women. As a result, many women accept the situation and tend to minimize the inequities in the workplace.

Structured mobility ladders in internal labor markets can explain the persistence of segregation. There are often "male ladders" and "female ladders" within companies. The female ladders are typically shorter, so that there is less increase of status and earnings over time for females than for males (England & McCreary, 1987).

Occupational desegregation, however, may not always be the positive step that it appears to be for women, since the more females in an occupation the lower the average wage (Reskin, 1988). The occupation may then become resegregated as a female occupation. One example of this is the occupation of bank telling which was predominantly male before World War II, and paid well relative to similar occupations. By 1981 the occupation was 94% female. The prestige and wages of bank telling, and opportunities to advance declined as the number of women in the occupation increased.

Pink Collar Jobs

More women work in clerical occupations than any other job category. These are stressful jobs with limited upward mobility. Pink collar jobs also include low paying service jobs.

Most women are in clerical or low-skilled service work, low paid **pink collar jobs**. Pink collar jobs do not require any college or professional training and are characterized by a high degree of sex segregation, and low pay. Jobs such as waitress and clerical worker are pink collar jobs. Clerical work is now divided and specialized into many different types of positions, ranging from a secretary with an individual boss to a woman seated in front of a computer terminal all day. More women are employed as clerical workers than they are in any other occupational category (Ferree, 1987). In 1990, approximately 15 million women, 28% of the female labor force, were in clerical and administrative support jobs (Gwartney-Gibbs & Lach, 1994).

In general, the clean office environment tends to disguise just how stressful and unpleasant most clerical jobs are. . . . The Framingham Heart Study found the highest levels of stress and stress-related heart disease among workers who had more than one person making work demands on them and little control over the pacing of their own work, both of which were seen as characteristic of clerical work. (Ferree, 1987, p. 230)

The resolution of *personality conflicts,* which is a term women clerical workers tend to use to describe conflicts over how tasks should be accomplished as well as interpersonal and emotional issues, are often a cause of emotional stress for women or of lateral transfers that reduces their human capital. In comparison, a study of men and women clerical workers in two companies found men clerical workers to openly challenge their supervisors or ignore the personality conflicts (Gwartney-Gibbs & Lach, 1994). Women clerical workers were found to be unlikely to use formal, dispute resolution forums. "To improve productivity and efficiency, unions and employers need to acknowledge the emotional aspect of workplaces. The emotional experiences of workers must be heard, contextualized, and affirmed as real" Gwartney-Gibbs & Lach, 1994, p. 635).

I think that another approach to improving the job climate for clerical workers would be to design training opportunities and career ladders. That would reduce feelings of powerlessness and provide opportunities for increased income. The upward mobility opportunities of clerical work have been substantially reduced in the computerized office as compared with the past, where clerical work provided some opportunity to advance to lower professional jobs.

Women's Representation in Male Dominated Blue Collar Jobs

The percentage of women in male-dominated blue collar jobs is low. Women are underrepresented in the better paid trades.

There has been a gradual entrance of women into male-dominated blue-collar jobs. One reason that more women are entering these jobs is because of **affirmative action** agreements between the federal government and private employers. A second reason is that, in general, such jobs pay more money and have better benefits, job security, training, and promotional opportunities than do female-dominated jobs (Palmer & Lee, 1990).

Despite the gains, the proportions of women in these fields remains low. For example, in 1988 only 8.7% of all craft, repair, and precision production workers were women. Women have gained larger numbers among bus drivers (48.5% in 1988), but many women are part-time bus drivers for school districts, whereas men are more often in better paying jobs as city bus drivers (England & McCreary, 1987; Palmer & Lee, 1990). In better-paying trades (e.g., the nation's construction trades), there has been very little change, with women holding just under 3% of these jobs in 1990; similarly, in the field of auto body repair, just over 4% of the jobs were held by women (D. Cohn & Vobejda, 1992).

Women's Treatment in Male Dominate Blue Collar Jobs

Women in male-dominate blue collar jobs are treated more negatively by male co-workers who also frequently sexually harass them. Women earn more money in male-dominated blue collar jobs, but have higher levels of satisfaction in pink collar jobs.

Women in male-dominated blue-collar jobs frequently face differential treatment and sexual harassment. In a study of 327 male co-workers and 53 supervisors of women employees of maintenance, utilities, transportation, and materials departments in male-dominated blue collar civilian jobs with the navy, men were less likely to predict that women would develop into good workers with training and work experience (Palmer & Lee, 1990). Men objected to working shift work with women and to working irregular hours with them. Men were significantly less likely to ask a female co-worker as compared with a male co-worker to help with hazardous duties and to lift a 40–50-pound object. They did give the edge to women over men in knowing when to ask for more information about a task and in ability to identify the tools needed to do a job. The male supervisors, however, held significantly more positive attitudes toward the female employees than did the male co-workers. Both the male co-workers and supervisors who had previous experience working with women held more favorable attitudes toward them.

Women make more money in male-dominated blue-collar occupations, but face more **sexual harassment** and have lower job satisfaction (P. K. Mansfield et al., 1991). Comparisons among 151 female city transit workers, 71 skilled tradeswomen, and 389 school secretaries found salary level to be much higher for the male-dominated occupations than for the secretarial jobs. The secretaries were much more likely to be married (83%) as compared with the transit workers (42%) and the tradeswomen (30%) and also more likely to have children. Half of the tradeswomen

Focus on Women   No Liberation in Sight for Blue-Collar Women

Did the women's movement leave us behind? Although there are more opportunities than ever before for women today, most of the focus is on young, upwardly mobile middle- or upper-class women.

We read many profiles of the harried young attorney or emergency room physician, but rarely do we hear of an overworked waitress or factory worker. While it is undeniably more glamorous to don a power suit than polyester, the fact remains that more women than ever before are stuck in low-paying dead-end jobs.

What is particularly ironic is that in the earliest days of the women's movement, the chief focus was on improving the plight of the female workers who toiled in the factories and sweatshops of our cities. Somehow, somewhere, we got lost in the shuffle. The very women who stood to gain the most, the women who desperately needed support, never quite latched on to the coattails of the current movement.

During the early '70s, at the height of the modern women's movement, I was a young divorced mother struggling to support a child on income earned from cleaning two houses a day. In the evening my friends and I would read *Ms.* or *New Woman* magazine and say, "What are they complaining about?" All the women featured had what we considered to be clean, easy, well-paying jobs. More than twenty years later, things haven't changed all that much.

The average woman today, working long hours in a factory, nursing home or service-related job, has a problem identifying with the woman who is college-educated and moving up the corporate ladder.

A woman is hardly liberated when she must work two jobs just to get by. Many of the entry-level positions open to blue-collar women do not even offer health insurance, a truly frightening situation when you consider that a lot of young women today are the sole providers for their children, as well as themselves.

As women near retirement age the picture grows even bleaker. After a lifetime of struggling, many older women face their so-called golden years trying to subsist on near poverty-level incomes.

While no one wants to see a return to the days when educational and career opportunities were the sole province of men, the fact remains that economically, many of us may as well be back in the '50s.

Perhaps the fault lies with all of us. We, as a society, do not place much value on menial labor. On the other side of the coin, a woman who has put in 8 (or 10) hours a day on the assembly line or passing out the bedpans is going to be less than enthusiastic about getting involved in any extracurricular activity, including the women's movement.

More attention must be paid to the fact that if we are to end discrimination in the workplace, we must start at the bottom rung of the ladder and work our way up, not the other way around, as has been the problem for all too long. Only then can we hope to achieve true equality for all women.

Serena Caswell-Patterson
Pawtucket, Rhode Island

---

were both unmarried and without children. The transit workers and the tradeswomen were more often single parents than were the secretaries.

The tradeswomen suffered significantly more sexual harassment (60%) and sex discrimination (55.7%) than either transit (36.2% and 38.3%, respectively) or clerical workers (6.4% and 8.1%, respectively). In all of the occupations, Blacks reported more sexual harassment and sex discrimination than did their White counterparts; they also reported more race discrimination.

The secretaries described their day-to-day jobs significantly more positively than either the transit workers or the tradeswomen:

> Cleaner, safer, more control over their work area, more interesting, more smoke free. Their supervisors were significantly more likely to give clear instructions, give helpful feedback, and seek their ideas; their co-workers were significantly more responsible, supportive, friendly, caring, and willing to listen than co-workers in the TM groups. (P. K. Mansfield et al., 1991 p. 73)

The secretaries scored significantly higher on satisfaction on all items except those relating to salary and opportunities for promotion in which they were less satisfied than the transit workers, but not the tradeswomen. Tradeswomen were particularly negative about their supervisors being sexist, unfair, and critical. Their co-workers were also characterized in very negative terms (lazy, disrespectful, prejudiced, sexist).

WOMEN IN THE PROFESSIONS

Women with college, graduate, and professional degrees are entering male-dominated professions in large numbers. Women have different career patterns from men in these professions.

Unlike women in pink collar occupations who are mired at the bottom of the job market, American women with college degrees made great strides in the professions during the last couple of decades. "The most lucrative occupations for women in 1990 were lawyers, physicians, engineers, computer systems analysts and scientists, college and university teachers, marketing, advertising and public relations managers, natural scientists and registered nurses" (U.S. Department of Labor, July, 1991). In fact, in 1993 more women were in professional specialties than were men (53.2% of professional specialists) (U.S. Bureau of the Census, 1994).

Physicians

One-third of medical school graduates are women. Women choose different specialties and are less likely than men to be in private practice. Women physicians have lower average incomes than male physicians.

Women are a rapidly growing proportion of the medical profession. For 50 years, until 1960, only 5% of medical school graduates were women. The feminist movement and antidiscrimination legislation brought an increasing number of women to medical school and into the profession. By 1985, 31% of medical school graduates and 15% of the physician population were women; by 1990, 21% of physicians were women. Female physicians, however, choose different specialties. Most female physicians were found in the specialties of (in descending order) internal medicine, pediatrics, psychiatry, family practice, and obstetrics-gynecology. Only 5% of female residents were training in surgery in 1985, although it was the second-most-common discipline for men. Females are also proportionately more likely than men to specialize in pediatrics (Bickel, 1990; Foreman, 1993).

Female physicians are less likely to be in private practice than are male physicians. Although 80% of men were in private practice in 1986, only 50% of women were self employed. Women are more likely to be found in health maintenance organizations and institutional settings. Although women settle more in urban areas, male physicians have higher average incomes than do female physicians. In part, the income differential is due to the fact that male physicians work more hours per week (58.2 hours per week for men and 52.2 hours per week for women), men earn more per hour, men spend less time per patient, and men see 15% more patients per week than do female physicians. Women physicians are underrepresented in positions of power in the profession. They are less likely to be board certified and to hold leadership positions in medical institutions or associations (Bickel, 1990; Foreman, 1993).

Lawyers

Dramatic increases have occurred since 1970 in the numbers of women attending law school. The legal profession, however is still stratified by gender.

In 1971, only 9% of law students in law schools approved by the American Bar Association (ABA) were women. Since 1987, women have comprised over 40% of students in ABA-approved schools of law. In 1993, 22.9% of lawyers in the United States were women (U.S. Bureau of the Census, 1994). Research on the entry of women into occupational settings indicates that structural settings of dominants and tokens influences three perceptual tendencies associated with being in the minority: visibility, polarization, and stereotyping (Kanter, 1977). Research on a randomly selected sample of male (48) and female (64) attorneys in Pima County, Arizona, where females were only 15% of practicing attorneys at the time of the survey, supported Kanter's thesis of tokenism (MacCorquodale & Jensen, 1993). Any visibility women may have by being in the minority did not work to their advantage in the courtroom or judge's chambers, where none of the attorneys reported women attorneys getting more attention and credibility, but 38% of female attorneys felt more attention and credibility was given to male attorneys. Interactions based on stereotypes were documented by female attorneys who reported receiving more compliments from male attorneys based on their appearance than on their handling of a case and legal reputation. Patronizing behavior by judges and attorneys toward female attorneys were reported by a number of the women in the sample. Sexist jokes and remarks are a means of polarizing gender divisions. The women attorneys reported hearing sexist jokes and remarks more frequently than did the men.

Evidence continues to show that the legal profession still tends to be stratified by gender. Women in law firms are less likely to become partners during their careers, to earn two-thirds the income of men, to have little decision-making power in law firms, and to be in lower-income specialties in private practice. Based on a survey of women attorneys ($N = 220$) in a midwestern state capital city, more women felt that gender had benefitted them in recruitment (27.1%) and hiring (35.0%) than had hurt them (20.5% and 20.0%, respectively) (J. Rosenberg, Perlstadt, & Phillips, 1993). When it came to on-the-job situations such as salary and promotion, however, women reported discrimination.

Overall, 40.8% of the women lawyers said they had been discriminated against in salary, 32.8% in promotion, and from 25.5% to 34.9% in various activities such as legal assignments. In addition, disparagement was common. "Approxi-

mately two-thirds of our respondents reported being addressed as 'honey' or 'dear' and being the butt of remarks emphasizing gender and sexuality ('nice to have a pretty face') in professional situations." (J. Rosenberg, et al., 1993, p. 422). Disparagement was more commonly directed at women under 35 (75%) than at older women (55%). Virtually all women under 35 working in private settings were targets of disparagement as compared with two-thirds of women in public settings and one-third of women in court settings. In addition, one-fourth of the lawyers reported being sexually harassed in a professional situation, by other lawyers (45%), clients (31.3%), judges (17.6%) or other legal personnel. Harassment was less-frequently directed at women with a feminist orientation as compared with women with other orientations. Sexism in the legal profession varies with the structure of the workplace and the perceived vulnerability of the woman attorney.

Engineers

Women in the male-dominated field of engineering are less likely to be married and have families, and more likely to be divorced than the men in the field. The parents and spouses of women engineers are more likely to be employed in professional careers.

Do women in male-dominated professions have it all? A national survey of engineers (the National Engineering Career Development Study) found women engineers to be less likely to be married and to have children than the men (Jagacinski, 1987). The divorce rate was very low for the men (5% or less separated or divorced per age group), but much higher for the women, 16% and 20% for the 10–15 and 16–20 years postdegree groups, respectively. Fathers and mothers of women engineers were more likely to be employed in professional positions than parents of male engineers. Similarly, husbands of women engineers were more likely to have completed college and to be professionally employed than were wives of male engineers. In fact, a majority of the women were married to engineers (53%) compared with only 3% of the men who married engineers. While the majority of women did not decide to become engineers until they were in college, the majority of men had made that decision in high school. The starting salaries for the younger women and men were the same, but the starting salaries had been higher for men among those who had graduated 10–20 years prior to the survey. In both their starting jobs and in their current positions, men reported more supervisory responsibilities than did women. Although the salaries were not different for men and women who had their degrees for zero to five years, as time from degree increased, salary differentials between men and women increased. Women more strongly endorsed the existence of opportunities for women in engineering than did men. The women in all of the different experience groups and the men who had received their degrees 16–20 years previously believed engineering to offer more opportunities to men than to women. Based on this research, it appears that women engineers do not have the same career advancement opportunities as do men in that field.

Analysis of questionnaire data from a matched sample of 51 male–female pairs of engineers reveals the women to have higher self-confidence and to attribute less importance to having a job that allows them to develop their technical expertise (Bailyn, 1994). For the men, success in all aspects of their lives is positively correlated: perceived success at work; perceived success outside of work; self-confidence; and importance of opportunity to develop technical expertise. For the women, there is a more-conflicted pattern, particularly for women in strictly technical jobs rather than in managerial positions. "For them self-confidence is most strongly correlated with perceived success in their lives *outside* of work, and is *negatively* correlated with the importance attached to the opportunity to develop technical expertise" (Bailyn, 1994, p. 304). It seems that this reflects ambivilence about technical competence that our society defines as "gender alien" for women.

Psychologists

Psychology is no longer a male-dominated field, but women earn less money and have different career experiences.

Increasing numbers of women have been entering the field of psychology. Female psychologists have different experiences throughout their careers (A. G. Cohen & Gutek, 1991). A random sample survey of the combined memberships of Divisions 9 (Society for the Psychological Study of Social Issues) and 35 (Psychology of Women) found that men earned more money from their current job in psychology than did women, and that they also had higher total personal annual incomes from all sources. When total family income for the sample subjects' spouses or significant others was included, however, there was no difference between the sexes (probably because wives of male respondents earn less than husbands of female respondents). A much higher percentage of men than women were currently married (80.7% vs. 55.7%), which is consistent with findings from other professions and business. The male psychologists published more papers in graduate school and throughout their academic careers. The men received more help from graduate faculty in finding jobs (60.5% of men compared with 49.6% of women). Men were also more likely to report having a role model while in graduate school (70.5% to 65.1%) and to have developed personal relationships with faculty (79.0% to 65.1%). Men were also more likely to have moved to go to graduate school and to have made more moves since receiving their Ph.D.s. Therefore, women's experiences differ from men's even when they are in the same career field.

Ethnicity/race also substantially influences professional experiences and advancement in psychology (Wyche & Graves, 1992). In 1980–1989 there were 1,780 full-time women faculty in psychology departments in academia, of which 191 (9%) were minority-status women (African, Asian, Hispanic, and Native American). European American men held most of the full-time faculty positions in psychology (N = 5,295), whereas only 259 (4.9%) of these men were minority.

Representation on editorial boards of journals published by the American Psychological Association (APA) also has an important influence on the field. By 1990, women were 23% of editors/associate editors and 25% of consulting editors of APA journals. Estimates from an APA member's survey indicates that about 20% of minority women served as consultants or reviewers on journals.

> Although the number of women Ph.D.-level psychologists has increased, they are less likely to be represented among the faculty at 4-year colleges, among the ranks of tenured faculty, on editorial boards, and in other positions of power within the field of psychology. Women who are members of racial/ethnic groups are even less likely to be represented in these areas. (Wyche & Graves, 1992, p. 434)

It is necessary to combat discriminatory practices in hiring, promotion, and tenure of women, particularly minority women in academic psychology. To do this may require social psychological intervention that breaks down stereotypes that prevent White men and women from mentoring, hiring, and promoting minority women.

Women Educational Administration

Women are very underrepresented in administrative positions in elementary, secondary, and higher education, which is due to situational rather than personality variables.

Despite the fact that most elementary school teachers are women, men greatly outnumber women in the policymaking positions in elementary education. Research by Erinakes (1980) sought to determine why women are so underrepresented as elementary school principals. In the year in which she conducted her study in Rhode Island, 1979–1980 academic year, there were 244 (85%) men and only 42 (15%) women serving as elementary school principals. A comparison of 158 women elementary school teachers who had been teaching for at least 10 years with women elementary school principals found principals to have less-traditional attitudes toward the role of women in society and a more-internal locus of control as compared with teachers. Those characteristics, however, were found to be low discriminators. Women principals were significantly more likely to indicate having a mentor than were teachers. Principals were less likely to be married, although those who were married were more likely to have husbands who had graduate or professional degrees than did teachers. Unlike research on women managers, the women principals were more likely to be youngest children and to have older brothers than were teachers.

As recently as 1971, there were few women in higher education administration. Of 1,500 persons who were presidents of four-year colleges and universities at that time, there were 95 women. Of these 84 were nuns and two were ex-nuns, leaving only nine other presidents (Chamberlain, 1988). In 1975–1976, the first national survey of employment and salary of women and minorities in higher education (including two year institutions) conducted by the College and University Personnel Association (CUPA) collected data on 18,035 administrators in first-line primary administrative positions. It was found that women held 16% of administrative positions, including 2% that were held by minority women. Women were paid about 80% of what men were paid in the same type of institution. A decade later CUPA conducted the 1985–1986 Administrative Compensation Survey. Of a total of 38,085 primary positions reported on, 28% were held by women, which showed a gain over the previous decade. Salary gaps, however, were shown to widen between men and women during that decade, with women's salaries approximately 43% lower in the mid-1980s than men's salaries, whereas in the mid-1970s salaries of women were 20% lower than those of men in similar positions. One reason given for this gap is that women are more likely to hold positions in lower-ranking and lower-paying institutions than men. Length of time in the position was not found to be a cause of the salary differential. It appears that men are often brought into administrative positions at salaries higher than that of women in those positions.

Female Faculty

Women faculty used to be discriminated against by nepotism rules. Now they are discriminated against by nontenure line part-time appointments.

When I began my doctoral work at the University of Oklahoma I had an assistantship with Muzafer Sherif, Professor of Psychology, on campus at the Institute of Group Relations. His research associate at the Institute was his wife, Carolyn Sherif, who had a Ph.D. from the University of Texas and was his coauthor on much of his research and writing. Carolyn Sherif, however, was unable to obtain a faculty position at the university except for a one year temporary position, because of nepotism rules, which prevented married couples from both being faculty members. Rules such as these kept many capable and qualified women from achieving faculty positions at many universities and shunted them into research associate positions that did not lead to any kind of promotion or tenure.

The rapid growth of women attending college and graduate and professional schools has not been matched by increasing numbers of women faculty. For example, in psychology, during the 1988–1989 academic year, there were 5,295 male faculty members, of which 259 (4.9%) were minority men. At the same time, there were 1,780 full-time women faculty, of which 161 (9%) were minority women. The number of minority women currently holding tenured psychology faculty positions is disproportionately small. During the 1980s, minority women represented only 4% of tenured faculty in psychology departments, although 8% of doctorates were awarded to minority women during this period (Wyche & Graves, 1992).

Although most colleges and universities no longer have nepotism rules, results from the 1987 National Survey of Postsecondary Faculty by the U.S. Department of Education reveal a large increase in part-time and even full-time non-tenure-track faculty appointments (Farrell, 1992). Between 40 and 45% of all nontenure-track appointments are filled by women.

Almost 17 percent of the total faculty in the prestigious research universities are part-timers. At doctoral and comprehensive universities combined, the percentage of part-time faculty goes up to 26.4%; at comprehensive institutions alone, part-time faculty constitute 29.8 percent of the entire faculty. At liberal arts colleges, the part-time figure rises to 32.6 percent. At the two-year institutions, the percentage of part-time faculty reaches 52.1 percent of the total faculty. (Farrell, 1992, p. 41)

While the growth of women in tenure-track faculty positions has been slow, increasing from 18.3 to 20.8% between 1975 and 1985, the percentage of women in non-tenure-track positions rose from 33.6 to 40.3% during that time. Women in the survey in both tenure- and nontenure-track positions were less satisfied than men with their perceptions of opportunities to advance (38% and 51% respectively). There is little basis for hope among nontenure-track faculty that their attainments and abilities will result in ever obtaining a tenure-track position or, for that matter, even a full-time position. Since salaries are significantly lower for part-time and other nontenure-track faculty, many of them teach at more than one institution in order to maintain a living wage. A woman Ph.D. teaching part-time at our college this year also teaches part-time at two other colleges and holds a part-time clerical position at a bank as well in order to make ends meet. This further undermines her ability to do research and writing that might improve her prospects for full-time tenure-track appointments.

Even though women are more likely than men to choose a path in academic medicine, they are promoted more slowly and given tenure less frequently. By the 1986–1987 academic year, fewer than 5% of medical school department chairs, 1.6% of medical school deans, 9.6% of associate deans, and 20% of assistant deans were women.

Similarly, women are still rare in top academic posts in the field of economics. "The glass ceiling for women in economics is rather thick: only a handful are tenured professors at the nation's top-ranked universities." (Uchitelle, 1993, p. A 10). At universities with the top 30 graduate economics programs, only 3.3% of tenured professors are women and 96.7% are men. During the past decade 22% of Ph.D. degrees in economics have gone to women and 20% of assistant professors at the 80 universities with graduate departments of economics are women, but only 8% are associate professors and less than 4% are tenured full professors at these schools.

Women in Science

Women have had to face many discriminatory barriers in science. Female scientists publish fewer but higher quality publications than male scientists.

It is not surprising that few women have achieved eminence in science, given the discriminatory barriers women have had to face in science. When they do achieve scientific breakthroughs, the credit is often not given to them. A glaring example of a woman's contribution being invisible is the lack of notice by the scientific community given to the role played by Rosalind Franklin in the discovery of the structure of the genetic molecule DNA (Sayre, 1978).

There is an immense variation in the productivity of scientists. As a group, female scientists have lower average productivity than male scientists. A multidimensional exploration of the differences in productivity of biochemists looked at the population of males and females who received Ph.D.s in biochemistry during selected years in the 1950s and 1960s (J. S. Long, 1992). Sex differences in productivity began in graduate school and continued during the 17 years of the follow-up period. In addition to frequency of publication and number of collaborators, the impact of the journals in which articles were published was also taken into account, as well as citations of the articles by other authors. Women publish fewer articles, particularly during their first postdoctoral decade, and increase their productivity during their second postdoctoral decade, while that of men levels off. The lower productivity of females is primarily due to the greater proportion of females who do not publish at all. It is interesting that throughout their careers, the articles published by females receive a greater number of citations per article in the work of other authors than do articles published by males. The number of citations is typically used as a measure of quality of research, indicating a higher level of quality of the women's publications.

It is necessary, however, to examine the kinds of barriers female scientists have had to overcome in order to publish at all. An excellent first-person account of some of the barriers faced by women in the sciences is given in a book chapter by Naomi Weisstein, an experimental psychologist doing research in vision. On her first day in graduate school at Harvard, one of the star professors announced: "Women don't belong in graduate school." After receiving her Ph.D., doing a year of postdoctoral research, and being promised an instructorship, she was informed 10 days before the start of the semester that she would not get the position because of nepotism rules that prevented her appointment because her husband had a faculty position in another department at the university. Instead, she was shunted into a lectureship, the rules of which forbade her from applying for research grants. Finally, she was able to overcome this barrier, too. This did not occur in the nineteenth century, but during the 1960s (Weisstein, 1979).

A colleague of mine in the biology department of the college in which I teach recounted to me how he came face to face with discrimination against women in science. He and a female colleague submitted a research article to a scientific journal for review for publication. His colleague was first author. The rejection of the article came back with the most scathing comments that he had ever received on any article he had submitted for publication—and he thought this was the highest-quality research and writing he had ever done. He could not understand the rejection until he attended a workshop sponsored by the American Federation of Teachers on sex discrimination in science. It dawned on him that this was the only article he coauthored with a female, who also happened to be first author of this article. The journal did not use blind review (in which the names of the authors would be removed before being sent out for review). This anecdote perhaps gives us an explanation of why females publish fewer articles in science, but why those that they do publish are of higher quality than those published by men.

WOMEN MANAGERS

The Glass Ceiling

There is a "glass ceiling" in corporate America that is a barrier to women reaching the highest levels of corporate officership.

As judged by their numbers in high-level management positions, there is considerable evidence that women do encounter a "glass ceiling" in corporate America.

A Korn/Ferry International (1982) survey reported that only 2% of 1,362 senior executives were women. A study of the Fortune 500, the Fortune Service 500, and the 190 largest health care organizations in the United States (Van Glinow & Krzyczkowska-Mercer, 1988) similarly found that only 3.6% of board directorships and 1.7% of corporate officerships in the Fortune 500 were held by women; the Fortune Service 500 and the health industry indicated that 4.4% of board members were women and that 3.8% and 8.5% of their corporate officers, respectively, were women. (A. M. Morrison & Von Glinow, 1990, p. 200)

Other data indicates an exodus of women from management due to differential treatment. Studies indicate that there are substantial pay differentials between men and women in management (Drazin & Auster, 1987). Women in executive, administrative and managerial positions had median weekly earnings in 1993 of $528 compared with median weekly earnings of $791 for men in

those positions (U.S. Bureau of the Census, 1994). In 1990, women made up only 3% of managers at the nation's 1,000 largest companies, and only two women were CEOs of these 1,000 largest public corporations (Schmittroth, 1991).

It is surprising, however, that an analysis of actual promotions to top managment positions for U.S. federal government Senior Executive Service positions in a cabinet—level department found that gender worked to women's advantage (Powell & Butterfield, 1994). The greatest influence on promotion decisions, however, was already being employed in the hiring department. Men were 88% of the total applicants.

Three theories explain the sexual and racial differences in management: deficiency theory; discrimination; and structural barriers.

The three general theories used to explain the sexual and racial differences within management are almost identical to the theories used to explain gender segregation, although the emphasis there was a little broader to include why women entered certain occupations and not others. The first set of theories postulates that deficiencies within the underrepresented groups themselves account for their disadvantaged position. The second set of theories cites discrimination on the part of White men as the cause of differential treatment. The third group of theories pinpoints structural barriers within organizations rather than individual behavior as the cause of the perpetuation of discrimination toward women and people of color (A. M. Morrison & Von Glinow, 1990).

Psychological Theories

Psychological theories explaining why men and women differ are addressed elsewhere in this book, but they have also been used to explain women's lack of progress in organizational hierarchies. "The person-centered explanations for the gender gap focus on factors internal to women and attribute those factors to causes such as gender-differentiated socialization practices (Hennig & Jardin, 1977), different early ways of constructing reality (Gilligan, 1982), and early gender identity formation (Chodorow, 1978; 1989)" (Hood & Koberg, 1994). We have also examined the fear of success literature and saw that overall women and men do not differ in fear of success, which discredited this as an explanation for women's current status in organizations. The psychological deficiency argument has not been supported by research.

Women have a lesser sense of personal entitlement than do men.

Research support is found for gender differences in pay allocation and also for gender differences in pay expectations. **Personal entitlement** is the sense of how much one should be paid in a particular job (Major, 1987). In laboratory experiments, women typically work longer, do more work, and work more accurately and efficiently than do men for the same pay (Major, McFarlin & Gagnon, 1984). Women allocate less pay to themselves for performing a task than do men, even when the outcomes of others are unaffected (Major & Deaux, 1982) and have expectations for less pay (Major, 1987).

After being informed of average salaries of previous graduates, men and women college seniors majoring in business administration were asked to estimate how much they themselves expected to be paid in their first job after graduation. Women expected to earn significantly less ($16,607) than did men (18,203) (B. A. Martin, 1989). Similarly, Major and Konar (1984) found women to expect lower career-entry starting salaries than did men.

Women workers are systematically paid less than men, even after being matched on occupational prestige, seniority, and other job-related dimensions (Crosby, 1982). It is surprising that women do not see themselves as victims of pay discrimination and do not differ from men in reported job satisfaction even though they perceive that other women are paid unfairly. As a result, women tend to be contented workers. Crosby (1982), however, found that women were unhappy about the underpayment of women in gen-

eral, but were contented with their own pay even though this represented underpayment.

In order to test reasons for women's lower sense of personal entitlement, Blysma and Major (1992) "examined whether social comparisons and performance feedback affected judgments of fairness and satisfaction indirectly via their effects on perceived entitlement or whether these factions affected judgments of fairness and satisfaction directly" (p. 195). Students read a scenario about a student hired to perform data-entry work for a professor during summer vacation. When students were not given either comparison information or performance feedback, men felt entitled to a significantly higher hourly wage than women. When the same comparison information about the hourly rate others were being paid or the same performance feedback was given, gender differences in personal entitlement were eliminated.

Performance and social comparison are independent determinants of personal entitlement. Women in the workforce are less likely than are men to indicate dissatisfaction with their pay (Jackson, 1989) and more likely to use other women as a comparison group for salary equity. Occupational gender segregation promotes lower personal entitlement of women because they are exposed to lower-waged women, and not men, who earn more. This finding is consistent with social comparison theory, which says that people generally compare themselves with similar others.

Male and female managers are very similar on many personality measures. Vocational interest patterns show some similarities but also differences between men and women.

Gender differences on paper-and-pencil personality tests and interest surveys of 100 women and 270 men who were engaged in a job search program revealed these middle- and upper-level-management men and women to be very similar on many measures including nurturance, succorance, and aggressiveness (Hatcher, 1991). On the Jackson Personality Research Form-E, men tested higher in physical risk, and women tested as more autonomous, more sentient, and more understanding (a scale measuring academic and abstract interests—a need to know). Further analysis revealed that these differences were due to gender rather than to other variables such as age, salary level, job tenure, and education.

On the Strong Campbell Interest Inventory, both men and women ranked the Enterprise theme as their primary area of occupational interest. Women's second occupational interest was Artistic, however, which was ranked last by men. Men ranked Conventional as their second preferred theme, which women ranked third. Men ranked Realistic as their third area of interest, which women ranked last. The women in this sample are not typical of women in general, as indicated by the differences between their responses on the measuring scales and the scores for women on the published normative data. To become a corporate manager in the 1990s is still a conforming role for men and a nonconforming role for women. It may be the traits of risk taking and independence that facilitate the decision to become a female manager. In conclusion, it does not appear that personality differences between men and women managers can account for the gender gap at higher levels in the organization.

Discrimination

Taller people achieve higher positions in the organization. Men have the advantage of being taller on average than women.

One of the physical deficiencies that women have is that generally they are shorter than men. Yes, I am writing this with a straight face. A number of studies have found a positive correlation between height or perceived height of men and the impression they make in job interviews (Hensley & Cooper, 1987), the starting salary of MBAs (Deck, 1968), and the prestige of their occupations (Morrow, 1984). Egoff and Corder (1991) evaluated the height of female and male corporate employees to see if height differentiated those of higher job status from those of lower. Two studies, one conducted with employees of a Fortune 500 company and the other with employees in a nonprofit, nonuniversity corporation, found that for both women and men, managers (high-status employees) are on average taller than same-sex nonmanagers (low status employees).

When women managers behave in a competent, expert, and task-oriented manner they are evaluated more negatively than men who exhibit the same behaviors.

The fact that discrimination toward women exists in large corporations is evident from the data indicating that women are well represented in managerial levels at smaller companies and nonprofit organizations. In 1993 42.0% of all civilian executive, administrative, and managerial positions were held by women (U.S. Bureau of the Census, 1994).

Discrimination against women as a reason for their not being more highly evaluated and promoted in corporate careers can be explained in part by expectation states theory (Berger, Fisek, Norman, & Zelditch, 1977). This theory was described in Chapter V as an explanation for gender differences in social behavior. In order to determine if the different relative status of the sexes in corporations is the result of differential evaluations of male and female managers, Wiley and Eskilson (1982) had 96 experienced managers evaluate the performance of a stimulus person in a script who is trying to persuade another person in the corporation (position unspecified) to adopt a specific plan of action. The male influencers were judged to hold higher positions in the corporation than the female influencers, and were seen as more powerful, particularly when influencing another male. Female influencers, when successful, were perceived as much colder than men, and created a less-positive impression. Persons influencing males were perceived as more competent, rational, and proper than persons influencing women. Females were evaluated more favorably, as more effective and active, when they use reward-based influence attempts rather than expert-based influence. Conversely, males were seen as more effective and active when they use expert-based rather than reward-based techniques.

> The differential expectations of men and women performing identical assertive roles result in less positive evaluations of women than men. This implies that attempts to reduce bias by training women to employ a "masculine interaction style will not reduce unequal evaluations." (Wiley & Eskilson, 1982, p. 8)

In fact, the case of Ann Hopkins, which went all the way to the United States Supreme Court, is a good example of how a corporation treated a woman whose style and behavior were characterized as masculine.

Ann Hopkins was a top performer at one of the nations leading accounting and consulting firms, Price Waterhouse (PW). In 1982, a year in which she had brought in $25 million worth of business to the firm, she was the only woman of 88 candidates proposed for partner. She did not make partner that year, and she was not proposed for partner the following year.

> According to some evaluators, this "lady partner candidate" was "macho," she "overcompensated for being a woman," and she needed a "course at charm school." A sympathetic colleague advised that she would improve her chances if she could "walk more femininely, talk more femininely, dress more femininely, wear make-up, have her hair styled, and wear jewelry." (Fiske, Bersoff, Borgida, Deaux & Heilman, 1991, p. 1050)

Although Ann Hopkins possessed the "competency cluster" of traits considered desirable in males and in managers and was considered hard-working and effective, she was negatively evaluated because her behavior was considered inappropriate for women. Ann Hopkins filed a complaint in district court alleging a violation of Title VII of the 1964 Civil Rights Act. Price Waterhouse v. Hopkins (1989) was the first Supreme Court case to use psychological research about sex stereotyping. The APA submitted an *amicus curiae* (friend of the court) brief to the Supreme Court that informed the Court of the

scientific validity of the sex stereotyping literature on which psychologist Susan T. Fiske's expert testimony in support of Hopkins was based. APA helped to establish that sex stereotyping was a form of sex discrimination. On May 1, 1989, the Supreme Court handed down a decision favorable to Hopkins declaring that it is not permissible for employers to use discriminatory criteria for promotion. However, the Court also said that PW had been held to too high a standard of proof, that their decision would have been the same if no impermissible discrimination had taken place. The case was remanded to district court Judge Gerhard Gesell to review the facts and to see whether PW could win under a less-stringent standard of proof. In his May 1990 ruling, Judge Gesell ruled that sex stereotyping played a role in the refusal of PW to make Ann Hopkins a partner. After being employed elsewhere for several years while her case was resolved by the courts, Ann Hopkins is once again in the employ of PW, now as a partner (Fiske et al., 1991).

The way that women's performances are evaluated by society also leads to discrimination in salary, hiring, and promotion.

> Women's performances are frequently regarded as less competent than identical performances by men (Deaux, 1976; Nieva & Gutek, 1981); successful performances by women often are attributed to external or unstable causes such as luck or temporary effort (Hansen & O'Leary, 1985); and a task or job labeled "feminine" is often seen as requiring less effort and ability, and as worth less, than an identical job given a masculine label (McArthur & Obrant, 1986; Deaux, 1984). (Major, 1989, p. 109)

As we saw in Chapter IV, not all of these biases are consistently found. To the extent that they operate, they can lead to women's work as being seen by persons in decision-making positions in the workforce as deserving of lower wages than men's.

Bias in hiring and promotion may involve a complex interaction of both person and situational factors. Research has shown implicit (without the person's awareness) gender stereotyping to influence evaluations of men and women even when they were performing identical behaviors (Banaji, Hardin, & Rothman, 1993). Implicit sterotyping may undermine the equality of treatment of diverse groups of individuals in the workplace.

Stereotypes of managers are similar to stereotypes of men. The form of address, Ms., evokes male images of competency and leadership.

Research in the 1970s found a link between the stereotypes of managers and the stereotypes of men. The characteristics used to describe men were also the characteristics used to describe managers (Schein, 1973, 1975). Research by Dion and Schuller (1990) found little difference in descriptions for a male stimulus person and a female with the title of Ms. rather than Miss or Mrs. The images evoked were of leadership and competency, and the typical male stereotype. The Ms. stimulus person, however, was perceived as less warm and likeable than a woman with a traditional title (Miss, Mrs.) or than a man. She was also evaluated as more masculine than the traditional woman, but less masculine than a man. Women managers may want to use the title Ms. to evoke a more leaderlike and competent image, but socially perhaps, use Miss or Mrs.

Structural Barriers

Business organizations are dominated by a White male culture in which women and minorities may be acculturated but not assimilated. Feminism challenges the impersonality and hierarchical relations of bureaucracies.

In the section on gender segregation, it was pointed out that structured mobility ladders favor White men. Women and minorities are more likely to be in staff positions such as personnel that are less likely to be ladders to top management. Historically, business organizations have been dominated by a White male culture (Hood & Koberg, 1994). Although minority members may become acculturated (adopting the dominant culture's patterns of behavior) they still might not be assimilated (fully accepted into the

cliques and social networks). "Evidently the issue is not women's actual leadership behavior or deservingness, but the willingness of the 'corporate tribe' to accept women as equal members of the group (Symons, 1986)" (Hood & Koberg, 1994, p. 166). Women and Blacks and other minorities may be excluded from informal relationships related to career success. Not knowing what is going on in the organization is a disadvantage of being excluded from the network. Cross-sex mentor relationships may be more difficult to manage because of sexual innuendo and, in the case of Black women, taboos of race as well (A. M. Morrison & Von Glinow, 1994).

Finally, feminism provides a critique of organizational bureaucracy and hierarchy. "The personal is political" ideology of the feminist movement challenges the impersonality and hierarchical power relations of bureaucratic norms and procedures. The goal of feminism is to create humane, egalitarian, and diverse workplaces. It involves the challenge of "reconceiving personnel as persons." (Morgen, 1994)

REPRODUCTIVE HAZARDS

Feminists and unions have argued that women of childbearing age should not be prohibited from working in certain areas considered hazardous. The United States Supreme Court agreed.

Early in the twentieth century, labor legislation was passed that mandated special treatment for women, limited hours, lifting, and night work, and even prohibited them from certain professions.

This legislation ameliorated the conditions under which women worked, but it also effectively limited women's opportunities and classified them as marginal workers. Because the legislation was designed to protect white, native-born women, it further marginalized racial-ethnic women such as African-American, Chinese-American, and Mexican-American women "who experienced the oppressions of a patriarchal society but were denied the protections and buffering of a patriarchal family (Dill, 1988, p. 418). (Baber & Allen, 1992, p. 191)

Concern over **reproductive hazards in the workplace** are relatively new. Prior to 1970, only seven studies were conducted on the topic (M. Rose, 1988). That is not because heavy manufacturing with its attendant chemical processes were a "safe" environment for women of reproductive age. Actually, the belief has been that as the economy turned toward "cleaner" information and service industries, jobs would become reproductively safer for women. Studies in high-tech industries, however, raise the specter of serious reproductive hazards from occupational exposures.

Lawsuits brought by women who worked on the semiconductor production lines at GTE Corporation claiming that exposure to job-site chemicals caused miscarriages, uncontrolled bleeding requiring hysterectomies, and children born mentally retarded and with learning disabilities, brought public attention to the problem. Corporations, particularly, begin to take notice when University of Massachusetts researchers released a study in 1986 that reported higher than normal miscarriage rates for women who worked on Digital Equipment Corporation's (DEC), Hudson, Massachusetts, chip production line. Both DEC and IBM responded by encouraging women of child-bearing age to transfer off the chip production line. AT&T went a step further by prohibiting women of child-bearing age from working in its "clean rooms"—those sterile rooms where workers manufacture computer chips. Labor unions and women's groups were concerned, however, that women may be excluded from jobs and promotions thorough this policy. Instead, they advocated a policy that would make the workplace safe for all of the workers (M. Rose, 1988).

A lawsuit was filed by the United Auto Workers (UAW) against the Johnson Controls Company of Milwaukee for excluding women of child-bearing age from certain areas where automobile batteries are manufactured because of exposure to airborne lead. The UAW charged that the policy constituted illegal sex discrimination under Title VII of the Civil Rights Act of 1964. Feminists and the union argued that the workplace should be made safe for all employees, and

that women of child-bearing age should not be segregated from other workers. In 1991, the Supreme Court ruled that barring women of child-bearing age from certain hazardous jobs violates antidiscrimination law (Baber & Allen, 1992). The arguments were within the legal framework of the Pregnancy Discrimination Act (PDA) of 1978. "The PDA extends the 1964 Civil Rights Act to cover discrimination on the basis of pregnancy and specifically mandates that employers treat pregnant workers the same as other workers who are comparably able or unable to work" (Vogel, 1990, p. 14).

AFFIRMATIVE ACTION AND COMPARABLE WORTH

Affirmative Action

Affirmative action prohibits discrimination in selection, promotion, and other personnel matters.

The Equal Pay Act of 1963 mandates equal pay for equal work and Title VII of the Civil Rights Act of 1964 prohibits discrimination in selection, promotion, and other personnel decisions based on race, religion, national origin, and sex. In addition, in 1965, President Johnson signed Executive Order 11246 requiring federal contractors to take affirmative action to ensure equal and fair access to employment and career opportunities. The purpose of affirmative action is to make up for past discrimination by increasing employment opportunities (Crosby & Clayton, 1990; Summers, 1991). Although women are still very underrepresented at the highest levels of management and academia, affirmative action policies have served to open the doors of management and the academy to women.

On a warm spring day in 1963 I walked into the personnel office of a Fortune 500 company in Oklahoma City. I had a master's degree and had experience for over a year as an Assistant Survey Director at Opinion Research Corporation in New Jersey. I had answered an ad for a management trainee position. The man who interviewed me looked at my resume and said, "You're too well educated to be a secretary and we don't hire women for management training positions. Goodbye." My husband had lost his job and we had two small children. It was at that point, that I decided to go into a doctoral program to prepare for a career teaching college, where I believed there would not be discrimination in hiring. Although it was not to impact on my career, little did I realize that discrimination in hiring and promotion of women was also a problem in academic settings. It was brought to my attention here in Rhode Island, where I have had a long academic career on the faculty of Rhode Island College, by separate, successful class action lawsuits against Brown University and the University of Rhode Island for sexist discrimination in hiring, tenure, and promotion decisions.

The goal of affirmative action, of removing racial and sexual discrimination in the workplace, is widely approved of by the American people. Many Americans, however, criticize affirmative action methods and programs. For example, Tougas and Veilleux (1989) found that both men and women view preferential treatment as unfair. An examination of the effects of sex-based selection procedures that impacted on their careers in field settings for 188 men and women MBAs, indicated that both men and women had more favorable job attitudes when their sex was preferentially treated (Graves & Powell, 1994). Increasing affirmative action led to more positive attitudes, greater organizational commitment and intent to remain for women, and somewhat more negative job attitudes for men.

Crosby and Clayton (1990) emphasize the necessity for organizations to educate about the nature and extent of race and sex bias and the dimensions of prejudice and discrimination. It can help to reduce the tendency to categorize and stereotype individuals based on race, ethnicity, or sex. "Only when the continuing extent of problems of sexism and racism becomes obvious does the pressing need for viable solutions become totally clear" (Crosby & Clayton, 1990, p. 74).

TARGET HIRING

Target hiring by gender is not a quota. When targets are in place, qualified women are no longer overlooked.

Minas (1993) supports gender targets in hiring, particularly at universities. It is not a quota. **Target hiring** is "setting in place goals of hiring certain percentages of women over a specified time, with the aim of increasing the numbers of women in certain positions" (Minas, 1993, p. 117). A gender target does not mean that a woman should be hired even if she is less qualified. If a target is not met, however, it requires an explanation in terms of recruitment qualifications of candidates and the judgment procedures used in selection. Minas argues that gender targets do provide maximum weight to the best qualified candidate because women who were previously neglected in hiring practices will then receive adequate consideration of their qualifications.

COMPARABLE WORTH

The concept of comparable worth is that employers should be required to pay workers in female-dominated occupations such as secretaries equal salaries to workers in male-dominated occupations such as maintenance workers.

Equal pay for equal work has been federal law since 1963, when Congress approved the Equal Pay Act as an amendment to the Fair Labor Standards Act. Nevertheless, women concentrated in female-dominated occupations earn less than men concentrated in male-dominated occupations (E. F. Paul, 1993). The concept of **comparable worth** is that employers should be required to pay workers in female-dominated occupations such as secretaries equal salaries to workers in male-dominated occupations such as maintenance workers, when these occupations are of comparable value to the organization. Comparable worth refers both to a theory that cites discrimination as a cause of the pay differential between males and females and a compensation policy that seeks to eliminate the pay disparities (S. H. Taylor, 1989).

> "Comparable" means that jobs are judged to be similar, based on composite ratings of requirements such as skill, effort, responsibility, or other factors valued by the organization. The comparable worth standard does not require that comparison jobs be equivalent in terms of individual factors or actual task content, thus distinguishing it from the "equal work" standard implied by the Equal Pay Act of 1963. (S. H. Taylor, 1989, pp. 24–25)

Kim (1989) analyzed the wage structure of the California State Civil Service, finding that the salaries established in the 1930s were explicitly lower in female-dominated jobs. The relative wage structure has been maintained, although the Civil Rights Act of 1964 outlawed underpaying female-dominated jobs. As a result, workers in female-dominated jobs have lost considerable amounts of money during the period since the 1930s. "Even if this agency did not deliberately discriminate after 1931, workers in female-dominated jobs collectively lost between $202–990 million in the period between 1973 to 1986, due to its policy of perpetuating the 1931 wage structure" (Kim, 1989, p. 48). Thus, one factor in the gender wage gap is due to practices established several decades ago that have not been challenged and changed.

ENTREPRENEURIAL WOMEN

> *Nearly one-third of businesses in the United States are owned by women. Female businesses are increasing at twice the rate of male businesses. Female businesses hire more women than do firms owned by men.*

Women in the United States have been making up for lost time by going into business for themselves at record rates. Before 1970, only 5% of businesses were owned by women. By the beginning of 1992, it stood at 30%. There are about 4.3 million businesses owned by women ("Women-owned businesses," 1992). In the 1990s female businesses are increasing at twice the rate of male-owned firms (P. L. Smith, Smits, & Hoy, 1992). Although most of these businesses are concentrated in stereotypically feminine fields such as retail trade and services, females have also emerged as owners of firms in male-dominated industries such as mining, construction, and manufacturing businesses. Opportunities for women business owners were enhanced by the Women's Business Ownership Act of 1988, which authorized $10 million over a three-year period for private organizations to provide expertise to women business owners in a variety of areas such as marketing and technical assistance (Facts on Working Women, 1989).

A comparison of 42 firms that were female owned and managed with 45 firms that were male owned and managed in three industries (construction, manufacturing, and wholesale distribution) found male and female business owners to be very similar in personality, obtaining similar nurturance and dominance scores. Both men and women entrepreneurs gave independence, autonomy, and personal fulfillment as the leading reasons for forming and operating their own businesses. Men were more likely to have completed college (89%) than the women (41%) and to be currently married (86% vs. 59%). Although firms owned by women were in operation significantly less time than those owned by men, there was no difference in the size of the firms operated by men and women. The female-owned firms hired significantly more female employees proportionately than did male owners. Female-owned businesses offer a road to greater independence and autonomy for women.

SEXUAL HARASSMENT

> *In 1980, the EEOC issued legal guidelines on sexual harassment in the workplace. Sexual harassment is unwelcome sexual advances, requests for sexual favors, and other verbal or physical conduct of a sexual nature.*

In the mid-1970s sexual harassment became defined as a social issue when the feminist movement labeled this previously unnamed problem of unwanted sexual attention in the workplace (M. B. Brewer & Berk, 1982; Livingston, 1982). The legal guidelines did not become established until 1980 when the Equal Employment Opportunity Commission (EEOC) issued Guidelines on Sexual Harassment in the Workplace based on Title VII of the Civil Rights Act of 1964 (Dzeich & Weiner, 1984). According to the EEOC sexual harassment involves "unwelcome sexual advances, requests for sexual favors, and other verbal or physical conduct of a sexual nature." Evidence accumulated over the past 15 years has shown sexual harassment to be a pervasive problem at work and in academic settings.

Sexual harassment did not really come to the forefront of public consciousness until October 1991, when the Senate Judiciary Committee conducted hearings for the confirmation of Clarence Thomas as an Associate Justice of the United States Supreme Court. Professor Anita F. Hill, of the University of Oklahoma Law School, testified that Judge Thomas had sexually harassed her when she worked with him at the Education Department of the federal government, and later, when he headed the EEOC and she worked for him as an attorney.

After three days of graphic televised public testimony by Professor Hill before the Senate Judiciary Committee, and denials by Judge Thomas, a poll reported in the New York Times showed that more than twice as many of the public (58%) believed Judge Thomas's account as believed Professor Hill (24%) (Kolbert, 1991). Professor Hill faced tough questioning as a result of coming forward with her charges, and her truthfulness, character, and even sanity were questioned by Republican Senators. Her very treatment by the Senate Judiciary Committee stands as testament as to why more women do not come forward with sexual harassment charges. When she returned to Oklahoma, Professor Hill summed up her feelings as follows:

It was suggested that I had fantasies, that I was a spurned woman and that I had a martyr complex,

. . . I will not dignify those theories except to assure you that I did not imagine the conduct to which I testified. I have been deeply hurt and offended by the nature of the attacks on my character. (A. Rosenthal, 1991, A-1)

She also went on to say that she hoped her experience would not stop other women from coming forward when they had been sexually harassed.

By a vote of 52 to 48 Judge Thomas's nomination to the United States Supreme Court was approved by the Senate. As happens in many sexual harassment and even rape cases, the man is believed, not the woman who accuses him. Her motives are suspect, and her character is derogated.

Anita Hill's televised testimony about sexual harassment, however, did raise the nation's consciousness. Reports indicate that sexual harassment complaints at the EEOC increased significantly between the last quarter of 1990 and the last quarter of 1992 (Sexual Harassment Claims on the Rise, 1993).

Four out of 10 women who work for the federal government are sexually harassed on the job within a two-year period.

Women are much more frequently the target of sexual harassment than are men. The U.S. Merit Systems Protection Board conducted a survey of federal employees in 1981, finding that 42% of the women and 15% of the men reported experiencing sexual harassment during the previous 24 months (Tangri, Burt & Johnson, 1982). An update of this survey in 1988 found the same percentage of women (42%) reporting that they had experienced unwanted and uninvited sexual attention. Ninety-five percent of the women and 22% of the men were harassed by men. Single women (53%) are most likely to be harassed, followed by divorced (39%), married (37%), and widowed women (31%). Both men and women report that their harasser has also harassed other victims. Most workers are harassed by co-workers (65% for female victims, 76% for males). Women are also much more likely to be harassed by supervisors (37%) than are men (14%). Sexual harassment also reinforces women's economic vulnerability by providing a barrier to women's economic independence (B. E. Schneider, 1982).

Sexual harassment is a fact of campus life that for too long has been kept quiet.

High rates of sexual harassment have also been found in educational institutions. A sexual insult, defined as "uninvited sexually suggestive, obscene or offensive remark, stare, or gesture," was reported as having occurred on campus by 40% of female respondents and 17% of male respondents who were part of a sample of 900 men and women at the University of Rhode Island (Lott, Reilly, & Howard, 1982).

A book that served to bring the problem of sexual harassment on campus to the attention of the general public was *The Lecherous Professor* (1984), by Billie Wright Dzeich and Linda Weiner. In this book they cite both numerous court cases and case studies of sexual harassment. They say that sexual harassment on campus of students by professors is a fact of campus life that has long been ignored and met with silence. If an incident was too bizarre, the faculty member may have been quietly asked to depart.

Faculty, as well, have tended to say nothing about sexual harassment that they might face. In one case, a female faculty member finally reported to the Dean that a professor who was charged by three students with second degree sexual assault in the mid-1980s had raped her in her office after an evening class 12 years earlier. She had not at the time said anything to anyone. The behavior of the perpetrator of sexual harassment is typically repetitive and the harassment has occurred many times before someone brings charges.

On campus, harassers are male professors. Most students do not report it.

Who is the harasser and why does he(she) harass? The harasser is likely to be male, in a position of authority over a female victim who is younger and in a subordinate status. Although male victimization does occur, it is much less frequent than female victimization. Both male and female students have rarely been subjected to sexual harassment by females. Although students who respond to vignette situations about sexual harassment say they would be likely to report it, most students do not report the incidents, particularly the less severe forms of sexual harassment (L. J. Rubin & Borgers, 1990).

Self-reports of sexually harassing behaviors of 235 male professors at a prestigious research-oriented university indicated that more than one-quarter of the professors admitted having sexual encounters or relationships with students (Fitzgerald & Weitzman, 1990). Over 25% of these men reported that they had dated students enrolled at their university. Nevertheless, only one of the professors believed he had ever sexually harassed a student.

In contrast to their male colleagues, only 7% of the 79 women faculty responding to the questionnaire reported dating a student, and even fewer reported having had a sexual encounter with a student. Thus, although the female professors held the same power as their male colleagues, it was a very rare occurrence for one to become sexually involved with a student, while one in four of the male professors did so.

There are a number of dimensions to the professor's power over students. Some of the power is real and concrete such as giving grades and writing recommendations for graduate school, jobs, and awards. The power, however, is also more ephemeral and illusive, such as the power gained by superior knowledge and wisdom, and the power gained over the minds of students by the expectation that the professor nurture the student's capacity to think and to mature intellectually and aesthetically (Zalk, 1990).

The American Psychological Association sent an anonymous survey to female members of their clinical psychology division asking about sexual intimacy with and sexual advances from psychology educators (Glaser & Thorpe, 1986). Thirty-one percent of the women reported sexual advances not leading to sexual contact, and 17% had sexual contact with at least one psychology educator during graduate training. Although at the time of the sexual contact, only 28% experienced it as coercive to some extent, 51% at the time of the study said their perception now is that it was a coercive relationship. Similarly, 36% felt it was ethically wrong when the relationship took place, whereas, 55% at the time of the survey saw an ethical problem with it.

Sexual harassment can be particularly damaging for women who have been previously sexually victimized or for lesbian women, and for women of color.

Sexual harassment can have damaging effects on both the individual and the organization, such as increased stress for the individual and lost productivity and increased turnover for the organization. For some women, sexual harassment is a replay of incestuous relations with their fathers, to which they were forced to submit as children. For such women the incident(s) may prove particularly traumatic.

Another group of women for whom sexual harassment may be perceived as particularly oppressive is lesbian women. B. E. Schneider (1982) surveyed lesbian and heterosexual women working mostly in professional or managerial level positions in human services, health, or educational fields finding a high percentage of both lesbian (82%) and heterosexual women (69%) reported experiencing one or more incidents (requests for dates, jokes about body or appearance, pinches or grabs, and sexual propositions) in the preceding year. The less serious behaviors are more frequently reported. Co-workers and recipients of services are the most frequent offenders. Lesbian women who are closed about their sexual identity reported more incidents than those who are open about it. Heterosexual women who are single, separated, or divorced also reported more of these incidents than married women. Lesbians were more likely than heterosexuals to apply the label "sexual harassment" to these incidents.

DeFour (1990) points out that in most of the studies the researchers have not asked for respondents to indicate their race or ethnicity. The result is that we do not have an accurate estima-

tion of the level of victimization of women of color. Women of color may be more vulnerable to harassment, however, because of having fewer financial resources and being more likely than White women to be in untenured academic positions or lower-level corporate positions, where they are supervised by male bosses. The stereotypes about women of color that describe them as hot-blooded (Hispanic women), or as highly sexed with low morals (Black women), or as exotic and submissive (Asian women) make them more likely targets of sexual harassment.

Men and women have differing ideas about what constitutes sexual harassment—and some men (mis)interpret friendly behavior by women as sexual interest.

Numerous studies have found gender differences in perceptions of what constitutes sexual harassment, and in the frequency that it occurs in the workplace (B. J. Benson & Thomson, 1982; Gutek & Morasch, 1982). In one study, women and men who were enrolled in a junior-level management course completed an anonymous questionnaire that included 18 scenarios depicting potentially sexually harassing situations (D. D. Baker, Terpstra, & Larntz, 1990). Sex of the respondent strongly affected reactions to eight of the scenes of sexual harassment, with a disproportionately high percentage of women indicating that they would report an incident to someone internal or external to the organization, or that they would physically or verbally react to the scenarios. The gender difference found for the eight scenarios may indicate that men and women have differing ideas about what constitutes appropriate sociosexual behavior in the workplace. Organizations may need to provide training sessions illustrating a range of sexually harassing behaviors and the negative reactions individuals are likely to have to them. (D. D. Baker et al., 1990).

Gender differences are also apparent in whether more responsibility for the sexual harassment is assigned to the woman who is being harassed or to the man who harasses her. Among men and women who were part of a representative sample of workers in Los Angeles County, men were more likely to assign responsibility to the women for sexual harassment (I. W. Jensen & Gutek, 1982). One of the questions asked was, "When a woman is asked by a man at work to engage in sexual relations, it's usually because she did something to bring it about." Significantly more males (54.5%) than females (44.7%) agreed with the statement.

Among women, women who themselves have not been victims of harassment and women who hold more traditional sex role attitudes are more likely to blame the woman for the harassment. Follow-up interviews with women who had been harassed show that 20–30% engaged in self-blame. Women with traditional sex role attitudes were more likely to blame themselves, and to feel anger and disgust about the incident than other victims who did not report self-blame. They were less likely to report it or tell anyone about it, but they were also more likely to have concern about protecting the harasser than victims not engaging in self-blame.

Both laboratory experiments and retrospective reports of naturally occurring incidents reveal that men perceive other people and relationships in a more sexualized manner than do women (Abbey, 1982, 1987; Shotland & Craig, 1988). After watching a videotaped role-played episode of the first meeting of two male and female students, men perceived both the male and female role players to show a greater degree of sexual interest than did the women observers (Shotland & Craig, 1988). This finding was further supported in videotaped interactions between a male store manager and a female cashier, and between a male professor and female student (Saal, Johnson, & Weber, 1989). The implication of this research is that men are likely to misjudge friendly behavior as a sign of sexual interest, whereas women are likely to judge sexual interest as a sign of friendly behavior (Shotland & Craig, 1988).

Although men view interpersonal interactions in more sexual terms than women, a videotaped male professor acting in a very harassing manner was viewed as more sexy and flirtatious by

women than by men. "Our findings suggest that men are less likely than women to differentiate between the sexual intentions of a more severe male harasser and those of a less severe one" (C. B. Johnson, Stockdale, & Saal, 1991). Female actors, however, whether in the role of student or professor, were viewed as behaving in a more promiscuous, seductive, and sexy manner by men than by women. Thus, the behavior of a female is viewed as sexual rather than friendly even when she is in the superior power position.

DUAL-EARNER COUPLES

Work-Home Role Conflict

Research on employed women and their spouses finds that work conflict and family conflict are highly correlated.

Research supports a spillover model in which the daily tensions and satisfactions experienced at work shape an employees's emotional state at the end of the workday. A study of 86 employed women and their employed spouses who were parents of young adolescents found that work overload and low rewards were related to work stress that was in turn related to global stress (H. A. Sears & Galambos, 1992). Higher levels of global stress were related to lower levels of marital adjustment.

> The links between women's work, women's stress, and women's marital adjustment are undoubtedly played out in couples' interactions after work. Exposure to strains at work may place employees in a negative mood or create preoccupations that may result in negative marital interactions. (H. A. Sears & Galambos, 1992, p. 795)

An implication of this research is that work and family life cannot be conceived as two mutually exclusive domains, but rather as systems whose reciprocal influence is mediated by the individual.

Job-role quality was found to be significantly negatively related to psychological distress for both men and women in a sample of 300 full-time employed, predominantly middle class, White, dual-earner couples (Barnett, Marshall, Raudenbush, & Brennan, 1993). Flying in the face of earlier beliefs that the job situation was a more important role for men than for women, this data demonstrates that, "Indeed, many of our beliefs about sex differences may turn out to be time-bound gender differences, more a reflection of the different social role contexts in which men and women operated in the past than of inherent 'sex' differences" (Barnett et al., 1993, p. 803). Women, however, indicated higher job-role quality than did their male partners, and women reported significantly higher levels of distress than did men.

Politics and lack of career progress were significantly related to each other, but unrelated to work–home conflict among 195 female personnel professionals (D. L. Nelson, Quick, Hitt, & Moesel, 1990). Although work–home conflict is related to distress symptoms, it is unrelated to job satisfaction. Both politics and lack of career progress were both negatively related to job satisfaction. Lack of career progress, but not politics, is also associated with dysfunctional health consequences.

Work–family conflict is a form of interrole conflict. The individual must deal with pressures from both the family and work domains. (Higgins, Duxbury & Irving, 1992, p. 53). Using questionnaire responses from 220 career employees, each with a "significant other" who was also employed full time and with children living at home, it was found that work and family domains are interdependent entities. "A highly significant, positive relationship was found between work conflict and family conflict" (Higgins et al., 1992, p. 68). Quality of work life was a better predictor of life satisfaction than was quality of family life.

A positive family climate is associated with reduced home–work conflict.

On the other hand, another study found the most important correlate of work–home conflict for both men and women to be family climate (Wiersma & Van den Berg, 1991). Work–home role conflict was studied by means of questionnaires distributed to working parents who were married, had employed spouses, and had one or more children in daycare. Positive family climate was indicated by endorsement of statements such as "'Our family talks things out . . . There are activities we all enjoy doing together . . . When things aren't going right at work, my spouse is always there to offer emotional and moral support'" (Wiersma & Van den Berg, 1991, p. 1210). Women reporting a better family climate spend less time on domestic responsibilities and more time socializing with friends. Men reporting a better family climate spend less free time on career-related activities. The more free time that both men and women spend in career related activities, the greater their role-conflict. Household chores performed during one's free time also correlates with role conflict for women. Domestic responsibilities of the spouses explain a significant portion of the variance in role conflict. Part of the reason women have greater role conflict is because of their greater domestic responsibilities.

Masculine women have higher self-efficacy and report lower levels of work strain and anxiety regardless of whether they are in nontraditional professional and managerial or pink collar jobs.

Are women in nontraditional professional and managerial positions under greater strain than women in more traditional pink collar clerical and secretarial occupations? The mediating variables of sex role orientation and self-efficacy (one's perception of ability to successfully bring about change) were examined in a sample of 104 women in traditional and 177 women in nontraditional occupations. Women who scored masculine on the BSRI, whether they were in professional, managerial, or pink collar occupations, reported lower levels of strain, anxiety, and work impairment, and more problem-focused and preventive coping and greater self-efficacy than did low masculine women. A masculine orientation, however, did not moderate interpersonal strain (problems with friends, family, or spouse). For high feminine women self-efficacy and coping did not differ by occupational role. For low feminine women, however, those in nontraditional occupations have greater self-efficacy and coping, compared with low feminine women in traditional occupations. The lesser strain and greater coping of masculine women was no longer found when self-efficacy was partialed out, suggesting that self-efficacy (people's perceptions of their capabilities) may account for the lesser strain and greater coping of high masculine women.

Married Women's Employment Patterns

The relative rewards of two-earner, two-parent families is greater for low-income as compared with middle- and high-income families. Nevertheless, a greater percentage of middle- and upper-income mothers are in the labor market.

Two-earner families have played an important role in keeping many families out of poverty. When there are young children in families, however, there are economic costs, particularly for babysitting and childcare, as well as rewards. In order to assess the economic costs and rewards of two-earner, two-parent families, data from an employed husband–wife subsample of the 1980–1983 Consumer Expenditure Survey (CE) conducted by the Bureau of the Census was analyzed (Hanson & Ooms, 1991). Income advantages were found for all families with employed wives. The advantages are greater for lower-income than for higher-income groups. For example, in lower-income families, dual-earner families are 39% more likely to own their own homes than single-earner families. For middle- and upper-income families the home ownership differential is 14% and 6%, respectively. When costs of a wife working are calculated, much of the income advantage of dual-earner families is lost. It is still the lower-income families that experience the fewest costs and greatest financial rewards of dual-earner status. Given the economic advantage, it is surprising that data from the Bureau of Labor Statistics show that a greater number of

middle- and upper-income mothers are in the labor market as compared with lower-income mothers. Perhaps it is due to lack of skills and less availability of paid work. The large difference in median household income in the United States among different racial/ethnic groups is, in part, the result of differential rates of two earner families (see Figure 6.3).

Influences on Married Women's Employment

Sex role behavior rather than family income determines women's employment patterns.

Married women's employment patterns were examined over a five-year period (1976–1981) (Avioli & Kaplan, 1992). The findings, based on a longitudinal study of 366 wives in dual-earner families, were that none of the husband variables (i.e., hours worked, labor income, nor work commitment) influenced wives' employment. The only exception to this pattern appeared in cases where the husband worked weekend or extra hours; their wives were more likely to work part-time rather than full-time. The women who spent a higher proportion of their adult life in the workforce and who were employed full-time in 1976 were more likely to be employed full-time during the subsequent five-year period. The authors of this study speculate that by the early 1980s women's employment behavior was determined more by changes in sex role behavior than by economic factors, as it had been in the past.

Students in traditional and nontraditional fields want to combine marriage, family, and careers. Women entering traditional careers plan to work part time rather than full time to accommodate family life to a greater extent than do women in nontraditional fields.

Female students in traditional (nursing) and nontraditional (engineering and veterinary medicine) fields were found to be similar in their plans for marriage and family and in their gender beliefs (O'Connell, Betz, & Kurth, 1989). They want to have it all—marriage, children, and careers.

Only a minority of women planning to enter either nontraditional (29%) or traditional (25%) fields planned to work full time, however, when they had preschool children. Women entering traditional fields were more likely to say that they intended to work part-time rather than full-time at every stage of family life.

Career and Marriage in Male- and Female-Dominated Professions

It is somewhat easier to combine career and marriage in a female-dominated profession than a male-dominated profession.

Can women have it all? Most college women today want it all (Baber & Monaghan, 1988). Can they successfully combine marriage, children, and a career? Is it easier to combine marriage and family with some careers than with others? Does it matter whether the career is a male-dominated or female-dominated profession?

A comparison of women librarians (MLS degrees) and women managers (MBA degrees) found that it is somewhat easier to combine career and marriage in the female-dominated profession of librarian than it is in management because of the greater availability of part-time work and the lesser negative effect of job interruptions on later salaries (J. E. Olson, Frieze, & Detlefesen, 1990). Overall, however, many of the women surveyed had not combined a career, marriage, family, and motherhood. Research has consistently found that women with strong career orientations such as female scientists and managers are more likely to be unmarried and childless than other women (Astin, 1969; Rollins & Lederberg, 1989).

THE UNPAID WORK OF WOMEN

Marital Inequality

As predicted by resource theory, wives who earn more than their husbands have more overall say than wives who earn less than their husbands. As predicted by cultural resource theory, however, high earning wives still have more responsibility for children and the household than do their husbands.

There are two forms of marital inequality: differential evaluation of husbands' and of wives' careers and unequal sharing of domestic tasks and domestic influence. Resource theory predicts that if women have status and generate income comparable to their husbands, then differential evaluating of careers and inequalities in domestic responsibilities will be eliminated. Cultural resource theory, on the other hand, takes into account social norms that place greater emphasis on the husband/father's role and predict that income and job status resources may work differently for husbands than for wives. Certain of the findings derived from interviews with 60 White couples ranging in age from 24 to 52 both working full time, in half of which the wives earned more than the husbands, were consistent with cultural resource theory: Men rated their careers as more important than women did theirs; regardless of wage-earner group, wives were significantly more likely than their husbands to say they would move for their husband's jobs than vice versa; husbands had more say than wives with regard to financial issues; wives in the high-earning group reported the most concern with issues of competitiveness; and wives had more responsibility for childcare and household issues than did husbands (Steil & Weltman, 1991). Consistent with the resource position, women who earned more than their husbands rated their careers as more important than women who were low wage earners, although they were more likely to say their careers were equal to rather than more important than their husband's career. Regardless of sex, high-wage earners had less responsibility for childcare than low-wage earners, and more overall say and more say with regard to financial issues.

Housework and Childcare

Housework, who does it? Wives spend three to five times as many hours per week on household tasks and childcare as do husbands.

Women have always worked, but often not gotten paid for it. That is probably because over the centuries the term *work* has increasingly been defined as what men do.

> Women's work is often trivialized, ignored, and undervalued, both in economic and political terms. It is not called work when women "only" care for their households and children. Much of the work women do does not appear in the Gross National Product (GNP) and hence has neither reality nor value in standard description of the economy. (Hubbard, 1988, pp. 4–5)

Although the numbers of women in the workforce has greatly increased over the years, there has not been a corresponding decrease in their household and childcare responsibilities (Berardo, Shehan, & Leslie, 1987; Coverman & Sheley, 1986; Ross, 1987). Wives spend 30–60 hours per week on household labor, while husbands spend 10–20 hours per week at household tasks (Berk, 1985; Denmark, Shaw, & Ciali, 1985).

If all the work women do is counted, including housework, volunteer work, and paid employment, then women actually spend more time working than do men. Men and women with children both spend more time on household labor, with women's time more affected by children than men's. Analyzing data from a representative national sample survey conducted in 1987, Shelton (1992) found that women with no children spend 28.2 hours per week on household tasks compared with 43.8 hours per week for women with one child and 51.2 hours per week for women with two children. On the other hand men without children spend 18.5 hours per week on household tasks as compared with 26.1 hours per week for men with one child and 23.8 hours per week for men with two children. Women's tasks are also less likely to be discretionary, such as preparing a meal, whereas men's, such as yardwork, may offer more flexibility of scheduling. If an employer expects an employee to work after hours with minimal notice, then this is more likely to disrupt a woman's life than a man's. Women's household responsibilities are therefore more likely to limit their paid labor opportunities.

Do women in high-level positions have more equality in sharing responsibilities at home than other women? Even in marriages where the partners are of relatively equal economic and professional status, there is considerable inequity in home chores and childcare responsibilities (Biernat & Wortman, 1991). On every childcare task, wives were more involved than their husbands, although husbands spent more time in "interactive fun" with the child. On every household chore except repairs, wives had greater responsibility than husbands. There was, however, somewhat greater equity in household chores than for childcare. Both partners reported satisfaction with their spouses contributions to childcare and household responsibilities. The women, however, were more critical of their own performance as wives and mothers than men were about their performance as husbands and fathers. The husbands rated their wives' role performance higher than the wives rated themselves. This research illustrates that even high-level professional women are socialized to follow traditional standards regarding home and childcare.

The research is very consistent in finding that women are *not* more dissatisfied with the amount of housework done by their husbands as compared with themselves (Pleck, 1985; Berk, 1985; Biernat & Wortman, 1991). The situation with housework is parallel with that of the contented woman worker who earns less than her male counterpart. Women have a lower sense of personal entitlement both in the workplace and at home.

> Specifically, women may not perceive the distribution of family work as unfair because the distribution (1) matches the comparison standards they use to evaluate what they are entitled to receive or expect in their relationship; (2) is perceived as justifiable (due, for example, to the application of a need rather than equity justice rule, or to the perception that they had a "voice" in how family labor is allocated), or (3) matches what they are socialized to want or value from their relationships (e.g., women do not want more help from their husbands with housework or childcare). (Major, 1993, p. 147)

Rather than comparing the amount of housework they do with the amount their husbands do,

Doonesbury

women often compare themselves with other working wives they know and with their mothers. They also use social norms about the priority of motherhood and homemaking in women's lives. When they look at the alternative, being a single mother who does all of the childcare and housework or having a husband who does some of the work, may make a woman think twice about creating conflict that may lead to divorce. Justice is considered to be done because the husband usually earns more money than the wife, so she feels she is doing her share by doing more of the housework and childcare. Finally, because of gender-role socialization, women may want to be responsible for seeing to the household chores and childcare.

Sex Role Orientation and Domestic Chores

Masculine men perform the fewest household chores, and feminine persons of both sexes perform more domestic chores. Androgynous persons have the least conflict surrounding domestic chores.

Sex role orientation as well as sex affects the domestic division of labor (J. Atkinson & Huston, 1984; Gunter & Gunter, 1990). Similar to other studies, among 139 dual-career couples, ranging in age from 22 to the late 50s, women performed more internal domestic chores than men; however, feminine and androgynous individuals of both sexes performed significantly more domestic tasks than did masculine individuals (Gunter & Gunter, 1990). This was particularly true for internal domestic functions and for maintenance of extended family contacts. The fewest domestic tasks are performed by masculine men, whose wives have the most duties to perform. Men who are androgynous or feminine shared more in tasks that were more frequent, repetitious, and pressing. When the husband is undifferentiated, both husbands and wives perform fewer domestic tasks. Androgynous people tended to have the lowest conflict surrounding domestic tasks, and have significantly less conflict than do undifferentiated individuals.

Similarly, a study of newlyweds found that masculine men were less likely to perform "feminine" household tasks, and feminine wives had husbands who performed fewer household tasks (J. Atkinson & Huston, 1984). The extent to which the newlyweds held liberal attitudes toward women predicted the degree to which wives, but not husbands, were employed outside of the home. The more hours of employment of the husband relative to that of the wife, the fewer "feminine" household tasks he performed. If we raise more androgynous men, the picture may begin to change in the direction of more equitable sharing of domestic responsibilities.

Household Responsibilities and the Life Cycle

Husbands and wives may differentially participate in housework during different stages in the family's life cycle, according to data from the ninth wave (1976) of a panel study (the same people were interviewed at different times over a number of years) of 5,000 White, intact families (Rexroat & Shehan, 1987). Wives spent five times as much time doing housework as did husbands (28.5 versus 5.2 hours per week). Wives were found to show differential domestic involvement, however, across the family life cycle. As expected, wives with children in the home spend significantly more time doing housework than wives in households where there are no children. This difference in housework when there are children is found from right after a child is born until they are grown and leave home. Men spend more time on housework during the times of least occupational involvement, when they are young and do not have children, and the most time when they are at retirement age. It is interesting to note that these two stages in the family life cycle are those during which the wives contribute proportionally more of the total family income. Among a Los Angeles community sample, however, Mexican American men at all age levels had a traditional pattern, whereas among Whites, older White women did proportionately more housework (Golding, 1990).

Housespouses

Few men have assumed the role of housespouse. Male housespouses are evaluated more negatively than female housespouses.

Despite the fact that male roles are also changing, albeit more slowly than female roles, few men have assumed the role of housespouse. In one vignette study, the sex as well as income from freelance writing was varied for the stimulus person (Rosenwasser, Gonzales, & Adams, 1985). Even males who were earning higher incomes were devalued. Female housespouses are more positively evaluated than are male housespouses. Androgynous students evaluated both male and female housespouses more favorably than did students of other sex role orientations. Men may not feel they have the choice of being a housespouse because of the negative evaluation of males in this role.

DISPLACED HOMEMAKERS

Displaced homemakers are women who performed the traditional role of wife and mother who have lost a spouse through separation, divorce, desertion, or death. These women suffer social dislocation as well as frequent financial hardship.

Displaced homemakers are women caught in the middle of the changing mores of society. They are women who performed the traditional role of wife and mother, dependent on their husbands for income, but who through death, divorce, separation, or desertion lost that spouse. These women are often too young for social security, and, in our youth-oriented society, considered too old for employment.

Women's labor-force participation increases significantly when a woman divorces. The labor-force participation rate increased for recently divorced women from 55% in 1967 to 81% in 1977. During that same period of time the labor-force participation of women continuously married increased from 44% in 1967 to 57% in 1977. The net increase in labor-force participation due to divorce, therefore, was about 13%. Compared with divorced women who remained unmarried, those who remarried generally had lower rates of labor-force participation (R. R. Peterson, 1989).

The economic consequences of divorce are not likely to be as severe today as they were for women even a decade ago. Work has become normative for young married women. Few plan to spend their lives as full-time homemakers, although young women continue to face problems of gender inequality in the labor market, and a lack of day care. (R. R. Peterson, 1989, p. 101)

The woman who gives priority to her homemaker and childcare roles faces serious disadvantages in the event of divorce or desertion. Following divorce, the full-time homemaker is more likely to have a lower standard of living and to receive public assistance than is the woman who worked at least intermittently. A number of constraints push women to invest in childcare rather than paid employment: low-paying jobs, lack of affordable childcare, traditional expectations on the part of husbands, jobs without mobility, and lack of sharing of childcare by husbands (Peterson, 1989).

REFLECTIONS

Barriers to equality in the workplace still exist for women. Women are encumbered by job stresses rarely encountered by men including: sexual harassment, pay inequality, role overload from the obligations of work and home, and discrimination based on sex. More needs to be done to adapt the workplace to the employee rather than the other way around. Utilizing women's unique talents requires innovative programs such as job sharing, comparable worth, and prosecution of cases of sexual discrimination, including sexual harassment. Part-time employment, which is often a necessity for women given their other responsibilities, should deserve recognition by being placed on the career ladder. The workplace needs to be made more humane and flexible for human beings.

The heroines in the struggle to attain equal employment opportunities are the women in male-dominated blue collar occupations. These are the women whose small numbers bespeak the discrimination and harassment these women are forced to endure in order to make a decent wage. Harassment also occurs in the professions, but not nearly to the extreme degree as that which blue collar women face. The income discrepancy is also greater between blue and pink collar jobs than it is between men's and women's salaries in the professions. Since women in male-dominated blue collar occupations are less likely to be mar-

ried and more likely to be single parents than are women in pink collar occupations, they often put up with outrageous harassment in order not to lose their income.

Despite the barriers for women that still exist in the workplace, women are making great strides. These advances are due primarily to two factors; women's greatly accelerated rate of obtaining college and professional degrees, and women opening their own businesses. The latter avenue is open to women who did not attend college; in fact, fewer women entrepreneurs have college degrees than men entrepreneurs. The future in the world of work is very bright for women.

Experiential Exercises

1. Interview a woman business owner about how she came to start her business. What are the difficulties and rewards and satisfactions of owning her own business?
2. Talk to full-time working mothers about juggling family and work. What strategies do they use? What is the division of household and childcare tasks in their homes?
3. Talk to married Black and Hispanic women about their reasons for working or not working outside of the home.
4. Interview a woman who holds a blue collar job. Has she faced any sexual harassment or discrimination on the job?

KEY TERMS

Affirmative Action   The Equal Pay Act of 1963 mandates equal pay for equal work and Title VII of the Civil Rights Act of 1964 prohibits discrimination in selection, promotion, and other personnel decisions based on race, religion, national origin and sex. In addition, the purpose of affirmative action is to make up for past discrimination by increasing employment opportunities for women and minorities.

Comparable Worth   The concept of comparable worth is that employers should be required to pay workers in female-dominated occupations such as secretaries equal salaries to workers in male-dominated occupations such as maintenance workers.

Discrimination An important cause of women's lower wages and salaries. In the workplace, discrimination would mean that a woman would be less likely to be hired, placed in an important position, or promoted.

Displaced Homemakers Women who performed the traditional role of wife and mother, dependent on their husbands for income, but through death, divorce, separation, or desertion lost that spouse.

Gender Gap in Pay The difference between the full-time wage and salary earnings of men and women.

Human Capital This theory looks at people as investments. Human capital can appreciate through educational investment or on-the-job training, but can also depreciate through nonuse, such as when a woman stays out of the labor force to be a full-time homemaker.

Labor Force Participation Rate The percentage of a particular group in the labor force. There has been a dramatic increase in the labor force participation rate of women since 1950.

Occupational Gender Segregation The concentration of males and females in certain occupations. For example, elementary schoolteaching and nursing are still 90% female.

Part-Time employment Less than full-time employment. Women are overrepresented in part-time employment.

Personal Entitlement The sense of how much one should be paid in a particular job.

Pink Collar Jobs Nonprofessional occupations that are composed primarily of women workers. Clerical occupations are a good example of pink collar jobs.

Reproductive Hazards in the Workplace Hazards in the workplace that may adversely affect the unborn child of a pregnant woman. In 1991, the Supreme Court ruled that barring women of child-bearing age from certain hazardous jobs violates antidiscrimination law.

Sexual Harassment Unwanted sexual attention in the workplace. According to EEOC guidelines, it involves "unwelcome sexual advances, requests for sexual favors, and other verbal or physical conduct of a sexual nature."

Social Reproduction or Reproductive Labor Both paid and unpaid work that includes activities involved with taking care of people, such as childcare, elder care, household tasks, and maintaining kin and community ties.

Structured Mobility Ladders The ladders leading to promotions within the organization. Within companies there are often "male" and "female" ladders, leading to less increase of status and earning over time for females than for males.

Target Hiring It is not a quota, but the goal of hiring certain percentages of women over a specified time for certain positions.

Underemployment People who are employed part time who would like to be employed full time, or who cannot find jobs in the field for which they have been trained.

Unemployment The percentage of people who are not in the paid labor force who are seeking employment.

SUGGESTED READINGS

Amott, T., & Matthaei, J. (1991). *Race, gender, and work: A multicultural economic history of women in the United States.* Boston, MA: South End Press. A fascinating, readable, history of culturally diverse women's experience of work in the United States.

Hood, J. N., & Koberg, C. S. (1994). Patterns of differential assimilation and acculturation for women in business organizations. *Human Relations, 47,* 159–181. This article develops a conceptual model of women's position in organizations that hypothesizes that women can acculturate to the organization but be prevented from assimilating to it.

Major, B. (1993). Gender, entitlement, and the distribution of family labor. *Journal of Social Issues, 49* (3), 141–159. In this article Major uses the concept of personal entitlement to explain why women are relatively contented doing most of the housework and childcare.

CHAPTER 7

Violence Against Women

> The anti-rape movement must not limit itself to training women to avoid rape or depending on imprisonment as a deterrent, but must aim its attention at changing the behavior and attitudes of men.
>
> Jacquelyn David Hall, 1992

Women's lives are touched by two sources of interpersonal violence: criminal violence, which includes stranger rape, assault, burglary, and homicide, and intimate violence, which is perpetrated by someone known to the victim and is often a family member, and includes child abuse, incest, date and marital rape, courtship violence, wife battering, and elder abuse (Koss, 1990). The two overlap since intimate violence is also a crime, but they are often treated very differently by society, with a shroud of secrecy surrounding intimate violence. Both types of violence, however, create a serious public health problem in the consequences for the mental and physical health of the women who are victims. Domestic violence is the leading cause of injury to women in the United States. One pregnant woman in six is abused. Battered women account for three out of ten of the women who use emergency room services (V. E. Parker, 1995).

RAPE

Definition of Rape

Rape was very much of a hidden crime until the women's movement focused attention on it in the 1970s.

Rape is the use of force or threat of force to have sexual intercourse (penile–vaginal penetration). Oral and anal penetration are also included in most legal definitions, making it possible for men to be raped as well as women. It is also rape if the individual is incapable of giving consent due to mental retardation, emotional disturbance, or intoxication (Koss, 1993). Different research studies have used different definitions of rape; therefore, they worded questions that were intended to elicit reports of rape by victims differently, leading to some confusion in the statistics and findings (Muehlenhard, Powch, Phelps, & Guisti, 1992).

Rape was very much of a hidden crime until the women's movement focused attention on the issue of rape in the early 1970s. The first rape crisis hotline was established in America in 1971, and it was in that same decade that rape crisis centers sprang up around the country. The Federal Government allotted an estimated $125 million for research on sexual assault between 1973 and 1981. Another federal initiative was the establishment of a National Center for the Prevention and Control of Rape within the Department of Health, Education and Welfare (Temkin, 1986).

Rape Statistics

Rape was the fastest growing crime of violence in the United States between 1960 and 1992. Rape is still one of the most underreported crimes. Females under 18 years of age are the victims of the majority of rapes.

Officially, 109,062 rapes of women occurred in the United States during 1992 and 104,806 during 1993 (U.S. Department of Justice, 1994). These are statistics from the Uniform Crime Report, based on cases of forcible rapes reported to the FBI (87% of the total) and of attempts or assaults to commit forcible rape. This represents a dramatic increase in reported rapes, which in 1960 numbered 16,860, representing a larger increase than for any other violent crime (Baron & Straus, 1989). However, there was a 3.9% decline in forcible rape between 1992 and 1993. It should be hoped that this is the beginning of a decline in rape in the United States.

Some of the increase in the rape statistics may be due to increased reporting of rapes, but even today many victims never tell their closest family or friends, never mind the police. Rape is still considered to be the most underreported serious crime. The government estimates that 3–10 rapes are committed for every one reported. Rape was an even more underreported crime in the past for reasons of social stigma and because of the stringent criteria for obtaining a conviction against a rapist. For example, to obtain a conviction of

rape in New York State in the 1970s, there had to be a witness who saw or heard the assault and would testify that the woman had resisted the attack (Donat & D'Emilio, 1992).

The **National Crime Victim Survey (NCVS)** is another method for estimating the number of crimes. The NCVS is a national representative sample of residents who are asked to indicate those crimes of which they, or anyone else in their household, have been victims during the preceding year. The NCVS Survey data reported here is based on approximately 400,000 interviews conducted between 1987 and 1991. According to NCVS statistics, the average annual rate of rape of women in the United States between 1987 and 1991 was 132,172, which is more than one-third higher than the figures provided by FBI statistics for those years. Since rape is a stigmatized crime, it is possible that a woman might not want to tell an interviewer in a face-to-face situation about the rape, so rape may still be underreported in NCVS statistics (Koss, 1992). Females suffer vastly more rape than males (8.1:1) (Finkelhor & Dziuba-Leatherman, 1994).

Based on a survey of a cross-section of 4,000 women in 1990 the National Victim Center estimated that 683,000 rapes had occurred during that year. It is very disturbing that the majority (61%) of the victims of rape were younger than 18, at the time of the attack, and 29.3% were younger than 11 years of age. Only 16% of these attacks were reported to the authorities. Only 22% of the rapes were committed by strangers, and most of the rapes were perpetrated by friends or relatives (National Victim Center, 1992).

The statistics in the preceding paragraphs were incidence data based on annual numbers of rapes. Lifetime prevalence rates are not collected by government sources, but research studies indicate prevalence rates among adult women typically to range between 14% and 25% (Koss, 1993). Differences in prevalence rates are found for women of different ages and in different regions of the country. The prevalence rate for sexual assault of a representative sample of women in North Carolina was only 5.9% as compared with 16.7% for a representative sample of women in Los Angeles County (George, Winfield, & Blazer,

1992). Prevalence rates were higher for women with some college education or more, living in urban as opposed to rural areas and younger than 45 years.

One out of four college women have been the victim of rape or attempted rape since the age of 14.

In order to determine realistic estimates of the actual prevalence of rape, *Ms.* magazine approached the National Institute for Mental Health to do a survey on "date rape." NIMH named Mary Koss, a psychologist then at Kent State University who had conducted research in the area, as director of the research project. She and her research team administered a self-report questionnaire to a national, random sample of 6,159 students (3,187 women and 2,972 men), at 32 institutions of higher education (Koss, Gidycz, & Wisniewski, 1987; Warshaw, 1988).

The rationale for selecting college students, in addition to the availability, was that they are a high-risk age group for rape. Responses of females to questions that were designed to detect victimization that met the legal definition of rape revealed that 15.4% had been raped and 12.1% had been victims of attempted rape since age 14. Nearly half of these women, however, did not recognize that they were victims of rape. Although rates of victimization did not differ by the size of the college or university, it did differ by the type of governance, with women attending private colleges and major universities twice as likely to have been raped as those attending religiously affiliated institutions. Only a very small percentage of these students had reported the rape to the police, therefore these rapes would not be included in the official crime statistics.

Kahn, Mathie, and Torgler (1994) found evidence that college women whose experiences had met the legal definition of rape but did not acknowledge it as such were more likely to have mental rape scripts in which the rapist was a stranger and the sexual experiences were more violent as compared with women who had acknowledged being raped. In addition, the unac-

knowledged rape victims had sexual histories, including the rape experience, that involved less force than what was experienced by the acknowledged victims.

Black and White Rape

Black women are somewhat more likely to be raped than White women—except on college campuses.

In the United States, certain demographic characteristics are associated with a higher risk of being raped. Based on the data collected by the NCVS the annual rate of rape (in 1987–1991) of White women was 1.1 per 1,000 women age 12 and older in the population, as compared with a rate of 2.0 for Black women (the difference is not statistically significant) (Bachman, 1994).

A stratified probability telephone sample of African American and White women 18–36 years of age in Los Angeles County found 25% of Black women and 20% of White women to have been victims of at least one incidence of rape since age 18 (a nonsignificant difference) (Wyatt, 1992). Black women were less likely to have reported the rape to the police or to disclose it to anyone until years later (64% for African American women as compared to 36% for White women). Black women may not perceive their credibility as rape victims to be established or the police to be supportive.

Despite their somewhat greater likelihood of being raped, media attention rarely focuses on Black victims of rape. Outrage seems to be reserved for White victims, particularly when the rape is interracial. When a White jogger was raped in Central Park in 1989 by a group of Black youths, it was the talk of the media for weeks, if not months. At the same time, brutal rapes were also being committed against Black women (one was even hung out of the window several floors above the ground by her assailant) with very little or no media attention.

Black women's literature is full of the pain of frequent assault, not only by a racist patriarchy, but also by Black men. Yet the necessity for and history

TABLE 7.1 Average Annual Rate of Rape Per 1,000 Females Age 12 or Older by Demographic Characteristics, 1987–1991

Characteristic	Rape
Race/Ethnicity	
White	1.1
Black	2.0
Hispanic	1.1
Age	
12–19	1.8
20–24	3.1
25–34	1.5
35–49	.7
50–64	.2
65 or over	.1
Marital Status	
Never married	2.9
Married	.3
Widowed	.3
Divorced/separated	2.8
Family Income	
Less than $9,999	2.4
$10,000–$19,999	1.4
$20,000–$49,999	1.0
$50,000 or more	.5

Source: Abstracted from "Violence Against Women: A National Crime Victimization Survey Report." by R. Bachman, 1994, U.S. Department of Justice, Annapolis Junction, MD.

of shared battle have made us, Black women, particularly vulnerable to the false accusation that anti-sexist is anti-Black. Meanwhile, womanhating as a recourse of the powerless is sapping strength from Black communities, and our very lives. Rape is on the increase, reported and unreported, and rape is not aggressive sexuality, it is sexualized aggression. (Lorde, 1992a, p. 500)

Only ending male domination will end rape.

Among college students in the *Ms.*-sponsored survey, White women were more likely to indicate that they had been forced to have sex (16%, *N* = 3,075), than Black women (10%, *N* = 215), or Hispanic women (12%, *N* = 106), or Asian women (7%, *N* = 79), or Native American women (4.0%, *N* = 20) (Koss, Gidycz, & Wisniewski, 1987). Among college men admitting sexual aggression, Black men were the largest percentage (10%), followed by Hispanic men (7%), White

men (4%), Asian men (2%), and Native American men (0%).

Black men do not seek out White women to rape—Black women are their most likely victims.

Black-on-White rape historically was severely sanctioned, with Black men the objects of lynchings or executions. "Despite its tenacity, however, the myth of the black rapist was never founded on objective reality" (J. D. Hall, 1992, p. 402). Fewer than one-quarter of the Black men lynched in the South were even accused of rape or attempted rape. At the present time, however, the rate of rape perpetrated by Black men is much higher than the rate of rape perpetrated by White men, although White men commit the majority of rapes in the United States. In 1993, 18,473 White men were arrested for rape as compared with 13,419 Black men.

Eldrege Cleaver depicted Black-on-White rape as an insurrectionary act (Cleaver, 1968). Others have suggested that Black men rape White women as a way of gaining revenge on their White male oppressor (Curtis, 1976; La Free, 1982). South and Felson (1990) used data on rapes reported in the National Crime Survey's (NCS) Cities Sample to examine the racial patterning of rape. No support was found for the conflict theories of rape, since interracial rapes were no more frequent in cities with high Black poverty, unemployment, or racial inequality.

Instead, the research supported Blau's macro-structural opportunity model. Living in a city with a relatively large Black population increases the probability that a White woman will be raped by a Black man rather than by a White man. Also, a White woman living in a city that is highly segregated by race reduces the probability of being raped by a Black man, compared with a White woman living in a mildly segregated city. These data illustrate that interracial rape is related to opportunities for interpersonal contact between Whites and Blacks.

There is no evidence that Black rapists prefer to rape White women. In fact, when robbing a woman, a White or Black robber has equivalent opportunities to rape a female victim. Actually, in robberies, there was a trend for Black robbers to be more likely to rape a Black rather than a White victim. White robbers were equally likely to rape a White or a Black victim. In stranger rapes, multiple Black offenders, however, are more likely to rape Whites than Blacks (South & Felson, 1990). The probability of an interracial rape is due largely to the opportunities provided by the properties of urban social structure rather than by a racial preference.

Historically, Black women were victimized by White men. "In the United States the fear and fascination of female sexuality was projected onto black women; the passionless lady arose in symbiosis with the primitively sexual slave" (J. D. Hall, 1992, p. 401). Black women slaves, already in chains, had no recourse to resist the white slave owner's rape. Rape of Black women by White men after the Civil War was a continued weapon of political subordination of Blacks. At the present time, however, rape is largely committed within the same race: 78% of White women are raped by White men and 98% of Black women are raped by Black men.

The rape of Black women is taken less seriously by the criminal justice system whether it is committed by White or by Black men. Most of the rape cases prosecuted involve Black or poor men and White victims (Wyatt, 1992). Racialized women "are considered inherently less innocent and worthy than white women, and the classic rape in legal discourse is the rape of a white woman. The rape script is thus inevitably raced whether it involves intraracial or interracial rape" (Razack, 1994, p. 899).

Hispanic Women and Rape

Non-Hispanic White women are two-and-a-half times more likely to have been victims of sexual assault than have Hispanic women.

A representative sample of over 3,000 residents of Los Angeles of Hispanic and non-Hispanic White ethnicity found the lifetime prevalence of sexual assault of Whites to be two-and-a-half times that of Hispanics (19.9% vs. 8.1%) (Sorenson & Siegel, 1992). The lifetime prevalence of sexual assault of women was greater than that for men (16.7% vs. 9.4%) for both ethnic groups. Hispanics were less likely than non-Hispanic Whites to use any health services following sexual assault. Sexually assaulted Hispanic women were much more likely to have sought mental health services during the six months preceding the survey compared with nonassaulted Hispanic women (21.2% vs. 7.2%).

The circumstances and consequences of the sexual assaults were very similar for non-Hispanic Whites and Hispanics. "Hispanics and non-Hispanic Whites were equally likely to resist assault, to report various specific reactions to the assault, to develop mental disorders subsequent to assault, and to talk to someone about the assault" (Sorenson & Siegel, 1992, p. 100). Most of the Hispanic respondents were Mexican Americans, whose culture includes norms against violence toward the in group, a sense of community, and protective restrictions on females, including dating that may serve to reduce rape.

Feminist Theory of Rape

Feminist theory of rape—rape expresses male dominance of women and exists within a culture of violence.

Susan Brownmiller (1975), in her groundbreaking book on rape, *Against Her Will,* focuses on the assaultive and hostile aspects of rape. Feminist critiques of theories of rape, however, have broadened the scope of understanding rape to include sociological and cultural forces rather than focusing on individual psychopathology, as did theories of rape within criminology. Feminist approaches also challenged psychodynamic theories that explained rape as sexual pathology. "In essence, the feminist theory views rape as a pseudosexual act motivated by male desires to maintain supremacy over women in sociopolitical and economic terms" (L. Ellis, 1991, p. 631). Rape is defined as an expression of either power or anger motivations where sex is only the vehicle of expression (Lisak, 1991). Rape can only be understood in the culture in which it is embedded.

Feminist research has focused on rape myths and rape-supportive attitudes in society. The double standard of sexuality that gives men more sexual freedom than women is also expressed in the belief that men want sex and it is up to women to control them. This leads to men forcing sex on their dates and women being blamed when they do not stop the man from raping her. The implication is also present that if she did not stop the rape, it is because she really wanted it and enjoyed it.

A number of college men have been asked by researchers if they would commit rape if they could be sure they would not be caught. In one study 51% of the men indicated some likelihood of committing rape if they could get away with it, but only 2% of women said they would enjoy being raped (Malamuth, Haber, & Feshbach, 1980). Some prevalent rape myths in American society are: victims are loose women who provoke rapists; no healthy woman can be raped, and any woman can avoid it; women charge rape to cover accidental pregnancies or to take revenge; otherwise decent men are spurred to rape by the clothing or behavior of women; and rapists act on uncontrollable sexual impulses (M. T. Gordon & Riger, 1989, p. 6). Men and women with more traditional attitudes toward women tend to believe rape myths to a greater extent than those who are more liberal.

Margaret T. Gordon and Stephanie Riger (1989) believe that the acceptance of rape myths heightens women's fear of rape and feelings of being responsible for attacks. Fear of rape was found to be a central concern of everyday life for about one-third of urban American women interviewed by telephone in three cities. For another third it is something they worry about occasionally, but it is still in the back of their minds. Another third say they never worry about being raped, but still take precautions to prevent being raped.

Women are twice as likely as men to feel unsafe out alone in their neighborhoods at night. Black women feel less safe than White women,

single women less safe than married, and old less safe than young women. This fear of being raped has led to annual marches of women to "Take Back the Night" to call for making the streets safe for women (M. Gordon & Riger, 1989).

Cross-Cultural Perspective on Rape

"Rape-prone" societies are those with an ideology of male dominance. The sexes are seen as equal in "rape-free" societies.

The sociocultural context was found by anthropologist Peggy Reeves Sanday, who examined 156 tribal societies, to be the determinant of whether a society could be classified as **rape prone** or **rape free** (Sanday, 1981). She designated societies as rape prone if the incidence of rape is high, rape is a ceremonial act, or rape is used to punish women. Rape is a product of a culture or subculture of violence. Rape is associated with an ideology that encourages men to be tough and aggressive. "Rape is not an integral part of male nature, but the means by which men programmed for violence express their sexual selves" (Sanday, 1981, pp. 25–26). When warfare is reported as being frequent or endemic (as opposed to absent or occasional), rape is more likely to be present. Raiding other societies for wives is also significantly associated with the incidence of rape.

The evidence supports the notion that "rape is an expression of a social ideology of male dominance." Women have less power in these societies as can be seen from their lesser role in decision making. There is also greater separation of the sexes in these societies. When the character of the father–daughter relationship is primarily indifferent, aloof, cold, and stern, rape is more likely to be present.

On the other hand, rape-free societies are those in which the sexes are seen as equal and complementary. Interpersonal violence is uncommon. The contribution of women is valued. Sanday cites West Sumatra as a rape-free society. In West Sumatra police reports noted 28 rapes for a population of 28 million during 1981–1982 (Sanday,

1986). "In West Sumatra, for example, a man who rapes demeans himself and everyone he is associated with. His masculinity is ridiculed and he faces assault, perhaps death, or he might be driven from his village never to return" (Sanday, 1986, p. 84).

The United States has the highest crime statistics on rape in the industrialized world. Most rape is normative and not considered a crime in most cultures.

American society is the most violent in the industrialized world. The United States has the highest rate of rape of any society in which statistics on crime are kept (M. Gordon & Riger, 1989). Many aspects of the American culture contribute to a climate that fosters rape, including the objectification of women in advertising, violent pornography, and the oppression of women in the legal system (Lisak, 1991).

Nonnormative rape, the only type that is prosecuted in cultures, is the stereotypical rape by a stranger on a virtuous woman (Koss, Heise, & Russo, 1994). In Pakistan, to determine if the woman is virtuous the court uses a finger test to see if her vagina will accommodate two fingers easily. Normative rapes are those that are against the woman's choice but are supported by social norms. These include acquaintance rape and marital rape (which is only illegal in the United States and Great Britain). In countries such as Algeria, very young girls in arranged marriages are restrained and forced to submit to intercourse on their wedding night. Rape is also used as a mechanism of social control, such as the gang rape of a woman leader in India who was organizing against child marriage. Rape has also been a weapon of war, as has been documented in conflicts in Liberia, Uganda, Peru, Cambodia, Somalia, and Bosnia. Normative rapes also include ceremonial rapes and status rapes where, for example, Asian servants in Kuwait are expected to be sexually available to their employers. Koss et al. view these rapes within the framework of the negative implications for women's health—both mental and physical.

Causes of Rape

Research as to the causes of rape supports feminist, pornography, and social disorganization theories.

Marked variations exist in the rate of rape in the different states in the United States (Baron and Straus, 1989). The Uniform Crime Reports (based on FBI data) indicate that the rate of rape per 100,000 population for 1980–1982, ranges from a high of 83.3 in Alaska to a low of 9.3 in North Dakota. Baron and Straus (1989) tested four theories of rape to explain the variation in the rate of rape from state to state: feminist theories; pornography; cultural support for violence; and social disorganization theory.

Feminist theories explain rape as an expression of patriarchy and subjugation of women in male-dominated societies. The antipornography movement contends that sexual violence is now commonplace in pornography and that it leads to rape. The cultural spillover theory cites the approval of violence in various institutions of society such as the mass media and sports (legitimate violence) as an important cause of violent behavior including rape. Social disorganization theory has been proposed by sociologists who argue that disorganizing factors in communities such as divorce and geographic mobility are related to crime and deviance including rape.

Three of the four theories were directly supported by the research—feminist theory, social disorganization theory, and pornography. Feminist theories were supported by the finding that as the status of women increases, the rate of rape decreases. Rape was also correlated with gender inequality, which is made up of economic, political, and legal equality measures. There was only an indirect relationship between legitimate violence and rape through its inverse relationship with gender equality.

In support of social disorganization theory, it was found that higher rates of rape occur in states where there are higher rates of geographical mobility, divorce, lack of religious affiliation, female-headed households, nonfamilied male householders with no female present, and higher tourist to resident ratios. The composite Social Disorganization Index is also higher in states with a high rate of rape.

Pornography, as measured by the sales of sex magazines in each state, was also directly related to the rate of rape. Baron and Straus say that they are very hesitant to interpret their findings linking sex magazine circulation with rape as reflecting a cause and effect relationship. They cite research data that showed no increase or decrease in the rate of rape following legalization and increase in circulation of pornography in the United States, Denmark, Sweden, and West Germany.

Rape Victims

Among college students there are no personality differences between women who are and are not raped. Although rape by a date or family member is not likely to be reported to the police or an agency, the postrape psychological symptoms are just as severe.

To determine if women with certain attitudinal and personality profiles are more likely to be victims of rape, a survey of sexual experiences was administered to 2,016 women in randomly selected classes at a midwestern university (Koss, 1985). Overall, 38% of women reported victimizations that met the legal definition of rape or attempted rape. The majority of these women had been raped by an acquaintance or romantic partner. When the victim and attacker were closely acquainted and had previously shared sexual intimacy, the assault was unlikely to be seen as rape. Only 4% of these victims reported the assault to the police. There were no significant personality differences or attitudinal differences between the women who had not been victims of rape and those who had been raped. In other words, anyone can be raped, it is the characteristics of the man and not the woman involved that determines who gets raped.

Comparisons of stranger and acquaintance rape, including date rape of female college students, finds that stranger rapes were more likely to involve multiple offenders, whereas acquaintance rapes were perpetrated by a single offender, but often involve a series of assaults by the same offender (Koss, Dinero, Seibel, & Cox, 1988). Both stranger and marital/family rapes were higher in violence than acquaintance or date rapes.

The women raped by strangers were more likely to seek crisis services, to report the rape to the police, and to label the assault as rape than were women raped by spouses, relatives, or acquaintances. A number of studies have reported that the severity of postrape psychological symptoms (fear, depression, social maladjustment) did not differ in stranger or acquaintance rapes (E. M. Ellis, Atkison, & Calhoun, 1981; Kilpatrick, Veronen, & Best, 1985; Koss, Dinero, Seibel, & Cox, 1988).

In a larger percentage of cases than is usually realized, the same woman is the victim of rape on different occasions. Are there characteristics of a woman or the situation that make rape more likely for her? A risk profile for vulnerability to rape was developed by Koss and Dinero (1989) based on data from a representative sample of 2,723 college students, but it only characterized 10% of the victims. For those women, however, the risk of rape was twice the rate of women who did not fit the profile. The vulnerability factors were previous traumatic experiences such as sexual abuse and family violence, sexual attitudes including sexual conservatism and acceptance of rape myths, and alcohol use in the situation in which the rape took place.

In the community, women who suffer from psychopathology are more vulnerable to being raped. The same women are often victimized repeatedly because the rapist is a husband, relative, or acquaintance with whom they have frequent contact.

The community mental health research, however, finds that those individuals who suffer from certain disorders are more likely to suffer sexual assault subsequent to the onset of the disorder (Burnam et al., 1988). The results of the community study suggested that major depression, substance abuse or dependence, antisocial personality, and phobia may increase risk for later sexual assault. The women in the community study are drawn from a heterogeneous population in terms of age, socioeconomic level, and mental health. The overall conclusion from these studies might be that in a normal population, such as a college student population, there is little difference between those who are and are not victims of rape. In a more heterogeneous population such as is found in the community, women who suffer from psychopathology are more vulnerable to being raped.

One in five (21%) of a sample of 2,291 women medical patients of a worksite-based health maintenance organization had been victims of rape at some point in their lives since age 14 (Koss, Koss, & Woodruff, 1991). Fifty-seven percent had been victims of crimes, 32% of which were violent crimes. Thirty-seven of the victims of forcible vaginal intercourse reported 216 incidents during the previous year. The large number of incidents within one year may be attributable to the proportion of this crime that was perpetrated by husbands, partners, or relatives of the victim with whom they continued having contact. Only 17.1% of the rapes could be classified as stranger rapes.

Gang Rape

Gang rapes are more violent, degrading, and brutal than single-offender rapes.

Gang rape—where two or more offenders attack one victim—are more brutal than single offender rapes. Sexual humiliation, such as repeated intercourse, fellatio, and/or cunnilingus are more common in gang rapes than they are in single rapes (Amir, 1971). When multiple rapists are involved, the offenders are more likely to have a previous criminal record than when there is a single rapist (Rozee-Koker & Polk, 1986). In the college student survey (Gidycz & Koss, 1990) it was found that group offenders were more

likely to use threats of physical force and actual physical force such as twisting the victim's arm, holding her down, hitting and slapping her, and having a weapon.

Group sexual assaults were also more likely to be one time occurrences, whereas individual assaults were more likely to have occurred twice. Group sexual assault victims were more likely to use crying and sobbing, running away, and pushing or hitting the offender(s). They were more likely to be assaulted by strangers and to seek crisis services and to report the assault to police as compared with individual assault victims. The victims of group sexual assault were also more likely to have considered suicide and to have sought therapy. Thus, the assault itself is more violent overall and the after-effects more severe when the woman is subjected to gang rape (Gidycz & Koss, 1990).

Group offenders tend to be younger, tend to plan the rape in advance, and tend to be using alcohol. A social psychological perspective explains group rape in terms of group dynamics, in which the planning and execution occurs in a group context. Each male commits a more atrocious act on the victim as a way of increasing his status in the group and demonstrating how macho he is. It is a microcosm of the male-dominant culture.

Male-dominant institutions, from the U.S. Senate to law enforcement to the exclusively Bohemia Club, provide the camaraderie, sense of belonging, and the shared sense of maleness (and "not-femaleness") necessary to maintain the authority structure. This androcentric pattern is simply reiterated within the group rape situation. (Rozee-Koker, & Polk, 1986, p. 58)

Thus, group rape helps maintain the feeling of power over femaleness by the individual and the group. Other males that may be observers to the group rape often wink and look the other way, or even may cheer and join in participation. A good example of that was the infamous pool table gang rape of a woman in a bar in New Bedford, Massachusetts.

Fraternity Gang Rape

Fraternities are rape prone.

According to anthropologist Peggy Reeves Sanday's book, *Fraternity Gang Rape* (1990), the sexual practices of fraternities on American university campuses encourage gang rape. The pattern is to seek out a "vulnerable" young woman, one seeking acceptance or high on alcohol. She may go to a room to have sex with one man and then may pass out or be too confused, frightened, or outnumbered to resist when his fraternity brothers take turns raping her. Recruitment of men whose masculinity corresponds to a narrow and stereotypical type, and norms and practices of fraternities predispose fraternity men to coerce women sexually, both individually and collectively (P. Y. Martin & Hummer, 1992).

Sorority women have been found to be at higher risk of rape or attempted rape than the women in the college student study. Of 140 randomly selected sorority members at a large public Midwestern university (Copenhaver & Grauerholz, 1991), 41% reported that they had experienced an act that met the legal definition of rape or attempted rape. Over half of these acts (57%) occurred either at a fraternity house or by a fraternity member. Sorority women have exposure to fraternity men who are part of a culture that debases women.

Another group of women even more likely to be sexually objectified and commodified by fraternity men than sorority women are fraternity little sisters (Stombler, 1994). Fraternity little sisters are undergraduate women affiliated with a men's fraternity and serve a "hostess" or "booster" function. They go through a rush and pledge process, but they do not enjoy full membership status in the fraternity.

Fraternity little sister programs consist of a structured inequality of relations in which men exploit little sisters' emotional labor (they expect women to act as their confidantes and to cheer them on at sporting events), physical labor (domestic chores, fundraising), and sexuality (among other things, the brothers photograph women in bathing suits to attract male pledges) (Martin & Hummer, 1989; Stombler & Martin, 1994). (Stombler, 1994, p. 300)

Based on in depth interviews with 21 little sisters, Stombler concludes that women become little sisters to meet high status men on campus, have fun, attend parties, and be a part of the Greek system. Little sisters tend to have reputations as either "buddies" (just pals with the fraternity men), or "slutties" (women who have sexual relations with them). A number of universities and fraternity organizations, however, have disbanded the little sister programs after media attention linking them to gang and acquaintance rapes by fraternity men, although many little sister programs are still in existence.

Unwanted Intercourse

Unwanted intercourse is more common than rape.

Unwanted intercourse occurs when one partner uses psychological pressure to induce a reluctant partner to engage in sexual intercourse, but without the use of force or threat of force (M. Lewin, 1985). Nearly one-third (30%) of senior women in a four-year liberal arts college reported at least one experience of unwanted intercourse (the median number of such experiences was four). M. Lewin proposes that four cultural norms account for the prevalence of unwanted intercourse: (1) The ideology of male supremacy; (2) The lack of positive norms about premarital sexual experience for women; (3) The man has the initiative; and (4) The stroking function of women who are brought up to believe they should put their man's needs above their own.

Marital Rape

Women are less likely to be raped by their husbands than by other men—but husbands who rape, do so repeatedly. Wives who stay in abusive situations are more traditional.

Until recently, a man could not be prosecuted in the United States for raping his wife. States had rape laws that specifically exempted the husband from a criminal charge for having sex with his wife against her will. The tradition of these laws goes back to British common law. In the late 1970s feminists begin to mount legal and political efforts to criminalize rape in marriage (Finkelhor & Yllo, 1985).

A random sample survey of households in the San Francisco Bay area, in which 930 women were interviewed, discovered that 44% of these women had been raped at some time in their lives, with 8% of the entire sample having been raped by a husband (D. E. H. Russell, 1982). The statistics were calculated so that multiple attacks by the same man counted as one "incident." When rapes and attempted rapes are combined, and the frequency of attacks for men who raped a woman on more than one occasion is counted, rapes by husbands and ex-husbands become by far the most prevalent incidents, followed by lovers and ex-lovers, acquaintances, other relatives, dates, authority figures, and boyfriends.

Raped wives were found to be no more traditional, as measured by whether she was self-supporting, had raised one or more or no children, or had worked most of the time during her adult life. The more traditional wives, however, did differ from the less traditional in their being more likely to stay in the marriage even though abused. Most women, however, do leave a marriage in which they have been raped. Only 22% of the eighty-seven raped wives were still married at the time of the interview.

Marital rape can be classified into three types: battering rapes; force only rapes; and obsessive rapes.

In order to learn more about the dynamics of rape in marriage Finkelhor and Yllo (1982; 1985) conducted case study interviews with women clients of family planning agencies who said that their husbands or former husbands had "used physical force or threat to try to have sex with them." They divided the case studies into three types of **marital rape**. They classified the first group as battering rapes. These were committed by men who beat their wives and would also rape them. Their husbands' behavior can be characterized as angry and belligerent toward them. The abuse was verbal as well as physical, often fueled by alcohol and drugs.

The second type of rape occurred in a marriage in which there was little or no other violence. These were classified as force only rapes. They grow out of sexual conflicts. The motive is power. As compared with victims of the battering rapes, the victims of force only rape were more likely to be more educated and middle class and less likely to come from a home where they had been victims of child abuse.

A third type of rape, the least common, was the obsessive rape. "Their sexual interests ran toward the strange and the perverse, and they were willing to use force to carry these activities out." These husbands not only forced intercourse, but frequently more unusual sexual activities such as anal intercourse, inserting objects into the wife's vagina, and tying her up. These men were also engrossed in pornography, particularly movies, books, and magazines about women being brutalized.

Women who are raped by husbands are just as likely to fear serious injury or even being killed as are women raped by strangers (Koss, 1993). Women raped by husbands, however, are much less likely to report the rape to the police or seek victim assistance.

Rape Avoidance

Women who fight back are more likely to avoid rape.

Women who are attacked and escape being raped are much more likely to run away, scream for help, and/or fight back. This has been found to be true for college students fending off date rape (Levine-MacCombie & Koss, 1986) as well as for women in the community, many of whom were attacked by strangers (Bart & O'Brien, 1985; Kleck & Sayles, 1990). The most effective method of resistance is with a weapon (gun, knife, or other weapon). "Physical resistance much more

Focus on Women   Prevention of Rape

Judith Kinzel has worked with victims of sexual assault for 10 years. In an interview she advocated a two-pronged approach to rape prevention: (1) societal—society must hold rapists accountable, and take a clear stand that rape is unacceptable; (2) individual—individuals can develop safety strategies to reduce their vulnerability.

Societal
We must start to understand more about rapists, rather than focussing on what a woman has done that is supposedly wrong. Rape does not happen by accident, it is a deliberate act of violence. Rapists mix sex and violence from an early age. Their behaviors are deliberate and planned. Rapists do not rape because a woman leads them on, instead they use rape as a weapon to gain power and control over another person. We need to put a spotlight on offenders: deny them the opportunity to hide behind the myths about sexual assault. For example, one judge recently said that, since the victim and accused knew each other, what happened between them could not have been rape. The reality is that most rapes happen between people who are acquainted, rather than between strangers. Not all men mix sex and violence. Men can take a stand by refusing to tolerate sexist jokes and images. As a society, we must stop blaming women for their victimization and hold offenders accountable.

Individual
We can develop safety strategies to decrease our vulnerability to rapists, and this should happen before any problem occurs. We need to understand that we are all vulnerable to a sexual assault—denial of the magnitude of the problem does not make us safer. We must believe that we have a right to say "no" to behaviors that make us uncomfortable. We should also know our own strengths and weaknesses, and the resources available to us. Finally, we should talk to each other about our success stories: many women have successfully escaped from dangerous situations.

---

frequently resulted in rape avoidance than a beating" (Bart & O'Brien, 1985; p. 111). Women's resistance is effective even in dangerous situations with highly aggressive offenders. Physical injury is related to offender aggression, but is unrelated to resistance. In other words, resistance decreases the likelihood of sexual assault, but does not increase the probability of physical injury (Ullman & Knight, 1991) (see Focus on Women).

Black women and White Catholic women, are most likely to avoid rape, while Jewish women are most likely to be raped. The success of Black women in escaping rape is particularly dramatic given that Black women are more likely to be attacked by multiple assailants, are as likely to escape an armed as an unarmed assailant, and, when raped, to be the victims of more brutal rapes (Bart & O'Brien, 1985). Black women were most likely to have "street smarts" and Jewish women were least likely to have been socialized for unprotected and dangerous situations. Other factors associated with avoiding rape were being tall, having been the oldest daughter, and having had major household responsibilities. These are all factors that socialize a woman to be more dominant and assertive.

In both the *Ms.*-supported college student survey, and an NIH-funded survey, arguing or pleading with the attacker did not help in avoiding rape (Levine-MacCombie & Koss, 1986). "Quarreling with the offender contributed significantly to the prediction of completed rape. On the other hand, crying and reasoning did make some contributions to the identification of rape avoiders" (Levine-MacCombie & Koss, 1986). In a third survey, threatening or arguing with the offender was associated with increased harm to the victim (Kleck & Sayles, 1990).

The research from all of the preceding studies is clear. Women should resist rape by screaming, fighting, and using a weapon. Women in our society are often socialized to be nurturing, passive, and subordinate to men. Females need assertiveness training and opportunities for training in self-defense techniques if they are to prevent themselves from being victimized by men. At the same time, women whose socialization makes it difficult for them to exhibit decisive and aggressive resistance should not be made to feel guilty for having been raped (Abarbanel, 1986).

Blaming the Victim

Men blame the rape victim more than women do, and men who believe in a just world are particularly likely to blame the victim.

The reason that so many rapes go unreported is that the victim is often blamed for the rape. She must go through the ordeal of being questioned by the police, appearing in court, and being interrogated by the rapist's defense attorney. States have begun to pass laws that prevent the defense attorney from questioning the victim in detail in open court about her sexual history. The victim's husband or boyfriend, if he believes rape myths, may see the rape as an act of infidelity on her part and reject her.

In response to rape depictions, women have been found to see stranger rape as more serious than acquaintance rape, to be more certain that the rape had occurred, and to attribute less responsibility to the victim. Men showed just the opposite pattern on these three variables. Any ambiguity in the situation in acquaintance rape, for example (Did she go willingly to his apartment? Did she allow him to kiss her?) leads to perceptions that are less favorable toward the victim and more lenient to the perpetrator (J. D. Johnson & Jackson, 1988). Rape is rated as significantly more justifiable "when the couple went to the man's apartment rather than to a religious function, when the woman rather than the man initiated the date (unless they went to a religious function), and when the man paid all the dating expenses rather than splitting the costs with the woman" (Muehlenhard, Friedman, & Thomas, 1985, p. 306).

Men are less favorable toward the victim and more lenient toward the perpetrator than are women in jury trials of rape (J. D. Johnson & Jackson, 1988; Kleinke & Meyer, 1990). Whether or not people hold a belief in a just world has been found to also influence perceptions of rape victims. According to Lerner (1980), people have a need to believe that the universe is orderly and that people will be rewarded if they are good and punished if they are bad. When a tragedy happens to someone, people look for a justification for what happened. In order to maintain their belief in a just world they blame the victim as either provoking or enjoying the violence, or as having been a flawed person in some way. High belief in a just world has been related to men blaming the victim, but not to increased derogation of the rape victim by women (Kleinke & Meyer, 1990). Women identify with a rape victim and are therefore less likely to blame her.

Rape Trauma

Women who are raped are at risk for posttraumatic stress disorder and psychopathology. Women who were assaulted as children are more likely to develp mental disorders than those whose assaults occurred in adulthood.

Ann W. Burgess and Lynda Holmstrom (1974a, 1974b), who counseled 146 women treated for rape at the Emergency Room at Boston City Hospital, described a **rape trauma syndrome** that consisted of two stages, an acute phase of immediate emotional crisis and a long-term reorganization phase. The long-term reorganization phase included nightmares, rape-related phobias, and restrictions in lifestyle. More recently, this has come to be recognized as posttraumatic stress disorder (PTSD), an anxiety disorder first used to describe the long-term reactions of veterans of the Vietnam war. Symptoms of PTSD include "reliving experiences, nightmares, flashbacks, avoidance of reminders and thoughts of the assault, less socializing with friends, sense of detachment, inhibited emotion, disturbed sleep, difficulty concentrating, hyperalertness, feelings of guilt, and increased fearfulness" (Foa, Rothbaum, Riggs, & Murdock, 1991). PTSD was diagnosed in 94% of rape victims an average of 12 days following assault, and in 46% of victims three months later (Rothbaum, Foa, Riggs, Murdock, & Walsh, 1992).

What are the factors that influence the severity of a woman's response to being raped? Both behavioral self-blame and characterological self-blame are associated with depression postrape (Frazier, 1990; C. B. Meyer, & Taylor, 1986). Characterological blame would include self statements such as, "I got what I deserved" or "I can't take care of myself." Behavioral self-blame would focus on behavior of the woman prior to the rape, such as, "I shouldn't have gone out at night by myself" or "I shouldn't have opened the door without knowing who it was." On the other hand, societal blame (i.e., There is too much violence on TV; There are not enough police on duty in this city) is unrelated to adjustment following rape.

A cross-sectional probability survey of 3,132 households representing two Los Angeles communities found that many victims of sexual assault develop symptoms of psychopathology (Burnam et al., 1988). The experience of having been sexually assaulted was predictive of later onset of major depressive episodes, substance abuse disorders (alcohol and drug abuse or dependence), and anxiety disorders (phobia, panic disorder, and obsessive–compulsive disorder). Those who were sexually assaulted as children (15 years and younger) were more likely to develop disorders than those whose assaults occurred in adulthood (16 years or older). This study thus indicates that sexual assault has severe and long-lasting mental health consequences.

Physical consequences of rape are also well recognized. Sexually transmitted diseases result from rape in 4–30% of cases and pregnancy in 5% (Koss, 1993). Other persisting conditions that are diagnosed disproportionately among rape victims include chronic pelvic pain, gastrointestinal disorders, headaches, and premenstrual symptoms (Koss, 1993). Women with a past history of physical or sexual assault visit physicians 6.9 times a year versus 3.5 times a year for nonvictimized women.

Coping with Rape

Many women make major changes in their lives after being raped. Therapy, particularly cognitive behavioral therapy or cognitive processing therapy, is effective in reducing the symptoms of depression and anxiety.

Many of the women in the Boston City Hospital study made major changes in their lives (A. W. Burgess & Holmstrom, 1974a, 1974b). For example, women stopped attending classes or changed schools or employment. Other studies show mod-

erate or severe depression as measured by standardized depression scales in significant numbers of rape victims within the weeks following rape (Frank, Turner, & Duffy, 1979). The rape often also puts a strain on the woman's relationship with her husband or boyfriend. Many of these men also go through a very difficult time. Unfortunately, reflecting society's traditional views of rape victims, some of these men blame their wives, leading to desertion or divorce.

In terms of coping strategies, staying at home and withdrawing from others is associated with experiencing depression, fear, and sexual dissatisfaction. Precautionary strategies, however, were associated with fewer sexual problems following rape. The use of stress-reduction techniques is also associated with good adjustment following rape. In answer to an open-ended question, coping responses mentioned as effective by women who had been raped, in order of effectiveness, were: counseling; use of precautionary behaviors; talking to friends and family; and making life changes such as moving or quitting work (C. B. Meyer & Taylor, 1986).

Although counseling is the most helpful option in coping with rape, the reality of the situation is that few of the victims receive any kind of assistance services immediately following the rape (Koss & Burkhart, 1989). Many rape victims suffer from chronic, posttraumatic stress disorder, which needs to be dealt with when the rape victim eventually seeks professional psychotherapy, as surveys indicate that 31–48% of rape victims eventually do. Successful cognitive reappraisals need to redefine the rape as not being their fault, and provide the client an opportunity to be guided into positive experiences and coping.

Therapy, particularly cognitive behavioral therapy (CBT) or cognitive processing therapy (CPT), which was developed to reduce the symptoms of PTSD in rape victims, can be effective (Foa et al., 1991; Resick & Schnicke, 1992). Two cognitive behavioral approaches, **stress inoculation techniques (SIT)** and **prolonged exposure (PE),** were found to be more effective than counseling or being on a waiting list to receive treatment (Foa et al., 1991). SIT, including breathing exercises, deep muscle relaxation, and thought stopping for obsessive thinking, was effective for immediate symptom relief. PE, which involves the victim retelling the rape event several times each therapy session into a tape recorder that she then listens to at home, was found to bring about improvement in anxiety, depression, and rape-related distress on a longer-term basis.

CPT is similar to CBT in many ways except that where CBT tends to deemphasize the expression of emotion (except for prolonged exposure), CPT encourages the expression of affect.

> Rather than involving induced imagery, the exposure component consists of writing and reading a detailed account of the rape. The cognitive component includes training in identification of thoughts and affect, techniques for challenging maladaptive beliefs, and specific modules for five areas of beliefs: safety, trust, power, esteem, and intimacy. (Resick & Schnicke, 1992, p. 750)

Significant improvement was noted in both PTSD and depressive symptomology in 19 sexual assault survivors who participated in 12 weekly group CPT sessions and were assessed at pretreatment, posttreatment and three- and six-month follow-up. Although the women had suffered their symptoms for a considerable period of time (average length of time from most recent rape was 6.4 years), the improvement was maintained at the six-month follow-up. A waiting list control group did not change from the pre- to posttreatment assessment.

Men Who Rape

Men who rape are from a variety of backgrounds, but are hostile, aggressive, impulsive, sexually promiscuous, have traditional sex role attitudes—and fathers who are either not involved with them or who are abusive.

Although rape is a product of a culture of violence, most men within a violent culture do not rape. What is it that differentiates those men who do rape women from those who do not? Rap-

ists are heterogeneous. They have widely varying backgrounds, psychological characteristics, and criminal histories. Rape is a multidetermined behavior—it has many causes, not just one. Antisocial personality and nonsexual criminal history, both of which reflect a lifestyle of impulsive behavior, is common among rapists, although many rapists have no previous criminal record. Low social competence (poor heterosexual and interpersonal skills) plays a role for a subgroup, but not for all rapists. Alcohol and drugs, which reduce an individual's inhibitions, are often present in the situation (Prentky & Knight, 1991). Sexual aggressors are men who score higher in authoritarianism, have more "prorape" attitudes, and are high in sex guilt (W. D. Walker, Rowe, & Quinsey, 1993).

Acceptance of the traditional male sex role and male dominance were found to be related to both verbal sexual coercion and forcible rape among a sample of 1,152 male college students (Muehlenhard & Falcon, 1990). The men in the *Ms.*-supported college student survey who were high in both sexual and nonsexual aggression were characterized as having a hostile home environment, a background of general delinquency, sexual promiscuity, and hostile, impulsive personalities (Malamuth, Sockloskie, Koss, & Tanaka, 1991).

A comparison of 15 unreported rapists and 15 control students at a Southeastern university found the rapists scored significantly higher than the controls in hostility toward women, underlying anger motivations, dominance as a motive for sexual interaction, and on two indices of hypermasculinity (Lisak, 1991). Three of the rapists described their fathers as physically abusive. The others described their fathers as physically or emotionally absent. They complained of their fathers not spending time alone with them, and of general noninvolvement with them.

Community Response to Rape

Rape crisis centers have dual goals of helping victims of rape and changing power relations between men and women in society.

The response to rape most rooted in the feminist movement is the rape crisis centers that have sprung up around the country over the past 20 or so years.

> While rape had been viewed as a crime carried out by pathological men, with women partially responsible (Amir 1971), feminists argued that power issues were central. From a feminist perspective, rape and other sorts of sexual violence reflect and contribute to gendered social structures (Bart 1979). In particular, rape forces women to depend on men for protection (Griffin 1971; Sheffield 1984) and it enforces oppressive relations (Brownmiller 1975; Donat & D'Emilio 1992). (A. Fried, 1994, pp. 562–563)

Rape crisis centers are organizational structures that have often demonstrated a tension between proponents of radical feminism and liberal feminism in the goals and functioning of the organization. Fried (1994) conceptualizes the radical feminist position as the politicized perspective and the liberal feminist position as the service perspective. The goal of the radical feminist approach is to try to change the power relations in society. The liberal feminist approach is to try to help victims of sexual violence. Obviously, rape crisis centers do focus on the short-term measure of helping victims of sexual violence, and on education about rape prevention. They can also play a slower, more incremental role in transforming gendered social structures.

A real threat to the provision of care for rape victims by rape crisis centers has been inadequate funding. In 1990, the average grant to a rape crisis program in the state of New York was $17,600 per year (Koss, 1993). Increased state and federal funding is needed for rape crisis centers for staff development and higher salaries in order to retain a highly qualified professional staff.

Since rape victims are more likely to be seen by a physician than a mental health worker, physicians need to be trained in sensitive care and the relationship between rape and physical symptoms. They should also be knowledgeable about referral resources in the community. "The repertoire of interventions for rape would benefit from further development especially of multicultural approaches, programs for adolescent victims, and treatments for victims with multiple diagnoses" (Koss, 1993, p. 1067).

PORNOGRAPHY

Pornography is writings, pictures, or films that are intended to cause sexual excitement. The 1970 report of the U. S. Presidential Commission on Obscenity and Pornography stated that there was no evidence that exposure to explicit sexual materials caused sex crimes. The Attorney General's Commission on Pornography issued a report in 1986, however, that reached the conclusion that the depictions of violence in a sexually explicit manner are likely to increase sexual violence. The different conclusions are based, in part, on a focus on different types of pornography in the two reports. Researchers as well as the U.S. Attorney General's Commission on Pornography (1986) have made a distinction among three types of sexually explicit material: (1) sexual violence; (2) nonviolent but degrading material; and (3) erotica (which is nonviolent and characterized by choice and mutuality) (Cowan & Campbell, 1994).

X-Rated Videos

Content analysis of X-rated videocassette finds them to be sexist and racist.

A content analysis of 45 widely available X-rated videocassettes determined that dominance and exploitation comprised the majority (54%) of the explicitly sexual scenes, compared with only 37% of scenes portraying sexual equality (Cowan, Lee, Levy, & Snyder, 1988). In most of the dominance scenes (78%) a man was dominating one or more women. In 23% of these scenes, physical violence was being directed toward women. In 14% of the scenes rape myths were reinforced by women being shown enjoying being forced to engage in sex.

A recent study by Cowan and Campbell (1994) found X-rated interracial videos to be racist as well as sexist. "One supposition is that race exaggerates sex roles in pornography. Women are dominated but Black women are particularly dominated. Men are shown as sex machines, but Black men are particularly so" (Cowan & Campbell, 1994, p. 335). The pornographic videos, therefore, served to reinforce racial as well as gender stereotypes.

Viewing violent pornography increases aggression toward women in the laboratory. Feminists are divided about whether or not to censor pornography.

Major changes that occurred between the two reports were the increase in violent pornography that had become available, and the increase in quantity and quality of research and publications by scholars. Based on this research the 1986 Commission concluded that sexually violent material leads to (1) acceptance of rape myths and violence against women; (2) has more pronounced effects when the victim is shown enjoying the use of force or violence; (3) is arousing for rapists and for some males in the general population; and (4) has resulted in sexual aggression toward women in the laboratory (U.S. Attorney General's Commission on Pornography, 1986, p. 1005).

It was Susan Brownmiller (1975) in her book on rape who first examined the connection between the history of rape and pornography, saying that acts of sexual hostility were ideologically encouraged by pornography. The appearance in 1975 of the porn film, "Snuff," which showed an actual rape, murder, and dismemberment of a woman, galvanized feminists to take action. Diana Russell helped form a San Francisco group called "Women against Violence in Pornography and Media" claiming that the proliferation of pornography, particularly violent pornography, is a backlash against the women's liberation movement (I. Diamond, 1980).

The controversy over pornography is further complicated by the fact that men and women's attitudes toward pornography differ. Men (332) and women (315) who viewed the antipornogra-

phy documentary film, "Not a Love Story," completed questionnaires before and after viewing it and over a five-week period (Bart, Freeman, & Kimball, 1991). The women were significantly more negative toward pornography than the men, and factor analysis found also that their attitudinal dimensions differed from those of men. "Pornography represents male interests. Women in pornography are required to behave as male fantasies would have them behave. Thus it is no accident that men are more propornography than women" (Bart et al., 1991, p. 191). Thus the test used in U.S. obscenity law—that to be pornographic the material violates community standards, is not a viable one because there are at least two community standards, male and female.

Whether there should be legal restrictions on violent pornography is dividing feminists, some of whom support legislation restricting violent pornography and others who do not want to infringe on First Amendment rights of free speech. Typically, it is the liberal feminists, those represented by groups such as the Feminist Anticensorship Taskforce (FACT), who take the position that censorship of pornography will infringe on the rights and freedom of women and men. On the other hand, radical feminists such as Andrea Dworkin and Catherine MacKinnon favor banning pornography. "Radical feminists view pornography as an extremely important means of enforcing men's control of women and their bodies and sustaining domination of women (I. Diamond, 1980)" (Cowan, 1992, p. 166). I agree with Dworkin and MacKinnon that violent pornography debases women; however, I do not agree that censorship is the solution. Crimes committed in making the films such as the use of underage girls and violence committed on women, however, should be vigorously prosecuted.

Laboratory Experiments

Men with a predisposition to rape show sexual arousal to rape depictions.

Regardless of one's position on censorship of pornography, the laboratory evidence, which has largely come out of social psychological research, shows that viewing violent pornography does influence aggressive behavior and desensitization to the crime of rape. In a series of experiments, Abel and his colleagues found that rapists showed a fairly high and about equal sexual arousal (as measured by penile tumescence) in response to audiotaped portrayals of rape depictions and consenting sexual depictions (Abel, Barlow, Blanchard, & Guild, 1977; Abel, Blanchard, Becker, & Djenderedjian, 1978). An experiment by Quinsey, Chaplin, & Upfold (1984), however, found that male nonrapists showed relatively little sexual arousal, as measured by both self-report and penile tumescence, to rape depiction as compared with consenting depictions.

In two experiments, Malamuth, Check, and Briere (1986) found that both male and female introductory psychology students reported more sexual arousal in response to nonaggressive than to aggressive sexual depictions. When the portrayals were nonsexual, however, more sexual arousal was reported from the aggressive than from the nonaggressive depictions. This indicates that aggression may be a sexual stimulant for some individuals in the general population. On the basis of their self-report of sexual arousal to the use of force, male subjects were divided into no arousal, moderate arousal, and high arousal from force groups. Although for the no arousal and moderate arousal from force groups, aggression inhibited sexual arousal; for the high level of arousal from force (about 30% of the subjects) aggression enhanced sexual arousal as measured by penile tumescence. Those indicating high levels of arousal from force were also more accepting of an ideology of male aggression and dominance over women in both sexual and nonsexual situations. In addition, arousal from force was also related to the belief that the individual himself might engage in such acts in the future.

Excitation Transfer Theory

Excitation transfer theory, which says that erotic stimuli can facilitate aggression, is supported by experimental research.

Zillmann (1978, 1984) developed **excitation transfer theory,** which says that the arousal caused by one stimulus is transferred to and added to arousal from a second stimulus, and the combined arousal is then attributed to the second stimulus. Donnerstein and Hallam (1978) conducted an experiment that illustrated this theory showing that erotic stimuli can facilitate aggression. Male participants were angered by male and female confederates and exposed to an erotic film, aggressive film, or nonfilm condition. They were then given an opportunity to aggress against the confederate immediately after exposure to the film. Erotic films did increase aggression as compared with that of the no-film controls. Although there was no difference in aggression toward male or female confederates during the initial aggression, aggressive responses were greater toward the female than the male when the male participants were given a second opportunity to aggress 10 minutes later.

Even erotic material that does not contain violence or force, simply consenting sex between adults, has been shown to have an effect on attitudes toward sentences for convicted rapists. Zillman and Bryant (1984) conducted a study in which male and female volunteers were shown 6 eight-minute films that were either pornographic or non-erotic. The more pornographic films watched by both the male and female participants, the shorter the sentences they recommended for a convicted rapist. Thus, the amount of pornography viewed by people can influence the seriousness with which they view sexual crimes.

Men shown violent films in a laboratory experiment showed less anxiety and depression and declines in negative affective responses with increased exposure to the violent films (Linz, Donnerstein, & Penrod, 1988). They were also less sympathetic to the victim in a sexual assault trial reenactment and less empathetic to rape victims in general even though the films used by them were feature films containing a myriad of other scenes and ideas about women in which they were depicted in a variety of other activities besides sex, such a going to work, and going out to dinner.

Laboratory experiments appear to conclusively demonstrate that viewing pornographic films can increase aggressive behavior in the laboratory, and that some men are particularly susceptible to the effects of violent pornography. Even pornography that is not violent may change attitudes toward women and rape, encouraging men to view rape as a less-serious crime.

What about the real world? Does pornography increase the incidence of rape and other violent crimes toward women? Because the research in the field is correlational, it makes it much more difficult to draw conclusions. Silbert and Pines (1984) conducted a study of 200 juvenile and adult, current and former, female street prostitutes in the San Francisco Bay area. The sample had an average age of 22: the youngest was 10 and the oldest 46 years of age. An unexpected finding of the study was the many open-ended comments made by the prostitutes that referred to the role played by pornography in the sexual abuse they had suffered. Out of the 193 cases of rape reported by the prostitutes, 24% mentioned the sex offender having referred to pornographic materials he had seen or read. He then insisted that the victims enjoyed the rape or extreme violence.

Spontaneously, without being questioned about it, 10% of the 200 respondents said they had been used in pornographic films and magazines when they were children. In 22% of the 178 cases in which the prostitutes had been sexually exploited as children, the adult had shown the children pictures of children engaged in sexual acts with adults as a way of showing the child that it was legitimate for the adult to have sexual relations with the child. Others of the abusers had used pornography to arouse themselves before sexually abusing the child. Questions about pornography had not been asked in the survey.

The solution advocated by Linz, Wilson, and Donnerstein (1992), who have conducted much laboratory research on the effects of violent pornography on eliciting aggressive behavior, is educational interventions with adolescents specifically directed to changing beliefs about rape and sexual violence. Adolescents would be taught about the inaccuracies in media depictions, such as the typical portrayal of women enjoying the violence directed toward them. Further research is necessary to determine the most effective type of educational program.

INCEST

It was not until the late 1970s that the feminist movement succeeded in raising public consciousness about incest. It was during 1978 that two books appeared on incest from a victim oriented perspective, Sandra Butler's *Conspiracy of Silence* and Louise Armstrong's *Kiss Daddy Goodnight*. Since that time, numerous books and articles have been written about incest. This previously hidden secret has also become part of the public consciousness via television talk shows, advice columns, and magazine articles.

Freud's Repudiation of His Seduction Theory

Freud at first believed his female clients that they had been "seduced" by their fathers, but he changed his mind, and wrote that these women were indulging in fantasies.

Perhaps the secret of incest would not have stayed hidden for so long if Freud had not concluded that his patients' accounts of early incestuous relations with their fathers were figments of their imaginations. Freud initially believed the women's accounts that they had been "seduced" by their fathers and attributed their neurotic symptoms to repression of these incidents. Later Freud, pressured by his clinical colleagues and believing that "such widespread perversions against children are not very probable" (Freud as cited in Masson, 1984) changed his mind that his patients had been molested by their fathers or other male relatives, and instead stated that their accounts must be based on their own sexual fantasies.

Freud was seduced into and seduced others into protecting the sexual offender and thus betrayed the sexual victim. Freud's failure in his reformulation of theory to validate the experience of his female clients led to his failure to develop a female psychology. (Westerlund, 1986, p. 308)

Freud's judgment that these accounts were unreal fantasies became the standard in psychoanalytic thought. Kinsey and his colleagues further contributed to keeping incest in the closet by downplaying the damaging consequences of incest to children (Masson, 1984).

Prevalence of Incest

One out of six women were sexually abused by age 18. Incest is more common among families with a higher rather than a lower socioeconomic level, social isolation, greater religiosity, incapacity of the mother, and pseudomaturity of the daughter.

Diana E. H. Russell (1986) found that one out of six (16%) women had been incestuously abused by the age of 18. This revelation is based on a probability sample survey of 930 women residents of San Francisco who participated in face to face interviews. Of these cases, 43% of the incestuous incidents occurred only one time, 31% occurred two to five times, 17% occurred 6–20 times, and 10% occurred over 20 times. The rate of sexual abuse was similar for White (17%), African American (16%), and Latina women (20%). Asian and Filipino women were, however, only half as likely to be sexually abused (8%), although this difference did not reach statistical significance. Jews (10%) were less likely to be incestuously abused than were Catholics (17%) or Protestants (18%), although, again, this difference was not statistically significant.

More of the victims of incestuous abuse came from higher-income families as compared with low socioeconomic families. This is the reverse of the pattern for other types of abuse such as battering. Certain characteristics of the families in which father–daughter incest occurs have been identified: (1) Social isolation—few social relationships outside the nuclear family; (2) Religiosity—the family tends to engage in rigorous religious participation; (3) Incapacity of the mother—she may be ill, physically handicapped, have mental illness, although the father may still be having sexual relations with her; and (4) Pseudomaturity of the daughter—she takes over adult roles such as childcare, housekeeping, and household budgeting (Storer, 1992).

Incestuous Activity

Incestuous activity occurs gradually in stages as the father engages in "courtship" with the daughter.

The incestuous activity occurs in stages, beginning with a presexual contact stage in which the father engages in "courtship" behavior, during which time he gives the girl a lot of attention. The first stage is fondling of the breasts, buttocks, and genitals. This is introduced gradually in the context of playing with the child or bathing or dressing her. The second stage graduates to mutual masturbation and oral and anal intercourse. The third stage is genital intercourse. The ongoing need for secrecy is handled by the fathers either through threats of punishment for telling anyone or the "Let's just keep this our secret" ploy. The incestuous family is typically a traditional father-centered one in which the father has the dominant role. Although there has been considerable speculation about how much the mother knows about the incestuous relationship, the mother did not admit to firm suspicion in any of the cases studied by Storer (1992). The behavior observed by the mother is not overtly sexual. Nevertheless, elements of jealousy and hostility develop between mother and daughter because of the heightened attention being paid to the daughter. The incest usually continues until the daughter leaves home or authorities find out about it because of something the daughter says to a friend, or teacher or other authority figure. "There is no institutional means of dealing with father–daughter incest while maintaining the family" (Storer, 1992, p. 96).

Attachment Theory of Incest

Father–daughter incest can be conceptualized as a failure of parent–child attachment. Only 5% of perpetrators of incest are women.

Attachment theory can also explain the familial antecedents of incest and the long-term consequences (P. C. Alexander, 1992). According to John Bowlby (1969, 1980, 1988) on the basis of early experience with the caregiver, the infant develops an attachment style that leads to expectations about relationships. Attachment style to parents continues to affect relationships in adulthood. Adults are classified into four attachment styles: secure; avoidant; anxious/ambivalent; and anxious or fearful. Alexander (1992) proposes that incest may develop out of insecure parent–child attachment. An emphasis on prevention would focus on father–child attachment and holding him responsible for the welfare of the child.

Consistent with common beliefs, Diana E.H. Russell's (1986) survey data revealed only 10 cases of incestuous abuse by females. This constituted only 5% of all incest perpetrators in their survey and affected only 1% of the 930 women interviewed. Many of the cases involving female abusers could also be considered only borderline in being described as incidents of abuse.

In patriarchal cultures incest with a daughter is not an offense against another man's rights.

Why are fathers so much more likely to commit incest than mothers? In patriarchal societies, incest with a daughter is not an offense against another man's rights. "Male supremacy invests fathers with immense powers over their children, especially their daughters. The sexual division of labor, in which women nurture children and men do not, produces fathers who are predisposed to use their powers exploitatively (Herman, 1981, p. 62). In cultures with greater male dominance, as in families with greater domination of the father, the greater the likelihood of father–daughter incest.

Mental Health Consequences of Childhood Sexual Abuse

Being sexually abused as a child has both immediate and long-term negative mental health consequences.

Reviews of the literature on the impact of child sexual abuse found both immediate and long-term negative mental health consequences (Browne & Finkelhor, 1986; Kendall-Tackett, Williams, & Finkelhor, 1993). Nevertheless, childhood sexual abuse is not associated with a specific set of symptoms that distinguish it from other types of abuse. One of the reasons for the diverse effects of childhood sexual abuse is the fact that the developmental stage of the child has not been taken into account. "Age-related variables, particularly the *age at first sexual contact* and the *number of developmental transitions during which the abuse persisted,* should be included with other factors in studies of effects of child sexual abuse" (Cole & Putnam, 1992, p. 180).

Initial reactions of the sexually abused child include fear, anxiety, depression, poor self esteem, anger, and hostility, aggression, sleep, and eating disorders and sexually inappropriate behavior. Although abused children have more symptomatic and pathological behavior than do nonabused children, with abuse accounting for 15–34% of the variance, there is no dominant and consistent set of symptoms. Approximately one-third of abused children are symptom-free. Characteristics of the abuse experience that increase symptomatology include molestation that involved some penetration (oral, anal, or vaginal), longer duration and greater frequency of the abuse, a perpetrator close to the child (i.e., father, stepfather), an abuser who is an adult rather than a teenager, and abuse involving force (Browne & Finkelhor, 1986; Kendall-Tackett, et al., 1993).

Long-term effects have found a link between child sexual abuse and depression. Victims of child sexual abuse have also been found to suffer from anxiety and tension, to continue to report feelings of isolation and to feel stigmatized as adults, and to have low self-esteem. Difficulties in interpersonal relations are common, including difficulty in trusting others, difficulty in parenting, and sexual maladjustment. Women who were sexually abused as children have a vulnerability to be revictimized as adults by rape and battering. Several studies also show a link between child sexual abuse and substance abuse disorders in women (G. R. Brown & Anderson, 1991) and eating disorders (Bulik, Sullivan, & Rorty, 1989).

Treatment for Incest Survivors

Effectiveness of treatment for incest varies with the sexual abuse history and pretreatment levels of distress.

How effective is treatment for incest survivors? The answer to this question has been found to vary with demographic variables, sexual abuse history, characteristics of the family of origin, and pretreatment levels of depression and distress. Follette, Alexander, and Follette (1991) evaluated 65 women who had been sexually abused by fathers, step-fathers, or another close male relative who participated in time-limited group therapy for incest survivors. Having less education, having experienced oral–genital abuse or intercourse rather than fondling alone, initial higher levels of general distress and depression, and being currently married rather than with no partner were variables predicting poorer treatment outcomes. The authors suggest that being in marital therapy at the same time as participating in an incest survivor's group would perhaps facilitate the therapy for those with a partner.

Repressed Memories

Memories of childhood sexual abuse can be repressed and recalled at a later date. Therapists and others can suggest memories of events that never occurred.

Controversy exists both in the media and among psychologists about the validity of repressed memories of childhood sexual abuse that are recovered, often in therapy. The accuracy of repressed memories has been readily accepted by many psychotherapists, but it has been questioned by experimental psychologists (Loftus, 1993).

> Public attention has focused on a large and steadily growing cadre of public figures, celebrities, and others who have revealed their own child sexual victimization experiences, many reporting they had at some time forgotten that the abuse had occurred. The laws in many states have changed to extend the statute of limitations, and recently recovered memories of abuse have figured prominently in some prosecutions and numerous civil cases (Loftus & Rosenwald, 1993). (L. M. Williams, 1994, p. 1167)

Only in the last few years have studies been conducted to try to ascertain the extent to which repression of childhood memories occurs. Overall, 54% of 105 women interviewed in an outpatient substance abuse program indicated they had experienced some form of childhood sexual abuse (Loftus, Polonsky, & Fullilove, 1994). Of those women recalling childhood sexual abuse, 69% claimed to have always remembered their abuse completely. According to Loftus et al., of those with some degree of forgetting, the memory was of a different quality; it was deteriorated in some respects and less of a "picture."

In the mid-1970s, 206 girls (86% African American) aged 10 months to 12 years were examined for sexual abuse in the emergency room of a large northeastern hospital and interviews were conducted with the child, the caregiver, or both (L. M. Williams, 1994). Seventeen years later, 129 of the women who had been examined in the emergency room as children were asked detailed questions about their abuse history. Overall, 38% of the women did not report the abuse documented in the hospital records, nor any other abuse by the same perpetrator. Abuse occurring at a younger age and perpetrated by someone they knew was more likely to be forgotten, although some of the younger victims had detailed memories of the abuse. Sixteen percent of the women reporting the abuse indicated that they had forgotten about it for some period of time. Physical force and violence associated with the abuse was not related to recall.

In another study, 450 adult women and men in treatment who had reported sexual abuse histories to their therapists were asked the question, "During the period of time between when the first forced sexual experience happened and your 18th birthday was there ever a time when you could not remember the forced sexual experience?" (Briere & Conte, 1993). A *yes* response (59% of those responding) was more likely to be given if the abuse involved multiple perpetrators and more severe violence. There was, however, a lack of association between recall and conflict as measured by guilt, shame, and enjoyment.

On the other hand, Loftus (1993) raises the issue of clinicians leading clients to believe that sexual abuse did occur in their childhood. She cites therapists who know of those who will ask a client, "You sound like the sort of person who must have been sexually abused. Tell me what that bastard did to you" (Loftus, 1993, p. 526). Loftus also cites many studies that have demonstrated that through exposure to misinformation false memories can be created. Individuals may also make many errors when recalling a traumatic event. She cites Jack Hamilton's recall of his pitch during a major league baseball game when his fastball severely injured opposing player Tony Conigliaro's face. Hamilton made a number of errors of recall, remembering it as occurring during a day game when it took place at night.

I think the reason there is so much controversy in the area of repressed memory and later recall of sexual abuse is because there is truth on both sides of the issue. I think it is apparent from the research that memories of childhood sexual assault can be repressed and recalled at some time in the future. Also, memories of past events can be subject to distortion due to suggestion such as from a therapist or from just plain inaccuracies in memories.

PROSTITUTION

Prostitution is female sexual slavery.

Some people might wonder why I would include **prostitution** in a chapter on "Violence against Women." After all, is prostitution not vol-

untary? Is it not just a profession that some women choose, albeit illegal in the United States except for a few counties in Nevada. If that is what you think, then you should read Kathleen Barry's groundbreaking book, *Female Sexual Slavery* (1979), in which she documents an international trade in women for the purpose of prostitution. Female sexual slavery, however, happens not only in exotic places like Bangkok and Zanzibar, but it also happens in the United States.

Barry includes incest, wife battery, and pornography as forms of female sexual slavery, along with forced prostitution.

> Many women and girls directly experience female sexual slavery without ever going out of their homes. For them home replaces brothel; they are wives or daughters who are the victims of husbands or fathers instead of pimps. I am speaking, of course, of wife battery and incest, practices which make the private family instead of the public street or "house" the location of female sexual slavery. In certain cultures these practices take the form of forced marriage, polygyny, veiling, and seclusion of women. (Barry, 1979, p. 139)

A history of rape and incest prior to becoming prostitutes has been documented in a number of studies. In a study of 200 street prostitutes 60% of the women reported exploitation as juveniles with abuse by an average of two males each, some with as many as 11 abusers (Silbert & Pines, 1983). Two-thirds of the prostitutes had been abused by their fathers or surrogate fathers. An attack by a stranger seemed to have affected the victim less traumatically, since it usually only occurred once. Silbert and Pines say that the questionnaires "generated an enormous amount of data, quantitative as well as qualitative documenting stunning amounts of sexual abuse of street prostitutes as part of their job, outside of their work environment, and in their childhood prior to entering prostitution." (Silbert & Pines, 1983, p. 863). Barry (1979) provides many examples of the brutality of pimps who force women and girls to sell their bodies.

It should be recognized, however, that prostitution is a heterogeneous category. Prostitution is "an institution or pattern of impersonal and/or time-limited transactions between socially unrelated individuals involving purchase and sale of sexual services at an acknowledged and agreed unit price" (de Zalduondo, 1991, p. 229). Just as in other occupations, prostitutes vary in social status from the street prostitute to the high-priced call girl.

Contemporary debate about prostitution within feminism focuses on the civil rights issue of whether women have the right to free sexual expression and entrepreneurial activity or the right to be protected from male subjugation and exploitation (Jolin, 1994). The radical feminist theorists Catherine MacKinnon and Andrea Dworkin oppose prostitution on the grounds that it is intrinsically exploitive. On the other hand, for egalitarian feminists, the freedom to choose is linked to equality. "Thus 'saving a woman from herself' by restricting her choice denies her equality, and with it, her status as a full human being" (Jolin, 1994, p. 77). On this issue, I tend to agree with the radical feminists about the exploitive nature of prostitution because most prostitutes in the United States are drug addicts with a history of physical and sexual abuse. I believe that free choice is a continuum, with choices at one end completely free and at the other end completely determined. When a woman is a drug addict, perhaps under the influence of a pimp, her free choice to prostitute herself is a dangerous illusion. On the other hand, feminist prostitutes' rights groups such as COYOTE (Call off Your Old Tired Ethics) and HIRE (Hooking is Real Employment) see prostitution as a labor issue. Other prostitutes who are members of the collective WHISPER (Women Hurt in Systems of Prostitution) acknowledge the ways they have been used and hurt by men and do not see prostitution as such a free choice. Pateman (1993) disagrees. "Prostitution is the public recognition of men as sexual masters; it puts submission on sale as a commodity in the market" (p. 388). Most women make this "choice" only after having suffered previous physical and sexual abuse. Rather than protecting prostitutes police see them as fair game for sexual abuse (Carmen & Moody, 1985).

In the 1980s, a postmodern perspective on prostitution emerged that views it as a plural subject with many meanings. "Specific experiences in prostitution have given rise to different and contested constructions of the postitute body: a site of work, a site of abuse, power, sex, addiction, and even pleasure" (S. Bell, 1994, p. 99). The diverse viewpoints of the prostitutes themselves are a needed part of the debate about prostitution, nevertheless, I tend to agree with the radical feminists that prostitution exploits and degrades women. As a pragmatist, however, I support the resolution passed by The Division of Psychology of Women of American Psychological Association calling for the decriminalization and destigmatization of prostitution (Resolution For, 1984). The resolution notes the discrimination against women of color in enforcement of the antiprostitution laws.

BATTERING

Violence occurs in dating relationships as a function of both impulsive, aggressive personality characteristics and patriarchal subcultural norms.

Sugarman and Hotaling (1989) define dating violence as "the perpetration or threat of an act of physical violence by at least one member of an unmarried dyad on the other within the context of the dating process" (p. 5). This definition excludes married and divorced couples, but it does include homosexual as well as heterosexual relationships. Their review of 20 studies of violence in dating relationships in high school and college samples found higher average prevalence rates for college ($M = 31.9\%$) than for samples of high school students ($M = 22.3\%$).

Females are only slightly more likely than males to report having been victimized at some point in their dating history, according to the Sugarman and Hotaling (1989) review. Victimization rates for both males and females in the context of dating were for males $M = 33.3\%$ and for females $M = 36.2\%$ Based on a more recent survey of 631 respondents from three midwestern high schools (urban, suburban, and inner-city), the proportion of girls reporting being victims of physical violence was 15.5% whereas only 7.8% of boys reported being victims of physical violence (Bergman, 1992). On the other hand, among a sample of 336 college students 27.5% of men and 29.6% of women disclosed that they had been targets of their partner's physical aggression within the past two years therefore not supporting the stereotype of male violence (Thompson, 1991). What this study did find, however, was that both women and men scoring masculine on the BSRI had aggressed against a dating partner significantly more often than men and women with feminine sex role orientations.

Across these various studies, males generally initiate more severe violence and inflict much more serious injuries on their female partners than females inflict on males. Certain factors emerge as being risk factors for dating violence. These are, primarily, lower family income, poorer academic performance, higher levels of stress, and the support of patriarchal norms. Regional differences in prevalence rates are also significant, with higher levels of violence in dating occurring in the South (43.8%), followed by the West (27.5%), then the Midwest (25.7%), and the least in the East (22.8%). The finding of differences in regional patterns probably reflect differences in subcultural norms, indicating that it is part of the patriarchal attitudes of some regions (Hotaling & Sugarman, 1989).

Riggs and O'Leary (1989) have developed a theoretical model of violence in dating relationships. The model includes both contextual (what factors will cause a person to behave aggressively toward any dating partner in any situation) and situational factors (what factors in the situation contribute to that person becoming aggressive in that instance). The contextual factors include: (1) models of aggression in intimate relationships; (2) having been subjected to parental aggression as a child, (3) aggressive–impulsive personality characteristics, (4) a history of prior use of aggression; (5) psychopathology; (6) arousability and emotionality; and (7) acceptance of aggression as a response to conflict.

The situational variables that have been found by Riggs and O'Leary (1989) to be predictors of courtship violence are: (1) the expectation of a positive outcome for aggression; (2) stress; (3) alcohol use; (4) partner's aggression; and (5) relationship conflict as manifest in severe and frequent disagreements. The contextual and situational components interact. Intervention potentially could be targeted through treatment programs helping couples to deal with stress, improve communication and problem solving skills, and deal with specific problem areas.

A theoretical model of interactive processes in predicting physical aggression in dating relations among young people, tested by means of a nationally representative telephone sample, found evidence that conflict is more likely when the respondent is low in role-taking and acts to control the other (Stets, 1992).

> The effect of role-taking on aggression confirms the notion that it is important to imagine the inner states of another, for through this imagination, feelings of guilt, shame, or embarrassment may be called up to deter aggressive behavior (Franks, 1985). The effect of interpersonal control supports the idea that those who act to control others are more likely to use aggression either as a last resort when other methods have failed or as a first response if the perpetrators have learned, over time, that aggression gets what they want (Stets & Pirog-Good, 1990). (Stets, 1992, p. 175)

Lack of consensus in the dating relationship over some issue also influences the occurrence of one-time minor aggression. Unlike Hotaling and Sugarman's review, this study found the interactive factors to be better predictors of dating violence than demographic variables.

Violence in Marriage

Three to four million American women are beaten every year by their partner.

Identified as a problem in the 1970s, wife beating became the focus of a proliferation of research in the 1980s. Historically, a husband had a right to hit his wife in order to chastise her and maintain his authority. It was not until the beginning of the twentieth century that **battering** was no longer sanctioned by law in the United States. Abuse, however, was still common and it remained a hidden problem until, inspired by the feminist movement, a "grassroots" battered women's movement emerged in the 1970s and shelters for battered women began to be opened. There are now more than 1,200 shelters, hotlines, and safe-home networks in this country. It is estimated that 3–4 million women are beaten every year by their spouse or intimate partner. Of these women, more than 1 million seek medical assistance each year for injuries inflicted on them by the battering (Diehm & Ross, 1988). More women sustain injuries from spousal abuse than from automobile accidents and muggings combined (Carden, 1994).

Family violence may be declining in the United States.

Family violence typically occurs in the home, so it is difficult to estimate the extent of its occurrence. National probability data on spousal and child abuse was obtained from a sample of 2,143 families in 1975 and 3,520 in 1985. The first survey was reported on in a book appropriately titled *Behind Closed Doors* (Straus, Gelles, & Steinmetz, 1980). The Conflict Tactics Scale, which was a part of the two surveys, measures violence by asking respondents to indicate how frequently they have engaged in each of eight types of violence against a family member. The scale ranges from throwing something, to pushing, grabbing, or shoving the person, to using a gun or knife.

The husband-to-wife violence rate declined from 121 incidents per 1,000 couples in 1975 to 113 per 1,000 couples in 1985, a decline of 6.6% (which is not statistically significant). The measure of severe violence, however, declined from 38 per thousand couples to 30 per thousand couples in 1985, which is a 26.6% decrease (this approached significance, $p < .10$). Applying this decrease to the 54 million couples in the United States in 1985 would mean 432,000 fewer severely beaten wives (Straus & Gelles, 1986, 1989).

This decrease in husband-to-wife violence may be attributed to hopeful factors such as the growth of paid employment of women, the growth of women's shelters, and the greater probability of being caught and punished for wife battering. Critics of Straus and Gelles' 1985 survey, however, point out that it was conducted by telephone, whereas the 1975 data was collected in face-to-face interviews. Another criticism is that in 1985 people may have been more reluctant to report severe marital violence because of public and media attention to it as a crime.

Egley (1991) reanalyzed the same survey data that Straus and Gelles (1986) used, adjusting for the difference in age distribution of the population at the second survey. Egley concludes that most of the reduction in family violence can be accounted for by changes in the age structure of the child and adult population, some due to methodological differences in the two surveys, and some to actual reduction in violent behavior.

Violence toward husbands was about the same in 1975 as it was in 1985. Severe violence toward husbands was 46 incidents per 1,000 couples in 1975 versus 44 per 1,000 couples in 1985. The same act (for example, a punch) may inflict much greater injury when delivered by a man, however, than when it is delivered by a woman because of the greater average size and strength of men. Another point to keep in mind is that a great deal of violence by wives against their husbands is retaliation or self-defense (Gelles & Straus, 1988, 1986).

The rate of wife abuse also declined significantly for African Americans. "Ten years ago the rate of severe violence toward black women was nearly four times greater than the rate of severe violence toward white women. In 1985 the rate of severe violence toward black women dropped substantially to slightly more than twice the rate of severe violence against white women" (Hampton, Gelles, & Harrop, 1991, p.10). Although the overall violence rate for Black women toward Black men increased by 33.3%, the change was not statistically significant. It is difficult to determine causes for the trend toward increasing wife-to-husband violence in African American families. It may be that Black women's improvement in education and economic conditions relative to that of Black men have decreased the economic and social costs of striking back.

Risk Markers for Battering

Husbands at high risk for beating their wives witnessed violence as children, are high school graduates, drink, have lower occupational and income status, are nonassertive, rape their wives, and beat their children. They also are somewhat deviant psychologically.

In order to draw a more scientific assessment of causes of wife beating, Hotaling and Sugarman (1986) reviewed the literature and identified 96 potential risk markers in husband-to-wife violence. Hotaling and Sugarman found only one consistent risk marker that was characteristic of the wife, which was witnessing violence as a child. Women who had witnessed violence in their homes as children or adolescents were at greater risk of being battered wives. For husbands, the consistent risk marker supported by the largest number of studies was witnessing violence as a child. Other consistent risk markers for husband characteristics were: educational level (curvilinear relationship, with high school graduates showing the greatest risk of violent behavior); alcohol usage; lower occupational status; lower income; lower levels of assertiveness; sexually aggressive behavior toward their wife/partner; and violence toward their children. Couple characteristics that were found to be consistent risk markers were: lower family income/social class; poorer marital adjustment/satisfaction; and marital status (married couples have a lower incidence of marital violence than do divorced, separated, cohabiting, or reconstituted couples). Although the frequency of wife abuse varies with the characteristics noted by Hotaling and Sugarman, family violence occurs in families of every race, religion, social class, and educational level.

Few studies have looked at personality characteristics and standard measures of psychopathology of batterers. One study, of 250 men enrolled in group treatment for wife abuse, supported the previous data linking alcoholism and violence in family of origin to current family violence. Level of violence was also related, however, to pathologies (anxiety, depression, schizoid tendencies, social nonconformity) as measured by standardized psychological tests. Although more than half of abusive men typically do not complete the treatment program, violence is less after treatment than before (Schuerger & Reigle, 1988).

Interaction Dynamics in Violent Marriages

Violent marriages are characterized by a high degree of husband control and jealousy.

Questionnaire data on interaction dynamics in 50 violent and 50 nonviolent marriages or cohabiting relationships revealed the husbands of battered women to be very controlling and lacking in trust of their wives (Whittle & Rollins, 1980). Although both the battered and nonbattered wives were European American and had similar levels of education, the husbands of the battered women also European American, had significantly less education than did the husbands of nonbattered women.

A majority of the battered wives said that their husbands did not trust them, and that they were not allowed to leave the house or talk on the phone without their husband's approval. None of the nonbattered wives reported such control by their husbands. Most surprising was the fact that 62% of the violent husbands had surreptitiously taken a day out of work to check up on their wive's activities.

Women are not masochists. They do not like to be beaten. Nearly two-thirds of the wives said they either disliked or hated their husbands after the abuse, whereas about one-third felt sympathetic toward him. They do not find violence sexually stimulating or their batterers attractive. When asked to rate their husband's attractiveness, the majority of battered wives reported them as not being physically attractive at all. The majority of nonbattered wives generally rated their husbands from somewhat good looking to very handsome.

Although the frequency of sexual intercourse was similar in both the control and critical marriages, the men who battered their wives were more likely to initiate sex, whereas the nonbat-

VIOLENCE

PHYSICAL / SEXUAL

USING COERCION AND THREATS
Making and/or carrying out threats to do something to hurt her • threatening to leave her, to commit suicide, to report her to welfare • making her drop charges • making her do illegal things.

USING INTIMIDATION
Making her afraid by using looks, actions, gestures • smashing things • destroying her property • abusing pets • displaying weapons.

USING ECONOMIC ABUSE
Preventing her from getting or keeping a job • making her ask for money • giving her an allowance • taking her money • not letting her know about or have access to family income.

USING EMOTIONAL ABUSE
Putting her down • making her feel bad about herself • calling her names • making her think she's crazy • playing mind games • humiliating her • making her feel guilty.

POWER AND CONTROL

USING MALE PRIVILEGE
Treating her like a servant • making all the big decisions • acting like the "master of the castle" • being the one to define men's and women's roles

USING ISOLATION
Controlling what she does, who she sees and talks to, what she reads, where she goes • limiting her outside involvement • using jealousy to justify actions.

USING CHILDREN
Making her feel guilty about the children • using the children to relay messages • using visitation to harass her • threatening to take the children away.

MINIMIZING, DENYING AND BLAMING
Making light of the abuse and not taking her concerns about it seriously • saying the abuse didn't happen • shifting responsibility for abusive behavior • saying she caused it.

PHYSICAL / SEXUAL

VIOLENCE

Source: Domestic Abuse Intervention Project, 206 West Fourth Street, Duluth, Minnesota 55806, 218-722-4134.

tered wives reported the initiative to be equal. The level of sexual satisfaction was also much less for the battered wives, with 38% rating their sex life as poor, whereas only 6% of the controls gave their sex lives such a low rating. Over half of the battered wives, compared with none of the others, said that from time to time their husbands had raped them. One-third of the battered wives also indicated that their husbands had sexually abused their children.

Why did they stay? The battered women were in shelters when they were interviewed, but nearly three-quarters of the battered wives re-

ported that the main reason they had stayed with their husbands was because of the need for financial support, whereas only 1 in 10 of nonbattered wives cite financial reasons for staying in the marriage. The majority of the nonbattered group said that the main reason they stayed with their husbands was because of love.

Violence in Lesbian Relationships

Violence in lesbian relationships is a hidden problem in most communities.

The most emotional paper session I have ever attended at a psychology conference was a session on lesbian relationships at the 1983 annual meeting of the Association for Women in Psychology. The final paper at the session dealt with violence in lesbian relationships. The author of the paper said she had been a victim of violence in a lesbian relationship, having been battered by her partner who was a college professor. The room was crowded with women. After the paper was presented, women in the audience begin speaking out about their own experience with battering in a lesbian relationship. Apparent from this session was that battering is a topic the lesbian community wanted to ignore. A book on the issue edited by Kerry Lobel, *Naming the Violence: Speaking Out about Lesbian Battering,* (1986), concurs that it is a hidden problem. "The wall of silence surrounding lesbian battering has been virtually impenetrable, as has the wall of isolation, keeping lesbian victims separate from and unsupported by our community" (B. Hart, 1986, p. 9).

According to Lydia Walker (1986) who has worked with battered women, the only difference between male-on-female and female-on-female violence is that the battered woman in lesbian couples reports fighting back more often than do women who are battered by men. Similar to heterosexual couples, lesbian batterers also have a "honeymoon phase" of remorse and promises that the violence will not happen again. It serves the same purpose of controlling the battered woman and keeping her from leaving or seeking help.

There is a need for staff, board, and volunteers in shelters to provide nondiscriminatory services for lesbians that involve revising counseling methods, intake procedures, and heterosexist language, and organizing support groups for lesbian women. It is also necessary to provide outreach to lesbians in need of their services (Porat, 1986). Ironically, although shelters may not be sensitive to lesbian victims, it is often lesbian women who organized and led the battle for providing shelters for battered women in the community.

Lesbians also face other issues such as the unresponsiveness of the criminal justice system. Lesbians who have not come out also face threats to their job security or child custody by seeking out police intervention and court remedies (Linda & Avreayl, 1986). The biological mother may be the batterer who has legal custody of the children. To assist in these cases, the lesbian community can provide temporary foster care by having homes licensed to do this.

Renzetti (1988) recruited lesbians who had been in battering relationships through brochures and ads in lesbian and gay newspapers. The majority of women in the sample (78%) sought help but did not perceive sources of help used by heterosexuals, such as women's shelters, attorneys, or police, as available or helpful to them. Counselors and friends were the sources from whom help was sought most often.

The batterers tended to be overdependent on their partners and used violence as a way of inhibiting their partner's attempts at independence. Power differentials, particularly differences in social class and intelligence, were highly correlated with severe forms of psychological and physical abuse. The responses of others in the lesbian community play a major role in whether the victim is able to free herself from the battering relationship.

Male Violence Against Lesbians

Lesbians are victims of violent crime because of their sexual orientation.

There has been a rise in antilesbian violence, violence in which the lesbianism of the victim was defined by the perpetrator as the reason for the assault (Brownworth, 1993). These women are treated by crime statistics as victims of violent crime and not as victims of antilesbian violence (as cited in Brownworth). According to Chezia Carraway, coordinator of the New York City Task Force Against Sexual Assault, lesbians are more uncomfortable about reporting rapes and reluctant to deal with a male authority structure.

In May 1988, when Rebecca Wight and Claudia Brenner went hiking on the Appalachian Trail near Gettysburg, neither expected to become statistics. But before the trip ended, Wight was shot to death and Brenner critically wounded. The killer's defense was that the women "teased him" by making love together in the isolated woods where he lived. (Brownworth, 1993, p. 323)

Lesbian women are the targets of both sexism and homophobia.

Ending the Violence

To end the violence women should seek outside help, preferably from the police, a shelter, or a lawyer—not from a priest or minister.

Of 1,000 battered women recruited through newspapers, television, and magazines who had experienced wife abuse at some time in a relationship, 49% had eliminated the problem but were still able to maintain the relationship with that husband or partner (Bowker, 1983; Bowker & Maurer 1986). The sample was predominantly White (906) and middle class. The violence suffered by these wives was extensive—the incidents had occurred weekly or even three or four times per week over a period of years. "Weapons involvement was reported in 406 families, child abuse in 543, marital rape in 562, assaults while pregnant in 479, and miscarriages due to the batterings in 72" (Bowker, 1983, p. 89). Jealousy was the most common provocation. The jealousy was not necessarily over another man, but also because husbands were jealous of women friends of their wives or even of their own children.

Sexual perversion and rape were often components of the abuse. Some of the husbands resorted to sadistic techniques such as burning their wives with cigarettes, cutting their hair, and using painful weapons in the beating. Psychological abuse was part of the pattern of overall abuse.

So how did nearly half of these women who were violently abused manage to stay in the relationship and diminish or end the battering? There are three types of forces that battered women can bring to bear to try to end the battering, including (1) Their own personal strategies and techniques such as trying to get him to promise to end the abuse, (2) Hiding from him, and (3) Threatening him with nonviolent action such as

calling the police and filing for divorce. "The more serious the violence, the less likely there is to be a sufficiently healthy relationship between husband and wife to allow these strategies to be successful in reducing marital violence" (Bowker, 1983, p. 73). The most potent personal strategy was threatening to call the police or a lawyer. Informal sources of help were also used by wives such as the wife's own family, in-laws, neighbors, and friends. In addition shelter services were also included as an informal help-source since not all of them were formal agencies. The formal help sources used were the police, social-service agencies, lawyers and district attorneys, clergy, and women's groups.

No single strategy or help source worked for the majority of women to end the battering following the last incident. Bowker (1983) concludes that the most crucial factor was the woman's determination that the violence *must stop now*. Bowker and Maurer (1986) do point out that not all counseling is equally effective.

The battered women rated women's groups more highly than social service counseling agencies, with the clergy a distant third. Women's groups were almost twice as likely as the clergy to be rated as very or somewhat effective, and less than half as likely to be rated as not effective at all. (Bowker & Maurer, 1986, p. 73)

The clergy were more likely to have a sexist tradition that was reflected in their counseling. "A clergyman suggested that maybe I wasn't pleasing my husband in bed and that was why he beat me," one woman wrote on her questionnaire.

Contrary to Bowker, Lenore E. Walker (1989), based on years of research, counseling, and expert testimony in battered women cases, strongly believes that battering relationships cannot be salvaged, that they are better off dissolved. Some battering relationships do end permanently, unfortunately, in death. "More than half of all women murdered in the United States during the first half of the 1980s (52%) were the victims of partner homicide (Browne & Williams, 1989). (Goodman, Koss, Fitzgerald, Russo, & Keita, 1993, p. 1055)

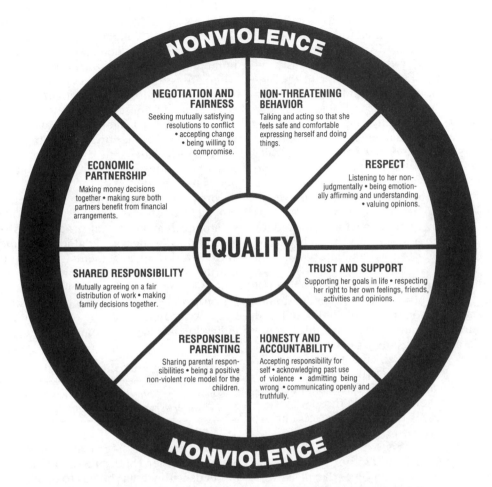

NONVIOLENCE

NEGOTIATION AND FAIRNESS
Seeking mutually satisfying resolutions to conflict • accepting change • being willing to compromise.

NON-THREATENING BEHAVIOR
Talking and acting so that she feels safe and comfortable expressing herself and doing things.

ECONOMIC PARTNERSHIP
Making money decisions together • making sure both partners benefit from financial arrangements.

RESPECT
Listening to her non-judgmentally • being emotionally affirming and understanding • valuing opinions.

EQUALITY

SHARED RESPONSIBILITY
Mutually agreeing on a fair distribution of work • making family decisions together.

TRUST AND SUPPORT
Supporting her goals in life • respecting her right to her own feelings, friends, activities and opinions.

RESPONSIBLE PARENTING
Sharing parental responsibilities • being a positive non-violent role model for the children.

HONESTY AND ACCOUNTABILITY
Accepting responsibility for self • acknowledging past use of violence • admitting being wrong • communicating openly and truthfully.

NONVIOLENCE

Source: Domestic Abuse Intervention Project, 206 West Fourth Street, Duluth, Minnesota 55806, 218-722-4134.

Legal Response

Arresting the husband may be the most successful short-term strategy for ending domestic violence. Mandatory arrest laws, however, may deter calling the police.

Police tend to respond slower to domestic disturbances than they do to other calls because it is dangerous work. Between 1972 and 1984, 6% of all officers killed in the line of duty were killed on domestic violence calls (Gelles, & Straus,

1988). This figure has been greatly exaggerated by the media, which in turn leads to an even greater reluctance of the police to respond in this kind of a situation. Police have also typically been reluctant to make arrests in domestic violence cases. Because of this, laws are now being passed in some jurisdictions requiring police to arrest the batterer when called, regardless of whether the woman is willing to press charges.

Does arresting the husband end the violence? To answer this question, the Minneapolis Police Department conducted a field experiment in which the responses by police officers called to the scene of domestic violence for simple assault were randomized so the officers made either an arrest, gave "advice" (which in some cases included mediation), or gave an order to the suspect to leave the house for eight hours (Sherman & Berk, 1984). The cases were found to be disproportionately unmarried couples, with lower than average educational levels, disproportionately minority and mixed race (black male, white female), and people who had previously come to police attention for prior violent incidents. The suspects also had the very high unemployment rate of 60% in a community where the rate was only 5% at that time. The suspect was tracked for six months after the police intervention by means of both official police reports and interviews with victims.

The statistical analysis of the 314 cases that fell within the definition of the experiment found that the arrest treatment significantly reduced repeat occurrences compared with the "separation" treatment. Results for the mediation treatment was in between and not statistically different from the other two. The victims reported that those arrested exhibited significantly less subsequent violence than did those who were advised. This indicates the effectiveness of arrest even when the courts dismiss the cases. Criticisms have been leveled at this experiment based on the fact that some officers did not adhere completely to the randomization on each call. Nevertheless, the data is suggestive that arrest of the violent husband/boyfriend may serve to reduce the violence in the situation. The results of the Sherman and Berk (1984) study, and of Bowker and Maurer's (1986) research on wives who were able to end the battering, indicate that the "cost" of being arrested or brought to the attention of the criminal justice system may be one of the best deterrents to wife battering.

Angela Browne (1993) points out, however, that mandatory arrest laws that have been adopted in many areas may actually work against deterrence of male violence toward women. "For example, mandatory arrest of male abusers given evidence that an assault has occurred removes a woman's choice of whether to press charges once the immediate danger is passed, and ramifications of arrest may deter women from calling for immediate protection or transportation to safety when an assault is in progress" (Browne, 1993, p. 1084). Police also arrest both the man and the woman if the abuser claims she also committed an aggressive act against him, which may be a way of his retaliation for calling the police. Browne advocates that legal protections and options be made available to all women. Society needs to provide for the economic necessities to be provided for all children so that mothers do not have to stay in an abusive relationship for economic reasons. Legal proceedings related to assault need to be coordinated with child custody and visitation arrangements so that mothers do not have to be in frequent proximity with a violent ex-spouse in order to comply with court visitation privileges. Legal professionals need to be better educated about the extent and severity of male violence against women.

Counseling and Shelter Services

Shelters for battered women provide safety, legal and other services and psychological counseling.

The most pressing need for the battered woman and her children is safety. The second set of needs with which she has to deal are related to transition issues, such as obtaining a restraining order against her partner, finding a place to live, finding a job, and filing for divorce. The third set of needs revolves around ameliorating the psychological effects caused by the trauma of abuse (PTSD) (Dutton-Douglas & Dionne, 1991). Battered women's shelters have become an important resource for assisting women with all three sets of needs.

It is important for community agencies such as hospital emergency rooms, or agencies that oversee welfare programs, or even schools to recognize battered women and make them aware of services and legal protection available to her. Outpatient community counseling programs for battered women are less common than shelters. Women are also seen for treatment in community mental health clinics.

> There is little evidence identifying the components of shelter and/or counseling interventions that are related to ameliorate outcomes. However, Berk et al.'s (1986) data indicate that for victims who use a shelter, each additional effort to obtain help (e.g., calling police, obtaining a restraining order, seeking prosecution, previous shelter stay, seeking help from an attorney or legal aid) reduces the number of subsequent violent episodes. (Dutton-Douglas & Dionne, 1991, p. 124)

Interventions must take into account the oppression faced by many battered women by the institutions of society based on race, sexual preference, language, and able-bodiedness. Battered women's shelters usually have a majority of staff who are volunteers, who may have a great deal of empathy, and who may have left a battering situation themselves, but it may also be necessary to refer the client to trained professionals for treatment of serious psychological problems.

THEORIES OF BATTERING

Why does she stay? That is the most frequently asked question about battered women. Further, the empirical research shows that about half of the women who seek aid return to live with the batterer again (Strube, 1988). This is a rather surprising figure since most women do not leave unless the abuse is severe. It is also probably an underestimation since most studies have had only a brief follow-up time. Strube reviewed both the empirical and theoretical literature addressing the decision to leave an abusive relationship with a man who beats her and classified the theories into four models: psychological entrapment; learned helplessness; a model derived from exchange theory that looks at relative costs and benefits; and reasoned action. The popular press has also developed a theory; women's masochism.

Entrapment

Entrapment occurs when a woman increases her efforts to make a relationship work because of her prior investments and the societal belief women are responsible for relationship success.

Psychological entrapment is a process whereby an individual increases commitment to a previously chosen, although failing course of action, in order to justify prior investments (Strube, 1988). The battered woman keeps trying to make the relationship work, believing that if she tries hard enough she will be successful. Society puts more of the burden for the success of relationships on women, so if the abuse continues she may feel it is because she is not doing a good enough job as a wife and with increased effort can attain the goal of a harmonious relationship. A woman who sees few alternatives to her present relationship because of financial dependence is more likely to take risks with her current relationship. If she grew up in a family where her mother was abused, she is also less likely to view other relationship possibilities.

Social Learning Theory

The social learning theories of intermittent reinforcement and learned helplessness which lead to the battered women's syndrome can help explain why women stay.

The social learning theory of **intermittent reinforcement** that was developed in laboratory experiments with rats and applied to people playing slot machines in the casinos of Las Vegas and Atlantic City, has demonstrated that behavior that is intermittently reinforced (rewarded only some of the time) is the most difficult behavior to extinguish. After the beating, the batterer is very loving (rewarding) to his wife. The random and variable unpredictability of the batterer's behavior is one variable that keeps the woman there, hoping he will be her "good" husband (L. E. Walker, 1989).

Another theory is PTSD, which was described as a reaction to rape. Many battered women also show the symptoms of PTSD. **The Battered Woman Syndrome** is a subcategory of this disorder (L. E. Walker, 1984). Battered women suffer both physical and psychological symptoms such as nightmares, startle response, anxiety and fearfulness. Individuals having undergone such trauma may begin to believe that anything they do might not have a positive effect. This theory is closely tied to that of **learned helplessness.**

The concept of learned helplessness was originated by Martin Seligman (1975), a psychologist at the University of Pennsylvania, who placed dogs in cages from which they could not escape and gave them electric shocks in a random and unpredictable fashion. He found, in a later experiment, that when these same dogs could escape, they did not avoid the shocks until they had been repeatedly dragged to the cage exits (Seligman, 1975). On the level of human beings, a reformulation of the learned helplessness model proposes that the kinds of attributions people make to themselves and others or the situation, determines whether they become helpless and depressed or try to escape from the situation (Abramson, Garber & Seligman, 1980). Attributions can be internal or external, stable or unstable, and global or specific. Learned helplessness would occur when a negative situation such as being beaten is attributed to internal, stable, and global causes. The woman who blames herself for being beaten—"I'm not a good wife"—is making an internal (to herself), stable (over a long period of time), and global (in general is not good at performing wifely duties) self attribution. Attributional retraining with battered women may be a promising intervention.

Lenore E. Walker (1984) studied over 400 battered women in the Rocky Mountain region to learn about the psychological sequelae, which she called the Battered Woman Syndrome, of living in a domestic violence situation. Actually Walker found a set of factors that resulted in childhood learned helplessness and included factors such as the number of critical life events before age 18 (i.e., parent's divorce, moving, sexual assault, etc.) and a child's relationship with father. Learned helplessness during the battering relationship was defined by variables such as the frequency of battering incidents, whether or not the woman thought the batterer might kill her and whether the woman's emotional reaction to the battering incident could be characterized by "fear," "depression," and so on.

Cycle of Violence

In battering relationships, husbands and wives are caught in a cycle of violence.

The pattern that evolves in battering relationships has been labeled by Lenore Walker (1989), the **Cycle of Violence.** She says that this pattern was found to occur in the more than 1,600 incidents of violence studied in her research on battered women. The Cycle of Violence is divided into three phases: the tension-building phase; the acute battering incident; and the tranquil phase.

During the tension-building phase, mild battering incidents such as slaps, pinches, and controlled verbal abuse occur. The wife exhibits placatory, docile, behavior, trying to prevent a sudden escalation of violence. The second phase is the acute battering incident. It is distinguished from the first phase by its savagery, destructiveness, and uncontrolled nature. During the tranquil phase there is an absence of tension and the husband often shows loving contrition.

Lenore E. Walker says that support for the cycle of violence theory and learned helplessness was found in a majority of the battering incidents described by the women in her sample. Although, over time, the pattern may change.

For first incidents, the proportion showing evidence of a tension-building phase is 56%, the proportion showing evidence of loving contrition is 69%. Over time, these proportions changed drastically. By the last incident, 71% of battering incidents were preceded by tension building but only 42% were followed by loving contrition. In other words, over time in a battering relationship, tension building becomes more common (or more evident) and loving contrite behavior declines. (L. E. Walker, 1984, p. 97)

The woman's state of functioning was related to both her childhood experiences and experiences in the battering relationship itself.

Social Exchange Theory

Social exchange theory (a cost–benefit analysis) can help explain both why women stay and why men beat their wives.

Gelles and Straus (1988) have applied **social exchange theory**, which is based on rewards and costs of being in a relationship, as well as the past history of the rewards and costs the individual has received in previous relationships (comparison level) and the prospect for alternatives if the person leaves the present relationship (comparison level for alternatives), to intimate violence. If a woman perceives the economic, social, and psychological costs to be greater by leaving than by staying in the relationship, then she is likely to stay (Strube, 1988).

A cost–benefit analysis can also be applied to the batterer's behavior. It is essentially saying that people hit family members because they can—because they do not suffer serious costs as a result.

> The proposition that people hit family members because they can is based on the principles of social exchange theory, which assumes that human interaction is guided by the pursuit of rewards and the avoidance of punishments and costs. (Gelles & Straus, 1988, p. 82)

Some of the rewards the violent individual gets from hitting are power, control, self-esteem, and just plain relief from anger and frustration. Another "reward" may be revenge; after their self-worth had been threatened or attacked, revenge is sweet. The risk of violence is greater in in-equitable relationships, where one person has all the power (Straus & Gelles, 1989).

Reasoned Action

The theory of reasoned action takes into account behavioral intentions and social influence in the decision to leave.

Strube (1988) also applies Ajzen and Fishbein's (1980) theory of reasoned action to answering the question of why women stay. According to reasoned action, decisions are related to behavioral intentions. "To the extent that an individual believes that a behavior has a high likelihood of producing valued outcomes, or avoiding undesirable outcomes, the intention to perform that behavior will be high" (Strube, 1988, p. 246). Antecedents of behavior that must be performed before the behavior takes place such as finding employment or childcare also must exist before the behavior in question will be performed. Another major component of the theory of reasoned action, subjective norm, takes into account the individual's normative belief about what significant others think about whether the behavior, such as leaving an abusive spouse, should be performed. According to this model, interventions could be effective which provide the woman with social influences supportive of the decision to leave, such as a peer support group.

The Myth of Women's Masochism

Women do not enjoy being beaten.

The heading for this section is taken from the title of a book by Paula Caplan (1985) in which she describes the history of the concept that women are masochistic, and through a scholarly examination of the support (or rather lack of empirical support) proceeds to debunk the **myth of women's masochism**. In most dictionaries of the English language, the first definition given of masochism is of sexual pleasure received from abuse, humiliation, and pain; the second is the

Focus on Women   Maria Correia

Early on the morning of August 7, 1988, 14-month-old Karen Correia crawled up into the big bed to lie beside her mother. By then 20-year-old Maria Correia was already dead or close to it. Police later found the baby physically unharmed lying in her mother's arms.

The night before when her aunt drove them to their home in Pawtucket, Karen began to cry and kept thrusting her head down, as if to stop her mother from lifting her out of the car. But Maria carried little Karen to their second-floor apartment, turning to smile at her sister in the car and reassure her that everything would be all right. The next day, police told her sister that the family should not look at Maria's body, because it had been beaten beyond recognition.

Although Maria feared her husband's violent outburst, she kept hoping the relationship would improve. She prided herself on being a good mother, and she longed for her daughter to grow up with both parents. Tragically, Karen now has neither parent, and she has been deeply scarred by the violence she witnessed as a baby.

Aries Correia was the only boyfriend Maria ever had when she married him in October 1986. From the beginning, it was an abusive relationship. According to Maria's older sister, Carmen, he would say hurtful things to her, and she would "just take everything and keep it inside. I think she was ashamed to open up and really tell us what was going on, as if we would think less of her, but she did say a few things."

Maria grew up in a closely knit family with her three sisters and three brothers. Their home still feels peaceful and serene, tastefully decorated in muted tones. "It was a big change for her when she married and moved out," says Carmen. "She missed the quietness of this house and the love, the way we treat each other. Here, nobody talks loud, everybody understands. There's no fights, no

arguments. That's what she wanted to provide for her daughter, the same things our parents did for us."

Maria was an outgoing, friendly girl who liked to tell jokes and make people laugh. "She was so nice. People were always attracted to her the minute they saw her," Carmen recalls.

Maria and Aries' families had both gone to a company picnic at Rocky Point that Saturday. Aries went off drinking with his friends, but he had spoken angrily to Maria before leaving, saying he would "fix her" when he got home. Later that night, his friends followed him home, worried that he would hurt her. When they knocked on the door, Aries turned off the lights and pretended to have gone to sleep.

"He could have let his friends help her by calling the ambulance," says Carmen, "but he chose to let her die." She offers her personal opinion: "He was very jealous, and he knew that if she lived, he would never see her again. He told police every detail," she says. Three times he stopped beating her, then started again. The next day his hands were swollen.

"The funeral director said he had seen bodies badly damaged from accidents, but he had never seen anything like this before. He said it would be very, very, bad for us to see her body."

The trial of Aries Correia took place in Superior Court in Providence. "Did you intend to hurt her?" prosecutor David Prior asked him. "No," Correia replied, saying he associated being beaten with discipline. "How many times did you hit her?" the defense attorney asked. "I hit her a few times," Correia said. "What were you trying to do?" "I was trying to like make her listen, you know" (Hulick, 1990b, p. A–8). Correia was convicted of second-degree murder. Judge Corrinne P. Grande sentenced him to life in prison. (Hulick, 1990a).

general tendency to seek and derive gratification from pain, deprivation, and abuse as a result of the actions of oneself or of others. Although pornographic materials—particularly bondage pornography—portray women as responding with pleasure to the horrifying acts of violence perpetrated on them, the evidence is that this is

very rare. In fact, Kinsey's statistics showed that far more men than women are "sexual masochists" (Caplan, 1985). Okay, so maybe women do not enjoy sexual abuse, but what about the battered women who stay, are they not masochists? Again, the evidence is overwhelming that a woman may stay in a battering relationship for many reasons, none of which is that she enjoys being beaten.

WOMEN AND CRIME

Gender Differences in Crime

It is a myth that the women's movement has brought about an increase in serious crime by women. Women commit fewer than one out of ten homicides and one out of eight assaults.

It has been argued that the women's movement has brought about greater criminal activity on the part of women. This is due in part to the view that if women stray from the straight and narrow path of traditional housewife and mother, then they will become corrupt versions of men.

The myth that there has been an extraordinary change in the extent and nature of women's criminal behavior since 1960 can be dispelled by a reading and interpretation of the statistics presented in the standard source for gauging criminal activity in the United States, the *Uniform Crime Reports* published since 1930 by the Federal Bureau of Investigation. (Feinman, 1994)

Increases in the number of men and women arrested since 1960 must take into account the baby boom generation who were in the high-risk 15–30-year-old age group in the 1960s, 1970s, and 1980s. During this same period, the drug epidemic led to a "war on drugs" and mandatory sentencing laws that affected women as well as men. In a study of women in New York City jails by Feinman (1994), approximately 85% were addicted to narcotics. The greatly expanded welfare programs since 1960 have provided a new means for women to commit fraud, and welfare fraud may account for one-third to one-half of the arrests for fraud (Feinman, 1994). A change in the pattern of women's criminality from property crimes to violent crimes has not been borne out. In 1993, women committed only 9.4% of the homicides and nonnegligiant manslaughters and 15.7% of aggravated assaults (U.S. Dept. of Justice, 1994). Neither were the women who were

arrested feminists involved in the women's movement. Imprisoned women were poor, uneducated, and unskilled women who often got involved in criminal activities because of their association with men.

The only crimes for which women represent a majority of those arrested are still prostitution and runaways (U.S. Department of Justice, 1994). Early drug use is associated with later prostitution. A comparison of female prostitutes and female arrestees ($N = 100$) in Hillsborough County, Florida, indicated that significantly more prostitutes had tried drugs and used drugs at younger ages and with greater frequency and had dropped out of school than had arrestees (Kuhns, Heide, & Silverman, 1992). This research underscores the necessity of early drug treatment for adolescent female substance abusers.

A life history approach to investigate the pattern of criminal activities of incarcerated women revealed the women to be survivors of family environments of physical and/or sexual abuse (Gilfus, 1992). Running away from home was typically the first delinquent behavior. Once on the streets, the women became victims again of violent crimes and battering relationships. Their criminal activities—mostly prostitution, drug possession, check fraud, and shoplifting—became their work. These women see themselves as survivors.

Women Who Kill Their Husbands

Women who kill their husbands have suffered more severe violence over a longer period of time and perceive their lives to be in danger.

A great deal of media publicity has been given to women who kill their abusive husbands. Psychologically there is no real difference between battered women who kill their abuser and those who do not. They are women like you and I, or your sister or your mother. "The difference lies, perhaps, in the extremely life-threatening nature of the violence to which they are subjected and from which some of them can escape alive only by ending their abusers' lives." (L. E. Walker, 1989, p. 7). Angela Browne (1987), who had be-

TABLE 7.2   Arrests by Sex for Selected Crimes, 1993

Crimes	Number of Persons Arrested		Percent Male	Percent Female
	Male	*Female*		
Murder and nonnegligent manslaughter	18,375	1,900	90.6	9.4
Forcible rape	32,107	416	98.7	1.3
Robbery	140,128	13,405	91.3	8.7
Aggravated assault	372,557	69,518	84.3	15.7
Burglary	304,702	33,536	90.1	9.9
Larceny-theft	842,658	408,619	67.3	32.7
Motor vehicle theft	148,932	19,863	88.2	11.8
Other assaults	792,848	172,470	82.1	17.9
Forgery and counterfeiting	58,425	31,062	65.3	34.7
Fraud	335,580	199,297	59.4	40.6
Weapons; carrying, possessing, etc.	206,990	17,405	92.2	7.8
Prostitution and commercialized vice	31,712	57,138	35.7	64.3
Drug abuse violations	811,493	157,113	83.8	16.2
Runaways	65,051	87,081	42.8	57.2
Disorderly conduct	481,553	125,919	79.3	20.7
Driving under the influence	1,056,544	173,427	85.9	14.1
Vandalism	229,424	31,858	87.8	12.2

Source: Adapted from "Uniform Crime Reports for the United States 1993." Federal Bureau of Investigation, U.S. Department of Justice. Washington, DC: U.S. Government Printing Office.

gan working with Lenore Walker in 1979, compared the 40 homicide cases they had collected by 1983 with a subsample of 100 battered women who had been living out of the battered relationship for less than one year. The main difference she found between the two groups was in the greater degree of violence experienced by the women who killed their abuser. The women who killed perceived their men as using greater violence, more frequently, resulting in graver injuries to them. The men also made death threats and used weapons to terrorize them. The women had become increasingly desperate in their attempts at survival. The men tended to abuse alcohol even more frequently than other batterers and seemed to be growing continually more dangerous toward the women, their children, and others.

Women in Prison

Special needs of women in prison relating to parenting, drug treatment, and psychotherapy should be addressed.

Despite an increased number of incarcerated women during the 1980s, special needs of incarcerated women have not been addressed relating to the fact that 41% of incarcerated women have a history of prior physical and/or sexual abuse and that two-thirds of women in prison have children under 18 (Morash, Haarr, & Rucker, 1994). Data from *The Survey of Inmates in State and Federal Prisons* conducted in 1986 and the *Census of State Adult Correctional Facilities* conducted in 1984 were analyzed by Morash et al. by sex. Women were somewhat more likely than men to be involved in academic educational programs in adult basic education and at the college level (there was no difference at the secondary school level). Women are more likely to have work assignments, and these are typically in cleaning and kitchen work. Women did not work in prison industries at all. Men were more often paid for prison work than were women. Women were more likely than men to receive medical attention and twice as likely to receive psychotropic medication. Women were less likely to receive drug treatment than men, but more likely than men to be offered the chance to see a mental health professional. Although somewhat more women than men had contact with an attorney after incarceration, fewer women had used law books provided by the prison. Only 4% of women received parenting education. That was very inadequate considering the high proportion of women who would assume responsibility for their children upon release.

REFLECTIONS

Different forms of violence against women— pornography, rape, wife battery, child sexual abuse, and sexual harassment—"form a system that is but one element in the larger social system of male dominance and female subordination" (H. Wheeler, 1985, p. 374). They are all a form of social (male) control of women. Women are seen as the providers of sexual services for men. In addition, sexual harassment reinforces women's economic vulnerability by providing a barrier to women's economic independence (B. E. Schneider, 1982). The goal of feminism—achieving equal status for females—will contribute to a reduction of violence against women.

More attention needs to be focused on the male perpetrators of violence against women. Most of the difference in violent and nonviolent families is due to the characteristics of the abusive husbands and not the characteristics of the wives (Holtzworth-Monroe & Stuart, 1994). Research indicates that abusive men are not a homogeneous group; therefore, multiple strategies are necessary for prevention of violence and rehabilitation of violent men—everything from more positive role models for boys by inducing more men to become elementary school teachers, to treating rape and battering as serious crimes, and providing rehabilitation programs for rapists and batterers.

We live in a culture of violence in the United States, and aggression against women is one manifestation of that violence. The voices of respected nonviolent men and women need to be heard to establish norms of nonviolence. A human relations course should be required for high school graduation in the United States. Students would receive training in role playing and learning to take the perspective of the other, conflict resolution through compromise and negotiation, assertiveness training and respect for the rights of others, and most importantly, parenting skills.

Experiential Exercises

1. Volunteer at a Rape Crisis Center.
2. Volunteer at a shelter for battered women.
3. Participate in a "Take Back the Night" march.
4. Discuss with your friends, relatives, and political representatives whether violent pornography should be censored.
5. Discuss with your friends, relatives, and political representatives the advantages and disadvantages of legalizing prostitution.
6. Take a course in self defense or martial arts so you can better protect yourself if attacked.

KEY TERMS

Battered Woman Syndrome A subcategory of posttraumatic stress disorder (PTSD) in which the woman suffers both physical and psychological symptoms such as nightmares, startle response, anxiety, and fearfulness. This theory is closely tied to that of learned helplessness.

Battering A pattern of physical abuse of a partner.

Cycle of Violence The pattern that evolves in battering relationships. It is divided into three phases: the tension-building phase; the acute battering incident; and the tranquil phase.

Excitation Transfer Theory The theory that the arousal caused by one stimulus can be transferred to and added to arousal from a second stimulus. For example, sexual arousal from pornography can be transferred to aggressive impulses stemming from receiving an electroshock, with the combined arousal leading to an aggressive act.

Gang Rape When two or more offenders sexually assault one victim. These rapes are generally more violent and degrading.

Intermittent Reinforcement   A principle of social learning theory that indicates that behavior that is rewarded only some of the time is the most difficult behavior to extinguish.

Learned Helplessness   A concept originated by a psychologist, Martin Seligman, from experiments on dogs and applied to the behavior of women suffering from "Battered Woman Syndrome."

Marital Rape   Rape in marriage that is further classified into three types: force only; battering; and obsessive.

Myth of Women's Masochism   The false belief that women are masochistic and derive pleasure from abuse, humiliation, and pain.

National Crime Victim Survey (NCVS)   A national representative sample of the population who are asked to indicate those crimes of which they, or anyone else in their household, have been victims during the preceding year.

Pornography   Writings, pictures, or films that are intended to cause sexual excitement. Distinctions have been made among three types of sexually explicit material: (1) sexual violence; (2) nonviolent erotica; and (3) erotica (nonviolent material characterized by choice and mutuality).

Prolonged Exposure   A form of cognitive behavioral therapy that involves the victim retelling the rape event several times each therapy session into a tape recorder that she then listens to at home. This has been found to bring about improvement in anxiety, depression, and rape-related distress on a longer-term basis.

Prostitution   Pattern of impersonal purchase and sale of sexual services between socially unrelated individuals. It is illegal in the United States except for two counties in Nevada.

Rape   The use of force or the threat of force to have sexual intercourse. Oral and anal penetration are also included in most legal definitions. It is still one of the most underreported crimes.

Rape-Free Society   One in which the sexes are seen as equal and complementary and where interpersonal violence is uncommon.

Rape-Prone Society   One in which the incidence of rape is high, rape is a ceremonial act, or rape is used to punish women.

Rape Trauma Syndrome   A two-stage reaction to having been raped: an acute phase consisting of immediate emotional crisis and a long-term reorganization phase.

Social Exchange Theory   A theory that assumes that human interaction is guided by the pursuit of rewards and the avoidance of punishments and costs and concludes that people hit family members because they can—because they do not suffer serious costs as a result of doing so.

Stress Inoculation Techniques (SIT)   A cognitive behavioral therapy that includes breathing exercises, deep muscle relaxation, and thought stopping for obsessive thinking. It has proven helpful in reducing symptoms of postrape trauma.

Unwanted Intercourse   The use of psychological pressure to induce a reluctant partner to engage in sexual intercourse, but without the use of force or threat of force.

SUGGESTED READINGS

Browne, B. (1993). Violence against women by male partners: Prevalence, outcomes, and policy implications. *American Psychologist, 48,* 1077–1087. This article links what is known about male violence against women with proposals for mental health and legal interventions.

Strube, J. J. (1988). The decision to leave an abusive relationship: Empirical evidence and theoretical issues. *Psychological Bulletin, 104,* 236–250. This article examines the complex psychological forces that serve to keep women in abusive relationships.

White, J. W., & Sorenson, S. B. (Eds.), (1992). Adult Sexual Assault. *Journal of Social Issues, 48*(1). This entire issue focuses on three aspects of rape and sexual assault: definitional and methodological issues; social-contextual factors and the prevalence of sexual assault; and policy implications.

CHAPTER 8

Mental Health

Victimization in interpersonal relationships is a significant risk factor in the development of depressive symptomatology in women. What is presented clinically as depressed mood may be long-standing posttraumatic responses to experiences of intimate violence and victimization, for example, childhood sexual or physical abuse, marital or acquaintance rape, woman battering, sexual harassment in the workplace, or sexual abuse by a therapist or health care provider.

Ellen McGrath, Gwendolyn Puryear Keita,
Bonnie R. Strickland, & Nancy Felipe Russo
1990

Significant gender differences appear in the patterns of mental illness. Two types of studies have been conducted to determine these differences—mental health delivery statistics, and community surveys of mental illness in the general population. Complex relationships exist among gender roles, marital status, race/ethnicity, and mental health. Biomedical models are not sufficient to explain the **epidemiology** (incidence and distribution of mental illness).

UTILIZATION OF MENTAL HEALTH SERVICES

Gender Differences in Utilization

Although more men are admitted to outpatient facilities, women receive more total outpatient services. Men make up the majority of patients receiving inpatient mental health treatment.

Men and women differ in the utilization of mental health services, by type of facility. Women predominate in the use of outpatient facilities in free-standing clinics, private psychiatric hospitals, and nonfederal general hospitals, whereas men predominate in the use of outpatient mental health facilities in state and county mental hospitals, VA medical centers, and multiservice mental health organizations. Overall, in 1986 men comprised 52.4% of admissions and 48.7% of total outpatients under care in outpatient mental health facilities, women comprised 47.6% of admissions and 51.3% of total outpatient services. Women stayed in treatment for a longer period of time than men. In that same year men ac-

237

counted for 56.7% of inpatient admissions and 59.1% of patients under care in comparison to women who were 43.3% of inpatient admissions and 40.9% of patients under care. Thus, it is apparent that men are more likely to receive inpatient treatment than are women (Manderscheid & Sonnenschein, 1992).

Mental Health and Marital Status

Rates of admission to mental institutions and mental health facilities vary by sex and marital status. Women are most frequently admitted for depression, men for alcoholism.

Service delivery statistics show that married women are more likely to receive treatment from mental health facilities than married men. Never-married and separated or divorced men, however, have higher rates of admission to mental health facilities than women of similar marital status. Both men and women who are married have markedly lower rates of treatment for mental illness than men and women who have never been married, widowed, or divorced (Gove, Style, & Hughes, 1990). This relationship is stronger for men, who seem to benefit more from marriage than women.

For all marital status categories, both Hispanic and non-Hispanic women who are inpatients predominate in the diagnosis of **affective disorder** (mood disorder). Male inpatients, of all marital statuses, predominate in the diagnosis of alcohol disorders. For Hispanics only, men receive a greater likelihood of diagnosis of schizophrenia for all marital status categories (Russo, 1990).

COMMUNITY MENTAL HEALTH

Patterns of Mental Illness by Sex

Community mental health surveys find men and women to have similar rates of mental illness, but different patterns of illness.

A major contribution to the understanding of the prevalence and patterns of mental illness in the United States in the 1980s was the Epidemiologic Catchment Area Study (ECA), supported by the National Institute of Mental Health (NIMH). It was a community survey of a sample of the noninstitutionalized population, 18,000 Americans in five research sites—New Haven, Connecticut; Baltimore, Maryland; St. Louis, Missouri; Raleigh, North Carolina; and Los Angeles, California (Eichler, & Parron, 1987). The survey questionnaire used the NIMH Diagnostic Interview Schedule (DIS), which could be used by lay interviewers and then computer scored for diagnosis according to the Diagnostic and Statistical Manual of Mental Disorders (DSM-III) (Belle, 1990).

The NIMH ECA Study found that although the overall lifetime mental illness rates were similar for men and women, there were significant gender differences in the prevalence of a lifetime diagnosis of the 15 illnesses studied (Eichler & Parron, 1987). Women were much more likely to have received diagnoses of **major depressive disorder**, **agoraphobia** (fear of open places and unfamiliar settings) and **simple phobia** (fear of a specific object, person or situation). Women were also more likely than men to predominate in the diagnosis of **dysthymia** (neurotic depression), obsessive-compulsive disorder, schizophrenia, somatization disorder (constant physical complaints such as headaches, nausea, abdominal pains, etc.), and **panic disorder**. Men, on the other hand, were more likely to be diagnosed as having antisocial personality and alcohol abuse/dependence. No sex differences appeared for manic episode or cognitive impairment (Robbins et al., 1984; Russo, 1990).

Survey data also mirrored the same pattern in mental illness by marital status of men and women that was found for admission to mental health treatment facilities. Married women scored higher than married men on measures of psychological dysfunction, but the psychological well-being of married men and women was substantially better than that of the unmarried (Gove, Style, & Hughes, 1990).

Race, Poverty and Mental Health

Poverty is related to psychological distress, but race is not.

A well-established finding, based on decades of community studies, is the higher level of mental health problems among low-income and low-socioeconomic status as compared to higher socioeconomic status groups. Community studies in the 1970s found that depressive symptoms were most common among women who are financially less well off, without confidants, child-rearing assistance, or employment. The ECA study conducted in the 1980s found that "the six-month prevalence of any DSM-III disorder is 2.86 times higher in the lowest socioeconomic status (SES) category than in the highest SES group, controlling for age and sex (Holzer et al., 1986)" (Belle, 1990, p. 386).

It is not surprising that poor women have poor mental health considering the stress they are under. Poor women are much more likely to experience crime and violence, the illness and death of children, and the imprisonment of husbands. In addition, poor women face discrimination, which is even greater toward women of color. Women of color are more likely to be poor than White women. (See Chapter XIII for a discussion of women and poverty).

Research has largely ignored the interactive effects of gender and ethnicity on mental health. Differences in socioeconomic factors also interact with race in creating distress. "Effects of powerlessness, dependency, and poverty, which have been associated with women's roles and which are linked to poor mental health, are expected to be even more extreme among minority women, and the relationship between marriage and mental health differs for women of different racial and ethnic groups" (Russo, 1987, p. 47).

Although some researchers conclude that race has an independent effect on psychological distress among lower socioeconomic individuals (i. e., lower-class Blacks have higher levels of distress than do lower-class Whites) (Kessler & Neighbors, 1986), research by Cockerham (1990) does not support the contention that race is a determinant of distress among lower-class individuals. Based on probability sample telephone interviews, Cockerham concluded that although low socioeconomic status, as measured by education and income, is significantly related to psychological distress, there is no general tendency for Blacks, because of their race, to suffer from greater distress than Whites. "These data clearly do not support the contention that blacks show a greater tendency toward more psychological distress than whites, either in general or within low-income groups" (Cockerham, 1990, p. 1325). The reason that Blacks have a higher rate of mental illness than Whites is because Blacks have a higher rate of poverty.

Homelessness

Homelessness is also a mental health stressor.

Homelessness is another stressor that results from poverty. Homelessness has been rapidly growing among women who made up only 3% of the homeless population in 1950 and now comprise about 20% of the adult homeless population (Burt & Cohen, 1989 as cited in Smith & North, 1994). Homeless families represent up to 25% of the homeless and most of these are single mothers with children. Nearly half of homeless women have had an abusive partner and many have had a family background of violence. Individuals are at risk for distress when they suffer a major life event such as the loss of one's home. "More often than domiciled women, homeless women are faced with significant and multiple external pressures, including residential instability, poverty, work and employment problems, and victimization" (Milburn & D'Ercole, 1991, p. 1162). It is therefore not surprising that one-third of a sample of 300 primarily African American (76%) homeless women in St. Louis were found to be suffering from (PTSD), and another one in four from major depression (E. M. Smith, North, & Spitznagel, 1993). In addition, nearly one in three had a history of substance abuse, and one-fourth had received inpatient psychiatric care. Shelter is only part of the answer for homeless women.

Of the homeless women studied in St. Louis, 90% were mothers, and four-fifths of the mothers of children under 16 had their children with them (E. M. Smith & North, 1994).

> The findings of this study suggest that homeless mothers with dependent children with them, compared to other homeless women, have greater social vulnerabilities (dependent children; lack of employment) and fewer personal vulnerabilities (substance abuse and other psychiatric problems) to homelessness. These mothers with dependent children have mostly depended on welfare, a system that seems to have failed them. (E. M. Smith & North, 1994, p. 609)

Mothers who do not have any children with them have a much higher rate of lifetime psychiatric disorder (72%) and are in need of psychiatric treatment. Mothers whose children are with them are primarily in need of supportive services, including training and skills that will enable them to find jobs that will make it possible for them to obtain and maintain housing.

Mental Health Consequences of Sexual Assault

Adults who had been sexually assaulted have two to four times the incidence of mental illness as those who had never been sexually assaulted. Women are much more likely than men to be the victims of sexual assault.

The Los Angeles ECA site obtained supplemental funds from the NIMH Center for the Prevention and Control of Rape to include questions regarding sexual assault in the survey (Burnam et al., 1988). Those who reported being sexually assaulted had a two- to four-fold increase for later onset of major depression, substance use disorders (alcohol and drug abuse), and anxiety disorders (phobia, panic disorder, and obsessive-compulsive disorder) than those who were not assaulted. Those who were assaulted in childhood (age 15 or younger) were more likely to develop these

disorders than were those assaulted as adults. Women were more likely to be victims of assault than men, but among those assaulted, men and women did not differ in the development of disorders except that assaulted men were more likely to develop alcohol abuse than women. Non-Hispanic Whites (19.9%) reported a higher lifetime frequency of sexual assault than Hispanics (8.1%).

DEPRESSION

Diagnosis of Depression

According to the fourth edition of the Diagnostic and Statistical Manual of Mental Disorders (DSM-IV), (American Psychiatric Association, 1994) there are several forms of mood disorders. For a diagnosis of Major Depressive Episode, five of the following symptoms must be present during the same two-week period, and one of the symptoms must be either depressed mood or loss of interest or pleasure: (1) depressed mood; (2) markedly diminished pleasure in all, or almost all, activities; (3) significant weight loss or weight gain when not dieting; (4) insomnia or hypersomnia; (5) psychomotor agitation or retardation; (6) fatigue or loss of energy; (7) feelings of worthlessness or excessive or inappropriate guilt; (8) diminished ability to think or concentrate, or indecisiveness; and (9) recurrent thoughts of death, recurrent suicidal ideation without a specific plan, or a suicide attempt or a specific plan for committing suicide.

Dysthymic Disorder is a depressed mood for more days than not over a period of two years accompanied by other depressive symptoms. This disorder is not as severe as major depressive episode. If the mood disorder is due to substance abuse or to a general medical condition a diagnosis of dysthymic disorder or major depressive disorder would not be made. For bipolar disorder, major depressive episodes alternate with one or more manic episodes that are characterized by elevated mood, or if wishes are thwarted, by irritability (DSM-IV, American Psychiatric Association, 1994).

Gender Differences in Rates of Depression

Women have twice the rate of depression that men do. This sex ratio is the same in other industrialized nations as well as the United States.

During the 1970s, studies of affective disorders were published concluding that the rates of depression are significantly higher in women than in men (Weissman & Klerman, 1977; Weissman & Myers, 1978). The ECA Study found an increase of females over males for six-month prevalence rates of major depression for three of the five communities studied (Myers et al., 1984). The six-month prevalence rates for bipolar disorder found equal sex ratios. A review of the literature on depression based on studies conducted in the United States found the mean female-to-male ratio across the studies of psychiatric patients with diagnosed unipolar depression was 1.95:1 (Nolen-Hoeksema, 1987). Community studies of depression that have used standardized scales of depression show a mean female-to-male ratio of 1.62:1. Similarly, a probability sample survey of residents of Puerto Rico found rates of depression to be more than twice as high in women as they are in men (Canino et al., 1987). Lifetime depressive symptoms were also found to be more prevalent among women than among men. When the methodologically stronger studies of patient populations from outside the United States were analyzed, the mean female-to-male ratio was 2.39:1. Several of these studies report comprehensive records of all psychiatric patients treated in a given geographic area. Women significantly outnumber men treated for depression in Denmark, Scotland, England, Wales, Australia, Canada, Iceland, and Israel (Nolen-Hoeksema, 1987).

Some researchers have suggested that the higher rates of depression found for women in community studies may be the result of women being more likely to admit to symptoms of depression than men. Based on their community surveys, Weissman and Klerman (1977) say they have found no evidence that women report symptoms of affective disorder more frequently than men because they feel less stigma or are seeking approval. Another argument is that since more males than females have alcohol problems, depressed men are identified as being alcoholics rather than as depressed. Studies of alcohol and depression transmission in families show that they are independent disorders. The hypothesis has also been put forward that antisocial behavior in men, which lands them in the criminal justice system rather than the mental health system, is an expression of depression in men.

Locus of Control

People who have a greater sense of perceived control over their lives have lower levels of depression. Research is not consistent on whether men have a more internal locus of control than women.

Perceptions of control were found to significantly decrease depression among people contacted by C. E. Ross and Mirowsky (1989) in a probability sample telephone survey in the Chicago area. Identification and measurement of the concept of **locus of control** was first developed by Rotter (1966), who said that the person who believes his/her actions play a major role in what happens to them has an internal locus of control and someone who perceives that what happens to them is determined by fate or luck has an external locus of control. Whites, persons with high levels of education and income, younger persons, and non-Catholics were more likely to feel in control of their lives than non-Whites, persons with lower levels of education and income, older persons, and Catholics (C. E. Ross & Mirowsky, 1989).

People with high levels of education and family income were found to have low levels of depression. The reason for this was found to be due to the feeling of being in control of their lives, which largely explained the association between socioeconomic status and depression. Men and women, however, did not differ in perceived control. However, in another study of 321 men and women divided among young, middle-aged, and older adults, men had significantly higher scores on internal control than women (Ryff, 1989). Persons who feel in control of their lives are more likely to attempt to solve problems and to have a decrease in depression.

The specific attribution of desired outcomes to internal causes was associated with the absence of depression in a study of 192 married women professionals with preschool children (Marshall & Lang, 1990). Optimism by itself—the expectation that desired outcomes are forthcoming—was not associated with the absence of depression. If a woman has a sense, however, that through her own actions she can bring about desired events in her life, then she will not be depressed.

Social Support

Although social support plays a role in decreasing depression, talking to others about one's problems may increase depression. A Wellesley project with mothers of young children, however, found peer contact and support to decrease depression.

Social support, however, has a more mixed effect on depression. Married persons, well-educated persons, younger persons, those with some religious preference, and women report higher levels of support. "Having supportive relationships decreases depression, but talking to others when faced with problems increases it" (C. E. Ross & Mirowsky, 1989, p. 213). The effectiveness of support in reducing depression is suppressed by the increased likelihood of talking to others about one's problems when greater social support is available. Why would talking to others about one's problems increase depression? Probably because the focus is on the problem itself and how bad one feels about it, rather than on alternatives and solutions. The lower levels of depression of married compared with unmarried persons found in this study is only partially explained by the higher level of support available to married people. Both support and control are alternative ways to decrease depression. "Control and support can substitute for one another to decrease depression; one can fill the gap if the

other is absent, and each has less of an effect if the other is present" (C. E. Ross & Mirowsky, 1989, p. 216).

A group of researchers at Wellesley College found peer support to decrease depression of mothers of young children (ages 1 to 6) (Genero, Goldstein, Unger, & Miller, 1993). Mothers who belonged to a Health Maintenance Organization in the Boston area and had at least three risk factors for depression, were included in either a peer-support group or a control group. In addition to being paired with a peer who was also a mother of a young child with whom they had to make contact two to three times per week, they attended eight group meetings that provided information about the program and facilitated their discussion of mutual problems in a larger group setting. Pre- and postdepression measures found the women who participated in the peer support intervention to have significantly lower depression scores following participation in the program. The depression symptoms for those in the control group were not significantly different over the same period of time. When asked if they would recommend this program to a friend, all of the women in the intervention group said *yes*.

Self-Focused Attention

Self-focused people have higher levels of depression than others. Women show a greater tendency to be self-focused. Feminine self-focused people, regardless of gender, are more depressed.

One factor that has been empirically associated with gender and with depression is **self-focused attention**. "Self focused attention refers to attention directed internally toward thoughts and feelings as opposed to outwardly toward the external environment" (Ingram, Cruet, Johnson, & Wisnicki, 1988, p. 967). A number of studies have shown that self-focused attention is related to both subclinical and clinical depression. Women have been shown to have a greater tendency to self focus in response to eliciting events in laboratory experiments (being in front of a large mirror, being videotaped) (Ingram et al., 1988). Sex role (using the BSRI) was found to play a mediating role in the relation between increased self-focused attention and gender. Self on video screen was used as a self-focused manipulation. Participants were then all exposed to an event designed to promote negative affect—after completing a task that supposedly measured empathy, they were told that they did not do well. The self-focused feminine participants (both male and female) responded with greater levels of self-focused attention. Also, "regardless of actual sex, feminine subjects who were self focused expressed significantly more negative affect than feminine non-self focused subjects, . . . and masculine self-focused subjects." (Ingram et al., 1988, p. 973). Other studies have also found an association between sex role and negative emotion. Generally, these studies have shown that feminine individuals have a greater degree of depression than do masculine or androgenous individuals.

Feminine Sex Role Orientation

Clinical depression in women is highly related to feminine sex role. Environmental stresses, however, may play a greater role in depression than sex role orientation.

As discussed in Chapter IV, more masculine people of both sexes have been found to have higher levels of general adjustment than individuals with other sex role orientations. Keep in mind, however, that Whitley's (1983) meta-analysis and the other studies mentioned were based on normal individuals rather then clinical populations.

A comparison of middle-aged women (35–50 years old), who had been diagnosed as clinically depressed or women who were not depressed, supported the hypothesis that depression in middle-aged females is related to the feminine sex role (Tinsley, Sullivan-Guest, & McGuire, 1984). Depression and femininity showed a significant positive correlation of .61. None of the clinically depressed women had a BSRI score in the masculine range, and only one of them had a score in the androgynous range. Our socialization practices need to be such that we allow individuals to develop their full potential rather than to be re-

stricted by stereotypes that allow only a narrow range of traits, characteristics, and behaviors for women that are maladaptive (passivity, dependence, helplessness) and exclude masculine sex role traits (self-reliance, assertiveness, independence). Life stress, however, is much more strongly related to depression in college students than to either masculinity or femininity (Stoppard & Paisley, 1987). The psychological literature perhaps overemphasizes internal causes while neglecting environmental factors.

Derived Identity

Derived identity is significantly related to depression in women.

Derived identity has also been found to be related to women's higher incidence of depression. "We define derived identity as a sense of self that is overly influenced by and dependent upon relationships with significant others" (Warren & McEachern, 1985). In other words, the woman who thinks of herself primarily as Mrs. John Jones, Mark and Sarah's mother, rather than as Sue Jones would be an example of someone high in derived identity. Among a sample of women in California, higher derived identity was significantly correlated with depression. Professional women with higher education reported lower levels of depression and showed less derived identity than either nonprofessionals or nonemployed women. Married women scored higher on derived identity than single women even when education and age were controlled.

Environmental Stressors

Women have more environmental stressors than men. There is a complex set of bidirectional relations between environmental stressors and depression.

Women earn less money than men and poverty is a very negative environmental stressor. Women are responsible for most of the childcare and housework, often in addition to paid laborforce participation. Women are more likely victims of incest, rape, and sexual harassment. Women are more likely to be living alone than are men. Society gives women a lower status position than men, which creates stress in many aspects of life. Women also face greater discrimination than men in the institutions of society such as the medical establishment, the legal system, and business corporations.

A longitudinal study of 267 disadvantaged mothers found a complex and bidirectional relationship between depression and stressful life events (Pianta & Egeland, 1994). Although environmental stressors contribute to depressive symptoms independent of previous stress, depressive symptoms contribute to interpersonal problems and health-related problems that then become environmental stressors. Health stress and family fights were found to contribute to depressive symptoms. On the other hand, health stress, family fights, marital or partner stress, financial stress, household changes, and stress due to substance abuse in the family may be based on the person's actions. Both loss and employment stress, however, did not predict subsequent depressive symptoms and were not predicted themselves by these symptoms. Both stress and depressive symptoms account for variance in each other, but not all events or stressors are predictive of subsequent depressive symptoms.

Depressive Explanatory Style

Individuals who make internal, stable, and global attributions for adverse events have a pessimistic (depressive) explanatory style and are at risk for depression.

In his book, *Learned Optimism* (1991), Martin Seligman describes his research projects for more than 25 years, beginning with his research on learned helplessness in dogs who could not escape from electroshocks to his reformulation along more cognitive lines. It is how people explain the cause of adverse events, not the negative events that occur in people's lives, that lead to depression.

Thus, a person may attribute the cause to something within the self (an internal, personal, causal explanation) or may attribute the cause to something about the situation or to a special set of circumstances (an external causal explanation). Second, the person may view the factor that has caused the adverse event as chronic, one that will persist for an unknown time (a stable cause) or may view the cause as acute, and thus, relatively transient in nature (an unstable causal explanation). Third, the cause of the bad event may be seen as likely to generalize to a great number of other situations (global causal explanation), or the cause may be thought of as applying only to the single bad event and, therefore, be relatively limited in its effect on the individual (specific causal explanation). (Colligan, Offord, Malinchoc, Schulman, & Seligman, 1994, pp. 72–73)

Individuals who make internal, stable and global attributions for adverse events have a **depressive explanatory style**. These individuals conversely explain good events in terms of external, unstable, and specific causes. A depressive explanatory style has been found to relate to proneness to depressive symptoms among individuals in adverse situations such as imprisonment, poor grades on a midterm exam among college freshmen, and parents of children with a chronic illness as compared with individuals who make external, unstable, and specific attributions for negative events (Colligan et al., 1994). Seligman has the hopeful message that optimism can be learned.

Seligman's model of depressive explanatory style is closely related to the cognitive model developed by Aaron T. Beck, father of cognitive therapy and Seligman's colleague at the University of Pennsylvania (A. T. Beck, 1991). A. T. Beck had noticed that his depressed patients, when asked what they were thinking, had a negative view of the past, present and future. "The negativity permeated 'internal communications' such as self-evaluation, attributions, expectancies, inferences and recall, and were manifested in low self-esteem, self-blame and self-criticism, negative predictions, negative interpretations of experiences, and unpleasant recollections" (A. T. Beck, 1991, p. 369).

EATING DISORDERS

The two major disturbances of eating behavior are anorexia nervosa and bulimia nervosa.

Anorexia nervosa and **bulimia nervosa**, but not obesity, are included in the DSM-IV (American Psychiatric Association, 1994) and are considered to be severe disturbances in eating behavior.

Anorexia Nervosa is characterized by a refusal to maintain a minimally normal body weight. **Bulimia Nervosa** is characterized by repeated episodes of binge eating followed by inappropriate compensatory behaviors such as self-induced vomiting; misuse of laxatives, diuretics, or other medications; fasting; or excessive exercise. A disturbance in perception of body shape and weight is an essential feature of both Anorexia Nervosa and Bulimia Nervosa. (DSM-IV, American Psychiatric Association, 1994, p. 539)

Current explanations for the causes of eating disorders can generally be included in one of three models: the cultural, the biomedical, or the psychological.

The cultural model examines trends in society and cultural norms to explain why we are seeing a high incidence of eating disorders at this time (Brumberg, 1988; C. S. Crandall, 1988). Biomedical models postulate a hormonal basis for the disorders and prescribe drug treatment. Psychological models fall into three basic groups: psychoanalysis; family systems theory; and social psychology.

Cultural Explanations for Eating Disorders

Cultural norms that equate beauty with thinness are bringing about eating disorders in American society.

Thin is beautiful in American society. One only needs to pick up a popular magazine aimed at adolescent girls such as *Seventeen* or *Young Miss,* or one aimed at older, more sophisticated women such as *Vogue,* to see society's emphasis on the thin female body. "The current standard of attractiveness portrayed in the mass media is slimmer for women than for men, and the standard is slimmer now than in the past" (M. E. Collins, 1988, p. 227). The shift of the ideal body type of the American woman to thinner dimensions from 1959 to 1978 has been documented through comparisons of the figures of *Playboy* magazine centerfolds and Miss America contest winners (D. M. Garner, Garfinkel, Schwartz, & Thompson, 1980). The weight and body measures of the contestants decreased during those years and the pageant winners were thinner still than the average contestant.

The cultural norms and stereotypes regarding weight and beauty in American society are bringing about the problem of eating disorders (J. Rodin, Silberstein, & Striegel-Moore, 1985). The underlying cause is that the cultural beauty ideal of thinness is at odds with the biologically normal weight for most women. Obesity is a stigmatized state in American society. Female biological markers such as menarche and menopause tend to increase fat. Dieting lowers metabolism, which means that the individual will gain more weight on fewer calories. This developed biologically as a survival mechanism, when a scarcity rather than an abundance of food was the norm, as it still is in countries such as Somalia, and in pockets of poverty in the United States. Pursuit of thinness becomes a form of competition for women. Unfortunately, the significant consequence of women's concern with attaining an ideal weight and appearance is, in some cases, the development of eating disorders.

Body Image

The body image literature finds that women are dissatisfied with their bodies. The majority of both Black and White women think they are too fat.

The literature on **body image** documents the dissatisfaction of American women with their bodies. Seventy-five percent of the 33,000 women who responded to a *Glamour* magazine questionnaire on body image felt they were too fat, although by weight–height tables, only 25% were overweight (Wooley & Wooley, 1984). Only 6% were completely positive about their bodies, and 16% said they were "just right." Teenage women had the poorest body images. As women moved up in their careers they felt more satisfied with their bodies. The readership of *Glamour* magazine is largely White, middle-class, and young, so despite the size of the sample, it cannot be construed to represent the female population.

The majority of a sample of middle-class Black women also felt they were too fat (60.4%) although a higher proportion (34.7%) felt they were just right as compared with the *Glamour* magazine survey (16%) (Thomas & James, 1988). The majority (55.8%) reported using moderate food intake for weight control, exercise (78.4%), and restrictive techniques such as crash diets (64.7%) and diet pills (74.5%). Masculine women weighed less than feminine women, were less likely to use restrictive dieting methods, and were happier with their bodies. Further research still needs to be done with a broader range of racial, ethnic, and socioeconomic groups.

Dieting and Overeating

Dieting may be a cause of binge eating. High school students at risk for overeating have a poorer relationship with the person closest to them, have parents who engage in addictive behaviors, have multiple stressors, early age at menarche, and depressive affect.

It is only very recent in evolutionary history that food deprivation is self-imposed in the form of a diet rather than as a result of ecological scarcity. Polivy and Herman (1985) argue both that **dieting** and binge eating go together and that dieting causes binge eating. Laboratory research has shown that normal dieters exhibit what is called counterregulation. They eat little food after not eating or being forced to eat a small amount (thus maintaining their diets), but eat a great deal after being forced to eat a large, high-calorie meal. The high-calorie forced eating ruins

their diet temporarily, and triggers their overeating. Nondieters, however, are able to regulate their eating behavior and eat much less after forced eating of large amounts and eat more after no or only a small amount of forced eating.

Other factors that ordinarily inhibit eating in nondieters increase eating in dieters. For example, nondieters eat less when they are anxious, but dieters eat more when they are anxious. In a laboratory experiment that manipulated anxiety levels, dieters ate more (even unpalatable food) when distressed than when calm, but nondieters ate nonsignificantly less when anxious than calm (Polivy, Herman, & McFarlane, 1994). Similarly, alcohol suppresses eating in nondieters, but dieters eat large amounts following alcohol administration. In clinical cases as well, bulimics reported a period of dieting just prior to the onset of bulimia (Polivy & Herman, 1985). In light of this research, should one diet?

Binge eating patterns have been identified in substantial percentages of obese individuals seeking treatment. In a study of overweight men and women who sought treatment, 55% had moderate problems with binge eating and 23% had serious problems with binge eating (Gormally, Black, Daston, & Rardon, 1982). Thus, obesity is a risk factor for the development of binge eating and bulimia.

A three-factor model of the effects of dieting on eating behavior was developed by Lowe (1993), who critiques restraint theory. "I argue that the eating behavior exhibited by restrained eaters stems from their frequent dieting and overeating in the past rather than from their current state of dietary or cognitive restraint" (Lowe, 1993, p. 100). Lowe proposes three factors as being important to eating behavior: (1) frequency of dieting and overeating in the individual's history; (2) Current dieting or ongoing effort to restrict caloric intake to lose weight; and (3) weight suppression, which is sustained weight reduction over a period of time. How each of these factors influence eating behavior is mediated by psychological, biological, and sensory mechanisms.

High school students at risk for overeating rate their life quality more poorly than the other students and indicate they have a less-positive relationship with the person closest to them (Marston, Jacobs, Singer, Widaman, & Little, 1988). At risk students also more frequently reported that their parents engaged in more addictive behaviors: alcohol, drugs (other than uppers or downers), gambling, and overeating. The at-risk students did not differ significantly from the others on general adjustment and health. The at-risk subsample reported less daydreaming, worrying, and insecurity, probably due to the defensive effects of overeating.

A cumulative stressor model of risk for eating disorders among adolescent girls proposes that the onset of menarche (along with weight/fat gain associated with advanced puberty), the onset of dating and the intensification of academic demands in interaction with a slender body ideal, create a risk for eating disturbances (M. D. Levine & Smolak, 1992). A test of this model with 382 middle school (almost all European American) girls supported the general aspects of the model, and suggested a complex threshold phenomenon wherein if a girl achieves menarche, begins dating during the same year, and also feels she is under academic pressure, then there is an increase for subclinical disturbed eating. Her mother's investment in slenderness and exposure to peer dieting techniques were also correlates of dieting.

An eight year longitudinal study of 116 adolescent girls who were assessed at a mean age of 14.3, 16.0 and 22.3 years, found that clinical or subclinical eating disorders were associated with a pattern of physical and psychological characteristics (Graber, Brooks-Gunn, Paikoff & Warren, 1994). Girls at risk for eating disorders had the earliest age at menarche and a higher percentage of body fat. At risk girls also reported higher rates of depressive affect in mid-adolescence and young adulthood.

Anorexia Nervosa

Anorexia nervosa is characterized by dieting to extreme weight loss. Ninety-five percent of anorectics are female. It is fatal in 10–15% of cases. Freud saw anorexia as denial of sexuality.

It is a culture-bound syndrome, found in some cultures and not others.

Adolescence, particularly, is characterized by a preoccupation with appearance and a dissatisfaction with size of hips, waist, thighs, and so on. Some adolescent females become so obsessed with body appearance that they diet to the extreme of anorexia nervosa. Over 90% of the reported cases of anorexia nervosa involve adolescent females (C. L. Grant & Fodor, 1986). The most tragic aspect of this illness is that, despite treatment, it is fatal in approximately 10–15% of cases, from either physical complications or suicide (Eckert, 1985). The symptoms of anorexia nervosa are:

A. Refusal to maintain body weight at or above a minimally normal weight for age and height.
B. Intense fear of gaining weight or becoming fat, even though underweight.
C. Disturbance in the way in which one's body weight or shape is experienced . . . or denial of the seriousness of the current low body weight.
D. In postmenarcheal females, amenorrhea, i.e., the absence of at least three consecutive menstrual cycles. (DSM-IV, American Psychiatric Association, 1994, p. 545)

The body image distortion is in the direction of seeing oneself as "too fat" or specific body parts (thighs) as being "fat" even though objectively the individual might be considered emaciated. Two subtypes of anorexics have been identified: the restricting type, in which weight loss is accomplished through dieting, fasting, and excessive exercise; and the binge eating/purging type, in which in addition to dieting the individual purges through self-induced vomiting, or abuse of laxatives and diuretics. Some individuals with this subtype may not binge eat, but purge after eating even small amounts of food (DSM-IV, American Psychiatric Association, 1994). As a result of the extreme weight loss, other symptoms may appear including low body temperature, abnormally slow heartbeat, low blood pressure, fluid retention, and lanugo—

a downy-like hair on the body, and a variety of metabolic changes.

The disorder typically occurs in adolescence (mean age of onset is 17) or early adulthood, and overwhelmingly in females (90%). About one-third of anorectics were mildly overweight before the onset of the illness, and what may begin with normal dieting becomes extreme, limiting intake to only 600–800 calories per day. Obsessive-compulsive behavior unrelated to food such as excessive handwashing or behavior related to food such as collecting recipes and hoarding food may also occur. As a further means of losing weight, anorectics often engage in vigorous exercise, sometimes even waking in the middle of the night to ride a stationary bicycle or do calisthenics. While they may prepare elaborate meals for others, they are severely limiting their own food intake and exhibiting other bizarre behavior with regard to food such as hoarding, concealing, or throwing away food (Brumberg, 1988; DSM-IV, American Psychiatric Association, 1994).

In the 1970s the popular press began to feature stories about anorexia nervosa. In 1978 psychiatrist Hilda Bruch published *The Golden Cage,* a book on anorexia for the lay audience that contributed to the popular perception of an epidemic. Anorexia nervosa, however, was named and identified during the Victorian era by physicians in England, France, and the United States (Brumberg, 1988).

Freud (as cited in Bruch, 1978) wrote that young girls with anorexia are suffering from a melancholia where sexuality is undeveloped. He also viewed anorexia as a fear of impregnation. The anorectic sees eating as a way of becoming pregnant. By refusing to eat, she eliminates the risk of becoming pregnant. Clinicians find, at the present time, that adolescents with anorexia are not usually sexually active. Bruch (1978) went further than Freud, saying that the anorectic is not prepared to cope with adult life in general, not just her sexuality. "Because of the anorectic's paralyzing sense of ineffectiveness and anxiety about her identity, she opts, furiously, for control of her body" (Bruch, 1978, p. 28).

Anorexia nervosa is what is called a "culture-bound syndrome." At the present time anorexia nervosa is only found in North America, Western Europe, Japan, and other areas experiencing rapid Westernization (Brumberg, 1988). The tragic death of thirty-two year old singer Karen Carpenter, disclosed in January 1983 to be due to heart failure resulting from low serum potassium—a consequence of long-term starvation—focused public attention on the disorder. The cultural model alone, however, fails to explain why so many young women do not develop anorexia.

Bulimia

Bulimia is characterized by binging and purging or binging and behaviors such as fasting and/or excessive exercise.

Bulimia Nervosa is characterized by binge eating. Although ashamed of their eating, individuals with this disorder feel a sense of lack of control over stopping their eating. Two subtypes can be used to distinguish bulimics: (1) Purging type who regularly use self-induced vomiting or misuse laxatives, diuretics or enemas; and (2) Nonpurging type in which the person uses other compensatory behaviors such as fasting or excessive exercise.

Sweet, high calorie food is often preferred for the binge, such as cake and ice cream, with a texture that can be gobbled down easily with little chewing. The bulimic may consume 4,000–5,000 calories per day, but because of the vomiting and abuse of laxatives, not gain weight. Unlike the anorectic, the bulimic is usually of normal weight, although there is a wide range of weights from underweight to overweight. Higher socioeconomic women are more susceptible to bulimia because they are more likely to emulate the trendsetters in fashion and beauty. (Striegel-Moore, Silberstein, & Rodin, 1986). Certain subcultures such as boarding schools and colleges, which are composed more of middle- and upper-class women, and members of certain professions such as dancers, models, and athletes have a higher incidence of bulimia.

Bulimia and Psychopathology

Bulimia is most frequently found among middle-class adolescent or young adult women. Bulimics have been found to have higher levels of psychopathology and drug and alcohol abuse than nonbulimics.

It is only in the past 20 years that a cluster of symptoms that have come to be identified as bulimia came to the attention of the mental health profession. Demographically and clinically a homogeneous pattern began to be revealed. At least 90% of the patients are female, with the onset of the disorder occurring in adolescence or early adulthood, in industrialized societies (DSM-IV, American Psychiatric Association, 1994). Researchers on bulimia have only had the benefit of standard diagnostic criteria since 1979 when bulimia was included in the classification system of the American Psychiatric Association.

Women with certain personality and individual behavioral patterns may also be more susceptible to bulimia. Clinical studies have found depressive and anxiety symptoms associated with bulimia. Substance abuse, most frequently involving sedatives, amphetamines, cocaine, or alcohol, is common among bulimics (DSM-IV, American Psychiatric Association, 1994; Striegel-Moore et al., 1986).

Undergraduate women who were normal-weight dieters displaying bulimic symptoms had greater restrained eating, but they also had lower expectations regarding their being able to sustain dieting (L. M. Zinn & Stanton, 1987). Low self-esteem was also associated with bulimic behavior. This data is consistent with that reported by Polivy & Herman (1985), who also found dieters to be at risk for bulimia.

Patients with bulimia nervosa and restrained eaters (dieters) are on a simple continuum going from unrestrained eaters (nondieters), restrained eaters, to bulimics (Laessle, Tuschl, Waadt, & Pirke, 1989). With regard to psychopathological measures such as perception of internal signals, depression, self-esteem, and fears about social re-

lationships and maturity, there does not appear to be a continuum. Bulimic patients differ significantly from both restrained and unrestrained eaters in psychopathology. Bulimics share specific features of psychopathology "such as ineffectiveness, distorted interoceptive awareness, and interpersonal distrust, which have been described as fundamental disturbances in eating disorders" (Laessle et al., 1989, p. 774). Bulimics are characterized by significantly more psychopathology than are the restrained eaters.

Bulimia and Sociocultural Norms

Bulimia is influenced by social norms. Bulimia may be declining among American adolescents.

A social psychological model of bulimia focuses on norms, shared expectations for behavior within a culture or in a particular group. Social psychologists have observed that social pressures may lead to eating disorders. In an investigation of two sororities C. S. Crandall (1988), traced how social norms and popularity patterns influence binge eating. In Sorority Alpha, the highest levels of popularity were among moderate bingers. The norm for binge eating was at the mean level, with deviance in either direction—binging too much or too little—associated with reductions in popularity. In Sorority Beta, on the other hand, the more binging the more popularity. Within that sorority, cliques with high levels of binging were the most prestigious. If a woman did not binge at the normative level in the fall, she moved toward it during the academic year, indicating that binge eating is a learned pattern of behavior, perhaps through modeling.

A cross-cultural study of Arab female undergraduate students attending London and Cairo universities, found a much greater prevalence of abnormal eating attitudes and behavior among the London university students (Nasser, 1986). In the London sample, 22% scored higher than the cut-off on The Eating Interview (EAT), which indicates the likelihood of bulimia nervosa; however, none fulfilled the criteria for anorexia nervosa. In the Cairo sample, although 12% scored above the cut-off for at least a partial syndrome of anorexia nervosa, none of the students fulfilled diagnostic criteria for either anorexia or bulimia.

The fact that there were no diagnosable cases of anorexia—only of bulimia among Arab females in London—would suggest that bulimia is more influenced by social norms than is anorexia. Some of the bulimic students in London gave a history of prior contact with bulimics suggesting some social contagion effects. Abnormal eating attitudes did occur in Cairo as well, but to a lesser extent, perhaps reflecting the beginning stages of Westernization, but the lesser influence as compared with London.

Research indicated a decline in the extent of bulimic behavior among high school students in the 1980s. Over 95% of the female population of a large, suburban, midwestern high school were administered a questionnaire designed to provide an estimate of bulimic behaviors in 1981 and in 1986. "The 1986 sample demonstrated a 50% reduction in bulimic behaviors, a marked decrease in the prevalence of dieting behavior, and reduction in preoccupation with thinness. Nevertheless, body dissatisfaction remained the same in the latter sample" (C. Johnson, Tobin, & Lipkin, 1989).

The researchers point to several sociocultural factors that may have accounted for the decline in bulimic behavior in the 1980s. The life-threatening ailment of AIDS is characterized by weight loss to the point of severe emaciation. Thinness, once associated with beauty, health, and success, may now be increasingly associated with having a contagious, fatal disease. In addition, young women are striving for athletic accomplishment and strength as a way of demonstrating mastery and control over their bodies and "pursuit of strength" is replacing a "drive for thinness." My daughter, who is a college student, tells me that working out in the gym is the "in thing" that everybody is doing. Also, an antidieting literature has emerged that indicates that weight lost through dieting is regained.

Eating Disorders and Family Systems Theory

According to **family systems theory** *anorectic daughters are overprotected by their parents and need greater autonomy, which they try to achieve through control over their bodies. Bulimics are hostilely enmeshed in their families.*

Research by family systems theorists support the view that eating disorders are a reflection of pervasive family problems. Nevertheless, the families of anorectics present a facade of perfection, self-sacrifice, and love. Bulimic families are more hostile, depriving, disorganized, and conflictual, as well as less nurturant, supportive, and empathic (Garner, Garfinkel, & O'Shaughnessy, 1985; Strober & Humphrey, 1987).

Mothers and fathers of classical, restricting anorectics are more nurturing and comforting, but also ignoring and neglecting of their daughters' needs to express themselves and their feelings than are parents of normal and bulimic adolescents. Humphrey (1989) arrived at this conclusion based on videotaped observations of 74 family triads—mother, father, and adolescent daughter (16 daughters were anorectic, 16 bulimic, 16 both anorectic and bulimic, and 24 were normal). Anorectic daughters are the most submissive and ambivalent about disclosing their feelings. Parents ignore and negate her individuality and developmental needs. "The anorectic daughter mirrors their mixed messages with her ambivalence about separating. She cannot seem to disclose her true self and feelings without also submitting to her parents' opinions and expectations" (Humphrey, 1989, p. 213). Bulimics are more hostilely enmeshed with their parents, as is seen by a greater percentage of mutual belittling and blaming as well as sulking and appeasing as compared with normal families.

In their book, *Unlocking the Family Door,* Stierlin and Weber (1989), systems theorists in Germany, describe families of anorectics as being bound by strong loyalty ties and having a fear of separation. The book title refers to their therapeutic goal, which is to unlock the family door so the daughter can separate from her parents and learn to lead a more independent life. The parents and daughter are caught in a charged state of deadlock over eating behavior. "Anorectic girls are frequently experienced by their parents as being defiant and obstinate, that is, in the final analysis as 'bad' whereas the parents are experienced by the girls as being domineering, demanding, and overpowering" (Stierlin & Weber, 1989, p. 84).

Eating-disordered women see their mothers and their fathers as less caring but their fathers as more protective than do normal women (Calem, Waller, Slade, & Newton, 1990). The result of this paternal overprotectiveness is that it prevents the child from developing autonomy. Anorectic and bulimic females, as compared with dieters and normal controls, have been found by psychiatrists and psychologists to have the (1) greatest external locus of control and (2) most self-directed hostility, but (3) least assertiveness and (4) least family encouragement of independence (G. Williams, Chamove, & Millar, 1990). Although the eating-disordered women differed significantly from the dieters and normal controls on these measures, they did not differ from psychiatric patients, except only on family independence.

Lesbians with Eating Disorders

Among college women lesbians do not differ from heterosexual women on symptoms of eating disorders.

The lesbian subculture has been reported to place less emphasis on physical attractiveness than does the heterosexual culture. Lesbian ideals challenge the culturally prescribed beauty ideals; it may be postulated that loving a woman may lead to greater acceptance of one's own female body. Thus, one might think that lesbian women would have fewer eating disorders than do heterosexual women of similar age and socioeconomic level. According to Laura S. Brown (1987) lesbians are underrepresented among bulimic women who are seen either in treatment or as research participants.

Nevertheless, lesbian and heterosexual undergraduate women did not differ on a multidimensional measure of body esteem and symptoms of eating disorders. Body esteem was more closely related to self-esteem for lesbian women than for heterosexual women. "Lesbian students reported lower self-esteem, more ineffectiveness, more interpersonal distrust, and more difficulties in identifying their own emotions than did heterosexual students" (Striegel-Moore, Tucker, & Hsu, 1990, p. 493). The researchers attribute these personality differences to the lesbian women's experience of living in a homophobic society. There was a trend for lesbians to engage in less dieting, but more binge eating than heterosexuals, but the difference did not reach statistical significance. Certainly, more research needs to be conducted on lesbians and eating disorders before any firm conclusions can be reached, but it appears that lesbian ideology may not be enough to overcome the already internalized standards and beliefs of society with regard to standards of physical beauty.

Women of Color with Eating Disorders

Middle class women of color also have eating disorders.

Much of the literature on eating disorders is written as if it is a problem exclusively of White middle- and upper-class females. As more social, economic, and vocational opportunities open up to women of color, they are under increased pressure both to conform to the White dominant culture's norms, and to be a test case, expected to act and look "perfect" (Root, 1990). There is also an increased pattern of outmarriage among ethnic women resulting from a desire to partner in the same way as White women, with someone of greater education, and financial solvency than she and also perhaps less chauvinistic than many men from traditional ethnic cultures. Root raises three key questions regarding women of color and eating disorders.

How might stereotypes about people of color and who gets eating disorders obfuscate clinical assessment of this possibility in people of color (especially women)? Given the increase in observation of eating disorders among African Americans are eating disorders actually increasing among other Americans of color? Lastly, what do we need to do to include people of color as subjects in research studies on and in treatment of eating disorders? (Root, 1990, p. 526)

Research indicates a broader prevalence of the disorder across the racial spectrum than was originally believed. Among the entire female population of a large suburban, midwestern community high school, students classified as Probably Bulimic on the Eating Disorder Inventory were found across all ethnic groups: 17% of the Anglos; 17% of the Blacks, and 15% of the others were classified as Probably Bulimic (Van Thorre & Vogel, 1985). The implication is that clinicians working with Black and other non-White middle-class adolescents should also be alert to the possibility that they may be bulimic. Although those identified as Probably Bulimic were identified at all age levels, the youngest group, the 14-year olds, actually had the highest percentage.

Recovery from Anorexia and Bulimia

The outcome for bulimics is significantly better than for anorexics or for anorexic/bulimics.

About 40 outcome studies of anorexia nervosa have been published in the past 30 years (Herzog et al., 1993). Follow-ups of from 4 to 20 years of anorectics show a recovery rate ranging from 17% to 77%. Although there are fewer follow-up studies of bulimia, long-term follow-up studies show a recovery rate ranging from 13% to 69%. The largest naturalistic, longitudinal study of women with eating disorders was conducted by Herzog et al. (1993), who followed up 225 women screened to meet DSM-III-R (American Psychiatric Association, 1987) criteria for anorexia and/or bulimia, who sought treatment for an eating

disorder at Boston-area eating disorder programs. The outcome for bulimics at one year was significantly better (56% full recovery rate) than it was for anorexic/bulimics (15% full recovery rate) or for anorexics (10% full recovery rate). A low percentage of ideal body weight at intake was also a predictor of poor outcome at one-year follow-up. The authors note that this calls for stringent efforts on the part of clinicians in limiting how much weight an anorexic patient loses. A high rate of other psychopathology was also found among this group of eating disordered women, with affective disorders the most frequent. Only personality disorders, however, were significant as outcome predictors; women with a personality disorder had significantly worse outcomes at one-year follow-up. Future research will continue to monitor the course of these women.

ANXIETY DISORDERS

Anxiety disorders is a general term under which a number of more specific disorders are subsumed. In this section I will focus on those anxiety disorders from which women suffer to a greater extent than do men.

The prevalence of phobias are more common among women than men in the general population, ranging from 55% to 90%, depending on the specific phobia. A person with a **specific phobia** becomes very anxious in the presence of a specific object, such as spiders, or a specific situation, such as flying (DSM-IV, American Psychiatric Association, 1994). The gender imbalance is particularly noticeable for panic disorder and **agoraphobia**. Panic attacks may occur in the context of several anxiety disorders, only one of which is agoraphobia.

Agoraphobia with and without History of Panic Disorder

Most agoraphobics are married and have a conflict between self-determination and managing alone. Panic disorder has been treated effectively by antidepressant medication and by psychotherapy.

Sheehan (1986) indicates that among women, phobias or pathological fears are the number one psychiatric disorder in all age groups. There is a large disproportion in female sufferers of agoraphobia. Estimates based on psychiatric clinic samples and surveys in both the United States and United Kingdom indicate that about 80–88% of agoraphobics are women (Chambless & Goldstein, 1980; Thorpe & Burns, 1983).

Technically, agoraphobia is from the Greek word, *agora,* meaning "open space" or "marketplace," and *phobia,* meaning fear. Agoraphobia is an incapacitating anxiety when traveling away from home, or fear of being home alone. Many agoraphobics suffer from a wide range of phobias. Agoraphobia is classified as either Agoraphobia Without History of Panic Disorder or as Panic Disorder with Agoraphobia (which occurs three times as often in women as in men). In the case of agoraphobia without history of panic disorder, the individual may have a fear of specific occurrences when venturing out of the house such as loss of bladder control, or a fear of fainting rather than of having a full-blown panic attack. Only 5% of the cases of agoraphobia occur without panic disorder (DSM-IV, American Psychiatric Association, 1994).

The symptoms of the **panic attack** include a sudden feeling of intense fear, and often a sense of impending doom and an urge to escape, rapid heart beat, shortness of breath, dizziness, choking, trembling or shaking, sweating, nausea or abdominal distress, depersonalization, numbness or tingling sensation, hot flashes or chills, chest pain, fear of dying, fear of going crazy, or doing something uncontrolled during the attack (DSM-IV, American Psychiatric Association, 1994). The sufferer of a panic attack begins to fear or avoid the situations that she comes to associate with the panic attacks. The victim becomes so afraid of having an attack, especially in a public place, that she stays home, literally becoming housebound. Agoraphobia thus restricts choices for the individual, forcing her into rigid and narrow behavior patterns that limit growth and everyday functioning (Chambless & Goldstein, 1980).

Theories of Agoraphobia and Panic Disorder

Various theories of agoraphobia and panic disorder include the cognitive model, the marital conflict theory, attachment theory, and biological theory.

One conceptualization of panic disorders is that it is fear of fear. It is a fear of having a panic attack, rather than of the open spaces that keeps a woman housebound. "The cognitive model of panic assumes that attacks develop from the misinterpretation of bodily sensations" (Black, Wesner, Bowers, & Gabel, 1993, p. 44). For example, someone may experience an increase in heartbeat and not pay any attention to it while another individual may believe it signals an impending heart attack. Theories of how this fear develops includes classical conditioning to one's own internal cues that precede a panic attack. The anxiety–sensitivity hypothesis says that some individuals have a tendency to "respond fearfully to anxiety symptoms."

A marital conflict theory contends that the majority of agoraphobics are married and the disorder can only be understood in terms of the dynamics of the marital relationship (R. J. Hafner, 1982). Within these marriages, there are conflicts between the agoraphobic's wish to become more self-determined and her fear of managing alone.

Within a framework of attachment theory developed by John Bowlby (1980) agoraphobia is viewed as a disorder resulting from insecurity of attachment in childhood.

Within this context, agoraphobia is conceived as a condition of anxious attachment, related to fear of separation from those with whom one has formed affectional bonds. Because of fear and anxiety over the availability and responsiveness of attachment figures, the person is prone to separation anxiety and clinging behavior, lacking confidence for exploring the world or dealing with stressful situations. (Sable, 1994, p. 370)

Research examining parental loss prior to age 17 years and adult psychopathology in 1,018 pairs of female twins from a population-based registry found the relation of parental loss to psychiatric disorders to be greatest for panic disorder (Kendler, Neale, Kessler, Heath, & Eaves, 1992). Panic disorder was equally associated with death of mother or father and with maternal, but not paternal, separation. The relationship of early parental loss and adult development of panic disorder further supports attachment theory.

SUICIDE

Suicide Rate for Men and Women

For over 100 years the suicide rate for men has been about three times the rate for women. Women, however, attempt suicide more often than men.

In 1881, it was noted that the suicide rate for men was about three times the rate for women (H. White and Stillion, 1988). The ratio is about the same today. In 1986 there were 24,200 deaths by suicide that year in the United States for males and 6,700 deaths by suicide for females, a ratio of 3.6:1 (U.S. Bureau of the Census, 1994). Although males commit suicide with a higher frequency than females, females attempt suicide more often than males. Females are reported to attempt suicide anywhere from 2.3 to 10 times more often than males (H. White & Stillion, 1988).

A number of explanations have been put forth in the literature to account for the sex difference in completed suicide. Men are said to use more lethal methods (e.g., shooting, hanging), whereas women use more passive and less-effective methods (e.g., drugs). Are there sex differences, however, in the psychological factors leading up to the suicide attempt? In a content analysis of sui-

cide notes of 20 males and 20 females, no gender differences were found in psychological variables and conscious intention and early life stresses (Leenaars, 1988). The author concluded that by implication, men's suicides are psychologically similar to women's.

In more recent years, there has been speculation that the Women's Movement and changing sex roles would lead women to behave more like men and show an increase in deviant behavior (alcoholism, crime, suicide). Steffensmeier (1984) examined the statistics on White suicide rates for men and women for the years 1960–1978. She used data that was made available by the Division of Vital Statistics of the National Center for Health Statistics to calculate a "sex differential" (SD). "The SD refers to the percentage that the female rate comprises of the combined male plus female rate for the total population and specific age groupings" (Steffensmeier, 1984, p. 615).

Overall, there has been a trend for a slight increase in suicide rates between 1960 and 1978. The findings show that the SD in suicide rates for 1960, 1967, 1972, and 1978, respectively, were 23.1, 27.9, 28.3, and 25.5. The data thus clearly indicates that male rates are still considerably higher than are female rates, accounting for nearly three-quarters of all suicides. Female suicide rates increased somewhat for women during the 1960s (except for women over 65), but remained stable during the 1970s. This would not be the pattern expected if the Women's Movement were responsible for an increase in female suicide, since the Women's Movement did not really impact on most women until the late 1960s and early 1970s. The overall increase in suicide rates are accounted for by young males, while suicide rates of males 40 years and over declined.

Suicide and Psychiatric Disorders

One out of four individuals suffering from panic disorder complicated with other psychiatric disorders or major depressive disorder complicated with other psychiatric disorders attempts suicide at some time.

A relationship was found between suicide attempts and psychiatric disorders in the ECA study of 18,011 adults described earlier (Eichler & Parron, 1987; Robbins et al., 1984). The lifetime rates of suicide attempts are similar for uncomplicated panic disorder and major depression (about 7% to 7.9%). Most cases of panic disorder or major depression were not uncomplicated (meaning that other disorders are also present). The lifetime rate of suicide attempts increases to 26.3% for those with panic disorders and other psychiatric disorders and 19.8% for those with major depression and other disorders. The combination of panic disorder–major depression was associated with a 19.5% rate of suicide attempts. The lifetime rate of suicide attempts for those with no psychiatric disorder in the ECA study was only 1%. Clinicians working with patients with panic disorder and/or depression need to be aware of the potential for suicide.

ALCOHOL AND DRUG ABUSE

Women and Men's Alcohol Use

Women have a lower rate of alcoholism than men. Alcoholism is a risk factor for homelessness.

Men use drugs and alcohol more than women (Gomberg, 1979; J. Harrison, 1978). Nor is there any indication that women's drinking is increasing, a conclusion supported by a national survey of women's drinking in 1981 (Wilsnack, Wilsnack, & Klassen, 1984). The respondents were selected based on a screening interview to include 500 moderate- to heavy-drinking women, 378 light-drinking or abstaining women, 39 women who were self-reported former drinkers, as well as 396 men. The data from this interview was compared with nine surveys conducted between 1971 and 1979. The authors conclude from their research that, in fact, "women drinkers remain predominantly light drinkers." Young women aged 21–34 had more adverse conse-

quences and episodes of drinking than women in other age groups. In 1981, however, more of the middle-aged women (ages 35–64) were drinkers than in previous surveys. Higher-status women are more likely to be drinkers than lower-status women, and to be heavier drinkers. Women with less than an eighth-grade education and with lower-income levels are the most likely group to be abstainers (Wilsnack, et al., 1984).

The fundamentalist Protestant women (62%), and more Black women compared with White women (45% vs. 38%) were abstainers. Heavier drinking varied by marital status with never married, separated, divorced, or cohabiting women more likely to be heavier drinkers and less likely to be abstainers than widowed, or married women working full-time as housewives or part-time or full-time for pay. Women with spouses, partners, siblings, or friends who were heavy drinkers were also more likely to be heavy drinkers (Wilsnack et al., 1984).

Husbands are less likely to stay with an alcoholic wife than wives are with an alcoholic husband. Through divorce and loss of financial support, alcoholism may indirectly play a role in women's homelessness. "Thus although alcohol and other drug abuse should not be construed as an explanation of family homelessness (Weitzman et al., 1990), it may serve as an important contributing risk factor for some women and children" (Robertson, 1991, p. 1198).

Childhood Sexual Abuse and Later Alcohol and Drug Abuse

Women who have been sexually abused as children have a higher rate of alcoholism than do women who had not been abused.

Being molested as a child may be a hidden contributor to adult alcohol and drug abuse in large numbers of women. Many victims turn to alcohol and drugs as a way of coping with the serious emotional consequences of having been sexually victimized as a child (Rohsenow, Corbett, & Devine, 1988).

Sexual victims who later turn to substance abuse may be using alcohol or drugs to cope with some of the long-term effects of sex abuse, such as the sense of powerlessness, low self esteem, and social isolation resulting from their damaged sense of self, impaired social skills and inability to trust others. (Rohsenow et al., 1988, p. 17)

Questions about child sexual abuse experiences should be asked upon admission of substance abusers to inpatient treatment programs. Before the question was routinely asked in one facility, 20% of adult women reported child sexual abuse histories, as compared with 74–77% after the question was routinely asked at different times during treatment (Demo et al., 1988). This was a far greater incidence of child sexual abuse compared with that typically reported in community surveys.

Alcoholic women are more passive and have a more negative view of their childhood than do nonalcoholic women. Depression and eating disorders are also linked to alcoholism in women.

"Alcoholic women are frightened people who view the world as a dangerous and hostile place that is made up of people who should be kept at a distance" (J. L. Hafner, Fakouri, & Chesney, 1988, p. 305). Those are the conclusions of Hafner et al., who found that early recollections of middle-class alcoholic women were significantly more negative than those of a control group of women. Nonalcoholic women mentioned mother and other relatives (e.g., uncles, aunts, grandparents) and pets more often than alcoholic women. Alcoholic women were more passive than the nonalcoholic women who reported initiating action significantly more frequently. The fundamental life view held by the alcoholic women was laden with much more unhappiness and distress than that of the nonalcoholic women.

Among women attending an alcohol treatment unit in England, 26% of the patients had symptoms of a current clinical eating disorder (Peveler & Fairburn, 1990). Another 19% of the sample had a history suggestive of anorexia nervosa. This research has implications for treatment

programs dealing with either alcohol abuse or eating disorders to be alert for evidence of the other problem.

During stressful times, women characterized by lower levels of success preoccupation reported greater use of mind-altering drugs, whereas women with higher levels of success preoccupation reported greater use of mind-altering drugs during less-stressful times (Snell, Belk, & Hawkins, 1987). One theory of causal factors of alcoholism in women is "sex role conflict." Sex role conflict has been hypothesized to lead to drinking as a way of reducing the stress associated with the conflict or by actually reducing the disparity between actual and ideal sex role behavior (C. S. Benson & Wilsnack, 1983). In a test of sex role conflict as a cause of alcoholism in women, however, Kroft & Leichner (1987) found that women who were classified as (1) abstainers, (2) social drinkers, (3) alcoholics, and (4) remitted alcoholics did not differ significantly in their actual and ideal scores on the BSRI. Thus, the research did not support a greater degree of sex role conflict of alcoholic women. "When the factors of age, socioeconomic status, and marital status were controlled, alcoholic women scored as more depressed and more sex role undifferentiated than the non-alcoholic women" (Kroft & Leichner, 1987, p. 685). Before the removal of an estimate of the effects of depression, alcoholic women were also significantly less satisfied with their roles of "housekeeper" and "woman." It may be depression that is accounting for the apparent sex role dissatisfaction in female alcoholics.

Moving into full-time careers has not increased women's drinking. Role deprivation is a predictor of women's drinking.

Some psychologists have speculated that women's moving into full-time careers may alter characteristic ways of females expressing distress (Lennon, 1987). Working women may begin to express distress in ways more characteristic of men (i.e., drinking). She used data from the National Center of Health Statistics' Health and

Nutrition Examination Survey (HANES I), a national multistage probability survey conducted between 1971 and 1975 that collected data on 28,000 individuals in 100 sampling areas across the United States.

The hypothesis was not supported. Working women do not have higher drinking levels than nonworking women. This was true even for women in "male" jobs, or "jobs that involve motor skills, undesirable working conditions, and physical demands, for full-time work status, for service jobs, and for the sex type of job" (Lennon, 1987, p. 298). Women in these jobs do not have higher levels of drinking than nonworking women, and they have lower levels of drinking than do men in these or any other jobs.

The lack or loss of stable, full-time roles, on the other hand, is related to problem drinking (Wilsnack, Klassen, Schur, & Wilsnack, 1991). Five year follow-ups were conducted with 143 problem drinkers and 157 non-problem drinkers identified in a 1981 national survey of women's drinking. Predictors of problem drinking included never having been married, becoming unemployed during the follow-up, or being employed part-time at the second interview. The authors of the study suggest that role deprivation may reduce women's self-esteem and also reduce contact with role partners who could provide both social support and negative feedback about drinking. Sexual dysfunction was the single best predictor of problem drinking, perhaps because the women were using alcohol for self medication, but alcohol has detrimental effects on physiological sexual functioning.

Heroin Addiction

Women heroin addicts often come from homes where there is an alcoholism problem. Most heroin-addicted women are involved in prostitution and other criminal activity.

Does heroin addiction stem from a pathological family environment? Although heroin use is commonly reported to begin at an early age, 17–20 (Cuskey & Wathey, 1982), Binion (1982) disputes the view of heroin-addicted women or men

as coming from pathological families of origin. The majority of both women (54.7%) and men (58.4%) interviewed in methadone maintenance and drug treatment facilities lived in families with both parents present up until the age of 12 years. Men (51.5%) were significantly more likely than women (41.2%) to be raised in poverty. The majority of both the women (68.5%) and the men (78.5%) perceived the adults in their family as getting along "very well or fairly well." Forty percent of the women and 60% of the men said they had a "good" mother.

The major problem found with a high frequency in the families of addicts was alcoholism, with 58% of the women and men reporting that they had family members with drinking problems. The women (57.6%) were more likely than the men (44.1%) to report having run away from home before age 16. Both men and women were likely to have begun drug use with marijuana, followed by barbiturates, heroin, and amphetamines. Women were more likely to have first been introduced to heroin by an opposite sex partner.

For ghetto women, there is a proximity to heroin and criminal activity in the community that is the result of poverty and discrimination. The young woman may be introduced to heroin at a party or by a boyfriend or husband.

> If addicts appear to be successful and addiction rewarding, a woman might intentionally become an addict. To a relatively poor young girl with few options, the fast life and heroin use may seem quite attractive. Involvement in this scene may be her only opportunity to wear expensive clothes and drive an expensive car; she may find the members of this world attractive and friendly, and experimenting with heroin may increase the opportunity of having an enduring relationship. (Rosenbaum, 1981, p. 32)

The majority of the addicted women turned to prostitution at some point. Far fewer women than men deal drugs. It is very difficult to combine legitimate work and heroin careers, unless the woman restricts heroin use to weekends. Many of the women were already involved in criminal activities before becoming addicted, but addiction to heroin also often necessitates criminal activity for its support.

Cuskey and Wathey (1982) reported on women treated by the Odyssey House Mabon Parents' Demonstration Program (MPDP) organized by Dr. Judianne Densen Gerber. Three hundred and four women, along with 158 children, were admitted over a three-year period, from 1974 to 1977. Although the majority of the White addicts (61.9%) were reared by both parents, and 42.9% of non-White addicts were reared by both parents, alcohol problems were present in nearly half of both the Black (45.2%) and White (47.6%) families. Approximately one-third of both the White (33%) and non-White (30.7%) addicts reported having been sexually abused as a child. Although the average age was in the early 20s at the time of their entry into the program, they had a history of multiple problems. Fifty-two percent had dropped out of high school, and 62% had been truant before reaching the tenth grade. Only 40% had held a job for at least six months prior to admission for treatment. Seventy-two percent had been arrested. The most common offenses were drug pushing (21.9%), prostitution (20.1%), robbery and burglary (13.1%), forgery (10.6%), and shoplifting (2.5%).

Cocaine Abuse

There are two distinct types of female cocaine users—poor and Black from the inner city and White and affluent.

There appears to be a bimodal distribution of the female cocaine abuser, poor and Black or White and affluent. The picture of the cocaine abuser is one of the polydrug-user from the inner city who is addicted to cocaine along with heroin and other drugs. In the Cuskey & Wathey (1982) study cited earlier, although 76.5% of the women were addicted to heroin, 62% also used cocaine, as well as barbiturates (54.4%), amphetamines (45.6%), and even LSD (44.1%).

On the other hand, another type of cocaine abuser presents a radically different picture from the heroin addict. Washton (1986) conducted a random sampling of 165 women callers to the 800-COCAINE helpline. The profile revealed by this sample was the following: "white, 85%; mean age 30; mean education 14 years; annual income over $25,000, 40%" (p. 57). Many of the callers were business or professional women who said they did not have a previous history of drug addiction or psychiatric illness. Many of them felt, however, that they had developed a serious dependency on cocaine. They had been using the drug an average of 4.6 years.

> Many women receive cocaine as a gift from men, as they would candy or flowers, and this practice has become incorporated to some extent in courtship rituals. Cocaine use among women is increasing and the use of the drug is often connected with issues of sexuality and relationships with men. (Washton, 1986, p. 57)

What may have started in romantic innocence has become a serious dependency when they call the helpline: "81% said they could not refuse cocaine; 75% experienced an irresistible craving and compulsion to use the drug; and 72% said they could not limit or control their drug intake" (Washton, 1986, p. 57). The average woman used 4.9 grams per week at a cost of about $450. Their habits were supported by their husbands or their boyfriends, or they dealt drugs (21%) or they stole from work, family, and friends (26%). Many negative consequences followed from their cocaine use: depression, insomnia, fatigue, irritability, memory loss, complete loss of sexual desire, suicide attempts, brain seizures, and automobile accidents.

PSYCHOTHERAPY

Psychotherapy involves the use of psychological methods to alleviate the symptoms of mental disorders or to help individuals cope during periods of stress in their lives. Psychologists and other mental health practitioners such as social workers, counselors, and psychiatrists do psychotherapy. In addition, psychiatrists who are also trained in medicine, may prescribe medication and in severe cases of depression also treat patients with electroconvulsive therapy (electrical current is passed through the patient's brain).

Beginning in 1970, with the publication of an article by Broverman, Broverman, Clarkson, Rosenkrantz, and Vogel, feminist-oriented psychologists and other psychotherapists began to question the underlying assumptions of psychotherapy with women and the nature of the therapeutic relationship, particularly between male therapists and female clients. In a further indictment of mental health professionals, particularly psychiatrists and clinical psychologists, Phyllis Chesler, in her book, *Women and Madness* (1972), charged that psychotherapists pity the dependence and fearfulness of women, while at the same time considering independent behavior to be masculine and unacceptable for women.

Race, Sex, and Psychiatric Diagnosis

Both sex and race have been found to influence diagnosis of mental health clients to be consistent with stereotypes.

In their classic study, Broverman et al. (1970) asked 79 psychologists, psychiatrists, and social workers (46 men and 33 women) to respond to 122 bipolar adjectives in order to describe a "mature, healthy socially competent" adult woman, adult man, and adult whose gender is not specified. Both male and female therapists were found to give similar descriptions for the healthy adult and the healthy adult man. However, their descriptions of the healthy, adult woman showed her to be significantly less healthy (e.g., very excitable in minor crises, more easily influenced, less adventurous, less independent, very illogical, very sneaky) than the healthy adult or the healthy adult man. Not all research, however, has arrived at similar results (Stricker, 1977).

Two studies conducted nearly 20 years later, (Loring & Powell, 1988) found that both sex and race still influence diagnosis. A case study approach was used in which a stratified random sample of 290 psychiatrists diagnosed persons, using DSM-III-derived criteria, described in two vignettes. Two written cases who were diagnosed by their psychiatrists as having an undifferentiated schizophrenic disorder with a dependent personality disorder, were manipulated so that approximately one-fifth of the clinicians evaluated a White male, a White female, a Black male, a Black female, or a client whose race and sex were not disclosed.

When the case study did not provide information about race and sex, psychiatrists, regardless of their sex and race, agreed with the original diagnosis. Similarly, when the race, and sex of the psychiatrist and the case study coincided, they also agreed with the original diagnosis. An exception to this was that when White female clinicians diagnosed White female clients, over one-half of the diagnoses were for "brief reactive psychosis," the least severe of the possible diagnoses. Male psychiatrists were more likely to diagnose females as being depressed, or, when diagnosing White females, to choose histrionic personality disorders. Black males and Black females were most likely to be diagnosed as having a paranoid schizophrenic disorder. "Clinicians appear to ascribe violence, suspiciousness and dangerousness to black clients even though the case studies are the same as the case studies for the white clients" (Loring & Powell, 1988, p. 18). This diagnosis was made by Black as well as White psychiatrists, and was most likely made for Black males. The serious implications of these results is that stereotypes can influence professional diagnostic judgment, which in turn influences the medication and treatment approach prescribed.

Clinical psychologists' perceptions of degree of psychological maladjustment have also been found to be related to whether the symptoms fit the prevailing gender-role stereotypes (Waisberg & Page, 1988). Female patients who had "masculine" symptoms (alcohol abuse or antisocial personality disorder) were rated as more seriously disturbed than were males with the same symptoms. Similarly, males with "feminine" symptoms (depression and anxiety) were rated as more disturbed than were their female counterparts. Stronger recommendations for drug treatment were made for females in all diagnostic categories except depression, with male psychologists more likely than female psychologists to recommend drug treatment. Female psychologists were more optimistic in their overall outlook for the patient's future progress.

Professional status as well as sex of a therapist also influences the severity of diagnosis of clients (C. T. Wright, Meadow, Abramowitz, & Davidson, 1980). Diagnostic evaluations made by 26 clinicians of male and female outpatients entering a community mental health center found that male nurses, social workers, psychologists, and psychiatrists, made increasingly higher proportions of psychotic diagnoses.

Consciousness-Raising Groups

Consciousness-raising groups were much more common in the late 1960s and 1970s than they are in the 1990s. Today, women are more likely to participate in self-help and therapy groups such as groups for incest survivors or battered women.

The method of a **consciousness-raising group** is for the same women to meet regularly to sit and listen to one another's stories, to share their lives. It is usually a group of 8 or 10 women who meet in the home of one of the women. There is no formal leader.

> Our relationship to everything—our bodies, our work, our sexuality, the men and women and children in our lives—emerged in a thoroughly new light. Together, we saw that the old terms used to describe politics, relationships, sexuality, power, and language itself were an outgrowth of male experience and had to be reinvented from our own point of view as women. For many of us, the overwhelming sense was of seeing the world through our own eyes for the very first time. (Greenspan, 1983, p. 233)

Consciousness-raising groups are less frequently formed by women in the 1990s than was true in the earlier days of the women's movement of the late 1960s and 1970s. **Self-help** groups, and therapy groups for women who are survivors of incest, of rape, or of family violence, or with eating disorders, or other problems have largely replaced the consciousness-raising groups.

Feminist Therapy

Feminist therapy is really a philosophical position that a major cause of women's problems is that they have less economic and political power than men.

Greenspan (1983) points out three myths of traditional therapy. The first myth is that, "It's all in your head." The meaning of this statement is that the personal, private realm of reality is derived largely from unconscious forces, and is divorced from the current social, historic, and economic context. The implication of this approach is that the individual needs to be fixed, not the society or the social organization of the family.

The second myth, Greenspan says, is the medical model of psychopathology. The medical model tells us that human emotional pain is a disease that must be diagnosed and treated. While high-class individuals get psychotherapy, the lower classes are likely to get only institutionalization and drugs.

The third myth is that if the person's pain is a psychic disease, only an expert can diagnose and treat it. "The myth of the Expert leads inevitably to a therapeutic relationship which is based on a fundamental inequality of power between doctor and patient" (Greenspan, 1983, p. 32). By implication, the patient is also taught to accept similar social relationships outside of therapy.

While traditional therapies have viewed people's problems as stemming primarily from internal factors, **feminist therapy** focuses on environmental stress as a major source of pathology. A major cause of the problems of women is viewed as their having less political and economic power than men. In a review of 80 years of psychotherapy, from Freud's treatment of a young woman patient named Dora, to 1980, Rachel T. Hare-Mustin (1983) concluded that, "What is apparent over and over again is that the psychological problems of women reflect societal conditions and attitudes, but the solutions offered, according to Albee (1981), are individual and part of the sexist texture of contemporary life" (p. 598). She discusses a number of problems of high concern for women that have been ignored or treated with bias by therapists: the basic inequality of the traditional family; women's reproductive experiences; physical and sexual abuse; misattribution of depression to stages such as the empty nest and menopause rather than to low social status, legal and economic discrimination and learned helplessness; diagnosis based on negative labels for conditions such as hysteria that may be due to environmental stress; and the need for research on the eating disorders. She mentions the alternatives available to women now, such as self-help groups, crisis models, and feminist therapy.

Feminist therapy does not want women to adjust to the status quo; rather, it encourages women to become economically and psychologically autonomous. The relationship with the therapist is egalitarian, and this is viewed as a model for other relationships including marriage, which should be equal in personal power (E. I. Rawlings & Carter, 1977). Feminist therapy is really a philosophy underlying the therapy rather than a specific therapeutic technique and can be integrated with other treatment approaches, such as cognitive–behavioral therapy (McGrath, Keita, Strickland, & Russo, 1990).

Jean Baker Miller (1986) points out the dangers that exist when one person has more power in a relationship. The less powerful person finds it more difficult to change the relationship, so she may instead change herself. The price of maintaining the relationship may be acting on her partner's wishes rather than her own. This immobilizing path may lead to depression and eating disorders. Women's desire for affiliation is a strength, but also a source of her current problems, according to Miller, because the kinds of connections available to women are subservient affiliations. The solution for women is to acquire "economic, political, and social power and authority." Self-determination can only come when women have attained this power.

Nonsexist Therapy

Therapy should be free of sex bias and gender stereotypes.

The task force on sex bias and sex role stereotyping of the American Psychological Association published principles for **nonsexist therapy** (American Psychological Association, 1975). According to nonsexist therapy, the therapeutic concepts employed should be free of gender stereotypes and the client should be treated as an equal. The therapist should respect the client's assertiveness.

The difference between nonsexist therapy and feminist therapy is that feminist therapy has an underlying political philosophy that women's problems have external causes and the women should not be made to adjust to behavior prescribed by cultural norms, but rather be encouraged to develop her own power, and to change society so it no longer oppresses women. While nonsexist therapy starts with the premise of the equality of the sexes, it is similar to traditional therapies in that it focuses on personal change.

Sexism in Drug- and Alcohol-Treatment Programs

Sexist attitudes are a major problem in drug-treatment programs. Lesbian women particularly suffer harsh discrimination.

Sexism has been a major problem in drug-treatment programs. It ranges from sexist attitudes toward women by both counselors and male clients, to rape. Drug-treatment programs fail to provide a supportive climate for women. Research by Leonard Murphy and Joan Rollins (1980) found that the counselors and male clients at three locations of an inpatient drug treatment facility in New England had very traditional attitudes on the Attitudes toward the Women Scale.

Mixed-sex drug-treatment groups have been found to average three men to one woman and to fail to provide a supportive environment for women.

Encounter sessions are employed by several programs as an intrinsic part of the treatment regimen. This technique aims to strip the addict of damaging pretenses and attack antisocial behavior in a manner that makes way for healthier reactions and more acceptable behavior. However, female addicts expect to be hurt and abused by men, and the use of such harsh "tearing down" techniques may serve to intensify their feeling of being victims, causing them to leave a program prematurely. (Cuskey & Wathey, 1982, p. 17)

In addition, in one study reported by Cuskey & Wathey, half of the women in treatment reported being propositioned by male staff members.

The impact of a structured, six-week assertiveness and sexuality workshop for women at three community-based methadone maintenance programs found women who participated frequently to show greater increases in self-esteem and knowledge compared with women who participated infrequently. Level of participation in the treatment program was related to continuation in the methadone-maintenance program (Bartholomew, Rowan-Szal, Chatham, & Simpson, 1994). Anecdotal evidence, such as that some of the women continued to meet informally after the session ended, indicated the social networking benefits of the groups.

The situation is even more difficult for lesbian women, who often receive harsh discrimination stemming from staff views of homosexuality as a sickness and suffer attempts to change their sexual orientation. "The stigma of homosexuality appears to be applied more severely to females perhaps because men feel threatened by homosexual women, who are perceived as rivals and as sources of rejection" (Cuskey & Wathey, 1982, p. 19). The lack of sensitivity to the needs of homosexual women is a major problem in drug treatment programs, since different samples report that the prevalence of homosexuality is 29–50% among female addicts.

Women with drinking problems have better outcomes in all female treatment groups than in male dominated groups.

Women with drinking problems may also benefit from different treatment settings and modalities than their male counterparts. A meta-analytic review of 20 outcome studies published between 1953 and 1991 found that women alcoholics tend to respond better in all-female group therapy than they do in male-dominated groups (Jarvis, 1992). Women tend to talk more in all-female groups and to be more self-revealing than they are in mixed-gender groups, whereas in mixed-sex groups women interact less with both men and women than they do with women in all female groups. Data showing that as high as 86% of women entering treatment had been sexually or physically abused, may account for some of the reluctance of women to be open in mixed-sex groups.

Cognitive Behavior Therapy

Cognitive behavior therapy corrects erroneous beliefs and changes behavior. It is equally as effective as psychopharmacology in treating depression. It has also been found to be effective for the treatment of binge eating.

Cognitive behavior therapy focuses on what the early American psychologist William James called stream of consciousness—the continuous dialogue that each of us carries on within oneself. It is these thoughts or meanings that we are continually giving to the events in our lives that determine our emotional reactions to them. For example, a woman suffering from agoraphobia might think, "If I am away from home something terrible might happen, and I won't be able to cope with it."

Cognitive behavior therapy corrects erroneous beliefs that are the source of the painful emotional reactions. Behavioral techniques are also used (e.g., assertiveness training in which the person is coached to be more assertive in situations that might inhibit or frighten her) (A. T. Beck, 1976). Depressed patients' interpretations seem to be shaped by certain underlying beliefs such as, "I am worthless" or "I can't do anything right" (A. T. Beck, 1991). For example, a woman loses her job about which she said "They (her employer) hated my work. I'm a failure," which was upsetting to her and may have some validity in that she did not succeed in that job. The therapist, however, works to change the underlying inferences, "I'm a failure" and "I'll never be any good." Changing these underlying cognitions brings about improvement in mood.

A literature review of mediators and moderators in cognitive behavior therapy (variables that are predictive of treatment outcome) provides tentative support for changes in depression related to changes in attributional style (Whisman, 1993). Some provisional supports also exist for behavioral mediation. Client involvement and engagement have also been associated with good outcome, as it is for psychotherapy in general.

The cognitive analysis of panic attack assumes that the attacks develop from misinterpretation of bodily sensations.

> The model proposes that a trigger stimulus (eg. palpitations, sweating, hot flashes) creates a perception of danger. This misperception leads to the development of additional anxiety and physical discomfort, all of which seem to verify the existence of a catastrophic event (e.g., a heart attack). This misattribution produces a further increase in physical symptoms and the psychological conviction of danger. This vicious cycle culminates in a panic attack. (Black, Wesner, Bowers, & Gabel, 1993)

Cognitive behavior therapy teaches the patient to understand the role of this misattribtion of bodily sensations in the developing panic attack and to use distraction and breathing exercises to prevent the attack. Systematic exposure to these feared internal sensations by inhalation of CO_2/O_2 over a period of time has also proved to be therapeutic (McNally, 1990).

Family Therapy for Anorexia

Weight gain and improvement in eating attitudes of anorectics is correlated with a shift in communication patterns during family therapy from covert to overt aggression.

Family dynamics of anorectics has already been discussed, focusing on the overprotective and domineering attitude of parents toward the anorexic adolescent. At the same time, the family maintains an outward appearance of family harmony. Family therapy conducted with 25 consecutive families with anorectic daughters (mean age 14.3 years) admitted to a psychiatric inpatient unit for 12–14 weeks, uncovered a dysfunctional pattern of suppression of hostility and aggression (Shugar & Krueger, 1995). Early in therapy, these families showed a pattern of a high proportion of covert agression (62% of interactions) and a low proportion of overt aggression (5% of interactions). Improved eating attitudes and weight gain of the anorectic daughters correlated highly with the increase in overt communication of aggression during the middle and end phases of therapy, whereas families with the most covert and indirect aggression during all three phases had daughters with the least weight gain and least improved eating attitudes. The therapeutic implications of this study are that "treatment that shifts families' communication style from suppressing aggression to expressing aggression will facilitate improvement in young anorexic patients" (Shugar & Krueger, 1995, p. 30).

Sex between Client and Therapist

Sex between client and therapist is against the code of ethics of the American Psychological Association, and against the law in several states. Nevertheless, nearly 1 out of 10 male psychologists admit to having sexual relations with clients.

The most frequently filed ethics complaint with the American Psychological Association is that of violation of the code of the Ethical Principles for Psychologists (American Psychological Association, 1981), which prohibits sexual intimacies with clients. The cases that get reported to the APA, however, represent only a tip of the iceberg. To determine the extent of the problem among psychologists, Pope, Keith-Spiegel, and Tabachnick (1986) mailed an anonymous questionnaire to a randomly selected sample of 500 male and 500 female members of Division 42 of APA (Psychologists in Private Practice). Of these, 585 were returned. Although survey data reveal that 87% (95% of men and 76% of women) had at least upon one occasion been attracted to a client, only 9.4% of men and 2.5% of women had actually engaged in sexual intimacies with clients.

Some psychiatrists as well as psychologists also are guilty of sexual involvement with clients. In a survey of psychiatrists 7.1% of male and 3.1% of female psychiatrists admitted to having sexual involvement with clients. Of these cases, 87.5% were between male psychiatrists and female patients, 7.6% between male psychiatrists and male patients, 3.5% between female psychiatrists and male patients, and 1.5% between female psychiatrists and female patients (Gartrell, Herman, Olarte, Feldstein, & Localio, 1986). A review of investigated ethics complaints filed with The Ethics Committee of the American Psychiatric Association over a five-year period revealed that 8 women and 85 men were accused of having sexual relationships with patients (Mogul, 1992). Two of the cases against the women and 12 against the men were dismissed. Six of the complaints against the female psychiatrists were involvement with female patients, whereas only 2 of the 85 complaints against male psychiatrists were for homosexual involvement. It would appear that females are much more likely to be victimized by therapists.

Other studies have investigated the types of patients and therapists who become involved in sexual intimacies. "The female clients were approximately 12 to 16 years younger than their therapists; many, but by no means all, were sexually dysfunctional and nonorgasmic. The studies described them as lonely, searching, unhappy, looking for acceptance and friendship (Bouhoutsos, 1984, p. 297). They were vulnerable women, many of whom had a prior history of sexual abuse by family members and/or other professionals. The patients were harmed in 90% of the cases and suffered damage ranging from hesitation in trusting men, to depression and suicide.

Since the 1970s, civil suits have been filed by clients alleging damage as a result of sexual intimacy with their therapist. A number of states now have legislation that states that sexual intimacy between client and therapist is illegal. The public attention brought to bear on the problem also serves to alert potential or present clients about the unethical and in many states illegal nature of sexual intimacies between client and therapist (Bouhoutsos, 1984).

Therapy with Lesbians

Therapists counseling lesbians need to be educated to understand that lesbianism is not a form of psychopathology and that lesbians can lead fulfilling lives.

The Daughters of Bilitis began as a secret social group in 1955, later becoming a well-known self-help organization for lesbians. The need for this organization is clear because of, until recently, adherence to the sickness theory of homosexuality by practicing psychiatrists and psychologists.

The client often spent her money and her time educating her therapist about lesbians. The best she got in return was pity and attempts to help her change her sexual orientation. . . . More common, however, was the male therapist who knew, without a doubt, that all a lesbian needed was intercourse with a man—and he was that man (D. Martin & Lyon, 1984, p. 151).

The Committee on Lesbian and Gay Concerns (CLGC) of the American Psychological Association established a task force on bias in psychotherapy with lesbians and gay men in 1984. The task force issued a final report in June 1991 based on a 1986 survey of 2,544 licensed psychologists. The report identified 25 themes that show "biased, inadequate, or inappropriate" practices. Examples of these themes are:

A therapist automatically attributes a client's problems to his or her sexual orientation without evidence that this is so.

A therapist expresses beliefs that trivialize or demean homosexuality and gay male or lesbian orientation or experience.

In an educational context, a therapist teaches information about lesbians or gay men that is inaccurate or prejudiced, or actively discriminates against gay male and lesbian students or colleagues. (Garnets, Hancock, Cochran, Goodchilds, & Peplau, 1991, p. 35)

The task force also described 20 themes of exemplary practices for therapists. Among them:

A therapist understands that homosexuality, in and of itself, is neither a form of psychopathology nor is necessarily evidence of psychopathology or developmental arrest, and recognizes that gay men and lesbians can live fulfilling lives.

A therapist does not attempt to change the sexual orientation of the client without strong evidence that this is the appropriate course of action and that the change is desired by the client. (Garnets et al., 1991, p. 35)

The task force also recommended that in order to sensitize psychologists to lesbian and gay issues, they need to be discussed in graduate training programs in psychology, as well as in inservice and continuing education courses.

Psychotherapy with Women of Color

White therapists need to broaden their understanding of their female clients' values and racial and ethnic subcultures.

From early childhood, women of color have been taught that self-disclosure to someone outside of the ethnic subculture is akin to treason (Boyd, 1990). In addition, ethnic normative values have not been included in the training of White psychotherapists. White feminist therapists are also ignorant of non-White, non–middle-class lifestyles. "As a feminist, the therapist will need to broaden her range of awareness in depth through reading, networking, and researching the lifestyles of women of color" (Boyd, 1990, p. 166).

Therapy with American Indian Women

The extended family is an important part of American Indian life. Native Americans first seek the extended family network, spiritual leaders and the tribal community rather than professional therapeutic help. The federal boarding school system in which girls received less classroom instruction than boys and had to do the cleaning of the schools while being away from their loved ones and unable to observe traditional parenting activities contributed to later anxiety while parenting. American Indian women have higher alcoholism rates than do women in the general U.S. population.

In Indian communities drugs and alcohol contribute to a high incidence of accidental deaths, homicide, suicide, sexual violence, child abuse and neglect, and fetal alcohol syndrome, and although it is declining, the death rate due to alcoholism is alarmingly high. (LaFramboise, Berman, & Sohi, 1994, p. 47)

A study of 28 female and 30 male American Indian clients of residential treatment programs found substances used and substance-use pattern to be very similar for males and females, except for marijuana, which all males and 77.8% of females reported using (Gutierres, Russo, & Urbanski, 1994). Females reported coming from families with more alcohol and drug problems and more emotional, physical, and sexual abuse. There was a higher treatment-completion rate for these clients (81%) than there was for completion rates for the general population. The high treatment-completion rate for this sample may be a reflection of the opportunity for clients to choose a range of alternative therapeutic services, including methods traditional in their culture (Gutierres et al., 1994). The treatment program allowed children to accompany their mothers, and it provided services for them as well. Psychological measures showed increased self-esteem, lower depression scores, and more stable, global, and internal attributions for positive events at treatment completion as compared with entry into treatment.

Traditionally, Indian women played a valued role in their tribes as transmitters of cultural knowledge and in many tribes both sexes were treated equally. A therapist must be aware of the cultural attitudes and customs of the Indian woman both self-disclosed and from other sources in the community. Network therapy developed by Carolyn Attneave, a Delaware Indian, draws on the strength of the Indian kin and social system by drawing the members of the individual's extended family as well as other unrelated individuals known to the client and the intervention team to prevent and deal with psychiatric problems. Group social skills training can also be effective in dealing with problems such as unplanned pregnancy, drinking behavior, and sexual abuse. Caregivers from the community need to be trained (LaFramboise, Berman, & Sohi, 1994).

Therapy with Asian American Women

Although the traditional Asian family is a patriarchy in which women are expected to be subservient, Asian American women are a very diverse group represented by recent immigrants from southeast Asia, to fifth-generation Chinese Americans with graduate and professional degrees.

The Asian American family has a tradition of patriarchy in which women are expected to play a passive, subservient role. Exposure to the Western ideology of greater equality between the sexes creates conflicts for them as their expectations undergo change (True, 1990). Also a source of stress for Asian American women are the negative stereotypes about them in American culture. The therapist dealing with Asian American female clients needs to use a family focused approach. At the same time, the therapist should be aware of the entrenched sexism of the Asian American family. In addition, Asian American women may need assertiveness training and exposure to positive Asian American women role models. An Asian American woman therapist needs to share more about herself with her female client in order to show the client that she has lived through similar experiences and survived. A number of Asian American women's groups are now being formed to provide auxiliary self-help or a therapeutic alternative.

Asian American women are a heterogeneous group, some are third- or fourth-generation well-educated Japanese or Chinese Americans, and

others such as the Hmong or Vietnamese recent immigrants coping with poverty and a new culture. Among the better-educated, acculturated Asian Americans concepts about mental health treatment and therapeutic process may not differ from that of other Americans. Depending on the client's cultural orientation, value conflicts may arise in psychotherapy. The therapist should be aware

that verbal expression and communication, especially of criticism or dissatisfaction may be indirect and restrained, whereas Western socialization encourages verbal expressiveness as a sign of honesty; that silence in the Asian tradition may reflect respect instead of resistance or repression; that Asian clients may expect that therapy will enhance their willpower to withstand morbid or ill thoughts, and on this basis may misunderstand the therapist's nondirectiveness when a client-centered or psychodynamic approach is taken. (Bradshaw, 1994, p. 101)

The therapist needs to pay attention to place of birth, degree of acculturation and assimilation, and ethnic identity and contact with extended family in order for psychotherapy to work with Asian Americans.

Therapy with Hispanics

Many Hispanics are recent immigrants. Acculturative stressors including their reception in the United States must be taken into account.

Hispanics are the second largest minority group in the United States (U.S. Bureau of the Census, 1994). Hispanics are a very diverse group in terms of historical, political, economic, and racial differences (Amaro & Russo, 1987). Because many Hispanics are recent immigrants, acculturative stressors are an important source of depressive symptomology. Factors such as skin color, age, and educational level affect the reception Hispanics receive in the United States.

Among Mexican immigrant women in Los Angeles, those who made the final decision to migrate to the United States were found to have significantly lower levels of depressive symptomology than those for whom the decision was made by someone else (Salgado de Snyder, 1987). Lack of English skills was also related to poor psychological adjustment.

Latina women who are refugees from Latin America may be suffering PTSD as a result of rape and torture suffered in conflicts going on in their homeland (Espin, 1987). In addition, issues of loss and grief are issues of primary concern in therapy with immigrant women.

> Not infrequently, the immigrant experiences feelings of guilt in relation to people and relationships left behind. New loyalties to individuals and relationships developed in the host country, including the therapeutic relationship, are frequently experienced as betrayal of the parents or the home country. (Espin, 1987, p. 500)

Feminist therapy is well suited to treatment of immigrant women in its approach to understanding the causative role of external factors in psychological distress.

Therapists must be vigilant of their own stereotypes about a racial/ethnic group. For example, White therapists may have sex role stereotypes of the Hispanic family as being dominated by a macho husband.

> Families that are relatively healthy and functional, where roles are traditionally assigned, exhibit a mutuality and respect for the ascribed roles. In those healthy families, the traditional roles (e.g., working father, homemaker mother) do not exclude equity in decision making and conflict resolution. However, in dysfunctional families, traditional roles are carried out in a more oppressive and pathological manner, with power battles, abusive behavior, poor conflict resolution, and low marital satisfaction. (Vasquez, 1994, p. 124)

The therapist's task is to separate out behavior consistent with traditional roles from that which is pathological and abusive.

Therapy with African American Women

Both societal racism and internalized racism are important issues for the Black woman in therapy.

African American culture is a derivative of African world views, the current dominant culture and the residual of the heritage of slavery. Although motherhood is central for African American women, strong kinship bonds as well as friendship create an extended network involved in the rearing of children (Greene, 1994). "Many African American women internalize the stereotype of the ubiquitous strong matriarch: In the tradition of the mammy, she acknowledges no personal pain, can bear all burdens, and will take care of everyone. Consequently, many African American women feel deficient if their burdens are too heavy, and will resist asking for help" (Greene, 1994, p. 21).

Racism on many levels, internalized as well as external, is an underlying issue to be dealt with in psychotherapy with Black women. Internalized racism may be a factor in the woman's body image resulting from socialization in a society that presents the White woman as the beauty ideal. Stereotypes about race may also be internalized, which may in turn influence the woman to either react against them and inhibit emotional responses or to act them out.

Racism in the dominant culture may make the African American woman less likely to call the police on an abusive husband or boyfriend because of empathy for the racism he faces in society as well as the more severe treatment he may receive from the police than a White man would receive. At the same time, the therapist must assist the client in protecting herself from abuse. "In feminist therapy, women of color can find their anger validated, examine their experience of anger, learn to manage it, and circumvent depression through freedom to express anger in productive action both in their personal lives and in their social worlds" (Espin, 1994, p. 273).

PSYCHOPHARMACOTHERAPY

Two-thirds of prescriptions for psychoactive drugs written in the United States are written for women.

American medicine is a profit-making business, and **psychopharmacotherapy**—the use of drugs in order to treat psychological and behavioral problems—is $1 billion business (Greenberg, Stiglin, Finkelstein, & Berndt, 1993). In order to bolster their sales, pharmaceutical corporations cultivate images of women among physicians and even among women themselves that increase sales of **psychoactive drugs** (drugs that affect psychological functioning and behavior). Advertisements in medical journals frequently depict women as suffering from anxiety, sleeplessness, and depression, or as "bored" housewives who are unreasonable, emotional, and shrewish (Travis, 1988b).

Nearly two-thirds (64%) of patients for whom psychoactive drugs are prescribed in the United States are women. When the prescribing physician is not a psychiatrist, 90% of psychoactive drug prescriptions are written for women (Russo, 1985). "In fact, 85% of those using psychoactive drugs had never seen a psychiatrist in their lives, and only about one-third of those given new prescriptions for psychotropic drugs had a documented diagnosis of any mental or emotional problems" (Ogur, 1986, p. 113). One of the results of this is that women are disproportionately addicted to prescription drugs. It is necessary to educate physicians on women's role in society and to alert them to the possibility of their "reinforcing the already passive role of women" (Ogur, 1986).

Treatment for Depression

Tricyclic antidepressants and monoamine oxidase inhibitors were for many years the standard treatment for depression. These drugs have potentially serious cardiovascular side effects.

The standard drug treatment for major depression for a number of years has been one of the **tricyclic antidepressants** (TCAs) such as imipramine (Tofranil and others) or desipramine (Norpramin and others) or, for people who are anxious as well as depressed, monoamine oxidase inhibitors (MAOIs) such as phenelzine (Nardil and others). Tricyclics increase the level of neurotransmitters in the brain by blocking their re-

uptake by brain cells, therefore prolonging their stimulatory effect on the brain. The most dangerous side effects of Tricyclics are related to the cardiovascular system such as elevated blood pressure, rapid heart beat, or, in the most extreme cases, heart attack or stroke (Medical Economics Data, 1995). MAIOs increase the level of neurotransmitters by blocking the action of an enzyme that breaks down neurotransmitters. MAIOs taken with foods rich in certain enzymes such as cheeses, beer, wine, liver, yeast, dry sausage, and yogurt can cause rapid rise in blood pressure.

A new generation of antidepressants, the best known of which is Prozac, are equally as effective as tricyclics for the treatment of depression and have fewer side effects.

A new generation of antidepressants that are now widely prescribed are more specific (Bech, 1993). For example, one group of the new generation of antidepressants are **serotonin selective reuptake inhibitors** (SSRIs), the best known of which is fluoxetine (Prozac). Fluoxetine blocks the reuptake by brain cells of the neurotransmitter serotonin, whereas the tricyclics block the reuptake of other neurotransmitters as well (Medical Economics Data, 1995). Another advantage of the newer antidepresssants is that patients do not feel "drugged" on them the way they do on tricyclics or MAOIs (Kramer, 1993).

Clinical lore among psychiatrists has suggested that these newer agents are less effective than standard tricyclics for major depression (Bech, 1993). A meta-analysis of well-controlled studies comparing imipramine (Tofranil and others) with three newer antidepressants—bupropion (Wellbutrin), fluoxetine (Prozac), and trazodone (Desyrel and others)—indicated that all four agents were effective (efficacy refers to the antidepressive effects) as compared with placebo (Workman & Short, 1993). The newer agents were not significantly different from imipramine in effectiveness.

In another meta-analysis comparing SSRIs, a specific MAOI, and tricyclics found the SSRIs and a specific MAOI equal to the tricyclics in treating depression (Bech, 1993). "The side effects of SSRIs . . . in the acute treatment of depression are very few indeed compared with tricyclics. Both from the patient's point of view and from the doctor's, the new drugs are much more acceptable than the tricyclics" (Bech, 1993, p. 26).

Cognitive therapy is equally effective as imipramine in remitting the symptoms of depression, but twice as effective as imipramine in preventing relapse.

Which is more effective, cognitive therapy or pharmacotherapy (antidepressant medication) for the treatment of major depression? To answer that question, and also to determine how cognitive therapy works, DeRubeis et al. (1990) randomly assigned patients, who met the criteria for major depressive disorder, to one of four treatment conditions for 12 weeks: cognitive therapy alone; imipramine pharmacotherapy alone; the combination of cognitive therapy with imipramine; and imipramine for 12 weeks plus maintenance imipramine for the following year. Four standardized measures of cognition and three measures of depression were used at each of three points of treatment: beginning, middle, and end. "Syndrome depression remitted significantly and substantially in all treatment groups during the acute (12 week) treatment period" (DeRubeis et al., 1990, p. 865). Imipramine and cognitive therapy were equally effective in improving the symptoms of depression, and the mediational role played by changed cognitive constructs in cognitive therapy was necessary to further improvement in cognitive therapy but not in pharmacotherapy.

Psychotherapists have argued that psychotherapy provides protection against relapse. After treatment has been terminated does psychotherapy reduce subsequent risk of return of symptoms as compared with pharmacotherapy? To answer this question, Evans et al. (1992) conducted a two-year posttreatment follow-up of patients successfully treated during a three-month period with either imipramine, cognitive therapy, or combined imipramine and cognitive therapy.

Half of the patients who were in the imipramine condition continued to receive medication for the first year of the follow-up, whereas half of the imipramine only patients and patients in the cognitive therapy and combined cognitive–imipramine conditions were discontinued in treatment at the end of the three-month acute treatment phase. "Patients treated with cognitive therapy (either alone or in combination with medication) evidenced less than half the rate of relapse shown by patients in the medication-no continuation condition, and their rate did not differ from that of patients provided with continuation medication" (Evans et al., 1992, p. 802). Providing cognitive therapy can be cost effective because of its role in preventing relapse.

Treatment of Panic Disorder

Panic disorder can be effectively treated by alprazolam (Xanax), imipramine, fluvoxamine (Luvox) and a variety of psychological approaches. The attrition rate for alprazolam is high and there are withdrawal difficulties.

A double-blind, placebo-controlled study comparing the effectiveness of alprazolam (Xanax) and imipramine in the long-term treatment of panic disorder, with or without agoraphobia, found that all patients who completed the acute eight-week treatment phase as well as the six-month maintenance treatment were panic free at the end of the study treatment (Schweizer, Rickels, Weiss, & Zavodnick, 1993). The attrition rate for the alprazolam-treated patients (11%) was much lower than for those receiving imipramine (41%) or the placebo (57%).

Both alprazolam and imipramine demonstrated efficacy during acute treatment of panic disorder on most measures of panic and nonpanic anxiety, as well as measures of phobic avoidance and panic-related social and occupational disability. These clinical benefits were achieved without any concomitant behavioral therapy or psychotherapy, and they were sustained throughout an 8-month course of maintenance therapy without any dose escalation. (Schweizer et al., 1993, p. 59)

The most frequent negative side effects of alprazolam and imipramine during treatment were sedation, dry mouth, constipation, increased appetite, decreased libido, and impaired coordination.

After eight months of maintenance on alprazolam, imipramine, or placebo, a gradual taper from medication over a four-week period resulted in a withdrawal syndrome in almost all alprazolam-treated patients, but only in a few of the imipramine- or placebo-treated patients (Rickels, Schweizer, Weiss, & Zavodnick, 1993). Fifty-nine percent of patients who tapered alprazolam reported a rebound in panic attacks that was at least 50% above baseline pretreatment. Both withdrawal and anxiety symptoms ran their course by the end of three weeks after the discontinuation of drug therapy, but 33% of the alprazolam patients were unable to tolerate taper and resumed drug therapy. The most potentially dangerous withdrawal effect of alprazolam is seizure (Medical Economics Data, 1995), but this did not occur among patients in the Rickels et al. study.

Fluvoxamine (Luvox) was more effective in treating panic disorder than either cognitive therapy or placebo.

A comparison of fluvoxamine, cognitive therapy, and placebo in the treatment of 75 outpatients with moderate to severe panic disorder found significantly greater improvement with fluvoxamine than either cognitive therapy or placebo at week 8 (Black, Wesner, Bowers, & Gabel, 1993). "By week 8, 90% of fluvoxamine-treated patients showed at least moderate improvement, compared with 50% of subjects receiving cognitive therapy and 39% of subjects receiving placebo" (Black et al., 1993, p. 46). Patients receiving fluvoxamine recorded a significantly greater reduction in panic attacks as compared with cognitive behavior therapy or placebo. This study ended at eight weeks and therefore does not address the long-term benefits of cognitive therapy relative to fluvoxamine. Panic attacks, however, can also be alleviated with other psychological approaches to therapy such as marital therapy, applied relaxation, respiratory control, and systematic exposure to feared bodily sensations (R. J. Hafner, 1982; McNally, 1990; Thorpe & Burns, 1983).

Treatment of Bulimia Nervosa

Cognitive behavior therapy is more effective than desipramine or imipramine for the treatment of bulimia. Fluoxetine (Prozac) is superior to placebo in decreasing binge eating and vomiting.

A comparison of cognitive behavior therapy alone, desipramine alone, and cognitive behavior therapy combined with desipramine (Norpramin and others) in the treatment of bulimia nervosa found cognitive behavior therapy alone to be more effective than desipramine alone (Leitenberg et al., 1993). At posttreatment and at six months follow-up there was no additional benefit derived from combining cognitive behavior therapy and desipramine. A study that conducted treatment for 16 weeks or 24 weeks and again measured treatment effectiveness at 32 weeks also found cognitive behavior therapy to be significantly more effective in reducing binging and purging than desipramine alone with no greater effectiveness achieved by combining desipramine and cognitive behavior treatment (Agras et al., 1992).

Cognitive behavior therapy in a 12-week group format for treatment of bulimia nervosa was more effective on multiple measures than was imipramine, although imipramine was more effective than was placebo (Mitchell et al., 1990). An eight week double-blind trial comparing fluoxetine (Prozac) with placebo in the treatment of bulimia nervosa in 387 bulimic women found fluoxetine superior to placebo in decreasing binge-eating and vomiting episodes (Fluoxetine Bulimia Nervosa Collaborative Study Group, 1992). Other symptoms such as depression, carbohydrate craving, and pathologic eating attitudes and behaviors also decreased in the fluoxetine condition. A number of side effects occurred more frequently in the fluoxetine condition, however, such as insomnia, nausea, and tremor.

Group cognitive behavior therapy resulted in a 94% decline in binge-eating episodes at posttreatment compared with no improvement for individuals on a waiting list.

Group cognitive behavior therapy has also been reported to be an effective treatment in reducing binge eating (Telch, Agras, Rossiter, Wilfley, & Kenardy, 1990). Forty-four female binge eaters were randomly assigned to either group cognitive-behavioral treatment for 10 weeks or a control waiting-list condition. All participants included in the study reported binge-eating episodes in which they consumed large amounts of food.

Group leaders explained to subjects that the focus of the treatment was on eradicating binge-eating patterns. They emphasized that treatment did not address weight reduction. They were told that binge-eating patterns result from restrictive dieting, which only makes the person feel hungry and deprived and leads to binge-eating, which makes the person resolve to go on yet another diet, beginning the cycle again (Telch et al., 1990). The results for cognitive behavior therapy were positive. At posttreatment the frequency of binge-eating episodes had declined by 94%, with 74% of those treated being abstinent from binge eating by the end of treatment. By comparison, there was no significant reduction in the frequency of binge eating for waiting-list controls, and 100% continued to binge eat. At a 20-week follow-up, although binge eating had significantly increased, it was still significantly below the pretreatment level.

MULTIPLE ROLES
AND MENTAL HEALTH

It is the quality rather than the quantity of roles women play that is most strongly related to mental health. Paid employment, however, is the one role related to mental health more than others for women. Generally, more roles enhance well-being.

One explanation for the greater levels of depression among women is a social roles explanation. The "scarcity" hypothesis assumes that the more roles one occupies, the greater the strain and impairment of well being. On the other hand, the "enhancement" hypothesis emphasizes the benefits of multiple roles such as status, increased self-esteem, and gratification. Actually, neither hypothesis was unequivocally supported, in a study of employed White women aged 35–55, because it was the quality of the roles rather than the quantity that was related to well-being (Baruch & Barnett, 1986). The women occupied four role categories: never-married, married without children, married with children, and divorced with children. Half of the married and all of the single women were employed.

Paid employment was the only role occupancy related to well being when other measures such as family income, age, and education were controlled. It was significantly related to self-esteem. This finding is consistent with other research that concludes that involvement in the role of paid worker is related to self-esteem of women and seems to protect against psychiatric symptomatology (G. W. Brown & Harris, 1978).

A decrease in male paid employment and an increase in female paid employment had led to a decrease in gender differences in distress, despite the fact that psychological distress appears to have increased in the population (McClanahan & Glass, 1985). This trend has also been documented with data from Canada and Sweden as well as the United States.

Men's as well as women's employment is significantly related to psychophysiological distress and also accounts for a large portion of the sex trend. While the coefficient for men's employment is larger than the female coefficient (indicating that employment is more important for men than for women), the variable itself accounts for slightly less of the sex trend than did women's employment (approx. 20% vs. 27%). This is due to the fact that changes in employment levels between 1957 and 1976 were much more dramatic for women than for men. (McClanahan & Glass, 1985, p. 332)

An important workplace variable that has been found to relate to general well being in women is the complexity of the job. Women in jobs of low complexity have lower levels of psychological well being, lower than that of women in more complex jobs and lower than that of men in low-complexity jobs. In highly complex jobs, however, women surpass men in their overall level of well being (Lennon, 1987). Contrary to other research, this study found that full-time work was associated with demoralization only among women. Other factors that Lennon found to relate significantly and negatively to general well being in both men and women are the number of persons in the household, and being separated, divorced, or widowed as compared with married.

The quality of the homemaking role in the lives of employed women has been a neglected area of research. A random stratified sample of 342 White and 61 Black women social workers and licensed practical nurses found that when the quality of the experience in the homemaking role is high, then psychological well being is high and distress is relatively low (Kibria, Barnett, Baruch, & Pleck, 1990). Similarly, low–homemaking-role quality is associated with less psychological well-being and greater distress. The aspects of homemaking-role quality that were related to positive psychological health were "a sense of autonomy or control as well as of 'helping' or connection to others" (Kibria et al. 1990, p. 344). This finding held for both Black and White women. Overall, Black women had higher levels of psychological distress. Low-paid work-role quality was also related to low psychological well being and high distress.

Research with a stratified random sample of 300 dual earner couples, predominantly White (in which the man is 25–40 years of age) found that marital role quality was significantly associated with marital distress for both men and women (Barnett, Brennan, Raudenbush, & Marshall, 1994). Although in this study the men and women occupied similar roles, women had higher levels of distress. "These findings challenge the dominant assumption that marital-role quality is more crucial to women's mental health than to men's (Barnett et al., 1994, p. 122).

Waldron and Jacobs (1989), using longitudinal data, tested the hypothesis that the greater number of roles has both harmful and beneficial effects, and that the outcome varies depending on the specific characteristics of the roles and of the women considered. Data from a national sample of noninstitutionalized women collected in 1977 and 1982 generally supports the finding that women who held more roles (labor force participant, spouse and parent) had better health trends described at the time of the second interviews.

The health effects of specific roles and role combinations differed, however, between White and Black women. For White women labor-force participation had beneficial effects on health for unmarried women, marriage had beneficial effects on health for women who were not in the labor force, and parental status did not affect health. For Black women those with children who were in the labor force had better health trends than did those who were not in the labor force; for women who were not in the labor force, women with children had worse health trends than did women without children; marital status was not significantly related to health trends. The authors conclude that for White women marriage or labor-force participation may substitute for one another in producing favorable health trends. Marriage does not, however, appear to have a beneficial effect on health for Black women. Although having children at home had harmful effects on health for Black women who were not in the labor force, this was not so for White women, probably because of the greater difficulties in raising children for Black women due to discrimination and lower socioeconomic levels. The reason there has been some conflicting research in this area of multiple roles and mental health is that some roles have different effects on the woman depending on other factors such as race.

Social roles per se, however, do not account for differences in anxiety and depression between men and women. Studies fail to support a social role approach to gender differences in reported psychological distress. A probability sample of 630 men and women between the ages of 18 and 65 found women to have higher levels of anxiety and depression as measured by the Psychiatric Epidemiology Research Interview (PERI). "Sex remains consistently and significantly related to anxiety and depression when role config-urations, satisfaction, and strains are included in the analyses" (Voydanoff & Donelly, 1989, p. 929).

Household labor may serve as a source of considerable strain. Golding (1990) hypothesized that household strain may be an indirect cause of the higher incidence of depression in women than in men since women have a disproportionate responsibility for housework. Her respondents were 668 Mexican American and 394 non-Hispanic Whites who were married or cohabiting, selected by means of a probability area sample in Los Angeles.

The sample as a whole had relatively low levels of household strain with 60% reporting none at all, and a relatively low average level of depressive symptoms. Only women who did more housework reported greater household strain, and this was associated with greater depressive symptomatology. Perhaps this was because men did a much lower level of housework and strain may be evident only if housework exceeds a certain amount of time per week. Men who reported greater household strain, however, had greater depressive symptomatology.

Positive Well Being

Married women are happier than married men.

Although, as we have seen above, married women have higher rates of depression and psychopathology than married men, a meta-analytic study by W. Wood, Rhode, & Whelan (1989) also shows that married women have greater positive well being than married men. They examined gender differences with regard to four measures: happiness, life satisfaction, positive affect, and general evaluation. Any measures of psychological adjustment, mental illness, psychosomatic symptoms or physical health were excluded.

Women were found to have significantly greater life satisfaction and happiness scores than men. Although positive affect scores were in the same direction, they were nonsignificant. The heterogeneous category labeled general evaluation yielded higher scores for men. "A basic assumption of the present analysis is that positive and negative aspects of well-being are independent and that well being is best represented as two unipolar dimensions rather than as a single bipolar construct" (W. Wood, Rhode, & Whelan, 1989, p. 257).

Greater emotionality is associated with the feminine rather than the masculine gender role, so that women are expected to reveal more extreme responses than men on both positive and negative dimensions. "More women than men were represented in the extremely high end of the distribution of happiness scores, but no sex differences were obtained on the extremely low end of the scales" (W. Wood et al., 1989, p. 259). This indicates that happiness is a unipolar dimension. Women's versus men's greater well being was found for married but not for unmarried respondents. Although for both sexes the married state was associated with favorable well being, the effect was stronger for women than it was for men. The authors also attribute the gender differences in positive well-being to differential roles in marriage, with wives serving as emotional specialists and having experiences with attitudes and skills that facilitate emotional well being. In other research women have been found to score higher in positive relations with others and in personal growth (Ryff, 1989).

People who report a high degree of satisfaction with their marriages, tend to have a high level of well being. On the other hand, people who are dissatisfied with their marriages have a low level of well-being (Gove, Hughes, & Style, 1983). Since surveys find that most people report a high level of satisfaction with their marriages, married people tend to be happier than unmarried people.

REFLECTIONS

Why are women being prescribed medication for depression and bulimia nervosa when cognitive behavior therapy has been experimentally shown to be equal to or more effective than psychopharmacotherapy for these disorders? In addition, cognitive therapy has been shown to be significantly more effective than drug treatment in preventing relapse during a two-year posttreatment period. Given the side effects of drugs, should cognitive behavior therapy not be the first treatment choice? Since cognitive behavior therapy in group format has also been shown to be effective, the cost of individual therapy could be greatly reduced by having patients with similar disorders participate in group therapy. Cognitive behavior therapy involves changing negative thoughts about oneself, as well as learning new behaviors such as assertiveness. When a woman seeks therapy, she should question the therapist about her/his theoretical orientation and training, ensuring that the therapist is trained in cognitive behavior therapy and has a feminist or nonsexist orientation. (I am a social psychologist and my advocacy of cognitive behavior therapy is based on reading the research literature that indicates its effectiveness in the treatment of emotional disorders, rather than by being a practitioner of this form of therapy myself).

One theme seems to run through this chapter, whether it relates to depression, eating disorders, anxiety disorders, or role conflict—that is a sense of control over one's life. Women have less power than men, and therefore less control. It is only by taking control of their lives, however, and taking action to improve their situation on an individual level, as well as gaining more power in the institutions of society by organizing together that women can improve their mental health. The medical establishment's overprescription of psychoactive drugs for women with emotional disorders should be challenged by individual women as well as by the women's movement.

Experiential Exercises

1. Attend a meeting of a self-help group. Look in your local newspaper to find one.
2. Ask the women you know if they are now, or in the past have ever been, on a diet. Did the diet work? For how long were they able to keep the weight off?
3. If you are currently experiencing any of the emotional problems discussed in this chapter, seek professional psychotherapy. A place to start would be to make an appointment at your campus counseling center, community mental health center, or get a referral from your state psychological association. Ask your therapist if she/he is a feminist or nonsexist therapist and if she/he has been trained in cognitive behavioral therapy.

KEY TERMS

Affective Disorders   Mood disorders.

Agoraphobia   An incapacitating anxiety when traveling away from home, or fear of being home alone. Agoraphobia may occur with or without a fear of having a panic attack when help may not be available. There is a large disproportion in female sufferers of agoraphobia.

Anorexia Nervosa   Dieting to extreme weight loss (20% or more below normal body weight). The disorder typically occurs in adolescence or early adulthood, and overwhelmingly in females (95%).

Anxiety Disorders   Disorders that are characterized by at least six months of persistent and excessive anxiety and worry. There are a number of specific anxiety disorders such as agoraphobia, specific phobia, and panic attack.

Body Image   The concept one has about her body. The majority of American women think they are too fat.

Bulimia Nervosa   An eating disorder characterized by binge eating (rapid consumption of a large amount of high calorie food in a short time), followed by purging (self-induced vomiting, use of laxatives, enemas, and/or diuretics). Bulimics may also engage in strict dieting or fasting and vigorous exercise.

Cognitive Behavior Therapy   This therapy focuses on changing erroneous beliefs. Behavioral techniques such as assertiveness training are also used. Research has shown cognitive behavioral therapy to be an effective treatment for major depression and bulimia.

Consciousness Raising Group   A leaderless group of women meeting regularly to sit and listen to one another's stories, seeing the world through women's experiences.

Derived Identity   A sense of self that is overly determined by relationships with significant others. It is correlated with depression in women.

Dieting   Self-imposed food restriction.

Environmental Stressors External stress affecting the individual. Women have more environmental stressors than men such as higher rates of poverty, greater responsibility for childcare and housework, often in addition to paid labor participation, and being single parents.

Epidemiology The incidence and distribution of an illness, such as mental illness, in a population according to gender, race/ethnicity, social class, and marital status.

Family Systems Theory The view that disorders of one individual within a family are due to pervasive family problems. According to family systems theory, anorectic daughters are overprotected by their parents and need greater autonomy that they try to achieve through control over their bodies. Bulimics are hostily enmeshed in their families.

Feminist Therapy A philosophy underlying therapy, rather than a specific therapeutic technique, that can be integrated with other treatment approaches. While traditional therapies have viewed people's problems as stemming primarily from internal factors, feminist therapy focuses on environmental stress as a major source of pathology.

Locus of Control The person who believes his/her actions play a major role in what happens to them has an internal locus of control and someone who perceives that what happens to them is determined by luck has an external locus of control. Women who are depressed or suffer from eating disorders tend to have an external locus of control.

Major Depressive Disorder A diagnostic category of mental illness, one of the symptoms of which must include depressed mood or loss of interest or pleasure for a period of two weeks or more. At least four other symptoms of depression must be present from among fatigue or loss of energy, inability to concentrate, significant weight loss or gain, feelings of worthlessness or excessive guilt, sleep disorders, psychomotor agitation, or retardation and recurrent thoughts of death.

Nonsexist Therapy Therapy that is free of sex bias and stereotypes and recognizes that the source of many of women's problems are external to her rather than due to internal psychological factors.

Panic Attack A discrete period during which the individual has a sudden intense fear and terror. During the attack the individual may have such symptoms as shortness of breath, rapid heart beat, chest pain or discomfort, choking or smothering sensations, and fear of "going crazy."

Pharmacotherapy The use of psychoactive drugs as a method of treatment for mental disorders.

Psychoactive Drugs Drugs that affect psychological functioning and behavior. Nearly two-thirds (64%) of patients for whom psychoactive drugs are prescribed are women.

Psychotherapy The use of psychological methods to alleviate symptoms of mental disorders or to help individuals cope during periods of stress in their lives.

Self-Focused Attention Attention directed internally to thoughts and feelings rather than externally toward the environment. It is related to depression.

Self-Help Groups Support groups whose members share a common problem (e.g., obesity being a survivor of incest or being recently widowed).

Serotonin Selective Reuptake Inhibitors (SSRI) One group of the new generation of antidepressants that act specifically to prevent the reuptake by the brain cells of the neurotransmitter serotonin. Fluoxetine (Prozac) is the most widely prescribed of these newer drugs.

Specific Phobia An intense anxiety provoked by exposure to a specific feared object or situation, which often leads to avoidance of that object or situation. Common examples of specific phobias are fear of spiders or fear of flying.

Tricyclic Antidepressants Drugs such as imipramine (Tofranil and others) and desipramine (Norpramin and others), which were the standard drug treatment for major depression for many years. These drugs have a number of negative side effects, the most serious of which affect the cardiovascular system.

SUGGESTED READINGS

Comas-Diaz, L., & Greene, B. (Eds.). (1994). *Women of color: Integrating ethnic and gender identities in psychotherapy.* New York: Guilford. This excellent book written by women of color applies cultural and psychological knowledge of women of color (Black, Asian, Southeast Asian, Women of the Indian Subcontinent, Hispanic, American Indian, and West Indian Women) to the practice of psychotherapy.

Graber, J. A., Brooks-Gunn, J., Paikoff, R. L., & Warren, M. P. (199). Prediction of eating problems: An 8-year study of adolescent girls. *Developmental Psychology, 30,* 823–834. This study followed the same 116 adolescent girls over an eight-year period in order to identify factors related to eating disorders.

Nolen-Hoeksema, S., & Girgus, J. S. (1994). The emergence of gender differences in depression during adolescence. *Psychological Bulletin, 115,* 424–443. This article tests three models of the development of gender differences in depression in early adolescence via a thorough review of the literature.

CHAPTER 9

Physical Health

The women's health movement has been one of the most visible and best received aspects of the women's movement. Since the late 1960s, groups of feminists throughout the United States and the world have critiqued curative medical systems that are based on the values of the male medical establishment.

Marianne H. Whatley &
Nancy Worcester, 1989

THE WOMEN'S HEALTH MOVEMENT AND PUBLIC POLICY

The women's health movement has impacted on public policy. NIH and ADAMHA now require the inclusion of both sexes in research.

During most of the twentieth century, women's health issues were not given as much attention in research as were men's. In 1987, The National Institutes of Health (NIH) and the Alcohol, Drug Abuse, and Mental Health Administration (ADAMHA) issued a policy requiring the inclusion of both genders in research so that the results may be applicable to the general population. Members of peer review groups that review grant proposals for scientific merit were also instructed to evaluate the gender composition of the study as well. Grants would be ap-

proved for research on only men only when there is a strong scientific rationale for excluding one gender (American Psychological Association, 1991). In 1991, a new Office of Women's Health Research was established at the NIH.

These changes in policy, to include women in research on health, have been the result of the women's health movement, which has been one of the most successful aspects of the women's movement.

Many of the key developments within health psychology—for example, behavioral prevention, compliance, coping, health promotion, locus of control, and social support—reflect essentially feminist principles that emphasize the legitimate authority and significance of the individual. Feminist principles of equity and inclusiveness are also represented in emerging concerns that the health needs of many underprivileged groups deserve more focused attention. (Travis, Gressley, & Crumpler, 1991)

The women's health movement, therefore, has increased awareness of the health concerns of the population as a whole, not just the focus on White, middle class men that had been the case with much of the previous research.

GENDER, MARITAL STATUS, AND RACE DIFFERENCES IN PHYSICAL HEALTH

Gender Differences

Women get sick more often than men, but with mild transitory illnesses. Men die earlier. Women have more illnesses because they get lower pay and spend more time doing housework and childcare. Women are also more likely to seek medical attention.

The irony about women's health is that women have more **morbidity** (illness) than men during their lives, but a lower **mortality** rate (death rate). Although approximately 125 males are conceived for every 100 females, more males are miscarried, and proportionately more males die at every age. During the first year of life 27% more males die than females. In 1993 the expectation of life in the United States was, on average, 72.0 years for baby boys and 78.7 years for girls (Kranczer, 1995). Five times as many women as men live to celebrate their one-hundredth birthdays (J. Rodin & Ickovics, 1990).

Women are more likely to report illnesses and to seek medical attention. Sixty percent of surgery in this country is performed on women, with gynecological operations leading the list. Women also generally have higher prevalence than men of chronic diseases such as diabetes, anemia, arthritis, and hypertension (Strickland, 1988). Even in the homeless population the gender difference persists, with females reporting more symptoms than males (Ritchey, La Gory, & Mullis 1991). Although men are sick less often, they have more severe injuries and higher rates of the chronic diseases that are the leading causes of death. Men have more than twice the rate of homicide,

respiratory cancer, suicide, chronic obstructive pulmonary disease, accidents, cirrhosis of the liver, and heart disease than do women, and the number of men who die of **coronary heart disease** (CHD) is greater than the number of women who die of CHD (J. Rodin & Ickovics, 1990).

The social roles of women, particularly nurturing demands, cause women to have more frequent illnesses than men. Based on a sample drawn from a survey conducted on a random sample of households in Chicago, Gove and Hughes (1979) concluded that the sex differences in illness are real, that women are ill more often, but with mild, transitory illnesses. Compared with married men, women had more variables associated with poor physical health such as having more chores, being unable to rest, and not receiving care. Bird and Fremont (1992) conclude from their research that women's slightly lower educational level, lower wages, and more time spent doing housework and caring for children account for why women get sick more than men. On the other hand, according to a survey of 1,648 adult members of a health maintenance organization, women are less inhibited about admitting illness and seeking help (Hibbard & Pope, 1986).

Marital Status, Marital Quality and Illness

Married persons have better health and lower mortality rates than do the unmarried. Marriage has a more positive influence on men's health than it does on women's. Marital status, marital quality, and marital interaction patterns all influence health.

Married individuals of both sexes have substantially lower **mortality rates** than unmarried, with the differences between the married and never married less than that between the formerly married and married (Gove, Style, & Hughes, 1990). Married people have the best health, followed by the never married, then the widowed, with separated and divorced persons having the poorest health. Men's health has been found to be even more favorably influenced by marriage than is women's. Never married women, divorced or separated women, and widowed women have better health, however, than men in each of those categories.

The quality of the marriage is an important variable, however, with unhappily married persons having greater physical and psychological health problems than unmarried persons. Since most persons report a high level of satisfaction with their marriages, marriage generally produces positive states of well being.

Based on a review of the literature, Burman and Margolin (1992) developed a hypothetical model of the association between marital relationships and health problems which includes marital variables grouped into three dimensions: marital status; marital quality; and marital interaction. These marital variables effect two components of health problems, etiology and course/outcome/treatment. Although it is also true that people with health problems are less likely to marry, there is sufficient data to conclude that being married, having high satisfaction in marriage and supportive interactions, improves health.

Widowers suffer more illness and have a higher mortality rate than widows.

The death of a spouse leads to more negative health consequences for men than for women. A review of the literature by Stroebe and Stroebe (1983) points to a convergence of findings from longitudinal and cross-sectional studies of both normal and pathological grief reactions, which supports the conclusion that men suffer more from both psychological and physical illness and have a higher mortality rate following the death of a spouse. Interpersonal protection theory, which emphasizes the role of social support in buffering individuals against the deleterious effects of life stress, seems to account for the greater mortality of widowers as compared to widows. Widows have greater networks of social support because men are more likely than women to rely exclusively on their wives as confidants. Widows are more prevalent than widowers; there-

fore, more same-sex friends are available. Men experience the greatest problems in the first six months following bereavement, while widows suffer most during the second year. Because of cultural norms, widowers do not usually find an opposite sex interest until at least after the first six months, but then the greater availability of widows makes their later adjustment easier.

Black Women and White Women's Health

The leading causes of death are the same for Black women and White women—heart disease, stroke, and cancer. The death ratio is higher for all of these diseases for Black women. White women have better primary prevention. Black women have better secondary prevention.

Black women have higher mortality rates than White women. In 1993 life expectancy at birth was 79.5 for White women and 73.7 for Black women (Kranczer, 1995). The leading causes of death for both Black and White women are heart disease, stroke, and cancer. The death ratio is higher for all of these diseases for Black women than for White women: 1.5 for heart disease; 1.8 for stroke; and 1.2 for cancer. Black women have twice the mortality rate from cervical cancer that White women do.

Why do Black women have higher mortality rates than White women? According to data from the 1985 Health Interview Survey (19,277 female respondents, 16.2% Black and 83.8% White) Black women are less likely to exercise, less likely to have favorable weight, and more likely to smoke than are White women (Duelberg, 1992). Generally, it can be said that White women have better **primary prevention** than do Black women, which refers to the extent to which individuals actively improve their health status.

Black women, however, were found to have better **secondary prevention**. Black women were more likely to get a Pap test and to have a breast exam than White women. This finding shows a change from the early 1980s when Black women were less likely than White women to receive a pap test or breast exam. Geographical differences in health behavior were also found. Urban Blacks are much more likely to get a pap test than are rural Blacks, but among Whites, urban residents are only slightly more likely to get a pap test than are rural residents. Implications of this research are that more education needs to be directed toward African American women for primary prevention and toward White women for secondary prevention (Duelberg, 1992).

CORONARY HEART DISEASE

Coronary heart disease is the leading cause of death for both men and women, but men die at earlier ages from heart disease. Occupational mobility is related to higher blood pressure and cholesterol levels, and lower exercise levels for men, but not for women.

The leading cause of death for both sexes is CHD, disease of the heart and/or arteries supplying blood to the heart. Currently, 52% of deaths of women are due to CHD. The age-adjusted mortality rate, however, is higher for men from CHD than it is for women. Both hypertension (high blood pressure) and atherosclerosis (hardening of the arteries) increase women's risk of heart disease.

Will the increase of women into the labor force increase their risk of heart disease? What is the relationship of work and health? To answer this question, Sorensen et al., (1985) analyzed data from approximately 2,500 employed persons (1,379 men and 1,133 women) from The Minnesota Heart Survey.

No significant differences emerged for leisure-time physical exercise or cigarette smoking between men and women. "Men work significantly more hours than women, report more deadlines and occupational mobility, and score higher on measures of job absorption, speed and impatience, and hard-driving behavior. Yet women report more symptoms of stress" (Sorensen et al., 1985, p. 385). Although the percentage of men and women who work 40 hours per week is simi-

lar, more women are working part-time (43%), and more men work more than 40 hours per week (47%). Blood pressure and blood cholesterol levels are higher among men than women, and both rise with increasing occupational mobility among men, but not among women. Occupational mobility is negatively related to men's exercise levels, but not to women's exercise levels. Although both men and women with occupational mobility showed greater job absorption, hard-driving and competitive behavior, there was no relation between stress symptoms and occupational mobility. This study did not find any support for the theory that women's job advancement and exposure to job pressures will increase their risk of CHD.

Alcohol Consumption and CHD

While heavy drinking has been shown to cause cardiovascular problems (heart disease and strokes), moderate drinking may be beneficial to the cardiovascular system.

There is considerable evidence that excessive alcohol consumption defined as two drinks per day or more, increases the risk of high blood pressure, and has toxic effects on the cardiovascular system (blood vessels and the heart) leading to stroke, arrhythmias (irregular heart beat), and other cardiac disorders and increases overall mortality (Criqui, 1987). Research has received wide publicity in the media which shows that at moderate levels alcohol may be beneficial to the cardiovascular system and reduce the risk of death from CHD. The mechanism by which moderate alcohol intake offers this protective effect was determined to be through an increase in levels of high-density lipoprotein cholesterol (Gaziano et al., 1993). The "French paradox"—the fact that the French eat a high-fat diet but have a low incidence of CHD—led researchers to test the protective effects of red wine, also a staple of French diets. The research demonstrates that ingestion of red wine is associated with significant reduction of low-density lipoprotein cholesterol levels (LDL) (Maxwell, Cruickshank, & Thorpe, 1994, p. 194).

Most of the studies examining the relation between alcohol intake and CHD have adjusted for age, sex, cigarette use, cholesterol level, blood pressure, and weight; however, few studies have controlled for physical activity level. As part of the South Carolina Cardiovascular Disease Prevention Project, analysis of data from 2,072 men and women revealed that women who were moderate or heavy drinkers engaged in the highest prevalence of regular physical activity (Barrett, Anda, Croft, Serdula, & Lane, 1995). Another confounding variable that has to be taken into account in studies of the relationship of alcohol consumption and CHD is that a sizeable proportion of the nondrinkers may represent "sick quitters," people who stopped drinking because of health problems. "In addition to considering the possibility that some non-drinkers may be people who quit drinking because of illness, . . . Increased physical activity levels among drinkers may account for some of the protective effect attributed to moderate alcohol use" (Barrett et al., 1995, p. 15).

A moderate dose of alcohol taken just prior to exercise for 30 minutes on a stationary bicycle by women aged 21–45 years was shown to increase blood pressure, oxygen consumption, and blood lactic of women as compared with a placebo group (Wang et al., 1995). "This can be interpreted as a negative effect on the cardiovascular system during exercise" (Wang et al., 1995, p. 20). It would appear that it is not a good idea for women to exercise while or shortly after drinking alcohol.

CANCER

Incidence of Breast Cancer

Breast cancer is the most common cause of cancer in women in the United States. Although breast cancer rates are higher for White women than for Black women, at diagnosis Black women are likely to have more advanced cancer.

Breast cancer is the most common cause of cancer among women in every major ethnic group in the United States. One-third of all cancers in women are breast cancers. About 180,000 new cases of breast cancers in women were diagnosed and about 46,000 deaths in women were attributable to breast cancer in 1992. The American Cancer society predicts that one in nine women in the United States will develop breast cancer at some time in her life (Kelsey & Horn-Ross, 1993).

The incidence of breast cancer has been rising in the United States during the past decade. Is increased detection due to mammographic screening or to other factors? Clinical and demographic data were collected by a cancer registry on all new cases of cancer among residents of five counties in metropolitan Atlanta, Georgia (Liff, Sung, Chow, Greenberg, & Flanders, 1991). Between 1979 and 1986, age-adjusted incidence rates of breast cancer more than doubled among Blacks and tripled among Whites. For invasive breast malignancies, there was an increase of 45% for Blacks and 26% for Whites. The researchers concluded that the mammographic detection of asymptomatic lesions could only account for 20–40% of the increase in incidence of breast cancer among Whites and only 13–25% of the increase among Blacks. Nationally, authorities have also attributed the increase in the number of women diagnosed with breast cancer to detection of smaller lesion. Overall, in the United States the breast cancer incidence is 20% higher in White women than it is in Black women (Cancer Incidence . . . , 1994). Among women younger than 40, however, incidence rates are higher in Black women than White women. It is not until after age 45 that the rate in breast cancer becomes higher in White women than in Black women.

Black women are more likely to be first diagnosed at a later stage of the disease than White women. Why? To try to answer this question, R. J. Coates et al., (1992) interviewed 410 Black women and 325 White women from Atlanta, New Orleans, and San Francisco/Oakland, who were newly diagnosed with invasive breast cancer. At diagnosis, the Black women were twice as likely to have more advanced cancer. "The women whose breast cancer was diagnosed prior to symptom occurrence were much more likely to have been White and older, to have lived in San Francisco/Oakland, and to have had smaller, earlier stage, and lower grade tumors" (R. J. Coates, et al., 1992, p. 941).

Risk Factors Associated with Breast Cancer

Variables related to a higher risk of breast cancer include earlier age at menarche, later age at menopause, later age of first giving birth, a female relative with breast cancer, benign breast disease, and high levels of alcohol consumption.

The younger a woman's age at menarche and the older her age at menopause, the higher her risk of breast cancer. The younger a woman is when she has her first full-term pregnancy, the lower her risk of breast cancer. Women who do not have a first birth until after age 30 have a higher risk of breast cancer than the woman who never gives birth. In the United States, some studies have shown a protective effect of breast-feeding on breast cancer. Decreasing breast cancer risk has been associated with increasing duration of breast-feeding in the United States and China, with the effect stronger in China, where more than half of the women breast-feed for at least 24 months, as compared with the United States, where only 5% of women breast-feed for that length of time. In the United States some studies find no effect of breast-feeding on risk of breast cancer. Some studies have shown positive associations between spontaneous and induced abortion and breast cancer risk, and other studies have shown inverse relationships. Inconsistent results have also been reported for the effect of oral contraceptives on breast cancer risk (Kelsey, Gammon, & John, 1993).

A woman with a female relative who developed breast cancer has a two to three times greater risk. Benign breast disease has also been found to be related to an increase in the incidence of breast cancer. Incidence of breast cancer in-

creases with age in women, with the increase less steep after around age 45–50 years (Kelsey & Horn-Ross, 1993). Breast cancer is also more common in women of high-socioeconomic status (L. Rosenberg, Metzker, & Palmer, 1993). It is possible that more women of higher socioeconomic level are detected with breast cancer because of better access to screening. A dose-response association between increasing alcohol consumption and increasing breast cancer risk has been found (Longnecker, 1994). It is known that women of higher-socioeconomic level drink more than lower-socioeconomic women, which may account for some of the higher risk of breast cancer among higher-socioeconomic level women.

Nutrition and Breast Cancer

Nutrition may play a role in the widely varying rates of breast cancer in different countries. The Nurses' Health Study found women at increased risk for breast cancer who have a lower intake of vegetables and inadequate vitamin A in the diet.

The rate of breast cancer varies greatly from one country to another (it is fivefold in some countries as compared with others). One factor accounting for this difference may be in the intake of vitamins through foods and supplements. The Nurses' Health Study, a prospective investigation of 89,494 women who were 34–59 years old in 1980, and who did not have diagnosed cancer, were studied for their intakes of vitamins C, E, and A from foods and supplements (D. J. Hunter et al., 1993). During the eight-year follow-up, 1,439 women were diagnosed as having breast cancer. Large intakes of vitamins C and E did not decrease women's risk of developing breast cancer. Among women with the lowest dietary intake of vitamin A, those who took vitamin A supplements had a significantly lower risk of breast cancer. "However, our data suggest that vitamin A supplements are unlikely to influence the risk of breast cancer among women whose dietary intake of this vitamin is already adequate" (D. J. Hunter et al., 1993, p. 240). Of the food groups studied, only the intake of vegetables was associated with a lowered risk of breast cancer. A number of other studies have also found an association between vitamin A in the diet and a reduced risk of breast cancer.

It has been observed that dietary fat intake in various countries in the world is associated with breast cancer. Correlations of this type, however, can be confounded with other factors such as food wastage, so that not all the dietary fat is actually being consumed. A meta-analysis of fat intake did find a positive associated for both daily total fat intake and saturated fat intake (Howe et al., as cited in D. J. Hunter & Willett). "The pooled relative risk was 1.35 for a 100-g increase in daily total fat intake, although the risk was somewhat stronger for postmenopausal women (relative risk [RR] = 1.48)" (D. J. Hunter & Willett, 1993, p. 112).

Breast Self Examination and Mammography

Women who conduct regular breast self-examinations detect breast cancer earlier and have higher survival rates.

Women who conduct regular breast self-examination (BSE) detect changes in the breast earlier. Among women who have cancer, those who conduct regular BSE's have higher survival rates than do women who rely exclusively on physician examinations for breast cancer. At present, over 90% of breast cancers are detected by BSE. Free pamphlets on BSE may be obtained from the American Cancer Society. When a woman finds a lump, however, she should not panic because approximately 80% of all breast tumors are **benign**. Other warning signs are changes in the nipple, such as the nipple being pulled askew. In addition, the woman should be seen by a physician if she notices changes in the normal shape of the breast or depressions, puckering or dimpling of the skin of the breast (Travis, 1988a; Whatley & Worcester, 1989).

Mammography has a lower rate of both false negative (a true cancer is not recognized) or false positive (a lump is recognized as cancer when it is in fact benign) than other screening technologies (Travis, 1988a). The "average" false negative rate of mammograms is placed at approximately 20%. The safety of mammography is still being debated because of radiation exposure during the mammogram. Today, doses of radiation are significantly lower than previously used.

When the mammography finds a possible cancer, other detection methods are necessary—aspiration cytology, the insertion of a fine hyperdermic needle that draws out fluid and cells that are tested for cancer, or excisional biopsy, in which the entire lump is removed. For many years, **radical mastectomy** was the treatment of preference for breast cancer. It involves removing the breast as well as the pectoral muscles (chest wall muscles) and the underarm lymph nodes.

At what age should a woman begin to have yearly mammographic screening? Based on 10-year results of mammography screening in Edinburgh and Sweden, a reduction of risk in women aged 40–49 years was 0.85 compared with 0.76 for women aged 50–74 years (A. P. Forrest & Alexander, 1995). The predictive value of mammography detection of cancer in women aged 40–49 is less than in women over age 50 because of the greater density of breast tissue of younger women. Age at menopause is highly relevant in the decision whether to have annual mammograms at ages 40–49 years. Since density of breast tissue is determined by hormonal status, mammograms would be more accurate for women in their 40s who have gone through either natural or surgical menopause. Women with a family history of breast cancer might also want to get mammography screening in their 40s.

Breast Cancer Treatment

Survival rates for early stage breast cancers are comparable for lumpectomy plus radiation and mastectomy.

During the past decade there has been a conservative trend (less radical surgery) in the treatment of early Stage I and II breast cancer. A number of studies with randomized clinical trials have found the survival rates and local control of Stage I and II breast cancer comparable for conservative surgery (**lumpectomy**) plus radiation treatment and for radical mastectomy (Sarrazin et al., 1989; Veronesi et al., 1986). Indication of misconduct by one of the investigators who admitted to falsification of data in one of the sites of a large study of breast cancer surgery comparing lumpectomy and mastectomy need not disquiet women about the survival rate of lumpectomy patients because a number of other studies, including studies conducted in Italy, have come to the same conclusions about the comparability of survival rates for lumpectomy patients for early-stage cancer (Bernard Fisher & Redmond, 1994).

Research has been comparing conservative surgery for small breast cancers with and without postsurgery radiotherapy. Researchers in Italy, who randomly assigned 567 women either to radiation or not following removal of the breast quadrant for small breast cancers, found a significantly lower recurrence rate with radiotherapy as compared with those not treated with postsurgical radiotherapy (8.8% versus 0.3%) (Veronesi et al., 1993). However, patients more than 55-years old did not differ significantly in four-year overall survival whether or not they were treated with postsurgical radiotherapy. For women over 55, breast irradiation after lumpectomy may not be necessary.

In premenopausal women, timing of breast cancer surgery during the follicular phase improves 10-year survival.

Can the timing of patient's breast cancer surgery in the menstrual cycle influence survival rates? A controversial study of 283 premenopausal breast cancer surgery patients found that 10-year survival was 43% for those who had surgery during the luteal phase of their cycle (days 15–30 following last onset) as compared with 49% of those whose surgery was performed during the follicular phase (days 1–14) (Senie, Rosen, Rhodes, & Lesser, 1991). The effect was

seen only in those whose cancer had spread to the lymph nodes. Other researchers are skeptical about the finding and do not feel surgeons should time breast cancer operations to the phase of the menstrual cycle (McGuire, 1991). If there is a possibility it could make a difference in saving a woman's life, why not?

Psychological Sequelae of Lumpectomy and Mastectomy

Patients who had mastectomy, but not lumpectomy, report less satisfactory postoperative sexual relationships. There are no differences in psychiatric pathology, however, between the two groups.

What are the psychological effects of having a mastectomy versus a lumpectomy? Interviews with 32 women one year after treatment for early breast cancer with either mastectomy or lumpectomy with radiation revealed that the patients who had mastectomy felt less attractive, less sexually desirable, and reported less satisfaction in their sexual relationships than they had before treatment (Margolis, Goodman & Rubin, 1990). The lumpectomy patients did not perceive any changes in these areas. Half of the mastectomy patients regretted not having had the more conservative lumpectomy with radiation. Nevertheless, there were no differences in psychiatric pathology between the two groups.

Coping with Breast Cancer

Most women with breast cancer tend to compare themselves with others they feel are not doing as well as they are.

Social psychological factors are involved in coping with breast cancer. According to Festinger's (1954) theory of social comparison, people have a drive to compare themselves with others in order to evaluate their opinions and abilities. Schachter (1959) extended this analysis by proposing that individuals seek social comparison in stressful situations to help them clarify their emotions. A number of research studies have been conducted to determine whether individuals are likely to make upward comparisons (others more successful than they are), similarity comparisons (others who are similar in relevant, dimensions), or downward comparisons (others who are worse off) (J. V. Wood, Taylor, & Lichtman, 1985). In their study of 87 breast cancer patients, J. V. Wood et al. found that most women made downward comparisons, not usually to specific persons, but said their adjustment was very good compared with other breast cancer patients, and tended to ignore the models in the media of "supercopers" when making their comparisons. These downward comparisons may help the patient minimize her sense of victimization.

Optimism about life is related to lower distress in women with breast cancer.

Women have been found to use a wide variety of coping responses when given a diagnosis of breast cancer, extensively using cognitive avoidance and positive reappraisal (Jarrett, Ramirez, Richards, & Weinman, 1992). Are some coping styles better than others in reducing distress levels? Overall optimism about life was measured at diagnosis for 59 breast cancer patients; their recent coping responses and distress levels were reported at 1 day presurgery, 10 days postsurgery, and at 3-, 6-, and 12-month follow-ups (Carver et al., 1993). Optimism about life was inversely related to distress at each measurement point. The effect of optimism on change in distress was found to be mediated by the coping styles of acceptance and humor. Positive reframing, although linked to low concurrent distress, did not play a role in prospective tests. Other coping styles, particularly denial and behavioral disengagement, predicted more distress.

Breast Cancer Mortality Rates

African American women have a higher mortality rate following diagnosis for breast cancer than European American women.

European American women have a lower fatality rate following diagnosis for breast cancer than African American women. The five year relative survival rate was 64% among Black women and 78% among White women between 1981 and 1986 (R. J. Coates et al., 1992) (see Table 9.1). Mortality rates among women under age 65 with breast cancer dropped 6% between 1973 and 1990, but mortality rates for those over age 65 rose by 15%. By 1990, five-year survival rates reached 79% of all breast cancer patients and 93% for patients diagnosed in an early stage of the disease (Cancer Incidence . . . , 1994).

Breast Implants

The largest product liability lawsuit in U.S. history was awarded for health problems caused by silicone breast implants. It is now certain that only a fraction of the $4.25 billion settlement will be paid out.

After a mastectomy, women may decide to wear an external prosthesis, and others have reconstructive plastic surgery at the time of the mastectomy or at a later time. Reconstructive surgery involves either moving tissue from the woman's own back, abdomen, or buttocks to the chest area or having a saline implant. Many problems arose with the use of silicone implants because of leakage of silicone oil, which can be

TABLE 9.1 Five-Year Relative Survival Rates (%) for Breast Cancer among U.S. White Women and Black Women by Age Group

Age Group	White	Black
<35	70.5	55.6
35–44	78.3	61.5
45–54	79.5	61.9
55–64	79.0	62.4
65–74	81.2	66.9
75≥	79.3	58.6
All Ages	79.3	60.1

Source: "Breast Cancer: Magnitude of the problem and descriptive epidemiology." by J. L. Kelsey & P. L. Horn-Ross, 1993, *Epidemiologic Reviews*, 15, p. 8.

transported by the lymph system and blood-stream to other parts of the body. The health hazards caused by silicone implants led to a major class action lawsuit. Final approval was granted by a federal judge in 1994 for a $4.25 billion agreement to compensate women whose health was impaired by silicone breast implants. Despite the fact that this was the largest product liability settlement in United States history, it is now certain that only a fraction of the settlement will be paid out.

The settlement is on the verge of collapse due to the bankruptcy of Dow Corning Inc., the company that originally agreed to contribute $2 billion of the $4.25 billion settlement. The number of women filing claims has far exceeded expectations—about 440,000. An offer in the case from three other companies that made implants would make partial payments to about 50,000 women, and would not include women who had inplants made by Dow Corning, Inc. (New Offer, 1995).

Disease of the esophagus is found in children breast-fed by mothers with silicone breast implants.

A study found disease of the esophagus in six of eight breast-fed children of mothers who had silicone breast implants (J. J. Levine & Ilowite, 1994). The abnormalities of the esophagus were not seen in three bottle-fed children of mothers with silicone implants. Women with silicone breast implants should not breast-feed their infants.

Funding of Breast Cancer Research

Breast cancer research has been inadequately funded.

The women's movement can learn some lessons from AIDS activism in bringing about changes in the funding for breast cancer research. AIDS activism has shaped health policy and led to increased funding. In 1990, 28,121 Americans died of AIDS (Centers for Disease Control, 1992). During 1990, 1.6 billion federal dollars were spent on AIDS. During that same year, $1.5 billion was spent on cancer of all types, a disease that killed 500,000 people in 1989. Breast cancer alone killed 43,000 Americans in 1990, but only $77 million in research money was spent on breast cancer (one-twentieth of the AIDS allocation) (Wachter, 1992). The moral of the story is not that advocates of AIDS and breast cancer should compete for health dollars; rather, they should "work in concert to improve access to health care for all Americans, expedite the approval process at the FDA for all drugs, and fight discrimination against victims of all diseases" (Wachter, 1992, p. 132).

Lung Cancer

Eighty-five percent of lung cancer is caused by smoking. Lung cancer is now the leading cause of cancer death in women.

The convergence in smoking is responsible for the narrowing gap in lung cancer rates between men and women, since 85% of lung cancer is caused by smoking. Beginning in 1986, the rate of death of women from lung cancer has surpassed the rate of death from breast cancer. The incidence of lung cancer in women in 1992 (77,000 cases) was still, however, less than half the incidence of breast cancer (180,000 cases) (Kelsey & Horn-Ross, 1993). Between 1979 and 1986 the rate of death from lung cancer rose 7% among men and 44% among women in the United States (J. Rodin & Ickovics, 1990).

Colorectal Cancer

Colorectal cancer can be prevented by removal of noncancerous polyps when found.

Colorectal cancer (cancers of the colon and rectum) is the third most common cancer in both women and men (U.S. Bureau of the Census, 1994). There was a 10% drop in the age-adjusted rate of colorectal cancer between 1985 and 1989. The survival rate is higher for Whites than it is for

Blacks. Research supports the practice of periodic examination for colorectal cancer and removal of noncancerous polyps when found (Winawer et al, 1993). Evidence indicates that these polyps progress to cancer over time.

Cervical Cancer

Cervical intraepithelial neoplasia, abnormal cells in the cervix, does not develop into cancer in most cases.

It is important to get an annual Pap test. Abnormal cells on or near the cervix will be detected by a routine Pap smear. **Cervical intraepithelial neoplasia (CIN)**, however, does not mean that the woman has cancer. CIN does not develop into cancer in most cases. "Cervical intraepithelial neoplasia class I, II, or III is best treated conservatively, with laser vaporization or excision, cone biopsy, loop electrosurgical excision procedures, or cryotherapy" (Carlson, Nichols, & Schiff, 1993, p. 858). CIN occurs along a continuum, at one end of which only a few abnormal cells appear, to the other end, which is invasive cancer. Invasive cervical cancer has spread beyond the surface layers of the tissue into the underlying lymph or blood systems.

A number of factors have been associated with cervical cancer (J. Bornstein, Rahat, & Abramovici, 1995). The two main risk factors that have been identified are the total number of sexual partners and early age at first sexual intercourse. A male partner with a greater number of sexual partners also poses a greater risk of cervical cancer for his wife (this finding is based on one study of husbands and wives). A causal association of Herpes Simplex Virus Type 2 (HSV-2) (genital herpes) and Human Papillomarvirus (HPV) (genital warts) have been found in the etiology of cervical cancer. Smoking is considered an independent risk factor. Protection against cervical cancer has been found for beta carotene, vitamin C, folic acid, and a diet rich in vegetables. Research has also consistently shown a protective effect against cervical cancer for use of the condom, diaphragm, and spermicidal agents.

Endometrial Cancer

Obesity, hypertension, and diabetes increase the risk of endometrial cancer in postmenopausal women.

Endometrial cancer (cancer of the lining of the uterus) is most frequent in postmenopausal women in their fifties. Conditions that increase the risk of endometrial cancer are hypertension, obesity, and diabetes. The most common symptom of uterine cancer is bleeding in postmenopausal women; in premenopausal women, it is heavy bleeding during menstruation and bleeding between periods. The Pap test is not a reliable indicator of uterine cancer. An endometrial biopsy and/or D and C are methods for diagnosis. Radical hysterectomy is the treatment most frequently used to treat uterine cancer, with radiation if it has spread to the lymph nodes (The Boston Women's Health Book Collective, 1992; Grimes & Economy, 1995).

Ovarian Cancer

Symptoms may not be present in ovarian cancer. Family history, a high-fat diet, and use of talcum powder in the genital area are causes of ovarian cancer.

Ovarian cancer was the fifth leading cause of cancer among women in the United States in 1992 (Kelsey & Horn-Ross, 1992). The Pap test is not a reliable test for ovarian cancer, and symptoms may not be present. "Symptoms may include indigestion, gas, constipation or diarrhea, loss of appetite or weight, a feeling of fullness, lower abdominal discomfort or pain, frequent urination, fatigue, backache, nausea, vomiting, nonmenstrual vaginal bleeding, enlargement or bloating of the abdomen or an unusual growth or lump" (The Boston Women's Health Book Collective, 1992, p. 627). A number of causes may be related to the development of ovarian cancer including a family history of ovarian cancer, a high-fat diet, and use of talcum powder in the genital area. Oral contraceptive use and multiple pregnancies may offer some protective effect.

A higher risk of ovarian cancer was found in a cohort of 3,837 women treated for infertility between 1974 and 1985 in Seattle as compared with women not undergoing fertility treatments (Rossing, Daling, Weiss, Moore, & Self, 1994). The increased risk was associated with treatment with the fertility drug, clomiphene, for a period of 12 or more monthly cycles, as compared with infertile women who had not taken the drug, or who had been treated with clomiphene for less than one year.

SMOKING

Smoking is the largest cause of preventable death and disease in the United States. More adolescent young women are smoking than young men.

The rates of smoking for men and women have been converging, with the rate of smoking of men declining substantially in recent years, while women's rate of smoking has been increasing. "Tobacco is the single largest cause of premature adult death throughout the world. Over the next 30 years tobacco-related deaths among women will more than double, so that by the year 2020 well over a million adult women will die every year from tobacco-related illnesses" (Chollat-Traquet, 1992, p. 3).

The U.S. Public Health Service has identified smoking as the single largest preventable cause of death and disease in the United States. Cigarette smoking is a causal factor in 225,000 cases of CHD and 100,000 cases of cancer (Tavris, 1988a). CHD is not reduced by smoking the low tar and nicotine cigarettes, but is directly related to the number of cigarettes smoked per day and how long the woman has been smoking. In countries where women have smoked for some time, it is estimated that smoking also accounts for 55% of deaths from cerebrovascular disease (stroke) in women under 65 (Chollat-Traquet, 1992). "Perhaps as much as 50% of observed sex differences in longevity may be attributable to differences in smoking patterns" (Tavris, 1988a, p. 20).

Advertising has been very effective in associating women who smoke with youth, good looks, and sophistication (Strickland, 1988). Advertisers have also tied themselves to the coattails of the feminist movement, "You've come a long way baby." Unfortunately, since the 1920s, cigarette smoking in women was associated with emancipation and equality. More adolescent women now begin to smoke than young men, although men and women are quitting at about the same rate. By 1988, 33% of men and 26% of women in the United States were smokers (Chollat-Traquet, 1992).

Data from the National Health Interview Surveys, a national probability survey of the U.S. population, which was conducted periodically since 1944, found trends in initiation of smoking by adolescent girls to be associated with advertising targeting them (J. P. Pierce, Lee, & Gilpin, 1994). The initiation of smoking in adolescent girls showed an only slightly increasing trend from the close of World War II through 1967. Beginning in 1967, peaking in 1973, the initiation rate in girls younger than 17 showed a dramatic rise. In 1967 women's brands of cigarettes were introduced, advertising budgets were increased, and advertising specifically aimed at women was begun. "Our findings add to the evidence that tobacco advertising plays an important role in encouraging young people to begin this lifelong addiction before they are old enough to fully appreciate its long-term health risks (J. P. Pierce et al., 1994, p. 611).

White girls and boys begin smoking earlier than Black girls and boys. Peer influence is greater for White females in initiation of smoking.

What is the process by which adolescents begin to smoke? According to a probability sample of 1,277 12–14 year olds followed-up for two years, in metropolitan areas in the southeastern United States, the correlates of cigarette smoking are different for male and female adolescents, and for Blacks and Whites (Headen, Bauman, Deane, & Koch, 1991). Whites started smoking earlier than Blacks. At age 12, 23.1% of White females but only 9.5% of Black females had begun to smoke. Among males, 26.6% of White 12-year olds, but only 7.1% of Blacks, had begun to smoke. By age 14, the Black–White difference had narrowed, with 20.6% of Black females and 26.7% of White females smoking. Among 14-year-old males, 17.9% of Blacks and 30.3% of Whites were smoking. The influence of best friend in initiating smoking was greater among Whites than among Blacks. Peer programs aimed at preventing smoking may therefore be more effective for White adolescents than for Black adolescents. The influence on initiation of smoking was related to mother's smoking only if the adolescent reported a close relationship with his/her mother.

FERTILITY-RELATED BEHAVIOR

U.S. Unintended Pregnancy Rates

The United States has the highest rate of unintended pregnancy and abortion in the Western world. Data from a 1992 national survey finds an increase in condom usage among unmarried sexually active women.

The United States has among the highest rates of unintended pregnancy and **abortion** in the Western world. Estimates are that more than half of the 6 million annual pregnancies in the United States are unintended, and one-quarter end in induced abortion. This unintended pregnancy rate appears to be due to the nonuse or inconsistent use of contraceptives by substantial portions of sexually active women and men in this country (J. D. Forrest, 1987; J. D. Forrest & Fordyce, 1993).

The proportion of births to ever married women increased between 1982 and 1988 according to a comparison of data from Cycles III (1982; 7,969 women interviewed) and Cycles IV (1988; 8,450 women interviewed) of the National Survey of Family Growth (NSFG) (G. Williams & London, 1994). The increases in unwanted childbearing was particularly pronounced among Black

women (even when income was controlled for), women living below the poverty level, and women with less than a high school education.

My own research among college students has identified several factors related to nonuse of contraceptives among sexually active college students. Concepts such as perceived availability, perceived dangerousness, and perceived effectiveness of contraceptives influence contraceptive behavior. Students have tended to overestimate the dangerousness to their health of contraceptives they consider most effective (The Pill), and to underestimate the effectiveness of contraceptives they consider the safest in terms of unwanted side effects (condoms). These cognitions, combined with lack of planning for sex, leads to "being swept away" by passion and failure to use contraception (L. R. Olson & Rollins, 1982).

A national survey of 6,955 women aged 15–44 in 1992, found an increase in the proportion of unmarried women who had had intercourse from 76% in 1987 (as measured by a previous survey) to 86% in 1992 (J. D. Forrest & Fordyce, 1993). The proportion of women exposed to the risk of unintended pregnancy not using any method was slightly higher for unmarried women (8%) than for married women (3%). The most frequently used method among married women is sterilization (48%), which is used by only 11% of unmarried women. Unmarried women are more likely to use the Pill (52%) compared with only 28% of married women. More unmarried women also use the condom (33%) than did married women (19%), and withdrawal (11% vs. 6%). The rhythm method is used by 5% of married and 4% of unmarried women. The same percentage of married and unmarried women use the diaphragm (4%) and the sponge (3%). More unmarried (40%) as compared with married women (13%) said they were using the condom in addition to other methods of contraception. This represented an increase in condom usage compared with a similar 1987 survey, probably the result of educational messages to prevent AIDS and other STD infections. Black women, and women with incomes over $50,000, were underrepresented in this survey.

CONTRACEPTIVES

Contraceptive research has been dominated by Western medicine, the population control establishment and the pharmaceutical industry.

The past 35 years have seen an explosion of contraceptive methods and technologies. The social forces shaping contraceptive choices are Western medicine, the population control establishment, which has greater concern with limiting the size of poor and Third World populations than with giving individual women choice over reproduction, and pharmaceutical companies whose goal is to maximize sales and increase profits. As a result of these goals, "Millions of women's lives have been adversely affected by following advice or orders to use such new 'miracle' technologies as the Dalkon Shield, oral contraceptives, Depo-Provera, or hormonal implants" (Yanoshik & Norsigian, 1989, p. 62). The pill was initially tested on poor women in Haiti and Puerto Rico in doses and combinations that are now known to be extremely dangerous to a woman's health. Most of the contraceptive research money has gone for "high-tech" methods such as oral contraceptives and steroid injectibles that concentrate on the female reproductive system with only 3% going toward female barrier methods, spermicides, and natural fertility control methods (Yanoshik & Norsigian, 1989).

Condoms

Condoms are widely available, safe, and effective and prevent venereal disease. Condom use is greater among monogamous men and women. More than two-thirds of unmarried Hispanic and Black women say they never use condoms.

Condoms have been in use for centuries. The replacement of the skin sheath by the rubber condom in the late nineteenth century made condoms less expensive and widely available. Unlike most other methods of contraception, condoms reduce the possibility of AIDS or other venereal infection. Condoms are highly effective, with failure rates ranging from as low as 1.6 per hundred

woman years to 7.5 per hundred woman years in various studies (J. F. Potts & Diggory, 1983). The only potential side effect of condom use is an allergic reaction in some people to latex condoms (Turjanmaa, 1994).

Condoms are the contraceptive method with the greatest capacity to prevent sexually transmitted diseases. Natural membrane condoms, however, are not impermeable. Studies show a consistent reduction in relative risk for use of latex condoms against gonococcal and HIV infection (d'Oro, Parazzini, Nalda, & LaVecchia, 1994).

Condom use is greater among sexually active men and women who are monogamous. Among 1,229 unmarried sexually active men and women in 16 San Francisco census tracts with high levels of sexually transmitted diseases and admission rates to drug programs, men and women who had one sexual partner in the previous year were twice as likely to always use condoms as compared with those who had two or more partners (12% and 11% vs. 6% and 5%) (Catania et al., 1992). Among heterosexuals, 45% of men and 30% of women said they sometimes use condoms and 46% and 61% say they never do so. Hispanic women are least likely to use condoms, 72% saying they never used condoms as compared with 69% of Black women and 49% of White women. In addition to monogamy, communicating well with their partner and enjoying using condoms were factors related to condom use.

The Female Condom

The female condom also offers protection against sexually transmitted diseases.

The **female condom** is a six-inch prelubricated polyurethane sheath, with a flexible ring on either end. The woman squeezes the ring at the closed end in order to insert it into the vagina (like insertion of a diaphragm). The ring at the closed end extends about an inch beyond the vaginal opening, covering the labia during sexual intercourse. Like the male condom, it offers protection against sexually transmitted diseases, including HIV/AIDS. The female condom has a

15% pregnancy failure rate. It requires no prescription and can be used once (B. Baker, 1993).

Oral Contraceptives

The Pill was an important impetus to the Sexual Revolution and to Women's Liberation. Nevertheless, only a minority of women of reproductive age are taking the Pill.

With the twentieth century came more reliable methods of contraception, such as the diaphragm. It was not until the 1960s that we had a readily available, easy to use method of birth control that did not in any way interrupt the sex act and was nearly 100 percent effective—oral contraceptives (the Pill). Many, including some feminists, welcomed the Pill as a means to liberated sexuality and reproductive freedom. Biology was no longer destiny. Women were freed from reproductive slavery. Nevertheless, other feminists, particularly those involved in the Women's Health Movement, pointed out the dangers of the high estrogen levels of the early Pill. It is my view that the Pill was an important part of the zeitgiest for large numbers of women going to work, even though most women were never on the Pill. Social change reflected in individual attitudes and behavior is the tidal wave that follows technological change. The wave is larger and floods into all aspects of our lives when the technology is one that changes our bodies rather than simply the physical environment. The Pill brought with it a new morality, the sexual revolution. Along with the freedom came side effects and drawbacks.

In addition, the liberalization of sexuality has brought new psychological problems, and again, it is mostly women who pay the price. Now it is women, for example, who become both more readily available and disposable, because the sexual relationship is "without consequences." Men, on the other hand, are relieved of even more responsibility than before. Not infrequently, the pressure of sexual expectations has increased, in some cases culminating in a "throwaway relationship" with a woman as sex object. (Beck-Gernsheim, 1989)

Many young women now feel they are expected to have sex on a date whether or not they really want to. Another repercussion of the Pill is that the whole society becomes geared for small families (apartment and car size, cost of raising a child, etc.), so that reproductive choice is influenced by all of these external factors, making the choice to have a large family very difficult.

Despite the changes brought about in sexual attitudes and behavior that may be attributed, at least in part, to the Pill, only a minority of women of reproductive age are taking the Pill. According to data from the 1988 NSFG, 10.7 million American women are currently using the Pill (30% of contraceptive users) (Williams-Deane & Potter, 1992). Most of the oral contraceptive users are young—80% under the age of 30. To the 23% of oral contraceptive users who have not graduated from high school, the instructions are often confusing. As a result, first year use failure rates have been shown to be as high as 20% among groups such as inner-city teenagers. The FDA has recommended standardized and simplified instructions to manufacturers of oral contraceptives.

For current users of oral contraceptives there is no significant increased risk of fatal heart attacks. The risk increases dramatically for women who smoke. The Pill reduces the risk of both endometrial and ovarian cancers.

What are risk factors associated with the Pill? One risk factor has been an increase in both fatal and nonfatal heart attacks (myocardial infarction). In a study of the relationship of newer low-dose oral contraceptive use to fatal heart attacks, it was found that the risk was 1.1 for current use of oral contraceptives. The overall risk for both current and past use of the Pill, was estimated to be 1.9. The relative risk was greatly increased for those using preparations containing 50 mg of estrogen (4.2) as compared with current use of any other oral contraceptive or nonuse. The risk for women who were currently smoking increased dramatically to 19.3 (Thorogood, Mann, Murphy, & Vessey, 1991). My advice to any woman who smokes is not to take oral contraceptives, or, better yet, use oral contraceptives but quit smoking. The relative risk of a fatal hemorrhage stroke associated with low-dose oral contraceptives was estimated to be 1.1 for current use and 1.3 for ever use (Thorogood, Mann, Murphy, & Vessey, 1992). The risk of an occlusive stroke (due to blockage of blood vessels) for current use was 1.3 and for ever use was 4.4.

The good news about that Pill is that it reduces the risk of both endometrial and ovarian cancers. The risk of endometrial cancer can be reduced by about 50% by the use of combination oral contraceptives (Grimes & Economy, 1995). Low dose estrogen and high dose progestin oral contraceptives confer the greatest protection against endometrial cancer. Oral contraceptives also reduce the risk of ovarian cancer by about 30% to 60%, the protective effect increasing with longer duration of use.

What is the relation of the use of oral contraceptives to sexually transmitted diseases?

The risk of cervical clamydial infections is higher among women who use oral contraceptives as compared with women who do not. On the other hand, sexually active women on the Pill are half as likely to be hospitalized for pelvic inflammatory disease (PID) than their counterparts not using contraceptives. The association between HIV infection and oral contraceptive use is not yet clear at this time. The research is conflicting, some of the studies showing higher incidence of acquisition of HIV among oral contraceptive users and other studies not showing such an association (D. M. Potts, 1992).

Norplant

An alternative to taking oral contraceptives is the Norplant subdermal implant system which lasts five years.

An alternative to taking oral contraceptives is the **Norplant subdermal implant system,** which consists of six silicone capsules containing levonorgestrel, a progestogen. Insertion into the arm

is done by a physician using local anesthesia. Contraceptive effects last for five years. After five years of use by 97 Singapore women, it was found that Norplant use does not appear to activate the coagulation system that has been related to increased risk of thromboembolic complications (such as heart attacks) (K. Singh, Viegas, Koh, & Ratnam, 1992). A problem that has arisen in the United States is difficulty in removing the Norplant, requiring surgery.

Depo-Provera

Depo-provera is a highly effective injectable contraceptive that is a progestin. It is typically given in three-month doses.

Depo-provera is an injectable contraceptive that is a progestin. It works by preventing gonadotropin production in the pituitary, which inhibits ovulation. Effects reducing fertility also act on the production of cervicle mucus, on the fallopian tubes, and on the lining of the uterus (Yanoshik & Norsigian, 1989). It is typically given in a three-month dosage of 150 mg, which gradually increases in concentration, peaking at around 13 weeks. Although it is a highly effective contraceptive, the disadvantage is that if a woman suffers from adverse effects, then she cannot withdraw it from her bloodstream, and must wait for the drug to gradually leave her system. The most common side effect is a disturbance of the menstrual cycle such as frequent bleeding and/or spotting or an absence of bleeding. "Other effects reported include headaches, backaches, abdominal discomfort, weight gain, skin disorders, tiredness, nausea, depression, hair loss, loss of libido, diarrhea, and delayed return to fertility. (Yanoshik & Norsigian, 1989, p. 80).

Intrauterine Device

The Dalkon Shield was associated with pelvic infection and even death.

The intrauterine device (IUD) has a long history. Anthropological evidence indicates that such devices were used by preliterate people.

Casanova recommended a gold ball. In the late nineteenth century some physicians tried its use, but it was not until the 1960s that IUDs began to be widely used (J. F. Potts & Diggory, 1983).

Between 1970 and 1975, a large IUD—the Dalkon shield, which covered most of the uterine cavity—was marketed. It had a low expulsion and pregnancy rate that made it a popular method. Within five years, however, use became associated with serious infection and in some cases death. In 1975 the Dalkon Shield was withdrawn from the market, but not before over 4,000 women had filed a lawsuit against A. H. Robbins, the manufacturer (J. F. Potts & Diggory, 1983). "In the United States alone the Shield killed at least twenty women, and worldwide tens of thousands of women have been seriously injured. In just five years over 4.5 million devices were distributed in eighty countries (Mintz, 1985)" (Yanoshik & Norsigian, 1989, p. 73). By the deadline for filing claims against the company, over 300,000 claims had been made by women from over 30 countries.

Among IUDs currently on the market in the United States are ParaGard T380A, which is a T-shaped plastic partially covered by copper and remains effective for eight years; and Progestasert, also T-shaped, which contains a progestin released over one year. The failure rate for both of these IUDs is 4–5% (M. S. Goldberg, 1993).

The rate of PID over the course of a year is the same for women using a regular IUD and women using a stringless IUD. In a multinational study, 1,265 women were randomly assigned to use a Copper T IUD with a polyethylene string and an identical IUD without a string. The same percentage of women in the two groups were diagnosed with a sexually transmitted disease (17% each) or with PID (4% each). The women with the standard IUD with the string were, however, more likely to have had their IUD removed for breakthrough bleeding or pain. The researchers believe that PID in IUD users is most likely due to contamination of the uterine cavity when the IUD is inserted rather than to contamination from the string in the cervical canal.

Although some problems have been associated with postpartum IUD insertion, research indicates that it is safe with a low incidence of infection, and low perforation rates. Unplanned pregnancy rates range from 2.0 to 2.8 per 100 users at 24 months for postpartum insertions (O'Hanley & Huber, 1992).

Spermicides

Spermicidal cream, jelly, or aerosol has a theoretical failure rate of 3% and an actual failure rate of 21%. It is recommended that spermicides be used with a condom.

Spermicidal cream, jelly, or aerosol foam are available without prescriptions at drugstores. The theoretical failure rate is 3%, with an actual failure rate of 21%. More spermicide must be inserted into the vagina every time the couple has intercourse, no matter how recent the last time was. The only side-effect is that spermicides may cause irritation to some vaginas and penises. When used with a condom, contraceptive effectiveness becomes nearly 100% (Boston Women's Health Book Collective, 1992).

Spermicides, particularly those containing non-oxynol-9, can reduce the risk of acquiring AIDS and a variety of sexually transmitted diseases (Bourinbaiar & Lee-Huang, 1994; d'Oro, et al., 1994). Many high-risk women are unfamiliar with spermicides. Minority women seeking services at a family planning clinic who were educated about spermicides and how to use them, subsequently used spermicides more than three times as often, on average, as a control group of women (D. Cohen, Reardon, Alleyne, Murthy, & Linton, 1995).

Barrier Methods

Diaphragms, cervical caps and contraceptive sponges are barrier methods of contraception combined with spermicides.

Diaphragms, cervical caps and contraceptive sponges are barrier methods to contraception that are used by about 2.4 million women in the United States (Trussell, Strickler, & Vaughn,

1993). They block sperm from going into the cervical canal. Diaphragms and cervical caps are used with spermicidal jelly or cream that kills the sperm. Diaphragms and cervical caps must be fitted by a physician. They reduce the probability of getting gonorrhea or trichomoniasis infections and increase protection against PID.

Clinical studies comparing the failure rate of the contraceptive sponge or the diaphragm (1,439 randomly assigned women) or the cervical cap or the diaphragm (1,394 randomly assigned women) found first year failure rates during typical use of 17% for the sponge, 18% for the cervical cap, and 13–17% for the diaphragm. "The probability of failure during perfect use is significantly higher among women who have given birth than among those who have not for users of the sponge (19–20% vs. 9–10%) and users of the cervical cap (26–27% vs. 8–10%), but not for users of the diaphragm" (Trussell et al., 1993). Among women who had a child, the diaphragm yielded perfect use first year failure rates of 3% and 14% in the two studies.

Women sometimes forget to use spermicide with the diaphragm, or forget to take it out of the drawer and insert it before intercourse which is called "the bureau drawer effect." Contraceptive sponges are no longer on the market.

Sterilization

Sterilization is accomplished by tubal ligation in women. Strict guidelines have been set up by medicaid to prevent poor women from being pressured into being sterilized.

Sterilization is the most common form of contraception for married couples in the United States. Female sterilization is usually accomplished by tubal ligation, in which the fallopian tubes are cut and tied or blocked. It is a nearly 100% effective method for preventing pregnancy. Poor and minority women have been frequently pressured into sterilization or even the recipients of tubal ligation or hysterectomy without their knowledge. Feminists have organized to prevent sterilization abuses, which led to federal guidelines as of March 9, 1979, regulating sterilization.

Medicaid has set up strict guidelines to prevent pressure for sterilization of poor women.

For example, Medicaid patients must be 21 years of age or older, must sign a lengthy consent form that is valid for only 180 days, and must wait 30 days after signing the form before undergoing the procedure (72 hours in the event of a preterm delivery). Medicaid regulations also explicitly require that the woman receive counseling about alternative methods of birth control. (Ramos & Huggins, 1991, p. 38)

Tubal sterilization has a failure rate of approximately 1 in 250–300. The mortality rate due to the procedure is approximately 3–4 per 100,000 cases. The risk of ectopic pregnancy if fertilization occurs is 15–20% and as high as 50% of pregnancies after laparoscopic tubal coagulation procedure. Estimates are that between 3% and 25% of sterilized women regret having the procedure. A risk factor for later regret is marital discord at the time of sterilization. Only 1–2% of women eventually request a reversal of the procedure, the most common reason cited being remarriage. Not all women making the request are candidates for reversal—only 30–70%, and the success rate among those women is about 70–80% (Ramos & Huggins, 1991).

ABORTION

Abortion Rates

About 1.5 million abortions are performed in the United States every year. During her lifetime, about one in five women will have an abortion.

About half of the unintended pregnancies in the United States every year are aborted. In 1992, 1,529,000 abortions were performed. Since 1979 there has been a gradual decline in the number of abortions performed each year. During the course of her lifetime, about one out of five women will have an abortion (Cohan, Dunkel-Schetter, & Lydon, 1993; Henshaw & Van Vort, 1994).

Abortion has been a politically charged issue since the 1960s, when pro-choice advocates begin lobbying to overturn the restrictive abortion laws in effect in almost all of the states in the United States. "The debate centers on the fundamental choice between competing rights: the government's right to protect human life and a woman's right to make one of the most important decisions of her life—whether and when to have a child" (Blumenthal, 1991, p. 17). In 1973, The Supreme Court, in its *Roe v Wade* decision, said that the abortion decision is protected by the right of privacy and made abortion legal for any reason during the first trimester of gestation (Adler et al., 1992). Later in pregnancy, however, the state was given the right to regulate abortion and to prohibit it unless it is necessary to preserve the life and health of the mother.

Abortion Clients

Who gets abortions? Mostly young unmarried women, the majority of whom are White, although minorities are disproportionately represented.

The women who get abortions are mostly young and unmarried. Over two-thirds (69%) are under 30. Sixty-three percent have never been married, 19% are married, 11% divorced, 6% separated, and 1% widowed. They are of poor to modest means. One-third (33%) have annual incomes of less than $11,000, and another third (34%) have incomes between $11,000 and $24,999. The overwhelming majority (86%) have abortions performed in clinics. Only 10% have abortions performed in hospitals, and 4% are performed in doctor's offices. More Whites (65%) have abortions than minorities (35%), but since Whites are 83% of the population in the United States and minorities 17%, a disproportionate number of minorities have abortions (Mauro, 1992).

The Decision to Abort

Four variables are predictive of the abortion decision: intendedness of conception; acceptability of abortion; adjustability of child-bearing; and independent decision making.

What is the decision-making process involved in terminating a pregnancy versus carrying to term an unintended pregnancy? A model of psychological antecedents of having an abortion has found support for four variables predictive of the abortion decision: intendedness of conception; acceptability of abortion; adjustability of child-bearing; and the decision process (W. B. Miller, 1992). Women who did not intend the conception, for whom abortion was acceptable both in her own viewpoint and that of her family, who were not married or who were but did not intend to have a child until far in the future, and women who were independent minded and therefore more likely to make an active decision, were more likely to have an abortion.

Eighty-seven women seeking pregnancy testing in a low-cost gynecologic and prenatal clinic were interviewed just prior to the pregnancy testing, a day after receiving positive test results, and one month later (Cohan et al., 1993). Prior to the pregnancy testing, the majority of the women (78%) said that they had already made their decision about whether to abort or carry to term, and 22% were undecided. Only one woman did not carry out her original decision. The undecided women who aborted their pregnancies and the decided aborters had more stress at the time of the pregnancy test and shortly after the results were received, as compared with those carrying their pregnancies. Negative feelings at the time of the pregnancy test by the aborters subsided, and there were no differences in negative affect between the aborters and those carrying the pregnancy by the one month follow-up.

Psychological Effects of Abortion

The psychological effects of abortion are not different from those for women postpartum. Women who have positive psychological outcomes are those who have good relationships and have high self esteem.

Women have elective abortions for three types of reasons. Some women have an abortion because they never want to have a child. For others, it is not the right time in their lives and they feel it would not be best for themselves or the child to continue the pregnancy, although at some time in the future they would like to have a child. The third group of women who get an abortion are the "tired" mothers who underwent sterilization after terminating a pregnancy (Minden & Notman, 1991). For another group of women abortion is labeled "therapeutic" when carrying the pregnancy to term would endanger the mother's health or even life. The 1989 Surgeon General's Report concluded that there was insufficient evidence to conclude that abortion did or did not cause negative psychological effects and called for longitudinal prospective research (Blumenthal, 1991; Wilmoth, de Alteriis, & Bussell, 1992).

A review of the psychological literature by an expert panel appointed by the American Psychological Association (APA) concluded that "abortion is not likely to be followed by severe psychological responses and that psychological aspects can best be understood within a framework of normal stress and coping rather than a model of psychopathology" (Adler et al., 1992, p. 1194). In Denmark, where highly accurate abortion and psychiatric hospitalization records are kept, David, Rasmussen, and Holst (1981) found that the psychiatric hospitalization rate of 1.8 per 1,000 for married and never-married women who had abortions was not significantly different from the rate of 1.2 per 1,000 married and never-married women who delivered. In Great Britain the rate of postabortion psychosis (.3 per 1,000) was found to be significantly less than the rate of postpartum psychosis (1.7 per 1,000) (C. Brewer, 1977).

Meta-analyses of studies of psychological effects of abortion found that across studies including both elective and therapeutic abortions, women having abortions had more negative psychological outcomes than women in the comparison groups. When the data was further analyzed by type of abortion (elective vs. therapeutic), it was found that although women having therapeutic abortions had more negative psychological outcomes, women having elective abortions had more positive psychological outcomes than women in comparison groups (Wilmoth et al., 1992).

Some women, however, are at greater psychological risk following an abortion than are others. These women are those who have negative relations with their mothers, children, husbands, or lovers; women who have strongly ambivalent feelings about pregnancy and abortion; women who are younger and unmarried and without children; women who have second trimester abortions; women who feel they were coerced into having the abortion by their husband/ boyfriend; women who suffer events subsequent to the abortion such as inability to get pregnant later; and women with poorer levels of psychological functioning prior to the abortion (Adler et al., 1992; Blumenthal, 1991; Major & Cozzarelli, 1992; W. B. Miller, 1992; Minden & Notman, 1991). Improved contraceptive practice following abortion was associated with the absence of postabortion regret. Counseling programs need to focus on the relationships of the woman, problems with her husband/boyfriend, her postabortion use of contraception, and what she learned from the experience.

What are the psychological factors that are predictors of effective coping with the abortion experience? A study of 291 English-speaking women who were obtaining a first-trimester abortion at a clinic and were followed-up a few weeks later found that optimism (the tendency to expect good things to happen), perceptions of perceived control (the tendency to feel personal control in coping with situations), and high self-esteem were all related to better postabortion adjustment. This relationship was mediated by self-efficacy, on both immediate and three-week postabortion psychological adjustment. Self-efficacy is the perception that one is capable of achieving desired outcomes in a specific situation or on a task (Bandura, 1977). Possessing one of the personality variables, optimism, perception of perceived control, and high self-esteem were highly intercorrelated, so that possession of one of these characteristics alone is nearly as effective in producing a favorable outcome as is possessing all three. More efforts need to be made in counseling women both pre-and postabortion to strive to develop feelings of optimism, high self-esteem, and self-efficacy in the women in a variety of dimensions.

Zabin, Hirsch, and Emerson (1989) compared 360 Black adolescents who received positive or negative pregnancy tests. Further comparisons were made between those who were pregnant and carried to term and those who chose abortion. All of the adolescents had higher levels of anxiety at the time of the initial interview as compared with the follow-up one to two years later. After two years, the teenagers who had obtained abortions were far more likely to have graduated from high school or still be in school at the appropriate grade level and to be better off economically. They were less likely to have experienced a subsequent pregnancy, and were slightly more likely to practice contraception. They were no more likely to have psychological problems. Thus, overall, the teenagers who had abortions were better off than those who carried to term.

Barriers to Abortion

Many barriers exist to obtaining abortions in the United States, such as lack of doctors and facilities performing abortions, and cost. A strong antiabortion bloc in the United States continues to fight to make abortion illegal.

Despite a high level of national support for abortion (67% in 1993 in the General Social Survey of the National Opinion Research Center, Chicago, supported a women's right to abortion for any reason), a bloc of Catholic and fundamental Protestant antiabortionists continue to fight to make it illegal. In the United States, many factors make it difficult to obtain an abortion (Henshaw & Van Vort, 1994). Unlike in most developed countries, where abortions are performed primarily in hospitals, about two-thirds of abortions in the United States are performed in specialized clinics where abortion is the main service provided. "As a proportion of all providers, hospitals decreased from 40% in 1988 to 36% in 1992; in 1973, 81% of all providers were hospitals" (Henshaw & Van Vort, 1994, p. 104). Hospitals tend to provide few abortions, usually

performing them when the mother's life or health is threatened.

The murders of two doctors and two Planned Parenthood receptionists and the shootings of Planned Parenthood clients and staff as well as the harassment by Right to Life groups who picket both clinics and the doctors' homes has led to fewer facilities performing abortions. As a result many women have to travel long distances to obtain an abortion because there are no abortion services in many rural and smaller metropolitan areas. In 1992, 82% of all U.S. counties had no abortion provider. Even among metropolitan counties, 51% had no abortion services. Between 1982 and 1992, the number of abortion providers declined by 18% (Henshaw & Van Vort, 1994).

In addition, the fees charged for abortions can put the procedure out of reach of many women. In 1989, the average fee for a nonhospital abortion was $251, and an abortion at 10 weeks gestation in a hospital cost an average of $1,757. Delay caused by time needed to acquire the money in order to obtain an abortion is one cause of seeking abortions past the first trimester. Only 43% of facilities will permit abortions past the first trimester. Also, 27–37% of abortion clinics say they will not treat patients who test positive for the human immunodeficiency virus (HIV). Antiabortion harassment is reported by 85% of clinics that serve 400 or more patients in a year (Henshaw, 1991). All of these factors serve as barriers for women in obtaining medical abortions.

Estimates of the American Public Health Association are that in the 1960s, before abortion was legalized in the United States, at least 1 million women a year had abortions. Many women had severe medical complications resulting from these abortions; in 1965, 235 (20%) of all maternal deaths were abortion-related. A decrease of approximately 90% in these adverse outcomes occurred following legalization of abortion. According to the U.S. Centers for Disease Control and the National Center for Health Statistics, the risk of dying from medical abortion is only one-twenty-fifth of that of dying from carrying a pregnancy to term (Stotland, 1991). Ninety percent of abortions are performed during the first trimester and only 1% are performed after 20 weeks.

RU-486

RU-486 is a pill that induces abortion.

The antiabortion bloc also delayed FDA approval of **RU-486** (mifepristone), a pill that induces abortion. RU-486, discovered in France by scientist Etienne-Emile Baulieu, has induced abortion in over 100,000 French women as well as in other countries such as China and Great Britain (Lader, 1991). RU-486 blocks the hormone progesterone and thus prevents preparation of the uterus for implantation of the ovum. Legalization of RU-486 in the United States would reduce the use of surgical abortion. The woman has to make a second trip to the doctor's office or clinic, however, to receive a follow-up prostaglandin (substance that causes uterine contractions).

MENOPAUSE

Menopausal Symptoms

There are widely differing reports by women of the prevalence of menopausal symptoms. Estrogen replacement therapy or hormone replacement therapy (estrogen and progesterone) can relieve the symptoms of menopause.

Menopause, also called the climacteric or in common parlance "change of life," is clinically defined as absence of menses for one year. Before menopause occurs, the ovaries produce less and less estrogen. The menstrual cycle usually becomes irregular and in some cycles no egg may be released. After menopause some estrogen continues to be produced by peripheral tissues such as blood, liver, and fat. Menopause normally occurs between 40 and 60, with the average age being 51. Two centuries ago only 30% of women lived long enough to even reach menopause, compared with 90% today. There are currently 30 million postmenopausal American women

with a life expectancy of 28 years beyond the climacteric (Plunkett & Wolfe, 1992).

How common are the physical symptoms of menopause? It is commonly reported in the literature that about 85% of women have some physiological symptoms, with only 10–30% seeking treatment for them. A much lower reporting of menopausal symptoms was found in a study of European American and Japanese American women in Hawaii (Goodman, Stewart, & Gilbert, 1977) found that 28% percent of 170 postmenopausal European American women and 24% of 159 postmenopausal Japanese American women reported traditional symptoms such as hot flashes, sweats, and so on, on general medical history forms completed at the time of an annual multiphasic health screening in connection with healthcare needs, not specifically associated with the menopausal state. Thus, approximately three-quarters of postmenopausal women did not report any menopausal physical symptoms. These same symptoms were also reported by 16% of 162 European American premenopausal women and 10% of 187 Japanese American premenopausal women.

Results from a survey responded to by 15,000 readers of *Prevention* magazine found that 58% described the menopause as "somewhat bothersome." The most frequently reported symptoms of menopause were weight gain, sleep problems and hot flashes. Women who reach menopause at a younger age report more symptoms than those who reach menopause later (Perlmutter, Hanlon, & Sangiorgio, 1994). Lifestyle factors associated with a more positive menopause experience were low levels of stress and exercising three or more times a week. Postmenopausal women, however, indicated a significantly higher frequency of arthritis, surgery for female disorder, and use of medication.

The most common symptoms of postmenopausal women are hot flashes—when a feeling of warmth comes over the woman and her face, neck, and chest may flush—and night sweats—where she may wake up at night sweating. Urogenital atrophy, which includes thinning and drying of the vaginal mucosa and complaints of urinary frequency and urgency, also eventually occurs in most women. The most serious result of menopause is the onset of osteoporosis, a decrease in skeletal bone mass (Stuenkel, 1989).

Estrogen-Replacement Therapy and Hormone-Replacement Therapy

Relief from menopausal symptoms can be achieved through estrogen replacement therapy (ERT) or hormone replacement therapy (HRT).

The book, *Feminine Forever,* by Robert Wilson appeared in 1966, trumpeting the benefits of estrogen replacement for postmenopausal women by promoting the idea that it would keep them feminine and sexual. Wilson was a prominent gynecologist who was also the head of the Wilson Foundation, which was supported by 1.3 millions in grants from pharmaceutical firms. Doctors began prescribing estrogen for postmenopausal women until two articles appeared in the *New England Journal of Medicine* linking estrogen with endometrial (lining of the uterus) cancer.

Low estrogen is the cause of menopausal symptoms described earlier, and relief can be achieved through **estrogen replacement therapy (ERT)** or **hormone replacement therapy (HRT)** estrogen and progestin in combination. It has been found that estrogen given without natural progesterone or synthetic progestin causes changes in the lining of the uterus that can progress to endometrial cancer. The relative risk can be as much as 12 times as great for someone taking estrogen for a period of years without progesterone. The addition of progesterone reduces the risk of uterine cancer to 1.0 or lower (Plunkett & Wolfe, 1992; Stuenkel, 1989).

HRT, however, can cause side effects. These side effects are very unpredictable. The most commonly reported side effect is fluid retention, causing about 2% of women to stop taking HRT. Breast tenderness is usually a temporary side effect when it occurs. Other symptoms such as anxiety, irritability, and depressed mood may be experienced by some women during the phase when they are taking progesterone. These symptoms may disappear after several months for many women. Weight gain is also reported by some women. This may be a result of fluid retention or the normal tendency to put on weight postmenopausally. A number of other symptoms may be fleetingly experienced by some women such as nausea, headaches, and increased vaginal discharge (Landau, Cyr, & Moulton, 1994). Any woman experiencing these symptoms when on HRT should discuss them with the prescribing physician.

Estrogen Administration

A more efficient route of HRT is transdermal therapy.

In addition to being taken in pill form, HRT may also enter the body transdermally (through a patch worn on the body). In a comparison of transdermal and oral estrogen–progestin replacement therapy, it was found that both methods reduced low-density lipoprotein cholesterol (LDL); high-density lipoproteins (HDL) were largely unchanged. Oral therapy, however, increased triglycerides, while this lipid was lowered with transdermal therapy (Crook et al., 1992). Oral estrogen is not the most efficient route because of poor gastrointestinal absorption. Oral estrogen administration has also been found to be related to a 2.5 times increased risk of gallbladder disease (Steunkel, 1989). The transdermal method bypasses both the intestine and the liver, and might be a preferable method (Gannon, 1990).

HRT and Heart Disease

Women who take postmenopausal estrogen have half the risk of dying from heart attacks as women who had never used estrogen.

A prospective (follow-up) study of 48,470 women observed from 1976 to 1986 by the Nurses' Health Study found that postmenopausal estrogen users had about half the risk of major coronary disease and/or fatal cardiovascular disease and no increase in the risk of stroke as compared with women who had never used estrogen (Stampfer et al., 1991). At the beginning of the study, women were excluded who had cancer or cardio-vascular disease.

A random sample survey of 2,000 Finnish women aged 45–64 years old compared past users and nonusers with current users of ERT or HRT and concluded that "there are two selection processes resulting in healthier women using hormone therapy: one involving the initiation and the other the continuation of therapy" (Hemminki, Malin & Topo, 1993, p. 217). Hemminiki et al. also review other studies that point to nonusers as having a poorer health prognosis to begin with based on factors such as higher cholesterol level, blood pressure and blood sugar levels. Thus, some of the effect of ERT on CHD may be due to selective factors for better health of those who go on ERT.

Review of the literature on ERT finds that 14 of 15 other prospective studies have also reported that postmenopausal estrogen use is associated with a decreased risk of coronary disease. Too few of the women in the study (2.7%) were taking progestin in combination with estrogen to determine the effects of taking estrogen alone as compared with estrogen combined with progestin. In analyses of total mortality, in women with any estrogen use, an age-adjusted relative risk of 0.81 and a multivariate relative risk of 0.89 was found (M. J. Stampfer et al., 1991).

HRT keeps LDL from rising.

How does HRT act on the body to reduce the risk of heart attack? A prospective study was conducted of 541 premenopausal women age 42–50, who returned for a follow-up clinic visit three years later (Egeland et al., 1990). The estrogen and estrogen–progestogen users had minimal increases in LDL cholesterol levels. Nonusers, however, had significant increases in LDL over that time period. Estrogen users had a nonsignificant increase in HDL cholesterol and estrogen-progestogen users maintained premenopausal HDL cholesterol levels. Nonusers, however, had slightly greater, but nonsignificant, increases in HDL cholesterol levels. A significant increase in triglycerides was found for the hormone-re-placement-therapy groups. This increase in triglycerides is difficult to interpret because the independent relationship of triglycerides to heart disease has not been established. Estrogen could provide cardiovascular benefits to postmenopausal women by protecting against the changes in LDL cholesterol observed among the nonusers.

Does progestin administration in any way interfere with the changes in lipids and lipoproteins as a result of estrogen administration? To answer this question, V. T. Miller et al. (1994) randomized 103 postmenopausal women into a control group and two groups receiving 0.625 mg or 1.25 mg of conjugated equine estrogen, respectively, for four months, and then added progestin along with the estrogen for eight months. The research confirmed previous findings that beneficial changes occur in the levels of LDL and HDL cholesterol and the LDL–HDL cholesterol ratio with both the 0.625-mg and the 1.25-mg estrogen doses, although they occur to a greater extent with the 1.25 dose. Addition of the progestin (medroxprogesterone) to either estrogen-treatment group reversed the estrogen-induced increase in HDL to near baseline levels by eight months. Cross-sectional studies have demonstrated, however, that women taking estrogen–progestin combination for three years or more did not have lower levels of HDL than women not taking estrogen (Barrett-Connor, Wingard, & Criqui, 1989; C. Christiansen & Riis, 1990; Gambrell & Teran, 1991).

Significant declines in total cholesterol levels and significant increases in the HDL cholesterol–LDL cholesterol ratio are found for both estrogen-replacement and exercise treatment groups.

Research evaluating the independent effects of exercise and estrogen found significant reductions in lipids and lipoproteins in postmenopausal women for both exercise and conjugated equine estrogen groups at six months compared with baseline (Lindheim et al., 1994). "All three treated groups (exercise, conjugated equine estrogen, and conjugated equine estrogen with exercise) had decreased LDL cholesterol levels compared to baseline and to the control group (-10%, $P < .01$; -14.1%, $P < .001$; -8.7%, $P < .001$; versus controls 6.3%, $P < .001$)" (Lindheim et al., 1994, p. 170). At the beginning of the study all women were sedentary and were not taking hormone replacement therapy of any kind. Participants randomized to the two exercise groups walked on a treadmill and pedaled a stationary bicycle three times per week for 30 minutes. During the study, participants did not take progestin. In addition to significant decreases from baseline in total cholesterol, significant increases for the HDL cholesterol–LDL cholesterol ratio were found for all groups except the control group. Significant decreases in systolic blood pressure were also found for all treatment groups. The exercise-alone group was the only one that showed significantly lowered triglyceride levels. Combined conjugated equine estrogen and exercise did not surpass exercise alone in cardiorespiratory fitness or in changes seen in lipids or lipoproteins. For women who cannot take estrogen replacement therapy, exercise can be an effective alternative.

Physicians greatly increased HRT prescriptions in the 1980s. Women on HRT still get periods. A new low dose HRT program eliminates monthly bleeding.

Physician's increased recognition of the benefits of HRT led to a 43% increase in estrogen prescriptions dispensed in the United States from 14 million in 1980 to 20 million in 1986. One survey found a current usage rate of 32 percent among women in the 50–65 age group (Harris et al., 1990 as cited in Brinton & Schairer, 1993). One of the reasons physicians do not prescribe it, however, is because there is a continuance of periods when progestin is also taken. Sometimes, the periods may be painful and the bleeding heavy. In the words of my gynecologist, "Little old ladies of 80 don't want to still be getting a period."

A new HRT program has been found, however, which virtually eliminates spotting and bleeding, but still provides the benefits of HRT in reducing morbidity and mortality from heart dis-

ease and osteoporosis-related fractures. To date this has been accomplished in a pilot study with 18 postmenopausal women with climacteric symptoms in which low doses of norgestrel (0.75 mg/day) were given daily and estradiol (1 mg/day) was given 25 out of 28 days for three years (Plunkett & Wolfe, 1992). This HRT program virtually eliminated spotting and bleeding. It also eliminated hot flashes, which may be recurrent during the 7 days off the estrogen during the typical HRT regimen. There was a 23% mean decrease in LDL cholesterol, as well as a 13% decrease in HDL cholesterol for an overall favorable decrease in the ratios of LDL cholesterol–HDL cholesterol. Blood levels of triglycerides fell 31%. There was no change in bone density over the three-year period, which is in contrast to the bone loss expected in postmenopausal women not receiving estrogen.

HRT and Breast Cancer

Long-term HRT use and HRT use by women with a family history of breast cancer increases the risk of breast cancer.

The good news about HRT is its role in the reduction of heart disease and prevention of osteoporosis. The bad news is its role in increased risk of breast cancer for women who have used HRT long term or who have a family history of breast cancer. A prospective study in Sweden of 23,244 women 35 years of age or older (median age, 53.7 years) who took noncontraceptive estrogen for menopausal symptoms were found to have an increased risk of breast cancer compared with those who did not take HRT (Bergvist, Adami, Persson, Hoover, & Schairer 1989). After their inclusion in the study, during the follow-up period (mean, 5.7 years), 253 women developed invasive breast cancer. Overall, there was a relative risk of 1.1 (10% greater risk) of breast cancer among women who had post-menopausal exposure to estrogens. This risk increased with the increase in the length of time of estrogen exposure, to an excess risk of 1.7 (70% greater risk) in women with more than nine years of use.

Risk was also calculated separately for the type of estrogen used and the presence of progestin. Estradiol, a potent form of estrogen, was the most common form used by the women in the study. Estradiol risk was greater than that for the overall estrogen risk, showing a doubling in the relative risk of breast cancer after six or more years of use. There was no association found, however, between weaker estrogens (estriols) and the development of breast cancer. Nor was there an increased risk of breast cancer with the use of conjugated estrogens (which are commonly used in the United States). The doses of conjugated estrogens in this cohort was lower (0.625 mg), however, than that commonly used in the United States (1.25 mg or more). The risk of breast cancer was highest (4.4) for those women who took estrogen and progestin in combination for more than six years. This group consisted of only a small subsample, so the authors point to the need for further research investigating the possibility that adding progestin to estrogen therapy may increase the risk of breast cancer.

A meta-analysis of the effect of estrogen replacement therapy on the risk of breast cancer, based on 16 studies in which the estrogen was prescribed for any menopausal (natural or surgical) and not contraceptive purposes, did not find an increased risk of breast cancer until at least five years of estrogen use (K. K. Steinberg et al., 1991). After 15 years of estrogen use the relative risk increased to 1.3 (30% greater risk). Women with a family history of breast cancer who had ever used estrogen replacement had a significantly higher risk (3.4 or 340% greater risk) than those who had not (1.5 or 50% greater risk).

The follow-up of participants on the Nurses' Health Study was extended to 1992, making it possible to include data on women taking estrogen and progestin preparations (Colditz et al., 1995). During 725,550 person-years of follow-up, 1935 new cases of invasive breast cancer occurred. The relative risk of breast cancer was significantly elevated among women currently using estrogens alone (adjusted relative risk 1.32) or estrogen plus progestin (adjusted relative risk 1.4) and progestins alone (adjusted relative risk 2.24). The relative risk of breast cancer was not significantly different among the three groups. The relative risk of breast cancer was at least as high at every age for women taking estrogen plus progestin as for those taking estrogen alone. The increase in risk for breast cancer was only for women who had been on hormone therapy for five or more years and was highest among the oldest women.

> As compared with postmenopausal women who had never taken hormones, and after controlling for the age at menopause, the type of menopause, and family history, the relative risk of breast cancer among postmenopausal women who used hormones was 1.54 . . . for those 55 to 59 years of age for those who had taken hormones for five or more years. For women 60 to 64 years of age, the relative risk was 1.71. (Colditz et al., 1995, p. 1591)

Women who had received hormone therapy in the past but were no longer taking it were not at increased risk.

A much lower risk of breast cancer was found by a meta-analysis of 27 studies, which revealed an overall relative risk of 1.06 (Sillero-Arenas et al., 1992). A higher risk was found for natural menopause, an overall relative risk of 1.13 as compared with surgical menopause (premenopausal surgical removal of ovaries and uterus) for which there was no significant increase of risk. Women with natural menopause who were on HRT for more than 12 years showed a significant 63% increase in breast cancer risk. The reason for the higher risk of HRT relative to breast cancer in women with natural menopause is that the ovaries gradually decline in estrogen production; therefore, postmenopausal women's ovaries are still producing some estrogen. Research has reported that women with breast cancer have higher serum estradiol levels and more urinary estradiol and estriol excretion than similar women who do not have breast cancer (Bernstein, Ross, Pike, Brown, & Henderson, 1990). It may be sensible to measure a women's blood levels of estrogens before making a decision whether to prescribe HRT. Research does show a 20–40% lower mortality rate from breast cancer among women on ERT compared with nonusers who developed breast cancer. This may be due to more frequent physical exams and mammography among ERT users (Lafferty & Fiske, 1994).

Mortality and HRT

On balance, death rates of postmenopausal women would decline with the use of long-term estrogen replacement therapy.

A hypothetical, population-based analysis to assess the value of estrogen replacement therapy among a cohort of 10,000 women at age 50 years concluded that estrogen use for 25 years would prevent 574 deaths as compared with nonuse.

Estrogen use for 25 years would decrease fatal coronary heart disease events by 48% (567 cases), decrease death from hip fracture by 49% (75), increase deaths from breast cancer by 21% (39), and increase deaths from endometrial cancer by 207% (29 excess deaths). . . . Sensitivity analysis suggests that the benefits of estrogen replacement therapy outweigh the risks under most assumptions. (Gorsky, Koplan, Peterson, & Thacker, 1994)

The model focused on estrogen replacement therapy without the use of progestins because of the lack of studies of the long-term health effects of progestin use after age 50. One problem that has been reported is that depression in menopausal women has been linked to progestogen, which is given along with estrogen in HRT. The symptoms of progestogen-induced depression may be severe, including suicidal ideation (Wheatley, 1991).

An alternative to estrogen for treatment of hot flashes is megestrol acetate, a progestational agent (Loprinzi et al., 1994). A trial of megestrol acetate with 97 women with a history of breast cancer found that hot flashes were reduced 85% as compared with only 21% for the placebo group. The megestrol acetate was well tolerated.

A review of the literature indicates that HRT may be given to women who are breast cancer survivors in order to improve quality of life as well as to reduce the mortality rate from cardiovascular disease. "A major concern over prescribing ERT for women with a history of breast

cancer is that dormant tumor cells might be activated. There is surprisingly little clinical information to substantiate such concern" (Cobleigh et al., 1994, p. 541).

Since the age-adjusted mortality rate from heart disease is about four times the rate for endometrial and breast cancer, it appears that the benefits of HRT outweigh the risk for most women (K. K. Steinberg et al., 1991). Conditions that prohibit the use of estrogen include a history of cancer of the genitalia, impaired liver function, acute liver disease, and a history of acute vascular thrombosis (Stuenkel, 1989). Prior ovarian cancer or cervical cancer, the presence of known cardiovascular disease, diabetes, or hypertension are not a contraindication to HRT (Shoupe & Mishell, 1994). Whether to use HRT is a decision each individual woman must make for herself in consultation with her physician. I have tried to provide enough research evidence in this chapter to assist a woman in making that choice.

Alternatives to HRT

Alternatives to HRT for menopausal women are improved nutrition, increased physical exercise and relaxation techniques.

If for some reason, a woman does not take HRT, other remedies are vitamin E, increased calcium intake, reduced fat in the diet, and increased physical exercise, which is particularly helpful in preventing osteoporosis and heart disease. A recent meta-analysis of diet and cancer of the breast found a significant relationship between total fat in the diet and breast cancer in both premenopausal and postmenopausal women. "There was a suggestive difference between the risks for the different types of fat, with risks being greater for saturated and monounsaturated fats than for polyunsaturated fat (p = 0.06)" (Doll, 1994, p. 237).

Relaxation techniques may be helpful in reducing hot flashes. To test the hypothesis that hot flashes are frequently associated with stress, Swartzman, Edelberg, and Kemmann (1990) recorded physiological measures (objective) as well as subjective measures of hot flashes during stressful and nonstressful laboratory sessions. There was a significantly greater number of physiological hot flashes recorded during the stress sessions than there were during the nonstress sessions, indicating that stress does increase the occurrence of hot flashes.

Symptoms such as vaginal dryness and irritation, which may make intercourse painful, can be remedied with vaginal creams. Estrogen vaginal creams, while very effective in maintaining the elasticity of the vagina, are absorbed into the body and should not be used by women if there is a contraindication for estrogen use. Nonestrogen moisturizing agents (Gyne-Moistrin, Shering-Plough or Replens, Warner-Lambert) can also be helpful for maintaining the elasticity of the vagina. Nonestrogen lubricants such as Personal Lubricant (Ortho) and Lubrin (Upsher-Smith) can provide the necessary lubrication for intercourse. Frequent sexual intercourse also seems to be a means of maintaining the elasticity and lubrication of the vagina (Nachtigall, 1994).

DIETHYLSTILBESTROL (DES)

DES, a synthetic estrogen, is linked to vaginal cancer, cervical cancer, and reproductive problems in daughters whose mothers used it during pregnancy.

Diethylstilbestrol (DES) is a synthetic estrogen that was first produced in 1938 and prescribed to women for complications of pregnancy and for menopausal symptoms (S. E. Bell, 1992). It has been linked with a rare form of vaginal cancer in daughters whose mothers used it during pregnancy. These daughters also have higher rates of infertility, miscarriage, premature birth, stillbirth, tubal pregnancy, and cervical cancer than do nonexposed daughters. Sons of mothers who took DES have increased risk of genital abnormalities such as undescended testes, low sperm count, and decreased sperm mobility. As part of the women's health movement, DES Action, a national organization, was formed to provide information and support for DES exposed people. It also engages in political activity to restructure

health care. DES argues that informed consent of the mothers was not given. The irony is that DES was not effective in preventing miscarriage.

OSTEOPOROSIS

Osteoporosis is related to half a million arm, vertebral, and hip fractures every year. HRT, calcium, and exercise can improve bone mass.

Osteoporosis, loss of bone mass, is the most serious of the menopausal symptoms. "Each year, 200,000 hip fractures, 100,000 forearm fractures, and 200,000 vertebral fractures are said to be related to osteoporosis" (Travis, 1988a). Osteoporosis, however, may not be the only cause of hip fractures. Among Black women 45 years old or older, other factors associated with hip fracture were a history of stroke, use of aids in walking, and alcohol consumption of seven or more drinks a week (Grisso et al., 1994).

Despite the fact that so many fractures in women over age 50 are due to osteoporosis, little was heard of this disease until recently. Beginning in 1982, however, Ayerst Laboratories sponsored an education campaign in the media to create public awareness of osteoporosis. Their motives were not purely altruistic, however, since Ayerst Laboratories is the maker of Premarin, a popular form of HRT (Whatley & Worcester, 1989). It is the thesis of Whatley and Worcester that the women's health movement has been coopted by the medical establishment when it proves profitable to them. An example is osteoporosis screening that consists of bone mass measurements.

It has been estimated that the majority of women consume less than 50% of the recommended daily allowance for calcium. Research has found that the use of calcium supplements in conjunction with HRT is effective in reducing bone loss at lower doses of estrogen than required without the calcium (Ettinger, Genant, & Cann, 1985). Vitamin D (found in sunshine, fatty fish, fortified milk, and fortified cereals) must be taken with calcium for prevention of osteoporosis. Calcium supplements combined with exercise may be particularly effective in bone protection. When 42 women aged 30–49, who had participated in a running program for two years were compared with 39 sedentary controls, it was found that the sedentary women experienced a significant bone loss, whereas the runners had either stable or increased bone mineral content during that time (C. Brewer, Meyer, Keefe, Upton, & Hagan, 1983). In a study of elderly women aged 69–95, sedentary controls lost a mean of 3.29% of bone mineral over 36 months compared with a mean increase in bone mineral of 2.29% for those in an exercise program (E. L. Smith, Redden, & Smith, 1981).

It has been demonstrated that ERT in postmenopausal women reduces the incidence of osteoporotic fractures (T. D. Spector et al., 1992). Can osteoporosis be reversed in women already suffering from the disorder? Yes. Median bone density increased 11.6% for the spine and 4.3% at the hip for 16 postmenopausal women with low bone mineral density who received percutaneous (under the skin) estradiol (E2) implants for one year (Holland et al., 1994). Biopsies also showed formation of a more mature collagen fiber.

Since menopause is associated with sharp reductions in progesterone as well as estrogen, the role of administration of progestogen on bone loss in postmenopausal women was compared for 35 women who received promegestone (a progestin) or a placebo in a two-year, blind, randomized study (Tremollieres, Pouilles, & Ribot, 1993). After two years, the mean bone mineral density was not different from baseline for the progestin treated women. In comparison, the placebo group had significant bone loss over the two-year period. Progestin treatment may be an alternative for some postmenopausal women who for a variety of reasons may not want to take estrogen.

A study of 980 postmenopausal White women aged 50–98 years found lifetime caffeinated coffee intake of two cups per day to be associated with decreased bone density, if the women do not drink one or more glasses of milk on a daily basis (Barrett-Connor, Chang, & Edelstein, 1994). Bone density was not related to caffeine intake if the women reported drinking at least one glass of milk during most of their adult lives. Previous research has been conflicting about the relationship of osteoporosis to caffeine use, but did not take into account calcium intake.

HYSTERECTOMY

Rates of Hysterectomy

The United States has the highest rate of hysterectomy of any country in the Western World.

Hysterectomy, the removal of the uterus, is second only to caesarean section as the most frequent major surgical procedure performed in the United States. Are all of the hysterectomies performed every year, approximately 590,000 in this country, really necessary? One-third of women will have had a hysterectomy by age 60 (Carlson, Nichols, & Schiff, 1993).

The United States has the highest rate of hysterectomy operations among Western nations, leading to a questioning of monetary motivation. Within the United States, hysterectomy rates are the highest in the South, followed by the Midwest, and higher among male than female gynecologists. Black women have a higher rate of hysterectomy operations than do White women. Do traditional attitudes toward women and racist attitudes play a role in hysterectomy rates? (Carlson et al., 1993; Zussman, Zussman, Sunley, & Bjornson, 1981).

Hysterectomy for Benign Conditions

Most hysterectomies are performed for benign conditions such as fibroids, endometriosis, and prolapse of the uterus. Many of these hysterectomies are not necessary.

A leading reason for hysterectomy is fibroid tumors (leiomyomas), which are solid tumors that are benign (not cancerous) in all cases. Fibroids account for about 30% of hysterectomies. For most women fibroids are symptom free, although some women with fibroids have excessive bleeding, pelvic pain, and symptoms related to pressure on related organs. Since fibroids are affected by estrogen, if a woman waits until menopause, the fibroids will shrink by themselves unless she uses HRT. Are fibroid tumors a good reason to have a hysterectomy? Not when there are no symptoms associated with the fibroids and possible adverse consequences of hysterectomy are considered.

> A range of long-term adverse effects of hysterectomy has been reported, including urinary symptoms, early ovarian failure, the retained ovary syndrome (a poorly understood syndrome of pelvic pain after hysterectomy), constipation, fatigue, changes in sexual interest and function, depression, and other psychiatric morbidity. (Carlson et al., 1993, p. 859)

Another benign condition for which hysterectomies are frequently performed is endometriosis. Approximately 20% of hysterectomies in the United States are performed for endometriosis (Carlson et al., 1993). Endometriosis is a condition in which the endometrial tissue (the tissue of the lining of the uterus) is disseminated by menstrual blood flowing back (retrograde menstruation) through the fallopian tubes into the abdominal cavity. These cells become attached to the organs such as the ovaries, fallopian tubes and broad ligaments and uterosacral ligaments and large bowel.

The most common symptoms of endometriosis are pelvic pain and dysmenorrhea. Pain during or following intercourse is also a frequently reported symptom. Endometriosis also frequently leads to infertility and miscarriage if the woman does get pregnant. The most accurate diagnosis is made by thorough examination of the pelvic cavity by means of a laparoscope.

The endometrial cells are responsive to estrogen and progesterone levels in the body. One treatment is a drug, danazol, which suppresses follicle-stimulating hormone (FSH) and luteinizing hormone (LH), which results in decreased estrogen production by the ovaries. Another pharmacologic approach is to administer GnRH agonists, which initially stimulates FSH and LH, although repeated administration begins to inhibit these hormones, leading to a decrease in estrogen and progesterone production and to a remission of endometriosis. These drugs, however, are not without side effects, which may include hot flashes, acne, weight gain, oily skin, hirsutism, and irregular vaginal bleeding. It is estimated that endometriosis occurs in from 1% to 7% of women aged 15–45 years of age (Apgar, 1992).

Hysterectomy, often including removal of the ovaries as well as the uterus, is frequently performed as a "cure" for endometriosis. At the present time, laser surgery can be used to remove endometrial implants, restore fertility, and relieve symptoms, although endometriosis will recur in patients.

Prolapse of the uterus may occur in women who have had several pregnancies. It is caused by relaxation of the broad ligaments holding the uterus in place and by poor abdominal muscle tone. It can be prevented by toning the muscles of the pelvic floor with exercises termed Kegel exercises, which the woman can learn initially by practicing the starting and stopping of the flow during urination. Some cases may be treated with a pessary, topical estrogen and exercises to strengthen the pelvic floor. It is the reason for approximately 15% of hysterectomies (Carlson et al., 1993).

Hysterectomies and **oophorectomies** (surgical removal of the ovaries) have been reported by as many as 33–46% of women to decrease sexual desire and responsiveness, so these operations should not be performed for benign conditions except in extreme cases (Zussman, Zussman, Sunley, & Bjornson, 1982). Premenopausal Black women (mean age 35.5 years) who were admitted to a hospital for hysterectomy due to a benign problem were interviewed prior to surgery, at the postoperative checkup, and three months after the surgery. Being given accurate knowledge about the anatomy and physiology of the reproductive system, wound healing, and sexual responses help women achieve positive sexual outcomes after hysterectomy (Bernhard, 1985).

Hysterectomy for the Treatment of Cancer

Hysterectomy is the treatment for cervical and often also for ovarian, tubal, colon, rectal, or bladder cancers.

Hysterectomy is the definitive treatment for cervical and uterine cancers. Oophorectomies may be performed along with a hysterectomy in women over 45. Hysterectomy is often also indicated in the course of treatment for ovarian and tubal cancers, and colon, rectal or bladder cancers (Carlson et al., 1993).

SEXUALLY TRANSMITTED DISEASES

Chlamydia

Chlamydia, a bacterial infection, is the most common sexually transmitted disease in the United States.

Chlamydia, a bacterial infection, is the most common sexually transmitted disease in the United States. Approximately 4 million cases are contracted annually. It is the infectious agent in about 50% of the 1 million cases of PID annually in this country. It is a cause of infertility and ectopic pregnancy due to obstruction of the fallopian tube. In pregnant women it can cause prematurity, pneumonia, and conjunctivitis of the newborn (J. F. Potts, 1992).

In women, chlamydia most commonly causes cervical infection, often without symptoms, but may be accompanied by lower abdominal pain, and cervical motion tenderness. It can be detected by direct specimen tests. If a woman does not have symptoms, why would she be tested? Certain groups of women are at high risk and should be tested when they visit a family planning clinic or gynecologist's office. These include women who are seen at clinics for sexually transmitted diseases; are seen at health care clinics where chlamydia is common, such as at family

planning clinics; report having multiple sex partners; are pregnant under age 20; have a history of sexually transmitted diseases (J. F. Potts, 1992). It is treated with the antibiotics Doxycycline or tetracycline. In pregnant patients it is treated with erythromycin. In men, chlamydia may also be symptom-free or be characterized by a scant mucoid discharge. Male partners of women patients who have the disease should also be treated.

Genital Herpes

Genital herpes is a viral disease with no known cure. It can be transmitted to the infant during childbirth, causing retardation, visual problems, or even death.

Genital herpes (HSV-2) is a sexually transmitted disease caused by a virus. It is chronic, with no known cure. Approximately 20 million Americans have the disease with 500,000 new cases diagnosed very year (Wheeler, 1988). The disease can be characterized as Primary genital herpes, which is the first and usually most severe occurrence, with genital and extragenital lesions present, but with no antibodies present in a serum culture. Initial genital herpes is diagnosed by presence of the Herpes Simplex Virus (HVS) antibodies in a serum culture. Persons with recurrent herpes have had a previous outbreak of lesions and a positive HVS serum culture (Jadack, Keller, & Hyde, 1990). Some people never experience a recurrence, but about 75% of people do, usually within 3–12 months of the outbreak.

Participants (34 females, 26 males) in a study of gender differences related to the disease found both men and women to report a wide range of disease-related stressors, such as fear of telling a new sexual partner, possible transmission to a sexual partner, fear of new intimate relationships, fear of reactions of friends and relatives, and loss of sexual spontaneity (Jadack, Keller, & Hyde, 1990). Women reported greater fear of negative effects on health, that the recurrences were more painful, and that herpes caused them concern daily. Men reported longer durations of recurrences.

Herpes may carry particular risks related to pregnancy. If an infant is delivered when the virus is shedding, the disease can be transmitted to the infant, causing mental retardation, visual problems, and a 50%–80% mortality rate. Caesarean section is necessary if the woman is having an outbreak at the time of delivery. Although there is no known cure for genital herpes, acyclovir is a drug given orally, intravenously, or topically that shortens the duration of genital herpes recurrences and relieves symptoms. Alternative treatments that may be helpful include taking 2,000 mg of vitamin C daily, taking 750–1,000 mg daily of lysine, taking 5–60 mg of zinc daily, and eating red grapes (Boston Women's Health Book Collective, 1992).

Genital Warts

Genital warts are a sexually transmitted disease caused by the human papillomavirus (HPV). In addition to the vagina, warts also occur in the entire genital area and on the cervix, where they may be lesions that are invisible to the naked eye. There are a number of treatments for genital warts, with laser therapy applied to the warts being perhaps the most effective. Any woman who has had HPV should get annual Pap tests because some HPV caused lesions are related to an increased risk of cervical cancer (Boston Women's Health Book Collective, 1992).

Syphilis

A new epidemic of syphilis, a bacterial infection, emerged in the late 1980s in the United States. It disproportionately affects minorities and is associated with the use of crack cocaine.

Following a decline in **syphilis** in the United States from 1982 to 1985, due primarily to a decrease in cases among gay and bisexual males, a new epidemic emerged with a 61% increase from 1985 to 1989. This new epidemic disproportionately affects African Americans and to a lesser extent Latino Americans, and is associated with

heterosexual transmission in urban areas (Balshem, Oxman, van Rooyen, & Girod, 1992).

Syphilis is a bacterial infection that is readily curable by antibiotics in adults. Fetal syphilis is associated with perinatal morbidity and mortality. Syphilis is associated with a greater risk for acquiring HIV infection, probably due to the ease with which the virus can be transmitted through syphilitic chancres in the genital area. The epidemic has been traced primarily to users of crack cocaine, which is relatively less expensive than cocaine and therefore concentrated in poor communities. Balshem et al. (1992) interviewed 40 respondents (22 female, 18 male) at high risk for syphilis. Ten women and two men admitted working as prostitutes, and 31 reported using crack cocaine.

> Respondents agree that in the crack houses, men are generally the purchasers of sexual services, offering a piece of crack (a "rock") or even just a hit on a pipe to a woman . . . Women who are heavily engaged in the trading of sex for crack are referred to as "strawberries," "rock stars," or "crack stars." (Balshem et al., 1992, p. 157)

The transmission of syphilis can spread because "rock" stars may have sex with men who also have sex with prostitutes, so the prostitutes and their customers are exposed to the STDs that are common among the crack users.

Hepatitis B

Over half of prostitutes in the United States have or have had Hepatitis B virus.

A survey of 1,368 prostitutes in different regions of the United States revealed that 56% had present or past **Hepatitis B** virus (HBV) infection compared with an estimated 6% among women in the general population of the United States (Rosenblum et al., 1992). Women at higher risk of HBV were women who: were injecting drug users (74%); had a history of anal intercourse; had tested positive for syphilis and HIV infection; had larger numbers of lifetime sexual partners; had partners who were from groups at high risk for HBV. Use of a diaphragm and/or spermicide was associated with a significantly lower risk of HBV among Blacks and Hispanics. Unfortunately, 83% of the prostitutes in the study never used female barrier contraceptives. Between 1982 and 1989 the spread of HBV through heterosexual contact increased from 15% to 26%. It is recommended that all prostitutes be vaccinated for HBV, which is effective in preventing the infection.

AIDS

HIV infection leads to the development of AIDS, a fatal disease with no known cure. Nearly half of AIDS cases in women are acquired through intravenous drug use.

The most serious sexually transmitted disease is **AIDS (acquired immune deficiency syndrome).** It is caused by HIV (human immunodeficiency virus). The two major modes of transmission are through penetrative sexual contact, anal or vaginal, and second, through the sharing of infected needles by intravenous drug users (Plant, 1990). A person who tests positive for HIV may not have any symptoms and appear to be perfectly healthy. However, it is possible to infect others even when no symptoms are present. AIDS is a disease of the immune system. "AIDS is officially diagnosed in an HIV-positive individual when a predetermined set of infections or cancers can be medically documented" (Osmond et al., 1993, p. 100). AIDS is a fatal disease with no currently known cure.

A study conducted at primary health care centers in 13 U.S. cities that tracked 768 women and 3,779 men with the AIDS virus for 15 months found women to be more likely to die than men who were comparably ill at the beginning of the study (Melnick et al., 1994). Causes of death were not reported, however, for nearly half of the women who died. Other causes, such as domestic violence (which is high among women with AIDS), could have been the cause of some of the deaths.

By December 1994, a total of 435,319 cases of AIDS in adolescents and adults in the United States had been reported to the Centers for Disease Control, of which 58,428 were women, representing approximately 13% of the AIDS cases. Of the cases of male adults and adolescents over the age of 13, homosexual men accounted for 228,954 (53%) of the cases and intravenous (IV) drug users for 109,393 (25%) of the cases. Heterosexual contact was determined to be the mode of transmission for 31,663 (7%) of the total number of cases. Among women, IV drug use accounted for 48% of the cases and heterosexual contact another 36% of cases. Black women (54%) and Hispanic women (20.5%) are disproportionately represented among AIDS victims (Centers for Disease Control, 1994). HIV infection also appears most prevalent in women of child-bearing age.

The geographic, racial, and age distributions of women with AIDs reflects its association with HIV drug use. The highest concentration of AIDS in women is found in states along the Atlantic coast, including the District of Columbia and Puerto Rico, and large metropolitan areas in other parts of the country.

The tragedy of the AIDS epidemic highlights the need to understand the complex interaction between human behavior, health, and disease. Women at highest risk for AIDS are mostly poor women of color who suffer from the "multiple jeopardy" of race, class, and gender (Osmond et al., 1993). Interviews with 694 women who exchanged sex for money and who also had a main sexual partner indicated that women were significantly more likely to negotiate condom use with a client than with a main partner.

As of June 1, 1992, the Food and Drug Administration (FDA) mandated that U.S. blood centers must implement testing for antibodies to HIV-2 in addition to testing for antibodies to HIV-1. The diseases associated with HIV-1 and HIV-2 are similar. HIV-2 is prevalent in Africa, but it is much rarer in other parts of the world. Through 1991, 17 case reports had been detected in the United States, and an additional 15 cases through serologic surveillance (analysis of blood samples). None of the cases of HIV-2 have been among homosexual men or intravenous drug users (T. R. O'Brien, George & Holmberg, 1992).

AIDS in Sub-Saharan Africa

In Sub-Saharan Africa, men and women are at equal risk of acquiring the HIV virus.

Unlike North America, men and women in Sub-Saharan African countries are at equal risk of acquiring HIV (Ulin, 1992). So far, no country has been successful in information and education campaigns that change heterosexual behavior impacting on the heterosexual spread of AIDS.

In Africa, both men and women are leaving rural areas, where economic survival is difficult, for urban centers in search of employment. The women often face limited economic opportunity. The practice of exchanging of sexual favors, for social and economic support, has become widespread. The women are not prostitutes, but the larger number of sexual partners increases their risk of AIDS. Also, female students sometimes resort to informal paid sex as a way of obtaining an education. Women are in the difficult position of trying to control and influence male sexual behavior, since the condom is the most effective means of preventing AIDS (Ulin, 1992).

AIDS Risk Behavior

It is necessary to understand the social and cultural context in which needle and syringe sharing and sexual risk-taking behavior takes place.

The social and cultural context within which the behavior is taking place provides a framework that influences the degree of sexual and needle-sharing, risk-taking behavior among women.

Many AIDS-related studies have shown a tendency to focus upon behaviors known to transmit HIV infection in isolation from their social context. Although understandable, there is some danger in this since HIV risk behavior patterns, such as needle and syringe sharing or unprotected sexual contact, do not occur within a vacuum, but as part of a much wider context of human relationships. (McKeganey & Barnard, 1992, p. 12)

It is also foolhardy to view drug injectors or male homosexuals as somehow separate from everyone else because AIDS is spreading among non-IV drug-using heterosexuals as well. This wider social context must be understood in order for effective AIDS prevention strategies to be developed.

Ethnic women face problems of poverty in finding money to purchase condoms as well as cultural norms that may make it difficult to implement the use of condoms once acquired.

Some ethnic women report experiencing verbal and physical abuse as a result of advocating condom usage by their sexual partners. The social context of a request for condom use not only can convey a message about suspicions of past sexual behaviors or drug use, but also represents a possible change in the power and decision-making balance in the relationship. (Cochran & Mays, 1989, p. 533)

The Black community and the Black media have been slow to address the issue of AIDS. "'the fear of a racial backlash against minorities as they become more identified with AIDS is one of the reasons the black community has been slow to address this issue'" (Hammonds, 1992, p. 336). The White media has also given little attention to AIDS in the Black and Hispanic communities. Increased funding is necessary for AIDS prevention programs for minority women as well as for facilities that provide care, comfort and counselling for minority women suffering from AIDS.

Reducing High-Risk Sex Behavior

Female IV drug users taught skills designed to reduce sexual risk behavior and needle risk behavior are more likely to practice these skills than are controls.

Both White and Black heterosexual IV drug users have not shown a change in behavior to reduce the risk of AIDS in the way that gay men have drastically changed their sexual behavior because of AIDS. Applied research has demonstrated that skills-training can be effective in reducing high-risk sexual behaviors. Ninety-one women in a methadone maintenance program were randomly assigned to a single information-only, or five skills-building sessions, focusing on skills necessary to negotiate safe sex with sexual partners (El-Bassel & Schilling, 1992). Significant posttest between-group differences were found favoring the skills-training groups in reports of feeling more comfortable in talking with partners about sex and in obtaining, carrying, and using condoms more frequently. A follow-up 15 months later found that most of the posttest gains were retained for the skills-training group. Skills-training women continued to use condoms more frequently, although they did not appear to obtain or carry them more than did controls. The skills-building participants still reported feeling more comfortable in talking about safe sex with their partners. There was, however, no difference between the groups in the number of sexual partners. To maintain the advantage of women attending these skills-training workshops, it may be necessary to have periodic booster sessions because some of the advantages do erode over time.

The Harlem AIDS project recruited 624 Black and Hispanic women not in drug treatment who were either drug injectors or sex partners of intravenous drug users and provided them with one session of information about AIDS transmission and risk reduction (Deren, Tortu, & Davis, 1993). Second and third sessions were held for half of the participants in which cognitive behavioral skills such as needle cleaning methods, condom use and various negotiations techniques were demonstrated, including role playing by participants. All clients were also given access to health referral services. Considerable risk reduction occurred in the women in both conditions. At the same time, contrary to expectations, they developed a more external AIDS locus of control and a decline in personal self-efficacy and well being.

Partners of Hemophiliacs

Partners of hemophiliacs have a higher condom use rate than other sexually active women at risk for the heterosexual transmission of HIV, but 27% use condoms only sometimes.

Even among a more middle class population, women in monogamous long-term relationships with HIV positive hemophiliacs, who had been counseled repeatedly about risk reduction, do not always use condoms during sexual intercourse. Although 60% always used condoms, and 13% did most of the time, 27% only used condoms sometimes. Frequency of condom use was not related to knowledge of AIDS, or their partner's HIV status. Factors related to women at high risk for acquiring HIV not to use condoms were: a desire to avoid being perceived as rejecting the partner; long-standing sexual behavior practices; a desire to share their partner's fate; and false reassurance based on their own HIV-negative test results (Mayes, Elesser, Schaefer, Handford, & Michael-Good, 1992).

PREVENTIVE HEALTH

AIDS Prevention

Provider referral is more successful than partner referral for AIDS patients.

A comparison of partner notification and health provider notification of sex partners and needle-sharing partners of HIV-infected patients (mostly male—69%, and mostly Black—87%) found that provider-referral was more successful than patient-referral (S. E. Landis et al., 1992). Provider-referral is when the names and addresses of sex partners and needle-sharing partners are given to health department counselors to notify them of their HIV risk. Patient-referral is when patients have the initial responsibility for notifying their partners. In the provider-referral group, 50% were successfully notified, whereas only 7% were successfully notified in the patient-referral group. Of those notified, 23% were HIV positive. Counselors who notify partners of HIV-infected patients can refer them to educational, medical, and support services for persons at high risk for HIV infection. Early medical intervention can also be provided for those who test HIV positive.

The majority of heterosexual college students engage in sexual behavior that puts them at high risk for sexually transmitted diseases and unplanned pregnancy.

The majority of college students in a sample of 642 undergraduate students at a large Midwestern university during 1988 were found to engage in heterosexual behavior that put them at high risk for sexually transmitted diseases (STDs) and unplanned pregnancy (Reinisch, Sanders, Hill, & Ziemba-Davis, 1992). The data showed that 85.6% of heterosexual males and 78.8% of heterosexual females were sexually experienced (defined as having engaged in vaginal or anal intercourse). At the time of the survey the mean age for the sexually experienced males was 21.1 years and 20.3 years for sexually experienced females. On average both males and females had four years of sexual experience. During that time males had an average of 11.2 sexual partners and females an average of 5.6. Although only one in five respondents had ever had an STD, over one-third of respondents had engaged in vaginal or anal intercourse at least once during the preceding year without using any method of contraception or a method that provided minimal or no protection from pregnancy or STDs (withdrawal or rhythm). Fewer than one-third had used condoms, which provide protection from both pregnancy and STDs, and fewer than 10% had used a barrier method that provides protection from pregnancy and some limited protection from STDs (i.e., foam, spermicide, the sponge, the diaphragm and the cervical cap).

The key question becomes one of getting the students to practice safer sex. Reinisch et al. (1992) suggest that the finding that students in exclusive relationships participated in more frequent sexual behavior than those who are sexually nonexclusive, may be pointed out as a benefit of involvement in lower-risk lifestyles. Emphasizing the greater frequency of sexual behavior in exclusive relationships, rather than pointing out the negative aspects of multiple sexual partners, may provide a positive strategy for encouraging sexually exclusive relationships.

Women need to be educated about the risk factors for transmission of AIDS.

Certain risk factors for women in the sexual transmission of HIV have been identified. An uninfected woman has a greater risk of acquiring HIV during sexual intercourse with an infected partner than does a man whose female partner is infected. A man whose disease is more advanced is a more efficient transmitter of the disease than a man who is clinically well. HIV, however, can be transmitted from a man who has no symptoms, and this has been the predominant case to date. Having another STD increases the risk of both acquiring and transmitting HIV infection. Approximately one-third of pregnancies in HIV-infected women result in HIV transmission to the child (J. R. Anderson, 1991).

Educational efforts need to educate women with basic information about AIDS. Women need to limit the number of sexual partners, avoid traumatic sexual practices, and go to a physician or clinic to receive prompt treatment for STDs. Sexually active women not in a monogamous relationship with an uninfected partner need to use latex condoms for each and every sexual encounter. Women should be given specific guidance in how to discuss condom use with partners, and, when appropriate, how to go about getting HIV-antibody testing. Spermicide (both spermicidally lubricated condoms and vaginal spermicide) can be used as additional protection should the condom break.

Douching

Douching is unnecessary, and it may lead to infections. African American women and women who did not complete high school are most likely to douche.

One-third of American women douche on a regular basis, according to the 1988 National Survey of Family Growth (Aral, Mosher, & Cates, 1988). Differences appear in douching by educational level, with women who did not graduate from high school being the most likely to douche regularly (56%) and women who graduated from college being the least likely to do so (17%). Large differences are also found between Black and White women in the rate of douching. African American women (67%) are twice as likely as White women (32%) to douche regularly.

Douching is not necessary because the woman's own natural secretions from membranes that line the vagina cleanse the vagina. Douching and the use of vaginal deodorants change the acidic and alkaline balance of the vagina, and may lead to infection. "Feminine hygiene sprays" may also cause allergic reactions (Boston Women's Health Collective, 1984). Women who prefer to douche can use cider vinegar and water rather than a commercial preparation. Cider vinegar is also a lot less expensive than commercial douches and deodorants.

Exercise

Physical exercise provides protection against some of the most frequent causes of illness and death. Older women benefit from even moderate exercise.

One of the most important elements in improving the quality of life, particularly as one ages, is exercise. As people live longer, the crucial challenge becomes extending the years of independence and mobility while forestalling morbidity and degeneration. Physical activity may provide protection against some of the most frequent causes of illness and death. Are older women as physically active as younger women? A descriptive study of the physical activity of 375 women (73% White, 22% Black and 5% other) aged 33–62 (mean age 47), found that peak in overall physical activity occurred between ages 25 and 39, with a steep decline after age 39 (Dan, Wilbur, Hedricks, O'Connor, & Holm, 1990).

Physical activity was measured by an instrument developed to measure occupation, leisure, and household levels of physical activity (LLPAQ).

Physiological benefits can be derived from even moderate exercise undertaken by elderly women with a typically inactive lifestyle. In one study, 80 sedentary women between the ages of 60 and 70 were randomly assigned to a training group or to a control group (Hamdorf, Withers, Penhall, & Haslam, 1992). The training group participated in a six-month twice-weekly program of warm-ups and flexibility, strengthening and calisthenic exercises followed by a walking program which increased from 16 minutes during the first week to 45 minutes by the nineteenth week and thereafter.

The training group showed significant declines in resting heart rate and exercising heart rate. Although there were no significant differences between the training group and the control group at the beginning of the study the training group had significantly lower heart rates after 26 weeks of training than did the control group both at rest and after five to six minutes of an ergometer work test. Improvement also occurred for the training group on the Human Activity Profile, which asks respondents about performance of a wide variety of activities such as vacuuming, walking, and climbing. The researchers concluded that a low-frequency training program can bring about positive changes in both physiological functioning and functional ability, lifestyle, and independence in older women.

Nutrition

Women should increase fruits and vegetables in their diets. Vitamin A prevents breast cancer and Vitamin E prevents CHD.

According to the National Cancer Institute, only 9% of the population eats the recommended five daily servings of fruits and vegetables. Limited fruit and vegetable intake also deprives the individual of necessary dietary fiber. American diets are low in vitamin C, which is found in oranges, grapefruit, lemons, green leafy vegetables, cabbage, and strawberries, among other fruits and vegetables. Nearly 47% of women ages 19–50 are not getting sufficient vitamin E in their diets (N. McVicar, 1994).

The Nurses' Health Study, in 1980, assessed the nutrients of 87,245 female nurses aged 34–59 who were then followed-up for eight years (M. J. Stampfer et al., 1993). The nurses who took vitamin E supplements during that period had a risk of coronary disease that was 40% lower than the risk in the women who did not take these supplements. Vitamin E is found in wheat germ, whole wheat breads, fortified cereals, almonds, hazelnuts, and sunflower seeds.

As was shown, vitamin A or beta carotene are linked to the prevention of breast cancer, and women's diets are deficient in this nutrient also. A nutritional diet does not need to be expensive. Carrots, an inexpensive vegetable, are high in Beta carotene as are sweet potatoes, collard greens, spinach, broccoli, mangoes, cantaloupe, and apricots. Increasing foods high in these vitamins and reducing high-fat foods such as hamburger, pies and pastries, potato chips, and ice cream can contribute to preventive health. "Dietary behaviours have been linked to both the development and prevention of the major causes of death and disability in the US, including cardiovascular diseases, diabetes, certain cancers, and osteoporosis" (Posner, Cupples, Franz, & Gagnon, 1993, p. 1014).

Smoking Prevention

Self-efficacy serves as a buffer against peer influence in the initiation of smoking among adolescents.

If we know the factors that are related to smoking in adolescence, it is possible to better prevent teens from beginning to smoke. A sample of 1,245 students in grades 9–12, 48% female, 59% white, 21% Hispanic, and 20% other completed questionnaires in class (Stacy, Sjussman, Dent, Burton, & Flay, 1992). A number of factors were found to have a direct effect on smoking behavior—self-esteem, stress, grade, self-efficacy, and social influence. Of the potential moderating variables tested, only self-efficacy was a significant moderator of social influences (peer smoking and peer approvals). The potential practical effects of this research are that prevention programs could be designed to enhance self-efficacy, students' belief in their ability to resist social influence.

REFLECTIONS

The women's health movement has had considerable impact on the inclusion of women in medical research. Another thrust of the women's health movement is to encourage every woman to be as informed a consumer as possible vis-à-vis the health care system. Women have to be assertive in asking questions and making choices about their own treatment. Many unnecessary hysterectomies are performed every year in the United States. At the very least, a woman should seek a second opinion before undergoing a hysterectomy.

Although overall mortality rates are lower for postmenopausal women taking HRT, a woman must consider her own health history and make her own decision. As I mentioned in an earlier chapter, I went through menopause while writing this book. My gynecologist prescribed HRT, which I took for 10 days and then stopped taking after reading some of the articles I summarized. I have a family history of breast cancer. My mother underwent radical mastectomy at age 63 (but fortunately, did not have a recurrence of cancer for 20 years). I also had fibroids. My gynecologist told me that his own wife is on HRT, even though her mother had breast cancer. I was not persuaded. I hesitated about writing of my personal case because I do not want to dissuade other women from taking HRT if that would be the best choice for them. Also, as more research continues to be conducted, I might change my mind at some point and decide to take HRT. I have tried to include enough current information in this chapter for women to make a more informed choice about HRT.

The physical health of women can be greatly improved by behavior change. The following actions, if followed by every woman, could significantly improve health:

Do not start smoking, and stop smoking if you do.

Eat a balanced diet—reduce fat, increase fruit, and vegetables.

Exercise regularly.

Do regular breast self-examinations.

Over age 50, get an annual mammography and pap test.

Do not use IV drugs.

If sexually active in a heterosexual relationship, use condoms with spermicides.

Participate in frequent interaction with friends and relatives or support groups.

If all of these are followed, the health of the nation's women will greatly improve. Women will also feel more empowered by a greater sense of control over their own bodies and lives.

Experiential Exercises

1. Get together with a friend to go walking, swimming, or participate in some other exercise.
2. Form a women's health consciousness-raising group to exchange nutritional recipes, support each other in stopping smoking, weight loss, or whatever health behavior members need to improve.
3. Attend a support group meeting for women survivors of breast cancer.

KEY TERMS

Abortion   Elective termination of a pregnancy.

AIDS (Acquired Immune Deficiency Syndrome)   A disease of the immune system. It is diagnosed when a predetermined set of infections or cancers are medically diagnosed in an HIV positive individual.

Benign Conditions   Noncancerous tumors and tissue changes.

Breast Cancer   The most common cause of cancer in women in the United States. It can be detected through breast self examination, mammography, or breast examination by a physician.

Cervical Intraepithelia Neoplasia (CIN)   Abnormal, precancerous cells in the cervix.

Chlamydia   A bacterial infection that is the most common sexually transmitted disease in the United States.

Coronary Heart Disease (CHD)   Disease of the heart and the arteries that supply the heart muscle with blood.

Depo-Provera   An injectable contraceptive that lasts three months. It is a highly effective contraceptive.

Endometrial Cancer   Cancer of the lining of the uterus.

Endometriosis   Condition in which cells from the lining of the uterus migrate to other areas and become attached to, for example, ovaries, Fallopian tubes, bladder, bowel, or lining of the abdominal cavity.

Estrogen Replacement Therapy (ERT)   Estrogen administered orally or transdermally to relieve the symptoms of menopause, such as hot flashes, and to prevent osteoporosis and coronary heart disease. Given without progestin, ERT greatly increases the risk of endometrial cancer.

Female Condom   A six-inch prelubricated polyurethane sheath, with a flexible ring on either end. It is inserted into the vagina, and like the male condom, it offers protection against pregnancy and sexually transmitted diseases.

Genital Herpes   A sexually transmitted disease caused by a virus.

Genital Warts   Warts in the genital area that are caused by the Human Papillomavirus. The virus causing genital warts also causes lesions on the cervix too small to be seen by the naked eye.

Gonorrrhea   Sexually transmitted disease caused by a bacterium.

Hormone Replacement Therapy (HRT)   Estrogen given in combination with progestin for menopausal symptoms and prevention of osteoporosis and coronary heart disease. HRT does not increase the risk of endometrial cancer.

Human Immunodeficiency Virus (HIV)   A slow-acting virus that is sexually transmitted and usually develops into AIDS.

Hysterectomy   Surgical removal of the uterus.

Lumpectomy   Removal of a cancerous tumor in the breast, leaving the rest of the breast intact.

Mammography   X-ray technique for the detection of tumors of the breast.

Menopause   The absence of menstruation for one year. Beginning before menopause, the ovaries produce less and less estrogen.

Morbidity   Illness.

Mortality Rate   Death rate.

Norplant Subdermal Inplant System A contraceptive method in which six silicone capsules containing a progestin are inserted into the arm. It can be effective for five years.

Oophorectomy Surgical removal of the ovaries.

Osteoporosis The loss of bone mass. It is the cause of many of the bone fractures in women over the age of 50.

Primary Prevention The extent to which individuals actively improve their health status through behaviors such as exercise and nutritional diet.

Radical Mastectomy Removal of the breast, underlying chest muscles and underarm lymph nodes as a treatment for breast cancer.

RU-486 (mifepristone) A drug taken in pill form that induces abortion. A second trip to the doctor's office is necessary to receive a prostaglandin (a substance that causes uterine contractions) in order to complete the abortion.

Secondary Prevention Getting preventive health exams such as pap tests and mammography screening.

Syphilis A sexually transmitted bacterial infection.

SUGGESTED READINGS

Burman, B., & Margolin, G. (1992). Analysis of the association between marital relationships and health problems: An interactional perspective. *Psychological Bulletin, 112,* 39–63. This article reviews the evidence on the relationship of marital status, marital adjustment, and marital interaction on health problems. It also looks at the effect that health problems have on marriage.

Lobo, R. A. (Ed.). (1994). *Treatment of the postmenopausal woman: Basic and clinical aspects.* New York: Raven Press. This is an edited book with 43 chapters. It can serve as a reference book on just about any medical aspect of menopause or diseases that are more common in postmenopausal women such as coronary heart disease and breast cancer.

Osmond, M. W., Wambach, K. G., Harrison, D. F., Byers, J., Levine, P., Imershein, A., & Quadagno, D. M. (1993). The multiple jeopardy of race, class, and gender for AIDS risk among women. *Gender & Society, 7,* 99–120. This article provides a feminist perspective in understanding the AIDS risk behavior of minority women as resulting from their subordinate status.

CHAPTER 10

Intimate Relationships

Each of us wants to be close to somebody else: to feel and to believe that—in some place, at some time, and in our own idiosyncratic way—we can connect with another person; we can come to know the other and reveal what can be known about ourselves.

Dan P. McAdams, 1989

This chapter is written at three levels of analysis, a psychological and a sociological level, and a feminist overview. At the psychological level I will be concerned with cognition and behavior that influence relationship quality such as patterns of attribution and attachment, and yes, that mysterious force—romantic love. Intimate relationships, however, do not occur within a vacuum; rather, they occur in a particular sociocultural context. Sociological factors such as the ratio of members of the opposite sex, and employment opportunities also determine whether two people will be attracted to one another and marry or cohabit and stay together. Ethnocultural background also influences love experiences, and whether marriage will be arranged, for example, or based on romantic love.

FEMINIST ANALYSIS

Feminist Analysis and New Family Structures

Feminist analysis attacks "love" as a woman's career. New family structures—single parent families, lesbian families, dual-career families— are transforming family life in America. These new family structures should be studied as alternative styles rather than as deviant families.

Feminist analysis has attacked the idea of "love" being a woman's career. In her 1965 book, *The Love Fraud,* Edith de Rahm wrote, "The fraud which has been imposed upon women in general through popularization of the notions that **being** is as satisfactory as **doing** and that love is a valid substitute for action" (de Rahm, 1965, p. 7). Vast structural changes are transforming family life in American society: increases in households headed by women; more dual earner families; decreases in the percentage of married couple families; increases in gay and lesbian households; and more commuting couples (M. L. Andersen, 1991). A feminist perspective argues that these families should be studied as new family structures rather than as examples of deviant family arrangements. Actually, the media is beginning to portray alternative families to the nuclear family. The presentation of conventional versus single-parent or "contrived" families on prime-time television across four decades (1947–1990) has changed to include more nonconventional families (Moore, 1992). The number of wives/mothers being employed outside the home has also increased during this time. Nevertheless, female single parents, Black families, and working-class families were underrepresented, while the role of male single parents as well as the role of the husband/father in the family was overemphasized. Despite all of the changes that have occurred in families, the traditional family ideal persists of the family as nuclear, consisting of a married heterosexual couple and their children. The White middle class conceptualization of family is as a private sphere where members are nurtured and protected from the outside world.

While some see these structural transformations as putting the family in crisis, others interpret them as providing increased autonomy for women and encouraging the growth of feminism as a social movement (Hartmann, 1989). "Structural transformations demand new explanations of family experience" (Andersen, 1991, p. 235). In a period of such transformation, it is inevitable that attitudes and values may lag behind structural changes, creating conflicts. This chapter, will examine friendship and dating relationships and alternative as well as traditional family styles and the experiences and behavior related to each.

FRIENDSHIP

Gender Differences in Friendships

Women spend more time with friends, sharing feelings and discussing personal relationships, whereas men spend more time sharing activities with friends.

Friendship is the most widely diffused form of love. Women have a greater number of close friends than men. Women also have a more communal or helping orientation than men (D. C. Jones, Bloys, & Wood, 1990). Men spend more time sharing activities and interests with their friends (P. H. Wright, 1982). Women's friendships, on the other hand, involve self-disclosure, sharing of feelings, and discussion of personal relationships (Caldwell & Peplau, 1982). Is this pattern characteristic of males and females across the life span? According to in-depth interviews with 31 men and women 18–22, 35–55, and 65–75, young men's friendships are characterized as instrumental, whereas young women are more expressive in their friendships (Fox, Gibbs, & Auerbauch, 1985). Men talk about sports and shared activities. Women reveal their thoughts and feelings to one another. This pattern among young women may develop from the relationship of girls with their mothers. Although four of the five young women named their mothers as close friends, none of the young men named their fathers. In fact, other research has found that a close relationship with one's mother is correlated with intimacy in female friendships (Gold & Yanof, 1985). Since lesbianism is stigmatized in our society, fear of being labeled as a lesbian acts as a brake on female friendships, particularly physical demonstrativeness (O'Connor, 1992).

Friendships of midlife men and women are deeper and more complex than friendships of young men and women, but midlife women still have greater intimacy in relationships than midlife men.

Although the instrumental/expressive dimension continues to differentiate the friendships of men and women at midlife, midlife men show greater complexity in their thoughts about the meanings of their friendships than young men. Midlife women are less confrontational with their friends than young women, wanting to talk out problems, and being more conciliatory rather than the "honesty at all costs" attitude of young women. The friends of the older men and women are frequently friends that have been there across the life span, so that the friendships are deeper and more complex than in the younger years. The friendships of older men, however, are still characterized by instrumental-

Focus on Women   "Birds of a Feather"

This participant observation of a group of three women written by a part-time graduate student, illustrates a type of friendship that has been left out of the research, female friendships that take place primarily in groups of three or more people rather than in dyads.

Randi, Pat, and Marge are a close-knit, informal friendship group in existence for about three years. All are life-long residents of the same New England city, in their late 20s, teachers, single, the second or third born in a family of three children. All were completing or had completed a master's degree at the time of the observation, which made them more educated than other members of their families. Other similarities are that each woman had a parent die when she was 10 years old, each has a tremendous fear of failure that overwhelms her at times, each is a doting, overindulgent aunt, and each has tremendous feelings of responsibility for other members of her family.

The group members respect each other's needs for privacy—to be alone at times without being questioned. Each has almost totally adopted the others' families. Each attends family gatherings such as birthdays, Sunday dinners, and holidays at the others' family homes.

A norm exists concerning behavior in mixed-sex group activities. Their behavior revolves around a concerted effort to establish rights as women, and their ability to think, feel, and act according to standards generally presumed to be "male." For example, all three women tend to be competitive and aggressive in playing intellectual games with men who appear arrogant and/or ignorant. At times, their efforts are combined; sometimes, if one is han-

dling a man well, the others observe. If one is having difficulty, the others jump in. When efforts are combined, and a man is nearly psychologically castrated, there is a sort of revelry that occurs. With regard to men, however, a norm exists about never discussing sexual relationships. Sexual activity has never been a topic for discussion in their three-year relationship. Each woman is totally loyal to the other members of the group. No one of the group will tolerate listening to anyone else speak in a derogatory manner about either of the other two group members. Each also fulfills emotional needs of the others.

Each member plays a different role in the group. Randi is extremely dependable. When she says she will do a particular task, the task is accomplished. She is also extremely considerate of other people's feelings. Marge is extremely logical and rational. When Randi and/or Pat are irrational in their handling of situations, Marge is the one who makes them sit down and analyze their behavior in an intelligent way. Pat provides psychological and emotional support for the other group members. Randi and Marge know that if they are feeling depressed or are experiencing a specific problem, Pat can help them feel better.

Randi generally is the initiator of activities. She is the person who suggests things to do, places to go, and so on. Pat generally knows that it is Randi who will bring the group together. If Randi does not initiate an activity within six or seven days, then Pat does. Randi's suggestions are generally accepted; many times, however, they are modified by Pat. Marge usually agrees to do just about anything that has been decided on by Randi and Pat.

---

ity, with the men still having greater problems with self-disclosure (M. Fox, Gibbs, & Auerbach, 1985).

Gender Differences in Self-Disclosure

Women disclose more to other women and to partners with whom they have a relationship (spouses, parents) than do men.

One of the operational definitions (defining something by how it is measured) of intimacy in relationships is **self-disclosure**, revealing private aspects of the self to others. A meta-analysis of 205 studies of gender differences in self-disclosure obtained an effect size of $d = -.18$, indicating women had somewhat higher self-disclosure than did men (Dindia & Allen, 1992). The magnitude of the gender difference in self-disclosure varied with the relationship. Women disclose more to other women than men do to other men, but women and men have about the same self-disclosure to a male partner, indicating that women disclose more to other women, but not to men. Women disclose more than men to strangers when self-disclosure was measured by observational data. Women also disclose more than men to partners with whom they have a relationship (friends, parents, and spouses).

Men indicate a desire to express their feelings more than they do. A significantly greater number of men than women say it is easier to feel close to a member of the opposite sex. Both men and women believe an opposite sex relationship, particularly a spousal relationship, should be the most intimate. It appears, however, that both men and women find it easier to relate to women (Reisman, 1990).

Similarly, among a sample of 65 female and 58 male predominantly White college students it was clear that friendships involving at least one woman were more satisfying than friendships between two men (Elkins & Peterson, 1993). Women's friendships with men, however, were not less satisfying than women's friendships with other women. Men held lower ideal friendship standards for their friendships with other men, but equally high standards were held by women for the friendships with men as with women, and by men for their friendships with women. Unhappiness was not associated with the number of friends and relatives, but with the degree of support received from them.

Same-Sex Married Women's Friendships

Same-sex confidant and companionate relationships are important for married women. These relationships help maintain the stability of their marriages.

A typology of very close same-sex relationships for married women as developed by O'Connor are: confidant relationships (a high level of intimate confiding); nurturant relationships (a high level of practical help or identity enhancement); purely companionable relationship; and latent (a high level of intimacy, but seen infrequently) (O'Connor, 1992). Approximately two-fifths of the relationships studied were confidant, two-fifths were latent, and approximately one-fifth were companionable. The purely nurturant type was very rare. Oliker (1989) argues that married women's friendships help to maintain the stability of their marriages by meeting intimacy needs not met in marriage and by diffusing anger and framing the marital situation in humorous terms. Some research indicates that the friendships of working-class men and women are sex segregated similar to those of premarital relationships, whereas middle- and upper-class friendships are more often based on couple relationships. In couple friendships, however, the women tend to confide in one another and the men in one another. Husbands are more likely to initiate these joint friendships than are wives (O'Connor, 1992).

Diane R. Brown and Lawrence E. Gary (1985) investigated social support among a probability sample of 274 Black women, 33.2% of whom were married and 66% of whom were unmarried (never married, separated, divorced, widowed). There were no significant differences in the number of relatives and friends in the social support group of married and unmarried women.

Women's Friendships After Divorce

Some of women's friendships are lost after divorce, but kin relationships become more important.

After divorce, there is a tendency for a substantial proportion of preseparation friendships to atrophy. Women with custody of children were more likely to intensify relationships with relatives rather than developing new friends. Studies have shown divorced women to have fewer friends than their married counterparts. Divorced women having fewer friends after the divorce is particularly true for women whose married friends were primarily those associated with their husbands in some way (O'Connor, 1992).

After writing the preceding paragraphs, I find myself reflecting that the research does not quite square with my own experiences and observations. The female friendship networks of the never-married and divorced women that I know are very important in their lives, as are their kinship networks. One of my heterosexual divorced friends says that her women friends are very important to her because the men she dates come and go, but her women friends are always there to provide her companionship and support.

Lesbian Friendships

Lesbians often maintain friendships with former lovers.

Ferguson (1990) argues that lesbians in the United States form a subculture, as they do in different societies and as they have in different historical periods. Many of these cultures are oppositional subcultures in the sense of being a force of resistance in a patriarchal culture as well as a source of empowerment of women. "Nonetheless, our society has unifying common social spaces for lesbians. Bars, women's bookstores, lesbian magazines and newsletters exist which allow any woman regardless of class, racial or ethnic background to find a common identification as lesbian" (Ferguson, 1990, p. 80). Lesbian friendships often take place within the context of the lesbian community.

> Lesbian communities are typically defined by geography and composed of groups or networks who are connected through social and political activity. In small towns or universities, there may be a sense of one large community; in larger cities, there may be many communities. The center of community can be one or more bars or coffee houses, a women's center, a social organization, self-help or discussion groups, or an occasional dance or musical event. (Pearlman, 1987, p. 314)

What defines the community is a sense of "groupness" rather than any formal organization or territory. These communities are a source of pride, joy, and camaraderie. As Pearlman points out, however, a sense of limitation and confinement can also develop within lesbian communities. Internalized homophobia and the burden of oppression of lesbians can create conflicts within lesbian communities and put stresses on friendships. "Friendships between lesbians are often intense and erotically charged so that minor disappointments can be experienced as if one's friend were a rejecting lover" (Pearlman, 1987, p. 315). Lesbian friendships, therefore, are often more highly charged and intimate, and also more conflictual, than are heterosexual women's same-sex friendships. Research from the *Hite Report* (1987) finds a high degree of permeability between sex and friendship among lesbian women, with almost two-thirds staying friends with serious ex-lovers.

Although homosexuality is less prevalent among females than it is among males, lesbians are well organized. The Daughters of Bilitis (formed in 1955) publish an informative monthly newsletter entitled "The Ladder." In addition to the national headquarters of Daughters of Bilitis in San Francisco, there are chapters in Los Angeles, New York City, and Chicago. These lesbian organizations facilitate friendships among lesbian women.

Elderly Women's Friendships

Mental health is positively related to friendships among the Elderly.

Although old age is a time of losing friendships through death, the overwhelming majority of elderly women make new friends. Health or mobility is very strongly related to maintaining contact with friends. In her study of 1,000 widows living in California, Lopata (1979) found education and income to be strongly positively related to friendships. Senior citizen centers and retirement communities also contribute to friendship formation among the elderly. Mental health among the elderly is facilitated by regular social interactions (O'Connor, 1992).

Disabled Women's Friendships

Friendships between disabled and nondisabled women need to be based on a realistic understanding of the disabled woman's capabilities.

Integrating the disabled into society allows for the development of intimate relationships.

Friendships between disabled and nondisabled women require a balancing that includes reciprocity and at the same time any special accommodations that need to be made by the nondisabled friend, depending on the situation. Disabled women want as much physical autonomy as possible. A friend of a disabled woman needs to take the time to get to understand the woman's capabilities. Berenice Fisher and Roberta Galler (1988) give an example, of a conflict that arose over whether Diane, a disabled friend of Ruth's, was capable of babysitting for Ruth's young child.

> Diane countered, with some bitterness, that her own parents had trusted her with the care of her siblings when she was only 12. From Diane's point of view, the most difficult aspect of this incident was the implication that she could not take care of children and should not, therefore become a mother. Such an implied judgment seemed a sort of betrayal, a lack of faith. (Berenice Fisher & Galler, 1988, p. 182)

Another problem that may arise between disabled and non-disabled friends is that certain sensitive topics may be shied away from, such as sexuality, courting, and child-bearing. Discussion of these topics is often censored because of the way society treats disabled people. Injustice often occurs in the treatment of disabled women in the areas of dating and marriage. By integrating the disabled into all of society's activities, they will have many more opportunities for intimate relationships.

Friendship and Sex Role Orientation

Femininity and androgyny are associated with maintaining close friendships, whereas being undifferentiated is related to friendship problems.

Are there differences in friendship styles of men and women based on sex role orientation, rather than on their biological sex? The expressive nurturant traits that are emphasized as female characteristics are optimal for the formation of friendships. It is, therefore, not surprising that individuals whose sex role orientations are feminine and androgynous have the most relationship success. Feminine and androgynous individuals have been found to have superior social support networks (Burda, Vaux, & Schill, 1984). Feminine individuals of both sexes are less lonely (L. Wheeler, Reis, & Nezlek, 1983).

Androgyny is associated with characteristics that contribute to the maintenance of close friendships, such as "a communal orientation, a sense of reliable trust in friends, a positive view of friends' attributes, lower loneliness, and greater friendship satisfaction" (D. C. Jones, Bloys, & Wood, 1990, p. 142). Androgyny seems to enhance same-sex friendships for males, whereas an androgynous pattern enhances cross-sex friendships for females. Androgynous women place greater value on the truthfulness and trustworthiness of male as compared with female friends. Androgynous women, however, rate female friends positively on activity and affective attribute measures. Sex role orientation relates to both quantitative and qualitative aspects of friendship.

Those with an undifferentiated sex role orientation have the most interpersonal difficulties. "They do not adequately recognize the needs of others, have a diminished sense of trust in their friends, do not feel positive about the characteristics of their friends, feel dissatisfied and isolated in their friendships" (D. C. Jones, Bloys & Wood, 1990).

DATING RELATIONSHIPS

Exchange Theory, Marriage Market Theory, and Sociobiology

Men seek physical attractiveness in a romantic partner to a significantly greater extent than do women. This finding supports both exchange theory and sociobiology. Women place more emphasis on earnings in a potential marriage partner.

Two sociodemographic theories of mate selection have been put forth: **exchange theory** and **marriage market theory** (South, 1991). Exchange theory stresses the resources that individuals trade in order to maximize their rewards. Traditionally, men have exchanged their socioeconomic resources for the woman's physical attractiveness. Marriage market theory focuses on the quantity and quality of potential mates as the primary influence on mate selection preferences. For example, since there are an overabundance of women over 45, women in that age group who want to marry might have to select men with less-desired characteristics in order to expand their field of eligible mates. The ratios of men to women vary for different racial groups, as well as for age. Among persons aged 18–34, there are 93 Black males for every 100 Black females, but the ratios for Whites and Hispanics are 124 and 138 males for every 100 females, respectively. If only 30–34-year olds are considered the gender ratio for Blacks is below 90, which is about equal to that of 64-year-old Whites (Hale, 1992).

An evolutionary theory of mate selection is sociobiology (see Chapter II). The theoretical framework of mate selection according to sociobiology is that since women can only reproduce a few offspring, they judiciously choose men who show social dominance (cues to resource acquisition), whereas men who can sire many children, select women who are young and attractive as cues to their reproductive health (Buss, 1988). Both exchange theory and sociobiology predict that physical attractiveness would be a more-desired characteristic for females than it would be for males.

A meta-analysis to test the hypothesis of a gender difference in preference for attractiveness using a mate selection questionnaire yielded $d = 0.54$, indicating men rate physical attractiveness as more important to them than do women (Feingold, 1990). Other meta-analyses found that:

- Men more often advertise in personal ads for an attractive partner than do women.
- Romantic popularity is higher for attractive women than for attractive men.

- A more attractive blind date is better liked by both sexes, but men show a greater liking for an attractive blind date than do women.
- More attractive opposite sex strangers are better liked. The effect of attractiveness is larger when the judgments are made by men rather than women.

Overall, the research is very consistent in finding that men place greater emphasis on physical attraction in mate selection than do women.

What type of women do men find attractive? Sociobiological theories postulate that men find women attractive whose body type provides reliable cues to a woman's reproductive success. Two studies by D. Singh (1993) found that men judge women attractive, healthier and with greater reproductive potential who have low waist-to-hip ratio (WHR) in other words, smaller waists relative to hips. Stimulus figures that were overweight or underweight were perceived as less attractive than normal weight figures. Contrary to what women think, this as well as other studies have found that men do not find underweight women attractive (Fallon & Rozin, 1985; Rozin & Fallon, 1988). Although the figures of Miss America contest winners and Playboy centerfolds have been getting thinner over the years (D. M. Garner, Garfinkel, Schwartz, & Thompson, 1980; Mazur, 1986), the WHR has remained the same (D. Singh, 1993).

The National Survey of Families and Households (a survey of over 2,000 unmarried, noncohabiting persons) similarly found men place higher value than do women on physical attractiveness and also on youth, while women put more emphasis on earnings (South, 1991; Sprecher, Sullivan, & Hatfield, 1994). Overall, this research provides better support for exchange theory than for marriage market theory.

Individuals with higher earnings and education are less willing to marry someone with non-normative or undesirable traits, which suggests that persons of high socioeconomic status seek to "exchange" their resources for a spouse with valued qualities. Men are more likely than women to attempt to translate high earnings into gaining a desirable mate. In contrast, individuals with fewer resources are more willing to marry outside of the normative marriage pool. (South, 1991, p. 937)

A marital search model demonstrated that both the quantity and quality of men available in a geographic area is related to women's likelihood of first marriage (Lichter, McLaughlin, Kephart, & Landry, 1992). Trends seem to indicate a growing interest of men in the woman's material resources. Data from the 1979–1986 waves of the National Longitudinal Survey of Youth found that women who are employed and have greater earnings are the most likely to marry.

Consistent with marriage market theory, Black men are less willing than White men to accept a marriage partner with less desirable characteristics. Black women are more willing to stay unmarried than are White women rather than marry a man with less-desirable characteristics.

Consistent with the higher ratios of African American women to men, Black men show less willingness than do White to consider marriage to someone who has previously married, who does not hold a job, and who has less earnings and education (South, 1991). Despite the less-traditional attitudes toward the role of women of Black women and men (Crovitz & Steinmann, 1980), equality may be difficult to achieve in Black relationships due to Black women's higher level of education and achievement relative to Black men (C. Bell, 1989). Contrary to marriage market theory, however, Black women are less willing than White women to marry younger men, men who have previously married, men with less education, and men who are not good-looking (South, 1991). It is more normative in the Black community for women to remain single, so perhaps Black women are more willing to choose that alternative rather than marry someone less desirable.

African American women are much less likely to marry than are European American women. The transition to first marriage of Black and White women who were followed from age 22 to age 28 (The National Longitudinal Survey of Youth, a nationally representative sample, $N =$ 6,288) (Lichter et al., 1992) found that there are half as many eligible males available for Black as for White women. By age 28, there are only .374 unmarried Black men with earnings above the poverty level for each Black woman, as compared with .762 unmarried White men with earnings above the poverty level for each White woman. Lack of available mates, however, does not account for all of the difference in marriage rates between Black and White women. "Even when exposed to similar marriage market conditions, the transition to first marriage among blacks is still roughly 50 to 60 percent of that of comparable white women" (Lichter et al., 1992 p. 796). For both Black and White women, economic independence as measured by education, employment, and earnings is positively associated with marriage. On the other hand, women who were cohabiting or who held traditional values were more likely to marry in a given year. Values, such as whether or not the woman is "searching" and expects to marry, are another important variable in her likelihood of marriage. Despite the suggestion of some that the solution to poverty among Black women and children is marriage, the fact that only one-third of Black men in their late 20s are earning above the poverty level makes that statement obviously false. "Creating jobs for men and women that pay a livable wage may be a better strategy for encouraging marriage and family formation" (Lichter et al., 1992, p. 797).

The declining rates of marriage in African American families are due to changes in environmental supports for marriage such as economic factors, and mate availability. Although unmarried, half of Black men and more than one third of Black women have a primary romantic relationship.

In 1993, 46.1% of Black men and 41.1% of Black women over the age of 18 were married. Marked changes occurred in the marital behavior of Black women between 1970 and 1993, the proportion aged 18 or over who had ever married dropped from 82.6% to 65.1%; (U.S. Bureau of the Census, 1994). A shortage of marriageable Black men due to differential mortality, migration, and patterns of intermarriage of Black men

Focus on Women

Below is a poem written by an African American college senior to her university newspaper relating the frustration and anger about the dateless situation of Black women on the campus of a state university.

A Poem to Our Strong Black Brothers?

As you walk up and down the hill of life, with one on your arm pale and white. You place her on a pedestal like they did long ago. What it feels to love a strong black sista you'll never know.

Her skin so dark, like a warm, clear night. But you choose to love the skin that is cold and white.

Da sista, she works and cleans to survive each day.

The "other" she shops with no bills to pay.

You gave up on your sista because she screams and yells.

She wants a commitment but you say "go to hell."

It's different when the "other" yells and acts to what you refer to as ignorant.

Because to you her loudness is regarded to as mean succulents.

Sometimes she smiles with no complaints. After all she's having fun. In four years she'll be through and done.

She can't bring you home to dinner, you best believe, daddy will kill her or call you a thief.

It angers me when you see the women with skin like honey chocolatey sweet and turn to one with skin so pale, so white, so weak.

Assure me this my brother, why is the Afro-American woman('s) ability to speak her mind freely regarded to you as a curse?

For the only difference between her and the "other" girl is a material thing called a purse.

Sure its true that the sista can't bring you instant fortune and fame.

But wouldn't you rather wait on her than to be lead on a leash and tamed?

You see my blood relative, my message is clear, these four years sistas hope to find a brother who is loving with a stong mind.

One that won't use her to get a piece and sees us in public and hold his speech.

After the club brothers boast and brag about the "others" they're sure to have.

Sista alone in her room at night, no big deal, she'll be all right.

You can't imagine the pain we feel, how can you know, to you, its no big deal.

Silently we weep inside trying to hold back the tears, sistas from long ago faced this for many, many years.

We thank you for the strength you gave us, now we know the game, in 10 years or so, brother, you'll still be the same.

It's not easy for me to say the truth to you my friend.

But its obvious our heritage is coming to an end.

What's happening to us is a disgrace and what needs to take place is reuniting our race.

We do not blame you, you want to have fun, but what happens when all your fame is done?

Myrtle D. Holder
and your Sistas of URI-'92

and women contributes to what sociologists call a "marriage squeeze" for Black women.

Although unmarried, many Black Americans have a primary, romantic relationship. According to a national probability sample of Black Americans, among those not married, half of the men (48.9%) and more than one-third of the women (38.6%) had a main romantic relationship. For both men and women there was a curvilinear relationship between age and marriage/romantic involvement, with middle-age respondents (35–54) more likely to be married or involved than younger or older individuals. Having a higher income was associated with marriage for men, indicating that Black men are less likely to marry until they can fulfill the provider role. On the other hand, higher income was negatively related to marriage for Black women. The most striking gender difference in the study was the case of women 55 and older, only 9% of whom were romantically involved, as compared with 40.2% of the men over 55. "Greater male involvement speaks to the premium placed on maleness (due to their more extreme shortage among the elderly) and on youthfulness in women [reinforced in a situation of an abundance of females]" (Tucker & Taylor, 1989). Given the high level of romantic involvement, it would appear that the declining rates of marriage are due to changes in environmental supports for marriage such as economic factors and mate availability.

An Investment Model of Romantic Relationships

The more individuals have invested in a relationship and the lesser the availability of alternative partners, the more likely a relationship is to last.

An investment model of the stability of a romantic relationship is a variant of exchange theory. According to this model, commitment is a function of level of satisfaction, the extent of desirable alternative partners and the level of investment (the resources the person has put into the relationship). The investment model was supported by longitudinal research investigating the romantic relationships of female and male undergraduate students (Simpson, 1987). Approximately three months after the initial questionnaire responses, 128 of the 234 participants were still dating the same person.

Analysis revealed five variables could predict relationship stability when all other predictors were controlled for—satisfaction with the relationship, length of the relationship, engaging in sexual relations, exclusivity of the relationship, and a restricted orientation toward sexual relations. The degree of emotional distress suffered among those whose relationships did break up could be predicted by being closer to their former partner, having dated the former partner for a longer period of time, and believing they could not easily acquire a satisfactory alternative.

Psychological Mechanisms for Relationship Maintenance

Psychological mechanisms, such as devaluing the attractiveness of other opposite-sex persons, help maintain the relationship.

Certain psychological mechanisms help maintain a dating relationship. Both male and female students who are engaged in an exclusive dating relationship rate opposite-sex persons in advertisements as less physically and sexually attractive than do students not involved in dating relationships (Simpson, Gangestad, & Lerma, 1990). This effect is not accounted for by differences in their own physical attractiveness, self-esteem, empathy, self-monitoring, or altruism. Thus, it is only when evaluating young opposite-sex persons that they view them as less attractive. "Once involved in a relationship, individuals may possess perceptual 'blinders' that effectively insulate them from the distracting and tempting lure of highly attractive persons whom they regularly may encounter" (Simpson et al., 1990, p. 1200).

Attachment Style in Relationships

Personality factors influence relationship satisfaction. Both men and women with secure attachment styles report greater interdependence, commitment, trust, and satisfaction in relationships. Men and women with avoidant or anxious attachment styles report more negative emotions in relationships.

John Bowlby (1988) suggests that the individual's experiences with his or her parents would be reflected in later attachment behavior. **Attachment styles** influence the satisfaction of a relationship and the emotional trauma suffered if a relationship should break up (N. L. Collins & Read, 1990; Feeney & Noller, 1990). The quality of romantic relationships were found to vary in nature with the attachment style of the partners of 144 undergraduate dating couples (Simpson, 1990). These styles represent affective/cognitive models that people develop about themselves and others that guide their social behavior.

People who possess a secure attachment style tend to develop mental models of themselves as being friendly good-natured, and likable and of significant others as being generally well intentioned, reliable, and trustworthy. Those who display an anxious style tend to develop models of themselves as being misunderstood, unconfident, and underappreciated and of significant others as being typically unreliable and either unwilling or unable to commit themselves to permanent relationships. And those who have an avoidant style typically develop models of themselves as being suspicious, aloof, and skeptical and of significant others as being basically unreliable or overly eager to commit themselves to relationships. (Simpson, 1990, p. 971)

Contrary to stereotypical thinking that portrays men as avoiding relationship commitment, the distribution of attachment styles does not seem to be related to gender (Hazen & Shaver, 1987). People with secure attachment styles indicated they were involved in relationships with greater interdependence (love for, dependency on, and self-disclosure), greater commitment, greater trust, and greater satisfaction. They also reported experiencing more-positive and less-negative emotion. People who scored high on the avoidant index had the reverse pattern in their relationships–lesser amounts of interdependence, commitment, trust, and satisfaction. People who manifest the anxious and avoidant styles reported experiencing fewer positive and more negative emotions in the relationship (Simpson, 1990).

For men, but not for women, attachment style was also related to the amount of distress experienced following the breakup of the relationship. Avoidant men experienced significantly less distress following the dissolution of the relationship than did other men.

About three-quarters of both men and women classified themselves as secure in a longitudinal study of 354 heterosexual couples in serious relationships (L. A. Kirkpatrick & Davis, 1994). None of the pairs consisted of couples both of whom had avoidant or anxious attachment styles. Anxious men tended to be paired with avoidant women and vice versa. The relationships of anxious men and avoidant women had the highest breakup rates across the three years of the research. Avoidant women are not likely to work to maintain a relationship. The more surprising finding was that the relationships that had the most negative ratings at the initiation of the study—those of avoidant men and anxious women—were as stable as those of the more satisfied secure couples.

Anxious women, for whom abandonment and relationship loss are central concerns, would be expected to be more accommodating and more active in relationship maintenance efforts and hence to have higher stability rates than their avoidant counterparts. Even though they may wish for the perfect romantic relationship, this desire may be overridden by dependency on the current relationship, fear of being abandoned, and pessimism regarding their ability to attract another (perhaps more desirable) partner. (L. A. Kirkpatrick & Davis, 1994, p. 510)

Another reason relationships with avoidant men may have lasted is that women with avoidant male partners give them higher passion ratings than those with anxious male partners. Consistent with previous research, both prior duration and commitment of relationships were independent contributors to relationship stability.

Empathy

People who are high in empathy, behave in more positive ways in relationships, leading to greater relationship satisfaction.

Empathy as a personality construct has also been found to be related to satisfaction in romantic relationships. Three distinct types of empathy are emphasized: perspective taking—being able to see things from another's point of view; empathic concern—feelings of sympathy and compassion for another; and personal distress—to experience personal feelings of discomfort and unease in the presence of someone who is distressed (Davis & Oatout, 1992).

Studies have found a substantial link between empathy and positive behavior in heterosocial relationships (Davis & Oatout, 1987, 1992). People high in empathy reported good communication, warmth, having an even temper, and a positive outlook, which in turn significantly influenced partner's perceptions of those behaviors and satisfaction in the relationship. Women high in empathy reported twice as many behaviors consistent with that personality characteristic than men high in empathy. Heterosocial anxiety, the fear that one will be judged negatively by members of the opposite sex, to some extent moderates the effect of dispositional empathy by disrupting the process by which empathic disposition is translated into positive social behavior.

The New Singles

Research on singles from 25 to 45 shows them to be involved in only one meaningful relationship at a time, to have members of the opposite sex as platonic friends, and to want to marry again. Black men are more likely to date White women than Black women are to date White men.

College students are not the only ones who date. Simenaur and Carroll's (1982) book, *Singles: The New Americans,* is crammed with statistics and insights from their survey of 3,000 single adults (never married, widowed, or divorced) between the ages of 25 and 45. The following is a sampling of findings that provide a brief glimpse of the single lifestyle.

- Over 90% of single men and women think that men and women can and should be platonic friends.
- Three quarters of men and over 90 percent of women say that they can only be meaningfully and sexually involved with one person at a time.
- Singles do not think that love is a prerequisite for good sex.
- Half of single parents say that their children have no problems about their dates.
- Three quarters of single men and women would like to marry (again).

Dating behavior of single, middle-class Black men and women is shaped by the excess of women in this group. Despite the prevailing societal stereotype of Blacks as morally loose, historically middle class Black women were held to an even more rigid moral code than that of the majority group. Virginity at marriage was often expected by middle-class Black males of their wives. "Due to the lingering effect of the past and the double sexual standard, it is the woman who is defined as sacrificing respectability and marriage chances in exchange for whatever a male can or is willing to offer" (Staples, 1981, p. 105).

A survey of the dating behavior of single, Black men and women aged 25–45 who had completed at least four years of college found that given the excessive number of women, few Black middle class men in the survey indicated any difficulty in getting their sexual needs met (Staples, 1981). A number of the women complained that the men would not even take them out or bring them gifts. They just wanted to come over, sit, watch TV, and have sex. Further limiting the availability of men is the fact that middle-class Black men are more likely to date White women than Black women are to date White men. In his survey, Staples (1981) reports that 85% of the men had at least one interracial dating experience ranging from a one-night fling to marriage. On the other hand, only 39% of Black women had any experience with a White man ranging from casual dating to marriage. Unlike the Black man–White woman relationship, many of the White man–Black woman relationships did not include sexual relations. Black women were often more likely to find White men with similar interests because of the shortage of well educated Black men, whereas, one of the reasons given by Black men for dating White women was their greater sexual liberation.

The tendency of Black men to be more likely to date White women than Black women are to date White men leads to many more marriages where the husband is Black and the wife is White than vice versa. In 1993, there were 182,000 married couples with Black husbands and White wives as compared to 60,000 married couples where the wife was Black and the husband White (U.S. Bureau of the Census, 1994). Opposite to the pattern in Black–White relationships, other female minority group members are more likely to marry Whites than are male minority members. Mexican American women in Arizona were found to be more likely to marry Anglos than were Mexican American men (Fernandez & Holscher, 1983). For the United States population as a whole, census data for 1991 showed Hispanic women to be more likely to be married to non-Hispanic men (610,000 married couples) than were Hispanic men to be married to non-Hispanic women (531,000 couples) (U.S. Bureau of the Census, 1992).

Disabled Women

Disabled women are often discriminated against in dating and marriage. Society needs to view disabled women as intact women with strengths and weaknesses just as other women have.

Due to societal constructions of the ideal body of a young woman, disabled women may find themselves stigmatized and discriminated against in dating and marriage. "Legal action can require an employer to hire a black or disabled person, but it cannot require a potential partner to date a disabled woman or man" (Rousso, 1988, p. 140). A myth in American society that disabled women are asexual further serves as a barrier to dating and marriage opportunities for them. Society's view needs to change in the direction of viewing disabled women as intact human beings with strengths and weaknesses, just as other women have strengths and weaknesses.

Dating in Lesbian Relationships

Friendship was the basis of romantic relationships for three-quarters of lesbians interviewed.

Friendship is often a basis for lesbian love relationships. Structured interviews with 23 lesbian women found that for 18 of the 23 women (78%), their first same-sex love relationship grew out of a basic friendship with another woman (Vetere, 1992). Contrary to the stereotypes, the first female love relationship was not with an older woman; rather, it was typically with a woman close to her own age (2 years 9 months average difference), and was equally as likely to be with a younger as with an older woman.

A majority of women (57%) in this study reported significant problems in the relationship, many stemming from feelings of fear and confusion related to family and upbringing, such as fear of parents finding out about their lesbian relationship and guilt about their homosexual behavior. Of their later relationships, 21 women (91%) had at some time had a friend become a lover. For three-quarters (77%) of the women, the friend-to-lover transition was more common

than the lover-to-friend transition. Several of the women felt that lover and friend are more often meshed for women-identified-women because there are no roles and no oppression as compared with heterosexual relationships.

A problem that lesbians have to deal with in relationships that heterosexuals do not, which can interfere with their intimate relationships, is internalized homophobia (Margolies, Becker, & Jackson-Brewer, 1987). One manifestation is restricting their attractions to unavailable women, heterosexuals, or women in committed relationships, which prevents their full expression of lesbianism. Another result of internalized homophobia is confining relationships to casual "dating" and avoiding commitment. In a committed relationship there are greater social risks such as questions of how to spend holidays that draw attention to the homosexual lifestyle. Erotophobia, fear of sexuality, which is a problem shared by many heterosexuals in our society, is often a particularly acute problem for lesbians because of the separation of homosexuality from procreation. "Because homophobia is a reflection of the way in which society views homosexuality, the nature of homophobia may change over time with society's changing attitudes toward sex and difference (Margolies et al., 1987, p. 240).

Breaking-Up in Heterosexual Relationships

Dating couples are less likely to break up who are similar in age, educational plans, intelligence, and physical attractiveness. When the woman is more in love, the relationship is more likely to last. The woman is more likely to break off the relationship.

Why do some dating relationships progress to marriage while others dissolve? One of the best-supported findings in all of social psychology is that people who are similar are attracted to one another (Bersheid & Walster, 1978). Consistent with other research, support was found for the "birds of a feather" hypothesis in the Boston Couples Study, a longitudinal study of 231 dating couples (C. T. Hill, Rubin, & Peplau, 1976). Two

Focus on Women   Dan and Dee and Al and Jan

Dan and Dee and Al and Jan have been going out on double dates for about a year. Al has the most influence in the group by making the most suggestions and taking the responsibility for calling everyone to inform them of the plans. He is able to get the others to agree with him and accept his suggestions. Dan is second in command, except when the group takes the camper to the shore for a weekend of scuba diving, then a shift in status occurs. Dan occupies the highest status position on these weekends because of his ownership of the camper, and his knowledge of and skill in scuba diving. Jan is Al's date. She has a stable third position in the hierarchy. She coordinates the suggestions of others to reach a consensus and sometimes mentions alternatives or clarifies the choices. Dee, Dan's date, is consistently the lowest status member because of her age (youngest in the group), her sex, and her passive acceptance of the suggestions of others.

Al and Dan were friends long before they started dating Jan and Dee and enjoy a number of activities together both with and without the women. Jan and Dee have known each other only since they have been dating Al and Dan. The power that Al and Dan have in the group can be traced to their being men and because of their long-standing, cohesive bond between them that strengthens their position of leadership.

Interaction in the group is characteristically casual and humorous. Work is valued and the group members take pride in their jobs. The group has developed separate informal norms for the men's behavior and for the women's behavior.

Expectations for the Women

The norms for the women are oriented toward the expectations the men have for their behavior.

Be on time.
Agree to and cooperate with plans that come out of the men's executive sessions.
Have beer or lunch ready when the men finish scuba diving.
Wear feminine dresses for more formal occasions and jeans and tops at other times.
Drink at the same rate as one another, and refuse more than one or two drinks.
Be frugal when taken out—choose less-expensive items on the menu, not ask for anything, enjoy a night at the movies as much as a "fancy night out."

Expectations for the Men

The norms of the men are oriented toward expectations each has for the other's behavior.

Comment freely on the physical desirability of women who are not in the group.
Split the cost of financing the activities of the group.
Highly value cars and devote a great deal of time caring for their cars and the camper.
Reinforce one another for drinking, keeping count of who has drunk the most, and brag about their drinking ability. Tell stories about situations where large amounts of liquor were consumed, and often tell the other "to catch up."
Through frequent compliments indicate they value the neat, feminine appearance of their dates.
Coordinate their clothing with one another, and the type of activity, although a coat and tie is only worn if absolutely necessary.

Negative Sanctions

The men apply negative sanctions to the women for violation of their norms. Tickling is the most common negative sanction. Al and Dan frequently tickle their respective dates as retaliation for not going along with something the men want to do. Actually, tickling is the mildest form of sanction, and is sometimes used instead to express affection. Another sanction is the threat of "walking home." For more serious deviations, the men use "expense guilt." "We take them out to dinner and what do we get," implies that the trouble the women give them is one more expense. The most severe form of negative sanction are threats to "leave the women at home," or to "get a new girl," which are potentially most disruptive to the integrity of the group. The kinds of behavior that are the most typically punished by these sanctions are being late, or disagreeing with higher-status members—the men.

This group was together during the 1970s, but broke up about a year after this observation was written. Writing the report, Jan said, made her realize how controlling the men were.

years later, those couples were less likely to break up who were similar in age, educational plans, intelligence, and physical attractiveness. On the other hand, the couples were no more or less likely to break up when they differed in social class, religion, sex role traditionalism, religiosity, or desired family size.

Couples were also more likely to stay together when the woman was more in love since women were more likely to break off the relationship. Consistent with other research, men were more likely to fall in love first and women to fall out of love first (T. L. Huston & Ashmore, 1986; Hatfield & Sprecher, 1986). The reason women may be slower to fall in love than men is that women have had to be more practical about mate selection since the wife's status, income, and life chances have traditionally been more dependent on the husband than vice versa.

Trends show that an increase in desire among women to marry for romantic love has been concomitant with women's liberation. In the 1960s, only one-fourth of female college students compared with two-thirds of male college students said that they would not marry someone unless they were in love (Kephart, 1967). Dramatic changes in female responses occurred in repetitions of Kephart's question in 1976 and 1984, when four-fifths of both male and female college students said that romantic love is a necessary prerequisite to marriage (Simpson, Campbell, & Berscheid, 1986).

Sex role attitudes also played a role in the dating relationships in the Boston Couples Study. Although sex role attitudes were not related to couple satisfaction, having traditional or moderate sex role attitudes was related to relationship stability over the two-year period, whereas having egalitarian sex role attitudes was related to the couples' breaking up (Peplau, Hill, & Rubin, 1993). A fifteen-year follow-up of the Boston Couples Study found that sex role attitudes played a significant role in what happened to the college dating relationships over time.

Fully 43% of traditionalist women married their boyfriend, and not a single one of these marriages ended in divorce! In contrast, only 26% of egalitar-

ian women married their boyfriend, and half these marriages ended in divorce. Similar but weaker trends were found for traditional, moderate, and egalitarian men. (Peplau, Hill, & Rubin, 1993, p. 49)

Women's sex role attitudes, however, were unrelated to number and timing of children, employment, and whether or not women married (although egalitarian women were much more likely to have married someone other than their boyfriend in the original study).

NEVER-MARRIED WOMEN

Over 90% of women have been married by age 54. Never-married women find satisfaction in their families of origin, friends, and work.

Most women do marry at some time in their lives. As a matter of fact, by age 50–54, 96.1% of all White women, 91.9% of all Black women, and 91.8% of all Hispanic women have been married (U.S. Bureau of the Census, 1994). Some women even marry after age 54 for the first time. One of my cousins married at age 62 for the first time to a 61-year-old widower. The marriage lasted until the death of the husband 20 years later.

Not too long ago, women often had to make a choice between marriage and career. In 1941 only 13% of school systems in the United States would hire a married woman as a teacher. Most public school systems would make teachers resign if they got married. In the 1950s Eleanor McMahon was required to resign from her tenured teaching position in Pawtucket, Rhode Island when she married. She went on to get a doctorate from Harvard University and become a dean and then vice president at Rhode Island College, and later Commissioner of Education for the state of Rhode Island. (Personal Communication, Eleanor McMahon, September 10, 1994). State and municipal governments also would not hire married female librarians and social workers, and banks and insurance companies would not hire married women and would require women to resign if they did marry (Simon, 1987).

There is a projected rising tide of never-married women in the United States (Simon, 1987), but the contemporary cohort of women who will never marry have a different profile than the current generation of never-married elderly women. The contemporary women who will never marry include many women who are mothers and who will have cohabited for long periods of their lives, as well as lesbian women in partnerships. These contemporary never-married women bear little resemblance to the spinster in fiction and poetry.

> William Wordsworth bemoaned "maidens withering on the stalk"; William Blake called prudence "a rich, ugly old maid, courted by Incapacity." Alexander Pope caught the image in a couplet: "My soul abhors the tasteless dry embrace/Of a stale virgin with a winter face." (Simon, 1987, p. 2)

The great majority (76%) of the 50 never-married women 66 years old from diverse racial, religious, and social-class backgrounds interviewed by Simon (1987) *chose* to remain single. Each had turned down marriage proposals, although 30 of the women considered seriously each marriage proposal with the idea that she would marry if she felt it were to the right person. Although the 12 Black women, 4 Puerto Rican, 1 Cuban, and 2 Asian women in the study came from different social class backgrounds, there was deep involvement with and reliance on family of origin, including extended family as well as parents and brothers and sisters, which was also true for a number of the White women. Some of these women supported their families in economic hard times and were caretakers in times of illness.

> Dad was a tree-trimmer. One day he fell and broke his back. His spine was hurt to such a degree that he never walked again. I was about twenty-eight at the time. From that terrible day on, I supported all three of us until there was only me left. (Simon, 1987, p. 81)

Friendships, particularly with other single women, also played a very important role in these women's lives. Fourteen of the 50 women shared a household over a period of years with another woman.

With one exception, the women all worked continuously from their first job to retirement. Paid work meant independence and economic survival. Work had a central place in their lives, providing them with an avenue for social utility and meaning.

MARRIED AND COHABITING COUPLES

Cohabiting Couples

Since 1970, the age of marriage has been increasing, but there has also been a sharp rise in the number of cohabiting couples. Previously divorced people are more likely to cohabit than never marrieds.

During the twentieth century, the age of marriage declined from 26.1 in 1890 to 22.8 years in 1950 for men, and for women from 22.0 years to 20.3 years. Since 1970, the age of marriage has reversed the trend, and is increasing (Googins, 1991). Concomitant with the rise in the age of marriage since 1970 has been a sharp rise in the number of **cohabiting** couples. In 1970, only 11% of individuals marrying for the first time had lived with a partner before marrying compared to nearly half in recent years (Bumpass, Sweet, & Cherlin, 1991). Since 40% of cohabitors have children, cohabitation is very much of a family status, but one which has less stability than marriage. Previously divorced individuals have an even higher rate of cohabitation than among the never married. Between 1980 and 1987, 60% of persons who remarried had lived with a partner between marriages.

Motivation for Marriage

Intrinsic motivation for entering a marriage or cohabiting relationship leads to greater consensus and cohesion in the relationship and higher satisfaction in western culture, but not in Israeli culture.

Why is an individual motivated to enter into and maintain a marital or cohabiting relationship? Does the motivation influence relationship behaviors and satisfaction? A motivational model of couple happiness based on **self-determination theory** was tested through a study of 63 married (77.4%) or nonmarried cohabiting (22.6%) French Canadian couples (Blais, Sabourin, Boucher, & Vallerand, 1990). Motivational styles in relationships were measured by the development of a Couple Motivation Questionnaire that assessed motivation on a continuum of self-determination. At one end was amotivation, or the person who is in a hopeless relationship, but who does not quite know why or what to do about it. Next to amotivation was external motivation, which is when the person is in the relationship to gain external rewards such as the status or standard of living the marriage would provide. At the other end of the continuum is intrinsic motivation in which the individual is in the relationship because of the pleasure of the day to day interaction with the other person.

The initial motivation serves to influence adaptive relationship behavior such as consensus, cohesion, and affectional expression, which in turn affects relationship satisfaction. The main finding of the study was that the more self-determined (intrinsically motivated) both partner's behavior, the greater their perceptions of positive adaptive behavior in the relationship and the greater their personal happiness with the relationship. A second important finding was that women's motivational style was the only significant predictor of women's perceptions of the relationship and had a greater influence on men's satisfaction than did men's own perspective-taking tendency.

The relationship of the motivation for entering the marriage and satisfaction in the marriage may vary with the cultural context. In a study conducted in Israel, whether or not the marriage was arranged had little effect on marital satisfaction (Shachar, 1991). The variables with the greatest effect on marital satisfaction for both spouses were the degree of liberalism of the husband and the husband's desire to marry. Husband's were most satisfied with the marriage when they had liberal attitudes and their wives had conservative views. The more-liberal males have less desire to marry, but once married, the husband's liberalism is associated with marital satisfaction for both partners.

> The findings of the present study . . . indicate that the less the husband's traditional expectations are fulfilled, the lower his marital satisfaction. Conversely, when his wife tends to meet such expectations, in keeping with the traditional family model and in opposition to his own declared gender ideology, his satisfaction rises. (Shachar, 1991)

Such findings reflect a society in transition, but where husband and wife are still perceived in nonegalitarian terms. Intrinsic motivation may be more importantly related to marital satisfaction in North America where romantic love is a strong ideal.

Perceived economic adequacy is the single most important factor in satisfaction in Black marriages.

Civil Rights legislation and Affirmative Action have helped increase the size of a viable, productive Black middle-class. While Blacks as a whole have a higher fertility rate than do Whites, the group with the lowest fertility rate in the United States are college-educated Black women. The Black middle-class is not having enough children to reproduce itself (Staples, 1981).

Researchers have often focused on negative aspects of Black heterosexual relationships, but research is beginning to focus on factors that relate to marital quality in Black families. To look at the relation of socioeconomic variables to marital satisfaction, 75 Black couples from urban areas representing a range of incomes were interviewed (Clark-Nicolas & Gray-Little, 1991). Objective measures of socioeconomic resources, such as income, education, and occupation, were not as consistently associated with marital satisfaction as were perceived economic adequacy.

Perceived economic adequacy was the single most important predictor of marital quality, being positively related to wives' marital satisfaction, reciprocity, and spousal evaluation, and to husband's marital satisfaction and reciprocity. Perceived social class was the second most important variable, predicting regard for the spouse among men and women and marital satisfaction for men. Education and occupation were not related to marital satisfaction for husbands or wives. Socioeconomic factors were more closely related to marital satisfaction for lower-income couples, but they were less relevant for middle-income relationships. The wives' role performance was more positively evaluated by husbands when there was a feeling of personal development, fewer children, and more income. Wives' evaluations of their husbands were positively related to perceived economic adequacy and personal development, followed by job satisfaction and fewer children. More attention needs to be devoted in research to those factors that enhance marital relationships.

Models of Satisfaction in Intimate Relationships

Three conceptual models guide much of the research on satisfaction in intimate relationships: the contextual model; the investment model; and the problem-solving model. Research supports all three models.

Three conceptual models guide much of the research on satisfaction in intimate relationships: the **contextual model**, the **investment model**, and the **problem-solving model** (Kurdek, 1991b). Contextual models describe proximal and distal individual difference variables that influence how information is processed. In the proximal context, individual differences in the way information is processed (e.g., attributions regarding a particular relationship event) is related to relationship satisfaction. In the distal context, individual differences in relatively stable traits (such as expressiveness) predict relationship satisfaction.

Patterns of attributions spouses make about the causes of one another's behavior have been found to be related to marital satisfaction (Bradbury & Fincham, 1990). In dissatisfied marriages, spouses make attributions for the partner's behavior that cast it in a negative light. "She wouldn't have sex with me because she is trying to get back at me for what I did at the party." Even positive behavior by the partner is viewed negatively. For example, "He only brought me flowers because all of his friends were buying gifts for their wives."

In nondistressed marriages, on the other hand, positive events are enhanced, "I have a wonderful, considerate husband who brought me flowers because he is so sweet and romantic." The impact of negative events is also lessened, "She was angry because she has been working so hard lately." Research from both experimental and clinical research including longitudinal data suggests that marital satisfaction is higher when individuals make positive attributions for their partner's behavior.

The investment model is one that explains the individual's satisfaction in a relationship as based on the rewards of the relationship minus the costs. For there to be rewards in the relationship, the level of rewards must be above an internal standard based on previous experience in relationships, the comparison level.

The problem-solving model predicts marital satisfaction based on the problem-solving strategies used during conflict resolution. Research has looked at problem-solving strategies in terms of accommodation processes in close relationships. When a partner acts badly in a relationship, how are people likely to react? Will people react destructively in return or will they try to sooth ruffled feathers with a constructive reaction? A willingness to stifle destructive reactions and to respond constructively is referred to as accommodation. Four responses to dissatisfaction in close relationships have been identified as:

Exit: Separating, moving out of a joint residence, actively abusing one's partner, getting a divorce, threatening to leave, or screaming at one's partner;

Voice: Discussing problems, seeking help from a friend or therapist, suggesting solutions, changing oneself, or urging one's partner to change;

Loyalty: Waiting and hoping that things will improve, supporting the partner in the face of criticism, or praying for improvement;

Neglect: Ignoring the partner or spending less time together, avoiding discussing problems, treating the partner poorly (being cross with him or her), criticizing the partner for things unrelated to the real problem or just letting things fall apart. (Rusbult, Verette, Whitney, Slovik, & Lipkus, 1991, p. 54)

Both voice and loyalty can be seen as constructive responses in a relationship, trying to solve the problems. On the other hand, exit and neglect are destructive to the relationship.

Kurdek (1991b) tested all three models by examining the relation between relationship satisfaction and variables derived from the contextual, investment, and problem-solving models of intimate relationships in 75 gay and 51 lesbian cohabiting couples. The research supported a mediational model in which relationship satisfaction is jointly influenced by contextual, investment, and problem-solving variables. Support was also found for the hierarchical nature of the model (i.e., that the processes related to each model are at different levels of generality).

> The problem-solving model is the most specific because it examines particular interactional styles of particular couples in a conflictual setting. The investment model is more general than the problem-solving model because it deals with broader features of relationships, including conflict and other costs in addition to perceived rewards and comparison levels. Finally, the contextual model is even more general than the investment model because it highlights stable personality traits that influence how relationship information is processed. (Kurdek, 1991b, p. 921)

The correlates for relationship satisfaction were very similar for gay and for lesbian couples, although lesbian couples reported more rewards from the relationship than did gay men, which is perhaps due to females' greater socialization for expressive and nurturing behavior.

Love for partner is related to staying in the relationship for heterosexual married, heterosexual cohabiting, and gay and lesbian relationships (Kurdek & Schmitt, 1986). Cohabiting heterosexual couples had both the lowest love for partner and relationship satisfaction scores of any of the four types of couples. Gay, lesbian, and heterosexual married partners did not differ from one another in love and relationship satisfaction scores.

Intimacy in Lesbian Relationships

Higher levels of intimacy are correlated with relationship satisfaction.

Erotic relationships unconsciously create the lost experience of sensuality and safety one knew as an infant in the mother's arms for the individuals involved. "In heterosexual relationships, the evocation is more direct and complete for a man than for a woman as he once again loses himself in loving physical contact with a woman" (Burch, 1987, p. 126). For the woman in a heterosexual relationship, she embodies to a greater extent the power of the mother within her, and vicariously enjoys the infant role that the man recapitulates. In a lesbian relationship, however, the woman has more direct experience of the connection with the mother, and the possibility of evoking lost intimacy.

This connection with the partner in lesbian relationships is sometimes considered to be overinvolvement that results in fusion or merging. There is some disagreement among psychologists whether the blurring of boundaries between two women is pathological or simply the result of female socialization to be concerned with the other.

> If being female has meant attending to others, maintaining a caretaking attitude toward others, and not asserting one's individual needs, as the new literature on women suggests, then two individuals following those rules together may well become involved in a circular process of orienting self toward the other. That two women in a relationship may consider their own and the other's interests in maintaining the relationship could well be the result of successful socialization and not indicative of any individual pathology. (Vargo, 1987, p. 165)

Autonomy, however, is often also an important value in lesbian relationships. By choosing a lesbian lifestyle, homosexual women are acting independently in a culture that prescribes a heterosexual female role. In a study of the relationships of 127 lesbians, most of the women reported a high degree of intimacy and satisfaction in their relationships (Peplau, Cochran, Rook, & Padesky, 1978). Concern about independence, however, was considered a major problem by 17% of the women and a minor problem for 37% of the women in their relationships.

Actually, that higher degrees of intimacy are correlated with greater satisfaction in lesbian relationships was found in a study of correlates of relationship satisfaction in 275 dual career lesbian couples, aged 20–59, who had been together in a primary relationship for at least two years (Eldridge & Gilbert, 1990). Partners tended to be similar in age and education. The couples were in the relationship for an average of 5.4 years and as long as 22 years. Almost all of the couples (90%) maintained a joint household, and 15% were raising children with their partners. The population was largely hidden, however, with regard to their lesbian orientation: 65% had not told their employers about their lesbianism; 37% had not disclosed it to anyone in their workplace; more than half had not told their fathers; more than one-third had not told their mothers; and more than three-quarters did not disclose their lesbianism and therefore their primary relationship to friends and neighbors. All of the intimacy scales were positively correlated with greater relationship satisfaction—emotional intimacy, intellectual intimacy, recreational intimacy, sexual intimacy, and social intimacy. Those women indicating a greater sense of power or influence in the relationship were also more satisfied in the relationship.

Partner Characteristics and Satisfaction

Although both heterosexuals and homosexuals prefer a partner who is physically attractive and athletic, these characteristics are negatively correlated with relationship satisfaction. Relationship satisfaction was related to having an ambitious and expressive partner.

It is interesting that sexual orientation has little effect on mate preferences. A study of 4,314 heterosexual married and cohabiting couples, 969 gay male couples, and 788 lesbian couples found similar characteristics to be preferred in a romantic partner (Howard, Blumstein, & Schwartz, 1987). Characteristics such as expressiveness, athleticism, ambition, and aggressiveness are preferred more in men than they are in women. Physical attractiveness is preferred more in women than it is in men. Among both the heterosexual and homosexual couples, there is a high degree of correspondence between mate preferences and characteristics of the actual partner. All of the within-couples correlations are significant and positive, indicating a high degree of similarity of preference between the two partners in both heterosexual and homosexual couples. The within-couples preferences for physical attractiveness and athleticism were the largest for the heterosexual couples. The within-couples preferences for ambitiousness and expressiveness were substantially smaller in the heterosexual couples than for the homosexual samples. Relationship satisfaction was positively correlated with expressive and ambitious partners.

On the other hand, preferences for attractive and athletic partners were negatively correlated with relationship satisfaction, which is quite a bombshell finding after all of the research showing that attraction to a romantic partner is often heavily influenced by physical attractiveness. It may be because if your partner is more attractive and athletic than you are, it puts you in a less-powerful position in the relationship. Thus, we all want good looking partners, but when we get one, we are not as happy with the relationship as when our partner is not so good looking. I was discussing this finding in my social psychology class one day. One woman in the class said that sure was true. She had a very handsome husband. Every other woman in the apartment complex where they lived also thought he was very handsome. He thoroughly enjoyed the attention, which led to marital conflicts. Anyway, they are now divorced and she is a single parent raising two children by herself and going to college.

Gender and Marital Satisfaction

Husbands have higher levels of marital satisfaction than wives. The degree to which husbands are willing to talk about the relationship with their wives is related to wife's satisfaction. Wives have greater positive well-being than husbands.

Are there two marriages, his and hers? The research on mental health has shown married men to be mentally healthier than married women (see Chapter VIII). It would be logical that men were receiving more rewards from marital interactions than women, which tends to foster their mental health and satisfaction. Marital satisfaction was indeed found to be higher for men than for women in a national sample of married couples (7,261 couples) who had completed psychological scales when they sought marital counseling or marital enrichment through counselors or clergy (Fowers, 1991). Husbands indicated greater satisfaction in the specific areas of finances, parenting, family and friends, communication, and their partner's personality. No significant differences were found, however, between husbands and wives ratings of leisure activities, their sexual relationship, and conflict resolution. Women were found to be more in favor of egalitarian roles in marriage than men. The difference in egalitarian attitudes was particularly large when the wife had more education than her husband, and did not differ among similarly educated spouses.

Improving wives' level of satisfaction in marriage may not be that difficult. Among young married couples, the degree to which husbands are willing to talk about their marital relationship is related to wives' level of satisfaction, although husbands' satisfaction was not related to wives' relationship talk (Acitelli, 1992). A couple's level of marital adjustment has been found to be related to husbands,' but not wives,' global level of intimacy maturity, maturity level in intimacy concern, sexuality, commitment, and communication.

Research on social support in marriage of 69 married couples (mean age = 74 years) indicated that perceptions of social support by one's spouse is more strongly related to the marital satisfaction and general well-being of wives than husbands (Acitelli & Antonucci, 1994). This finding is consistent with other studies, including one conducted with young couples, which also found husbands' interpersonal skills more predictive of relationship satisfaction than these skills in wives (K. M. White, Speisman, Jackson, Bartis, & Costos, 1986). It may be because wives are more finely tuned to the qualitative aspects of the relationship than are husbands that their marital satisfaction is more dependent on their husband's expressiveness, intimacy, and maturity.

What makes some marriages go on to golden wedding anniversaries while others are breaking up? To answer that question, Lauer and Lauer (1985) surveyed 351 married couples who had been married for 15 years or more. The great majority of these couples reported being happily married. When asked why their marriages were successful, the most frequent response was that their relationship was based on friendship, "My spouse is my best friend." They also stressed commitment to marriage, and the sacredness of marriage. They also said the marriage lasted because of similarity in aims and goals in life, and agreement about many aspects of life from a philosophy of life to sex. They also find each other interesting, laugh together, and are proud of their spouse and his/her achievements.

Another study of long-term marriage made an effort to include couples of varying degrees of satisfaction with their relationship (Levenson, Carstensen, & Gottman, 1993). They recruited 156 couples varying in spouses' age (40–50 years or 60–70 years). The old couples reported lower levels of conflict than did middle-aged couples (money, religion, and children). This was particularly true of disagreement related to children because in almost all of the older couples the children had grown up and left home. Wives were found to have lower physical and psychological health than did husbands in dissatisfied marriages, but not those in satisfied marriages. The husbands were more highly educated than were wives in old couples, but not in middle-aged couples. Middle-aged couples had known one another longer before marriage than old couples. This study is the first report in what is planned to be a longitudinal study of these couples.

MARITAL CONFLICT

What causes the most fights in marriage? Money. Men early in marriage are most upset about sexual rejection. In addition, a wide range of variables predict marital distress.

It is inevitable that when two people with different personalities and from unique backgrounds marry that there will be some conflict. What causes most conflict in marriage? The source of most fights in marriage has stayed remarkably stable over the past quarter-century. In rank order of importance the causes of conflict in marriage are: money; children; household chores; in-laws; being away from home too much; personalities and habits; time spent together as a couple; condition of house/furniture; plans for the future; and affection/sexual relations (Jorgensen, 1986).

From the vantage point of sociobiology, Buss (1989) tested hypotheses about sex differences in marital and sexual dissatisfaction. In a sample of undergraduates and newlyweds, men were found to be most upset about the female reproductive strategy involving sexual withholding and rejection. In the undergraduate sample, but not the newlywed sample, women were most upset about male sexual aggressiveness. It may be that men are more sexually aggressive toward women with whom they are not pair bonded. The evolutionary model, however, did not predict the wide variety of other behavior that elicits upset in the opposite sex discovered in this study, such as being condescending, possessive, neglecting, abusive, inconsiderate, moody, and self-centered. Further research, preferably longitudinal research, needs to be conducted on the elicitors of conflict during different stages of marriage and on the reasons for men and women terminating relationships.

What accounts for high levels of distress in a marriage? A three-year longitudinal study with 310 couples (97% White) beginning shortly after their marriage found husbands who at Year 1 had lived with their wives only a few months, had few years of education, and did not pool finances showed increasing marital distress over the course of the study (Kurdek, 1991a). A wider range of Year 1 variables predicted wives' marital distress over three years—few years of education, earned low income, stepchildren, perception of many rewards from the relationship and few costs, pooled finances, and a large emotional investment in the marriage. These variables, however, only accounted for a small amount of the variance in marital distress. Other factors that were not considered in the research such as interaction patterns during conflict probably contribute significantly to marital distress.

In distressed marriages, wives have more egalitarian attitudes than husbands.

In distressed couples, the wives have been found to have much more egalitarian attitudes than the husbands. In the study by Fowers (1991) previously cited, couples were divided into distressed and nondistressed categories depending on whether or not either partner had considered divorce. Distressed wives scored significantly higher on the Equalitarian Roles scale than did all husbands or nondistressed wives. In distressed couples, the wives' dissatisfaction with communication, parenting responsibilities, and the sexual relationship was much greater than the husband's dissatisfaction. Nondistressed wives had indicated higher sexual satisfaction than their husbands had.

The wife/demand–husband/withdraw pattern is more common than the reverse.

Gender and social structure both influence the demand–withdraw interaction pattern found in marital conflict. Andrew Christiansen and Christopher L. Heavey (1990) videotaped 31 predominantly White, middle-class parents engaging in two marital conflicts, one where the husband wanted to change the wife and one where the wife wanted to change the husband. The wife-demand–husband-withdraw interaction was significantly more likely to occur than the reverse. The situation also influenced the interaction. When mother wanted a change in father, the mother-demand–father-withdraw interaction pattern was significantly more likely to occur than the reverse. When father wanted a change in mother, however, the father-demand–mother-withdraw pattern increased to where the mother's and father's demands were no longer significantly different. Women, therefore, are more likely to be in the demand position and men in the withdraw position, but situational variables also influence this pattern with the one who wants a change in the other being demanding while the other withdraws. "If differences in sex role socialization make women seek more closeness and men seek more autonomy in relationships . . . then these personality differences may lead to a situation where the woman wants more changes in the relationship than the man" (A. Christiansen & Heavey, 1990, p. 80).

Although femininity in both husbands and wives is associated with negative interaction behavior, wives' femininity is related to a more positive outcome.

Sex role orientation rather than biological sex may be a factor in relating in distressed couples (Sayers & Baucom, 1991). A study of 60 maritally distressed couples found both husbands' and wives' femininity to be associated with negative interaction behavior. Sequential analyses of observed and coded communication showed femininity in wives related to exhibiting negative reciprocity. Femininity in husbands was associated with a tendency to terminate fewer negative sequences of behavior than their wives. Wives' masculinity, on the other hand, was related to shorter average sequences of negative behavior. It was found that wives' femininity, however, was associated with a more positive outcome for distressed couples. This may be due to feminine wives pressing their concerns in interaction and thus dealing with rather than avoiding conflictual issues in the relationship.

DIVORCE

Divorce Rate

The United States has the highest divorce rate of any industrialized nation. African Americans and people of low socioeconomic level have higher divorce rates. Women with bachelor's degrees are the least likely to get divorced.

Although the high divorce rate is a recent phenomenon in American society (in 1970 less than 3% of women and 4% of men had been divorced) there was a high rate of marital disruption in the nineteenth century due to death (Googins, 1991). The United States has the highest divorce rate in the industrialized world. The sharp increase in divorce in the 1970s stabilized in the 1980s. The divorce rate increased from 2.5 per 1,000 population in 1965 to 5.3 in 1980, then declined slightly to 4.6 per 1,000 population in 1989 (Benson-von der Ohe, 1987; McKenry & Price, 1991). The rate of divorce is now the lowest it has been since 1974.

About one in three divorces occur within the first four years of marriage. Although the figure that half of all marriages end in divorce is widely quoted in the media, this is not exactly correct. One out of two marriages are expected to end in divorce sometime in the future (Weed, 1980, cited in Kahn & London, 1991).

African Americans have a divorce rate about twice the White divorce rate. This can largely be accounted for by Blacks being overrepresented in low-socioeconomic groups, which have a higher divorce rate (Price & McKenry, 1988). The divorce rate also varies with education. Women who graduate from college have a lower divorce rate than do women with high school diplomas. Women who do graduate work, however, are more likely to get divorced than women who graduate from college and stop there. Houseknecht and Spanier (1980) explain that women with graduate training are more likely to be working than women with less education and that they may find their commitment to a career competing with their commitment to marriage. Their greater financial independence also makes it easier for them to maintain a household. They are also likely to develop separate social relationships through their careers that may put a strain on the marital relationship. Highly educated Black women are even more likely to be divorced than similar White women.

Risk Factors for Divorce

Premarital sex and cohabiting before marriage increases the risk of divorce. Couples with the highest risk of divorce are those who are less than 30 years old, had a child before marriage, and are in second or subsequent marriages.

Data from the 1988 National Survey of Family Growth indicated that women who were virgin brides had a considerably lower risk of marital disruption, at least for White couples married since the 1960s (J. R. Kahn & London, 1991). The lower risk of divorce of virgins remains even after taking into account other background variables such as coming from a nonintact family. "The positive relationship between premarital sex and the risk of divorce can be attributed to prior unobserved differences (e.g., the willingness to break traditional norms) rather than to a direct causal effect" (J. R. Kahn & London, 1991, 845). Thus, it appears to be because people who refrain from premarital sex have more traditional attitudes and values that they have a lower divorce rate, not because premarital sex causes divorce. One argument put forth for the higher divorce rate of couples who had previously cohabited was that it is accounted for by the longer time the cohabitors have been together. A test of this theory using data from the longitudinal study of the 1972 high school senior cohort found that those who cohabited before marriage were more likely to get divorced. This effect cannot be explained by the length of time the couple had been together because "cohabitors are significantly more likely to dissolve their marriages at any given duration" (DeMaris & Rao, 1992, p. 187).

Duration of marriage has been found to be less related to divorce than age. Because of the quality and detail of record keeping on divorce in Finland, it was possible to compare how basic demographic variables (age, duration of marriage, number of children born, and interval elapsed since last birth) were related to divorce (Lutz, Wils, & Nieminen, 1991). A surprising finding was that although divorce was likely to peak at 4–6 years of marriage, most of this was due to the young age of the couple rather than to the duration of the marriage (i.e., when the couple is older the marriage is likely to last longer). The more recent marriages were less likely to end in divorce than the marriages that took place during an earlier period. Women under 25 were much less likely to marry in the 1980s than they had been previously. The probability of divorce was lowest for families with two or three children and highest for those with no children, if age and duration of marriage are controlled. Otherwise, women with one child were at highest risk of divorce. Those at highest risk of divorce were individuals less than 30 years old, couples with children born before the marriage, and those in second or subsequent marriages.

Social Integration and Divorce

Both communicative and normative social integration deters divorce. If the wife has a nontraditional occupation and/or higher status job than her husband, divorce is more likely to occur than if this is not the case.

A major sociological concept, **social integration**, can partially explain the divorce rate in American society. Two forms of social integration, communicative (as measured by the number of friends and organizational affiliations) and normative (absence of divorce among reference-group members), were found to deter divorce in a national survey of married persons (Booth, Edwards, & Johnson, 1991). Communicative integration was found to have a negative effect on divorce only for those couples married less than seven years. Although functional integration (sharing friends and organizational affiliation) was related to lower divorce rates, most of it could be accounted for by marital happiness; in other words, happier couples would seek out common friends and organizational activities.

Wife's Occupation and Divorce

Wives who have a higher status occupation than their husbands are likely to get divorced or change occupations.

What if the wife has a higher status occupation than her husband? Does this put a strain on the marriage? If she is in a position primarily occupied by men, does that have different implications for the marriage than a position primarily occupied by women? To answer these questions, Philliber and Hiller (1983) analyzed data from a 1967 national probability sample survey of White women who were working and were married to men in the labor force. They were again interviewed in 1974.

The strongest predictor of change in marital or occupation status of women was their being employed in a nontraditional (primarily male) occupation. "Women in nontraditional jobs were more likely to become divorced, to leave the labor force, or move to a lower status position than were women in traditional positions. The consistency of this finding is dramatic" (Philliber & Hiller, 1983, p. 168). All of these changes were less likely to occur if the wife was in a nontraditional position of lower status than that of her husband. The wife's having a higher status job than her husband did not matter if she was in a traditional position. For example, it did not predict divorce, if she was a nurse and he was a carpenter, but if she was an engineer and he was a carpenter, that would predict divorce and/or her changing to a more traditional occupation such as a teacher or leaving the job market altogether.

Personality and Divorce

The personality characteristic of neuroticism is related to divorce or to dissatisfaction if the couple stays together. Among a select group of college women, a desire for autonomy, achievement, and assertion were related to divorce.

Psychologists have demonstrated that personality also plays an important role in marital satis-faction and dissolution. Personality antecedents of marital stability and marital satisfaction were investigated in a panel study of 300 couples who were followed from their engagements in the 1930s until 1980 (E. L. Kelly & Conley, 1987). Three aspects of personality—neuroticism of the husband, neuroticism of the wife, and the impulse control of the husband—accounted for more than half of the predicted variance in marital outcome. Both men and women who divorced early were more puritanical in their attitudes and had more premarital romantic and sexual experience than the stably married. Women who divorced early also had more tense, less close, and more unstable families of origin.

The marital satisfaction of those who stayed married resembled a J curve, with the majority of respondents indicating a high level of marital satisfaction, and a small group who were still married in 1980 but had been consistently dissatisfied with the marriage. High neuroticism of both spouses was significantly higher for the stably married but dissatisfied group than it was for the stably married who were satisfied with the marriage. "In marital relationships, neuroticism acts to bring about distress, and the other traits of the husband help to determine whether the distress is brought to a head (in divorce) or suffered passively (in a stable but unsatisfactory marriage)" (E. L. Kelly & Conley, 1987, p. 34). Whether the person saves regularly, changes jobs frequently, and other economic items that other studies have found to be related to marital stability are often a reflection of personality characteristics.

Among a group of 141 women studied during their senior year of college and again when they were in their early 40s, 20% had divorced (Helson, Mitchell, & Moane, 1984). The divorcing subgroup had a different profile of scores on the California Personality Inventory, which they had taken in college, that distinguished them from the group as a whole. Those who were to later divorce expressed greater impulsivity, less awareness and internalization of conventional values and socialization, and less motivation to achieve socially structured goals. While still in college, they indicated greater intention of entering graduate school, and afterwards were less likely to have chosen their first job after college because of the opportunity it afforded for doing something of social value. "These data suggest that, even before marriage, the divorcing women held attitudes and manifested traits that reflected a desire for autonomy, direct achievement, and assertion of individual priorities" (Helson, Mitchell, & Moane, 1984, p. 1087).

Dissolution of Lesbian Relationships

Since lesbians cannot marry or divorce, courts rarely deal with conflicts in lesbian relationships.

Lesbians cannot marry; therefore, they cannot legally divorce. The courts may deal with conflicts between lesbians, but not without "punishing" the partners for their homosexuality (Engelhardt & Triantafillou, 1987). The case of the famous tennis star, Martina Navratilova, however, illustrates a case of at least the financial aspects of the dissolving of a lesbian relationship being handled by the court system. Englehardt and Triantafillou created a mediation service to deal with the emotional and legal ramifications of lesbians separating. Englehardt is a licensed clinical social worker and Triantafillou is a family lawyer and civil rights attorney.

Initiating Divorce

Although wives are seen as having more control in initiating divorce, both husbands and wives tend to see themselves as the victim and the other partner as the villain.

Research on 45 former spouses' divergent perspectives in coping with their divorce was consistent with previous literature in finding that both partners rated the women as having more control in the initiation of the separation and divorce than did the men. (Gray & Silver, 1990). It was a heterogeneous sample of divorced couples in terms of education and income. They had been married on average 10 years and the average age of men was 42 and of women 39. Both husbands

and wives tended to see themselves in a more favorable light and the other partner as the villain.

> Overall, our results provide strong support for the use of predictable and systematic cognitive biases that facilitate a self-enhanced appraisal of a potentially stressful situation. Specifically, ex-spouses tended to see themselves in a positive light and to see their former spouse in a negative light. We found no differences in the degree to which husbands or wives were susceptible to this bias. (Gray & Silver, 1990, p. 1187)

Each spouse tended to minimize his/her part in the breakup and to see themselves as the victim. At the same time, the more one saw an ex-spouse as responsible for the breakup, the greater the distress. Despite both spouses' perceptions of the breakup being biased in an ego-enhancing fashion, the reality of the events set limits, and the more spouses report the ex-partner having been in control over the breakup, the lower the level of psychosocial adjustment they reported.

Data from national samples in 1957 and 1976 showed a decrease in attributions for problems of marriages to be made to oneself or one's spouse (McRae & Kohen, 1988). The authors interpret this as part of a trend of secularization of marital values in which responsibilities are transferred to other external factors. "The avoidance of attributing problems to the spouse was most pronounced in both years among men, the better educated, and the young, groups which simply are more exposed to secular stimuli" (McRae & Kohen, 1988, p. 79). The decrease was also especially pronounced among divorced respondents when talking about previous marriages. This is related to decreased religiosity among those who divorced.

Personal Consequences of Divorce

Divorce is linked to higher rates of illness and death.

Divorce is one of the most stressful life experiences. Stress relating to divorce has been linked to premature death rates, which are greater for men than for women (Price & McKenry, 1988). The formerly married, compared with those married, "are more often hospitalized, more frequently visit physicians, have more acute illnesses, including terminal cancer, have higher rates of illness and disability, and miss more days of work due to illness" (Price & McKenry, 1988, p. 59).

Despite the trauma of divorce, it is a period of ego development for some women.

Despite the trauma of divorce, it is a period of positive growth and development for some women. Bursik (1991) studied 104 White, middle- or upper-middle-class women, aged 22–62, who were adapting to marital separation and divorce. A follow-up interview was conducted one year later. Some of the women found the divorce disequilibrating, but were able to make a successful adjustment by the following year. Adjustment was measured by self-esteem, life satisfaction, mood disturbance, stress symptoms, and physical health. Those women who adjusted within a year also showed an increase in ego development level (25% of the sample). Ego development is a separate construct from adjustment.

Bursik bases her concept of ego development on Loevinger's model.

> This conceptualization of ego development takes account of a person's integrative processes and overall frame of reference. The theory assumes that a person has a customary orientation toward the self and the world and that there exists a continuum—ego development—along which these frames of reference can be arrayed. The process of ego development is characterized by a more differentiated perception of one's self, the social world, and the relations of one's feelings and thoughts to those of others (Bursik, 1991, p. 300).

Other women experienced the separation process as disequilibrating and failed to make a successful adaptation. This group showed considerable variability in ego level—34% increased ego level, 50% remained unchanged, and 16% decreased in ego level between the first and second interviews. Finally, some women did not experience the sep-

aration as disequilibrating but were low in adjustment one year later, also showing a decrease in ego development (12% of the sample).

Black mothers cope better than White mothers with divorce.

Black women with children tend to cope better with divorce than do their White counterparts. Despite large drops in income for both Black and White mothers, Black mothers report significantly less distress than White mothers. White mothers have greater feelings of loneliness, being hassled, and not having enough time, whereas Black mothers indicate that they had more social supports (Geerkin & Gove, 1974).

Social Support for Divorcing/ Divorced Individuals

Financial and emotional support is often given by family members to the divorcing/divorced individuals.

Although researchers have typically focused on the hardships of divorce, there are a number of potential sources of support for divorcing/divorced individuals. Family members, often parents, provide both financial and emotional support. Women in particular are likely to increase interaction with their relatives after divorce. Because women are more likely to have custody of the children, they are more likely than men to maintain relationships with in-laws. Maternal grandparents often perform important childcare duties. In some cases paternal grandparents play a childcare role, particularly if the divorcing couple have joint custody. In other cases, the paternal grandparents may have difficulty in obtaining visitation with the grandchildren, although a number of states have mandated grandparent visitation.

Alimony

Only 15% of divorcing women are awarded alimony.

Alimony is much less common than most people realize. Of the 17 million divorced or separated women in 1982, only 15% had been awarded alimony. The alimony awarded tended to be short-term, with the average duration of the award 25 months in California. The mean amount of the alimony award in 1981 was only $3,000 a year—despite what we read about the amounts a Johnny Carson or other famous stars pay (Price & McKenry, 1988). See Chapter XIII for the allocation and payment of child support.

REMARRIAGE

Remarriage Rates

Men are more likely to remarry than women.

Along with the high-divorce rate in American society is a high-remarriage rate. Every day, 1,300 stepfamilies come into existence when previously widowed or divorced people remarry (Whitsett & Land, 1992). Men are more likely to remarry than women. In the twenties the remarriage rate is fairly equal. Probability of remarrying are greatest for a woman in her 20s (76%), then progressively declines in the 30s (56%), 40s (32%) and 50s (12%) (Benson-von der Ohe, 1987).

Satisfaction in Remarriage

Couple satisfaction is not significantly different in first marriages and remarriages. Having a baby decreases happiness for wives in first marriages, but not in remarriages.

Are there differences in satisfaction between first and second marriages? No, not really. A longitudinal study of White middle-class couples entering a first or a second marriage found that although second marriages reported fewer everyday satisfactions, they had fewer everyday dissatisfactions or tensions (Benson-von der Ohe, 1987). Couple happiness based on his and her self-reports were not significantly different. The majority of people in second marriages, however, said it was "a great deal happier" than their first marriage.

Among second marriages, happiness was greater if the husband's previous marriage had lasted longer (over six years). Both stability of the marriage (staying together) and couples' happiness could be predicted by a higher than average income of husbands at the outset of marriage and the husband's perception that his wife pulls more than her share of the joint burden of taking initiative and of sharing both the paid and unpaid work (having a job plus doing more of the work at home). Couples who begin marriage with stepchildren in the home had similar marital happiness scores to other couples.

A study of couples in first and second marriages found that stepparents did not become closer to the stepchildren during the first few years of the marriage. The presence of a new baby in the marriage was associated with lower happiness among women in first marriages, but not among remarried women; men tended to be happier with new babies (Benson-von der Ohe, 1987). Stepmothers report significantly more role strain than stepfathers (Whitsett & Land, 1992). Despite changes in women's roles, women are still expected to fulfill the nurturer and caretaker role in the family, and her discrepant feelings toward her stepchildren may create strain in the form of self-role incongruence. Avoidant strategies were found by Whitsett and Land to do little to alleviate the role strain of stepmothers. Women higher in self-esteem and self-efficacy had lower role strain. Marital satisfaction was inversely related to role strain. Counseling may be particularly helpful for stepparents if it increases the parents' sense of control over life.

Dual-career couples in both first and second marriages are more likely to report high levels of happiness.

Dual-career couples, for both first and second marriages, were three times more likely to be represented among those reporting high couple happiness. The best attitudinal predictors of later equality as measured by the division of household tasks, were attitudes about careers for wives and, more specifically, for the wife in that marriage. Equal task power, equality of influence over the division of household tasks, was more frequent among couples who were better educated, had no children (or at most one child at home), and where the wife was employed full time at the beginning of the marriage. The marriage was not any happier if the couple shared equal housework and equal influence.

During the course of the study, 17 marriages dissolved. A short courtship (dating less than one year) and very low religious participation in the year prior to the marriage were associated with marital breakup. Couples who had cohabited before the marriage were slightly more likely to breakup, but not significantly so. Overall, the differences were small between couples in first and second marriages.

Conflict in Remarriages

Conflict is endemic in marriage and remarriages often have additional issues to deal with such as ex-spouses, stepchildren and soon, making these marriages particularly vulnerable to conflict. Data from a survey of 232 remarried and 102 first-married couples with at least one child under 18 years of age found that although the remarried do not report more conflict over handling money than those first married, they do more frequently mention economic difficulties than the first married (Hobart, 1991). Both husbands and wives reported more conflict over "rearing and disciplining" children than do first-married couples. This issue had the highest mean disagreement score for the remarried respondents, with an item asking about stepchildren issues and favoritism with the second-highest score. The remarried wives have more difficulty with their husband's children from a prior marriage than the husband's have with their wive's prior-marriage children. They have the most positive relations with the children that were born of the remarriage. Remarried couples have no greater difficulties with in-laws than do first-married couples. Despite the difficulties with children from prior marriages, the Marital Adjustment

Scores of remarried husbands and wives were not significantly different from that of individuals in first marriages. One explanation is that remarried husbands were found to accommodate to their wives more often than first-married men. This may be due to the emotional difficulties faced by divorced men, who want to preserve the remarriage and not be divorced again.

REFLECTIONS

This chapter has revealed how important women's relationships with other women are throughout their lives, whether they are married or single. Women self-disclose to each other, sharing feelings as well as companionship. Women have greater intimacy in same-sex friendships than do men.

The new wave of feminism is about caring, sharing, and trust in relationships between men and women as well as between women. The new feminism means men and women working together to build better lives for themselves and future generations. "Women, apart from lesbian separatists, consider it a necessity to deal with the issue of men; it is difficult to change the role of women, ultimately, if men are not prepared to change too" (T. Gordon, 1990. p. 117). This chapter has provided some clues as to what factors lead to greater satisfaction in intimate relationships. One important factor is equality between the two partners. We also need to socialize men and women so that they can develop secure attachment styles and to socialize men in particular to be more expressive and to communicate with women better because that seems to improve heterosocial relationships.

Experiential Exercises

1. Discuss with your parents their dating relationships. How did they differ from yours?
2. Do you have any friends who have recently become engaged? If so, discuss with them how they met, what attracted them to each other, what made them decide to marry, and why they think the

marriage has a good chance of success given the present divorce rate.

3. Ask people you know about their friendships. Do they have opposite-sex friendships? What are the differences between their same-sex and opposite-sex friendships in self disclosure, satisfaction and length of time the friendships last?

4. Attend a meeting of a support group for divorced persons. What are some of the greatest difficulties they face?

5. Talk to your grandparents or another couple married over 30 years. What advice do they have for achieving marital happiness?

KEY TERMS

Attachment Styles   Affective/cognitive models of relationships developed in childhood that influence the pattern and satisfaction of adult relationships. The three basic styles are secure, anxious, and avoidant.

Cohabiting   Living with a member of the opposite sex as a couple.

Contextual Model   A model specifying that proximal (temporary—such as attributions about a particular relationship event) and distal (individual differences in relatively stable traits such as expressiveness) contexts predict relationship satisfaction.

Empathy   A personality characteristic which allows the person to see things from another's point of view, feel compassion for another, and feel discomfort in the presence of someone who is distressed.

Exchange Theory   A theory of marital selection based on the resources individuals trade in order to maximize their rewards. Men have traditionally exchanged their socioeconomic resources for the woman's physical attractiveness.

Investment Model   A variant of exchange theory that says that commitment to a relationship is a function of level of satisfaction, the extent of desirable alternative partners, and the level of investment

(resources such as time and effort the person has put into the relationship).

Marriage Market Theory   The primary influence on mate selection preferences, according to this theory, is the quantity and quality of potential mates.

Problem-Solving Model   This model predicts relationship satisfaction when the problem-solving strategies of voice and loyalty are used to resolve conflict in close relationships rather than exit and neglect.

Self-Determination Theory   A theory describing the motivation for entering or maintaining a relationship. Relationships are characterized as being either intrinsic—the pleasure of interacting with the partner—or extrinsic—to gain rewards such as money or status.

Self-Disclosure   Revealing private aspects of the self to others.

Social Integration   There are two forms, communicative (as measured by the number of friends and organizational affiliations) and normative (absence of divorce among reference-group members), both of which are found to be related to a lower divorce rate.

SUGGESTED READINGS

Acitelli, L. K., & Antonucci, T. C. (1994). Gender differences in the link between marital support and satisfaction in older couples. *Journal of Personality and Social Psychology, 67,* 688–698. This article reviews the literature as well as conducts research with older married couples to answer the question, "What makes a marriage satisfying?"

O'Connor, P. (1992). *Friendships between women.* New York: Guilford. An excellent overview is provided of women's same-sex friendships and the meaning of these friendships in the lives of women.

Simon, B. L. (1987). *Never married women.* Philadelphia: Temple University Press. This book is based on in-depth interviews with 50 never-married women who were all older than 66 years at the time of the interviews. It presents a rich tapestry of their lives.

CHAPTER 11

Female Sexuality

Female sexuality emerges slowly and can reach full expression only when intimate interaction is guided by symmetrical interpersonal relations.

Joan Rollins, 1995

Heterosexual female sexuality must be studied through the prism of the nature of the relations between the sexes. "A good part of the initial excitement in women's studies consisted of this discovery, that what had been taken as 'natural' was in fact man-made, both as social order and as description of that order as natural and physically determined" (Kelly-Gadol, 1983, p. 16). If we look at female sexuality across historical periods and cross-culturally, then we see that sexual attitudes and behavior vary at a given time and in a given place. What is considered normal is **socially constructed sexuality** within the context of roles and relations between the sexes.

Changes in assumptions about female sexuality have occurred across the centuries. "Well into the eighteenth century, both popular notions and medical understanding retained vestiges of the belief that women were as passionate, lewd, and lascivious as men were" (Groneman, 1994). The rise of evangelical Christianity in the late eighteenth century began to attribute a noble character to females that was passionless and therefore morally superior. The sexual division of labor in the middle classes, brought about by urban, in-

dustrial capitalism, gave rise to theories about women's differences from men including smaller brains, more-passive nature, and lesser-sexual desire (Groneman, 1994).

THE SOCIAL CONSTRUCTION OF FEMALE SEXUALITY

Female sexuality is socially constructed and has primarily been viewed through male lenses. Sexual inequality has been eroticized by society's dictum that the man play a more dominant role in the relationship.

Human sexuality should be viewed from a social constructionist approach, which emphasizes the role of concepts and categories in shaping human sexuality (Tiefer, 1987). Refocusing on social and personality dimensions of sexuality provides a more-penetrating understanding of sexuality. How do we come to view certain activities as sexual and others as not sexual? What personal meanings do these sexual activities have for people? How do these constructions change within the lifetime of the person or during the course of a relationship? For example, sexual acts between "inappropriate" partners has consistently been devalued and degraded. Research on social construction of sexuality will have political implications.

Female sexuality has been described through male lenses almost exclusively. The term *foreplay,* for example, reflects the male perspective that it is simply preliminary to the main event, penetration and ejaculation. For many women, however, foreplay is the source of their primary sexual satisfaction. Tiefer (1987) has criticized much of the research and writing by psychologists as being limited by a **medicalized perspective of sexuality.** Why is sexuality still so beholden to the body when other aspects of human conduct have long since been disengaged?" (Tiefer, 1987, p. 81). She cites the establishment of female "anorgasmia" in DSM-III (American Psychiatric Association, 1980) as another example of medicalization. Tiefer agrees with the anthropologist Margaret Mead who saw female orgasm as a potentiality that may or may not be developed depending on the cultural context and individual life history, rather than as a health disorder if it is not forthcoming.

Bem (1993) argues that **sexual inequality** has been eroticized by what is considered normal heterosexuality.

> First, although neither women or men in American society tend to like heterosexual relationships in which the woman is bigger, taller, stronger, older, smarter, higher in status, more experienced, more educated, more talented, more confident, or more highly paid than the man, they do tend to like heterosexual relationships in which the man is bigger, taller, stronger, and so forth, than the woman. (Bem, 1993, p. 163)

Similarly, the female is also expected to play a less-dominant and less-assertive role in the relationship in everything from initiating the first date to guiding sexual encounters.

Self-Esteem and Sexual Behavior

For women, self-esteem and sexual behavior fluctuates with the social norms.

Research conducted in the 1960s found that sexually permissive subjects were lower in self-esteem than were those with more conservative sexual behavior (Stratton & Spritzer, 1967). During the 1970s as the sexual revolution began to sweep the nation, high–self-esteem subjects reported significantly more sexual partners than did those low in self-esteem (Perlman, 1974). A study later in the 1970s found no difference between high– and low–self-esteem subjects and number of sexual partners (MacCorquodale & DeLamater, 1979). Among university students in the late 1980s, it was found that high and low self-esteem was identical for female virgins and sexually experienced females (A. Walsh, 1991). High–self-esteem females, however, had a greater number of sexual partners than did low self-esteem females. For females, unlike for males, the older the woman, the greater the number of her sexual partners. For males, however, the males who had never experienced sexual intercourse had the lowest self-esteem and those who were sexually active had high self-esteem. The greater the number of partners, the higher the self-esteem of males. What all of this research seems to indicate is that for females, if their sexual behavior conforms to the norms, then they have high self-esteem, whereas if their pattern of sexual behavior deviates from the current normative sexual behavior for females, their self-esteem suffers. At the present time, with the emphasis on AIDS and pregnancy prevention, we are post–sexual revolution, but the norms have not reverted to pre–sexual revolution standards for females, so social norms for premarital sexual behavior are less clearcut than they were in the past. Women can now have high self-esteem whether or not they engage in premarital sex.

Sexual Meaning in Women's Lives

American culture ignores the female as a sexually desiring person.

American culture implicitly imposes a male perspective on the female body as an object of male sexual desire, which is why a woman's physical attractiveness is given such emphasis. On the other hand, the female as a sexually desiring agent is ignored (Bem, 1993). What is the meaning of sexuality in the lives of women? In order to answer this question, 10 psychologically healthy women aged 30–66 years, including the researcher, participated in an approximately three-hour meeting once a week for 11 weeks during which time each woman told her sexual and reproductive history. Unfortunately, both medicine and religion, institutional sources perceived as influential in their conceptualization of sexuality, created shame, fear, and self-blame. "The women were shamed by the language of medicine and experienced objectification in the medical processes and procedures ostensibly employed in the name of health/and or healing" (Daniluk, 1993, p. 58). Sexual violence, including incest, rape, sexual harassment, and verbal abuse, also translated into fear and self-blame in the lives of the women. Although the media had a subtle influence, its pervasive standard of female beauty left the women feeling inadequate. Sexual development within a patriarchal culture has left women feeling that their sexual needs and desires were secondary to those of men. "Lack of information and both implicit and explicit proscriptions against female sexual enjoyment resulted in the *Experience of Invalidation of Self, Body, and Pleasure* for the women" (Daniluk, 1993, p. 61). For the few women in the group for whom early sexual experiences were positive, sexual expression was characterized as the *Experience of Connection, Mutuality, and Pleasure*. Women are able to experience healing and integration of self in the context of mutually caring relationships with both friends and lovers. Relationships with children were also important in the women's own self-acceptance and growth.

Women's Sexual Self-Schema

Women with a positive sexual self-schema have a higher mean lifetime number of sexual relationships and a more secure attachment style than do women with a negative sexual self-schema.

Schemas are a concept from social cognition that represents our mental frameworks based on past experiences. We have schemas for other persons that provide expectations for their behavior and we have self-schemas for our own behavior (Fiske & Taylor, 1991). Self-schemas refer to our cognitions about ourselves and how we expect to behave in a variety of situations. Just as we have self-schemas relating to how honest or hardworking we think we are, we have **sexual self-schemas**, cognitive generalizations about our sexuality and sexual expressiveness (B. L. Andersen & Cyranowski, 1994). Sexual self-schemas help process relevant social information and serve as a guide for sexual behavior.

Barbara L. Andersen and Jill M. Cyranowski (1994) developed a Sexual Self-Schema Scale that measures two positive aspects, "an inclination to experience passionate-romantic emotions and a behavioral openness to sexual experience, and a negative aspect, embarrassment or conservatism, which appears to be a deterrent to sexually relevant affects and behaviors" (p. 1094). Women with a positive sexual self-schema were open to sexual relationships and experiences, and reported a significantly higher mean lifetime number of sexual relationships. Positive sexual self-schema women were also more likely to describe themselves in terms of a secure attachment style, whereas women with a negative sexual self-schema were avoidant or overly eager to commit to a relationship.

Erotophobia and Erotophilia

People who are erotophobic have negative attitudes toward sex and high sex guilt. Erotophobic women have a lower frequency of sexual activity and are less likely to use contraceptives during premarital sex. They are also less likely to do breast self-examinations and get gynecological exams.

Whether or not one responds positively to sex (**erotophilia**) is often influenced by the attitudes conveyed by family, religion, and culture about sex and sexual expression. Individuals responding with fear, guilt, and anxiety about their sexual fantasies and behavior are people who have **erotophobia**. Two scales that have been developed by psychologists to measure the extent of positive versus negative sexual attitudes are the Sex Guilt Scale (Mosher, 1968) and the Sexual Opinion Survey (W. A. Fisher, Byrne, White & Kelley, 1989). These scales classify individuals as erotophilic (relatively low in sex guilt) or as erotophobic (relatively high in sex guilt). Erotophobes generally report family backgrounds consisting of sexual restrictiveness, religious training, and political conservatism to a greater degree than erotophilics (W. A. Fisher & Byrne, 1978).

Scores on sexual attitude scales are predictive of behavior in many areas relating to sex. For example, psychologists have found that erotophobic parents are less likely to provide sex information to their children (Yarber & Whitehill, 1981). Erotophobia is associated with a lower level of sexual activity among college students as well as among individuals across the lifespan (DiVasto, Pathak, & Fishburn, 1981; W. A. Fisher, et al. 1989). As compared with erotophilics, erotophobes have a lower frequency of orgasm, masturbation, marital intercourse, and are less likely to use contraceptives when engaging in premarital intercourse. Females who are erotophobic are also less likely to do breast self-examination and to have regular gynecological visits (Byrne, 1983). The importance of individual differences in sexual attitudes and behavior is clear from this brief review.

A probability sample of African American and White American women in Los Angeles county found African American women to have higher mean sex guilt scores than White women (Wyatt & Dunn, 1991). The best predictor of sex guilt, however, was not race, but religiosity. Even at lower levels of religious service attendance, however, African American women had significantly higher sex guilt than did the White women. This is somewhat surprising in view of the fact that African American females begin sexual activity at an earlier age on average than do White females.

The Double Standard

The double standard says that premarital sex is acceptable for men but not for women. The sexual double standard may lead some women to deny their desire for sex.

According to the **double standard**, premarital sexual intercourse is more acceptable for males than it is for females. The underlying assumption of the double standard is that men have a stronger sex drive than women, and their sexual needs are more important. In general, research in the 1950s and 1960s found that the double standard was prevalent, although a conditional double standard was emerging that was tolerant of sexual activity for females in love relationships. In one study in the 1980s, it was found that university students evaluating a female or male stimulus person in a written description, perceived a female more negatively than a male when she had first coitus in a casual relationship (rather than in a close relationship) or at age 16 (rather than at age 21).

The sexual double standard may in some situations lead women to deny their desire for sexual intercourse. It puts women in a double bind because if she acknowledges her desire for sex she risks being labeled "loose," "easy," or worse, but if she follows a scripted refusal, she says she does not want to have sex when she really does. A study of 403 college women found that neither personality characteristics nor acceptance of traditional sex roles differentiated women who had or had not engaged in scripted refusal (Muehlenhard & McCoy, 1991). Women who had used scripted refusal, however, did believe that their partners accepted the sexual double standard. This indicates that it is the cultural context that leads women to deny their desire for sex. The authors note that the majority of women have not engaged in scripted refusal, and those that have, have done so infrequently. This research should not be construed as giving men an excuse for rape. It is rape if she does not consent.

The double standard makes it less likely that females will accept sexual propositions from strangers than will men. In studies conducted in 1978, and again in 1982, college students were approached by an attractive stranger of the opposite sex and asked one of the following questions: "Would you go out tonight?" "Will you come over to my apartment?" or "Would you go to bed with me?" (R. Clark & Hatfield, 1989). Men were much more likely to accept the invitations than were women. In fact, not one woman agreed to have a sexual encounter with the man who asked them, whereas the majority of men agreed to sex. In addition to the double standard, women are probably also constrained by the fear of violence on the part of a strange man. Women also have to worry about getting pregnant.

It is surprising that in a meta-analysis of gender differences in sexual attitudes and behavior, a negative *d* value, indicating greater acceptance by females than by males, was found for the double standard (Oliver & Hyde, 1993). The samples regarding the double standard were all conducted in 1977 or before, which may color the results. The age groups of the respondents were also young, with the oldest being 20 years of age.

Sexuality of Women with Disabilities

Parental attitudes shape sexuality of women with disabilities.

Women with disabilities are double minorities in American society. It is only recently that the women's movement has considered the experience of gender and disability. Disabled men are much more likely to marry than disabled women, and women already in marriages when the disability occurs are more likely than men to be divorced. The stereotypes of women and disabilities is that they are not sexual beings, and that no man would want to marry them. (Asch & Fine, 1988; Fine & Asch, 1981).

The sexual development of women with disabilities is shaped by parental attitudes and expectations for them. A study of 43 women with physical and sensory disabilities found that many of the parents had expectations that their daughters would be unable to fulfill a wife and mother role and therefore should/would not become involved in heterosexual relationships (Rousso, 1988). Some of these daughters rebelled sexually and others became isolates. On the other hand, if parents treated their daughters as sexually normal, the daughters were likely to have normal social and sexual relationships.

HUMAN SEXUAL RESPONSE

Stages of Physiological Responsiveness to Sexual Stimulation

The pioneering research of William Masters and Virginia Johnson measured physiological responses during sexual activity. Both men and women have four stages of physiological responsiveness to sexual stimulation: excitement; plateau; orgasm; and resolution.

Until the 1960s the study of the physiology of sexual response was considered a taboo topic. The pioneering work of William Masters and Virginia Johnson, *Human Sexual Response* (1966), reported on laboratory research that measured and photographed the physiological responses of 382 women and 312 men while engaged in autoerotic and heterosexual behavior.

Both men and women were found to have the same four stages of physiological responsiveness to sexual stimulation: excitement, plateau, orgasm, and resolution.

Excitement. A variety of stimuli, both internal to the individual such as fantasies, or external such as the voice or touch of a lover, may trigger sexual arousal. Vasocongestion, or increased blood flow to the genital organs occurs. In females, the increased blood flow causes fluid to seep from the walls of the vagina lubricating it. The lips of the vagina swell and the upper two thirds of the vagina expand. The clitoris glans, which is located just in front of the urethra, swells. In males, vasocongestion causes erection of the penis. The glans of the clitoris and the glans (head) of the penis develop from the same embryonic tissue, and both are densely packed with nerve endings. The clitoris is a highly sensitive organ, and the only organ of the body whose sole purpose is sexual pleasure.

Other physiological responses also occur. Various muscle fibers contract (myotonia), resulting

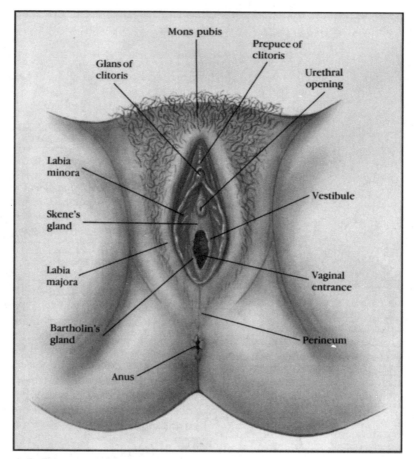

Mons pubis

Prepuce of clitoris

Glans of clitoris

Urethral opening

Labia minora

Vestibule

Skene's gland

Labia majora

Vaginal entrance

Bartholin's gland

Perineum

Anus

FIGURE 11.1   External Female Genitalia.

in hardening of the nipples and other responses such as elevation of the testes in males. Heart rate, blood pressure, pulse, and rate of breathing all increase.

Plateau. Vasocongestion and myotonia increase to a peak level bringing about the "orgasmic platform." This refers to the narrowing of the outer third of the vagina caused by engorgement with blood. The vagina thus holds the penis more tightly, increasing the pleasure of the male (if arousal is occurring during sexual intercourse). The clitoris retracts, but is still highly sensitive. Heart rate, blood pressure, pulse, and rate of breathing increase further.

Orgasm. Orgasm is a series of involuntary rhythmic neuromuscular contractions of the vagina and uterus, and in some women of the rectal and urethral sphincters as well. These contractions occur at about 0.8 second intervals and vary in intensity and number for different women and with different sources of stimulation.

Resolution. During the resolution phase there is a release of tension throughout the body, and blood is released from the engorged blood vessels. This process is slower in the female than in the male. It may also be reversed at any point with renewed stimulation, so that females may have multiple orgasms within a short time period. In the absence of further stimulation, the process of pulse rate, breathing, blood pressure, and heart rate returning to normal usually takes about 15–30 minutes, but may take longer if the woman did not reach orgasm. Men, on the other hand, enter a refractory period following orgasm, during which they do not respond with erection and orgasm to stimulation. There is a great deal of variation in the length of time of the refractory period depending on the age of the man and his physical health as well as psychological factors. The refractory period may be anywhere from a few minutes to 24 hours, during which the man cannot be stimulated to erection and orgasm.

Some feminists have been critical of the research of Masters and Johnson (1966) on the human sexual response cycle. "At a time when women were beginning to make known their desires in sexual relationships, a male model of sexual response was generalized to define sexuality for women as well as men (Hare-Mustin & Marecek, 1994). The central focus of the model is physiological response rather than psychological experience.

Vaginal versus Clitoral Orgasms

According to Freud, clitoral orgasm is immature and vaginal orgasm mature. Masters and Johnson's research found that the physiological response of orgasm is exactly the same whether the stimulus is clitoral or vaginal stimulation.

According to Freudian theory, females can experience two distinct kinds of orgasm, one due to clitoral stimulation and the other in response to vaginal stimulation during sexual intercourse. Freud (1938b) believed that the **vaginal orgasm** was more mature and **clitoral orgasm** "immature." Research in Masters and Johnson's laboratory showed that the physiological response was exactly the same regardless of whether the orgasm occurred during sexual intercourse or as a result of oral or manual stimulation of the clitoris. Masters and Johnson further said that clitoral stimulation is involved in all orgasms. The vagina has relatively few nerve endings and also has the reproductive function of serving as the birth canal.

It is however sensitive to pressure, the distention by the erect penis thereby causing pleasure.

Vaginal Orgasm

Stimulation of the Grafenberg spot in the vagina elicits orgasm. Research on women in the Sudan who reach orgasm even when the clitoris has been surgically removed, would indicate that vaginal orgasms can be achieved independent of the clitoris.

Is there really only one kind of orgasm? The rediscovery of the **Grafenberg spot** (G-Spot) again raised the question of one or two types of orgasm (only clitoral, or vaginal, too). The Grafenberg spot has been located two-thirds of the way toward the cervix in the vagina. Direct stimulation of the Grafenberg spot in laboratory research has brought about orgasmic response, and, in some women, a spurt of liquid from the urethra that is chemically similar to seminal fluid (D. C. Goldberg et al., 1983).

Research in the Sudan on women who have been genitally circumcised and infibulated indicates that vaginal orgasms can be achieved even when the clitoris has been surgically removed. In Sudanese society, which is patriarchal and patrilineal, circumcision is as old as recorded history. **Genital circumcision** distinguishes the respectable woman from the prostitute or slave. "Without circumcision, a girl can not marry and is thereby unable to fulfill her intended role, i.e., to produce legitimate sons to carry on her husband's patrilineate" (Lightfoot-Klein, 1989, p. 375). Although it was declared illegal under Sudanese law dating from 1956 when Sudan became an independent state, the law has not been enforced. As practiced in the Sudan, circumcision involved the excision of the clitoris, the labia minora, and the inner layers of the labia majora. The outer layers of the labia majora are then sewn together, leaving only a pinhole-sized opening.

Women are considered by the Sudanese to be naturally sexually voracious and promiscuous. The purpose of the circumcision is to decrease sexual sensitivity and dampen their sex drive. Despite the circumcision, and custom that decrees that a woman remain passive during the sex act, nearly 90% of the over 300 women interviewed by Lightfoot-Klein (1989) said that they experienced orgasm (climax) or had experienced it at various times in their marriage.

This research on genitally circumcised women seems to question the assertion that the clitoris needs to be stimulated in order for a woman to reach orgasm. Whether or not women are capable of achieving one or two types of orgasm, what would be unfortunate is if society went back to the Freudian notion that vaginal orgasm is an "ideal" and women are made to feel that they are somehow inadequate if they typically reach orgasm with clitoral but not vaginal stimulation.

SEXUAL SURVEYS

Most sexuality surveys have relied on nonprobability methods of sample selection.

Most of the research on sexuality that has attracted widespread media and academic attention has been conducted on nonprobability samples. In order to conduct a probability (scientific) sample survey, the researcher must first define the population about whom generalizations will be made. The next step is choosing a method for selecting a representative sample of that population.

Included among nonprobability surveys are those by Kinsey (Kinsey, Pomeroy, & Martin, 1948; Kinsey, Pomeroy, Martin & Gebhard, 1953; Hite, 1979; 1981); M. Hunt's *Playboy* survey, (1974), as well as *Redbook* and *Cosmopolitan* magazine surveys. Some of these surveys included large numbers of people, the *Redbook* survey was of 100,000 married women. All of the surveys just mentioned were of volunteers, who may not reflect the general population in a variety of characteristics.

A scientific survey is designed so that the incidence and prevalence of sexual attitudes and practices can be accurately generalized to a designated population. Some scientifically designed surveys have dealt with specific aspects of sexual behavior on one segment of the population such as those of Zelnik and Kantner (1972; 1980) and Zelnik, Kantner, and Ford (1981), who focused on sexual activity and pregnancy prevention behavior of adolescents. The surveys I am most frequently citing in this chapter are those of Alfred C. Kinsey and his associates (Kinsey et al., 1953), who analyzed data on 5,940 White women and 12,214 men secured during the late 1930s and 1940s through their organizational memberships and the National Health and Social Life Survey (NHSLS), a nationwide probability sample survey of 3,432 American men and women between the ages of 18 and 59 conducted in 1992 (Laumann, Gagnon, Michael, & Michaels, 1994). Most of the data in both surveys were collected by means of face to face interviews, by male interviewers in the Kinsey surveys and by same sex as respondent interviewers in the NHSLS survey. Most of Kinsey's female respondents ranged in age from 16 to 50 years, although the total age range was from 2 to 90. Kinsey's sample greatly overrepresented women with higher levels of education, with 75% of the women having attended and/or graduated from college. Why am I citing data from a 50-year-old, nonprobability sample survey? Because it has been used as the gold standard against which all other surveys have been compared during the past 40 years. It was the first major survey of sexual behavior.

First Intercourse

Nearly one out of three women were forced or coerced into losing their virginity.

In the NHSLS survey, only 71% of women wanted first intercourse to happen when it did (Laumann, et al. 1994). Of those women, nearly half (47.5%) said the reason was affection for their partner; one-quarter (24.3%) said they were curious. About one-fourth (24.5%) of female respondents, however, answered that they went along with it without really wanting to, and 4% of the women said they had actually been forced to have first intercourse. Younger women in the survey were much more likely to report not wanting intercourse the first time than were older women.

Many of the older women had first intercourse on their wedding night. Black women (41%) were much more likely than other women (29%) to report not wanting their first experience of sexual intercourse to happen when it did.

Is first intercourse painful for women? Yes, for most women.

One of the components of folk wisdom about female sexuality is that first intercourse is painful. Is it? In a survey of college women about their experience of "loss of virginity" of the 130 women who had sexual intercourse, at least once, 28% of the women reported no pain, 40% experienced moderate pain, and 32% experienced severe pain during first sexual intercourse (Weis, 1985). Other experiences that were as likely as pain were pleasure, guilt, and anxiety.

Surveys of Frequency of Orgasm

There is a great deal of variability in whether a woman reaches none or one or more orgasms. Women who are orgasmic most likely have sex in the context of marriage or an intimate relationship rather than casual sex.

Surveys show that many women do not reach orgasm during intercourse or heterosexual lovemaking. In the 1974 survey of 100,000 married women readers of *Redbook* magazine, when asked if they reach orgasm 7% said never, 10.6% said once in awhile, 19.1% said sometimes, 48.2% said most of the time, and 15.0% said all of the time (Tavris & Sadd, 1975). The women in the *Redbook* survey were less likely, however, to have reached orgasm during premarital sexual activity. One-third (34.2%) of the respondents said they never had an orgasm during premarital sexual experience, 36.5% said sometimes, 34.2% said most of the time, and only 6.7% said all of the time. An intimate relationship, rather than casual sex, is most conducive to a woman's reaching orgasm during premarital sex. Among those who reported a series of one night stands, 77% said they never reached orgasm. Of those reporting

on a stable premarital relationship, only 23% said they never reached orgasm.

The NHSLS survey shows that only 28.3% of women reporting always having an orgasm during lovemaking with a partner as compared with 75% of men (Laumann et al., 1994). Age differences indicate the youngest women, 21.5% of 18–24 year olds, least likely to always reach orgasm during sex with a partner, and women in their 40s and early 50s (45.9% and 44.9%, respectively) most likely to always reach orgasm. It is interesting that men overestimate by about 15% their partner's always reaching orgasm.

Others who may have one orgasm during lovemaking do not have multiple orgasms. Masters and Johnson (1966) reported that women during masturbation sometimes would have 5–20 orgasms and even 50 with a vibrator. What are some factors that are related to whether or not a woman has none or one or more orgasms? In a study of 24 orgasmic and 10 nonorgasmic women ages 21–40, the women who reached orgasm were significantly older than the nonorgasmic women, were better able to communicate with a partner regarding direct clitoral stimulation, had less negative attitudes about masturbation, greater sex knowledge, and lesser sex guilt (M. P. Kelly, Strassberg, & Kircher, 1990).

The differences observed in this study strongly suggest that those therapeutic techniques aimed at changing attitudes, guilt and knowledge (i.e., cognitive changes), and those designed to explore couples' communication difficulties and improve communication comfort with regard to sex, may be of particular value in the treatment of anorgasmia. (M. P. Kelly et al., 1990, p. 175)

An anonymous questionnaire completed by 2,175 professional female nurses in 15 states indicated that 42.7% of these women usually experienced multiple orgasms during masturbation, petting, and/or sexual intercourse (Denney, Field, & Quadagno, 1984). Only a small percentage experienced multiple orgasms during all three types of stimulation. Comparison of those who usually experienced multiple orgasm with those who experienced single orgasm during sexual activity found that multiorgasmic women were more likely to have initiated sexual activities such as masturbation at an earlier age. They were also more likely to have examined their clitoris and to have more often explored other techniques such as mental stimulation through sexual fantasies and erotic films and literature. With regard to partner sexual activity, multiorgasmic women were more likely to have given and received oral–genital stimulation, and to have had partners who orally and manually stimulated their nipples. Multiorgasmic women appear to have been able to overcome to some extent societally restrictive social norms regarding female sexuality.

Surveys and Laboratory Research of Female Arousal to Erotica

Women who were surveyed by Kinsey reported less arousal to erotica than men did. More recent laboratory research finds that women are as physiologically aroused by erotica as are men. Some women, however, are not aware of their own sexual arousal.

Kinsey et al. (1953) concluded that women were not as aroused by erotic materials as were men. The women surveyed by Kinsey had reported a low level of sexual arousal to **erotic** materials such as watching burlesque shows or reading erotic literary materials, or hearing stories that were deliberately intended to cause sexual arousal.

The NHSLS survey found twice as many men (23%) reported watching X-rated movies or videos as women (11%) within the past month (Laumann et al., 1994). Only 4% of women had gone to a club that has nude or seminude dancers and 4% reported having read sexually explicit books or magazines as compared with 22% and 16% of men, respectively.

Laboratory research, however, which measures physiological as well as subjective arousal, finds women to be aroused by erotic pictures and stories. The sexual double standard may make women reluctant to admit their arousal or to buy erotic materials, or even to be aware of their arousal. In more recent years, researchers have

devised physiological measures of sexual arousal. Blood volume in the penis is measured by a device called a penile strain gauge, which is a loop that fits around the base of the penis, and blood volume in the vagina is measured by a photoplethysmograph, a tampon-like cylinder that fits inside the entrance to the vagina. In an experiment by Julia Heiman (1977) male and female students listened to one of four kinds of tapes: (1) erotic (descriptions of heterosexual sex); (2) romantic (a couple who were expressing love and tenderness to one another but not engaging in sexual activity; (3) erotic-romantic (a couple expressing love and affection as well as engaging in sexual activity); and (4) control (neutral conversation). Both physiologically and in self-reports, males and females showed the most arousal to the tapes containing explicit sex, the erotic and erotic-romantic tapes. Neither men nor women were aroused by the romantic or neutral tapes.

Using physiological devices in her research, Heiman (1977) discovered that self-report of females and physiological sexual arousal in response to erotica was in many cases quite different. Some women lacked awareness of their own physiological sexual arousal. Although 100% of men who showed high-physiological arousal also reported feeling sexually aroused, only 58% of women whose physiological measures indicated high arousal reported being aroused. The other 42% reported experiencing no arousal during their greatest genital response to erotica.

Women may not attend to cues of genital response because females are socialized not to touch their genitals and not to focus attention on their genitals. Second, society presents ambivalent messages about sex to women, that although a woman is to please her husband she should be less interested in gratification of her own sexual needs (Morokoff, 1988).

Sexual Daydreaming

Sexual daydreaming is closely related to sexual drive, sexual activity, and a positive sexual attitude.

Sexual daydreaming is defined as sexual thoughts that occur spontaneously whereas **sexual fantasies** may be conscious, deliberately manipulated thoughts (Purifoy, Grodsky, & Giambra, 1992). Among 117 women in three age groups, 26–39 years, 40–55 years and 56–78 years, it was found that sexual daydreaming was closely related to sexual drive and sexual activity and with a positive sexual attitude. Although increased age was associated with lower reported sexual interest and activity, much of this relationship was due to the fact that most of the women with no sexual partner were in the oldest age group, and not having a partner was related to lower sexual daydreaming. "In fact, some of these women explained during the interview that they had adapted to the lack of a sexual partner, e.g. through widowhood, divorce, or estrangement within the marriage, by 'not thinking about it.'" (Purifoy, Grodsky, & Giambra, 1992). Thus, one way of adapting to being without a partner is to reduce sexual stimulation and to deliberately refrain from thinking about it.

Masturbation

The largest gender difference in sexual behavior is for masturbation. Men have a much greater incidence of masturbation than women.

Masturbation is typically a solitary sexual activity that requires no partner. This is a sexual behavior where significant gender differences have been found. Kinsey had found that the percentage of men and women reporting having masturbated varied by education: college graduates—96% of males and 57% of females; high school graduates—95% of males and 59% of females; and for those ending education with grammar school—89% of males and 34% of females (Kinsey, et al., 1953). A higher rate of frequency of masturbation was also found for men who masturbated as compared with women who masturbated.

In the *Redbook* magazine survey of 100,000 married women, when asked how often they masturbated since their marriage, 16% said frequently, 52% occasionally, 7% once, and 26%

never. However, for these married women, the more often a woman masturbates, the less satisfying her marital sex was likely to be. Those who did so often were compensating for bad sex in their marriage (Tavris & Sadd, 1978).

A meta-analysis of 239 independent samples and 490 effect sizes testing gender differences in sexual attitudes and behaviors found the largest gender difference to be in the incidence of masturbation, with males significantly more likely to engage in masturbation ($d = +.96$) (Oliver & Hyde, 1993). Differences in incidence of masturbation were smaller for the youngest samples (under age 18) ($d = +.44$), and much greater for the older samples (over age 25) ($d = +1.33$). Gender differences in the incidence of masturbation were also greater during the 1960s than they were in the 1980s, although they still remained large in the 1980s ($d = .60$).

The difference in attitudes toward masturbation, however, was trivial, although men did indicate somewhat more favorable attitudes. The gender difference in attitudes toward masturbation was related to age, with females younger than 18, having more favorable attitudes than males ($d = -.20$), whereas the reverse was true for the oldest samples ($d = +.15$).

Female masturbation, however, seems to be coming out of the closet in the 1990s, with articles appearing such as the one in the April 1994 issue of *Cosmopolitan*, "The M Word We Dare Not Say: (It Isn't Marriage, Money, or Mother) . . . it's *masturbation*, silly! Everybody knows self-love is normal, healthy, fun, so what's to be uptight about?" The article goes on to extol the pleasures of masturbation and discuss techniques (Meade, 1994).

Frequency of Sexual Activity

Couples living together two years or less, cohabiting heterosexual couples, and male homosexual couples, have sex more frequently than do couples in relationships of more than two years, married couples, and lesbian couples.

According to the NHSLS survey, the single most important determinant of the frequency of sexual activity is whether an individual is married or cohabiting or not living with a partner. Among those not cohabiting, 30.2% of the never married and 34.4% of the divorced/separated/widowed did not have sex in the past year, as compared with 1.4% of the never married, cohabiting, 0% of the divorced/separated/widowed cohabiting, and 3% of the married respondents.

> About 35% of the total have sex with a partner at least two or more times a week, and nearly 30 percent have partnered sex only a few times a year or not at all. The remaining 35% have partnered sex once or several times a month. (Laumann, et al., 1994, p. 89)

Age differences in the frequency of sexual activity among females is also large. The most sexually active women are the 25–29-year olds, only 4.5% of whom reported no sexual activity during the past year as compared to 40.8% of the 55–59 year olds.

In a nonprobability sample survey conducted by *Cosmopolitan* magazine, the frequency of sexual relations was found to vary with whether or not the couple is married, the gender of the partners, and the duration of the relationship (Bowe, 1993). Single women who live with a man have sex more frequently (40% make love once a day or more) than married (23% once a day) or dating women (7% once a day) (Bowe, 1993). In their study of heterosexual and homosexual couples Blumstein and Schwartz (1989) found that couples living together two years or less had sex more frequently than couples living together for longer durations of time. Among couples living together two years or less, the percentage of those having sex three times a week or more were 45% of married couples, 61% of heterosexual cohabiting couples, 67% of male couples, and only 33% of lesbian couples. Men were found to initiate sex more frequently than women in heterosexual relationships. This is most likely due to females' sexual socialization that teaches women to be the recipient rather than the leader in sexual relations. It may also account at least partially for the lower rate of sex among lesbians, since neither is socialized to be the initiator. "Additionally, themes in some lesbian subcultures stigma-

tize sexual aggressiveness as 'powerplays' and male-type sexuality, and place a lower premium on genital sexuality, with a corresponding emphasis on other forms of physical intimacy" (Blumstein & Schwartz, 1989, p. 127).

Human sexual behavior is embedded in a context and not simply the expression of individual sexual desires. Lesbian criticism of the Blumstein and Schwartz study is that a question about the frequency about "having sex" has different meaning for lesbians than it does for a heterosexual couple (Frye, 1990). The concept is a "phallic concept" that pertains to heterosexual intercourse in which the male ejaculates. "My guess is that neither the women's pleasure nor the women's orgasms were pertinent in most of the individuals' counting and reporting the frequency with which they 'had sex'" (Frye, 1990, p. 308).

Consistent with sex role scripts (and sociobiological explanations) men were found to initiate sex more frequently among married and cohabiting couples (Byers & Heinlein, 1989). More initiations also occurred by participants who were younger, were cohabiting rather than married, who had a relationship of shorter duration, and were satisfied with the relationship and reported greater sexual satisfaction. The partners responded positively to the sexual initiation three-quarters of the time.

Reasons for Engaging in Sex

Men attach most importance to pure pleasure; women attach most importance to emotional closeness.

Sexual desires of women are often not met in heterosexual sex. In Hite's (1979) research, she found dissatisfaction of women with the amount of foreplay that occurs during sexual interaction. A study of college students found that women indicated that foreplay was the most important part of a sexual encounter for them, and said that they wanted to spend more time in foreplay and afterplay (Denney, Field, & Quadagno, 1984). Men, on the other hand, reported enjoying intercourse more than foreplay and afterplay.

Men and women also differ in their reasons for engaging in sexual activities. A mail questionnaire on sexuality based on a systematic random sample of households in San Francisco yielded a 24% response rate, which included 445 women and 477 men (Leigh, 1989). Men attached more importance to pure pleasure, pleasing one's partner, conquest, and relief of tension than did women. The most important reason given by women for engaging in sex was to express emotional closeness. These gender differences appeared in both heterosexual and homosexual relationships. Men, however, also rated emotional closeness as an important reason, just after pleasure. It is interesting that men were more likely than women to say they engaged in sexual activities to please their partner. Differences also emerged between gays and straights with conquest and relief of sexual tension rated more highly by gay men and lesbians than by heterosexual men and women.

The Sexual Revolution

The sexual revolution began in the 1960s and is continuing in the 1990s. The rate of premarital sexual activity has increased dramatically. Economic and political equality of women is a necessary but not yet achieved concomitant of the sexual revolution.

The **sexual revolution** was largely a revolution in female sexual behavior. Men did not change their premarital sexual behavior all that much, but their partners were now likely to be the girl next door rather than a prostitute or woman of "sullied" reputation. "In the fifties, sleeping with a 'nice girl' was like walking through a china shop: 'You break it, you buy it' held true in both cases, and 'shotgun' marriages were common" (Ehrenreich, Hess, & Jacobs, 1986, p. 168).

The downside of the sexual revolution is that true sexual liberation cannot come until women have equality with men in every other domain. Feminism has challenged the narrow, heterosexual definition of sex, but more fundamental social change must accompany changes in sexual mores. The sexual revolution has been separated from the feminist movement.

The result is, to us, an odd and disturbing separation of goals: Women have won a new range of sexual rights—to pleasure, to fantasy and variety—but we have not yet achieved our full human rights. This disjuncture between feminism and women's sexual revolution affects both movements. (Ehrenreich, Hess, & Jacobs, 1986, pp. 5–6)

Women still bear children and undertake a disproportionate share of their rearing, particularly if they are never married or divorced. Women still have financial vulnerability since they still earn less income than men. Sexual freedom also removed the institutional supports linking sex, marriage, and financial support from a husband. Economic and political equality are a necessary (but not yet attained) concomitant of the sexual revolution.

The sexual revolution began in the late 1960s and is continuing into the 1990s. During this time, the rate of premarital sexual activity in the United States has increased dramatically. The Centers for Disease Control (1991) reported a survey they conducted in 1988 in which they asked 8,450 women between the ages of 15–44 years old when they had first had sex. Based on this data, average age at first intercourse was calculated for the years between 1970 and 1988. The rate of sexual activity increased steadily from 1970 to 1988. In 1988, 25.6% of 15 year olds were already sexually active, which was more than five times the rate of sexual activity for 15 year olds in 1970 (4.6%). For 19 year olds, the 1988 rate of sexual activity was 75.3%, which was more than 50% greater than the rate in 1970 (48.2%).

The Oliver and Hyde (1993) meta-analysis of research on sexual attitudes and behavior found a large gender difference in attitudes toward casual sex ($d = .81$) with males much more permissive in these attitudes. It is surprising that although males also had a greater number of sexual partners, the gender difference ($d = .25$) was small. Oliver and Hyde speculate that this smaller gender difference in behavior is best explained by social psychological models (situational determinants) so that females involved in dating relationships will engage in sexual inter-

TABLE 11.1 Meta-Analyses of Gender Differences in Sexual Attitudes and Behavior

	Effect Size *d*	*Study*
Attitudes toward:		Oliver & Hyde 1993
Anxiety or guilt about sex	−.35	
Casual premarital sex	.81	
Sexual permissiveness	.57	
Premarital sex in a committed relationship	.49	
Extramarital sex	.29	
Behavior		
Masturbation	.96	
Age at first intercourse	.38	
Incidence of sexual intercourse	.33	
Frequency of sexual intercourse	.31	
Number of sexual partners	.25	

course, although they may have negative attitudes toward casual sex.

Sociosexuality

Those who score high in sociosexuality have a larger number of partners and less commitment in sexual relationships than do those scoring low in sociosexuality. High scorers in sociosexuality have an avoidant attachment style.

Individual differences exist in the willingness to engage in uncommitted sexual relations (Simpson & Gangestad, 1991). Variability in **sociosexual** behavior occurs in frequency of sexual intercourse, number of partners, number of concurrent partners, including extramarital affairs, number of different partners foreseen in the future and frequency of sexual fantasies about partners other than the current one. Simpson and Gangestad (1991) developed a Sociosexual Orientation Inventory (SOI) that identifies the extent to which individuals possess a restricted as opposed to an unrestricted orientation toward engaging in uncommitted sex.

Two hundred and forty-one couples involved in dating relationships responded to the SOI and other measures within the survey. Unrestricted individuals compared with restricted ones typically engaged in sex at an earlier point in their relationship, engaged in sex with more than one partner at a time, and had less investment, less

commitment, and weaker affectional ties. Among sexually active couples, however, SOI scores did not correlate with absolute frequency of sex, indicating that an unrestricted approach to sex is not related to a high sex drive. Neither are SOI scores appreciably correlated with measures of sexual satisfaction, anxiety, and guilt. Thus, restricted individuals as compared with unrestricted ones are more likely to become involved in long-term relationships involving greater commitment.

What is the origin of sociosexuality? Research indicates that unrestricted individuals are more likely to adopt an avoidant attachment style (Simpson & Gangestad, 1989, as cited in Simpson & Gangestad, 1991). Sociosexuality also correlates moderately (.20 to .50) with the personality measures of social potency, harm-avoidance, aggression, and absorption (Tellegen et al., 1988, as cited in Simpson & Gangestad, 1991).

Despite the sexual revolution, the majority of men and women are monogamous.

The National Opinion Research Center's (NORC's) survey given during the winter of 1988 to 1,500 adults who were selected from a national probability sample of households in the United States found the majority of Americans to be monogamous. Among all adults, 86% were monogamous during the preceding 12 months, and 82% were monogamous among those who were sexually active. Women (90%) were more likely to be monogamous than men (81%). Monogamy increases with age, with 61% of 18–24-year olds reporting monogamy as compared with 98% of those over 70. Married men and women have particularly high rates of monogamy, with 96% saying they had only one partner during the previous year (Greeley, Michael, & Smith, 1990).

In the study of male homosexual, female homosexual, heterosexual married couples, and heterosexual cohabiting couples describe in Chapter X, Blumstein and Schwartz (1989), found married couples to be more monogamous than either cohabiting heterosexual couples or homosexual couples. Among married couples, 11% of husbands and 9% of wives reported at least one non-monogamous instance in the previous year. Among heterosexual cohabitors the instance of nonmonogamy was 25% for males and 22% for females; for homosexual males the frequency of nonmonogamy was 79% and for lesbians 19%. Marriage as an institution provides rules of monogamous conduct that shape people's behavior.

Extramarital Sex

Adultery is tolerated in men but punished in women, historically and cross-culturally.

The double standard for adultery is much stronger than the double standard for premarital sex. **Adultery** (extramarital sex) by men is tolerated but punished in women both historically and cross-culturally as well as in literature. In Jewish law, for example, a married woman is considered to be adulterous if she has sexual intercourse with any man other than her husband, but a married man is only guilty of adultery if he has sexual intercourse with another man's wife. It is not the violation of the wife's honor that is at issue, but a property crime against the other man.

The anthropologist Suzanne Frayser (1985) reports on the study of sexuality in 62 cultures, finding that in none of the cultures is adultery allowed for women but not for men. On the other hand, in 26% of the cultures the husband is allowed extramarital sex, although the wife is not. Of the 48 societies for which data was available,

more than half allowed the husband to kill his unfaithful wife.

In present day American culture, a wife's crime of adultery is all too frequently still punished by death. The tendency of jealous husbands to kill their wives—along with their children and their wives' lover—fill the pages of literature just as it fills pages of newspapers. Murder may be a dramatic breach of the marriage vows, but not so unthinkable that even the merest suspicion of extramarital sex cannot instantaneously provoke and even justify it (Heyn, 1992, p. 6).

Age, Employment, and Extramarital Sex

Women who work are twice as likely to engage in extramarital sex as compared with women who are housewives.

The NHSLS survey reports that over 90% of the women and 75% of the men are monogamous while married or cohabiting during the entirety of the relationship (Laumann et al., 1994). The number who were married or cohabiting at the time of the interview were less likely to have reported an extramarital affair during the union than were those whose relationships had ended.

According to Kinsey's data, the peak of extramarital sexual intercourse for females in the sample was when they were in their mid-30s and early 40s. About 85% of those who were engaging in extramarital activity were responding with orgasm at least some of the time, which was comparable to orgasm during marital coitus (Kinsey, et al., 1953).

In the *Redbook* sample of 100,000 married women (Tavris & Sadd, 1978) 29% of the wives had had extramarital sex. Employment of the wife nearly doubled the likelihood of having extramarital sex. Of wives in their late 30s, 53% of full-time employed women had had an extramarital affair, compared with only 24% of full-time housewives. The major theory as to why this occurs is the opportunity theory, that employment increases the opportunity to meet men. This theory seems to be supported by the data showing that women who do volunteer work or work part-time are halfway between full-time employed and part-time employed or volunteer workers in their level of extramarital affairs.

In the *Cosmopolitan* survey of female sexuality (Bowe, 1993) 39% of the married women admitted to having "cheated" on their husbands, mostly with just one man. Two-thirds of the husbands, however, did not know about it.

A survey of married individuals (148 males and 155 females) found that attitudes toward extramarital involvement vary according to justifications given for the relationship (Glass & Wright, 1992). Men were more approving of sexual justifications and women of emotional justifications as reasons for extramarital affairs. For example, sexual excitement was endorsed by 75% of the men as compared with 53% of the women in the sample who had engaged in extramarital intercourse. On the other hand, 77% of the women involved in extramarital relationships reported "falling in love" as a justification for extramarital sex as compared with 43% of the men. Men are more likely to separate sex and love than are women. Attitude–behavior congruence was found in that men and women who have engaged in extramarital relationships have more approving attitudes toward them.

Divorce and Sex

Being male and under 35 are the two variables most related to being involved in a sexual relationship among divorced persons. Recent research indicates a lower level of sexual activity among the divorced in the late 1980s as compared to the early 1970s.

Despite the fact that divorced people now constitute 9% of the population in the United States, we know very little about the sex lives of divorced people. Data from the 1988 and 1989 General Social Survey (GSS), a full probability sample of noninstitutionalized, English-speaking persons 18 years of age and older in the U.S. population, included 340 divorced respondents (Stack & Gundlach, 1992). Divorced women are more likely to have no sex partners (34%) as compared with divorced men (16%). Age was also related

to having sex partners, with only 4% of those under 35 reporting no sex partner compared with 35% of those over 35 reporting no sex partner. Lower religiosity, higher education, and political liberality, and absence of children were significant predictors of increased number of sex partners. These variables were, however, unrelated to sex frequency, with being male and under rather than over 35 the only two variables related to higher sexual frequency. This survey reports lower levels of sexual activity among the divorced as compared to previous research such as that of M. Hunt (1974). The previous surveys, however, were not probability sample surveys, so this is more accurate data. It may also be that since divorce has become more common, people with generally conservative attitudes also get divorced now.

Hispanic Women's Sexuality

Hispanic women generally have more conservative attitudes toward sex than nonHispanic women. They are less likely to be sexually active in high school and college, but are equally likely to become premaritally pregnant and are more likely to give birth.

Although there are shared aspects to culture and history for Latin women, their attitudes toward sex roles and sexuality are diverse. Some Latin women have embraced modern sex roles and sexual attitudes, whereas others maintain very traditional positions concerning sexual behavior. Hispanic women living in the United States, however, share the factors of immigration, language, and shared experience of oppression in the United States. Oppression further increases subordination to Latin men, as women may be suitable displacements for anger of oppressed men and victims of rape and wife beating (Espin, 1984).

Among Hispanics, women's sexual behavior is a reflection of the family's honor. The importance of maintaining virginity until marriage is still emphasized. Nevertheless, Hispanic unwed mothers are usually accepted by their families. As part of the message of subservience to men, combined with the emphasis on sexual purity, enjoying sexual pleasure may indicate a woman's lack of purity.

> To shun sexual pleasure and to regard sexual behavior exclusively as an unwelcome obligation toward her husband and a necessary evil in order to have children may be seen as a manifestation of virtue. In fact, some women even express pride at their own lack of sexual pleasure or desire. (Espin, 1984, p. 156)

The "macho" Hispanic man is still in existence and his inconsiderate behavior toward women may serve to reinforce her negative attitudes toward sex.

Research comparing sexual, contraceptive, pregnancy, abortion, and live-birth rates for Anglo and Mexican American college students (Padilla & O'Grady, 1987) and adolescents in a community-based probability sample (Aneshensel, Fielder, & Becerra, 1989) both found the two groups to differ significantly, largely due to a more traditional value system of Mexican American females. Mexican Americans had experienced intercourse less frequently, had fewer dating partners, had masturbated less frequently, had used condoms more frequently, and had used the pill less frequently. Mexican Americans had more conservative attitudes than Anglos concerning autoeroticism, abortion, and heterosexual relations. Mexican Americans also possessed less factual knowledge. Although Mexican Americans were no more likely to have been pregnant, they were more likely to have had a live birth, while Anglos were more likely to have had an abortion.

African American Women's Sexuality

Although sexually active at an earlier age than White females, Black females engage in less variety of sexual behavior, sexual intercourse being their primary sexual outlet. Open communication and an overall satisfying relationship with her partner is related to sexual satisfaction for African American women.

Sexuality for Black females is complex, created by a history of sexual and economic exploitation by White men and the frustrated rage of Black men dispossessed of their power.

> Because poor and systematically exploited Black and third world women do not seem to place great emphasis on sexuality in the manner of more comfortable Western women, does not mean our sexual feelings are not important to us. But it should be understood that if you're starving to death along with your children and your men are dead, have migrated or are waging a guerrilla war, sexual pleasure cannot be a primary consideration. (P. M. Robinson, 1984, p. 262)

Men in this world become more important for their role in impregnation and having children, which are very important to Black women emotionally. The children become a compensation for the exploitation and disparagement of society and relations with men who are restricted by their own oppression.

Given the past and present oppression, what are present sexual attitudes and behavior among young African American women? Sexual activity and contraceptive use among African American urban, low-income females was studied via questionnaire measures administered to clients of an inner city health care clinic (Keith, McCreary, Collins, Smith, & Bernstein, 1991). Not sexually active young women tended to be younger, to be more career motivated, to have a father at home, and to be more conservative in their attitudes toward adolescent sexual activity, which had been influenced by family values, as compared with sexually active adolescents.

Comparisons between African American and White adolescent females show that White females from two-parent families were most likely to be virgins, but once sexually active, White females had a higher level of sexual activity than Black females from two-parent homes (E. W. Young, Jensen, Olsen, & Cundick, 1991). Although for females, a two-parent home had less influence than it did for males, females from two-parent families were also less likely to be sexually active and to be older at first intercourse than females from single parent homes. For females from single parent homes, the boyfriend may in part be a father substitute. She may need and crave male attention that may have been lacking in her life, and find that sexuality is a way of receiving that male attention.

As part of a larger study of a probability sample of African American and White American women 18–36 years of age in Los Angeles County, African American women were interviewed in order to understand the circumstances in which women engage in sex and the elements of their sexual satisfaction (Wyatt & Lyons-Rowe, 1990). They were asked to respond to the questions in terms of the longest relationship with the primary partner.

Sex for African American women was highly dependent on a partner, since 42% said they never masturbated. Sexual satisfaction for African American women was related to open communication and a satisfying overall relationship. The women's sexual satisfaction was related to communicating sexual needs verbally and nonverbally, and a high frequency of sexual intercourse. When the woman initiated sex with her partner, a high percentage of the time, she felt that intercourse with her partner brought new and exciting feelings and was one of the best experiences she had ever had. In relation to background variables, women with mothers who had higher educational levels reported higher sexual interest/enthusiasm. A high level of church attendance in childhood was related to less sexual responsiveness in adulthood. A satisfaction scale that was devised for this study found no relationship between fellatio and anal intercourse and satisfaction, as these were behaviors only infrequently engaged in—55% and 21% of African American women had ever engaged in these activities, respectively. They were less sexually satisfied when they "were unsure if engaging in intercourse was right or wrong; felt guilty; were fearful of the consequences of intercourse with their primary partner; did not feel sexual relations with their partner was a rewarding experience; and were orgasmic less than 25 percent of the time" (Wyatt & Lyons-Rowe, 1990, pp. 517–518).

SEXUAL ORIENTATION

Bisexual Women

Married bisexual women have a high level of sexual and marital satisfaction when their lesbian experiences take place within the context of "swinging," but not when they participate in lesbian activities outside of the marriage.

A **bisexual** woman is one who is sexually attracted by members of both sexes. A sample of 45 bisexual women (average age 35.9) who were currently (4) or previously married (41) were surveyed regarding lesbian experiences before marriage, sexual problems in marriage, and sexual orientations (Coleman, 1985). Twenty-one (47%) of the women had some awareness of their lesbian feelings before marriage. Since the average age of marriage of these women was 21.6 years, 27 (60%) did not have their first lesbian experience until after they were married. Sexual difficulties were very common in these marriages, with 40 (89%) reporting some degree of sexual problems, primarily lack of sexual desire for their spouse (62%). Nine percent of the wives sought psychotherapy for the purpose of eliminating their homosexual feelings. None was able to do this. Their marriages lasted an average of 8.5 years. They moved in sexual behavior, fantasy, and emotional attachments along Kinsey's continuum from the heterosexual end toward the homosexual end before marriage, during, and after marriage.

In terms of developing an integrated sexual orientation identity, these women seem to be further delayed developmentally than the average population of exclusively homosexual women or men. One reason for this delay may be that these individuals seem to have an extensive bisexual history, which in turn might delay the process of developing an integrated identity (Coleman, 1985, p. 97).

Another factor in their delay in developing their sexual orientation identity may be that while mainstream society supports heterosexual orientation and homosexual groups provide support for lesbians, there is little in the way of support for bisexuals. This was not a random survey and sought participants from among clients of psychotherapists, so further research needs to be conducted with bisexual women to better understand their development.

One way in which women become introduced to same sex sexual activities is through "swinging" with their husbands. Research reports on women swingers find that a high percentage (60–92%) of the females engage in genital sexual activities with other women (Dixon, 1985). In-depth personal interviews with 50 married women who, with their spouses, engaged in consensual swinging activities, including sexual activities with another woman, found the average length of time in which they engaged in the swinging lifestyle before they engaged in sex with another female was three years. The median number of sex partners was 12, although the range was from 3 to 250. For none of the women was their first or current sexual activities with other women limited to situations where the two females were alone. The vast majority (82%) were receivers in their first multifemale sexual activity. They rated their first multifemale sexual experience from "excellent" (16%), "fair" (36%), neutral (24%), "somewhat negative" (14%), and "very negative" (10%). They became increasingly positive about multifemale sexual activities as they gained more experience with it. Their fantasy lives changed as well as their behavior.

I never before fantasized about women. My whole fantasy world has changed . . . I learned how great they (women lovers) are.

Now I fantasize women together sometimes—before I had no fantasies.

Now while masturbating I fantasize two women actively involved . . . never had women in fantasies before (Dixon, 1985, p.123).

It is interesting that sexual satisfaction was rated high within the marriage, with 76% rating it as excellent or good. They rated their marital compatibility as excellent or good (80%). This sample differs from the Coleman study in that they already were swingers and had open marriages, and so did not have to deal with issues of

nonmonogamy in initiating woman-to-woman sexual relationships. They maintained a high level of coital activity with their spouses (mean = 3.5 times per week), and shared at least five other (nonsexual) activities with their spouses as well.

Despite their history of heterosexual behavior, all of the respondents self-identified as bisexual at the time of the interview. None of the women, however, had changed her overall preference for males. For many of the women, their involvement in multifemale sexual activity improved their relationships with other women and increased their interest in the women's movement. Prior to their bisexuality only 4% indicated that they were in any way involved in the women's movement, whereas 22% became active after their first multifemale experience. Their attitudes toward themselves also changed positively. Keep in mind that these women were already engaged in a lifestyle with few sexual inhibitions or restrictions and were not a representative sample of the female population.

Lesbian Women

Homosexuality and heterosexuality is a continuum, with most people exclusively heterosexual, but others have had both heterosexual or homosexual relationships at different periods in their lives, and some people have been exclusively homosexual.

Homosexuality refers to sexual attraction to and genital sexuality practiced with persons of the same sex. **Lesbians** are female homosexuals. Disapproval in American society is stronger towards male homosexuals than it is toward lesbians. The Oliver and Hyde (1993) meta-analysis found no gender difference in attitudes towards homosexuals.

Kinsey and his colleagues (1953) devised a heterosexuality–homosexuality scale ranging from 0 to 6 on which individuals were categorized on a continuum between exclusively heterosexual at one end and exclusively homosexual at the other end.

0 Completely heterosexual
1 Predominantly heterosexual, incidental homosexual responses
2 Predominantly heterosexual, more than incidental homosexual responses
3 Equally heterosexual and homosexual
4 Predominantly homosexual, but more than incidental heterosexual responses
5 Predominantly homosexual, only incidental heterosexual responses
6 Exclusively homosexual

Heterosexuality, homosexuality, and bisexuality may coexist, a homosexual phase of development may be antecedent to heterosexuality, or homosexuality may occur after heterosexuality over a period of time. **Primary lesbians** are those who from an early age experienced sexual attraction to other females that lasts a lifetime. **Elective lesbians** are those who have chosen homosexuality after having lived in heterosexual relationships in the past (Golden, 1987).

Klein (1990) has developed a complex model of sexual behavior that takes into consideration sexual attraction, sexual fantasies, self-identification, lifestyle, emotional preference, and social preference. One feature of this model is that it accounts for change over time. Each individual could be placed on a continuum from exclusively heterosexual to exclusively homosexual, but sexual fantasies, emotional preference, and so on, would be included as well as behavior.

An example of an elective lesbian is a friend, who was married for over 20 years and during that marriage had two children. After divorcing her husband, she said she fell in love with another woman and entered a lesbian relationship with her. She said that over the many years of her marriage she was not aware of being sexually attracted to other women. Her experience of a prolonged period of engagement in one or more heterosexual relationships prior to becoming a lesbian is not unusual. Falling in love with another woman was the marker of transition to lesbianism for three-quarters of the 80 participants in a research study of lesbian identity (Kitzinger & Wilkinson, 1995). All of the women had a minimum of 10 years active heterosexual behavior, including intercourse, before defining themselves

as lesbians. Girls are taught to value femininity and heterosexuality, so a lesbian identity is one that is considered abnormal and perverse and one that girls are taught to avoid.

> The first time I fell in love with a woman I was 25 and pregnant with my second child. I thought, "What's this? Are you bisexual or what? And then I pushed it to the back of my mind. There was no way I could deal with it because I had these children, and a husband, and no way of supporting myself. So I just didn't think about it. (Kitzinger & Wilkinson, 1995, p. 98)

So some women postponed their development of a lesbian identity until later in their lives, whereas others did not become aware of a lesbian orientation until much later in life. The coming-out process was a mixture of pain and of joy and excitement, as they lost privilege, safety, and status, but gained a sense of freedom and of community with other lesbians. This research was conducted within a social constructionist framework, that women construct their lesbian identities. This is quite different from the essentialist view that lesbianism is a biological given.

Support exists for both the social construction and biological approaches to the development of homosexuality. As I stated in Chaper II in this book, the reason psychologists cannot decide on the percentage of intelligence due to heredity or environment is because the percentage due to heredity or environment varies from one individual to another. The same holds true for sexual behavior. For some individuals becoming homosexual or heterosexual is primarily due to genetics, whereas for others the decision is primarily due to environmental influences. Also to be kept in mind is that biological factors are not all hereditary and biological influences may be environmental as well. An investigation of women with a history of prenatal exposure to DES, a synthetic estrogen prescribed for their mothers during pregnancy, found the DES daughters to be more likely to rate themselves as bisexual or homosexual (Meyer-Bahlburg et al., 1995). For some individuals homosexuality is largely the result of biological forces, whereas for other individuals, the psychosocial factors are more important in the construction of a lesbian identity.

The answers to the development of heterosexuality, homosexuality, or bisexuality are found in the influence of prenatal hormones and brain structure (see Chapter II) and postnatal experience (Money, 1987). Which of these is the more influential element in the individual's sexual orientation is going to vary from one individual to another. According to A. P. Bell, Weinberg, and Hammersmith (1981) about two-thirds of exclusively homosexual men and women exhibited atypical gender-role behavior during childhood. To gain insight into the determinants of homosexuality (and heterosexuality), Van Wyck and Geist (1984) reanalyzed the original Kinsey data. Demographic variables and variables such as mother or father absence accounted for less than 1% of the variance in the Kinsey scale scores. Females who had elevated homosexuality scores on the Kinsey scale were found to be more likely to have had prepubertal sexual contact with an adult male and to have been aroused by it. By the age of 18 the women with higher homosexual scores had found the thought or sight of females, but not males, arousing. Lesbians had fewer girl companions at age 10 and fewer male companions at age 16 than did women with a heterosexual orientation. They were also more likely to have learned to masturbate by being masturbated by a female. This data analysis thus indicates that early sexual experience is predictive of later homosexual behavior.

According to Kinsey's data, 20% of females reported homosexual experience by age 45. Among single women, 26% reported some homosexual experience, but among married females only 3% reported homosexual experience, and among the formerly married, the percentage rose to 10% (Kinsey, et al., 1953). On the other hand, the NHSLS (1994) survey reports that only 3.8% of women and 7.1% of men had at least one same sex partner since puberty. When asked on the self-administered questionnaire, which the respondent placed in a sealed envelope before giving to the interviewer, about specific acts with same sex partners, 4.3% of women and 9.1% of the men indicated ever having a same-sex sexual

experience. Of the men, for 42% of the men who reported a same sex-experience, it occurred before they turned 18 and not after. Probability sample surveys conducted in Great Britain and France find similar percentages of homosexual experience.

Data from the Blumstein and Schwartz (1983) study, *American Couples,* finds that lesbian couples have sex less frequently than gay men or heterosexual couples. Two-thirds of lesbians in relationships of two years or longer had sex less than once a week, and 47% had sex only once a month or less. In contrast, two-thirds of heterosexual couples had sex once a week or more, and only 15% of those in long-term relationships had sex once a month or less. Lesbians interviewed by Blumstein and Schwartz preferred hugging and cuddling rather than genital sex.

Some lesbians cohabit in long-term relationships, whereas others remain unattached and seek partners in gay bars and at lesbian dances. Some gay women may have long-term lovers but maintain separate residences. Lesbian couples have a median relationship duration of 3–4 years and a mean of less than two years. Why are lesbian relationships of shorter duration than heterosexual relationships? "Reasons hypothesized have been lack of kin and peer support, societal stigma and oppression, lack of role congruence, and different value systems" (Laws & Schwartz, 1977).

A problem that lesbians have to deal with in relationships that heterosexuals do not, which can interfere with their sexual relationships, is internalized homophobia (Margolies, Becker, & Jackson-Brewer, 1987). One manifestation is restricting their attractions to unavailable women, heterosexuals, or women in committed relationships, which prevents their full expression of lesbianism. Another result of internalized homophobia is confining relationships to casual "dating" and avoiding commitment. In a committed relationship there are greater social risks such as questions of how to spend holidays, that draw attention to the homosexual lifestyle. Erotophobia, fear of sexuality, which is a problem shared by many heterosexuals in our society, is often a particularly acute problem for lesbians because of the separation of homosexuality from procreation. "Because homophobia is a reflection of the way in which society views homosexuality, the nature of homophobia may change over time with society's changing attitudes toward sex and difference (Margolies et al., 1987, p. 240).

"Coming out" is a complex process, but appears to be related to higher levels of physical and mental health.

The theory that coming out is a complex process, resulting from an interaction of internal and external factors, was supported by research with a highly educated sample of lesbians (M. J. Kahn, 1991). Holding feminist attitudes was associated with lower levels of internalized homophobia and more openness. Lesbians who had a more intimate relationship with their family of origin were less likely to be open in general and with their family. One risks loss of the relationship with disclosure. Being out, however, appears to be related to higher levels of physical and mental health and more authenticity in interpersonal relationships and less guilt (Graham et al., as cited in M. J. Kahn, 1991).

Attitudes toward Homosexuals

Homosexuals can be legally discriminated against in most states in the United States. Homophobic attitudes are most strongly held by church-going, older, male, uneducated, married, southerners.

Many people in society display homophobia, a strong negative attitude towards and irrational fear of homosexuals. This attitude is carried so far that in most states homosexuals can be discriminated against in housing, employment, and credit. In 1955, the Rhode Island State legislature passed a law to end discrimination against homosexuals, after it had been defeated in the legislature every year for the 12 previous years. Based on a national telephone survey of 2,308 adult respondents conducted by the *Los Angeles Times*, political viewpoints are the most predictive variable for homophobic attitudes (Seltzer, 1992), with political conservatives holding more antihomosexual attitudes. People who attend church frequently or who are reborn Christians hold more antihomosexual attitudes, except among Blacks where weekly church attendance was unrelated to antihomosexual attitudes. More antihomosexual attitudes were also held by those who are less educated, older, married, and Southern. Among the college educated, there is a "civil rights generation" effect with those between 30 and 49 more liberal than those who are either older or younger. Similarly, with Blacks, those respondents between the ages of 30 and 49 (of all educational levels) are more liberal in homosexual attitudes.

Although Oliver and Hyde (1994) found no gender difference in attitudes toward homosexuality in their meta-analysis, another meta-analysis by Whitley and Kite (1995) reported an effect size of $d = +.26$ showing males to be more homophobic than females. Whitley and Kite added a number of studies with college students who show a much larger gender difference in attitudes toward homosexuality than does the general population. Whitley (1987) found that heterosexuals' negative attitudes toward gay men and lesbians was related to more traditional sex role beliefs, sex role self-concept, and sex role behavior patterns as well as to being younger. A more recent study again found gender role attitudes to mediate the relationship between negative attitudes toward gay men and lesbians (Kerns & Fine, 1994). No gender differences were found in attitudes toward lesbians among heterosexual college students, but men had more negative attitudes toward gay men than did women. The attitudes toward gay men, however, were more strongly related to gender role attitudes than to gender.

SEX AND THE REPRODUCTIVE LIFECYCLE

The Menstrual Cycle

Research on the sex activity of women during the menstrual cycle provides conflicting results.

Does the sex drive of women vary with phases of the menstrual cycle? The research in this area has not been consistent. At least in part this has been due to methodological problems. Many of the studies have tested women only once during each phase of the menstrual cycle. We do not know, for example, what the time relationship is between hormonal and behavioral changes. Sexual behavior is also influenced by external stimuli. The presence of a partner and the nature of the relationship with that partner is the overriding determinant of sexual motivation and behavior in women.

When tested on a Sexual Arousal Inventory on a daily basis during the menstrual cycle, no differences were found in sexual arousal scores of women (1) who were not on the pill and married, (2) who were on the pill and married, and (3) who were not married and were celibate. An interaction effect was found, however, between the three groups and phases of the cycle. All three groups reported an increase in arousal from the menses to the early follicular phase, during which time estrogen levels would be increasing. After that, the nonpill married group reported a second increase during the ovulatory phase. This group and the celibate group declined in sexual arousal during the luteal phase. The difference in sexual arousal for the different phases was significant, however, only for the celibate group, not the married nonpill group. The pill taking group did not report a luteal trough. A replication of this research with larger numbers of women is warranted.

When Jarvis and McCabe (1991) asked undergraduate women to rate their present level of sexual arousal, they found no difference between ratings for women in different phases of the menstrual cycle. When asked about their usual level of sexual arousal, however, the highest ratings were given by those in the ovulatory phase, and lowest for those in the premenstrual phase. Being in the experimental situation probably inhibited their ratings for current sexual arousal. Since there was no difference in ratings of sexual arousal by those on oral contraceptives and those not taking them, estrogen levels cannot explain their higher-reported usual sexual arousal.

Sexual Desire and Satisfaction during Pregnancy

In general, women report less sexual desire and satisfaction during pregnancy, particularly during the third trimester, but some women report greater sexual responsiveness.

A number of studies have reported a decrease in sexual desire, frequency, and satisfaction of intercourse during pregnancy (W. E. Miller & Friedman, 1988; Ryding, 1984). This decline occurred even in normal pregnancies where the physicians following the women placed no limitations on their sexual activity (Tolor & DiGrazia, 1976). A longitudinal study of women who were seen as many as eight times during pregnancy and six times in the postnatal year indicated a decrease in the desire for and satisfaction with intercourse as pregnancy progressed (Elliot & Watson, 1985). There was, however, a high degree of individual variation. In a longitudinal study of couples expecting their first child, the greatest decline in sexual desire, frequency, and satisfaction for both men and women was in the third trimester. Women experienced significantly more decline in sexual desire than did men during the first trimester. Women who were over 25, who had at least a high school education, and who were married had decreased sexual desire and frequency during the first and third trimester. Women with sexual aversion before pregnancy more often had decreased sexual satisfaction during the first trimester compared to before pregnancy whereas women who did not have previous sexual aversion showed no decline. Women who had a good relationship with both their mother and father during childhood were more likely to have unchanged sexual desire and frequency during pregnancy compared to other women.

As Masters and Johnson (1966) pointed out, some women may find heightened sexual responsiveness during pregnancy due to an increased blood supply to the pelvic area. W. A. Fisher and Gray (1989) have found a difference between women who were erotophobic or erotophilic, with erotophilic women showing more sexual interest, activity, and satisfaction during pregnancy.

Many conflicting emotions may arise during pregnancy regarding sexuality by both the woman and her partner.

Saunders (1983) views sex in pregnancy from a feminist perspective—from her own journals and from in-depth interviews with six other women. She criticizes social sciences for looking at only what can be measured, leaving out the experiences of women. Many conflicting emotions may arise during pregnancy regarding sexuality on the part of both the woman and her partner.

"I felt particularly 'safe' being pregnant—safe from being leered at or wolf-whistled at or attacked, and I wanted to be seen as being pregnant." As we know this safety is hypothetical. "I wanted sexual contact but my husband saw me as somehow untouchable, the Virgin Mary syndrome." The woman who felt safe while pregnant also reveals: "My husband often jokingly made uncomplimentary comments about the shape and size of my stomach and although I wasn't seriously affected by these, I occasionally saw myself as someone totally undesirable sexually." (Saunders, 1983, p. 91)

Although some women take refuge in pregnancy from sexuality, in other cases it may be the husband rather than the wife who no longer desires sex because he does not find his pregnant wife sexually attractive.

Sex and Motherhood

There is a widespread ideology that once a woman becomes a mother she is no longer a sexual being. The conflict over asexual motherhood is highlighted during breast-feeding. Some authors point out that breast-feeding can be sexually arousing (Kitzinger, 1983; Lawrence, 1980). One reason some women do not breast-feed in our society is because of guilt and fear about sexual arousal during breast-feeding. Some women may feel guilty about this kind of experience because they do not realize this arousal is normal. Research does show that women high in sex guilt are less likely to breast-feed their infants (W. A. Fisher et al., 1989).

Myths about women categorize women as either madonna or whore. The madonna is supposed to be silent about sexuality. Masters and Johnson (1966) report, however, that mothers are more likely to be orgasmic during sexual intercourse than women who have never borne a child. Nevertheless, a comparison of two matched groups of military wives (beyond one year postpartum), 50 of whom were mothers and 50 who were not, found the mothers to have more negative attitudes toward sex and a lower frequency of sexual activity (Apt & Hurlbert, 1992).

Sex and Aging

Generally, the quality of sex remains high over 40, but frequency usually declines.

A survey of readers of *Family Circle* magazine who were over 40 found that the women reported that sex gets better as they get older, but that the frequency declines (C. R. Rubenstein, 1985). The women said that quality is more important than quantity. Research going back to Kinsey's survey data suggests that women get more orgasmic as they get older.

Actually, women are likely to enjoy sexual activity in middle age more than they did in adolescence and young adulthood (C. G. Adams & Turner, 1985). On the other hand, Kinsey also found that there is a steady decline in sexual activity of females for each advancing decade (i.e., 30s, 40s, 50s, 60s, etc). The extent that the decline in sexual activity is a function of the male partner's lowered sexual activity with declining age is difficult to determine.

To better assess changes in women's sexual desire at midlife, 497 urban women in Sweden who were married or cohabiting were interviewed about their sexual desire on two occasions six years apart (Hallstrom & Samuelsson, 1990). Women were aged 38, 46, 50, and 54 at the initiation of the study. A change in sexual desire between the first and second interviews was found for 37% of the sample, with 27% noticing a decrease of sexual desire and 10% experiencing an increased desire. A decrease in sexual desire was positively related to: age; higher sexual desire at the first interview; lack of a confiding relationship; insufficient support from spouse; alcoholism in spouse; and major depression. A decrease in sexual desire was also related to mental disorder, anxiety neurosis, use of psychotropic medication, duration of mental disorder, and life-event stress. Increased sexual desire was related to weaker sexual desire and greater mental disability at first interview (over the six years mental health was likely to improve among the more disturbed), and negative marital relations at first interview. Nearly two-thirds of the respondents reported no change in sexual desire from the first to the second interview.

Morokoff (1988) considered sexuality of postmenopausal women in terms of four dimensions: desire; arousal; orgasm; and pain. She reviewed the literature, concluding that most women continue to enjoy sexual activity during and after menopause. Postmenopausal women, however, do show a decline in sexual functioning including decrease in the frequency of sexual intercourse, decreased desire, decreased frequency of orgasm, and lack of vaginal lubrication. There is conflicting data in the literature about the relationship of hormone levels to sexual functioning in postmenopausal women. Dyspareunia (painful intercourse) may be related to lowered estrogen levels because of its relation to vaginal dryness. Testosterone appears to be related to women's sexual desire. More research has been done on the effect of hormone levels on women who have undergone surgical menopause (removal of uterus and ovaries) than on women who have gone through a natural menopause.

The Starr-Weiner Report on Sex & Sexuality in the Mature Years (1981) explodes some of the myths about sexuality and aging. The book reports on a survey of 800 men (35%) and women (65%) between the ages of 60 and 91. Many of the women (41%) said that sex is better than ever. Orgasm is still considered "very important" (63%) or "somewhat important" (29%) by the female respondents. In fact, 98.5% of the women said that they were orgasmic during lovemaking. This is a higher percentage than that reported in any other study, all of which have used samples of younger women. When asked how sex has changed since the menopause, 31.1% said better, 35.3% said no change, and 13.6% said worse.

Despite the high interest in and responsiveness to sex of the women in the Starr and Weiner survey, the majority of the women (61%) were widows or single and divorced women. For the sample as a whole, 30% of the women (as compared with only 7% of the men) were not currently sexually active. For the women that were not involved in a sexual relationship with a man, developing new patterns of nonsexual intimacy with women friends, masturbation, communal living, and lesbianism were alternatives for some women.

SEXUAL DYSFUNCTION

Primary and Secondary Orgasmic Dysfunction

The most common sexual dysfunctions are primary orgasmic dysfunction, inhibited sexual desire, vaginismus and dyspareunia. Sex guilt, acceptance of myths about sex and relationship problems are the major causes of sexual dysfunction, except for dyspareunia which most frequently has a physical cause.

Primary orgasmic dysfunction is used to describe women who have never experienced orgasm under any circumstances—foreplay, intercourse, masturbation, vibrator, and so on. The incidence of women reporting primary orgasmic dysfunction apparently has not changed much over the years, with about 10–20% reporting in various surveys that they are nonorgasmic. Females who do not reach orgasm span the range of responsivity, from absolute unresponsiveness to considerable responsivity, up to, but not including orgasm. Both Masters and Johnson (1970) and Kaplan (1974) rely on physiological measures of vaginal contractions to describe the clinical phenomena of inorgasmia.

If a woman has had orgasms, but is concerned about the frequency or is not reaching orgasm during intercourse or under other circumstances in which she would like to, then the difficulty is called **secondary orgasmic dysfunction**. Orgasmically dysfunctional women have been found to report greater difficulty in communicating with a partner about clitoral stimulation, to have more negative attitudes toward masturbation, greater acceptance of myths about sex and greater sex guilt (M. P. Kelly, Strassberg, & Kircher, 1990).

Inhibited sexual desire (ISD) disorders refer to the lack of interest in sexual activity. In clinical settings, arousal phase disorders are the most common presenting problem of females, followed by orgasmic dysfunction (I. P. Spector & Carey, 1990; Stuart, Hammond, & Pett, 1987). In the 1970s females were more likely than were males to seek help for inhibited sexual desire, but the pattern reversed in the 1980s, with males more likely to seek help for this disorder than females. The incidence of this disorder also had an overall increase in the 1980s.

Psychological and relationship factors appear to be more important influences on female sexual desire than are biological factors. Research on 17 women aged 27–39 suffering from inhibited sexual desire were found not to significantly differ from 13 healthy, sexually active women in their level of reproductive hormones: testosterone, SHBG, estradiol, progesterone, prolactin, and luteinizing hormone (Schreiner-Engel, Schiavi, White, & Ghizzani, 1989).

One study compared 59 married women seeking treatment for inhibited sexual desire from a marital therapy clinic with 31 married women expressing normal sexual desire but seeking treatment for other marital problems (Stuart et al., 1987).

> In order to receive the diagnosis of ISD, at least three of the following criteria (Kaplan, 1979) need to be present: a lifelong history of asexuality, phobic avoidance of sex, low level of initiation or sexual receptivity, low frequency of sexual activity, a consistent negative reaction to sexual activity, verbal expression of a lack of interest in sex, significant decrease in libido from a past norm for that particular individual, engaging in sex for reasons other than desire (e.g., to avoid hurting a partner's feelings), and partner complaint. (Stuart et al., 1987, p. 95)

No significant differences were found between the ISD and non-ISD groups in endocrine factors, personality adjustment as measured by the 10 clinical scales of the MMPI, or in background characteristics. Significant differences were found, however, in past and present sexual history. The largest differences were found between the two groups in the quality of the marital relationship. Despite the fact that ISD women refused sexual intercourse more than half of the time, and 50% of the husbands stopped initiating sex, the ISD women reported a sexual frequency that did not differ from that of the non-ISD women, which in part may be due to the persistence of the 50% of the ISD husbands who do continue to initiate intercourse, and the possible sexual difficulties of the non-ISD husbands. It is apparent that the ISD women engage in sexual intercourse for reasons other than sexual desire, such as the desire to be held, out of the guilt of depriving their husband of sexual intercourse, because of the husband's persistence, or the fear of infidelity. Non ISD women also perceived their parents as having a more affectionate interaction with one another, which may indicate that parental modeling may have an effect later in life. The implications of this research for sex therapy is that the couple rather than the individual must be treated.

Patricia Morokoff and Julia Heiman (1980) simultaneously measured subjective and physiological sexual response of vaginal vasocongestion of 11 patients at a sexual dysfunction clinic and 11 sexually nondysfunctional women. Although there was no significant difference in the physiological arousal of the two groups of women when watching and listening to erotic video and audio tapes and engaging in sexual fantasy, the sexually dysfunctional women were often not aware of their sexual arousal.

Vaginismus is contractions of the outer third of the vagina, which may constrict the opening of the vagina to such an extent that it may even be impossible to engage in sexual intercourse. Vaginismus ranges from 12% to 17% of those seeking help from sexual dysfunction clinics (I. P. Spector & Carey, 1990). It may be caused by having been raped during an earlier period, by having painful intercourse over a period of time, or by having been raised to believe that sex is dirty and sinful.

Dyspareunia refers to pain during sexual intercourse. This problem is usually reported to general practitioners or gynecologists rather than to sex therapists. The cause of pain in the pelvic region is almost always an underlying medical problem such as PID, and a gynecological exam should be performed. Vaginal pain may be the result of failure to lubricate, particularly in post menopausal women, and can be ameliorated by use of a lubricant. In some cases, however, the cause may be psychogenic.

Sex Therapy

Newer sex therapies are more effective in treating problems of sexual dysfunction than is traditional psychotherapy.

Traditional psychotherapy was ineffective in treating problems of sexual dysfunction. In more recent years, several major treatment approaches have appeared on the scene to treat sexual dysfunction with more demonstrable success—systematic desensitization, sensate focus, directed masturbation, and hypnosis. The publication of the book *Human Sexual Dysfunction* by Masters and Johnson (1970) introduced a new short-term sex therapy approach for patients with sexual dysfunction. The sexual dysfunction was treated as a problem of the couple rather than an individual problem. A couple would spend two weeks at Masters' and Johnson's clinic, staying at a nearby hotel. During the first few days the couple would be told not to have sexual intercourse, but to instead use the technique of sensate focus, in which partners would touch and massage parts of the body of their partners while receiving feedback from the partner about how the touching felt. One method women are advised to use to enhance sexual pleasure and increase the frequency of orgasm are Kegel exercises (voluntary vaginal contractions). The woman is told to learn to contract the vaginal muscle by imagining she is urinating and to voluntarily stop the flow of urine. In an experiment with college women, the group of women who were given information about the

exercises and practiced them in a private chamber in the laboratory and between sessions had higher levels of arousal, both subjectively and physiologically, than did the women who were given the information about Kegel exercises but did not practice tensing during or between recording sessions (Messe & Geer, 1985). When also instructed to combine the exercises with self-generated fantasy, tensing further increased arousal. It thus appears that practice of the Kegel contractions can enhance sexual pleasure.

Masturbation has been advocated as a method of becoming orgasmic.

Therapists advise masturbation to cure frigidity, teach women about their bodies, promote happy orgasms, express one's full sexual potential, learn about multiple climaxes, and survive sexually without a partner. Masturbation is the all-purpose tonic. And, as the wag said, you don't have to look your best. (Tavris & Sadd, 1975, p. 94)

Many women with sexual dysfunctions turn to self-help books, including books about masturbation, rather than to sex therapists to treat their problem. Bibliotherapy—the use of these books—has been shown to produce significant increases in women's frequency of orgasm during sexual intercourse (Dodge, Glasgow, & O'Neill, 1982).

Until recently the vast majority of erotica was written by men from a male perspective. Concomitant with the feminist movement has been a call for the reawakening of female sexuality. For such a long time in patriarchal society, female sexuality was for the service of male sexual needs rather than an expression of the female's desires. Among the works from a female perspective is *Erotic Interludes,* edited by Lonnie Barbach (1986), a therapist who put together the volume of fictional erotica written by women writers for women in her therapy groups to read during their sexual-arousal exercises.

Novelists have made us aware of female sexuality used in the service of getting something else, such as by the prostitute who exchanges sex for money, and also by the respectable housewives portrayed in Marilyn French's (1977) novel, *The Women's Room,* for whom sex is a requirement of the job of wife. The feminist movement seeks equality of female sexuality as a fundamental requirement for overturning the system of male supremacy. There are many disparate elements involved in achieving equality of female sexuality, including ending sexual violence. Female sexuality is socially constructed and has been restricted by the roles and relations between the sexes that have subordinated female desires.

REFLECTIONS

Female sexuality is complex. The content of this chapter should be integrated with other chapters in the book, particularly Chapter VII, "Violence Against Women," Chapter VIII, "Mental Health," and Chapter X "Intimate Relationships," to achieve a more holistic view of female sexuality. The repercussions of women's victimization by rape and incest on female sexuality is only hinted at in this chapter, but may supply part of the answer as to why many women do not psychologically experience their own sexual arousal and orgasm. The objectification of women's bodies as described in Chapter VIII, "Mental Health," that leads to eating disorders is an area for further investigation in its relation to sexuality. Of course, Chapter X, "Intimate Relationships," provides an understanding of the relationship context for the expression of female sexuality.

All of the research in this chapter, whether based on probability sample surveys or nonprobability sample surveys, is consistent in showing that female sexuality best reaches its full flower within a committed, caring relationship, whether heterosexual or homosexual. In contrast to media portrayals of sexuality, most people are monogamous or celibate according to the national probability sample survey, the NHSLS (Laumann et al., 1994). America is not a paradise of sexual license. Since the great majority of women are heterosexual, it is clear that equality in relationships between the sexes is necessary in order for women to develop a consciousness of self in the exploration of their sexuality. The goal is for female sexuality to be an expression of the personality and of mutual choice of the partners, rather than as a vehicle for eroticized power relations. How do cultural views about gender shape sexual relationships and females' experience of their sexuality?

Experiential Exercises

1. Talk to your mother about her sexual values. If there were sexual topics she did not discuss with you while you were growing up, ask her about them now and why she never taught you about sexuality.
2. Discuss with your friends the impact that the AIDS epidemic has had on their sexual behavior.
3. Talk with women who are heterosexual and who are homosexual about at what age they were first aware of their sexual orientation and how they knew. Did their sexual orientation change at any point in their lives?

KEY TERMS

Adultery   Extramarital sexual relationships.

Bisexual   A woman (or man) who is sexually attracted to and engages in sex with both men and women.

Clitoral Orgasm   Orgasm brought about by stimulation of the clitoris. Masters and Johnson said all orgasm involves clitoris.

Double Standard   The norm that premarital sexual intercourse is more acceptable for males than for females.

Dyspareunia   Pain during sexual intercourse. The cause is almost always an underlying medical problem such as PID.

Elective Lesbians   Women who have chosen homosexuality after having lived in heterosexual relationships during some periods in their past.

Erotophilia   Positive response to sex and low sex guilt.

Erotophobia   Sex guilt and negative attitudes toward sexuality.

Genital Circumcision   Surgical removal of the clitoris, and as practiced in the Sudan, removal of the labia minora, and the inner layers of the labia majora as well.

Grafenberg Spot   Located two-thirds of the way to the cervix, direct stimulation brings about orgasmic response.

Homosexuality   Sexual attraction to and genital sexuality practiced with persons of the same sex.

Inhibited Sexual Desire (ISD)   Lack of interest in sexual activity.

Lesbians   Female homosexuals.

Masturbation   Solitary sexual behavior that requires no partner.

Medicalized Perspective of Sexuality   The view that sexual behavior is determined by biological rather than sociopsychological factors and that sexual dysfunctions should be treated medically.

Primary Lesbians   Women who from an early age were sexually attracted to other females and continue to be throughout their lives.

Primary Orgasmic Dysfunction   Never having experienced orgasm under any circumstances—foreplay, intercourse, masturbation, and so on.

Secondary Orgasmic Dysfunction   Reaching orgasm under some circumstances, such as masturbation, but not under other circumstances in which the woman would like to, such as during intercourse.

Sexual Daydreaming   Sexual thoughts that occur spontaneously.

Sexual Fantasies   Consciously guided sexual thoughts.

Sexual Inequality   Society expects women to play a less-dominant and assertive role in everything from initiating the first date to guiding sexual encounters.

Sexual Revolution   Earlier age and greater premarital sexual activity of females that has occurred since the 1960s.

Sexual Self-Schema   Cognitive generalizations about our sexuality and sexual expressiveness based on past experience.

Socially Constructed Sexuality   Female sexuality is embedded in the social context of roles and relations between the sexes that describe the normal limits. What is considered appropriate or normal sexual desires and behavior varies from one historical period to another and within different cultures.

Sociosexuality   A personality dimension that ranges from unrestricted sexual orientation that involves a willingness to engage in uncommitted sex to a restricted orientation that describes a willingness to engage in sex only in a committed relationship.

Vaginal Orgasm   Orgasm brought about by vaginal stimulation. Freud considered it more "mature" than clitoral orgasm.

Vaginismus   Contractions of the outer third of the vagina that may constrict the opening of the vagina to such an extent that it may even be impossible to engage in sexual intercourse.

SUGGESTED READINGS

Kitzinger, C., & Wilkinson, S. (1995). Transitions from heterosexuality to lesbianism: The discursive production of lesbian identities. *Developmental Psychology, 31,* 95–104. This article deals with the process of becoming lesbian for women who had at least 10 years prior heterosexual relations.

Laumann, E. O., Gagnon, J. H., Michael, R. T., & Michaels, S. (1994). *The Social Organization of Sexuality: Sexual practices in the United States.* Chicago: The University of Chicago Press. This is the most recent and comprehensive probability sample survey of sexual behavior in the United States.

Oliver, M. B., & Hyde, J. S. (1993). Gender differences in sexuality: A meta-analysis. *Psychological Bulletin, 114,* 29–51. A meta-analysis based on a literature search of studies of gender differences in both sexual behavior and attitudes toward various aspects of sexuality.

CHAPTER 12

Pregnancy, Childbirth, Breast-Feeding, and the New Reproductive Technologies

Homebirthers ... use rich images to describe pregnancy, labor and birth that work to humanize, personalize, feminize, and naturalize the processes of procreation. They speak of mothers and babies as unified beings, complementary coparticipants in the creative mysteries, entrained and joyous dancers in the rhythms and harmonies of life.

Robbie Davis-Floyd, 1994

Pregnancy, childbirth, breast-feeding, and motherhood are the events in a woman's life, which along with menstruation, differentiate her from men. Woman's unique capability of bearing children has been the overriding determinant of her relationship to men and of her role in society. This chapter will examine the physiological and psychological interactions occurring during pregnancy, childbirth, and breast-feeding. Also explored will be the brave new world of reproductive technologies as applied to infertility problems and pregnancy and childbirth.

PREGNANCY

Pregnancy begins with the fertilization of the female ovum by the male sperm cell, forming the zygote. The normal ejaculation contains about 200 million to 1,200 million spermatozoa. A few dozen of the original sperm reach the fallopian tube, the small tube that connects the ovary with the uterus, that is the site of fertilization. A powerful enzyme helps one sperm penetrate the outer membrane of the ovum. After the sperm fuses with the maternal cell nucleus, a coating forms round the fertilized egg and prevents other sperm cells from entering (Begley, Firth, & Hoult, 1980).

First Trimester

The first trimester of pregnancy is characterized by rapid hormonal changes that cause the cessation of menstrual periods and morning sickness.

The average length of pregnancy is 266 days or nine months, which is typically divided by obstetricians into three trimesters. Within a week these first two cells, the fertilized zygote (egg), multiply into a cluster of more than 100 cells, and have implanted on the inner lining of the uterus. Shortly after, a **placenta** forms that is connected to the growing embryo by the umbilical cord. The placenta develops from both maternal and fetal tissue. Through the placenta passes oxygen, nutrients, antibodies, and drugs if the mother takes any, and in the other direction from the developing embryo, waste materials.

The placenta also functions as an endocrine gland producing estrogen, progesterone, and **human chorionic gonadotropin (HCG)**, which assist in the maintenance of the pregnancy. The pregnancy is maintained by the interaction of maternal, fetal and placental hormones (Challis & Mitchell, 1983). HCG is secreted by the embryo early in pregnancy and later by the placenta. HCG levels are particularly high early in pregnancy, and early tests of pregnancy are aimed at detecting this hormone (Begley et al., 1980). Placental progesterone production is sufficient to maintain pregnancy after about 35–40 days. Before that time the corpus luteum, formed after the ovum ruptures from the ovary, is the major source progesterone. The placenta synthesizes estrogen using fetal and maternal precursors. Hormone levels of estrogen and progesterone rise dramatically in the pregnant woman (Begley et al., 1980).

By the end of the first month, a recognizable embryo has formed. Although it is only 1 cm long, it is forming rudimentary organs. An **amnion** or bag of waters surrounds it. During this period of rapid cell growth, the embryo is particularly vulnerable to physical and chemical influences and any diseases which the mother may contract. If the embryo is failing to grow properly, nature may "correct" this mistake through a miscarriage. Miscarriages are most likely to occur during the first trimester, and are more common among older mothers (over age 40) (Begley et al., 1980). A prospective research study on 13,643 pregnancies in Germany showed a two-thirds reduction in rates of early miscarriage in women who had taken vitamin supplements as compared with those who had not (Koller, 1988).

The first sign of pregnancy for a woman is usually that of missing her period, although some women may have some menstrual bleeding for the first two or three months when their periods would be due. Nausea during the first two or three months of pregnancy is probably one of the best known symptoms. In most cases, this feeling of sickness (nausea) occurs most frequently just after arising in the morning and may be followed by actual vomiting. Studies vary in the incidence reported for morning sickness. In a large sample of British women Fairweather (1968) found that 50% reported nausea and 50% did not. In a U.S. survey of women in their sixth month of pregnancy, 72% reported having had morning sickness during their first trimester and 35% said they continued to have nausea during their second trimester (Hofmeyr, Marcos, & Butchart, 1990).

Although the exact mechanism is not known, hormonal changes are certainly thought to be involved in morning sickness. One of the incidental effects of progesterone, unrelated to its role in pregnancy, is to relax the smooth muscle of the intestinal tract which increases the length of time that food remains in the stomach. The hormone HCG is also implicated in nausea during pregnancy. Women with a tumor that excretes this hormone suffer more severe nausea and vomiting in pregnancy. Women who are about to abort, and in whom the placenta has ceased normal functioning, have an abrupt cessation of nausea (Wolkind, 1981).

Nausea and vomiting during the first trimester of pregnancy is perfectly normal. No psychiatric differences have been found between women who do and do not experience nausea and vomiting early in pregnancy (Wolkind, 1981). Many studies link both external stress and internal psychological factors, however, to nausea and vomiting later in pregnancy. Married women who experience prolonged morning sickness, continuing after the first trimester, were found to have much less social support from both husbands and parents. The single women with prolonged sickness were found to have a significantly higher rate of psychiatric disorder than those who experienced sickness only during the first trimester.

Other symptoms of first trimester pregnancy include: frequent urination because of hormonal changes and the pressure of the enlarging uterus on the bladder; increased fatigue; some swelling of the breasts; darkening of the nipples and the area around them (areola); and some constipation because of the effect of progesterone in relaxing the smooth muscles (Boston Women's Health Collective, 1992).

Second Trimester

During the second trimester the woman becomes visibly pregnant, and most women have a sense of well being.

The woman becomes visibly pregnant. Although the fetus has been moving for months, it is during the fourth or fifth month that the pregnant woman begins to feel the movement. Indigestion (heartburn) and constipation may occur because of the slowed movement of the digestive system. The feet, ankles, hands, and fingers may swell (edema) because of increased water retention. Leg cramps may also occur in some women. Veins in the rectum (hemorrhoidal) veins may become dilated, and veins in the legs may become enlarged (varicose veins). Nosebleeds and nasal congestion may also occur in some women (Boston Women's Health Collective, 1992).

Women typically have a sense of well being during the second trimester. They no longer have the frequent urination, fatigue, and nausea symptoms of the first trimester and have not yet gotten so large that movement and sleep are difficult. Some women, however, begin to worry about whether the baby will be born healthy and begin to be afraid of what they will go through during childbirth.

Third Trimester

During the third trimester, the fetus becomes very active. The mother may have a variety of physical problems. Weight gain is rapid, but infant out-come is more favorable with a high rather than low weight gain.

The uterus becomes very large and feels hard to the touch. The fetus within the uterus becomes very active, and the movements are visible to someone observing the woman's abdomen, or felt by placing a hand on the abdomen. Some women may be susceptible to varicose veins or hemorrhoids. Because of the pressure of the enlarged uterus on the lungs and diaphragm, the third trimester woman may experience shortness of breath. Water retention increases during the third trimester causing swelling of the hands, feet, and ankles to be common. Pregnancy-associated hypertensive disorders (increased blood pressure) are common in first pregnancies and women with chronic hypertension, diabetes or multifetal gestations. Research in a randomized trial of placebo or 60 mg aspirin daily, however, found that the aspirin group had significantly reduced occurrence of high blood pressure (Hauth et al., 1993).

Increased appetite and rapid weight gain also occur during the last trimester. For years obstetricians cautioned their patients to try to limit weight gain in pregnancy, and many told their patients not to gain more than 20 pounds. Research is questioning the wisdom of this advice. Low infant birth weight is the most important factor in adverse infant outcome. Research analyzing the relationship between maternal weight gain and preterm delivery in 2,163 women indicated that the risk of spontaneous preterm birth increased 60% in women with a low rate of weight gain (less than 0.27 kg/week) compared with those with an average rate (0.27–0.52 kg/week). Those with a high gain (0.52 kg/week) were only half as likely to have preterm birth, compared with the group with a low gain (B. Abrams, Newman, Key, & Parker, 1989). It appears, therefore, that infant outcome is more favorable with high rather than low weight gain.

Ectopic Pregnancy

An ectopic pregnancy is one in which the zygote implants outside of the uterus. Minority women are at higher risk.

Any implantation away from the endometrium of the uterus is considered by strict definition to be an ectopic implantation. In an **ectopic pregnancy,** the fertilized ovum implants in the fallopian tube, in the abdominal cavity (including the ovary), or in the cervical canal. The most common site for these pregnancies is the fallopian tube. Implantation of the zygote outside of the uterus occurs in about 1 in 50 pregnancies.

Because low levels of HCG may be found in unruptured ectopic pregnancies, a uterine pregnancy may take place (although this occurs only rarely) even though there exists an ectopic pregnancy (Keyser, 1986). Mechanical factors such as blockage in a fallopian tube are frequently cited in the medical literature as factors in the cause of a tubal pregnancy. The fact that women who have infertility problems or have suffered from menstrual disorders are more likely to suffer an ectopic pregnancy suggests that endocrine factors may also play a role.

> Factors known to be conducive to endocrine imbalance, such as high maternal age, nutritional deficiency, heavy physical work, and low socioeconomic status are known to be present with relative frequency in the background of ectopic gestations. (Iffy, 1986, p. 87)

Ectopic pregnancies usually do not progress beyond six to eight weeks. An abdominal pregnancy, however, may go to term, but these are very rare, occurring in about only 1 in 3,000 or 4,000 deliveries (Poland & Kalousek, 1986).

Rupture of the wall of the fallopian tube, and resulting hemorrhage, is the most serious complication of ectopic pregnancy. The ovary, however, is usually unaffected by ectopic pregnancy (Philippe, Bilenki, & Warter, 1986). Although pregnancy tests may detect ectopic pregnancy, a positive pregnancy test gives no information as to the site of the implantation. False negative pregnancy tests occur more often in ectopic pregnancy because of the lower levels of HCG that may be present as compared with the levels that would be found in a normal pregnancy. Ultrasound does provide an effective tool for diagnosis of ectopic pregnancy (Gottesfeld, 1986; Saxena

& Singh, 1986). The symptoms of ectopic pregnancy may include abnormal uterine bleeding (a menstrual period lasting 10 or 12 days), which usually appears earliest, abdominal pain and amenorrhea (absence of menstruation), which may or may not be present (A. Langer, 1986).

Data gathered by the National Center for Health Statistics (NCHS) show that the rate of ectopic pregnancies more than doubled between 1970 and 1981, going from 4.5 to 13.6 per 1,000 reported pregnancies (Frau, MacKay, Hughes, & Cates, 1985). Studies in both the United States and other developed nations report a similar increasing incidence in ectopic pregnancy. The increase in a wide variety of populations in many developed countries qualifies as an epidemic (Greiss, 1986).

Ectopic pregnancies are a higher proportion of pregnancies for older women as compared with younger women. Black women also have a higher rate of ectopic pregnancy at every age level than do White women. Although the reasons for the higher incidence of ectopic pregnancy in Black women is not clear, Frau et al. (1986) speculate that it might be due to two factors: (1) the higher reported frequency of STDs and PID among Black women; and (2) the lower rate of physicians visits among Black women, which means that health care may be less available to Black than to White women (see Figure 12.1).

There is no clear cause for the increase in ectopic pregnancies. Various hypotheses have been put forth, including PID, use of intrauterine contraceptive devices (IUD), douching, and earlier age at menarche, which leads to earlier sexual activity and increased risk of PID. Women sterilized by various tubal interruption procedures also have a one to six per 1,000 chance of becoming pregnant, often in the fallopian tube. None of these has been clearly identified as a cause of the increase in ectopic pregnancy (Frau et al., 1986).

Deaths from Ectopic Pregnancy

Ectopic pregnancy is the leading cause of maternal deaths in the United States.

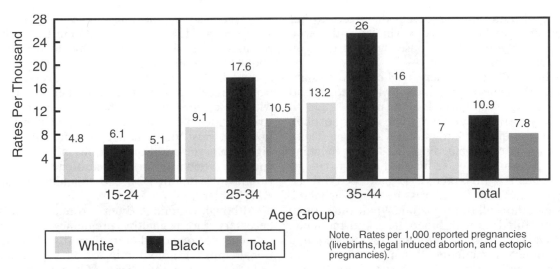

FIGURE 12.1   Ectopic Pregnancy By Age And Race. Adapted from Frau, MacKay, Hughes and Cates, 1986, p. 185.

Deaths from ectopic pregnancy are a significant and increasing proportion of reproductive mortality. Although the death-to-case rate has declined, the increase in the incidence of ectopic pregnancy has lessened the decrease in the absolute number of deaths. Ectopic pregnancy is the leading cause of maternal mortality in the United States (Greiss, 1986).

The risk of dying from ectopic pregnancy is significantly greater than that from childbirth and from legal induced abortion.

Of the factors analyzed thus far, race appears to have the greatest effect on risk of death . . . in addition to a 3.2 times greater death-to-case rate than white women, black women have a 1.6 times greater chance of having an ectopic pregnancy or almost a five times greater chance of dying. (Greiss, 1986, pp. 201–202)

Education about ectopic pregnancy needs to be provided to both primary health care workers and to women. Any woman of reproductive age who is seen in an emergency room or physician's office who is complaining of abdominal pain should be given a pregnancy test. Women need to be educated about the necessity of seeking medical care for any abnormal bleeding or abdominal pain.

The traditional treatment of prompt surgical removal of the involved fallopian tube has been replaced by nonsurgical methods of treatment for early unruptured tubal pregnancies (Pansky et al., 1993). The latest technique is use of the laparoscope and injection of a single low dose of methotrexate (MTX) directly into the pregnancy site. A follow-up of 77 women treated with local MTX injection found the probability of conception was 91% after a year among those trying to conceive. An intrauterine pregnancy rate of 67% was achieved and an ectopic pregnancy rate of 13%.

Few women know about ectopic pregnancy, but ignorance of it could cost a woman her life. It almost cost me mine. Soon after getting into my car, after teaching a late afternoon class, I suddenly got terrific abdominal cramps. Since I lived only a mile from the college, I continued to drive home. After pulling into my driveway and stopping, I realized I felt very weak, too weak to get out of the car and walk into the house by myself. I leaned on the horn and in a few minutes, Barbara, the teenager who was babysitting for my two children came out. I said "Barbara, please help me into the house, I don't know what's wrong, but I feel very weak." When I stood up and put my arm around her shoulder, I slumped to the ground. She ran across the street to her home and quickly came back with her father who half carried me into my house and placed me on the living room couch.

After calling another neighbor, who summoned the general practitioner who lived around the corner, I found myself in the rescue squad on the way to the emergency room of the hospital. The intern did not know what was wrong. There was no external bleeding, but after checking other possibilities, he summoned the gynecological resident who asked if I could possibly be pregnant. When I said yes, he stuck a needle through the wall of my vagina. When the syringe quickly filled up with blood, he asked the name of my gynecologist and told me I would be going into surgery immediately. When I awoke the next morning, my gynecologist was standing over me. He told me that I had a ruptured ectopic pregnancy. He said he suctioned two quarts of blood out of my abdomen, and removed the remains of the ruptured fallopian tube, and while he was in there also removed my appendix. If there had been a longer delay in my getting to a hospital emergency room, I would have hemorrhaged to death.

I did not have any of the risk factors for ectopic pregnancy—I had never used an IUD, had never had PID, had never had abdominal surgery, had no infertility problem, but I did, like so many other women (poor and uneducated as well as educated and middle-class), ignore warning signs such as abnormal bleeding, and had not sought medical care until it was an emergency.

Nutrition during Pregnancy

A well-balanced diet including milk and dairy products, fish, meat, and fruits, and vegetables is necessary during pregnancy. Folic acid in the diet prevents neural tube disorders. Too much vitamin A, however, can cause birth defects.

Diet has long been known to be important during pregnancy. During the second half of pregnancy the total calcium transfer from maternal to fetal blood increases, requiring about a 50% increase in calcium intake from normal prepregnancy levels. A good vitamin D supply is required for utilization of the calcium, requiring about a 100% increase in vitamin D. During the second half of pregnancy the turnover rate of iron increases almost fourfold when compared with the requirements of the nonpregnant menstruating woman. The additional recommendations for most vitamins and minerals are much higher than the additional requirements for food energy, particularly for beta carotene vitamin C, riboflavin (vitamin B2), and thiamine (vitamin B1) (Kubler, 1988).

Although vitamin A (beta-carotene, retinol) is necessary for a healthy pregnancy, babies of women who consumed more than 10,000 International Units (IU) of vitamin A from supplements or food had an increased risk of babies born with malfunctions of the head, heart, brain and spinal cord (J. Brody, 1995). Women who are pregnant or may become pregnant should not take multi vitamin supplements that exceed 4,000 to 8,000 IU. The consumption of beef liver which contains very high levels of vitamin A, as much as 30,000 IU of vitamin A in a three-ounce serving, should be restricted during pregnancy. Beta-carotene, which the body converts into vitamin A, is not associated with increased birth defects. Women can continue to eat plenty of fruits and vegetables which contain high levels of beta-carotene.

An international, multicenter, double-blind, trial involving 1,817 women at high risk of having a pregnancy with a neural tube defect, because of a previous affected pregnancy, who were planning another pregnancy were randomly assigned to one of four conditons: (1) folic acid; (2) other vitamins; (3) folic acid plus other vitamins; and (4) no supplement (MRC Vitamin Study Research Group, 1991). The results show that 72% of neural tube defects were prevented by taking folic acid supplements.

Rich sources of folic acid, thiamine, vitamin A, vitamin C, and calcium in the diet are green, leafy vegetables, citrus fruit, milk and dairy products, potatoes, nuts, dried beans, peas, egg yolks, whole grain or enriched cereals and breads, brown rice, pasta, liver, meat, fish, and most fruits and vegetables. Basically, a pregnant woman needs to throw out the junk food and eat a nutritionally balanced diet and take vitamin supplements.

Pseudocyesis

Pseudocyesis—she looks pregnant, she acts pregnant, she believes she is pregnant, but she is not.

Pseudocyesis is a condition in which women imagine themselves to be pregnant. As far back as ancient Greece, Hippocrates described women who thought they were pregnant, but were not. They have many of the symptoms of pregnancy such as abdominal enlargement, menstrual disturbance, and breast changes including swelling and tenderness. The enlargement of the abdomen is usually due to gaseous distention or weight gain. Psychologically, pseudocyesis occurs with depression. The belief in the pregnancy may be a way of reducing life stresses. Pregnancy tests and a physical examination can easily determine that the woman is not pregnant; however, the doctor needs to establish rapport with the patient and perhaps enlist family in order to convince the woman that she is not pregnant (Lorentz, & LaFerla (1991).

Attitudes about Pregnant Women

Although people stand farther away from a pregnant woman than from other women, they are more likely to help her.

Psychologists have speculated that treatment of pregnant women may be similar to treatment of individuals with a stigma of some type. Shelly Taylor and Ellen Langer (1977) conducted an experiment in which two confederates rode an elevator together. One was padded so as to appear pregnant and the other carried a small box in front of her at abdomen level. Although both women took up the same amount of space, people tended to stand further away from the pregnant woman and to stand closer to the woman with the box. Men, in particular, avoided proxim-

ity to the pregnant woman. Staring at her was another common reaction.

To more directly test the hypothesis of the pregnant role being a stigmatized one, Walton et al. (1988) recorded helping behavior (assistance in helping to pick up scattered keys) toward a pregnant, nonpregnant, or facially disfigured women. Each woman was alone, with a female companion, or with a male companion in an elevator. The findings were that pregnant women were helped significantly more than nonpregnant or facially disfigured women, except when accompanied by a male, in which condition all three women received very little help. There was a low rate of helping in this experiment, and women were particularly unlikely to offer assistance. Overall, the authors conclude that the notion of stigma is not a good explanation for the behavior of others toward the pregnant woman, since she is more likely to receive help than a woman with a stigma.

Pregnancy has a more glamorous image among the upper-class.

Social class differences also exist in attitudes toward pregnant women and pregnancy. Horgan (1983) looked at where maternity clothes were placed in high-status (such as Lord & Taylor or Saks) and in low-status (such as Sears or J.C. Penney) department stores as a way of inferring attitudes toward pregnant women. In the high-status department stores, the maternity clothes were adjacent to lingerie or loungewear, whereas in low-status stores the maternity clothes were near the large women's sizes and the uniforms. The higher-class stores portray the image of luxury, femininity, delicacy, and privacy as appropriate to pregnancy, whereas the message conveyed by the lower-status stores is of the functional aspect of the clothes and the women as fat.

A follow-up study of pregnant women by Horgan (1983) confirmed these class differences. The upper-middle-class women reported feeling sexier and more attractive than did the working-class women. They also reported planning to return to work sooner.

PRENATAL SCREENING

Alpha-Fetoprotein Test (AFP)

Alpha-fetoprotein test (AFP) screens for neural tube disorder.

Alpha-Fetoprotein Test (AFP) is a test of a small amount of the mother's blood to screen for neural tube disorder (NTD), such as spina bifida. Approximately 2 in 1,000 infants are born with this disorder in the United States each year. High levels of AFP are found in the blood of women who are carrying a fetus with NTD. This blood test may give false positives and further tests such as ultrasound or amniocentesis are conducted (Boston Women's Health Collective, 1992).

Amniocentesis

Amniocentesis can screen for a large number of birth disorders.

A process called **amniocentesis** can be used during the second trimester, usually the sixteenth week of pregnancy, to test for genetic birth defects. A long needle is inserted into the pregnant woman's abdomen, where it withdraws fluid from the amniotic sack surrounding the fetus. The cells are cultured in the laboratory in order to derive information about the chromosomes and biochemistry of the fetus. Amniocentesis can potentially be used to screen for hundreds of genetic disorders. Women over 35 account for 80–90% of amniocentesis procedures. It is also used when there is a known family history of chromosomal disorders or birth defects in a previous child to the mother. Disorders typically screened by amniocentesis are cystic fibrosis, Down's syndrome, sickle cell anemia (malformed red blood cells, which is found more frequently among Blacks), Tay-Sachs disease (a degenerative disease of the nervous system that is more often found among Jews), hemophilia, and many others. Screening for NTDs (incompletely formed spinal canal and/or brain), although it is based on chemical composition of amniotic fluid and not on chromosome patterns, can also be done with amniocentesis. The increased risk of spontaneous abortion resulting from the amniocentesis is quite low, about 1% increase (Nicolaides, Brizot, Patel, & Snijders, 1994; Travis, 1988a). In the late 1980s, early amniocentesis was introduced, but four studies reported a somewhat increased risk of fetal loss ranging from 3.3% to 6.6%.

Another study of 693 early amniocenteses performed between 11 and 15 weeks, however, found a spontaneous miscarriage rate to 28 weeks of 1.5%. During the same time period a control group of women who had standard amniocentesis at 15–20 weeks had a spontaneous miscarriage rate of 0.6% (B. F. Crandall, Kulch, & Tabsh, 1994). Crandall et al. suggest early amniocentesis as an alternative to **chorionic villus sampling**.

Ultrasound

Obstetric application of ultrasound can be used to determine if the pregnancy is normal, the age of the gestation (fetus) and multiple gestations. Research does not provide support for routine ultrasound screening of women with normal pregnancies.

Ultrasound can be used to diagnose a variety of conditions of pregnancy. Intermittent high-frequency sound waves are transmitted from a probe that is inserted into the vagina or run back and forth across the abdomen to a computer, which translates the sound waves into pictures on a video screen. When the patient has bleeding in early pregnancy, ultrasound can be used to determine if the pregnancy is normal. It can detect ectopic pregnancy. It also can detect if there is a normal amniotic sac and an embryo with cardiac activity, or if there are abnormalities that may signal an impending miscarriage. If there is a discrepancy between the patient's last menstrual date and the uterine size as felt by the physician, ultrasound can be used to determine gestational age (age of the fetus). Or, ultrasound may detect multiple gestation (twins, triplets, etc.). Abnormalities of fetal anatomy also may be detected (Sarti, 1984).

Research on over 22,000 low-risk women entering a study of prenatal ultrasound screening between November 1, 1989, and May 31, 1991, found a rate of adverse perinatal outcome for 5.0% in the ultrasound-screening group and 4.9% in the control group (Ewigman et al., 1993). The study was designed to test the hypothesis that routine screening of pregnant women with standardized ultrasonography would reduce perinatal morbidity and mortality. This study demonstrates that routine ultrasound screening of pregnant women does not improve pregnancy outcome as compared with a control group of women who received ultrasound screening only when there is a medical indication. Considerable health care costs could be saved without risk for mothers and babies by using ultrasound only when there is a medical reason to do so.

Chorionic Villus Sampling

Chorionic villus sampling increases the risk of babies born with limb defects.

Chorionic Villus Sampling (CVS) is a prenatal diagnostic test that can be used earlier than amniocentesis. It is done between 8 and 13 weeks. Ultrasound is used to guide a catheter that is inserted through the vagina and cervix into the chorionic villi (fingerlike projections of the cells that become the placenta), where a small amount is aspirated via suction (Bogart, 1992; Boston Women's Health Collective, 1992).

A comparison of CVS with early amniocentesis (EA) done during the first trimester at 10–13 weeks of gestation found a 5.9% spontaneous loss rate (intrauterine or neonatal) after EA as compared with a 1.2% loss rate after CVS among 1,301 women (Nicolaides et al., 1994). Both procedures were equally efficient in obtaining the fetal information.

Some studies have reported an increased incidence of babies born with limb abnormalities associated with CVS. In a study of 75 babies with limb defects who were exposed to CVS in utero, the earlier during the pregnancy that CVS was done, the more severe the limb abnormalities

(Firth et al., 1994). A case control study was conducted in Italy controlling for maternal age, a possible confounder with limb deficiencies since older women are more likely to have CVS (Mastroiacovo & Botto, 1994). The overall risk estimate of limb deficiencies associated with CVS was 12.63, and was not explained by advanced maternal age. Given this information, a woman and her physician must carefully weigh the benefits of CVS with the possible risks.

Psychological Aspects of Prenatal Screening

Prenatal testing creates anxiety and ambivalence in pregnant women. People with disabilities can lead quality lives.

Research has pointed out the anxiety and ambivalence that couples experience regarding the prenatal diagnostic procedures of anniocentesis, CVS, and alpha fetoprotein testing (Sandelowski, 1993).

> The prevailing concerns that women generally have about prenatal testing involve the risk of miscarrying a normal fetus in the course of testing and the very limited availability of therapeutic interventions to treat an impaired fetus. Tests such as amniocentesis have been called "search and destroy missions" (Drugan, Johnson, & Evans, 1990, p. 288), with abortion the only option typically available to women carrying an impaired fetus other than carrying the fetus to term. (Sandelowski, 1993, p. 142)

As was pointed out in Chapter IX, the psychological consequences of abortion are more severe for women who wanted the pregnancy and had a therapeutic abortion because of a health risk to themselves or to the fetus. Infertile couples who had become pregnant after years of trying or with the aid of in vitro fertilization were particularly ambivalent about prenatal testing and the decision to abort a fetus with abnormalities.

Others view negative attitudes toward having a child with a disability as resulting from prejudices against the disabled.

A eugenic ideology prevails in this and other countries that finds its political expression in a neglect of the needs and civil rights of people with disabilities. As a result, people who have a disability confront unnecessary and arbitrary barriers to education and employment, which make it difficult for them to live ordinary lives. (Hubbard, 1988, p. 225)

The assumption that prenatal screening increases our quality of life is challenged by those who question whether most women have insufficient knowledge about disability and the disabled individuals who lead productive, independent lives. The more important challenge than to eliminate disability is acceptance of all people with disabilities (Saxton, 1988).

Prenatal Screening and Low Income Women

Low income and minority women do not have equal access to prenatal screening and abortion.

A concern is that low-income women and minority women do not have equal access to prenatal diagnostic procedures and counseling. A second issue is that the cultural background of the woman of color would differ from her physician or counselor, and if a genetic condition is diagnosed, would she be pressured into having an abortion because of her race, or maybe denied one because of her economic level. "A woman dependent upon Medicaid . . . may be able to learn about the physical condition of her fetus but may be unable to afford an abortion, the only 'treatment' alternative in most cases" (Nsiah-Jefferson & Hall, 1989, p. 101).

SUBSTANCE ABUSE DURING PREGNANCY

Use of Drugs during Pregnancy

At least 11% of women use illegal drugs during their pregnancy.

With the drug problem reaching epidemic proportions in the United States, many babies are being born cocaine addicted, with fetal alcohol syndrome, heroin addicted, or of low birth weight due to smoking. It is during the first six weeks of development that the neurological system of the embryo is developing most rapidly. Unfortunately, it is during this period that a woman may be unaware that she is pregnant. Nevertheless, often the most serious damage may be caused at this stage of development.

Drug use by pregnant women increased during the 1980s. According to a survey by the National Association for Perinatal Addiction Research (NAPARE), at least 11% of pregnant women in the United States use illegal drugs (Aronson, Hunt & Madison, 1990). There is also ample use of legal drugs during pregnancy, particularly alcohol and cigarettes.

Alcohol Abuse

Sustained drinking of alcohol during pregnancy causes fetal alcohol syndrome.

The pattern of birth defects associated with sustained drinking of alcoholic beverages during pregnancy are called **Fetal Alcohol Syndrome (FAS)**. It is defined by a cluster of potential birth defects including: deficient growth; a pattern of facial malformation consisting of a small head, misshaped eyes, and flattened midface; central nervous system defects, the most serious of which is mental retardation; and other symptoms such as hyperactivity and sleep disturbances (Sokol, 1981; Travis, 1988a). In addition to FAS, increased stillbirth and miscarriage rates are found for women who drink regularly during pregnancy.

A critical aspect of drinking during pregnancy is that during the first weeks after conception the organ systems are differentiated, and it is an especially vulnerable period for the developing fetus (D. W. Smith, 1980). Since safety limits for consumption of alcohol during pregnancy have not been established, the professional advice to women of child-bearing age is do not drink if you are pregnant, or have been engaging in unprotected sexual intercourse.

Smoking

Smoking during pregnancy is associated with low birth weight infants.

A number of negative findings have been associated with smoking during pregnancy including premature delivery, ectopic pregnancy, low Apgar scores, and early childhood illness such as respiratory illnesses. Numerous studies have documented the finding that smoking during pregnancy is associated with term low birth weight of the baby, shortened gestation, and higher rates of spontaneous abortion and infant mortality (for example, sudden infant death syndrome) (Chandra, 1995; Shiono et al., 1995). "Low birth weight is perhaps the single most important determinant of the survival chances of a newborn and a good predictor of the infant's prospects for healthy growth and development" (Kane & Smith, 1987, p. 109). Data collected by Family Health International between 1977 and 1984 in 40 countries found that the risk of low birth weight increases with whether and how much the mother smokes during pregnancy. When the same mother smoked during one pregnancy but not another, a lighter infant was produced in the pregnancy where she smoked (Witter & King, 1980).

Cocaine

Research is conflicting about whether cocaine use during pregnancy is associated with premature birth, but comprehensive prenatal care can improve the outcome.

It is estimated that in 1990 2.1 million American women used cocaine (Shiono et al., 1995). A study of 1,226 women in a Boston inner-city prenatal clinic found that 18% had used cocaine during their pregnancies (B. Zuckerman et al., 1989). The use of cocaine during pregnancy causes constriction of uterine and placental blood vessels, thereby reducing the flow of nutrients and oxygen to the fetus. Cocaine may stimulate prema-

ture uterine contractions, which may result in miscarriage or premature births. Cocaine crosses the fetal blood–brain barrier and accumulates in the central nervous system of the fetus, which may have a particularly deleterious effect during the first several weeks of pregnancy. Because fetal enzymes that metabolize cocaine are not fully developed in the liver, cocaine reaches higher blood levels in the fetus than in the mother, and stays in the fetal system longer (up to four to six days). "The exchange of sex for crack has led to a near epidemic of spontaneous abortions, preterm deliveries, fetal anomalies, and other lethal complications in pregnant drug users" (Christmas, 1992, p. 36). A study of 7,470 pregnant women (of whom 2.3% had used cocaine) contrary to other research did not find low birth weight associated with cocaine use, but did find an association between cocaine use and abruptio placentae (Shiono et al., 1995).

A multidisciplinary approach for prenatal care may improve outcome of the pregnancies among cocaine-abusing pregnant women. Those women who had used cocaine and had little or no prenatal care did have a significantly greater infant morbidity compared with those receiving comprehensive care in a special program at Northwestern University (MacGregor, Keith, Bachicha, & Chasnoff, 1989). The group receiving little prenatal care had lower mean gestational age at delivery, lower mean birthweight, and higher incidence of preterm delivery. A comparison group of non–drug users had fewer low birth weight and preterm infants than the comprehensive care group. Thus, while comprehensive prenatal care may reduce negative outcomes of cocaine abusing mothers (two-thirds of whom continued to use cocaine throughout pregnancy) it cannot eliminate the problems associated with cocaine use.

Heroin

Heroin use in pregnancy is associated with withdrawal syndrome at birth and later hyperactivity of the child.

Heroin and methadone both cause prenatal growth retardation, with the effect of heroin more severe (Gewolb & Warshaw, 1983). Infants who have suffered intrauterine growth retardation are at higher risk of perinatal asphyxia. Although heroin does not appear to produce gross structural defects in humans, it does, however, ". . . produce behavioral effects that occur in two phases: a neonatal withdrawal syndrome at birth characterized by tremors, hyperreflexia, irritability, excessive high-pitched crying, and disturbed sleep, and later, long-term neurobehavioral impairments that appear to include hyperactivity and short attention span" (Hutchings, 1980, p. 110).

Should pregnant drug users be sent to prison? No, drug treatment programs should be provided for them instead.

The seriousness of the consequences of drug use during pregnancy has raised questions about maternal and fetal rights. Across the United States judges are beginning to sentence women to jail who are found to be abusing drugs during pregnancy. In one example, Brenda Vaughn, a 29-year-old Washington woman, pleaded guilty to forging about $700 worth of checks. It was her first offense and one that would normally have brought probation. Because Ms. Vaughn was pregnant, however, and tests showed she had used cocaine, the judge sent her to jail until the date the baby was due, saying he wanted to protect her fetus from drug abuse. (T. Lewin, 1989b). Punitive measures against pregnant women may discourage at-risk mothers from seeking prenatal care. The irony is that very few cities and counties in the United States have drug abuse treatment facilities for pregnant women, and existing drug treatment programs often discriminate against pregnant women.

A lawsuit filed on December 4, 1989, by the Women's Rights Project of the American Civil Liberties Union and by the New York Civil Liberties Union, charged North General Hospital in East Harlem, New York, and three other drug-treatment programs in New York City with illegally discriminating against pregnant women, who were refused treatment for drug abuse. The Executive Director of North General Hospital admitted that the hospital had a policy of not tak-

ing pregnant women in their drug detoxification program because, he said, they do not have adequate facilities to treat pregnant women. A study by Dr. Wendy Chavkin of Columbia University conducted in 1987 found that about 54% of the state-financed drug treatment programs in New York City refused to treat pregnant women (T. Lewin, 1989b).

There is something very shortsighted about a society that would prefer to punish drug using pregnant women by putting them in jail, while at the same time turning them away from drug treatment programs. In my own state of Rhode Island, a drug treatment facility exclusively for pregnant women has opened. It should be hoped that the provision of drug treatment facilities for pregnant women is a trend that will rapidly spread in the United States.

Pregnancy and HIV Infection

Most pregnant women with HIV infection acquired it through intravenous drug use, or sex with an IV drug user. The drug zidovudine (AZT) given during pregnancy or after birth can reduce maternal-infant transmission of HIV.

Unlike the majority of cases among men, as noted in Chapter IX, the women most likely to acquire HIV infection are intravenous drug users. "Because HIV infection in women is so often inextricably tied to substance abuse, particular attention should be paid to resolving the current problems women, and particularly pregnant women, face in receiving substance abuse treatment" (Hardy, 1991, p. 54).

It is estimated that more than 80% of children with AIDS acquired it perinatally. HIV-infected pregnant women have roughly a 30–50% chance of transmitting the virus to their infant (P. J. Boyer et al., 1994). For this reason, AIDS among children mirrors the geographic and racial and ethnic distribution among women, with Black and Hispanic children overrepresented in children with AIDS. Unfortunately, there is systematic exclusion of HIV infected pregnant women from some reproductive health care facilities. "For example, HIV infected pregnant women who elect to terminate their pregnancies may discover that their access to abortion services is restricted. Some areas report outright exclusion of HIV-infected women by abortion clinics" (Hardy, 1991, p. 51).

Fortunately, research indicates that the drug, zidovudine (AZT) given during pregnancy and to the infant after birth can reduce maternal–infant transmission of immunodeficiency virus type 1 (HIV). A study in which 26 out of 63 HIV-1 positive mothers received AZT during pregnancy and/or delivery found a significant protective effect of AZT in preventing maternal–fetal HIV-1 transmission (P. J. Boyer et al., 1994). A randomized, double-blind, placebo-controlled trial of the efficacy of AZT given to HIV-positive pregnant women and to their infants for six weeks after birth found a 67.5% reduction in relative risk of HIV transmission in the AZT group (180 babies were in the AZT group and 183 in the placebo group) (Connor et al., 1994).

Ethical issues are raised by AZT treatment related to mandatory testing of pregnant women and/or infants for HIV. Does the case for screening and treatment of newborns outweigh the privacy rights of the mother? The Public Health Service task force convened to consider the implications of AZT treatment concluded that efforts be made to persuade pregnant women to be tested for HIV and to undergo AZT treatment, but rejected compulsory testing and treatment of pregnant women (Bayer, 1994).

BABIES AT RISK

Infant Mortality

The United States ranks nineteenth in the world in infant mortality. The Black infant mortality rate is more than twice the rate for Whites. Inadequate prenatal care and shorter interval between pregnancies account for the Black–White difference.

The United States of America, the most affluent nation in the world, has a disgraceful infant mortality rate, ranking below most other industrialized nations. The United States ranks nine-teenth of nations of the world in infant mortality rates (Hoyert, 1995). What are the characteristics of mothers, and of the type of obstetrical care they receive, that disproportionately accounts for infant death or premature babies or babies with birth defects? The high infant mortality rate of Black babies in the United States as compared with Whites accounts for the U.S. ranking. When we look at the 1991 Black infant mortality rate (15.7 per 1,000 live births) we see that it is more than twice the rate for Whites (7.4 per 1,000 live births) in that year. The infant mortality rate for the Hispanic population (7.9) was 11% higher than that of the non-Hispanic White population.

A study by the Alan Guttmacher Institute found that from 1984–1988, 16% of American women who gave birth each year had inadequate care. Inadequate prenatal care was defined as starting care in the fifth month or later or by making fewer than half of the recommended doctor's visits. Teenage mothers and unmarried women were least likely to receive adequate prenatal care, with about 33% receiving inadequate care. Minority women were also more likely to receive inadequate care. While only 13% of White women received inadequate care, the rates were 30% for Hispanic women and 27% for Black women (T. Lewin, 1989a). Considerable variation exists in the level of care in different states and also from one county to another within the same state. The highest percentage of women receiving inadequate care is found in the District of Columbia and New Mexico (more than 25%), whereas in the New England states (except for Vermont), Iowa, and Wisconsin, 10% or fewer of pregnant women receive inadequate care.

Black mothers who had inadequate or intermediate prenatal care were found to be three times more likely to experience infant death as those receiving adequate care (Ahmed, McRae, & Ahmed, 1990). Mothers who are younger, unmarried, and less educated received less adequate care than their older, married, and better educated counterparts. Ahmed et al. suggest that provision of postpartum care to high-risk women and pediatric care to their infants can provide a link for maintaining continuous contact with them. Such programs for these women should also include social workers and public health nurses, who could provide social support, counseling, and referrals.

Having a high number of previous pregnancies and a short interval between terminations and/or births also constitute a high-risk group, regardless of marital status (Ahmed et al., 1990; J. S. Rawlings, Rawlings, & Read, 1995). The higher infant mortality rate among Black infants than among White infants in the United States is due largely to a greater frequency of low birth weight and preterm infants. In a study of Black and White women in military families who had access to free, high-quality health care, results indicated that low birth weight and preterm delivery were associated with shorter intervals between pregnancies. "Our findings reveal a clear association among black women between interpregnancy intervals of less than nine months and a significantly higher prevalance of preterm delivery of low-birth-weight infants" (J. S. Rawlings et al., 1995, p. 73). Among White women, the increase in preterm and low birth weight infants was associated with intervals of three months or less between birth and the conception of the next pregnancy. Among Black women nearly half (46.3%) had interpregnancy intervals of less than nine months; 4.2% of White women had interpregnancy intervals of less than three months. The implications of this study are that Black women require a longer time between pregnancies to achieve optimal birth outcome than do White women. "Because prenatal events may have lifelong effects on health, the adverse outcomes observed by investigators may reflect the cumulative effects of poverty over a number of generations" (Lieberman, 1995, p. 118).

Black teenagers are the most vulnerable group for adverse infant outcome according to a large scale longitudinal study of obstetrical patients (45,142 patients studied for eight years) at 14 university hopitals in different areas of the United States (E. A. Friedman & Neff, 1987). According to the National Collaborative Perinatal Project, which began in 1958, "Strong adverse effects were documented for patients with a low socioeconomic index, low family income, high housing density, and limited income. If the father of the baby was absent, the results tended to be worse" (E. A. Friedman & Neff, 1987, p. 499). A previous premature birth and premature or postdate delivery also adversely affected outcome. Patients who began prenatal care late or who only had a small number of prenatal visits were at serious risk as well. Male fetuses were at greater risk than were female fetuses.

Among the drug and anesthesia agents used in labor and delivery, paracervical block and general inhalation anesthesia carried potentially serious risk. Spinal anesthesia was not associated with any adverse effects. Analgesics such as meperidine (Demerol) and hydroxyzine (Vistaril, Atarax) generally had negligible effects.

Prenatal Care

Situational and psychosocial barriers reduce a woman's likelihood of seeking prenatal care.

Considerable literature exists linking no or little prenatal care to premature and/or low birthweight infants and higher infant mortality rates (Goldenberg, Patterson, & Freese, 1992). Situational barriers that prevent mothers from getting prenatal care include lack of childcare, transportation problems, rural residence, difficulty attending during clinic hours, and lack of knowledge of community resources. Psychosocial barriers that reduce a woman's likelihood of seeking prenatal care include an unplanned pregnancy, not knowing they are pregnant, denial of the pregnancy, lack of understanding of the importance of prenatal care, a lack of commitment toward preventive care for children, a fear of doctors and medical procedures, and lack of a support person.

Research on factors related to decision making about prenatal care by low-income women (approximately half White and half minority women) indicates that the most important rewards of prenatal care are the health of the baby and maternal health (Schaffer & Lia-Hoagberg, 1994). In the choice to seek prenatal care, the support of family members and having health care professionals willing to talk about problems and get them checked out were found to be important. Women who have children indicated more psychological costs of obtaining prenatal care. The most frequently mentioned health-care provider cost was seeing someone different on each visit. "The availability of affordable prenatal care does not guarantee that low-income women will seek it. Personal, family, and health-care-provider rewards and costs influence perceptions of gain from prenatal care" (Schaffer & Lia-Hoagberg, 1994, p. 157). Among the recommendations to increase participation of women in prenatal care are education for partners and family members of the pregnant women in the clinic setting while she is being seen by the health-care provider. Play areas for children in the clinics would help reduce costs of prenatal care for mothers. A woman seen by the same health-care provider is more likely to develop a trusting relationship that will increase her continuation of care. Of course, providing financially subsidized prenatal care to low-income women is necessary.

MIDLIFE CHILD-BEARING

Good news! Child-bearing is no riskier for mothers over 35. The bad news is that there is an increase in genetic defects, particularly Down's syndrome, for infants born to midlife mothers.

One of the social trends of the 1980s was the increase in the percentage of women postponing child-bearing until a more advanced maternal age. "Between 1970 and 1986 the rate of first births in the United States more than doubled among women 30 to 39 years of age, and it increased by 50 percent for women 40 to 44" (Berkowitz, Skovron, Lapinski, & Berkowitz, 1990). Factors accounting for this increase in the numbers of older first-time mothers included women's career priorities, advanced education, financial concerns, delayed or unstable marriage, and an increase in the number of women in the 35–44 age group as the baby boom generation aged (Kirz, Dorchester, & Freeman, 1986).

The medical "wisdom" has been that women over 35 are "high risk." Mansfield (1988) con-

ducted a critical review of all U.S. studies of advanced maternal age and eight reproductive outcomes conducted up to 1983 and a small number of studies conducted since that date. Nearly two-thirds of the studies were found to suffer from serious methodological flaws. Maternal age was confounded with other factors such as poverty, multiparity (having had more than one pregnancy), disease, caesarean sections, prior fetal loss, and labor medications. Mansfield concluded that the pessimistic assessment of midlife child-bearing by the medical community is not warranted for current midlife mothers, who may in fact, have many favorable factors operating such as middle-class status and good prepregnancy health.

Well-designed studies comparing the pregnancy complications, labor complications, delivery factors, and neonatal outcome of women who were 35 years and older with women in their 20s have found no increases in negative outcomes for the infants (Kirz et al., 1986; Mansfield, 1988). These studies of predominantly White women, however, have found an increased incidence of diabetes among the older mothers, and pregnancy induced hypertension.

More of the younger women had spontaneous vaginal deliveries, whereas the older women had significantly more operative deliveries (low forceps, cesarean, and vacuum extractors). This may be the result of self-fulfilling prophecies on the part of physicians, since there were no statistically significant differences in the medical indications for these procedures for the older group.

There were no significant differences in neonatal outcome between the older or younger primiparous pregnant women. Among the parous women, however, the older women had an increased incidence of exceptionally large babies. The data is not consistent on whether older or younger mothers have babies of lower birthweight, and complications associated with that. Nor do the older women have an increased risk of having an infant who was small for gestational age, or had a low Apgar score (a composite of five measures that reflect infant health at one and five minutes). Even among older women with diabetes and hypertension, there was no increase in stillbirths or neonatal death as compared with the younger women. "Perhaps it is time to eradicate the offensive labels of elderly, dangerous, or postmature and consider these women as mature—the mature gravida" (Mansfield, 1988, p. 11).

There is a higher incidence, however, of genetic defects, particularly Down's Syndrome, a major cause of mental retardation and congenital heart disease, that does increase with advanced maternal age. A Down's syndrome child has an extra chromosome in every cell in his/her body. Down's Syndrome is found in all cultures. The finding that the incidence of Down's Syndrome increases steadily with age, and dramatically over age 40, is found for all cultures where it has been studied. The risk of giving birth to a Down's Syndrome baby is 1 in 384 births at age 35 increasing to 1 in 112 births at age 40 and to 1 in 11 births and by age 48 (Bogart, 1992; Hassold et al., 1992; Travis, 1988a). Despite the increased risk, however, the odds are still much greater that the infant will not have Down's Syndrome even in the highest risk age group (over 40 mothers). Research also indicates that 5–25% of cases of Down's syndrome may be due to paternal rather than maternal chromosomal error (Bricarelli et al., 1988; Hassold et al., 1992). Since mothers over 35 account for only 7% of births each year, screening the over 35 pregnant population will only detect about 20–25% of Down's Syndrome pregnancies (Bogart, 1992).

CHILDBIRTH

Medicalization of Childbirth

The trend in this century has been the medicalization of childbirth. This creates a feeling of powerlessness in women. In recent years there has been an effort to give back some control of the childbirth process to women.

Cross-culturally and historically, the practices surrounding labor and delivery have varied radically. The revolution in this century pertaining to childbirth in industrialized societies has been the introduction of medical technology, which placed childbirth in the hands of physicians and hospitals. For centuries, childbirth took place in the home surrounded by midwife, family, and friends. In 1900, less than 5% of births in the United States took place in hospitals (Wertz & Wertz, 1977).

The shift from home to hospital births was almost total by 1979, when 99% of American babies were born in hospitals (Mackey & Brouse, 1988). "During this shift in the location of birth, the view of childbirth also changed from that of a normal physiological family event to an illness that needed to be treated" (Mackey & Brouse, 198, p. 109). In the past couple of decades, technological interventions have increased, particularly in fetal monitoring and caesarian deliveries.

Feminist Perspective

A feeling of powerlessness and alienation is enhanced in the mother by the medicalization of birth. One of the harmful effects is a process of infantilization by others through downgrading her abilities and sense of autonomy. The second effect is akin to sexual assault through her treatment by the (typically) male doctor.

The (male) doctor's total access to a woman's breasts, vagina and womb as she lies semi-naked looks suspiciously like a sexual power-game. Yet both the sexuality and the assault are denied: to admit one would be to admit the other. We are forced to deny it, too, by dissociating ourselves to a degree from what is really happening and by rationalizing it in terms of medical practice. (Saunders, 1983, p. 93)

As a reaction to the medicalization of birth, however, has come a social construction of birth as a natural process and a movement to put the woman and baby back at the center of attention. Four social movements converged to bring about this trend: "l) the natural childbirth movement; 2) feminism; 3) consumerism; 4) 'back to nature' romanticism" (K. K. Nelson, 1986, p. 170). Women began to question obstetrical practices and demand the right to participate actively in the child-bearing experience. Women developed health-care services and women began to give birth at home again (Mackey & Brouse, 1988).

Natural Childbirth Classes

Participation in natural childbirth classes may be beneficial both physically and psychologically for mother and infant.

For both nonhuman primates and human beings, the contractions leading to childbirth cause pain. "Indications of such in primates included grimacing, moaning, grasping 'blindly' at objects, unusual postures, and occasionally loud cries" (Trevathan, 1987, p. 102). In different parts of the world, there have been numerous remedies for dealing with this pain, including herbal medicines, sympathetic magic, heat, and massage. Modern medicine's answer has been analgesics and anesthetics. Because of increasing concern with the effect of pain medication on the baby, many women in modern society have begun to rely on psychoprophylaxis (some form of relaxation training).

During the 1950s two methods of natural childbirth began to become popularized, the method developed by Grantly Dick-Read, a British physician, and the LaMaze method. Dick-Read first published his book, *Natural Childbirth* in 1933, and further developed his ideas in revisions. Dick-Read reasoned that the severe pain women experience during labor and delivery are a result of fear and apprehension arising from the sociocultural attitudes and expectations communicated by mothers to daughters. His method emphasizes training in female anatomy and physiology, exercises designed to improve general fitness, and instruction in breathing and relaxation training. At the same time, Dick-Read minimizes medical interference in the birth process (Calhoun, Selby, & Calhoun, 1980).

The **Lamaze** method of childbirth preparation stems from the work of several Russian and other European physicians. It began in the 1800s with the use of hypnosis during childbirth. Later Russian physicians adapted Pavlov's ideas of classical conditioning to childbirth preparation. The method was adopted as the official method of childbirth in the Soviet Union in 1951. In that same year, a French obstetrician Ferdinand Lamaze visited the Soviet Union to observe this method. Lamaze made modifications, including rapid breathing during the second stage of labor, and panting during crowning and delivery. The approach, which came to be known as the Lamaze method, was well received, and was sanctioned for use by Catholics by Pope Pious XII in 1959. The woman attends six to eight prenatal childbirth classes in the last trimester along with a labor coach, often her husband. She is taught to substitute breathing techniques for grimacing and writhing responses to labor contractions. In addition, she and her coach are given instruction in anatomy and physiology of pregnancy and childbirth, controlled neuromuscular relaxation, and visual focusing (Calhoun et al., 1980).

Measurable physical advantages have been reported for Lamaze preparation. Hughey, McElin, and Young (1978) compared the charts of 500 LaMaze-prepared women and an equal number of charts of controls matched for age, parity, race, and educational level. The outcomes were far more positive for the LaMaze births as compared with the others. Women who had LaMaze births had one-fourth as many caesarian sections, one-fifth as many cases of fetal distress, one-third as many cases of post partum depression, one-third as many cases of toxemia, half as many premature births, and fewer instances of postpartum hemorrhage, or perinatal mortality and fewer peritoneal lacerations. In addition, the babies of Lamaze-prepared women had higher Apgar scores in both the one and five-minute ratings. Based on the research, Hughey et al. conclude that the Lamaze method is not harmful, and may be beneficial both physically and psychologically for mother and infant.

Another study comparing birth statistics of 64 women who attended prepared childbirth classes with a matched sample of 64 women who did not found no significant differences to mother or baby in maternal or neonatal outcomes (Patton, English, & Hambleton, 1985). It should be kept in mind that the Hughey et al. (1978) study, which did find positive outcomes of natural childbirth, was conducted on a much larger sample, leading to greater confidence in the results. It can be concluded that "natural" childbirth at best is of benefit in decreasing some of the adverse outcomes of childbirth, at worst it will make no difference.

Walking around and sitting during labor, and squatting during childbirth are associated with shorter labor, decreased pain, and greater satisfaction for mothers.

The typical position for labor in the American hospitals is to have the woman lying in bed. When the birth approaches, she is wheeled into the delivery room and her feet put in stirrups while she lies flat on her back. In most primitive cultures, women give birth in a squatting position. Research has found that an upright position—standing, sitting, or walking around during labor is associated with increased intensity of uterine contractions, shorter labor, decreased pain, and greater satisfaction and comfort on the part of the mother (Lupe & Gross, 1988; Romond & Baker, 1985). Some hospitals have introduced a birthing chair that women can sit in while giving birth instead of delivering while lying flat on a table.

Episiotomy

Episiotomy is routinely performed by most obstetricians in the United States. Research results do not support its routine use in childbirth.

At the present time there is considerable controversy in the United States about the routine use of **episiotomy** in childbirth. Episiotomy was used in 62.5% of vaginal deliveries in the United States in 1976. During that same year, the episiotomy rate was only 28.2% in France and 8% in Holland. Episiotomy is the cutting of the perineum, the area between the vagina and the anus, during labor and delivery to enlarge the opening for the baby to get out (Graham, Catanzarite, Bernstein & Varela-Gittings, 1990).

The New Our Bodies Ourselves (1992), written by the Boston Women's Health Collective, has condemned the routine use of episiotomy, charging that it prevents women from experiencing

birth as a sexual event, is genital mutilation, and is extremely painful for several weeks after birth as the stitches heal up. It also may make intercourse very painful for a period of time when resumed. Is episiotomy medically necessary?

Physicians advocate performing episiotomies by claiming that the procedure prevents tearing, allows less traumatic delivery of the baby's head, protects the pelvic floor (from becoming too stretched and allowing the uterus to fall into the vagina later in life) (Graham et al., 1990). Another reason some doctors have for performing an episiotomy is to give a woman a "tight" vagina for her husband's pleasure.

I saw my doctor at the checkup six weeks after my baby was born. Full of male pride, he told me during my pelvic exam, "I did a beautiful job sewing you up. You're as tight as a virgin; your husband should thank me." (The Boston Women's Health Collective, 1992, p. 458)

A study in New Mexico of episiotomy attitudes and practices among different types of health-care providers found that most obstetricians favor routine use of episiotomy. It is less favored by family physicians, less yet by nurse midwives, and least favored by lay midwives. As stated by a nurse midwife, "if God meant for every woman to have an episiotomy, He would have given women a zipper down there" (Graham et al., 1990, p. 191).

A randomized, controlled study conducted with 356 first-time mothers and 341 who had previously given birth found that early and three-month postpartum localized pain was least for women who did not have an episiotomy (M. C. Klein et al., 1994). Women also had less pain who had spontaneous perineal tears rather than episiotomy. Sexual functioning was better for women who had not had the episiotomy, even if they had spontaneous perineal tears. Third- and fourth-degree tears were causally linked to episiotomy. Three-month postpartum examination revealed that those with episiotomy had the weakest pelvic floor musculature, whereas those with an intact perineum had the strongest. "The current practice of using episiotomy at routine and high rates should be abandoned, and methods for protecting and preserving the perineum intact, or with small perineal tears, should become a formal part of medical education (M. C. Klein et al., 1994, pp. 597–598).

Nurse Midwives

Nurse midwives pay more attention to the social and emotional aspects of pregnancy and childbirth. Research finds the birth outcomes to be just as favorable as for physician deliveries.

An alternative birth movement began in the United States in the early 1970s as a way of reclaiming birth for the home and family and away from the sick-care approach of the medical establishment. Changes set into motion "involving midwives, home births, birth centers, and a new appreciation and awareness of the social and emotional aspects of birth, were fueled by a generation of women who wanted more from their childbirth experiences than traditional physicians and hospitals were able to provide" (D. Young, 1986, p. 47). Midwife based care focuses on the whole woman and encourages her to actively participate in all aspects of pregnancy and birth. Nurse-midwives pay more attention to the psychological experience of childbirth and pregnancy. Most nurse-midwives also try to serve the needs of the people who accompany and support the mother. A certified nurse-midwife (CNM) is trained in both nursing and midwifery. The certification agency is the American College of Nurse-Midwives (ACNM). An ACNM survey of nurse-midwifes found that they are well educated, with two-thirds holding master's degrees or higher (C. J. Adams, 1986).

Nurse-midwives practice in six types of settings: publically supported hospitals; private practice with physicians; private practices of nurse-midwives which utilize hospitals for births; free standing birth centers; nurse-midwifery within health maintenance organizations; and nurse-midwife home-birth services. Most nurse-midwives deliver in hospitals, with only 14% conducting any deliveries in private homes and 12% conducting deliveries in free-standing birthing centers. Despite the number of types of prac-

tices, the number of nurse-midwives in the United States numbers fewer than 3,000, and only about four percent of pregnant women receive nurse-midwife services (C. J. Adams, 1986). In other industrialized countries, such as England, Japan, Sweden and the Netherlands, a large percentage of pregnant women use midwifery services.

Although there has been a lack of well-controlled studies of the safety and effectiveness of nurse midwifery care, the research that exists finds positive benefits of nurse midwifery practice. Of course, where nurse midwives were practicing, there often was a relative lack of care by obstetricians. Even more recent studies, however, support the claim of reduction in maternal and infant mortality and morbidity in areas where other care providers also practice (J. B. Thompson, 1986).

Rates of Caesarean Section

Nearly one in four births in the United States is now by caesarean section. Research indicates that a substantial number of these are not required for the health and welfare of the mother and baby.

When risk factors are present for the mother or baby, **caesarean section** (surgical removal of the fetus by abdominal incision) is often performed. The caesarean section rate increased fivefold in the United States between 1965 and 1988. The rate of caesarean section deliveries finally leveled off in 1991 at 23.5% of all births (Flamm, 1995a). There has been a shift away from the idea that "once a caesarean always a caesarean," with an increase in vaginal deliveries for women with a previous caesarean. Nevertheless, repeat operations accounted for 36% of all caesareans in 1990 (Flamm, 1995b).

Medical sources have attributed the fall in infant death rates that occurred during this same time to increases in caesarean section. O'Driscoll and Crowley (1985), examined the infant death rate for infants delivered at the National Maternity Hospital, Dublin, Ireland, where the caesarean section rate remained unchanged at 4.2% in 1970, 4.8% in 1980, and 4.4% in the first half of 1984.

During the decade 1970–80 the perinatal mortality rate for infants over 500 grams fell from 36.5 per 1000 in 1970 to 16.8 per 1000 in 1980. This fall in perinatal mortality rates compares favorably with that experienced in United States centres with a 3–4-fold higher caesarean section rate. (O'Driscoll & Crowley, 1985, pp. 155–156)

O'Driscoll and Crowley conclude that this data invalidates the hypothesis that the improved perinatal mortality rates experienced in the United States over the same period can be attributed to the increase in caesarean section rate.

A chart review study was carried out to determine the rate of diagnosis of dystocia (difficult labor) and the use of caesarean section to treat dystocia among 3,887 primiparous women who gave birth to a single baby at four hospitals in the Ottawa–Carleton region of Canada in 1984 (P. J. Stewart, Dulberg, Arnill, Elmslie, & Hall, 1990). Almost one-third of the women in the study were given a diagnosis of dystocia. The authors conclude that since 41% of the caesareans for dystocia were performed during the latent phase of labor, before effective labor started, then fetal distress rather than dystocia be used as a criterion for performing a caesarean section.

If all the elective cesarean sections for disproportion and the cesarean sections for dystocia without fetal distress were eliminated the overall cesarean section rate for primiparous women with a single baby in the vertex presentation could drop from 16.4% to 8%. (P. J. Stewart et al., 1990, p. 463)

Therefore it appears that a substantial number of the caesarean sections performed in the United States and Canada every year are not necessary to the health and welfare of the mother and baby.

Of the 966,000 caesarean sections performed in 1991, 349,000 or 36.1% were unnecessary according to a report from the Centers for Disease Control (as cited in E. A. Friedman, 1995). The additional expenditure for increased hospital costs alone for the unnecessary caesareans performed is more than 1 billion dollars annually.

Postpartum Adjustment and Caesarean Delivery

Although there is less satisfaction with a caesarean delivery, there is no difference in postpartum psychological adjustment for mothers who had caesarean or vaginal delivery.

The existing research on the emotional and psychological effects of caesarian births has consistently suggested negative emotional reactions to the labor and delivery experience for those women having caesarean sections. Women who deliver vaginally report greater satisfaction with the birth experience. This is true for both White middle-class and for poor Black women (Padawer, Fagan, Janoff-Bulman, Strickland, & Chorowski, 1988; Sandalowski & Bustamente, 1986).

No differences have been found, however, in postpartum psychological adjustment between women who delivered by emergency caesarean or vaginally. Results show that although the caesarian delivery mothers were negative about the delivery mode, they were not more anxious, depressed, or less confident in mothering ability than women who delivered vaginally. There was no indication of decreased mental health or psychological distress among those who had a caesarean delivery. The poor Black women said that although they had not expected or prepared for a caesarean section, it was "ok" because their focus was on the outcome, the baby, and not the experience of birth itself.

PSYCHOSOCIAL ASPECTS OF PREGNANCY AND CHILDBIRTH

Pregnant women are not more depressed than nonpregnant women.

No large-scale studies have been conducted of psychological well-being during pregnancy. Kaplan (1986) argues that typical symptoms of a normal pregnancy, such as weight gain, need for more sleep, fatigue, slower movements, increased bodily concerns, and some mood fluctuation, are also symptoms of depression. B. J. Kaplan seems to think of the stereotype of the happy placid pregnant woman as a myth and calls for research on the normal affective course of pregnancy.

Lips (1982) did conduct a study in which she compared responses of 108 pregnant women in their second to fifth month of pregnancy with those given by their husbands and nonpregnant women and their husbands. On the Beck Depression Inventory, the women scored significantly more depressed than did the men; however, the women who were pregnant were no more depressed than were the nonpregnant women. On a factor labeled Negative Emotional State, expectant parents scored significantly lower (less negative) than did nonpregnant couples. Expectant parents also reported significantly less Performance Decrement than did the other couples. On two of the factors, Feeling Overweight and Feeling Ill, pregnant women did score higher than the other three groups. I think Lips' study refutes Kaplan's thesis that pregnant women are more depressed.

Psychosocial Factors and Abnormal Birth Outcome

Among pregnant women, those who have negative birth outcomes have less support from husbands, mothers, and friends, and exhibit more psychological problems during pregnancy.

Social psychological factors have been found during pregnancy that differentiate women who later deliver a premature baby from those who deliver at term. A prospective psychological study of 47 pregnant women, beginning around the twenty-fourth week of pregnancy, found significant differences between preterm and term mothers in responses to multiple choice questions (DeMuylder & Wesel, 1988). There were no differences in age, parity, marital situation, and socioeconomic level between the 11 women who delivered a premature baby and the 36 who went to term. The preterm mothers more frequently declared

that pregnancy has been difficult to accept; they have poor communication with their baby (or even no communication at all); their husband offers little help or support; they reacted negatively when the first menses started. (DeMuylder & Wesel, 1988, p. 89)

This study suggests that there could be important differences in mental attitude between women who later deliver preterm and those who go to term.

Psychosocial factors have also been found to differentiate mothers who have normal and abnormal birth outcome in studies with low-risk patients of a certified nurse midwifery practice group who deliver patients at a hospital (Mehl, Donovan, & Peterson, 1988; G. Peterson, Mehl, & McRae, 1988). The women were interviewed and completed psychological tests prior to childbirth. Abnormal birth outcome, as defined by longer first-stage labor length and poorer Apgar scores at one and five minutes, was related to negative maternal self-identity, negative beliefs, and lack of support from mother and from friends. The two factors that more strongly discriminated between normal and abnormal birth outcome groups were that abnormal outcome mothers had greater fear and reported a lack of support from their partners.

Character disorder and/or defenses of denial, repression, projection, and somatization were more commonly found among women with uterine dysfunction or caesarean section. The caesarean group had the highest anxiety rating and had husbands who had more negative attitudes toward the pregnancy. Hypnotherapy was useful in reducing abnormal birth outcome. The normal delivery group had the lowest anxiety scores and the lowest mean total life stress rating. The implications of this body of research are that the participation of mental health professionals in prenatal care could reduce some of the negative outcomes of the childbirth process.

Low-income pregnant women who receive prenatal social support have better labor progress and babies with higher Apgar scores, and less postpartum depression than women who recieve less social support.

Different dimensions of social support—amount of support received, quality of support received, and social network resources—were all found to be related to maternal and infant health and well-being in a prospective study of a sample of ethnically diverse low-income pregnant women ($N = 129$) (N. L. Collins, Dunkel-Schetter, Lobel, & Scrimshaw, 1993). Women who received more prenatal social support experienced fewer difficulties in labor and had babies who had higher Apgar ratings. Independent of the amount of support they received, women who had higher quality support had babies with higher Apgar scores and experienced less postpartum depression. "When broken down by type of support received, prenatal task, material, and informational support appeared most important for infant Apgar score, whereas prenatal task, material, and confiding support contributed disproportionally to labor progress" (N. L. Collins et al., 1993, p. 1253). Larger social support networks were associated with higher birthweight. Significantly less stress during pregnancy, less prenatal substance use, and earlier initiation of prenatal care were associated with satisfaction with the support received by the pregnant women. Larger resource networks were related to more prenatal clinic visits. Interventions need to be designed to provide social support for low-income, socially disadvantaged pregnant women in order to improve the health and well-being of mothers and their infants.

POSTPARTUM ADJUSTMENT

Most women suffer from some form of postpartum depression, ranging in seriousness from the "blues" to depression to psychosis.

The days and weeks following childbirth may be stressful for women, particularly the first-time mother. Profound social and psychological changes are occurring in the woman's life during this period, as well as sharp drops in the level of hormones, particularly estrogen and progesterone. The **postpartum** period is a life transition requiring intrapsychic and interpersonal reorganization and adaptation (Hopkins, Marcuse, & Campbell, 1984).

Changes have been found in four important self-definitional areas between the pregnancy state and the postpartum-period, relationship to husband, pain tolerance, interest in sex, and social boredom. There are, however, also areas that show remarkable consistency between pregnancy and postpartum responses—relationship with mother, body image, attitude toward breast-feeding, and feelings of dependency (Ruble et al., 1990).

Given the number of changes occurring in a woman's life after childbirth, it is not surprising that researchers estimate that 39–85% of women experience some form of postpartum depression (Hopkins, Marcuse, & Campbell, 1984; O'Hara, 1987). The severity of the symptoms varies on a continuum from the **blues,** which lasts only a few days, to a "neurotic" postpartum depression, which lasts a few weeks to several months, and finally to postpartum "psychosis," which effects fewer than 1% of women (Hopkins, Marcuse, & Campbell, 1984; O'Hara, 1987). Just as some women do not experience dysmenorrhea, or morning sickness, some women do not experience the blues. The same woman may also experience postpartum depression following the birth of one child, but not following the birth of other children. I went through a period of the blues for a few days with my first child, but not after the births of my second and third children.

Although there are sharp drops in progesterone and estrogen levels during the first few days following childbirth, the results of studies of hormone levels of women who do or do not experience some level of postpartum depression are mixed and inconclusive (O'Hara, 1987). There is an increase in psychiatric treatment postpartum that is due largely to affective disorders (Kendell, Wainwright, Hailey, & Shannon, 1976).

The Blues

The blues only last a few days. There is more crying one week after birth than either three weeks before birth or one month after birth, but also more positive emotion.

The mildest psychological disturbance is the "**maternity blues,**" which usually last from 24 to 48 hours. The woman may cry easily and be on somewhat of an emotional roller coaster. She may also have difficulty sleeping, and be tense, irritable, and angry. It is more common among first-time mothers. Estimates are that 50–80% of postpartum women suffer from the blues. For a subgroup of women, it may represent the onset of a clinical or postpartum depression.

L. C. Garner and Tessler (1989) found no increase in blues symptoms of "crying, feeling mildly depressed or in low spirits, feeling particularly vulnerable to criticism, and being mildly confused as to everyday things" between three weeks before birth, one week after birth, and one month after birth, when the symptoms are treated as a cluster. There was more crying, however, one week after birth than at either of the other two time periods, but there was also more positive emotion—feeling excited, proud, pleased. Negative emotion, on the other hand, was reported to be higher before birth. Levels of depressed mood were lowest one month postpartum.

Women who had more obstetrical technologies during labor and delivery were also found to have more negative emotion one week after the birth (L. C. Garner & Tessler, 1989). "The loss of personal control, a frequent by-product of the new birth technologies, may influence the incidence of postpartum moods (L. C. Garner & Tessler, 1989, p. 119). The technologies employed ranged from caesarean section, to vaginal delivery with forceps, to fetal monitoring to drugs for pain.

Postpartum Depression

Postpartum depression, having the typical symptoms of depression, affects about 7–20% of new mothers.

Postpartum depression is a mild-to-moderate depression that is less common than the blues, affecting about 7–20% of new mothers. The aver-

age duration appears to be six to eight weeks, although for some women it can last as long as a year, during which time the mother may have such typical symptoms of depression as sleep and appetite disturbance, fatigue, loss of interest in sex, and guilt. It is more likely to recur in a woman who suffered postpartum depression in a previous pregnancy. Three sets of variables explained 35.5% of the variance in depression of 84 White, married mothers after the delivery of their first-born children (Hock, Schirtzinger, & Lutz, (1992). Parental rejection and/or overprotection of the mother during her childhood, heightened levels of anxiety about separation, and dissatisfaction with the marriage were all risk factors for depression.

Women who have a history of previous emotional problems have a higher incidence of postpartum depression. In terms of personality and attitudinal variables, it has been found that high anxiety, high hostility, and an external locus of control (a sense that one is not in control of one's life) during pregnancy correlate with postpartum depression (Cutrona, 1982).

In one study (Pfost, Lum, and Stevens 1989) the strongest predictor of postpartum depression, as measured by the Beck Depression Inventory (BDI), was depression during pregnancy. The severity of the depression actually declined shortly after childbirth. Women who scored feminine on the BSRI had lower depression scores, indicating that expressive behaviors facilitate the mothering role. Masculinity scores, however, did not predict level of postpartum depression. More depression was reported by undifferentiated women than those of other sex role orientations. The women who had plans for returning to work also had fewer depressive symptoms.

Postpartum Psychosis

Depressive psychosis is rare, afflicting fewer than 1% of new mothers.

Postpartum depressive psychosis has many of the same signs and symptoms of an acute psychosis not associated with childbirth. It includes such severe symptoms as delusions (persistent false beliefs) paranoid symptoms, anxiety, depressed mood and suicidal thoughts. Delusions of postpartum psychosis, however, often represent themes relating to childbirth, guilt from thoughts of infanticide or concern about not being able to care for the child. Treatment is the same as for other affective psychosis (therapy, medication) (Rhode & Maneros, 1993).

Among women with a history of mental illness, fifty-one percent were found to relapse within 6 months postpartum. All of the cases of postpartum psychosis were in women who had a previous history of bipolar or schizoaffective psychosis. Only 7% of control women developed non-psychotic depressive disorders (Marks, Wieck, Checkley & Kumar, 1992). In a longitudinal study involving 86 cases of postpartum psychosis over a follow-up period of 26 years, 64% of the 61 women on whom data was available had recurrences of mental illness (49% schizoaffective disorder, 28% schizophrenic disorder) (Rhode & Maneros, 1993). Some researchers suggest that postpartum psychosis is a variant of bipolar affective disorder (Strouse, Szuba, & Baxter, 1992).

Factors Related to Postpartum Depression

There is no one cause of postpartum depression, but it is associated with a number of factors including a more difficult labor and delivery and lack of social support.

A number of factors do, however, correlate with postpartum depression. These risk factors include: a more difficult labor and delivery; being single; lack of social support from others; prior history of psychiatric symptoms; and a history of severe menstrual distress (Cutrona, 1982; Hopkins et al. 1984). None of these causal factors in postpartum depression, however, have been unambiguously supported in the literature (O'Hara, 1987). Research shows that women for whom the postpartum depression was a recurrence of depression were at increased risk of further non-postpartum depression. However, women for whom the postpartum depression was the first occurrence of depression were at increased risk

of only of a future postpartum depression, but not for other nonpostpartum episodes (Cooper & Murray, 1995).

MOTHER–INFANT BONDING

Mother–infant bonding occurs within a few days after delivery.

The reciprocal interaction of mother and infant during the hours and days following childbirth leads to an attachment that ensures the mother's commitment to seeing that the infant's needs are met during the months and years of dependency.

> The process of forming an attachment between mother and child is a process which begins long before the infant is born. For most mothers it is quite natural to begin to incorporate the baby into their everyday thinking and, during the second trimester, into the way they view themselves. For most mothers the third trimester is a time of coming to see the baby as a separate human being. (Jernberg, 1988, p. 253)

The father, however, also forms an early attachment with the infant. A conversation I had with two fathers underscored that attachment for me. One man said he was jealous of his wife being able to breast-feed their month-old baby, of her ability to provide that kind of nurturing, and to form such a close bond with the baby. The other father had to be absent from home during the week because of his job, and wished he had as much time with his four-year-old daughter as did his wife.

Age of the mother, and psychosocial factors related to age, may also influence mother–infant interaction patterns. Culp, Appelbaum, Osofsky, and Levy (1988) conducted a longitudinal study of 130 adolescent mothers (aged 13–17 years) and 86 married first-time nonadolescent mothers (aged 18–35 years). The birth weights and gestational age of the babies did not differ between the two groups. Psychosocial differences, however, did appear between the two groups. Adolescents were less happy about being pregnant, had less social support, and reported less support from the father of the infant. Adolescents were also observed to vocalize less to their infants during feeding than nonadolescent mothers.

BREAST-FEEDING

The medicalization of birth during the first half of the twentieth century led to a steep decline in breast-feeding. The La Leche League, the Women's Health Movement, and awareness of the nutritional benefits of breast-feeding led to sharp increases in breast-feeding during the 1970s and early 1980s, at least among White, middle-class women.

The switch from breast-feeding to use of commercial infant formula for bottle feeding babies accompanied the medicalization of birth during the first half of the twentieth century. The mothers who did want to nurse during this time were given little or no information about it. "The founding of the **La Leche League** in 1956 suggests a growing reaction against the widespread employment of physician-directed bottle feeding" (Apple, 1987, p. 177). The purpose of the organization was to enable mothers who had successfully breast-fed their infants to provide information and support to others who wished to breast-feed. In more recent years, both the women's movement and the advanced knowledge of the nutritional superiority of human milk over formula or cow's milk for babies triggered increases in the prevalence of breast-feeding, although a decline again occurred in the last half of the 1980s.

Both the American Academy of Pediatrics and the Surgeon General of the United States have advocated that mother's breast-feed their babies. The Surgeon General stated, "We must identify and reduce the barriers which keep women from beginning or continuing to breast-feed their infants" (R. Lawrence, 1980, p. 6). Despite the backing of these august medical institutions, only about half of pediatricians interviewed in one study routinely recommend breast-feeding to new mothers or offered them any specific assistance for or education about breast-feeding (Michelman, Faden, Gielsen, & Buxton, 1990). Nevertheless, the pediatricians had positive attitudes about offering new mothers information about breast-feeding.

A resurgence of breast-feeding began in this country in the 1970s. Ross Laboratories have been conducting ongoing surveys since 1955 on large, nationally representative samples of mothers to assess the trend in the incidence of breast-feeding (G. A. Martinez & Krieger, 1985; Ryan, Rush, Krieger, & Landowski, 1991). In 1970, fewer than 25% of infants one week of age were receiving breast milk. By 1984, that figure had increased to 61% of infants being breast-fed at one week old. There was also an increase in the duration of breast-feeding from the early 1970s to mid-1980s. In 1971, only 8.1% of babies were still breast-fed at ages three or four months, compared with 37% of babies still being breast-fed at three or four months in 1984. Comparing rates for 1984 and 1989, however, a decline occurred of 7.5% (from 59.7% to 52.2%) in initiation of breast-feeding. The decline was 24% (from 23.8% to 18.1%) for mothers still breast-feeding at six months of age (Ryan et al., 1991).

In terms of background characteristics of the 1984 sample, the woman least likely to breast-feed her infant was a Black teenager of low income and educational level. The decline in breast-feeding between 1984 and 1989 was also largest for that group. White, college-educated mothers, and mothers not in the labor force are most likely to breast-feed their infants and this group also showed the least decline in rates of breast-feeding in 1989. Mothers who breast-feed are also more likely to be older, multiparous, live in the western portion of the United States, and not be enrolled in the government-subsidized Women, Infants, and Children program for low income mothers, which provides free infant formula (Ryan et al., 1991). A similar decline in breast-feeding between 1984 and 1988 was also documented in the United Kingdom (Emery, Scholey, & Taylor, 1990).

Although research does show that employed mothers can successfully breast-feed, it takes a high level of motivation to do so. Seventeen women who successfully breast-fed their infants while employed said that initially they did so because of concern for the baby's health and well being, but after four months of breast-feeding, closeness with the infant was also an important motivation (Rafsnider & Myers, 1985). Factors cited as important by employed breast-feeding mothers were a good diet, support from family, use of a breast pump and manual expression, and the use of formula when necessary. Many of the women did, however, cite fatigue and other hindering factors such as the baby being far from work and inability to use a breast pump. Support networks were particularly important, both within the family and with other breast-feeding mothers (Rafsnider & Myers, 1985).

Nutritional Advantages of Breast-Feeding

Breast-feeding has nutritional advantages for the baby. Breast-fed babies have fewer illnesses during the first year of life. Some doctors criticize the research on methodological grounds and say that there are no differences in infections in breast-fed and bottle-fed babies.

A nursing baby is sure to receive food at the correct temperature and consistency and with the right nutritional content. Although cow's milk has three times the protein of human milk, the protein in cow's milk is mostly casein, while the protein in human milk is mostly lactalbumin, which is more easily digested by infants. The fat content of human milk is predominantly long-chain unsaturated fatty acids and polyunsaturated fatty acids, while saturated fatty acids are mainly found in cow's milk (Goldfarb, & Tibbetts, 1980). Breast-fed babies also have more control over their feeding situation and may, therefore, limit their intake and keep their weight down because they are not encouraged to finish the bottle. Bottle-fed babies often have disproportionalities in weight and length gains that may be an outgrowth of their lesser control over feeding. Bottle-feeding provides the temptation for a busy mother to prop the bottle on some diapers while the baby feeds, and to continue with other chores. Research does show that mothers ended 75% of feeding rounds when bottle-feeding compared with breast-feeding mothers whose babies were as equally likely to end the feeding.

Antibodies are present in **colostrum**, the yellowish protein-rich substance secreted from the breast during the first few days after childbirth. Over the first four weeks there is a transition from colostrum to milk. One study that monitored the health of 238 babies, half of whom were nursing, found two or three times more gastrointestinal and respiratory illnesses in bottle-fed as compare with breast-fed babies (Bond, Filer, Leveille, Thomson, & Weil, 1981). In a prospective study of infants under age six months in a pediatric practice, it was found that acute gastrointestinal illness was six times greater in bottle-fed infants than in infants who were breast-fed. The increased risk of illness of the bottle-fed infants could not be explained by numerous control factors (Koopman, Turkish, & Monto, 1985).

A study that followed 1,220 infants in Tucson, Arizona, during their first year of life, found that those who were exclusively breast-fed during their first four months of life developed half as many ear infections as did those fed formula, and 40% less than infants whose breast-feeding was supplemented with other foods prior to four months (Duncan, et al., 1993). Those infants breast-fed exclusively for six months or more had only 10% as many recurrences of ear infections.

A dissenting voice, however, is heard from Bauchner, Leventhal, and Shapiro (1986), who criticize the methodology of studies of the association between breast-feeding and immunity to infections in infants. They do not feel the research has scientifically supported the claim that "breast is best."

Studies of the anti-infectious properties of breast milk in vitro, as well as most of the clinical studies of the effects of breast-feeding against infections in underdeveloped countries, have provided convincing evidence that breast-feeding protects against infections. In contrast, clinical studies in industrialized countries have produced conflicting results about the protective effects of breast-feeding. (Bauchner, Leventhal, & Shapiro, 1986, p. 887)

One of the major drawbacks of these studies is that they are not experimental (i.e., they do not randomly assign infants to either breast- or bottle-feeding). Obviously, that is an impossibility from an ethical and practical perspective, but Bauchner et al., who reviewed 20 studies, claim that when confounding variables such as size of the family, cigarette smoking, and mother's education are controlled for, breast-feeding is no longer found to be protective against infections. It is important to note, however, that none of the studies reported higher rates of infection among breast-fed babies.

Breast-Feeding and Baby's IQ

Breast-feeding provides the baby with more stimulation and is related to higher IQ and developmental level.

Breast-feeding has been found to have psychological advantages for the child as well. Breast-feeding provides the baby with more sensory stimulation than does bottle-feeding. Nursing mothers are more likely to touch, rock, and sleep or rest with their babies than are mothers who bottle-feed. Eye contact between mother and baby is more likely when the baby is held at the breast than in the lap (Jelliffe & Jelliffe, 1978).

Breast-feeding of infants has also been correlated with greater developmental and intellectual performance of children. A study of 1,037 children at age three, 991 at age five, and 957 at age seven in New Zealand found that children who were breast-fed for four months or more scored significantly higher in IQ scores than did children who were bottle-fed (Fergusson, Beautrais, & Silva, 1982). Investigators controlled for maternal intelligence, maternal education, childhood experiences, and training in child-rearing, as well as family socioeconomic status, birth weight, and gestational age. The authors attribute this to

the superior proteins in breast milk for brain growth.

Similarly, a large-scale study in Great Britain found that at age five, children who had been breast-fed for longer durations scored higher on developmental tests (B. Taylor & Wadsworth, 1984). This study is consistent with one in the United States that correlated developmental progress at ages one and two with breast-feeding (Morrow-Tlucak, Haude, & Ernhart, 1988). A study in the United States found that breast-fed children have an eight point average IQ advantage over bottle-fed children at age eight (Rogan & Gladen, 1993). The breast-fed youngsters also had moderately higher English grades and slightly higher math grades.

Mothers' Reasons for Breast-Feeding

Women choose to breast-feed because of a belief in benefits to the baby, and not to breast-feed because of personal inconvenience, physical discomfort, and erotophobia. Husbands and mothers have an influence on the decision to breast-feed.

Given the physical and psychological advantages of breast-feeding, why do so many women choose not to breast-feed? Social and psychiatric factors independently associated with the intention of 483 pregnant women not to breast-feed were being young, already having children, and not having a stable relationship (A. Stein, Cooper, Day, & Bond, 1987).

Beliefs about the benefits to infants and personal inconvenience were the factors most related to breast- or bottle-feeding for low socioeconomic, young (under 25) Black American and Anglo American mothers in a Texas study (Baronowski, Rassin, Richardson, Brown, & Bee, 1986). Personal inconvenience alone was the single predictor for not breast-feeding among a similar group of Mexican American mothers.

No significant difference in sex role orientation was found for mothers who were and were not breast-feeding their infants (Rollins, Scorpio,

& Cragin, 1991). Women who breast-fed were somewhat older, had a higher educational level, were more likely to have been breast-fed themselves, to be Protestant rather than Catholic, to have husbands who were supportive of breast-feeding, and to have a better relationship with their partner than women who were bottle-feeding. They were also more likely to breast-feed female (73%) rather than male (27%) infants. A slight tendency to breast-feed female infants more than male infants has also been reported in other research (Travis, 1988a). In a review of studies on breast-feeding, it was noted that father's attitudes may influence breast-feeding in a number of ways. One of the mothers in a study was quoted as saying, "I changed to bottle-feeding because my son's father was jealous and did not like me feeding a little boy. I gave in to keep the peace" (Woollett, 1987, p. 129).

Although women report that breast-feeding is a pleasant experience that arouses a feeling of warmth and openness (S. Kitzinger, 1983), women also report nipple pain and pain from uterine contractions during the first couple of weeks as reasons for not continuing breast-feeding. In one study of breast-feeding mothers, 39% experienced some nipple pain, which also coincided with uterine pain. Although for most mothers the pain was mild, some reported the worst pain as excruciating (Drewett, Kahn, Parkhurst, & Whitely, 1987).

Whether the mother breast- or bottle-feeds has also been found to be related to her responsiveness to the signals that the baby emits. In an experiment to determine the respective responsiveness of breast- and bottle-feeding mothers to their infants' signals, nursing mothers differed from their formula-feeding counterparts according to several self-report variables, in physiological responses, and in observed behavioral interactions (Weisenfeld, Malatesta, Whitman, Granrose, & Uili, 1985). Bottle-feeders had higher resting electrical skin levels, and while viewing videotapes of their infants' emotional signals, more extreme heart-rate accelerations, whereas breast-feeders initially showed deceleratory and then a secondary acceleration in cardiac response to the same scenes.

The researchers favor the explanation for these differences in a higher level of generally anxious and reactive behavior by bottle-feeders in the laboratory situation. Bottle-feeders reported less desire to pick up their infants than did the nursing mothers. When asked about their decision for having chosen a method of feeding, bottle-feeders gave more reasons that were mother-centered, particularly the greater freedom allowed by bottle-feeding in terms of travel and work. The breast-feeders showed the reasons for their choice to be centered more equally between self and baby.

> Over-all breastfeeders seemed to be more personally invested in their feeding choice; their evaluations of the feeding experience indicated that they enjoyed feedings more than the bottle-feeders, found it more relaxing, and felt more strongly that their choice was beneficial for the baby, both physically and emotionally. (Weisenfeld et al., 1985, p. 84)

Empathy and facial expression measures, however, did not differentiate breast- and bottle-feeders.

The advice given by pediatricians to breast-feeding mothers in twentieth century America has also often served as an impediment to breast-feeding. The factory model of efficiency in breast-feeding, where feedings are scheduled by the clock and limited in duration according to timetables, has provided the main frame of reference for pediatric advice about breast-feeding.

> In rural central Mexico for example, breast-feeding schedules simply are not an issue, and there as in most non-Western societies, expertise tends to be located formally in lay women. In many non-Western societies, particularly in rural areas, women universally breastfeed (up to 98%), infants rarely cry, and childrearing tends to be congruent with women's daily routines and with social interaction in general. (Millard, 1990, p. 211)

I successfully breast-fed my first child by feeding on demand and for much longer durations of time than the literature would allow. It was convenient for my schedule at the time because I was studying for my comprehensive exams for my Master's degree. I would, therefore, have the baby in one arm breast-feeding for long periods of time while I was reading a book, which I held in the other arm. With my second child, I was a full-time housewife, so I could follow the advice books and feed the baby only every four hours—unsuccessfully. She was a very good baby who did not cry much. She was not gaining enough weight when, on the advice of the pediatrician, I switched her to formula at four months old. With my third child I was teaching college, and two weeks after she was born returned to classes and 150 term papers to read. Again, I fed the baby for long periods of time at short intervals while I read my term papers. After the semester ended I still breast-fed her frequently, gazing into her beautiful blue eyes. She thrived. The longer and more frequently the baby nurses, the greater the mother's milk supply. If you are having problems, talk to friends, relatives, or members of the LaLeche League who have successfully breast-fed their infants.

Breast-Feeding Advantages for Mother's Body

Breast-feeding has physical advantages for the mother, too.

Breast-feeding also has physical advantages for the mother. Breast-feeding triggers the release of hormones that stimulate uterine contractions that aid in returning the uterus to its normal size and shape. Vaginal contractions also occur during breast-feeding that aid the vagina in returning to its prechildbirth state. Breast-feeding also helps rid the body of excess fluid buildup that occurred in the body during pregnancy.

Breast-feeding burns additional calories, about 750 extra per day, making it easier for the mother to lose weight after childbirth. Just as it is necessary to the developing fetus during pregnancy, a high-protein, high-calcium diet and drinking of fluids is necessary to sustain milk production. A study of the caloric intake of 22 primiparous, six week postpartum lactating women with nonlactating controls (matched for pre pregnancy weight and current weight), found lactating women not to differ in their total caloric daily intake or meal patterns (Heck & de Castro, 1993). Lactating women, however, were consuming a significantly lower percentage of the recommended dietary allowance (RDA) per day than did the nonlactating controls. Lactating women do not increase their caloric intake to compensate for breast-feeding. "Yet most of the women studied who consumed less than the recommended amounts continued to lactate successfully and maintain their own health" (Heck & de Castro, 1993, p. 642). Other research has shown that when maternal diet is severely restricted, vitamin content and the content of immunological substances in human milk is adversely affected (Miranda et al., 1983).

Society and Breast-Feeding

Societal institutions should be organized to facilitate breast-feeding.

Because of the physical and psychological advantages of breast-feeding for mothers and babies, our institutions should be organized to facilitate breast-feeding. This would include encouragement and instruction in hospitals, paid maternity leave for new mothers, and education in school health programs about the nutritional and psychological benefits of breast-feeding. Since father's encouragement of their partner's breast-feeding is important, males as well as females need to be educated about the advantages of breast-feeding.

It should also be recognized that many mothers still might not choose to breast-feed for a variety of reasons. These mothers should not be made to feel as if they were failures as mothers. The child can still be held while being fed, the mother can still bond with the child, and the child may develop a closer relation with the father who may also take turns with the mother feeding the infant.

INFERTILITY AND REPRODUCTIVE TECHNOLOGY

We are on the brink of a revolution. Technology was first applied to reconstructing the physical environment—the steam engine, skyscrapers, jet planes, television, fax machines, computers. A new age of technology is dawning that has begun to reconstruct the human being. Many troubling ethical questions arise in the context of engineering human beings. Who will have the control and authority to develop what kind of person for whose purposes? The experiments on reproductive technology that are currently ongoing are done largely under the guise of treating infertility.

Causes of Infertility

One out of 10 couples suffer from infertility. In addition to physical causes, smoking and anxiety may be related to infertility. For most women, however, blocked fallopian tubes and hormonal problems are the causes of infertility.

Infertility is experienced by about 10% of couples of child-bearing age who actively seek pregnancy (S. Johnson, 1988). Infertility is the inability to conceive a child after one year of regular sexual relations or the inability to carry a pregnancy to term (Menning, 1980). Although there are more out-of-wedlock pregnancies than ever before, abortion rates are also higher than ever before, and unwed mothers keep their babies. Thus, adoption of a healthy infant is also more difficult than ever.

When the male is infertile, many couples turn to donor artificial insemination. Menning, based on her work counseling infertile couples, says that it is a life crisis that typically involves going through stages of surprise, anger, denial, isolation, guilt, and grief. When the female is infertile, couples may turn to adoption if possible, or to reproductive technology to try to solve their problem.

Less well known than the risk of smoking in pregnancy is that smoking may reduce fertility in women. Researchers in King County, Washington, sought to identify and interview all female residents between the ages of 20–39 who were evaluated by their physicians for infertility between 1979 and 1981 (Daling, Weiss, Spadoni, Moore, & Voigt, 1987). Each woman was matched with a paired control. "A higher percentage of the cases (39%) than controls (16%) were smokers at the time they started trying to conceive. . . . Former smokers, however, had little increase in risk compared with women who had never smoked" (Daling et al., 1987, p. 40).

Tubal blockage is the most common form of female infertility, accounting for about 25% of cases. It results from venereal diseases, PID, abdominal surgery, ectopic pregnancies, appendicitis, and endometriosis (Bonnicksen, 1989).

Coping with Infertility

Infertility is perceived as more stressful for women than it is for men.

Infertile wives perceive their fertility problem as more stressful and their lives as more disrupted than their husbands. Women desire a child more and engage in more coping responses (Abbey, Andrews, & Halman, 1991). Wives take the lead in seeking medical treatment (Greil, Leitko, & Porter, 1988). Although women in general are more likely to seek medical treatment than are men, another reason for this initiative is that "wives were mostly more likely than husbands to see infertility as a devastating experience. The wives often said they experienced infertility as role failure, interpreting it as a challenge to their "womanhood" (Abbey et al., 1991, p. 180). The husbands saw it as a disappointment, but one that could be gotten over and ignored. Greil et al. conclude that there are two infertilities, his and hers. The research on infertility to date has been based on White, middle-class couples and cannot be generalized to minorities.

Artificial Insemination

Artificial insemination by donor (AID) has a success rate of about 70–75%, with no increase in congenital birth defects or other complications. Although couples are usually very pleased they had AID, they often keep it a secret.

Artificial insemination by donor (AID) is the oldest of the alternative methods of reproduction. Sperm, other than the husband's, was first used for artificial insemination by John Hunter, a Scottish physician, in 1884. The development of techniques for storing sperm at very low temperatures has expanded and simplified the use of AID. In the United States alone, as many as 300,000 children are believed to have been conceived by AID, and that number is increasing by 10,000–20,000 births a year (Moghissi, 1989).

Pregnancy rates from fresh semen, when patients over 40 are eliminated, are about 70–75%. With frozen semen, pregnancy rates are about 10–20% lower. Frozen semen offers the advantage, however, of immediate availability, more convenience in timing of insemination, and, thus, greater possibility of a better match between donor and recipient.

Although AID is so widely used, few people hear about it from their friends and relatives because of the greater secrecy surrounding its use than that of any other reproductive technology. A study of attitudes toward secrecy among individuals who use one of the reproductive technologies found that the most secretive were people who had or contemplated AID, 62% responding that it was important to keep secret from others (Lasker & Borg, 1989). Fifty percent of people using AID, however, did say they planned to tell the child. When the husband's sperm was used for artificial insemination the number of people planning to keep it secret dropped to 36%. Even fewer planned to keep in vitro fertilization a secret (23%). Couples who hired surrogates generally planned to be open about it with others. Of course, it is much easier to keep AID secret. One thesis is that because AID is exclusively for male fertility—a "condition with greater stigma attached to it than female infertility"—that the secrecy exists.

An evaluation of the pregnancies and children and family relations of 427 women who conceived through AID found that the great majority of couples were pleased that they had gone through the AID process. AID children had no higher incidence of congenital anomalies than normally conceived children—this was true whether fresh or frozen semen was used. Nor was there a higher spontaneous abortion rate for the AID group. The divorce rate among those with AID children, however, was 7.2%, which was significantly less than that for a matched population (Amuzu, Laxova, & Sanders, 1990).

Surrogacy

Surrogacy raises many legal and ethical issues. Radical feminists consider surrogate motherhood to be reproductive slavery.

The internationally famous case of "Baby M" created a dialogue among the courts, lawyers, and feminists about the legal and social aspects of surrogacy. The case involved Mary Beth Whitehead, a 29-year-old New Jersey housewife, who was made pregnant through artificial insemination with the sperm of William Stern, a 40-year-old biochemist. Stern's wife, Elizabeth, a 41-year-old pediatrician, was unwilling to become pregnant because she feared the pregnancy would exacerbate a mild case of multiple sclerosis. William Stern and Marybeth Whitehead signed a "surrogate parenting agreement" on February 6, 1985, at the Infertility Center of New York (ICNY), a profit-making business founded by Noel Keane, a surrogacy advocate. Under the terms of the contract, Mary Beth Whitehead agreed to surrender the child at birth to William Stern, and to terminate all parental rights. At the time of surrender of the child, Mary Beth Whitehead was to receive the sum of $10,000.

Following delivery and seeing her baby, Mary Beth Whitehead changed her mind about relinquishing her to William Stern and his wife. She said she wanted to keep the child and not accept the $10,000. Throughout the contract William Stern was referred to as the natural father, but Mary Beth Whitehead was referred to as Surrogate. On March 31, 1987, New Jersey Superior Court Judge Harvey Sorkow ruled that the surrogacy contract was legal and gave custody to William Stern and deprived Mary Beth Whitehead of her parental rights.

Feminist groups criticized the court's ruling and on August 31, 1987 launched, at a press conference in Washington, D.C., the National Coalition Against Surrogacy (Arditti, 1988). Among the founders of the Coalition were members of the Feminist International Network of Resistance to Reproductive and Genetic Engineering (FINRRAGE) as well as some "surrogate" mothers such as Elizabeth Kane, the first surrogate mother in the U.S., who was inseminated with only male sperm because the donor wanted a son. Gena Corea, speaking at the press conference announcing the coalition raised some disquieting questions about surrogacy.

> The real questions are: Is reproductive slavery appropriate for women: Is this good public policy? Should we create a class of paid breeders, calling the women, as Dr. Lee Salk did in his testimony at the Baby M trial, "surrogate uteruses," or, as Harvey Sorkow did in his Baby M judgment, "alternative reproduction vehicles," or, as the American Fertility Society did in its recent ethics report, "therapeutic modalities"? . . .
>
> Another public policy question: As a society do we want to industrialize reproduction? Is absolutely everything grist for the capitalist mill? Are there any limits to what can be bought and sold? (Arditti, 1988, p. 61)

On February 3, 1988, the New Jersey Supreme Court overruled the lower court decision in the baby M case. The New Jersey Supreme Court found the surrogacy contract unenforceable, declaring that commercial surrogacy is baby selling. Although the Court allowed William Stern to maintain custody of the infant, it permitted Mary Beth Whitehead unsupervised visitation rights (Garcia, 1989).

In another case in California, however, a surrogacy contract was upheld by the California Supreme Court ("Surrogate mother contracts upheld," 1993). On May 20, 1993, the California Supreme Court said that surrogacy contracts are enforceable, and do not violate public policy. In a contract entered into in January 1990, Mark and Crispina Calvert agreed to pay Anna Johnson $10,000 to bear a child for them. Anna Johnson was implanted with the couple's already fertilized egg. Johnson's attorney said he planned to

appeal the ruling to the U.S. Supreme Court, which has yet to rule on a surrogacy case.

Although the rulings in these two cases may appear to be quite different they reflect an underlying ideology of the value of the "seed." Patriarchy was concerned with genetic relationships because they were the basis for inheritance. In more modern times, the rights of women to children were also recognized because of the contribution of the female "seed." In the Baby M case, Mary Beth Whitehead was recognized by the New Jersey Supreme Court as the mother and did get visitation rights because she was the genetic mother, as William Stern was the genetic father. In the California case, Anna Johnson was not given any rights to the child, probably because the child was not genetically related to her. In our society the genetic connection is most highly valued because of historical patriarchy. The nurturing relationship that develops between mother and child during pregnancy and childbirth is ignored, as it was in the case of Anna Johnson, because the mother is viewed in a mechanistic way as the means of production only if it is not her ovum that is fertilized.

Radical feminists have issued dire warnings that the new reproductive technologies may lead to "reproductive brothels" (Corea, 1987; Dworkin, 1983). "While sexual prostitutes sell vagina, rectum and mouth, reproductive prostitutes sell other body parts: wombs; ovaries; eggs" (Corea, 1987, p. 39). Feminists fear an exploitation of poor women.

Egalitarian feminists, however, argue that the gestational mother has a right to undertake whatever work she chooses, including surrogacy. In the liberal tradition, individual freedom and contract law is highly valued. Liberal feminists do propose some safeguards to insure the pregnancy is noncoercive, such as counseling for the surrogate mother and perhaps limiting it to women who already bore a child so that they would know the emotional and physical experience involved. They further argue that payment is not for the child, but for gestational services which is work analogous to other types of paid labor. Shanley (1993) contends, however, that the interrelatedness of mother and fetus makes gestational labor unlike any other type of work. "Contract pregnancy entails a very high degree of self-alienation, because the work of pregnancy involves women's emotional, physical, and sexual experiences and understandings of themselves as women" (Shanley, 1993, p. 627). The analogy she makes is to consensual slavery or marriage contracts, saying that the woman cannot know ahead of time how the relationship with the fetus will change her. What is her free choice at one point in time, just as in a marriage, may not be one's choice at a later point in time.

Sex Selection

Sex selection is already widespread in India, creating a sex imbalance in favor of males.

Of the many different methods proposed for determining the sex of the child, only one at this writing is essentially 100% reliable, amniocentesis. Searches for other less-expensive methods and which may be conducted during the first trimester continue in laboratories around the globe. Efforts are also underway to develop technology for selection for X or Y sperm. Feminists are alarmed by the possibility of widespread sex selection because of a preference for sons in both developed and developing nations.

> The real heart of the problem is that sex choice technologies would nurture patriarchy. All current forms of government are patriarchal: they foster competitiveness and have hierarchies of power and privilege; 'masculine' traits, such as aggressiveness are rewarded. 'Feminine' qualities such as compassion and co-operation are disparaged. (Holmes & Hoskins, 1987, p. 23)

Since the early 1980s physicians in India, after studying in the United States, have set up clinics for amniocentesis and abortion for sex selection purposes. "They advertise through leaflets, newspapers and magazines: 'Come for this test so that you don't have an unwanted daughter born to you'" (Kishwar, 1987, p. 34). In India there already is a sex imbalance in favor of males, which has increased from 972 females per 1,000 males to

935 females per 1,000 males during this century. There is a 50% higher mortality rate for baby girls than for baby boys due in some cases to infanticide, but in most instances to systematic neglect such as not seeking medical treatment for the girl when ill (Kishwar, 1987).

Feminists in India are fighting for special government incentives for families to raise and educate daughters. Among the incentives being sought are universal free education with stipends given to families who educate girls. Because families see girls as economic liabilities, it is also necessary to fight for access to more remunerative forms of employment. Since the large majority of women work on family farms, effective land rights for women are also essential in that country.

In Vitro Fertilization

In vitro fertilization has a low success rate and a high cost both in monetary and human terms for most infertile women. Although minority women have higher rates of infertility, they are less likely to receive infertility treatments.

The first scientific paper reporting the results of **in vitro fertilization** (IVF) were published by a British physiologist, Robert Edwards, and a gynecologist, Patrick Steptoe, in 1969. It was not until 1978 that Edwards and Steptoe announced an ongoing pregnancy from an external fertilization. That pregnancy culminated in the birth of a healthy baby girl, Louise Brown.

IVF is the process of removing an ovum from a woman's body, fertilizing it in a petri dish, and implanting it in the uterus of a woman. "In the most popular method, women receive local anesthetic, gonadotropin injections, and ultrasound monitoring of the ovaries. The reproductive technologist punctures through a woman's abdominal wall, filled bladder, and ovary to obtain an enlarged follicle containing an egg" (J. Murphy, 1984, p. 70). If it is implanted in the uterus of the same woman from which the egg was removed, it is called "embryo replacement." If it is implanted in the uterus of a different woman from which it was taken, it is called "embryo transfer" (ET). To feminist Julie Murphy, this practice is seen as "egg farming," which gives patriarchal scientists more complete control of reproduction.

IVF and ET as a solution for infertility raise serious questions about efficacy, safety, and costs, including indirect expenditures on treatment of side effects in relation to benefits. The efficacy is low. If efficacy is defined as live-birth pregnancies, the estimates based on a U.S. congressional survey of 146 clinics are of only 4–5% per stimulation cycle (Wagner & St. Clair, 1989).

Based on a National Registry of 189 U.S. clinics performing assisted reproduction procedures in 1990, more than 19,000 women were treated that year. The procedures resulted in 5,150 proven pregnancies and 3,950 live births. About 16,400 IVF procedures were attempted, 19% of which resulted in a pregnancy and 14% produced a birth. Of 3,750 gamete intrafallopian transfers (GIFT) (the insertion of an egg and sperm inside the fallopian tube), 29% ended in pregnancy and 22% in live births. Almost 3,300 frozen embryos were transferred, 12% of which culminated in a pregnancy and 9% in a live birth (Medical Research International, Society for Assisted Reproductive Technology [SART], & The American Fertility Society, 1992). Thus, the large majority of women who endure the procedures do not achieve their goal of giving birth to a baby.

Adverse outcomes among babies born after (IVF/ET) is higher than after normal conception, in part due to the increased occurrence of multiple pregnancies. Data from the Australia and New Zealand register showed a perinatal mortality rate for IVF/ET babies of 42.2 per 1,000 total births, four times the population rate (Wagner & St. Clair, 1989). Women are also at risk from IVF/ET. Complications linked to superovulation by fertility drugs include ovarian cancer, cyst, heart attack, and stroke (Wagner & St. Clair, 1989).

Economic costs associated with IVF/ET are high. Ethical and social issues are raised by these costs. Other hidden costs include those associated with subsequent procedures that may occur, such as caesarean section and neonatal intensive care.

In countries with a large, private health sector, receipt of IVF/ET hinges on the woman's ability to pay. When government subsidies cover some or all costs, all taxpayers shoulder the burden of paying for a service that benefits only a few. In either case, the direct and indirect costs of IVF/ET increase per-capita health care expenditures without significantly improving the health of the population. (Wagner & St. Clair, 1989, p. 1028)

The media stories written about the new reproductive technologies portray them as technological breakthroughs. According to Janice Raymond (1990), the articles written about IVF are promotional, focusing on the promise of the technology, often in hyperbolic terms. It is therefore not surprising that there is a demand for in vitro fertilization by infertile couples. By 1987 there were 167 clinics in the 48 states and the District of Columbia offering IVF.

The stated need revolves around an "epidemic" of tubal infertility and a dearth of treatments for it, a shortage of adoptable babies and a desperate clientele. The number of visits to physician's offices for infertility treatment nearly tripled from 1968 (600,000) visits to 1984 (1.6 million visits). (Bonnicksen, 1989, pp. 22–23)

Feminists are concerned about the dangers reproductive technology bring, both on the individual level of painful and dehumanizing procedures and failed attempts at conception, and on the societal level of babies becoming a product of the capitalist manufacturing process like any other commodity. According to Sandelowski (1990) questioning the motherhood motives of infertile women, however, shatters sisterhood, and further alienates women who may already feel alienated from their fertile friends and relatives.

Infertile woman's desire to have children are suspect by radical feminists as an expression of patriarchy's mandate that she reproduce. Research, however, has shown the motivation for motherhood to be based on many psychodynamic factors. Neither demographic variables, nor feminism scores, as measured by a scale designed to tap sympathy for the principles of the women's liberation movement, are related to motivation for motherhood (Gerson, 1986). Feminists are providing a service to infertile women, however, because they need to be made aware of the actual probability of success (a live, healthy baby) of the procedures to which they submit themselves. Also, despite the fact that married Black women have an infertility rate about one-and-a-half times that of married White women, the needs of minority women for infertility services are ignored by the for-profit health care system of the United States (Gerson, 1986).

REFLECTIONS

In an article, "The technocratic body: American Childbirth as cultural expression," Robbie Davis-Floyd (1994) points out that the core value system of a culture is displayed in the rituals that surround birth. "In contemporary Western society, that mythology—the mythology of the technocracy—is enacted through obstetrical procedures, the rituals of hospital birth" (Davis-Floyd, 1994, p. 1125). Technocracy has the separation of mind and body as an underlying philosophical basis. We have seen in this chapter, however, over and over again the importance of social psychological support for the mother during pregnancy, childbirth, and the postpartum period. We have seen that many technological medical procedures during childbirth are often performed when there is no medical reason in terms of the mother's and/or baby's health to perform them—ultrasound, caesarean section, episiotomy. Other less-technical hospital procedures are also detrimental to the mother's and baby's emotional experience of birth and the early postpartum period, such as having the mother lying down during labor and delivery, and the baby separated in a nursery after birth.

The Women's Health Movement has played an important role in making childbirth more humane for women, families, and babies. Babies are no longer whisked away to a nursery right after birth. The baby can stay in the mother's room during the entire hospital stay. Birthing chairs are an option in many hospitals. Midwives with their greater concern for the psychological and emo-

tional aspects of childbirth are increasingly available to women. When I had my first child I was given gas, although I had asked for no anesthesia, and high forceps were used in the delivery. By the time I had my third child, 13 years later, I had taken LaMaze classes, I was awake, had no anesthesia during delivery, except for a shot of novocaine locally for the episiotomy (about which I was not given a choice), and my husband was in the delivery room.

A high infant mortality rate continues in the United States, because of poverty, lack of prenatal care, and short interval between pregnancies, particularly for Black and teenaged mothers. This requires an educational and medical outreach to these women.

We are on the brink of a revolution in which reproductive technologies will in the near future be able to incubate babies the way we now do chicks. We will be able to pick and choose those characteristics that we want our baby to have. "To what extent do we desire to give up those processes that since the beginning of the species have defined us as women, in order to merge into the technocracy and succeed on its terms?" (Davis-Floyd, 1994, p. 1138). How will a supermarket approach to reproduction affect the mother child bond? Will there be an imbalanced sex ratio?

Experiential Exercises

1. Attend a LaMaze childbirth class.
2. Attend a meeting of the LaLeche League.
3. Interview your own mother about her experience with pregnancy and childbirth with you.
4. Interview your own grandmother, if she is living, or a woman past middle age about her experience with pregnancy and childbirth.
5. Attend a meeting of RESOLVE, a support group for infertile people.

KEY TERMS

Alpha-Fetoprotein Test (AFP) A test of a small amount of the mother's blood to screen for neural tube disorder (NTD), such as spina bifida.

Amniocentesis A process that can be used during the second trimester, usually between the sixteenth and twentieth week of pregnancy, to test for genetic birth defects. It involves using a long needle to aspirate a sample of the amniotic fluid for chromosomal and other tests.

Amnion The medical term for the bag of waters surrounding the embryo and later the fetus during pregnancy.

Artificial Insemination by Donor (AID) The oldest of the alternative methods of reproduction. It involves using sperm other than the husband's to impregnate the woman.

Caesarean Section Surgical removal of the fetus by abdominal incision.

Chorionic Villus Sampling A prenatal diagnostic test that is usually done between eight and 12 weeks of gestation. It involves the aspiration of a small sample by a catheter from the chorionic villi (the fingerlike projections of the cells that eventually become the placenta).

Colostrum The yellowish protein-rich substance secreted from the breast during the first few days after childbirth. It is the precursor of breastmilk. Colostrum contains antibodies that increase the infant's immunity to infection.

Ectopic Pregnancy Any implantation of the fertilized egg (zygote) outside of the uterus, most commonly in the fallopian tube. It occurs in about 1 in 50 pregnancies.

Episiotomy The medical term for the cutting of the perineum, the area between the vagina and the anus, during labor and delivery to enlarge the opening for childbirth.

Fetal Alcohol Syndrome (FAS) A pattern of birth defects associated with sustained drinking of alcoholic beverages during pregnancy that includes: deficient growth; facial malformation consisting of a small head, misshaped eyes, and flattened midface; central nervous system defects, the most serious of which is mental retardation; and behavioral disturbances such as hyperactivity and sleep problems.

Human Chorionic Gonadotropin (HCG) A hormone secreted by the embryo early in pregnancy and later by the placenta that assists in the maintenance of the pregnancy.

Infertility The inability to conceive a child after one year of regular sexual relations or the inability to carry a pregnancy to term.

In vitro fertilization The process of removing an ovum from a woman's body, fertilizing it in a petri dish, and implanting it in the uterus of a woman.

La Leche League An organization founded in 1956, to enable mothers who had successfully breast-fed their infants to provide information and support to new mothers who wished to breast-feed.

Lamaze Method A method of childbirth preparation that includes rapid breathing during the second stage of labor and panting during crowning and delivery, controlled neuromuscular relaxation, and visual focusing. Through attendance at classes, the pregnant woman and her a labor coach are taught these techniques and are given instruction in the anatomy and physiology of pregnancy and childbirth.

Maternity blues The mildest, most short-lived and transient of postpartum symptoms that may include crying, feeling mildly depressed or in low spirits, feeling particularly vulnerable to criticism, and being mildly confused as to everyday things.

Placenta The organ that develops during pregnancy from both maternal and fetal tissue and is connected to the growing embryo by the umbilical cord. It functions as an endocrine gland producing pregnancy sustaining hormones and also allows oxygen, nutrients, antibodies, and drugs to pass through it to the developing embryo and likewise returns waste materials back to the mother's system.

Postpartum The period of transition following childbirth.

Postpartum depression A mild to moderate depression that is less common than the blues and may last six to eight weeks, although for some women it can last as long as a year.

Postpartum depressive psychosis This has many of the same signs and symptoms of an acute psychosis not associated with childbirth and can include such severe symptoms as delusions (persistent false beliefs) and suicidal and/or homicidal thoughts.

Pseudocyesis A condition in which women imagine themselves to be pregnant.

Ultrasound The diagnostic use of intermittent high-frequency sound waves to diagnose a variety of conditions or abnormalities of pregnancy.

SUGGESTED READINGS

Collins, N. L., Dunkel-Schetter, C., Lobel, M., & Scrimshaw, C. M. (1993). Social support in pregnancy: Psychosocial correlates of birth outcomes and postpartum depression. *Journal of Personality and Social Psychology, 58.* 1243–1258. This article discusses research that demonstrates the importance of social support during pregnancy for positive mental and physical health outcomes for mother and baby.

Davis-Floyd, R. E. (1994). The technocratic body: American childbirth as cultural expression. *Social Science & Medicine, 38,* 1125–1140. This article presents a feminist view of American customs of chiildbirth and reproductive technology.

Sandelowski, M. (1993). *With child in mind: Studies of the personal encounter with infertility.* Philadelphia: University of Pennsylvania Press. This is a sensitively written and comprehensive book about the medical and psychological aspects of infertility.

CHAPTER 13

Mothers and Children

Being a mother is an experience of body and soul
which ties one to the source of our life and all life.
Naomi Ruth Lowinsky, 1992

Motherhood can be viewed as an institution of society. It can also be viewed as a relationship between a woman and her child. This chapter will examine motherhood from both perspectives. Motherhood as an institution of society differs for women by marital status, race, class, and ethnic group. The relationship of a woman and her child is a unique interpersonal relationship.

THEORIES OF MOTHERHOOD

Feminist Perspective

Feminists of the 1960s and 1970s viewed motherhood as an institution of society that oppressed women.

From the fear of this unique ability of women to bear children, men have, according to Adrienne Rich (1977), made motherhood into an institution that makes women powerless and dependent. She sees the reason for social and individual powerlessness of women in social motherhood. Simone de Beauvoir (1961) and Schulamith Firestone (1970) think the fact of biological motherhood makes women powerless. According to Firestone, the origins of the sex/class system lie in the bio-

logically reproductive roles of men and women. Because women bear and nurse infants and because of the long dependency of human children, women have been relegated to being breeders and have been excluded from any real participation in culture. Now that reliable birth control methods are available, women are no longer at the mercy of their biology that made women dependent on males for their physical survival. The inherently unequal power distribution of the family is the prototype of all power relationships and the origin of power psychology—the desire to dominate others. Firestone calls for a revolution to free women from their reproductive biology and to diffuse child-bearing and child-rearing to the society as a whole.

Black Women's Views on Motherhood

Black women would have liked to spend more time with their children rather than working in demeaning jobs.

These feminist views reflected those of White middle class, college-educated women. They were not the expression of the views of Black or lower class women.

Had black women voiced their views on motherhood, it would not have been named a serious obstacle to our freedom as women. Racism, availability of jobs, lack of skills or education and a number of other issues would have been at the top of the list-but not motherhood. Black women would not have said motherhood prevented us from entering the world of paid work because we have always worked. (hooks, 1984, p. 133)

The long hours and menial jobs Black women have historically held in the fields, factories, and homes of Whites were degrading and dehumanizing. Many Black women would have liked to spend more time in the context of the caring environment inside the home with their children.

Current Feminist Thinking about Motherhood

In more recent years, feminists have begun to put more emphasis on motherhood as a relationship with a child and to consider the influence of this relationship on both mother and child.

There has been a major shift in feminist thinking about motherhood since the writings of de-Beauvoir, Rich, and Firestone in the 1960s and 1970s. Rather than viewing motherhood solely as a source of oppression, mothering has moved to center stage in debates about women's "difference" from and "similarity" with men (Bower, 1991). Books such as the one by feminist Phyllis Chesler, *With Child: A Diary of Motherhood,* extol the pleasures of childbirth and motherhood.

Oakley (1980b) notes the paradox of "the logic of the male perspective" carried to its most extreme formulation—that women would no longer be oppressed if they did not have children. Her conclusion contains a "maternal revivalist" thesis—that reproduction is not a handicap, but an achievement of women. (T. Gordon, 1990, p. 49)

The social as well as biological nature of motherhood is now celebrated in feminist thinking about motherhood that is occurring in the 1990s.

Motherhood is not simply another kind of production. It is an emotionally demanding labor—a labor of love. "For without love, without close interpersonal relationships, human beings, and it would seem especially small human beings, cannot survive" (H. Rose, 1987, p. 275). The relationship of mother and child begins during pregnancy and continues throughout life.

Chodorow's Theory

According to Nancy Chodorow, the desire to be a mother springs from the early intense relationship of mother and daughter.

In her book, *The Reproduction of Mothering* (1978), Nancy Chodorow integrates psychoanalytic theory, sociological theory, and a feminist perspective to answer the questions of why women want to be mothers and why motherhood is ultimately devalued. In **Chodorow's theory**, unlike Freud's, the central relationship is that of mother and child rather than of father and child. For Chodorow, the desire to be a mother springs from early socialization, from being taken care of by a mother, from the early intense relationship of mother and child. "Because women are themselves mothered by women, they grow up with the relational capacities and needs, and psychological definition of self-in-relationship, which commits them to mothering" (Chodorow, 1978, p. 209). This relationship with the mother is never entirely broken for the girl.

Boys, who must develop a masculine identity, must deny the maternal attachment and identification. In order to separate himself from his mother, the boy devalues the mother and everything female and feminine. This occurs as Freud had postulated with the resolution of the Oedipus complex (by age five or six). The basis of the division of labor in society is women's exclusive child-rearing, which further contributes to her second class status. Chodorow's solution to women's inequitable position is to have men participate equally in child-rearing. Chodorow's prescription of male child-rearing is contradictory with her theory, however, since the socialization of boys by mothers, and their having to develop abstract identifications with more distant male figures produces a more impersonal style of being that is not conducive to caring for and nurturing the young.

Studies conducted to test Chodorow's theory of the relationship between mothering and social connectedness (a sense of self in relation to others) have found support for the theory (Tolman, Dickmann, & McCartney, 1989). Young adult daughters whose mothers were absent since early childhood (prior to age five) due to death or divorce, scored lower on measures of social connectedness than daughters who had never been separated from their mothers, or separated from their mothers after age five, or even than daughters who had a mother substitute. Also consistent with Chodorow's theory, there was no effect of maternal absence on social connectedness of sons. Maternal employment, however, did not affect daughter's social connectedness. Further research needs to examine differences in the sexes in styles of parenting as well as the affect of mother/father parenting on children.

Ideologies Shaping Motherhood

Rothman posits that three ideologies shape modern American motherhood: the ideology of patriarchy, the ideology of technology, and the ideology of capitalism.

In her book, *Recreating Motherhood,* Rothman (1989) posits that three deeply rooted ideologies shape modern American motherhood: the **ideology of patriarchy**, the **ideology of technology**, and the **ideology of capitalism**. The key of patriarchy was the concept of the "seed," and women's role in that system is as the nurturer of the "seed." This right of patriarchy has been extended to women in recognition of the contribution of their "seed."

This does not end patriarchy, and it does not end the domination of the children of women by men. Instead, by maintaining the centrality of the seed, the ideology maintains the rights of men in their children, even as it recognizes something approaching equal rights of women in their children. Since men's control over women and the children of

women is no longer based simply on men's (no longer) unique seed, men's economic superiority and the other privileges of a male-dominated social system become increasingly important. (Rothman, 1989, p. 36)

The ideology of technology, which is the application of science to everything, when combined with the ideology of patriarchy creates a "depersonalized mother-machine being manipulated to efficiently produce babies out of valued sperm" (Rothman, 1989, pp. 38–39). Separation and compartmentalization occur. Motherhood, as the physical embodiment of connectedness, is lost. The ideology of technology paves the way for surrogacy.

Under capitalism, everything is for sale. The body is seen as a collection of parts that can be sold. A very precious commodity in American society is the healthy White baby. The mother is the laborer and the baby is her product. "The combination of patriarchy and capitalism explains the powerful reluctance to engage in the open sale of babies by their mothers, while permitting surrogacy" (Rothman, 1989, p. 73). In surrogacy the "seed" will still be given back to the biological father after it has been fertilized and gestation has taken place. Patriarchy is disrupted by the sale of babies, but not by surrogacy.

Rothman provides an alternative vision to the way motherhood is being re-created in American society. She says we need to value the social relationship that is pregnancy. Children belong to the mother at birth, because of the "unique nurturant relationship" that existed between mother and child up to that moment, not because of genetic claims. After six weeks, custody should go to the person doing the parenting. Where two people are genuinely sharing that parenting, then joint custody would be appropriate. Since adoption agreements could take place only after the birth of a child, surrogacy would be outlawed. If men want to have children, they could do so only through a relationship with a woman in which they coparent or coadopt a child. America must follow the lead of other countries in which economic responsibility for children is shared by society.

The Motherhood Mandate

Societal pressure on women to have children has been called the motherhood mandate.

Women's role in producing children has been considered their chief role in life. It is the primacy of this role that has created what Russo (1976) calls the **Motherhood Mandate**—"which requires having at least two children and raising them well." Phyllis Chesler (1986) elaborates on the expectations of the "fit" mother.

Traditionally, an ideal mother is expected to choose married motherhood for her future at a very young age. She is expected to become pregnant, give birth, psychologically "bond" with, and assume bottom-line responsibility for her children's physical and emotional needs.
  She is also expected to behave in physically non-violent and psychologically self-sacrificing ways. This female socialization into and practice of motherhood is devalued and taken for granted. (Chesler, 1986, p. 63)

Women who have no children are somehow viewed as deficient by society. (Although during my lifetime, I have noticed that childless women are no longer treated with the disdain they used to be). Russo (1976) argues that it is necessary to attack the motherhood mandate in order to eliminate sex role stereotypes and sex-typed behaviors. Not all women desire to be mothers or would make good mothers. The Motherhood Mandate limits educational and job opportunities for women who are socialized to think of their future only in terms of motherhood.

In the feminist movement at the present time, marriage and motherhood are neither denigrated, nor viewed as expected of a woman.

Feminists want to help women free themselves from traditional norms sufficiently so that they can accept at an emotional level their rights to control their own bodies and comfortably reject, at any given time, and for any period of time, either a maternal, life-nurturing role or marriage inextricably tied to birth of a child. (Rosen, 1982, p. 254)

If the women chooses marriage and/or motherhood, this no longer denies her right to develop her intelligence and to self-determination.

Motivations for Motherhood

College women today seem to be emphasizing the positive aspects of parenting in their desire to have children.

Have there been changes in the motivations for having children among young adults between 1976 when Russo named the "motherhood mandate" and more recent years? Morahan-Martin (1991) compared the motivations for childbearing of male and female undergraduates in 1977 and 1986. She found an increase in the positive aspects of parenthood and a decrease in the negative aspects of parenthood during this nine-year period. For example, the young people in 1986 were less likely to emphasize the cost factors of parenthood. They were more likely to agree with the positive role of children providing goals and incentives, to their parents, and seeing children as providing for continuity, tradition, and security. Men rated many of these motivations for parenthood significantly higher than did women: children for continuity, tradition, security, role motivations, goals and incentives, and social status from children. These gender differences were found in both 1977 and 1986. The author sees these results as supporting the view that females are "increasingly rejecting the stereotype of woman as mother" (Morahan-Martin, 1991, p. 312). (Even among women, however, there is a greater acceptance of beliefs about the positive role of parenthood in 1986 as compared with 1977.) The views of males, then, appear to be somewhat more traditional than that of women with their emphasis on children providing continuity, tradition, and security.

The Male Parent

Men are capable of being the primary parent. A feminist analysis says that men do not want to share equally in parenting because they prefer to devote their energies to competitive achievement.

If men are more traditional in their desire for children, then are men willing to parent equally? A minority of feminists in the late 1960s, instead of rejecting marriage, men, and motherhood, opted for shared parenting within the family context (Ehrensaft, 1983). The small group of men and women who tried shared parenting were not representative of the families in America. They tended to be White, middle-class graduates of the new left. Before them, however, other men have occasionally served as primary parents. Growing up in New York City's Greenwich Village, I remember playmates whose fathers served as the primary parent. One playmate's father stayed home and took care of her and did the cooking and other housework while her mother worked as a successful executive. Another father worked midnight to 8 A.M. and the mother from 3 P.M. to midnight, so the father was the primary parent when the children came home from school. It seemed to work well, both fathers seemed to be close to their children, and were good parents. My own maternal grandfather was the sole parent to his six young children after his wife died of tuberculosis at the age of 28. He did not remarry and alone raised five daughters and one son on a Massachusetts farm.

Men, therefore, are capable of parenting. Why do they tend to shy away from it? According to Polatnick (1983), it is because a feature of the child-rearing job is that the "mother" must devote herself to others and put aside her personal objectives for power and success. "Males primed for competitive achievement show no eagerness to suppress their personal ambitions and sacrifice their own interests to attend to others' immediate wants" (Polatnick, 1983, p. 35). Women, on the other hand are socialized in interpersonal nurturing skills. The fact that these attributes are devalued by society also contributes to males lack of interest in childrearing.

I recently interviewed a man for research I am conducting, whose wife left him with a son aged 10 and a daughter aged eight. He was in a program director engineering position at the time. He asked for a demotion in order to spend more time at home with his children and so he would no longer have to travel on business. I interviewed him 15 years after his wife had left. He had still not received a promotion to the position he had held before requesting the demotion, although he was still working for the same organization. We come to view certain interactions as gendered because women are far more likely to encounter certain situations and men others, but juggling family and career may require some sacrifices of men or women who have the primary responsibility for child-rearing.

Rothman (1989) makes a powerful argument that men should mother. She sees a better world if men become involved in the intimate, daily, nurturing of children. She goes on to say that if women are not to drop from exhaustion in this world of work and home responsibilities, they need the help of the person(s) with whom they are sharing their lives. Nurturing children also teaches one to be nurturing to others, the person with whom one is living as well as elderly parents. Men should take care of children so that the world of care and of power are not separated, so that the gender and class system are not continually re-created.

Women Who Do Not Want to be Mothers

Not all women want to be mothers. Women who are supportive of feminism or who have greater psychological distance from their parents have less interest in child-rearing. The decision to have a child is also based on marriage, career, and financial determinants.

Not all women in American society want to be mothers, or would be good mothers. Women who have a feminine sex role orientation tend to want and to have larger families than do women who are masculine in their orientation (Scott & Morgan, 1983). I found in research I have been conducting on women leaders and managers, however, that women managers who are masculine in sex role orientation are significantly more likely to have children and to have more children than women managers with other sex role orientations (Rollins & Lederberg, 1989). Perhaps, this is because masculine women are better able to cope with multiple roles. Women who are more supportive of feminism have less interest in child rearing than women who are more traditional (Biaggio, Mohan, & Baldwin, 1985). There is an inverse relationship between age of marriage and fertility. Women who marry at young ages and/or have their first child at young ages subsequently have more children during their lifetimes (Sweet, 1982).

Sometimes it is the husband rather than the wife who wants children. A friend in his mid-30s who got divorced told me that the reason for the divorce was that he very much wanted children, but his wife did not. She did not see motherhood as compatible with her career as a successful attorney. They had married right out of college and had not really discussed having children at that time. As Brownmiller writes in her book, *Femininity* (1984), "Motherhood and ambition have been opposing forces for thousands of years" (Brownmiller, 1984, p. 129). She goes on to say that the feminine dilemma for many women is the conflict between motherhood and personal ambition. On the other hand, the desire to be a mother can itself be a powerful ambition.

> Responsive to the ticking of the biological clock, the motivation to produce and raise a child of one's own (for whatever reason, and the reason's are legion) and the gratifications that a child may bring are spurred by an urgency that is as unique to femaleness as motherhood itself. (Brownmiller, 1984, p. 230)

A growing trend is for successful career women to suddenly awaken to the ticking of their biological clocks and have children in their late 30s and early 40s.

Socialization for motherhood is continuous over the reproductive life span, with some women deciding relatively early in life to remain childless and others not deciding until they are married that they do not want to have children. Women who decided early that they did not want to have children were characterized by greater psychological distance from parents during adolescence, significantly lower levels of warmth in their family of orientation, parents who stressed higher levels of achievement orientation, and

parents who were less likely to use principled discipline and who were less likely to encourage assertive autonomy than parents of women who postponed the decision of whether or not to have a child (Houseknecht, 1979).

In an intensive study of 24 White, middle class, childless, dual-career women ranging in age from 27 to 35, Wilk (1986) developed a dual-career couple child-bearing decision model consisting of feminine intrapsychic determinants, marriage determinants and career determinants. The most dramatic finding relative to the women who were voluntarily childless was an early negative relationship with their father and a lack of satisfactory resolution of the oedipal conflict. The women who decided to have children had a generally satisfactory relationship with their mothers, whereas six out of the eight women who had decided not to have children felt a sense of maternal rejection. Only the women who decided to have children included elements of both sexuality and nurturance in their feminine self-concept, indicating having fully identified with mother and accepting her as a model for nurturance.

A sense of marital stability and permanence was also required for an unconflicted desire to have children. A host of career factors such as considering it the "right" time to have a child, the philosophy and professional demands of their work setting, and the attitudes of colleagues, among other issues, impact on the child-bearing decision. Finally, a series of lifestyle issues (i.e., financial issues) are combined with the personality, marriage, and career issues in reaching the decision to bear a child.

Although women experience pleasure in maternal love and welcome the responsibility, conflicts and guilt feelings arise in the context of modern American society. "They are aware that they carry out their responsibilities in a social, material and cultural environment which does not privilege children and mothers, and in a world centered around production, not reproduction" (T. Gordon, 1990, p. 106). The guilt is both in terms of the different roles women play as well as a guilt that centers on the world children have to grow up in and the mothers' sense of powerlessness in trying to change that world.

Careers, Marriage, and Motherhood

Today's college-educated young women want it all, careers, husbands, and children.

What do today's generation of young women want, careers or motherhood, or both? According to research with 250 unmarried undergraduates, today's college women want it all, husbands, children, and careers (Baber & Monaghan, 1988). Only three (1.2%) of the women planned to remain single, and only six (2.5%) planned to remain child-free. The women planned to have an average of 2.9 children, and over half of the women planned to have three or more children. All of the women planned to have careers after graduation. I continue to get a similar pattern of responses from the students in my psychology of women classes.

Women planning innovative careers, however, were less child oriented than were those planning more traditional careers. In terms of contingency strategies for managing career and family, nearly three-quarters (71%) of the women wanted to establish their careers before having a child. The majority also said that when they returned to work after the birth of their first child, they would work only part time, and they expected to have a spouse who assumes equal responsibility for parenting and domestic chores.

Some of these beliefs are unrealistically optimistic. College women in our society receive formal preparation for careers, but not for parenting or combining career and family obligations. "Even among feminists there is no consensus regarding the role of motherhood in women's lives, how it affects efforts to achieve gender equality, or the most effective strategies for addressing the responsibilities of mothering" (Baber & Monaghan, 1988, p. 202).

MOTHERING

Feelings about Motherhood

How do women really feel about being mothers? It may be exhausting and heart-breaking and/or one of life's most rewarding experiences.

Motherhood is the best of jobs and the worst of jobs. When a mother has to shoulder all of the responsibility herself as a single parent it may be exhausting, or when her children get into trouble and do not turn out the way she wanted, it can be heartbreaking. On the other hand, motherhood may be among life's most rewarding experiences. How do women really feel about motherhood and their experiences as mothers? To answer that question, Genevie & Margolies (1987) mailed questionnaires to a nationally representative sample of women. Questionnaires were returned by 79% of the sample and consisted of 1,100 mothers from 18 to 80 who were currently raising children or whose children were grown. The authors say that their research dispelled a number of myths about motherhood. Their findings include the following:

- Infancy was second to adolescence as the stage most disliked by mothers.
- Twice as many women said their marriages changed for the worse after having children as said their marriages changed for the better.
- The empty nest is a myth. Most mothers reported feeling good about it when their children left home. Marriages improved.
- Women who had felt least accepted by their own mothers made the greatest effort to be good mothers and not make the same mistakes their own mothers had made.
- Women who are performing the most roles often find motherhood more gratifying than the mother who feels less harried.
- Working mothers did feel a lot of conflict about their dual role.
- Mothers who had the most conflict about being full-time homemakers, had the most negative feelings about motherhood, their marriages, and families.
- Women who had the most conflict about being full-time homemakers often had felt the most accepted by their own mothers.
- Some children are less likeable than others and mothers feel less loving toward those children.

Sylvia

Copyright 1994 by Nicole Hollander

- Fathers still do not play much of a role in house-work or childcare. Nurturing, active fathers were just as likely to be old as young (Genevie & Margolies, 1987).

Mothers of Daughters

Male-dominated theories distort the mother–daughter relationship. Mother–daughter close-ness is lifelong.

According to Nice (1992), a distortion of mother–daughter relationships take place through interpretation by male dominated theories of development. The issue of mother–daughter sep-aration, for example, is colored by Western in-dividualism, middle-class ideology, and male domination.

> Individuation, separation, independence—the lan-guage of the individualized, competitive, hierarchi-cal male—are considered developmentally mature, whereas women's connectedness, mutuality, con-cern with relationships are seen as developmentally immature. (Nice, 1992, p. 9)

In order to liberate women, the artificial barriers erected in the mother–daughter relationship need to be torn down. The mother can be the pro-totype of the female friend, which holds out hope of sisterhood with other women.

Relationships of adult daughters is closer with mothers than with fathers (Fischer, 1987). Retro-spective accounts of adolescence of 43 young adult daughters with their mothers indicate more continuity of the relationship with mothers than with fathers. The mother–daughter closeness is illustrated by the fact that daughters were much more likely to confide in mothers than in fath-ers. Conflict also occurs between the adolescent daughter and her mother as the daughter "re-bels" by asserting herself or withdrawing as a way of detaching from the mother. Heterosex-uality also creates a problem in the mother–daughter relationship. Whereas four-fifths of the mothers had talked to their daughters about menstruation, almost one half had learned noth-ing about sexuality from their mothers. Even after adolescence, sexuality is not talked about between mothers and daughters, at least not until the daughter experiences pregnancy and birth.

A turning point in the relationship of mothers and daughters seems to be when the daughter becomes a mother. They tend to elevate their mothers as role models. Married daughters with children talk on the telephone much more fre-quently than childless daughters, and geographi-cally near daughters with children interact more frequently with their mothers than childless daughters. The mother also typically helps the daughter on childcare and household chores af-ter the birth of her child, if only coming to stay for a week or two after the birth. Most mothers did at least some occasional babysitting. Thus, the closest relationship seems to develop when the cycle is complete and the daughter herself becomes a mother.

Daughters play an important role for mothers when the mother becomes elderly and the daughter a caregiver (A. J. Walker, Pratt, & Wood, 1993). One aspect of caregiving of middle-aged daughters that previous research had overlooked was the relationship between the daughter and mother. "A serendipitous finding has been the significance of the care receiver as a contributor to the relationship with the caregiver: Elderly care receivers play an active role in their relationships with caregivers, particularly in the provision of socioemotional support" (A. J. Walker, et al., 1993, p. 83). An agist belief has been the passive dependence of the elderly mother on her daughter. Many of the mothers and daughters described each other as best friends. The caregiving daughters worked to maintain their mothers' autonomy.

Mothers of Sons

Mothers are typically blamed for whatever goes wrong with offspring, particularly mothers of sons. Daughters occupy more center stage in mother's lives than sons.

Many "mother-blaming" books and articles have been written, particularly blaming mothers of sons. "Since early in this century, mental health professionals have legitimized the tendency of both lay-people and professionals to blame mothers for whatever goes wrong with their offspring" (Caplan & Hall-McCorquodale, 1985, p. 345). A review of articles in major clinical journals in 1970, 1976, and 1982 found very few changes across those years in mother-blaming despite the efforts of the women's movement during that time period. A wide range of problems, 72 different kinds of psychopathology, were identified in the literature as being attributable to mothers, (i.e., schizophrenia, aggressiveness, sexual dysfunction, minimum brain dysfunction, arson, sleepwalking) (Caplan & Hall-McCorquodale, 1985).

Unlike most of the preceding books on mother–son relationships the feminist book by Lina Forcey, *Mothers of Sons* (1987), looks at this relationship from the mother's perspective. The book is based on open-ended interviews of over 102 women of differing socioeconomic backgrounds and age groups who indicated a willingness to talk about their relationships with their sons. Forcey develops a rich narrative telling the mothers' stories about themselves and their sons, often in their own words. She does find certain themes, however, that transcend ethnic, religious, class, or sexual preference differences. First and foremost, mothers consider themselves to be the primary parent throughout their son's lives. It is a lifetime commitment. Mothers are the more caring parent. Mothers are showing ambivalence about nurturing sons to develop a traditional masculine identity. It does not appear, as was previously thought, that mothers seek fulfillment through the lives of their sons. Daughters seem to occupy more center stage in mothers' lives than sons. "Women's search for the balance between selfhood and caring is contributing to the transformation of Western culture and the shattering of the mother-son myth." (Forcey, 1987, p. 149) Mothers more typically have friendships with adult daughters, but are beginning to open lines of communication with sons as one human being to another.

A topic that has been even less written about than the mother–son relationship from the mother's perspective is the mother–son relationship when the mother is a lesbian, or in the case of Audre Lorde, a Black lesbian. Lorde's philosophy of child rearing is to be genuine with her son and to encourage his personhood.

The strongest lesson that I can teach my son is the same lesson I teach my daughter: how to be who he wishes to be for himself. And the best way I can do this is to be who I am and hope that he will learn from this not how to be me, which is not possible, but how to be himself. And this means how to move to that voice from within himself, rather than to those raucous, persuasive, or threatening voices from outside, pressuring him to be what the world wants him to be. (Lorde, 1992b, p. 257)

Lorde thus provides guidance that would be useful for any mother—not just a lesbian mother, not just a Black mother, but any mother.

Changes in Mothers

Children change mothers. According to Ruddick, feminist maternal thinking leads to a politics of peace.

No one questions that mothers have an influence on their children. Much less thought about and researched, however, is that children change mothers. According to Ruddick (1983) mothers respond to three demands of raising children: preserving their lives; nurturing and fostering their growth; and socializing them to be decent human beings. This process of mothering leads to developing greater concern for others, seeking cooperative solutions to problems, and healing rather than harm doing. Feminist maternal thinking leads to antimilitarist attitudes and a politics of peace (Ruddick, 1989).

Longitudinal research finds that mothers develop more responsibility, self-control, tolerance, and femininity, but less acceptance and sociability than women who are not mothers.

Significant personality changes have been found at a five-year follow-up of college women among those who had become mothers (Helson, Mitchell, & Moane, 1984). Changes on three California Personality Inventory factors appeared: a rise in responsibility, self-control, and tolerance. There was also an increase on the femininity scale which reflects maturity, warmth, nurturance, and feelings of vulnerability. There was a drop on self-acceptance, and sociability indicating less involvement in social activity. Thus, personality changes did occur in those women who became mothers that were not seen in those who were still childless.

It has been well documented that mothers of young children have higher depressive symptomatology than do women who do not have children or do men. B. S. Zuckerman and Beardslee

(1987) found that mother's level of separation anxiety from her child was related to her level of depressive symptoms. To further explore factors related to depression in mothers, Hock, Schirtzinger, and Lutz (1992) studied 84 married mothers raising first-born children at the time the children reached six years of age. Factors that were found to elevate the risk of depression were maternal separation anxiety, recollections of disturbed parental relationships, and dissatisfaction in the marriage.

Children and Marital Satisfaction

Women are less satisfied with their marriages after a child is born than they were before. Some of this dissatisfaction is attributable to less household and childcare help from husbands than they had expected to receive.

While the personality changes in women may be positive following motherhood, the changes in women's lives often are not. One of the most consistent findings of research on marital satisfaction is the decline in satisfaction after the birth of the first child, particularly for the wife/mother (Belsky, 1985; N. D. Glenn & McLanahan, 1982; Grossman, Eichler, & Winickoff, 1980). Why would mothers be less satisfied with their marriages than women who are childless? The answer to that question seems to be that expectations for division of household labor and childcare, once the child is born, are violated (Ruble, Fleming, Hackel, & Stangor, 1988). Cross-sectional samples of 670 women (98% White) responded to questionnaires when they were married/cohabiting and planning pregnancy or when the women were in their first, second, or third trimester, or one or three months postpartum. In addition, 48 women were interviewed late in pregnancy and again at three months postpartum. This research again found that women were less satisfied with their marriage during the postpartum months than they were during pregnancy. The division of household tasks was found to be more unequal than the pregnant women had reported or than they had expected after the birth.

The most dramatic differences occurred in child-care; relatively few of the pregnant women in either sample expected to be doing much more of the childcare than their husbands, but in fact, more than 40% of the postpartum women reported a large discrepancy in childcare division of labor. (Ruble et al., 1988, p. 84)

The analysis did find that expectancy violations were predictive of negative feelings postpartum for the longitudinal sample.

Perceptions of Mothers

Married mothers are rated as more competent and responsible as well as happier and better adjusted than divorced mothers. Employed mothers are seen as more competent but less dedicated to their families.

Do people perceive a woman differently if they know she is a mother? Do they view a woman differently if she is a divorced mother rather than a married mother? The public's view still seems to be that women should be mothers, and that they should be married mothers and stay home with their families. Among male and female shoppers at a mall, married mothers were rated more favorably in competence, sociability, security, stability, happiness, and personal adjustment (Etaugh & Nikolny, 1990). Married mothers were also seen as more nurturant than were divorced mothers. Perceptions of the mothers were also influenced by their employment status, with employed mothers being seen as more dedicated to career, competitive, influential, reliable, and sociable. Although employed mothers were described as being more competent, they were seen as more tense, less sensitive to the needs of others, and less dedicated to family than nonemployed mothers. The authors indicate that these evaluations of women based on their marital and parental status could, for example, unconsciously influence a supervisor's rating of the woman's job performance (i.e., an unmarried mother perceived as less competent) even though her marital status may have no bearing on her job performance.

MATERNAL EMPLOYMENT

Trends in Employment of Mothers

A major trend of the twentieth century has been the employment of married women and of mothers of children under 18. The majority of mothers of preschool children are in the labor force.

One of the major trends of the twentieth century has been the employment of married women and of mothers with children under 18 years of age. Married mothers, who traditionally stayed home, have returned to work in increasing numbers (Reifman, Biernat, & Lang, 1991). As was shown in Chapter VI, the most dramatic change in women's employment has been the return of married women to work who are mothers of preschool children.

Major differences emerge, however, when comparing employment of mothers by marital status. A higher percentage of married mothers (59.6%) of children under six are employed than never-married mothers (47.4%), but divorced, separated, or widowed mothers (60.0%) are just as likely to be employed as are the married mothers. Women who are divorced, separated or widowed who have children aged 6–17 are more likely to be working (78.3%) than are women who are married (74.9%) or who have never married (70.2%) ("Diverse living arrangements," 1993).

Employment also varies with the race of the mother. "In 1992 fully 90 percent of single white mothers with children 12–17 years of age were in the labor force. By comparison, the proportion was 63 percent for African-American mothers and 57 percent for mothers of Hispanic origin" ("Diverse living arrangements," 1993, pp. 6–9). The profile of families in the United States is one evolving from a two-parent to a single-parent, primarily mother-only family, particularly for African Americans.

The United States is the only one of the 75 industrialized nations that does not have a comprehensive family policy that assists families with some form of paid maternity benefits, parental leave, and subsidized childcare (Silverstein, 1991).

The Family and Medical Leave Act of 1993 was signed into law by President Clinton on February 5, 1993. It has minimal provisions that allow workers to take up to 12 weeks of unpaid leave during any 12-month period because of the birth or adoption of a child; the need to care for a child, spouse, or parent with a serious health condition; or the worker's own serious illness. Businesses that employ fewer than 50 persons, the majority of businesses in this country, are exempt from the law. Critics have said that poor people cannot afford to take off from work without pay. The reality of American life in the 1990s is that mothers of young children do work outside of the home in large numbers (Moses-Zirkes, 1993).

Women perceive greater rewards relative to costs of maternal employment than do men.

Two studies using the scale, Beliefs about the Consequences of Maternal Employment for Children (BACMEC), which measures perceptions of the benefits and costs of maternal employment, found that women perceive more benefits relative to costs of maternal employment than do men (Greenberger, Goldberg, Crawford, & Granger, 1988; Hyde & McKinley, 1993). This confirms the results of other research that men hold more traditional views about women's roles than do women. Age is a better predictor, however, than sex with older respondents perceiving maternal employment to have more negative consequences for children than do younger respondents (Greenberger et al., 1988). In a sample of 570 pregnant women and 550 of their husbands/partners, first-time mothers and fathers believed that there were more benefits for children of maternal employment than did experienced mothers and fathers (Hyde & McKinley, 1993). It is not surprising that women who work and those who work longer hours are more favorable to maternal employment than are women who are housewives.

Those who return to work within a year after the birth of a child are likely to have careers such as teaching that provide better hours, to have an-

other preschool child, and to have less separation anxiety.

Who are the women who return to work within a year after the birth of a child? Why do they work and what is the pattern of that work? An Index of Work Attachment that measured the proportion of time worked since the birth of the first child, was used to study the work attachment of mothers in 166 families in the Sydney, Australia, area who had at least one preschool-aged child (Cotton, Antill & Cunningham, 1990). The study found support for previous research concerning the "diverse and often intermittent nature of the work involvement of mothers with young children." After the birth of their first child, some of the women had worked part time, some part time for a period of time, then full time, some had not worked, or worked less than 10% of the time. Characteristic of women with high work attachment was older age at time of marriage and smaller family size. The high work attachment women were in teaching or secretarial-clerical positions. Teaching in Australia provides maternity leave, school holidays and summer vacation, and school hours—all of which facilitate full-time employment for mothers.

This same question of mothers returning to work was investigated in a diverse American sample using a longitudinal approach to investigate decisions of mothers of healthy infants to work or stay home at infant birth and at 3, 8, and 12 months of infant's age (Hock, Morgan, & Hock, 1985). The work/work mother who planned to return to work and did so usually by three months of infant age is least likely to have other children at home, and is least anxious of all mothers about separation from her infant. She is also most career-oriented. The work/home mothers who planned to work after the birth of the child but then stayed home differs from mothers in the other groups in the likelihood of being Black, lower-socioeconomic status, younger, single, and the least likely to have planned her pregnancy. Like the home/home mother, who planned to stay home and does, she has a 50% likelihood of having an infant at home. The home/home mother has the greatest anxiety of all of the mothers about separation from her infant and ascribes more importance to the homemaker role than do the others. The home/work mother who planned to stay home but goes back to work is strongly career-oriented. She is similar in race, socioeconomic status, age, and education to the sample. Although she is positive about the maternal role, when interviewed in the hospital, she becomes less positive by three months postpartum. She is more susceptible to mothering stress and sees her infant as less-securely attached to her than mothers who continue to stay home. No one theory is able to organize the diverse results for these different mothers.

Mothers' messages to daughters are more influential in the daughter's career vs. homemaker role choice than the mother's own choice.

"Do as I say, not as I do" seems to be the moral of the story when it comes to women's role choices in relation to those of their mothers. A study of primary role decisions of career, noncareer work, or homemaking of 67 married women who were mothers of preschool children revealed that daughters did not model their mothers' work role choices. For example, a homemaker mother was just as likely to have a daughter with a career or as a homemaker (Sholomskas & Axelrod, 1986). The messages given daughters by mothers, however, was related to daughters' role preferences. Career women reported mothers having told them to "do something with their lives." Although the daughters did not directly model the mother's choices, what the mother said was influential in the daughter's primary role choice and sense of self. This research supports my own life experience. My mother was a full-time homemaker until I was in high school, when she worked part-time in my father's business. She always encouraged me, however, to go to college and have a career, which I have done except for a period of two-and-one-half years I spent as a homemaker, during which time I gave birth to two children.

CHILDCARE

Are children harmed by having mothers who work? No. Employed mothers spend more of their time at home with their child in direct interaction. Children whose mothers work score as high in school competence as do children with mothers at home, unless the mother only interacts infrequently with the child.

Research in psychology has been influenced by the popular culture's idealization of motherhood by searching for the negative consequences for children of mothers who work (Silverstein, 1991; Zaslow, 1991). It has not been able to find them. Mothers employed more than 20 hours per week do spend less time with the preschool child or infant than do nonemployed mothers. Employed mothers, however, spend more of their time at home with the child in direct interaction.

Based on detailed time diary data collected from married couples with children, Nock and Kingston (1988) found that unemployed mothers with preschoolers spend an average of nine hours per day with their children, which is twice the amount of time of employed mothers. Mothers who are full-time homemakers spend an average of six hours with their school age children on workdays as compared with a little less than four hours for employed mothers. Regardless of whether their wives are employed, fathers spend less time with children than do mothers, averaging 2.5 hours per workday. It is not surprising that employed fathers and mothers spend more time on weekends with their children. Employed fathers with wives who are also employed spend more time on weekends with their children than do fathers of unemployed wives.

Shared mother–child activities may be a linking mechanism between maternal employment and child outcomes (Moorehouse, 1991). Consistent with the literature on the relation between close mother–child interactions and children's development, Moorehouse (1991) found that children whose mothers experienced changes in work hours or worked full-time scored as high or higher in school competence as did children with mothers at home. When mothers only engaged infrequently with the child in activities, however, and worked long hours on a stable basis or changed their job status such as by taking on a full-time job, the cognitive and social outcomes were lower for the child as compared with children whose mothers did not work.

Women with high interrole conflict and dissatisfaction with the employed mother role, however, do have a negative effect on their children.

The mothers' experiences of employment is more crucial to the child's adjustment than whether or not the mother works. MacEwen and Barling (1991) developed a four-stage model of how mother's interrole conflict and satisfaction with the employed mother role affected children's behavior. Female employees of a hospital who had at least one school-age child at home completed a number of psychological scales. Mother's age and education were controlled.

Interrole conflict directly affected both cognitive difficulties (concentration, mental alertness), and negative mood. Role satisfaction exerted a direct effect on negative mood, but not on cognitive difficulties. In turn, mothers with cognitive difficulties exhibited rejecting but not punishing behavior toward their children. Negative mood, however, directly affected both rejecting and punishing behavior. In fact, there was a direct relationship between negative mood and both conduct disorder and attention/immaturity of children.

Infant Day Care

Although some research does indicate that infants in extensive nonmaternal care do have less-secure mother–infant attachment, a meta-analytic study concludes that nonmaternal care has little or no influence on mother–child attachment.

Another line of research has focused on the security of infant–parent attachment in infants in nonmaternal care in the first year of life. A number of studies have reported that extensive nonmaternal care (20 or more hours per week) in the first year of life is associated with more avoidance of mother on reunion and more insecure patterns of maternal attachment (Barglow, Vaughn, & Molitar, 1987; Belsky & Rovine, 1988). It is also true, however, that more than 50% of the infants in extensive daycare do establish secure relationships with their mothers. The more insecurely attached infants

> were more likely to be boys, to be characterized as fussy/difficult by their mothers, and to have mothers who evinced limits in their interpersonal sensitivity, expressed less satisfaction with positive aspects of their marriages, and had strong career-oriented reasons for working; whereas those who developed secure relationships with their mothers were more likely to be cared for by their fathers. (Belsky & Rovine, 1988, p. 165)

A meta-analysis by McCartney & Phillips (1988) examined 25 studies on substitute child-care and attachment. Fourteen of the studies used the Strange Situation or a variation of it where four attachment behaviors of the child in a strange situation were recorded: exploratory behavior, crying, proximity to the mother, and avoidance of the mother. The effect size estimates for two of the behaviors were practically zero, $-.01$ for crying and $-.01$ for proximity to mother. A small effect size was found for exploratory behavior (.10) and for avoiding mother (.16). Meta-analysis allows for examination of methodological moderators to see the effects of the research design on the results. When six research factors were examined, experimenter's knowledge of group status, experimenter sex, mean age of the children, age range of the children, any modification to the Strange Situation paradigm, and length of time of child in substitute care, only one was found to be significantly related to attachment behaviors. Experimenters who were not blind to which child was in day care had a larger effect size for avoidance of mother for day care children, indicating an experimenter expectancy effect. Based on this research we can conclude that day care has little or no influence on the child's attachment to the mother.

Preschool Daycare and Mother Child Relations

Controversy surrounds research finding that three-to-five-year olds whose mothers are employed are less compliant than three-to-five-year olds whose mothers are at home.

Belsky and Eggebeen (1991) further sought to extend the research on children's socioemotional development by collecting data on the development of children from four to six years old whose mothers were studied as part of the **National Longitudinal Survey of Labor Market Experience of Youth (NLSY)**, a national probability sample of 12,686 men and women who were aged 14–21 in 1979, and who have been interviewed annually since. Included in the sample is an oversample of Black and Hispanic, and of White disadvantaged youths. A subsample of all White and Black mothers who had four-to-six-year-old children (*N* = 1,248) were interviewed. Analyses of the NLSY data found that children whose mothers were employed full-time beginning in the child's first or second year of life scored more poorly on a composite adjustment measure than children whose mothers were not employed during their first three years. The three component parts of the adjustment measure were behavior problems, attachment security, and compliance. It was only on the index of compliance, however, that a reliable association between early and extensive maternal employment and child functioning was obtained. This effect was general as it was not modified by the child's gender, race, or class. Of course, it is possible to view the behavior of noncompliance in the more positive light of increased assertiveness in the behavior of the children whose mothers worked during their first and second year. The authors suggest that they might even be called "precociously independent." It also should be kept in mind that early and extensive maternal employment accounted for only a small amount of the variance in the adjustment measure.

The Belsky and Eggebeen (1991) research has been criticized on several grounds. There was lack of representativeness of the sample since the mothers were younger, less educated, and dispro-

portionately unmarried and poor as compared with mothers in the general population (Scarr, 1991). The employed mothers and unemployed mothers in the sample were not comparable because the unemployed mothers were more likely to be Black, have lower self-esteem, have lower intelligence scores, have more than one child, be teenage mothers, have not finished high school, have larger households, have fewer working adults in the household, and live in rural areas. The research has also been criticized on the basis of the statistical analyses (Vandell, 1991).

Results appear to vary as a function of characteristics of both the family environment and the childcare/employment environments. For those infants whose family environments are high in quality but who experience poor-quality alternate care, early and extensive maternal employment may lead to problematic functioning. For other infants, such as those with adolescent mothers, early maternal employment may result in better child functioning. For these infants, staying home with their mothers may not be advantageous, especially if it consigns the family to poverty. (Vandell, 1991, p. 1102)

Research therefore needs to take into account both the quality as well as quantity of home care and other care of children, and the level of functioning of the mother.

Effects on Children of Childcare Centers or Home Care

Children in childcare centers tend to score higher in social and intellectual skills than children in home care. Center care givers are better trained and less authoritarian and directive than are home care givers.

Clarke-Stewart (1991) reported on research conducted with two- and three-year-old children in six different childcare arrangements ranging from care at home with parents to full-time care in a center. Children in center care performed at higher levels on "social and intellectual skills—verbal ability, nonverbal cognition, social cognition, creativity with materials, cooperation with the examiner, cooperation with an unfamiliar peer, and overall social competence (Clarke-Stewart, 1991, p. 108).

These research findings are consistent with other studies reviewed by Clarke-Stewart that found children in day centers and preschool programs to be socially and intellectually more advanced than children in home care whether in their own homes or in day care homes. Although not all of the research shows children in centers to be superior to children in home care, none of the studies favored children in home care. Why are these differences generally favoring children in center care found?

Analysis of those variables that relate to higher-level social and cognitive skills in centers as compared with home care, finds center care givers are better trained and are less directive and authoritarian. Authoritarian discipline has been found to relate to lower social and intellectual skills and competence. In addition, the more structured educational curriculum of day care centers and preschool programs appear to contribute to the advanced cognitive development of children in these programs. Research shows that children in those programs that are more educationally oriented score higher on intelligence and achievement tests than do those in less-educationally oriented programs. Another possibility that was investigated was in differences in parents themselves who are likely to send their children to centers as opposed to having them in home care. Although large overlap has been found in the characteristics of the groups of parents, when differences are observed, they tend to show greater verbal stimulation and less authoritarian direction among parents who send their children to center care.

Swedish children entering day care during the second half of their first year of life perform better on aptitude tests and are better adjusted socially and emotionally at ages 8 and 13 than are children who entered day care at a later stage.

What about children's later development, are there long-lasting effects of having been in day care? A Swedish study of the effects of early day care experience on cognitive and socioemotional

competence found that at eight years of age, children who had entered day care during the second half of their first year of life performed better on aptitude tests than did children who entered day care at a later stage or remained at home (Andersson, 1989). The children who entered day care during their first year of life were also more verbally facile, independent, and persistent than other children. They were also less anxious and more socially competent. Even after statistical control of home background and gender, their entrance from preschool to school was a less-problematic process. None of the measures indicated negative effects for the group having entered day care during the second half of their first year of life. A further follow-up of these same children at age 13 found that school performance was rated highest among those children who entered day care prior to age one. The lowest school performance was found among those who had not had out-of-home experience. Similar results were found for social competence, with those having the highest social competence being the ones who entered day care prior to age one, and those with the lowest social competence being those who had not had out-of-home care. Two factors must be kept in mind about this research. One is that "family characteristics, such as type of family, family's socioemotional status, and mother's educational level, influence the time of first entry into day-care" (Andersson, 1992, p. 20). Second, day care in Sweden is subsidized by the state and of high quality. Taking these factors into account, it is still possible that this research uncovered a long-term positive effect of day care.

The second wave of research on day care has begun to investigate the variations in quality of different day care programs and the implications for children's development. Zaslow (1991) examined the research on the quality-development linkage. High-quality care centers are characterized by a lower caregiver–child ratio, and caregiver training.

Quality of Childcare

Now, the bad news about childcare. Most childcare in the United State is of poor quality.

A four-state study conducted by economists and child psychologists from four universities who examined 400 childcare centers in California, Colorado, Connecticut, and North Carolina and tested 826 children attending those centers concluded that "only 1 in 7 offered the kind of warm relationships that teach children how to trust adults and the intellectual stimulation that helps children become ready for school" (Chira, 1995, p. A-12). About 12% of the childcare centers were unsafe or unsanitary. High-quality centers received extra money from state, federal, or employer funding. Although most of the childcare centers were rated poor or mediocre, 90% of parents whose children were in these centers rated the childcare their child was receiving as good. Childcare centers were of higher quality in states that had stricter regulations for childcare.

Childcare Arrangements of Aid to Families with Dependent Children (AFDC) Mothers

Since there are advantages and disadvantages to different forms of childcare, welfare mothers should be empowered to choose their childcare arrangements.

AFDC mothers' use of childcare was studied over a 14-month period in 1983–1984 (Sonenstein & Wolf, 1991). The sample consisted of 382 AFDC mothers with children under age six randomly drawn from welfare rolls in four metropolitan areas. Nearly two-thirds (63%) of these mothers used childcare arrangements at least once during this time. Of these, 43% were employed, 24% were participating in a training program, 12% were seeking work, and 36% were not engaged in any of these activities. Mothers rated their recent childcare arrangements on convenience, quality, and cost. Mothers using group care (centers, nursery schools, Head Start programs, or schools) and in-home sitters were the most satisfied, whereas those using care by a relative outside of the home were the least satisfied. When asked about how the children felt about the care-giving person and how happy the children were, care by relatives both inside and out-

side of the home received significantly superior ratings. Sitters in the child's home had the lowest ratings. Although group care arrangements were rated worst in terms of child-to-adult ratios, the mothers felt that group care workers were the best-trained care givers. Mothers also rated group care as the best in terms of the availability of learning opportunities for the child and in that it most closely matched the mother's ideal care. Mothers whose children were in group care also had to stay home, however, because of the child's illnesses six times as often as mothers using other forms of care. One of the implications of this research is that welfare mothers should be empowered to choose their own childcare arrangements. Since many parents work at other than 9 to 5 jobs, and there are benefits and drawbacks to different arrangements, alternative arrangements to group care are also needed.

Solutions to the Childcare Crisis in America

Childcare centers should become incorporated into elementary schools. Welfare mothers should be trained to be teachers and teacher's aides.

One solution for improving childcare in American society would be to include childcare centers within elementary schools. They could be under the overall supervision of the school principal. Each childcare room would have one teacher certified in early childcare education and certified teacher's aides to assist her. Welfare mothers could be trained to become teachers or teacher's aides. The training would provide welfare mothers with skills that would ensure high-quality childcare in these school-based centers at the same time that it gave welfare mothers jobs and skills for better parenting. Some of the money now going to AFDC could be used toward salaries of the teachers and teacher assistants in the childcare centers. Further monies would come from local, state and federal governments. Employers of over 50 persons who did not have an on-site childcare center would pay a tax toward operation of the public childcare centers.

Valerie Polakow (1993) conducted field observations of preschool programs and kindergarten classes and 11 in-depth interview studies with poor, single mothers, both those who are working and those on welfare. The solutions proposed by Polokow include school-based health clinics, nutrition programs for women and infants, community and migrant health centers, and viable housing. She also advocates for an early childhood education system accredited by the National Association for the Education of Young children and a child allowance paid to mothers. The disparity of funds available to rich and poor school districts needs to be changed so that funding is equitable.

School-Age Children

School-age children of mothers who work are better adjusted, more independent, and perform more household chores than do children of mothers who do not work.

Looking at school-age children, one negative finding that has been reported is that boys whose mothers work were found to have slightly lower grade point averages in school than did boys whose mothers do not work (Silverstein, 1991). This lower cognitive performance in middle-class sons has not been confirmed in more recent research (Hoffman, 1989).

In blue-collar families, however, the sons whose mothers work have tended to score higher on measures of cognitive development and socioemotional adjustment as compared with sons of mothers who stay home. Adjustment scores have also been higher for sons and daughters of middle-class families with employed mothers. Sons and daughters of employed mothers, from kindergarten through adulthood, have less-traditional views of sex roles. Employed mothers also seem to emphasize independence training more than mothers who are full-time homemakers (Hoffman, 1989). Research has also been consistent in finding that children of mothers who work perform more chores at home than do children of mothers who do not work. Since it is a fact of life

that most women with children work, the research that would be helpful in developing public policy would focus on documenting the negative consequences of not providing high-quality affordable day care (Silverstein, 1991).

SINGLE-PARENT FAMILIES

Dramatic increases have occurred in the number of single-parent families during the past two decades. Two-thirds of Black children now live in single-parent families. The total monthly income for female-headed households is less than one-half the income for male-headed households.

The number of children living in female-headed households has increased dramatically during the past two decades. The increase in single-parent families is due to both an increase in divorce and an increase in births to unmarried mothers. In 1960 only 2.3% of White births were to unmarried women; 23% of Black births were to unmarried women. By 1991, 18% of White births were to unmarried women; 68.2% of Black births were to unmarried women (Seebach, 1993; U.S Bureau of the Census, 1994). American Indian, Eskimo, and Aleut births to unmarried women were 55.3% in 1991. Among Americans of Asian and Pacific Islander origin the percentage of births to unmarried mothers varied depending upon the particular group, ranging from 5.5% for Chinese Americans to 45% for Hawaiian Americans. The percentage of births for Hispanics also varies according to cultural group, but the average percentage of births to unmarried Hispanic women was 38.5% in 1991 (See Figure 13.1) (U.S. Bureau of the Census, 1994).

In 1970, 13% of children were living in one-parent families; by March 1992, the percentage living in single-parent families had risen to 27% (Horton, 1990; Diverse living arrangements of children, 1993). The increase in single-parent households is particularly pronounced for African-American families in which, in 1993, 63% of Black families with children had a single parent ("Typical family slipping further away," 1994). In that year, 24.5%

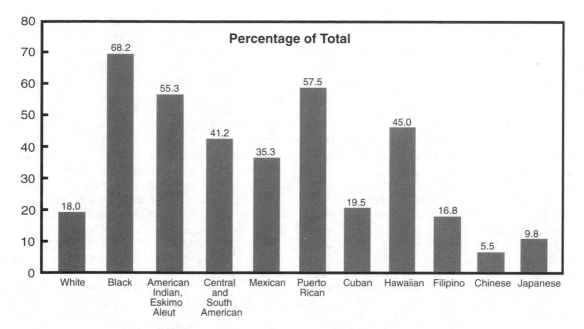

FIGURE 13.1 Births to Unmarried American Mothers by Race and Ethnic Origin, 1991. (*Source:* Abstracted from U.S. Bureau of the Census, 1994. Statistical Abstract of the United States, 1994. Washington, DC: U.S. Government Printing Office).

of White children and 35% of Hispanic children resided with a single-parent. As with Blacks, those in White and Hispanic single-parent families usually lived with the mother. Single White mothers differ from single Black and Hispanic mothers in having a higher level of educational attainment and income. Educational attainment is higher in two-parent families than it is for single parents. Single-parent families are often lumped together in statistical analyses.

High divorce rates do not, as many alarmists fear, spell doom for a society. High divorce rates instead appear to be related to an idealized view of marriage and acceptance of remarriage (Price & McKenry, 1988). Divorce does not necessarily mean the end of the nuclear family, particularly when children are involved. It means moving to a postdivorce "binuclear" family that involves co-parenting. It may also mean alimony and child support be given by the ex-husband or ex-wife to the former spouse.

Effects of Divorce on Children

Meta-analytic research finds children of divorce to score lower in overall well being than children in intact families, although this difference is relatively small.

Every year in the United States, 1 million children experience the divorce of their parents. At the current rate, 38% of White children and 75% of Black children who are born to married parents will experience the divorce of their parents by age 16. What are the effects on children of being raised in a single-parent family as compared with an intact family or a reconstituted family? To answer this question, Featherstone, Cundick, and Jensen (1992) compared 530 students, of whom 159 were from single-parent families, 78 from reconstituted families, and 293 from intact families, who were in grades six through nine in two schools in Salt Lake City, Utah. The great majority (490) of these children were Caucasian, 24 were Spanish, 8 Asian, and 8 "other" students. Students from intact families scored more favorably, followed by children from reconstituted families, and then by children from single-parent families on all of the variables investigated, which were: grade point averages; the number of tardies and absences; citizenship ratings of honors; citizenship ratings of needs improvement and unsatisfactory; and teacher behavioral ratings. Social class, race, grade level, and age were controlled for in the analysis. The authors conclude that the continuous presence of two parents appears advantageous for both social-emotional and scholastic development.

A meta-analysis involving 92 studies found that children of divorce score lower in overall well being (mean effect size = -0.19 without control variables) than do children from continuously intact families (Amato & Keith, 1991). This difference is relatively small. The strongest difference between the two groups of children were for father–child relations and conduct.

Methodologically strong studies tended to find less difference between children from divorced and intact families than did methodologically weak studies (studies, for example, that failed to used matching of subjects) because the weaker studies may have been confounding income with divorce, since income tends to drop after divorce for the mother, who usually has custody of the children. Earlier studies also tended to find greater differences in favor of children from intact families than did more recent studies. This is probably due to the increase in divorce and attitudes of greater acceptance of divorce today than in the past. More recent studies are also more likely to use better methods. Why do children of divorce have lower well being? The most support was found for conflict theory, with some lesser support for parental absence and for economic disadvantage.

Intact families with higher levels of conflict have more negative impact on adolescents than families who separate or divorce.

In view of the lower well being in children in divorced families, should parents stay together for the sake of the children? Children's problems appear to result largely from high levels of marital discord. Amato and Keith's (1991) meta-analysis found that children in high-conflict intact families score lower in measures of well being than do children in divorced families. The effect size for psychological adjustment of children in high-conflict intact families is $-.31$ compared with children in divorced families, and measures of self-esteem show an effect size of $-.35$ favoring the children in divorced families as compared with those in high-conflict intact families. The answer, therefore, is *no,* parents should not stay together for the sake of the children. If the parents are fighting, then the children are worse off than if they divorced.

Various research studies have supported increases in problems in late adolescence and early adulthood in people whose parents divorced when they were children compared with children from intact families. Studies of the impact of divorce show that adolescents and adults whose parents divorced have lower educational attainment; earn less income; are more likely to be dependent on welfare; are more likely to bear a child out of wedlock; get divorced; and be the head of a single-parent family (Amato & Keith, 1991). Not all studies, however, have reported poorer adjustment for children of divorce. Gabardi and Rosen (1991) found no differences between college students from divorced and intact families in depression, anxiety, and self-esteem.

A three-year longitudinal study of adolescents in seventh, ninth, and eleventh grades in five communities in New Jersey found higher levels of family conflict to have more negative effects than divorce or separation (Mechanic & Hansell, 1989). Children of divorce living in relatively conflict-free settings had fewer problems than did those living in intact families characterized by high levels of conflict. Thus, it is not the divorce per se that has damaging consequences for adolescents; rather, it is the conflict that typically accompanies divorce. There was no evidence that divorce and family conflict affected boys and girls differently. There is some evidence, however, that the sex of the custodial parent may influence the child's overall adjustment. Father-custody boys and mother-custody girls have been found to be better adjusted than children with opposite-sex custodial parents (Warshak & Santrock, 1983). Stronger negative effects on adolescents have been found for family conflict and divorce for Hispanic and Asian American adolescents (Mechanic & Hansell, 1989). It could reflect the greater value placed on the family in these cultures and the more devastating effect of disruption when the family is tightly knit.

In a longitudinal study comparing children from nondivorced homes, divorced single-mother homes, and remarried homes, four to six years after the divorce, parents, teachers, and children all reported that the adolescents in divorced single-mother homes were still exhibiting difficulties in adjustment, both at home and at school. In remarried families, although parents still reported difficulties, the teachers and the children themselves did not (Lindner, Hagan, & Brown, 1992). The difficulties reported in divorced and remarried homes included higher levels of acting-out antisocial behavior, and deficiencies in scholastic, social, and general competence.

In a comprehensive review article, Barber and Eccles (1992) point out that in the research literature on how divorce affects adolescent development is often confounded with the effects of living with a single mother. Many other variables are also confounded with family constellation in the research.

> Although there seem to be some small differences between children in divorced and intact families in cognitive performance, delinquency, and self-esteem, these differences frequently disappear when confounding and mediating variables are controlled. The research on children of divorce is frequently flawed by serious methodological problems, reducing generalizability of findings and leading to the possibility that the negative outcomes attributed to divorce may, in fact, be due to economic struggle or parent conflict. (Barber & Eccles, 1992, p. 122)

Barber and Eccles present a model of the possible influences of mediating variables of maternal employment, family processes, and parental expectations on the relationship of family structure to adolescent identity development in educational and occupational contexts and on gender-role values. They state that it is time to go beyond searching for the negative outcomes of divorce and focus instead on a better understanding of the positive and negative processes that influence development in different family types.

Black Single-Parent Families

The Black single-parent family has more societal stress than do other types of families.

All families inevitably encounter stresses, but some types of families, the Black single-parent family, in particular, has more societal stress than do other types of families. A comparison of Black, single-mother families, 70 of which were classified as functional and 56 as dysfunctional, found both the dysfunctional and functional families to have a high frequency of life event change during the previous two years as compared with families in community surveys (Lindblad-Goldberg, Dukes, & Lasley, 1988). The dysfunctional families, who were being treated at an outpatient clinic, were similar demographically to the functional families. About 50% of both groups had become mothers as teenagers, but most were in their early 30s at the time of the study. Differences in stressors were found between functional and dysfunctional families with dysfunctional families experiencing more legal problems, more short- and long-term physical, emotional, and behavior problems, more job changes, more family arguments, and more problems with boyfriends or ex-spouses.

Dysfunctional families tended to be more involved with family and relatives, something that was particularly true when family network members were younger. The stress was probably due to the fact that the mother had to give more than she got back in these family interactions. There were also significant differences in the way life stressors were perceived by the families. "Non-clinic families appeared to be more adaptive in that they perceived life events more positively and less negatively than clinic families" (Lindblad-Goldberg et al., 1988, p. 117).

Poverty

It is poverty rather than "nontraditional" living arrangements that creates risks for children. Two-thirds of Black female-headed households with a child under 18 years of age live below the poverty level.

Demo (1992) argues that the effects on children of changes transforming "traditional" living arrangements for children—divorce, single parent families, employed mother—has been greatly exaggerated. Poverty, however, greatly increases for single-parent families. Female-headed households have significantly lower income levels than do households in which two parents are present. In 1993, the median income of Black married-couple families with children under 18 was $36,660 as compared with $10,380 for Black female-headed households with no spouse present and children under 18 years of age. The median income of White, non-Hispanic married-couple families with children under 18 was $48,630 as compared with $17,890 for White female-headed households with no spouse present and children under 18 years of age. In female-headed households with at least one related child under 18 present, the percentage of families below the poverty level rises to 39.0% of White families and 65.9% of Black families (Bennett, 1995). Serious economic deprivation creates many risks for children.

What are the characteristics of women receiving AFDC? The majority are White (55%), although African Americans are disproportionately represented (40% although Blacks are only 13% of the population), and only 5% are of other races. They are overwhelmingly young: 30% are under 22 years of age and 71% are under 30 years of age. The implications are that the teenagers bearing children are the most likely to end up on AFDC. One-third are separated (32%), 28% are divorced, 29% are single, and 8% are widowed (Green, 1992). One question is, Where is the child support?

Child Support

Nonpayment of child support is one cause of poverty of mothers and children. The need of the mother and the number and ages of the children are not related to receipt of child support. Payment of child support is linked to the motivations and circumstances of the father.

Although the issues are complex relating to the feminization of poverty, nonpayment of child support plays a central role in discussions about the causes of poverty of mothers and children. Actually, only about 60% of mothers heading single-parent families have received a child-support award from a court. Of these only 48% receive the full award, and 26% receive nothing (Teachman, 1991). Teachman analyzed data from the fifth round of the National Longitudinal Study (NLS) of the High School Class of 1972, (NLS) which followed respondents from their senior year in college until 1986. The fifth follow-up in 1986 contained a subsample of 14,489 men and women. Of the mothers in the sample who were divorced, 78% were due child support. About 50% of these actually received the support during the month previous to the survey. The socio-economic characteristics of mothers and the number and ages of children were not related to whether child support is received or the amount received. Fathers with a voluntary support agreement, who visit their children at least as often as consistent with the divorce agreement, who were ordered to pay a larger amount of award at divorce, who have higher incomes, and who have remarried are more likely to pay child support than are other fathers. The longer the time since the divorce and the farther away a father lives from his ex-wife and their children, the less likely he is to pay child support. Teachman concludes that these findings are consistent with the theory that child support is linked to the motivation of absent fathers to provide the support. The receipt of child support is largely dependent on the circumstances of fathers, and not on the circumstances of mothers and children. Generally, it has been found that fathers either pay no support or they are likely to pay the amount due or nearly full support.

Welfare Assistance

In 1989 and 1990, two major pieces of federal legislation were passed that provided direct childcare assistance to welfare-dependent parents and to low-income, single, working parents.

Approximately 11% of this nation's children have mothers on AFDC. A chief component of the Family Support Act of 1988 was to require mothers with children over the age of two to participate in approved-employment directed activities including education or job training under the Job Opportunities and Basic Skills Training (JOBS) Program, and to provide for childcare. A state may lower the cutoff to mothers with a child over one year of age. Prior to this law, welfare mothers were not required to seek employment if they had a child under six years of age (Sonenstein & Wolf, 1991).

The Childcare and Development Block Grant, passed in October 1990, "provided grants to states and refundable tax credits for low-income single working parents" (Hofferth & Phillips, 1991). The childcare debate has shifted from whether the federal government should provide funding for childcare to what role should the government play and at what cost.

Welfare mothers are under considerable pressures from the welfare bureaucracy, the general public, and sometimes from ex-husbands or boyfriends. "We have in effect married the state. To comply with the conditions of our recipient status, we cannot make any personal decisions ourselves. We must consult the Welfare Department first, and the final decision is theirs. The state is a domineering, chauvinistic spouse" (Dujon, Gradford, & Stevens, 1992, p. 260). The welfare mother is faced with many catch-22 situations. The welfare mother has to feed, clothe, and house her children on a budget that is two-thirds of the amount established as the poverty level. There are few legal ways, however, for the welfare mother to earn extra income and maintain her eligibility. Medicaid

benefits are highly valued by the mothers, but doctors, hospitals, and druggists often refuse to accept medicaid patients. Food stamps typically buy enough food to last only 10 days. Welfare recipients are hounded for minor infractions of the rules, such as earning a little money to buy Christmas presents, while the white-collar professionals such as doctors, dentists, druggists, and nursing home operators who commit Medicaid fraud are seldom investigated or taken to court (Dujon, Gradford, & Stevens, 1992).

Poverty of Single Mothers in Europe

In contrast to the United States, only a small percentage of single mothers are living below the poverty level in Europe.

There is a better way to deal with the problems of single mothers and their children who are living in poverty. All we have to do is to look to Europe to find the answers. The poverty rate of single parents in the United States is at least twice as high as in any European country. In the United States three times as many single-parent families (53.3%) live in poverty as families headed by married couples (17.9%). In contrast, in the United Kingdom, the Netherlands, and Sweden single-parent families have only a slightly higher rate of poverty than do families headed by married couples (McFate, 1991).

In the United States and Sweden, single mothers and married mothers are equally likely to be working at paid employment. In Sweden, although 85% of poor single mothers work, most work part-time, and less than 8% rely on their income for over half of their total support. In Sweden there is a continuum between income earned from work and that provided by welfare. Although there is a much lower participation in the labor force of mothers in other European countries, "the low rates of poverty among lone-parent families result from the combined effects of advance child-support payments, relatively generous income support 'packages' for families with children in general, and support services—particularly publicly funded childcare—that allows mothers to remain in the labor force during their child-rearing years" (McFate, 1991). Family policies are such that families with children receive support even when the father and mother are both present in the household. Sweden has also reduced gender pay inequity, instituted child-support collection, and made available publicly supported childcare, all of which help provide income security for mothers.

Older Single Mothers

An increasing phenomenon are single mothers by choice who are in their late 20s, 30s, and 40s.

Another group of single mothers have also been increasing in recent years, a group which is quite separate from the poor, unwed teenager who is unprepared for motherhood. These new single mothers are unmarried women in their late 20s, 30s, and 40s who have decided to either bear a child or adopt a child and raise the child as a single parent. Although the media has described the single mother over 30 as a White career woman, Black women are disproportionately represented in this group. This is due to the greater "marriage squeeze" for Black women as compared with White women (see Chapter X).

Most single women who choose to become mothers are happy with their choice. People perceive adoption by a single mother as more acceptable than bearing a child.

Through a New York–based organization called Single Mothers by Choice and other informal contacts, 20 single mothers were contacted and interviewed in depth (Mechaneck, Klein, & Kuppersmith, 1987). The women were White, well educated, had an average annual income of $39,000, and all but one was heterosexual. One-third of the women had been previously married, but the marriages had terminated prior to conception. Ten of the women had become pregnant through sexual intercourse with a man of their acquaintance, four had AID, and six adopted a child. Fifteen of the women lived alone with their

children, while three had live-in housekeepers and two had communal living arrangements. The women reported being happy with their decision to become single mothers. "However, those women who were involved with men at the time of conception and expected them to share parenthood responsibilities expressed the most dissatisfaction when their expectations were not met" (Mechaneck et al., 1987, p. 279).

A survey of attitudes of 151 men and women and high school students toward single women having children revealed that people had the most favorable responses to adoption by a single woman and the least favorable to intercourse with an unknown man for the purpose of becoming pregnant (Mechaneck et al., 1987). The child of the unmarried mother was seen at a disadvantage as compared with the child of divorced parents by 39% of the women and 47% of the men. Men tended to be concerned of the lack of a father figure in the child's life, more so than women.

Mothers without a spouse present are much more likely than other mothers to report their child's health as poor, often as poorer than does a physician who examines the child.

Two health surveys were conducted by the NCHS and a survey of well being conducted by the Bureau of the Census to determine the health effects on children of being raised in single-parent households (Angel & Worobey, 1988). Single-parent families were found to be more dependent on welfare (AFDC, food stamps, Medicaid, SSI, other transfers) than were the two-parent families. Mothers without a spouse present were much more likely than mothers with a spouse present to report their children's health as poor. For Mexican Americans, however, female headship was not related to mothers' reports of children's health over and above the other social class correlates of health. "It is clear that much of the stress associated with single motherhood results from economic deprivation" (Angel & Worobey, 1988, p. 47). Analyses revealed significant differences between physicians' and mothers' ratings of the children's health, with mothers rating the child's health as poorer. The mothers who report their child's health as poorer than do the physicians tend the have depressive disorders.

Increased Earnings and Self-Efficacy

Increased earnings are associated with increased self-efficacy for single mothers.

Increased earnings have been found to be associated with increased self-efficacy. Self-efficacy was defined "as a generalized belief in one's own efforts to control desired outcomes, as opposed to luck or the effects of powerful others" (G. Downey & Moen, 1987, p. 320). Self-efficacy was the focus of a study of a representative sample of 5,000 households (60% Black and 40% White) that were female-headed in 1972 and were followed up in 1976 (G. Downey & Moen, 1987). Seventeen percent had married at the latter time. Although income is associated with self-efficacy, employment apart from income had no influence on self-efficacy. In fact, income had an equally great effect on self-efficacy regardless of its source. Marriage had a marginally significant impact on efficacy, but decreased when family income is controlled. The transition to the "empty nest" has a marginal but negative effect on efficacy, indicating the effect of the loss of a role.

LESBIAN MOTHERS

Gender Role and Adjustment of Children of Lesbian Mothers

Lesbian mothers number between 1.5 and 5 million in America. There are no differences between children raised by lesbian and heterosexual mothers in gender identification, cognitive functioning, or incidence of emotional problems.

Until the past 10 years or so, lesbian mothers were unrecognized in American society, most people believing that lesbianism and motherhood were mutually exclusive categories. My first consciousness raising about lesbian mothers was at a session at the 1983 conference of the Associ-

ation of Women in Psychology in New York. The session on lesbian mothers was attended almost exclusively by lesbian women, most of whom were considering motherhood at the time. Some of the women were pregnant through donor insemination, and one woman said she was impregnated by a gay male friend with whom she had sexual intercourse for the purpose of getting pregnant. Other women had adopted or were in the process of doing so. A few of the lesbian women had children by a previous marriage. This session took place at the beginning of what has come to be called a "baby boom" among lesbian mothers (Patterson, 1994). Estimates of the number of lesbian mothers range from 1.5 million to 5 million in American society (Falk, 1990).

Lesbian mothers often have difficulty in obtaining custody of their children in divorce or child-protection proceedings. In a number of cases, custody was awarded to the father when the mother's sexual preference was made known to the court (Gottman, 1990). In cases that have come before the courts, a number of assumptions about lesbian mothers have been used when denying them custody. These include the assumptions that lesbian mothers are mentally ill, that lesbian women are less maternal than heterosexual women, that their children will be more likely to have mental problems, that the children will be sexually molested by the lesbian mother or her partner, that the child's gender-role development will be impaired, or that the child will be likely to grow up to be homosexual, and that the child will be stigmatized by society or other children. In her review of the research literature, Falk (1990) does not find support for any of these assumptions, with the possible exception that children of lesbian mothers may be subject to some stigma. Similarly, a review of the literature by Patterson (1992) found no support for the belief that the children of lesbian or gay parents are different from the children of heterosexual parents in outcome measures. The courts, however, are perpetuating the stigma of being raised in a lesbian family if they deny custody to a lesbian mother simply because she is a lesbian.

Lesbian communities often provide the children of lesbians an extended network, created beyond the ties of kinship and marriage, that provides support emotionally, financially, and in other ways (Ainslie & Feltey, 1991). Within this network, lesbian feminist mothers strive to transform motherhood. They see motherhood as political work, teaching children feminist values and affecting social change by raising "politically aware, open-minded children."

> Lesbian feminist mothers seek to "forge new forms" of family, in which the institution serves the individual. These new forms are based on the possibility for the adult members of the family to fill multiple roles—as providers, nurturers, and receivers, of familial support and love. . . . "In families of choice, each person is there as a person, not as a role." (Ainslie & Feltey, 1991, p. 72

A lesbian community provides a social context in which the children can feel secure, realizing that although their family may be different from those in mainstream society, they are not alone.

Is there a difference in the sex role acquisition of children whose mothers are lesbian or heterosexual? A study by Hoeffer (1981) of the only or oldest six- through nine-year-old child of 20 lesbian and 20 heterosexual single mothers found the children to be similar in their sex role acquisition regardless of their mother's sexual orientation. Boys of both groups of mothers preferred a majority of sex typed masculine toys and activities. Girls of both lesbian and heterosexual mothers preferred a larger percentage of neutral toys and activities. Lesbian mothers did try to encourage their children to play more with a mixture of masculine and feminine toys than did heterosexual mothers, but this was not reflected in children's preferences.

Do children raised by lesbian mothers differ in cognitive functioning or have more emotional problems than children raised by heterosexual mothers? No significant differences were found on IQ and behavioral adjustment measures between six- to nine-year-old children born to lesbian couples by donor insemination and the same age children in matched heterosexual parent families (Flaks, Ficher, Masterpasqua, & Joseph, 1995). The relationship quality of lesbian or het-

erosexual couples were found to be similar. The lesbian parents were found to have significantly more parental awareness skills, however, than did the heterosexual parents. This difference was due to the significantly lower scores of the fathers as compared with either the lesbian or heterosexual biological mothers or the nonbiological lesbian mothers. "Healthy developmental outcomes for the children in this and other studies of lesbian families support the view of Patterson (1992) and others that neither father presence nor parental heterosexuality is crucial for healthy child development" (Flaks et al., 1995, pp. 112–113).

A study comparing the adult daughters of divorced lesbian mothers with adult daughters of divorced heterosexual mothers found no significant differences between the two groups in gender identity, gender role (when older brothers were partialed out—women with older brothers score more masculine), or in sexual orientation (Gottman, 1989). On the Well-Being scale, which measures the "individual's sense of feeling secure in the world and in relationships," daughters of lesbian mothers tended to score the highest. On the other hand, daughters of non-remated (neither married nor co-habiting) mothers scored the lowest. It seems that having another parent figure is important regardless of the sex of that person.

STEPMOTHERS AND NONCUSTODIAL MOTHERS

There is a period of disruption and increased conflict when a stepparent enters the home, which is more difficult for a stepmother than it is for a stepfather. There are accommodations that can help ease the adjustment.

A study of couples in first and second marriages found that stepparents did not become closer to the stepchildren during the first few years of the marriage. The presence of a new baby in the marriage was associated with lower happiness among women in first marriages, but not among remarried women, and men tended to be happier with new babies (Benson-von der Ohe,

1987). Stepmothers report significantly more role strain than did stepfathers (Whitsett & Land, 1992).

Despite changes in women's roles, women are still expected to fulfill the nurturer and caretaker role in the family and her discrepant feelings toward her stepchildren may create strain in the form of self-role incongruence. Avoidant strategies do little to alleviate the role strain of stepmothers (Whitsett & Land, 1992). Women higher in self-esteem and self-efficacy had lower role strain. Marital satisfaction was inversely related to role strain. Counseling may be particularly helpful for stepparents if it increases the parents sense of control over life.

Since 75% of divorced mothers and 80% of divorced fathers remarry, many stepfamilies are created (Hetherington, Stanley-Hagan, & Anderson, 1989). Stepmothers who live with stepchildren appear to take a more active role in parenting than do residential stepfathers (Santrock & Sitterle, 1987). The adjustment is more difficult when a custodial father remarries and a stepmother enters the family as compared with a family where a custodial mother remarries and a stepfather enters the home (Clingempeel, Brand, & Ievoli, 1988). Frequent visits by the biological mother creates additional problems, particularly for daughters. Unlike the Brady Bunch, families in which both parents bring children have the greatest degree of behavior problems (Santrock & Sitterle, 1987).

There is usually a temporary period of disruption and an increase in conflict between the custodial mother and her children following remarriage. After about two years there is little difference between divorced mothers and remarried mothers and their children (Hetherington, 1992). The stepparent may become increasingly distant and disengaged from the stepchildren as a result of resentment and resistance on the part of the stepchildren.

A family therapist and stepparent who has conducted therapy with many stepfamilies, Emily Visher (1994) has proposed three strategies for stepfamilies based on a study of 292 stepfamilies who have been in therapy. "These lessons are: 1) dealing productively with losses and changes;

2) accepting and appreciating differences; and 3) enhancing relationships by increasing dyadic interactions." (J. S. Visher, 1994, p. 335). The adults have to accept the grieving and sense of loss of the children for their original family, listen to each other and share feelings, but then move on to recognize the gains to the family. The children in stepfamilies have different heredity and different family experiences. Learning to accept and appreciate someone who is different—whether in types of music, hairstyles, recreational activities—is a task for all family members. Helping to smooth the way is parent–child alone time for each child in the family. "Positive memories of *dyadic* moments as well as family moments strengthen bonds and deepen relationships" (J. Visher, 1994, p. 335). John Visher (1994) provides additional guidelines for stepparents that include stepmothers coming in gradually, the biological parent enforcing the rules, the biological parent requiring respectful treatment of the stepparent, cooperation between the parents and stepparents in raising the children, and obtaining educational input in the form of books and/or support groups.

African American Stepfamilies

Although African American stepfamilies are far fewer than White stepfamilies, it appears that they are quite similar. Fewer adjustment problems are reported by African American parents than by White parents in both intact and stepfamilies.

As noted previously, African American families are more likely to be disrupted by divorce in both first and second marriages than are White families (T. C. Martin & Bumpass, 1989). Black women, however, are less likely to remarry than White women, so there are proportionately fewer African American stepfamilies. Data from a subsample of families from the National Survey of Families and Households (M. A. Fine, McKenry, Donnelly, & Voydanoff, 1992) of 82 African American and 415 White stepfather families, and 394 African American and 2,312 White intact families were analyzed for perceived adjustment of parents and children. Black males reported less life satisfaction than did White males in both intact and stepfather families. Black respondents in stepfather families, compared with those in White stepfather families, were more depressed. Statistical controls for lower family incomes, less education, and more people living in the household, characteristic of African American families, could partially explain racial differences in respondent adjustment. The only statistically significant difference remaining was in respondent adjustment. "However, given that these racial demographic differences are also present in the general population, analyses that use demographic controls mask actual racial differences and should be interpreted with caution" (M. A. Fine, et al., 1992, p. 124).

A statistically significant effect for both Black and White families was that respondents in stepfather families reported being less satisfied with their lives. In both White and Black families respondents reported that their children's lives were not going as well, and that their children were experiencing more distress and that they had poorer quality (step)parent relations than in intact families. This difference in children's adjustment was found even after controls for demographic variables. African American respondents, however, in both intact and stepfamilies perceived their children as less psychologically distressed than did White respondents. The authors conclude that overall the parent and child adjustment are similar in African American and White stepfather families.

Noncustodial Mothers

A mother is considered noncustodial if she has one or more children living away from her. The most frequent reason for noncustody is money. Mothers whose children have been kidnapped live in a continual state of mourning.

Although the census bureau does not count **noncustodial mothers**, estimates can be made from charting the number of custodial fathers. Grief and Pabst (1988) estimate that there are over 1 million mothers living away from their children. Mothers may be considered noncusto-

dial if they have one child living away from them even if they have one or more children living with them. Mothers with joint shared custody are not considered in these statistics. In most of the arrangements, fathers are the custodian.

Historically, mothers without custody have been with us for a variety of reasons. In her book, *Mothers on Trial* (1986), Phyllis Chesler recounts the tragic stories of female slaves who were separated from their children when they or she were sold to different plantation owners. As recently as the 1800s, children were considered the property of the father. Mothers were also unlikely to have a sufficient income to support a family, and in the event of a divorce custody of the children were given to the father (Grief & Pabst, 1988). With the industrial revolution and fathers working outside of the home while mothers cared for children in the home, and an increase in women's rights, custody of children was given to women following divorce, during most of the twentieth century.

It was not until the 1970s that the courts began to question whether mothers should be given sole custody of children. Grief and Pabst (1988) conducted a survey of 517 noncustodial mothers (mostly White and middle class) drawn largely from Parents Without Partners and Mothers Without Custody, two self-help organizations. In addition, 100 phone or personal interviews were conducted with these women. The most frequent reason these women gave for why they do not have custody is money. "'I could not afford to raise them,' 'He could provide for them better financially than I could,' 'He threatened me with not paying alimony and/or child support if I took custody,' I could not afford a good lawyer.'" (Grief & Pabst, 1988, p. 73). The next most frequently given reasons for not having custody were that the children chose the father, so the children would not have to move, the mother had problems, and the mother lost them after a court battle.

Noncustodial mothers report experiencing much more discrimination than do noncustodial fathers.

Our contention is that these mothers are harshly judged and that judgment comes from a lack of understanding regarding how mothers become noncustodial and from the common belief that children need to be with their mothers. It also comes from the belief that a father cannot be an adequate parent. (Grief & Pabst, 1988, p. 257)

Mothers have a range of emotions about not being the custodial parent, from being pleased with how the children are adjusting to serious pain about the situation. The mothers who are having a difficult time are likely to be mothers who lost custody against their will, and to have had acrimonious divorces. They may not be on good terms with their children.

Chesler (1986) studied 60 custodially challenged, predominantly White mothers who were similar demographically to the majority of divorced White mothers in America, and 50 minority mothers. She also interviewed 55 fathers who had been involved in custody decisions. Of the custodially challenged mothers, 70% lost custody to the fathers. These custody decisions went against these mothers despite the fact that 83% of the fathers had not previously been involved in primary childcare, 67% had not paid any child support, 62% had physically abused their wives, 57% had engaged in antimother campaigns with the children, and 37% had kidnapped their children (Chesler, 1986).

Psychologically, the mothers whose children have been kidnapped are never the same again. If the children are returned, they live in constant fear of it happening again. For those whose husbands fled the country or otherwise covered their tracks so they are not found, the mothers live in a constant state of mourning.

Mothers have lost custody for "crimes" ranging from going out on a date while the divorce was proceeding to being a lesbian. Mothers also lost custody because the father was better able to support the children. For some fathers, the custody battle was a way of retaining the marital home and other assets. About half of the mothers in Chesler's study became welfare recipients upon separation. In two-thirds of the cases, however, the fathers who fought for custody were not paying child support (Chesler, 1986).

Noncustodial mothers are treated more negatively by family, friends, and the church. Many of these mothers are "haunted by guilt." Mothers whose children chose not to live with them suffer the most emotional distress. How well the noncustodial mother adjusts to the situation is dependent on a number of factors, particularly the ability of the father to parent, the children's adjustment, her job situation, how the noncustodial decision was made, and the reaction of family, friends, and co-workers (Grief & Pabst, 1988).

MOTHERS IN MINORITY SUBCULTURES

Changes in the Black family have come about for structural rather than cultural reasons.

The Black family in America has been the focus of heated debate since Daniel Patrick Moynihan's 1965 labor report, "The Negro Family: The Case for National Action," which became known as "The Moynihan Report." Moynihan warned of the disintegration of the African American family and painted a bleak picture for Black America. Twenty-one years later, a documentary televised as Bill Moyers's special report, "The Vanishing Family: Crisis in Black America," sounded the same theme of moral decay in African Americans that, he says, is leading to deteriorating conditions of the African American family (P. H. Collins, 1989).

Both reports blame inappropriate gender roles as a cause of the plight of the Black family. The Moynihan report emphasizes what he considers to be the unnatural power of Black women in Black families as leading to its destruction, and encourages Black men to reestablish patriarchy. Moyers's documentary suggests that Black women stop depending on government assistance and instead depend on Black men. Patricia H. Collins (1989) points out that this is hardly a solution when Black males are economically marginal.

The political and economic structures that shape the industries, organizations, and jobs offered to

Black men and women and influence the social institutions such as transportation and schooling that assist Blacks in gaining access to jobs are absent from this analysis. (P. H. Collins, 1989, p. 883)

The Black family is diverse in American society, consisting of married couples and their children, as well as single-parent families and lesbian couples, just as White families are diverse. What differs between White and Black families are the percentages of different types of families, and the average socioeconomic levels of Black and White families. A strong relationship exists between out-of-wedlock births and joblessness rather than cultural beliefs about ideal family structure. Discrimination in education and employment are the root cause of the cycle of poverty of the Black family. Another very important point to understand is that many of the current problems of Black America are being created by the contraction of the manufacturing sector of the economy, which leads to limited job opportunities and resulting poverty, which creates dependency on a welfare system that promotes single-parent families. Young men without jobs tend not to marry. "African American children—particularly poor children in poor neighborhoods—are faced early with restrictions that result from segregated housing, inferior schools, and lack of access to appropriate role models. These conditions limit opportunities to succeed" (McAdoo, 1990, p. 84).

Patricia H. Collins (1989) criticizes both the Moynihan Report and the Moyers documentary on a variety of grounds, such as not taking into account working- and middle-class Black families. They did not deal with alternative family arrangements such as extended families, lesbian couples who head families, and male single-parent families. The role of racism and discrimination as causes of Black poverty were underemphasized. Black females, being a double minority, can often expect only minimum wage and no health benefits in jobs they might get. The welfare system in many states pays only when there is no man in the home, further encouraging female-headed households.

The inner city is now cut off from the economic mainstream of American society. If Ameri-

can society wants to bolster the African American family, then the solution is business investment and jobs in the inner city, supported by childcare, health care, and an excellent school system. These same solutions would also allow Black single mothers to raise themselves and their children out of poverty.

The Extended Black Family

The Black extended family includes both relatives and nonrelatives.

Black family life is characterized by an extended family system. Black families, to a greater extent than White families, are involved in day to day interactions with extended family.

Extended families represent a significant proportion of families in the Black community. The Black child is surrounded by a kin organization of significant family associations and family influences that go beyond mother, father, and children to include parental, sibling, avuncular, and cousin links of spouses and offspring. (M. N. Wilson, 1989, p. 380)

Black families also change frequently, particularly extended, low-income and one-parent families. Many single mothers live with their family of origin. Single motherhood is a major factor in the formation of the extended family. For low-income families, sharing residence with extended family members is a way of reducing costs.

The boundaries of motherhood are also fluid in African American communities. "Organized, resilient, women-centered networks of blood-mothers and othermothers are key in understanding this centrality; Grandmothers, sisters, aunts, or cousins acted as othermothers by taking on childcare responsibilities for each other's children" (P. H. Collins, 1995, p. 201). Providing economic resources for the Black family was integrated into the mothering role for Black women, whereas the provider role was seen as incompatible with motherhood for White women.

Black mothers are primarily responsible for the household chores and childcare responsibilities.

Focus on Women   Rain

Rain is an African American woman with a quick, broad smile, sparkling eyes and a deep throaty laugh. Rain was raised by her Catholic mother and Muslim father in an inner-city area. The family of eight was poor in material goods but rich in spiritual and moral values. Rain saw education as the way to a better life and studied hard in school, winning a scholarship to a prestigious state university. It was during college that Rain met her husband, Paul, a promising young artist. Their son, Michael, was born while they were still in college.

After Paul and Rain graduated, Paul informed Rain that he felt that family life was limiting him as an artist. He wanted to live in an artist's colony in New York or Paris. Essentially, he wanted his freedom. Still very much in love, Rain gave Paul the freedom he wanted. They divorced, with the idea that Rain would wait for him and Paul would return when he was ready to settle down again.

Shortly thereafter, Rain moved east after obtaining a fellowship at an ivy league university. After completing her master's degree, Rain found a job and stayed in the east. Rain is now 37 and Michael 15. Rain works three jobs supporting herself and Michael, living in a small but immaculate apartment with Michael in a racially mixed neighborhood.

In addition to her full-time job doing editorial work, Rain works part-time doing freelance typing and editing, as well as at a minimum wage job in a bookstore from four until midnight three days a week in order to earn tuition to send Michael to a private school. Her son has a mild case of attention deficit disorder (ADD) and would not be able to function as well in a large public school classroom. She leads a very spartan life in order to give Michael the opportunities many young Black men in our society do not have. Michael is a pleasant, smiling lad who is polite to his elders. His mother has taught him that to be a responsible man means that you have to work hard. He plans to "up" his mom one by getting an M.D. His aspiration is to become a neurosurgeon. Michael will do her proud. Rain, herself, is a talented writer who has written three novels, one of which was recently published. She suffers from exhaustion, but she feels it is worth it to work so hard to make a better life for her son.

Paul never returned to the family, nor kept in contact with them, and Rain never remarried. Mobutu, a Nigerian man, who once asked Rain to marry him, but is now married to a White woman, is a surrogate father to Michael. Mobutu visits Rain and Michael once a week, when possible. When Mobutu speaks to Michael it is like God speaking and Michael does whatever Mobutu asks. Rain has focused her life on making a better life for Michael.

Grandmothers are most likely to perform household tasks when residing with their adult daughters.

Are Black families more egalitarian than White families? Is there more sharing of childcare and household chores between mothers and fathers, and do Black grandmothers provide substantial childcare and housework for Black mothers? Sixty-four lower-middle-class Black families participated in a study of perceived childcare activities, parental punishment behaviors, and household duties of various family members (M. N. Wilson, Tolson, Hinton, & Kiernan, 1990). Four types of households were included in the study; single-parent with grandmothers living in the home or in the community, and dual-parent with grandmothers living in the home or in the community. Each family had at least one child between 7 and 14 years of age and an average of 2.4 children. Overall, mothers performed the 12 household duties most often, 60% of the time. Mothers were also nominated as doing most of the childcare tasks (24%), although "no one does this task" was the most frequently used category. Mothers in single-parent families with grandmothers residing in the community performed significantly more of the household tasks than in any other type of family. Grandmothers were most likely to perform household duties when residing with their single adult daughters. It is not surprising that residential fathers performed significantly more household tasks and childcare than did nonresidential fathers. The hypothesis of role flexibility and sharing with regard to household tasks and childcare in the Black family was not supported in this study (M. N. Wilson et al., 1990). Black mothers are primarily responsible for care of the house and children.

Dual-Earner Black Families

A study of 63 middle- to lower-middle-income dual-earner African American mothers' and fathers' involvement in childcare (of infants below 24 months of age) and housework revealed traditional gender patterns of involvement in childcare and housework. In families in which the mother worked full-time, the father provided about one-third as much time as did mothers in primary care-giving. By contrast, when the mother worked part-time, fathers spent about 50% as much time as mothers in primary care-giving. This was not due to fathers' increased time in care-giving; rather, it was due to mothers' decrease in primary care-giving when working part-time. It is not clear, however, why mothers working part-time spend proportionately less time in childcare than mothers working full-time (Hossain & Roopnarine, 1993).

Black Lesbian Mothers

Black lesbian mothers are more tolerant of transgressions, the child's sexuality, and have more masculine sex role expectations for their daughters than do Black heterosexual mothers.

A group of 26 Black self-identified lesbian mothers and a group of 26 Black heterosexual mothers, who were the biological mothers of at least one child between the ages of 4 and 13, were participants in a study of child-rearing attitudes (M. Hill, 1987). Lesbian mothers were found to be significantly more tolerant of transgressions and more flexible about child-rearing rules. Lesbian mothers also demonstrated more tolerance of the child's sexuality, as measured by the mother's being more permissive about modesty, about sex play, and about showing greater open-

ness in giving information. The lesbian mothers viewed boys and girls as more similar than did heterosexual mothers. The lesbian mothers also had more traditional masculine role expectations for their daughters than did their heterosexual counterparts. In other areas, such as a tendency to interfere with their children's relationships with their fathers and independence training, there were no differences between the two groups of mothers. This study is a pioneering one on the topic of Black lesbian mothers. Further research certainly needs to be done to examine the many questions that could be asked.

American Indian Mothers

In American Indian culture, the mother role was greatly valued. Women, however, were also allowed flexibility in assuming more masculine occupational and social roles.

In traditional American Indian cultures, the mother role was greatly valued and rooted in biological, spiritual, and social worlds (LaFramboise, Heyle, & Ozer, 1990).

Biologically, they valued being mothers and raising healthy families, spiritually, they were considered extensions of the Spirit Mother and keys to the continuation of their people (Allen, 1986; Jenks, 1986); and socially, they served as transmitters of cultural knowledge and caretakers of their children and relatives. (LaFramboise, Heyle, & Ozer, 1990, p. 457)

At the same time, within the cultures, females were allowed to express alternative roles such as the "manly hearted" and "warrior woman" roles that allowed them to engage in masculine occupations without dressing as men. An even more extreme role change was the "bedarche," which was a complete shift to both the male social and occupational roles. Thus, while motherhood was revered, women were also allowed the flexibility of assuming more masculine roles.

Educational and occupational disadvantages make it more difficult for Native American single-parents. In 1980, nearly one-quarter of Native American families were headed by women, and

47% of these single-parent families had incomes below the federal poverty guidelines. Even more shocking was that the poverty rate was 82% for single Native American mothers with children under age six.

Hispanic Families

Despite strong family and marriage values, Hispanics also have a higher percentage of female-headed households than do Whites. It is because Blacks and Hispanics are trapped in cities that no longer have an adequate employment base.

Hispanic is a hybrid category encompassing Mexican Americans, Latin Americans, South Americans, Cubans, and Puerto Ricans. Three-quarters of the Hispanics in the United States are of Mexican American and Puerto Rican origin. The number of Mexican Americans was about 12 million in 1988, which was about five times the size of the Puerto Rican American population, which was about 2.3 million. Most of the Puerto Rican Americans reside in the large metropolitan areas of the Northeast, whereas 90% of all Mexican origin Hispanics live in the Southwestern section of the country—California, New Mexico, Arizona, Texas, and Colorado (Aponte, 1991).

Because of the differential pattern of geographic residence of the Hispanic subgroups, not all Hispanic groups have been equally hard hit by the macrostructural changes in the national economy that has particularly affected manufacturing industries in the North and Midwest (M. B. Zinn, 1989). Among Latinos, the highest incidence of female-headed households is among the Puerto Ricans (43.3%) who live in the Rustbelt cities, which have lost factories and jobs. The percentage of female-headed households declined to 25.5% for Central and South Americans and 19.2% for Mexicans Americans.

Motherhood was traditionally seen as the central role of women among Puerto Ricans.

Their concept of motherhood is based on the female capacity to bear children and on the notion of *marianismo*, which presents the Virgin Mary as a role model (Stevens, 1973). *Marianismo* presup-

poses that it is through motherhood that a woman realizes herself and derives her life's greatest satisfactions. (Sanchez-Ayendez, 1992, p. 240)

The bond between the mother and child is viewed as stronger than the father–child bond. The mother is in charge of the domestic domain and creates and maintains family unity and interdependence. The older women also expect to be taken care of during their old age by their children. They prefer to live in their own households and maintain as much independence as possible, but receive support from their children. Daughters in particular are relied on for emotional support, and for help during times of illness.

Mexican American families are larger and more stable than are Black or White families. Acceptance/rejection of their children by migrant Mexican American mothers is related to the amount of support they have from partner or friends and relatives.

Mexican American families are larger than White families (Jorgensen & Adams, 1988). Traditionally, they have been cohesive families with stable marriages and a lower divorce rate than either Black or White marriages (Staples & Mirande, 1980). Mexican American children are particularly close to their mothers, and the extended family is common (E. A. Martinez, 1988; Markides, Hoppe, Martin, & Timbers, 1983).

Correlates of maternal acceptance of preschool children was studied in a sample of 100 Mexican American mothers (89% married, 90% migrant workers) of normal preschool children aged three to five who were enrolled in the Texas Migrant Council's Headstart Program (Siantz, 1990). More of the variance (75%) in mother's acceptance/rejection of their children was accounted for by total amount of social support received from spouse/partner, family, or friends, than from problems in life conditions alone. "The findings of the present research underscore the importance of social support to maternal warmth and acceptance in the presence of problematic life conditions" (Siantz, 1990, p. 253). Mothers can be warmer, more loving mothers if they receive love and support themselves.

Asian American Families

There is great diversity within Asian American families. The family structure of Asian Americans also varies as a function of place of origin, when the immigration occurred, and reasons for immigrating, whether as refugees from a war torn country or for educational and economic improvement. Asian Americans have higher marriage rates than do White or Black Americans. Asian women are more likely to marry White men, however, than are Black women. As noted in Chapter V, even the new Hmong immigrants marry before becoming teenage mothers. In general, Asian American families have been patriarchal with husbands in a position of authority and women being responsible for childcare and housekeeping tasks (Kitano & Daniels, 1988). Children are socialized to have values of cooperation, obedience, and responsibility to family (Huang & Ying, 1989). Third- and fourth-generation Asian American women have high levels of education and are frequently employed in professional and managerial positions, creating less hierarchical structure in the Asian American family.

THE POSTMODERN FAMILY

In his book, *Ties that Stress: The New Family Imbalance,* David Elkind (1994) writes about the **postmodern family.** Modernity arose as a revolt against the autocracy of medieval forms of government, religion, science, art, and education. According to Elkind, modernism had three conceptual foundations: the belief in the progress of society and the individuals within it; the belief in universal principles of nature that could be discovered and understood; and the notion of regularity, predictability. Within modernism, the nuclear family developed based on "romantic love (the tie of parents to one another), maternal love (the tie of parents to offspring), and domesticity (the tie of family to community)" (Elkind, 1994, p. 39).

Consensual love has replaced romantic love. Romantic love was ushered in by modernism, which allowed individuals rather than the family to choose their own marital partners. Widespread uncommitted premarital sex has changed the contingencies of the marital agreement. The marriage may no longer be life-long, and each other's autonomy and need for growth and change is respected.

The family in the postmodern period is characterized by a transition from unilateral to mutual authority. Shared parenting and the deconstruction of the sentiment of maternal love in the modern sense of the exclusive mother child bond is another shift occurring in the family. Parenting is shared between mothers and fathers, grandparents, and nonrelatives in day care centers and home care. In the postmodern family, concerns of gender, race, and class diversity are supported. Finally, the sentiment of urbanity has replaced domesticity. "In relation to the larger society, the postmodern home is no longer a haven, a place for nurturance and protection. Rather it is more like a railway station, with parents and children pulling in and out as they go about their busy lives" (Elkind, 1994, p. 57). Elkind does not think that children and adolescents are given enough time and space as were modern children and that their needs are less well met than are those of adults.

Elkind is hopeful, however, of the emergence of what he calls the vital family. Committed love is a merging of romantic love with consensual love. In committed love both partners have equality.

> The vital family still takes many different kinship forms, from the traditional nuclear pattern to that of single parents, adoptive families, blended families, and more. What distinguishes the vital family is its emphasis on lifespan human development—its recognition that both children and adults undergo continuous change and growth—and its adaptive melding of unilateral and mutual authority. (Elkind, 1994, p. 211)

Community is also a part of the vital family, whether it involves parents who are leaders in Cub scouting and Brownies or community programs for teenage or drug addicted mothers. Electronic communities are also expanding via the personal computer and electronic bulletin boards. Movements are also occurring in the schools for parents, teachers, and administrators to cooperate and share authority in schools such as in the Coalition for Essential Schools led by Ted Sizer, dean of education at Brown University. Interdependence that acknowleges difference while at the same time supports family members is emerging in the vital family and its interface with community.

REFLECTIONS

What matters far more than the family structure in which children grow up is that there be adults who love the child, and treat the child with respect. The parent(s) must be willing to teach the child how to take care of himself/herself and the realities of the world, teach the child values, encourage him/her to develop skills and abilities and praise his/her accomplishments. Poverty, neglect, physical and sexual abuse, and inadequate day care and schools are detrimental to children.

What can society do to ensure that children will grow up both mentally and physically healthy? How is motherhood changing? What should society do to ensure that mothers and fathers are prepared to asssume their awesome responsibilities? Do we need to change the traditional role of the school? Should schools offer evening classes in parenting to the mothers and fathers of the children in the school? Should schools offer joint evening programs for parents and their children that focus on everything from learning to use computers to sex education? Would such school based programs be too expensive? What are the costs to society of not providing such programs?

American society needs public policies that support children, whether those children are in a family that consists of husband and wife both working and caring for the children, or the family as headed by a single mother, whether lesbian or heterosexual. I have raised three children (my youngest just graduated from college) and much of the time I did so as a single parent. I received a great deal of help from my aunt, my mother and father, and my sister, as well as from a warm neighbor family.

I became a grandmother this year for the first time. My older daughter, who works in human resources management, has gone back to work three ten hour days a week at four-fifths salary. Her husband, who works in hotel management, works on Sundays and stays home on Mondays to care for the baby. I am able to arrange my class schedule in order to go to their home in nearby Massachusetts two days a week to take care of my granddaughter. (Although sometimes her other grandmother gives me a day off.) We are fortunate in being able to have sufficient flexibility of schedules to work out this arrangement. Since American society does not have a system of federally funded daycare as do other western countries, organizations should make available flexible scheduling so that individuals can meet the needs of their families.

"Family" is not just a buzz word for reaction; for women, as for men, it is the symbol of that last area where one has any hope of individual control over one's destiny, of meeting one's most basic human needs, of nourishing that core of personhood threatened now by vast impersonal institutions and uncontrollable corporate and government bureaucracies and the bewildering, accelerating pace of change. Against these menaces, the family may be as crucial for survival as it used to be against the untamed wilderness and the raging elements, and the old, simple kinds of despotism. (Friedan, 1981, p. 178)

According to Betty Friedan (1981) in her book, *The Second Stage,* this phase of the women's movement must concentrate on domestic evolution within the home, and even on extending the physical boundaries of the home. For example, in Sweden Friedan visited "service housing" in which people had their own apartments but shared a childcare center, nursery, and after-school program, as well as a kitchen, a common dining room, and cleaning, gardening and laundry services. Eating in the common dining room helped develop new extended family like bonds. Structuring the environment in "user friendly" ways can help to foster intimate and supportive relationships.

Experiential Exercises

1. Visit a day care center.
2. Interview your mother and grandmothers about their parenting and grandparenting experiences.
3. Interview a mother who has both sons and daughters about her relationships with them.
4. Observe children in a playground and their interactions with mothers, fathers or other caretakers. Do mothers play differently with their children than fathers?
5. What was the family constellation in which you were raised, two biological parents? mother only? father only? other relatives living in the home? biological parent and stepparent? lesbian parents? Ask a close friend about their family constellation when growing up, and discuss how your different family constellations may have influenced your personality and behavior.

KEY TERMS

Aid to Families with Dependent Children (AFDC)   A government program providing cash subsidies and medical and other benefits to the mothers of approximately 11% of this nation's children.

Chodorow's Theory   The desire to be a mother springs from the early intense relationship of mother and daughter.

Ideology of Capitalism   It is the view that everything is a commodity that can be bought and sold, including a child. One of the three deeply rooted ideologies claimed by Rothman to shape modern American motherhood.

Ideology of Patriarchy   The concept of the "seed" and women's role in a patriarchal system as the nurturer of the "seed." It is one of the three ideologies claimed by Rothman to shape modern American motherhood.

Ideology of Technology   The application of science to everything including motherhood, and one of the three ideologies, claimed by Rothman to shape modern American motherhood.

Motherhood Mandate   Society's imperative that women have children and raise them well.

National Longitudinal Survey of Labor Market Experience of Youth (NLSY)   A national probability sample of 12,686 men and women who were aged 14–21 in 1979, and who have been interviewed annually since, which also included an oversample of Black and Hispanic, and of White disadvantaged youths.

Noncustodial Mothers   Mothers may be considered noncustodial if they have one child living away from them even if they have one or more children living with them. This does not apply to mothers with joint shared custody arrangements.

Postmodern Family   It is characterized by mutual authority, shared parenting among relatives and non-relatives, and diversity of structure.

SUGGESTED READINGS

Amato, P. R., & Keith, B. (1991). Parental divorce and the well-being of children: A meta-analysis. *Psychological Bulletin, 110,* 26–46. This meta-analysis examines the effects of divorce, single parenting and remarriage on children.

Elkind, D. (1994). *Ties that stress: The new family imbalance.* Cambridge, MA: Harvard University Press. Elkind conceptualizes the changes occurring in contemporary families in the United States within the framework of postmodernism.

Flaks, D. K., Ficher, I., Masterpasqua, F., & Joseph, G. (1995). Lesbians choosing motherhood: A comparative study of lesbian and heterosexual parents and their children. *Developmental Psychology, 31,* 105–114. This article explodes some of the myths about lesbian parenting. It briefly reviews the literature and also reports on a study using a variety of assessment measures comparing children of 15 lesbian and 15 heterosexual couples.

CHAPTER 14

Women and Power/ Empowering Women

> Women make up only a small portion of public office holders not because they win less often than men, but because they have made up only a small portion of those running for office.
>
> Jody Newman, 1994

This chapter analyzes the gender politics of the 1990s in the context of its historical past. It focuses on the shaping of women's use of **power** within the political structure of American society as well as on the interpersonal level.

> Throughout history and across cultures, males have generally been allocated more power over females than vice versa—in private and in public, in the bedroom and in the boardroom, academically and vocationally, economically and politically, morally and legally. In consequence, insofar as women have had power over men, it has of necessity been achieved deviously by stratagems of obduracy and neglect, conspiracy, seduction, and subterfuge—the sources of the proverbial power behind the throne. (Money, 1988, p. 69)

Mary Daly (1993) points out that there is a universal sexual caste system, which differs only by degree in New York and Saudi Arabia. This distribution of power is the most basic gender inequality.

THE RIGHT TO VOTE

> *The Nineteenth Amendment to the Constitution finally gave women the right to vote in 1920. Women's organizations that made up the Suffrage Movement disintegrated and other women's organizations such as the PTA and the NACW took it's place.*

The Nineteenth Amendment to the Constitution was ratified in 1920, finally giving women the right to vote. After 1920, the large coalition women's movements disintegrated. Other women's organizations arose to take the place of ones that went out of existence (Cott, 1990). The National Congress of Parents and Teachers Associations (PTA) more than quintupled its membership during the 1920s, for example, working to establish playgrounds, libraries, and health clinics as well as working for international peace and, of course, improved schools.

Although Black women had played an active role during the early decades of the twentieth century in the politics of women's suffrage, particularly through suffrage clubs of Black women in the states that had given women the vote prior to 1920, large numbers of Black women in the South were turned away from the voting booth after ratification of the Nineteenth Amendment. Hundreds of thousands of Black migrants through the 1920s headed north to factory and domestic jobs, making possible greater political opportunity for Black women. The National Association of Colored Women (NACW), which had been actively working for the suffragist cause, became a springboard for political work of Black women (Higgenbotham, 1990).

Women are heterogeneous and have not mobilized into a cohesive political voting bloc.

The addition of women to the ranks of voters, however, did not significantly alter voting patterns. Heterogeneity on the issues has continued to the present time. The women's movement has tried to mobilize women into a cohesive political voting bloc. This has not taken place. Data from a 2,257-representative sample of American voters was able to test women's interests in relation to other variables. The reason for women's fragmentation on issues is that women are split on religion, political party preferences, and political ideology. These divisions go back to symbolic political predispositions resulting from early socialization rather than from interest-based cleavages (D. O. Sears & Huddy, 1990).

It was not until almost 50 years after winning the right to vote that as many women as men voted in a Presidential election. Now more women than men vote. President Clinton was the first president elected where women were the majority of those electing the president.

The rise of the second women's movement in the late 1960s led to greater roles for women in the Republican and Democratic national conventions. Women were only a small percentage of convention delegates prior to World War II. The pattern continued during the 1950s and 1960s,

with women averaging only 15% of delegates for the Republicans and 13% for the Democrats during this time. Beginning in 1972, however, women begin to far exceed their earlier presence as delegates to the political conventions. In 1988 women represented 37% of delegates to the Republican convention and 49% to the Democratic convention (Jennings, 1990).

For the first few decades of the **franchise**, far fewer women turned out to vote than men. In the Presidential election in 1920, the first in which women were eligible to vote, only one-third of the eligible women voted. In fact, it was not until 1968 that women voted in equal numbers to men (Lips, 1991). Voter turnout is very similar for women and men. In local elections 33% of women and 35% of men vote (Verba, 1990). In 1992, 60.2% of men and 62.3% of women reported they voted in the Presidential election (U.S. Bureau of the Census, 1994). Since there are more women than men in this country, particularly as age increases, this represented an actual vote of almost 2 million more women than men. More men than women, however, actively work for a party or candidate, persuade others how to vote, and attend political meetings or rallies (Verba, 1990).

With the election of Ronald Reagan in 1980, political analysts pointed to a gender gap, since 55% of male voters, but only 47% of female voters had voted for Reagan (Verba, 1990). "By the 1984 campaign, the Republicans had responded with the nomination of Sandra Day O'Connor to the Supreme Court, the appointment of Jeanne Kirkpatrick as ambassador to the United Nations and of Margaret Heckler and Elizabeth Dole to cabinet positions" (C. Mueller, 1993, p. 460). Although Democrats nominated Geraldine Ferraro as Walter Mondale's running mate in 1984, it appeared to make little difference in the women's vote in that election. In the 1988 election, Michael Dukakis, the Democratic candidate for President, had an unprecedented 15–20% lead with women voters in the polls in the spring, but by the election the Bush–Quayle ticket had been able to reduce the gender gap so that only 8% more women than men voted for Dukakis and 7% more men voted for Bush (C. Mueller, 1993).

The 1992 election of President Clinton, however, put women in the majority of those electing the President.

WOMEN IN POLITICAL OFFICE

Numbers of Women in Political Office

Women officeholders in top federal and statewide positions and local governments are increasing. Nevertheless, women are still significantly underrepresented in elected positions at all levels in the United States.

Although women have made substantial gains over the years in holding political office, in the 1994 Congress they were still a mere 11% of the membership of the House of Representatives and 7% of the Senate (Newman, 1994). Looking at the statewide elective executive offices in the 50 states in 1993, including offices such as governor, lieutenant governor, secretary of state, and treasurer, 72 were held by women. A total of 1,524 women were serving as elected state legislators in 1993 (U.S. Bureau of the Census, 1994).

It was not until 1988 that Arizona voters in the general election voted to remove the requirement that holders of state office be male. The law had not been enforced in recent years, since at the time of the vote the governor was a woman, Rose Mofford (Lips, 1991). Nevertheless, nearly one out of five of those voting opted to keep the male-only requirement law. Across the nation, however, there was a 22% increase in women in top statewide positions between 1990 and 1991 (Ogletree, Coffee, & May, 1992).

Although women have also shown large increases in their representation in local government, they are still significantly underrepresented as elected officials. Between 1971 and 1991, the percentage of elected mayors who were women increased from 1% to 17% (Ries & Stone, 1992). Local government in my home state of Rhode Island and nearby southeastern Massachusetts is still largely a "boy's club." In 1993, Rhode Island had its first female mayor in 209 years of mayoral elections. The town in which I live has a five-member town council with no women represented. In 1993, 78% of the town councils in Rhode Island and 80% of city councils and boards of selectmen in Southeastern Massachusetts were composed only of men (McVickar, 1993).

The Success of Men and Women Candidates

Women candidates running in general elections for their state legislature, Governor, U.S. House, or U.S. Senate are as likely as men candidates to win their races. at every level of government, incumbents are much more likely to get elected.

Are women candidates less likely to win political office than men running for office? A poll conducted by the National Women's Political Caucus (NWPC) found that two-thirds of voters believe that it is more difficult for a woman to get elected to public office than for a man. The reason so few women hold political office is because so few women run for political office. A study conducted by the NWPC found a similarity between the number of women who run for political office and those who hold political office (Newman, 1994). "Based on the overwhelming weight of the data gathered, the conclusion is clear: **a candidate's sex does not affect his or her chances of winning election**" (Newman, 1994, p. 2). This is true for candidates running for local, state, and federal offices.

One factor that does strongly influence the election of a candidate is whether or not that candidate is an incumbent. Incumbency provides an enormous advantage in an election, and women are much less likely to be an incumbent. At every level of government, incumbents have a much greater success rate in the election. The percentages of general elections won by incumbents were: 94% for state representive; 92% for state senator; 95% for U.S. House; 82% for U.S. Senator; and 77% for governor. Since most officeholders are men, male candidates are much more likely to be incumbents than female candidates. "But when male incumbents were compared to female incumbents, men running for open seats

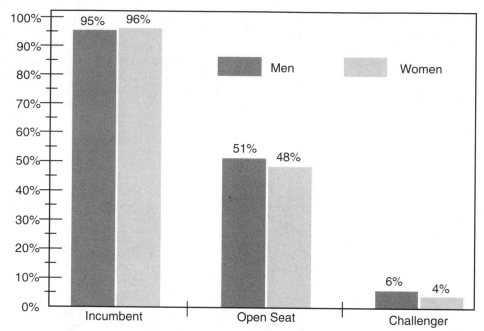

FIGURE 14.1   Success rates for men and women running in general elections for the U.S. House of Reprentatives, 1972–1992. *Source:* Adapted from "Perception and Reality: A Study Comparing the Success of Men and Women Candidates" by J. Newman, 1994, National Women's Political Caucus, Washington, DC.)

to women running for open seats, and male challengers to female challengers, **women won as high a percentage of their races as men**" (Newman, 1994, p. 1). More women should run for political office, particularly for open seats where an incumbent is not running.

African American Women Politicians

There is a predominance of African American women who hold political office when compared with other minority women.

Women of color, particularly African American women, are beginning to seek political office with tenacity and determination. Despite the oppression of society and poverty, Black women are the original feminists and embody androgyny (characteristics of self-reliance, independence, assertiveness, and strength). Several traditional African religions have a respect for women and their independent roles that is not seen in Western religions (C. R. Robinson, 1983).

Carol Mosely Braun became the first African American to sit in the U.S. Senate in 1993. Minority women are beginning to make greater inroads in local politics. In 1990, 133 women of color served in state legislatures, which was 10.5% of the 1,273 women state legislators (Natividad, 1992). African American women officeholders have been mayors of Washington, D.C., and Hartford, Connecticut.

The predominance of African American women in politics when compared to other women of color is an outgrowth of their longer-term experiences as community leaders, church leaders, and as "leaders" of families often bereft of men. Having had to enter the workplace far earlier than white women, African American women have also "tended to be more assertive with their men" as Shirley Chisholm accurately points out. (Natividad, 1992, p. 129)

Women of color face an uphill battle because they have less access to campaign money and they are less likely to receive support from male politicians.

Ideological Positions of Women Politicians

Women officeholders are more likely than men to be supporters of humanistic issues.

Once women achieve political office, do they make a difference? A research monograph on women in Congress between 1917 and 1976 found them to be supporters of humanist issues such as peace, childcare, health, and welfare. Research on women officeholders in the 1980s finds them more likely to support feminist or liberal policies regardless of political party (Mandel & Dodson, 1992). Women and men typically come to public office by different routes. For example, women are less likely to be lawyers and more often to be teachers, nurses, or social workers, broadening the experiences of those holding political office. Black women in political office also differ from their White female colleagues in being less likely to support the death penalty and more likely to support government-subsidized childcare, and to believe that local taxes should be raised to support social services.

Women, unlike other minorities, live intermixed with men, making gender a very complex political variable. Women are spread throughout the population and all geographic regions. Although identification with feminism has implications for attitudes on issues, a larger group of women do not identify themselves as feminists. Nevertheless, there is a pattern of women's positions on certain policy issues that appears with regularity.

WOMEN IN EUROPEAN POLITICS

Women's political participation varies among western democratic countries. Women in Norway have more equal roles in government and in intimate relationships than do women in France.

There have been major differences among Western democratic countries in the participation of women in political life. In Norway, there is almost equal representation of women and men in political bodies. "Since 1986, 40% of the Norwegian cabinet ministries in each succeeding government have been held by women, and the representation of women in the Parliament or in municipal elections is over 30%" (Apfelbaum, 1993, p. 413). In contrast, in France, women make up a small percentage of the political parties, and in 1993 only 5.7% of the parliamentary deputies and 4.3% of the senators were women.

In-depth interviews were conducted with 50 women leaders in France and Norway. The women were at the cabinet or subcabinet level, head of municipal government agencies, trade unions, or national corporations or institutions. The concept and exercise of power in Norway is one of "passing the torch" in which power is seen as transitory, a function of the position rather than the person. Viewing power in this way may help explain why Norwegian men are less threatened by women's participation in decision making. The Norwegian women expressed their experiences in their positions in a much more positive way than did the French women. The French women who came into office during the 1970s had a very different profile than did those emerging in the 1980s. The 1970s women saw themselves as token women who were conscious of the role of historical circumstances leading to their present position. The women who came into highly visible positions in the 1980s arrived at those positions at a much younger age and they felt legitimized in their positions by the women leaders who had come before. "In their accounts, Norwegian women expressed a deeply anchored sense of legitimacy that was totally alien to the French women of the first generation and just evolving for the second" (Apfelbaum, 1993, p. 419). French women were also quick to deny being feminists, although espousing a concern with women's issues, and were lacking the support of an organized feminist movement. The Norwegian women acknowledged the influence of feminism in their political roles.

The women's role in the political structure of the society has implications for the personal lives of women in high positions. Among the French women leaders, seeking political power jeopardized their intimate relations with male partners—only 5 of the 30 French women were married when interviewed as compared with 18 of the 20 Norwegian women.

> Women's positions on matters of public policy, in contrast to those of men, are more likely to be compassionate than "tough," communitarian than individualistic, public-interested than self interested. Whether the issue is arms control or capital punishment or welfare and social service programs, women differ systematically from men in their political views. (Verba, 1990, pp. 561–562)

Thus, there is reason to believe that changes in laws in a more humanistic direction will come about by increased representation of women in state and federal legislatures.

Evaluating Male and Female Candidates

Women and men use the same criteria in evaluating male candidates. Women rate female candidates as more attractive and competent than men rate them. Men are strongly influenced by a female politician's attractiveness in evaluating her competence.

Do men and women use the same "decision rules" in evaluating the attractiveness of male and female politicians? Sex differences in ratings of attractiveness and competence of 44 members of the U.S. House of Representatives by 117 undergraduate and graduate students (39% male; 61% female) indicated that they use the same decision rules for male politicians, but not for female politicians (K. E. Lewis & Brierly, 1990). No differences were found between men and women in ratings of attractiveness and competence of male politicians. Women rated female politicians, however, as more attractive and more competent than did men. Men's judgments of female politician's competence were highly influ-

enced by their level of attractiveness (accounting for 53% of the variance). Women's ratings of female politician's attractiveness, on the other hand, only accounted for 15% of the variance in the competence ratings. This research indicates that female politicians may benefit from women's votes, particularly when running against a male politician. An extremely attractive female politician, however, would be seen as more competent by men.

Female candidates need to be more "squeaky clean" than male candidates. Masculine characteristics are considered more important in candidates than feminine traits.

When a personal or family issue becomes problematic during a campaign, is a male or female candidate more at risk of losing an election? The behavior of a candidate's spouse or child did not differentially affect the likelihood that a college student would vote for a male or female candidate (Ogletree, Coffee, & May, 1992). Male candidates with previous psychological problems had a better chance, however, of being elected than did a female candidate with past psychological problems. A male candidate with past financial problems was also potentially more electable than a female candidate with past financial problems. It is apparent from these research studies that stereotypes impact on male and female candidates' likelihood of being elected. Female candidates need to be more "squeaky clean" than male candidates.

According to a study with college students, "masculine" traits from the BSRI were considered more important characteristics for local, state or national office than "feminine" traits (Rosenwasser & Dean, 1989). Candidates with "masculine" characteristics were rated more competent on "masculine" presidential tasks such as dealing with terrorism than on "feminine" presidential tasks such as solving problems in our educational system. Men were perceived as being more likely to win the office of president even when the women and men candidates had the same background, qualifications, and attributes.

POWER

Defining Power

Power is defined in terms of both the ability to exert power and to defend against power. Men have had greater access to the five bases of power (reward, coercive, referent, expert, and legitimate) than women have had.

What is power? Social psychologists define power in terms of "the ability to **exert** power, in the sense of controlling others and events, and the capacity to **defend** against power" (Hollander, 1985, p. 488). Most people do not appreciate the significance of the importance of defending against power. The women's movement has sought to empower women, which means to make inroads in male-dominated institutions such as the U.S. Senate, but also to defend against male power as exhibited in "take back the night" marches and the establishment of women's shelters for battered women, which seek to defend women against male violence.

The classic theory on power in the social psychological literature is J. R. P. French and Raven's model of the bases of power. They point out that an individual's ability to exert power derives from one or more of five bases of power: **reward power; coercive power; legitimate power; referent power; and expert power** (J. R. P. French & Raven, 1959). Reward power refers to a wide range of reinforcers that give a person what she/he needs, wants and values. Coercive power depends on fear. One is influenced by this power out of the fear of the negative consequences that might result if one fails to do what is requested. Expert power refers to the possession of valuable information, particularly when that information is unique or not widely shared. Legitimate power springs from one's position in society, the organization, or the group. A car pulls over to the side of the road when flagged down by a police officer. Referent power depends on identification with the person. Reference groups are groups with which the individual identifies. The individual internalizes the attitudes, beliefs, and behavior of referent persons or groups. Applying

French and Raven's bases of power to the relations between women and men, it is clear that men possess more bases of power. Men earn more money and therefore have greater material reward power at their disposal, which is perhaps why women rely more on socioemotional reward power, such as nurturing and love.

Men hold far more positions of authority in society; therefore, they have much greater legitimate power. Men have higher levels of professional and technical education and therefore have more expert power. The expert possesses superior skills, ability, and information, so that persons who think they are inferior will accept the influence attempts of the expert. Since male characteristics are more valued than female traits in our society (see Chapter IV) males therefore have greater referent power. With the advent of the women's movement, women have been encroaching on some of the traditional male bases of power. For example, women are entering graduate and professional schools in large numbers, creating women who are experts in many fields such as psychology, medicine, and law. Women are slowly increasing their numbers in positions that confer legitimate power. For example, two women now sit on the U.S. Supreme Court. There is still a large shortfall in the number of women who are power holders in legitimate positions compared with their percentages in the population. As far as coercive power goes, women have much greater fear of men than vice versa (rape, battering, homicide). Since men are more likely to be in positions of authority such as being the boss, women also fear such consequences as the loss of a job if they are not compliant.

Women also have traditional forms of power that they have always used. Nurturant power is the power to take care of others and to influence others because of the need they develop for the nurturer. Cooperative power is the ability to influence outcomes through cooperation with others. Socialization power is the power to mold children to develop specific skills, abilities, and characteristics through the socialization process. Sexual power has always been a potent source of women's influence over men. Reproductive power emanates from women's child-bearing capacity, which is valued in a patriarchal society. The recent acquisition of powers that were previously monopolized by men (expert, legitimate, reward) added to women's traditional powers will give women an increasingly powerful position in society.

THEORIES OF POWER

Theories of power locate power either within the individual or within the social structure. Experimental research shows that it is structural differences in power that can explain gender differences in power use. Women use power strategies associated with people in weaker positions.

Two different kinds of theories address the issue of gender and power, those that locate differences of power use within the individual, and those that locate it within the social structure (Molm & Hedley, 1992). A conceptualization of power taking into account both types of theories would include **structural power**, **power strategies,** and **power outcomes**. Structural power refers to an individual's control over resources or events that others value. "It is structural power that males have greater access to, in organizations, families, and political and economic relations" (Molm & Hedley, 1992, p. 2). The behavior of individuals takes place within this "macro" or structural level of power. Strategic power is the exercise of power by individuals that takes into account the behavior of other actors (the "micro" level of power). Power outcomes (does the person get what he/she wants in the relation) are a product of both the structure and the strategies of power use.

A series of experiments were conducted to test the effect of different dimensions of structural power on both power strategies and power outcomes, and how gender affects strategies of power use either alone or in interaction with structural power (Molm & Hedley, 1992). The four structural dimensions varied in these experiments were average reward power, average punishment power, reward-power imbalance, and punishment-power imbalance. The results of the study show that structural power explains substantially more of the variation in power outcomes than does gender. Power strategies of males were more influenced by structural power than were power strategies of females. "Females, like power-disadvantaged males, do not vary the contingency of their rewards or punishments with structural power imbalance" (Molm & Hedley, 1992, p. 18). On the other hand, powerful males decrease reciprocal reward or punishment strategies and increase nonreciprocal reward or punishment strategies as their reward or punishment power advantage increases. Males in a disadvantaged position reward their partners more than do females in that position. It is women's structural disadvantage that accounts for gender differences in power use. "To the extent that women are structurally disadvantaged, they are seriously impaired in their capacity to use power and to obtain more power resources through exchange." (Molm & Hedley, 1992, p. 23).

To view power differentials between men and women as an outcome of structural power is more hopeful than viewing power as an inherent part of the male personality in the way that Adrienne Rich (1976) implies.

It would seem therefore that from very ancient times the identity, the very personality, of the man depends on power, and on power in a certain, specific sense: that of power over others, beginning with a woman and her children. The ownership of human beings proliferates: from primitive or arranged marriage through contractual marriage-with-dowry through more recent marriage "for love" but involving the economic dependency of the wife, through the feudal system, through slavery and serfdom.

A review of the empirical literature (Sagrestano, 1992) concluded that gender is inextricably linked to power and status. Women use influence strategies associated with people in weaker positions. It is power in the organizational hierarchy, however, or society that is related to choice of influence tactics rather than gender.

Difficulty has arisen in the study of power due to the person–society dualism (Griscom, 1992). "A nondualistic perspective moves beyond interactionism to attend to the fact that individuality and sociality are part of each other" (Griscom, 1992, p. 390). By understanding that individual and society are part of each other, issues of race, ethnicity, class, sexuality, and other differences besides gender are not ignored. Much of psychology of women has also fallen into this trap by treating White, middle-class women as representative of all women.

Stereotyping a group of people is a way of exerting power over them. Power and control over a group of people is maintained and justified by stereotypes. The interaction between power and stereotyping is mediated by attention. In a study in which undergraduates made judgments about high school students' summer job applications, Goodwin and Fiske (as cited in Fiske, 1993) found as their power to make the decision increased, their attention to the applications decreased. On the other hand, a number of studies have shown that people pay attention to others who control their outcomes. In another laboratory study conducted by Depret and Fiske, (as cited in Fiske, 1993), undergraduates who expected to complete a task under the watchful eye of someone who had power to judge, reward, punish, or interfere with their performance paid more attention to them as their power increased. The attention level was highest for the person with power who was from an outgroup (in this case someone with a very different major). The powerful are not stereotyped, but the powerless are.

INFLUENCE STRATEGIES

Female Influence Strategies

The psychiatrist, Jean Baker Miller, describes female indirect influence strategies as based on the dominant–subordinate relationship between men and women. Inequality prevents open conflict around real differences.

Do women use weak influence strategies and men use strong influence strategies? Psychiatrist Jean Baker Miller, in her best-selling book, *Toward a New Psychology of Women* (1976, 1986), describes female influence strategies based on the dominant–subordinate relationship between men and women. The dominant group holds the power.

It follows that subordinates are described in terms of, and encouraged to develop, personal psychological characteristics that are pleasing to the dominant group. These characteristics form a certain familiar cluster: submissiveness, passivity, docility, dependency, lack of initiative, inability to act, to decide, to think, and the like. (J. B. Miller, 1986, p. 7)

On the other hand, when subordinates develop qualities like assertiveness and initiative they are defined as deviant. Many women have pretended to be dumb to remain in the good graces of the dominant group (men). Women use an indirect mode of influence because they live by trying to please men. They are attuned to and responsive to the needs of men. They attempt to transform their drives into achieving the desires of men.

Inequality generates hidden conflict. According to Jean Baker Miller (1986) inequality prevents open engagement around real differences. The woman may get what she wants by making it seem that it is what her husband wants. There is a considerable amount of manipulation and deception in such a relationship. In other relationships, the wife accepts the dominant group's depiction of her as inferior. She depends on the man to fulfill her needs, which may be unclear even to her.

When women reject inequality, it can lead to open conflict. Women who see their own needs as equally valid to that of men, may be accused of not living up to men's images of "true womanhood." "This can lead to discomfort, anxiety, and even more serious reactions for both parties. The hope, however, is that interaction between two resourceful and competent adults can bring the needs of both people closer to fulfillment" (J. B. Miller, 1986, p. 17). According to Jean Baker Miller, women need to stop suppressing conflict, which is difficult to do when you are dependent on the other person, and engage in productive conflict that can lead to change.

Influence strategies can be categorized along a strong/weak dimension. Some experimental research has supported Miller's clinical observations that women use weak influence strategies.

Falbo and Peplau (1980) developed a two-dimensional model of power strategies that defined power according to whether it is (1) **direct (versus indirect)** and (2) **bilateral (versus unilateral)**. Direct–unilateral strategies would be considered strong strategies, whereras indirect–bilateral would be considered weak strategies. In a direct–unilateral strategy the person would tell the other person what she/he wants her/him to do. A person using a direct–bilateral strategy would state her/his wishes, but also modify the request based on the other person's stated desires. In an indirect–unilateral strategy the person may use many kinds of strategies such as supplication, crying, and manipulating circumstances, such as taking a walk with her husband by a department store window in which the coat she wants is on display and commenting on how beautiful it would look on her, and so on. In an indirect–bilateral strategy the woman might first cook her husband his favorite meal to get him in a good mood and then bring up the subject of the coat she wants and elicit his response and perhaps work out something about how she could get it.

A number of researchers have used a strong–weak dichotomy in describing influence strategies (Cowan & Avants, 1988; Howard, Blumstein, & Schwartz, 1986). Bullying and autocracy would be considered strong strategies, while manipulation and supplication would be considered weak. Although some experimental research has supported Jean Baker Miller's clinical observations that women have less power than men and are therefore more likely to use indirect, manipulative strategies whereas men are more likely to employ rational, direct strategies

(Kipnis, 1984), other research has not supported these observations.

Dunn and Cowan (1993) compared Japanese and American college women in their use of strong and weak strategies. Japanese culture is one in which there is greater ascription to traditional gender roles. Contrary to their expectations, the researchers found that American women reported significantly more weak strategies overall than did Japanese women. American women used manipulation more frequently and reasoning less frequently than did the Japanese college women.

Because the primary role of women in Japan is that of mother (Long, 1986), the Japanese woman's role in the domestic sphere, traditional as it may be, may allot her a different, albeit equal, status to that of Japanese men. In contrast, American women have not yet achieved equality in the employment sphere nor are they valued in the private sphere. (Dunn & Cowan, 1993, p. 49)

A Eurocentric view that status and power only resides in the economic sphere, and that devalues the domestic sphere, may not be applicable in Eastern cultures.

Not all research, however, finds American college women to use weak influence strategies. A cross cultural comparison in the United States, Korea, and Japan found that men and women college students in all three cultures display a strong preference for direct versus indirect power strategies. No gender differences were found in any of the cultures in use of direct and indirect strategies. Students who perceived themselves as having greater power were less likely to employ indirect strategies. Perceived power did not vary by sex or cultural group. The Korean and Japanese students, however, did use less confrontational strategies than did the Americans. "Asian students were less likely to convince and more likely to acquiesce and accept opposition from both parents and friends than were their American counterparts" (Steil & Hillman, 1993, p. 462). This was a reflection of the Japanese and Korean students' concerns for politeness.

THE POWER MOTIVE

The Power Motive and Careers

Both men and women with a high need for power are likely to seek careers in teaching, psychology and therapy, and business management. Unlike women, men with a high need for power also may display an impulsive, profligate pattern of behavior. Socialization can direct the power motive into more useful channels.

Does power as a personality variable take different forms in women and men? A review of the research literature on the power motive (**n Power**) by Winter (1988) reveals that there are few gender differences in the "socially appropriate" exercise of power. Women and men with high *n* Power are likely to obtain formal social power such as by holding office, whether on campus or later in the community. Women with high *n* Power are likely to seek similar careers to those of men with high *n* Power (teaching, psychology and therapy, journalism, business management—the only exception being clergy, which no women studied entered). These are all careers in which one can influence others. These occupations, however, differ in certain structural features, whether they influence many or few people, whether the change is transient or lasting and the extent to which feedback is immediate or not.

> The roles of journalist, "pulpit clergy," lecturing faculty, and business executive are classified as directive power roles. Directive power jobs require influencing many people to a lesser extent, provide less immediate feedback, and require relatively more time in administration and paperwork than in influential actions like policymaking and persuading. In contrast, the relational power roles of teacher and psychologist (and of clergy in pastoral counseling) require inducing much (and quite personal) change in a few people, provide immediate feedback, and relatively large amounts of work days are spent exercising influence. (Jenkins, 1994, p. 157)

Both men and women with high *n* Power seek prestige and visibility, and the display of power symbols. There are, however, several striking gender differences in behavior of *n* Power women and men, with the men likely to display a pattern of behaviors labeled "expansive, profligate impulse."

> Thus, among men, n Power usually predicts drinking, drug use, physical and verbal aggression, gambling, precocious and exploitative sexuality, and reading "vicarious" or sexually oriented magazines. Further, as would be expected from these results, power-motivated men also have difficult and less stable intimate relationships with women and tend to oppress women both psychologically and economically. (Winter, 1988, p. 512–513)

Women high in *n* Power do not display this cluster of behaviors. The explanation for the difference in impulsive, profligate behaviors lie in traditional sex roles. "Thus, women who act in profligate ways might actually lose their power, be humiliated, locked up, abused, or even murdered" (Winter, 1988, p. 513). Predictive of responsible behavior for both men and women with high *n* Power is having younger siblings and/or having children. The differences in the impulsive/profligate dimension of power motivation appears to be the result of socialization rather than sex. The implications of this research is that early socialization in responsibility training such as early childcare can direct power motives into more socially useful channels such as responsible leadership while at the same time protecting society from the bad effects of profligate power.

Women high in n power show career progression 14 years after college graduation only when in power-relevant positions. Women in relational power careers and women who report job satisfaction in power careers show an increase in power motivation over time.

Career progression of 118 college seniors 14 years after graduation was predicted by *n* Power only for women in power relevant careers (teaching, including college; psychotherapy; journalism; and business management) (Jenkins, 1994).

Women in relational power careers showed an *n* Power increase over time, whereas those in directive power careers were more likely to decrease in *n* Power than were women in low power careers. People in directive power careers get less immediate feedback than women in relational power careers. "Using Jenkin's nomenclature, directive power careers appear more motive congenial in that they offer more visibility, prestige, opportunities for alliance, and autonomy and attract high *n* Power women, but they are not motive arousing" (Jenkins, 1994, p. 163). Women high in *n* Power reported more power-relevant job satisfaction and dissatisfaction. Those women who reported greater overall job satisfaction in job roles with power attributes (whether task role or hierarchal demands) showed an increase in *n* Power during the 14 years since college. "If the job situation requires power behavior but frustrates the attainment of power rewards as directive power roles appear to do (Jenkins, 1992), it increases dissatisfaction among high n Power-workers and lowers n Power arousal" (Jenkins, 1994, p. 164).

Women's Subordinate Role in Society

Theories of women's subordinate roles carry a political agenda.

Four types of subordination theories have been put forth to explain women's subordinate role in society: (1) early adaptation or the "hunting hypothesis" assumes that early humans lived on the savannas of eastern and southern Africa and males did most of the hunting and shared the meat with their females and offspring, which made the females dependent on the males; (2) technical-environmental theories postulate that to avoid overpopulation, cultural institutions emerged such as warfare in which men went to battle and female infanticide as a means of birth control giving males superior status; (3) sociobiological theory is based on reproductive differences, that a female has very few eggs, which gives her greater investment in her young than does a male who produces many sperm; there-

fore, she must attract and persuade a male to take care of her and her offspring; and (4) structural theories argue that women have lower status and authority because women's child-bearing and childcare responsibilities tie women to home and hearth, while men are involved in the public sphere conferring on them greater power (Gailey, 1987).

According to Gailey, theories of women's subordination carry a political agenda.

The sociobiological approaches suggest that movements for women's equality are senseless, even destructive, because they fly in the face of inclusive fitness and sexual selection as natural laws. . . . Technico-environmentalists would offer technological solutions, such as reducing women's subordination through birth control and population planning . . . The dependency of females and children—assumed to be primal—could be redirected to the state, presumably, instead of to husband or fathers. (Gailey, 1987, pp. 60–61)

Sociobiological theory, in particular, has been attacked on many grounds. Several of these criticisms were discussed in Chapter II. Gender hierarchy may be explained simply in terms of our capacity to create symbols according to Gailey (1987). Subordinate groups are relatively powerless groups.

POWER IN INTIMATE RELATIONSHIPS

Resource Theory

The person with greater resources generally has greater power in marriage.

Resource theory is one of the most popular theories to explain power in relationships. The person who has higher education, income, and occupational prestige generally has more power relative to their spouses (Blood & Wolfe, 1960). In a marriage, because women are expected to find someone with more resources, women often turn to other means of power such as love. In dating and marriage, the partner less in love has

Focus on Women   The LaPiere Family

Ed and Lynn are a couple in their 40s. They are the parents of Paul and Marie and grandparents to Andy. Paul is married to Diane and they are the parents of Andy, age 11 months. Marie is single, and has been going steady for two years with Ken. For Ed, Lynn, Paul, and Diane, this family group is their most important reference group. Ed and Lynn and Paul and Diane share many of the same traditional values and beliefs about the roles of husband and wife. Ken and Marie have many other reference groups that have aided in their developing differing beliefs. Despite these differences, the group as a whole is still very cohesive.

Ed owns his own used-car business and is a very hard worker. Ed does not have a high school education, and is very proud of what he has accomplished without an education and of his "breadwinner" role. He is also very dedicated to his family. Lynn, Ed's wife, was forced by her mother to quit school at the age of 16 to help support the family. Lynn is ashamed of her lack of education and encourages Marie to go as far as she can with her education. Since Ed is the sole provider (Lynn has been working since Paul and Marie grew up, but what she earns is considered her money, not the family's), he is unquestioningly granted the highest status in the group.

Marie has followed her mother's advice and is now a graduate student, although she still lives at home and commutes to classes. Marie is liberal in her attitudes, and is career and goal oriented. She values equality between the sexes and refuses to be referred to as anyone's possession (i.e., "My girl"). Her brother, Paul, challenges her from time to time by expecting her to wait on him. When sitting at the table, he will tell her to get up to get him a soda or a piece of cake. Marie refuses to do so until the demand is phrased as a polite request. Often, the result of Paul's demand that Marie get something for him is that Lynn will perform the task and verbally or with eye contact reprimand Marie. On the other hand, Ken, Marie's boyfriend, believes in equality between the sexes and is the only male who will do anything in the house such as pitch in to clean the table after the weekly family

Sunday dinner. Ed and Paul tell Ken he should not allow himself to be dominated and controlled by Marie. Ken is a likeable guy with a good sense of humor, and often breaks the tension within the group by making funny comments. Ken has recently returned to college and works as a truck driver and cook in the summer.

Paul does not value education and dropped out of high school in the ninth grade. Although immature and irresponsible for several years, now in his early 20s, with a wife and baby, he is a dedicated worker at a job he loves. His wife, Diane, was extremely shy when she first joined the group. She is a very dedicated mother and considers it her first duty to care for her husband and child. Recently, she has taken a home-based computer job and claims that Paul will be expected to help out in the house more now.

Because of the "breadwinner ethic" of the family, Ed gives most of the orders, and is not challenged by other group members and receives the most respect. Lynn often makes suggestions, such as the one she recently made about the group's going to Newport for the day. Ken and Marie, who were present, agreed, and then Ed was asked if it was okay. If Ed had decided not to go, the group would not have gone. When they left the house, Ed stopped at Paul and Diane's and asked them if they wanted to go, too. They said they did, if the others would wait while they got ready. Without consulting Lynn, Marie, and Ken who were sitting in the car, Ed said they would wait. This is just on everyday example that what Ed decides is the action to be taken is then executed by the group.

Lynne's most important role, in her opinion, is taking care of her husband. She also plays a socioemotional role for the group as a whole. If Paul and Diane have a fight, they will often separately go to Lynn for advice about the situation. If Marie needs extra gas money during the week, she is more likely to ask Lynn than to go to Ed. Whenever there are problems, members of the group go to Lynn. Lynn really enjoys this role because she loves to know everything that is going on in the group members' lives. Lynn is a very good listener.

more power in the relationship (Sprecher, 1985; Peplau & Campbell, 1989).

When married couples have equal responsibility for providing financially for the family, wives use fewer power strategies to get their way, and they are more satisfied than traditional wives (Aida & Falbo, 1991). In their study of 42 nonstudent married couples, there were no differences among equal-partner husbands and wives in use of power strategies and marital satisfaction. Satisfied marital partners were significantly less likely to use indirect strategies (dropping hints, crying, acting helpless, withdrawal, etc.) to get their way. Being in an imbalanced resource relationship, such as a traditional marriage where the husband works and the wife stays home, may lead to the greater use of power strategies.

Although women gain economically from marriage, marriage decreases women's perceived control.

Women gain economically from marriage. Compared with unmarried women, married women are in an economically advantaged position. Although higher household income is associated with higher perceived control in one's life (the expectation that one's behavior will affect outcomes), marriage decreases women's sense of perceived control. For men, marriage is less related to sense of control in their lives. "Marriage presents a trade-off for women's sense of control: on the one hand it increases it by way of increased household income, but on the other hand it decreases it, probably by way of subordination, dependence or lack of autonomy" (C. E. Ross, 1991, p. 837).

Both heterosexual and homosexual partners of males use weak influence tactics such as manipulation and supplication. The partner who controls fewer resources also uses weak influence strategies.

Sex is a status characteristic in society. Men and women have differential access to power.

Both women and homosexual men are found to use "weak" influence tactics of manipulation and supplication with male partners (Howard, Blumstein, & Schwartz, 1986). The authors attribute the use of these strategies to the characteristics of the male partner. "The power associated with being male thus appears to be expressed in behavior that elicits weak strategies from one's partner" (Howard et al., 1986, p. 107). Controlling fewer resources, such as having less income and seeing oneself as the less attractive partner, was also related to "weak" influence tactics, but could not account for the influence styles used with male partners. Lesbians report more shared decision making than did married or cohabiting heterosexual couples, or male homosexual partners (Kurdek & Schmitt, 1986).

Egalitarian Couples

When husbands and wives contribute equally to financial resources they use fewer power strategies and have higher levels of marital satisfaction.

Research studies of husband–wife power interactions have consistently indicated that highest levels of satisfaction are most often found among egalitarian couples (Gray-Little & Burks, 1983). Greater levels of marital satisfaction are also found for individuals reporting equality of decision making among Mexican American couples (Bean, Curtis, & Marcum, 1977). The most likely marriages to be unhappy are where the wife is dominant (Gray-Little & Burks, 1983). This is true for Black as well as for White couples (Gray-Little, 1982). Of 12 post-1960 studies reviewed by Gray-Little and Burks (1983) eight reported that the highest levels of marital satisfaction were linked to egalitarian decision making and two to husband-dominated decisions.

What are marriages like between couples who espouse a feminist ideology? Ten White, educated, couples married for five or more years who were self-identified feminists prior to marriage and at the time of interviews confirmed even in feminist marriages a distinction between the ide-

Focus on Women   Share and Share Alike

George, a college science professor, and Ellie, a college administrator, met the first week of their freshman year in college. They will celebrate their thirty-first wedding anniversary this year. Four-and-a-half years later, after graduation, they married. George went into a doctoral program and Ellie taught school while pursuing a master's degree at night. They say their marriage has been egalitarian from the beginning and has become stronger with the years. From the beginning George and Ellie shared the household responsibilities. They also shared the same checking account, with both putting their paychecks into it. George and Ellie even share the same den at home—he has his desk, and she her table.

George and Ellie's only child, Melissa, was born six years after they married. Both participated in childcare, changing diapers, reading to her, bathing her, feeding her, and playing with her. Life became somewhat more hectic after Melissa was born, so when she was about two or three years old, they sat down and made a list of household responsibilities. The list had about 25 items ranging from chores such as cooking to cutting the grass

and cleaning the toilets and balancing the checkbooks. Each took a turn selecting an item as they went down the list. That chore became the person's responsibility who chose it and has remained so over the years. Now that the couple is financially better off, each may decide to hire someone to perform the chore, such as cutting the grass or hiring a cleaning woman to come in every other week, but that person still has the responsibility of overseeing that the chore gets done. George admits, however, that since they both grew up in working class families, he feels somewhat uncomfortable about hiring someone to come in to do housework, even if it is only for one day every other week.

George and Ellie have had an open and honest relationship with Melissa. They had few rules when she was growing up, and she was not a rebellious teenager. Their most difficult time with Melissa was after she graduated from college and came home to live, but did not seem to know in which direction she wanted to go or what she wanted to do. After a few years, Melissa enrolled in law school where she is currently a student, living in her own apartment.

ology and practice of equality (Blaisure & Allen, 1995). Although there was not a complete sharing of "the second shift," these couples did engage in many behaviors that served to upgrade the marriage experience for women.

> Couples reported the practice of vigilance, defined as an attending to and a monitoring of equality, within and outside of their relationship. This vigilance of equality appeared as five processes: (a) critique of gender injustices, (b) public acts of equality, (c) support of wives' activities, (d) reflective assessment, and (e) emotional involvement. (Blaisure & Allen, 1995, p. 5)

All of the couples reported the first three processes, but only four of the couples used all five processes. The four couples who used all five processes of vigilance also reported equal sharing of parenting, household, and domestic tasks.

This research suppports the view that feminist women can achieve equality in heterosexual marriage with a partner who shares beliefs in gender equality.

Power in Violent Marriages

Husbands in violent marriages use violence as a power strategy.

A comparison study of 137 self-identified battered and 137 comparison wives found that husbands in violent marriages used violence as a power strategy that led to higher levels of decision making by them (Frieze & McHugh, 1992). Women in violent marriages made use of most of the influence strategies with less use of positive indirect strategies and more use of indirect strategies of ignoring and withdrawing. They also made more use of the direct strategies of saying they were an expert and of coercive strategies. They did not, however, make more use of direct positive strategies of talking things over and of using past (informational) experience. "The use of physical coercion and ignoring in the women in our study married to violent men was predictive of low decision-making power for these women, which suggests that such strategies are reactive or defensive, rather than direct attempts to influence the partner" (Frieze & McHugh 1992, p. 462). Husband violence was a significant predictor of lower levels of wives' satisfaction.

Age and Power

Although women are perceived as more powerful as they age, that may not be based on any actual changes in behavior of women.

A number of studies have noted a shift in power between men and women as they age, with women being perceived as relatively more powerful and men as relatively less powerful in their second half of life (Gutmann, 1987; V. Mitchell & Helson, 1990; Todd, Friedman, & Kariuki, 1990). Gutmann (1987) argued that the "parental emergency" caused by females taking care of children develops their empathy and nurturing side while men become competitive and aggressive to earn the families' living.

A study conducted in Israel with 60 members from two kibbutzim and 60 from an urban center confirmed the findings of previous research of a shift in perceived power with age (A. Friedman, Tzukerman, Weinberg & Todd, 1992). The research, based on stories told to a picture from the Thematic Apperception Test (TAT) of a man and a woman, was conducted with married participants, with the younger group having a mean age of 33 years and the older group a mean age of 62 years. The behavior of men and women were not seen to change with age, but the evaluation of the behavior changed. "Furthermore, older women used traditionally feminine power strategies, but their behavior was evaluated as more powerful than the same behavior in younger women" (A. Friedman et al., 1992, p. 513). This study,

therefore, does not support the notion that men become more "feminine" and women more "masculine" with age; rather, it showed that the same power strategies are used by older men and women, but now are perceived differently.

Cybernetic Theory

Cybernetic theory, a feedback process of maintaining a desired state of control, can explain increased attempts at control over one's partner in dating relationships in situations of high conflict or low-perspective taking.

Cybernetic theory, a feedback process of monitoring one's own behavior so that one's perceived state approximates one's desired state of control, has been used to explain the process of power in dating relationships (Stets, 1992).

It is argued that individuals act to increase their level of control over others in those stages of dating relationships where control over the situation has been threatened or disturbed by others either because of high conflict or lack of perspective taking. (Stets, 1992, p. 673)

Data obtained from a random telephone sample of 7,000 respondents of never-married persons between the ages of 18 and 30 supports cybernetic theory. Respondents were asked questions about their current or most recent dating relationship. A nine-item scale with items relating to making partners do what they want or stop doing something was used to measure control.

It was found that low-perspective taking increased conflict and control over another. Involvement in serious relationships was also related to conflict and increased control. Therefore, increased control over one's partner occurs when one perceives levels of control in the situation to be below some desired level. Under conditions of both low-perspective taking and high conflict, one increases one's attempt to control the situation. A surprising finding of the research was that women were more likely than men to act to control their partners. The researchers suggest that it may be due to the fact that women have greater control over love.

Power in Black and White Marriages

Although there has been conflicting research, it has been suggested that men have greater power in both Black and White marriages. Wives greater use of negative affect in marriage may be tied to husbands' having more power.

A number of studies have examined power structures within Black and White families. Black families have traditionally depended on the wife's income more than White families have, leading some researchers to suggest that Black women are more powerful in their families than are White women (Landry & Jendrick, 1978; Scanzoni, 1975). The research is conflicting about whether Black husbands perform more of the household chores than do White husbands (Broman, 1988; Willie, 1985).

Interaction in marital relations was studied by means of interviews with a representative sample of urban, newlywed couples (199 Black and 174 White) in first marriages in which the wife was under 35 years of age (Oggins, Veroff, & Leber, 1993). White, but not Black, husbands reported significantly less self-disclosure than did their wives. White wives also reported less self-disclosure than did Black wives. Black husbands reported receiving more affirmation from their wives than did White husbands, and more than the Black wives felt they received from their husbands. Husbands were less likely than wives to report using destructive ways of resolving conflicts and more likely to report using constructive styles such as trying to compromise. "Wives' use of negative affect in conflict may also be tied to husbands' greater power in marriage" (Oggins et al., 1993, p. 507).

Men thought they helped out in the home more than wives thought they did. Women were somewhat more likely to report doing the housecleaning than their husbands. Men reported more power in decision making than did wives. "It ap-

pears that for Blacks and Whites alike, men's greater power in American society is also reflected in marriage" (Oggins et al., Veroff & Leber, 1993, p. 507). The presence of children in the home was associated with "a more traditional assignment of childcare . . . more destructive conflict . . . finding one's spouse less supportive . . . and reporting less affective affirmation" (Oggins et al., 1993, pp. 503–504). Overall, marital well-being was strongly predicted by marital interactions that affirmed one's sense of identity.

Racial differences appear in men's attitudes about gender roles. Data analysis from the NLS of the Labor Market Experiences, a probability sample survey, found little evidence of maternal influence on son's attitudes toward gender roles (Blee & Tickamyer, 1995). African American young men were found to be significantly more liberal than were White young men on attitudes toward wives working. On more general gender-role issues, however, African American men had more conservative attitudes than did White men. Over time, both groups of men showed increasingly liberal attitudes. Among White men, but not among Black men, education and income were positively associated with more liberal gender-role attitudes.

LEADERSHIP

Dominance

Research findings support the belief that males are more dominant than females. Research conducted with Black participants, however, does not find males to be more dominant than females.

Research findings, with both humans and other primates, support the belief that males are more dominant than females. Studies on group interaction document that men display more dominance and are more likely to achieve high status in a group than are women, even when the females have been preselected for dominance (Megargee, 1969; Fleischer & Chertkoff, 1986; Nyquist & Spence, 1986). In these studies, participants were pretested (California Personality Inventory, Dominance) to determine their level of dominance. A person low in dominance was then paired with another who was high in dominance. The pair was instructed to determine which of them was to be the leader, and to engage in a reasoning task. When interacting in a same-sex pair, 73% of the high dominant partners became the leader. This percentage rose to 90% in mixed-sex pairs in which the man was high in dominance. However, in mixed-sex dyads in which the woman was high in dominance, a woman became the leader only 35% of the time (Nyquist & Spence, 1986).

On personality inventories that measure dominance, males consistently score higher than females in high school, college, and adult groups (Anastasi, 1958). In mixed-gender groups, men dominate the discussion, talking more than females, interrupting females, or ignoring them (Lockheed & Hall, 1976). This behavior is characteristic of a person who has higher status in a group. Bernice Lott (1987) found that when performing a task with a stranger, men tended to make more negative comments, turn away from their partner more, and less frequently follow their advice when they were women than when they were men.

Race, another status characteristic in society—one that determines the status ascribed to someone in a group when it first comes together—interacts with gender in influencing dominance behavior. Although Black females may be expected to show the least dominance, because they are a double minority and have low status in terms of both sex and race, this prediction is not supported by research. In a laboratory experiment in which the number of challenges a student sustained was used as a measure of dominance, Black females were more dominant than either White females or Black males (K. A. Adams, 1983). White males were more dominant than Black males. These results suggest less status differential in Black male–female relationships than in White male–female relationships. Sweeping generalizations about male dominance cannot be made. Male dominance appears to be true of White, but not Black, male–female relationships, at least among strangers in laboratory situations.

Leadership Emergence

Men emerge more often as leaders than do women. On measures of social leadership women emerge more frequently than do men.

The earlier research on gender and leadership focused on leadership emergence. Are men or women more likely to emerge as leaders in small, initially leaderless, mixed-sex groups? It was found that men emerged as leaders much more frequently than did women. In classic studies of mock juries, (Strodtbeck & Mann, 1956) found that men were much more likely to be selected as jury foremen than were women.

Eagly and Karau (1991) conducted a meta-analysis on gender differences in emergence of leadership in initially leaderless mixed sex-groups, finding that men emerge more often as leaders than do women on general leadership (mean weighted $d = +0.32$). When the type of leadership was task leadership, men were also more likely to emerge as leaders (mean weighted $d = +0.41$), and similarly for unspecified leadership (mean weighted $d = +.29$). Women, however, emerge more frequently than do men on measures of social leadership (mean weighted $d = -.18$). This tendency for men to become leaders lessened the longer the group interaction prior to leader selection. This could be a reflection of the lesser influence of the person's gender and the greater role of task-relevant competence as more information is gained through the process of interaction. Male leadership was particularly likely when the tasks on which the groups were working did not require complex social interactions. Women's social interaction skills became more relevant to tasks requiring negotiation and sharing of ideas. Eagly and Karau conclude that these findings are consistent with Eagly's gender-role theory of sex differences.

The tendency for men to emerge as leaders was less for more recently published studies than for earlier studies in groups with a male or female majority, but not in groups with an equal sex composition.

Perhaps in a modern cultural context the impact of an unequal sex ratio is not merely to increase the salience of members of the numerically rare sex but also to increase the salience of gender-equality issues. (Eagly & Karav, 1991, p. 704)

Men were particularly likely to emerge as leaders in short-term groups and those not requiring complex social interactions. Male leadership emergence was also more pronounced for groups with older persons. Raising the consciousness of women and men about the tendency to defer leadership to men, however, can result in men and women sharing leadership equally.

Leadership Style

Women leaders are more concerned with interpersonal relationships in assessment studies and laboratory experiments, but no gender differences in leadership style emerge in organizational studies. Women in all three types of studies are more democratic and participative leaders than are men.

Much of the research on gender and leadership has been conducted on leadership style. The research findings most frequently cited by textbooks fit the stereotypes, indicating that men are more likely to initiate a higher proportion of their acts in task-oriented categories, and women to concentrate their behavior in social–emotional categories (Lockheed & Hall, 1976; Nemeth, Endicott, & Wachtler, 1976; R. T. Stein & Heller, 1979; Strodtbeck & Mann, 1956). A meta-analysis on the leadership style question compared two different facets of leadership style: (1) task style versus interpersonal style; and (2) autocratic versus democratic style (Eagly & Johnson, 1991). The data showed a small but significant difference in the direction of women being more interpersonally oriented than men ($d = -13$). However, a small but significant difference was also found, contrary to the stereotype, in the direction of women being more task-oriented than men ($d = -0.06$).

Because of the considerable variability between the studies included in the meta-analysis, the data was partitioned into separate studies of organizational leaders and managers, assessment studies (in which people simply respond to a paper and pencil questionnaire about their leadership style), and laboratory experiments conducted with college students (Eagly & Johnson, 1991). In contrast to the stereotypes that women have a more interpersonally oriented style of leadership, there were no gender differences in interpersonal style in organizational settings. However, consistent with stereotypic expectations, women were more concerned with social relationships than were men in assessment studies ($d = -0.25$) and in laboratory experiments ($d = -0.37$). These results are in line with Eagly's gender-role theory predictions that although behavior tends to be stereotypic in experimental settings, it should be much less so for men and women who occupy the same roles in organizations.

The criteria organizations use for selecting managers and the forces they maintain for socializing managers into their roles minimize tendencies for the sexes to lead or manage in a stereotypic manner. Yet these data also suggest that people not selected or trained for leadership roles do manifest stereotypic leadership behavior when placed in these roles, as shown by the data from the assessment and the laboratory studies. (Eagly & Johnson, 1991, p. 247)

The largest gender difference ($d = -0.27$) showed women to be more democratic and participative in their approach to leadership, and men to be more autocratic. This finding held up across all three types of studies (laboratory, assessment, and organizational). Eagly and Johnson suggest that this difference stems from women's greater interpersonal skills that make it easier for them to be participative—asking for suggestions and inviting subordinates to take part in decision making.

Sex role orientation of the leader, rather than sex per se, also influences the leader's style (Jose & McCarthy, 1988). Men and women who had high scores in masculinity were perceived to have talked more and to have better ideas than men and women with other sex role orientations.

Women and feminine individuals were rated as being more concerned about group members' feelings, than men and individuals low in femininity. Androgynous individuals were marginally perceived to have displayed both more task-related and social behaviors.

Leadership Effectiveness

Overall, men and women are equally effective leaders.

A meta-analysis averaged across 76 studies of gender differences in leader effectiveness aggregated across both organizational and laboratory experimental research found a mean weighted effect size that did not differ from 0.00 (Eagly, Karau, & Makhijani, 1995). Thus, there was no overall gender difference in leadership effectiveness. Certain conditions, however, were associated with greater effectiveness of leadership for men or women. "Specifically, sex differences in leaders' effectiveness were significantly correlated with the congeniality of their roles for men or women, as indexed by our questionnaire respondents' judgments of competence and interest in relation to the roles" (Eagly et al., 1995, p. 137). Although gender differences in leaders' effectiveness did not vary depending on whether the study's setting was an organization or an experimental laboratory, the type of organization did relate to effectiveness. Findings from one type of organization—the military—differed from all others, significantly favoring male leaders. Military roles were masculine on a number of dimensions, including numerical dominance by men. Differences were also found in male and female leadership effectiveness by hierarchical position. Effectiveness comparisons favored men for first-level or line leadership ($d = 0.19$), and favored women for second or middle-level leadership ($d = -0.18$). Men were also more effective as leaders as the percentage of men among the leaders and the percentage of men among subordinates increased. These findings are consistent with Eagly's social-role theory as applied to leadership, which predicts that individual's generally favor gender role consistent behavior and are more motivated to act in those roles.

> If the trend of the past decades continues so that more women enter managerial roles, including at the highest levels, the shaping of people's expectations according to the gender of leaders and managers should weaken . . . Thus, the entry of a substantial proportion of women into managerial roles may itself change the perception of these roles in an androgynous direction. Alternatively, for reasons unrelated to women's participation in management, many organizations may be changing to favor styles of management that are less autocratic and more participative, producing managerial roles that tend to be more congenial to women (see Offerman & Gowing, 1990). (Eagly et al., 1995, pp. 140–141)

The overall finding of no gender difference in effectiveness between men and women leaders shows that despite barriers and prejudice toward women as leaders, women who serve in leadership and managerial positions do succeed in those roles.

Evaluations of Male and Female Leaders

Females' intellectual assertiveness elicits negative nonverbal reactions from fellow group members in mixed-sex groups. Overall, female leaders are evaluated somewhat more negatively than are male leaders.

In a laboratory experiment, it was found that competent assertiveness on the part of women leaders elicits nonverbal cues of negative affect from others that are misinterpreted as evidence of poor contributions (D. Butler & Geis, 1990). Discussion groups consisted of one male and one female náive participant and one male and one female confederate, one of whom assumed leadership in each group. Female leaders' intellectual assertiveness also elicited fewer positive nonverbal responses from fellow group members than did men offering the same suggestions and arguments. "These data provide evidence that leadership and gender expectations are prescriptive as well as descriptive" (D. Butler & Geis, 1990, p. 54). In other words, women leaders exhibiting the same behaviors as men are punished rather than rewarded as are the men, which is a way of telling women that they should not be behaving that way.

A number of experiments have held the characteristics of the leader constant while varying only sex to determine followers' reactions to the leader. For example, a study of four-person problem-solving groups, in which either a male or a female confederate played an active role in solving all four problems, found that the male leaders were evaluated higher in competence than were the female leaders, although their performance was identical (Rollins, et al., 1982). Eagly, Makhijani, and Klonsky (1992), in their meta-analysis of experiments using this type of design, found that there was a small overall tendency for female leaders to be evaluated less favorably than male leaders. The tendency was greater under certain conditions: when leadership was stereotypically masculine (autocratic or directive); when leaders occupied male-dominated roles; and when the evaluators were men.

SUCCESSFUL WOMEN LEADERS

Women who are very successful in their positions have high ambition, love their work, have "megavision," have perseverance, and combine business and people skills.

What are successful women leaders really like? How did they get there? To answer these questions Gardenswartz and Rowe (1987) interviewed 100 women who fit their definition of success: women who were top officers of large corporations; entrepreneurs who started businesses that achieved over $5 million worth of business a year; public servants in high elected or appointed political offices; and pioneers or groundbreakers in a field. Among these women were Shirley Hufstedler, who was the first Secretary of the U.S. Department of Education; Congresswoman Pat Schroeder of Colorado; Eileen Ford, co-owner of Ford Models, Inc.; then-Mayor of San Francisco

and now U. S. Senator from California, Dianne Feinstein; and Mary Kay Ash, whose company has more women earning over $50,000 a year than any other in the country.

Culled from their interviews with these 100 women, Gardenswartz & Rowe, 1987, concluded that there are five factors common to these women: (1) The women all have compelling ambition, in other words, a high need to achieve; (2) They love their business or profession and work very hard at it; (3) They have "megavision"—they dream on a grand scale and they have a deeply rooted belief in themselves; (4) These successful women have a "no excuses, just results" attitude that is marked by the ability to overcome obstacles and persevere in achieving their goals; (5) they use "practical magic," which is a combination of business savvy and interpersonal skills and zealous learning.

A book by Cantor and Bernay, *Women in Power, The Secrets of Leadership (1992)*, describes the leadership secrets of 25 prominent women politicians in the United States. The women did not report having faced obstacles. They related how their confidence in their own abilities had enabled them to succeed. Based on these interviews, the authors developed the following equation: Leadership = Competent Self + Creative Aggression + Woman Power.

Just as women are redefining other aspects of life such as sexuality, knowledge, family, and justice, women are redefining leadership. Helen Astin and Carole Leland (1991) studied 77 women leaders during the span of three decades (the 1950s, 1960s, and 1970s). These women were leaders of educational institutions, foundations, government agencies, heads of programs about women, and women who provided leadership through their scholarly work on women. Based on the data they gathered, Astin and Leland propose a new model to examine leadership. "The model identifies four key elements in any study of leadership: (1) the leader, (2) the context, (3) the leadership processes, and (4) the outcomes" (Astin & Leland, 1991, p. 156). The women they studied conceived of leadership as a process of collective action, passionate commitment and consistent performance.

In another study of successful career women in diverse occupational fields, Northcutt (1991) identified the personal and demographic characteristics as well as the differences in achievement/motivation and self-esteem of these women. Participants in her research were 249 successful career women in a large city in southern Arizona who had received recognition by a professional organization, civic group, women's recognition event, or their employers.

The three largest occupational fields of the successful women were business, 91 (36.6%); health services, 52 (20.9%), and education 36 (14.5%). The great majority had one or more child (70.7%). Although 58.6% of the women were married, nearly half of these women (49.9%) were the primary support for themselves and their families, while 30.5% equally shared primary financial support for self/family and 19.7% did not provide the primary financial support. Among men, this probably would not be considered a particularly successful group, at least financially. Mentors played an important role for most of these women.

EMPOWERING WOMEN AND MINORITIES

Transforming Education

Kreisberg suggests developing the concept of power "with" rather than power "over" in order to transform the schools and empower women and minorities.

Kreisberg (1992) criticizes the dynamics of authoritarian education and argues for the importance of developing a liberating or emancipatory pedagogy for our schools. Although feminist postmodernism has began to address some of the issues of education and society, its weakness has been a failure to move beyond the conceptualization of power as domination. If educators want to end oppression of women and minorities, and expand opportunities for individuals based on mutual action, they need to develop the concept of power in order to fulfill the potential of educa-

tion. "The themes of voice, synergy, synergistic community, balance of assertiveness and openness, vulnerability, assertive mutuality, co-agency, integration, dialogue, and shared decision making are essential in the discourse of empowerment and a reconceived notion of power" (Kreisberg, 1992, pp. 194–195).

An organization devoted to transforming schools is Educators for Social Responsibility which was founded in 1982 by educators concerned about addressing concerns about the possibility of nuclear war. The organization was broadened by teachers and educators to have the mission of educating students to develop the values and skill necessary for creating a more just and humane world. Kreisberg (1992) studied the methods used by the steering committee of the Boston Area Educators for Social Responsibility (BAESR) as ways of fostering empowerment of students. In all of the classes students were given a say in decision making. "In Gene's classroom, decision making occurred in town meetings with regard to the everyday rules, problems, and issues involved in the functioning of the community. In town meetings teachers and students had an equal vote, and a two-thirds majority was needed for a measure to be approved" (Kreisberg, 1992, p. 170).

The implementation of the decisions and taking responsibility for the consequences was equally as important as the decision making. Students develop interpersonal skills in the process of shared decision making and working together to put the decision into action. They come to identify with the group, and in so doing come to care about themselves and about other people in the class.

In a reexamination of power, Kreisberg (1992) proposes power **with** rather than power **over**. In this formulation she draws on the work of Jean Baker Miller, who suggests that women can gain power to advance their own development, but not use this power to infringe on the rights and potential of others. It is a power that enhances both ourselves and others. It is power based on the reward structure of cooperation rather than competition. Power has traditionally been viewed in terms of domination of individuals or groups by other individuals or groups. A new age is dawning in which empowerment is proposed as an antidote to powerlessness.

> On one level empowerment is described as a psychological process. It is intimately connected with individual's feelings of self-worth and self-confidence and sense of efficacy. But empowerment is also inseparably linked to the social and political conditions in which people live. (Kreisberg, 1992, p. 19)

Kreisberg emphasizes the importance of a democratic education as necessary for empowerment of students. A key of this democratic education is in the relationship of teacher and students.

Reclaiming Women's Souls

The male God in the world's religions represents power over women's souls and the legitimation of patriarchy. Although women are ministers in most protestant churches, they are still not permitted to be Catholic priests or Orthodox Jewish rabbis. Some women worship the goddess as a symbol of female power.

Religion represents a power not just over one's mind, but over one's soul as well. According to Mary Daly (1993) God is male in all of the major world religions, and this serves to legitimize patriarchy. Women are objectified as "the other." The priesthood and other positions of authority in the Roman Catholic church are reserved for men, as it was until very recently in most other Judeo-Christian churches. The United Church of Christ, the American Baptist Churches, and the Disciples of Christ, however, had women ministers since the ninteenth century. Reform Judaism ordained the first woman rabbi in 1972, but Orthodox Jews still do not allow women to be rabbis. Nevertheless, by the early 1980s women were a majority in some of the leading theological seminaries (J. W. Carroll, Hargrove, & Lummis, 1983; Lehman, 1985).

One response to the marginalization of women within the Judeo-Christian tradition is a return to the Goddess symbol. The symbol of the Goddess is an affirmation of female power.

> The symbol of Goddess has much to offer women who are struggling to be rid of the "powerful, pervasive, and long-lasting moods and motivations" of devaluation of female power, denigration of the female body, distrust of female will, and denial of the women's bonds and heritage that have been engendered by patriarchal religion. (C. P. Christ, 1993, p. 246)

Women around the country stand on rocky hills at the time of the full moon or solstice paying tribute to the Goddess symbol of the cyclical energies of the universe and in themselves. That may seem far out to some readers, but in order to truly value women is it not necessary to confront patriarchal thinking in the religious sphere as well as other spheres of life?

"There is a great multiplicity of ways in which women's spiritual experience is being expressed and named" (Tulip, 1990, p. 259). Many Christian women in the United States are in the process of forming Women-Church, which is a coming together of women to challenge the patriarchal authority figures of male dominated churches. In her book, *Women-Church*, Rosemary Reuther (1985) says that it is not enough to engage in an ideology of criticism of the Christian church. Women cannot wait for institutional reform in contemporary churches; rather, they must form their own communities with their own symbols, rituals, theology, and practice. Women-Church is only one of the groups of feminist theologizing taking form throughout the world (Tulip, 1990).

WOMEN AND POVERTY

Psychology needs to design more adequate research with poor women and ethnic women.

Poor women have not only been excluded from the resources of society, they have also largely been excluded from psychological research. Single-parent female householders represent nearly half of all poor households in the

United States. Poor women are also found in households with a male present.

> Poor women are elderly with inadequate medical care and emotional support. Poor women are teenage mothers and high-school dropouts. They are welfare recipients and underpaid employees. They are clerical workers, receptionists, sales clerks, waitresses, babysitters, hotel maintenance staff, and domestic workers. (P. T. Reid, 1993, p. 136)

In 1990, 33 million people in the United States lived below the poverty level. More women and girls than boys and men were in this group. Being poor is a context for other psychological dimensions, such as aspirations, parenting styles, language, and social perception (P. T. Reid, 1993). There is also a need to disentangle ethnicity, race, and class. Reid makes suggestions for psychology to achieve feminist goals relative to poor women. Psychologists need to conduct research that analyzes gender in the context of poor women and ethnic women. We must expand our own knowledge to include multiple perspectives and then teach this knowledge to our students and colleagues.

Women and Community Organization

Women organizing at the community level can be successful in achieving their goals and transcending both race and class.

Women have played a role in community organization that transcends both race and class. An example of the role of community organization played by a group of women was documented by Sandra Morgen (1988) who examined a nine-month campaign by a cross-class, multiracial group of women who opposed the local hospital's closing of outpatient gynecological and prenatal clinics for low-income women. The community was a New England city of 100,000 with higher than average unemployment and poverty, and a large minority population. The women formed an organization called Citizen Action for Health (CAFH), which fluctuated in size from 7 to 30

and was a multiracial and multiethnic group of women ranging in age from the 20s to the 50s, who were from working- and middle-class backgrounds. Over a period of eight months the group used a variety of tactics to win the reopening of the clinics.

> These included public meetings, pickets and demonstrations at the hospital, a petition campaign, meeting with the hospital board of trustees, taking their concerns to the local council of the Health Systems Agency (HSA), conducting a survey of patients utilizing the private practices of the obstetrician-gynecologists, and filing a "Ten Taxpayers," suit against the hospital. (Morgen, 1988, p. 99)

The campaign was successful in getting the hospital to reopen the prenatal clinic and to open a community health center within two years.

The response of the City University of New York (CUNY) to the Black power movement of the 1960s, was the establishment of Medgar Evers College in the heart of Brooklyn, New York, which has one of the largest Black populations in the United States. By early 1976, however, the CUNY Board of Trustees was proposing the closing of several CUNY colleges including Medgar Evers. The Student–Faculty Coalition to save Medgar Evers College was founded. By September 1976, the college had been stripped of its four-year status and reduced to a two-year community college. It was viewed as a racist measure, particularly in view of the fact that two community colleges in White communities were upgraded to four-year college status in 1976 and 1980. The college was 95% Black and three-quarters were women and 69% were mothers. Also, in 1976, the CUNY system ended its 129-year tradition of free tuition. Broad-based support in the central Brooklyn community lent support to the faculty–student coalition in demonstrations. A broad-based coalition was formed including student groups from other colleges in the State University of New York (SUNY) system, women's groups and community churches and business persons. It was a protracted struggle, including a sit-in the President's office and student strike, taking several years. Finally, several goals were achieved, such as the forming of a Child Development Center and a Center for Women's Development. The President of the college was replaced, although with a Black male rather than the Black female.

> Many of the women involved in the struggle at Medgar Evers later went on to lead community tenant associations, parent–teacher associations, women's organizations, food co-ops, coalitions for political prisoners, and welfare rights groups, and to organize significant cultural programs, community demonstrations against injustice, forums, film series, and conferences. (Nicola-McLaughlin & Chandler, 1988, p. 192)

Perhaps one of the most important outcomes of the struggle was the empowerment of Black women who were engaged in it.

Body Politics

Both first-world and third-world feminism focus on "body politics," the previously private world of abortion, rape, and battering.

Both the first and the second waves of the feminist movement have brought women's quest for power out of the closet, which was often characterized by more devious strategies in the past, and into the forefront of public consciousness by making direct demands for equal rights of women and minorities. The second wave of the feminist movement has spread worldwide. First-world feminism (in industrialized societies) and third-world feminism (in developing countries) have continuity in their focus on "body politics," the previously private arena of abortion, rape, and battering (Luthra, 1993).

The very different experiences of first- and third-world women (and also of women of color and lower class women in the first world) create many dilemmas of "choice," or the decision-making process as it relates to reproduction. Structural constraints in the lives of many third-world and minority and lower-class women restrict what might appear to be the availability of choice. *Roe* vs. *Wade* made abortion legal in the United States, but the Hyde amendment was

soon passed, which restricted federal funding for abortion, putting it out of the reach of many poor women. Among minority women, the concern is just as great concerning issues of pregnancy and childbirth. "In the context of a racist and classist society, forced sterilization, high infant mortality, and high maternal mortality rates are just as much a reality for working class women of color as the lack of access to abortion and other health services" (Luthra, 1993, p. 44). In the third world, the concerns of women may not be lack of availability of contraceptives; rather, it may be the dumping of high-risk contraceptives. Regardless of the specific issue, the feminist movement worldwide has made women's control over their own bodies a priority.

HUMAN RIGHTS VIOLATIONS AGAINST WOMEN

Violence against women exists as a sociopolitical linchpin in women's subordination.

Brinton Lykes and her colleagues, in her studies of women in Guatemala, Chile, and Argentina, has developed the concept of **social individuality,** which combines self, other selves, and society. Women are the target of many of the human rights violations occurring in the world today. War has become an increasingly devastating experience for women and children. During World War I, only 5% of the casualties were civilians, whereas during World War II civilians constituted 50% of the casualties. In recent wars such as the one in Bosnia, civilian massacres and razing of villages are systematically carried out, and the rape of women by members of the military is a policy (Lykes, Brabeck, Ferns, & Radan, 1993).

> The psychological effects of private and structural acts of violence and abuse are seen in individuals, families, and communities. Many psychologists have identified individual effects that range from feelings of discomfort, annoyance, and anger to physical complaints, lowered self-esteem, and weakened self-confidence, and more severe clinical diagnoses

such as depression, rape trauma syndrome, and posttraumatic stress (Loo, 1993). (Lykes et al., 1993, p. 527)

This violence against women is a sociopolitical linchpin in maintaining women in a demeaned state.

In South America, the most horrific forms of state-sponsored torture have been used against women and men who were kidnapped and put in clandestine jails. The Argentine Mothers of the Plaza de Mayo began informally after the military coup of 1976. Angry at the disappearance of their children, the Mothers began to demonstrate in Buenos Aires in the Plaza de Mayo in front of the Presidential palace despite encounters with the ever present security police.

> Their numbers soon swelled to the hundreds and included a network of Mothers in the interior provinces and support groups staffed by exiles and nationals throughout Western Europe. At a time when any opposition was banned and even friends and family members of people suspected to be opponents of the regime were being disappeared, the Mothers not only continued to demonstrate in the plaza de Mayo but also, in 1979, openly constituted themselves as an organization promoting democratic values. (Bouvard, 1994, p. 2)

The mothers shaped political dialogue at a time when others lived in fear of a repressive regime. They published their own newspaper, spoke throughout the country, and created an organization that established a network of international support groups. They paved the way for the return of a constitutional government in 1983. The Mothers have continued as a political organization to pave the way for a political process that allows a voice for all social groups and working for the elimination of the military presence in Argentina to prevent the reccurrence of another coup (Bouvard, 1994).

The American Psychological Association Division 35 has established a task force that has been collecting resources to aid women living in situations of war and/or state-sponsored violence in Latin America. It has been working with women's groups, progressive organizations, and individual women in areas of human rights and mental health. The task force has concluded that responses in terms of political action as well as community-based mental health programs are necessary for refugees who have escaped from the political violence as well as for those living under oppression.

REFLECTIONS

After reviewing voluminous research, it is clear that the transformation of traditional sex roles and political structures is necessary for creating a more humane world that provides opportunities for development and utilization of talents of all people. This transformation requires cooperative efforts by women and men. Girls must be socialized differently, as fully competent and capable in all spheres of life. Women, men, and children can benefit from changes such as increased involvement of men in childcare, and greater representation of women in elected offices at the local, state, and national levels.

Women collectively have great power to affect change in their own lives and in society as well. It is clear that structural differences in power define the strategic interactions between the sexes rather than any innate differences in uses of power. Women and men are equally capable of being effective leaders. Further, the Argentine Mothers of the Plaza de Mayo have shown the world that women are capable of taking hold of their destiny and transforming a nation.

Can power in American society be transformed from power over to power with? Will electing more women to political office help develop a more humane society?

Experiential Exercises

1. Attend a meeting of the city or town council where you live. Are there any women on the council? Are there any differences in the concerns expressed by women and men council members? Are there differences in the way women are treated by the voters attending the meeting?
2. Run for local office such as school board or town or city council.

3. Work to achieve passage of a bill in your state legislature that you support.
4. Participate in a community organization that is trying to improve the lives of women and children.

KEY TERMS

Coercive Power One is influenced by this power out of the fear of the negative consequences that might result if one fails to do what is requested.

Direct–Indirect Power Strategies When a person is using a direct strategy, she/he states what is wanted or tells the other person what to do. When a person is using an indirect strategy, she/he uses supplication, crying, manipulation or other such strategies.

Expert Power Possession of valuable information, particularly when that information is unique or not widely shared.

Franchise The right to vote.

Legitimate Power derived from one's position in the society, organization, and group.

n Power The motive to achieve power.

Power The ability to control and influence others and events, and to defend against the control and influence attempts of others.

Power Outcomes Does the person get what he/she wants in the relation? The outcomes are a product of both the structure and the strategies of power use.

Power Strategies The exercise of power by individuals, taking into account the behavior of other actors.

Referent Power Groups or individuals with which the individual identifies have greater influence on that person than other individuals and groups.

Reward Power Reinforcers that give a person what she/he needs, wants and values.

Social Individuality The combination of self, other selves and society. The violence, particularly toward women, in some societies have very destructive effects on the self.

Structural Power An individual's control over resources or events that other's value.

Unilateral–Bilateral Power Strategies The person who acts in a unilateral fashion makes decisions without consulting others. A person acting in a bilateral fashion takes into account the wishes and desires of the other person.

SUGGESTED READINGS

Bouvard, M. G. (1994). *Revolutionizing motherhood: The Mothers of the plaza de Mayo*. Wilmington, DE: SR Books. The mothers of Plaza de Mayo were an informal group of mothers searching for their disappeared children, but with the courage to demand civil rights and stand up to a brutal dictatorship. They changed a nation.

Eagly, A. H., Karau, S. J., & Makhijani, M. G. (1995). Gender and the effectiveness of leaders: A meta-analysis. *Psychological Bulletin, 117,* 125–145. This article provides theoretical analyses as well as a meta-analysis of gender differences in leadership effectiveness.

Jenkins, S. R. (1994). Need for power and women's careers over 14 years: Structural power, job satisfaction, and motive change. *Journal of Personality and Social Psychology, 66,* 155–165. This article reports on a 14-year longitudinal study of college women and their satisfaction/dissatisfaction with careers in relation to their initial level of *n* Power and the type of power expression allowed by the career.

Kreisberg, S. (1992). *Transforming power: Domination, empowerment, and education*. Albany, NY: State University of New York Press. This book describes an approach to education which empowers students.

REFERENCES

Abarbanel, G. (1986). Rape and resistence. *Journal of Interpersonal Violence, 1,* 101–105.

Abbey, A. (1982). Sex differences in attributions for friendly behavior: Do males misperceive females friendliness? *Journal of Personality and Social Psychology, 32,* 830–838.

Abbey, A. (1987). Misperception of friendly behavior as sexual interest: A survey of naturally occurring incidents. *Psychology of Women Quarterly, 11,* 173–194.

Abbey, A., Andrews, F. M., & Halman, L. J. (1991). Gender's role in responses to infertility. *Psychology of Women Quarterly, 15,* 295–316.

Abraham, G. E., & Rumley, R. E. (1987). Role of nutrition in managing the premenstrual tension syndromes. *Journal of Reproductive Medicine, 32,* 405–422.

Abel, G. G., Blanchard, E. B., Becker, F. V, & Djenderedjian, A. (1978). Differentiating sexual aggressiveness with penile measures. *Criminal Justice and Behavior, 5,* 315–332.

Abel, G. G., Barlow, D. H., Blanchard, E. & Guild, D. (1977). The components of rapists sexual arousal. *Archives of General Psychiatry, 34,* 895–903.

Abrams, B., Newman, V., Key, T., & Parker, J. (1989). Maternal weight gain and preterm delivery. *Obstetrics and Gynecology, 74,* 577–583.

Abrams, D. (1989). Differential association: Social developments in gender identity and intergroup relations during adolescence. In S. Skevington & D. Baker (Eds.), *The social identity of women* (pp. 59–83). London: Sage.

Abramson, L. Y., Garbner, J., & Seligman, M. E. P. (1980). Learned helplessness in humans: An attributional analysis. In J. Garbner & M. E. P. Seligman (Eds.), *Human Helplessness: Theory and applications.* New York: Academic Press.

Acitelli, L. K. (1992). Gender differences in relationship awareness and marital satisfaction among young married couples. *Personality and Social Psychology Bulletin, 18,* 102–110.

Acitelli, L. K., & Antonucci, T. C. (1994). Gender differences in the link between marital support and satisfaction in older couples. *Journal of Personality and Social Psychology, 67,* 688–698.

Acker, J., Barry, K., & Esseveld, J. (1991). Objectivity and truth: Problems in doing feminist research. In M. M. Fonow & J. A. Cook (Ed.), *Beyond methodology: Feminist scholarship as lived research* (pp. 133–153). Bloomington, IN: Indiana University Press.

Adams, C. G., & Turner, B. F. (1985). Reported change in sexuality from young adulthood to old age. *Journal of Sex Research, 21*(2), 126–141.

Adams, C. J. (1986). Profile of the current nurse-midwifery workforce and practice. In J. Rooks & J. E. Haas (Eds.), *Nurse-midwifery in America* (pp. 21–23). Washington, DC: American College of Nurse-Midwives Foundation.

Adams, K. A. (1983). Aspects of social context as determinants of black women's resistance to challenges. *Journal of Social Issues, 39*(3), 69–78.

Adelmann, P. K. (1993). Psychological well-being and homemaker vs. retiree identity among older women. *Sex Roles, 29,* 195–212.

Adler, N. E., David, H. P., Major, B. N., Roth, S. H., Russo, N. F., & Wyatt, G. E. (1992). Psychological factors in abortion: A review. *American Psychologist, 47,* 1194–1204.

Agras, W. S., Rossiter, E. M., Arnow, B., Schneider, J. A., Telch, C. F., Raeburn, S. D., Bruce, B., Perl, M., & Koran, L. M. (1992). Pharmaco-logic and cognitive-behavioral treatment for bulimia nervosa: A controlled comparison. *American Journal of Psychiatry, 149,* 82–87.

Ahmed, F., McRae, J. A., & Ahmed, N. (1990). Factors associated with not receiving adequate prenatal care in an urban Black population: Program planning implications. *Social Work in Health Care, 14* (3), 107–122.

Aida, Y., & Falbo, T. (1991). Relationships between marital satisfaction, resources, and power strategies. *Sex Roles, 24,* 43–56.

Ainslie, J., & Feltey, K. M. (1991). Definitions and dynamics of motherhood and family in lesbian communities. *Marriage and Family Review, 17,* 63–85.

Ajzen, I., & Fishbein, M. (1980). *Understanding attitudes and predicting social behavior.* Englewood Cliffs, NJ: Prentice Hall.

Alexander, G. M., & Hines, M. (1994). Gender labels and play styles: Their relative contribution to children's selection of playmates. *Child Development, 65,* 869–879.

Alexander, P. C. (1992). Application of attachment theory to the study of sexual abuse. *Journal of Consulting and Clinical Psychology, 60,* 185–195.

Allen, K. R., & Baber, K. M. (1992). Ethical and epistemological tensions in applying a postmodern perspective to feminist research. *Psychology of Women Quarterly, 16,* 1–15.

Allen, S. G., & Hubbs, J. (1987). Outrunning Atalanta: Feminine destiny in alchemical transmutation. In S. Harding & J. F. O'Barr (Eds.), *Sex and Scientific Inquiry.* (pp. 79–98). Chicago: University of Chicago Press.

Almagor, M., & Ben-Porath, Y. S. (1991). Mood changes during the menstrual cycle and their relation to the use of oral contraceptive. *Journal of Psychosomatic Research, 35,* 721–728.

Amaro, H., & Russo, N. F. (1987). Hispanic women and mental health: An overview of contemporary issues in research and practice. *Psychology of Women Quarterly, 11,* 393–407.

Amato, P. R., & Keith, B. (1991). Parental divorce and the well-being of children: A meta-analysis. *Psychological Bulletin, 110,* 26–46.

American Psychiatric Association. (1980). *Diagnostic and statistical manual of mental disorders* (3rd ed.). Washington, DC: Author.

American Psychiatric Association. (1987). *Diagnostic and statistical manual of mental disorders* (3rd ed. rev.). Washington, DC: Author.

American Psychiatric Association. (1994). *Diagnostic and statistical manual of mental disorders* (4th ed.). Washington, DC: Author.

American Psychological Association. (1975). Report on the task force on sex bias and sex-role stereotyping in psychotherapeutic practice. *American Psychologist, 30,* 1169–1175.

American Psychological Association. (1981). *Ethical principles of Psychologists* (Rev. ed.). Washington, DC: Author.

American Psychological Association. (1991, June). Grant proposals to include women. *APA SPAN.*

Amir, M. (1971). *Patterns in forcible rape.* Chicago: University of Chicago Press.

Amott, T., & Matthaei, J. (1991). *Race, gender and work: A multicultural economic history of women in the United States.* Boston, MA: South End Press.

Amuzu, B., Laxova, R., & Sanders, S. S. (1990). Pregnancy outcome, health of children and family adjustment after donor insemination. *Obstetrics and Gynecology, 75,* 899–905.

Anastasi, A. (1958). *Differential psychology: Individual and group differences in behavior* (3rd ed.). New York: MacMillan.

Anastasi, A. (1985). Reciprocal relations between cognitive and affective development-with implications for sex differences. In T. E. Sonderegger (Ed.), *Psychology and gender. Nebraska Symposium on Motivation, 1984* (pp. 1–35). Lincoln, NE: University of Nebraska Press.

Andersen, B. L., & Cyranowski, J. M. (1994). Women's sexual self-schema. *Journal of Personality and Social Psychology, 67,* 1079–1100.

Andersen, M. L. (1991). Feminism and the American family ideal. *Journal of Comparative Family Studies, 22,* 235–246.

Anderson, J. (1994). Separatism, feminism, and the betrayal of reform. *Signs, 19,* 437–448.

Anderson, J. R. (1991). HIV in women: Factors that increase their risk. *Medical Aspects of Human Sexuality, 25*(5), 20–27.

Anderson, R. H., Fleming, D. E., Rhees, R. W., & Kinghorn, E. (1986). Relationships between sexual activity, plasma testosterone, and the volume of the sexually dimorphic nucleus of the preoptic area in prenatally stress and nonstressed rats. *Brain Research, 370,* 1–10.

Anderson, S. A., & Fleming, S. M. (1986). Late adolescents' home-leaving strategies: Predicting ego identity and college adjustment. *Adolescence, 2,* 453–459.

Andersson, B. (1989). Effects of public day-care—a longitudinal study. *Child Development, 60,* 857–866.

Andersson, B. (1992). Effects of day-care on cognitive and socio-emotional competence of thirteen-year-old Swedish schoolchildren. *Child Development, 63,* 20–36.

Aneshensel, C. S., Fielder, E. P., & Becerra, R. M. (1989). Fertility and fertility-related behavior among Mexican-American and non-Hispanic white female adolescents. *Public Opinion Quarterly, 53,* 548–562.

Angel, R., & Worobey, J. L. (1988). Single motherhood and children's health. *Journal of Health and Social Behavior, 29,* 38–52.

Apfelbaum, E. (1993). Norwegian and French women in high leadership positions. *Psychology of Women Quarterly, 17,* 409–429.

Apgar, B. S. (1992). Endometriosis: Diagnostic clues and new treatment options. *Postgraduate Medicine, 92,* 283–299.

Aponte, R. (1991). Urban Hispanic poverty: Disaggregations and explanations. *Social Problems, 38,* 516–528.

Apple, R. D. (1987). *Mothers and Medicine: A social history of infant feeding, 1890–1950.* Madison, WI: University of Wisconsin Press.

Apt, C., & Hurlbert, D. F. (1992). Motherhood and female sexuality beyond one year postpartum: A study of military wives. *Journal of Sex Education and Therapy, 18,*(2), 104–114.

Aral, S. O., Mosher, W. D., & Cates, W. Jr., (1988). Vaginal douching among women of reproductive age in the United States: 1988. *American Journal of Public Health, 82,* 210–214.

Archer, J. (1976). The organization of aggression and fear in vertebrates. In P. P. G. Bateson & P. Klopfer (Eds.), *Perspectives in ethology* (2nd ed., pp. 231–298). New York: Plenum.

Archer, J. (1988). *The behavioural biology of aggression.* Cambridge: Cambridge University Press.

Arditti, R. (1988). A summary of some recent developments on surrogacy in the United States. *Reproductive and Genetic Engineering, 1,* 51–64.

Armstrong, L. (1978). *Kiss daddy goodnight.* New York: Hawthorne Press.

Aronson, R. A., & Hunt, L. H., & Madison, (1990). Cocaine use during pregnancy: Implications for physicians. *Wisconsin Medical Journal, 89,* 105-110.

Asch, A., & Fine, M. (1988). Introduction: Beyond pedestals. In M. Fine & A. Asch (Eds.). *Women with disabilities: Essays in psychology, culture, and politics* (pp. 1–37). Philadelphia: Temple University Press.

Ashton, E. (1983). Measures of play behavior: The influence of sex-role stereotyped children's books. *Sex Roles, 9,* 43–47.

Asso, D. (1983). *The real menstrual cycle.* New York: Wiley.

Asso, D. (1986). Psychology degree examinations and the premenstrual phase of the menstrual cycle. *Women & Health, 10,* 91–104.

Astin, H. S. (1969). *The woman doctorate in America: Origins, career, and family.* New York: Russell Sage Foundation.

Astin, H. S., & Leland, C. (1991). *Women of influence, women of vision. A cross generational study of leaders and social change.* San Francisco: Jossey-Bass.

Atkinson, J., & Huston, T. L. (1984). Sex role orientation and division of labor early in marriage. *Journal of Personality and Social Psychology, 46,* 330–345.

Atkinson, J. W. (Ed.). (1958). *Motives in fantasy, action and society.* Princeton, NJ: Van Nostrand.

Atkinson, J. W., & Feather, N.T. (Eds.). (1966). *A theory of achievement motivation.* New York: Wiley.

Aube, J., & Koestner, R. (1992). Gender characteristics and adjustment: A longitudinal study. *Journal of Personality and Social Psychology, 63,* 485–493.

Avioli, P. S., & Kaplan, E. (1992). A panel study of married women's work patterns. *Sex Roles, 26,* 227–241.

Baber, K. M., & Allen, K. R. (1992). *Women & families: Feminist reconstructions.* New York: Guilford Press.

Baber, K. M., & Monaghan, P. (1988). College women's career and motherhood expectations: New options, old dilemmas. *Sex Roles, 19,* 189–203.

Bachman, R. (1994, January). *Violence against women: A National Crime Victimization Survey report.* NCJ-145325. U.S. Department of Justice, Rockville, MD: Bureau of Justice Statistics. Washington, DC: U.S. Government Printing Office.

Bachrach, C. A., Stolley, K. S., & London, K. A. (1992). Relinquishment of premarital births: Evidence from national survey data. *Family Planning Perspectives, 24,* 27–32, 48.

Backstrom, T., & Hammarback, S. (1991). Premenstrual syndrome-Psychiatric or gynaecological disorder? *Annals of Medicine, 23,* 625–633.

Bailey, J. M., & Pillard, R. C. (1991). A genetic study of male sexual orientation. *Archives of General Psychiatry, 48,* 1089–1096.

Bailey, J. M., Pillard, R. C., Neale, M. C., & Agyei, Y. (1993). Hereditable factors influence sexual orientation in women. *Archives of General Psychiatry, 50,* 217–223.

Bailyn, L. (1994). Experiencing technical work: A comparison of male and female engineers. *Human Relations, 40,* 299–312.

Bakan, A. B., & Stasiulis, D. K. (1995). Making the match: Domestic placement agencies and the racialization of women's household work. *Signs, 20,* 303–335.

Bakan, D. (1966). *The duality of human existence.* Chicago: Rand McNally.

Baker, B. (1993, March/April). The female condom. *Ms.* 80–81.

Baker, D. D., Terpstra, D. E., & Larntz, K. (1990). The influence of individual characteristics and severity of harassing behavior on reactions to sexual harassment. *Sex Roles, 22,* 305–325.

Ballard-Reisch, D., & Elton, M. (1992). Gender orientation and the Bem sex role inventory: A psychological construct revisited. *Sex Roles, 27,* 291–306.

Ballinger, C. B. (1990). Psychiatric aspects of menopause. *British Journal of Psychiatry, 156,* 773–787.

Balshem, M., Oxman, G., van Rooyen, D., & Girod, K. (1992). Syphilis, sex and crack cocaine: Images of risk and morality. *Social Science & Medicine, 35,* 147–160.

Banaji, M. R., Hardin, C., & Rothman, A. J. (1993). Implicit stereotyping in person judgment. *Journal of Personality and Social Psychology, 65,* 272–281.

Bandura, A. (1977). *Social learning theory.* Englewood Cliffs, NJ: Prentice-Hall.

Barba, R., & Cardinale, L. (1991). Are females invisible students: An investigation of teacher-student questioning interactions. *School Science and Mathematics, 91,* 306–310.

Barbach, L. (Ed.), (1986). *Erotic interludes: Tales told by women.* Garden City, NY: Doubleday.

Barber, B. L., & Eccles, J. S. (1992). Long-term influence of divorce and single parenting on adolescent family- and work-related values, behaviors, and aspirations. *Psychological Bulletin, 111,* 108–126.

Barer, B. M. (1994). Men and women aging differently. *International Journal of Aging & Human Development, 38,* 29–40.

Barglow, P., Vaughn, B. E., & Molitar, N. (1987). Effects of maternal absence due to employment on the quality of infant-mother attachment in a low-risk sample. *Child Development, 58,* 945–954.

Barnett, R. C., Brennan, R. T., Raudenbush, S. W., & Marshall, N. L. (1994). Gender and the relationship between marital-role quality and psychological distress: A study of women and men in dual-earner couples. *Psychology of Women Quarterly, 18,* 105–127.

Barnett, R. C., Marshall, N. L., Raudenbush, S. W., & Brennan, R. T. (1993). Gender and the relationship between job experiences and psychological distress: A study of dual-earner couples. *Journal of Personality and Social Psychology, 64,* 794–806.

Baron, L., & Straus, M. A. (1989). *Four theories of marital rape in American Society: A state-level analysis.* New Haven, CT: Yale University Press.

Baronowski, T., Rassin, D. D., Richardson, C. J., Brown, J. P., & Bee, D. E. (1986). Attitudes toward breastfeeding. *Developmental and Behavioral Pediatrics, 7,* 367–372.

Barrett, D. H., Anda, R. F., Croft, J. B., Serdula, M. K., & Lane, M. J. (1995). The association between alcohol use and health behaviors related to the risk of cardiovascular disease: The South Carolina cardiovascular disease prevention project. *Journal of Studies on Alcohol, 56,* 9–15.

Barrett-Connor, E., Chang, J. C., & Edelstein, S. L. (1994). Coffee-associated osteoporosis offset by daily milk consumption. The Rancho Bernardo Study. *Journal of the American Medical Association, 271,* 280–283.

Barrett-Connor, E., Wingard, D. L., & Criqui, M. H. (1989). Postmenopausal estrogen use and heart disease risk factors in the 1980s. *Journal of the American Medical Association, 261,* 2095–2100.

Barry, K. (1979). *Female sexual slavery.* Englewood Cliffs, NJ: Prentice-Hall.

Bart, P. B., Freeman, L. N., & Kimball, P. (1991). The different worlds of women and men: Attitudes toward pornography and responses to not a love story—A film about pornography. In M. M. Fonow & J. A. Cook (Eds.), *Beyond methodology: Feminist scholarship as lived research* (pp. 171–196). Bloomington, IN: Indiana University Press.

Bart, P. B., & O'Brien, P. H. (1985). *Stopping rape: Successful survival strategies.* New York: Pergamon Press.

Bartholomew, N. G., Rowan-Szal, G. A., Chatham, L. R., & Simpson, D. D. (1994). Effectiveness of a specialized intervention for women in a methadone program. *Journal of Psychoactive Drugs, 26,* 249–255.

Barton, S. (1994). Chaos, self-organiztion, and psychology. *American Psychologist, 49,* 5–14.

Baruch, G. K., & Barnett, R. (1986). Role quality, multiple role involvement, and psychological well-being in midlife women. *Journal of Personality and Social Psychology, 51,* 578–585.

Basow, S. A., & Medcalf, K. L. (1988). Academic achievement and attributions among college students: Effects of gender and sex typing. *Sex Roles, 19,* 555–557.

Bauchner, H., Leventhal, J. M., & Shapiro, E. D. (1986). Studies of breast-feeding and infections: How good is the evidence? *Journal of the American Medical Association, 256,* 887–892.

Baucom, D. H., Besch, P. K., & Callahan, S. (1985). Relation between testosterone concentration, sex role identity, and personality among females. *Journal of Personality and Social Psychology, 48,* 1218–1226.

Bayer, R. (1994). Ethical challenges posed by *zidovudine* treatment to reduce vertical transmission of HIV. *New England Journal of Medicine, 331,* 1223–1225.

Bean, F. D., Curtis, R. L., Jr., & Marcum, J. P. (1977). Familism and marital satisfaction among Mexican Americans: The effects of family size, wife's labor force participation, and conjugal power. *Journal of Marriage and the Family, 19,* 759–767.

Bech, P. (1993). Acute therapy of depression. *Journal of Clinical Psychiatry, 54,*(8), [suppl], 18–27.

Beck, A. T. (1976). *Cognitive therapy and the emotional disorders.* New York: International Universities Press.

Beck, A. T. (1991). Cognitive therapy. *American Psychologist, 46,* 368–375.

Beck, B. L. (1991, April). *PMS as an excuse? The effects of dispositional self-handicapping, premenstrual syndrome, and success contingency on situational self-handicapping.* Paper presented at the annual meeting of the Eastern Psychological Association, New York.

Beck-Gernsheim, E. (1989). From the pill to test-tube babies: New options, new pressures in reproductive behavior. In K. S. Ratcliffe, M. M. Ferree, G. O. Mellow, B. D. Wright, G. D. Price, K. Yanoshik, & M. S. Freston (Eds.), *Healing technology: Feminist perspectives* (pp. 23–40). Ann Arbor: University of Michigan Press.

Becker, J., & Breedlove, S. M. (1992). Introduction to behavioral endocrinology. In J. B. Becker, S. M. Breedlove, & D. Crews (Eds.), *Behavioral endocrinology,* (pp. 3–37). Cambridge, MA: The MIT Press.

Becker, J., Breedlove, S. M., & Crews D. (Eds.). (1992). *Behavioral endocrinology,* Cambridge, MA: MIT Press.

Begley, D. J., Firth, J. A., & Hoult, J. R. S. (1980). *Human reproduction and developmental biology.* London: MacMillan.

Belenky, M. F., Clinchy, B. M., Goldberger, N. R., & Tarule, J. M. (1986) *Women's ways of knowing: The development of self, voice, and mind.* New York: Basic Books.

Bell, A. P., Weinberg, M. S., & Hammersmith, S. K. (1981). *Sexual preference: Its development in men and women.* New York: Simon & Schuster.

Bell, C. (1989). The effects of affirmative action on male-female relationships among African Americans. *Sex Roles, 21,* 13–24.

Bell, S. (1994). *Reading, writing, and rewriting the prostitute body.* Bloomington, IN: Indiana University Press.

Bell, S. E. (1989). The meaning of risk, choice, and responsibility for a DES daughter. In K. S. Ratcliffe, M. M. Ferree, G. O. Mellow, B. D. Wright, G. D. Price, K. Yanoshik, & M. S. Feston (Eds.), *Healing technology: Feminist perspectives* (pp. 245–261). Ann Arbor: University of Michigan Press.

Belle, D. (1990). Poverty and women's mental health. *American Psychologist, 45,* 385–389.

Belsky, J. (1985). Exploring individual differences in marital change across the transition to parenthood: The role of violated expectations. *Journal of Marriage and the Family, 47,* 795–803.

Belsky, J., & Eggebeen, D. (1991). Early and extensive maternal employment and young children's socioemotional development: Children of the National Longitudinal Survey of Youth. *Journal of Marriage and the Family, 53,* 1083–1110.

Belsky, J., & Rovine, M. J. (1988). Nonmaternal care in the first year of life and the security of infant-parent attachment. *Child-Development, 59,* 157–167.

Bem, S. L. (1974). The measurement of psychological androgyny. *Journal of Consulting and Clinical Psychology, 42,* 155–162.

Bem, S. L. (1981). Gender schema theory: A cognitive account of sex-typing. *Psychological Review, 88,* 354–364.

Bem, S. L. (1987). Gender schema theory and the romantic tradition. In P. Shaver, & C. Hendrick (Eds.), *Sex and gender* (pp. 251–271). Newbury Park: CA: Sage.

Bem, S. L. (1993). *The lenses of gender: Transforming the debate on sexual inequality.* New Haven, CT: Yale University Press.

Benbow, C. P., & Stanley, J. C. (1980). Sex differences in mathematical ability: Fact or artifact? *Science, 210,* 1262–1264.

Benbow, C. P., & Stanley, J. C. (1983) Sex differences in mathematical reasoning ability: More facts. *Science, 222,* 1029–1031.

Benson, C. S., & Wilsnack, S. C. (1983). Gender differences in alcoholic personality characteristics and life expectancies. In W. V. Cox (Ed.), *Identifying and measuring alcoholic personality characteristics.* San Francisco: Jossey-Bass.

Benson, D. J., & Thomson, G. (1982). Sexual harassment on a university campus: The confluence of authority relations, sexual interest, and gender stratification. *Social Problems, 29,* 236–251.

Benson-von der Ohe, E. (1987). *First and second marriages.* New York: Praeger.

Berardo, D., Shehan, C. & Leslie, G. (1987). A residue of tradition: Jobs, careers, and spouses' time in housework. *Journal of Marriage and the Family, 49,* 381–390.

Berenbaum, S. A., & Hines, M. (1992). Early androgens are related to childhood sex-typed toy preferences. *Psychological Science, 3,* 203–206.

Berger, J., Cohen, B. P., & Zelditch, M., Jr. (1972). Status characteristics and social interaction. *American Sociological Review, 37,* 241–255.

Berger, J., Fisek, M. H., Norman, R. Z., & Zelditch, M., Jr. (1977). *Status characteristics and social interaction: An expectation states approach.* New York: Elsevier.

Berger, J., Rosenholz, S. J., and Zelditch, M. (1980). Status organizing processes. *Annual Review of Sociology, 6,* 479–508.

Berger, J., Webster, M., Jr., Ridgeway, C., & Rosenholtz, S. J. (1986). Status cues, expectations, and behavior. In E. J. Lawler (Ed.), *Advances in group processes, Vol. 3,* (pp. 1–22). Greenwich, CT: JAI Press.

Bergin, D. J., & Williams, J. E. (1991). Sex stereotypes in the United States revisited: 1972–1988. *Sex Roles, 24,* 413–424.

Bergman, L. (1992). Dating violence among high school students. *Social Work (37),* 21–27.

Bergvist, L., Adami, H., Persson, I., Hoover, R., & Schairer, C. (1989). The risk of breast cancer after estrogen replacement. *The New England Journal of Medicine, 321,* 293–297.

Berk, S. F. (1985). *The gender factory: The apportionment of work in American households.* New York: Plenum.

Berkowitz, G. S., Skovron, M. L. Lapinski, R. H., & Berkowitz, R. L. (1990). Delayed childbearing and the outcome of pregnancy. *The New England Journal of Medicine, 322*(10), 669–653.

Bernhard, L. A. (1986). Sexuality expectations and outcomes in women having hysterectomies. *Chart, 83,* 11.

Bernstein, B. (1977). Effect of menstruation on academic performance among college women. *Archives of Sexual Behavior, 6,* 65–68.

Bernstein, L., Ross, R. K., Pike, M. C., Brown, J. B., & Henderson, B. E. (1990). Hormone levels in older women: A study of post-menopausal breast cancer patients and healthy population controls. *British Journal of Cancer, 61,* 298–302.

Bersheid, E., & Walster, E. (1978). *Interpersonal attraction* (2nd ed.). Reading, MA: Addison-Wesley.

Beyer, S. (1990). Gender differences in the accuracy of self-evaluations of performance. *Journal of Personality and Social Psychology, 59,* 960–970.

Biaggio, M. K., Mohan, P. J., & Baldwin, C. (1985). Relationships among attitudes toward children, women's liberation, and personality characteristics. *Sex Roles, 12,* 47–62.

Bickel, J. (1990). Women in medical school. In S. Rix (Ed.), *The American woman 1990–91: A status report* (pp. 211–221). New York: Norton.

Bielert, C. (1984). Estradiol benzoate treatment of an XY gonadal dysgenetic chacma baboon. *Hormones and Behavior, 18,* 191–205.

Bierman, B. R., & Streett, R. (1982). Adolescent girls as mothers: Problems in parenting. In I. R. Stuart & C. F. Wells, (Eds.), *Pregnancy in adolescence: needs, problems, and management* (pp. 407–426). New York: Van Nostrand Reinhold.

Biernat, M., & Manis, M. (1994). Shifting standards and stereotype-based judgments. *Journal of Personality and Social Psychology, 66,* 5–20.

Biernat, M., Manis, M., and Nelson, T. E. (1991). Stereotypes and standards of judgement. *Journal of Personality and Social Psychology, 60,* 485–499.

Biernat, M., & Wortman, C. B. (1991). Sharing of home responsibilities between professionally employed women and their husbands. *Journal of Personality and Social Psychology, 60,* 844–860.

Bigler, R. S., & Liben, L. S. (1992). Cognitive mechanisms in children's gender stereotyping: Theoretical and Educational implications of a cognitive-based intervention. *Child Development, 63,* 1351–1363.

Billy, J. O. G., & Brewster, K. L., & Grady, W. R. (1994). Contextual effects on the sexual behavior of adolescent women. *Journal of Marriage and the Family, 56,* 387–404.

Bindra, D. (1972). Weeping: A problem of many facets. *Bulletin of the British Psychology Society. 25,* 281–284.

Binion, V. J. (1982). Sex differences in socialization and family dynamics of female and male heroin users. *Journal of Social Issues, 38*(2). 43–57.

Binion, V. J. (1990). Psychological androgyny: A black female perspective. *Sex Roles, 22,* 487–507.

Bird, C. E., & Fremont, A. M. (1992). Gender, time use, and health. *Journal of Health and Social Behavior, 32,* 114–129.

Black, D. W., Wesner, R., Bowers, W., & Gabel, J. (1993). A comparison of fluvoxamine, cognitive therapy, and placebo in the treatment of panic disorder. *Archives of General Psychiatry, 50,* 44–50.

Blais, M. R., Sabourin, S., Boucher, C., & Vallerand, R. J. (1990). Toward a motivational model of couple happiness. *Journal of Personality and Social Psychology, 59,* 1021–1031.

Blaisure, K. R., & Allen, K. R. (1995). Feminists and the ideology and practice of marital equality. *Journal of Marriage and the Family, 57,* 5–19.

Blee, K. M., & Tickamyer, A. R. (1995). Racial differences in men's attitudes about women's gender roles. *Journal of Marriage and the Family, 57,* 21–30.

Blood, R. O., & Wolfe, D. M. (1960). *Husbands and wives.* Glencoe, IL: The Free Press.

Blumenthal, P. D. (1991). Abortion. *Current Opinion in Obstetrics and Gynecology, 3,* 496–500.

Blumstein, P., & Schwartz, P. (1989). Intimate relationships and the creation of sexuality. In B. J. Risman & P. Schwartz (Eds.), *Gender in intimate relationships: A microstructural approach* (pp. 120–129). Belmont, CA: Wadsworth.

Blumstein, P., & Schwartz, P. (1983). *American Couples.* New York: William Morrow.

Blysma, W. H., & Major, B. (1992). Two routes to eliminating gender differences in personal entitlement: Social comparisons and performance evaluations. *Psychology of Women Quarterly, 16,* 193–200.

Bogart, M. H. (1992). Current and future modes of prenatal diagnosis. In I. T. Lott & E. E. McCoy (Eds.), *Down syndrome: Advances in medical care* (pp. 13–22). New York: Wiley-Liss.

Bogren, L. Y. (1991). Changes in sexuality in women and men during pregnancy. *Archives of Sexual Behavior, 20*(1), 35–45.

Bohan, J. S. (1993). Regarding gender: essentialism, constructionism, and feminist psychology. *Psychology of Women Quarterly, 17,* 5–21.

Bond, J. T., Filer, L. J., Leveille, G. A., Thomson, A. M., & Weil, W.B. (1981). *Infant and child feeding.* New York: Academic Press.

Bonilla-Santiago, G. (1990). A portrait of Hispanic women in the United States. In S. Rix (Ed.), *The American woman 1990–91: A status report* (pp. 249–257). New York: Norton.

Bonnicksen, A. L., (1989). *In vitro fertilization: Building policy from laboratories to legislatures.* New York: Columbia University Press.

Bonson, K. R., & Winter, J. C. (1992). Reversal of testosterone-induced dominance by the serotonergic agonist quipazine. *Pharmacology, Biochemistry and Behavior, 42,* 809–813.

Booth, A., Edwards, J. N., & Johnson, D. R. (1991). Social integration and divorce. *Social Forces, 70,* 207–224.

Bornstein, J., Rahat, M. A., & Abramovici, H. (1995). Etiology of cervical cancer: Current concepts. *Obstretrical and Gynecological Survey, 50,*(2), 146–154.

Boston Women's Health Book Collective. (1984). *The new our bodies, ourselves.* New York: Simon & Schuster.

Boston Women's Health Book Collective. (1992). *The new our bodies, ourselves: A book by and for women* (rev. ed.). New York: Simon & Schuster.

Bouhoutsos, J. C. (1984). Sexual intimacy between psychotherapists and clients: Policy implications for the future. In L. E. Walker (Ed.), *Women and mental health policy* (pp. 207–227). Beverly Hills, CA: Sage.

Bourinbaiar, A. S., Lee-Huang, S. (1994). Comparative in vitro study of contraceptive agents with anti-HIV activity: Gramicidin, nonoxynol-9, and gossypol. *Contraception, 49,* 131–137.

Bowe, C. (1993, April). The Cosmo girl's sex survey. *Cosmopolitan,* pp. 202–205.

Bower, L. C., (1991). "Mother" in law: Conceptions of mother and the maternal in feminism and feminist legal theory. *Differences: A Journal of Feminist Cultural Studies, 3,* 20–38.

Bowers, C. A., & LaBarba, R. C. (1988). Sex differences in the lateralization of spatial abilities: A spatial component analysis of extreme group scores. *Brain and Cognition, 8,* 165–177.

Bowker, L. H. (1983). *Beating wife-beating.* Lexington, MA: D.C. Heath.

Bowker, L. H., & Maurer, L. (1986). The effectiveness of counseling services utilized by battered women. *Women and Therapy, 5,* 65–82.

Bowlby, J. (1980). *Loss: Sadness and depression (Vol. 3), of Attachment and loss.* New York: Basic Books.

Bowlby, J. (1988). *A secure base: Parent-child attachment and healthy human development.* New York: Basic Books.

Boyd, J. A. (1990). Ethnic and cultural diversity: Keys to power. *Women & Therapy, 9,* 151–167.

Boyer, D., & Fine, D. (1992). Sexual abuse as a factor in adolescent pregnancy and child maltreatment. *Family Planning Perspectives, 24* (1), 4–11, 19.

Boyer, P. J., Dillon, M., Navaie, M., Deveikis, A., Keller, M., O'Rourke, S., & Bryson, Y. J. (1994). Factors predictive of maternal-fetal transmission of HIV-l: Preliminary Analysis of zidovudine given during pregnancy and/or delivery. *Journal of the American Medical Association. 271,* 1925–1930.

Brabant, S. (1976). Sex role stereotyping in the Sunday comics. *Sex Roles, 2,* 331–337.

Brabant, S., & Mooney, L. (1986). Sex role sterotyping in the Sunday comics: Ten years later. *Sex Roles, 14,* 141–148.

Bradbury, T. N., & Fincham, F. D. (1990). Attributions in marriage: Review and critique. *Psychological Bulletin, 107,* 3–33.

Bradshaw, C. K. (1994). Asian and Asian American women: Historical and political considerations in psychotherapy. In L. Comas-Diaz & B. Greene (Eds.), *Women of color: Integrating ethnic and gender identities in psychotherapy* (pp. 72–113). New York: Guilford.

Brand, T., & Slob, A. K. (1988). Peripubertal castration of male rats, adult open field ambulation and partner preference behavior. *Behavioural Brain Research, 30,* 111–117.

Brandon, P. (1991). Gender differences in young Asian Americans' Educational Attainments. *Sex Roles, 25,* 45–61.

Breinlinger, S., & Kelly, C. (1994). Women's responses to status inequality. *Psychology of Women Quarterly, 18,* 1–16.

Brell, D. J., & Cantor, J. (1988). The portrayal of men and women in U.S. television commercials: A recent content analysis and trends over 15 years. *Sex Roles,* 595–609.

Brewer, C. (1977). Incidence of post-abortion psychosis: A propective study. *British Medical Journal, 1,* 476–477.

Brewer, M. B., & Berk, R. A. (1982). Beyond nine to five: Introduction. *Journal of Social Issues, 38*(4), 1–4.

Brewer, V., Meyer, B. M., Keefe, M.S., Upton, S. J., Hagan, R. D. (1983). Role of exercise in prevention of involutional bone loss. *Medicine and Science in Sports and Exercise, 15,* 445–449.

Bricarelli, F. D., Pierluigi, M., Perroni, L., Grasso, M., Arslanian, A., & Sacchi, N. (1988). High efficiency in the attribution of parental origin of non-disjunction in trisomy 21 by both cytogenetic and molecular polymorphisms. *Human Genetics, 79,* 124–127.

Bridgeman, B., & Wendler, C. (1991). Gender differences in predictors of college mathematics performance and in college mathematics course grades. *Journal of Educational Psychology, 83,* 275–284.

Bridges, J. S. (1989). Sex differences in occupational values. *Sex Roles, 20,* 205–211.

Briere, J., & Conte, J. R. (1993). Self-reported amnesia for abuse in adults molested as children. *Journal of Traumatic Stress, 6,* 21–31.

Brinton, L. A., & Schairer, C. (1993). Estrogen replacement therapy and breast cancer risk. *Epidemiologic Reviews, 15*(1), 66–79.

Brody, C. M. (1990). Women in a nursing home: Living with hope and meaning. *Psychology of Women Quarterly, 14,* 579–592.

Brody, J. (1995, October 7). Birth defects, high vitamin A use linked. *Providence Journal-Bulletin,* A-1, A-7.

Brody, L. H. & Hall, J. A., (1993). Gender and emotion. In M. Lewis & J. M. Haviland (Eds.), *Handbook of emotions.* New York: Guilford Press.

Broman, C. L. (1988). Household work and family life satisfaction of blacks. *Journal of Marriage and the Family, 50,* 743–748.

Bronfenbrenner, U., & Ceci, S. J. (1994). Nature-nurture reconceptualized in developmental perspective: A bioecological model. *Psychological Review, 101,* 568–586.

Brooks-Gunn, J. (1988). Antecedents and conquences of variations in girls' maturational timing. *Journal of Adolescent Health Care, 9,* 365–363.

Brooks-Gunn, J., & Ruble, D. (1980). The menstrual attitude questionnaire. *Psychosomatic Medicine, 42,* 503–511.

Brophy, J. (1985). Interactions of male and female students with male and female teachers. In L. C. Wilkinson & C. B. Marrett (Eds.), *Gender influences in classroom interaction* (pp. 115–142). Orlando, FL: Academic Press.

Broverman, I. K., Broverman, D. M., Clarkson, F. E., Rosenkrantz, P. S., & Vogel, S. R. (1970). Sex-role stereotypes and clinical judgments of mental health. *Journal of Consulting Psychology, 34,* 1–7.

Broverman, I. K., Vogel, S. R., Broverman, D. M., Clarkson, F. E., & Rosenkrantz, P. S. (1972). Sex role stereotypes: A current appraisal. *Journal of Social Issues, 28*(2), 59–78.

Brown, D. R., & Gary, L. E. (1985). Social support network differentials among married and nonmarried black females. *Psychology of Women Quarterly, 9,* 229–241.

Brown, G. R., & Anderson, B. (1991). Psychiatric morbidity in adult inpatients with childhood histories of sexual and physical abuse. *American Journal of Psychiatry, 140,* 55–61.

Brown, G. W., & Harris, T. (1978). *Social origins of depression: A study of psychiatric disorder in women.* New York: Free Press.

Brown, L. S. (1987). Lesbians, weight, and eating: New analyses and perspectives. In the Boston Lesbian Psychologies Collective (Ed.), *Lesbian psychologies: Explorations and challenges* (pp. 294–309). Urbana, IL: University of Illinois Press.

Brown, L. S. (1989). New voices, new visions: Toward a lesbian/gay paradigm for psychology. *Psychology of Women Quarterly, 13,* 445–458.

Brown, R. (1965). *Social Psychology.* New York: Free Press.

Brown, R. M. (1976). The shape of things to come. In *A plain brown rapper* (pp. 109–117). Oakland, CA: Diana Press.

Browne, A. (1987). *When battered women kill.* New York: Free Press.

Browne, A. (1993). Violence against women by male partners: Prevalence, outcomes, and policy implications. *American Psychologist, 48,* 1077–1087.

Browne, A., & Finkelhor, D. (1986). The impact of child sexual abuse: A review of research. *Psychological Bulletin, 99,* 66–77.

Brownmiller, S. (1975). *Against our will.* New York: Simon & Schuster.

Brownmiller, S. (1984). *Femininity.* New York: Linden Press/Simon & Schuster.

Brownworth, V. A. (1993). Not invisible to attack. In V. Cyrus (Ed.), *Experiencing race, class, and gender in the United States* (pp. 323–326). Mountain View, CA: Mayfield.

Bruch, H. (1978). *The golden cage: The enigma of anorexia nervosa.* Cambridge, MA: Harvard University Press.

Brumberg, J. J. (1988). *Fasting girls: The emergence of anorexia nervosa as a modern disease.* Cambridge, MA: Harvard University Press.

Bryden, M. P., McManus, I. C., & Bulman-Fleming, M. B. (1994). Evluating the empirical support for the Geschwind-Behan-Galaburda model of cerebral lateralization. *Brain and Cognition, 26,* 103–167.

Budoff, P. W. (1981). *No more menstrual cramps and other good news.* New York: Penquin Books.

Budoff, P. W. (1982). Zomepirac sodium in the treatment of primary dysmenorrhea syndrome. *New England Journal of Medicine, 307,* 714–719.

Bulik, C. M., Sullivan, P. F., & Rorty, M. (1989). Childhood sexual abuse in women with bulimia. *Journal of Clinical Psychiatry, 50,* 460–464.

Bumpass, L. L., Sweet, J. A., & Cherlin, A. (1991). The role of cohabitation in declining rates of marriage. *Journal of Marriage and the Family, 53,* 913–927.

Bunch, C. (1993). Lesbians in revolt. In M. Pearsall (Ed.), *Women and values: Readings in recent feminist philosophy* (2nd ed., pp. 140–144). Belmont, CA: Wadsworth.

Burch, B. (1987). Barriers to intimacy: Conflicts over power, dependency, and nurturing in lesbian relationships. In the Boston Lesbian Psychologies Collective (Eds.), *Lesbian Psychologies: Explorations and challenges* (pp. 126–141). Urbana, IL: Univeristy of Illinois Press.

Burda, P. C. Jr., Vaux, A., & Schill, T. (1984). Social support resources: Variation across sex and sex role. *Personality and Social Psychology Bulletin, 10,* 119–126.

Burgess, A. W., & Holmstrom, L. L. (1974a). Rape trauma syndrome. *American Journal of Psychiatry, 131,* 981–986.

Burgess, A. W., & Holmstrom, L. L. (1974b). *Rape: Victims of crisis.* Bowie, MD: Robert J. Brady Co.

Burgess, N. J. (1994). Gender roles revisited: "Woman's Place among African American women in the United States." *Journal of Black Studies, 24,* 391–401.

Burman, B., & Margolin, G. (1992). Analysis of the association between marital relationships and health problems: An interactional perspective. *Psychological Bulletin, 112,* 39–63.

Burnam, M. A., Stein, J. A., Golding, J. M., Siegel, J. M., Sorenson, S. B., Forsythe, A. B., & Telles, C. A. (1988). Sexual assault and mental disorders in a community population. *Journal of Consulting and Clinical Psychology, 56,* 843–850.

Bursik, K. (1991). Adaptation to divorce and ego development in adult women. *Journal of Personality and Social Psychology, 60,* 300–306.

Buss, D. M., (1988). The evolution of human intrasexual competition: Tactics of mate attraction. *Journal of Personality and Social Psychology, 54,* 616–628.

Bussey, K., & Bandura, A. (1984). Influence of gender constancy and social power on sex-linked modeling. *Journal of Personality and Social Psychology, 47,* 1292–1302.

Butler, D., & Geis, F. (1990). Nonverbal affect responses to male and female leaders: Implications for leadership evaluations. *Journal of Personality and Social Psychology, 58,* 48–59.

Butler, M., & Paisley, W. (1980). *Women and the mass media.* New York: Human Science Press.

Butler, S. (1978). *Conspiracy of silence: The trauma of incest.* San Francisco: New Glide Publications.

Bybee, J., Glick, M., & Zigler, E. (1990). Differences across gender, grade level, and academic track in the content of the ideal self-image. *Sex Roles, 22,* 349–358.

Byers, S. E., & Heinlein, L. (1989). Predicting initiations and refusals of sexual activites in married and cohabiting heterosexual couples. *Journal of Sex Research, 26*(2), 210–231.

Byrne, D. (1983). The antecedents, correlates, and consequents of erotophobia-erotophilia. In C. M. Davis (Ed.), *Challenges in sexual science: Current theoretical issues and research advances* (pp. 53–75). Lake Mills, IA: Graphic.

Byrnes, J. P., & Takahira, S. (1993). Explaining gender differences on SAT-math items. *Developmental Psychology, 29,* 805–810.

Cacioppo, J. T., & Berntson, G. G. (1992). Social psychological contributions to the decade of the brain: Doctrine of multilevel analysis. *American Psychologist, 47,* 1019–1028.

Calcium subdues menstrual blues. (1991, July 20). *Science News, 140,* 45.

Caldwell, M. A., & Peplau, L. A. (1982). Sex differences in same-sex friendship. *Sex Roles, 8,* 721–732.

Calem, R., Waller, G., Slade, P. & Newton, T. (1990). Eating disorders and perceived relationships with parents. *International Journal of Eating Disorders, 9,* 479–485.

Calhoun, L. G., Selby, J. W., & Calhoun, M. L. (1980). The psychological value of prepared childbirth. In J. W. Selby, L. G. Calhoun, A. V. Vogel, & H. E. King (Eds.), *Psychology and human reproduction* (pp. 39–54). New York: Free Press.

Cancer incidence, mortality and survival: Trends in four leading sites. (1994). *Statistical Bulletin, 75*(3), 19–27.

Canino, G. J., Rubio-Stipec, M., Shrout, P., Bravos, M., Stolberg, R., & Bird, H. R. (1987). Sex differences and depression in Puerto Rico. *Psychology of Women Quarterly, 11,* 443–459.

Cannon, K. G. (1993). Moral wisdom in the black women's literary tradition. In M. Pearsall (Ed.), *Women and values: Readings in recent feminist philosphy* (2nd ed., pp. 401–409). Belmont, CA: Wadsworth.

Cannon, L. W., Higginbotham, E., & Leung, M. L. A. (1991). Race and class bias in qualitative research on women. In M. M. Fonow, & J. A. Cook, (Eds.), *Beyond methodology: Feminist scholarship as lived research* (pp. 107–118). Bloomington, IN: Indiana University Press.

Cantor, D. W., & Bernay, T. (1992). *Women in power: The secrets of leadership.* New York: Houghton Mifflin.

Caplan, P. J. (1985). *The myth of women's masochism.* New York: Dutton.

Caplan, P. J. (1993). Premenstrual syndrome DSM-IV diagnosis: The coalition for a scientific and responsible DSM-IV. *Psychology of Women: Newsletter of Division 35, 20*(3), pp. 4–5, 13.

Caplan, P. J., & Hall-McCorquodale, I. (1985). Mother-blaming in major clinical journals. *American Journal of Orthopsychiatry, 55,* 345–353.

Carden, A. D. (1994). Wife abuse and the wife abuser: Review and recommendations. *The Counseling Psychologist, 22,* 539–582.

Cardoza, D. (1991). College attendance and persistence among Hispanic women: An examination of some contributing factors. *Sex Roles, 24,* 133–147.

Carli, L. L. (1989). Gender differences in interaction style and influence. *Journal of Personality and Social Psychology, 56,* 565–576.

Carli, L. L. (1990). Gender, language, and influence. *Journal of Personality and Social Psychology, 59,* 941–951.

Carlson, K. J., Nichols, D. H., & Schiff, I. (1993). Indications for hysterectomy. *New England Journal of Medicine, 328,* 856–860.

Carmen, A., & Moody, H. (1985). *Working women: The subterranean world of street prostitution.* New York: Harper & Row.

Carroll, J. W., Hargrove, b., & Lummis, A. (1983). *Women of the cloth.* New York: Harper & Row.

Carver, C. S., Pozo, C., Harris, S. D., Noriega, V., Scheier, M. F., Robinson, D. S., Ketcham, A. S., Moffat, F. L. Jr., & Clark, K. C. (1993). How coping mediates the effect of optimism on distress: A study of women with early stage breast cancer. *Journal of Personality and Social Psychology, 65,* 375–390.

Castellano, O. (1992). Canto, locura y poesia. In M. L. Andersen, & P. H. Collins (Eds.), *Race, class and gender: An anthology* (pp. 376–385). Belmont, CA: Wadsworth.

Castro, G. (1990). *American feminism: A contemporary history* (E. Loverde-Bagwell, Trans.). New York: New York University Press. (Original work published 1984).

Catania, J. A., Coates, T. J., Kegeles, S., Fullilove, M. T., Peterson, J., Marin, B., Siegel, D., & Hulley, S. (1992). Condom use in multi-ethnic neighborhoods of San Francisco: The population-based AMEN (AIDS in Multi-Ethnic Neighborhoods) Study. *American Journal of Public Health, 82,* 284–287.

Centers for Disease Control. (1991). Premarital sexual experience among adolescent women-United States, 1970–1988. *Morbidity and Mortality Weekly Report, 39,* Nos. 51 & 52. Atlanta, GA: Author.

Centers for Disease Control. (1994, December). *HIV/AIDS Surveillance Report, 6*(2), Atlanta, GA: Author.

Challis, J. R. G., & Mitchell, B. F. (1983). Endocrinology of pregnancy and parturition. In J. B. Warshaw (Ed.). *The biological basis of reproductive and developmental medicine.* New York: Elsevier Biomedical.

Chamberlain, M. K. (Ed.), (1988). *Women in academe: Progress and prospects.* New York: Russell Sage Foundation.

Chambless, D. L., & Goldstein, A. J. (1980). Anxieties: Agoraphobia and hysteria. In Brodsky, A. M., & Hare-Mustin, R. T. (Eds.), *Women and psychotherapy: An assessment of research and practice* (pp. 113–134). New York: Guilford Press.

Chandra, A. (1995). Health aspects of pregnancy and childbirth: United States, 1982–88. *Vital Health Statistics* (DHHS Publication No. PHS 95–1994). Washington, DC: U.S. Government Printing Office.

Changes in U.S. Life Expectancy. (1994). *Statistical Bulletin, 75,*(3). 11–17.

Chapman, J. R. (1988). Women in prison. In S. E. Rix (Ed.), *The American Woman 1988–1989): A status report* (pp. 303–309). New York: Norton.

Chavez, D. (1985). Perpetuation of gender inequality: A content analysis of comic strips. *Sex Roles, 13,* 93–102.

Cherry, F., & Deaux, K. (1978). Fear of success versus fear of gender-inappropriate behavior. *Sex Roles, 4,* 97–101.

Chesler, P. (1972). *Women and madness.* New York: Doubleday.

Chesler, P. (1986). *Mothers on trial: The battle for children and custody.* New York: McGraw Hill.

Chira, S. (1995, February 7). Care at most daycare centers rated as poor. *The New York Times,* p. A12.

Chodorow, N. (1978). *The reproduction of mothering: Psychoanalysis and the sociology of gender.* Berkeley, CA: University of California Press.

Chodorow, N. J. (1995). Gender as a personal and cultural construction. *Signs, 20,* 516–544.

Chollat-Traquet, C. (1992). Tobacco or health: A WHP programme. *European Journal of Cancer, 28,* 311–315.

Chrisler, J. C., Johnston, I. K., Champagne, N. M., & Preston, K. E. (1994). Menstrual joy: The construct and its consequences. *Psychology of Women Quarterly, 18,* 375–387.

Chrisler, J. C., & Levy, K. B. (1990). The media construct a menstrual monster: A content analysis of PMS articles in the popular press. *Women & Health, 16,* 89–104.

Christ, C. P. (1993). Why women need the Goddess: Phenomenological, psychological, and political reflections. In M. Pearsall (Ed.), *Women and values: Readings in recent feminist philosophy* (2nd ed., pp. 239–247). Belmont, CA: Wadsworth.

Christiansen, A., & Heavey, C. L. (1990). Gender and social structure in the demand/withdraw pattern of marital conflict. *Journal of Personality and Social Psychology, 59,* 73–81.

Christiansen, C., & Riis, B. J. (1990). Five years with continuous oestrogen/progestogen therapy: Effects on calcium metabolism, lipoproteins and bleeding pattern. *British Journal of Obstetrics and Gynecology, 97,* 1087–1092.

Christiansen, K., & Knussmann, R. (1987). Sex hormones and cognitive functioning in men. *Neuropsychobiology, 18,* 27–36.

Christmas, J. T. (1992). The risks of cocaine use in pregnancy. *Medical Aspects of Human Sexuality, 26*(2), 36–43.

Ciancanelli, P., & Berch, B. (1987). Gender and the GNP. In B. B. Hess and M. M. Ferree (Eds.), *Analyzing gender: A handbook of social science research* (pp. 244–266). Newbury Park, CA: Sage.

Clark, R., & Hatfield, E. (1989). Gender differences in receptivity to sexual offers. *Journal of Psychology and Human Sexuality, 2*(1), 39–55.

Clark-Nicolas, P., & Gray-Little, B. (1991). Effect of economic resources on marital quality in black married couples. *Journal of Marriage and the Family, 53,* 645–655.

Clarke-Stewart, K. (1991). A home is not a school: The effects of child care on children's development. *Journal of Social Issues, 47*(2), 105–123.

Cleaver, E. (1968). *Soul on ice.* New York: McGraw-Hill.

Clingempeel, W. G., Brand, C., & Ievoli, R. (1984). Stepparent-stepchild relationships in stepmother and stepfather families: A multimethod study. *Family Relations, 33,* 465–473.

Coates, D. L. (1987). Gender differences in the structure and support characteristics of Black adolescents' social networks. *Sex Roles, 17,* 719–136.

Coates, R. J., Bransfield, D. D., Wesley, M., Hankey, B., Eley, J. W., Greenberg, R. S., Flanders, D., Hunter, C. P., Edwards, B. K., Forman, M., Chen, V., Reynolds, P., Boyd, P., Austin, D., Muss, H., Blacklow, R. S. (1992). Differences between Black and White women with breast cancer in time from symptom recognition to medical consultation. *Journal of the National Cancer Institute, 84,* 938–950.

Cobleigh, M. A., Berris, R. F., Bush, T., Davidson, N. E., Robert, N. J., Sparano, J. A., Tormey, D. C., & Wood, W. C. (1994). Estrogen replacement therapy in breast cancer survivors: A time for a change. *Journal of the American Medical Association, 272,* 540–545.

Cochran, S. D., & Mays, V. M. (1989). Women and AIDS-Related concerns: Roles for psychologists in helping the worried well. *American Psychologist, 44,* 529–535.

Cockerham, W. C. (1990). A test of the relationship between race, socioeconomic status, and psychological distress. *Social Science and Medicine, 31,* 1321-1326.

Cohan, C. L., Dunkel-Schetter, C., & Lydon, J. (1993). Pregnancy decision making: Predictors of early stress and adjustment. *Psychology of Women Quarterly, 17,* 223–239.

Cohen, A. G., & Gutek, B. A. (1991). Sex differences in the career experiences of members of two APA divisions. *American Psychologist, 46,* 1292–1298.

Cohen, D., Reardon, K., Alleyne, D., Murthy, S., & Linton, K. (1995). Influencing spermicide use among low-income minority women. *Journal of the American Medical Women's Association, 50,* 11–13.

Cohen, J. (1977). *Statistical power analysis for the behavioral sciences* (Rev. ed.). New York: Academic Press.

Cohn, D. & Vobejda, B. (1992, December 7). Women advancing, by degrees. *The Providence Journal (Evening Bulletin),* pp. A-1, A-11.

Cohn, L. (1991). Sex differences in the course of personality development: A meta-analysis. *Psychological Bulletin, 252*–266.

Colditz, G. A., Hankinson, S. E., Hunter, D. J., Willett, W. C., Manson, J. E., Stampfer, M. J., Willett, W. C., Manson, J. E., Stampfer, M. J., Hennekens, C., Rosner, B., & Speizer, F. E. (1995). The use of estrogens and progestins and the risk of breast cancer in postmenopausal women. *The New England Journal of Medicine, 332,* 1589–1593.

Cole, P. M., & Putnam, F. W. (1992). Effect of incest on self and social functioning: A developmental psychopathology perspective. *Journal of Consulting and Clinical Psychology, 60,* 174–184.

Coleman, E. (1985). Bisexual women in marriages. *Journal of Homosexuality, 11,* 87–99.

Coleman-Burns, P. (1989). African American women—education for what? *Sex Roles, 21,* 145–160.

Colligan, R. C., Offord, K. P., Malinchoc, M., Schulman, P., & Seligman, M. (1994). CAVEing the MMPI for an optimism-pessimism scale: Seligman's attributional style and the assessment of explanatory style. *Journal of Clinical Psychology, 50,* 71–95.

Collins, M. E. (1988). Education for healthy body weight: Helping adolescents balance the cultural pressure for thinness. *Journal of School Health, 58,* 227–231.

Collins, N. L., Dunkel-Schetter, C., Lobel, M., & Scrimshaw, C. M. (1993). Social support in pregnancy: Psychosocial correlates of birth outcomes and postpartum depression. *Journal of Personality and Social Psychology, 65,* 1243–1258.

Collins, N. L., & Read, S. J. (1990). Adult attachment, working models, and relationship quality in dating couples. *Journal of Personality and Social Psychology, 58,* 644–663.

Collins, P. H. (1989). The social construction of Black feminist thought. *Signs, 14,* 745–773.

Collins, P. H. (1991). Learning from the outsider within: The sociological significance of Black feminist thought. In M. M. Fonow & J. A. Cook (Eds.), *Beyond methodology: Feminist scholarship as lived research* (pp. 35–59). Bloomington, IN: Indiana University Press.

Collins, P. H. (1995). The meaning of motherhood in Black culture. In A. Kesselman, L. D. McNair, & N. Schniedewind (Eds.), *Women images and realities: A multicultural anthology* (201–204). Mountain View: CA: Sage.

Coltrane, S., & Ishu-Kuntz, M. (1992). Men's housework: A life course perspective. *Journal of Marriage and the Family, 54,* 43–57.

Comas-Diaz, L., & Greene, B. (Eds.) (1994). *Women of color: Integrating ethnic and gender identities in psychotherapy.* New York: Guildford.

Connor, E. M., Sperling, R. S., Gelber, R., Kiselev, P., Scott, G., O'Sullivan, M. J., VanDyke, R., Bey, M., Shearer, W., Jacobson, R. L., Jimenez, E., O'Neill, E., Bazin, B., Delfraissy, J-F., Culnane, M., Coombs, R., Elkins,M., Moye, J., Stratton, P., & Balsley, J. (1994). Reducton of maternal-infant transmission of human immunodeficiency virus type 1 with zidovudine treatment. *The New England Journal of Medicine, 331,* 1173–1180.

Constantinople, A. (1973). Masculinity-femininity: An exception to a famous dictum? *Psychological Bulletin, 80,* 389–407.

Cooper, P. J., & Murray, L. (1995). Course and recurrence of postnatal depression: Evidence for the specificity of the diagnostic concept. *British Journal of Psychiatry, 166,* 191–195.

Copenhaver, S., & Grauerholz, E. (1991). Sexual victimization among sorority women: Exploring the link between sexual violence and institutional practices. *Sex Roles, 24,* 31–41.

Corbier, P. (1985). Sexual differentiation of positive feedback: Effect of hour of castration at birth on estradiol-induced luteinizing hormone secretion in immature male rats. *Endocrinology, 116,* 142–147.

Corea, G. (1987). The reproductive brothel. In G. Corea, D. R. Klein, J., Hanmer, H. B., Holmes, B., Hoskins, M., Kishwar, J. Raymond, R. Rowland, & R. Steinbacher (Eds.). *Man-made women: How new reproductive technologies affect women* (pp. 38–51). Bloomington, IN: Indiana University Press.

Cott, N. F. (1990). Across the great divide: Women in politics before and after 1920. In L. A. Tilly & P. Gurin (Eds.), *Women politics and change* (pp. 153–176). New York: Russell Sage Foundation.

Cotton, S., Antill, J. K., & Cunningham, J. D. (1990). The work attachment of mothers with preschool children. *Psychology of Women Quarterly, 14,* 255–270.

Coverman, S., & Sheley, J. F. (1986). Change in men's housework and child-care time, 1965–1975. *Journal of Marriage and the Family, 48,* 413–422.

Cowan, G. (1992). Feminist attitudes toward pornography control. *Psychology of Women Quarterly, 16,* 165–177.

Cowan, G., & Avants, S. K. (1988). Children's influence strategies: Sex differences, and bilateral mother-child influence. *Child Development, 59,* 1303–1313.

Cowan, G., & Campbell, R. R. (1994). Racism and sexism in interracial pornography, *Psychology of Women Quarterly, 18,* 323–338.

Cowan, G., Lee, O., Levy, D., & Snyder, D. (1988). Dominance and inequality in x-rated videocasettes. *Psychology of Women Quarterly, 12,* 299–311.

Cozzarelli, C. (1993). Personality and self-efficacy as predictors of coping with abortion. *Journal of Personality and Social Psychology, 65,* 1224–1236.

Crandall, C. S. (1988). Social contagion of binge eating. *Journal of Personality and Social Psychology, 55,* 588–598.

Crandall, V. C. (1969). Sex differences in expectancy of intellectual and academic reinforcement. In C.P. Smith (Ed.), *Achievement-related motives in children* (pp. 11–45). New York: Russell Sage Foundation.

Crandall, B. F., Kulch, P., & Tabsh, K. (1994). Risk assessment of amniocentesis between 11 and 15 weeks: Comparison to later amniocentesis controls. *Prenatal Diagnosis, 14,* 913–919.

Crawford, M. & MacLeod, M. (1990). Gender in the college classroom: An assessment of the "chilly climate" for women. *Sex Roles, 23,* 101–122.

Criqui, M. H. (1987). The roles of alcohol in the epidemiology of cardiovascular diseases. *Acta Medica Scandinavia, 717,* [Suppl.], 73–85.

Crockett, L. J., & Petersen, A. C. (1987). Pubertal status and psychosocial development: Findings from the early adolescent study. In R. M. Lerner & T. T. Foch (Eds.), *Biological-psychosocial interactions in early adolescence* (pp. 173–188). Hillsdale, NJ: Erlbaum.

Crook, D., Cust, M. P., Gangar, K. F., Worthington, M., Hillard, T. C., Stevenson, J. C., Whitehead, M. I., & Wynn, V. (1992). Comparison of transdermal and oral estrogen-progestin replacement therapy: Effects on serum lipids and lipoproteins. *American Journal of Obstetrics and Gynecology, 166,* 950–955.

Crosby, F. (1982). *Relative deprivation and the working woman.* New York: Oxford University Press.

Crosby, F., & Clayton, S. (1990). Affirmative action and the issue of expectancies. *Journal of Social Issues, 46*(2), 61–79.

Crossman, R.K., Stith, S.M., & Bender, M.M. (1990). Sex role egalitarianism and marital violence. *Sex Roles, 22,* 293–304.

Crovitz, E., & Steinmann, A. (1980). A decade later: Black-White attitudes toward women's familial role. *Psychology of Women Quarterly, 5,* 170–176.

Culp, R. E., Appelbaum, M.I., Osofsky, J. D., & Levy, J. A. (1988). Adolescent and older mothers: Comparison between prenatal maternal variables and newborn interaction measures. *Infant Behavior and Development, 11,* 353–362.

Cumming, D. C., Cumming, C. E., Krausher, J. R., & Fox, E. E. (1991). Towards a definition of PMS II: A factor analytic evaluation of premenstrual change in women with symptomatic premenstrual change. *Journal of Psychosomatic Research, 35,* 713–720.

Cupach, W. R., & Comstock, J. (1990). Satisfaction with sexual communication in marriage: Links to sexual satisfaction and dyadic adjustment. *Journal of Social and Personal Relationships, 7,* 179–186.

Curtis, L. (1976). Rape, race and culture: Some speculations in search of a theory. In M. J. Walker & S. L. Brodsky (Eds.), *Sexual Assault: The victim and the rapist* (pp. 117–134). Lexington, MA: Lexington Books.

Cuskey, W. R., & Wathey, R. B. (1982). *Female addiction: A longitudinal study.* Lexington, MA: Lexington Books.

Cutrona, C. E. (1982). Nonpsychotic postpartum depression: A review of recent research. *Clinical Psychology Review, 2,* 487–503.

Dabbs, J. M., Jr., de La Rue, D., & Williams, P. M. (1990). Testosterone and occupational choice: Actors, ministers, and other men. *Journal of Personality and Social Psychology, 5,* 1261–1265.

Dabbs, J. M., Jr., Frady, R. L., Carr, T. S., & Besch, N. F. (1987). Salvia testosterone and criminal violence in young adult prison inmates. *Psychosomatic Medicine, 49,* 174–182.

Dabbs, J. M., Jr., & Morris, R. (1990). Testosterone, social class, and antisocial behavior in a sample of 4,462 men. *Psychological Science, 3,* 209–211.

Dabbs, J. M., Jr., Ruback, R. B., Frady, R., Hopper, C. H., & Sgoutas, D. S. (1988). Salvia testosterone and criminal violence among women. *Personality and Individual Differences, 1,* 103–110.

Daling, J., Weiss, N., Spadoni, L., Moore, D. E. & Voigt, L. (1987). Cigarette smoking and primal tubal infertility. In M. J. Rosenberg (Ed.). *Smoking and reproductive health* (pp. 40–46). Littleton, MA: PSG Publishing Co.

Dalton, K. (1964). *The premenstrual syndrome.* Springfield, IL: Charles C.Thomas.

Dalton, K. (1977). *The premenstrual syndrome and progesterone therapy.* London: W. Heineman Medical Books.

Dalton, K. (1980). Cyclical criminal acts in premenstrual syndrome. *Lancet,* 1070–1071.

Daly, M. (1993). The qualitative leap beyond patriarchal religion. In M. Pearsall (Ed.) *Women and values*: Readings in recent feminist philosophy (2nd ed., pp. 227–238). Belmont, CA: Wadsworth.

Dambrot, F. H., Watkins-Malek, M. A., Silling, S. M., Marshall, R. S., and Garver, J. A. (1985). Correlates of sex differences in attitudes toward and involvement with computers. *Journal of Vocational Behavior, 27,* 71–86.

Dan, A. J., Wilbur, C. H., Hedricks, C., O'Connor, E. & Holm, K. (1990). Lifelong physical activity in midlife and older women. *Psychology of Women Quarterly, 14,* 531–542.

Daniluk, J. C. (1993). The meaning and experience of female sexuality. *Psychology of Women Quarterly, 17,* 53–69.

Darling, C. A., Davidson, J. K., & Jennings, D. A. (1991). The female sexual responsere visited: Understanding the multiorgasmic experience in women. *Archives of Sexual Behavior, 20,* 527–540.

Deren, S., Beardsley, M., Davis, R., & Tortu, S. (1993). HIV risk factors among pregnant and non-pregnant high-risk women in New York City. *Journal of Drug Education, 23,* 57–66.

David, H. P., Rasmussen, N., & Holst, E. (1981). Postpartum and postabortion psychotic reactions. *Family Planning Perspectives, 13,* 88–92.

Davis, M. H., & Oatout, H. A. (1987). Maintenance of satisfaction in romantic relationships: Empathy and relationship competence. *Journal of Personality and Social Psychology, 53,* 397–410.

Davis, M. H., & Oatout, H. A. (1992). The effect of dispositional empathy on romantic relationship behaviors: Heterosocial anxiety as a moderating influence. *Personality and Social Psychology Bulletin, 18,* 76–83.

Davis-Floyd, R. E. (1994). The technocratic body: American childbirth as cultural expression. *Social Science & Medicine, 38,* 1125–1140.

Deaux, K. (1979). Self-evaluation of male and female managers. *Sex Roles, 5,* 571–580.

Deaux, K. & Lewis, L. L. (1984). Structure of gender stereotypes: Interrelationships among components and gender label. *Journal of Personality and Social Psychology, 46,* 991–1004.

Deaux, K., White, L., & Farris, E. (1975). Skill versus luck: Field and laboratory studies of male and female preferences. *Journal of Personality and Social Psychology, 32,* 629–636.

de Beauvoir, S. (1961). *The second sex.* (Original work published in 1949). New York: Bantam.

Deck, L. P. (1968). Buying brains by the inch. *The Journal of College and University Personnel Association, 19,* 33–37.

DeFour, C. C. (1990). The interface of racism and sexism on college campuses. In M. A. Paludi (Ed.), *Ivory Power: Sexual harassment on campus* (pp. 45–52). Albany, NY: State University of New York Press.

De Jonge, F. H., Muntjewerff, M. W., Louwerse, A. L., & Van de Poll, N. E. (1988). Sexual behavior and sexual orientation of the female rat after hormonal treatment during various stages of development. *Hormones and Behavior, 22,* 100–115.

de Lacoste, M. C., Horvath, D. S., & Woodward, D. J. (1991). Possible sex differences in the developing human fetal brain. *Journal of Clinical and Experimental Neurobiology, 13,* 831–846.

de Lacoste-Utamsing, C. & Holloway, R. L. (1982). Sexual dimorphism in the human corpus callosum, *Science, 216,* 1431–1432.

DeMaris, A. & Rao, K. V. (1992). Premarital cohabitation and subsequent marital stability in the United States: A reassessment. *Journal of Marriage and the Family, 54,* 178–190.

Dembo, R., Williams, L., Wish, E. D., Dertke, M., Berry, E., Getreu, A., Washburn, M., & Schmeidler, J. (1988). The relationship between physical and sexual abuse and illicit drug use: A replication among a new sample of youths entering a juvenile detention center. *The International Journal of the Addictions, 23,* 1101–1123.

Demo, D. H. (1992). Parent-child relations: Assessing recent changes. *Journal of Marriage and the Family, 54,* 104–117.

DeMuylder, X., & Wesel, S. (1988). Maternal attitudes and preterm labor. In P. Feydor-Freybergh & M. L. V. Vogel (Eds.). *Prenatal and perinatal psychology and medicine: Encounter with the unborn* (pp. 87–97). The Parthenon Publishing Group.

Denmark, F. L. (1993). Women, leadership, and empowerment. *Psychology of Women Quarterly, 17,* 343–356.

Denmark, F. L., Shaw, J. S., & Ciali, S. D. (1985). The relationship among sex roles, living arrangements, and the division of household responsibilities. *Sex Roles, 12,* 617–625.

Denney, N. W., Field, J. K., & Quadagno, D. (1984). Sex differences in sexual needs and desires. *Archives of Sexual Behavior, 13,* 233–245.

Deren, S., Tortu, S., & Davis, W. R. (1993). An AIDS risk reduction project with inner-city women. In C. Squire (Ed.), *Women and AIDS: Psychological perspectives* (pp. 73–89). London: Sage.

de Rham, E. (1965). *The love fraud.* New York: Pegasus.

De Rubeis, R. J., Evans, M. D., Hollon, S. D., Garvey, M. J., Grove, W. M., & Tuason, V. B. (1990). How does cognitive therapy work? Cognitive change and symptom change in cognitive therapy and pharmacotherapy for depression. *Journal of Consulting and Clinical Psychology, 58,* 862–869.

Deutsch, F. (1990). Status, sex, and smiling: The effect of smiling in men and women. *Personality and Social Psychology bulletin, 16,* 531–540.

De Vincenzi, I., (1994). A longitudinal study of human immunodeficiency virus transmission by heterosexual partners. *The New England Journal of Medicine, 331,* 341–346.

deWolf, V. A. (1981). High school mathematics preparation and sex differences in quantitative abilities. *Psychology of Women Quarterly, 5,* 555–567.

de Zalduondo, B. O. (1991). Prostitution viewed cross-culturally: Toward recontextualizing sex work in AIDS intervention research. *Journal of Sex Research, 28,* 223–248.

Diamond, I. (1980). Pornography and repression.: A reconsideration of "who" and "what." In L. Lederer (Ed.), *Take back the night* (pp. 187–203). New York: William Morrow.

Diamond, M. C. (1988). *Enriching heredity: The impact of the environment on the anatomy of the brain.* New York: Free Press.

Dick-Read, G. (1933). *Natural childbirth.* London: Heinemann Medical Books.

Diehm, C., & Ross, M. (1988). Battered women. In S. E. Rix (Ed.), *The American woman 1988–1989: A status report* (pp. 292–302). New York: Norton.

Dindia, K., & Allen, M. (1992). Sex differences in self-disclosure: A meta-analysis. *Psychological Bulletin, 112,* 106–122.

Dines-Levy, G. (1988). An analysis of pornography research. In A. W. Burgess (Ed.), *Rape and sexual assault II.* New York: Garland Publishing.

Dion, K. L., & Schuller, R. A. (1990). Ms. and the Manager: A tale of two stereotypes. *Sex Roles, 22,* 569–577.

DiVasto, P. V., Pathak, D., & Fishburn, W. R. (1981). The interrelationship of sex guilt, sex behavior, and age in an adult sample. *Archives of Sexual Behavior, 10,* 119–122.

Diverse living arrangements of children. (1993). *Statistical Bulletin, 74,* (3), 2–9.

Dixon, J. K. (1985). Sexuality and relationship changes in married females following the commencement of bisexual activity. *Journal of Homosexuality, 11,* 115–133.

Dixson, A. F. (1993). Effects of testosterone propionate upon the sexual and aggressive behavior of adult male marmosets (Callithrix jacchus) castrated as neonates. *Hormones and Behavior, 27,* 216–230.

Dodge, L. J. T., Glasgow, R. E., & O'Neill, H. K. (1982). Bibliotherapy in the treatment of female orgasmic dysfunction. *Journal of Consulting and Clinical Psychology, 50,* 442–443.

Doll, R. (1994). The use of meta-analysis in epidemiology: Diet and cancers of the breast and colon. *Nutrition Reviews, 52,* 233–237.

Donat, P. L. N., & D'Emilio, J. (1992). A feminist redefinition of rape and sexual assault: Historical foundations and change. *Journal of Social Issues, 48,*(1) 9–22.

Donnerstein, E., & Hallam, J. (1978). Facilitating effects of erotica on aggression against women. *Journal of Personality and Social Psychology, 36,* 1270–1277.

Donovan, J. (1985). *Feminist theory: The intellectual traditions of American feminism.* New York: Frederick Ungar.

d'Orban, P. T., & Dalton, K. (1980). Violent crime and the menstrual cycle. *Psychological Medicine, 10,* 353–359.

d'Oro, L. C., Parazzini, F., Naldi,L., & LaVecchia, C. (1994). *Genitourinary Medicine, 70,* 410–417.

Dovidio, J. F., & Ellyson, S. L. (1985). Patterns of visual dominance behavior in humans. In S. L. Ellyson & J. F. Dovidio (Eds.), *Power, dominence, and nonverbal behavior* (pp. 129–149). New York: Springer-Verlag.

Dowling, C. (1981). *The cinderella complex: Women's hidden fear of independence.* New York: Summit.

Downey, G., & Moen, P. (1987). Personal efficacy, income, and family transitions: A longitudinal study of women heading households. *Journal of Health and Social Behavior, 28,* 320–333.

Drazin, R., & Auster, E. R. (1987). Wage differences between men and women: Performance appraisal ratings vs. salary allocation as the locus of bias. *Human Resource Management, 26,* 157–168.

Drewett, R. F., Kahn, H., Parkhurst, S., & Whiteley, S. (1987). Pain during breastfeeding: The first three months postpartum. *Journal of Reproductive and Infant Psychology, 5,* 183–186.

DuBois, D. L., & Hirsch, B. J. (1990). School and neighborhood friendship patterns of blacks and whites in early adolescence. *Child Development, 61,* 524–536.

Duelberg, S. I. (1992). Preventive health behavior among black and white women in urban and rural areas. *Social Science and Medicine 34,* 191–198.

Dujon, D., Gradford, J., & Stevens, D. (1992). Reports from the front: Welfare mothers up in arms. In M. L. Andersen & P. H. Collins (Eds.), *Race, class, and gender: An anthology* (pp. 259–266). Belmont, CA: Wadsworth.

Duncan, B., Ey, J., Holberg, C. J., Wright, A. L., Martinez, F. D., & Taussig, L. M. (1993). Exclusive breast-feeding for at least 4 months protects against otitis media. *Pediatrics, 91,* 867–871.

Dunn, K. F., & Cowan, G. (1993). Social influence strategies among Japanese and American College Women. *Psychology of Women Quarterly, 17,* 39–52.

Dutton-Douglas, M. A., & Dionne, D. (1991). Counseling and shelter services for battered women. In M. Steinman (Ed.), *Woman battering: Policy responses* (pp. 113–130). Cincinnati, OH: Anderson.

Dworkin, A. (1983). *Right-wing women.* New York: Perigee Books.

Dzeich, B., & Weiner, L. (1984). *The lecherous professor: Sexual harassment on campus.* Boston: Beacon.

Eagly, A. H. (1978). Sex differences in influenceability. *Psychological Bulletin, 85,* 86–116.

Eagly, A. H. (1987). *Sex differences in social behavior: A social role interpretation.* Hillsdale, NJ: Erlbaum.

Eagly, A. H. & Carli, L. L. (1981). Sex of researchers and sex-typed communications as determinants of sex differences in influenceability: A meta-analysis of social influence studies. *Psychological Bulletin, 90,* 1–20.

Eagly, A. H. & Crowley, M. (1986). Gender and helping behavior: a meta-analytic review of the social psychological literature. *Psychological Bulletin, 100,* 283–308.

Eagly, A. H. & Johnson, B. T. (1991). Gender and leadership style: A meta-analysis. *Psychological Bulletin, 108,* 233–256.

Eagly, A. H. & Karau, S. J. (1991). Gender and the emergence of leaders: A meta-analysis. *Journal of Personality and Social Psychology, 60,* 685–710.

Eagly, A. H., Karau, S. J., & Makhijani, M. G. (1995). Gender and the effectiveness of leaders: A meta-analysis. *Psychological Bulletin, 117,* 125–145.

Eagly, A. H., Makhijani, M. G., & Klonsky, B. G. (1992). Gender and the evaluation of leaders: A meta-analysis. *Psychological Bulletin, 111,* 3–22.

Eagly, A. H., Mladinic, A., & Otto, S. (1991). Are women evaluated more favorably than men? An analysis of attitudes, beliefs, emotions. *Psychology of Women Quarterly, 15,* 203–216.

Eagly, A. H., & Steffen, V. J. (1986). Gender and aggressive behavior: A meta-analytic review of the social psychological literature. *Psychological Bulletin, 100,* 283–308.

Eagly, A. H., & Wood, W. (1991). Explaining sex differences in social behavior: A meta-analytic perspective. *Personality and Social Psychology bulletin, 17,* 306–315.

East, P. L., & Felice, M. E. (1990). Outcomes of parent-child relationships of former adolescent mothers and their 12-year-old children. *Journal of Developmental and Behavioral Pediatrics, 11*(4), 175–183.

Eaton, W. O. and Enns, L. R. (1986). Sex differences in human motor activity level. *Psychological Bulletin, 100,* 19–28.

Eaton, W. O. & Yu, A. P. (1989). Are sex differences in child motor activity a function of sex differences in maturational status? *Child Development, 60,* 1005–1011.

Eccles, J. S. (1985). Sex differences in achievement patterns. In T. E. Sonderegger (Ed.), *Psychology and gender. Nebraska Symposium on Motivation 1984* (pp. 99–132). Lincoln, NE: University of Nebraska Press.

Eccles, J. S. (1987). Gender roles and women's achievement-related decisions. *Psychology of Women Quarterly, 11,* 135–172.

Eccles, J. S., & Blumenfeld, P. (1985). Classroom experiences and student gender: Are there differences and do they matter? In L. C. Wilkinson and C. B. Marrett (Eds.), *Gender influences in classroom interaction* (pp. 79–114). Orlando, FL: Academic Press.

Eccles, J. S. and Jacobs, J. E. (1986). Social forces shape math attitudes and performance. *Signs, 11,* 367–389.

Echols, A. (1989). The new feminism of Yin and Yang. In B. J. Risman and P. Schwartz (Eds.), *Gender in intimate relationships* (pp. 48–57). Belmont, CA: Wadsworth.

Eckert, E. D. (1985). Characteristics of anorexia nervosa. In J. E. Mitchell (Ed.), *Anorexia nervosa & bulimia: Diagnosis and treatment* (pp. 3–28). Minneapolis, MN: University of Minnesota Press.

Egeland, G. M., Kuller, L. H., Matthews, K. A., Kelsey, S. F., Cauley, J., Guzick, D. (1990). Hormone replacement therapy and lipoprotein changes during early menopause. *Obstetrics & Gynecology, 76,* 776–782.

Egley, L. C. (1991). What changes the societal prevalence of domestic violence? *Journal of Marriage and the Family, 53,* 885–897.

Egoff, D. B., & Corder, L. E. (1991). Height differences of low and high job status, female and male corporate employees. *Sex Roles, 24,* 365–373.

Ehrenreich, B., Hess, E., & Jacobs, G. (1986). *Re-making love: The feminization of sex.* Garden City, NY: Anchor Press/Doubleday.

Ehrensaft, D. (1983). When women and men mother. In J. Trebilcot (Ed.), *Mothering: Essays in feminist theory* (pp. 41–61). Totowa, NJ: Rowman & Allanheld.

Eichler, A., & Parron, D. L. (1987). *Women's mental health: Agenda for research.* Rockville, MD: National Institute of Mental Health.

Eisenberg, N., & Lennon, R. (1983). Sex differences in empathy and related capacities. *Psychological Bulletin, 94,* 100–131.

Eisenhart, M. A., & Holland, D. C. (1992). Gender constructs and career commitment: The influence of peer culture on women in college. In T. L. Whitehead & B. V. Reid (Eds.), *Gender constructs and social issues* (pp. 142–180). Urbana, IL: University of Illinois Press.

El-Bassel, N., & Schilling, R. F. (1992). 15-month followup of women methodone patients taught skills to reduce heterosexual HIV transmission. *Public Health Reports, 107,* 500–504.

Eldridge, N. S., & Gilbert, L. A. (1990). Correlates of relationship satisfaction in lesbian couples. *Psychology of Women Quarterly, 14,* 43–62.

Elkind, D. (1994). *Ties that stress: The new family imbalance.* Cambridge, MA: Harvard University Press.

Elkins, L. E., & Peterson, C. (1993). Gender differences in best friendships. *Sex Roles, 29,* 497–508.

Elliott, S. A., & Watson, J. P. (1985). Sex during pregnancy and the first postnatal year. *Journal of Psychosomatic Research, 29,* 541–548.

Ellis, E. M., Atkison, B. M., & Calhoun, K. S. (1981). An assessment of long-term reaction to rape. *Journal of Abnormal Psychology, 90,* 263–266.

Ellis, L. (1991). A synthesized (biosocial) theory of rape. *Journal of Consulting and Clinical Psychology, 59,* 631–642.

Ellyson, S. L., Carson, C. M., DeBlasio, C. L., Morrison, S. K., Riley, M. E., Dovidio, J. F., Brown, C. E. (1991, April). *Positions of power and visual dominance behavior in females.* Paper presented at the the annual meeting of the Eastern Psychological Association. New York City.

Emery, J. L., Scholey, S., Taylor, E. M. (1990). Decline in breast feeding. *Archives of Diseases in Childhood, 65,* 369–372.

Engelhardt, B. J., & Triantafillou, K. (1987). Mediation for lesbians. In the Boston Lesbian Psychologies Collective (Eds.), *Lesbian psychologies: Explorations and challenges* (pp. 327–343). Urbana, IL: University of Illinois Press.

England, P. (1992). *Comparable worth: Theory and evidence.* New York: Aldine de Gruyter.

England, P., & McCreary, L. (1987). Gender inequality in paid employment. In Hess, B. B. & M. M. Ferree (Eds.). *Analyzing gender: A handbook of social science research* (pp. 286–320). Newbury Park, CA: Sage.

Entwisle, D. R., & Baker, D. P. (1983). Gender and young children's expectations for performance in arithmetic. *Developmental Psychology, 19,* 200–209.

Epple, G. (1978). Lack of effects of castration on scent marking, displays and aggression in a South American primate (Saguinus fuscicollis). *Hormones and Behavior, 11,* 139–150.

Epple, G., Alveario, M. C., & St. Andre, E. (1987). Sexual and social behavior of adult saddle-back Tamarins (Saguinus fascicollis), castrated as neonates. *American Journal of Primatology, 13,* 37–49.

Ericsson, K. A., & Charness, N. (1994). Expert performance: Its structure and acquisition. *American Psychologist, 49,* 725–747.

Erikson, E. (1968). *Identity: Youth and Crisis.* New York: Norton.

Erinakes, D. M. (1980). An analysis of women elementary school principals and long term women teachers in relation to selected psychological and situational variables. (Doctoral dissertation, University of Connecticut, 1980).

Eskey, J. (1993, April 10). Most elderly are homeowners. *The Providence Journal Bulletin*, p. B-l.

Espin, O. M. (1984). Cultural and historical influences on sexuality in Hispanic/Latin women: Implications for psychotherapy. In C. S. Vance (Ed.), *Pleasure and danger: Exploring female sexuality* (pp. 149–164). Boston: Routledge & K. Paul.

Espin, O. M. (1987). Psychological impact of migration on Latinas: Implications for psychotherapeutic practice. *Psychology of Women Quarterly, 11,* 489–503.

Espin, O. M. (1994). Feminist approaches. In L. Comas-Diaz & B. Greene (Eds.), *Women of color: Integrating ethnic and gender identities in psychotherapy* (pp. 265–286). New York: Guilford.

Espin, O. M. & Warner, B. (1982). Attitudes toward the role of Cuban women attending a community college. *International Journal of Social Psychiatry, 28,* 233–239.

Etaugh, C., & Nekolny, K. (1990). Effects of employment status and marital status of mothers. *Sex Roles, 23,* 273–280.

Ettinger, B., Genant, H. K., & Cann, C. E. (1985). Long-term estrogen replacement therapy prevents bone loss and fractures. *Annals of Internal Medicine, 102,* 319–324.

Evans, M. D., Hollon, S. D., DeRubeis, R. J., Piasecki, J., Grove, W. M., Garvey, M. J., & Tuason, V. B. (1992). Differential relapse following cognitive therapy and pharmacotherapy for depression. *Archives of General Psychiatry, 49,* 802–808.

Ewigman, B. G., Crane, J. P., Frigoletto, F. D., LeFevre, M. L., Bain, R. P., McNellis, D., & the RADIUS Study Group (1993). Effect of prenatal ultrasound screening on perinatal outcome. *The New England Journal of Medicine, 329,* 821–827.

Exline, R. V., Ellyson, S. L., & Long, B. (1975). Visual behavior as an aspect of power-role relationships. In P. Pliner, L. Krames, & T. Alloway (Eds.), *Nonverbal communication of aggression* (pp. 21–53). New York: Plenum Press.

Fairweather, D. V. I. (1968). Nausea and vomiting in pregnancy. *American Journal of Obstetrics and Gynecology, 102,* 135-175.

Falbo, T., & Peplau, L. A. (1980). Power strategies in intimate relationships. *Journal of Personality and Social Psychology, 38,* 618–628.

Falk, P. J. (1989). Lesbian mothers: Psychosocial assumptions in family law. *American Psychologist, 44,* 941–947.

Fallon, A. E., & Rozin, P. (1985). Sex differences in perceptions of desirable body shape. *Journal of Abnormal Psychology, 94,* 102–105.

Farrell, G. J. (1992). How to kill higher education. *Academe, 78,* 30–48.

Fausto-Sterling, A. (1985). *Myths of gender: Biological theories about women and men.* New York: Basic Books.

Fausto-Sterling, A. (1987). Society writes biology/biology constructs gender. In J. K. Conway, S. C. Bourque, & J. Scott (Eds.), *Learning about women: Gender, politics, and power* (pp. 61–76). Ann Arbor, MI: University of Michigan Press.

Fausto-Sterling, A. (1992). *Myths of gender: Biological theories about men and women* (2nd ed.). New York: Basic Books.

Featherstone, D. R., Cundick, B. P., & Jensen, L. C. (1992). Differences in school behavior and achievement between children from intact, reconstituted, and single-parent families. *Adolescence, 27,* 1–12.

Feeney, J. A., & Noller, P. (1990). Attachment style as a predictor of adult romantic relationships. *Journal of Personality and Social Psychology, 58,* 281–291.

Feingold, A. (1988). Cognitive gender differences are disappearing. *American Psychologist, 43,* 95–103.

Feingold, A. (1990). Gender differences in effects of physical attractiveness on romantic attraction: A comparison across research paradigms. *Journal of Personality and Social Psychology, 59,* 981–993.

Feingold, A. (1992a). Gender differences in mate selection preferences: A test of the parental investment model. *Psychological Bulletin, 112,* 125–139.

Feingold, A. (1992b). Sex differences in variability in intellectual abilities: A new look at an old controversy. *Review of Educational Research, 62,* 61–84.

Feingold, A. (1994). Gender differences in personality: A meta-analysis. *Psychological Bulletin, 116,* 429–456.

Feinman, C. (1994). *Women in the Criminal Justice System* (3rd ed.). Westport, CT: Praeger.

Feiring, C., & Lewis, M. (1987). The child's social network: Sex differences from 3 to 6 years. *Sex Roles, 17,* 621–636.

Fennema, E., & Sherman, J. (1977). Sex-related differences in mathematics achievement, spatial visualization, and related factors. *American Educational Research Journal, 4,* 51–71.

Ferguson, A. (1990). Is there a lesbian culture? In J. Allen (Ed.), *Lesbian philosophies and culture.* Albany, NY: State University of New York Press.

Fergusson, D. M., Breautrais, A. L., & Silva, R. A. (1982). Breastfeeding and cognitive development in the first 7 years. *Social Science and Medicine, 16,* 1705–1708.

Fernandez, C., & Holscher, L. (1983). Chicano-Anglo intermarriage in Arizona, 1960–1980: An exploratory study of eight counties. *Hispanic Journal of Behavioral Sciences, 5,* 291–304.

Ferree, M. M. (1987). She works hard for a living: Gender and class on the job. In B. B. Hess & M. M. Ferree (Eds.), *Analyzing gender: A handbook of social science research* (pp. 221–236). New York: Academic Press.

Festinger, L. (1954). A theory of social comparison processes. *Human Relations, 7,* 117–140.

Fetler, M. (1985). Sex differences on the California statewide assessment of computer literacy. *Sex Roles, 13,* 181–191.

Fine, M., & Asch, A. (1981). Disabled women: Sexism without the pedestal. *Journal of Sociology and Social Welfare, 8*(2), 233–248.

Fine, M. A., McKenry, P. C., Donnelly, B. W., & Voydanoff, P. (1992). Perceived adjustment of parents and children: Variations by family structure, race, and gender. *Journal of Marriage and the Family, 54,* 118–127.

Finegan, J., Bartleman, B., & Wong, P. Y. (1989). A window for the study of prenatal sex hormone influences on postnatal development. *Journal of Genetic Psychology, 150,* 101–112.

Finkelhor, D. (1984). *Child sexual abuse: New theory and research.* New York: Free Press.

Finkelhor, D., & Browne, A. (1985). The traumatic impact of child sexual abuse: A conceptualization. *American Journal of Orthopsychiatry, 55,* 530–543.

Finkelhor, D., & Dziuba-Leatherman, J. (1994). Victimization of children. *American Psychologist,* 173–183.

Finkelhor, D., & Yllo, K. (1982). Forced sex in marriage: A preliminary research report. *Crime & Delinquency, 28,* 459–478.

Finkelhor, D., & Yllo, K. (1985). *License to rape: Sexual abuse of wives.* New York: Holt, Rinehart & Winston.

Fiorentine, R. (1988). Sex differences in success expectancies and causal attribtions: Is this why fewer woman become physicians? *Social Psychology Quarterly, 51,* 236–249.

Firestone, S. (1970). *The dialectic of sex: The case for feminist revolution.* New York: William Morrow.

Firth, H. V., Boyd, P. A., Chamberlain, P. F., MacKenzie, I. Z., Morriss, K. G. M., & Huson, S. M. (1994). Severe limb abnormalities after chorion villus sampling at 56–66 days' gestation. *The Lancet, 337,* 762–763.

Fischer, L. R. (1987). *Linked lives: Adult daughters and their mothers.* New York: Harper & Row.

Fisher, Berenice, & Galler, R. (1988). Friendship and fairness: How disability affects friendship between women. In M. Fine & A. Asch *Women with disabilities: Essays in psychology, culture and politics* (pp. 172–194). Philadelphia: Temple University Press.

Fisher, Bernard, Costantino, J., Redmond, C., Fisher, E., Margolese, R., Dimitrov, N., Wolmark, N., Wickerham, D. L., Deutsch, M., Ore, L., Mamounas, E., Poller, & Kavanah, M. (1993). Lumpectomy compared with lumpectomy and radiation therapy for the treatment of intraductal breast cancer. *The New England Journal of Medicine, 328,* 1581–1586.

Fisher, W. A., & Byrne, D. (1978). Individual differences in affective, evaluative, and behavioral responses to an erotic film. *Journal of Applied Social Psychology, 8,* 355–365.

Fisher, W. A., Byrne, D., White, L. A., & Kelley, K. (1989). Erotopho-bia-erotophilia as a dimension of personality. *Journal of Sex Research, 25,* 123–151.

Fisher, W. A., & Gray, J. (1988). Erotophobia-erotophilia and sexual behavior during pregnancy and postpartum. *Journal of Sex Research, 25,* 379–396.

Fiske, S. T. (1993). Controlling other people: The impact of power on stereotyping. *American Psychologist, 48,* 621–628.

Fiske, S. T., Bersoff, D. N., Borgida, E., Deaux, K. & Heilman, M. E. (1991). Social science research on trial: Use of sex stereotyping research in Price Waterhouse v. Hopkins. *American Psychologist, 46,* 1049–1060.

Fiske, S. T., & Taylor, S. E. (1991). *Social cognition* (2nd ed.). Reading, MA: Addison-Wesley.

Fitzgerald, L. F., & Weitzman, L. M. (1990). Men who harass: Speculation and data. In M. A. Paludi (Ed.), *Ivory power: Sexual harassment on campus* (pp. 125–140). Albany, NY: State University of New York Press.

Flaks, D. K., Ficher, I., Masterpasqua, F., & Joseph, G., (1995). Lesbians choosing motherhood: A comparative study of lesbian and heterosexual parents and their children. *Child Development, 31,* 105–114.

Fleischer, R. A., & Chertkoff, J. M. (1986). Effects of dominance and sex on leadership selection in dyadic work groups. *Journal of Personality and Social Psychology, 50,* 95–99.

Fluoxetine Bulimia Nervosa Collaborative Study Group. (1992). Fluoxetine in the treatment of bulimia nervosa: A multicenter, placebo-controlled, double-blind trial. *Archives of General Psychiatry, 49,* 139–147.

Foa, E. B., Rothbaum, B. O., Riggs, D. S., & Murdock, T.B. (1991). Treatment of posttraumatic stress disorder in rape victims: A comparison between cognitive behavioral procedures and counseling. *Journal of Consulting and Clinical Psychology, 59,* 715–723.

Follette, V. M., Alexander, P. C., & Follette, W. C. (1991). Individual predictors of outcome in group treatment for incest survivors. *Journal of Consulting and Clinical Psychology, 59,* 150–155.

Forcey, L. R. (1987). *Mothers of sons: Towards an understanding of responsibility.* New York: Praeger.

Ford, M. R., & Lowery, C. R. (1986). Gener differences in moral reasoning: A comparison of the use of justice and care orientations. *Journal of Personality and Social Psychology, 50,* 777–783.

Ford, T. E., & Stangor, C. (1992). The role of diagnosticity in stereotype formation: Perceiving group means and variances. *Journal of Personality and Social Psychology, 63,* 356–367.

Foreman, J. (November 1, 1993). Study shows women earn less teaching medicine. *Boston Globe,* p. 18.

Forrest, A. P., & Alexander, F. E. (1995). A question that will not go away: At what age should mammographic screening begin? *Journal of the National Cancer Institute, 87,* 1195–1197.

Forrest, J. D. (1987). Unintended pregnancy among American women. *Family Planning Perspectives, 19,* 76–77.

Forrest, J. D., & Fordyce, R. R. (1993). Women's contraceptive attitudes and use in 1992. *Family Planning Perspectives, 25,* 175–179.

Fowers, B. J. (1991). His and her marriages: A multivariate study of gender and marital satisfaction. *Sex Roles, 24,* 209–221.

Fowler, R. D. (1991, Spring). Running commentary. *The APA Monitor, 2*(4), 3.

Fox, G. L. (1983). The familiy's role in adolescent sexual behavior. In T. Ooms (Ed.), *Teenage pregnancy in a family context* (pp. 73–130). Philadelphia: Temple University Press.

Fox, M., Gibbs, M., & Auerbach, D. (1985). Age and gender dimensions of friendship. *Psychology of Women Quarterly, 9,* 489–502.

Frank, E., Turner, S. M., & Duffy, B. (1979). Depressive symptoms in rape victims. *Journal of Affective Disorders, 1,* 269–297.

Frau, L. M., MacKay, H. T., Hughes, J. M. & Cates, W. (1986). Epidemiologic aspects of ectopic pregnancy. In A. Langer & L. Iffy (Eds.), *Extrauterine pregnancy* (pp. 179–203). Littleton, MA: PSG Publishing Co.

Frayser, S. (1985). *Varieties of sexual experience: An anthropological perspective.* New Haven, CT: HRAF Press.

Frazier, P. A. (1990). Victim attributions and post-rape trauma. *Journal of Personality and Social Psychology. 59,* 298–304.

Freeman, E. W., Rickels, K., & Sondheimer, S. J. (1992). Course of premenstrual syndrome symptom severity after treatment. *American Journal of Psychiatry, 149,* 531–533.

French, J. R. P., Jr., & Raven, B. (1959). The bases of social power. In D. Cartwright (Ed.), *Studies in social power.* Ann Arbor, MI: University of Michigan Press.

French, M. (1977). *The women's room.* New York: Summit Books.

Freud, S. (1938a). Infantile Sexuality. In *The basic writings of Sigmund Freud* (pp. 580–603) (A. A. Brill Trans.). New York: Random House.

Freud, S. (1938b). The transformation of puberty. In A. A. Brill (Ed. and Trans.), *The basic writings of Sigmund Freud* (pp. 604–629). New York: Random House.

Freud, S. (1925/1989). Some psychical consequences of the anatomical distinction between the sexes. In P. Gay (Ed.), *The Freud reader* (pp. 670–678). New York: Norton.

Freud, S. (1948). Some psychological consequences of the anatomical distinction between the sexes. In *Collected papers* Vol. V pp. 186–197. London, Hogarth.

Fried, A. (1994). "It's hard to change what we want to change": Rape crisis centers as organizations. *Gender & Society, 8,* 562–583.

Friedan, B. (1963). *The feminine mystique.* New York: Dell.

Friedan, B. (1981). *The second stage.* New York: Summit Books.

Friedman, A., Tzukerman, Y., Wienberg, H., & Todd, J. (1992). The shift in power with age: Changes in perception of the power of women and men over the life cycle. *Psychology of Women Quarterly, 16,* 513–525.

Friedman, E. A. (1995). Dystocia and "failure to progress" in labor. In B. L. Flamm, & E. J. Quilligan (Eds.), *Cesarean section: Guidelines for appropriate utilization* (pp. 23–42). New York: Springer-Verlag.

Ford, M. R., & Lowery, C. R. (1986). Gender differences in moral reasoning: A comparison of the use of justice and care orientations. *Journal of Personality and Social Psychology, 50,* 777–783.

Friedman, E. A., & Neff, R. K. (1987). *Labor and delivery: Impact on offspring.* Littleton, MA: PSG Publishing Co.

Friedman, W. J., Robinson, A. B., & Friedman, B. L. (1987). Sex differences in moral judgments? A test of Gilligan's theory. *Psychology of Women Quarterly, 11,* 37–46.

Frieze, I. H., & McHugh, M. C. (1992). Power and influence strategies in violent and nonviolent marriages. *Psychology of Women Quarterly, 16,* 449–465.

Frieze, I. H., Whitley, B. E., Jr., Hanusa, B. H., & McHugh, M. C. (1982). Assessing the theoretical models for sex differences in causal attributions for success and failure. *Sex Roles, 8,* 333–343.

Frisch, R. E. (1983). Fatness, puberty, and fertility: The effects of nutrition and physical training on menarche and ovulation. In J. Brooks-Gunn & A. C. Petersen (Eds.), *Girls at puberty.* New York: Plenum Press.

Frye, M. (1990). Lesbian "sex." In J. Allen (Ed.), *Lesbian philosophies and cultures* (pp. 305–315). Albany, NY: State University of New York Press.

Frye, M. (1993). Some reflections on separatism and power. In M. Pearsall (Ed.), *Women and values: Readings in recent feminist philosophy* (2nd ed., pp. 144–150). Belmont, CA: Wadsworth.

Fullerton, H. N. Jr. (1992). Evaluation of labor force projections to 1990. *Monthly Labor Review, 115*(8), 3–14.

Furguson, A. (1990). Is there a lesbian culture? In J. Allen (Ed.), *Lesbian philosophies and cultures* (pp. 63–88). Albany, NY: State University of New York Press.

Furstenberg, F. F. Jr., Brooks-Gunn, J., & Chase-Lansdale, L. (1989). Teenaged pregnancy and childbearing. *American Psychologist, 44,* 313–320.

Gabardi, L., & Rosen, L. A. (1991). Differences between college students from divorced and intact families. *Journal of Divorce and Remarriage. 15*(3/4), 175–191.

Gailey, C. W. (1987). Evolutionary perspectives on gender hierarchy. In B. B. Hess & M. M. Ferree (Eds.), *Analyzing gender: A handbook of social science research* (pp. 32–67). Newbury Park, CA: Sage.

Gambrell, R. D. Jr., & Teran, A. Z. (1991). Changes in lipids and lipoproteins with long-term estrogen deficiency and hormone replacement therapy. *American Journal of Obstetrics and Gynecology, 165,* 307–317.

Gannon, L. (1990). Endocrinology of menopause. In R. Formanek (Ed.), *The meanings of menopause: Historical medical and clinical perspectives* (pp. 179–237). Hillsdale, NJ: The Analytic Press.

Gannon, L, & Ekstrom, B. (1993). Attitudes toward menopause: The influence of sociocultural paradigms. *Psychology of Women Quarterly, 17,* 275–288.

Gannon, L., Luchetta, T., Rhodes, D., Pardie, L. & Segrist, D. (1992). Sex bias in psychological research: Progress or complacency? *American Psychologist, 47,* 389–396.

Garcia, S. A. (1989). The baby M case: A class struggle over undefined rights, unenforceable responsibilities, and inadequate remedies. In L. M. Whiteford & M. L. Poland (Eds.). *New approaches to human reproduction: Social and ethical dimensions* (pp. 198–216). Boulder, CO: Westview Press.

Gardenswartz, L., & Rowe, A. (1987). *What it takes: Good news from 100 of America's top professional and business women.* New York: Doubleday.

Garfinkel, P. E. & Garner, D. M. (1982). *Anorexia nervosa: A multidimensional perspective.* New York: Bruner/Mazel.

Garner, D. M., Garfinkel, P. E., & O'Shaughnessy, M. (1985). The validity of the distinction between bulimia with and without anorexia nervosa. *American Journal of Psychiatry, 142,* 581–587.

Garner, D. M., Garfinkel, P. E., Schwartz, D., & Thompson, M. (1980). Cultural expectations of thinness in women. *Psychological Reports, 47,* 483–491.

Garner, L. C., & Tessler, R. C. (1989). Technology in childbirth: Effects on postpartum moods. In K. S. Ratcliff, M. M. Ferree, G. O. Mellow, B. D. Wright, G. D. Price, K. Yanoshik, & M. S. Freston (Eds.), *Healing technology: Feminist perspectives* (pp. 119–134). Ann Arbor, MI: University of Michigan Press.

Garnets, L., Hancock, K. A., Cochran, S. D., Goodchilds, J., & Peplau, L. A. (1991). Issues in psychotherapy with lesbians and gay men. *American Psychologist, 46,* 964–972.

Gartrell, N., Herman, J., Orarte, S., Feldstein, M., & Localio, R. (1986). Psychiatrist-patient sexual contact: Results of a national survey, I: Prevalence. *American Journal of Psychiatry, 143,* 1126–1131.

Gaziano, M. M., Buring, J. E., Breslow, J. L., Goldhaber, S. Z., Rosner, B., VanDenburgh, M., Willett, W., & Hennekens, C. H. (1993). Moderate alcohol intake, increased levels of high-density lipoprotein and its subfractions, and decreased risk of myocardial infarction. *The New England Journal of Medicine, 329,* 1829–1834.

Geerkin, M., & Gove, W. R. (1974). Race, sex, and marital status: Their effect on mortality. *Social Problems, 21,* 567–580.

Gelles, R. J., & Straus, M. (1988). *Intimate violence: The causes and consequences of abuse in the American family.* New York: Touchstone.

Genero, N., Goldstein, L. H., Unger, R., & Miller, J. B. (1993, October). Evaluating and implementing a peer support intervention: Can mutual confiding relationships promote well being in high risk mothers? In N. Genero (Chair), Symposium conducted at the annual meeting of the New England Psychological Association, Manchester, NH.

Genevie, L., & Margolies, E. (1987). *The motherhood report: How women feel about being mothers.* New York: Macmillan.

George, L. K., Winfield, I., & Blazer, D. G. (1992). Sociocultural factors in sexual assault: Comparison of two representative samples of women. *Journal of Social Issues 48*(1), 105–125.

Gergen, M. M. (1988). Toward a feminist metatheory and methodology in the social sciences. In M. M. Gergen (Ed.), *Feminist thought and the structure of knowledge* (pp. 87–104). New York: New York University Press.

Gergen, M. M. (1990). Finished at 40: Women's development within the patriarchy. *Psychology of Women Quarterly, 14,* 471–493.

Gerson, M. J. (1986). The prospect of parenthood for women and men. *Psychology of Women Quarterly, 10,* 49–62.

Geschwind, N. & Behan, P. (1982). Left-handedness: Association with immune disease, migraine, and developmental learning disorder. *Proceedings of the Natural Academy of Science, 79,* 5097–5100.

Geschwind, N., & Galaburda, A. M. (1987). *Cerebral lateralization: Biological mechanisms, associations, and pathology.* Cambridge, MA: MIT Press.

Gewolb, I. H., & Warshaw, J. B. (1983). Influences on fetal growth. In J. B. Warshaw (Ed.), *The biological basis of reproductive and developmental medicine* (pp. 365–389). New York: Elsevier Biomedical.

Gibbons, J. L., Lynn, M., Stiles, D. A., de Berducido, E. J., Richter, R., Walker, K., & Deane, W. (1993). Guatemalan, Filipino, and U.S. adolescents' images of women as office workers and homemakers. *Psychology of Women Quarterly, 17,* 373–388.

Gidycz, C. A., & Koss, M. P. (1990). A comparison of group and individual sexual assault victims. *Psychology of Women Quarterly, 14,* 325–342.

Gilfus, M. E. (1992). From victims to survivors to offenders: Women's routes of entry and immersion into street crime. *Women and Criminal Justice, 4,* 63–89.

Gillespie, M. A. (1988, November). Winfrey takes all. *Ms., 17,* 50–54.

Gilligan, C. (1982). *In a different voice: Psychological theory and women's development.* Cambridge, MA: Harvard University Press.

Gilligan, C., Lyons, N. P., & Hammer, T. J. (1990). *Making connections: The relational worlds of adolescent girls at Emma Willard School.* Cambridge, MA: Harvard University Press.

Glaser, R. D., & Thorpe, J. S. (1986). Unethical intimacy: A survey of sexual contact and advances between psychology educators and female graduate students. *American Psychologist, 41,* 43–51.

Glass, S. P., & Wright, T. L. (1992). Justifications for extramarital relationships: The association between attitudes, behaviors, and gender. *Journal of Sex Research, 29,* 361-387.

Gleick, J. (1987). *Chaos: Making a new science.* New York: Penquin Books.

Glenn, E. N. (1992). From servitude to service work: Historical continuities in the racial division of paid reproductive labor. *Signs, 18,* 1–40.

Glenn, N. D., & McLanahan, S. (1982). Children and marital happiness: A further specification of the relationship. *Journal of Marriage and the Family, 44,* 63–72.

Gold, M., & Yanof, D. S. (1985). Mothers, daughters, and girlfriends. *Journal of Personality and Social Psychology, 49,* 654–659.

Goldberg, D. C., Wipple, B., Fishkin, R. E., Waxman, H., Fink, P. J., & Weisberg, M. (1983). The Grafenberg spot and female ejaculation: A review of initial hypotheses. *Journal of Sex and Marital Therapy, 9,* 27–37.

Goldberg, E., Podell, K., Harner, R., Riggio, S., & Lovell, M. (1994). Cognitive bias, functional cortical geometry, and the frontal lobes: Laterality, sex, and handedness. *Journal of Cognitive Neuroscience, 63,* 276–296.

Goldberg, M. S. (1993). Choosing a contraceptive. *FDA Consumer,* 18–25.

Goldberg, P. A. (1968). Are women prejudiced against women? *Transaction, 5,* 28–30.

Golden, C. (1987). Diversity and variability in women's sexual identities. In Boston Lesbian Psychologies Collective (Eds.), *Lesbian psychologies* (pp. 19–34). Urbana, IL: University of Illinois Press.

Goldenberg, R. L., Patterson, E. T., & Freese, M. P. (1992). Maternal demographic, situational and psychosocial factors and their relationship to enrollment in prenatal care: A review of the literature. *Women & Health, 19,* 133–151.

Goldfarb, J., & Tibbetts, E. (1980). *Breastfeeding handbook: A practical reference for physicians, nurses and other health professionals.* Hillsdale, NJ: Enslow.

Goldfoot, D. A., & Wallen, K. (1978). Development of gender role behaviors in heterosexual and isosexual groups of infant rhesus monkeys. In D. J. Chivers & J. Hebert (Eds.), *Recent Advances in Primatology Vol. 1, Behavior* (pp. 155–159). New York: Academic Press.

Golding, J. M. (1990). Division of household labor, strain, and depressive symptoms among Mexican Americans and non-Hispanic whites. *Psychology of Women Quarterly, 14,* 103–117.

Golub, S. (1976). The effect of premenstrual anxiety and depression on cognitive function. *Journal of Personality and Social Psychology, 34,* 99–104.

Golub, S. (1992). Menarche: The beginning of menstrual life. In N. J. Kenney, M. D. Brot, K. E. Moe, & K. Dahl (Eds.), *The complexities of women: Integrative essays in psychology and biology* (pp. 15–28). Dubuque, IA: Kendall/Hunt.

Gomberg, E. S. (1979). Problems with alcohol and other drugs. In E. S. Gomberg & V. Frank (Eds.), *Gender and disordered behavior: Sex differences in psychopathology* (pp. 204–240). New York: Brunner/Mazel.

Gonzalez, J. T. (1988). Dilemmas of the high-achieving chicana: The double-bind factor in male/female relationships, *Sex Roles, 18,* 367–380.

Goodfellow, P. N., Davies, K. E., & Ropers, H. H. (1985). Human gene mapping. 8. Report of the committee on the genetic condition of the X and Y chromosomes. *Cytogenetics and Cellular Genetics, 40,* 295–252.

Goodlin, R. C., Keller, D. W., & Raffin, M. (1971). Orgasm during late pregnancy, possible deleterious effects: *Obstetrics and Gynecology, 38,* 916–920.

Goodman, L. A., Koss, M. P., Fitzgerald, L. F., Russo, N. F., & Keita, G. P. (1993). Male violence against women: Current research and future directions. *American Psychologist, 48,* 1054–1058.

Goodman, M. J., Stewart, C. J., & Gilbert, F. Jr. (1977). Patterns of menopause: A study of certain medical and phsyiological variables among Caucasian and Japanese women living in Hawaii. *Journal of Gerontology, 32,* 291–298.

Goodwin, R. (1990). Sex differences among partner preferences: Are the sexes really very similar? *Sex Roles, 23,* 501–513.

Googins, B. K. (1991). *Work/family conflicts: Private lives-lives-public responses.* New York: Auburn House.

Gordon, M. T. & Riger, S. (1989). *Female fear.* Springfield, IL: Collier.

Gordon, T. (1990). *Feminist mothers.* New York: New York University Press.

Gormally, J., Black, S., Daston, S., & Rardin, D. (1982). The assessment of binge eating severity among obese persons. *Addictive Behaviors, 7,* 47–55.

Gorsky, R. D., Koplan, J. P., Peterson, H. B., & Thacker, S. B. (1994). Relative risks and benefits of long-term estrogen replacement therapy: A decision analysis. *Obstetrics & Gynecology, 83,* 161–166.

Gottesfeld, K. R. (1986). Sonographic diagnosis of extrauterine pregnancy. In A. Langer, & L. Iffy (Eds.). *Extrauterine Pregnancy* (pp. 225–234). Littleton, MA: PSG Publishing Co.

Gottman, J. S. (1990). Children of gay and lesbian parents. *Marriage and Family Review, 14,* 177–196.

Gouchie, C. T., & Kimura, D. (1991). The relationship between testosterone levels and cognitive ability patterns. *Psychoneuroendocrinology, 16,* 323–334.

Gould, S. J. (1981). *The mismeasure of man.* New York: Norton.

Gould, S. J. (1987). *An urchin in the storm.* New York: Norton.

Gove, W. R., & Hughes, M. (1979). Possible causes of the apparent sex differences in physical health. *American Sociological Review, 44,* 126–146.

Gove, W. R., Hughes, M. & Style, C. B. (1983). Does marriage have positive effects on the psychological well-being of the individual? *Journal of Health and Social Behavior, 24,* 122–131.

Gove, W. R., Style, C. B., & Hughes, M. (1990). The effect of mariage on the well-being of adults: A theoretical analysis. *Journal of Family Issues, 11,* 4–35.

Goy, R. W., Bercovitch, F. B., & McBrair, M. C. (1988). Behavioral masculinization is independent of genital masculinization in prenatally androgenized rhesus macques. *Hormones and Behavior, 22,* 552–571.

Graber, J. A. Brooks-Gunn, J., Paikoff, R. L., & Warren, M. P. (1994). Prediction of eating problems: An 8-year study of adolescent girls. *Developmental Psychology, 30,* 823–834.

Graham, S. B., Catanzarite, V., Bernstein, J., & Varela-Gittings, F. (1990). A comparison of attitudes and practices of episiotomy among obstetrical practitioners in New Mexico. *Social Science and Medicine, 31,* 191–201.

Grant, A. (1989). *Women's Center of Rhode Island Newsletter 1*(3), 1–3.

Grant, C. L., & Fodor, I. G. (1986). Adolescent attitudes toward body image and anorexic behavior. *Adolescence, 21,* 269–281.

Grant, L. (1985). Race-gender status, classroom interaction, and children's socialization in elementary school. In L. C. Wilkinson & C. B. Marrett (Eds.), *Gender influences in classroom interaction* (pp. 57–77). Orlando, FL: Academic Press.

Graves, L. M., & Powell, G. M. (1994). Effects of sex-based preferential selection and discrimination on job attitudes. *Human Relations, 47,* 133–157.

Gray, J. D., & Silver, R. C. (1990). Opposite sides of the same coin: Former spouses' divergent perspectives in coping with their divorce. *Journal of Personality and Social Psychology, 39,* 1180–1191.

Gray-Little, B. (1982). Marital quality and power processes among black couples. *Journal of Marriage and the Family, 44,* 633–646.

Gray-Little, B., & Burks, N. (1983). Power and satisfaction in marriage: A review and critique. *Psychological Bulletin, 93,* 513–537.

Greeley, A. M., Michael, R. T., & Smith, T. W. (1990). Americans and their sexual partners. *Society, 27*(5), 36–42.

Green, L. (1992). (1992, April 23). Profile of AFDC Mothers. *The Providence Journal-Bulletin,* p. A-1, A-5.

Greenberg, P. E., Stiglin, L. E., Finkelstein, S. N., & Berndt, E. R., (1993). The economic burden of depression in 1990. *Journal of Clinical Psychiatry, 54,* 405–418.

Greenberger, E., Goldberg, W. A., Crawford, T. J., & Granger, J. (1988). Beliefs about the consequences of maternal employment for children. *Psychology of Women Quarterly, 12,* 35–59.

Greene, B. (1994). African American Women. In L. Comas-Diaz & B. Greene (Eds.), *Women of color: Integrating ethnic and gender identities in psychotherapy* (pp. 10–29). New York: Guilford.

Greeno, C. G., & Maccoby, E. E. (1986). How different is the "Different Voice"? *Signs, 11,* 310–316.

Greenspan, M. (1983). *A new approach to women and therapy.* New York: McGraw-Hill.

Greil, A. J., Leitko, T. A., & Porter, L. K. (1989). Infertility: His and hers. *Gender and Society, 2,* 172-179.

Greiss, F. C. Jr. (1986). Ectopic pregnancy: Maternal mortality trends. In A. Langer and L. Iffy (Eds.), *Extrauterine pregnancy* (pp. 195–223). Littleton, MA: PSG Publishing Co.

Grief, G. L., & Pabst, M. S. (1988). *Mothers without custody.* Lexington, MA: Lexington Books.

Grimes, D. A., & Economy, K. E. (1995). Primary prevention of gynecologic cancers. *American Journal of Obstetrics and Gynecology, 172,* 227–235.

Griscom, J. L. (1992). Women and power: Definition, dualism, and difference. *Psychology of Women Quarterly, 16,* 389–414.

Grisso, J. A., Kelsey, J. L., Strom, B. L., O'Briien, L. A., Maislin, G., LaPann, B. A., Samelson, L., Hoffman, kS., and the Northeast Hip Fracture Study Group (1994). Risk factors for hip fracture in Black women. *The New England Journal of Medicine, 330,* 1555–1559.

Groggar, J., & Bronars, S. (1993). The socioeconomic consequences of teenage childbearing: Findings from a natural experiment. *Family Planning Perspectives, 25,* 156–161, 174.

Groneman, C. (1994). Nymphomania: The historical construction of female sexuality. *Signs, 19,* 337–367.

Grossman, F. K., Eichler, L. S., & Winickoff, S. A. (1980). *Pregnancy, birth, and parenthood.* San Francisco: Jossey-Bass.

Grudzinskas, J. C., Watson, C., & Chard, T. (1979). Does sexual intercourse cause fetal distress? *Lancet, 2,* 692–693.

Gunter, N. C., & Gunter, B. G. (1990). Domestic division of labor among working couples: Does androgyny make a difference? *Psychology of Women Quarterly, 14,* 355–370.

Gutek, B. A., & Morasch, B. (1982). Sex-ratios, sex-role spillover, and sexual harassment of women at work. *Journal of Social Issues. 38*(4), 55–74.

Gutierres, S. E., Russo, N. F., & Urbanski, L. (1994). Sociocultural and psychological factors in American Indian drug use: Implications for treatment. *The International Journal of the Addictions, 29,* 1761– 1786.

Guttmann, D. (1987). *Reclaimed powers: Toward a new psychology of men and women in later life.* New York: Basic Books.

Gwartney-Gibbs, P. A., & Lach, D. H. (1994). Gender differences in clerical workers' disputes over tasks, interpersonal treatment, and emotion. *Human Relations, 47,* 611–636.

Habib, M., Gayraud, D., Oliva, A., Regis, J., Salamon, G., & Khalil, R. (1991). Effects of handedness and sex on the morphology of the corpus callosum. A study with brain magnetic resonance imaging. *Brain and Cognition, 16,* 41–61.

Hafner, R. J. (1982). The marital context of the agoraphobic syndrome. In D. L. Chambless & A. J. Goldstein (Eds.), *Agoraphobia: Multiple perspectives on theory and treatment* (pp. 77–117). New York: Wiley.

Hafner, J. L., Fakouri, E., & Chesney, S. M. (1988). Early recollections of alcoholic women. *Journal of Clinical Psychology, 44,* 302–306.

Hale, C. B. (1992). A demographic profile of African Americans. In R. L. Braithwaite & S. E. Taylor, (Eds.), *Health issues in the Black Community* (pp. 6–19). San Francisco: Jossey-Bass Publishers.

Hall, E. G. (1990). The effect of performer gender, performer skill level, and opponent gender on self-confidence in a competitive situation. *Sex Roles, 23,* 33–41.

Hall, E. T. (1966). *The Hidden Dimension.* New York: Doubleday.

Hall, G. S. (1904). *Adolescence,* vol. 2. New York: Appleton.

Hall, J. A. (1978). Gender effects in decoding nonverbal cues. *Psychological Bulletin, 85,* 845–848.

Hall, J. A. (1984). *Nonverbal sex differences: Accuracy of Communication and expressive style.* Baltimore, MD: Johns Hopkins University Press.

Hall, J. A. (1987). On explaining gender differences: The case of nonverbal communication. In P. Shaver & C. Hendrick (Eds.), *Sex and Gender* (pp. 177–200). Newbury Park, CA: Sage.

Hall, J. A., & Halberstadt, A. G. (1981). Sex roles and nonverbal communication skill. *Sex Roles, 7,* 273–287.

Hall, J. A., & Halberstadt, A. G. (1986). Smiling and gazing. In J. S. Hyde & M. C. Linn (Eds.), *The psychology of gender: Advances through meta-analysis* (pp. 136–158). Baltimore, MD: Johns Hopkins University Press.

Hall, J. A., & Veccia, E. M. (1990). More "touching" observations: New interpersonal touch. *Journal of Personality and Social Psychology, 59,* 1155–1162.

Hall, J. A., & Veccia, E. M. (1992). Touch asymmetry between the sexes. In C. L. Ridgeway (Ed.), *Gender, interaction, and inequality* (pp. 81–96). New York: Springer-Verlag.

Hall, J. D. (1992). The mind that burns in each body: Women, rape and racial violence. In M. L. Andersen & P. H. Collins (Eds.), *Race, class, and gender: An anthology* (pp. 397–412). Belmont, CA: Wadsworth.

Hall, R. M., & Sandler, B. R. (1982). *The classroom climate: A chilly one for women?* Washington, DC: Project on the Status of Women, Association of American Colleges.

Hallstrom, T., & Samuelsson, S. (1990). Changes on women's sexual desire in middle life: The longitudinal study of women in Gothenburg. *Archives of Sexual Behavior, 19,* 259–268.

Halpern, D. F. (1989). The disappearance of cognitive gender differences: What you see depends on where you look. *American Psychologist, 44,* 1156–1158.

Halpern, D. F. (1992). *Sex differences in cognitive abilities* (2nd ed.). Hillside, NJ: Lawrence Erlbaum.

Hamdorf, P. A., Withers, R. T., Penhall, R. K., & Haslam, M. V. (1992). Physical training effects on the fitness and habitual activity patterns of elderly women. *Archives of Physical Medicine and Rehabilitation, 73,* 603–608.

Hamer, D. H., Hu, S., Magnuson, V. L., Hu, N., & Pattatucci, A. M. L. (1993, July 16). A linkage between DNA markers on the X chromosome and male sexual orientation. *Science, 261,* 321–327.

Hammonds, E. (1992). Race, sex, AIDS: The construction of "other." In M. L. Anderson & P. H. Collins (Eds.), *Race, class, and gender: An anthology* (pp. 329–340). Belmont, CA: Wadsworth.

Hampson, E. (1990a). Estrogen-related variations in human spatial and articulatory-motor skills. *Psychoneuroendocrinology, 15*(2), 97–111.

Hampson, E. (1990b). Variations in sex-related cognitive abilities across the menstrual cycle. *Brain and Cognition, 14*(1), 26–43.

Hampson, E., & Kimura, D. (1988). Reciprocal effects of hormonal fluctuations on human motor and perceptual-spatial skills. *Behavioral Neuroscience, 102,* 456–459.

Hampton, R. L., Gelles, R. J., & Harrop, J. (1991). Is violence in black families increasing? A comparison of 1975 and 1985 national survey rates. In R. L. Hampton (Ed.), *Black family violence: Current research and theory* (pp. 1–18). Lexington, MA: Heath.

Hansen, C. H., & Hansen, R. D. (1988). How rock music videos can change what is seen when boy meets girl: Priming stereotypic appraisal of social interactions. *Sex Roles, 19,* 287–316.

Hanson, S. L., & Ooms, T. (1991). The economic costs and rewards of two-earner, two-parent families. *Journal of Marriage and the Family, 53,* 622–634.

Harding, S. (1986a). The instability of analytical categories in feminist theory. *Signs, 11,* 645–666.

Harding, S. (1986b). *The science question in feminism.* Ithaca: Cornell University Press.

Harding, S. (1993) After the science question in feminism. In L. Richardson & V. Taylor (Eds.), *Feminist frontiers III* (pp. 12–20). New York: McGraw-Hill.

Hardy, L. M. (Ed.), (1991). *HIV Screening of pregnant women and newborns.* Washington, DC: National Academy Press.

Hare-Mustin, R. T. (1983). An appraisal of the relationship between women and psychotherapy: 80 years after the case of Dora. *American Psychologist, 38,* 593–601.

Hare-Mustin, R. T., & Marecek, J. (1986). Autonomy and gender: Some questions for therapists. *Psychotherapy, 23,* 203–212.

Hare-Mustin, R. T, & Marecek, J. (1988). The meaning of difference: Gender theory, postmodernism, and psychology. *American Psychologist, 43,* 455–464.

Hare-Mustin, R. T., & Marecek, J. (1994, August). Feminism & postmodernism: Dilemmas and points of resistance. In B. T. Fowers, (Chair), *Problems with postmodernism: Historical, critical and feminist perspectives.* Symposium conducted at the annual meeting of the American Psychological Association, Los Angeles, CA.

Harlap, S. (1987). Smoking and spontaneous abortion. In M. J. Rosenberg (Ed.), *Smoking and reproductive health* (pp. 75–80). Littleton, MA: PSG Publishing Co.

Harrison, J. (1978). Male sex role and health. *Journal of Social Issues, 34*(1), 65–86.

Harrison, W. M., Endicott, J., & Nee, J. (1990). Treatment of premenstrual dysphoria with alprazolam. *Archives of General Psychiatry, 47,* 270–275.

Hart, B. (1986). Preface. In K. Lobel (Ed.), *Naming the violence: Speaking out about lesbian battering* (pp.9–16). Seattle, WA: Seal Press.

Hart, N. (1990). Lesbian desire as social action. In J. Allen (Ed.), *Lesbian philosophies and cultures* (pp. 295–303). Albany, NY: State University of New York Press.

Hartmann, S. M. (1989). *From margin to mainstream: American women and politics since 1960.* Philadelphia: Temple University Press.

Hassold, T., Freeman, S., Phillips, C., Sherman, S., & Takaesu, N. (1992). Analysis of non-disjunction in human autosomal trisomies. In I. T. Lott, & E. E. McCoy (Eds.), *Down syndrome: Advances in medical care.* New York: Wiley-Liss.

Hatcher, M. A. (1991). The corporate woman of the 1990s: Maverick or innovator. *Psychology of Women Quarterly, 15,* 251–259.

Hatfield, E., & Sprecher, S. (1986). *Mirror, mirror . . . The importance of looks in everyday life.* Albany: State University of New York Press.

Hauth, J. C., Goldenberg, R. L., Parker, R. Jr., Philips, J. B. III, Copper, R. L., DuBard, M. B., & Cutter, G. R. (1993). Low-dose aspirin therapy to prevent preeclampsia. *American Journal of Obstetrics and Gynecology, 168,* 1083–1091.

Hawkins, J. (1985). Computers and girls: Rethinking the issues. *Sex Roles, 13,* 165–180.

Hazen, C., & Shaver, P. (1987). Romantic love conceptualized as an attachment process. *Journal of Personality and Social Psychology, 42,* 511–524.

Hcadcn, S. W., Bauman, K. E., Deane, G. D., & Koch, G. G. (1991). Are the correlates of cigarette smoking initiation different for Black and White adolescents? *American Journal of Public Health, 81,* 854–857.

Heck, H., & de Castro, J. M. (1993). The caloric demand of lactation does not alter spontaneous meal patterns, nutrient intakes, or moods of women. *Physiology & Behavior 54,* 641–648.

Hedges, L. V., & Becker, B. J. (1986). Statistical methods in the meta-analysis of research on gender differences. In J. Hyde & M. C. Linn (Eds.), *The Psychology of gender: Advances through meta-analysis* (pp. 14–50). Baltimore, MD: Johns Hopkins University Press.

Hedges, L. V., & Olkin, I. (1985). *Statistical methods for meta-analysis.* Orlando, FL: Academic Press.

Heider, F. (1958). *The psychology of interpersonal relations.* New York: Wiley.

Heilbrun, A. B., Friedberg, D. W., Wydra, D., & Worobow, A. L. (1990). The female role and menstrual distress: An explanation for inconsistent evidence. *Psychology of Women Quarterly, 14,* 403–417.

Heiman, J. R. (1977). A psycholo-physiological exploration of sexual arousal patterns in females and males. *Psychophysiology, 14,* 266–274.

Heister, G., Landis, T., Regard, M., & Schroeder-Heister, P. (1989). Shift of functional cerebral asymmetry during the menstrual cycle. *Neuropsychologia, 27,* 871–880.

Helson, R. (1992). Women's difficult times and the rewriting of the life story. *Psychology of Women Quarterly, 16,* 331–347.

Helson, R., Mitchell, V., & Moane, G. (1984). Personality and patterns of adherence and nonadherence to the social clock. *Journal of Personality and Social Psychology, 46,* 1079–1096.

Hemminki, E., Malin, M., & Topo, P. (1993). Selection to post-menopausal therapy by women's characteristics. *Journal of Clinical Epidemiology, 46,* 211–219.

Henley, N. (1973). Power, sex and nonverbal communication. *Berkeley Journal of Sociology, 18,* 1–26.

Henley, N. M. (1977). *Body politics: Power, sex, and nonverbal communication.* Englewood Cliffs, NJ: Prentice-Hall.

Henley, N. M. (1989). Molehill or mountain? What we do know and don't know about sex bias in language. In M. Crawford & M. Gentry (Eds.), *Gender and thought* (pp. 59–78). New York: Springer-Verlag.

Henshaw, S. K. (1991). The accessibility of abortion services in the United States. *Family Planning Perspectives, 23,* 246–253.

Henshaw, S. K., & Van Vort, J. (1994). Abortion services in the United States, 1991 and 1992. *Family Planning Perspectives, 26,* 100–112.

Hensley, W. E., & Cooper, R. (1987). Height and occupational success: A review and critique. *Psychological Reports, 60,* 843–849.

Herman, J. L. (1981). *Father-daughter incest.* Cambridge, MA: Harvard University Press.

Hertz, R. (1991). Dual career couples and the American dream: Self-sufficiency and achievement. *Journal of Comparative Family Studies, 22,* 247–263.

Herzog, D. B., Sacks, N. R., Keller, M. B., Lavori, P. W., von Ranson, K. B., & Gray, H. M. (1993). Patterns and predictors of recovery in anorexia nervosa and bulimia nervosa. *American Academy of Child & Adolescent Psychiatry, 32,* 835–842.

Heshka, S., & Nelson, Y. (1972). Interpersonal speaking distance as a function of age, sex, and relationship. *Sociometry, 35,* 491–498.

Hess, R. D., & Miura, I. T. (1985). Gender differences in enrollment in computer camps and classes. *Sex Roles, 13,* 193–203.

Hester, M. (1992). *Lewd women and wicked witches: A study of the dynamics of male domination.* London: Routledge.

Hetherington, E. M. (1972). Effects of father absence on personality development in adolescent daughters. *Developmental Psychology, 7,* 313–326.

Hetherington, E. M., Stanley-Hagan, & Anderson, E. R. (1989). Marital transitions: A child's perspective. *American Psychologist, 44,* 303–312.

Heyn, D. (1992). *The erotic silence of the American wife.* New York: Turtle Bay Books.

Hibbard, J. H., & Pope, C. R. (1986). Another look at sex differences in the use of medical care: Illness orientation and the types of morbidities for which services are used. *Women & Heath, 11,*(2), 21–36.

Higgenbotham, E. B. (1990). In politics to stay: Black women leaders and party politics in the 1920s. In L. A. Tilly & P. G. Gurin (Eds.), *Women politics and change* (pp.199–220). New York: Russell Sage Foundation.

Higgenbotham, E. B. (1992). African-American women's history and the metalanguage of race. *Signs, 17,* 251–275.

Higgins, C. A., Duxbury, L. E., & Irving, R. H. (1992). Work-family conflict in the dual-career family. *Organizational Behavior and Human Decision Processes, 51,* 51–75.

Hill, C. T., Rubin, Z., & Peplau, L. A. (1976). Break-ups before marriage: The end of 103 affairs. *Journal of Social Issues, 32*(1), 147–167.

Hill, M. (1987). Child-rearing attitudes of Black lesbian mothers. In the Boston Lesbian Psychologies Collective (Eds.), *Lesbian psychologies: Explorations and challenges* (pp. 215–226). Urbana, IL: University of Illinois Press.

Hines, M., & Kaufman, F. R. (1994). Androgen and the development of human sex-typical behavior: Rough-and-tumble play and sex of preferred playmates in children with congenital adrenal hyperplasia (CAH). *Child Development, 65,* 1042–1053.

Hite, S. (1976). *The Hite Report: A nationwide study of female sexuality.* New York: Macmillan.

Hite, S. (1981). *The Hite report on male sexuality.* New York: Knopf.

Hite, S. (1987). *Women & Love: A cultural revolution in progress.* New York: St. Martin's Press.

Hobart, C. (1991). Conflict in remarriages. *Journal of Divorce and Remarriage, 15,* 69–85.

Hock, E., Morgan, K. C., & Hock, M. D. (1985). Employment decisions made by mothers of infants. *Psychology of Women Quarterly, 9,* 383–402.

Hock, E., Schirtzinger, M. B., & Lutz, W. (1992). Dimensions of family relationships associated with depressive symptomatology in mothers of young children. *Psychology of Women Quarterly, 16,* 229–241.

Hoeffer, B. (1981). Children's acquisition of sex-role behavior in lesbian-mother families. *American Journal of Orthopsychiatry, 51,* 536–544.

Hofferth, S. L., & Phillips, D. A. (1991). Child care policy research. *Journal of Social Issues, 47*(2), 1–13.

Hoffman, L. W. (1977). Fear of success in 1965 and 1974: a follow-up study. *Journal of Consulting and Clinical Psychology, 45,* 310–321.

Hoffman, L. W. (1989). Effects of maternal employment in the two parent family. *American Psychologist, 44,* 283–292.

Hofmeyr, G. J., Marcos, E. F., & Butchart, A. M. (1990). Pregnant women's perceptions of themselves: A survey. *Birth, 17*(4), 205–206.

Hogan, H. W. (1978). IQ self-estimates of males and females. *Journal of Social Psychology, 106,* 137–138.

Hogg, M. A. (1985). Masculine and feminine speech in dyads and groups: a study of speech style and gender salience. *Journal of Language and Social Psychology, 4,* 99–111.

Holder, M. C. (1992). A poem to our strong black brothers? *The good 5c Cigar 23 (19),* 7. Kingston, RI: The University of Rhode Island.

Holland, E. F. N., Studd, J. W. W., Mansell, J. P., Leather, A. T., & Bailey, A. J. (1994). Changes in collagen composition and cross-links in bone and skin of osteoporotic postmenopausal women treated with percutaneous estradiol implants. *Obstetrics & Gynecology, 83,* 180–183.

Hollander, E. P. (1985). Leadership and power. In G. Lindzey & E. Aronson (Eds.) *Handbook of social psychology* (Vol 2, 3rd ed.), pp. 485–537). New York: Random House.

Holmes, H. B., & Hoskins, B.B. (1987). Prenatal and preconception sex choice technologies: A path to femicide. In G. Corea, R. D. Klein, J. Hanner, H. B. Holmes, B. Hoskins, M. Kishwar, J. Raymond, R. Powl & R. Steinbacker (Eds.), *Man-made woman: How new reproductive technologies affect women* (pp. l5–29). Bloomington, IN: Indiana University Press.

Holtzworth-Munroe, A., & Stuart, G. L. (1994). Typologies of male batterers: Three subtypes and the differences among them. *Psychological Bulletin, 116,* 476–497.

Hong, L. K., & Duff, R. W. (1994). Widows in retirement communities: The social context of subjective well-being. *The Gerontologist, 34,* 347–352.

Honig, A. S., & Park, K. J. (1993). Effects of day care on preschool sex-role development. *American Journal of Orthopsychiatry, 63,* 481–86.

Hood, J. N., & Koberg, C. S. (1994). Patterns of differential assimilation and acculturation for women in business organizations. *Human Relations, 47,* 159–181.

Hood, K. E. (1992). Contextual determinants of menstrual cycle effects in observations of social interactions. In A. J. Dan, & L. L. Lewis (Eds.), *Menstrual health in women's lives* (pp. 83–97). Urbana, IL: University of Illinois Press.

Hook, E. B. (1979). Extra sex chromosomes and human behavior: The nature of the evidence regarding XYY, XXY, XXYY, and XXX genotypes. In H. L. Vallet & I. H. Proter (Eds.), *Genetic mechanisms of sexual development* (pp. 437–464). New York: Academic Press.

hooks, b. (1984). *Feminist theory: From margin to center.* Boston: South End Books.

hooks, b. (1990). *Yearning: Race, gender, and cultural politics.* Boston: South End Press.

hooks, b. (1993). Black women and feminism. In L. Richardson & V. Taylor (Eds.), *Feminist frontiers III* (pp. 499–507). New York: McGraw-Hill. (Reprinted from *Ain't I a woman: Black women and feminism* 1981). Boston: South End Books.

Hopkins, J., Marcues, M., & Campbell, S. B. (1984). Postpartum depression: A critical review. *Psychological Bulletin, 95,* 498–515.

Hoptman, M. J., & Davidson, R. J. (1994). How and why do the two cerebral hemispheres interact? *Psychological Bulletin, 116,* 195–219.

Horgan, D. (1983). The pregnant woman's place and where to find it. *Sex Roles, 9,* 333–339.

Horner, M. S. (1968). *Sex differences in achievement motivation and performance in competitive and non-competitive situations.* Unpublished doctoral dissertation, University of Michigan.

Horner, M. S. (1969, June). Fail bright women. *Psychology Today,* p. 36.

Horner, M. S. (1978). The measurement of behavioral implications of fear of success in women. In J. W. Atkinson, and J. O. Raynor (Eds.), *Personality, motivation and achievement* (pp. 41–70). Washington, DC: Hemisphere.

Horney, K. (1967). The flight from womanhood: The masculinity-complex in women as viewed by men and by women. In H. Kelman (Ed.), *Feminine psychology* (pp. 54–70). New York: Norton.

Horney, K. (1980). *The adolescent diaries of Karen Horney* [Diaries written 1899–1911]. New York: Basic Books.

Hossain, Z., & Roopnarine, J. L. (1993). Division of household labor and child care in dual-earner African-American families. *Sex Roles, 29,* 571–583.

Hotaling, G. T., & Sugarman, D. B. (1986). An analysis of risk markers in husband to wife violence: The current state of knowledge. *Violence and Victims, 1,* 101–124.

Houseknecht, S. K. (1982). Voluntary childlessness in the 1980s: A significant increase? *Marriage and Family Review, 5,* 51–69.

Houseknecht, S. K., & Spanier, G. B. (1980). Marital disruption and higher education among women in the United States. *Sociological Quarterly, 21,* 375–389.

Howard, J. A., Blumstein, P. & Schwartz, P. (1986). Sex, power, and influence tactics in intimate relationships. *Journal of Personality and Social Psychology, 51,* 102–109.

Howard, J. A., Blumstein, P., & Schwartz, P. (1987). Social or evolutionary theories? Some observations on preferences in human mate selection. *Journal of Personality and Social Psychology, 53,* 194–200.

Hoyenga, K. B., & Hoyenga, K. T. (1993). *Gender-related differences: Origins and outcomes.* Boston: Allyn & Bacon.

Hoyert, D. L. (1995, August). Perinatal mortality in the United States: 1985–91. *Vital and Health Statistics* (DHHS No. PHS 95–1854). Washington, DC: U.S. Government Printing Office.

Huang, L. N., & Yin, Y. (1989). Chinese American children and adolescents. In J. T. Gibbs, L. N. Huang, & Associates (Eds.), *Children of color.* San Francisco: Jossey Bass.

Hubbard, R. (1979). Have only men evolved? In R. Hubbard, M. S. Henifin & B. Fried (Eds.), *Women look at biology looking at women* (pp. 7–36). Cambridge, MA: Schenkman.

Hubbard, R. (1988). Some thoughts about the masculinity of the natural sciences. In M. M. Gergen (Ed.), *Feminist thought and the structure of knowledge* (pp. 1–15). New York: New York University Press.

Hubbard, R. (1990). *The politics of women's biology.* New Brunswick, NJ: Rutgers University Press.

Hughey, M., McElin, T., & Young, T. (1978). Maternal and fetal outcome of Lamaze-prepared patients. *Obstetrics and Gynecology, 51,* 643–647.

Hulick, M. (1990b, March 6). Defendant Aries Correia says he hit his wife Maria to make her listen. *The Providence Journal Bulletin,* p. A-8.

Hulick, M. (1990a, May 17). Aries Correia sentenced to life in beating death of wife Maria. *The Providence Journal Bulletin,* p. B-1.

Humphrey, L. L. (1989). Observed family interactions among subtypes of eating disorders using structural analysis of social behavior. *Journal of Consulting and Clinical Psychology, 57,* 206–214.

Hunt, M. (1974). *Sexual behavior in the 1970s.* Chicago: Playboy Press.

Hunt, M. G. (1993). Expressiveness does predict well-being. *Sex Roles, 29,* 147–169.

Hunter College Women's Studies Collective. (1983). *Women's realities, women's choices: An introduction to women's studies.* New York: Oxford University Press.

Hunter, D. J., Manson, J. E., Colditz, G. A., Stampfer, M. J., Rosner, B., Hennekenns, C. H., Speizer, F. E., & Willett, W. C. (1993). A prospective study of the intake of vitamins C, E, and A and the risk of breast cancer. *The New England Journal of Medicine, 329,* 234–240.

Hunter, D. J., & Willett, W. C. (1993). Diet, body size, and breast cancer. *Epidemiologic Reviews, 15,* 110–128.

Hunter, J. E., & Schmidt, F. L. (1990). *Methods of meta-analysis: Correcting error and bias in research findings.* Newbury Park, CA: Sage.

Hunter, S., Schraer, R., Landers, D., Buskirk, E., & Harris, D. (1979). The effects of total oestrogen concentration and menstrual-cycle phase on reaction time performance. *Ergonomics, 22,* 263–268.

Hurt, S. W., Schnurr, P. P., Severino, S. K., Freeman, E. W., Gise, L. H., Rivera-Tovar, A., & Steege, J. F. (1992). Late luteal phase dysphoric disorder in 670 women evaluated for premenstrual complaints. *American Journal of Psychiatry, 149,* 525–530.

Huston, A. C. (1983). Sex-typing. In E. M. Hetherington (Ed.), P. H. Mussen (Series Ed.), *Handbook of Child Psychology: Vol. 4, Socialization, personality and social development* (pp. 387–467). New York: Wiley.

Huston, T. L., & Ashmore, R. (1986). Women and men in personal relationships. In R. D. Ashmore & F. K. Del Boca (Eds.) *The social psychology of female-male relations: A critical analysis of central topics* (pp. 167–210). New York: Academic Press.

Hutchings, D. E. (1980). Neurobehavioral effects of prenatal origin: Drugs of use and abuse. In R. H. Schwarz, & S. J. Yaffe (Eds.), *Drug and chemical risks to the fetus and newborn: Vol. 36 Progress in Clinical and Biological Research* (pp. 109–114). New York: Alan R. Liss.

Hutchison, R., & McNall, M. (1994). Early marriage in a Hmong cohort. *Journal of Marriage and the Family, 56,* 579–590.

Hyde, J. S. (1984a). Children's understanding of sexist language. *Developmental Psychology, 20*(4), 697–706.

Hyde, J. S. (1984b). How large are gender differences in aggression? A developmental meta-analysis. *Developmental Psychology, 20,* 722– 736.

Hyde, J. S. (1986). Gender differences in aggression. In J. S. Hyde and M. C. Linn (Eds.), *The psychology of gender: Advances through meta-analysis* (pp. 51–66). Baltimore: John Hopkins University Press.

Hyde, J. S., & Fennema, E. (1989, August). *Gender differences in mathematics performance and attitudes/affect: A meta-analysis.* Paper presented at the 97th annual meeting of the American Psychological Association. New Orleans.

Hyde, J. S., Fennema, E., & Lamon, S. J. (1990). Gender differences in mathematics performance: A meta-analysis. *Psychological Bulletin, 107,* 139–155.

Hyde, J. S., Fennema, E., Ryan, M., Frost, L. A., & Hopp, C. (1990). Gender comparisons of mathematics attitudes and affect. *Psychology of Women Quarterly, 14,* 299–324.

Hyde, J. S., Krajnik, M., & Skuldt-Niederberger, K. (1991). Androgyny across the life span: A replication and longitudinal follow-up. *Developmental Psychology, 27,* 516–519.

Hyde, J. S., & Linn, M. C. (1988). Gender differences in verbal ability: A meta-analysis. *Psychological Bulletin, 104,* 53–69.

Hyde, J. S., & McKinley, N. M. (1993). Beliefs about the consequences of maternal employment for children: Psychometric analyses. *Psychology of Women Quarterly, 17,* 177–191.

Ickovics, J. R., Morrill, A. C., Beren, S. E., Walsh, U., & Rodin, J. (1994). Limited effects of HIV counseling and testing for women: A prospective study of behavioral and psychological consequences. *Journal of the American Medical Association, 272,* 443–448.

Iffy, L. (1986). Etiology and pathologic mechanism of ectopic implantation. In A. Langer & L. Iffy (Eds.). *Extrauterine pregnancy* (pp. 73–95). Littleton, MA: PSG Publishing Co.

Imperato-McGinley, J., (1979). Male pseudohermaphroditism secondary to 5-alpha-reductase deficiency: A model for the role of androgens in both the development of the male phenotype and the evolution of a male gender identity. *Journal of Steroid Biochemistry, 11,* 637–645.

Imperato-McGinley, J., Peterson, R. E., Gautier, T., & Sturla, E. (1979). Androgens and the evolution of male gender identity among male pseudohermaphrodites with a 5-alpha-reductase deficiency. *New England Journal of Medicine, 300,* 1236–1237.

Individual Committee on Adolescent Abortion. (1987). *American Psychologist, 42,* 73–78.

Ingram, R. E., Cruet, D., Johnson, B. R., & Wisnicki, K. G. (1988). Self-focused attention, gender, gender role, and vulnerability to negative affect. *Journal of Personality and Social Psychology, 55,* 967–978.

Jacklin, C. N. (1989). Female and male: Issues of gender. *American Psychologist, 44,* 127–133.

Jackson, L. A. (1989). Relative deprivation and the gender wage gap. *Journal of Social Issues, 45*(4), 117–133.

Jacobs, B. L. (1994). Serotonin, motor activity and depression-related disorders. *American Scientist, 82,* 456–463.

Jacobs, J. E. (1991). Influence of gender stereotypes on parent and child mathematics attitudes. *Journal of Educational Psychology, 83,* 518–527.

Jacobs, J. E., & Eccles, J. S. (1985). Science and the media: Benbow and Stanley revisited. *Educational Researcher, 14,* 20–25.

Jacobs, J. E., & Eccles, J. S. (1992). The impact of mothers' gender-role stereotypic beliefs on mothers' and children's ability perceptions. *Journal of Personality and Social Psychology, 63,* 932–944.

Jadack, R. A., Keller, M. L., & Hyde, J. S. (1990). Genital herpes: Gender comparisons and the disease experience. *Psychology of Women Quarterly, 14,* 419–434.

Jagacinski, C. M. (1987). Engineering careers: Women in a male-dominated field. *Psychology of Women Quarterly, 11,* 97–110.

James, D., & Clarke, S. (1993). Women, men, and interruptions: A critical review. In D. Tannen (Ed.), *Gender and conversational interaction* (pp. 231–280). New York: Oxford University Press.

James, D., & Drakich, J. (1993). Understanding gender differences in amount of talk: A critical review of research. In D. Tannen (Ed.), *Gender and conversational interaction* (pp. 281–312). New York: Oxford University Press.

James, W. H. (1989). The norm for perceived husband superiority: A cause of human assortive marriage. *Social Biology, 36,* 271–277.

Jarett, L. R. (1984). Psychosocial and biological influences on menstruation: Synchrony, cycle length, and regularity. *Psychoneuroendocrinology, 9,* 21–26.

Jarrett, S. R., Ramirez, A. J., Richards, M. A., & Weinman, J. (1992). Measuring coping in breast cancer. *Journal of Psychosomatic Research, 36,* 593–602.

Jarvis, T. J. (1992). Implications of gender for alcohol treatment research: A quantitative and qualitative review. *British Journal of the Addictions, 87,* 1249–1261.

Jarvis, T. J., & McCabe, M. P. (1991). Women's experience of the menstrual cycle. *Journal of Psychosomatic Medicine, 35,* 651–660.

Jayaratne, T. E., & Stewart, A. J. (1991). Quantitative and qualitative methods in the social sciences: Current feminist issues and practical strategies (pp. 85–106). In M. M. Fonow, & J. A. Cook (Eds.), *Beyond methodology: Feminist scholarship as lived research* (pp. 85–106). Bloomington, IN: Indiana University Press.

Jellife, D. B. & Jelliffe, E. F. P. (1978). *Human milk in the modern world.* Oxford: Oxford Press.

Jenkins, S. R. (1994). Need for power and women's careers over 14 years: Structural power, job satisfaction, and motive change. *Journal of Personality and Social Psychology, 66,* 155–165.

Jenness, V., & Broad, K. (1994). Antiviolence activism and the (in)visibility of gender in the gay/lesbian and women's movements. *Gender & Society, 8,* 4402–423.

Jennings, M. K. (1990). Women in party politics. In L. A. Tilly & P. Gurin (Eds.), *Women politics and change* (pp. 221–248). New York: Russell Sage Foundation.

Jensen, B. K. (1982). Menstrual cycle effects on task performance examined in the context of stress research. *Acta Psychologia, 50,* 159–178.

Jensen, I. W., & Gutek, B. A. (1982). Attributions and assignments of responsibility in sexual harassment. *Journal of Social Issues, 38*(4), 121–136.

Jernberg, A. M. (1988). Promoting prenatal and perinatal mother-child bonding: a psychotherapeutic assessment of parental attitudes. In P. Fedor-Freybergh, and M. L. V. Vogel (Eds.), *Prenatal and perinatal psychology and medicine* (pp. 253–259). Park Ridge, NJ: Parthenon.

Jessor, R. (1993). Successful adolescent development among youth in high-risk settings. *American Psychologist, 48,* 117–126.

Johnson, C., Tobin, D. L., & Lipkin, J. (1989). Epidemiologic changes in bulimic behavior among female adolescents over a five-year period. *International Journal of Eating Disorders, 8,* 647–655.

Johnson, C. B., Stockdale, M. S., & Saal, F. E. (1991). Persistence of men's misperceptions of friendly cues across a variety of interpersonal encounters. *Psychology of Women Quarterly, 15,* 447–461.

Johnson, C. L. (1994). Differential expectations and realities: Race, socioeconomic status and health of the oldest-old. *International Journal of Aging & Human Development, 38,* 13–27.

Johnson, D. J., & Rusbult, C. E. (1989). Resisting temptation of alternative partners as a means of maintaining commitment in close relationship. *Journal of Personality and Social Psychology, 57,* 967–980.

Johnson, J. D., & Jackson, L. A. (1988). Assessing effects of factors that might underlie the differential perception of acquaintance and stranger rape. *Sex Roles, 19,* 37–45.

Johnson, S. (1988). Reproductive health. In C. J. Leppa and C. Miller (Eds.), *Women's health perspectives: An annual review Vol. 1.* Phoenix, AZ: Oryx Press.

Jolin, A. (1994). On the backs of working prostitutes: Feminist theory and prostitution policy. *Crime & Delinquency, 40,* 69–83.

Jones, D. C., Bloys, N., & Wood, M. (1990). Sex roles and friendship patterns. *Sex Roles, 23,* 133–155.

Jones, E. F. (1986). *Teenage pregnancy in industrialized countries.* New Haven, CT: Yale University Press.

Jones, J. C., & Barlow, D. H. (1990). Self-reported frequency of sexual urges, fantasies and masturbatory fantasies in heterosexual males and females. *Archives of Sexual Behavior, 19*(3), 269–279.

Jorgensen, S. R., & Adams, R. P. (1988). Predicting Mexican-American family planning intentions: An application and test of a social psychological model. *Journal of Marriage and the Family, 560,* 107–119.

Jorgensen, S. R. (1986). *Marriage and family, development and change.* New York: Macmillan.

Jose, P. E. & McCarthy, W. J. (1988). Perceived agentic and communal behavior in mixed-sex group interactions. *Personality and Social Pschology bulletin, 14,* 57–67.

Jost, A., & Magre, S. (1984). Testicular development phases and dual hormonal control of sexual organogenesis. In M. Serio, M. Motta, M. Zanisi, & L. Martini (Eds.), *Sexual differentiation: Basic and clinical aspects* (pp. 1–15). Serono Symposia Publications from Raven Press (Vol. II). New York: Raven Press.

Kahn, A. S., Mathie, V. A., Torgler, C. (1994). Rape scripts and rape acknowledgement. *Psychology of Women Quarterly, 18,* 53–66.

Kahn, A. S., & Yoder, J. D. (1989). The psychology of women and conservatism: Rediscovering social change. *Psychology of Women Quarterly, 13,* 417–432.

Kahn, J. R., & London, K. A. (1991). Premarital sex and the risk of divorce. *Journal of Marriage and the Family, 53,* 845–855.

Kahn, M. J. (1991). Factors affecting the coming out process for lesbians. *Journal of Homosexuality, 21,* 47–70.

Kalichman, S. C. (1990). Sex roles and sex differences in adult spatial performance. *The Journal of Genetic Psychology, 150,* 93–100.

Kalisch, P., & Kalisch, B. (1984). Sex role stereotyping of nurses and physicians on prime-time television: A dichotomy of occupational portrayals. *Sex Roles, 10,* 533–553.

Kamerman, S. B., & Kahn, A. J. (1988). *Mothers alone: Strategies for a time of change.* Dover, MA: Auburn House.

Kane, T. T., & Smith, J. B. (1987). Maternal smoking and birthweight: An international perspective. In M. J. Rosenberg (Ed.). *Smoking and Reproductive Health* (pp. 109–117). Littleton, MA: PSG Publishing Co.

Kanter, R. M. (1977). *Men and women of the corporation.* New York: Basic Books.

Kaplan, H. S. (1974). *The new sex therapy.* New York: Bruner/Mazel.

Kaplan, B. J. (1986). A psychobiological review of depression during pregnancy. *Psychology of Women Quaterly, 10,* 35–48.

Kazdin, A. E. (1993). Adolescent mental health. Prevention and treatment programs. *American Psychologist, 48,* 155–168.

Kearns, J. R., & Christopherson, V. A. (1992). Mexican-American women's perceptions of menopause. In A. J. Dan, & L. L. Lewis, (Eds.), *Menstrual health in women's lives* (pp. 191–197). Urbana, IL: University of Illinois Press.

Keith, J. B., McCreary, C., Collins, K., Smith, C. P., & Bernstein, I. (1991). Sexual activity and contraceptive use among low-income urban black adolescent females. *Adolescence, 26,* 769–785.

Kellam, S. G., Ensminger, M. A., & Turner, J. T. (1977). Family structure and the mental health of children. *Archives of General Psychiatry, 34,* 1012–1022.

Keller, E. F. (1985). *Reflections on gender and science.* New Haven, CT: Yale University Press.

Keller, E. F. (1987). Women scientists and feminist critics of science. In J. K. Conway, S. C. Bourque, & J. W. Scott (Eds.), *Learning about women: Gender, politics, and power* (pp. 77–91). Ann Arbor, MI: The University of Michigan Press.

Kelly, E. L., & Conley, J. J. (1987). Personality and compatibility: A prospective analysis of marital stability and marital satisfaction. *Journal of Personality and Social Psychology, 52,* 27–40.

Kelly, M. P., Strassberg, D. S., & Kircher, J. R. (1990). Attitudinal and experiential correlates of anorgasmia. *Archives of Sexual Behavior, 19,* 165–177.

Kelly-Gadol, J. (1983). The social relation of the sexes: Methodological implications of women's histotry. In E. Abel & E. K. Abel (Eds.), *The Signs reader women, gender & scholarship* (pp. 11–25). Chicago: University of Chicago Press.

Kelsey, J. L., Gammon, M. D., & John, E. M. (1993). Reproductive factors and breast cancer. *Epidemiologic Reviews, 15,* 36–46.

Kelsey, J. L., & Horn-Ross, P. L. (1993). Breast cancer: Magnitude of the problem and descriptive epidemiology. *Epidemiologic Reviews, 15,* 7–16.

Kendall-Tackett, K., Williams, L. M., & Finkelhor, D. (1993). Impact of sexual abuse on children: A review and synthesis of recent empirical studies. *Psychological Bulletin, 113,* 164–180.

Kendell, R. E., Wainwright, S., Hailey, A., & Shannon, B. (1976). The influence of childbirth on psychiatric morbidity. *Psychological Medicine, 6,* 297–302.

Kendler, K. S., Neale, M. C., Kessler, R. C., Heath, A. C., & Eaves, L. J. (1992). Childhood parental loss and adult psychopathology in women: A twin study perspective. *Archives of General Psychiatry, 49,* 109–116.

Kenrick, D. T. (1987). Gender, genes, and the social environment: A biosocial interactionist perspective. In P. Shaver & C. Hendrick (Eds.), *Sex and gender* (pp. 14–43). Newbury Park, CA: Sage.

Kephart, W. (1967). Some correlates of romantic love. *Journal of Marriage and the Family, 29,* 470–479.

Kerns, J. G., & Fine, M. A. (1994). The relation between gender and negative attitudes toward gay men and lesbians: Do gender role attitudes mediate this relation? *Sex Roles, 31,* 297–307.

Kessler, R., & Neighbors, H. (1986). A new perspective on the relationships among race, social class, and psychological distress. *Journal of Health and Social Behavior, 27,* 107–115.

Keyser, H. H. (1986). Physiology and pathology of ovulation: Relevance to ectopic implantation. In A. Langer & L. Iffy (Eds.). *Extrauterine pregnancy* (pp. 57–72). Littleton, MA: PSG Publishing Co.

Kibria, N., Barnett, R. C., Baruch, G. K., & Pleck, J. H. (1990). Homemaking role quality and the psychological well-being and distress of employed women. *Sex Roles, 22,* 327–347.

Kilpatrick, D. G., Veronen, L. J., & Best, C. L. (1985). Factors predicting psychological distress among rape victims. In C. R. Figley (Ed.), *Trauma and its wake: The study and treatment of post-traumatic stress disorder* (pp. 113–141).

Kimura, D. (1993). Sex differences in the brain. In *Mind and brain: Readings from Scientific American magazine* (pp. 79–89). New York: W. H. Freeman.

Kim, M. (1989). Gender bias in compensation structures: A case study of its historical basis and persistence. *Journal of Social Issues, 45*(4), 39–49.

Kimball, M. M. (1989). A new perspective on women's math achievement. *Psychological Bulletin, 105,* 198–214.

Kimble, G. A. (1993). Evolution of the nature-nurture issue in the history of psychology. In R. Plomin & G. E. McLearn (Eds.), *Nature nurture & psychology* (pp. 3–25). Washington, DC: American Psychological Association.

Kinsey, A. C., Pomeroy, W. B., & Martin, C. E. (1948). *Sexual behavior in the human male.* Philadelphia: Saunders.

Kinsey, A. C., Pomeroy, W. B., Martin, C. E., & Gebhard, P. H. (1953). *Sexual behavior in the human female.* Philadelphia: Saunders.

Kipnis, D. (1984). The use of power in organizations and in interpersonal settings. In S. Oskamp (Ed.), *Applied social psychology annual vol. 5* (pp. 179–210). Newbury Park, CA: Sage.

Kirby, D., Barth, R. P., Leland, N., & Fetro, J. V. (1991). Reducing the risk: Impact of a new curriculum on sexual risk-taking. *Family Planning Perspectives, 23,* 253–263.

Kirkpatrick, L. A., & Davis, K. E. (1994). Attachment style, gender, and relationship stability: A longitudinal analysis. *Journal of Personality and Social Psychology, 66,* 502–512.

Kirz, D. S., Dorchester, W., & Freeman, R. K. (1986). Advanced maternal age: The mature gravida. *American Journal of Obstetrics and Gynecology, 152,* 7–12.

Kishwar, M. (1987). The continuing deficit of women in India and the impact of amniocentesis. In G. Corea, R. D. Klein, J. Hanner, H. B. Holmes, B. Hoskins, M. Kishwar, J. Raymond, R. Powl, & R. Steinbacher (Eds.), *Man-made woman: How new reproductive technologies affect women* (pp. 30–37). Bloomington, IN: Indiana University Press.

Kitano, H. H. L., & Daniels, R. (1988). *Asian Americans: Emerging minorities.* Englewood Cliffs, NJ: Prentice Hall.

Kite, M. E., Deaux, K., & Miele, M. (1991). Stereotypes of young and old: Does age outweigh gender? *Psychology and Aging, 6,* 19–27.

Kitzinger, C., & Wilkinson, S. (1995). Transitions from heterosexuality to lesbianism: The discursive production of lesbian identities. *Developmental Psychology, 31,* 95–104.

Kitzinger, S. (1983). *Women's experience of sex.* New York: Putnam.

Klebanov, P. K., & Jemmott III, J. B. (1992). Effects of expectations and bodily sensations on self reports of premenstrual symptoms. *Psychology of Women Quarterly, 16,* 289–310.

Kleck, G., & Sayles, S. (1990). Rape and resistance. *Social Problems, 37,* 149–161.

Klein, F. (1990). The need to view sexual orientation as a multivariable dynamic process: A theoretical perspective. In D. P. McWhirter, S. A. Sanders, & J. M. Reinisch (Eds.), *Homosexuality/Heterosexuality* (pp. 277–282). New York: Oxford Univerity Press.

Klein, M. C., Gauthier, R. J., Robbins, J. M., Kaczorowski, J., Jorgensen, S. H., Franco, E. D., Johnson, B., Waghorn, K., Gelfand, M. M., Guralnick, M. S., Luskey, G. W., & Joshi, A. K. (1994) Relationship of episiotomy to perineal trauma and morbidity, sexual dysfunction, and pelvic floor relaxation. *American Journal of Obstetrics and Gynecology, 171,* 591–598.

Kleinke, C. L., & Meyer, C. (1990). Evaluation of rape victim by men and women with high and low belief in a just world. *Psychology of Women Quarterly, 14,* 343–353.

Kohlberg, L. (1966). A cognitive-developmental analysis of children's sex-role concepts and attitudes. In E. E. Maccoby (Ed.), *The development of sex differences* (pp. 82–173). Stanford, CA: Stanford University Press.

Kohlberg, L. (1969). Stage and sequence: The cognitive-development approach to socialization. In D. A. Goslin (Ed.), *Handbook of socialization theory and research* (pp. 347–480). Chicago: Rand McNally.

Kolbe, R., & LaVoie, J. (1981). Sex-role stereotyping in preschool children's picture books. *Social Psychology Quarterly*, 369–374.

Kolbert, E. (1991, October 15). Survey finds most of public believes nominee's account. *The New York Times*, p. A-1.

Koller, S. (1988). Preventive effects of vitamins and minerals on early abortion. In H. Berger (Ed.), *Vitamins and minerals in pregnancy and lactation* (27–28). New York: Raven.

Komnenich, P., Lane, D. M., Dickey, R. P., & Stone. (1978). Gonadal hormones and cognitive performance. *Physiological Psychology, 6*, 115–120.

Koopman, J. S., Turkish, V. J., & Monto, A. S. (1985). Infant formulas and gastrointestinal illness. *American Journal of Public Health, 75*, 477–480.

Koss, M. P. (1985). The hidden rape victim: Personality, attitudinal, and situational characteristics. *Psychology of Women Quarterly, 9*, 193–212.

Koss, M. P. (1990). The women's mental health research agenda: Violence against women. *American Psychologist, 45*, 374–380.

Koss, M. P. (1992). The underdetection of rape: Methodological choices influence incidence estimates. *Journal of Social Issues, 48*(1), 61–75.

Koss, M. P. (1993). Rape: Scope, impact, interventions, and public policy responses. *American Psychologist, 48*, 1062–1069.

Koss, M. P., & Burkhart, B. R. (1989). A conceptual analysis of rape victimization: Long-term effects and implications for treatment. *Psychology of Women Quarterly, 13*, 27–40.

Koss, M. P., & Dinero, T. E. (1989). Discriminant analysis of risk factors for sexual victimization among a national sample of college women. *Journal of Consulting and Clinical Psychology, 57*, 242–250.

Koss, M. P., Dinero, T. E., Seibel, C. A., & Cox, S. L. (1988). Stranger and acquaintance rape: Are there differences in the victim's experience? *Psychology of Women Quarterly, 12*, 1–24.

Koss, M. P., Gidycz, C. A., & Wisniewski, N. (1987). The scope of rape: Incidence and prevalence of sexual aggression and victimization in a national sample of higher education students. *Journal of Consulting and Clinical Psychology, 55*, 162–170.

Koss, M. P., Heise, L., & Russo, N. P. (1994). The global health burden of rape. *Psychology of Women Quarterly, 18*, 509–537.

Koss, M. P., Koss, P. G., & Woodruff, W. J. (1991). Deleterious effects of criminal victimization on women's health and medical utilization. *Archives of Internal Medicine, 151*, 342–347.

Kramer, P. D. (1993). *Listening to prozac: A psychiatrist explores antidepressant drugs and the remaking of the self.* New York: Viking Penguin.

Kramer, P. E., & Lehman, S. (1990). Mismeasuring women: A critique of research on computer ability and avoidance. *Signs, 165*, 158–172.

Kranzer, S. (1995). U. S. Longevity unchanged. *Statistical Bulletin, 76*(3), 12–22.

Kreisberg, S. (1992). *Transforming power: Domination, empowerment, and education.* Albany, NY: State University of New York Press.

Kroft, C., & Leichner, P. (1987). Sex-role conflicts in alcoholic women. *International Journal of the Addictions, 22*, 685–693.

Kubler, W. (1988). Vitamin and mineral requirements of pregnant and lactating women. In H. Berger (Ed.). *Vitamins and minerals in pregnancy and lactation.* (pp. 15–23). New York: Raven.

Kuhns, J. B., Heide, K. M., & Silverman, I. (1992). Substance use/misuse among female prostitutes and female arrestees. *International Journal of the Addictions, 27*, 1283–1292.

Kurdek, L. A. (1991a). Correlates of relationship satisfaction in cohabiting gay and lesbian couples: Integration of contextual, investment, and problem-solving models. *Journal of Personality and Social Psychology, 61*, 910–922.

Kurdek, L. A. (1991b). Predictors of increases in marital distress in newlywed couples: A 3-year prospective longitudinal study. *Developmental Psychology, 27*, 627–636.

Kurdek, L. A., & Schmitt, J. P. (1986). Relationship quality of partners in heterosexual married, heterosexual cohabiting, and gay and lesbian relationships. *Journal of Personality and Social Psychology, 51*, 711–720.

La Free, G. D. (1982). Male power and female victimization: Toward a theory of interracial rape. *American Journal of Sociology, 88*, 311–328.

Lader, L. (1991). *RU 486: The pill that could end the abortion wars and why American women don't have it.* Reading MA: Addison-Wesley.

Ladner, J. A. (1987). Introduction to tomorrow's tomorrow: The black woman. In S. Harding (Ed.), *Feminism and methodology: Social science issues* (pp. 74–83). Bloomington, IN: Indiana University Press.

Ladner, J. A., & Gourdine, R. M. (1992). Adolescent pregnancy in the African-American community. In R. L. Braithwaite, & S. E. Taylor (Eds.), *Health issues in the Black community* (pp. 206–221). San Francisco: Jossey-Bass.

Laessle, R. G., Tuschl, R. J., Waadt, S., & Pirke, K. M. (1989). The specific psychopathology of bulimia nervosa: A comparison with restrained and unrestrained (normal) eaters. *Journal of Consulting and Clinical Psychology, 57*, (6), 772–775.

Lafferty, F. W., & Fiske, M. E. (1994). Postmenopausal estrogen replacement: A long-term cohort study. *The American Journal of Medicine, 97*, 72–77.

LaFramboise, T. D., Berman, J. S., & Sohi, B. K. (1994). American Indian women. In L. Comas-Dias & B. Greene (Eds.), *Women of color: Integrating ethnic and gender identities in psychotherapy* (pp. 30–71). New York: Guilford.

LaFramboise, T. D., Heyle, A. M., & Ozer, E. J. (1990). Changing and diverse roles of women in American Indian cultures. *Sex Roles, 22*, 455–476.

LaFrance, M., & Banaji, M. R. (1992). Towards a reconsideration of the gender emotion relationship. In M. S. Clark (Ed.), *Emotion and social behavior.* Newbury Park, CA: Sage.

Lakoff, R. T. (1973). Language and woman's place. *Language and Society, 2*, 45–79.

Lakoff, R. T. (1975). *Language and woman's place.* New York: Harper and Row.

Lambert, H. H. (1987). Biology and equality: A perspective on sex differences. In S. Harding & J. F. O'Barr (Eds.), *Sex and scientific inquiry* (pp. 125–145). Chicago: University of Chicago Press.

Landau, C., Cyr, M. G., & Moulton, A. W. (1994). *The complete book of menopause: Every woman's guide to good health.* NY: G. P. Putnam's Sons.

Lander, L. (1988). *Images of bleeding: Menstruation as ideology.* New York: Orlando Press.

Landis, S. E., Schoenbach, V. J., Weber, D. J., Mittal, M., Krishan, B., Lewis, K., & Koch, G. G. (1992). Results of a randomized trial of partner notification in cases of HIV infection in North Carolina. *The New England Journal of Medicine, 326*(2), 101–133.

Landrine, H. (1985). Race x class stereotypes of women. *Sex roles, 13*, 65–75.

Landrine, H., Klonoff, E. A., & Brown-Collins, A. (1992). Cultural diversity and methodology in feminist psychology: Critique, proposal, empirical example. *Psychology of Women Quarterly, 16*, 145–163.

Landry, B., & Jendrek, M. P. (1978). The employment of wives in middle-class Black families. *Journal of Marriage and the Family, 40*, 787–797.

Langer, A. (1986). Clinical presentation of tubal pregnancy. In A. Langer & L. Iffy (Eds.), *Extrauterine Pregnancy* (pp. 235–244). Littleton, MA: PSG Publishing Co.

Langer, E. J., & Rodin, J. (1976). The effects of choice and enhanced personal responsibility for the aged: A field experiment in an institutional setting. *Journal of Personality and Social Psychology, 34*, 191–198.

Lasker, J. N., & Borg, S. (1989). Secrecy and the new reproductive technologies. In L. M. Whitesford & M. L. Poland (Eds.). *New approaches to human reproduction: Social and ethical dilemmas* (pp. 134-144). Boulder, CO: Westview Press.

Lauer, J. C., & Lauer, R. H. (1986). *Till death do us part: How couples stay together.* New York: Haworth Press.

Laumann, E. O., Gagnon, J. H., Michael, R. T., & Michaels, S. (1994). *The social organization of sexuality: Sexual practices in the United States.* Chicago: The University of Chicago Press.

Laws, J. L., & Schwartz, P. (1977). *Sexual scripts.* Hinsdale, IL: Dryden.

Lawrence, R. A. (1986). Toward understanding maternal choices for infant feeding. *Development and Behavioral Pediatrics, 7,* 373–374.

Lawrence, R. A. (1980). *Breastfeeding.* St. Louis: C. V. Mosby.

Leahy, T. (1994). Taking up a position: Discourses of femininity and adolescence in the context of man/girl relationships. *Gender & Society, 8,* 48–72.

Leenaars, A. A. (1988). Are women's suicides really different from men's? *Women's Health, 14,* 17–33.

Lehman, E. C. Jr., (1985). *Women clergy: Breaking through gender barriers.* New Brunswick, NJ: Transaction Books.

Leigh, B. C. (1989). Reasons for having and avoiding sex: Gender, sexual orientation, and relationship to sexual behavior. *Journal of Sex Research, 26,* 199–209.

Leitenberg, H., Rosen, J. C., Wolf, J., Vara, L. S., Detzer, M. J., & Srebnik, D. (1993). Comparison of cognitive-behavior therapy and desipramine in the treatment of bulimia nervosa. *Behavior Research and Therapy, 32,* 37–45.

Lenney, E. (1977). Women's self-confidence in achievement settings. *Psychological Bulletin, 84,* 1–13.

Lennon, M. C. (1987). Sex differences in distress: The impact of gender and work roles. *Journal of Health and Social Behavior, 28,* 290–305.

Lerner, M. (1980). *The belief in a just world: A fundamental delusion.* New York: Plenum.

LeVay, S. (1991). A difference in hypothalamic structure between heterosexual and homosexual men. *Science, 253,* 1034–1037.

Levenson, R. W., Cartensen, L. L., & Gottman, J. M. (1993). Long-term marriage: Age, gender, and satisfaction. *Psychology and Aging, 8,* 301–313.

Levin, H., & Hunter, W. A. (1982). Children's use of a social speech register: Age and sex differences. *Journal of Language and Social Psychology, 1,* 63–72.

Levine, J. J., & Ilowite, N. T. (1994). Sclerodermalike esophageal disease in children breast-fed by mothers with silicone breast implants. *Journal of the American Medical Association, 271,* 213–216.

Levine, M. P., & Smolak, L. (1992). Toward a developmental psychopathology of eating disorders: The example of early adolescence. In J. H. Crowther, S. E. Hobfoll, M. A. P. Stephens, & D. L. Tennebaum (Eds.), *The etiology of bulimia: The individual and familial context* (pp. 59–80). Washington, D.C.: Taylor & Francis.

Levine, M. P., Smolak, L., Moodey, A. F., Shuman, M., & Hessen, L. D. (1994). Normative developmental challenges and dieting and eating disturbances in middle school girls. *International Journal of Eating Disorders, 15,* 11–20.

Levine-MacCombie, J., & Koss, M. P. (1986). Acquaintance rape: Effective avoidance strategies. *Psychology of Women Quarterly, 10,* 311–320.

Levit, D. B. (1991). Gender differences in ego defenses in adolescence: Sex roles as one way to understand the differences. *Journal of Personality and Social Psychology, 61,* 992–999.

Levy, G. D. (1994a). Aspects of preschoolers' comprehension of indoor and outdoor gender-typed toys. *Sex Roles, 30,* 391–405.

Levy, G. D. (1994b). High and low gender schematic children's release from proactive interference. *Sex Roles, 30,* 93–108.

Levy, J. (1972). Lateral specialization of the human brain: Behavioral manifestation and possible evolutionary basis. In J. A. Kiger (Ed.), *The biology of behavior.* Eugene, OR: Oregon University Press.

Lewin, M. (1985). Unwanted intercourse: The difficulty of saying no. *Psychology of Women Quarterly, 9,* 184–192.

Lewin, T. (1989a, November 2). Study cites lack in prenatal care. *The New York Times,* p. A25.

Lewin, T. (1989b, January 9). When courts take charge of the unborn. *The New York Times,* pp. A1, A11.

Lewis, J. (1993). Feminism, the menopause and hormone replacement therapy. *Feminist Review, 43,* 39–56.

Lewis, K. E., & Brierly, M. (1990). Toward a profile of the female voter: Sex differences in perceived physical attractiveness and competence of political candidates. *Sex Roles,* 1–12.

Lewis, M. (1987). Early sex role behavior and school age adjustment. In J. M. Reinisch, L. A. Rosenblum, & S. A. Sanders (Eds.), *Masculinity/Femininity: Basic Perspectives* (pp. 202–239). New York: Oxford University Press.

Lewis, V. G., & Money, J. (1983). Gender-identity/role: G-I/R Part A: XY (androgen-insensitivity syndrome) and XX (Rokitansky syndrome) vaginal atresia compared. In L. Dennerstein & G. Burrows (Eds.), *Handbook of Psychosomatic Obstetrics and Gynaecology.* New York: Elsevier Biomedical press.

Libby, M. N., & Aries, E. (1989). Gender differences in preschool children's narrative fantasy. *Psychology of Women Quarterly, 13,* 293–306.

Lichter, D. T., McLaughlin, K. K., Kephart, G., & Landry, D. J. (1992). Race and the retreat from marriage: A shortage of marriageable men? *American Sociological Review, 57,* 781–799.

Lieberman, E., (1995). Low birth weight—not a Black-and-White issue. *The New England Journal of Medicine, 332,* 117–118.

Liebowitz, M. R. (1989). Antidepressants in panic disorders. *British Journal of Psychiatry, 155,* 46–52.

Liff, J. M., Sung, J. F., Chow, Wh. H., Greenberg, R. S., & Flanders, W. D. (1991). Does increased detection account for the rising incidence of breast cancer? *American Journal of Public Health, 81,* 462–465.

Lightdale, J. R., & Prentice, D. A. (1994). Rethinking sex differences in aggression: Aggressive behavior in the absence of social roles. *Personality and Social Psychology Bulletin, 20,* 34–44.

Lightfoot-Klein, H. (1989). The sexual experience and marital adjustment of genitally circumcised and infibulated females in the Sudan. *The Journal of Sex Research, 26,* 375–392.

Linda & Avreayl (1986). Organizing safe space for battered lesbians: A community based program. In K. Lobel (Ed.), *Naming the violence: Speaking out about lesbian battering* (pp. 103–110). Seattle, WA: The Seal Press.

Lindblad-Goldberg, M., Dukes, J. L., & Lasley, J. H. (1988). Stress in black, low-income, single-parent families: Normative and dysfunctional patterns. *American Journal of Orthopsychiatry, 58,* 104–120.

Lindheim, S. R., Notelovitz, M., Feldman, E.B., Larsen, S., Khan, F. Y., & Lobo, R. A. (1994). The independent effects of exercise and estrogen on lipids and lipoproteins in postmenopausal women. *Obstetrics & Gynecology, 83,* 167–172.

Lindner, M. S., Hagan, M. S., & Brown, J. C. (1992). The adjustment of children in nondivorced, divorced, single-mother, and remarried families. *Monographs of the Society for Research in Child Development, 57*(2), 35–72.

Linn, M. C., & Petersen, A. C. (1985). Emergence and characterization of sex differences in spatial ability: A meta-analysis. *Child Development, 56,* 1479–1498.

Linn, M. C., & Petersen, A. C. (1986). A meta-analysis of gender differences in spatial ability: Implications for mathematics and science achievement. In J. S. Hyde & M. C. Linn (Eds.), *The psychology of gender: Advances through meta-analysis.* (pp. 67–101). Baltimore, MD: Johns Hopkins University Press.

Linz, D., Donnerstein, E., & Penrod, S. (1988). The effects of long-term exposure to violent and sexually degrading depictions of women. *Journal of Personality and Social Psychology, 55,* 758–767.

Linz, D., Wilson, B. J., & Donnerstein, E. (1992). Sexual violence in the mass media: Legal solutions, warnings, and mitigation through education. *Journal of Social Issues, 48*(1), 145–171.

Lippa, R. (1991). Some psychometric characteristics of gender diagnosticity measures: Reliability, validity, consistency across domains, and relationship to the big five. *Journal of Personality and Social Psychology, 61,* 1000–1011.

Lips, H. M. (1982). Somatic and emotional aspects of the normal pregnancy experience: The first five months. *American Journal of Obstetrics and Gynecology, 142,* 524–529.

Lips, H. M. (1991). *Women, men, and power.* Mountain View, CA: Mayfield.

Lisak, D. (1991). Sexual aggression, masculinity, and fathers. *Signs, 16,* 238–262.

Livingston, J. A. (1982). Responses to sexual harassment on the job: Legal, organizational, and individual actions. *Journal of Social Issues, 38*(4), 5–22.

Lobo, R. A. (Ed.). (1994). *Treatment of the postmenopausal woman: Basic and clinical aspects.* New York: Raven Press.

Lobel, K. (1986). Introduction. In K. Lobel (Ed.), *Naming the violence: Speaking out about lesbian battering* (pp. 1–7). Seattle, WA: Seal Press.

Lobel, T. E., Bempechat, J., Gewirtz, J. C., Shoken-Topaz, T., & Bashe, E. (1993). The role of gender-related information and self-endorsement of traits in preadolescents' inferences and judgments. *Child Development, 64,* 1285–1294.

Lockheed, M. E. (1985). Women, girls and computers: A first look at the evidence. *Sex Roles, 13,* 115–121.

Lockheed, M. E., & Hall, K. P. (1976). Conceptualizing sex as a status characteristic: Applications to leadership training strategies. *Journal of Social Issues, 32*(3), 111–124.

Locksley, A., Borgida, E., Brekke, N., & Hepburn, C. (1980). Sex stereotypes and social judgement. *Journal of Personality and Social Psychology, 39,* 821–831.

Loftus, E. F. (1993). The reality of repressed memories. *American Psychologist, 48,* 518–537.

Loftus, E. F., Polonsky, S., & Fullilove, M. T. (1994). Memories of childhood sexual abuse: Remembering and repressing. *Psychology of Women Quarterly, 18,* 67–84.

Lombardo, W. K., Crester, G. A., Lombardo, B., & Mathis, S. L. (1983). For cryin out loud-there is a sex difference. *Sex Roles, 9,* 987–995.

Long, B. C. (1989). Sex-role orientation, coping strategies, and self-efficacy of women in traditional and nontraditional occupations. *Psychology of Women Quarterly, 13,* 307–324.

Long, J. S. (1992). Measures of sex differences in scientific productivity. *Social Forces, 71,* 159–178.

Longnecker, M. P. (1994). Alcoholic beverage consumption in relation to risk of breast cancer: Meta-analysis and review. *Cancer Causes Control, 5,* 73–82.

Lopata, H. Z. (1979). *Women as widows.* New York: Elsevier.

Loprinzi, C. L., Michalak, J. C., Quella, S. K., O'Fallon, J. R., Hatfield, A. K., Nelimark, R. A., Dose, A. M., Fischer, J., Johnson, C., Klatt, N. E., et al. (1994). Megestrol acetate for the prevention of hot flashes. *The New England Journal of Medicine, 331,* 347–352.

Lorde, A. (1992a). Age, race, class, and sex: Women redefining difference. In M. L. Andersen, & P. H. Collins (Eds.), *Race, class, and gender: An anthology* (pp. 495–502). Belmont, CA: Wadsworth.

Lorde, A. (1992b). Man child: A Black lesbian feminist's response. In M. L. Andersen and P. H. Collins, *Race, class, and gender: An anthology* (pp. 253–259). Belmont, CA: Wadsworth.

Lorentz, P., & LaFerla, J. J. (1991). The deceptive symptoms of pseudocyesis. *Medical Aspects of Human Sexuality, 48*–51.

Loring, M., & Powell, B. (1988). Gender, race, and DSM-III: A study of the objectivity of psychiatric diagnostic behavior. *Journal of Health and Social Behavior, 29,* 1–22.

Lott, B. (1987a). Sexist discrimination as distancing behavior: I. A laboratory demonstration. *Psychology of Women Quarterly, 11,* 47–58.

Lott, B. (1987b). *Women's Lives: Themes and variations in gender learning.* Monterey, CA: Brooks/Cole.

Lott, B. (1991). Social psychology: Humanist roots and feminist future. *Psychology of Women Quarterly, 15,* 505–519.

Lott, B., Reilly, M. E., & Howard, D. R. (1982). Sexual assault and harassment: A campus community case study. *Signs, 8,* 296–319.

Lowe, M. R. (1993). The effects of dieting on eating behavior: A three-factor model. *Psychological Bulletin, 114,* 100–121.

Lowinsky, N. R. (1992). *Stories from the motherline: Reclaiming the mother-daughter bond, finding our feminine souls.* Los Angeles: J. P. Tarcher.

Lugones, M. C., & Spelman, E. V. (1983). Have we got a theory for you! Feminist theory, cultural imperialism and the demand for the 'woman's voice'. *Women's Studies International Forum, 6,* 573–581.

Lupe, P. J., & Gross, T. L. (1986). Maternal upright posture and mobility in labor: A review. *Obstetrics and Gynecology, 67,* 727–734.

Luthra, R. (1993). Toward a reconceptualization of "choice": Challenges by women at the margins. *Feminist Issues,* 41–53.

Lutz, W., Wils, A. B., & Nieminen, M. (1991). The demographic dimensions of divorce: The case of Finland. *Population Studies, 45,* 437–453.

Lykes, M. B., Brabeck, M. M., Ferns, T., & Radan, A. (1993). Human rights and mental health among Latin American women in situations of state-sponsored violence. *Psychology of Women Quarterly, 17,* 525–544.

Lytton, H., & Romney, D. M. (1991). Parents' differential socialization of boys and girls: A meta-analysis. *Psychological Bulletin, 109,* 267–296.

Maccoby, E. E. (1966). Sex differences in intellectual functioning. In E. E. Maccoby (Ed.), *The development of sex differences.* Stanford, CA: Stanford University Press.

Maccoby, E. E. (1990). Gender and relationships: A developmental account. *American Psychologist, 45,* 513–520.

Maccoby, E. E., & Jacklin, C. N. (1974). *The psychology of sex differences.* Stanford, CA: Stanford University Press.

Maccoby, E. E. (1988). Gender as a social category. *Developmental Psychology, 24*(6), 755–765.

MacCorquodale, P., & DeLamater, J. (1979). Self-image and premarital sexuality. *Journal of Marriage and the Family, 41,* 327–339.

MacCorquodale, P., & Jensen, G. (1993). Women in the law: Partners or tokens? *Gender & Society, 7,* 582–593.

MacEwen, K. E., & Barling, J. (1991). Effects of maternal employment experiences on children's behavior via mood, cognitive difficulties, and parenting behavior. *Journal of Marriage and Family, 53,* 635–644.

MacGreagor, S. N., Keith, L. G., Bachicha, J. A., & Chasnoff, I. J. (1989). Cocaine abuse during pregnancy: Correlation between prenatal care and perinatal outcome. *Obstetrics and Gynecology, 74,* 882–885.

Mackey, M., & Brouse, S. (1988). Childbearing. In C. J. Lippa & C. Miller (Eds.), *Women's health perspectives: An annual review, Vol. 1,* (pp. 109–122). Phoenix, AZ: The Oryx Press.

MacKinnon, C. A. (1987). Feminism, marxism, method, and the state: Toward feminist jurisprudence. In S. Harding (Ed.), *Feminism and methodology: Social science issues* (pp. 135–156). Bloomington, IN: Indiana University Press.

MacKinnon, C. A. (1992). Francis Biddle's sister: Pornography, civil rights, and speech. In T. L. Whitehead and B. V. Reid (Eds.), *Gender constructs and social issues* (pp. 261–321). Urbana, IL: University of Illinois Press.

Magnusson, D., Strattin, H., & Allen, V. L. (1985). Biological maturation and social development: A longitudinal study of some adjustment problems from mid-adolescence to adulthood. *Journal of Youth and Adolescence 14,* 267–283.

Mahoney, M. A., & Yngvesson, B. (1992). The construction of subjectivity and the paradox of resistance: Reintegrating feminist anthropology and psychology. *Signs, 18,* 44–73.

Major, B. (1987). Gender, justice, and the psychology of entitlement. In P. Shaver & C. Hendrick (Eds.), *Review of personality and social psychology: Sex and gender* (Vol. 7, pp. 124–148). Beverly Hills, CA: Sage.

Major, B. (1989). Gender differences in comparisons and entitlement: Implications for comparable worth. *Journal of Social Issues 45*(4), 99–115.

Major, B. (1993). Gender, entitlement, and the distribution of family labor. *Journal of Social Issues, 49*(3), 141–159.

Major, B., & Cozzarelli, C. (1992). Psychosocial predictors of adjustment to abortion. *Journal of Social Issues, 48*(3), 121–142.

Major, B., & Deaux, K. (1982). Individual differences in justice behavior. In J. Greenberg & R. L. Cohen (Eds.), *Equity and justice in social behavior.* New York: Academic Press.

Major, B., & Konar, E. (1984). An investigation of sex differences in pay expectations and their possible causes. *Academy of Management Journal, 27,* 777–792.

Major, B., McFarlin, D., & Gagnon, D. (1984). Overworked and underpaid. *Journal of Personality and Social Psychology, 47,* 1399–1412.

Major, B., Schmidlin, A. M., & Williams, L. (1990). Gender patterns in social touch: The impact of setting and age. *Journal of Personality and Social Psychology, 58,* 634–643.

Malamuth, N. M. (1986). Predictors of naturalistic sexual aggression. *Journal of Personality and Social Psychology, 50,* 953–962.

Malamuth, N. M., Check, J. V. P., & Briere, J. (1986). Sexual arousal in response to aggression: Ideological, aggressive, and sexual correlates. *Journal of Personality and Social Psycholgy, 50,* 330–340.

Malamuth, N. M., Haber, S., & Feshbach, S. (1980). Testing hypotheses regarding rape: Exposure to sexual violence, sex differences, and the "normality" of rapists. *Journal of Research in Personality, 14,* 121–137.

Malamuth, N. M., Sockloskie, R. J., Koss, M. P., & Tanaka, J. S. (1991). Characteristics of Aggressors against women: Testing a model using a national sample of college students. *Journal of Consulting and Clinical Psychology, 59,* 670–681.

Manderscheid, R. W., & Sonnenschein, M. A. (Eds.), (1992). *Mental health, United States, 1992.* U. S. Department of Health and Human Services. Washington, DC: U.S. Government Printing Office.

Mandel, R. B., & Dodson, D. L. (1992). Do women officeholders make a difference? In Ries, P., & Stone, A. J. *The American woman 1992–1993* (pp. 149–177). New York: Norton.

Mansfield, P. K. (1988). Midlife childbearing: Strategies for formed decisionmaking. *Psychology of Women Quarterly, 12,* 445–460.

Mansfield, P. K., Koch, P. B., Henderson, J., Vicary, J. R., Cohn, M., & Young, E. W. (1991). The job climate for women in traditionally male blue-collar occupations. *Sex Roles, 25,* 63–79.

Marazziti, D. Rotondo, A., Presta, S. Pancioli-Guadagnucci, M. L., Palego, L., & Conti, L. (1993). Role of serotonin in human aggressive behaviour. *Aggressive Behavior, 19,* 347–353.

Marecek, J. (1989). Introduction: Theory and method in feminist psychology. *Psychology of Women Quarterly, 13,* 367–377.

Marecek, J., & Hare-Mustin, R. T. (1991). A short history of the future: Feminism and clinical psychology. *Psychology of Women Quarterly, 15,* 521–536.

Margolies, L., Becker, M., & Jackson-Brewer, K. (1987). Internalized homophobia: Identifying and treating the oppressor within. In the Boston Lesbian Psychologies Collective (Ed.), *Lesbian psychologies: Explorations and challenges* (pp. 229–241). Urbana, IL: University of Illinois Press.

Margolis, G., Goodman, R. L., & Rubin, A. (1990). Psychological effects of breast-conserving cancer treatment and mastectomy. *Psychosomatics, 31,* 33–39.

Markides, K. S., Hoppe, S. W., Martin, H. W., & Timbers, D. M. (1983). Sample respresentativeness in a three generation study of Mexican Americans. *Journal of Marriage and the Family, 45,* 911–916.

Marks, M. N., Wieck, A., Checkley, S. A., & Kumar, R. (1992). Contribution of psychological and social factors to psychotic and non-psychotic relapse after childbirth in women with previous histories of affective disorder. *Journal of Affective Disorder, 24,* 253–263.

Marshall, G. N., & Lang, E. L. (1990). Optimism, Self-mastery, and symptoms of depression in women professionals. *Journal of Personality and Social Psychology, 59,* 132–139.

Marston, A. R., Jacobs, D. R., Singer, R. D., Widaman, K. F., & Little, T. D. (1988). Characteristics of adolescents at risk for compulsive overeating on a brief screening test. *Adolescence, 23,* 59–65.

Martin, B. A. (1989). Gender differences in salary expectations when current salary information is provided. *Psychology of Women Quarterly, 13,* 87–96.

Martin, C. L. (1987). A ratio measure of sex stereotyping. *Journal of Personality and Social Psychology. 52,* 489–499.

Martin, D., & Lyon, P. (1984). Lesbian women and mental health policy. In L. E. Walker (Ed), *Women and mental health policy* (pp. 151–179). Beverly Hills, CA: Sage.

Martin, P. Y., & Hummer, R. A. (1992). Fraternities and rape on campus. In M. L. Andersen & P. H. Collins (Eds.), *Race, class, and gender: An anthology.* Belmont, CA: Wadsworth.

Martin, T. C., & Bumpass, L. L. (1989). Recent trends in marital disruption. *Demography, 26,* 37–51.

Martinez, E. A. (1988). Child behavior in American/Chicano families: Maternal teaching and child-rearing practices. *Family Relations, 37,* 275–280.

Martinez, G. A., & Krieger, F. W. (1985). 1984 milk-feeding patterns in the United States. *Pediatrics, 76,* 1004–1008.

Masson, J. (1984). *The assault on truth: Freud's suppression of the seduction theory.* New York: Farrar, Straus & Giroux.

Masters, W. H., & Johnson, V. E. (1966). *Human sexual response.* Boston: Little Brown.

Masters, W. H., & Johnson, V. E. (1970). *Human sexual dysfunction.* Boston: Little Brown.

Mastroiacovo, P., & Botto, L. D. (1994). Chorionic villus sampling and transverse limb deficiencies: Maternal age is not a confounder. *American Journal of Medical Genetics, 53,* 182–186.

Matthews, K. A., Wing, R. R., Kuller, L. H., Meilahn, E. N., Kelsey, S. F., Costello, E. J., & Caggiula, A. W. (1990). Influences of natural menopause on psychological characteristics and symptoms of middle-aged healthy women. *Journal of Consulting and Clinical Psychology, 58,* 345–351.

Mauro, J. (1992, May 3). Who gets abortions? *The Providence Journal-Bulletin,* p. A-2.

Maxwell, S., Cruickshank, A., & Thorpe, G. (1994). Red wine and antioxidant activity in serum. *The Lancet, 344,* 193–194.

Mayes, S. D., Elesser, V., Schaefer, J. H., Handford, H. A., & Michael-Good, L. (1992). Sexual practices and AIDS knowledge among women partners of HIV-infected hemophiliacs. *Public Health Reports, 107,* 504–514.

Mazur, A. (1986). U.S. trends in feminine beauty and overadaptation. *Journal of Sex Research, 22,* 281–303.

McAdams, D. P. (1989). *Intimacy: The need to be close.* New York: Doubleday.

McAdams, D. P., Lester, R. M., Brand, P. A., McNamara, W. J., & Lensky, D. B. (1988). Sex and the TAT: Are women more intimate than men? Do men fear intimacy? *Journal of Personality Assessment, 52,* 397–409.

McAdoo, H. P. (1990). A portrait of African American families in the United States. In S. E. Rix (Ed.), *The American Woman 1990–91: A status report* (pp. 71–93). New York: Norton.

McCarty, P. A. (1986). Effects of feedback on the self-confidence of men and women. *Academy of Management Journal, 29,* 840–849.

McClanahan, S. S., & Glass, J. L. (1985). A note on the trend in sex differences in psychological distress. *Journal of Health and Social Behavior, 26,* 328–336.

McClelland, D.C. (1961). *The achieving society.* New York: Van Nostrand.

McClintock, M. K. (1971). Menstrual synchrony and suppression. *Nature, 229,* 244–245.

McComb, H. G. (1989). The dynamics and impact of affirmative action process of higher education, the curriculum, and black women. *Sex Roles, 21,* 127–143.

McFarland, C., Ross, M., & DeCourville, N. (1989). Women's theories of menstruation and biases in recall of menstrual symptoms. *Journal of Personality and Social Psychology, 57,* 522–531.

McFarlane, J. M. & Williams, T. M. (1994). Placing premenstrual syndrome in perspective. *Psychology of Women Quarterly, 18,* 339–373.

McFate, K. (1991). *Poverty, inequality and the crisis of social policy: Summary of findings.* Washington, DC: Joint Center for Political and Economic Studies.

McGrath, E., Keita, G. P., Strickland, B. R., & Russo, N. F. (1990). *Women and depression: Risk factors and treatment issues.* American Psychological Association: Washington, DC.

McGuire, W. L. (1991). The optimal timing of mastectomy: Low tide or high tide? (editorial comment). *Annals of Internal Medicine, 115,* 401–403.

McHugh, M. C., Frieze, I. H., & Hanusa, B. H. (1982). Attributions and sex differences in achievement: Problems and new perspectives. *Sex Roles, 8,* 467–479.

McKeganey, N., & Barnard, M. (1992). Providing drug injectors with easier access to sterile injecting equipment: A description of a pharmacy based scheme. *British Journal of the Addictions, 87,* 987–992.

McKenry, P. C., & Price, S. J. (1991). Alternatives for support: Life after divorce-A literature review. *Journal of Divorce and Remarriage, 15,* 1–19.

McKinlay, J. B., McKinlay, S. M., & Brambilla, D. (1987). The relative contributions of endocrine changes and social circumstances to depression in mid-aged women. *Journal of Health and Social Behavior, 28,* 345–363.

McLaughlin, S. d., Manninen, D. L., & Winges, L. D. (1988). Do adolescents who relinquish their children fare better or worse than those who raise them? *Family Planning Perspectives, 20*(1), 911–916.

McNally, R. J. (1990). Psychological approaches to panic disorder. *Psychological Bulletin, 108,* 403–419.

McRae, J. A., & Kohen, J. A. (1988). Changes in attributions of marital problems. *Social Psychology Quarterly, 51,* 74–80.

McVicar, D. M. (1993, December 23). Changing the political dynamic. *The Providence Jounal Bulletin,* pp. D-1, D-3.

McVicar, N. (1994, April 6). Do vitamins fight disease? The FDA is still deciding. *The Providence Journal-Bulletin* (Evening Edition) E1, E3.

Meade, W. W. (1994, April). The M word we dare not say: (It isn't marriage, money, or mother). *Cosmopolitan,* 207–209.

Mechaneck, R., Klein, E., & Kuppersmith, J. (1987). Single mothers by choice: A family alternative. *Women and Therapy, 6,* 263–281.

Mechanic, D., & Hansell, S. (1989). Divorce, family conflict, and adolescents' well being. *Journal of Health an Social Behavior, 30,* 105–116.

Medical Economics Data (1995). *Physicians Desk Reference.* Oradell, NJ: Medical Economics Co.

Medical Research International, Society for Assisted Reproductive Technology (SART), & The American Fertility Society (1992). In vitro fertilization-embryo transfer (IVF-ET) in the United States: 1990 results from the IVF-ET registry. *Fertility and Sterility, 57,* 15–24.

Mednick, M. T. (1989). On the politics of psychological constructs: Stop the bandwagon, I want to get off. *American Psychologist, 44,* 1118–1123.

Megargee, E. I. (1969). Influence of sex roles on the manifestation of leadership. *Journal of Applied Psychology, 53,* 377–382.

Mehl, L., Donovan, S., & Peterson, G. (1988). The role of hypnotherapy in facilitating normal birth. In P. Fedor-Freybergh & M. L. V. Vogel (Eds.), *Prenatal and Perinatal psychology and medicine: Encounter with the unborn* (pp. 189–214). Park Ridge, NJ: The Parthenon Publishing Group.

Melnick, S. L., Sherer, R., Louis, T. A., Hillman, D., Rodiguez, E. M., Lackman, C., Capps, L., Brown, L. S., Carlyn, M., Korvick, J. A., Dayton, L., for the Terry Beirn Community Programs for Clinical Research on AIDS (1994). Survival and disease progression according to gender of patients with HIV infection. *Journal of the American Medical Association, 272,* 1915–1921.

Menning, B. E. (1980). The emotional needs of infertile couples. *Fertility and Sterility, 34,* 313–314.

Messé, M. R., & Geer, J. H. (1985). Voluntary vaginal musculature contractions as an enhancer of sexual arousal. *Archives of Sexual Behavior, 14,* 13–28.

Metcalf, M. G., Braiden, V., Livesey, J. H., & Wells, J. E. (1992). The premenstrual syndrome: Amelioration of symptoms after hysterectomy. *Journal of Psychosomatic Research, 36,* 569–584.

Meyer, C. B., & Taylor, S. E. (1986). Adjustment to rape. *Journal of Personality and Social Psychology, 50,* 1226–1234.

Meyer, J. (1988). Feminist thought and social psychology. In M. M. Gergen (Ed.), *Feminist thought and the structure of knowledge* (pp. 105–123). New York: New York University Press.

Meyer-Bahlburg, H. F. L. (1984) Psychoendocrine research on sexual orientation. Current status and future options. *Progress in Brain Research, 61,* 375–398.

Meyer-Bahlburg, H. F. L., Ehrhardt, A. A., Rosen, L. R., Gruen, R. S., Veridiano, N. P., Vann, F. H., & Neuwalder, H. F. (1995). Prenatal estrogens and the development of homosexual orientation. *Developmental Psychology, 31,* 12–21.

Micevych, P., & Ulibarri, C. (1992). Development of the limbic-hypothalamic cholecystokinin circuit: A model of sexual differentiation. *Developmental Neuroscience, 14*(1), 11–34.

Michelman, D. F., Faden, R. R., Gielsen, A. C., & Buxton, K. S. (1990). Breastfeeding promotion: Attitudes, beliefs, and practices. *American Journal of Health Promotion, 4,* 181–186.

Mickelson, R. A. (1989). Why does Jane read and write so well? The anomaly of women's achievement. *Sociology of Education, 62,* 47–63.

Milburn, N., & D'Ercole, A. (1991). Homeless women: Moving toward a comprehensive model. *American Psychologist, 46,* 1161–1169.

Mill, J. S. (1970), The subjection of women. In J. S. Mill & H. S. Mill *Essays on Sex Equality* (pp. 123–215). A. S. Rossi (Ed.). (Original work published in 1869). Chicago: The University of Chicago Press.

Millard, A. V. (1990). The place of the clock in pediatric advice: Rationales, cultural themes, and impediments to breast-feeding. *Social Science and Medicine, 31,* 211–221.

Miller, J. B. (1976). *Toward a new psychology of women.* Boston: Beacon Press.

Miller, J. B. (1986). *Toward a new psychology of women* (2nd ed.). Boston: Beacon Press.

Miller, V. T., Muesing, R. A., LaRosa, J. C., Stoy, D. B., Fowler, S. E., & Stillman, R. J. (1994). Quantitative and qualitative changes in lipids, lipoproteins, apolipoprotein A-1, and sex hormone-binding globulin due to two doses of conjugated equine estrogen with and without a progestin. *Obstetrics & Gynecology, 83,* 173–179.

Miller, W. B. (1992). An empirical study of the psychological antecedents and consequences of induced abortion. *Journal of Social Issues, 48*(3), 67–93.

Miller, W. E., & Friedman, S. (1988). Male and female sexuality during pregnancy: Behavior and attitudes. *Journal of Psychology and Human Sexuality 1*(2), 17–37.

Millet, K. (1970). *Sexual politics.* New York: Ballantine Books.

Minas, A. (1993). Target hiring. In A. Minas (Ed.), *Gender basics: Feminist perspectives on women and men* (pp. 117–121). Belmont, CA: Wadsworth.

Minden, S. L., & Notman, M. T. (1991). Psychotherapeutic issues related to abortion. In N. L. Stotland (Ed.), *Psychiatric aspects of abortion* (pp. 119–133). Washington, DC: American Psychiatric Press.

Minton, H. L., & Schneider, F. W. (1980). *Differential Psychology,* Monterey, CA: Brooks/Cole.

Miranda, R., Saravia, N. G., Ackerman, R., Murphy, N., Berman, S., McMurray, D. M. (1983). Effects of maternal nutritional status on immunological substances in human colostrum and milk. *American Journal of Clinical Nutrition, 37,* 632–640.

Mitchell, J. E., Pyle, R. L., Eckert, E. D., Hatsukami, D., Pomeroy, C., Zimmerman, R. (1990). A comparison study of antidepressants and structured intensive group psychotherapy in the treatment of bulimia nervosa. *Archives of General Psychiatry, 47,* 149–157.

Mitchell, V., & Helson, R. (1990). Women's prime in life: Is it the 50's? *Psychology of Women Quarterly, 14,* 451–470.

Moghissi, K. S. (1989). The technology of AID and surrogacy. In L. M. Whiteford & M. L. Poland (Eds.), *New Approaches to human reproduction: Social and ethical dilemmas* (pp. 117–232). Boulder, CO: Westview Press.

Mogul, K. M. (1992). Ethics complaints against female psychiatrists. *American Journal of Psychiatry, 149* (5), 651–53.

Molina, M. L. P. (1994). Fragmentations: Meditations on separatism. *Signs, 19,* 449–457.

Molm, L. D., & Hedley, M. (1992). Gender, power, and social exchange. In C. L. Ridgeway, (Ed.), *Gender, interaction, and inequality* (pp. 1–28). New York: Springer-Verlag.

Monaghan, E. P., & Glickman, S. E. (1992). Hormones and aggressive behavior. In J. B. Becker, S. M. Breedlove, & D. Crews (Eds.), *Behavioral endocrinology* (pp. 261–285). Cambridge, MA: MIT Press.

Money, J. (1987). Sin, sickness, or status? Homosexual gender idenity and psychoneuroendocrinology. *American Psychologist, 42,* 384– 399.

Money, J. (1988). *Gay, straight, and in-between: The sexology of erotic orientation.* New York: Oxford University Press.

Money, J., & Ehrhardt, A. A. (1972). *Man and woman, boy and girl.* Baltimore, MD: Johns Hopkins University Press.

Mooney, L., & Brabant, S. (1987). Two martinis and a rested woman: "Liberation" in the Sunday comics. *Sex Roles, 17,* 409–420.

Moore, M. L. (1992). The family as portrayed on prime-time television, 1947–1990: Structure and characteristics. *Sex Roles, 26,* 41–61.

Moorehouse, M. J. (1991). Linking maternal employment patterns to mother-child activities and children's school competence. *Developmental Psychology, 27,* 295–303.

Morahan-Martin, J. (1991). Consider the children: Is parenthood being devalued? *The Psychological Record, 41,* 303–314.

Morash, M., Haar, R. N., & Rucker, L. (1994). A comparison of programming for women and men in U.S. prisons in the 1980s. *Crime & Delinquency, 40,* 197–221.

Morawski, J. G. (1987). The troubled quest for masculinity, femininity, and androgeny. In P. Shaver and C. Hendrick (Eds.), *Sex and Gender* (pp. 44–69). Newbury Park, CA: Sage.

Morgan, L. A. (1976). A re-examination of widowhood and morale. *Journal of Gerontology, 31,* 687–695.

Morgan, S. (1982, March). Sex after hysterectomy—What your doctor never told you. *Ms,* (pp. 82–85).

Morgan, S. (1988). "It's the whole power of the city against us!": The development of political consciousness in a women's health care coalition. In A. Bookman & S. Morgen (Eds.), *Women and the politics of empowerment* (pp. 180–201). Philadelphia: Temple University Press.

Morgen, S. (1994). Personalizing personnel decisions in feminist organizational theory and practice. *Human Relations, 47,* 665–684.

Morokoff, P. J. (1988). Sexuality in perimenopausal and postmenopausal women. *Psychology of Women Quarterly, 12,* 489–511.

Morokoff, P. J., & Heiman, J. R. (1980). Effects of erotic stimuli on sexually functional and dysfunctional women: Multiple measures before and after sex therapy. *Behaviour Research and Therapy, 18,* 127–137.

Morrison, A. M., & Von Glinow, M. A. (1990). Women and minorities in management. *American Psyhcologist, 45,* 200–208.

Morrison, T. (1987). *Beloved.* New York: Knopf.

Morrow, J. (1984). Deviational salience: Application to short stature and relation to perception of adolescent boys. *Perceptual and Motor Skills, 59,* 623–633.

Morrow-Tlucak, M., Haude, R. H., & Ernhart, C. B. (1988). *Social Science and Medicine, 26,* 635–639.

Moses-Zirkes, S. (1993). The family leave act—is it the doughnut or the hole? *APA Monitor,* pp. 52–53.

Mosher, D. L. (1968). Measurement of guilt in females by self-report inventories. *Journal of Consulting and Clinical Psychology, 32,* 690–695.

Most first births are marital among young women of Mexican origin (1987). *Family Planning Perspectives, 19,* 30.

Moyer, K. E. (1974). Sex differences in aggression. In R. C. Friedman, R. M. Richart, & R. L. Vande Wiele (Eds.), *Sex differences in behavior* (pp. 335–372). Huntington, NY: Robert E. Krieger.

Moyers, B. (1986). The vanishing family: Crisis in Black America. TV documentary. Columbia Broadcasting System Special Report.

Moynihan, D. P. (1965). The Negro family: The case for national action. Washington, DC: Department of Labor, Office of Policy Planning & Research.

MRC Vitamin Study Research Group. (1991). Prevention of neural tube defects: Results of the Medical Research Council Vitamin Study. *Lancet, 338,* 131–137.

Muehlenhard, C. L., & Falcon, P. L. (1990). Men's heterosexual skill and attitudes toward women as predictors of verbal sexual coercion and forceful rape. *Sex Roles, 23,* 241–259.

Muehlenhard, C. L., Friedman, D. E., & Thomas, C. M. (1985). Is date rape justifiable? The effects of dating activity, who initiated, who paid and men's attitudes towards women. *Psychology of Women Quarterly, 9,* 297–310.

Muehlenhard, C. L., & McCoy, M. L. (1991). Double standard/double bind: The sexual double standard and women's communication about sex. *Psychology of Women Quarterly, 15,* 447–461.

Muehlenhard, C. L., Powch, I. G., Phelps, J. L., & Giusti, L. M. (1992). Definitions of rape: Scientific and political implications. *Journal of Social Issues, 48,*(1), 23–44.

Mueller, C. (1993). The gender gap and women's political influence. In L. Richardson & V. Taylor (Eds.), *Feminist Frontiers III* (pp. 459–470). New York: McGraw-Hill.

Mulac, A. (1989). Men's and women's talk in same-gender and mixed-gender dyads: Power or polemic? *Journal of Language and Social Psychology, 8,* 249–270.

Mulac, A., Studley, L. B., & Blau, S. (1990). The gender-linked language effect in primary and secondary student impromptu essays. *Sex Roles, 23,* 439–469.

Murphy, L., & Rollins, J. H. (1980). Attitudes toward women in co-ed and all female drug treatment programs. *Journal of Drug Education, 11,* 319–323.

Murphy, J. (1984). Egg farming and women's future. In R. Arditti, R. D. Klein, & S. Mindin (Eds.). *Test-tube women: What future for motherhood:* (pp. 68–75). London: Pandora Press.

Murrell, A. J., Frieze, I. H., & Frost, J. L. (1991). Aspiring to careers in male–and female-dominated professions: A study of black and white college women. *Psychology of Women Quarterly, 15,* 103–126.

Myers, J. K., Weissman, M. M., Tischler, G. L., Holzer, C. E., Leaf, P. J., Orvaschel, H., Anthony, J. C., Boyed, J. H., Burke, J. D., Kramer, M., & Stoltzman, R. (1984). Six-month prevalence of psychiatric disorders in three communities. *Archives of General Psychiatry, 41,* 959–967.

Nabulsi, A. A., Folsom, A. R., White, A., Palsh, W., Heiss, G., Wu, K. K., & Szklo, M. (1993). Association of hormone replacement therapy with various cardiovascular risk factors in postmenopausal women. *The New England Journal of Medicine, 328,* 1069–1075.

Nachtigall, L. E. (1994). Sexual function in the menopause and postmenopause. In R. A. Lobo (Ed.), *Treatment of the postmenopausal woman: Basic and clinical aspects* (pp. 301–312). New York: Raven Press.

Nanko, S., Saito, S., & Makino, M. (1979). X and Y chromatin survey among 1,581 Japanese juvenile delinquents. *Japanese Journal of Human Genetics, 24,* 21–25.

Nasser, M. (1986). Comparative study of the prevalence of abnormal eating attitudes among Arab female students of both London and Cairo universities. *Psychological Medicine, 16,* 621-625.

National Victim Center (1992). *Rape in America: A report to the nation.* Arlington, VA: National Victim Center.

Natividad, I. (1992). Women of color and the campaign trail. In P. Ries & A. J. Stone (Eds.), *The American woman 1992–93* (pp. 127–148). New York: Norton.

Naylor, G. (1982). *The Women of Brewster Place.* New York: Viking.

Nelson, D. L., Quick, J. C., Hitt, M. A., & Moesel, D. (1990). Politics, lack of career progress, and work/home conflict: Stress and strain for working women. *Sex Roles, 23,* 169–185.

Nelson, K. K. (1986). Birth and social class. In P. S. Eakins (Ed.). *The American way of birth* (pp. 142-174). Philadelphia, PA: Temple University Press.

Nemeth, C. J., Endicott, J., & Wachtler, J. (1976). From the '50s to the '70s: Women in jury deliberations. *Sociometry, 39,* 293–304.

Neville, M. C., & Neifert, M. R. (1983). *Lactation: Physiology, nutrition, and breastfeeding.* New York: Plenum Press.

New offer emerges for breast implant settlement. (1995, October 3). *The Providence Journal Bulletin,* A9.

Newman, J. (1994). *Perception and reality: A study comparing the success of men and women candidates.* Washington, DC: National Women's Political Caucus.

Nice, V. E. (1992). *Mothers and daughters: The distortion of a relationship.* New York: St. Martin's Press.

Nicolaides, K., Brizot, M. de L., Patel, F., Snijders, R. (1994). Comparison of chorionic villus sampling and amniocentesis for fetal karyotyping at 10–13 weeks' gestation. *Lancet, 344,* 435–439.

Nicola-McLaughlin, A., & Chandler, Z. (1988). Urban politics in the higher education of Black women. In A. Bookman & S. Morgen (Eds.), *Women and the politics of empowerment* (pp. 180–201). Philadelphia: Temple University Press.

Nicolson, P. (1992). Menstrual-cycle research and the construction of female psychology. In J. T. E. Richardson (Ed.), *Cognition and the menstrual cycle* (pp. 174–199). New York: Springer-Verlag.

Noble, K. D. (1987). The dilemma of the gifted woman. *Psychology of Women Quarterly, 11,* 367–378.

Nock, S. L., & Kingston, P. W. (1988). Time with children: The impact of couples' worktime commitments. *Social Forces, 67,* 59–85.

Nolen-Hoeksema, S. (1987). Sex differences in unipolar depression: Evidence and theory. *Psychological Bulletin, 101,* 259–282.

Nolen-Hoeksema, S., & Girgus, J. S. (1994). The emergence of gender differences in depression during adolescence. *Psychological Bulletin, 115,* 424–443.

Norris, A. E. (1992). Cognitive analysis of contraceptive behavior. In N. J. Kenney, M. D. Brot, K. E. Moe & K. Dahl (Eds.), *The complexities of women: Integrative essays in psychology and biology* (pp. 154–164). Dubuque, IA: Kendall/Hunt.

Norris, A. E., & Devine, P. G. (1992). Linking pregnancy concerns to pregnancy risk avoidant action: The role of construct accessibility. *Personality and Social Psychology Bulletin, 18,* 118–127.

Northcutt, C. A. (1991). *Successful career women: Their professional and personal characteristics.* New York: Greenwood.

Nsiah-Jefferson, L., & Hall, E. J. (1989). Reproductive technology: Perspectives and implications for low-income women and women of color. In K. S. Ratcliff, M. M. Ferree, G. O. Mellow, B. D. Wright, G. D. Price, K. Yanoshik, & M. S. Freston (Eds.), *Healing technology: Feminist perspectives* (pp. 93–117). Ann Arbor, MI: University of Michigan Press.

Nyborg, H. (1983). Spatial ability in men and women: review and new theory. *Advances in Behaviour Research and Therapy, 5,* 89–140.

Nyborg, H. (1984). Performance and intelligence in hormonally different groups. In G. J. de Vries, J. P. L. de Bruyn, H. B. M. Uylings & M. A. Corner (Eds.), *Sex differences in the brain. The relation between structure and function* (pp. 491–508). New York: Elsevier.

Nyborg, H. (1988). Mathematics, sex hormones, and brain function. *Behavioral and Brain Sciences, 11,* 206–207.

Nyborg, H. (1990). Sex hormones, brain development, and spatio-perceptual strategies in women with Turner's syndrome and in school girls. In B. Bender & D. Birch (Eds.), *Sex chromosome abnormalities and behavior.* Boulder, CO: Westview Press.

Nyquist, L. V., & Spence, J. T. (1986). Effects of Dispositional dominance and sex role expectations of leadership behaviors. *Journal of Personality and Social Psychology, 50,* 87–93.

O'Boyle, M. W., & Benbow, C. P. (1990). Handedness and its relationship to ability and talent. In S. Coren (Ed.), *Handedness and its relationship to ability and talent* (pp. 343–372). North Holland: Elsevier.

O'Brien, M., & Huston, A. C. (1985). Development of sex-typed play behavior in toddlers. *Developmental Psychology, 21,* 866–871.

O'Brien, T. R., George, R., & Holmberg, S. D. (1992). Human immunodeficiency virus type 2 infection in the United States: Epidemiology, diagnosis, and public health implications. *Journal of the American Medical Association, 267,* 2775–2770.

O'Connell, L., Betz, M., & Kurth, S. (1989). Plans for balancing work and family life: Do women pursuing nontraditional and traditional occupations differ? *Sex Roles, 20,* 35–45.

O'Connor, P. (1992). *Friendships between women.* New York: Guilford Press.

O'Driscoll, K. & Crowley, P. (1985). Cesarean section and perinatal mortality rates. In J. Clinch & T. Matthews (Eds), *Perinatal Medicine* (pp.155–159). Boston: MIT Press.

Oggins, J., Veroff, J., & Leber, D. (1993). Perceptions of marital interaction among Black and White newlyweds. *Journal of Personality and Social Psychology, 65,* 494–511.

Ogletree, S. M., Coffee, M. C., & May, S. A. (1992). Perceptions of female/male presidential candidates: Familial and personal situations. *Psychology of Women Quarterly, 16,* 201–208.

O'Hanley, K., & Huber, D. H. (1992). Postpartum IUDS: Keys for success. *Contraception, 45,* 351-361.

O'Hara, M. W. (1987). Post-partum 'blues,' depression, and psychosis: a review. *Journal of Psychosomatic Obstetrics and Gynecology, 7,* 205–227.

O'Heron, C. A., & Orlofsky, J. L. (1990). Stereotypic and monsterotypic sex role trait and behavior orientations, gender identity, and psychological adjustment. *Journal of Personality and Social Psychology, 58,* 134–143.

Ogletree, S. M., & Williams, S. W. (1990). Sex and sex-typing effects on computer attitudes and aptitude. *Sex Roles, 23,* 703–712.

Ogur, B. (1986). Long day's journey into night: Women and prescription drug abuse. *Women & Health, 11,* 99–115.

Oliker, S. J. (1989). *Best friends and Marriage: Exchange among women,* CA: University of California Press.

Oliver, M. B., & Hyde, J. S. (1993). Gender differences in sexuality: A meta-analysis. *Psychological Bulletin, 114,* 29–51.

Olson, J. E., Frieze, I. H., & Detlefesen, E. G. (1990). Having it all? Combining work and family in a male and female profession. *Sex Roles, 23,* 515–533.

Olson, L. R., & Rollins, J. (1982). Psychological barriers to contraceptive use among adolescent women. In I. R. Stuart & C. F. Wells (Eds.), *Pregnancy in adolescence: Needs, problems, and management* (pp. 177–193). New York: Van Nostrand Reinhold.

Osmond, M. W., Wambach, K. G., Harrison, D. F., Byers, J., Levine, P., Imershein, A., & Quadagno, D. M. (1993). The multiple jeopardy of race, class, and gender for AIDS risk among women. *Gender & Society, 7,* 99–120.

Otten, C. M. (1985). Genetic effects on male and female development and on the sex ratio. In R. L. Hall (Ed.), *Male-female differences: A bio-cultural perspective* (pp. 155–217). New York: Praeger.

Oz, S., & Fine, M. (1988). A comparison of childhood backgrounds of teenage mothers and their non-mother peers: A new formulation. *Journal of Adolescence, 11,* 251–261.

Padawar, J. A., Fagan, C., Janoff-Bulman, Strickland, B. R., & Chorowski, M. (1988). Women's psychological adjustment following emergency cesaraen versus vaginal delivery. *Psychology of Women Quarterly, 12,* 25–34.

Padilla, E. R., & O'Grady, K. E. (1987). Sexuality among Mexican Americans: A case of sexual stereotyping. *Journal of Personality and Social Psychology, 52,* 5–10.

Paige, K. E., & Paige, J. M. (1981). *The politics of reproductive technology.* Berkeley, CA: University of California Press.

Palmer, H. T., & Lee, J. A. (1990). Female workers' acceptance in traditionally male-dominated blue-collar jobs. *Sex Roles, 22,* 607–626.

Paludi, M. A. (1984). Psychometric properties and underlying assumptions of four objective measures of fear of success. *Sex Roles, 10,* 765–781.

Pansky, M., Langer, Bukovsky, J., Weinraub, Z., Golan, A., Caspi, E., & Avrech, O. (1993). Reproductive outcome after laparoscopic local methotrexate injection for tubal pregnancy. *Fertility and Sterility, 60,* 85–87.

Parlee, M. B. (1983). Menstrual rhythms in sensory processes: A review of fluctuations in vision, olfaction, audition, taste, and touch. *Psychological Bulletin, 89,* 454–465.

Parsons, T. (1961). General introduction II: An outline of the social system. In T. Parsons, E. Shils, K. D. Naegele, & J. R. Pitts (Eds.), *Theories of society: Foundations of modern sociological theory* (pp. 30–97). New York: The Free Press.

Paset, P. S. & Taylor, R. D. (1991). Black and white women's attitudes toward interracial marriage. *Pychological Reports, 69,* 753–754.

Pateman, C. (1993). Defending prostitution: Charges against Ericsson. In A. Minas (Ed.), *Gender basics: Feminist perspectives on women and men* (pp. 387–389). Belmont, CA: Wadsworth.

Patton, L. L., English, E. C., & Hambleton, J. D. (1985). Childbirth preparation and outcomes of labor and delivery in primiparous women. *The Journal of Family Practice, 20*(4), 375–378.

Patterson, C. J. (1992). Children of lesbian and gay parents. *Child Development, 63,* 1025–1042.

Patterson, C. J. (1994). Children of the lesbian baby boom: Behavioral adjustment, self-concepts, and sex-role identity. In B. Greene & G. Herik (Eds.). *Contemporary perspectives on gay and lesbian psychology: Theory, research, and applications* (pp. 156–175). Beverly Hills, CA: Sage.

Paul, E. F. (1993). The comparable worth debate. In A. Minas (Ed.), *Gender basics: Feminist perspectives on women and men* (pp. 121–128). Belmont, CA: Wadsworth.

Pearlman, S. E. (1987). Distancing and connectedness: Impact on couple formation in lesbian relationships. *Women and Therapy, 8*(1–2), 77–88.

Pellegrini, A. D., & Perlmutter, J. C. (1989). Classroom contextual effects on children's play. *Developmental Psychology, 25,* 289–296.

Peplau, L. A., & Campbell, S. M. (1989). The balance of power in dating and marriage. In J. Freeman (Ed.), *Women a feminist perspective* (4th ed., pp. 121–137). Mountain View, CA: Mayfield.

Peplau, L. A., & Campbell, S. M. (1989). The balance of power in dating and marriage. In J. Freeman (Ed.), *Women: A feminist perspective.* 4th ed. (pp. 121–137). Mountain View, CA: Mayfield.

Peplau, L. A., Cochran, S., Rook, D., & Padesky, C. (1978). Loving women: Attachment and autonomy in lesbian relationships. *Journal of Social Issues, 34*(3), 7–27.

Peplau, L. A., & Conrad, E. (1989). Beyond nonsexist research: The perils of feminist methods in psychology. *Psychology of Women Quarterly, 13,* 370–400.

Peplau, L. A., Hill, C. T., & Rubin, Z. (1993). Sex role attitudes in dating and marriage: A 15-year follow-up of the Boston couples study. *Journal of Social Issues, 49*(3), 31–52.

Perkins, K. (1992). Psychosocial implications of women and retirement. *Social Work, 37,* 526–532.

Perlman, D. (1974). Self-esteem and sexual permissiveness. *Journal of Marriage and the Family, 36,* 470–473.

Perlmutter, C., Hanlon, T., & Sangiorgio, M. (1994, August). Triumph over menopause. *Prevention,* 78–87, 142.

Perusse, D. (1993). Cultural and reproductive success in industrial societies: Testing the relationship at the proximate and ultimate levels. *Behavioral and Brain Sciences, 16,* 267–322.

Pesmen, C. (1991, November). Love and sex in the 90s: Our national survey. *Seventeen,* pp. 63–68.

Peterson, D. L., & Pfost, K. S. (1989). Influence of rock videos on attitudes to violence against women. *Psychological Reports, 64,* 319–322.

Peterson, G., Mehl, L., & McRae, J. (1988). Relationship of psychiatric diagnosis, defenses, anxiety and stress with birth complications. In P. Fedor-Freybergh & M.L.V. Vogel (Eds.), *Prenatal and perinatal psychology and medicine: Encounter with the unborn* (pp. 399–416). Park Ridge, NJ: Parthenon.

Peterson, R. R. (1989). *Women, work, and divorce.* Albany, NY: State University of New York Press.

Peveler, R., & Fairburn, C. (1990). Eating disorders in women who abuse alcohol. *British Journal of Addiction, 85,* 1633–1638.

Pfost, K. S., Lum, C. U., & Stevens, M. J. (1989). Femininity and work plans protect women against postpartum dysphoria. *Sex Roles, 21,* 423–431.

Pheterson, G. I., Kiesler, S. B., & Goldberg, P. A. (1971). Evaluation of the performance of women as a function of the sex, achievement and personal history. *Journal of Personality and Social Psychology, 19,* 114–118.

Philippe, E., Bilenki, I., & Warter, A. (1986). Pathology of ectopic pregnancy. In A. Langer & L. Iffy (Eds.), *Extrauterine pregnancy* (pp. 107–155). Littleton, MA: PSG Publishing Co.

Philliber, W., & Hiller, D. (1983). Relative occupational attainments of spouses and later changes in marriage and wife's work experience. *Journal of Marriage and the Family, 45,* 161–170.

Piaget, J. (1952). *The origins of intelligence in children.* New York: International Universities Press.

Piaget, J. (1965). *The moral judgement of the child.* New York: Free Press. (Original work published 1932).

Pianta, R. C., & Egeland, B. (1994). Relation between depressive symptoms and stressful life events in a sample of disadvantaged mothers. *Journal of Consulting and Clinical Psychology, 62,* 1229–1234.

Piedmont, R. L. (1988). An interactional model of achievement motivation and fear of success. *Sex Roles, 19,* 467–490.

Pierce, J. P., Lee, L., & Gilpin, E. (1994). Smoking initiation by adolescent girls, 1944 through 1988: An association with targeted advertising. *Journal of the American Medical Association, 271,* 608–611.

Pierce, K. (1990). A feminist theoretical perspective on the socialization of teenage girls through *Seventeen* magazine. *Sex Roles, 23,* 491–500.

Pingree, S. (1978). The effects of nonsexist TV commercials and perceptions of reality on children's attitudes about women. *Psychology of Women Quarterly, 2,* 262–277.

Plant, M. A. (1990). Alcohol, sex and AIDS. *Alcohol and Alcoholism, 25,* 293–301.

Pleck, J. H. (1985). *Working wives/working husbands.* Beverly Hills, CA: Sage.

Plomin, R. (1989). Environment and genes: Determinants of behavior. *American Psychologist, 44,* 105–111.

Plunkett, E. R., & Wolfe, B. M. (1992). Prolonged effects of a novel, low-dosage continuous progestin-cyclic estrogen replacement program in postmenopausal women. *American Journal of Obstretrics and Gynecology, 166,* 117–121.

Polakow, V. (1993). *Lives on the edge: Single mothers and their children in the other America.* Chicago: University of Chicago Press.

Poland, B. J., & Kalousek, D. K. (1986). Embryonic development in ectopic pregnancy. In A. Langer & L. Iffy (Eds.). *Extrauterine pregnancy* (pp. 97–106). Littleton, MA: PSG Publishing Co.

Polatnick, M. R. (1983). Why men don't rear children: A power analysis. In J. Trebilcot (Ed.), *Mothering: Essays in Feminist Theory* (pp. 21–40). Totowa, NJ: Rowman & Allanheld.

Polivy, J., & Herman, C. P. (1985). Dieting and binging: A causal analysis. *American Psychologist, 40,* 193–201.

Polivy, J., & Herman, C. P. (1989). Dietary restraint and binge eating: Response to Charnock. *British Journal of Clinical Psychology, 28,* 341–343.

Polivy, J., Herman, C. P., & McFarlane, T. (1994). Effects of anxiety on eating: Does palatability moderate distress-induced overeating in dieters? *Journal of Abnormal Psychology, 103,* 505–510.

Pope, K. S., Keith-Spiegel, P., & Tabachnick, B. G. (1986). Sexual attraction to clients: The human therapist and the (sometimes) inhuman training system. *American Psychologist, 41,* 147–158.

Porat, N. (1986). Support groups for battered lesbians. In K. Lobel (Ed.), *Naming the violence: Speaking out about lesbian battering* (pp. 80–94). Seattle, WA: The Seal Press.

Porter, M. E., Gardner, H. A., DeFeudis, P., & Endler, N. S. (1988). Verbal deficits in Klinefelter (XXY) adults living in the community. *Clinical Genetics, 33,* 246–253.

Posner, B. M., Cupples, L. A., Franz, M. M., Gagnon, D. R. (1993). Diet and heart disease risk factors in adult American men and women: The Framingham Offspring-Spouse nutrition studies. *International Journal of Epidemiology, 22,* 1014–1025.

Potts, J. F. (1992). Chlamydial infection: Screening and management update, 1992. *Postgraduate Medicine, 9,* 120–126.

Potts, D. M. (1991). IUD's and PID: A comparative trial of strings versus stringless devices. *Advances in Contraception, 7,* 231.

Potts, M., & Diggory, P. (1983). *Textbook of contraceptive practice* (2nd ed.). Cambridge, U.K: Cambridge University Press.

Powell, G. N., & Butterfield, D. An. (1994). Investigating the "*glass ceiling*" phenomenon: An empirical study of actual promotions to top management. *Academy of Management Journal, 37,* 68–86.

Powlishta, K. K., Serbin, L. A., & Moller, L. C. (1993). The stability of individual differences in gender typing: Implications for understanding gender segregation. *Sex Roles, 29,* 723–737.

Prentky, R. A., & Knight, R. A. (1991). Identifying critical dimensions for discriminating among rapists. *Journal of Consulting and Clinical Psychology, 59,* 643–661.

Price, S. J., & McKenry, P. C. (1988). *Divorce.* Newbury Park, CA: Sage.

Purcell, P., & Stewart, L. (1990). Dick and Jane in 1989. *Sex Roles, 22,* 177–185.

Purifoy, F. E., & Koopmans, L. H. (1980). Androstenedione, T and free T concentrations in women of various occupations. *Social Biology, 26,* 179–188.

Purifoy, F. E., Grodsky, A., & Giambra, L. M. (1992). The relationship of sexual daydreaming to sexual activity, sexual drive, and sexual attitudes for women across the life-span. *Archives of Sexual Behavior, 21,* 369–385.

Quina, K., Wingard, J. A., & Bates, H. G. (1987). Language style and gender stereotypes in person perception. *Psychology of Women Quarterly, 11,* 111–122.

Quinsey, V. L., Chaplin, T. C., & Upfold, D. (1984). Sexual arousal to nonsexual violence and sadomasochistic themes among rapists and non sex offenders. *Journal of Consulting and Clinical Psychology, 52,* 651–657.

Rafsnider, E., & Myers, S. T. (1985). Employed mothers can breastfeed, too! *American Journal of Maternal Child Nursing, 10,* 256–259.

Ramos, A. A., & Huggins, G. R. (1991). Tubal sterilization: When is it the right choice? *Medical Aspects of Human Sexuality 25*(12), 38–45.

Raskin, P. A., & Israel, A. C. (1981). Sex-role imitation in children: Effects of sex of child, sex of model, and sex-role appropriateness of modeled behavior. *Sex Roles, 7,* 1067–10

Rawlings, E. I., & Carter, D. K. (1977). Feminist and nonsexist psychotherapy. In E. I. Rawlings & D. Carter (Eds). *Psychotherapy for women.* Springfield, IL: Charles C. Thomas.

Rawlings, J. S., Rawlings, V. B., & Read, J. A. (1995). Prevalence of low birth weight and preterm delivery in relation to the interval between pregnancies among white and black women. *New England Journal of Medicine, 332,* 69–74.

Raymond, J. G. (1990). At Issue the marketing of the new reproductive technologies: Medicine, the media, and the idea of progress. *Issues in Reproductive and Genetic Engineering, 3,* 253–26l.

Razack, S. (1994). What is to be gained by looking white people in the eye? Culture, race, and gender in cases of sexual violence. *Signs, 19,* 894–923.

Reid, B. V., & Whitehead, T. L. (1992). Introduction. In T. L. Whitehead & B. V. Reid (Eds.), *Gender constructs and social issues* (pp. 1–9). Urbana, IL: University of Illinois Press.

Reid, P. T. (1991). Preface. *Psychology of Women Quarterly, 15,* 493–494.

Reid, P. T. (1993). Poor women in psychological research: Shut up or shut out. *Psychology of Women Quarterly, 17,* 207–221.

Reid, P. T., & Trotter, K. H. (1993). Children's self-presentations with infants: Gender and ethnic comparisons. *Sex Roles, 29,* 171–181.

Reifman, A., Biernat, M., & Lang, E. L. (1991). Stress, social support, and health in married professional women with small children. *Psychology of Women Quarterly, 15,* 431–445.

Reinharz, S. (1992). *Feminist methods in social research.* New York: Oxford University Press.

Reinisch, J. M., Sanders, S. A., Hill, C. A., & Ziemba-Davis, M. (1992). High-risk sexual behavior among heterosexual undergraduates at a midwestern university. *Family Planning Perspectives, 24,* 116–121, 145.

Reisman, J. M. (1990). Intimacy in same sex friendships. *Sex Roles, 23,* 65–90.

Rejeski, W. J., Brubaker, P. H., Herb, H. A., Kaplan, J. R., & Koritnik, D. (1988). Anabolic steroids and aggressive behavior in cynomolgus monkeys. *Journal of Behavioral Medicine, 11,* 95–105.

Renzetti, C. M. (1988). Violence in lesbian relationships: A preliminary analysis of causal factors. *Journal of Interpersonal Violence, 3,* 381–399.

Resick, P. A., & Schnicke, M. K. (1992). Cognitive processing therapy for sexual assault victims. *Journal of Consulting and Clinical Psychology, 60,* 748–756.

Reskin, B. F. (1988). Occupational resegregation. In S. E. Rix (Ed.), *The American woman 1988–1989* (pp. 258–263). New York: Norton.

Resolution for the decriminalization and destigmatization of prostitution. (1984, August). Adopted by Division 35, Psychology of Women,

at the 92nd annual convention of the American Psychological Association, Toronto.

Rest, R. (1979). *Development in judging moral issues.* Minneapolis, MN: University of Minnesota Press. A review/preview of women's reproductive biology. (1992). In N. J. Kenney, M. D. Brot, K. E. Moe & K. Dahl (Eds.), *The complexities of women: Integrative essays in psychology and biology* (pp. 1–8). Dubuque, IA: Kendall/Hunt.

Reuther, R. R. (1985). *Women church: Theology and practice of feminist liturgical communities.* San Francisco: Harper & Row.

Rexroat, C., & Shehan, C. (1987). The family life cycle and spouse's time in housework. *Journal of Marriage and the Family. 49,* 737–750.

Reynosa, T. C., Felice, M. E., & Shragg, P. G. (1993). Does American acculturation affect outcome of Mexican-American teenage pregnancy? *Journal of Adolescent Health, 14,* 257–261.

Rhode, A., & Maneros, A. (1993). Postpartum psychoses: Onset and long-term course. Psychopathology, 26, 203–209.

Rich, A. (1977). *Of woman born.* New York: Bantam.

Richardson, J. T. E. (1992). The menstrual cycle, cognition, and paramenstrual symptomatology. In J. T. E. Richardson (Ed.), *Cognition and the menstrual cycle* (pp. 1–39). New York: Springer-Verlag.

Rickels, K., Schweizer, E., Weiss, S., & Zavodnick, S. (1993). Maintenance drug treatment for panic disorder: II. Short- and long-term outcome after drug taper. *Archives of General Psychiatry, 50,* 61–67.

Ridgeway, C. L., & Diekema, D. (1992). Are gender differences status differences? In C. L. Ridgeway (Ed.), *Gender, interaction, and inequality* (pp. 157–180). New York: Springer-Verlag.

Ries, P., & Stone, A. J. (Eds.). (1992). *The American Woman 1992–93: A status report.* New York: Norton.

Riger, S. (1992). Epistemological debates, feminist voices: Science, social values, and the study of women. *American Psychologist, 47,* 730–740.

Riggs, D. S., & O'Leary, K. D. (1989). A theoretical model of courtship aggression. In M. A. Pirog-Good & J. E. Stets (Eds.), *Violence in dating relationships: Emerging social issues* (pp. 53–71). New York: Praeger.

Ritchey, F. J., LaGory, M., & Mullis, J. (1991). Gender differences in health risks and physical symptoms among the homeless. *Journal of Health and Social Behavior, 32,* 33–48.

Rix, S. E. (Ed.), (1990). *The American woman, 1990–91.* New York: Norton.

Robbins, L. N., Helzer, J. E., Weisman, M. M., Orvashel, H., Gruenberg, E., Burke, J. D., & Reiger, D. A. (1984). Lifetime prevalence of specific psychiatric disorders in three sites. *Archives of General Psychiatry, 41,* 949–958.

Roberts, T. (1991). Gender and the influence of evaluations on self-assessments in achievement settings. *Psychological Bulletin, 19,* 297–308.

Roberts, T., & Nolen-Hoeksema, S. (1989). Sex differnces in reactions to evaluative feedback. *Sex Roles, 21,* 725–747.

Roberts, S. (1994, November 23). Among black college grads, women now outearn men. . . . . . but will wage gap discourage marriage? *Hers, A Weekly publication of the Providence Journal Bulletin, 1*(5), p. 15.

Robertson, M. J. (1991). Homeless women with children: The role of alcohol and other drugs. *American Psychologist, 46,* 1198–1204.

Robinson, C. R. (1983). Black women: A tradition of self-reliant strength. *Women & Therapy, 2,* 135–144.

Robinson, P. M. (1984). The historical repression of women's sexuality. In C. S. Vance (Ed.), *Pleasure and danger: Exploring female sexuality* (pp. 251–266). Boston, MA: Routledge & Kegan Paul.

Robinson-Stavely, K., & Cooper, J. (1990). Mere presence, gender, and reactions to computers: Studying human-computer interaction in the social context. *Journal of Experimental Social Psychology, 26,* 168–183.

Rodin, J., & Ickovics, J. R. (1990). Women's health: Review and research agenda as we approach the 21st century. *American Psychologist, 45,* 1018–1034.

Rodin, J., & Langer E. J. (1977). Long-term effects of a control-relevent intervention with the institutionalized aged. *Journal of Personality and Social Psychology, 35,* 897–902.

Rodin, J., Silberstein, L. R., & Striegel-Moore, R. H. (1985). Women and weight: A normative discontent. In T. B. Sonderegger (Eds.), *Ne-*

braska *Symposium on motivation 1984: Vol. 32. Psychology and Gender* (pp. 267–307). Lincoln, NE: University of Nebraska Press.

Rodin, M. (1992). The social construction of premenstrual syndrome. *Social Science and Medicine, 35,* 49–56.

Rodriquez, C. Jr., & Moore, N. B. (1995). Perceptions of pregnant/parenting teens: Reframing issues for an integrated approach to pregnancy problems. *Adolescence, 30,* 685–706.

Rogan, W. J., & Gladen, B. C. (1993). Breast-feeding and cognitive development. *Early Human Development, 31*(3), 181–193.

Rogers, A. (1993). Voice, play, and a practice of ordinary courage in girls' and women's lives. *Harvard Educational Review, 63,* 265–295.

Rohsenow, D. J., Corbett, R., & Devine, D. (1988). Molested as children: A hidden contribution to substance abuse. *Journal of Substance Abuse Treatment, 5,* 13-18.

Rollins, J. H., Hennen, F. H., Scorpio, E., Kanarian, M., Marzullo, B., & Morand, L. (1982, August). *Attributions about informal leaders: Does sex make a difference?* Paper presented at the annual meeting of the American Psychological Association. Washington, DC.

Rollins, J. H., & Lederberg, V. S. (1989, June). *Gender role attributes and family relationships of female managers.* Poster session presented at the annual meeting of the International Council of Psychologists. Halifax, NS.

Rollins, J. H., Scorpio, E., & Cragin, K., (1991, October). *Self and other's perceptions of breast- and bottle-feeding mothers.* Poster session presented at the annual meeting of the New England Psychological Association. Portland, ME.

Romond, J. L., & Baker, I. T. (1985). Squatting in childbirth: A new look at an old tradition. *Journal of Obstetric, Gynecologic, and Neonatal Nursing, 14,* 406–411.

Rook, K. S. (1987). Reciprocity of social exchange and social satisfaction among older women. *Journal of Personality and Social Psychology, 52,* 145–154.

Root, M. P. P. (1990). Disordered eating in women of color. *Sex Roles, 22,* 525–536.

Rose, H. (1986). A feminist epistemology for the sciences. In R. Bleir (Ed.), *Feminist Approaches to Science* (pp. 57–76). New York: Pergamon.

Rose, H. (1987). Hand, brain, and heart: A feminist epistemology for the natural sciences. In S. Harding & J. F. O'Barr (Eds.), *Sex and scientific inquiry* (pp. 265–282). Chicago: The University of Chicago Press.

Rose, M. (1988). Reproductive hazards for high-tech workers. In S. E. Rix (Ed.), *The American Woman 1988–1989: A Status Report* (pp. 277–285). New York: W. W. Norton.

Rosen, R. H. (1982). Pregnancy resolution decisions: A review and appraisal of research. In G. L. Fox (Ed.), *The childbearing decision: Fertility attitudes and behavior* (pp.247–266). Beverly Hills, CA: Sage.

Rosenbaum, M. (1981). *Women on heroin.* New Brunswick, NJ: Rutgers University Press.

Rosenberg, J., Perlstadt, H., & Phillips, W. R. F. (1993). Now that we are here: Discrimination, disparagement, and harassment at work and the experience of women lawyers. *Gender & Society, 7,* 415–433.

Rosenberg, L., Metzger, L. S., & Palmer, J. R. (1993). Alcohol consumption and risk of breast cancer: A review of the epidemiologic evidence. *Epidemiologic Reviews, 15,* 136–143.

Rosenblum, L., Darrow, W., Witte, J., Cohen, J., French, J., Gill, P., Potterat, J., Sikes, K., Reich, R., & Hadler, S. (1992). Sexual practices in the transmission of hepatitis B virus and prevalence of hepatitis delta virus infection in female prostitutes in the United States. *Journal of the American Medical Association, 267,* 2477–2481.

Rosenkrantz, P. S., Vogel, S. R., Bee, H., Broverman, I. K., & Broverman, D. M. (1968). Sex role stereotypes and self concepts in college students. *Journal of Consulting and Clinical Psychology, 32,* 287–295.

Rosenthal, A. (1991, October 15). Thomas's edge steady, vote due today. Each side seeks to get benefit of the doubt. *The New York Times,* p. A-1.

Rosenthal, R. (1984). *Meta-analytic procedures for social research.* Beverly Hills, CA: Sage.

Rosenthal, R. (1991). *Meta-analytic procedures for social research* (2nd ed.). Beverly Hills, CA: Sage.

Rosenthal, R., Hall, J. A., DiMatteo, M. R., Rogers, P. L., & Archer, D. (1979). *Sensitivity to nonverbal communication: The PONS test.* Baltimore: The Johns Hopkins University Press.

Rosenwasser, S. M., & Dean, N. G. (1989). Gender role and political office: Effects of perceived masculinity/femininity of candidate and political office. *Psychology of Women Quarterly, 17,* 77–85.

Rosenwasser, S. M., Gonzales, M. H., & Adams, V. (1985). Perceptions of a house-spouse: The effects of sex, economic productivity, and subject background variables. *Psychology of Women Quarterly, 9,* 258–264.

Ross, C. E. (1987). The division of labor at home. *Social Forces, 65,* 816–833.

Ross, C. E., (1991). Marriage and the sense of control. *Journal of Marriage and the Family, 53,* 831–838.

Ross, C. E., & Mirowsky, J. (1989). Explaining the social patterns of depression: Control and problem solving—or support and talking. *Journal of Health and Social Behavior, 30,* 206–219.

Ross, S. I., & Jackson, J. M. (1991). Teachers' expectations for black males' and black females' academic achievement. *Personality and Social Psychology bulletin, 17,* 78–82.

Rossing, M. A., Daling, J. R., Weiss, N. S., Moore, D. E., & Self, S. G. (1994). Ovarian tumors in a cohort of infertile women. *The New England Journal of Medicine, 33,* 771–776.

Rothbaum, B. O., Foa, E. B., Riggs, D. S., Murdock, T., & Walsh (1992). A prospective examination of post-traumatic stress disorder in rape victims. *Journal of Traumatic Stress, 5,* 455–475.

Rothenberg, P. S. (1988). How it happened: The legal status of women and people of color in the United States. In P. S. Rothenberg (Ed.), *Racism and Sexism: An integrated study* (pp. 177–184). New York: St. Martin's Press.

Rotheram-Borus, M. J., & Wyche, K. F. (1994). Ethnic differences in identity development in the United States. In S. Archer (Ed.), *Interventions for adolescent identity development* (pp. 62–83). Thousand Oaks, CA: Sage.

Rothman, B. K. (1989). *Recreating motherhood: Ideology and technology in a patriarchal society.* New York: Norton.

Rotter, J. B. (1966). Generalized expectancies for internal versus external control of reinforcement. *Psychological Monographs, 80,* (Whole No. 609).

Rousso, H. (1988). Daughters with disabilities: Defective women or minority women? In M. Fine & A. Asch (Eds.), *Women with disabilities: Essays in psychology, culture, and politics* (pp. 139–171). Philadelphia: Temle University Press.

Rowland, R., & Klein, R. D. (1990). Radical feminism: Critique and construct. In S. Gunew (Ed.), *Feminist knowledge: Critique and construct* (pp. 271–303). New York: Routledge.

Rozee-Koker, P., & Polk, G. C. (1986). The social psychology of group rape. *Sexual Coercion and Assault, 1,* 57–65.

Rozin, P., & Fallon, A. (1988). Body image, attitudes to weight, and misperceptions of figure preferences of the opposite sex: A comparison of men and women in two generations. *Journal of Abnormal Psychology, 97,* 342–345.

Rubenstein, C. (1982, November). Real men don't earn less than their wives. *Psychology Today, 16,* 36–41.

Rubenstein, C. R. (1985, March). Sex after 40 (The best-kept secret). *Family Circle,* pp. 60, 62, 64, 157.

Rubin, Z. (1973). *Liking and loving: An invitation to social psychology.* New York: Holt, Rinehart and Winston.

Rubin, L. J., & Borgers, S. B. (1990). Sexual harassment in universities during the 1980's. *Sex Roles, 23,* 397–411.

Ruble, D. N., Brooks-Gunn, J., Fleming, A. S., Fitzmaurice, G., Stangor, C., & Deutsch, F. (1990). Transition to motherhood and the self: Measurement, stability and change. *Journal of Personality and Social Psychology, 58,* 450–463.

Ruble, D. N., Fleming, A. S., Hackel, L. S., & Stangor, C. (1988). Changes in the marital relationship during the trransition to first time motherhood: Effects of violated expectations concerning division of household labor. *Journal of Personality and Social Psychology, 55,* 78–87.

Rudd, N. M., & McKenry, P. C. (1986). Family influences on the job satisfaction of employed mothers. *Psychology of Women Quarterly, 10,* 363–372.

Ruddick, S. (1983). Thinking about mothering—and putting maternal thinking to use. *Women's Studies Quarterly. 11,* 4–7.

Ruddick, S. (1989). *Maternal thinking: Towards a politics of peace.* Boston: Beacon Press.

Rusbult, C. E. (1983). A longitudinal test of the investment model: The development (and deterioration) of satisfaction and commitment in heterosexual involvements. *Journal of Personality and Social Psychology, 45,* 101–117.

Rusbult, C. E., Verette, J., Whitney, G. A., Slovik, L. F., & Lipkus, I. (1991). Accommodation processes in close relationships: Theory and preliminary empirical evidence. *Journal of Personality and Social Psychology, 60,* 53–78.

Russell, D. E. H. (1982). *Rape in marriage.* New York: Macmillan.

Russell, D. E. H. (1984). *Sexual exploitation: Rape, child sexual abuse and workplace harassment.* Beverly Hills, CA: Sage.

Russell, D. E. H. (1986). *The secret trauma: Incest in the lives of girls and women.* New York: Basic Books.

Russell, M. J., Switz, G. M., & Thompson, K. (1980). Olfactory influences on the human menstrual cycle. *Pharmacology, Biochemistry & Behavior, 13,* 737–738.

Russo, N. F. (1976). The motherhood mandate. *Journal of Social Issues, 32*(3), 143–153.

Russo, N. F. (Ed.), (1985). *Women's Mental Health Agenda.* Washington, D.C: American Psychological Association.

Russo, N. F. (1987). Position paper. In Eichler, A., & Parron, D. L. (Eds.), *Women's mental health: Agenda for research* (pp. 42–56). Rockville, MD: National Institute of Mental Health.

Russo, N. F. (1990). Overview: Forging research priorities for women's mental health. *American Psychologist, 45,* 368–373.

Rutter, M., Silberg, J., & Simonoff, E. (1993). Whither behavioral genetics?—A developmental psychopathological perspective. In R. Plomin & G. E. McClearn (Eds.), *Nature, nurture & psychology* (pp. 433–456). Washington, DC: American Psychological Association.

Ryan, A. S., Rush, D., Krieger, F. W., & Lewandowski, G. E. (1991). Recent declines in breast-feeding in the United States, 1984 through 1989. *Pediatrics, 88*(4), 719–727.

Ryding, E. L. (1984). Sexuality during and after pregnancy. *Acta Obstetrica Gynecolica Scandinavia 63,* 679–682.

Ryff, C. (1989). Happiness is everything, or is it? Explorations on the meaning of psychological well-being. *American Psychologist, 57,* 1069–1081.

Saal, F. E., Johnson, C. B., & Weber, N. (1989). Friendly or sexy? It may depend on who you ask. *Psychology of Women Quarterly, 13,* 263–276.

Sable, P. (1994). Separation anxiety, attachment and agoraphobia. *Clinical Social Work Journal, 22,* 369–383.

Sadker, M., & Sadker, D. (1986, March). Sexism in the classroom: From grade school to graduate school. *Phi Delta Kappan,* 512–515.

Sadker, M., & Sadker, D. (1994). *Failing at fairness: How America's schools cheat girls.* New York:Scribner.

Sagrestano, L. M. (1992). The use of power and influence in a gendered world. *Psychology of Women Quarterly, 16,* 439–447.

Salgado de Snyder, V. N. (1987). Factors associated with acculturative stress and depressive symptomatology among married Mexican immigrant women. *Psychology of Women Quarterly, 11,* 475–488.

Sanchez-Ayendez, M. (1992). Puerto Rican elderly women: Shared meanings and informal supportive networks. In M. L. Anderson & P. H. Collins *Race, class, and gender: An anthology* (pp. 238–252). Belmont, CA:Wadsworth.

Sanday, P. R. (1981). The socio-cultrual context of rape: A cross-cultural study. *Journal of Social Issues, 37*(4), 5–27.

Sanday, P. R. (1990). *Fraternity gang rape: Sex, brotherhood and privilege on campus.* New York: New York University Press.

Sandelowski, M. (1990). Fault lines: Infertility and imperiled sisterhood. *Feminist Studies, 16,* 33–51.

Sandelowski, M. (1993). *With child in mind: Studies of the personal encounter with infertility.* Philadelphia: University of Pennsylvania Press.

Sandelowski, M., & Bustamante, R. (1986). Cesarean birth outside the natural childbirth culture. *Research in Nursing and Health 9,* 81–88.

Sanders, C. M. (1980). A comparison of adult bereavement in the death of a spouse, child, and parent. *Omega, 10,* 303–322.

Sanders, C. M. (1988). Risk factors in bereavement outcome. *Journal of Social Issues, 44*(3), 97–111.

Santrock, J. W., & Sitterle, K. A. (1987). Parent-child relationships in stepmother families. In K. Pasley & M. Ihinger-Tallman (Eds.), *Remarriage and stepparenting: Current research and theory* (pp. 135–154). New York: Guilford Press.

Sapolsky, S., Tabarlet, J. O. (1991). Sex in primetime television: 1979 versus 1989. *Journal of Broadcasting and Electronic Media, 35,* 505–516.

Sapolsky, R. M. (1987). Stress, social status, and reproductive physiology in free-living baboons. In D. Crews (Ed.), *Psychobiology of reproductive behavior: An evolutionary perspective.* Englewood Cliffs, NJ: Prentice Hall.

Sarrazin, D., Le, M. G., Arriagada, R., Contesso, G., Fontaine, F., Spielmann, M., Rochard, F., Le Chevalier, T., & Lacour, J. (1989). Ten-year results of a randomized trial comparing a conservative treatment to mastectomy in early breast cancer. *Radiotherapy Oncology, 14*(3), 177–184.

Sarti, D. A. (1984). *Atlas of obstetric and gynecologic ultrasound.* Boston: G. K. Hall Medical Publishers.

Saunders, L. (1983). Sex and childbirth. In S. Cartledge & J. Ryan (Eds.), *New thoughts on old contradictions* (pp. 89 –104). London: The Women's Press.

Saxena, B. B., & Singh, M. (1986). Current pregnancy tests and their clinical application in diagnosis and management of pregnancy. In A. Langer & L. Iffy (Eds.), *Extrauterine pregnancy* (pp. 157–178). Littleton, MA: PSG Publishing Co.

Saxton, M. (1987). Prenatal screening and discriminatory attitudes about disability. *Women & Health, 13,* 217–224.

Sayers, S. L., & Baucom, D. H. (1991). Role of femininity and masculinity in distressed couples' communication. *Journal of Personality and Social Psychology, 61,* 641–647.

Sayre, A. (1978). *Rosalind Franklin and DNA.* New York: Norton.

Scanzoni, J. H. (1975). Sex roles, economic factors, and marital solidarity in White marriages. *Journal of Marriage and the Family, 37,* 130–144.

Scarr, S. (1991). On comparing apples and oranges and making inferences about bananas. *Journal of Marriage and the Family, 53,* 1099–1100.

Schachter, S. (1959). *The psychology of affiliation.* Stanford. CA: Stanford University Press.

Schaefer, F., Burgard, P., Batzler, U., Rupp, A., Schmidt, H., Gilli, G., Bickel, H., & Bremer, H. J. (1994). Growth and skeletal maturation in children with phenylketonuria. *Acta Paediatrica, 83,* 534–541.

Schaffer, M. A., & Lia-Hoagberg, B. (1994). Prenatal care among low-income women. *Families in Society: The Journal of Contemporary Human Services, 75,* 152–159.

Schein, V. E. (1973). The relationship between sex-role stereotypes and requisite management characteristics. *Journal of Applied Psychology, 57,* 95–100.

Schein, V. E. (1975). Relationships between sex-role stereotypes and requisite management characteristics. *Journal of Applied Psychology, 60,* 340–344.

Schiebinger, L. (1987). The history and philosophy of women in science: A review essay. In S. Harding & J. F. O'Barr (Eds.), *Sex and scientific inquiry* (pp. 7–34). Chicago: University of Chicago Press.

Schmittroth, L. (Ed.). (1991). *Statistical record of women worldwide.* Detroit, MI: Gale Research.

Schneider, B. (1993). Peril and promise: Lesbians' workplace participation. In L. Richardson & V. Taylor *Feminist Frontiers III* (pp. 223–234). New York: McGraw-Hill.

Schneider, B. E. (1982). Consciousness about sexual harassment among heterosexual and lesbian women workers. *Journal of Social Issues, 38*(4), 75–98.

Schreiner-Engel, P., Schiavi, R. C., White, D., & Ghizzani, A. (1989). Low sexual desire in women: The role of reproductive hormones. *Hormones and Behavior, 23,* 221–234.

Schuerger, J. M., & Reigle, N. (1988). Personality and biographic data that characterize men who abuse their wives. *Journal of Clinical Psychology, 44,* 75–81.

Schuster, D. T. (1991). Fulfillment of potential, life satisfaction, and competence: Comparing four cohorts of gifted women at midlife. *Journal of Educational Psychology, 82,* 471–478.

Schwartz, F. N. (1989). Management women and the new facts of life. *Harvard Business Review, 89,* 65–76.

Schweizer, E., Rickels, K., Weiss, S., & Zavodnick, S. (1993). Maintenance drug treatment of panic disorder: I. Results of a prospective, placebo-controlled comparison of alprazolam and imipramine. *Archives of General Psychiatry, 50,* 51–60.

Scott, W. J., & Morgan, C. S. (1983). An analysis of factors affecting traditional family expectations and perceptions of ideal fertility. *Sex Roles, 9,* 901–914.

Sears, D. O., & Huddy, L. (1990). On the origins of political disunity among women. In L. A. Tilly & P. Gurin (Eds.), *Women politics and change* (pp. 249–277). New York: Russell Sage Foundation.

Sears, H. A., & Galambos, N. L. (1992). Women's work conditions and marital adjustment in two-earner couples: A structural model. *Journal of Marriage and the Family, 54,* 789–797.

Seebach, L. (1993, April, 11). Jumping onto the safety net mostly because it is there. *Providence Sunday Journal.* D-9.

Selby, J. W., Calhoun, L. G., Vogel, A. V., & King, H. E. (1980). *Psychology and human reproduction.* New York: The Free Press.

Seligman, M. E. P. (1975). *Helplessness: On depression, development and death.* San Francisco: Freeman.

Seligman, M. E. P. (1991). *Learned optimism.* New York: Knopf.

Sells, L. W. (1978). Mathematics—a critical filter. *The Science Teacher, 45*(2), 28–29.

Sells, L. W. (1980). The mathematics filter and the education of women and minorities. In L. H. Fox, L. Brody & D. Tobin (Eds.), *Women and the Mathematical Mystique* (pp. 66–75). Baltimore: Johns Hopkins University Press.

Seltzer, R. (1992). The social location of those holding antihomosexual attitudes. *Sex Roles, 26,* 391–398.

Senie, R. T., Rosen, P. P., Rhodes, P., & Lesser, M. L. (1991). Timing of breast cancer excision during the menstrual cycle influences duration of disease free survival. *Annals of Internal Medicine, 115,* 337–342.

Serbin, L. A., Zelkowitz, P., Doyle, A., Gold, D., & Wheaton, B. (1990). The socialization of sex differentiated skills and academic performance: A mediational model. *Sex Roles, 23,* 613–628.

Sexual harassment on the rise. (1993, August). *Personnel Pride,* Providence, RI: The Rhode Island Office of Personnel Administration (OPA).

Shachar, R. (1991). His and her marital satisfaction: The double standard. *Sex Roles, 25,* 451–467.

Shanley, M. L. (1993). "Surrogate mothering" and women's freedom: A critique of contracts for human reproduction. *Signs, 18,* 618–639.

Shaywitz, B. A., Shaywitz, S. E., Pugh, K. R., Constable, R. T., Skudlarski, P., Fulbright, R. K., Bronen, R. A., Fletcher, J. M., Shankweller, D. P., Katz, L., & Gore, J. C. (1995). Sex differences in the functional organization of the brain. *Nature, 373,* 607–609.

Sheehan, D. L. (1986). Tricyclic antidepressants in the treatment of panic and anxiety disorders. *Psychosomatics, 27,* 10–16.

Shelton, B. A. (1992). *Women, men and time: Gender differences in paid work, housework and leisure.* New York: Greenwood Press.

Sherif, C. W. (1979). Bias in psychology. In J. A. Sherman & E. T. Beck (Eds.), *The prism of sex: Essays in the sociology of knowledge* (pp. 93–133). Madison, WI: University of Wisconsin Press.

Sherif, C. W. (1982). Needed concepts in the study of gender identity. *Psychology of Women Quarterly, 6,* 375–398.

Sherif, M., Harvey, O. J., White, V. J., Hood, W. E., & Sherif, C. W. (1961). *Intergroup conflict and cooperation: The Robbers Caver experiment.* Norman, OK: University of Oklahoma Press.

Sherman, L. W., & Berk, R. A. (1984). The specific deterrent effects of arrest for domestic assault. *American Sociological Review, 49,* 261–272.

Shields, S. A. (1987). The variability hypothesis: the history of a biological model of sex differences in intelligence. In S. Harding & J. F.

O'Barr (Eds.), *Sex and scientific inquiry* (pp. 187–215). Chicago: University of Chicago Press (Original work published 1982).

Shiono, P. H., Klebanoff, M. A., Nugent, R. P., Cotch, M. F., Wilkins, D. G., Rollins, D. E., Carey, J. C., & Behrman, R. E. (1995). The impact of cocaine and marijuana use on low birth weight and preterm birth: A multicenter study. *American Journal of Obstetrics & Gynecology, 172,* 19–27.

Sholomskas, D., & Axelrod, R. (1986). The influence of mother-daughter relationships on women's sense of self and current role choices. *Psychology of Women Quarterly, 10,* 171–182.

Shotland, R. L., & Craig, J. M. (1988). Can men and women differentiate between friendly and sexually interested behavior? *Social Psychology Quarterly, 51,* 66–75.

Shotter, J., & Logan J. (1988). The pervasiveness of patriarchy: On finding a different voice. In M. M. Gergen (Ed.), *Feminist thought and the structure of knowledge* (pp. 69–86). New York: New York University Press.

Shoupe, D., & Mishell, D. R. (1994). Contraindications to hormone replacement. In R. O. Lobo (Ed.), *Treatment of the postmenopausal woman: Basic and clinical aspects* (pp. 415–418). New York: Raven Press.

Shugar, G., & Krueger, S. (1995). Aggressive family communication, weight gain, and improved eating attitudes during systemic family therapy for anorexia nervosa. *International Journal of Eating Disorders, 17,* 23–31.

Shute, V. J., Pellegrino, J. W., Hubert, L., & Reynolds, R. W. (1983). The relationship between androgen levels and human spatial abilities. *Bulletin of the Psychonomic Society, 21,* 465–468.

Siantz, M. L. de L. (1990). Maternal acceptance/rejection of Mexican migrant mothers. *Psychology of Women Quarterly, 14,* 245–254.

Signorella, M. L., & Jamison, W. (1986). Masculinity, femininity, androgyny, and cognitive performance: A meta-analysis. *Psychological Bulletin, 100,* 207–228.

Silbert, M. H., (1988). Compounding factors in the rape of street prostitutes. In A. W. Burgess (Ed.), *Rape and sexual assault II* (pp. 75–90). New York: Garland Publishing.

Silbert, M. H., & Pines, A. M. (1983). Early sexual exploitation as an influence in prostitution. *Social Work, 28,* 285–289.

Silbert, M. H., & Pines, A. M. (1984). Pornography and sexual abuse of women. *Sex Roles, 10,* 857–867.

Sillero-Arenas, M., Delgado-Rodriquez, M., Rodigues-Canteras, et al. (1992). Menopausal hormone replacement therapy and breast cancer: a meta-analysis. *Obstetrics Gynecology, 79,* 286–294.

Silverstein, L. B. (1991). Transforming the debate about child care and maternal employment. *American Psychologist, 46,* 1025–1032.

Simenauer, J., & Carroll, D. (1982). *Singles: The new Americans.* New York: Simon and Schuster.

Simkins-Bullock, J. A., & Wildman, B. G. (1991). An investigation into the relationships between gender and language. *Sex Roles, 24,* 149–160.

Simon, B. L. (1987). *Never married women.* Philadelphia: Temple University Press.

Simpson, J. A. (1987). The dissolution of romantic relationships: Factors involved in relationship stability and emotional distress. *Journal of Personality and Social Psychology, 53,* 683–692.

Simpson, J. A. (1990a). Influence of attachment styles on romantic relationships. *Journal of Personality and Social Psychology, 59,* 971–980.

Simpson, J. A. (1990b). Perception of physical attractiveness: Mechanisms involved in the maintenance of romantic relationships. *Journal of Personality and Social Psychology, 59,* 1192–1201.

Simpson, J. A., Campbell, B., & Bersheid, E. (1986). The association between romantic love and marriage: Kephart (1967 twice revisited. *Personality and Social Psychology Bulletin, 12,* 363–372.

Simpson, J. A., & Gangestad, S. W. (1991). Individual differences in sociosexuality: Evidence for convergent and discriminant validity. *Journal of Personality and Social Psychology, 60,* 870–882.

Simpson, J. A., Gangestad, S. W., & Lerma, M. (1990). Perception of physical attractiveness: Mechanisms involved in the maintenance of romantic relationships. *Journal of Personality and Social Psychology, 59,* 1192–1201.

Singer, B., & Toates, F. M. (1987). Sexual motivation. *The Journal of Sex Research, 23,* 481–501.

Singer, J. M., & Stake, J. E. (1986). Mathematics and self-esteem: Implications for women's career choice. *Psychology of Women Quarterly, 10,* 339–352.

Singh, D. (1993). Adaptive significance of female physical attractiveness: Role of waist-to-hip ratio. *Journal of Personality and Social Psychology, 65,* 293–307.

Singh, K., Viegas, O. A. C., Koh, S. C. L., & Ratnam, S. S. (1992). Effect of long-term use of Norplant implants on haemostatic function. *Contraception, 45,* 203–219.

Sisto, G. W., & Maker, M. C. (1989). Therapeutic foster homes for teenage mothers and their babies. *Child and Youth Services, 12,* 195–203.

Six, B., & Eckes, T. (1991). A closer look at the complex structure of gender stereotypes. *Sex Roles, 24,* 57–71.

Slade, P., & Jenner, F. (1980). Performance tests in different phases of the menstrual cycle. *Journal of Psychosomatic Research 24,* 5–8.

Smith, A. (1983). Nonverbal communication among black female dyads: An assessment of intimacy, gender, and race. *Journal of Social Issues, 39*(3), 55–67.

Smith, D. W. (1980). Alcohol effects on the fetus. In R. H. Schwartz & S. J. Yaffe (Eds.), *Drug and chemical risks to the fetus and newborn* (pp. 73–82). New York: Alan R. Liss.

Smith, E. L., Reddan, W., & Smith, P. E. (1981). Physical activity and calcium modalities for bone mineral increase in aged women. *Medical Science in Sports & Exercise, 13,* 60–64.

Smith, E. M., & North, C. S. (1994). Not all homeless women are alike: Effects of motherhood and the presence of children. *Community Mental Health Journal, 30,* 601–610.

Smith, E. M., North, C. S., & Spitznagel, E. L. (1993). Alcohol, drugs, and psychiatric comorbidity among homeless women: An epidemiologic study. *Journal of Clinical Psychiatry, 54,* 82–87.

Smith, P. L., Smits, S. L., & Hoy, F. (1992). Female business owners in industries traditionally dominated by males. *Sex Roles, 26,* 485–496.

Snell, W. E., Jr., Belk, S. S., & Hawkins, R. C., II (1987). Alcohol and drug use in stressful times. *Sex Roles, 16,* 359–373.

Snell, W. E., Jr., & Godwin, L. (1993). Social reactions to depictions of casual and steady acquaintance rape: The impact of AIDS exposure and stereotypic beliefs about women. *Sex Roles, 29,* 599–616.

Sohn, D. (1982). Sex differences in achievement self-attributions: An effect-size analysis. *Sex Roles, 8,* 345–357.

Sokol, R. J. (1981). Alcohol and abnormal outcomes of pregnancy. *Canadian Medical Association Journal, 125,* 143–148.

Solberg, D. A., Butler, J., & Wagner, N. N. (1973). Sexual behavior in pregnancy. *The New England Journal of Medicine, 220,* 1098–1103.

Sommer, B. (1983). How does menstruation affect cognitive competence and psychophysiological response? *Women & Health, 8,* 53–90.

Sommer, B. (1992). Cognitive performance and the menstrual cycle. In J. T. E. Richardson (Ed.), *Cognition and the menstrual cycle* (pp. 39–66). New York: Springer-Verlag.

Sonenstein, F. L., & Wolf, D. A. (1991). Satisfaction with child care: Perspectives of welfare mothers. *Journal of Social Issues, 47*(2), 15–31.

Sorensen, G., Pirie, P., Folsom, A., Luepker, R., Jacobs, D., & Gillum, R. (1985). Sex differences in the relationship between work and health: The Minnesota Heart Survey. *Journal of Health and Social Behavior, 26,* 379–394.

Sorenson, S. B., & Siegel, J. M. (1992). Gender, ethnicity, and sexual assault: Findings from a Los Angeles study. *Journal of Social Issues, 48*(1), 93–104.

Sorosky, A. D. (1977). The psychological effects of divorce on adolescents. *Adolescence, 12,* 123–136.

South, S. J., & Felson, R. B. (1990). The racial patterning of rape. *Social Forces, 69,* 71–93.

South, S. J. (1991). Sociodemographic differentials in mate selection preferences. *Journal of Marriage and the Family, 53,* 928–940.

Spanier, G. B., & Glick, P. C. (1980). Mate selection differentials between whites and blacks in the United States. *Social Forces, 58,* 707–725.

Spector, I. P., & Carey, M. P. (1990). Incidence and prevalence of the sexual dysfunctions: A critical review of the empirical literature. *Archives of Sexual Behavior, 19*(4), 389–408.

Spector, T. D., Brennan, P., Harris, P. A., Studd, J. W. W., Silman, A. J. (1992). Do current regimes of hormone replacement therapy protect against subsequent fractures? *Osteoporosis International, 2,* 219–224.

Spence, J. T. (1993). Gender-related traits and gender ideology: Evidence for a multifactorial theory. *Journal of Personality and Social Psychology, 64,* 624–635.

Spence, J. T., Helmreich, R. L., & Stapp, (1975). Ratings of self and peers on sex-role attributes and their relations to self-esteem and conceptions of masculinity and femininity. *Journal of Personality and Social Psychology, 32,* 29–39.

Sperry, R. W. (1982). Some effects of disconnecting the cerebral hemispheres. *Science, 217,* 1223–1226.

Spitze, G. (1988). Women's employment and family relations: A review. *Journal of Marriage and the Family, 50,* 595–618.

Sprecher, S. (1985). Sex differences in bases of power in dating relationships. *Sex Roles, 12,* 449–462.

Sprecher, S., McKinney, K., & Orbuch, T. L. (1987). Has the double standard disappeared? An experimental test. *Social Psychology Quarterly,* 24–31.

Sprecher, S., Sullivan, Q., & Hatfield, E. (1994). Mate selection preferences: Gender differences examined in a national sample. *Journal of Personality and Social Psychology, 66,* 1074–1080.

Stack, S., & Gundlach, J. H. (1992). Divorce and sex. *Archives of Sexual Behavior, 27,* 359–357.

Stacy, A. W., Sjussman, S., Dent, C. W., Burton, D., & Flay, B. R. (1992). Moderators of peer social influence in adolescent smoking. *Personality and Social Psychology bulletin, 18,* 163–172.

Stampfer, M. J., Colditz, G. A., Willet, W. C., Manson, J. E., Rosner, B., Speizer, F. E., & Hennekens, C. H. (1991). Post menopausal estrogen therapy and cardiovascular disease: Ten year follow up from the nurses' health study. *The New England Journal of Medicine, 325,* 756–762.

Stampfer, M. J., Hennekens, C. H., Manson, J. E., Colditz, G. A., Rosner, B., & Willett, W. C. (1993). Vitamin E consumption and the risk of coronary disease in women. *The New England Journal of Medicine, 328,* 1444–1449.

Stangor, C., & Ruble, D. N. (1987). Development of gender role knowledge and gender constancy. In L. S. Liben & M. L. Signorella (Eds.), *Children's gender schemata* (pp. 5–22). San Francisco: Jossey-Bass.

Stanley, J. C., & Benbow, C. P. (1982). Huge sex ratios at upper end. *American Psychologist, 37,* 972.

Stanley, L., & Wise, S. (1991). Feminist research, feminist consciousness, and experiences of sexism. In M. M. Fonow & J. A. Cook (Eds.), *Beyond methodology: Feminist scholarship as lived research* (pp. 265–283). Bloomington, IN: Indiana University Press.

Staples, R. (1981). *The world of black singles: Changing patterns of male/female relationships.* Westport, CT: Greenwood Press.

Staples, R., & Mirande, A. (1980). Racial and cultural variation among American families. A decennial review of the literature among minority families. *Journal of Marriage and the Family, 42,* 887–903.

Starr, B. D., & Weiner, M. B. (1981). *The Starr-Weiner report: On sex & sexuality in the mature years.* New York: Stein & Day.

Steckler, N., & Rosenthal, R. (1985). Sex differences in nonverbal and verbal communication with bosses, peers, and subordinates. *Journal of Applied Psychology, 70,* 157–163.

Steffensmeier, A. H. (1984). Suicide and the contemporary woman: Are male and female suicide rates converging? *Sex Roles, 10,* 613–629.

Steil, J. M., & Hillman, J. L. (1993). The perceived value of direct and indirect influence strategies: A cross-cultural comparison. *Psychology of Women Quarterly, 17,* 457–462.

Steil, J. M., & Weltman, K. (1991). Marital inequality: The importance of resources, personal attributes, and social norms on career valuing and the allocation of domestic responsibilities. *Sex Roles, 24,* 161–179.

Stein, A., Cooper, P. J., Day, A., & Bond, A. (1987). Social and psychiatric factors associated with the intention to breastfeed. *Journal of Reproductive and Infant Psychology, 5,* 161–167.

Stein, R. T., & Heller, T. (1979). An empirical analysis of the correlations between leadership status and participation rates reported in the literature. *Journal of Personality and Social Psychology, 37,* 1993–2002.

Steinberg, K. K., Thacker, S. B., Smith, J., Stroup, D. F., Zack, M. M., Flanders, W. D., & Berkelman, R. L. (1991). A meta-analysis of the effect of estrogen replacement therapy on the risk of breast cancer. *Journal of the American Medical Association, 265,* 1985–1990.

Steinberg, L., Dornbusch, S. M., & Brown, B. B. (1992). Ethnic differences in adolescent achievement: An ecological perspective. *American Psychologist, 47,* 723–729.

Stern, L. (1990). Conceptions of separation and connection in female adolescents. In C. Gilligan, N. P. Lyons & T. J. Hanmer (Eds.), *Making connections: The relational worlds of adolescent girls at Emma Willard school* (pp. 73–87). Cambridge, MA: Harvard University Press.

Stern, M., & Karraker, K. H. (1989). Sex stereotyping of infants: A review of gender labeling studies. *Sex Roles, 20,* 501–522.

Stets, J. E. (1992). Interactive processes in dating aggression: A national study. *Journal of Marriage and the Family, 54,* 165–177.

Stuenkel, C. A. (1989). Menopause and estrogen replacement therapy. *Psychiatric Clinics of North America, 12,* 133–152.

Stewart, A. J., & Chester, N. L. (1982). Sex differences in human motives: Achievement, affiliation and power. In A. J. Stewart (Ed.), *Motivation and Society* (pp. 172–218). San Francisco: Jossey-Bass.

Stewart, A. J., & Ostrove, J. M. (1993). Social class, social change, and gender: Working-class women at Radcliffe and after. *Psychology of Women Quarterly, 17,* 475–497.

Stewart, D., & Vaux, A. (1986). Social support resources, behaviors, and perceptions among black and white college students. *Journal of Multicultural Counseling and Development, 14,* 65–72.

Stewart, P. J., Dulberg, C., Arnill, A. C., Elmslie, T., & Hall, P. F. (1990). Diagnosis of dystocia and management with cesarean section among primiparous women in Ottawa-Carlton. *Canadian Medical Association Journal, 142,* 459–463.

Stierlin, H., & Weber, G. (1989). *Unlocking the family door: A systematic approach to the understanding and treatment of anorexia nervosa.* New York: Brunner/Mazel.

Stipek, D. J., & Gralinski, J. H. (1991). Gender differences in children's achievement-related beliefs and emotional responses to success and failure in mathematics. *Journal of Educational Psychology, 83,* 361-371.

St. Lawrence, J. S., & Joyner, D. J. (1991). The effects of sexually violent rock music on males' acceptance of violence against women. *Psychology of Women Quarterly, 15,* 49–63.

Stockard, J., & Wood, J. W. (1984). The myth of female underachievement: A re-examination of sex differences in academic achievement. *American Educational Research Journal, 21,* 825–838.

Stombler, M. (1994). "Buddies" or "Slutties:" The collective sexual reputation of fraternity little sisters. *Gender & Society, 8,* 297–323.

Stoppard, J. M., & Paisley, K. J. (1987). Masculinity, femininity, life stress, and depression. *Sex Roles, 16,* 489–495.

Storer, J. H. (1992). Gender and kin role transposition as an accommodation to father-daughter incest. In T. L. Whitehead & B. V. Reid *Gender constructs and social issues* (pp. 70–102). Urbana, IL: University of Illinois Press.

Stotland, N. L. (1991). Psychiatric issues in abortion, and the implications of recent legal changes for psychiatric practice. In N. L. Stotland (Ed.), *Psychiatric Aspects of Abortion* (pp. 1–16). Washington, DC: American Psychiatric Press.

Stout, A. L., Steege, J. F., Blazer, D. G., & George, L. K. (1986). Comparison of lifetime psychiatric diagnoses in premenstrual syndrome clinic and community samples. *Journal of Nervous and Mental Disease, 174,* 517–522.

Stratton, J., & Spritzer, S. (1967). Sexual permissiveness and sexual behavior: A question of substance and a question of method. *Journal of Marriage and the Family, 29,* 434–441.

Straus, M. A., & Gelles, R. J. (1986). Societal change and change in family violence from 1975 to 1985 as revealed by two national surveys. *Journal of Marriage and the Family, 48,* 465–479.

Straus, M., & Gelles, R. (1989). *Physical abuse in American families: Risk factors and adaptations to violence in 8,145 families.* Transaction Books.

Straus, M. A., Gelles, R. J., & Steinmetz, S. K. (1980). *Behind closed doors: Violence in the American family.* Garden City, NY: Anchor Press/Doubleday.

Strause, T. B., Szuba, M. P., & Baxter, R. R. Jr. (1992). Response to sleep deprivation in three women with postpartum psychosis. *Journal of Clinical Psychiatry, 53,* 204–206.

Stricker, G. (1977). Implications of research for psychotherapeutic treatment of women. *American Psychologist, 32,* 14–23.

Strickland, B. R. (1988). Sex-related differences in health and illness. *Psychology of Women Quarterly, 12,* 381–389.

Striegel-Moore, R. H., Silberstein, L. R., & Rodin, J. (1986). Toward an understanding of risk factors for bulimia. *American Psychologist, 41,* 346–363.

Striegel-Moore, R. H., Tucker, N., & Hsu, J. (1990). Body image dissatisfaction and disordered eating in lesbian college students. *International Journal of Eating Disorders, 9,* 493–500.

Strober, M., & Humphrey, L. L. (1987). Familial contributions to the etiology and course of anorexia nervosa and bulimia. *Journal of Consulting and Clinical Psychology, 55,* 654–659.

Strodtbeck, F. L., James, R. M., & Hawkins, C. (1957). Social status in jury deliberations. *American Sociological Review, 22,* 713–719.

Strodtbeck, F. L., & Mann, R. D. (1956). Sex role differentiation in jury deliberations. *Sociometry, 19,* 3–11.

Stroebe, M. S., & Stroebe, W. (1983). Who suffers more? Sex differences in health risks of the widowed. *Psychological Bulletin, 93,* 279–301.

Strube, M. J. (1988). The decision to leave an abusive relationship. *Psychological Bulletin, 104,* 236–250.

Stuart, F. M., Hammond, D. C., & Pett, M. A. (1987). Inhibited sexual desire. *Archives of Sexual Behavior, 16*(2), 91–106.

Stuenkel, C. A. (1989). Menopause and estrogen replacement therapy. *Psychiatric Clinics of North America, 12,* 133–152.

Sue, S., & Okazaki, S. (1990). Asian-American educational achievements: A phenomenon in search of an explanation. *American Psychologist, 45,* 913–920.

Sugarman, D. B., & Hotaling, G. T. (1989). Dating violence: Prevalence context, and risk markers. In M. A. Pirog-Good and J. E. Stets (Eds.), *Violence in dating relationships: Emerging social issues* (pp. 3–32). New York: Praeger.

Summers, R. J. (1991). The influence of affirmative action on perceptions of a beneficiary's qualifications. *Journal of Applied Social Psychology, 21,* 1265–1276.

Sun, S. W., & Lull, J. (1986). The adolescent audience for music videos and why they watch. *Journal of Communication, 29*(1), 116–124.

Surrogate mother contracts upheld by Calif. court. (1993, May 21). *The Providence Journal-Bulletin* (Evening Edition), p. A-4.

Swartzman, L. C., Edelberg, R., & Kemmann, E. (1990). Impact of stress on objectively recorded menopausal hot flushes and on flush report bias. *Health Psychology, 9,* 529–545.

Sweet, J. A. (1982). Work and Fertility. In G. L. Fox (Ed.), *The childbearing decision: Fertility attitudes and behavior* (pp. 197–218). Beverly Hills, CA: Sage Publications.

Swim, J., Borgida, E., Maruyama, G., & Myers, D. G. (1989). Joan McKay versus John McKay: Do gender stereotypes bias evaluations? *Psychological Bulletin, 105,* 409–429.

Swim, J. K. (1994). Perceived versus meta-analytic effect sizes: An assessment of the accuracy of gender stereotypes. *Journal of Personality and Social Psychology, 66,* 21–36.

Szapocznik, J., & Kurtines, W. M. (1993). Family psychology and cultural diversity: Opportunities for theory, research, and application. *American Psychologist, 48,* 400–407.

Taeuber, C. (Ed.), (1991). *Statistical handbook on women in America.* Phoenix, AZ: Oryx Press.

Tajfel, H., & Turner, J. C. (1986). The social identity theory of intergroup behaviour. In W. G. Austin & S. Worshel (Eds.), *The psychology of intergroup relations* (2nd ed.), (pp. 7–24). London: Academic Press.

Tallen, B. S. (1990). How inclusive is feminist political theory? Questions for lesbians. In J. Allen (Ed.), *Lesbian philosophies and cultures* (pp. 241–257). Albany, NY: State University of New York Press.

Tangri, S. S., Burt, M. R., & Johnson, L. (1982). Sexual harassment at work: three explanatory models. *Journal of Social Issues, 38,* 33–54.

Tannen, D. (Ed.). (1993). *Gender and conversational interaction.* New York: Oxford University Press.

Tavris, T. (1992). *The mismeasure of woman.* New York: Simon & Schuster.

Tavris, T., & Sadd, S. (1975). *The Redbook report on female sexuality: 100,000 married women disclose the good news about sex.* New York: Delacorte Press.

Taylor, B., & Wadsworth, J. (1984). Breast feeding and child development at five years. *Developmental Medicine and Child Neurology, 26,* 73–80.

Taylor, S. E., & Langer, E. J. (1977). Pregnancy: A social stigma? *Sex Roles, 3,* 27–35.

Taylor, S. H. (1989). The case for comparable worth. *Journal of Social Issues, 45*(4), 23–37.

Taylor, V., & Rupp, L. J. (1991). Researching the women's movement: We make our own history, but not just as we please. In M. M. Fonow & J. A. Cook (Eds.), *Beyond methodology: Feminist scholarship as lived research* (pp. 119–132). Bloomington, IN: Indiana University Press.

Taylor, V., & Whittier, N. (1993). The new feminist movement. In L. Richardson & V. Taylor (Eds.), *Feminist frontiers III* (pp. 533–548). New York: McGraw-Hill.

Teachman, J. D. (1991). Who pays? Receipt of child support in the United States. *Journal of Marriage and the Family, 53,* 759–772.

Telch, C. F., Agras, W. S., Rossiter, E. M., Wilfley, D., & Kenardy, J. (1990). Group cognitive-behavioral treatment for the nonpurging bulimic: An initial evaluation. *Journal of Consulting and Clinical Psychology, 58,* 629–635.

Temkin, J. (1986). Women, rape and law reform. In S. Tomaselli & R. Porter, (Eds.), *Rape* (pp. 16–40). New York: Blackwell.

Terman, L. M., & Miles, C. C. (1936). *Sex and personality: Studies in masculinity and feminity.* New York: McGraw-Hill.

Terman, L. M., & Oden, M. H. (1947). *The gifted child grows up.* Stanford, CA: Stanford University Press.

Tetrault, P. A., & Barnett, M. A. (1987). Reactions to stranger and acquaintance rape. *Psychology of Women Quarterly,* 353–358.

Theilgaard, A. (1986). Psychologic study of XY and XXY men. In S. Ratcliff & N. Paul (Eds.), *Prospective studies of children with sex chromosome aneuploidy* (pp. 277–292). New York: Alan Liss.

Thoma, S. J. (1986). Estimating gender differences in the comprehension and preference of moral issues. *Developmental Review, 6,* 165–180.

Thomas, V. G., & James, M. D. (1988). Body image, dieting tendencies, and sex role traits in urban black women. *Sex Roles, 18,* 523–529.

Thompson, E. H. (1991). The maleness of violence in dating relationships: An appraisal of stereotypes. *Sex Roles, 24,* 271–278.

Thompson, J. B. (1986). Safety and effectiveness of nurse-midwifery care: Research review. In J. P. Rooks & J. E. Haas (Eds.), *Nurse-Midwifery in America* (pp. 40–44). Washington, DC: American College of Nurse-Midwives Foundation.

Thornton, A. (1990). The courtship process and adolescent sexuality. *Journal of Family Issues, 11,* 239–273.

Thorogood, M., Mann, J., Murphy, M., & Vessey, M. (1991). Is oral contraceptive use still associated with an increased risk of fatal myocardial infarction? Report of a case-control study. *British Journal of Obstetrics and Gynaecology, 98,* 512–514.

Thorogood, M., Mann, J., Murphy, M., & Vessey, M. (1992). Fatal stroke and use of oral contraceptives: Findings from a case-control study. *American Journal of Epidemiology, 136,* 35–45.

Thorpe, G. L., & Burns, L. E. (1983). *The agoraphobic syndrome.* New York: Wiley.

Thornton, A. (1990). The courtship process and adolescent sexuality. *Journal of Family Issues, 11,* 239–273.

Tiedje, L. B., Wortman, C. B., Downey, G., Emmons, C., Biernat, M., & Lang, E. (1990). Women with multiple roles: Role-compatibility perceptions, satisfaction, and mental health. *Journal of Marriage and the Family, 52,* 63–72.

Tiefer, L. (1987). Social constructionism and the study of human sexuality. In P. Shaver & C. Hendrick (Eds.), *Sex and Gender* (pp. 70–94). Newbury Park: CA: Sage.

Timonen, S., & Procope, B. J. (1971). Premenstrual syndrome and physical exercise. *Actda Obstetricia et Gynecologica Scandinavica, 50,* 331–337.

Tinsley, E. G., Sullivan-Guest, S., & McGuire, J. (1984). Feminine sex role and depression in middle aged women. *Sex Roles,* 25–32.

Tobias, S. (1976, September). Math anxiety: Why is a smart girl like you counting on your fingers? *Ms, 5,* 56–59ff.

Tobias, S. (1978). *Overcoming math anxiety.* New York: Norton, 1978.

Todd, J., Friedman, A., & Kariuki, P. (1990). Women growing stronger with age: The effect of status in U.S.A. and Kenya. *Psychology of Women Quarterly, 14,* 567–577.

Tolman, A. E., Diekmann, K. A., & McCartney, K. (1989). Social connectness and mothering: Effects of maternal employment and maternal absence. *Journal of Personality and Social Psychology, 56,* 942–949.

Tolor, A., & DeGrazia, P. V. (1976). Sexual attitudes and behavior patterns during and following pregnancy. *Archives of Sexual Behavior, 5,* 539–551.

Top, T. (1991). Sex bias in the evaluation of performance in the scientific, artistic, and literary professions: A review. *Sex Roles, 24,* 73–106.

Tougas, F., & Veilleux, F. (1989). Who likes affirmative action?: Attitudinal processes among men and women. In F. Blanchard and F. Crosby (Eds.), *Affirmative action in perspective* (pp. 111–124). New York: Springer-Verlag.

Travis, C. B. (1988a). *Women and health psychology: Biomedical issues.* Hillsdale, NJ: Lawrence Erlbaum.

Travis, C. B. (1988b). *Women and health psychology: Mental health issues.* Hillside, NJ: Lawrence Erlbaum.

Travis, C. B., Gressley, D. L., & Crumpler, C. A. (1991). Feminist contributions to health psychology. *Psychology of Women Quarterly, 15,* 557–566.

Tremollieres, F., Pouilles, J. M., & Ribot, C. (1993). Effect of long-term administration of progestogen on post-menopausal bone loss: Result of a two-year, controlled randomized study. *Clinical Endocrinology, 38,* 627–631.

Trevathan, W. R. (1987). *Human birth: An evolutionary perspective.* New York: Aldine De Gruyter.

Trevathan, W. R., & Burleson, M. H., & Gregory, (1993). No evidence for menstrual synchrony in lesbian couples. *Psychoneuroendocrinology, 18,* 425–435.

Trussell, J., Strickler, J., & Vaughan, B. (1993). Contraceptive efficacy of the diaphragm, the sponge and the cervical cap. *Family Planning Perspectives, 25,* 100–105, 135.

True, R. H. (1990). Psychotherapeutic issues with Asian American women. *Sex Roles, 22,* 477–486.

Tucker, M. B., & Taylor, R. J. (1989). Demographic correlates of relationship status among Black Americans. *Journal of Marriage and Family, 51,* 655–665.

Tulip, M. (1990). Religion. In S. Gunew (Ed.), *Feminist knowledge: Critique and construct* (pp. 229–268). London: Routledge.

Turjanmaa, K. (1994). Allergy to natural rubber latex: A growing problem. *Annals of Medicine, 26,* 297–300.

Turkheimer, E. (1991). Individual and group differences in adoption studies of IQ. *Psychological Bulletin, 110,* 392–405.

Turner J. S., & Rubinson, L. (1993). *Contemporary human sexuality.* Englewood Cliffs, NJ: Prentice Hall.

Turner, R. H., & Killian, L. M. (1972). *Collective behavior* (2nd ed.). Englewood Cliffs, NJ: Prentice Hall.

Tuttle, G. E., & Pillard, R. C. (1991). Sexual orientation and cognitive abilities. *Archives of Sexual Behavior, 20,* 307–318.

Tyler, L. E. (1965). *The psychology of human differences.* New York: Appleton-Century-Crofts.

"Typical" family is slipping further away. (1994, August 10). *The Providence Journal Bulletin,* p. A-10.

Uchitelle, L. (1993, January 11). In economics, a subtle exclusion. *The New York Times,* D-1.

Udry, J. R., & Talbert, L. M. (1988). Sex hormone effects on personality at puberty. *Journal of Personality and Social Psychology, 54,* 291–295.

Ulin, P. R. (1992). African women and AIDS: Negotiating behavioral change. *Social Science and Medicine, 34,* 63–73.

Ullman, S. E., & Knight, R. A. (1991). A multivariate mode for predicting rape and physical injury outcomes during sexual assaults. *Journal of Consulting and Clinical Psychology, 59,* 724–731.

Unzelman, R. F. (1992). Advanced epithelial ovarian carcinoma: Long-term survival experience at the community hospital. *American Journal of Obstetrics and Gynecology, 166,* 1663–1672.

U. S. Attorney General's Commission on Pornography (1986). *Final Report.* Washington, DC: U.S. Government Printing Office.

U. S. Bureau of the Census. (1989). Marital status and living arrangements: March 1988. *Current population reports,* Series P-20, No. 433. Washington, DC: U.S. Government Printing Office.

U.S. Bureau of the Census (1992, November). The rising cost of child care. *Monthly News From the U.S. Bureau of the Census: Census and You, 27*(11), p. 9. Washington, DC: U.S. Government Printing Office.

U.S. Bureau of the Census (1992, December). Our nation's elderly—A portrait. *Monthly News From the U.S.Bureau of the Census: Census and You, 27* (12), p. 8. Washington, DC: U.S. Government Printing Office.

U.S. Bureau of the Census. (1993, April). Education is the ticket to higher earnings. *Monthly News From the U. S. Bureau of the Census: Census and You 28*(4), 1–2. Washington, DC: U.S. Government Printing Office.

U.S. Bureau of the Census. (1993, August). College educated women return to work sooner after childbirth. *Monthly News From the U.S. Bureau of the Census: Census and You, 28*(8), pp. 1–2. Washington, DC: U.S. Government Printing Office.

U.S. Bureau of the Census. (1994). *Statistical abstract of the United States: 1994* (114th ed.). Washington, DC: U.S. Government Printing Office.

U.S. Bureau of the Census. (1994, February). New racial and ethnic information debunks stereotypes. *Monthly News From the U.S. Bureau of the Census: Census and You, 29*(2), pp. 4–5.

U. S. Bureau of the Census. (1995). *Statistical abstract of the United States: 1995* (115th ed.). Washington, DC: U.S. Government Printing Office.

U. S. Department of Justice (1991). *Sourcebook of Criminal Justice Statistics-1990.* Washington, DC: U.S. Government Printing Office.

U.S Department of Justice. (1994). Federal Bureau of Investigation, *Uniform Crime Reports for the United States, 1993.* Washington, DC: U.S. Government Printing Office.

U.S. Department of Justice. (1994, January). *Violence against women: A National crime victimization survey report.* NCJ-145325. Rockville, MD: Bureau of Justice Statistics Clearinghouse.

U.S. Department of Labor. (1990, October). Earnings differences between women and men. *Facts on working women.* (Report no. 90–3). Washington, DC: U.S. Government Printing Office.

U.S. Department of Labor. (1989, December). Women business owners. *Facts on Working Women, 89*(5), 4. Washington, DC: U.S. Department of Labor, Women's Bureau.

U.S. Department of Labor. (1991, March). Office of Employment and Public Affairs. The employment situation: February 1991. *Women & work.* Washington, DC: U.S. Government Printing Office.

U.S. Department of Labor (1991, July). Office of Employment and Public Affairs. Ratio of women'-to-men's earnings rise. *Women & work.* Washington, DC: U.S. Government Printing Office.

U.S. Department of Labor. (1992, September). *The American Workforce.* Washington, DC: U.S. Government Printing Office.

U.S. Department of Labor. (1993, May). Office of Employment and Public Affairs. *Women & work.* Washington, DC: U.S. Government Printing Office.

Vance, C. S. (1984). Pleasure and danger: Toward a politics of sexuality. In C. S. Vance (Ed.), *Pleasure and danger: Exploring female sexuality* (pp. 1–27). Boston: Routledge & Kegan Paul.

Vandell, D. L. (1991). Belsky and Eggebeen's analysis of the NLSY: Meaningful results or statistical illusions? *Journal of Marriage and the Family, 53,* 1100–1102.

Van den Bergh, B. R. H., Mulder, E. J. H., Mulder, E. J. H., Visser, G. H. A., Poelmann-Weesjes, G., Bekendam, D. J., & Prechtl, H. F. R. (1989). The effect of (induced) maternal emotions on fetal behaviour: A controlled study. *Early Human Development, 19,* 9–19.

Vandenberg, S. G. (1987). Sex differences in mental retardation and their implications for sex differences in ability. In J. M. Reinisch, L. A. Rosenblum & Sanders, S. A. (Eds.), *Masculinity/femininity: Basic perspectives* (pp. 157–171). New York: Oxford University Press.

Van Thorre, M. D., & Vogel, F. X. (1985). The presence of bulimia in high school females. *Adolescence, 20,* 45–51.

Van Wyck, P. H., & Geist, C. S. (1984). Psychosocial development of heterosexual, bisexual, and homosexual behavior. *Archives of Sexual Behavior, 13,* 505–544.

Vargo, S. (1987). The effects of women's socialization on lesbian couples. In the Boston Lesbian Psychologies Collective (Eds.), *Lesbian psychologies: Explorations and challenges* (pp. 161–173). Urbana, IL: University of Illinois Press.

Vasquez, M. J. T. (1994). Latinas. In L. Comas-Diaz & B. Greene (Eds.), *Women of Color: Integrating ethnic and gender identities in psychotherapy* (114–138). New York: Guilford.

Ventura, S. J. (1994). Recent trends in teenage childbearing in the United States. *Statistical Bulletin 75*(4), 10–17.

Verba, S. (1990). Women in American politics. In L. A. Tilly & P. Gurin (Eds.), *Women and political change* (pp. 555–572). New York: Russell Sage Foundation.

Veronesi, U., Banfi, A., Del Vecchio, M., Saccozzi, R., Clemente, C., Greco, M., Luini, A., Marubini, E., Muscolino, G., Rilke, F., Sacchini, V., Salvadori, B., Zecchini, A., & Zucali, R. (1986). Comparison of Halsted mastectomy with quadrantectomy, axillary dissection, and radiotherapy in early breast cancer: Long-term results. *European Journal of Cancer & Clinical Oncology, 22,* 1085–1089.

Vetere, V. A. (1982). The role of friendship in the development and maintenance of lesbian love relationships. *Journal of Homosexuality, 8*(2), 51–65.

Veronesi, U., Luini, A., Del Vecchio, M., Greco,M., Galimberti, V., Merson, M., Rilke, F., Sacchini, V., Saccozzi, R., Savio, T., Zucali, R., Zurrida, S., & Salvadori, B. (1993). Radiotherapy after breast-preserving surgery in women with localized cancer of the breast. *The New England Journal of Medicine, 328,* 1587–1591.

Visher, E. B. (1994) Lessons from remarriage families. *The American Journal of Family Therapy, 22,* 327–336.

Visher, J. S. (1994). Stepfamilies: A work in progress. *The American Journal of Family Therapy, 22,* 337–344.

Von Glinow, M. A., & Krzyczkowska-Mercer, A. (1988, Summer). Women in corporate America: A caste of thousands. *New Management, 6,* 36–42.

Vogel, L. (1990). Debating difference: Feminism, pregnancy, and the workplace. *Feminist Studies, 16,* 9–32.

Voydanoff, P., & Donnelly, B. W. (1989). Work and family roles and psychological distress. *Journal of Marriage and the Family, 51,* 923–932.

Voyer, D., Voyer, S., & Bryden, M. P. (1995). Magnitude of sex differences in spatial abilities: A meta-analysis and consideration of critical variables. *Psychological Bulletin, 117,* 250–270.

Wachter, R. M. (1992). Sounding board: AIDS, activism, and the politics of health. *The New England Journal of Medicine, 326,* 128–133.

Wagner, M. G., & St. Clair, P. A. (1989). Are in-vitro fertilization and embryo transfer of benefit to all? *The Lancet,* II, l027-l030.

Waisberg, J., & Page, S. (1988). Gender role nonconformity and perception of mental illness. *Women & Health, 14,* 3–16.

Waldron, I., & Jacobs, J. A. (1989). Effects of multiple roles on women's health-evidence from a national study. *Women & Health, 15,* 3–18.

Walker, Alice (1985). *The color purple.* New York: Pocket Books.

Walker, Anne (1994). Mood and well-being in consecutive menstrual cycles. *Psychology of Women Quarterly, 18,* 271–290.

Walker, A. J. (1994). You can't be a woman in your mother's house: Adult daughters and their mothers. In D. L. Sollie & L. A. Leslie *Gender, families, and close relationships: Feminist research journeys.* (pp. 74–96). Thousand Oaks, CA: Sage.

Walker, A. J., Pratt, C. C., & Wood, B. (1993). Perceived frequency of role conflict and relationship quality for caregiving daughters. *Psychology of Women Quarterly, 17,* 207–221.

Walker, L. (1986). Battered women's shelters and work with battered lesbians. In K. Lobel (Ed.), *Naming the violence: Speaking out about lesbian violence.* (pp. 73–76). Seattle, WA: Seal Press.

Walker, L. E. (1984). *The battered woman syndrome.* New York: Springer.

Walker, L. E. (1989). *Terrifying love: Why battered women kill and how society responds.* New York: Harper & Row.

Walker, L. J. (1984). Sex differences in the development of moral reasoning: A critical review. *Child Development, 55,* 677–691.

Walker, L. J. (1986). Sex differences in the development of moral reasoning: a rejoinder to Baumrind. *Child Development, 57,* 522–526.

Walker, W. D., Rowe, R. C., & Quinsey, V. L. (1993). Authoritarianism and sexual aggression. *Journal of Personality and Social Psychology, 65,* 1036–1045.

Walling, M., Andersen, B. L., & Johnson, S. R. (1990). Hormonal replacement therapy for postmenopausal women: A review of sexual outcomes and related gynecologic effects. *Archives of Sexual Behavior, 19,* 119–137.

Walsh, A. (1991). Self-esteem and sexual behavior: Exploring gender differences. *Sex Roles,* 441–467.

Walsh, M. R. (1993). Anita Hill and new research on trauma and recovery. *Psychology of Women,* Newsletter of Division 35, American Psychological Association, *20*(3), 5–6.

Walsh, R. T. (1989). Do research reports in mainstream feminist psychology journals reflect feminist values? *Psychology of Women Quarterly, 13,* 433–444.

Walton, M. B., Sachs, D., Ellington, R., Hazlewood, A., Griffin, S., & Bass, D. (1988). Physical stigma and the pregnancy role: Receiving help from strangers. *Sex Roles, 18,* 323–333.

Wang, M. Q., Nicholson, M. E., Richardson, M. T., Fitzhugh, E. C., Reneau, P., & Westerfield, C. R. (1995). The acute effect of moderate alcohol consumption on cardiovascular responses in women. *Journal of Studies of Alcohol, 56,* 16–20.

Ward, N. J. (1991). Occupational suitability bias for full-time and part-time employment in sex-typed jobs. *Sex Roles, 25,* 81–89.

Warren, L. W., & McEachern, L. (1985). Derived identity and depressive symptomatology in women differing in marital and employment status. *Psychology of Women Quarterly, 9,* 133–144.

Warshak, R. A., & Santrock, J. W. (1983). *New Directions for Child Development,* 29–46.

Warshaw, R. (1988). *I never called it rape: The Ms. report on recognizing, fighting, and surviving date and acquaintance rape.* New York: Harper & Row.

Washton, A. M. (1986). Women and cocaine. *Medical Aspects of Human Sexuality, 20,* 57.

Weiner, B. (1986). *An attributional theory of emotion and motivation.* New York: Springer-Verlag.

Weir, L. (1993) Anti-racist feminist pedagogy, self-observed. *RFR/DFR, 20,* 19–26.

Weis, D. L. (1985). The experience of pain during women's first sexual intercourse: Cultural mythology about female sexual initiation. *Archives of Sexual Behavior, 14,* 421–438.

Weisenfield, A. R., Malatesta, C. Z., Whitman, P. R., Granrose, C., & Uili, R. (1985). Psycho-physiological response of breast and bottle-feeding mothers to their infants' signals. *Psychophysiology, 22,* 78–86.

Weiss, R. S. (1988). Loss and recovery. *Journal of Personality and Social Psychology, 44,* 37–52.

Weissman, M. M., & Klerman, G. L. (1977). Sex differences in the epidemiology of depression. *Archives of General Psychiatry, 34,* 98–111.

Weissman, M. M., & Myers, J. K. (1978). Affective disorders in a United States Community: The use of research diagnostic criteria in an epidemiological survey. *Archives of General Psychiatry, 35,* 1304–1311.

Weisstein, N. (1979). Adventures of a woman in science. In R. Hubbard, M. S. Henifin & B. Fried (Eds.), *Women look at biology looking at women: A collection of feminist critiques* (pp. 187–203). Cambridge, MA: Schenkman.

Weitzman, L., Eifler, D., Hokada, E., & Ross, C. (1972). Sex role socialization in picture books for preschool children. *American Journal of Sociology, 77,* 1125–1150.

Welch, R., Gerrard, M., & Huston, A. (1986). Gender-related personality attributes and reaction to success/failure: An examination of mediating variables. *Psychology of Women Quarterly, 10,* 221–233.

Weller, A., & Weller, L. (1992). Menstrual synchrony in female couples. *Psychoneuroendocrinology, 17,* 171–177.

Weller, A., & Weller, L. (1993). Menstrual synchrony between mothers and daughters and between rommates. *Physiology and Behavior, 53,* 943–949.

Weller, L., & Weller, A. (1993). Human menstrual synchrony: A critical assessment. *Neuroscience and Biobehavioral Reviews, 17,* 427–439.

Wentling, R. M. (1992). Women in middle management: Their career development and aspirations. *Business Horizons, 35,* 47–54.

Wertz, R. W., & Wertz, D. C. (1977). *Lying-In: A history of childbirth in America* (Expanded ed.). New Haven, CT: Yale University Press.

Westerlund, E. (1986). Freud on sexual trauma: An historical review of seduction and betrayal. *Psychology of Women Quarterly, 10,* 297–310.

Whatley, M. H., & Worcester, N. (1989). The role of technology in the co-optation of the women's health movement: The cases of osteoporosis and breast cancer screening. In K. S. Ratcliff, M. M., Ferree, G. O. Mellow, B. D. Wright, G. D. Price, K. Yanoshik, & M. S. Freston (Eds.), *Healing technology: Feminist perspectives* (pp. 199–220). Ann Arbor: The University of Michigan Press.

Wheatley, D. (1991). Depression and the menopause. *British Journal of Psychiatry, 158,* 431–432.

Wheeler, C. E., Jr. (1988). The herpes simplix problem. *Journal of the Academy of Dermatology, 18,* 163–168.

Wheeler, H. (1985). Pornography and rape: A feminist perspective. In A. W. Burgess (Ed.), *Rape and sexual assault: A research handbook.* New York: Garland Publishing.

Wheeler, L., Reis, H., & Nezlek, J. (1983). Loneliness, social interactions, and sex roles. *Journal of Personality and Social Psychology, 45,* 943–953.

Whisman, M. A. (1993). Mediators and moderators of change in cognitive therapy of depression. *Psychological Bulletin, 114,* 248–265.

White, H., & Stillion, J. M. (1988). Sex differences in attitudes toward suicide: Do males stigmatize males. *Psychology of Women Quarterly, 12,* 357–366.

White, J. K., & Kowalski, R. M. (1994). Deconstructing the myth of the nonaggressive woman: A feminist analysis. *Psychology of Women Quarterly, 18,* 487–508.

White, K. M., Speisman, J. C., Jackson, D., Bartis, S., & Costos, D. (1986). Intimacy maturity and its correlates in young married couples. *Journal of Personality and Social Psychology, 50,* 152–162.

Whitley, B. E., Jr. (1983). Sex-role orientation and self-esteem: A critical meta-analytic review. *Journal of Personality and Social Psychology, 44,* 765–768.

Whitley, B. E., Jr. (1987). The relationship of sex-role orientation to heterosexuals' attitudes toward homosexuals. *Sex Roles, 17,* 103–113.

Whitley, B. E., Jr. (1988). Masculinity, Femininity, and self-esteem: A multitrait-multimethod analysis. *Sex Roles, 18,* 419–431.

Whitley, B. E., Jr., & Kite, M. E. (1995). Sex differences in attitudes toward homosexuality: A comment on Oliver and Hyde. *Psychological Bulletin, 117,* 146–154.

Whitsett, D., & Land, H. (1992). Role strain, coping, and marital satisfaction of stepparents. *Families in Society, 73,* 79–92.

Whittle, B. S., & Rollins, J. H. (1980, March), *Interpersonal dynamics in violent and nonviolent marriages.* Paper presented at the annual meeting of the Eastern Psychological Association. New York.

Wiersma, U. J., & Van den Berg, P. (1991). Work-home role conflict, family climate, and domestic responsibilities among men and women in dual-earner families. *Journal of Applied Social Psychology, 21,* 1207–1217.

Wiley, M. G., & Eskilson, A. (1982). Coping in the corporation: Sex-role constraints. *Journal of Applied social Psychology, 12,* 1-11.

Wilk, C. A. (1986). *Career women and childbearing: A psychological analysis of the decision process.* New York: Van Nostrand Reinhold.

Wilkerson, M. B. (1988). The critical moment: The educational status of black women. In S. E. Rix (Ed.), *The American Woman 1988–89: A status report* (pp. 207–225). New York: Norton.

Williams, G., Chamove, A. S., & Millar, H. R., (1990). Eating disorders, perceived control, assertiveness and hostility. *British Journal of Clinical Psychology, 29,* 327–335.

Williams, J. E., & Best, D. L. (1982). *Measuring sex stereotypes: A thirty-nation study.* Beverly Hills, CA: Sage.

Williams, L. B., & London, K. A. (1994). Changes in the planning status of births to ever-married U.S. women, 1982–1988. *Family Planning Perspectives, 26,* 121–124.

Williams, L. M. (1994). Recall of childhood trauma: A prospective study of women's memories of child sexual abuse. *Journal of Consulting and Clinical Psychology, 62,* 1167–1176.

Williams-Deane, M., & Potter, L. S. (1992). Current oral contraceptive use instructions: An analysis of patient package inserts. *Family Planning Perspectives, 24,* 111–115.

Willie, C. V. (1985). *Black and white families.* Bayside, NY: General Hall.

Wilmoth, G. H., de Alteriis, M., & Bussell, D. (1992). Prevalence of psychological risks following legal abortion in the U.S.: Limits of the evidence. *Journal of Social Issues, 48*(3), 37–66.

Wilsnack, R. W., Wilsnack, S. C., & Klassen, A. D. (1984). Women's drinking and drinking problems: Patterns from a 1981 national survey. *American Journal of Public Health, 74,* 1231–1238.

Wilsnack, S. C., Klassen, A. D., Schur, B. E., & Wilsnack, R. W. (1991). Predicting onset and chronicity of women's problem drinking A five-year longitudinal analysis. *American Journal of Public Health, 81,* 305–318.

Wilson, E. O. (1975). *Sociobiology: The new synthesis.*

Wilson, M. N. (1989). Child development in the context of the Black extended family. *American Psychologist, 44,* 380–385.

Wilson, M. N., Tolson, T. F. J., Hinton, I., & Kiernan, M. (1990). Flexibility and sharing of childcare duties in Black families. *Sex Roles, 22,* 409–425.

Wilson, R. A. (1966). *Feminine forever.* London: W. H. Allen.

Wink, P., & Helson, R. (1993). Personality change in women and their partners. *Journal of Personality and Social Psychology, 65,* 597–605.

Winawer, S. J., Zauber, A. G., Ho, M. N., O'Brien, M. J., Gottlieb, L. S., Sternberg, S. S., Waye, J. D., Schapiro, M., Bond, J. H., Panish, J. F., Ackroyd, F., Shike, M., Kurtz, R. C., Hornsby-Lewis, L., Gerdes, H., Steward, E. T., & The National Polyp Study Workgroup (1993). Prevention of colorectal cancer by colonoscopic polypectomy. *The New England Journal of Medicine, 329,* 1977–1981.

Winstead, B. A. (1986). Sex differences in same-sex friendships. In V. J. Derlega & B. A. Winstead (Eds.), *Friendship and social interaction.* New York: Springer Verlag.

Winter, D. G. (1988). The power motive in women—and men. *Journal of Personality and Social Psychology, 54,* 510–519.

Winter, D. G. (1993). Power, affiliation, and war: Three tests of a motivational model. *Journal of Personality and Social Psychology, 65,* 532–545.

Witkin, H. A., Mednick, S. A., Schulsinger, F., Bakkestrom, E., Christiansen, K. O., Goodenough, D. R., Hirschhorn, K., Lundsteen, C., Owen, D. R., Philip, J., Rubin, D. B., & Stocking, M. (1976). Criminality in XYY and XXY men. *Science, 193,* 547–555.

Witkin, H. A., Dyk, R. B., Paterson, H. F., Goodenough, D. R., & Karp, S. A. (1962). *Psychological Differentiation.* New York: Wiley.

Witter, F., & King, T. M. (1980). Cigarettes and pregnancy. In R. H. Schwartz & S. J. Yaffe (Eds.), *Drug and chemical risks to the fetus and newborn* (pp. 82–92). New York: Alan R. Liss.

Wittleson, S. F. (1985). The brain connection: The corpus callosum is larger in left-handers. *Science, 229,* 665–668.

Wittleson, S. F. (1989). Hand and sex differences in the isthmus and genu of the human corpus callosum. *Brain, 112,* 799–835.

Wittig, M. A., & Skolnick, P. (1978). Status versus warmth as determinants of sex differences in personal space. *Sex Roles, 4,* 493–503.

Wolkind, S. (1981). Nausea and vomiting of pregnancy. In S. Wolkind & E. Zajicek, (Eds.), *Pregnancy: A psychological and social study* (pp. 75–88). New York: Grune & Stratton.

Women in the labor force. (1994). *Statistical Bulletin, 75,* 2–10.

Women-owned businesses. (1992, February 3). *The Providence Journal Bulletin* (Evening Edition). p. A6.

Wonderlich, S. A., Swift, W. J., Slotnick, H. B., & Goodman, S. (1990). DSM-III-R personality disorders in eating-disorder subtypes. *International Journal of Eating Disorders, 9,* 607–616.

Wong, M., & Csikszentmihalyi, M. (1991). Affiliation motivation and daily experience: Some issues of gender differences. *Journal of Personality and Social Psychology, 60,* 154–164.

Wood, F. B., Flowers, D. L., & Naylor, C. E. (1991). In F. L. Kitterle (Ed.), *Cerebral Laterality: Theory and research* (pp. 103–115). Hillsdale, NJ: Lawrence Erlbaum.

Wood, J. V., Taylor, S. E., & Lichtman, R. R. (1985). Social comparison in adjustment to breast cancer. *Journal of Personality and Social Psychology, 49,* 1169–1183.

Wood, W. (1987). Meta-analytic review of sex differences in group performance. *Psychological Bulletin, 102,* 53–71.

Wood, W., Rhodes, N., & Whelan, M. (1989). Sex differences in positive well-being: a consideration of emotional style and marital status. *Psychological Bulletin, 106,* 249–264.

Woody, B. (1992). *Black women in the workplace: Impacts of structural change in the economy.* New York: Greenwood Press.

Wooley, S. C., & Wooley, O. W. (1984, February). Feeling fat in a thin society. *Glamour, 82,*198–201, 251–252.

Woollett, B. A. (1987). Who breastfeeds? The family and cultural context. *Journal of Reproductive and Infant Psychology, 5,* 127–131.

Workman, E. A., & Short, D. D. (1993). Atypical antidepressants versus imipramine in the treatment of major depression: A meta-analysis. *Journal of Clinical Psychiatry, 54,* 5–12.

Would be rapist's sentence is upheld. (1993, April 17). *The Providence Journal Bulletin,* p. A-9.

Wright, C. T., Meadow, A., Abramowitz, S. I., & Davidson, C. V. (1980). Psychiatric diagnosis as a function of assessor profession and sex. *Psychology of Women Quarterly, 5,* 240–254.

Wright, P. H. (1982). Men's friendships, women's friendships and the alleged inferiority of the latter. *Sex Roles, 8,* 1–20.

Wyatt, G. E. (1992). The sociocultural context of African American and White American women's rape. *Journal of Social Issues, 48*(1), 77–91.

Wyatt, G. E., & Dunn, K. M. (1991). Examining predictors of sex guilt in multiethnic samples of women. *Archives of Sexual Behavior, 20,* 471–485.

Wyatt, G. E., & Lyons-Rowe, S. (1990). African American women's sexual satisfaction as a dimension of their sex roles. *Sex Roles, 22,* 509–524.

Wyche, K. F., & Graves, S. B. (1992). Minority women in academia: Access and barriers to professional participation. *Psychology of Women Quarterly, 16,* 429–437.

Yahr, P. (1988). Sexual differentiation of behavior in the context of developmental psychobiology. *Handbook of behavioral neurobiology* (pp. 197–243). New York: Plenum Press.

Yanoshik, K., & Norsigian, J. (1989). Contraception, control, and choice: International perspectives. In K. S. Ratcliff, M. M. Ferree, G. O. Mellow, B. D. Wright, G. D. Price, K. Yanoshik & M. S. Freston (Eds.), *Healing technology: Feminist perspectives* (pp. 61–92). Ann Arbor, MI: University of Michigan Press.

Yarber, W. L., & Whitehill, L. L. (1981). The relationship between parental affective orientation toward sexuality and responses to sex-related situations of pre-school-age children. *Journal of Sex Education and Therapy, 7,* 36–39.

Yates, A. (1989). Current perspectives on the eating disorders: I history, psychological and biological aspects. *Journal of the American Academy of Child Psychiatry, 28,* 813–827.

Yoder, J. D., & Kahn, A. S. (1993). Working toward an inclusive psychology of women. *American Psychologist, 48,* 846–850.

Yoder, J. D., & Kahn, A. S. (1992). Toward a feminist understanding of women and power. *Psychology of Women Quarterly, 16,* 381–388.

York, K. L., & John, O. P. (1992). The four faces of Eve: A typological analysis of women's personality at midlife. *Journal of Personality and Social Psychology, 63,* 494–508.

Young, D. (1986). Nurse-midwives, consumers and childbirth educators: The need to work together. In J. Rooks & J. E. Haas (Eds.), *Nurse-Midwifery in America* (pp. 47–49). Washington, DC: American College of Nurse-Midwives Foundation.

Young, E. W., Jensen, L. C., Olsen, J. A., & Cundick, B. P. (1991). The effects of family structure on the sexual behavior of adolescents. *Adolescence, 26,* 977–986.

Young-Eisendrath, P. (1988). The female person and how we talk about her. In M. M. Gergen (Ed.), *Feminist thought and the structure of knowledge* (pp. 152–172). New York: New York University Press.

Youngstrom, N. (1991). Lesbians and gay men still find bias in therapy. *The APA Monitor, 22,* p. 35.

Zabin, L. S., Hirsch, M. B., & Emerson, M. R. (1989). When urban adolescents choose abortion: Effects on education, psychological status and subsequent pregnancy. *Family Planning Perspectives, 21,* 248–255.

Zabin, L. S., Hirsch, M. B., Smith, E. A., Streett, R., & Hardy, J. B. (1986). Evaluation of a pregnancy prevention program for urban teenagers. *Family Planning Perspectives, 18,* 119–126.

Zabin, L. S., Hirsch, M. B., Streett, R., Emerson, M. R., Smith, M, Hardy, J. B., & King, T. M. (1988). The Baltimore pregnancy prevention program for urban teenagers: I. How did it work? *Family Planning Perspectives, 20,* 182–187.

Zalk, S. R. (1990). Men in the academy: A psychological profile of harassment. In M. A. Paludi (Ed.), *Ivory power: Sexual harassment on campus* (pp. 8–175). Albany, NY: State University of New York Press.

Zaslow, M. J. (1991). Variation in child care quality and its implications for children. *Journal of Social Issues, 47,* 125–138.

Zelnik, M., & Kantner, J. F. (1972). Sexual experience of young unmarried women in the United States. *Family Planning Perspectives, 4*(4), 9–18.

Zelnik, M., & Kantner, J. F. (1980). Sexual activity, contraceptive use and pregnancy among metropolitan area teenagers: 1971–1979. *Family Planning Perspectives, 12*(5), 230–237.

Zelnik, M., Kantner, J. F., & Ford, K. (1981). *Sex and pregnancy in adolescence.* New York: Sage.

Zelnik, M., & Kim, Y. J. (1982). Sex education and its association with teenage sexual activity, pregnancy and contraceptive use. *Family Planning Perspectives, 14,* 117–119, 123–126.

Zillman, D., & Bryant, J. (1984). Effects of massive exposure to pornography. In N. M. Malamuth & E. I. Donnerstein (Eds.), *Pornography and sexual aggression* (pp. 115–138). New York: Academic Press.

Zillmann, D. (1978). Attribution and misattribution of exitatory reactions. In J. H. Harvey, W. Ickes & R. F. Kidd (Eds.), *New directions in attribution research Vol 2* (pp. 335–368). Hillsdale, NJ: Erlbaum.

Zillmann, D. (1984). *Connections between sex and aggression.* Hillsdale, NJ: Erlbaum.

Zillmann, D., Schweitzer, K. J., & Mundorf, N. (1994). Menstrual cycle variation of women's interest in erotica. *Archives of Sexual Behavior, 23,* 579–597.

Zimmerman, D. H., & West, C. (1975). Sex roles, interruptions and silences in conversation. In B. Thorne & N. Henley (Eds.), *Language and sex: Differences and dominance.* Rowley, MA: Newbury House.

Zinn, L. M., & Stanton, A. L. (August, 1987). *Restraint, diet-related cognitions, and bulimia in college women.* Paper presented at the 95th Annual Meeting of the American Psychological Association, New York.

Zinn, M. B. (1989). Family, race, and poverty in the eighties. *Signs, 14,* 856–874.

Zinn, M. B. (1987). *Minority families in crisis: The public discussion.* Working Paper no. 6. Memphis, TN: Memphis State University, Center for Research on Women.

Zuckerman, B., Frank, D. A., Hingson, R., Amaro, H., Levenson, S. M., Kayne, H., Parker, S., Vinci, R., Aboagye, K., Fried, L. E., Cabral, H., Timperi, R., & Bauchner, H. (1989). Effects of maternal marijuana and cocaine use on fetal growth. *The New England Journal of Medicine, 320,* 762–768.

Zuckerman, B. S., & Beardslee, W. R. (1987). Maternal depression: A concern for pediatricians. *Pediatrics, 79,* 110–117.

Zussman, L., Zussman, S., Sunley, R., & Bjornson, E. (1981). Sexual response after hysterectomy-oophorectomy: Recent studies and reconsideration of psychogenesis. *American Journal of Obstetrics and Gynecology, 140,* 725–729.

AUTHOR INDEX

Abarbanel, G., 208
Abbey, A., 187, 406
Abel, G.G., 214
Aboagye, K., 387
Abraham, G.E., 55
Abramovici, H., 287
Abramowitz, S.I., 260
Abrams, B., 379
Abrams, D., 128
Abramson, L.Y., 230
Acitelli, L.K., 337
Acker, J., 13
Ackerman, R., 405
Ackroyd, F., 287
Adami, H., 301
Adams, C.G., 370
Adams, C.J., 395
Adams, K.A., 468
Adams, R.P., 447
Adams, V., 193
Adelman, P.K., 151
Adler, N.E., 295, 296
Agras, W.S., 270–71
Agyei, 40
Ahmed, F., 389, 390
Ahmed, N., 389, 390
Aida, Y., 464
Ainslie, J., 439–40
Ajzen, I., 231
Alexander, F.E., 283
Alexander, G.M., 131, 132
Alexander, P.C., 217, 218
Allen, K.R., 7, 8, 9, 10, 180,
   181, 464–65
Allen, M., 319
Allen, S.G., 125
Allen, V.L., 137
Alleyne, D., 293
Almagor, M., 53
Alveario, M.C., 29
Amaro, H., 266, 387
Amato, P.R., 434
Amir, M., 205, 212
Amott, T., 82, 157, 158, 159,
   161, 162, 164, 165
Amuzu, B., 407
Anastasi, A., 11, 25, 62, 66,
   67, 468
Anda, R.F., 281
Andersen, B.L., 349
Andersen, M.L., 317, 318

Anderson, B., 218
Anderson, E.R., 441
Anderson, J., 5
Anderson, J.R., 312
Anderson, R.H., 39
Anderson, S.A., 145
Andersson, B., 430
Andrews, F.M., 406
Aneshensel, C.S., 143, 363
Angel, R., 438
Anthony, J.C., 241
Antill, J.K., 426
Antonucci, T.C., 337
Apfelbaum, E., 455
Apgar, B.S., 306
Aponte, R., 447
Appelbaum, M.I., 400
Apple, R.D., 401
Apt, C., 370
Aral, S.O., 313
Archer, D., 119, 120
Arditti, R., 408
Aries, E., 132
Armstrong, L., 215
Arnill, A.C., 396
Arnow, B., 271
Aronson, R.A., 386
Arriagada, R., 284
Arslanian, A., 392
Asch, A., 351
Ashmore, R., 331
Ashton, E., 135
Asso, D., 46, 49
Astin, H.S., 190, 471
Atkinson, J., 192
Atkinson, J.W., 85
Atkison, B.M., 204
Aube, J., 134
Auerbach, D., 318–19
Auster, E.R., 176
Austin, D., 281, 282, 285
Avants, S.K., 460
Avioli, P.S., 189
Avreayl, 225
Avrech, O., 381
Axelrod, R., 427

Baber, K.M., 7, 8, 9, 10, 180,
   181, 190, 421
Bachicha, J.A., 387
Bachman, R., 199

Bachrach, C.A., 144
Backstrom, T., 54
Bailey, A.J., 305
Bailyn, L., 171
Bain, R.P., 385
Bakan, A.B., 159
Bakan, D., 99
Baker, B., 290–91
Baker, D.D., 186
Baker, D.P., 87
Baker, I.T., 394
Bakkestrom, E., 41
Baldwin, C., 420
Ballard-Reisch, D., 101
Ballinger, C.B., 149
Balshem, M., 308
Balsley, J., 389
Banaji, M.R., 112, 180
Bandura, A., 126, 296
Barba, R., 73, 74
Barbach, L., 374
Barber, B.L., 435
Barer, B.M., 153
Barglow, P., 428
Barling, 428
Barlow, D.H., 214
Barnard, M., 310
Barnett, R.C., 188, 271, 272
Baron, L., 198, 203, 204
Baronowski, T., 403
Barrett, D.H., 281
Barrett-Connor, E., 300, 305
Barry, K., 13, 219
Bart, P.B., 207, 208, 213
Bartholomew, N.G., 262
Bartis, S., 337
Bartleman, B., 27
Barton, S., 18
Baruch, G.K., 271, 272
Bashe, E., 134
Basow, S.A., 102
Bass, D., 383
Bates, H.G., 113
Batzler, U., 23
Bauchner, H., 387, 402–3
Baucom, D.H., 34, 339
Bauman, K.E., 288
Baxter, R.R., Jr., 400
Bayer, R., 389
Bazin, B., 389
Bean, F.D., 464

Beardslee, W.R., 424
Beautrais, 403
Becerra, R.M., 143, 363
Bech, P., 268, 269
Beck, A.T., 55, 244, 262
Becker, B.J., 61
Becker, F.V., 214
Becker, J., 27
Becker, M., 329, 367
Beck-Gernsheim, E., 291
Bee, D.E., 403
Bee, H., 94
Begley, D.J., 377, 378
Behan, 33
Behrman, R.E., 387
Bekendam, D.J., 39
Belenky, M.F., 8, 72–73
Belk, S.S., 256
Bell, 41
Bell, A.P., 367
Bell, C., 324
Bell, S., 220
Bell, S.E., 304
Belle, D., 238, 239
Belsky, J., 424, 428, 429
Bem, S.L., 14, 29, 34, 42, 43,
   99, 100, 127, 128, 348–49
Bempechat, J., 134
Benbow, C.P., 38, 63, 66
Ben-Porath, Y.S., 53
Benson, C.S., 256
Benson, D.J., 186
Benson-Von Der Ohe, E.,
   339, 344, 440–41
Berardo, 191
Berch, B., 166
Bercovitch, F.B., 29
Berenbaum, S.A., 43
Berger, J., 130, 178
Bergin, D.J., 94
Bergman, L., 221
Bergvist, L., 301
Berk, R.A., 184, 228
Berk, S.F., 190, 191
Berkelman, R.L., 302, 303
Berkowitz, G.S., 391
Berkowitz, R.L., 391
Berman, J.S., 265, 266
Bernay, T., 471
Berndt, E.R., 268
Bernhard, L.A., 306

Bernstein, B., 49
Bernstein, I., 363
Bernstein, J., 8, 394
Bernstein, L., 302
Berntson, G.G., 18
Berris, R.F., 303
Bersheid, E., 329, 331
Bersoff, D.N., 179
Besch, N.F., 31
Besch, P.K., 34
Best, C.L., 204
Betz, M., 189
Bey, M., 389
Beyer, S., 87
Biaggio, M.K., 420
Bickel, H., 170
Bielert, C., 29
Biernat, M., 96, 97, 191, 425
Bigler, R.S., 127
Bilenki, I., 380
Billy, J.O.G., 140
Bindra, D., 112
Binion, V.J., 103, 257
Bird, C.E., 278
Bird, H.R., 241
Bjornson, E., 305, 306
Black, D.W., 253, 263, 270
Black, S., 246
Blacklow, R.S., 281, 282, 285
Blais, M.R., 333
Blaisure, K.R., 465
Blanchard, E.B., 214
Blau, S., 114, 115
Blazer, D.G., 53, 198–99
Blee, K.M., 467
Blood, R.O., 462
Bloys, N., 318, 322
Blumenfeld, P., 73
Blumenthal, P.D., 295, 296
Blumstein, P., 336, 358, 361, 367, 460, 464
Blysma, W.H., 176
Bogart, M.H., 385, 392
Bohan, J.S., 9
Bond, A., 403
Bond, J.H., 287
Bond, J.T., 402, 403
Bonilla-Santiago, G., 160
Bonnicksen, A.L., 406, 410
Bonson, K.R., 31
Booth, A., 340
Borg, S., 407
Borgers, S.B., 185
Borgida, E., 96, 97, 179
Bornstein, J., 287
Botto, L.D., 385
Boucher, C., 333
Bouhoutsos, J.C., 264
Bourinbaiar, A.S., 293
Bouvardi, 476
Bowe, C., 358, 362
Bower, L.C., 416
Bowers, C.A., 38
Bowers, W., 253, 263, 270
Bowker, L.H., 226, 228

Bowlby, J., 217, 253, 326
Boyd, J.A., 265
Boyd, P., 281, 282, 285
Boyd, P.A., 385
Boyed, J.H., 241
Boyer, D., 142
Boyer, P.J., 388, 389
Brabant, S., 134, 135
Brabeck, M.M., 475–76
Bradbury, T.N., 334
Bradshaw, C.K., 266
Braiden, V., 55
Brambilla, D., 148, 149
Brand, C., 441
Brand, P.A., 107
Brand, T., 29
Brandon, P., 81, 82
Bransfield, D.D., 281, 282, 285
Bravos, M., 241
Breautrais, A.L., 403
Breedlove, S.M., 27
Breinlinger, S., 129
Brekke, N., 96
Brell, D.J., 136
Bremer, H.J., 23
Brennan, P., 305
Brennan, R.T., 187, 272
Breslow, J.L., 280
Brewer, C., 296
Brewer, M.B., 183
Brewer, V., 305
Brewster, K.L., 140
Bricarelli, F.D., 392
Bridgeman, B., 65
Bridges, J.S., 166
Briere, J., 214, 219
Brierly, M., 456
Brinton, L.A., 301
Brizot, M.De L., 384
Brody, C.M., 154
Brody, J., 382
Brody, L.H., 112
Broman, C.L., 467
Bronars, S., 141
Bronen, R.A., 37
Bronfenbrenner, U., 25–26
Brooks-Gunn, J., 50, 137, 143, 247, 398
Brophy, J., 73, 74
Brouse, S., 392–93
Broverman, D.M., 94, 114, 259
Broverman, I.K., 94, 114, 259
Brown, C.E., 117
Brown, D.R., 320
Brown, G.R., 218
Brown, G.W., 271
Brown, J.B., 302
Brown, J.C., 435
Brown, J.P., 403
Brown, L.S., 11, 251, 309
Brown, R., 94
Brown, R.M., 4
Brown-Collins, A., 10, 11

Browne, A., 217, 226, 228, 233
Brownmiller, S., 201, 212, 213, 420
Brownworth, V.A., 225, 226
Brubaker, P.H., 30
Bruce, B., 271
Bruch, H., 248
Brumberg, J.J., 245, 248
Bryant, J., 214
Bryden, M.P., 33, 69, 70, 72
Bryson, Y.J., 388, 389
Budoff, P.W., 48
Bukovsky, J., 381
Bulik, C.M., 218
Bulman-Fleming, M.B., 33
Bumpass, L.L., 332
Bunch, C., 4
Burch, B., 335
Burda, P.C., Jr., 322
Burgard, P., 23
Burgess, 40, 436
Burgess, A.W., 209, 210
Burgess, N.J., 159
Buring, J.E., 280
Burke, J.D., 238, 241, 254
Burkhart, B.R., 210
Burks, N., 464
Burleson, M.H., 48
Burman, B., 279
Burnam, M.A., 205, 210, 240
Burns, L.E., 253, 270
Bursik, K., 343
Burt, M.R., 184
Burton, D., 314
Bush, T., 303
Buskirk, E., 50
Buss, D.M., 323, 338
Bussell, D., 296
Bussey, K., 126
Bustamante, R., 396
Butchart, A.M., 378
Butler, D., 470–71
Butler, M., 136
Butler, S., 215
Butterfield, D.An., 176
Buxton, K.S., 401
Bybee, J., 145
Byers, J., 309
Byers, S.E., 358
Byrne, D., 350
Byrnes, J.P., 65

Cabral, H., 387
Cacioppo, J.T., 18
Caggiula, A.W., 150
Calam, R., 251
Caldwell, M.A., 318
Calhoun, K.S., 204
Calhoun, L.G., 393
Calhoun, M.L., 393
Callahan, S., 34
Campbell, 462–64
Campbell, B., 331
Campbell, R.R., 212, 213

Campbell, S.B., 398
Canino, G.J., 241
Cann, C.E., 304
Cannon, K.G., 11
Cannon, L.W., 16
Cantor, D.W., 471
Cantor, J., 136
Caplan, P.J., 51, 231, 232, 423
Capps, L., 309
Carden, A.D., 222
Cardinale, L., 73, 74
Cardoza, D., 79
Carey, J.C., 387
Carey, M.P., 372
Carli, L.L., 106, 111, 113, 131
Carlson, K.J., 287, 305, 306, 307
Carlyn, M., 309
Carmen, A., 220
Carr, T.S., 31
Carroll, D., 328
Carroll, J.W., 473
Carson, C.M., 117
Cartensen, L.L., 337
Carter, D.K., 261
Carver, C.S., 285
Caspi, E., 381
Castellano, O., 80
Castro, G., 2, 3, 4
Catania, J.A., 290
Catanzarite, V., 8, 394
Cates, W., 380
Cates, W., Jr., 313
Cauley, J., 300
Ceci, S.J., 25–26
Challis, J.R.G., 378
Chamberlain, M.K., 82, 83, 173
Chamberlain, P.F., 385
Chambless, D.L., 253
Chamove, A.S., 251
Champagne, N.M., 52
Chandler, Z., 475
Chandra, A., 387
Chang, J.C., 305
Chaplin, T.C., 214
Chapman, J.R., 105
Charness, N., 24
Chase-Lansdale, L., 143
Chasnoff, I.J., 387
Chatham, L.R., 262
Chavez, D., 135
Check, J.V.P., 214
Checkley, S.A., 400
Chen, V., 281, 282, 285
Cherlin, A., 332
Cherry, F., 86
Chertkoff, J.M., 467
Chesler, P., 259, 416, 418, 442, 443
Chesney, S.M., 256
Chester, N.L., 107
Chira, S., 431
Chodorow, N., 8, 9, 138, 177, 416–17

Chollat-Traquet, C., 288
Chorowski, M., 396
Chow, Wh.H., 281
Chrisler, J.C., 50, 52
Christ, C.P., 473
Christiansen, A., 338–39
Christiansen, C., 300
Christiansen, K., 33
Christiansen, K.O., 41
Christmas, J.T., 387
Ciali, S.D., 191
Ciancanelli, P., 166
Clark, K.C., 285
Clark, R., 350–51
Clarke, S., 116
Clarke-Stewart, K., 429–30
Clark-Nicolas, P., 333
Clarkson, F.E., 94, 114, 259
Clayton, S., 181, 182
Cleaver, E., 200
Clinchy, B.M., 8, 72–73
Clingempeel, W.G., 441
Coates, D.L., 138
Coates, R.J., 281, 282, 285
Coates, T.J., 290
Cobleigh, M.A., 303
Cochran, S., 335
Cochran, S.D., 264, 310
Cockerham, W.C., 239
Coffee, M.C., 453, 456
Cohan, C.L., 294, 295
Cohen, 239
Cohen, A.G., 171
Cohen, B.P., 130
Cohen, D., 293
Cohen, J., 61, 117, 308
Cohn, D., 168
Cohn, L., 139
Colditz, G.A., 282, 299, 300, 302
Cole, P.M., 217
Coleman, E., 364, 365
Coleman-Burns, P., 81
Colligan, R.C., 244
Collins, K., 363
Collins, M.E., 245
Collins, N.L., 326, 398
Collins, P.H., 10, 443–44
Conley, J.J., 341
Connor, E.M., 389
Conrad, E., 6, 7
Constable, R.T., 37
Constantinople, A., 99
Conte, J.R., 219
Contesso, G., 284
Conti, L., 32
Coombs, R., 389
Cooper, J., 83, 84
Cooper, P.J., 400, 403
Cooper, R., 178
Copenhaver, S., 206
Copper, R.L., 379
Corbett, R., 255–256
Corbier, P., 29
Corder, L.E., 179

Corea, G., 408
Costello, E.J., 150
Costos, D., 337
Cotch, M.F., 387
Cott, N.F., 451
Cotton, S., 426
Coverman, S., 191
Cowan, G., 212, 213, 460
Cox, S.L., 204
Cozzarelli, C., 296
Cragin, K., 403–4
Craig, J.M., 187
Crandall, B.F., 384
Crandall, C.S., 245, 249
Crandall, V.C., 86, 87
Crane, J.P., 385
Crawford, M., 75
Crawford, T.J., 426
Crester, G.A., 112
Criqui, M.H., 280, 300
Crockett, L.J., 137
Croft, J.B., 281
Crook, D., 299
Crosby, F., 177, 182
Crovitz, E., 324
Crowley, M., 106, 107
Crowley, P., 395, 396
Cruet, D., 242, 243
Cruickshank, A., 281
Crumpler, C.A., 277
Csikszentmihalyi, M., 107
Culnane, M., 389
Culp, R.E., 400
Cumming, C.E., 53
Cumming, D.C., 53
Cundick, B.P., 363, 433
Cunningham, J.D., 426
Cupples, L.A., 314
Curtis, L., 200
Curtis, R.L., Jr., 464
Cuskey, W.R., 257, 258, 261–262
Cust, M.P., 299
Cutrona, C.E., 399, 400
Cutter, G.R., 379
Cyr, M.G., 299
Cyranowski, J.M., 349

Dabbs, J.M., Jr., 31, 35
Daling, J., 406
Daling, J.R., 288
Dalton, K., 54
Daly, M., 451, 473
Dambrot, F.H., 83
Dan, A.J., 313
Daniels, R., 448
Daniluk, J.C., 349
Darrow, W., 308
Daston, S., 246
David, H.P., 295, 296
Davidson, C.V., 260
Davidson, N.E., 303
Davidson, R.J., 39
Davies, K.E., 26
Davis, 311

Davis, K.E., 327
Davis, M.H., 327
Davis-Floyd, R.E., 411
Day, A., 403
Dayton, L., 309
De Alteriis, M., 296
Dean, N.G., 456
Deane, G.D., 288
Deane, W., 145
Deaux, K., 86, 89, 96, 151, 177, 178
de Beauvoir, S., 415, 416
De Berducido, E.J., 145
DeBlasio, C.L., 117
De Castro, J.M., 405
Deck, L.P., 178
DeCourville, N., 51
DeFeudis, P., 40
DeFour, C.C., 186
DeGrazia, P.V., 369
De Jonge, F.H., 29
de Lacoste, M.C., 36
de Lacoste-Utamsing, C., 35
DeLamater, J., 348
De La Rue, D., 35
Delfraissy, J-F., 389
Delgado-Rodriquez, M., 302
Del Vecchio, M., 284
DeMaris, A., 340
D'Emilio, J., 198, 212
Demo, D.H., 436
DeMuylder, X., 397
Denmark, F.L., 191
Denney, N.W., 355, 358
Dent, C.W., 314
D'Ercole, A., 239
Deren, 311
de Rham, E., 317
DeRubeis, R.J., 269
Detlefesen, E.G., 190
Detzer, M.J., 270
Deutsch, F., 116, 398
Deveikis, A., 388, 389
Devine, D., 255–256
Devine, P.G., 144
de Wolf, V.A., 65
de Zalduondo, B.O., 220
Diamond, I., 213
Diamond, M.C., 39
Dickey, R.P., 50
Dickmann, K.A., 417
Dick-Read, G., 393
Diehm, C., 222
Diggory, P., 290, 293
Dillon, M., 388, 389
DiMatteo, M.R., 119, 120
Dindia, K., 319
Dinero, T.E., 204
Dion, K.L., 180
Dionne, D., 228, 229
DiVasto, P.V., 350
Dixon, J.K., 365
Dixson, A.F., 30
Djenderedjian, A., 214
Dodge, L.J.T., 373

Dodson, D.L., 455
Doll, R., 303
Donat, P.L.N., 198, 212
Donnelly, B.W., 273, 441–42
Donnerstein, E., 214, 215
Donovan, J., 1, 5, 125
Donovan, S., 397
d'Orban, P.T., 54
Dorchester, W., 391
d'Oro, L.C., 290, 293
Dose, A.M., 303
Dovidio, J.F., 117
Dowling, C., 108
Downey, G., 41, 439
Doyle, A., 75
Drakich, J., 115
Drazin, R., 176
Drewett, R.F., 404
DuBard, M.B., 379
DuBois, D.L., 138
Duelberg, S.I., 279, 280
Duff, R.W., 153
Duffy, B., 210
Dujon, D., 437
Dukes, J.L., 435–36
Dulberg, C., 396
Duncan, B., 402
Dunkel-Schetter, C., 294, 398
Dunn, K.F., 460
Dunn, K.M., 350
Dutton-Douglas, M.A., 228, 229
Duxbury, L.E., 188
Dworkin, A., 213, 220, 408
Dyk, R.B., 69
Dzeich, B., 183, 184, 185
Dziuba-Leatherman, J., 198

Eagly, A.H., 61, 95, 104, 105, 106, 107, 111, 120, 129, 130, 468, 470, 471
East, P.L., 142
Eaton, W.O., 106, 109
Eaves, L.J., 254
Eccles, J.S., 66, 73, 76, 77, 78, 102, 166, 435
Echols, A., 4
Eckert, E.D., 247
Eckes, T., 95, 96
Economy, K.E., 287, 292
Edelberg, R., 303–4
Edelstein, S.L., 305
Ederly, G., 28
Edwards, B.K., 281, 282, 285
Edwards, J.N., 340
Egeland, B., 244
Egeland, G.M., 300
Eggebeen, D., 429
Egley, L.C., 222
Egoff, D.B., 178
Ehrenreich, B., 359
Ehrensaft, D., 419
Ehrhardt, A.A., 41, 366
Eichler, A., 238, 255
Eichler, L.S., 424

Eifler, D., 135
Eisenberg, N., 113, 119
Eisenhart, M.A., 145
Ekstrom, B., 150
El-Bassel, N., 310–11
Eldridge, N.S., 336
Elesser, V., 311
Eley, J.W., 281, 282, 285
Elkind, D., 448
Elkins, L.E., 320
Elkins, M., 389
Ellington, R., 383
Elliott, S.A., 369
Ellis, E.M., 204
Ellis, L., 201
Ellyson, S.L., 117
Elmslie, T., 396
Elton, M., 101
Emerson, M.R., 145, 297
Emery, J.L., 401
Endicott, J., 55, 469
Endler, N.S., 40
Engelhardt, B.J., 342
England, P., 164, 166, 167, 168
English, E.C., 393
Enns, L.R., 106, 109
Entwisle, D.R., 87
Epple, G., 29, 30
Ericsson, K.A., 24
Erikson, E., 138
Erinakes, D.M., 173
Ernhart, C.B., 403
Eskey, J., 153
Eskilson, A., 179
Espin, O.M., 267, 362, 363
Esseveld, J., 13
Etaugh, C., 425
Ettinger, B., 304
Evans, M.D., 269
Ewigman, B.G., 385
Exline, R.V., 117
Ey, J., 402

Faden, R.R., 401
Fagan, C., 396
Fairburn, C., 256
Fairweather, D.V.I., 378
Fakouri, E., 256
Falbo, T., 460, 464
Falcon, P.L., 211
Falk, P.J., 439
Fallon, A.E., 323
Farrell, G.J., 174
Farris, E., 89
Fausto-Sterling, A., 23, 28, 35, 39, 40, 45
Feather, N.T., 85
Featherstone, D.R., 433–34
Feeney, J.A., 326
Feingold, A., 44, 62–63, 67, 68, 72, 106, 108, 109, 112, 113, 323
Feinman, C., 233
Feiring, C., 132

Feldman, E.B., 300–301
Feldstein, M., 264
Felice, M.E., 142, 143
Felson, R.B., 200, 201
Feltey, K.M., 439–40
Fennema, E., 63, 64, 66
Ferguson, A., 321
Fergusson, D.M., 403
Fernandez, C., 328
Ferns, T., 475–76
Ferree, M.M., 166, 167
Feshbach, S., 202
Festinger, L., 284
Fetler, M., 83
Ficher, I., 440
Field, J.K., 355, 358
Fielder, E.P., 143, 363
Filer, L.J., 402, 403
Fincham, F.D., 334
Fine, D., 142
Fine, M.A., 142, 351, 368, 441–42
Finegan, J., 27
Fink, P.J., 353
Finkelhor, D., 198, 207, 217
Finkelstein, S.N., 268
Fiorentine, R., 76, 89
Firestone, S., 415, 416
Firth, H.V., 385
Firth, J.A., 377, 378
Fischer, L.R., 422
Fischer, T., 303
Fisek, M.H., 178
Fishbein, M., 231
Fisher, B., 322, 370
Fisher, W.A., 350, 369
Fishkin, R.E., 353
Fiske, M.E., 302–3
Fiske, S.T., 127, 179, 349, 459
Fitzgerald, L.F., 185, 226
Fitzhugh, E.C., 281
Fitzmaurice, G., 398
Flaks, D.K., 440
Flamm, 395
Flanders, D., 281, 282, 285
Flanders, W.D., 281
Flay, B.R., 314
Fleischer, R.A., 467
Fleming, A.S., 398, 424, 425
Fleming, D.E., 39
Fleming, S.M., 145
Fletcher, J.M., 37
Flowers, D.L., 36
Foa, E.B., 209, 210
Fodor, I.G., 247
Follette, V.M., 218
Follette, W.C., 218
Folsom, A., 280
Fontaine, F., 284
Forcey, L.R., 423
Ford, K., 354
Ford, M.R., 110
Ford, T.E., 98
Fordyce, R.R., 289
Foreman, 170

Forman, M., 281, 282, 285
Forrest, A.P., 283
Forrest, J.D., 289
Forsythe, A.B., 205, 210, 240
Fowers, B.J., 337, 338
Fowler, R.D., 79
Fowler, S.E., 300
Fox, E.E., 53
Fox, G.L., 141
Fox, M., 318–19
Frady, R.L., 31
Franco, E.D., 394–95
Frank, D.A., 387
Frank, E., 210
Franz, M.M., 314
Frau, L.M., 380
Frayser, S., 361
Frazier, P.A., 209
Freeman, E.W., 51, 54
Freeman, L.N., 213
Freeman, R.K., 391
Freeman, S., 392
Freese, M.P., 390
Fremont, A.M., 278
French, J., 308
French, J.R.P., Jr., 457
French, M., 373
Freud, S., 124, 125, 139, 155, 215–16, 246, 248, 260, 353, 416
Fried, A., 212
Fried, L.E., 387
Friedan, B., 2, 3, 449–50
Friedberg, D.W., 50
Friedman, A., 466
Friedman, B.L., 110
Friedman, D.E., 209
Friedman, E.A., 390, 396
Friedman, S., 369
Friedman, W.J., 110
Frieze, I.H., 81, 89, 190, 465, 466
Frigoletto, F.D., 385
Frisch, R.E., 137
Frost, J.L., 81
Frost, L.A., 66
Frye, M., 4, 358
Fulbright, R.K., 37
Fullerton, H.N., Jr., 158
Fullilove, M.T., 218, 290
Furstenberg, F.F., Jr., 143

Gabardi, L., 434
Gabel, J., 253, 263, 270
Gagnon, D., 177
Gagnon, D.R., 314
Gagnon, J.H., 354, 355, 356, 358, 361, 374
Gailey, C.W., 462
Galaburda, A.M., 33, 38
Galambos, N.L., 187
Galimberti, V., 284
Galler, R., 322, 370
Gambrell, R.D., Jr., 300
Gammon, M.D., 282

Gangar, K.F., 299
Gangestad, S.W., 326, 360
Gannon, L., 15, 150, 299
Garbner, J., 230
Garcia, S.A., 408
Gardenswartz, L., 471
Gardner, H.A., 40
Garfinkel, P.E., 245, 250, 323
Garner, D.M., 245, 250, 323
Garner, L.C., 399
Garnets, L., 264, 265
Gartrell, N., 264
Garver, J.A., 83
Garvey, M.J., 269
Gary, L.E., 320
Gauthier, R.J., 394–95
Gautier, T., 43
Gayraud, D., 38
Gaziano, M.M., 280
Gebhard, P.H., 354, 356, 357, 361, 365, 367
Geer, 373
Geerkin, M., 343
Geis, F., 470–71
Geist, C.S., 367
Gelber, R., 389
Gelfand, M.M., 394–95
Gelles, R.J., 222, 227, 231
Genant, H.K., 304
Genero, N., 242
Genevie, L., 421–22
George, L.K., 53, 198–99
George, R., 309
Gerdes, H., 287
Gergen, M.M., 9, 14, 146
Gerrard, M., 103
Gerson, M.J., 411
Geschwind, N., 33, 38
Gewirtz, J.C., 134
Gewolb, I.H., 388
Ghizzani, A., 372
Giambra, L.M., 357
Gibbons, J.L., 145
Gibbs, M., 318–19
Gidycz, C.A., 199, 200, 205
Gielsen, A.C., 401
Gilbert, F., Jr., 298
Gilbert, L.A., 336
Gilfus, M.E., 233
Gill, P., 308
Gilli, G., 23
Gilligan, C., 8, 93, 109–10, 137, 138, 177
Gillum, R., 280
Gilpin, E., 288
Girod, K., 308
Gise, L.H., 51
Giusti, L.M., 198
Gladen, B.C., 403
Glaser, R.D., 185
Glasgow, R.E., 373
Glass, J.L., 271
Glass, S.P., 362
Gleick, J., 18
Glenn, E.N., 157, 159

Glenn, N.D., 424
Glick, M., 145
Glickman, S.E., 30, 31
Golan, A., 381
Gold, D., 75
Gold, M., 318
Goldberg, D.C., 353
Goldberg, E., 38
Goldberg, M.S., 293
Goldberg, P.A., 97, 98
Goldberg, W.A., 426
Goldberger, N.R., 8, 72–73
Golden, C., 366
Goldenberg, R.L., 390
Goldfarb, J., 402
Goldfoot, D.A., 29
Goldhaber, S.Z., 280
Golding, J.M., 193, 205, 210, 240, 273
Goldstein, A.J., 253
Goldstein, L.H., 242
Golub, S., 49, 137
Gomberg, E.S., 255
Gonzales, M.H., 193
Gonzalez, J.T., 80
Goodchilds, J., 264
Goodenough, D.R., 41, 69
Goodfellow, P.N., 26
Goodman, L.A., 226
Goodman, M.J., 298
Goodman, R.L., 284
Googins, B.K., 332, 339
Gordon, M.T., 202, 203
Gordon, T., 345, 416, 420
Gore, J.C., 37
Gormally, J., 246
Gorsky, R.D., 303
Gottesfeld, K.R., 380
Gottlieb, L.S., 287
Gottman, J.M., 337
Gottman, J.S., 439, 440
Gouchie, C.T., 32
Gould, S.J., 23, 24–25
Gourdine, R.M., 142, 143
Gove, W.R., 238, 273, 278, 343
Gowing, 470
Goy, R.W., 29, 30
Graber, J.A., 247
Gradford, J., 437
Grady, W.R., 140
Graham, S.B., 8, 394
Gralinski, J.H., 89
Granger, J., 426
Granrose, C., 404
Grant, C.L., 247
Grant, L., 74, 75
Grasso, M., 392
Grauerholz, E., 206
Graves, L.M., 181
Graves, S.B., 172, 173, 174
Gray, H.M., 252
Gray, J., 369
Gray, J.D., 342
Gray-Little, B., 333, 464

Greco, M., 284
Green, 436
Greenberg, 41
Greenberg, P.E., 268
Greenberg, R.S., 281
Greenberger, E., 426
Greene, B., 267
Greeno, C.G., 110
Greenspan, M., 260
Gregory, 48
Greil, A.J., 406
Greiss, F.C., Jr., 380, 381
Gressley, D.L., 277
Greyser, 114
Grief, G.L., 442–43
Griffin, S., 383
Grimes, D.A., 287, 292
Griscom, J.L., 459
Grisso, J.A., 304
Grodsky, A., 357
Groggar, J., 141
Groneman, C., 347
Gross, T.L., 394
Grossman, F.K., 424
Grove, W.M., 269
Gruen, R.S., 366
Gruenberg, E., 238, 254
Guild, D., 214
Gundlach, J.H., 362
Gunter, B.G., 192
Gunter, N.C., 192
Guralnick, M.S., 394–95
Gutek, B.A., 172, 186, 187, 193
Gutierres, S.E., 265
Guttmann, D., 466
Guzick, D., 300
Gwartney-Gibbs, P.A., 167, 168

Haar, R.N., 234
Haber, S., 202
Habib, M., 38
Hackel, L.S., 424, 425
Hadler, S., 308
Hafner, J.L., 256
Hafner, R.J., 253, 270
Hagan, M.S., 435
Hagan, R.D., 305
Hailey, A., 398
Halberstadt, A.G., 116, 117
Hale, C.B., 323
Hall, E.G., 84
Hall, E.J., 386
Hall, E.T., 119
Hall, G.S., 59
Hall, J.A., 106, 108, 109, 112, 116, 117, 118, 119, 120
Hall, J.D., 197, 200, 201
Hall, K.P., 468, 469
Hall, P.F., 396
Hall, R.M., 75
Hallam, J., 214
Hall-McCorquodale, I., 423
Hallstrom, T., 370

Halman, L.J., 406
Halpern, D.F., 23, 38, 39, 62, 68
Hambleton, J.D., 393
Hamdorf, P.A., 313
Hamer, D.H., 40
Hammarback, S., 54
Hammer, T.J., 137
Hammersmith, S.K., 367
Hammond, D.C., 372
Hampson, E., 49
Hampton, R.L., 222
Hancock, K.A., 264
Handford, H.A., 311
Hankey, B., 281, 282, 285
Hankinson, S.E., 302
Hanlon, T., 150, 298
Hansell, S., 434, 435
Hansen, C.H., 136
Hansen, R.D., 136
Hanson, S.L., 189
Hanusa, B.H., 89
Hardin, C., 179
Harding, S., 7, 8, 9
Hardy, J.B., 144
Hardy, L.M., 388–89
Hare-Mustin, R.T., 9, 10, 17, 111, 260, 353
Hargrove, B., 473
Harner, R., 38
Harris, D., 50
Harris, P.A., 305
Harris, S.D., 285
Harris, T., 271
Harrison, D.F., 309
Harrison, J., 255
Harrison, W.M., 55
Harrop, J., 222
Hart, B., 225
Hart, N., 11
Hartmann, S.M., 2, 3, 5, 318
Harvey, O.J., 98
Haslam, M.V., 313
Hassold, T., 392
Hatcher, M.A., 177
Hatfield, A.K., 303
Hatfield, E., 323, 331, 350–51
Hatsukami, D., 271
Haude, R.H., 403
Hauth, J.C., 379
Hawkins, J., 83
Hawkins, R.C., II, 256
Hazen, C., 327
Hazlewood, A., 383
Headen, S.W., 288
Heath, A.C., 254
Heavey, C.L., 338–39
Heck, H., 405
Heckler, M., 452
Hedges, L.V., 61
Hedley, M., 458
Hedricks, C., 313
Heide, K.M., 233
Heider, F., 88
Heilbrun, A.B., 49

Heilman, M.E., 179
Heiman, J.R., 356, 372
Heinlein, L., 358
Heise, L., 203
Heister, G., 37
Heller, T., 469
Helmreich, R.L., 99, 100
Helson, R., 147, 148, 341, 342, 424, 466
Helzer, J.E., 238, 254
Hemminki, E., 300
Henderson, B.E., 302
Henderson, J., 168, 169
Henley, N.M., 9, 113, 116, 118, 120, 136
Hennekenns, C.H., 282
Hennekens, C., 302
Hennekens, C.H., 280, 299, 300, 313–14
Henshaw, S.K., 294, 297
Hensley, W.E., 178
Hepburn, C., 96
Herb, H.A., 30
Herman, C.P., 246, 249
Herman, J., 264
Herman, J.L., 217
Herzog, D.B., 252
Heshka, S., 119
Hess, E., 359
Hess, R.D., 83
Hester, M., 4
Hetherington, E.M., 441
Heyle, A.M., 446
Heyn, D., 361
Hibbard, J.H., 278
Higgenbotham, E.B., 6, 452
Higginbotham, E., 16
Higgins, C.A., 188
Hill, A.F., 184
Hill, C.A., 312
Hill, C.T., 329, 331
Hill, M., 446
Hillard, T.C., 299
Hiller, D., 341
Hillman, D., 309
Hillman, J.L., 460
Hines, M., 42, 43, 131, 132
Hingson, R., 387
Hinton, I., 445, 446
Hirsch, B.J., 138
Hirsch, M.B., 144, 297
Hirschhorn, K., 41
Hite, S., 354, 358
Hitt, M.A., 188
Ho, M.N., 287
Hobart, C., 345
Hock, E., 399, 424, 426
Hock, M.D., 426
Hoeffer, B., 440
Hofferth, S.L., 437
Hoffman, K.S., 304
Hoffman, L.W., 86, 432
Hofmeyr, G.J., 378
Hogan, H.W., 86
Hogg, M.A., 114

Hokada, E., 135
Holberg, C.J., 402
Holder, M.C., 325
Holland, D.C., 145
Holland, E.F.N., 305
Hollander, E.P., 457
Hollon, S.D., 269
Holloway, R.L., 35
Holm, K., 313
Holmberg, S.D., 309
Holmes, H.B., 409
Holmstrom, L.L., 209, 210
Holscher, L., 328
Holst, E., 296
Holtzworth-Munroe, A., 235
Hong, L.K., 153
Hood, J.N., 177, 180
Hood, K.E., 51, 54
Hood, W.E., 98
Hook, E.B., 41
hooks, b., 3, 5, 6, 416
Hoover, R., 301
Hopkins, J., 398, 400
Hopp, C., 66
Hoppe, S.W., 447
Hopper, C.H., 31
Hoptman, M.J., 39
Horgan, D., 383
Horner, M.S., 85, 86
Horney, K., 126
Horn-Ross, P.L., 281, 282,
    285, 286, 287
Hornsby-Lewis, L., 287
Horvath, D.S., 36
Hoskins, B.B., 409
Hotaling, G.T., 220, 221, 223
Hoult, J.R.S., 377, 378
Houseknecht, 339
Houseknecht, S.K., 420
Howard, D.R., 185
Howard, J.A., 336, 460, 464
Hoy, F., 183
Hoyenga, K.B., 26, 28, 29
Hoyenga, K.T., 26, 28, 29
Hoyert, D.L., 389
Hsu, J., 251
Hu, N., 40
Hu, S., 40
Huang, L.N., 448
Hubbard, R., 6, 12, 44, 191,
    386
Hubbs, J., 125
Huber, D.H., 293
Hubert, L., 32
Huddy, L., 452
Huggins, G.R., 294
Hughes, J.M., 380
Hughes, M., 238, 273, 278
Hughey, M., 393
Hulick, M., 232
Hulley, S., 290
Hummer, R.A., 206
Humphrey, L.L., 250
Hunt, L.H., 386
Hunt, M., 354, 362

Hunt, M.G., 101
Hunter, C.P., 282
Hunter, D.J., 282, 283, 302
Hunter, J.E., 61
Hunter, S., 50
Hunter, W.A., 114
Hurlbert, D.F., 370
Hurt, S.W., 51
Huson, S.M., 385
Huston, A., 103
Huston, A.C., 126
Huston, T.L., 192, 331
Hutchings, D.E., 388
Hutchison, R., 82
Hyde, J.S., 8, 63, 64, 66, 68,
    104, 105, 106, 136, 153,
    307, 351, 357, 359–60, 365,
    368, 426

Ickovics, J.R., 278, 286
Ievoli, R., 441
Iffy, L., 380
Ilowite, N.T., 286
Imershein, A., 309
Imperato-McGinley, J., 43
Ingram, R.E., 242, 243
Irving, R.H., 188
Israel, A.C., 126

Jacklin, C.N., 67, 68, 69, 106,
    108, 109, 112, 120, 133
Jackson, D., 337
Jackson, J.M., 74
Jackson, L.A., 179, 209
Jackson-Brewer, K., 329, 367,
    368
Jacobs, B.L., 32
Jacobs, D., 280
Jacobs, D.R., 247
Jacobs, G., 359
Jacobs, J.A., 272
Jacobs, J.E., 66, 76, 78
Jacobson, R.L., 389
Jadack, R.A., 307
Jagacinski, C.M., 171
James, D., 115, 116
James, M.D., 246
Jamison, W., 102
Janoff-Bulman, 396
Jarett, L.R., 48
Jarrett, S.R., 285
Jarvis, T.J., 369
Jayaratne, T.E., 8, 12, 13
Jellife, D.B., 403
Jelliffe, E.F.P., 403
Jemmott III, J.B., 52
Jendrek, M.P., 467
Jenkins, S.R., 461, 462
Jenner, F., 50
Jennings, M.K., 452
Jensen, B.K., 50
Jensen, G., 171
Jensen, I.W., 187
Jensen, L.C., 363, 433
Jernberg, A.M., 400

Jessor, R., 140
Jimenez, E., 389
John, E.M., 282
John, O.P., 147
Johnson, B., 394–95
Johnson, B.R., 242, 243
Johnson, B.T., 469
Johnson, C., 250, 303
Johnson, C.B., 187
Johnson, C.L., 153
Johnson, D.R., 340
Johnson, J.D., 209
Johnson, L., 184
Johnson, S., 62, 406
Johnson, V.E., 351, 353, 355,
    369, 370, 371, 373
Johnston, I.K., 52
Jolin, A., 220
Jones, D.C., 318, 322
Jones, E.F., 142
Jorgensen, S.H., 394–95
Jorgensen, S.R., 338, 447
Jose, P.E., 469
Joseph, G., 440
Joshi, A.K., 394–95
Jost, A., 27
Joyner, D.J., 136

Kaczorowski, J., 394–95
Kahn, A.J., 141, 142, 143
Kahn, A.S., 17, 18, 20, 199
Kahn, H., 404
Kahn, J.R., 339, 340
Kahn, M.J., 368
Kalichman, S.C., 102
Kalisch, B., 136
Kalisch, P., 136
Kalousek, D.K., 380
Kamerman, S.B., 141, 142,
    143
Kane, T.T., 387
Kanter, R.M., 171
Kantner, J.F., 354
Kaplan, B.J., 396–97
Kaplan, E., 189
Kaplan, H.S., 371
Kaplan, J.R., 30
Karau, S.J., 468, 470
Kariuki, P., 466
Karp, S.A., 69
Karraker, K.H., 131
Katz, L., 37
Kaufman, F.R., 42
Kayne, H., 387
Kazdin, A.E., 140
Keefe, M.S., 305
Kegeles, S., 290
Keita, G.P., 226, 237, 261
Keith, B., 434
Keith, J.B., 363
Keith, L.G., 387
Keith-Spiegel, P., 263
Keller, E.F., 7
Keller, M., 388, 389
Keller, M.B., 252

Keller, M.L., 307
Kelley, K., 350
Kelly, C., 129
Kelly, E.L., 341
Kelly, M.P., 355, 372
Kelly-Gadol, J., 347
Kelsey, J.L., 281, 282, 285,
    286, 287, 304
Kelsey, S.F., 150, 300
Kemmann, E., 303–4
Kenardy, J., 271
Kendall-Tackett, K., 217
Kendell, R.E., 398
Kendler, K.S., 254
Kenrick, D.T., 28
Kephart, G., 324
Kephart, W., 331
Kerns, J.G., 368
Kessler, R., 239
Kessler, R.C., 254
Ketcham, A.S., 285
Key, T., 379
Keyser, H.H., 380
Khalil, R., 38
Khan, F.Y., 300–301
Kibria, N., 272
Kiernan, M., 445, 446
Kiesler, S.B., 98
Killian, L.M., 3
Kilpatrick, D.G., 204
Kim, M., 183
Kim, Y.J., 141
Kimball, M.M., 65
Kimball, P., 213
Kimble, G.A., 25
Kimura, D., 32, 37, 49
King, T.M., 145, 387
Kinghorn, E., 39
Kingston, P.W., 427
Kinsey, A.C., 354, 356, 357,
    361, 365, 367
Kipnis, D., 460
Kircher, J.R., 355, 372
Kirkpatrick, L.A., 327
Kirz, D.S., 391
Kiselev, P., 389
Kishwar, M., 409
Kitano, H.H.L., 448
Kite, M.E., 151, 368
Kitzinger, C., 366
Kitzinger, S., 370, 404
Klassen, A.D., 255, 257
Klatt, N.E., 303
Klebanoff, M.A., 387
Klebanov, P.K., 52
Kleck, G., 207, 208
Klein, E., 438
Klein, F., 366
Klein, M.C., 394–95
Klein, R.D., 4
Kleinke, C.L., 209
Klerman, G.L., 241
Klonoff, E.A., 10, 11
Klonsky, B.G., 471
Knight, R.A., 208, 211

Knussmann, R., 33
Koberg, C.S., 177, 180
Koch, G.G., 288, 311
Koch, P.B., 168, 169
Koestner, R., 134
Koh, S.C.L., 292
Kohen, J.A., 342
Kohlberg, 110, 155
Kohlberg, L., 109, 127
Kolbe, R., 135
Kolbert, E., 184
Koller, S., 378
Komnenich, P., 50
Konar, E., 177
Koopman, J.S., 402
Koopmans, L.H., 34
Koplan, J.P., 303
Koran, L.M., 271
Koritnik, D., 30
Korvick, J.A., 309
Koss, M.P., 197, 198, 199, 200,
    203, 204, 205, 207, 208,
    210, 211, 212, 226
Koss, P.G., 205
Kowalski, R.M., 105
Krajnik, M., 151
Kramer, M., 241
Kramer, P.D., 268
Kramer, P.E., 83
Kranczer, 278, 279
Krausher, J.R., 53
Kreisberg, S., 472, 473
Krieger, F.W., 401
Krishan, B., 311
Kroft, C., 256
Krueger, S., 263
Krzyczkowska-Mercer, 176
Kubler, W., 382
Kuhns, J.B., 233
Kulch, P., 384
Kuller, L.H., 150, 300
Kumar, R., 400
Kuppersmith, J., 438
Kurdek, L.A., 334, 335, 338,
    464
Kurth, S., 189
Kurtines, W.M., 17
Kurtz, R.C., 287

La Barba, R.C., 38
Lach, D.H., 167, 168
Lackman, C., 309
Lacour, J., 284
Lader, L., 298
Ladner, J.A., 13, 142
Laessle, R.G., 249
LaFerla, J.J., 383
Lafferty, F.W., 302–3
LaFramboise, T.D., 265, 266,
    446
LaFrance, M., 112
La Free, G.D., 200
LaGory, M., 278
Lakoff, R.T., 113
Lamaze, F., 393

Lambert, H.H., 23
Lamon, S.J., 63, 64
Land, H., 344, 441
Landau, C., 299
Lander, L., 47
Landers, D., 50
Landis, S.E., 311
Landis, T., 37
Landowski, 401
Landrine, H., 10, 11, 95
Landry, B., 467
Landry, D.J., 324
Lane, D.M., 50
Lane, M.J., 281
Lang, E.L., 242, 425
Langer, A., 380, 381
Langer, E.J., 154, 383
LaPann, B.A., 304
Lapinski, R.H., 391
Larntz, K., 186
LaRosa, J.C., 300
Larsen, S., 300–301
Lasker, J.N., 407
Lasley, J.H., 435–36
Lauer, 337
Laumann, E.O., 354, 355,
    356, 358, 361, 374
LaVecchia, C., 290
LaVoie, J., 135
Lavori, P.W., 252
Lawrence, R.A., 370, 401
Laws, J.L., 367
Laxova, R., 407
Le, M.G., 284
Leaf, P.J., 241
Leahy, T., 138
Leather, A.T., 305
Leber, D., 467
Lederberg, V.S., 190, 419
Lee, C., 212
Lee, J.A., 168
Lee, L., 288
Lee-Huang, S., 293
Leenaars, A.A., 254
LeFevre, M.L., 385
Lehman, E.C., Jr., 473
Lehman, S., 83
Leichner, P., 256
Leigh, 359
Leitenberg, H., 270
Leitko, T.A., 406
Leland, C., 471
Lenney, E., 87
Lennon, M.C., 256, 257, 272
Lennon, R., 112, 113, 119
Lensky, D.B., 107
Leonard, 40, 436
Lerma, M., 326
Lerner, M., 209
Leslie, 191
Lesser, M.L., 284
Lester, R.M., 107
Leung, M.L.A., 16
LeVay, S., 40

Leveille, G.A., 402
Levenson, R.W., 337
Levenson, S.M., 387
Leventhal, J.M., 402–3
Levin, H., 114
Levine, J.J., 286
Levine, M.P., 247
Levine, P., 309
Levine-MacCombie, J., 207,
    208
Levit, D.B., 139
Levy, D., 212
Levy, G.D., 132
Levy, J., 38
Levy, J.A., 400
Levy, K.B., 50
Lewandowski, G.E., 401
Lewin, M., 206
Lewin, T., 388, 389
Lewis, K., 311
Lewis, K.E., 456
Lewis, L.L., 96
Lewis, V.G., 42
Lia-Hoagberg, B., 390, 391
Libby, M.N., 132
Liben, L.S., 127
Lichter, D.T., 324
Lichtman, R.R., 285
Lieberman, E., 390
Liff, J.M., 281
Lightdale, J.R., 105, 130
Lightfoot-Klein, H., 353, 354
Lindblad-Goldberg, M.,
    435–36
Lindheim, S.R., 300–301
Lindner, M.S., 435
Linn, M.C., 8, 65, 68, 69, 70,
    72
Linton, K., 293
Linz, D., 214, 215
Lipkin, J., 250
Lipkus, I., 334–35
Lippa, R., 98
Lips, H.M., 397, 452, 453
Lisak, D., 202, 203, 211
Little, T.D., 247
Livesey, J.H., 55
Livingston, J.A., 184
Lobel, K., 225
Lobel, M., 398
Lobel, T.E., 134
Lobo, R.A., 300–301
Localio, R., 264
Lockheed, M.E., 83, 468, 469
Locksley, A., 96
Loftus, 218
Logan, J., 7
Lombardo, B., 112
Lombardo, W.K., 112
London, K.A., 144, 289, 339,
    340
Long, B., 117
Long, J.S., 175
Longnecker, M.P., 282
Lopata, H.Z., 321

Loprinzi, C.L., 303
Lorde, A., 199–200, 423
Lorentz, P., 383
Loring, M., 59
Lott, B., 16, 185, 468
Louis, T.A., 309
Lovell, M., 38
Lowe, M.R., 246
Lowery, C.R., 110
Lowinsky, N.R., 415
Luchetta, T., 15
Luepker, R., 280
Lugones, M.C., 7
Luini, A., 284
Lull, J., 136
Lum, C.U., 399
Lummis, A., 473
Lundsteen, C., 41
Lupe, P.J., 394
Luskey, G.W., 394–95
Luthra, 475
Lutz, W., 340, 399, 424
Lydon, J., 294, 295
Lykes, M.B., 475–76
Lynn, M., 145
Lyon, P., 264
Lyons, N.P., 137
Lyons-Rowe, S., 364
Lytton, H., 131

McAdams, D.P., 107, 317
McAdoo, H.P., 444
McBair, M.C., 29, 30
McCabe, M.P., 369
McCarthy, W.J., 469
McCartney, K., 417, 428
McCarty, P.A., 87
McClanahan, S.S., 271
McClelland, D.C., 85
McClintock, M.K., 46
Maccoby, E.E., 67, 68, 69,
    106, 108, 109, 110, 112,
    120, 133
McComb, H.G., 78
MacCorquodale, P., 171,
    348
McCoy, M.L., 350
McCreary, C., 363
McCreary, L., 166, 167, 168
McEachern, L., 243
McElin, T., 393
MacEwen, 428
McFarland, C., 51
McFarlane, J.M., 52
McFarlane, T., 246
McFarlin, D., 176
McFate, K., 437–38
McGrath, E., 237, 261
MacGreagor, S.N., 387
McGuire, J., 243
McGuire, W.L., 284
McHugh, M.C., 89, 465, 466
MacKay, H.T., 380, 381
McKeganey, N., 310

McKenry, P.C., 339, 342–43, 344, 433, 441–442
MacKenzie, I.Z., 385
Mackey, M., 392–93
McKinlay, J.B., 148, 149
McKinlay, S.M., 148, 149
McKinley, N.M., 426
MacKinnon, C.A., 5, 213, 220
McLanahan, S., 424
McLaughlin, K.K., 324
McLaughlin, S.D., 143
MacLeod, M., 75
McManus, I.C., 33
McMurray, D.M., 405
McNall, M., 82
McNally, R.J., 263, 270
McNamara, W.J., 107
McNellis, D., 385
McRae, J., 397
McRae, J.A., 342, 389, 390
McVicar, D.M., 453
McVicar, N., 314
Madison, 386
Magnuson, V.L., 40
Magnusson, D., 137
Magre, S., 27
Mahoney, M.A., 9
Maislin, G., 304
Major, B., 118, 177, 179, 191, 296
Major, B.N., 295, 296
Makhijani, M.G., 470, 471
Makino, M., 41
Malamuth, N.M., 202, 211, 214
Malatesta, C.Z., 404
Malin, M., 300
Malinchoc, M., 244
Mandel, R.B., 455
Manderscheid, R.W., 238
Maneros, A., 400
Manis, M., 96, 97
Mann, J., 291, 292
Mann, R.D., 468, 469
Manninen, D.L., 143
Mansell, J.P., 305
Mansfield, P.K., 168, 169, 391, 392
Manson, J.E., 282, 299, 300, 302, 313–14
Marazziti, D., 32
Marcos, E.F., 378
Marcuse, M., 398, 400
Marcum, J.P., 464
Marecek, J., 9, 10, 17, 111, 353
Margolies, E., 421–22
Margolies, L., 329, 367, 368
Margolin, G., 279
Margolis, G., 284
Marin, B., 290
Markides, K.S., 447
Marks, M.N., 399
Marshall, G.N., 242
Marshall, N.L., 188, 272

Marshall, R.S., 83
Marston, A.R., 247
Martin, B.A., 177
Martin, C.E., 354, 356, 357, 361, 365, 367
Martin, C.L., 98
Martin, D., 264
Martin, H.W., 447
Martin, P.Y., 206
Martin, T.C., 441
Martinez, E.A., 447
Martinez, F.D., 402
Martinez, G.A., 401
Maruyama, G., 97
Masson, J., 215, 216
Masterpasqua, F., 440
Masters, W.H., 351, 353, 355, 369, 370, 371, 373
Mastroiacovo, P., 385
Mathie, V.A., 199
Mathis, S.L., 112
Matthaei, J., 82, 157, 158, 159, 161, 162, 164, 165
Matthews, K.A., 149, 150, 300
Maurer, L., 226, 228
Mauro, 295
Maxwell, S., 281
May, S.A., 453, 456
Mayes, S.D., 311
Mays, V.M., 310
Meadow, A., 260
Mechaneck, R., 438
Mechanic, D., 434, 435
Medcalf, K.L., 102
Mednick, M.T., 8, 86, 110–11
Mednick, S.A., 41
Messé, 373
Megargee, E.I., 467
Mehl, L., 397
Meilahn, E.N., 150
Melnick, S.L., 309
Menning, B.E., 406
Merson, M., 284
Metcalf, M.G., 55
Metzger, L.S., 282
Meyer, B.M., 305
Meyer, C.B., 209, 210
Meyer, J., 13–14
Meyer-Bahlburg, H.F.L., 40, 366
Micevych, P., 27
Michael, R.T., 354, 355, 356, 358, 361, 374
Michael-Good, L., 311
Michaels, S., 354, 355, 356, 358, 361, 374
Michalak, J.C., 303
Michelman, D.F., 401
Mickelson, R.A., 79
Miele, M., 151
Milburn, N., 239
Miles, C.C., 99
Milgram, 14
Mill, J.S., 1

Millar, H.R., 251
Millard, A.V., 404
Miller, J.B., 8, 242, 261, 459–60, 472
Miller, V.T., 300
Miller, W.B., 295, 296
Miller, W.E., 369
Millet, K., 125
Minas, A., 182
Minden, S.L., 296
Minton, H.L., 107, 108
Miranda, R., 405
Mirande, A., 447
Mirowsky, J., 241, 242
Mishell, D.R., 303
Mitchell, B.F., 378
Mitchell, J.E., 270
Mitchell, V., 148, 341, 342, 424, 466
Mittal, M., 311
Miura, I.T., 83
Mladinic, A., 95
Moane, G., 341, 342, 424
Moen, P., 41, 439
Moesel, D., 188
Moffat, F.L., Jr., 285
Moghissi, K.S., 407
Mogul, K.M., 264
Mohan, P.J., 420
Molina, M.L.P., 4
Molitar, N., 428
Moller, L.C., 134
Molm, L.D., 458
Monaghan, E.P., 30, 31, 189, 421
Money, J., 28, 39, 42, 367, 451
Monto, A.S., 402
Moody, H., 220
Mooney, L., 135
Moore, D.E., 288, 406
Moore, M.L., 317–18
Moore, N.B., 142, 144
Moorehouse, M.J., 427
Morahan-Martin, J., 418
Morasch, B., 186
Morash, M., 234
Morawski, J.G., 59, 100
Morgan, C.S., 419
Morgan, K.C., 426
Morgan, L.A., 153
Morgen, S., 180, 474
Morokoff, P.J., 356, 371, 372
Morris, R., 31
Morrison, A.M., 175, 176, 180
Morrison, S.K., 117
Morrison, T., 6
Morriss, K.G.M., 385
Morrow, J., 178
Morrow-Tlucak, M., 403
Mosher, D.L., 350
Mosher, W.D., 313
Moulton, A.W., 299
Moye, J., 389
Moyer, K.E., 105

Moyers, B., 443
Moynihan, D.P., 443
Muehlenhard, C.L., 198, 209, 211, 350
Mueller, C., 452
Muesing, R.A., 300
Mulac, A., 114, 115
Mulder, E.J.H., 39
Mullis, J., 278
Muntjewerff, M.W., 29
Murdock, T., 209
Murdock, T.B., 209, 210
Murphy, J., 409–10
Murphy, L., 261
Murphy, M., 291, 292
Murphy, N., 405
Murray, L., 400
Murrell, A.J., 81
Murthy, S., 293
Muskie, E., 112
Muss, H., 281, 282, 285
Myers, D.G., 97
Myers, J.K., 241
Myers, S.T., 402

Nachtigall, L.E., 304
Naldi, L., 290, 293
Nanko, S., 41
Nasser, M., 249
Natividad, I., 454
Navaie, M., 388, 389
Naylor, C.E., 36
Naylor, G., 6
Neale, M.C., 254
Nee, J., 55
Neff, R.K., 390
Neifert, M.R., 405
Neighbors, H., 239
Nekolny, K., 425
Nelson, D.L., 187, 188
Nelson, K.K., 392
Nelson, T.E., 96
Nelson, Y., 119
Nemeth, C.J., 469
Neuwalder, H.F., 366
Neville, M.C., 405
Newman, J., 451, 453, 454
Newman, V., 379
Newton, T., 251
Nezlek, J., 322
Nice, V.E., 422
Nichols, D.H., 287, 305, 306, 307
Nicholson, M.E., 281
Nicolaides, K., 384, 385
Nicola-McLaughlin, A., 475
Nicolson, P., 46
Nieminen, M., 340
Noble, K.D., 84
Nock, S.L., 427
Nolen-Hoeksema, S., 88, 241
Noller, P., 326
Noriega, V., 285
Norman, R.Z., 115, 178
Norris, A.E., 144, 145

Norsigian, J., 290, 292, 293
North, C.S., 239, 240
Northcutt, C.A., 147
Norton, E.H., 3
Notelovitz, M., 300–301
Notman, M.T., 296
Nsiah-Jefferson, L., 386
Nugent, R.P., 387
Nyborg, H., 32
Nyquist, L.V., 467, 468

Oatout, H.A., 327
O'Boyle, M.W., 38
O'Brien, M., 126
O'Brien, M.J., 287
O'Brien, P.H., 207, 208
O'Brien, T.R., 309
O'Briien, L.A., 304
O'Connell, L., 189
O'Connor, E., 313
O'Connor, P., 318, 320, 321
Oden, M.H., 62, 84
O'Driscoll, K., 395, 396
O'Fallon, J.R., 303
Offerman, 470
Offord, K.P., 244
Oggins, J., 467
Ogletree, S.M., 84, 453, 456
O'Grady, K.E., 363
Ogur, B., 268
O'Hanley, K., 293
O'Hara, M.W., 398, 400
O'Heron, C.A., 101
Okazaki, S., 82
O'Leary, K.D., 221
Oliker, S.J., 320
Oliva, A., 38
Oliver, M.B., 351, 357, 359–60, 365, 368
Olkin, I., 61
Olsen, J.A., 363
Olson, J.E., 190
Olson, L.R., 289
O'Neill, E., 389
O'Neill, H.K., 373
Ooms, T., 189
Orarte, S., 264
Orlofsky, J.L., 101
O'Rourke, S., 388, 389
Orvaschel, H., 241
Orvashel, H., 238, 254
O'Shaughnessy, M., 250
Osmond, M.W., 309
Osofsky, J.D., 400
Ospina, 40, 436
Ostrove, J.M., 148
O'Sullivan, M.J., 389
Otten, C.M., 26
Otto, S., 95
Owen, D.R., 41
Oxman, G., 308
Oz, S., 142
Ozer, E.J., 446

Pabst, M.S., 442–43
Padawar, J.A., 396
Padesky, C., 335
Padilla, E.R., 363
Page, S., 259
Paige, J.M., 137
Paige, K.E., 137
Paikoff, R.L., 247
Paisley, K.J., 243
Paisley, W., 136
Palego, L., 32
Palmer, H.T., 168
Palmer, J.R., 282
Paludi, M.A., 86
Pancioli-Guadagnucci, M.L., 32
Panish, J.F., 287
Pansky, M., 381
Parazzini, F., 290
Pardie, L., 15
Parker, J., 379
Parker, R., Jr., 379
Parker, S., 387
Parker, V. E., 197
Parkhurst, S., 404
Parlee, M.B., 50
Parron, D.L., 238, 255
Parsons, T., 94
Patel, F., 384
Pateman, 220
Paterson, H.F., 69
Pattatucci, A.M.L., 40
Patterson, C.J., 439, 440
Patterson, E.T., 390
Patton, L.L., 393
Paul, E.F., 182
Paulsen, 40, 436
Pearlman, S.E., 321
Pellegrino, J.W., 32
Penhall, R.K., 313
Penrod, S., 214
Peplau, 462–64
Peplau, L.A., 6, 7, 264, 318, 329, 331, 335, 460
Perkins, K., 151
Perl, M., 271
Perlman, D., 348
Perlmutter, C., 150, 298
Perlstadt, H., 171
Perroni, L., 392
Persson, I., 301
Perusse, D., 45
Petersen, A.C., 65, 69, 70, 72, 137
Peterson, C., 320
Peterson, D.L., 136
Peterson, G., 397
Peterson, H.B., 303
Peterson, J., 290
Peterson, R.E., 43
Peterson, R.R., 193, 194
Pett, M.A., 372
Peveler, R., 256
Pfost, K.S., 136, 399
Phelps, J.L., 198

Pheterson, G.I., 98
Philip, J., 41
Philippe, E., 380
Philips, J.B., III, 379
Philliber, W., 144, 341
Phillips, 428
Phillips, C., 392
Phillips, D.A., 437
Phillips, W.R.F., 171
Piaget, J., 109, 127, 155
Pianta, R.C., 244
Piasecki, J., 269
Piedmont, R.L., 86
Pierce, J.P., 288
Pierce, K., 135
Pierluigi, M., 392
Pike, M.C., 302
Pines, A.M., 215, 219
Pingree, S., 136
Pirie, P., 280
Pirke, K.M., 249
Plant, M.A., 309
Pleck, J.H., 191, 272
Plomin, R., 25
Plunkett, E.R., 298, 299, 301
Podell, K., 38
Poelmann-Weesjes, G., 39
Polakow, V., 432
Poland, B.J., 380
Polatnick, M.R., 419
Polivy, J., 246, 249
Polk, G.C., 205
Polonsky, S., 218
Pomeroy, C., 271
Pomeroy, W.B., 354, 356, 357, 361, 365, 367
Pope, C.R., 278
Pope, K.S., 263
Porat, N., 225
Porter, L.K., 406
Porter, M.E., 40
Posner, B.M., 314
Potter, L.S., 291
Potterat, J., 308
Potts, J.F., 307
Potts, M., 282, 290, 293
Pouilles, J.M., 305
Powch, I.G., 198
Powell, B., 59
Powell, G.N., 176, 181
Powlishta, K.K., 134
Pozo, C., 285
Pratt, C.C., 150, 423
Prechtl, H.F.R., 39
Prentice, D.A., 105, 130
Prentky, R.A., 211
Presta, S., 32
Preston, K.E., 52
Price, S.J., 339, 342–43, 344, 433
Pugh, K.R., 37
Purcell, P., 135
Purifoy, F.E., 34, 357
Putnam, F.W., 217
Pyle, R.L., 271

Quadagno, D., 355, 358
Quadagno, D.M., 309
Quella, S.K., 303
Quick, J.C., 188
Quina, K., 113
Quinsey, V.L., 211, 214

Radan, A., 475–76
Raeburn, S.D., 271
Rafsnider, E., 402
Rahat, M.A., 287
Ramirez, A.J., 285
Ramos, A.A., 294
Rao, K.V., 340
Rardin, D., 246
Raskin, P.A., 126
Rasmussen, N., 296
Rassin, D.D., 403
Ratnam, S.S., 292
Raudenbush, S.W., 188, 272
Raven, B., 457
Rawlings, E.I., 261
Rawlings, J.S., 390
Rawlings, V.B., 390
Raymond, J.G., 410
Razack, S., 201
Read, J.A., 390
Read, S.J., 326
Reardon, K., 293
Reddan, W., 305
Regard, M., 37
Regis, J., 38
Reich, R., 308
Reid, B.V., 123
Reid, P.T., 11, 17, 132, 474
Reifman, A., 425
Reiger, D.A., 238, 254
Reigle, N., 223
Reilly, M.E., 185
Reinharz, S., 13, 15, 17
Reinisch, J.M., 312
Reis, H., 322
Reisman, J.M., 320
Rejeski, W.J., 30
Reneau, P., 281
Renzetti, C.M., 225
Resick, P.A., 210, 211
Rest, R., 110
Reuther, R.R., 473
Rexroat, C., 193
Reynolds, P., 281, 282, 285
Reynolds, R.W., 32
Reynosa, T.C., 143
Rhees, R.W., 39
Rhode, A., 399–400
Rhode, N., 273
Rhodes, D., 15
Rhodes, P., 284
Ribot, C., 305
Rich, A., 415, 416, 458
Richards, M.A., 285
Richardson, C.J., 403
Richardson, J.T.E., 46, 48
Richardson, M.T., 281
Richter, R., 145

Rickels, K., 54, 270
Ridgeway, C., 130
Ries, P., 453
Riger, S., 7, 10, 12, 16, 17, 202, 203
Riggio, S., 38
Riggs, D.S., 209, 210, 221
Riis, B.J., 300
Riley, M.E., 117
Rilke, F., 284
Ritchey, F.J., 278
Rivera-Tovar, A., 51
Robbins, J.M., 394–95
Robbins, L.N., 238, 254
Robert, N.J., 303
Roberts, T., 88
Robertson, M.J., 255
Robinson, A.B., 110
Robinson, C.R., 454
Robinson, D.S., 285
Robinson, P.M., 363
Robinson-Stavely, K., 83, 84
Rochard, F., 284
Rodigues-Canteras, et al., 302
Rodriguez, E.M., 309
Rodin, J., 154, 155, 245, 248, 249, 278, 286
Rodin, M., 50, 51
Rodriquez, C., Jr., 142, 144
Rogan, W.J., 403
Rogers, A., 137
Rogers, P.L., 119, 120
Rohsenow, D.J., 255
Rollins, 474
Rollins, D.E., 387
Rollins, J., 289
Rollins, J.H., 189, 223, 261, 403–4, 419
Romney, D.M., 131
Romond, J.L., 394
Rook, D., 335
Rook, K.S., 152
Root, M.P.P., 251–52
Ropers, H.H., 26
Rorty, M., 218
Rose, H., 1, 416
Rose, M., 180
Rosen, J.C., 270
Rosen, L.A., 434
Rosen, L.R., 366
Rosen, P.P., 284
Rosen, R.H., 418
Rosenbaum, M., 257
Rosenberg, J., 171
Rosenberg, L., 282
Rosenblum, L., 308
Rosenholtz, S.J., 130
Rosenkrantz, P.S., 94, 114, 259
Rosenthal, A., 60, 184
Rosenthal, R., 61, 62, 114, 119
Rosenwasser, S.M., 193, 456

Rosner, B., 280, 282, 299, 300, 302, 313–14
Ross, C., 135
Ross, C.E., 191, 241, 242, 464
Ross, M., 51, 222
Ross, R.K., 302
Ross, S.I., 74
Rossing, M.A., 288
Rossiter, E.M., 271
Roth, S.H., 295, 296
Rothbaum, B.O., 209, 210
Rothenberg, P.S., 158
Rotheram-Borus, M.J., 139
Rothman, A.J., 180
Rothman, B.K., 12, 417, 419
Rotondo, A., 32
Rotter, J.B., 241
Rousso, H., 329, 351
Rovine, M.J., 428
Rowan-Szal, G.A., 262
Rowe, A., 471
Rowe, R.C., 211
Rowland, R., 4
Rozee-Koker, P., 205
Rozin, P., 323
Ruback, R.B., 31
Rubenstein, C.R., 370
Rubin, A., 284
Rubin, D.B., 41
Rubin, L.J., 185
Rubin, Z., 329, 331
Rubio-Stipec, M., 241
Ruble, D., 50
Ruble, D.N., 127, 398, 424, 425
Rucker, L., 234
Ruddick, S., 424
Rumley, R.E., 55
Rupp, A., 23
Rupp, L.J., 2
Rusbult, C.E., 334–35
Rush, D., 401
Russell, D.E.H., 15, 207, 216, 217
Russell, M.J., 48
Russo, N.F., 226, 237, 238, 239, 261, 265, 266, 268, 295, 296, 418
Russo, N.P., 203
Rutter, M., 24
Ryan, A.S., 401
Ryan, M., 66
Ryding, E.L., 369
Ryff, C., 242, 273

Saal, F.E., 186, 187
Sable, P., 253–54
Sabourin, S., 333
Sacchi, N., 392
Sacchini, V., 284
Saccozzi, R., 284
Sachs, D., 383
Sacks, N.R., 252
Sadd, S., 355, 361, 373
Sadker, D., 73, 74

Sadker, M., 73, 74
Sagrestano, L.M., 458
St. Andre, E., 29
St. Clair, P.A., 410
St. Lawrence, J.S., 136
Saito, S., 41
Salamon, G., 38
Salgado De Snyder, V.N., 267
Salvadori, B., 284
Samelson, L., 304
Samuelsson, S., 370
Sanchez-Ayendez, M., 447
Sanday, P.R., 202–3, 206
Sandelowski, M., 385, 396, 410
Sanders, C.M., 152, 153
Sanders, S.A., 312
Sanders, S.S., 407
Sandler, B.R., 75
Sangiorgio, M., 150, 298
Santrock, J.W., 435, 441
Sapolsky, S., 136
Saravia, N.G., 405
Sarrazin, D., 284
Sarti, D.A., 384
Saunders, L., 370, 392
Savio, T., 284
Saxena, B.B., 380
Saxton, M., 386
Sayers, S.L., 339
Sayles, S., 207, 208
Sayre, A., 174
Scanzoni, J.H., 467
Scarr, S., 429
Schachter, S., 284
Schaefer, F., 23
Schaefer, J.H., 311
Schaffer, M.A., 390, 391
Schairer, C., 301
Schapiro, M., 287
Scheier, M.F., 285
Schein, V.E., 180
Schiavi, R.C., 372
Schiebinger, L., 6
Schiff, I., 287, 305, 306, 307
Schill, T., 322
Schilling, R.F., 310–11
Schirtzinger, M.B., 399, 424
Schmidlin, A.M., 118
Schmidt, F.L., 61
Schmidt, H., 23
Schmitt, J.P., 335, 464
Schmittroth, L., 175
Schneider, B.E., 185, 186, 235
Schneider, F.W., 107, 108
Schneider, J.A., 271
Schnicke, M.K., 210, 211
Schnurr, P.P., 51
Schoenbach, V.J., 311
Scholey, S., 401
Schraer, R., 49
Schreiner-Engel, P., 372
Schroeder, P., 112, 471
Schroeder-Heister, P., 37
Schuerger, J.M., 223

Schuller, R.A., 179
Schulman, P., 244
Schulsinger, F., 41
Schur, B.E., 257
Schuster, D.T., 84, 85
Schwartz, D., 245, 323
Schwartz, P., 336, 358, 361, 367, 460, 464
Schweizer, E., 269–70
Scorpio, E., 403–4
Scott, G., 389
Scott, W.J., 419
Scrimshaw, C.M., 398
Sears, D.O., 452
Sears, H.A., 187
Seebach, L., 432
Segrist, D., 15
Seibel, C.A., 204
Selby, J.W., 393
Self, S.G., 288
Seligman, M.E.P., 230, 244
Sells, L.W., 66, 67
Seltzer, R., 368
Senie, R.T., 284
Serbin, L.A., 75, 134
Serdula, M.K., 281
Serdula, M.K., 281
Severino, S.K., 51
Sgoutas, D.S., 31
Shachar, R., 333
Shankweller, D.P., 37
Shanley, M.L., 408, 409
Shannon, B., 398
Shapiro, E.D., 402–3
Shaver, P., 327
Shaw, J.S., 191
Shaywitz, B.A., 37
Shaywitz, S.E., 37
Shearer, W., 389
Sheehan, D.L., 253
Shehan, 191, 193
Sheley, J.F., 191
Shelton, B.A., 161, 190
Sherer, R., 309
Sherif, C.W., 12, 17, 98, 111, 129
Sherman, J., 63
Sherman, L.W., 228
Sherman, S., 392
Shields, S.A., 62, 112
Shike, M., 287
Shiono, P.H., 387
Shoken-Topaz, T., 134
Sholomskas, D., 427
Short, D.D., 268
Shotland, R.L., 187
Shotter, J., 7
Shoupe, D., 303
Shragg, P.G., 143
Shrout, P., 241
Shugar, G., 263
Shute, V.J., 32
Siantz, M.L.De L., 447
Siegel, D., 290
Siegel, J.M., 201, 205, 210, 240

Signorella, M.L., 102
Sikes, K., 308
Silberg, J., 24
Silberstein, L.R., 245, 248, 249
Silbert, M.H., 215, 219
Sillero-Arenas, M., 302
Silling, S.M., 83
Silman, A.J., 305
Silva, R.A., 403
Silver, R.C., 342
Silverman, I., 233
Silverstein, L.B., 425, 427, 432
Simenauer, J., 328
Simkims-Bullock, J.A., 114
Simon, B.L., 331, 332
Simonoff, E., 24
Simpson, D.D., 262
Simpson, J.A., 326–27, 331, 360
Singer, J.M., 66, 67
Singer, R.D., 247
Singh, D., 323
Singh, K., 292
Singh, M., 380
Sitterle, K.A., 441
Six, B., 95, 96
Sjussman, S., 314
Skolnick, P., 119
Skovron, M.L., 391
Skudlarski, P., 37
Skuldt-Niederberger, K., 151
Slade, P.L., 50, 251
Slob, A.K., 29
Slovik, L.F., 334–35
Smith, A., 117
Smith, C.P., 363
Smith, D.W., 386
Smith, E.A., 145
Smith, E.L., 305
Smith, E.M., 239, 240
Smith, J., 302, 303
Smith, J.B., 387
Smith, M., 144
Smith, P.E., 305
Smith, P.L., 183
Smits, S.L., 183
Smolak, L., 247
Snell, W.E., Jr., 256
Snijders, R., 384, 385
Snyder, D., 212
Sockloskie, R.J., 211
Sohi, B.K., 265, 266
Sohn, D., 89
Sokol, R.J., 386
Sommer, B., 49, 50
Sondheimer, S.J., 54
Sonenstein, F.L., 431, 437
Sonnenschein, M.A., 238
Sorensen, G., 280
Sorenson, S.B., 201, 205, 210, 240
South, S.J., 200, 201, 323–24
Spadoni, L., 406

Spanier, 339
Sparano, J.A., 303
Spector, I.P., 372
Spector, T.D., 305
Speisman, J.C., 337
Speizer, F.E., 282, 299, 300, 302
Spelman, E.V., 7
Spence, J.T., 99, 100, 128, 467, 468
Sperling, R.S., 389
Sperry, R.W., 35
Spielmann, M., 284
Spitznagel, E.L., 239
Sprecher, S., 323, 331, 462–64
Spritzer, S., 348
Srebnik, D., 270
Stack, S., 362
Stacy, A.W., 314
Stake, J.E., 66, 67
Stampfer, M.J., 282, 299, 300, 302, 314
Stangor, C., 98, 127, 398, 424
Stanley, J.C., 63, 66
Stanton, A.L., 249
Staples, R., 328, 333, 447
Stapp, 99, 100
Starr, B.D., 371
Stasiulis, D.K., 159
Steckler, N., 114
Steege, J.F., 53
Steffen, V.J., 104, 105, 106
Steffensmeier, A.H., 254
Steil, J.M., 190, 460
Stein, A., 403
Stein, J.A., 205, 210, 240
Stein, R.T., 469
Steinberg, K.K., 302, 303
Steinmann, A., 324
Steinmetz, S.K., 222
Steptoe, P., 409
Stern, M., 131
Sternberg, S.S., 287
Stevens, D., 437
Stevens, M.J., 399
Stevenson, J.C., 299
Steward, E.T., 287
Stewart, A.J., 8, 12, 13, 107, 148
Stewart, C.J., 298
Stewart, D., 138
Stewart, L., 135
Stewart, R.J., 396
Stierlin, H., 250–51
Stiglin, L.E., 268
Stiles, D.A., 145
Stillion, J.M., 254
Stillman, R.J., 300
Stipek, D.J., 89
Stockard, J., 65
Stockdale, M.S., 187
Stocking, M., 41
Stolberg, R., 241
Stolley, K.S., 144
Stoltzman, R., 241

Stombler, M., 206
Stone, 50
Stone, A.J., 453
Stoppard, J.M., 243
Storer, J.H., 216
Stotland, N.L., 297
Stout, A.L., 53
Stoy, D.B., 300
Strassberg, D.S., 355, 372
Strattin, H., 137
Stratton, J., 348
Stratton, P., 389
Straus, M., 222, 227, 231
Straus, M.A., 198, 203, 204, 222
Streett, R., 144
Stricker, G., 259
Strickland, B.R., 237, 261, 278, 288, 396
Strickler, J., 293, 294
Striegel-Moore, R.H., 245, 248, 249, 251
Strober, M., 250
Strodtbeck, F.L., 468, 469
Stroebe, M.S., 153, 279
Stroebe, W., 153, 279
Strom, B.L., 304
Stroup, D.F., 302, 303
Strouse, T.B., 400
Strube, M.J., 229, 231
Stuart, F.M., 372
Stuart, G.L., 235
Studd, J.W.W., 305
Studley, L.B., 114, 115
Stuenkel, C.A., 298–99, 303
Sturla, E., 43
Style, C.B., 238, 273, 278
Sue, S., 82
Sugarman, D.B., 220, 221, 223
Sullivan, P.F., 218
Sullivan, Q., 323
Sullivan-Guest, S., 243
Summers, R.J., 181
Sun, S.W., 136
Sung, J.F., 281
Sunley, R., 305, 306
Swartzman, L.C., 303–4
Sweet, J.A., 332, 420
Swim, J., 97
Swim, J.K., 98–99
Switz, G.M., 48
Symons, 180
Szapocznik, J., 17
Szuba, M.P., 400

Tabachnick, B.G., 263
Tabarlet, J.O., 136
Tabsh, K., 384
Tajfel, H., 128
Takaesu, N., 392
Takahira, S., 65
Talbert, L.M., 34
Tanaka, J.S., 211
Tangri, S.S., 184

Tarule, J.M., 8, 72–73
Taussig, L.M., 402
Tavris, T., 12, 51, 355, 361, 373
Taylor, B., 403
Taylor, E.M., 401
Taylor, R.J., 325–26
Taylor, S.E., 127, 209, 210, 285, 349, 383
Taylor, S.H., 183
Taylor, V., 2, 3
Teachman, J.D., 436
Telch, C.F., 271
Telles, C.A., 205, 210, 240
Temkin, J., 198
Teran, A.Z., 300
Terman, L.M., 62, 84, 99
Terpstra, D.E., 186
Tessler, R.C., 399
Thacker, S.B., 302, 303
Thoma, S.J., 106, 110
Thomas, C., 184
Thomas, C.M., 209
Thomas, V.G., 246
Thompson, E.H., 221
Thompson, J.B., 395
Thompson, K., 48
Thompson, M., 245, 323
Thomson, A.M., 402, 403
Thomson, G., 186
Thornton, A., 138
Thorogood, M., 291, 292
Thorpe, G.L., 253, 270, 281
Thorpe, J.S., 185
Tibbetts, E., 402
Tickamyer, A.R., 467
Tiefer, L., 347, 348
Timbers, D.M., 447
Timperi, R., 387
Tinsley, E.G., 243
Tischler, G.L., 241
Tobias, S., 66
Tobin, D.L., 250
Todd, J., 466
Tolman, A.E., 417
Tolor, A., 369
Tolson, T.F.J., 445, 446
Top, T., 97, 98
Topo, P., 300
Torgler, C., 199
Tormey, D.C., 303
Tortu, 311
Tougas, F., 181
Travis, C.B., 268, 277, 283, 288, 304, 384, 386, 392, 404
Tremollieres, F., 305
Trevathan, W.R., 48, 393
Triantafillou, K., 342
Trotter, K.H., 132
True, R.H., 266
Trussell, J., 293, 294
Tuason, V.B., 269
Tucker, M.B., 325–26
Tucker, N., 251
Tulip, M., 473

Turjanmaa, K., 290
Turkheimer, E., 25
Turkish, V.J., 402
Turner, B.F., 370
Turner, J.C., 128
Turner, R.H., 3
Turner, S.M., 210
Tuschl, R.J., 249
Tuttle, G.E., 40
Tyler, L.E., 67
Tzukerman, Y., 466

Udry, J.R., 34
Uili, R., 404
Ulibarri, C., 27
Ulin, P.R., 310
Ullman, S.E., 208
Unger, R., 242
Upfold, D., 214
Upton, S.J., 305
Urbanski, L., 265

Vallerand, R.J., 333
Vance, C.S., 347
Vandell, 429
Van Den Berg, P., 188
Vandenberg, S.G., 62
Van Den Bergh, B.R.H., 39
VanDenburgh, M., 280
Van De Poll, N.E., 29
VanDyke, R., 389
Vann, F.H., 366
Van Rooyen, D., 308
Van Thorre, M.D., 252
Van Vort, J., 294, 297
Van Wyck, P.H., 367
Vara, L.S., 270
Varela-Gittings, F., 8, 394
Vargo, S., 335
Vasquez, M.J.T., 267
Vaughan, B., 293
Vaughn, B.E., 428
Vaux, A., 138, 322
Veccia, E.M., 119
Veilleux, F., 181
Ventura, S.J., 141, 142
Verba, S., 452, 456
Verette, J., 334–35
Veridiano, N.P., 366
Veroff, J., 467
Veronen, L.J., 204
Veronesi, U., 284
Vessey, M., 291, 292
Vetere, V.A., 329
Vicary, J.R., 168, 169
Viegas, O.A.C., 292
Vinci, R., 387
Visher, E.B., 441
Visher, J.S., 441
Visser, G.H.A., 39
Vobejda, B., 168
Vogel, F.X., 252
Vogel, S.R., 94, 114, 259

Voigt, L., 406
Von Glinow, M.A., 175, 176, 180
Von Ranson, K.B., 252
Voydanoff, P., 273, 441–42
Voyer, D., 69, 70, 72
Voyer, S., 69, 70, 72

Waadt, S., 249
Wachter, R.M., 286
Wachtler, J., 469
Wadsworth, J., 403
Waghorn, K., 394–95
Wagner, M.G., 410
Wainwright, S., 398
Waisberg, J., 259
Waldron, I., 272
Walker, 6
Walker, A.J., 53, 150, 423
Walker, K., 145
Walker, L., 106, 110, 225
Walker, L.E., 226, 229, 230–31, 233
Walker, W.D., 211
Wallen, K., 29
Waller, G., 251
Walsh, 209
Walsh, A., 348
Walsh, R.T., 16
Walster, E., 329
Walton, M.B., 383
Wambach, K.G., 309
Wang, M.Q., 281
Ward, N.J., 162
Warren, L.W., 243
Warren, M.P., 247
Warshak, R.A., 435
Warshaw, J.B., 388
Warshaw, R., 199
Warter, A., 380
Washton, A.M., 258
Wathey, R.B., 257, 258, 261–62
Watkins-Malek, M.A., 83
Watson, J.P., 369
Waxman, H., 353
Waye, J.D., 287
Weber, D.J., 311
Weber, G., 250–51
Weber, N., 187
Webster, M., Jr., 130
Weil, W.B., 402, 403
Weinberg, M.S., 367
Weiner, B., 88
Weiner, L., 183
Weiner, M.B., 371
Weinman, J., 285
Weinraub, Z., 381
Weir, L., 10
Weis, D.L., 355
Weisberg, M., 353
Weisenfeld, A.R., 404
Weisman, M.M., 238, 254
Weiss, N., 406

Weiss, N.S., 288
Weiss, R.S., 152
Weiss, S., 269–70
Weissman, M.M., 241
Weisstein, N., 175
Weitzman, L., 135
Weitzman, L.M., 185
Welch, R., 103
Weller, A., 46, 48
Weller, L., 46, 48
Wells, J.E., 55
Weltman, K., 190
Wendler, C., 65
Wertz, D.C., 392
Wertz, R.W., 392
Wesel, S., 397
Wesley, M., 281, 282, 285
Wesner, R., 253, 263, 270
West, C., 115
Westerfield, C.R., 281
Westerlund, E., 216
Whatley, M.H., 277, 283, 304
Wheatley, D., 303
Wheaton, B., 75
Wheeler, C.E., Jr., 307
Wheeler, H., 235
Wheeler, L., 322
Whelan, M., 273
Whisman, M.A., 263
White, D., 372
White, H., 254
White, J.K., 105
White, K.M., 337
White, L., 89
White, L.A., 350
White, V.J., 98
Whitehead, M.I., 299
Whitehead, T.L., 123
Whitehill, L.L., 350
Whiteley, S., 404
Whitley, B.E., Jr., 89, 100, 243, 368
Whitman, P.R., 404
Whitney, G.A., 334–35
Whitsett, D., 344, 441
Whittier, N., 2, 3
Whittle, B.S., 223
Widaman, K.F., 247
Wieck, A., 399
Wienberg, H., 466
Wiersma, U.J., 187, 188
Wilbur, C.H., 313
Wildman, B.G., 114
Wiley, M.G., 179
Wilfley, D., 271
Wilk, C.A., 420
Wilkerson, M.B., 80
Wilkins, D.G., 387
Wilkinson, S., 366
Willet, W.C., 299, 300
Willett, W.C., 283, 313–14
Williams, 226
Williams, G., 251
Williams, J.E., 94

Williams, L., 118
Williams, L.B., 289
Williams, L.M., 218
Williams, P.M., 35
Williams, S.W., 84
Williams, T.M., 52
Williams-Deane, M., 291
Willie, C.V., 467
Wilmoth, G.H., 296
Wils, A.B., 340
Wilsnack, R.W., 255, 257
Wilsnack, S.C., 255, 256, 257
Wilson, B.J., 215
Wilson, E.O., 43, 45
Wilson, M.N., 444, 445, 446
Wilson, R.A., 299
Winawer, S.J., 287
Winfield, I., 198–99
Wing, R.R., 150
Wingard, D.L., 300
Wingard, J.A., 113
Winges, L.D., 143
Winickoff, S.A., 424
Wink, P., 147
Winter, D.G., 461
Winter, J.C., 31
Wipple, B., 353
Wisnicki, K.G., 242, 243
Wisniewski, N., 199, 200
Withers, R.T., 313
Witkin, H.A., 41, 69
Witte, J., 308
Witter, F., 387
Wittig, M.A., 119
Wittleson, S.F., 38
Wolf, D.A., 431, 437
Wolf, J., 270
Wolfe, B.M., 298, 299, 301
Wolfe, D.M., 462
Wolkind, S., 378
Wollstonecraft, M., 1
Wong, M., 107
Wong, P.Y., 27
Wood, B., 150, 423
Wood, F.B., 36, 37
Wood, J.V., 285
Wood, J.W., 65
Wood, M., 318, 322
Wood, W., 120, 273
Wood, W.C., 303
Woodruff, W.J., 205
Woodward, D.J., 36
Woody, B., 159, 160
Wooley, O.W., 246
Wooley, S.C., 246
Woollett, B.A., 404
Worcester, N., 277, 283, 304
Workman, E.A., 269
Worobey, J.L., 438
Worobow, A.L., 50
Worthey, 114
Worthington, M., 299
Wortman, C.B., 191
Wright, A.L., 402

Wright, C.T., 260
Wright, P.H., 318
Wright, T.L., 362
Wunt, W., 11
Wyatt, G.E., 199, 201, 295, 296, 350, 364
Wyche, K.F., 139, 172, 173, 174
Wydra, D., 50
Wynn, V., 299

Yahr, P., 27, 28
Yanof, D.S., 318

Yanoshik, K., 290, 292, 293
Yarber, W.L., 350
Yin, Y., 448
Yllo, K., 207
Yngvesson, B., 9
Yoder, J.D., 17, 18, 20
York, K.L., 147
Young, D., 395
Young, E.W., 168, 169, 363
Young, T., 393
Young-Eisendrath, P., 9
Yu, A.P., 109

Zabin, L.S., 144, 297
Zack, M.M., 302, 303
Zalk, S.R., 185
Zaslow, M.J., 427, 430
Zauber, A.G., 287
Zavodnick, S., 269–270
Zelditch, M., Jr., 115, 130, 178
Zelkowitz, P., 75
Zelnik, M., 141, 354
Ziemba-Davis, M., 312
Zigler, E., 145

Zillman, D., 214
Zillmann, D., 214
Zimmerman, D.H., 115
Zimmerman, R., 271
Zinn, L.M., 249
Zinn, M.B., 447
Zucali, R., 284
Zuckerman, B., 387
Zuckerman, B.S., 424
Zurrida, S., 284
Zussman, L., 305, 306
Zussman, S., 305, 306

SUBJECT INDEX

Ability
  self-estimates of, 86-87
  success and failure based on, 88-90
Abortion, 142, 289, 294–98
  barriers to, 297–98
  clients for, 295
  decision to have, 295
  psychological effects of, 295–97, 385
  rates of, 294–95
  RU-486, 298
Abuse, sexual. See Sexual abuse, child-
    hood
Academic achievement, 78–83
  of African American women, 80–81
  of Asian American female students,
    81–82
  of Hispanic female students, 79–80
  of re-entry women, 82–83
Academic demands, eating disorders
    and, 247
Achievement motivation, 85
Acquaintance rapes, 204, 209
ACTH, 27
Activity level, gender differences in, 109
ADAHMA, 277
Addiction, heroin, 257–58
Adjustment
  at midlife, 148–49
  post partum, 396, 398–400
Adolescents
  anorexia nervosa among, 247
  divorce and, 435
  gender construction of, 137–46
    defense mechanisms, 139
    ego development, 139
    females' ideal self-image, 145–46
    girls' loss of voice, 137
    identity development, 139
    independence in relationship,
      138–39
    poverty and, 140
    puberty, 137
    racial and gender friendship pat-
      terns in junior high, 137–38
    romance and, 138
    teenage sexual activity and preg-
      nancy, 140–45
Adoption, race and, 144
Adrenal cortex, 27
Adrenal testosterone, 42–43
Adrenocorticotrophin (ACTH) hor-
    mone, 27
Adrenogenital syndrome, 42–43

Adultery, 361
Advertising, tobacco, 288
AFDC, 431, 436
Affective disorder (mood disorder), 238
Affiliation, gender differences in, 107
Affiliation motivation, 107, 108
Affirmative action, 78, 168, 181, 333
Africa, AIDS in, 310
African American families
  gender role differentiation in, 132
  marriage in, 324–25
  stepfamilies, 441–42
African American feminism, 5–6
African Americans
  divorce rate among, 339
  friendship patterns among, 138
  labor force participation of, 159
  oldest old, 154
  teacher expectations of, 74
  wife abuse among, 222–23
African American women. See also
    Black women
  douching by, 312–13
  income of, 164–65
  psychotherapy with, 267
  separatist, 4–5
  sexuality of, 363–64
Afrocentric feminist epistemology,
    10–11
Age
  extramarital sex and, 361–62
  labor force participation and, 161–62
  mother-infant bonding and, 400–401
  power in intimate relations and, 466
Agency, 99
Aggression
  defined, 104
  erotic stimuli and, 214–15
  gender role theory of, 130
  hormones and, 30–32
  role-taking and, 221
Aggressiveness, gender differences in,
    104–5, 120
Aging
  gender construction and, 150–54
    oldest old, 153
    perceptions of aging women,
      151–52
    residence of elderly, 153–54
    retirement, 151
    widowhood, 152–53
  sexuality and, 370–71
  women's attitudes toward, 150

Agoraphobia, 238, 252–54
AIDS, 250, 309–12
  partners of hemophiliacs and, 311
  prevention of, 311–12
  risk behavior for, 310–11
  risk factors for transmission of, 312
  in Sub-Saharan Africa, 310
AIDS activism, 286
Aid to Families with Dependent Chil-
    dren (AFDC), 431, 436
Alcohol and drug abuse. See Substance
    abuse
Alcohol consumption
  breast cancer risk and, 282
  coronary heard disease and, 280–81
Alcoholism among American Indian
    women, 265
Alcohol-treatment programs, sexism in,
    261–62
Alimony, 343–44
Alpha bias, 18
Alpha-Fetoprotein Test (AFP), 384
Alpha reductase deficiency, 43
Alprazolam (Xanax), 55, 269–70
Altruism, 106
Ambition, motherhood and, 420
Ambivalence in pregnant women, 385
American Indian women. See Native
    American women
American Psychiatric Association, 51
Amniocentesis, 384, 409
Amnion (bag of waters), 378
Amotivation, 333
Anal stage, 124
Androcentrism, 11–14
Androgen insensitivity syndrome,
    41–42
Androgens, 27, 32–33
Androgyny, 99, 100. See also Sex role
    orientation
  among Black women, 103
  friendships and, 322
Anorexia nervosa, 245, 247–48
  family therapy for, 263
  recovery from, 252
Antiandrogens, 31
Antimullerian hormone, 27
Antiprostaglandin drugs, 48
Antisocial behavior, testosterone and,
    31
Anxiety
  castration, 124
  gender differences in, 112

Anxiety *(cont.)*
math, 66
in pregnant women, 385
Anxiety disorders, 252–54
Anxious attachment style, 326–27
Argentine Mothers of the Plaza de
Mayo, 476
Aromatization, 32
Arrests
for battering, 227–28
by sex (1993), 234
Artificial insemination, 406–7
Asian American families, 448
Asian American women
income of, 165
psychotherapy with, 266
Asian family, traditional, 266
Assertiveness, 470
gender differences in, 108–9
Atrophy, urogenital, 298–99
Attachment
parent-child
agoraphobia and, 253
father-daughter incest and, 217
infant-parent, 428
in relationships, 326–27
Attachment theory of incest, 217
Attention
menstrual cycle and, 49
self-focused, 242–43
Attitudinal factors, math performance
and, 66
Attributions
learned helplessness and, 230
marital satisfaction and, 334
for success and failure, 88–90, 102–3
Auditory cues, 113
Autonomy in lesbian relationships,
335–36
Autosomes, 26
Avoidant attachment style, 327
AZT, 388, 389

Babies. *See also* Breast-feeding
marital satisfaction and, 334
premature, 387, 397
at risk, 389–91
infant mortality, 389–90
prenatal care, 390–91
"Baby M" case, 407–8
Bag of waters (amnion), 378
Barrier methods of contraception,
293–94
Battered Woman Syndrome, 229,
230
Battering, 219, 220–32
counseling and shelter services for,
228–29
ending, 226–27
interaction dynamics in violent marriages, 223–24
legal response to, 227–28
in lesbian relationships, 224
of lesbians by males, 225–26
in marriage, 219, 221–23
risk markers for, 223

theories of, 229–32
cycle of violence, 230–31
entrapment, 229
myth of women's masochism,
231–32
reasoned action, 213
social exchange, 231
social learning, 229–30
Battering rapes, 207
Bedarche, 446
Behavior, 19
Bem Sex Role Inventory (BSRI), 99
Benign breast disease, 282
Beta-carotene, 314, 382
Bias. *See also* Discrimination; Sexism
alpha, 18
androcentric, 11–14
in hiring and promotion, 179
media, 89, 90
in performance evaluation, 96–98
in research process, 12–13
in volunteer samples, 16
Bibliotherapy, 373
Binge eating, 246, 249
Bioecological model, 25–26
Biology, 23–58
heredity and environment, 23–26
hormonal influences on animal
brains, 29–31
human brain, 35–40
environmental influence on, structure of, 39
hemispheres of, 35
homosexuality and, 39–40
lateralization of, 35–39
menstrual cycle, 46–56
cognition and, 49
menstrual cramps (dysmenorrhea),
48
menstrual synchrony, 46–48
perceptual abilities and, 49–50
premenstrual syndrome, 50–56
reaction time and attention and, 49
sex role attitudes and menstrual
distress, 50
sex chromosome anomalies, 26, 40–43
sex hormones in humans, 26–29, 31–35
aggression and, 31–32
cognitive functioning and, 32–33
occupation and, 34–35
personality and, 33–34
sociobiology, 43–46
Biomedical models of eating disorders,
245
Birth. *See* Childbirth
Birth weight, low, 387
Bisexual women, 364–65
Black families
dual-earner, 446
extended, 444–46
single-parent, 432–33, 435–36
Black-on-White rape, 200
Blacks. *See also* African Americans;
Race
AIDS issue and, 310, 311
focus of research on, 13

marital satisfaction among, 333
middle class, 333
structural barriers in business and,
179–80
Black women
androgyny among, 103
with eating disorders, 251–52
ectopic pregnancy in, 380
as experimental subjects, 16
gender stereotypes of, 95
lesbian, 446
on motherhood, 415–16
older single mothers, 438
in politics, 454–55
psychotherapy with, 265
rape avoidance by, 208
rape of, 199–201
unemployment rates of, 159–60
voting rights and, 451–52
Blue collar jobs, 168–69
Body esteem, 251
Body image, eating disorders and,
245–46
Body image distortion, 247
Body politics, 475
Bonding, mother-infant, 400–401
Boston Area Educators for Social Responsibility (BAESR), 472
Brain
animal, hormonal influence on, 29–31
human, 35–40
environmental influence on structure of, 39
hemispheres of, 35
homosexuality and, 39–40
injury to, 37
lateralization of, 35–39
Breaking-up of relationships, 329–31
Breast cancer, 281–86
breast implants, 285–86
breast self examination and mammography, 283
coping with, 284–85
hormone-replacement therapy and,
301–3
incidence of, 281–82
mortality rates, 285
nutrition and, 282–83
research funding, 286
risk factors associated with, 282
treatment for, 283–84
Vitamin A and, 313–14
Breast-feeding, 282, 370, 401–5
advantages for mother's body, 405
baby's I.Q. and, 403
mothers' reasons for, 403–5
nutritional advantages of, 402–3
society and, 405
Broca's area, 37
BSRI, 99
Bulimia nervosa, 245, 248–50
norms and, 249–50
recovery from, 252
treatment of, 270–71
Bupropion (Wellbutrin), 269
Bureaucracy, feminist critique of, 180

Caesarean section, 395–96
Calcium, 55, 304–5
Call Off Your Old Tired Ethics (COY-OTE), 220
Cancer, 281–88
  breast, 281–86
    breast implants, 285–86
    breast self examination and mammography, 283
    coping with, 284–85
    hormone-replacement therapy and, 301–3
    incidence of, 281–82
    mortality rates, 285
    nutrition and, 282–83
    research funding, 286
    risk factors associated with, 282
    treatment for, 283–84
    Vitamin A and, 313–14
  cervical, 287, 304, 307
  colorectal, 286–87
  DES and, 304
  endometrial, 287, 292, 299
  hysterectomy to treat, 307
  lung, 286
  ovarian, 287–88, 292
  uterine, 307
Capitalism, 5
  ideology of motherhood and, 417
Career planning by Black women, 81
Careers
  alcohol abuse and, 256–57
  motherhood and, 421
  peer culture and commitment to, 146–47
  power motive and, 461–62
Caregiving by middle-aged daughters, 151, 423
Care justification for morality, 110
Castration anxiety, 124
Causality, 18
CBT (cognitive behavioral therapy), 210–11, 262–63
Censorship, 213
Cervical cancer, 287, 304, 307
Cervical caps, 293–94
Cervical intraepithelial neoplasia (CIN), 287
Chaos theory, 18
CHD. *See* Coronary heart disease (CHD)
Chicana Conference (1971), 3
Child-bearing, midlife, 391–92
Child-bearing decision model for dual-career couple, 420
Childbirth, 392–401
  caesarean section, 395–96
  episiotomy, 394–95
  feminist perspective on, 392–93
  medicalization of, 392, 401
  mother-infant bonding, 400–401
  natural, 393–94
  nurse midwives, 395
  post partum adjustment, 396, 398–400
  premature, 387
  psychosocial aspects of, 396–98

Childcare, 161, 190–92, 427–32, 437
  for AFDC mothers, 431
  centers vs. home care, 429–30
  division of labor in, 424–25
  infant day care, 428–29
  quality of, 430–31
  solutions to crisis in, 431–32
Child Care and Development Block Grant (1990), 437
Childhood
  gender construction in, 131–34
    infants nurtured by children, 132–34
    narrative fantasies, 132
    play and playmate preferences, 131–32, 133–34
    socialization by adults, 131
    tomboys and feminine boys, 134
  sexual abuse in
    adolescent pregnancy and, 142
    alcohol and drug abuse and, 255–57
    mental health consequences of, 217–18
  social interaction in, 133
Child-rearing, 131
  conflict over, 345
  by males, 416–17
Children. *See also* Childcare; Motherhood; Mothers
  custody of, 439, 443
  of divorce, 433–35
  kidnapped, 442, 443
  labor force participation and, 161–62
  language of, 114–15
  marital satisfaction and, 424–25
Child support, 436–37
Chlamydia, 307
Choice reaction time, 49
Cholesterol, low-density lipoprotein, 280–81, 300–301
Chorionic villus sampling (CVS), 384, 385
Chromosomes, 26, 40–43
CIN, 287
Circumcision, genital, 353–54
Citizenship status of household workers, 159
Civil Rights legislation, 2, 181, 333
Class bias in volunteer samples, 16
Classroom, gender in, 73–76
Clerical jobs, stress in, 167–68
Climacteric. *See* Menopause
Clitoral orgasms, 353
Coalition for Essential Schools, 449
Cocaine, crack, 308
Cocaine abuse, 258, 387
Coercive power, 457
Cognition
  hormones and, 32–33
  menstrual cycle and, 49
Cognitive abilities, sex role orientation and, 102
Cognitive analysis of panic attack, 263
Cognitive behavioral therapy (CBT), 210–11, 262–63

Cognitive developmental model, 127
Cognitive gender differences, 59–91
  academic achievement and, 78–83
    of African American women, 80–81
    of Asian American female students, 81–82
    of Hispanic female students, 79–80
    of re-entry women, 82–83
  academic decision making and, 76–78
  in computer competence, 83–84
  gender in the classroom and, 73–76
  gifted women, 84–85
  intelligence, 62–63
  mathematics ability, 63–67
  statistical analysis of, 59–62
    meta-analysis, 60–62
    normal curve distribution, 59–60
  success and failure, 85–90
  verbal ability, 67–69
  visual spatial ability, 69–72
  women's ways of knowing, 72–73
Cognitive model of teenage pregnancy, 144–45
Cognitive processing therapy (CPT), 210–11
Cognitive therapy
  for bulimia nervosa, 270–71
  for panic disorder, 270
  psychopharmacotherapy vs., 269
Cohabiting couples, 332, 335, 336, 340
Collaborative research, 15
College classroom, gender in the, 75–76
College experience, 146
Colorectal cancer, 286–87
Colostrum, 402
Comic strips, gender construction and, 134–35
Coming out, 368
Committed love, 448–49
Committee on Lesbian and Gay Concerns (CLGC), 264–65
Common sense, 10
Communicative integration, 340
Communion, 99
Community, 448–49
Community mental health, 238–40
  homelessness, 239–40
  mental illness by sex, 238
  race, poverty, and, 239
  sexual assault and, 240
Community organization, 474
Community response to rape, 211–12
Companionable relationship, 320
Comparable worth, 182
Computer competence, gender differences in, 83–84
Condoms, 289, 290
  female, 290–91
  users of, 310, 311
Confidant relationships, 320
Conflict
  in families, 434
  interrole, 187–88
    children and, 428
  marital, 338–39

Conflict *(cont.)*
    personality, 167–68
    in remarriages, 345
Conflict Tactics Scale, 222
Conformity, group pressure, 111
Congruence model, 100
Consciousness-raising groups, 260
Consensual love, 448
Constancy, gender, 127
Context, emphasis on, 17
Contextual model of satisfaction in inti-
    mate relationships, 334–35
Contraceptives, 143, 144, 145, 280–94
    barrier methods, 293–94
    condoms, 289, 290, 310, 311
    Depo-provera, 292
    female condom, 290–91
    intrauterine device (IUD), 292–93
    media and, 136
    Norplant, 292
    oral, 53, 289, 291–92
    sexual arousal and, 369
    spermicides, 293
    sterilization, 289, 294
Control, locus of, 241–42
Cooperative power, 457
Coronary heart disease (CHD), 280–81,
    299–301
    gender difference in, 278
    Vitamin E and, 313–14
Corporate America, glass ceiling in,
    175–76
Corpus callosum, 35
Cortical function, lateral symmetry of,
    36–37
Cost-benefit analysis of batterer's be-
    havior, 231
Counseling for battered women, 226
COYOTE, 220
Crack cocaine, 308
Cramps, menstrual (dysmenorrhea), 48,
    306
Creams, vaginal, 304
Crime, 233–35. *See also* Violence
        against women
    gender differences in, 233
    PMS and, 54
    violent, 105
    by women, 233–35
        husband murder, 233–34
        imprisonment, 234–35
Crying, 111–12
Cultural feminists, 8
Cultural model of eating disorders,
    245
Cultural resource theory, 189–90
Cultural spillover theory, 203
Cultural success, 45
Culture
    interpersonal distance and, 119
    rape and, 202–3
Culture-bound syndrome, 248
Custodial parents, 435
Custody of children, 439, 443
CVS, 384, 385
Cybernetic theory, 466

Cycle of violence theory of battery,
    230–31

Dalkon Shield, 292
Danazol, 306
Date rape, 199, 204
Dating, 138, 322–31
    attachment style in, 326–27
    breaking-up in heterosexual relation-
        ships, 329–31
    by disabled women, 329
    eating disorders and, 247
    empathy in, 327–28
    investment model of, 326
    in lesbian relationships, 329
    new singles, 328
    psychological mechanisms for rela-
        tionship maintenance, 326
    sex-role attitudes and, 331
    theories of, 322–26
    violence in, 220
Daughter-mother relationship, 151,
    422–23
Daughters of Bilitis, 264, 321
Day care, infant, 428–29
Daydreaming, sexual, 356–57
Death instincts, 124
Decoding cues of nonverbal behavior,
    119–20
Defense mechanisms in adolescence,
    139
Demand-withdraw interaction pattern,
    338–39
Dependency, gender differences in, 108
Depo-provera, 292
Depression, 240–44
    depressive explanatory style and, 244
    derived identity and, 243
    diagnosis of, 240
    environmental stressors, 243
    feminine sex role orientation and,
        243
    gender differences in rates of, 241
    among Hispanics, 267
    locus of control and, 241–42
    menopause and, 149–50, 303
    multiple roles and, 271
    postpartum, 398–400
    pregnancy and, 396–97, 399
    psychopharmacotherapy for, 268–69
    self-focused attention and, 242–43
    social support for, 242
    victimization and, 237
Depressive psychosis, postpartum, 400
Derived identity, 243
Desipramine, 268, 270
Desyrel, 269
Developmental psychology, feminist in-
        fluence on, 17
Diabetes, endometrial cancer and, 287
Diagnosticity, gender, 98
Diaphragms, 289, 293–94
Dichotomous thinking, 19
Dietary fat intake, breast cancer and,
    283
Diethylstilbestrol (DES), 304, 366–67

Dieting, 246–47
Differential Aptitude Tests (DAT), 63,
    67
Diffuse status characteristics, 130
Digital Equipment Corporation
    (DEC), 180
Direct-bilateral power strategy, 460
Directive power careers, 462
Direct-unilateral power strategies, 460
Disabled women
    dating by, 329
    friendship among, 321–22
    pregnancy and, 385–86
    sexuality of, 351
Discrimination. *See also* Bias; Sexism
    in employment, 160, 167
        in academic settings, 181
        hiring and promotion, 179
        in legal profession, 170
        in science, 174–75
        women managers, 177–79
    against homosexuals, 368
Diseases, sexually transmitted. *See* Sex-
        ually transmitted diseases
Displaced homemakers, 193
Distance, interpersonal, 119
Division of labor, 166. *See also* Child-
        care; Housework; Working
        women
Divorce, 108, 320, 339–44, 433. *See also*
        Single-parent families
    alimony, 343–44
    children of, 433–35
    friendships after, 320–21
    initiating, 342
    labor-force participation and, 193
    occupation of wife and, 341
    personal consequences of, 342–43
    personality and, 341–42
    rates of, 339
    risk factors for, 340
    sex and, 362
    social integration and, 340
    social support and, 343
Domestic division of labor, 192, 424–25.
        See also Childcare; Housework
Domestic violence, 197. *See also* Vio-
        lence against women
    police response to, 227–28
Dominance, 467–68
Dominant-subordinate relationship, 459
Double standard, sexual, 350–51, 356,
    361
Douching, 312–13
Down's Syndrome, 392
Doxycycline, 307
Drug abuse. *See* Substance abuse
Drugs, psychoactive, 268
Drug-treatment programs, sexism in,
    261–62
Dual-earner couples, 187–90
    career and marriage in male- and fe-
        male-dominated professions, 189
    child-bearing decision model for, 420
    influences on married women's em-
        ployment, 189

marital satisfaction of, 344–45
relative costs and rewards of, 188–89
work-home role conflict, 187–88
Dysmenorrhea (menstrual cramps), 48, 306
Dyspareunia, 371, 373
Dysthymia, 238
Dysthymic Disorder, 240
Dystocia (difficult labor), 396

Earnings, self-efficacy and, 439
Eating disorders, 245–52
anorexia nervosa, 245, 247–48
family therapy for, 263
recovery from, 252
body image and, 245–46
bulimia nervosa, 245, 248–50
recovery from, 252
treatment of, 270–71
cultural explanations for, 245
dieting and overeating, 246–47
family systems theory and, 250–51
lesbians with, 251
women of color with, 251–52
Economic adequacy, marital satisfaction and, 333–34
Economics profession, 174
Economic theory of human capital, 166–67
Ectopic pregnancy, 379–82
Educational administrators, women, 172–73
Educational institutions, sexual harassment in, 184
Education/educational status
divorce rate and, 339
douching and, 312–13
empowerment and, 472–73
income and, 162–63, 164–65
labor force participation and, 161–62
Educators for Social Responsibility, 472
Effect size (*d*), 61
Effort, success and failure based on, 88–90
Egalitarian attitudes in distressed marriages, 338
Egalitarian couples, 464–65
Egalitarian (liberal) feminism, 3, 212, 408–9
Ego, 124
Ego development, 139, 343
Elderly. *See also* Aging
friendship among, 321
poverty rates for, 152
residence of, 154–55
Elective lesbians, 366
Electra complex, 125
Elementary school classroom, teacher attention in, 73
Embryo, 378
Embryo transfer (ET), 409–10
Emic, 10–11
Emotionality
gender differences in, 111–12
sex role orientation and, 273
Empathy, 112–13, 327–28

Empiricism, feminist, 7
Employment. *See also* Working women
discrimination in, 160, 167
in academic settings, 181
in legal profession, 170
in science, 174–75
women managers, 177–79
extramarital sex and, 361–62
of married women, 188–89
maternal, 425–27
part-time, 162
self-esteem and, 271–72
Empowerment, 451–56, 472–73
of minorities, 472–73
psychology of women and, 17–18
right to vote, 451–53
teen pregnancy prevention and, 140
women in political office, 453–56
African American, 454–55
European, 455–56
ideological positions of, 455
numbers of, 453
success of candidates, 453–54
Endocrine, ectopic pregnancy and, 380
Endocrine glands, 26–27
Endometrial cancer, 287, 292, 299
Endometriosis, 306
Engineers, women, 171
Entitlement, personal, 176–77
Entrapment theory of battery, 229
Entrepreneurial women, 183
Environment, 23–26
brain structure and, 39
depression and, 243
hormones, body structure, and, 28–29
sexual differentiation and, 28
Environmental selection, 24
Epidemiologic Catchment Area Study (ECA), 238
Epidemiology, 237
Episiotomy, 394–95
Epistemological positions, feminist, 6–11
Equal Employment Opportunity Commission (EEOC), 183
Equality, 359
of female sexuality, 374
Equal Pay Act of 1963, 2, 181, 182
Equal Rights Amendment of 1972 (ERA), 3
Erotica, 373–74
female arousal to, 356
Erotic stimuli, aggression and, 214–15
Erotophilia, 349–50
Erotophobia, 329, 349–50, 367–68
Esophagus, disease of, 286
Essentialism, 8
Estradiol, 32, 54, 302
Estrogen, 27, 28, 378
Estrogen replacement therapy (ERT), 299, 305
ET, 409–10
Ethical issues
in AZT treatment, 389
in human engineering, 406
therapist-client sex, 263–64

Ethnicity. *See also* Race; *specific ethnic groups*
adolescent sexual activity and, 143–44
AIDS risk and, 310
condom use and, 290
identity development and, 139
mathematics ability and, 64–65
mental health and, 239
psychology career and, 172
single-parent families and, 432–33
working women and, 158–61
Etic, 10–11
Europe
poverty of single mothers in, 437–38
women politicians in, 455–56
Evaluations, gender stereotypes and, 96–98
Exchanges, nonreciprocal, 153
Exchange theory of dating relationships, 322
Excitation transfer theory, 214–15
Excitement, sexual, 351–52
Executive Order 11246, 78, 181
Exercise, 313
Kegel, 306, 373
PMS and, 55
postmenopausal women or, 300–301
Exit response to dissatisfaction in relationships, 334–35
"Expansive, profligate impulse," 461
Expectations states theory, 115–16, 123–24, 130–31
Experimental method, 17
Expert power, 457
Explanatory style, depressive, 244
Extended family, 265
External motivation, 333
Extramarital sex, 361–62

Facial cues, 113
Faculty, women, 173–74
Failure, attributions for, 88–90
Family(ies). *See also* Battering; Mothers; Sexual abuse, childhood; Single-parent families
Asian American, 448
Black, 444–46
conflict in, 434
extended, 265
heroin addiction and, 257
Hispanic, 447–48
home-work conflict and, 187–88
new structures of, 317–18
postmodern, 448–49
support from divorced person's, 343
traditional Asian, 266
violence in, 222, 244
vital, 448–49
Family and Medical Leave Act of 1993, 426
Family Support Act (1988), 437
Family systems theory, eating disorders and, 250–51
Family therapy for anorexia, 263

Fantasies
  children's narrative, 132
  sexual, 357
Fat, dietary
  breast cancer and, 283
  ovarian cancer and, 287–88
Fear of success, 85–86
Female condom, 290–91
Feminine boys, 134
Feminine hygiene sprays, 313
Feminine women, 33–34, 99. *See also*
    Sex role orientation
  coping, 188
  friendships and, 322
  marital conflict and, 339
  self-efficacy of, 188
Feminism, 1–22
  African American, 5–6
  androcentric bias in psychology and,
    11–13
  critique of organizational bureau-
    cracy and hierarchy, 180
  egalitarian (liberal), 3, 212, 408–9
  epistemological positions of, 6–11
  first feminist movement, 1–2
  Marxist, 5
  philosophical base of, 1
  political lesbianism, 4–5
  prostitution issue and, 220
  radical, 3–4, 20, 212
  research methods, 13–15
  second wave of, 2–3, 475
  socialist, 5
  suicide role and, 254
  transformation of psychology, 15–19
  violent pornography and, 213
Feminist perspectives
  on childbirth, 392–93
  on intimate relationships, 317–18
  on motherhood, 415, 416
  on rape, 201–3
Feminist psychology, 16–18, 19
Feminist psychotherapy, 260–61
Feminization of poverty, 436
Fertility, marriage age and, 420
Fertility-related behavior, 289
Fertilization, in vitro, 409–11
Fetal alcohol syndrome (FAS), 386
Fetal rights, 388
Fetal syphilis, 308
Fibroid tumors (leiomyomas), 305–6
First wave of feminist movement, 1–2
First-world feminism, 475
Fluoxetine (Prozac), 268, 269
Fluvoxamine (Luvox), 269–70
Folic acid, 382
Follicle-stimulating hormone (FSH),
    27, 46, 306
Force, sexual arousal from, 214–15
Force only rapes, 207
Foreplay, 348, 358
Fragile X syndrome, 62
France, women politicians in, 455–56
Franchise, 452
Fraternity gang rape, 206
Fraternity little sisters, 206

French paradox, 280
Friendliness, 98
Friendship, 318–22
  of disabled women, 321–22
  after divorce, 320–21
  of elderly women, 321
  gender differences in, 318–19
  in groups of three or more, 319
  in junior high school, 137–38
  lesbian, 321, 329
  same-sex married women's, 320
  self-disclosure in, 319–20
  sex role orientation and, 322
FSH, 27, 46, 306
Furies, 4

Gang rape, 205–6
Gay males, 11. *See also* Homosexuality
Gaze, 117–18
Gender
  in classroom, 73–76
  friendship patterns and, 137–38
  race and, 6
  teacher interactions and, 74–75
Gender constancy, 127
Gender construction, 9–10, 19, 123–56
  in adolescence, 137–46
    defense mechanisms in, 139
    ego development in, 139
    females' ideal self-image, 145–46
    girls' loss of voice, 137
    identity development in, 139
    independence in relationship,
      138–39
    poverty in, 140
    puberty, 137
    racial and gender friendship pat-
      terns in junior high, 137–38
    romance and, 138
    teenage sexual activity and preg-
      nancy, 140–45
  aging and, 151–55
    oldest old, 154
    perceptions of aging women,
      152–53
    residence of elderly, 154–55
    retirement, 151–52
    widowhood, 153–54
  in childhood, 131–34
    infants nurtured by children,
      132–34
    narrative fantasies, 132
    play and playmate preferences,
      131–32, 133–34
    socialization by adults, 131
    tomboys and feminine boys, 134
  language and, 136–37
  media and, 134–36
    books and magazines, 135–36
    comic strips, 134–35
    television, 136
  in middle age, 147–51
    adjustment at midlife, 148–49
    personality at midlife, 147–48
    psychological effect of menopause,
      149–51

    sandwich generation, 151
    women's attitudes toward aging,
      151
  theories of gender development,
    123–31
    cognitive developmental model, 127
    expectations states theory, 123–24,
      130–31
    gender schema theory, 127–28
    multifactorial gender identity the-
      ory, 128
    psychoanalytic theory of, 124–26
    reference group theory, 129
    social identity theory, 128–29
    social learning theory, 126
    social roles theory, 129–30
  in young adulthood, 146–47
Gender diagnosticity, 98
Gender differences. *See also* Biology;
    Cognitive gender differences
  in alcohol and drug abuse, 255
  in attitudes toward casual sex, 359–60
  in attitudes toward homosexuality,
    368
  in children's nurturing of infants,
    132–34
  in crime, 233
  defined, 59
  in depression rates, 241
  existence of, 120
  in friendships, 318–19
  in genital herpes, 307–8
  in interracial dating, 328
  in language, 113–16
    children's language, 114–15
    talking in groups, 115–16
  in leadership, 469–70
  in management, 175–80
  in marital satisfaction, 336–37
  in masturbation, 357
  in mental health services utilization,
    237–38
  in motivations for parenthood, 418
  in perceptions of sexual harassment,
    186
  in personality, 103–13
    activity level, 109
    affiliation, 107
    aggressiveness, 104–5, 120
    anxiety, 112
    assertiveness, 108–9
    dependency, 108
    emotion, 111–12
    empathy, 112–13
    helping behavior, 105–7
    influenceability, 111
    morality, 109–11
    self-esteem, 108
    sociability, 107–8
  in physical health, 278
  in preference for attractiveness, 323
  in psychological distress, 272–74
  in self-disclosure, 319
  in sexual attitudes and behavior,
    350–51
  in smoking, 288–89

Gender gap in pay, 163–64
Gender roles. *See also* Role(s); Sex role
    orientation
    in African American families, 132
    psychiatric diagnosis and, 259–60
    racial differences in men's attitudes
        about, 467
    socialization into, 76–77, 166. *See also*
        Gender construction
Gender role theory, 130
Gender schema theory, 127–28, 132
Gender segregation, occupational,
    165–69
    blue collar jobs, 168–69
    female occupations, 165–66
    personal entitlement and, 177
    pink collar jobs, 167–68
    theories of, 166–67
Gender stereotypes, 93–99, 120
    accuracy of, 98–99
    of Black and White women, 95
    evaluations and, 96–98
    gender diagnosticity and, 98
    as multicomponent social categories,
        95–96
General Trait Covariance—Andro-
    gen/Estrogen (GTC-A/E) Bal-
    ance Model, 32
Genes, rearrangement of, 24–25
Genetics of sex determination, 26. *See*
    also Biology
Genital circumcision, 353–54
Genital herpes, 307–8
Genital warts, 308
Genotypes, 24
Geschwind-Behan-Galaburda (GBG)
    model of cerebral lateralization,
    33
Gifted women, 84–85
Glands, 26–27
Glass ceiling, 175–76
GnRH agonists, 306
Goddess symbol, 473
Gonadotrophin releasing hormone
    (GnRH), 46
Gonads, 27
Grades, mathematics, 65
Grafenberg spot (G-Spot), 353
Grandparents, 343, 445–46
Grief, 153
Group and individual differences,
    heredity of, 25
Group pressure conformity, 111
Groups
    consciousness-raising, 260
    friendships in, 319
    talking in, 115–16
Growth hormone, 27
Growth retardation, prenatal, 387–
    88
Guidelines on Sexual Harassment in
    the Workplace, 183

Handedness, 38, 39
Harassment, sexual, 168, 183–87
HCG, 378

Health. *See* Mental health; Physical
    health
Health stress, 244
Heart attacks, oral contraceptives and,
    291
Heart disease
    coronary heart disease (CHD), 278,
        280–81, 313–14
    hormone-replacement therapy and,
        299–301
    HRT and, 301
Heavy-metal rock music, 136
Height, career advancement and, 177
Helping behavior, 105–7, 130
Helplessness, learned, 230
Hemispheres of brain, 35
Hemophiliacs, AIDS and partners of,
    311
Hepatitis B, 308–9
He pronoun, 136–37
Heredity, 23–26
Heroin abuse during pregnancy, 387–88
Heroin addiction, 257–58
Herpes, genital, 307–8
Herpes Simplex Virus (HVS), 307
Heterosexuality, mother-daughter rela-
    tionship and, 422
Heterosexual love, 4
Higher education, affirmative action in,
    78
Higher Education Guidelines to Exec-
    utive Order 11246, 78
Hiring. *See also* Employment; Working
    women
    bias in, 179
    target, 181–82
Hispanics
    depression among, 267
    families of, 447–48
    psychotherapy with, 266–67
Hispanic women
    income of, 164
    labor force participation of, 160
    rape among, 201
    sexuality of, 362–63
HIV infection, 292, 297, 309
    pregnancy and, 387–88
    risk factors for, 312
Hmong females, 82
Home care, 429–30
Homelessness, 239–40
Homemakers, displaced, 193
Homemaking role of employed
    women, 272
Home-work role conflict, 187–88
Homophobia, 329, 367–68
Homosexuality. *See also* Lesbians
    attitudes toward, 368
    defined, 365
    discrimination against, 368
    human brain and, 39–40
Hooking is Real Employment (HIRE),
    220
Hormone-replacement therapy (HRT),
    299–304
    alternatives to, 303–4

breast cancer and, 301–3
    diethylstilbestrol (DES), 304, 366–67
    heart disease and, 299–301
    mortality and, 303
Hormones, 26. *See also* Sex hormones
    influence on animal brains, 29–31
    pregnancy and, 378
    sexual functioning and, 371
    sexual orientation and, 366–67
Hot flashes, 303–4
Housespouses, 192–93
Housework
    division of, 192, 424–25
    life cycle and, 193
    psychological strain from, 273
    role conflict and, 188
    as unpaid labor, 190–92
HRT. *See* Hormone-replacement ther-
    apy (HRT)
Human Activity Profile, 313
Human capital, economic theory of,
    166–67
Human chorionic gonadotrophin
    (HCG), 378
Human engineering, 406
Human immunodeficiency virus. *See*
    HIV infection
Humanistic issues, 455
Human papillomavirus (HPV), 308
Human rights violations against
    women, 475
Husband murder, 233–34
HVS, 307
Hyde amendment, 475
Hygiene sprays, feminine, 313
Hypertension, endometrial cancer and,
    287
Hypertensive disorders, pregnancy-
    associated, 379
Hypothalamus, 27
Hysterectomy, 287, 305–7
    for benign conditions, 305–6
    for cancer treatment, 307
    PMS and, 55
    rates of, 305

IBM, 180
Id, 124
Identity, derived, 243
Identity development in adolescence,
    139
Ideologies
    shaping motherhood, 417
    of women politicians, 455
Imipramine, 268, 269, 270
Imitation, 126
Imperatives, use of, 114–15
Implantation, ectopic, 380
Implants, breast, 285–86
Imprisonment of women, 234–35
Impulse control, 341
Impulsive/profligate behavior, 461
Incest, 215–19
    attachment theory of, 217
    Freud's repudiation of seduction the-
        ory, 215–16

Incest *(cont.)*
  incestuous activity, 216
  mental health consequences of, 217–18
  prevalence of, 216
  repressed memories of, 218–19
  treatment of survivors of, 218
Income
  education and, 164–65
  prenatal care and, 390–91
  of working women, 162–65
    African Americans, 164–65
    Asian Americans, 165
    education and, 162–63
    gender gap in, 163–64
    Hispanics, 164
Incumbency, political, 453–54
Indirect-bilateral power strategy, 460
Indirect-unilateral power strategy, 460
Individual differences, hereditability of, 25
Individuality, social, 475
Individuating information, 96
Inequality. *See also* Bias; Discrimination; Working women
    marital, 189–90
    sexual, 348
Infant day care, 428–29
Infant mortality, 389–90
  caesarian section and, 395–96
Infant-mother bonding, 400–401
Infant-parent attachment, 428
Infants
  low birth weight, 387
  nurtured by children, 132–34
Infertility, 406–11. *See also* Reproductive technology
  artificial insemination and, 406–7
  causes of, 406
  coping with, 406
  surrogacy and, 407–9
  in vitro fertilization, 409–11
Influenceability, gender differences in, 111
Influence strategies, 459–60, 464
Inhibited sexual desire (ISD), 372
Insemination, artificial, 406–7
Instincts, 124
Intellectual skills, academic performance and, 75
Intelligence, 25, 62–63, 98
Intercourse, sexual, 354–55
  unwanted, 206
Intermittent reinforcement, 229
Interpersonal construction of gender, 9–10
Interpersonal distance, 119
Interpersonal protection theory, 279
Interracial rape, 201
Interrole conflict, 187–88
  children and, 428
Interruptions in conversation, 115–16
Intimate relationships, 317–46
  cohabiting couples, 332, 335, 336, 340
  dating, 138, 322–31
    attachment style in, 326–27

breaking-up in heterosexual relationships, 329–31
  by disabled women, 329
  eating disorders and, 247
  empathy in, 327–28
  investment model of, 326
  in lesbian relationships, 329
  new singles, 328
  psychological mechanisms for relationship maintenance, 326
  sex-role attitudes and, 331
  theories of, 322–26
  violence in, 220
divorce, 108, 320, 339–44, 433
  alimony, 343–44
  children of, 433–35
  friendships after, 320–21
  initiating, 342
  labor-force participation and, 193
  occupation of wife and, 341
  personal consequences of, 342–43
  personality and, 341–42
  rates of, 339
  risk factors for, 340
  sex and, 362
  social integration and, 340
  social support and, 343
feminist analysis of, 317–18
friendship, 318–22
  of disabled women, 321–22
  after divorce, 320–21
  of elderly women, 321
  gender differences in, 318–19
  in groups of three or more, 319
  in junior high school, 137–38
  lesbian, 321, 329
  same-sex married women's, 320
  self-disclosure in, 319–20
  sex role orientation and, 322
lesbian, 335–36
  dissolution of, 342
  intimacy in, 335–36
  violence in, 225
marriage, 332–34
  in African American families, 324–25
  age of, 332
  conflict in, 338–39
  gender and satisfaction with, 336–37
  mental health and, 272–74
  motherhood and, 421
  motivation for, 332–34
  power relations in, 462–67
  rape in, 206–7
  social class and, 149
  unpaid labor in, 189–90
  violent, 221–23
models of satisfaction in, 334–35
never-married women, 331–32
power in, 261, 462–67
  age and, 466
  Black and White marriages, 467
  cybernetic theory of, 466
  egalitarian couples, 464–65
  resource theory of, 462–64

violent marriages, 465–66
  remarriage, 344–45
Intrauterine device (IUD), 292–93
Intrinsic motivation, 333
Investment model
  of dating, 326
  of satisfaction in intimate relationships, 334
In vitro fertilization, 409–11
IQ scores, individual differences in, 25
IQ tests, 62
ISD, 372

Japanese women, influence strategies of, 460
Job Opportunities and Basic Skills Training (JOBS) Program, 437
Jobs. *See* Employment; Working women
Johnson Controls Company, 180
Judeo-Christian tradition, marginalization of women within, 473
Junior high school, friendship patterns in, 137–38

Kegel exercises, 306, 373
Kidnapped children, 442, 443
Klinefelter syndrome, 40–41

Labor
  childbearing, 396
  division of, 166. *See also* Housework; Working women
  reproductive, 157–58
Labor force participation. *See* Working women
La Leche League, 401
LaMaze method, 393–94
Language
  gender construction and, 136–37
  gender differences in, 113–16
    children's language, 114–15
    talking in groups, 115–16
Latency period, 125
Lateralization of brain, 35–39
  antecedents of, 38–39
Lateral symmetry of cortical function, 36–37
Lawyers, women, 170
Leadership, 467–72
  dominance, 467–68
  effectiveness of, 470
  emergence of, 468–69
  evaluations of, 470–71
  style of, 469–70
  successful women leaders, 471–72
  visual dominance behavior and, 117–18
Learned helplessness, 230
Learned Optimism, 244
Learning, observational, 126
Leeds Revolutionary Feminist Group, 4
Legitimate power, 457
Leiomyomas (fibroid tumors), 305–6
Lesbianism
  epistemology of, 11
  political, 4–5

Lesbian relationships, 335–36
   dating, 329
   dissolution of, 342
   frequency of sexual activity in, 358
   friendships, 318, 321
   intimacy in, 335–36
   violence in, 225
Lesbians, 365–68
   defined, 365
   in drug-treatment groups, 262
   with eating disorders, 251
   elective, 366
   homophobia and, 367–68
   male violence against, 225–26
   as mothers, 439–40
   primary, 366
   psychotherapy with, 264–65
   relationship with sons, 423–24
   sexual harassment of, 185
Levonorgestrel, 292
Liberal (egalitarian) feminism, 3, 212, 408–9
Libido, 124
Life cycle, household responsibilities and, 192. *See also* Reproductive life cycle
Life instincts, 124
Life stress, depression and, 243
Linguistic style, 113–15
Locus of control, 241–42
Logical positivism, 6
Love
   types of, 448–49
   as a woman's career, 317
Low birth weight infants, 387
Low-density lipoprotein cholesterol, 280–81, 300–301
Low-income women, prenatal screening of, 386. *See also* Single-parent families; Working women
Lubricants, nonestrogen, 304
Luck, success and failure based on, 88–90
Lumpectomy, 284
Lung cancer, 286
Luteinizing hormone (LH), 27, 46, 306
Luvox (fluvoxamine), 269–70

Macho Hispanic man, 363
Magazines, gender construction and, 135–36
Major depressive disorder, 238
Male-dominant culture, gang rape and, 205
Male reproductive success and resources, 44–45
Male supremacy, incest and, 217
Mammography, 283
Management, sexual and racial differences in, 175–80
Managers, women, 175–80
   discrimination against, 178–80
   glass ceiling, 175–76
   psychological deficiency theory and, 176–77
   structural barriers facing, 179–80

Mandate, motherhood, 418
MAOIs, 268
Marital status
   labor force participation and, 161–62
   mental health and, 238
   physical health and, 278–79
Marriage, 332–34. *See also* Dual-earner couples
   in African American families, 324–25
   age at, 332
      fertility and, 420
   conflict in, 338–39
   gender and satisfaction with, 336–37
   inequality in, 190
   mental health and, 272–74
   motherhood and, 421
   motivation for, 332–34
   power relations in, 462–67
      age and, 466
      Black and White marriages, 467
      cybernetic theory of, 466
      egalitarian couples, 464–65
      resource theory of, 462–64
      violent marriages, 465–66
   rape in, 206–7
   satisfaction with, 333, 424–25
   social class and, 149
   unpaid labor in, 189–90
   violent, 221–23
Marriage market theory, 322
Marriage squeeze, 325
Marxist feminism, 5
Masculine women. *See also* Sex role orientation
   self-efficacy of, 188
   work strain among, 188
Masculinity, 99, 125. *See also* Sex role orientation
   self-esteem and, 100–101
Masochism, women's, 229, 231–32
Mastectomy, 283, 284
Masturbation, 355, 357, 373
Maternal rights, 388
Maternity blues, 399
Mate selection, 45, 323–26
Math anxiety, 66
Mathematics ability, gender differences in, 63–67
Mechanical reasoning, 72
Mechanistic psychological research, 12
Media
   bias in reporting, 89, 90
   contraception and, 136
   gender construction and, 134–36
      books and magazines, 135–36
      comic strips, 134–35
      television, 136
   math performance and, 66
Medicaid, 437
Medical degrees, women with, 79
Medicalization of birth, 392, 401
Medicalized perspective of sexuality, 348
Medical model of psychopathology, 260
Megestrol acetate, 303
Memories of incest, repressed, 218–19

Men
   as feminist researchers, 17
   as "norm," 19
Menarche, 137, 247
Menopause, 298–304
   estrogen replacement therapy (ERT), 299, 305
   hormone-replacement therapy (HRT), 299–304
      alternatives to, 303–4
      breast cancer and, 301–3
      diethylstilbestrol (DES), 304, 366–67
      heart disease and, 299–301
      mortality and, 303
   psychological effects of, 148–49, 303
   symptoms of, 298–99
Menstrual Attitude Questionnaire (MAQ), 52
Menstrual cycle, 46–56
   breast cancer surgery and, 284
   cerebral asymmetry during, 37
   cognition and, 49
   menstrual cramps (dysmenorrhea), 48, 306
   menstrual synchrony, 46–48
   perceptual abilities and, 50
   premenstrual syndrome, 50–56
      behavior and, 54
      estradiol and, 54
      factors in, 53
      methodological issues in researching, 51–52
      methods for reducing, 54–55
      occurrence of, 50
      oral contraceptives and, 53
      percentage of sufferers, 53
      political issues of, 51
      popular press' depiction of, 50
      self-handicapping with, 55–56
   reaction time and attention and, 49
   sex role attitudes and menstrual distress, 50
   sexuality and, 368–69
Menstrual Distress Questionnaire (MDQ), 52
Menstrual Joy Questionnaire (MJQ), 52
Mental health, 237–76, 337
   alcohol and drug abuse, 255–58
      childhood sexual abuse and, 255–57
      cocaine abuse, 258
      gender differences in, 255
      heroin addiction, 257–58
      during pregnancy, 386–89
   anxiety disorders, 252–54
   community mental health, 238–40
      homelessness, 239–40
      mental illness by sex, 238
      race, poverty, and, 239
      sexual assault and, 240
   depression, 240–44
      depressive explanatory style and, 244
      derived identity and, 243

Mental health, depression *(cont.)*
　diagnosis of, 240
　environmental stressors, 243
　feminine sex role orientation and,
　　243
　gender differences in rates of, 241
　among Hispanics, 267
　locus of control, 241–42
　menopause and, 149–50, 303
　multiple roles and, 271
　postpartum, 398–400
　pregnancy and, 396–97, 399
　psychopharmacotherapy for,
　　268–69
　self-focused attention and, 242–43
　social support for, 242
　victimization and, 237
eating disorders, 245–52
　anorexia nervosa, 245, 247–48, 252,
　　263
　body image and, 245–46
　bulimia nervosa, 245, 248–50, 252,
　　270–71
　cultural explanations for, 245
　dieting and overeating, 246–47
　family systems theory and, 250–51
　lesbians with, 251
　women of color with, 251–52
friendships and, 321
incest and, 217–18
marital status and, 238
multiple roles and, 271–74
psychopharmacotherapy, 268–71
　for bulimia nervosa, 270–71
　for depression, 268–69
　for panic disorder, 269–70
psychotherapy, 258–68
　with African American women,
　　267–68
　with American Indian women,
　　265–66
　with Asian American women, 266
　cognitive behavior therapy, 262–63
　consciousness-raising groups, 260
　family therapy for anorexia, 263
　feminist, 260–61
　with Hispanics, 266–67
　with lesbians, 264–65
　nonsexist, 261
　race, sex, and psychiatric diagnosis,
　　259–60
　sex between client and therapist,
　　263–64
　sexism in drug- and alcohol-treat-
　　ment programs, 261–62
　with women of color, 265
suicide, 254–55
utilization of mental health service,
　237–38
Mental retardation, 62
Mental rotation, 70–72
Meta-analysis, 8
Methadone, 387
Methotrexate (MTX), 381
Mexican American adolescents, sexual
　activity among, 143

Middle age, gender construction in,
　146–50
　adjustment at midlife, 148–49
　personality at midlife, 147–48
　psychological effects of menopause,
　　149–51
　sandwich generation, 151
　women's attitudes toward aging, 151
Middle class, Black, 333
Midwives, nurse, 395
Mifepristone (RU-486), 298
Military roles, 470
Ministers, testosterone levels of, 35
Minority women. *See also specific racial
　and ethnic minorities*
　empowerment of, 472–73
　in feminist movements, 2–3
Miscarriages, 378, 384
Moclobemide, 269
Modeling, 126
Modernism, 448
Monkey, androgenized female, 29–30
Monoamine oxidase inhibitors
　(MAOIs), 268
Monogamy, 45, 360–61
Mood disorder (affective disorder), 238
Morality, gender differences in, 109–11
Morbidity, 278
Morning sickness, 378
Mortality, 278
　from ectopic pregnancy, 380–82
　hormone-replacement therapy and,
　　303
　infant, 389–90, 395–96
Mortality rates, 278
　for breast cancer, 285
　for CHD, 280
　race and, 279
Mother-blaming, 423
Mother-child relationship
　daughters, 151, 422–23
　in Hispanic families, 447
　preschool daycare and, 429
　sons, 423–24
Motherhood, 415–21
　ambition and, 420
　Black women's views on, 415–16
　careers, marriage, and, 421
　Chodorow's theory of, 416–17
　feelings about, 421–22
　feminist perspective on, 415, 416
　ideologies shaping, 417
　motherhood mandate, 418
　motivations for, 418
　myths about, 421–22
　power and, 415
　sex-role orientation and, 419–20
　sexuality and, 370
　social connectedness and, 416
　women's normative personality and,
　　148
Mother-infant bonding, 400–401
Mothers, 421–25. *See also* Single-parent
　families; Working women
　AFDC, child-care arrangements of,
　　431

　changes in, 424
　earnings and self-efficacy of single,
　　439
　employment of, 425–27
　lesbian, 439–40
　in minority subcultures, 443–48
　　American Indian, 446
　　Asian American families, 448
　　Black lesbians, 446
　　dual-earner Black families, 446
　　extended Black family, 444–46
　　Hispanic families, 447–48
　noncustodial, 442–43
　older single, 438–39
　perceptions of, 425
　teenage, 141, 142–43
　on welfare, 431, 437
Motivation, achievement, 85
Moynihan Report, 443, 444
Mullerian structures, 27
Multifactorial gender identity theory,
　128
Murder, husband, 233–34
Myotonia, 351–52
Myths
　about motherhood, 421–22
　about rape, 202
　about traditional therapy, 260
　about women's masochism, 231–32

Nardil, 268
Narrative fantasies, children's, 132
National Association of Colored
　Women (NACW), 452
National Center for the Prevention and
　Control of Rape, 198
National Congress of Parents and
　Teachers Association (PTA), 451
National Crime Victim Survey (NCVS),
　198
National Health and Social Life Survey
　(NHSLS), 354, 355, 356
National Institutes of Health (NIH),
　277
National Longitudinal Survey of Labor
　Market Experience of Youth
　(NLSY), 429
National Organization for Women
　(NOW), 2, 3
National Victim Center, 198
National Women's Political Caucus
　(NWPC), 2
Native American women
　labor force participation of, 160–61,
　　162
　mothers, 446
　psychotherapy with, 265–66
Natural childbirth, 393–94
Nausea during pregnancy, 378
Needle–sharing, 310
Neglect response to dissatisfaction in
　relationships, 334–35
"Negro Family: The Case for National
　Action, The" (Moynihan Re-
　port), 443, 444
Nepotism rules, 173, 175

Netherlands, single–parent families in, 437
Networks, support, 153–54
Neural tube disorder (NTD), 384
Neuroticism, 341
NHSLS, 354, 355, 356
Nineteenth Amendment to the Constitution, 2, 451
NLSY, 429
Noncustodial mothers, 442–43
Nonlinear dynamics, 18
Nonprobability samples, 354
Nonverbal behavior, 116–20
　decoding cues of, 119–20
　gaze, 116–17
　interpersonal distance, 119
　smiling, 116
　touch, 117–18
Nonverbal cues, 113
Normative barriers, 76
Normative rapes, 203
Normative social integration, 340
Norms, bulimia and, 249–50
Norplant, 292
Norpramin, 268, 270
North American Indian Women's Association, 2
Norway, women politicians in, 455–56
NOW, 2, 3
n Power, 461
Nurse midwives, 395
Nurses' Health Study, 282, 299
Nursing homes, 154–55
Nursing profession, 166
Nurturant power, 457
Nurturant relationships, 320
Nutrition, 313–14
　cancer and, 282–83
　for menopausal women, 303
　PMS and, 55
　during pregnancy, 382–83

Obesity, 245, 246
　endometrial cancer and, 287
Observational learning, 126
Obsessive rapes, 207
Occupation. *See also* Gender segregation, occupational; Working women
　coronary heart disease and, 280
　divorce and, 341
　hormones and, 34–35
Oedipal complex, 124–25
Oldest old, 154
Oophorectomies, 306, 307
Opportunity theory, 361–62
Optimism, breast cancer and, 285
Oral contraceptives, 53, 289, 291–92
Oral stage, 124
Organizational bureaucracy, feminist critique of, 180
Orgasm, 352, 353–54
　frequency of, 355–56
　primary and secondary orgasmic dysfunction, 371–72

Osteoporosis, 27, 299, 304–5
　HRT and, 301
Ovarian cancer, 287–88, 292
Ovaries, 27
Overeating, 246–47

Panic attack, cognitive analysis of, 263
Panic disorder, 238, 252–54
　psychopharmacotherapy for, 269–70
Pap smears, 287, 308
PAQ, 99, 100
ParaGard T380A, 293
Parental investment model, 44
Parents. *See also* Family(ies); Motherhood; Mothers; Single-parent families
　caring for aging, 151
　custodial, 435
　independence from, 146
　loss of, 253
Partner referral for AIDS patients, 311
Part-time employment, 162
Patriarchy, 4, 5, 266, 408
　ideology of motherhood and, 417
　incest and, 217
　male God and, 473
Peer contacts, teacher and, 74
Peer culture, women's career commitment and, 146–47
Peer support, depression and, 242
Pelvic inflammatory disease (PID), 292, 293
Pelvic pain, 306
Penile strain gauge, 356
Penis envy, 125
Percentage overlap, 60
Perception, spatial, 69–70
Perceptual abilities, menstrual cycle and, 49–50
Performance
　bias in evaluation of, 96–98
　self-expectations for, 87–88
Personal and interpersonal construction of gender, 9–10
Personal Attributes Questionnaire (PAQ), 99, 100
Personal entitlement, 176–77
Personality
　conflicts of, 167–68
　divorce and, 341–42
　Freud's concept of, 124
　gender differences in, 103–13
　　activity level, 109
　　affiliation, 107
　　aggressiveness, 104–5, 120
　　anxiety, 112
　　assertiveness, 108–9
　　dependency, 108
　　emotion, 111–12
　　empathy, 112–13
　　helping behavior, 105–7
　　influenceability, 111
　　meta-analysis of, 106
　　morality, 109–11
　　self-esteem, 108
　　sociability, 107–8

hormones and, 33–34
　of managers, 177
　at midlife, 147–48
Personal space, 119
Persuasion studies, 111
Phallic stage, 124–25
Phenelzine, 268
Phenotypes, 24
Phenylpyruvic amentia (PKU), 23
Pheromones, 47–48
Phobias, 238, 252
Phonological (rhyming) tasks, 37
Physical abuse, adolescent pregnancy and, 142
Physical attractiveness, mate selection and, 322–24
Physical health, 277–316
　abortion, 142, 289, 294–98
　　barriers to, 297–98
　　clients for, 295
　　decision to have, 295
　　psychological effects of, 295–97, 385
　　rates of, 294–95
　　RU-486, 298
　cancer, 281–88
　　breast, 281–86, 301–3, 313–14
　　cervical, 287, 304, 307
　　colorectal, 286–87
　　endometrial, 287, 292, 299
　　lung, 286
　　ovarian, 287–88, 292
　of children with one parent, 438–39
　contraceptives, 143, 144, 145, 280–94
　　barrier methods, 293–94
　　condoms, 289, 290, 310, 311
　　Depo-provera, 292
　　female condom, 290–91
　　intrauterine device (IUD), 292–93
　　Norplant, 292
　　oral, 53, 289, 291–92
　　spermicides, 293
　　sterilization, 289, 294
　coronary heart disease, 278, 280–81, 299–301
　　Vitamin E and, 313–14
　fertility and, 406
　　lung cancer and, 286
　　oral contraceptives and, 291–92
　　during pregnancy, 387
　　prevention, 314
　fertility-related behavior, 289
　gender differences in, 278
　hysterectomy, 287, 305–7
　　for benign conditions, 305–6
　　for cancer treatment, 307
　　rates of, 305
　marital status and, 278–79
　menopause, 298–304
　　estrogen replacement therapy (ERT), 299, 305
　　hormone-replacement therapy (HRT), 299–304, 366–67
　　symptoms of, 298–99
　osteoporosis, 27, 299, 301, 304–5

Physical health *(cont.)*
  preventive health, 311–14
    AIDS prevention, 311–12
    douching, 312–13
    exercising, 313
    nutrition, 313–14
    smoking prevention, 314
  race differences in, 279–80
  sexually transmitted diseases, 210,
      307–11
    AIDS, 250, 309–12
    chlamydia, 307
    genital herpes, 307–8
    genital warts, 308
    hepatitis B, 308–9
    syphilis, 308
    smoking, 288–89
  women's health movement and
      public policy, 277–78
Physicians, women, 169–70
Pill, the, 289, 291–92
Pink collar jobs, 167–68
Pituitary gland, 27
PKU, 25
Placenta, 378
Plateau, sexual, 352
Play, gender construction and, 131–32,
    133–34
Political lesbianism, 4–5
Politics. *See also* Empowerment; Power
  body, 475
  of PMS, 51
  women in, 453–56
    African American, 454–55
    European, 455–56
    ideological positions of, 455
    numbers of, 453
    success of candidates, 453–54
Pornography, 203, 204, 212–15, 219,
    231–32
  definition of, 212
  excitation transfer theory of, 214–15
  laboratory experiments on, 213–14
  X-rated videos, 212–13
Positivism, logical, 6
Postmenopausal women, sexuality of,
    371
Postmodern family, 448–49
Postmodernism, feminist, 9
Postnatal hormones, 30
Postpartum adjustment, 396, 398–400
Postpartum psychosis, 399
Poststructuralism, 10
Posttraumatic stress syndrome (PTSD),
    209, 210, 229–30
Poverty, 243, 473–75
  in adolescence, 140
  community organization and, 474
  elderly in, 152
  feminization of, 436
  mental health and, 239
  single-parent families and, 436, 437–38
Power, 457. *See also* Empowerment;
    Leadership
  body politics and, 475
  community organization and, 474–75

  defining, 457–58
  gazing and, 117–18
  influence strategies, 459–60, 464
  in intimate relationships, 261, 462–67
    age and, 466
    Black and White marriages, 467
    cybernetic theory of, 466
    egalitarian couples, 464–65
    resource theory of, 462–64
    violent marriages, 465–66
  motherhood and, 415
  rape and, 212
  theories of, 458–59
  touching and, 118–19
Power motive, 461–62
Power outcomes, 458
Power strategies, 458, 460
Pregnancy, 377–92
  attitudes about pregnant women, 383
  babies at risk, 389–91
    infant mortality, 389–90
    prenatal care, 390–91
  depression and, 396–97, 399
  ectopic, 379–82
    deaths from, 380–82
  first trimester, 377–79
  midlife child-bearing, 391–92
  nausea during, 378
  nutrition during, 382–83
  prenatal screening, 384–86
    low income women, 386
    psychological aspects of, 385–86
    types of, 384–85
  pseudocyesis, 383
  psychosocial aspects of, 396–98
  second trimester, 379
  sexual desire and satisfaction during,
      369–70
  substance abuse during, 386–89
    alcohol abuse, 386–87
    cocaine, 387
    heroin, 387–88
    HIV infection, 388–89
    smoking, 387
  teenage, 140–45
    physical abuse and, 142
    rates of, 141–42
  third trimester, 379
  unintended, 284
  vomiting during, 378
Pregnancy Discrimination Act (PDA)
    of 1978, 180–81
Preliminary Scholastic Aptitude Test
    (PSAT), 63, 67
Premarin, 304
Premarital sexual activity, 340, 350, 359
Premature baby, 387, 397
Premed students, self-attributions of,
    89–90
Premenstrual Assessment Form, 53
Premenstrual syndrome, 50–56
  behavior and, 54
  estradiol and, 54
  factors in, 53
  methodological issues in researching,
      51–52

  methods for reducing, 54–55
  occurrence of, 50
  oral contraceptives and, 53
  percentage of sufferers, 53
  political issues of, 51
  popular press' depiction of, 50
  self-handicapping with, 55–56
Premenstrual tension, 50
Prenatal care, 390–91
Prenatal hormones, 29–30
Prenatal screening, 384–86
  low income women, 386
  psychological aspects of, 385–86
  types of, 384–85
Prevention, primary and secondary,
    279–80
Preventive health, 311–14
  AIDS prevention, 311–12
  douching, 312–13
  exercising, 313
  nutrition, 313–14
  smoking prevention, 314
Price Waterhouse v. *Hopkins*, 178
Primary lesbians, 366
Primary orgasmic dysfunction, 371–72
Primary prevention, 279
Principals, women, 172
Prison, women in, 234–35
Professional women, 79, 170–76
  educational administrators, 173–74
  engineers, 171
  faculty, 174–75
  lawyers, 170
  managers, 176–80
    discrimination against, 178–80
    glass ceiling, 175
    psychological theories, 176–78
    structural barriers facing, 180
  physicians, 170
  psychologists, 172–73
  scientists, 175–76
Progestasert, 293
Progesterone, 28, 54, 299, 378
Progestin, 205, 300–301, 302
Progestogen, 305
Prolactin, 27
Prolonged exposure (PE), 210–11
Promotion, bias in, 179
Prostaglandins, 48
Prostitutes with Hepatitis B virus,
    308–9
Prostitution, 219–20, 257
Provider referral for AIDS patients,
    311
Proximal processes, 25
Prozac (fluoxetine), 268, 269
PSAT, 63, 67
Pseudocyesis, 383
Psychiatric disorders, suicide and,
    254–55
Psychoactive drugs, 268
Psychoanalytic theory of gender devel-
    opment, 124–26
Psychological deficiency theory, 176–77
Psychological models of eating disor-
    ders, 245

Psychologists, women, 171–72
Psychology
   feminist transformation of, 15–19
   sexual harassment in, 185
Psychopathology
   bulimia and, 249
   medical model of, 260
   rape and, 205, 210
   recovery from eating disorder and, 252
Psychopharmacotherapy, 267–71
   for bulimia nervosa, 270–71
   for depression, 268–69
   for panic disorder, 269–70
Psychosexual stages, 124
Psychosis, postpartum, 400
Psychotherapy, 258–68
   with African American women, 267–68
   with American Indian women, 265–66
   with Asian American women, 266
   cognitive behavior therapy, 262–63
   consciousness-raising groups, 260
   family therapy for anorexia, 263
   feminist, 260–61
   with Hispanics, 266–67
   with lesbians, 264–65
   nonsexist, 261
   race, sex, and psychiatric diagnosis, 259–60
   sex between client and therapist, 263–64
   sexism in drug- and alcohol-treatment programs, 261–62
PTSD, 209, 210, 230
Puberty, 28, 137
Public health policy, 277–78
Purging type of bulimia, 248

Qualitative vs. quantitative methods, 7–8

Race. See also African Americans; African American women; Blacks; Black women; Ethnicity
   adoption and, 144
   bias in volunteer samples, 16
   breast cancer and, 281–82, 285
   dominance behavior and, 468
   ectopic pregnancy and, 381
   friendship patterns and, 137–38
   gender and, 6
   mental health and, 239
   mortality rates and, 279
   multiple roles and, 272–73
   power relations and, 467
   psychotherapy and, 259–60
   rape and, 199–201
   sex role orientation and, 103
   sexual harassment and, 185
   single-parent families and, 432–33
   social construction of, 6
   structural barriers in business and, 179–80
   teacher interactions and, 74–75

teen sexual activity and, 140–41
   working women and, 158–61
Racial differences
   in breast-feeding, 401
   in children's nurturing of infants, 132–34
   in condom use, 290
   in erotophobia/erotophilia, 350
   in gazing, 117
   in infant mortality, 389–90
   in management, 175–80
   in men's attitudes about gender roles, 467
   in physical health, 279–80
   in smoking, 288–89
Racial feminists on surrogacy, 408
Racism
   therapy with African American women and, 267–68
   in X-rated videos, 212–13
Radical feminism, 3–4, 20, 212
Radical lesbians, 4
Radical mastectomy, 283
Radical political lesbian feminists, 20
Rape, 197–212
   acquaintance, 204, 209
   avoidance of, 207–8
   Black and White, 199–201
   blaming victim of, 208–9
   causes of, 203–4
   community response to, 211–12
   coping with, 210–11
   cross-cultural perspective on, 202–3
   date, 199, 204
   definition of, 197–98
   feminist theory of, 201–2
   gang rape, 205–6
   Hispanic women and, 201
   marital, 206–7
   mental health and, 240
   nonnormative, 203
   normative, 203
   power and, 212
   psychopathology and, 205, 210
   rapists, 211
   statistics on, 198–99
   stranger, 204, 209
   theories of, 203–4
   trauma of, 209–10
   unwanted intercourse, 206
   victims of, 204–5
Rape crisis centers, 198, 212
Rape crisis hotline, 198
Rape-free and rape-prone societies, 202
Rape trauma syndrome, 209
Reaction time, menstrual cycle and, 49
Reasoned action theory of battery, 231
Reciprocity, 153
Re-entry women, 82–83
Reference group theory, 129
Referent power, 457
Refractory period, 353
Reinforcement, 126
   gender-based, 126
   intermittent, 229
Relational power careers, 462

Relaxation techniques, 303
Religion, 473
Remarriage, 344–45
Reproductive hazards at work, 180–81
Reproductive labor, 157–58
Reproductive life cycle, 368–71
   aging and sex, 370–71
   menstrual cycle and, 368–69
   motherhood and sex, 370
   sexual desire and satisfaction during pregnancy, 369–70
Reproductive power, 457–58
Reproductive technology, 406–11
   artificial insemination, 406–7
   sex selection, 409
   surrogacy, 407–9, 417
   in vitro fertilization, 409–11
Research
   bias in, 12–13
   collaborative, 15
   inclusion of both genders in, 277
   mechanistic psychological, 12
   on premenstrual syndrome, 51–52
Research methods, feminist, 13–15
Residence of elderly, 154–55
Resource theory, 462–64
Retirement, 151–52
Retroviruses, 25
Reverse transcriptase, 24–25
Reward power, 457
Right to Life, 297
Rock music videos, 136
Roe v. *Wade*, 295, 475
Role(s). *See also* Gender roles; Sex role attitudes; Sex role orientation; Sex roles
   choices, 427
   mental health and, 271–74
   military, 470
   subordinate, 462
Role conflict, work-home, 187–88
Role deprivation, 256
Role-taking, aggression and, 221
Romance, adolescent, 138
Romantic love, 448
Rotation, mental, 70–72
RU-486 (mifepristone), 298

Sandwich generation, 150
Schemas, 349
Scholastic Aptitude Test (SAT), 63, 65, 67
Science, feminist criticism of, 6–7
Scientists, women, 174–75
Secondary orgasmic dysfunction, 371–72
Secondary prevention, 279–80
Secondary sex characteristics, 137
Second wave of feminist movement, 2–3, 475
Secretaries, 169
Secure attachment style, 326–27
Seduction theory, Freud's repudiation of, 215–16
Segregation. *See* Gender segregation, occupational

Selection, environmental, 24
Self-blame, rape and, 209–10
Self-confidence, 87
Self-determination theory, 333
Self-disclosure in friendship, 319–20
Self-efficacy, 188, 296
  earnings and, 439
  of feminine women, 188
  smoking and, 314
Self-esteem
  employment and, 271–72
  gender differences in, 108
  of lesbians, 251
  masculinity and, 100–101
  sexual behavior and, 348
Self-focused attention, 242–43
Self-handicapping with premenstrual
    syndrome, 55–56
Self-help groups, 260
Self-image, ideal, 145–46
Self organization, 18
Self-schema, sexual, 349
Seneca Falls Convention (1848), 1–2
Separatism, 4
Serotonin, 30–31, 32
Serotonin selective reuptake inhibitors
    (SSRIs), 268, 269
Sex, psychotherapy and, 259–60
Sex bias in performance evaluation,
    96–98
Sex characteristics, secondary, 137
Sex chromosome anomalies, 26, 40–43
Sex determination, genetics of, 26
Sex differences, 15–16. *See also* Biology
Sex education, 141
Sex Guilt Scale, 350
Sex hormones, 26–29, 31–35, 46, 306
  aggression and, 31–32
  cognitive functioning and, 32–33
  occupation and, 34–35
  personality and, 33–34
Sexism, 4
  in drug- and alcohol-treatment pro-
    grams, 261–62
  in legal profession, 170
  in psychology, 15–16
  in science, 7–8
  in X-rated videos, 212–13
Sex role attitudes
  dating relationships and, 331
  menstrual distress and, 50
Sex Role Inventory (BSRI), 100, 101–2
Sex role orientation, 99–103, 120
  depression and, 243
  domestic chores and, 192
  emotionality and, 273
  friendships and, 322
  of leader, 469–70
  marital conflict and, 339
  motherhood and, 419–20
  political office and, 456
  psychological adjustment and,
    100–102
  self-focused attention and, 242–43
Sex roles
  alcoholism and conflict in, 256

for Chinese women, expectations of,
    80
  lesbian mothers and acquisition of,
    440
  self-focused attention and, 242–43
Sex segregation of the workforce. *See*
    Gender segregation, occupa-
    tional
Sex selection, 409
Sex stereotyping, use of concept in
    court, 178–79
Sexual abuse, childhood
  adolescent pregnancy and, 142
  mental health consequences of,
    217–18
  substance abuse and, 255–57
Sexual activity. *See also* Sexuality, fe-
    male
  between client and therapist, 263–64
  extramarital, 361–62
  premarital, 340, 350, 359
  teenage, 140–45
Sexual assault. *See* Rape
Sexual differentiation, 27–28
Sexual double standard, 350–51, 356,
    361
Sexual dysfunction, problem drinking
    and, 257
Sexual fantasies, 357
Sexual harassment, 168, 183–87
Sexual inequality, 348
Sexuality, female, 347–75
  of disabled women, 351
  dysfunction, 371–74
    dyspareunia, 371, 373
    inhibited sexual desire (ISD), 372
    primary and secondary orgasmic
      dysfunction, 371–72
    sex therapy, 373–74
    vaginismus, 372–73
  equality of, 374
  human sexual response, 351–54
    orgasm, 352, 353–54
    stages of, 351–53
  medicalized perspective on, 348
  reproductive life cycle and, 368–71
    aging and sex, 370–71
    menstrual cycle, 368–69
    motherhood and sex, 370
    sexual desire and satisfaction dur-
      ing pregnancy, 369–70
  sexual orientation, 364–68
  social construction of, 347–51
    double standard, 350–51
    erotophobia and erotophilia,
      349–50
    self-esteem and sexual behavior,
      348
    sexual meaning in women's lives,
      348–49
    sexual self-schema, 349
  surveys of, 354–64
    African American women's sexual-
      ity, 363–64
    divorce and sex, 362
    extramarital sex, 361–62

  female arousal to erotica, 356
  first intercourse, 354–55
  frequency of orgasm, 355–56
  frequency of sexual activity, 357–58
  Hispanic women's sexuality,
    362–63
  masturbation, 357
  reasons for engaging in sex, 358–59
  sexual daydreaming, 356–57
  sexual revolution, 359–60
  sociosexuality, 360–61
Sexually transmitted diseases, 210,
    307–11
  AIDS, 250, 309–12
    partners of hemophiliacs and, 311
    prevention of, 311–12
    risk behavior for, 310–11
    risk factors for transmission of, 312
    in Sub-Saharan Africa, 310
  chlamydia, 307
  genital herpes, 307–8
  genital warts, 308
  hepatitis B, 308–9
  oral contraceptives and, 292
  syphilis, 308
Sexual orientation, 364–68. *See also*
    Homosexuality; Lesbians
  bisexual women, 364–65
  hormones and, 366–67
Sexual power, 457
She pronoun, 136–37
Shifting standards model, 97
Short Bem Sex Role Inventory (SB-
    SRI), 101
Simple phobia, 238
Simple reaction time, 49
Single Mothers by Choice, 438
Single-parent families, 432–39. *See also*
    Mothers
  Black, 432–33, 435–36
  child support, 436–37
  poverty and, 436, 437–38
  race/ethnicity and, 432–33
  single mothers, 438–39
  welfare assistance for, 437
Singles, new, 328
Skills-training, AIDS risk reduction
    through, 310–11
Slavery, female sexual, 219
Smiling, 116–17
Smoking, 288–89
  fertility and, 406
  lung cancer and, 286
  oral contraceptives and, 291–92
  during pregnancy, 387
  prevention, 314
Sociability, gender differences in, 107–8
Social behavior, gender differences in,
    106
Social circumstances perspective, 149
Social class
  attitudes toward pregnant women
    and, 383
  marriage and, 149
Social comparison, breast cancer and,
    284–85

Social connectedness, mothering and, 416
Social construction of homosexuality, 366. *See also* Gender construction
Social context, animal aggression and, 30
Social disorganization theory of rape, 203–4
Social exchange theory of battery, 231
Social identity theory, 128–29
Social individuality, 475
Social integration, divorce and, 340
Social interaction in childhood, 133
Socialist feminism, 5
Socialization, gender role, 76–77. *See also* Gender construction
Socialization power, 457
Social learning theory, 126
   of battery, 229–30
Social reproduction, 157–58
Social roles theory, 129–30
Social skills, academic performance and, 75
Social support
   for depression, 242
   divorce and, 343
Sociobiology, 43–46
   on dating relationships, 322
   on marital conflicts, 338
   on subordination, 462
Sociocultural norms, bulimia and, 249–50
Socioeconomic status, widowhood adjustment and, 153
Sociosexuality, 360–61
Son-mother relationship, 423–24
Sorority women, 206
Southeast Asian women, educational achievement of, 82
Southern University, 146–47
Spatial ability, math ability and, 65
Spatial visualization, 37–38
Specific phobia, 254
Specific-status characteristics, 130
Speech styles, 113
Spelling, 37
Spermicides, 293
Splenium, 35
Sponges, contraceptive, 289, 293–94
SSRIs, 268, 269
Standard deviation, 60
Standpoint theory, feminist, 8
Status, 118
   cues allocating, 130
   women's normative personality and, 148
Status approach, 131
Stepfamilies
   African American, 441–42
   stepparents, 344, 440–42
Stereotypes, 93–94, 98. *See also* Gender stereotypes
Stereotyping
   power and, 459
   use of concept in court, 178–79

Sterilization, 289, 294
Stranger rape, 204, 209
Strategic power, 458
Stratification by gender, 170
Stress
   in clerical jobs, 167–68
   from divorce, 342–43
   from infertility, 406
   prenatal, 39
   from work-home role conflict, 187
Stress inoculation techniques (SIT), 210–11
Structural barriers, 76
Structural power, 458
Structured mobility ladders, 167, 179
Subordinate-dominant relationship, 459
Subordinate role of women, 462
Substance abuse, 255–58
   by bulimics, 249
   childhood sexual abuse and, 255–57
   cocaine abuse, 258, 387
   gender differences in, 255
   heroin, 257–58, 387–88
   during pregnancy, 386–89
      alcohol abuse, 386–87
      cocaine, 387
      heroin, 387–88
      HIV infection, 388–89
      smoking, 387
Success
   attributions for, 88–90, 102–3
   cultural, 45
   fear of, 85–86
Suffrage, women's, 451–52
Suicide, 254–55
Suicide attempters, 32
Superego, 124
Support networks, 153–54
Surrogacy, 407–9, 417
Sweden
   day care children in, 430
   single-parent families in, 437
"Swinging," 365
Syphilis, 308

Talcum powder, ovarian cancer and, 287–88
Talking in groups, 115–16
Target hiring, 182
Task leadership, 468
Teacher and peer contacts, 74
Teacher attention in elementary school classroom, 73
Teacher expectations for performance, 74
Teaching profession, 166
Technical-environmental theories of subordination, 462
Technology
   ideology of, 417
   reproductive, 406–11
      artificial insemination, 406–7
      sex selection, 409
      surrogacy, 407–9, 417
      in vitro fertilization, 409–11
Teenage mothers, 141, 142–43

Teenage pregnancy, 140–45
   physical abuse and, 142
   rates of, 141–42
Teen sexual activity, race and, 140–41
Television, gender construction and, 136
Tension, premenstrual, 50
Testes, 27
Testosterone, 18, 27, 28, 30, 371
   adrenal, 42–43
   antisocial behavior and, 31
   brain lateralization and, 38
   cognitive functioning and, 32, 33
   occupation and, 34–35
   in women, 33–34
Testosterone propionate (TP), 30
Tetracycline, 307
Therapist, sexual relations with client, 263–64
Therapy, myths of traditional, 260
Third-world feminism, 475
Thyroid stimulating hormone (TSH), 27
Title VII of the Civil Rights Act of 1964, 2, 181
Tobacco advertising, 288
Tofranil, 268
Tokenism, 170
Tomboys, 134
Touch, 118–19
Toys, play with, 133
Tradeswomen, 168–69
Trauma of rape, 209–10
Trazodone, 269
Tricyclic antidepressants (TCAs), 268, 269
Trimesters of pregnancy, 377–79
Tubal ligation, 294
Tumors, fibroid (leiomyomas), 305–6
Turner's syndrome, 41

Ultrasound, 384–85
Underemployment, 160, 162
Undifferentiated individual, 99
Unemployment rates of Black women, 159
Uniform Crime Report, 198
United Kingdom, single-parent families in, 437
Unpaid work by women, 189–93
   housespouses, 192–93
   housework and childcare, 190–92
   marital inequality, 189–90
Urogenital atrophy, 298–99
Uterine cancers, 307
Uterine pregnancy, 380
Uterus, prolapse of, 306

Vaginal cancer, DES and, 304
Vaginal creams, 304
Vaginal orgasm, 353–54
Vaginismus, 372–73
Values, teen pregnancy and, 145
Variability in intelligence, 62–63
Vasocongestion, 351–52
Verbal ability, gender differences in, 67–69

Victimization, depression and, 237
Videos
    rock music, 136
    X-rated, 212–13
Vigilance, 465
Violence against women, 197–236
    battering, 220–32
        counseling and shelter services for, 228–29
        ending, 226
        interaction dynamics in violent marriages, 223–24
        legal response to, 227–28
        in lesbian relationships, 224
        of lesbians by males, 225–26
        in marriage, 219, 221–23
        risk markers for, 223
        theories of, 229–32
    human rights violations, 475
    incest, 215–19
        attachment theory of, 217
        Freud's repudiation of seduction theory, 215–16
        incestuous activity, 216
        mental health consequences of, 217–18
        prevalence of, 216
        repressed memories of, 218–19
        treatment of survivors of, 218
    pornography, 203, 204, 212–15, 219, 231–32
        definition of, 212
        excitation transfer theory of, 214–15
        laboratory experiments on, 213–14
        X-rated videos, 212–13
    prostitution, 219–20, 257
    rape, 197–212
        acquaintance, 204, 209
        avoidance of, 207–8
        Black and White, 199–201
        blaming victim of, 208–9
        causes of, 203–4
        community response to, 211–12
        coping with, 210–11
        cross-cultural perspective on, 202–3
        date, 199, 204
        definition of, 197–98
        feminist theory of, 201–2
        gang rape, 205–6
        Hispanic women and, 201
        marital, 206–7
        mental health and, 240
        nonnormative, 203
        normative, 203
        power and, 212
        psychopathology and, 205, 210
        rapists, 211
        statistics on, 198–99
        stranger, 204, 209

        theories of, 203–4
        trauma of, 209–10
        unwanted intercourse, 206
        victims of, 204–5
    rock music and, 136
Violent crime, 105
Violent marriages, power in, 465–66
Visual dominance behavior, 117–18
Visual spatial ability, gender differences in, 69–72
Vital family, 448–49
Vitamin A, 282, 313–14, 382
Vitamin D, 304, 382
Vitamin E, CHD and, 313–14
Vocal cues, 113
Voice, girls' loss of, 137
Vomiting during pregnancy, 378
Voter turnout, 452
Voting right, 451–53

Warts, genital, 308
Welfare assistance, 431, 437
Wellbutrin (bupropion), 269
Wernicke's area, 37
WHISPER (Women Hurt in Systems of Prostitution), 220
White-on-Black rape, 201
Widowhood
    gender construction and, 153–54
    men in, 108, 279
    physical health and, 279
Wife battering. *See under* Battering
Wolffian duct system, 27
Womb envy, 126
Women of color. *See* African American women; Black women
Women's Business Ownership Act of 1988, 183
Women's Equity Action League (WEAL), 2
Women's health movement, 277–78
Women's Movement. *See* Feminism
Women's Rights Project, 388
Work/home mother, 426–27
Working women, 157–95
    affirmative action and, 181
    breast-feeding and, 402
    comparable worth, 182
    displaced homemakers, 193
    dual-earner couples, 187–89
        career and marriage in male- and female-dominated professions, 189
        child-bearing decision model for, 420
        influences on married women's employment, 189
        marital satisfaction of, 344–45
        relative costs and rewards of, 188–89
        work-home role conflict, 187–88

    entrepreneurial women, 182–83
    income of, 162–65
        African Americans, 164–65
        Asian Americans, 165
        education and, 162–63
        gender gap in pay, 163–64
        Hispanics, 164
    labor force participation, 158–62
        age, marital status, children, and, 161–62
        part-time employment, 162
        racial-ethnic dimensions of, 158–61
        rates of, 158
    managers, 175–80
        discrimination against, 177–79
        glass ceiling, 175–76
        psychological deficiency theory and, 176–77
        structural barriers facing, 179–80
    mothers, 425–27
    occupational gender segregation, 165–69
        blue collar jobs, 168–69
        female occupations, 165–66
        personal entitlement and, 177
        pink collar jobs, 167–68
        theories of, 166–67
    occupational level of, children's academic success and, 75
    professional, 79, 169–75
        educational administrators, 172–73
        engineers, 171
        faculty, 173–74
        lawyers, 170
        physicians, 169–70
        psychologists, 171–72
        scientists, 174–75
    reproductive hazards facing, 180–81
    reproductive labor, 157–58
    school-age children of, 432
    sexual harassment, 168, 183–87
    target hiring and, 181–82
    unpaid work, 189–93
        housespouses, 192–93
        housework and childcare, 190–92
        marital inequality, 189–90
Workplace. *See* Discrimination
Work/work mother, 426

Xanax (Alprazolam), 55, 269–70
X chromosome, 40
X-rated videos, 212–13
XXX females, 41
XYY males, 41

Young adulthood, gender construction in, 145–46

Zidovudine (AZT), 388, 389
Zinc, 55